Kerrie Meyler
Byron Holt
Greg Ramsey

with Jason Sandys
Cameron Fuller
Anthony Puca

System Center Configuration Manager 2007

UNLEASHED

SAMS | 800 East 96th Street, Indianapolis, Indiana 46240 USA

System Center Configuration Manager 2007 Unleashed

Copyright © 2010 by Sams Publishing

ISBN-13: 978-0-672-33023-0

ISBN-10: 0-672-33023-7

Library of Congress Cataloging-in-Publication Data:

Meyler, Kerrie.
   System center configuration manager 2007 unleashed / Kerrie Meyler, Byron Holt, Greg Ramsey ; with Jason Sandys, Cameron Fuller, and Anthony Puca.
      p. cm.
   Includes bibliographical references.
   ISBN-13: 978-0-672-33023-0
   ISBN-10: 0-672-33023-7
   1. Computer networks–Management–Computer programs.   2. Software configuration management–Computer programs.   3. Microsoft System center configuration manager–Computer programs.   I. Holt, Byron.   II. Ramsey, Greg.   III. Title.
   TK5105.5.M488 2009
   005.36–dc22
                                                            2009020058

Printed in the United States of America

First Printing July 2009

Trademarks

All terms mentioned in this book that are known to be trademarks or service marks have been appropriately capitalized. Sams Publishing cannot attest to the accuracy of this information. Use of a term in this book should not be regarded as affecting the validity of any trademark or service mark.

Warning and Disclaimer

Every effort has been made to make this book as complete and as accurate as possible, but no warranty or fitness is implied. The information provided is on an "as is" basis. The authors and the publisher shall have neither liability nor responsibility to any person or entity with respect to any loss or damages arising from the information contained in this book or from the use of the programs accompanying it.

Bulk Sales

Sams Publishing offers excellent discounts on this book when ordered in quantity for bulk purchases or special sales. For more information, please contact

   U.S. Corporate and Government Sales
   1-800-382-3419
   corpsales@pearsontechgroup.com

For sales outside of the U.S., please contact

   International Sales
   international@pearsoned.com

Editor-in-Chief
Karen Gettman

Executive Editor
Neil Rowe

Development Editor
Mark Renfrow

Technical Editor
Steve Rachui

Managing Editor
Kristy Hart

Project Editors
Lori Lyons
Anne Goebel

Copy Editor
Bart Reed

Indexer
Publishing Works, Inc.

Proofreader
Williams Woods Publishing Services

Publishing Coordinator
Cindy Teeters

Cover Designer
Gary Adair

Composition
Jake McFarland

Contents at a Glance

Table of Contents

Foreword

To all of our customers...

Wow—it's been almost 15 years now since the announcement was made for this new product from Microsoft: Microsoft Systems Management Server (SMS) 1.0. The original charter was to "provide easier and more cost-effective management of desktop hardware and software throughout large-scale computing systems, easing what has been one of the most expensive and time-consuming aspects of client-server computing, and enabling customers to run their businesses more effectively." Sound applicable today? That charter still applies, even though the characteristics and importance for those features have taken on different meanings over the past 15 years, and we are so proud of what we think System Center Configuration Manager (SCCM) 2007 and SCCM 2007 R2 add to this long history. Quite frankly, this is the most significant release of SMS/SCCM ever, and the value we believe it will bring to you, our customers, is tremendous. Fifteen years ago, deploying Windows wasn't as hard—you just put in six floppy diskettes! Sarbanes-Oxley and HIPAA were just part of the "golden rule"—not governmental and corporate obligations. And software distribution was "good enough" if it did just slightly better than you could do if you went from machine to machine manually. Now...you bet your business success on the ability to get software to the right systems at the right time. The core disciplines have remained the same, but the world has evolved to place further demands on those cores. That is what SCCM 2007 is all about: continuing to solidify and extend that core discipline of change and configuration management to today's business problems, with the reliability you've come to expect.

But the greatest thing in those 14+ years is not the 1's and 0's we've shipped to the market—it's the relationships we've made with you, the tens of thousands of SCCM administrators around the world. We are very aware that a large degree of the SMS/SCCM success over the years is attributable to you, your passion and commitment to the problem of systems management and our product. What we've built, you've tweaked. What we've omitted, you've filled in. What we've gotten wrong, you've worked around—and let us know how to do it right next time. It's this relationship in working with you, in building our software and solving your needs, that makes us most proud to come to work every day.

What we've all learned in the software industry is that software is never perfect. We obviously continue to strive for perfection when it comes to quality and security, but we know with as large and diverse a group of customers that we have, there will be no way we get every feature you need, or every feature done in the way you need it. However, our "luxury" is that we have the *best* people on the planet using our product on a daily basis. You—our SCCM administrators—share the same passion in solving your problems and helping your fellow administrators, that we do in building the product. This book is just another testament to that dedication and spirit. We want to thank the authors (SCCM administrators, like you) for their ongoing support of our product and this community. And we look forward to continuing this relationship for years (and releases) to come!

With greatest admiration,
The System Center Configuration Manager Product Group

About the Authors

Kerrie Meyler, MVP, is the lead author of *Microsoft Operations Manager 2005 Unleashed* and *System Center Operations Manager 2007 Unleashed* (Sams Publishing). She is an independent consultant and trainer with over 15 years of Information Technology experience. Kerrie was responsible for evangelizing SMS while a Sr. Technology Specialist at Microsoft, and has presented on System Center technologies at TechEd and MMS.

Byron Holt, an IT professional for over 15 years, has been a lead SMS and Configuration Manager engineer for several Global 5000 corporations and was part of the Active Directory and Enterprise Manageability support teams while working at Microsoft. Byron's experience includes software development, security architecture, and systems management. Byron currently works for McAfee, in the security engineering team.

Greg Ramsey, Configuration Manager MVP, has worked with SMS and desktop deployment since 1998. He currently works for Dell, Inc., as a ConfigMgr administrator, and previously was a sergeant in the United States Marine Corps. Greg is a columnist for myITforum.com, cofounder of the Ohio SMS User Group and Central Texas Systems Management User Group, and creator of SMSView. Greg previously coauthored *SMS 2003 Recipes: A Problem-Solution Approach* (Apress, 2006).

About the Contributors

Jason Sandys, a Senior Consultant at Catapult Systems, has over 10 years of experience in development and systems management. Jason concentrates on implementing and supporting Microsoft-centric solutions for a wide variety of customers, focusing primarily on Configuration Manager and Operations Manager. Jason presented at MMS and TechEd in 2009 on ConfigMgr native mode.

Cameron Fuller, MVP, is a Managing Consultant for Catapult Systems, an IT consulting company and Microsoft Gold Certified Partner. He focuses on management solutions, with 15 years of infrastructure experience. Cameron is the coauthor of *Microsoft Operations Manager 2005 Unleashed* and *System Center Operations Manager 2007 Unleashed*.

Anthony Puca, MVP, is a Senior Solution Architect for EMC, a Global System Integrator and Gold Certified Partner focused on information infrastructure. Anthony concentrates on management technologies, and presents frequently on System Center management technologies.

Peter Zerger, MVP, is a consulting partner with AKOS Technology Services. He has 10 years of experience in the IT industry. Pete is webmaster of System Center Central (http://systemcentercentral.com), a popular community site focusing on the Microsoft System Center suite.

Jannes Alink, ConfigMgr consultant, works at Inovativ, a European consultancy with a dedicated focus on the System Center family. Jannes began as a support engineer and now consults in infrastructure management with System Center, with a primary focus on SMS 2003 and Configuration Manager 2007.

Dedication

To my father
—Kerrie Meyler

Acknowledgments

Writing a book is a huge project, and ConfigMgr is a massive topic. This book would not be possible without the help of many individuals. I would like to particularly thank Cameron Fuller, my coauthor since 2005 in the *Operations Manager Unleashed* series, for developing the Configuration Manager Visio template used in this book and stepping in as a contributing author. I would also like to thank Pete Zerger and AKOS Technology Services for contributing the lab resources used throughout *System Center Configuration Manager 2007 Unleashed*. Maintaining a ConfigMgr hierarchy requires a considerable amount of resources; without Pete's assistance, it would have been far more challenging than it was! Thank you also to Scott Weisler of AKOS, for supporting our lab environment.

Additional thanks go to Byron Holt for his inspiration, dedication, and effort throughout this entire project. Thanks to Raymond Chou and Allen Wat for their research on App-V, to Hamid Yusuff for his thoughts on Asset Intelligence, to Panu Saukko, to Maarten Goet, and to the ConfigMgr community for their dedication and commitment to Microsoft's flagship configuration management product. And, of course, thanks to the ConfigMgr team at Microsoft!

Thanks also go to the staff at Pearson and Sams Publishing, in particular to Neil Rowe.

Last but definitely not least, thanks to my coauthors and contributors, for their patience and work in developing the material for this book, and to Steve Rachui, an awesome technical editor, for vouching for the technical accuracy of the material.

—Kerrie Meyler

We Want to Hear from You!

As the reader of this book, *you* are our most important critic and commentator. We value your opinion and want to know what we're doing right, what we could do better, what areas you'd like to see us publish in, and any other words of wisdom you're willing to pass our way.

You can email or write me directly to let me know what you did or didn't like about this book—as well as what we can do to make our books stronger.

Please note that I cannot help you with technical problems related to the topic of this book, and that due to the high volume of mail I receive, I might not be able to reply to every message.

When you write, please be sure to include this book's title and authors as well as your name and phone or email address. I will carefully review your comments and share them with the authors and editors who worked on the book.

E-mail: feedback@samspublishing.com

Mail: Neil Rowe
Executive Editor
Sams Publishing
800 East 96th Street
Indianapolis, IN 46240 USA

Reader Services

Visit our website and register this book at www.samspublishing.com/register for convenient access to any updates, downloads, or errata that might be available for this book.

Introduction

With the release of System Center Configuration Manager 2007, Microsoft continues to enhance its premier systems management software product, used to manage large groups of Windows-based computer systems. Configuration Manager (ConfigMgr) 2007, formerly known as SMS or Systems Management Server, is a wide and diverse product. It enables you to deploy, assess, and update servers, clients, and devices across physical, virtual, distributed, and mobile environments, as well as manage clients that connect only over the Internet (IBCM). Configuration Manager provides software distribution, patch management, operating system deployment, hardware and software inventory, asset management, and desired configuration management. Perhaps it is not surprising that writing this book has been just about as wide and diverse a project as the software itself. *System Center Configuration Manager 2007 Unleashed* provides in-depth technical information about the capabilities and features of ConfigMgr 2007, including information on other products and technologies on which Configuration Manager features and components depend. Our purpose is to go beyond just describing the product and its features, however, and provide insight and examples of how ConfigMgr can be used to help solve real-world problems. The book begins by describing a methodology and framework for solutions-based deployments, and then maps the numerous ConfigMgr feature areas to the architecture, design, and implementation requirements for that topic. Information is current as of Configuration Manager 2007 Release 2 (R2).

Regarding the domain name used in the examples in this book—the official abbreviation of Configuration Manager is "ConfigMgr," which is the abbreviation we use for the product throughout the book. However, because we were unsuccessful in registering a domain name that had ConfigMgr or some permutation of it, the domain name is SCCMUnleashed.com, because SCCM is another commonly used abbreviation.

Part I: Configuration Management Overview and Concepts

System Center Configuration Manager 2007 Unleashed begins with an introduction to configuration management, including initiatives and methodologies such as Dynamic Systems Initiative (DSI), the IT Infrastructure Library (ITIL), Microsoft Operations Framework (MOF), and Microsoft Solutions Framework (MSF). Although some consider this to be more of an alphabet soup of frameworks than constructive information, these strategies and approaches give a structure to managing one's environment—from system configuration and inventory management to proactive management and infrastructure optimization. Moreover, implementing Configuration Manager is a project, and as such should include a structured approach with its own deployment. Chapter 1, "Configuration Management Basics," starts with the big picture and brings it down to the pain points that system administrators deal with on a daily basis, showing how Microsoft's System Center suite plans to address these challenges.

Chapter 2, "Configuration Manager 2007 Overview," shows how Configuration Manager has evolved from its first days in 1994 as SMS 1.0, and introduces key concepts and feature dependencies. In Chapter 3, "Looking Inside Configuration Manager," we peel back the layers of the onion to discuss the design concepts behind ConfigMgr 2007, the major ConfigMgr components, its relationship with Windows Management Instrumentation (WMI), and the ConfigMgr database.

Part II: Planning, Design, and Installation

Before installing any software, one needs to spend time planning and designing its architecture. ConfigMgr 2007 is no exception. Chapter 4, "Configuration Manager Solution Design," begins this discussion with envisioning the solution and tying into the MSF process phases. In Chapter 5, "Network Design," Chapter 6, "Architecture Design Planning," and Chapter 7, "Testing and Stabilizing," we step through the network and architectural concepts to consider when planning and prototyping a Configuration Manager architecture and deployment. Finally, it is time to implement that design, and Chapter 8, "Installing Configuration Manager 2007," and Chapter 9, "Migrating to Configuration Manager 2007," walk you through the process of installing a new environment or upgrading an SMS 2003 infrastructure to ConfigMgr 2007.

Part III: Configuration Manager Operations

The third part of the book deals with Configuration Manager operations. This is where the bulk of time is spent using ConfigMgr 2007. Our discussion of operations starts with using the console, discussed in Chapter 10, "The Configuration Manager Console." Chapter 11, "Related Technologies and References," introduces some of the related technologies used with the product. Using ConfigMgr requires an installed client on managed systems, as covered in depth in Chapter 12, "Client Management." Day-to-day operations include software packaging and distribution (Chapter 13, "Creating Packages," and Chapter 14,

"Distributing Packages") and activities such as patch management (Chapter 15, "Patch Management"), desired configuration management (Chapter 16, named appropriately enough, "Desired Configuration Management"), running queries (Chapter 17, "Configuration Manager Queries"), reporting (Chapter 18, "Reporting"), and operating system deployments (Chapter 19, "Operating System Deployment").

Part IV: Administering Configuration Manager 2007

The last part of the book discusses Configuration Manager administration. This includes security requirements (Chapter 20, "Security and Delegation in Configuration Manager 2007") as well as backups and maintenance (Chapter 21, "Backup, Recovery, and Maintenance").

Part V: Appendixes

This book contains two appendixes:

▶ Appendix A, "Configuration Manager Log Files," describes the usage of the myriad log files used by Configuration Manager 2007 that are helpful when trying to troubleshoot assorted issues. It also discusses how to enable those log files not enabled by default, and setting debug and verbose logging levels.

▶ Appendix B, "Reference URLs," includes references and descriptions for many URLs helpful for ConfigMgr administrators, also included as live links under the Downloads tab at the InformIT website at http://www.informit.com/store/product.aspx?isbn=0672330237.

Disclaimers and Fine Print

We do have several disclaimers. Although several chapters include information on using Configuration Manager 2007 for meeting various regulatory compliances, this book does not provide legal advice. It only provides factual and technical information related to regulatory compliance. Do not rely exclusively on this book for advice about how to address your regulatory requirements. For specific questions, consult your legal counsel or auditor.

In addition, the information we provide is probably outdated the moment the book goes to print. Microsoft is continually publishing Knowledge Base (KB) and TechNet articles, Service Pack 2 is in development, and as we continue to work with the product, we will always find yet another wrinkle in it. The authors and contributors of *System Center Configuration Manager 2007 Unleashed* have made every attempt to present information that is accurate and current, as we know it. Updates and corrections will be provided as errata on the InformIT website.

Who Should Read This Book

This book is targeted toward the systems professional who wants to be proactive in managing his or her Windows computing environment. This audience is cross–industry, ranging from a single system administrator in a smaller organization, to larger businesses where multiple individuals are responsible for managing servers, clients, and Windows devices. By providing insight into Configuration Manager's many capabilities, discussing tools to help with a successful implementation, and sharing real-world experiences, this book strives to enable a more widespread understanding and use of System Center Configuration Manager.

PART I

Configuration Management Overview and Concepts

IN THIS PART

CHAPTER 1

Configuration Management Basics

System Center Configuration Manager (ConfigMgr) 2007 represents a significant maturation in Microsoft's systems management platform. Configuration Manager is an enterprise management tool that provides a total solution for Windows client and server management, including the ability to catalog hardware and software, deliver new software packages and updates, and deploy Windows operating systems with ease. In an increasingly compliance-driven world, Configuration Manager delivers the functionality to detect "shift and drift" in system configuration. ConfigMgr 2007 consolidates information about Windows clients and servers, hardware, and software into a single console for centralized management and control.

Configuration Manager gives you the resources you need to get and stay in control of your Windows environment and helps with managing, configuring, tuning, and securing Windows Server and Windows-based applications. For example, Configuration Manager includes the following features:

▶ **Enterprisewide control and visibility**—Whether employing Wake On LAN to power up and apply updates, validating system configuration baselines, or automating client and server operating system deployment, Configuration Manager provides unprecedented control and visibility of your computing resources.

▶ **Automation of deployment and update management tasks**—ConfigMgr greatly reduces the administrative effort involved in deployment of client and server operating systems, software applications, and software updates. The scheduling features in software and update deployment ensure minimal interruption to the business. The ConfigMgr summary screens and reporting features provide a convenient view of deployment progress.

▶ **Increased security**—Configuration Manager 2007 provides secure management of clients over Internet connections, as well as the capability to validate Virtual Private Network–connected client configurations and remediate deviations from corporate standards. In conjunction with mutual authentication between client and server (available in Configuration Manager native mode only), Configuration Manager 2007 delivers significant advances in security over previous releases.

This chapter serves as an introduction to System Center Configuration Manager 2007. To avoid constantly repeating that very long name, we utilize the Microsoft-approved abbreviation of the product name, Configuration Manager, or simply ConfigMgr. ConfigMgr 2007, the fourth edition of Microsoft's systems management platform, includes numerous additions in functionality as well as security and scalability improvements over its predecessors.

This chapter discusses the Microsoft approach to Information Technology (IT) operations and systems management. This discussion includes an explanation and comparison of the Microsoft Operations Framework (MOF), which incorporates and expands on the concepts contained in the Information Technology Infrastructure Library (ITIL) standard. It also examines Microsoft's Infrastructure Optimization Model (IO Model), used in the assessment of the maturity of organizations' IT operations. The IO Model is a component of Microsoft's Dynamic Systems Initiative (DSI), which aims at increasing the dynamic capabilities of organizations' IT operations.

These discussions have special relevance in that the objective of all Microsoft System Center products is in the optimization, automation, and process agility and maturity in IT operations.

Ten Reasons to Use Configuration Manager

Why should you use Configuration Manager 2007 in the first place? How does this make your daily life as a systems administrator easier? Although this book covers the features and benefits of Configuration Manager in detail, it definitely helps to have some quick ideas to illustrate why ConfigMgr is worth a look!

Here's a list of 10 scenarios that illustrate why you might want to use Configuration Manager:

1. The bulk of your department's budget goes toward paying for teams of contractors to perform OS and software upgrades, rather than paying talented people like you the big bucks to implement the platforms and processes to automate and centralize management of company systems.

2. You realize systems management would be much easier if you had visibility and control of all your systems from a single management console.

3. The laptops used by the sales team have not been updated in 2 years because they *never* come to the home office.

4. You don't have enough internal manpower to apply updates to your systems manually every month.

5. Within days of updating system configurations to meet corporate security requirements, you find several have already mysteriously "drifted" out of compliance.

6. When you try to install Vista for the accounting department, you discover Vista cannot run on half the computers, because they only have 256MB of RAM. (It would have been nice to know that when submitting your budget requests!)

7. Demonstrating that your organization is compliant with regulations such as Sarbanes-Oxley (SOX), the Health Insurance Portability and Accountability Act (HIPAA), the Federal Information Security Management Act (FISMA), or *<insert your own favorite compliance acronym here>* has become your new full-time job.

8. You spent your last vacation on a trip from desktop to desktop installing Office 2007.

9. Your production environment is so diverse and distributed that you can no longer keep track of which software versions should be installed to which system.

10. By the time you update your system standards documentation, everything has changed and you have to start all over again!

While trying to bring some humor to the discussion, these topics represent very real problems for many systems administrators. If you are one of those people, then you owe it to yourself to explore how Configuration Manager can be leveraged to solve many of these common issues. These pain points are common to almost all users of Microsoft technologies to some degree, and Configuration Manager holds solutions for all of them.

However, perhaps the most important reason for using Configuration Manager is the peace of mind it brings you as an administrator, knowing that you have complete visibility and control of your IT systems. The stability and productivity this can bring to your organization is a great benefit as well.

The Evolution of Systems Management

The landscape in systems and configuration management has evolved significantly since the first release of Microsoft Systems Management Server, and is experiencing great advancements still today. The proliferation of compliance-driven controls and virtualization (server, desktop, and application) has added significant complexity and exciting new functionality to the management picture.

Configuration Manager 2007 is a software solution that delivers end-to-end management functionality for systems administrators, providing configuration management, patch management, software and operating system distribution, remote control, asset management, hardware and software inventory, and a robust reporting framework to make sense of the various available data for internal systems tracking and regulatory reporting requirements.

These capabilities are significant because today's IT systems are prone to a number of problems from the perspective of systems management, including the following:

- ▶ Configuration "shift and drift"
- ▶ Security and control
- ▶ Timeliness of asset data
- ▶ Automation and enforcement
- ▶ Proliferation of virtualization
- ▶ Process consistency

This list should not be surprising—these types of problems manifest themselves to varying degrees in IT shops of all sizes. In fact, Forrester Research estimates that 82% of larger IT organizations are pursuing service management, and 67% are planning to increase Windows management. The next sections look at these issues from a systems management perspective.

Hurdles in the Distributed Enterprise

You may encounter a number of challenges when implementing systems management in a distributed enterprise. These include the following:

- ▶ **Increasing threats**—According to the SANS Institute, the threat landscape is increasingly dynamic, making efficient and proactive update management more important than ever (see http://www.sans.org/top20/).

- ▶ **Regulatory compliance**—Sarbanes-Oxley, HIPAA and many other regulations have forced organizations to adopt and implement fairly sophisticated controls to demonstrate compliance.

- ▶ **OS and software provisioning**—Rolling out the operating system (OS) and software on new workstations and servers, especially in branch offices, can be both time consuming and a logistical challenge.

- ▶ **Methodology**—With the bar for effective IT operations higher than ever, organizations are forced to adapt a more mature implementation of IT operational processes to deliver the necessary services to the organization's business units more efficiently.

With increasing operational requirements unaccompanied by linear growth in IT staffing levels, organizations must find ways to streamline administration through tools and automation.

The Automation Challenge

As functionality in client and server systems has increased, so too has complexity. Both desktop and server deployment can be very time consuming when performed manually. With the number and variety of security threats increasing every year, timely application of security updates is of paramount importance. Regulatory compliance issues add a new burden, requiring IT to demonstrate that system configurations meet regulatory requirements.

These problems have a common element—all beg for some measure of automation to ensure IT can meet expectations in these areas at the expected level of accuracy and efficiency. To get IT operational requirements in hand, organizations need to implement tools and processes that make OS and software deployment, update management, and configuration monitoring more efficient and effective.

Configuration "Shift and Drift"

Even in those IT organizations with well-defined and documented change management, procedures fall short of perfection. Unplanned and unwanted changes frequently find their way into the environment, sometimes as an unintended side effect of an approved, scheduled change.

You may be familiar with an old philosophical saying: *If a tree falls in a forest and no one is around to hear it, does it make a sound?*

Here's the configuration management equivalent: *If a change is made on a system and no one knows, does identifying it make a difference?*

The answer to this question is absolutely "yes." Every change to a system has some potential to affect the functionality or security of the system, or that system's adherence to corporate or regulatory standards.

For example, adding a feature to a web application component may affect the application binaries, potentially overwriting files or settings replaced by a critical security patch. Or, perhaps the engineer implementing the change sees a setting he or she thinks is misconfigured and decides to just "fix" it while working on the system. In an e-commerce scenario with sensitive customer data involved, this could have potentially devastating consequences.

At the end of the day, your selected systems management platform must bring a strong element of baseline configuration monitoring to ensure configuration standards are implemented and maintained with the required consistency.

Lack of Security and Control

Managing systems becomes much more challenging when moving outside the realm of the traditional LAN (local area network)-connected desktop or server computer. Traveling users who rarely connect to the trusted network (other than to periodically change their password) can really make this seem an impossible task.

Just keeping these systems up to date on security patches can easily become a full-time job. Maintaining patch levels and system configurations to corporate standards when your roaming users only connect via the Internet can make this activity exceedingly painful. In reality, remote sales and support staff make this an everyday problem. To add to the quandary, these users are frequently among those installing unapproved applications from unknown sources, subsequently putting the organization at greater risk when they finally do connect to the network.

Point-of-sale (POS) devices running embedded operating systems pose challenges of their own, with specialized operating systems that can be difficult to administer—and for many systems management solutions, they are completely unmanageable. Frequently these systems perform critical functions within the business (such as cash register, automated teller machine, and so on), making the need for visibility and control from configuration and security perspectives an absolute necessity.

Mobile devices have moved from a role of high-dollar phone to a mini-computer used for everything: Internet access, Global Positioning System (GPS) navigation, and storage for all manner of potentially sensitive business data. From the Chief Information Officer's perspective, ensuring that these devices are securely maintained (and appropriately pass-word protected) is somewhat like gravity. It's more than a good idea—it's the law!

But seriously, as computing continues to evolve, and more devices release users from the strictures of office life, the problem only gets larger.

Timeliness of Asset Data

Maintaining a current picture of what is deployed and in use in your environment is a constant challenge due to the ever-increasing pace of change. However, failing to maintain an accurate snapshot of current conditions comes at a cost. In many organizations, this is a manual process involving Excel spreadsheets and custom scripting, and asset data is often obsolete by the time a single pass at the infrastructure is complete.

Without this data, organizations can over-purchase (or worse yet, under-purchase) soft-ware licensing. Having accurate asset information can help you get a better handle on your licensing costs. Likewise, without current configuration data, areas including Incident and Problem Management may suffer because troubleshooting incidents will be more error prone and time consuming.

Lack of Automation and Enforcement

With the perpetually increasing and evolving technology needs of the business, the need to automate resource provisioning, standardize, and enforce standard configurations becomes increasingly important.

Resource provisioning of new workstations or servers can be a very labor-intensive exercise. Installing a client OS and required applications may take a day or longer if performed manually. Ad-hoc scripting to automate these tasks can be a complex endeavor. Once deployed, ensuring the client and server configuration is consistent can seem an insur-mountable task. With customer privacy and regulatory compliance at stake, consequences can be severe if this challenge is not met head on.

Proliferation of Virtualization

There's an old saying: *If you fail to plan, you plan to fail.* In no area of IT operations is this truer than when considering virtualization technologies.

When dealing with systems management, you have to consider many different functions, such as software and patch deployment, resource provisioning, and configuration management. Managing server and application configuration in an increasingly "virtual" world, where boundaries between systems and applications are not always clear, will require considering new elements of management not present in a purely physical environment.

Virtualization as a concept is very exciting to IT operations. Whether talking about virtualization of servers or applications, the potential for dramatic increases in process automation and efficiency and reduction in deployment costs is very real. New servers and applications can be provisioned in a matter of minutes. With this newfound agility comes a potential downside, which is the reality that virtualization can increase the velocity of change in your environment. The tools used to manage and track changes to a server often fail to address new dynamics that come when virtualization is introduced into a computing environment.

Many organizations make the mistake of taking on new tools and technologies in an ad-hoc fashion, without first reviewing them in the context of the process controls used to manage the introduction of change into the environment. These big gains in efficiency can lead to a completely new problem—inconsistencies in processes not designed to address the new dynamics that come with the virtual territory.

Lack of Process Consistency

Many IT organizations still "fly by the seat of their pants" when it comes to identifying and resolving problems. Using standard procedures and a methodology can help minimize risk and solve issues faster.

A *methodology* is a framework of processes and procedures used by those who work in a particular discipline. You can look at a methodology as a structured process defining the who, what, where, when, and why of one's operations, and the procedures to use when defining problems, solutions, and courses of action.

When employing a standard set of processes, it is important to ensure the framework you adopt adheres to accepted industry standards or best practices as well as takes into account the requirements of the business—ensuring continuity between expectations and the services delivered by the IT organization. Consistently using a repeatable and measurable set of practices allows an organization to quantify more accurately its progress to facilitate the adjustment of processes as necessary for improving future results. The most effective IT organizations build an element of self-examination into their service management strategy to ensure processes can be incrementally improved or modified to meet the changing needs of the business.

With IT's continually increased role in running successful business operations, having a structured and standard way to define IT operations aligned to the needs of the business is critical when meeting the expectations of business stakeholders. This alignment results in improved business relationships in which business units engage IT as a partner in developing and delivering innovations to drive business results.

The Bottom Line

Systems management can be intimidating when you consider the fact that the problems described to this point could happen even in an ostensibly "managed" environment. However, these examples just serve to illustrate that the very processes used to manage change in our environments must themselves be reviewed periodically and updated to accommodate changes in tools and technologies employed from the desktop to the datacenter.

Likewise, meeting the expectations of both the business and compliance regulation can seem an impossible task. At the end of the day, as technology evolves, so must IT's thinking, management tools, and processes. This makes it necessary to embrace continual improvement in those methodologies used to reduce risk while increasing agility in managing systems, keeping pace with the increasing velocity of change.

Systems Management Defined

Systems management is a journey, not a destination. That is to say, it is not something achieved at a point in time. Systems management encompasses all points in the IT service triangle, as displayed in Figure 1.1, including a set of processes and the tools and people that implement them. Although the role of each varies at different points within the IT service life cycle, the end goals do not change. How effectively these components are utilized determines the ultimate degree of success, which manifests itself in the outputs of productive employees producing and delivering quality products and services.

FIGURE 1.1   The IT service triangle includes people, process, and technology.

At a process level, systems management touches nearly *every* area of your IT operations. It can continually manage a computing resource, such as a client workstation, from the initial provisioning of the OS and hardware to end-of-life, when user settings are migrated to a new machine. The hardware and software inventory data collected by your systems management solution can play a key role in incident and problem management, by providing information that facilitates faster troubleshooting.

As IT operations grow in size, scope, complexity, and business impact, the common denominator at all phases is efficiency and automation, based on repeatable processes that conform to industry best practices. Achieving this necessitates capturing subject matter expertise and business context into a repeatable, partially or fully automated process. At the beginning of the service life cycle is the service provisioning, which from a systems management perspective means OS and software deployment. Automation at this phase can save hours or days of manual deployment effort in each iteration.

After resources are in production, the focus expands to include managing and maintaining systems, via ongoing activities IT uses to manage the health and configuration of systems. These activities may touch areas such as configuration management, by monitoring for unwanted changes in standard system and application configuration baselines.

As the service life cycle continues, systems management can affect release management in the form of software upgrades. Activities include software-metering activities, such as reclaiming unused licenses for reuse elsewhere. If you are able to automate these processes to a great degree, you achieve higher reliability and security, greater availability, better asset allocation, and a more predictable IT environment. These translate into business agility, more efficient, less expensive operations, with a greater ability to respond quickly to changing conditions.

Reducing costs and increasing productivity in IT Service Management are important because efficiency in operations frees up money for innovation and product improvements. Information security is also imperative because the price tag of compromised systems and data recovery from security exposures can be large, and those costs continue to rise each year.

Microsoft's Strategy for Service Management

Microsoft utilizes a multifaceted approach to IT Service Management. This strategy includes advancements in the following areas:

▶ Adoption of a model-based management strategy (a component of the Dynamic Systems Initiative, discussed in the next section, "Microsoft's Dynamic Systems Initiative") to implement synthetic transaction technology. Configuration Manager 2007 delivers Service Modeling Language–based models in its Desired Configuration Management (DCM) feature, allowing administrators to define intended configurations.

▶ Using an Infrastructure Optimization (IO) Model as a framework for aligning IT with business needs and as a standard for expressing an organization's maturity in service management. The "Optimizing Your Infrastructure" section of this chapter discusses the IO Model further. The IO Model describes your IT infrastructure in terms of cost, security risk, and operational agility.

▶ Supporting a standard Web Services specification for system management. WS-Management is a specification of a SOAP-based protocol, based on Web Services, used to manage servers, devices, and applications (SOAP stands for *Simple Object Access Protocol*). The intent is to provide a universal language that all types of devices can use to share data about themselves, which in turn makes them more easily managed. Support for WS-Management is included with Windows Vista and Windows Server 2008, and will ultimately be leveraged by multiple System Center components (beginning with Operations Manager 2007).

▶ Integrating infrastructure and management into OS and server products, by exposing services and interfaces that management applications can utilize.

▶ Building complete management solutions on this infrastructure, either through making them available in the operating system or by using management products such as Configuration Manager, Operations Manager, and other components of the System Center family.

▶ Continuing to drive down the complexity of Windows management by providing core management infrastructure and capabilities in the Windows platform itself, thus allowing business and management application developers to improve their infrastructures and capabilities. Microsoft believes that improving the manageability of solutions built on Windows Server System will be a key driver in shaping the future of Windows management.

Microsoft's Dynamic Systems Initiative

A large percentage of IT departments' budgets and resources typically focuses on mundane maintenance tasks such as applying software patches or monitoring the health of a network, without leaving the staff with the time or energy to focus on more exhilarating (and more productive) strategic initiatives.

The Dynamic Systems Initiative, or DSI, is a Microsoft and industry strategy intended to enhance the Windows platform, delivering a coordinated set of solutions that simplifies and automates how businesses design, deploy, and operate their distributed systems. Using DSI helps IT and developers create operationally aware platforms. By designing systems that are more manageable and automating operations, organizations can reduce costs and proactively address their priorities.

DSI is about building software that enables knowledge of an IT system to be created, modified, transferred, and operated on throughout the life cycle of that system. It is a commitment from Microsoft and its partners to help IT teams capture and use knowledge to design systems that are more manageable and to automate operations, which in turn reduce costs and give organizations additional time to focus proactively on what is most important. By innovating across applications, development tools, the platform, and management solutions, DSI will result in

▶ Increased productivity and reduced costs across all aspects of IT;

▶ Increased responsiveness to changing business needs;

► Reduced time and effort required to develop, deploy, and manage applications.

Microsoft is positioning DSI as the connector of the entire system and service life cycles.

Microsoft Product Integration

DSI focuses on automating datacenter operational jobs and reducing associated labor through self-managing systems. Here are several examples where Microsoft products and tools integrate with DSI:

► Configuration Manager employs model-based configuration baseline templates in its Desired Configuration Management feature to automate identification of undesired shifts in system configurations.

► Visual Studio is a model-based development tool that leverages SML, enabling operations managers and application architects to collaborate early in the development phase and ensure applications are modeled with operational requirements in mind.

► Windows Server Update Services (WSUS) enables greater and more efficient administrative control through modeling technology that enables downstream systems to construct accurate models representing their current state, available updates, and installed software.

NOTE

SDM and SML—What's the Difference?

Microsoft originally used the System Definition Model (SDM) as its standard schema with DSI. SDM was a proprietary specification put forward by Microsoft. The company later decided to implement SML, which is an industrywide published specification used in heterogeneous environments. Using SML helps DSI adoption by incorporating a standard that Microsoft's partners can understand and apply across mixed platforms. Service Modeling Language is discussed later in the section "The Role of Service Modeling Language in IT Operations."

DSI focuses on automating datacenter operations and reducing total cost of ownership (TCO) through self-managing systems. Can logic be implemented in management software so that the management software can identify system or application issues in real time and then dynamically take actions to mitigate the problem? Consider the scenario where, without operator intervention, a management system moves a virtual machine running a line-of-business application because the existing host is experiencing an extended spike in resource utilization. This is actually a reality today, delivered in the quick migration feature of Virtual Machine Manager 2008; DSI aims to extend this type of self-healing and self-management to other areas of operations.

In support of DSI, Microsoft has invested heavily in three major areas:

► **Systems designed for systems management**—Microsoft is delivering development and authoring tools—such as Visual Studio—that enable businesses to capture the knowledge of everyone from business users and project managers to the architects, developers, testers, and operations staff using models. By capturing and embedding this knowledge into the infrastructure, organizations can reduce support complexity and cost.

▶ **An operationally aware platform**—The core Windows operating system and its related technologies are critical when solving everyday operational and service challenges. This requires designing the operating system services for manageability. Additionally, the operating system and server products must provide rich instrumentation and hardware resource virtualization support.

▶ **Virtualized applications and server infrastructure**—Virtualization of servers and applications improves the agility of the organization by simplifying the effort involved in modifying, adding, or removing the resources a service utilizes in performing work.

NOTE

The Microsoft Suite for IT Operations

End-to-end automation could include update management, availability and performance monitoring, change and configuration management, and rich reporting services. Microsoft's System Center is a family of system management products and solutions that focuses on providing you with the knowledge and tools to manage your IT infrastructure. The objective of the System Center family is to create an integrated suite of systems management tools and technologies, thus helping to ease operations, reduce troubleshooting time, and improve planning capabilities.

The Importance of DSI

There are three architectural elements behind the DSI initiative:

▶ That developers have tools (such as Visual Studio) to design applications in a way that makes them easier for administrators to manage after those applications are in production

▶ That Microsoft products can be secured and updated in a uniform way

▶ That Microsoft server applications are optimized for management, to take advantage of Operations Manager 2007

DSI represents a departure from the traditional approach to systems management. DSI focuses on designing for operations from the application development stage, rather than a more customary operations perspective that concentrates on automating task-based processes. This strategy highlights the fact that Microsoft's Dynamic Systems Initiative is about building software that enables knowledge of an IT system to be created, modified, transferred, and used throughout the life cycle of a system. DSI's core principles of knowledge, models, and the life cycle are key in addressing the challenges of complexity and manageability faced by IT organizations. By capturing knowledge and incorporating health models, DSI can facilitate easier troubleshooting and maintenance, and thus lower TCO.

The Role of Service Modeling Language in IT Operations

A key underlying component of DSI is the XML-based specification called the Service Modeling Language (SML). SML is a standard developed by several leading information technology companies that defines a consistent way for infrastructure and application architects to define how applications, infrastructure, and services are modeled in a consistent way.

SML facilitates modeling systems from a development, deployment, and support perspective with modular, reusable building blocks that eliminate the need to reinvent the wheel when describing and defining a new service. The end result is systems that are easier to develop, implement, manage, and maintain, resulting in reduced TCO to the organization. SML is a core technology that will continue to play a prominent role in future products developed to support the ongoing objectives of DSI.

NOTE

SML Resources on the Web

For more information on Service Modeling Language, view the latest draft of the SML standard at http://www.w3.org/TR/sml/. For additional technical information on SML from Microsoft, see http://technet.microsoft.com/en-us/library/bb725986.aspx.

IT Infrastructure Library (ITIL) and Microsoft Operations Framework (MOF)

ITIL is widely accepted as an international standard of best practices for operations management, and Microsoft has used ITIL v3 as the basis for Microsoft Operations Framework (MOF) v4, the current version of its own operations framework. Warning: Fasten your seatbelt, because this is where the fun really begins!

What Is ITIL?

As part of Microsoft's management approach, the company relied on an international standards-setting body as its basis for developing an operational framework. The British Office of Government Commerce (OGC) provides best-practices advice and guidance on using Information Technology in service management and operations. The OGC also publishes the IT Infrastructure Library, known as ITIL.

ITIL provides a cohesive set of best practices for IT Service Management (ITSM). These best practices include a series of books giving direction and guidance on provisioning quality IT services and facilities needed to support Information Technology. The documents are maintained by the OGC and supported by publications, qualifications, and an international users group.

Started in the 1980s, ITIL is under constant development by a consortium of industry IT leaders. The ITIL covers a number of areas and is primarily focused on ITSM; its IT Infrastructure Library is considered to be the most consistent and comprehensive documentation of best practices for IT Service Management worldwide.

ITSM is a business-driven, customer-centric approach to managing Information Technology. It specifically addresses the strategic business value generated by IT and the need to deliver high-quality IT services to one's business organization. ITSM itself has two main components:

▶ Service support

▶ Service delivery

A New Version of ITIL

ITIL has recently undergone a refresh, and the core books for version 3 (ITIL v3) were published on June 30, 2007. The major difference between v3 and its v2 predecessor is that v3 has adopted an integrated service life cycle approach to IT Service Management, as opposed to organizing itself around the concepts of IT service delivery and support.

ITIL v2 was a more targeted product, explicitly designed to bridge the gap between technology and business, with a strong process focus on effective service support and delivery. The v3 documents recognize the new service management challenges brought about by advancements in technology, such as virtualization and outsourcing, as well as emerging challenges for service providers.

The framework has been repositioned from its previous emphasis on the process life cycle and alignment of IT to an emphasis on "the business" (that is, managing the life cycle of the services provided by IT and the importance of creating business value rather than just the execution of processes). As an example, it is a publicly stated aim of the refresh to include more references to return on investment (ROI).

There are five core volumes of ITIL v3:

▶ **Service Strategy**—This volume identifies market opportunities for which services could be developed to meet a requirement on the part of internal or external customers. Key areas here are Service Portfolio Management and Financial Management.

▶ **Service Design**—This volume focuses on the activities that take place to develop the strategy into a design document that addresses all aspects of the proposed service and the processes intended to support it. Key areas of this volume are Availability Management, Capacity Management, Continuity Management, and Security Management.

▶ **Service Transition**—This volume centers on implementing the output of service design activities and creating a production service (or modifying an existing service). There is some overlap between Service Transition and Service Operation, the next volume. Key areas of the Service Transition volume are Change Management, Release Management, Configuration Management, and Service Knowledge Management.

▶ **Service Operation**—This volume involves the activities required to operate the services and maintain their functionality as defined in Service Level Agreements (SLAs) with one's customers. Key areas here are Incident Management, Problem Management, and Request Fulfillment.

> ▶ **Continual Service Improvement**—This volume focuses on the ability to deliver continual improvement to the quality of the services that the IT organization delivers to the business. Key areas include Service Reporting, Service Measurement, and Service Level Management.
>
> ITIL v3 really is a repackaging of what was in v2, with an additional layer of abstraction.

Philosophically speaking, ITSM focuses on the customer's perspective of IT's contribution to the business, which is analogous to the objectives of other frameworks in terms of their consideration of alignment of IT service support and delivery with business goals in mind.

Although ITIL describes the what, when, and why of IT operations, it stops short of describing how a specific activity should be carried out. A driving force behind its development was the recognition that organizations are increasingly dependent on IT for satisfying their corporate objectives relating to both internal and external customers, which increases the requirement for high-quality IT services. Many large IT organizations realize that the road to a customer-centric service organization runs along an ITIL framework.

ITIL also specifies keeping measurements or metrics to assess performance over time. Measurements can include a variety of statistics, such as the number and severity of service outages, along with the amount of time it takes to restore service. These metrics can be used to quantify to management how well IT is performing. This information can be particularly useful for justifying resources during the next budget process!

What Is MOF?

ITIL is generally accepted as the "best practices" for the industry. Being technology-agnostic, it is a foundation that can be adopted and adapted to meet the specific needs of various IT organizations. Although Microsoft chose to adopt ITIL as a standard for its own IT operations for its *descriptive* guidance, Microsoft designed MOF to provide *prescriptive* guidance for effective design, implementation, and support of Microsoft technologies.

MOF is a set of publications providing both descriptive (what to do, when and why) and prescriptive (how to do) guidance on IT Service Management. The key focus in developing MOF was providing a framework specifically geared toward managing Microsoft technologies. Microsoft created the first version of the MOF in 1999. The latest iteration of MOF (version 4) is designed to further

- ▶ Update MOF to include the full end-to-end IT service life cycle;

- ▶ Let IT governance serve as the foundation of the life cycle;

- ▶ Provide useful, easily consumable best practice–based guidance;

- ▶ Simplify and consolidate service management functions (SMFs), emphasizing workflows, decisions, outcomes, and roles.

MOF is designed to complement Microsoft's previously existing Microsoft Solutions Framework (MSF), which provides guidance for application development solutions.

Together, the combined frameworks provide guidance throughout the IT life cycle, as shown in Figure 1.2.

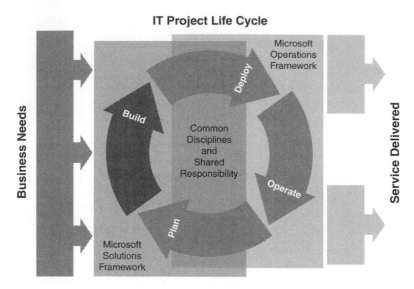

FIGURE 1.2   The IT life cycle and Microsoft frameworks

TIP

Using MSF for ConfigMgr Deployment

Microsoft uses MOF to describe IT operations and uses Configuration Manager as a tool to put that framework into practice. However, Configuration Manager 2007 is also an application and, as such, is best deployed using a disciplined approach. Although MSF is geared toward application development, it can be adapted to support infrastructure solution design and deployment, as discussed in Chapter 4, "Configuration Manager Solution Design."

At its core, the MOF is a collection of best practices, principles, and models. It provides direction to achieve reliability, availability, supportability, and manageability of mission-critical production systems, focusing on solutions and services using Microsoft products and technologies. MOF extends ITIL by including guidance and best practices derived from the experience of Microsoft's internal operations groups, partners, and customers worldwide. MOF aligns with and builds on the IT Service Management practices documented within ITIL, thus enhancing the supportability built on Microsoft's products and technologies.

MOF uses a process model that describes Microsoft's approach to IT operations and the service management life cycle. The model organizes the core ITIL processes of service support and service delivery, and it includes additional MOF processes in the four quadrants of the MOF process model, as illustrated in Figure 1.3.

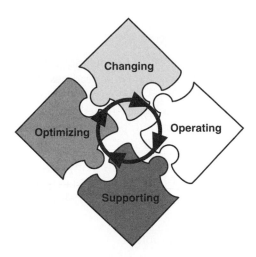

FIGURE 1.3   The MOF process model

It is important to note that the activities pictured in the quadrants illustrated in Figure 1.3 are not necessarily sequential. These activities can occur simultaneously within an IT organization. Each quadrant has a specific focus and tasks, and within each quadrant are policies, procedures, standards, and best practices that support specific operations management–focused tasks.

Configuration Manager 2007 can be employed to support operations management tasks in different quadrants of the MOF Process Model. Let's look briefly at each of these quadrants and see how one can use ConfigMgr to support MOF:

▶ **Changing**—This quadrant represents instances where new service solutions, technologies, systems, applications, hardware, and processes have been introduced.

   The software and OS deployment features of ConfigMgr can be used to automate many activities in the Changing quadrant.

▶ **Operating**—This quadrant concentrates on performing day-to-day tasks efficiently and effectively.

   ConfigMgr includes many operational tasks that you can initiate from the Configuration Manager console, or that can be automated completely. These are available through various product components, such as update management and software deployment features. The Network Access Protection feature can be utilized to verify clients connecting to the network meet certain corporate criteria, such as antivirus software signatures, before being granted full access to resources.

▶ **Supporting**—This quadrant represents the resolution of incidents, problems, and inquiries, preferably in a timely manner.

Using the Desired Configuration Management feature of ConfigMgr in conjunction with software deployment, widespread shifts in system configurations can be identified and reversed with a minimum of effort.

▶ **Optimizing**—This quadrant focuses on minimizing costs while optimizing performance, capacity, and availability in the delivery of IT services.

ConfigMgr reporting delivers in a number of functional areas of IT operations. For example, out of the box reports provide instant insight into hardware readiness for operating system deployment to help minimize the hands-on aspects of hardware assessment in upgrade planning. In conjunction with the software metering and asset intelligence features of Configuration Manager, reports can provide insight into unused software licenses that can be reclaimed for use elsewhere.

Service Level Agreements and Operating Level Agreements (OLAs) are tools many organizations use in defining accepted levels of operation and ability. Configuration Manager includes the ability to schedule software and update deployment, as well as to define maintenance windows in support of SLAs and OLAs.

Additional information regarding the MOF Process Model is available at http://go.microsoft.com/fwlink/?LinkId=50015.

MOF Does Not Replace ITIL

Microsoft believes that ITIL is the leading body of knowledge of best practices; for that reason, it uses ITIL as the foundation for MOF. Rather than replacing ITIL, MOF complements it and is similar to ITIL in several ways:

▶ MOF (with MSF) spans the entire IT life cycle.

▶ Both MOF and ITIL are based on best practices for IT management, drawing on the expertise of practitioners worldwide.

▶ The MOF body of knowledge is applicable across the business community—from small businesses to large enterprises. MOF also is not limited only to those using the Microsoft platform in a homogenous environment.

▶ As is the case with ITIL, MOF has expanded to be more than just a documentation set. In fact, MOF is now intertwined with another System Center component, Operations Manager 2007!

Additionally, Microsoft and its partners provide a variety of resources to support MOF principles and guidance, including self-assessments, IT management tools that incorporate MOF terminology and features, training programs and certification, and consulting services.

Service Management Mastery: ISO 20000

You can think of ITIL and ITSM as providing a framework for IT to rethink the ways in which it contributes to and aligns with the business. ISO 20000, which is the first international standard for IT Service Management, institutionalizes these processes. ISO 20000 helps companies to align IT services and business strategy, to create a formal framework for continual service improvement, and provides benchmarks for comparison to best practices.

Published in December 2005, ISO 20000 was developed to reflect the best-practice guidance contained within ITIL. The standard also supports other IT Service Management frameworks and approaches, including MOF, Capability Maturity Model Integration (CMMi) and Six Sigma. ISO 20000 consists of two major areas:

▶ Part 1 promotes adopting an integrated process approach to deliver managed services effectively that meets business and customer requirements.

▶ Part 2 is a "code of practice" describing the best practices for service management within the scope of ISO 20000-1.

These two areas—what to do and how to do it—have similarities to the approach taken by the other standards, including MOF.

ISO 20000 goes beyond ITIL, MOF, Six Sigma, and other frameworks in providing organizational or corporate certification for organizations that effectively adopt and implement the ISO 20000 code of practice.

TIP

About CMMi and Six Sigma

CMMi is a process-improvement approach that provides organizations with the essential elements of effective processes. It can be used to guide process improvement—across a project, a division, or an entire organization—thus helping to integrate traditionally separate organizational functions, set process improvement goals and priorities, provide guidance for quality processes, and provide a point of reference for appraising current processes.

Six Sigma is a business management strategy, originally developed by Motorola, which seeks to identify and remove the causes of defects and errors in manufacturing and business processes.

Optimizing Your Infrastructure

According to Microsoft, analysts estimate that over 70% of the typical IT budget is spent on infrastructure—managing servers, operating systems, storage, and networking. Add to that the challenge of refreshing and managing desktop and mobile devices, and there's not much left over for anything else. Microsoft describes an Infrastructure Optimization Model that categorizes the state of one's IT infrastructure, describing the impacts on cost, security risks, and the ability to respond to changes. Using the model shown in Figure 1.4, you can identify where your organization is, and where you want to be:

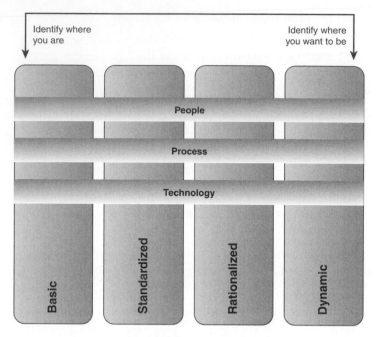

FIGURE 1.4   The Infrastructure Optimization Model

- ▶ **Basic**—Reactionary, with much time spent fighting fires
- ▶ **Standardized**—Gaining control
- ▶ **Rationalized**—Enabling the business
- ▶ **Dynamic**—Being a strategic asset

Although most organizations are somewhere between the basic and standardized levels in this model, typically one would prefer to be a strategic asset rather than fighting fires. Once you know where you are in the model, you can use best practices from ITIL and guidance from MOF to develop a plan to progress to a higher level. The IO Model describes the technologies and steps organizations can take to move forward, whereas the MOF explains the people and processes required to improve that infrastructure. Similar to ITSM, the IO Model is a combination of people, processes, and technology.

More information about Infrastructure Optimization is available at http://www.microsoft.com/technet/infrastructure.

About the IO Model

Not all IT shops will want or need to be dynamic. Some will choose, for all the right business reasons, to be less than dynamic! The IO Model includes a three-part goal:

- ▶ Communicate that there are levels.
- ▶ Target the desired levels.

    ▶ Provide reference on how to get to the desired levels.

Realize that infrastructure optimization can be by application or by function, rather than a single ranking for the entire IT department.

Items that factor into an IT organization's adoption of the IO model include cost, ability, and whether the organization fits into the business model as a cost center versus being an asset, along with a commitment to move from being reactive to proactive.

From Fighting Fires to Gaining Control

At the Basic level, your infrastructure is hard to control and expensive to manage. Processes are manual, IT policies and standards are either nonexistent or not enforced, and you don't have the tools and resources (or time and energy) to determine the overall health of your applications and IT services. Not only are your desktop and server management costs out of control, but you are in reactive mode when it comes to security threats. In addition, you tend to use manual rather than automated methods for applying software deployments and patches. To try to put a bit of humor into this, you could say that computer management has you all tied up, like the system administrator shown in Figure 1.5.

FIGURE 1.5   The Basic level can leave you feeling tied up in knots.

Does this sound familiar? If you can gain control of your environment, you may be more effective at work! Here are some steps to consider:

    ▶ Develop standards, policies, and controls.

- ▶ Alleviate security risks by developing a security approach throughout your IT organization.

- ▶ Adopt best practices, such as those found in ITIL, and operational guidance found in MOF.

- ▶ Build IT to become a strategic asset.

If you can achieve operational nirvana, this will go a long way toward your job satisfaction and IT becoming a constructive part of your business.

From Gaining Control to Enabling the Business

A Standardized infrastructure introduces control by using standards and policies to manage desktops and servers. These standards control how you introduce machines into your network. As an example, using Directory Services will manage resources, security policies, and access to resources. Shops in a Standardized state realize the value of basic standards and some policies, but still tend to be reactive. Although you now have a managed IT infrastructure and are inventorying your hardware and software assets and starting to manage licenses, your patches, software deployments, and desktop services are not yet automated. Security-wise, the perimeter is now under control, although internal security may still be a bit loose.

To move from a Standardized state to the Rationalized level, you will need to gain more control over your infrastructure and implement proactive policies and procedures. You might also begin to look at implementing service management. At this stage, IT can also move more toward becoming a business asset and ally, rather than a burden.

From Enabling the Business to Becoming a Strategic Asset

At the Rationalized level, you have achieved firm control of desktop and service management costs. Processes and policies are in place and beginning to play a large role in supporting and expanding the business. Security is now proactive, and you are responding to threats and challenges in a rapid and controlled manner.

Using technologies such as lite-touch and zero-touch operating system deployment helps you to minimize costs, deployment time, and technical challenges for system rollouts. Because your inventory is now under control, you have minimized the number of images to manage, and desktop management is now largely automated. You also are purchasing only the software licenses and new computers the business requires, giving you a handle on costs. Security is now proactive with policies and control in place for desktops, servers, firewalls, and extranets.

Mission Accomplished: IT as a Strategic Asset

At the Dynamic level, your infrastructure is helping run the business efficiently and stay ahead of competitors. Your costs are now fully controlled. You have also achieved integration between users and data, desktops and servers, and the different departments and functions throughout your organization.

Your Information Technology processes are automated and often incorporated into the technology itself, allowing IT to be aligned and managed according to business needs.

New technology investments are able to yield specific, rapid, and measurable business benefits. Measurement is good—it helps you justify the next round of investments!

Using self-provisioning software and quarantine-like systems to ensure patch management and compliance with security policies allows you to automate your processes, which in turn improves reliability, lowers costs, and increases your service levels.

According to IDC research, very few organizations achieve the Dynamic level of the Infrastructure Optimization Model—due to the lack of availability of a single toolset from a single vendor to meet all requirements. Through execution on its vision in DSI, Microsoft aims to change this. To read more on this study, visit http://download. microsoft.com/download/a/4/4/a4474b0c-57d8-41a2-afe6-32037fa93ea6/IDC_ windesktop_IO_whitepaper.pdf.

Relating the IO Model to Desktop Management

The June 2008 issue of *Redmond Magazine* includes an article by Greg Shields titled "5 Rules for Managing User Desktops." Greg makes the following points:

▶ If you leave any component of desktop management to the user, you are no longer managing that machine—abdicating responsibility means you are effectively rescinding proactive control over that environment you are supposed to control and manage.

▶ Never interrupt the user's workflow—only distribute software and patches when users are logged out of their workstations.

▶ Never ask for the user's opinion when it comes to desktop management—giving users choices is often giving them enough rope to hang themselves.

▶ Computing equipment belongs to the business, not IT and not the user.

▶ Moving desktop management from reactive to proactive can initially involve quite a bit of work—jumping from firefighting to measured and calculated change requires a systems management toolset to help with automating tasks, and you will need the knowledge and experience to implement broad changes with minimal impact.

You can read Greg's article in full at http://redmondmag.com/columns/article.asp?editorialsid=2635.

Bridging the Systems Management Gap

System Center Configuration Manager 2007 is Microsoft's software platform for addressing systems management issues. It is a key component in Microsoft's management strategy and System Center that can be utilized to bridge many of the gaps in service support and delivery. Configuration Manager 2007 was designed around four key themes:

▶ **Security**—ConfigMgr delivers numerous security enhancements over its predecessor, such as the mutual authentication of native mode and Network Access Protection (NAP), which in conjunction with the NAP feature available with Windows 2008 protects assets connecting to the network by enforcing compliance with system health requirements such as antivirus version.

▶ **Simplicity**—ConfigMgr delivers a simplified user interface with fewer top-level icons, organized in a way that makes resources easier to locate. Investments in simplicity have been made throughout the user interface (UI) in several features, such as the simplified wizard-based UI and common rule templates in DCM 2.0. Such improvements are also evident in the areas of software deployment and metering, as well as OS deployment. Improvements in branch office support also serve to not only simplify management of the branch office, but also reduce ConfigMgr infrastructure costs in these scenarios.

▶ **Manageability**—Some of the most important improvements in ConfigMgr come in the form of manageability improvements in common "fringe" scenarios where bandwidth or connectivity are in short supply. Offline OS and driver packages can now be created to support OS deployment in scenarios with no or low-bandwidth connectivity. Native Wake On LAN support makes patching workstation after hours a more hands-off scenario. Internet-Based Client Management (ICBM) is now a reality, providing management for remote clients not connected to the corporate network. Finally, the update management feature of ConfigMgr supports scans the WSUS Server as opposed to distributing a local copy of the catalog to each client.

▶ **Operating system deployment**—Systems Management Server (SMS) 2003's OS deployment feature (OSD) has been integrated into the product, and Microsoft investments in this area have made the feature truly enterprise-ready. For instance, OSD now supports both client and server OS deployment from the same interface, eliminating the need for a separate tool for server deployment.

The driver catalog feature available with OS deployment eliminates the need for a separate OS image for each driver set. Likewise, the task sequencer accommodates configuration of software deployment in conjunction with OS deployment through a wizard more easily than ever before.

Additionally, OEM and offline scenarios are now fully supported through OS deployment using removable media.

Central Control in the Distributed Enterprise

While centralized management and visibility are benefits of the platform, ConfigMgr 2007 employs a distributed architecture that delivers an agent-based solution. This brings numerous advantages:

▶ Once client policy is passed to the ConfigMgr client by the management point, data collection is managed locally on each managed computer, which distributes the load of collecting and handling information. This type of distributed management offers a clear scalability advantage, in that the load on the ConfigMgr server roles is greatly reduced. From the perspective of network load, because all the script execution,

Windows Management Instrumentation (WMI) calls, and such are local to the client, network traffic is reduced as well.

Data is then passed from the ConfigMgr client back to the management point and is ultimately inserted into the site database, and can then be viewed through the ConfigMgr console.

▶ A distributed model also enables fault tolerance and flexibility in the event of interruptions in network connectivity. If the network is unavailable, the local client agents still collect information. This model also reduces the impact of data collection on the network by forwarding only information that needs forwarding.

▶ With a distributed server topology that allows clients to connect to the ConfigMgr server in their local site, clients can access resources no matter where they may roam. This model can reduce response time and improve compliance in a large enterprise, where a traveling client might otherwise attempt to pull software across a slow wide area network (WAN) link, or even require manual intervention to receive needed software applications or updates.

The functionality implemented at the ConfigMgr client is determined by the client agents that are enabled for that client. There are 10 client agents, each of which delivers a subset of ConfigMgr functionality. The client agents, displayed in Figure 1.6, include the following:

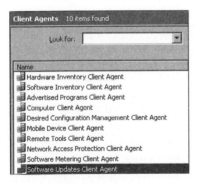

FIGURE 1.6   Client agents available in the ConfigMgr Setup Wizard

▶ Hardware Inventory

▶ Software Inventory

▶ Advertised Programs

▶ Computer

- ▶ Desired Configuration Management

- ▶ Mobile Device

- ▶ Remote Tools

- ▶ Network Access Protection

- ▶ Software Metering

- ▶ Software Updates

Data is forwarded from the client to the ConfigMgr site server, which inserts data into the ConfigMgr database. From here, data is available for use in a variety of reporting and filtering capacities, allowing granular customization in terms of how data is presented to administrators in the Configuration Manager console.

Automation and Control

In an environment with hundreds or even thousands of client and server systems, automating common software provisioning activities becomes a critical component to business agility. Productivity suffers when resources cannot be deployed in a timely manner with a consistent and predictable configuration. Once resources are deployed, ensuring systems are maintained with a consistent and secure configuration can be not only of operational importance, but of legal importance as well. ConfigMgr has several features to address the layers of process automation required to provision and maintain systems in a distributed enterprise. The following sections peel back the layers to explore common issues in each phase and examine how ConfigMgr 2007 addresses them.

Software Deployment

One process frequently automated in large IT environments is software deployment. Software deployment can be a time-consuming process, and automating the installation or upgrade of applications such as the Microsoft Office suite can be a huge timesaver. What is perhaps most impressive about the software deployment capabilities of ConfigMgr is the flexibility and control the administrator has in determining what software to deploy, to whom it is deployed, and how it is presented. The software deployment capabilities of ConfigMgr include a range of options, such as the ability to advertise a software package for installation at the user's option and to assign and deploy by a target deadline. The feature handles software upgrades as easily as new deployments, making that Office 2007 upgrade much less laborious.

Let's take software deployment a step further. Have you ever asked yourself, "Who is actually using application X among the users for whom it is installed?" Well, by using the software metering functionality in ConfigMgr, it is possible to report on instances of a particular application that have not been used in a certain period of time. This allows administrators to reclaim unused licenses for reuse elsewhere, saving the organization money on software licensing.

In ConfigMgr 2007 Release 2 (R2), software deployment takes another leap forward with adding support for deployment of virtual applications (using Microsoft Application

Virtualization version 4.5) to ConfigMgr clients from the ConfigMgr distribution points. You can read a detailed accounting of software deployment in ConfigMgr in Chapter 14, "Distributing Packages."

Operating System Deployment

If manually deploying applications is painful from a time perspective, operating system deployment would be excruciating. You can move a step beyond software deployment to operating system deployment in ConfigMgr, which allows configuring of the automated deployment for both the client and server OS using the same interface in the Configuration Manager console.

One of the most common areas of complexity in OS deployment is device drivers. In the past, drivers have forced administrators to maintain multiple OS images, each image containing the drivers for a particular system manufacturer and model. OS deployment in ConfigMgr 2007 introduces a new feature called *driver catalogs*. Using driver catalogs lets you maintain a single OS image. Here's how it works: A scan of driver catalogs is performed at runtime to identify and extract the appropriate drivers for a target system. This allows the teams responsible for desktop and server deployment to maintain a single golden OS image along with multiple driver catalogs for the various hardware manufacturers and systems models. There are some limitations here, which are discussed in Chapter 19, "Operating System Deployment."

Task sequences take automation of OS and software deployment yet one step further, allowing administrators, through a relatively simple wizard interface, to define a sequence of actions, incorporating both OS and software deployment activities into an ordered sequence of events. This enables nearly full automation of the resource-provisioning process.

While on the topic, the value of task sequences in advertisements is often overlooked. Task sequences can be deployed as advertisements, allowing administrators to control the order of software distribution and reboot handling, and as diagnostic actions to analyze and respond to those systems with configurations out of compliance with corporate standards.

A detailed walkthrough of operating system deployment in ConfigMgr is included in Chapter 19.

Compliance and Enforcement

Once you automate the provisioning process, what can be done to ensure system configurations remain consistent with corporate standards throughout the environment? With the proliferation of legislated regulatory requirements, ensuring configurations meet a certain standard is critical. The fines levied against an organization for noncompliance and breaching these requirements when sensitive client data is involved can be quite costly. This is an area that cannot be addressed by simple hardware and software inventory, making visibility in this area historically quite challenging. This is where the new Desired Configuration Management feature of ConfigMgr comes into play.

DCM allows administrators to define a list of desired settings (called *configuration items*) into a group of desired settings for a particular set of target systems. This is known as a *configuration baseline.* To facilitate faster adoption, Microsoft provides predefined configuration baselines (templates, so to speak) called *configuration packs,* available as free downloads from Microsoft's website at http://technet.microsoft.com/en-us/configmgr/cc462788.aspx. Microsoft provides configuration packs as a starting point to help organizations evaluate Microsoft server applications against Microsoft best practices or regulatory compliance requirements, such as Sarbanes-Oxley or HIPAA.

With DCM reports (available by default), administrators can identify systems that have "drifted" out of compliance and take corrective action. Although there is no automated enforcement functionality in this version of DCM, noncompliant systems can be dynamically grouped in a collection and then targeted for software deployment, providing some measure of automation in bringing systems back into compliance.

You can read more about Desired Configuration Management in ConfigMgr in Chapter 16, "Desired Configuration Management."

Securing Systems

The update management and network access protection features in ConfigMgr provide a platform for securing clients more effectively than ever before. The following sections discuss these capabilities.

Update Management

Microsoft overhauled the entire patch management process for ConfigMgr 2007, and the product uses WSUS 3.0 as its base technology for patch distribution to clients. However, ConfigMgr extends native WSUS capabilities, grouping clients based on user-defined criteria (in collections) and updates, as well as scheduling update packages of desired patches, providing more control than with WSUS alone. Using the maintenance window feature of ConfigMgr, you can define a window of time during which a particular group of clients should receive updates, thus ensuring the application of updates does not interrupt normal business. Microsoft recommends a four-phase patch management process to ensure your environment is appropriately secured (see Figure 1.7). You can read more about update management in ConfigMgr in Chapter 15, "Patch Management."

Internet Client Management

Many organizations have client machines, such as those belonging to sales staff working remotely, that rarely access the corporate network and make timely application of updates to the OS and applications very challenging. Using the Internet-Based Client Management feature in ConfigMgr in conjunction with an Internet-based management point, you can still deliver updates to clients that never attach to the corporate network. This ensures that clients outside the intranet on the local area network maintain patch levels similar to clients inside the network.

However, when Internet-based clients do attach to the trusted network, updates can resume seamlessly on the intranet. This intelligent roaming capability works in both directions, allowing clients to move seamlessly between Internet and intranet connectivity.

You can read more on IBCM in ConfigMgr in Chapter 6, "Architecture Design Planning."

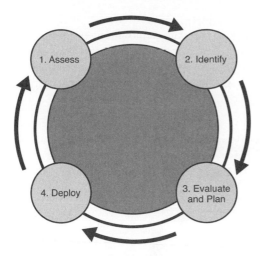

FIGURE 1.7   Microsoft's recommended four-phase update management process

Securing Remote Access Clients

As the saying goes, "one rotten apple can spoil the barrel." To that effect, clients connecting to the corporate network with computers that are not appropriately patched or perhaps not running antivirus software are always a concern. When integrated with the Network Access Protection functionality delivered in Windows Server 2008, the NAP feature in ConfigMgr can help IT administrators dynamically control the access of clients that do not meet corporate standards for patch levels, in addition to antivirus and other standard configurations.

NAP allows network administrators to define granular levels of network access based on who a client is, the groups to which the client belongs, and the degree to which that client is compliant with corporate governance policy. Here's how it works: If a client is not compliant, NAP provides a policy mechanism to compare client settings to corporate standard settings, and then automatically restricts the noncompliant client to a quarantine network where resources can be used to bring the client back into compliance, thus dynamically increasing its level of network access as the required configuration criteria are met.

Chapter 15 provides additional information about Network Access Protection.

Visibility

You cannot use information you cannot see. The ability to view the state and status of both the resources and processes in your environment is a critical component of IT operations because it helps to understand where attention is needed. One of the most powerful aspects of the Configuration Manager console (a Microsoft Management Console [MMC] 3.0 application) in ConfigMgr 2007 is the visibility it brings to all status of software, OS and update deployment, and inventory and configuration compliance of client agents deployed in the environment.

Home Pages

The *home pages* capability provides at-a-glance status of software deployment progress, application of patches, and so on. Each of the root nodes in the Configuration Manager console provides a home page displaying the status of activity related to that particular feature. For example, the Software Updates home page, shown in Figure 1.8, displays the progress of patch distribution.

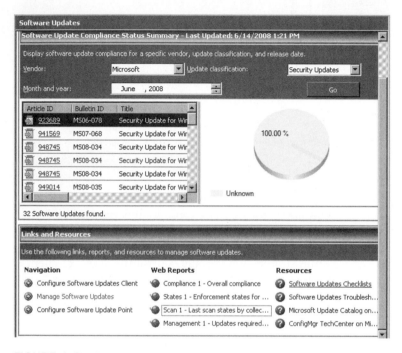

FIGURE 1.8   Software Updates home page

Search Folders

If you like having your surroundings organized, you will love search folders. Search folders provide a way to organize collections of similar objects in your ConfigMgr environment, such as packages, advertisements, boot images, OS installation packages, task sequences, driver packages, software metering, reports, configuration baselines, and configuration items. You can create custom search folders based on your own criteria. This makes it really easy to keep track of the resources deployed in your environment in a way that is meaningful to you.

Queries

Queries are a convenient way to facilitate ad-hoc retrieval of data stored in the ConfigMgr SQL Server database. Queries can be constructed using a wizard interface, which allows selection of criteria through the UI, thus minimizing the need for knowledge of the WMI Query Language (WQL) in which these queries are written. However, if you are familiar with WQL or Transact SQL (T-SQL), you can easily access the query directly to make changes to the query syntax and criterion.

For example, you could create a query that retrieves a list of all computers with hard drives containing less than 2GB of free space. This sort of logic could be used in determining client readiness for an upgrade to a new version of Microsoft Office.

Reporting in Configuration Manager

The default set of reports in ConfigMgr is huge. The product comes with more than 300 reports in 20 categories, out of the box (see Figure 1.9). The Reporting area also provides a filtering feature to display only the reports that match your criteria, making the reports you care about easier to locate. Reports are categorized by feature, with reporting categories including Asset Management, Desired Configuration Management, Hardware, Network Access Protection, Software Updates, and several others. Each category is then organized further into subcategories. For example, the Software Updates category includes approximately 40 reports in six subcategories:

▶ Compliance

▶ Deployment Management

▶ Deployment States

▶ Scan

▶ Troubleshooting

▶ Distribution Status for SMS 2003 Clients

Authoring new reports is quite easy, as is repurposing existing reports. You can actually clone an existing report, allowing you to make the desired changes to suit your particular situation without affecting the original report. You can even import and export reports between sites, allowing ConfigMgr administrators to easily share their customizations with other administrators of other sites.

You can view reports either through the Configuration Manager console or through the Configuration Manager Report Viewer.

NOTE

ConfigMgr Reporting and SRS

ConfigMgr reporting is fully integrated into the ConfigMgr console, and incorporates the Report Viewer that was present in SMS 2003. Reports are accessed using the ConfigMgr user interface and rendered in Internet Explorer.

However, in ConfigMgr 2007 R2, administrators have the option of moving from the existing reporting environment to SQL Reporting Services as the reporting engine. This requires converting existing reports, but once this is completed, the reports function as they did before and can continue to be administered through the ConfigMgr console. The conversion process is discussed in Chapter 18, "Reporting."

The Dashboard feature provides additional flexibility in that it allows administrators to group multiple default or custom reports into a single view. This can be used for a number of common scenarios, such as grouping reports that display a certain type of information (for example, hardware and software inventory). This is also very handy for grouping process-related reports, such as the current evaluation and installation state of software and updates. You could further filter your data by site, using a dashboard-per-site strategy to display the status of these processes at individual ConfigMgr sites, each in its own dashboard. All reports are accessible and searchable through the Reports home page, displayed in Figure 1.9.

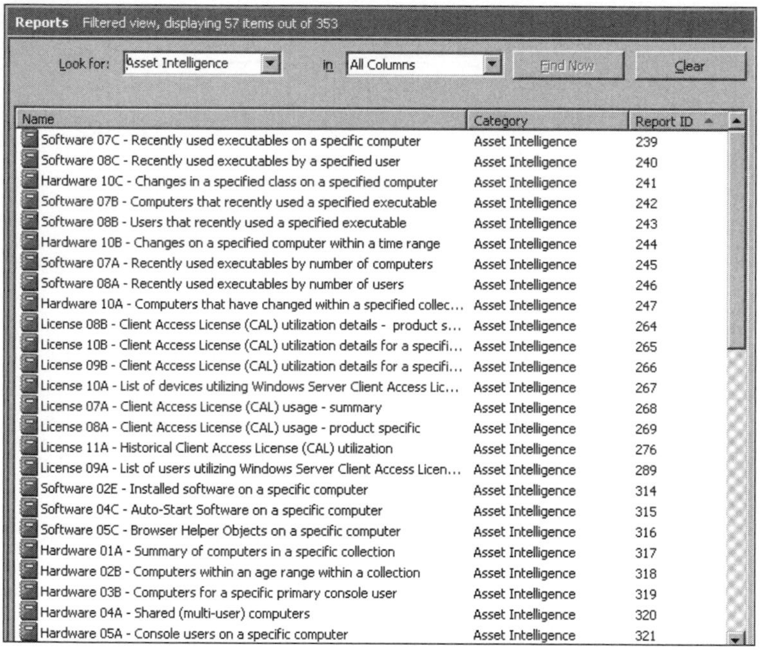

FIGURE 1.9   The ConfigMgr Reports home page

You can read more about the reporting capabilities in Configuration Manager 2007 in detail in Chapter 18.

Benefits

Configuration Manager is quite flexible in that it also allows deployment in an incremental fashion. You can begin by managing a specific group of servers or a department. Once you are comfortable with the management platform and understand its features and how those work, you can then deploy to the rest of your organization.

With ConfigMgr as the core component of your systems management toolset handling your systems management objectives, you can take comfort in knowing the tools are available to meet the high expectations of business stakeholders. It plays the role of a trusted partner, helping your IT organization improve service delivery and build a better relationship with the business, while working smarter, not harder.

Overview of Microsoft System Center

Beginning with SMS 2003, Configuration Manager has been a component of Microsoft's System Center strategy. System Center is the brand name for Microsoft's product suite focused on IT service delivery, support, and management. As time passes (and Microsoft's management strategy progresses), expect new products and components added over time. System Center is not a single product; the name represents a suite of products designed to address all major aspects of IT service support and delivery.

As part of a multiyear strategy, System Center is being released in "waves." The first wave included SMS 2003, MOM 2005, and System Center Data Protection Manager 2006. In 2006, additions included System Center Reporting Manager 2006 and System Center Capacity Planner 2006. The second wave includes Operations Manager 2007, Configuration Manager 2007, System Center Essentials 2007, System Center Service Manager, Virtual Machine Manager, and new releases of Data Protection Manager and System Center Capacity Planner. Presentations at popular Microsoft conferences in 2008 included discussions of a third wave, expected to begin around 2010-2011.

Microsoft System Center products share the following DSI-based characteristics:

- ▶ Ease of use and deployment
- ▶ Based on industry and customer knowledge
- ▶ Scalability (from the mid-market to the large enterprise)

Reporting in System Center

The data gathered by Configuration Manager 2007 is collected in a self-maintaining SQL Server database and comes with numerous reports viewable using the Configuration Manager console. ConfigMgr delivers more than 300 reports out of the box for categories including asset intelligence, agent health and status, hardware and software inventory, and several others. Using the native functionality in SQL Reporting Services (SRS) in ConfigMgr 2007 R2, reports can also be exported to a variety of formats, including a Report Server file share, web archive format, Excel, and PDF. You can configure ConfigMgr to schedule and email reports, enabling users to open these reports without accessing the Configuration Manager console.

Together with the reporting available in Operations Manager 2007, administrators will find a very complete picture of present system configuration and health, as well as a detailed history of changes in these characteristics over time.

Ultimately, the integrated reporting feature for System Center is moving under the to-be-released System Center Service Manager product and then will no longer be a separate product.

Operations Management

Microsoft rearchitected MOM 2005 to create System Center Operations Manager 2007, its operations management solution for service-oriented monitoring. Currently in its third release, the product is completely rewritten. The design pillars in Operations Manager (OpsMgr) include a focus on end-to-end service monitoring, best-of-breed manager of Windows, reliability and security, and operational efficiency. Features in OpsMgr 2007 include the following:

▶ **Active Directory Integration**—Management group information and agent configuration settings can be written to Active Directory, where they can be read by the OpsMgr agent at startup.

▶ **SNMP-enabled device management**—OpsMgr can be employed to discover and perform up/down monitoring on any SNMP-enabled server or network device.

▶ **Audit Collection Services (ACS)**—ACS provides centralized collection and storage of Windows Security Event Log events for use by auditors in assessment and reporting of an organization's compliance with internal or external regulatory policies.

▶ **Reporting enhancements**—Reporting has been retooled to support reporting targeted to common business requirements such as availability reporting. Data is automatically aggregated to facilitate faster reporting and longer data retention.

▶ **Command shell**—Based on PowerShell, the OpsMgr Shell provides rich command-line functionality for performing bulk administration and other tasks not available through the Operations console UI.

▶ **Console enhancements**—The console interfaces of MOM 2005 have been consolidated into a single Operations console to support all operational and administrative activities. The new console has an Outlook-like look and feel to minimize the need for training users how to navigate the interface. (A separate console is provided for in-depth management pack authoring.)

▶ **Network-Aware Service Management (NASM) and cross-platform monitoring**—In Operations Manager 2007 R2, Microsoft delivers network-aware service management using technology acquired from EMC Smarts, along with native cross-platform monitoring for a number of common Linux and Unix platforms.

System Center Essentials

System Center Essentials 2007 (Essentials for short) is a System Center application, targeted to the medium-sized business, that combines the monitoring features of OpsMgr with the inventory and software distribution functionality found in ConfigMgr into a single, easy-to-use interface. The monitoring function utilizes the form of the OpsMgr 2007 engine that utilizes OpsMgr 2007 management packs, and Essentials brings additional network device discovery and monitoring out of the box. The platform goes beyond service-oriented monitoring to provide systems management functionality, software distribution, update management, as well as hardware and software inventory, all performed using the native Automatic Updates client and WSUS 3.0. Using Essentials, you can centrally manage Windows-based servers and PCs, as well as network devices, by performing the following tasks:

▶ Discovering and monitoring the health of computers and network devices and viewing summary reports of computer health

▶ Centrally distributing software updates, tracking installation progress, and troubleshooting problems using the update management feature

▶ Centrally deploying software, tracking progress, and troubleshooting problems with the software deployment feature

▶ Collecting and examining computer hardware and software inventory using the inventory feature

Although Essentials 2007 provides many of the same monitoring features as OpsMgr (and ConfigMgr to some degree), the product lacks the granularity of control and extensibility required to support distributed environments, as well as enterprise scalability. The flip side of this reduced functionality is that Essentials greatly simplifies many functions compared to its OpsMgr and ConfigMgr 2007 counterparts. Customization and connectivity options for Essentials are limited, however. An Essentials deployment supports only a single management server; all managed devices must be in the same Active Directory forest. Reporting functionality is included, but only accommodates about a 40-day retention period.

Essentials 2007 also limits the number of managed objects per deployment to 30 Windows server-based computers and 500 Windows non-server-based computers. There is no limit to the number of network devices.

Service Manager: A Complete Service Desk Solution

Using System Center Service Manager (not yet released) will implement a single point of contact for all service requests, knowledge, and workflow. The Service Manager (previously code-named "Service Desk") incorporates processes such as incident, problem, change, and asset management, along with workflow for automation of IT processes. From an MOF perspective, Service Manager will be an anchor for the MOF Supporting quadrant. Figure 1.10 illustrates the mapping between the quadrants of the MOF Process Model and System Center Components.

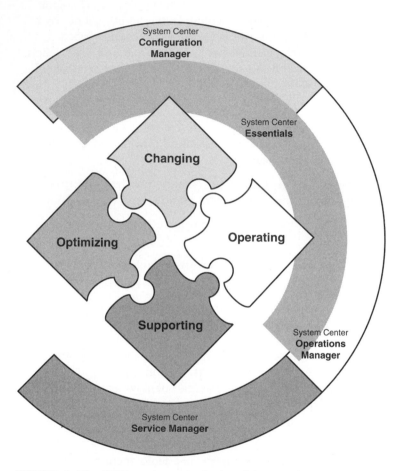

FIGURE 1.10   MOF quadrants and related System Center applications

Service Manager is Microsoft's new help desk product and fills a gap in Operations Manager—What do you do when OpsMgr detects a condition that requires human intervention and tracking for resolution? Until Service Manager, the answer was to create a ticket or incident in one's help desk application, which generally required a third-party product connector to facilitate data exchange between OpsMgr and the ticketing system. Now, within the System Center framework, OpsMgr can hand off incident management to

Service Manager. Similarly, you can use Service Manager in conjunction with ConfigMgr for software distribution. Design goals of Service Manager include the following:

- Incorporating Self-Service Portal technologies to help organizations reduce support costs, including providing the administrator with a view into the overall performance of the IT environment using reports and dashboards.

- Ready-to-use process-automated workflows based on processes defined in the Microsoft Operations Framework, using DSI models.

- A Service Manager Solution Pack framework, similar to the Operations Manager management packs, to enable customers and partners to develop additional custom functionality for the Service Manager.

- A Configuration Management Database (CMDB) based on SML and XML schema. Microsoft is positioning the CMDB as the foundation of its asset and change management capability, which parallels the CMDB function as defined in ITIL.

Supported scenarios include the following Service Management Functions (SMFs) and capabilities from the MOF Operating and Supporting quadrants:

- **Incident management**—Creating incident records based on information in management tools

- **Problem management**—Identifying problems by searching common incidents

- **Asset management**—Tracking movement and ownership of hardware assets

- **Change management**—Reviewing and approving change requests

- **Self-Service Portal**—Resolving an issue without calling the help desk

The console interface of Service Manager in style mirrors that of OpsMgr and Essentials, which have an appearance similar to Outlook. It uses the OpsMgr agent, and the console will have the ability to run OpsMgr tasks. Service Manager brings the "designed for operations" moniker full circle by providing a means to feed production and user data back into the development process using Visual Studio through incident and problem tracking.

Protecting Data

System Center's Data Protection Manager (DPM) 2007 is a disk-based backup solution for continuous data protection supporting servers running Windows 2003 Service Pack 1 and above. DPM provides byte-level backup as changes occur, utilizing Microsoft's Virtual Disk Service and Shadow Copy technologies.

Microsoft describes DPM 2007 as a "best of breed" product, adding support for tape media. The Enterprise Edition offers native protection for Windows applications such as Microsoft SQL Server, Exchange, SharePoint Portal Server, plus bare-metal restore capability. This means that in addition to selecting file shares, you can back up SQL Server databases and

Exchange Server storage groups. Via online snapshots, disk-based recovery can maintain backup points to a 15-minute window.

To support the burgeoning presence of virtual machines, DPM supports host-based backups of virtual machines using a single agent on the host. To support branch office and low-bandwidth scenarios, DPM advances de-duplication technology and block-level filter technology that only moves changed data during full backups.

Capacity Planning

System Center Capacity Planner is designed to provide tools and guidance to determine an optimal architecture for successful deployments, while also incorporating hardware and architecture "what-if" analyses for future planning. The Capacity Planner assists with planning deployments of Operations Manager, Exchange Server, and Microsoft Office SharePoint 2007.

In conjunction with the second "wave" of System Center, the newest version of Capacity Planner includes a model for OpsMgr 2007, which supports modeling the following areas:

- ▶ All core server and database components
- ▶ Gateway servers
- ▶ Backup servers for the Operations database, Root Management Server (RMS), and data warehouse
- ▶ 64-bit hardware support
- ▶ Database sizing recommendations
- ▶ Support for background loads
- ▶ Trusted and untrusted agents
- ▶ An enhanced predeployment wizard

The OpsMgr model for Capacity Planner only supports those OpsMgr 2007 installations running SP 1 and above.

The Capacity Planner creates models with information on topology, hardware, software, and usage profiles. It also allows you to run iterative simulations on the models for performance information. Capacity Planner ties into the DSI strategy by identifying when systems deviate from a defined performance model, providing guidance to correct those variations.

Virtual Machine Management

System Center Virtual Machine Manager (VMM) 2008 is Microsoft's management platform for heterogeneous virtualization infrastructures, providing centralized management of virtual machines across several popular platforms, specifically Virtual Server 2005 R2, Windows Server 2008 Hyper-V, and VMware ESX 3.x. VMM enables increased utilization of physical servers, centralized management of a virtual infrastructure, delegation of administration in distributed environments, and rapid provisioning of new virtual machines by system administrators and users via a Self-Service Portal.

VMM also delivers advanced functionality for enterprise environments, such as guidance in placement of Microsoft and VMware virtual guests (called intelligent placement), reliable physical-to-virtual (P2V) conversion, as well as virtual-to-virtual (V2V) transfer of VMware hosts. Integration with OpsMgr 2007 provides VMM access to historical performance data in the System Center data warehouse to augment intelligent placement decisions.

The Value Proposition of Configuration Manager 2007

The value of Configuration Manager lies in these areas:

- ▶ Increasing the agility of the IT organization in service delivery to the business

- ▶ Improving the organization's ability to monitor and manage change across client systems and server infrastructure

- ▶ Reducing the cost to deliver services as well as reducing the cost of maintenance throughout the life of the service

As a tool for managing system provisioning, configuration, and security, Configuration Manager is designed as a best-of-breed systems management solution for the Windows Server platform, providing enterprise scale for distributed environments. By incorporating rich OS and software deployment functionality, along with configuration compliance monitoring, it brings simplicity and automation to previously complex tasks.

As an enterprise-grade solution, ConfigMgr provides redundancy and high availability with an open architecture—a requirement for computing enterprises that include critical infrastructure. Configuration Manager is extensible, so it can integrate with other Microsoft technologies, such as SoftGrid Application Virtualization, as well as third-party infrastructure partner solutions.

The goal for the IT manager considering ConfigMgr is to lower the cost of deploying, maintaining, and managing Windows solutions. This can include a variety of areas within IT operations, such as providing systems configuration insight to reduce time-to-resolution problem and incident management, and numerous functions within the configuration management realm, such as monitoring system configuration baselines or deployment of software updates. Its broad functionality makes Configuration Manager 2007 a key component of DSI.

Out of the box, Configuration Manager 2007 reduces manual configuration effort through integration with Active Directory, and it ensures secure communications through mutual authentication (native mode only) and encryption. Comprehensive configuration compliance and update management functionality serve to ensure that the configurations of clients connected to your network are secure and up to date.

Many of the enterprise management platforms provide an infrastructure that has the potential to do great things, and they are sold based on that promise. Frequently though, the complexity of configuration renders these products permanent shelfware that will never be implemented, resulting in wasted IT dollars and missed opportunities.

ConfigMgr introduces a shift in the complexity paradigm with a platform that can be configured by IT pros without the need for extensive professional services engagements. This instant return on investment provides a huge win when the process improvements can be introduced with only hours of effort, with little or no IT effort.

Summary

The purpose of this chapter was to introduce the challenges of systems management and to discuss what Configuration Manager 2007 brings to the table to meet those challenges. You learned that systems management is a process that touches many areas within ITIL and MOF, such as change and configuration management, asset management, security management, and, indirectly, release management. You also learned about the functionality delivered in ConfigMgr that you can leverage to meet these challenges more easily and effectively.

The chapter discussed ITIL v3, which is an internationally accepted framework of best practices for IT Service Management. ITIL describes what should be accomplished in IT operations, although not actually how to accomplish it and how the processes are related and affect one another. To provide additional guidance for its own IT and other customers, Microsoft chose ITIL as the foundation for its own operations framework, the Microsoft Operations Framework. The objective of MOF was to provide both descriptive (what to do and why) as well as prescriptive guidance (how to do it) for IT service management as they relate to Microsoft products.

Microsoft's management approach, which incorporates the processes and software tools of MOF and DSI, is a strategy or blueprint intended to build automation and knowledge into datacenter operations. Microsoft's investment in DSI includes building systems designed for operations, developing an operationally aware platform, and establishing a commitment to intelligent management software.

Configuration Manager is a tool for managing Windows systems in a way that increases the quality of service IT delivers while reducing the operational cost of service delivery. Together with OpsMgr and the other members of the System Center family of products, ConfigMgr is a critical component in Microsoft's approach to system management that can increase your organization's agility in delivering on its service commitments to the business.

Systems management is a key component in an effective service management strategy. Throughout this book, you will see this functionality described and demonstrated, as the authors hope to illustrate the full value of Configuration Manager as a platform for improving the automation, security, and efficiency of service support and delivery in your IT organization.

The next chapter includes an overview of ConfigMgr terminology and discusses key concepts, feature dependencies, and what's new in Configuration Manager 2007.

CHAPTER 2

Configuration Manager 2007 Overview

Welcome to the newest version of Systems Management Server—System Center Configuration Manager (ConfigMgr) 2007. Chapter 1, "Configuration Management Basics," discussed the hurdles in systems management and configuration management. This chapter looks at the history of Configuration Manager and discusses terminology, key concepts, changes through Configuration Manager 2007 R2 and Service Pack 2, and feature dependencies Configuration Manager has on other technologies.

The History of Configuration Manager

There have been four major versions of the product, beginning with Systems Management Server (SMS) 1.0, launched by Microsoft in 1994. Since then, Microsoft has released versions 1.1, 1.2, 2.0, 2003 and now version 2007, which the company rebranded as System Center Configuration Manager 2007. Figure 2.1 displays a timeline showing the various versions of SMS and Configuration Manager.

The Earliest Versions

Microsoft introduced the first version of its desktop management software, Systems Management Server 1.0 (code-named *Hermes*), in January 1994. SMS 1.1 came out in mid 1995, and SMS 1.2, discussed in the next section, followed in 1996.

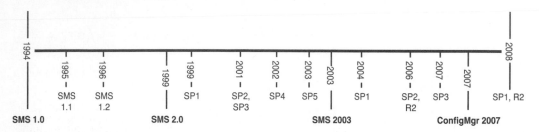

FIGURE 2.1   SMS and Configuration Manager versions from 1994 through 2008

NOTE

About the Versions of SMS 1.x

SMS 1.1 and 1.2 were initially intended as service packs to the base release of SMS 1.0, but became feature-heavy enough to call real releases. The fact that each year Microsoft had a new version of SMS points to the fact that the 1.x product needed some serious work, hence, the annual updates.

Systems Management Server 1.2

Microsoft touted SMS 1.2 as a systems management solution that provided an array of tools—from remote control to software distribution—helping local area network (LAN) administrators to monitor and manage their networks. In reality, SMS 1.2 was behind the competition for the following reasons:

▶ The software was cumbersome to use, with SMS site servers requiring installation on a Windows NT 4.0 backup domain controller (BDC).

▶ SMS 1.2 could only manage the domain it resided in.

▶ The end-user experience was very poor; you can still hear people joke today about the extremely long logon times in SMS 1.2. These long logins were due to the product inventorying the client systems during their network login, using a login script.

▶ SMS 1.2 was Microsoft's management software during the latter part of the 1990s, but the console only ran on a Windows NT 4.0 workstation. This was at a time when NT 4.0 was competing with Windows 95 and 98, two systems that were able to run on laptop computers much more efficiently. The console platform limitations further limited the adoption of SMS 1.2.

Systems Management Server 2.0

Microsoft released SMS 2.0 (code-named *Opal*) in January 1999, and shortly after that, its first service pack (SP). The product was one of the first management tools utilizing the Microsoft Management Console (MMC), and it incorporated major changes for SMS administrators and the worldwide community. Enhancements included the following:

▶ **Logon experience**—Eliminating the use of login scripts (although smsls.bat was still used with logon points).

▶ **Software discovery**—Removing the requirement to specify the software files to inventory (a poor way to determine what exists because you obviously don't know the information to begin with).

▶ **Site server placement**—Eliminating the requirement for the site server to reside on a BDC or domain controller (DC).

▶ **Subnet targeting**—Targeting a group of subnets as its management scope. Targeting subnets made the tool much more flexible and allowed managing multiple domains from a single SMS site.

The following sections discuss additional enhancements.

Inventory

SMS 2.0 introduced separate Hardware and Software Inventory Agent components. The agents were configurable independently of one another and able to run on completely different schedules. Most noticeably for the end-user experience, inventories did not run at login time. These changes allowed administrators to become aggressive and run inventories based on business requirements, without affecting end users' systems.

Microsoft listened to the SMS community's feedback and coded the Hardware Inventory Agent to run 15 minutes after the SMSExec service started if inventory was scheduled. The Software Inventory Agent was coded to behave similarly, 30 minutes after the service started.

Software Metering and License Enforcement

SMS 2.0 introduced software metering and license enforcement. Although the initial implementation was not as successful as Microsoft hoped, SMS 2.0's software metering served as a learning opportunity for what corporations considered acceptable regarding license management. The SMS 2.0 version allowed administrators to track applications, ensure license compliance, and monitor software usage throughout their organization.

The component required its own database, did not support mobile computing, and was generally intrusive on the user experience. The issues associated with metering, which grew exponentially as laptops became increasingly prevalent in the workplace, ultimately shut down most deployments.

Software Updates and Patches

SMS 2.0 released in early 1999, just prior to Y2K (Year 2000). One of the product's biggest draws—a feature used by SMS administrators worldwide—was its ability to implement Y2K patches. Y2K patching was a huge milestone for SMS and led to a large adoption rate for version 2.0. The flip side of this was that the quick adoption rate created a situation where many bugs were uncovered, some quite serious, almost immediately.

Data Discovery Record Processing

The most noteworthy feature in Service Pack 5, released in 2003, was its vast improvement in data discovery record (DDR) processing. SMS uses DDRs to report discovery information to the site database. Prior to SP 5, a DDR took approximately 1 second to process. (Because

SP 5 was only a service pack, Microsoft did not update official numbers about the improved scalability.)

Total Rewrite

The SMS product team and veteran SMS administrators still remember the hectic early days of SMS 2.0. SMS 2.0 was a complete rewrite from the ground up and had numerous bugs. There is still debate today over whether SMS 2.0 became a truly stable platform with Service Pack 2 (released June 2000) or until SP 3 (released in August 2001). Service Pack 4 for SMS 2.0 became available in August 2002, and Microsoft released SP 5 in April 2003.

However, one of SMS 2.0's largest failings was that none of its service packs included integration with Active Directory (AD), which released with Windows 2000 just a year after the base release of SMS 2.0.

SMS 2003

Microsoft launched SMS 2003 (code-named *Emerald*) in November 2003. Two major and three minor changes to SMS 2003 helped set it apart as the dominant systems management suite for Windows:

▶ The two major changes were Active Directory Integration and the Advanced Client.

▶ The minor, not-so-well-recognized changes included the following:

  ▶ Implementing software metering in a passive, silent fashion

  ▶ Adding a built-in reporting system

  ▶ Leveraging Background Intelligent Transfer Service (BITS) to handle bandwidth throttling

    Incorporating BITS helped minimize the impact of software updates and downloads on the user experience.

Active Directory Integration

SMS 2003 had the capability to extend and store key configuration data about its hierarchy in AD, using a small handful of schema extensions that were an optional part of the installation. This led to a number of benefits:

▶ **Site boundaries**—Using Active Directory let SMS administrators use AD sites rather than specify subnets for site boundaries.

  Using Active Directory sites as site boundaries added flexibility to SMS and saved hours of painstaking and tedious work. Incorporating AD sites also let SMS 2003 implementations easily adapt to network changes, because SMS could automatically detect changes when network administrators changed subnets at various locations and in Active Directory.

▶ **Schema extensions**—SMS schema extensions are a series of classes and attributes stored within AD and replicated among global catalog servers. Schema extensions facilitate client installation, site assignment, and global roaming.

► **Advanced security**—Advanced security allowed administrators to use machine accounts in AD to grant permissions across the organization.

Using machine accounts eliminated a plethora of problems, including account lockout issues, password resets, site resets, and broken clients due to corporate password change policies. (Security problems were such an issue in SMS 2.0 that Microsoft's only workaround for account-related issues was recommending SMS administrators place sites in resource domains with looser security!)

With advanced security, only one service account was necessary to push clients from the server, allowing a cleaner security implementation.

► **Discovery process**—AD Integration allowed SMS administrators to be selective about the objects they discovered. Administrators could target any Organizational Unit (OU) or Lightweight Directory Access Protocol (LDAP) path possible for any system, user, or group discovery process. This eliminated maintaining unneeded objects in the site, database, or collections because of product limitations.

► **Distribution points**—Distribution points (DPs) were also able to leverage AD, by using AD sites defined as their boundaries.

SMS administrators could define who could and could not connect to a DP by specifying permitted AD sites. This stopped clients from pulling content from a remote DP, improved the overall end-user experience with fast package installation times, and minimized the risk of saturating wide area network (WAN) links due to a package installation occurring across a slow link.

► **Roaming boundaries**—Roaming boundaries were a new concept in SMS 2003 and took advantage of AD integration as well.

Roaming boundaries allowed clients to move from one Internet Protocol (IP) network to another without uninstalling the client, a major drawback with SMS 2.0. Roaming always involves an IP network change for the client, either between offices or from an office to the user's home network. SMS 2.0 uninstalled the client and then reinstalled it when the computer returned to the corporate network, initiating new full hardware and software inventories and potentially package installations, depending on their configuration. Although there were some workarounds for this behavior in version 2.0, they did not really address the roaming issue as well as the Advanced Client did in SMS 2003.

Advanced Client

The single biggest improvement in SMS 2003 was undoubtedly the Advanced Client, referred to as the *Mobile Client* during the beta test cycle. The Advanced Client had a completely new architecture, which included the following features:

► Sending inventories using a compressed eXtensible Markup Language (XML) format.

► Not automatically uninstalling clients.

► Easily building clients into an image, without concern of duplicating the client Globally Unique Identifier (GUID).

▶ AD site-aware clients.

▶ Clients checking into AD themselves and storing their history in Windows Management Instrumentation (WMI), not in the file system like the 2.0 client. Therefore, uninstalling and reinstalling a client did not mean the user got all the applications he or she previously received, again.

The Advanced Client used BITS and downloaded packages from DPs using the Hypertext Transfer Protocol (HTTP). Using BITS allowed a download to pick up where it left off if the connection was broken during the download (also known as *checkpoint restarting*). BITS increased package deployment success rates and minimized deployment times for the following reasons:

▶ Clients now could download the package to their local cache in the background, during daily activity.

▶ At execution time, the clients could be configured to run the package from a local disk, thus reducing server disk contention on DPs and allowing clients to run packages when not connected to the infrastructure.

If an Advanced Client traversed the WAN, it would still only receive policy from its own site, thus addressing another issue SMS 2.0 was plagued with—the traveling corporate user. No longer would these users automatically be reassigned to a site because they spent time working there.

SMS 2003 also included a Legacy Client, which was purely for backward compatibility to support Microsoft operating systems unable to run the Advanced Client. These systems included Windows 95 and 98, Windows NT 4.0 SP 6a, and Windows 2000 systems prior to SP 4.

SMS 2003 Service Packs and R2

Service Pack 1 for SMS 2003 was released in September 2004. Although primarily a hotfix rollup, the service pack included new functionality:

▶ SP 1 limited legacy support to Windows 98 and Windows NT 4.0 SP 6a only—support was removed for Windows 95, Windows NT 4.0 SP5, and earlier versions. Optionally, administrators could publish a child site server in the hierarchy running an older version of SMS to support these clients if necessary.

▶ The service pack dropped the requirement for the Windows Internet Naming Service (WINS) if the AD schema was extended and DNS was configured to enable SMS clients and servers to resolve each other's NetBIOS names.

▶ The service pack provided SMS administrators the ability to categorize and organize objects in the SMS Administrator console using folders, a new feature with SP 1.

▶ SP 1 provided SMS support for managing systems that were members of a workgroup.

Microsoft released SMS 2003 Service Pack 2 in June 2006. SP 2 included hotfix rollups and new functionality, including querying AD security groups, Fully Qualified Domain Name (FQDN) support, support for x64, IA64, and R2-based Windows Server 2003 installations, multithreaded software inventory processing, replicating decommissioned DDRs up the hierarchy, and updates to the Inventory Tool for Microsoft Updates (ITMU).

In late 2006, Microsoft announced its first SMS version using the branding *R2* (for Release 2). SMS 2003 R2 built on SMS 2003 SP 2, with enhancements that included the Inventory Tool for Custom Updates (ITCU) and the Scan Tool for Vulnerability Assessment.

Service Pack 3 for SMS 2003 was released in April 2007. Microsoft's acquisition of AssetMetrix introduced Asset Intelligence for SMS 2003, included in the service pack. Asset Intelligence brings categorization of over 400,000 software titles in over 100,000 categories. SP 3 also gave SMS administrators the ability to deploy Windows Vista using the Operating System Deployment (OSD) feature pack. Administrators could also deploy updates to Vista clients and applications as well as perform hardware and software inventory on Vista clients.

Configuration Manager 2007

Microsoft released System Center Configuration Manager 2007 in August 2007. Known as *SMS v4* during beta testing days, the product was rebranded toward the end of the development phase. This version is the first to include the previously separate "feature packs" directly in the product. Using SMS 2003, one might install four to eight different feature packs to incorporate various capabilities, but then some of these items did not show up on the administrator's console without running a local installation!

In Configuration Manager 2007, Desired Configuration Management, Operating System Deployment, Device Management, Patch Management and other features come built in to every ConfigMgr console—these components previously required multiple, separate installations. ConfigMgr 2007 no longer has a Legacy Client; there is only one ConfigMgr client for all supported operating systems, starting with Windows 2000 Professional.

ConfigMgr 2007 has a concept of native mode as the security mode. Native mode allows using Public Key Infrastructure (PKI) to secure client-to-server communication, as discussed in detail in Chapter 6, "Architecture Design Planning." ConfigMgr also supports an implementation model known as Internet-Based Client Management (IBCM). IBCM allows managing clients across numerous firewalls, including unmanaged ones. This implementation allows ConfigMgr administrators to push software or updates to clients surfing the Web from home or a hotel. Chapter 6 also discusses IBCM.

Table 2.1 compares the SMS 2003 and ConfigMgr 2007 feature sets.

TABLE 2.1   SMS 2003 and Configuration Manager 2007 Comparison Matrix

Feature	SMS 2003	ConfigMgr 2007
Product installation	Good	Prerequisite checking added
Console drag-and-drop, multiselect, Actions pane, Preview pane, home pages	No	Yes
Wizards	Some	Pervasive

TABLE 2.1   SMS 2003 and Configuration Manager 2007 Comparison Matrix

Feature	SMS 2003	ConfigMgr 2007
Folders	Organizational	Search added, replication to child sites
OSD Automation	No	Yes
OSD Bare-Metal deployment with PXE (Preboot Execution Environment)	Loose integration with RIS (Remote Installation Services)	Built-in integration with WDS (Windows Deployment Services)
OSD Side-by-Side	BDD (Business Desktop Deployment) scripts	Built-in SMP (Symmetric Multiprocessing)
OSD Full Server Deployment, Fully Offline Deployment, Integrated Vista Upgrade Planning, Device Driver Management, Boot Image Management	No	Yes
OSD Security	Good	Improved
OSD Flexibility/Customizability, Vista/Windows 2008 (requires SP 1) Compatibility	Good	Excellent
OSD Task Sequencing	No	Yes
Asset Management Inventory	Good	Improved
Asset Management Integration with Usage Monitoring	No	Yes
Asset Management Database Updates	Service packs	Service packs, online updates
Desired Configuration Management	Solution Accelerator add-on	Integrated
Predefined configuration packs	No	Yes
Quarantine support (Network Access Protection [NAP] integration)	No	Yes
Manage over Internet	Requires Virtual Private Network (VPN)	VPN not required
Smartphone/PDA (Personal Digital Assistant) support	When cradled	Wireless and over-the-air
Patch and update management	Good, add-on pack	Excellent, integrated with Windows Software Update Services (WSUS) 3.0

Microsoft released Service Pack 1 for Configuration Manager 2007 in May 2008. SP 1 includes hotfix rollups and adds support for Vista SP 1 and Windows Server 2008. The service pack also provides support and integration with the Intel Active Management Technology (AMT), which allows remotely powering on and off systems as well as remote diagnostic capabilities. Asset Intelligence-related changes in the service pack include its addition as an independent node in the ConfigMgr console, an expanded catalog, new customization capabilities, new reports, hardware and software inventory enhancements, software license management capabilities, Client Access License-related data for Windows Server and Exchange Server, and Key Management Servers (KMS) for Windows Vista activation.

The R2 release of ConfigMgr 2007 (August 2008) incorporates a number of new features:

- ▶ Application virtualization

- ▶ Client status reporting

- ▶ Multicast delivery of images

- ▶ Forefront client monitoring using a new Desired Configuration Management (DCM) configuration pack

- ▶ OSD unknown computer support

- ▶ Run As capability in the run command-line option of the Task Sequence Wizard

- ▶ The ability to convert from the traditional ConfigMgr reporting environment to using SQL Reporting Services for reports

System Center Configuration Manager 2007 Service Pack 2

Microsoft has announced development of a second service pack for ConfigMgr 2007, which will not be released until after this book is published. The service pack is expected to encompass the following areas:

- ▶ **New operating system support**—With SP 2, ConfigMgr 2007 will support Windows 7, Windows Server 2008 R2 and SP 2, and Windows Vista SP 2. The support will include native 64-bit counters, thus enabling System Center Operations Manager (OpsMgr) 2007 SP 1 / R2 to monitor the 32-bit ConfigMgr client on 64-bit systems.

- ▶ **Improved integration with Intel's AMT**—The service pack will improve on the integration first provided in SP 1. SP 2 will add full feature support for computers with the Intel vPro chip set and iAMT firmware versions 4 and 5. In addition to providing feature parity with SP 1 and iAMT firmware versions 3.2.1, 4.0, and 5.0, Microsoft is adding support for the following features:

  - ▶ **Out of Band (OOB) wireless management**—Wireless profile management (mobile only)

  - ▶ **End-point access control**—802.1x support

  - ▶ **Persistent data storage**—Nonvolatile memory or third-party data store (3PDS)

▶ **Access Monitor**—Enabling/disabling the Audit Log and viewing it through the OOB console

▶ **Remote power management**—Power state configuration

Microsoft currently plans release of SP 2 approximately 90 days after Release to Manufacturing (RTM) of Windows 7.

Now that you have had a glimpse of the history of Configuration Manager, it is time to look at some key terminology for the product.

Configuration Manager Technology and Terminology

Configuration Manager uses terminology that is unique and specific to its management infrastructure and the actions it can carry out among its clients; these clients can be servers, workstations, or mobile devices such as PDAs and smartphones. The next sections of this chapter describe site, hierarchy, and role terms, providing a foundation to understand how these objects interact with one another, ConfigMgr clients, and the infrastructure.

Site Servers

The *site server* is a site system role assigned to the server where the Configuration Manager setup program runs. By definition, each ConfigMgr site has at least one site server. This system has the ConfigMgr binary files installed on it, and can have clients assigned to it for management purposes. The site server manages all components belonging to its site, including management points and distribution points.

Site servers are divided out into two types:

▶ Primary site servers

▶ Secondary site servers

Although both are types of site servers, there are significant differences between the two, differences you will need to understand to place them properly in your organization. The next sections discuss these differences.

Primary Site Servers

Primary site servers reference a SQL Server installation and store their configurations, client inventories, statuses, and other attributes in a SQL Server site database. SQL Server is typically installed locally, and Microsoft recommends this as a best practice. A local database installation provides the following advantages:

▶ Simplified management

▶ Reduced chance of resource contention

▶ Allows implementing the most secure and simple installation of SQL Server, thus safeguarding the client's inventory data

Primary site servers can scale to approximately 100,000 clients per server, although political or organizational reasons may mandate more than one site server and a lower client count per site. Primary site servers require a Microsoft Configuration Manager 2007 license for each site. (Chapter 4, "Configuration Manager Solution Design," discusses ConfigMgr licensing.)

Every Configuration Manager implementation has a minimum of one primary site, also known as the *central site*. The central site is the top primary site in the hierarchy. Whether there is one Configuration Manager site or multiple sites, the top of the hierarchy is always the central site. All inventory rolls up the hierarchy, making this site server the central repository for all client configuration data in the enterprise.

Scalability in ConfigMgr 2007 has increased substantially from SMS 2003 to support some of the largest and most complex enterprise environments around the world. Because ConfigMgr has so many unique roles, each of them has its own respective scalability limits due to the type of traffic involved.

Microsoft made public the scalability figures listed in Table 2.2 at the 2008 Microsoft Management Summit.

TABLE 2.2   Scalability Numbers for Configuration Manager 2007

Site Role	Maximum Number of Client Systems
Hierarchy (central site)	200,000
Primary site	100,000
System Health Validator	200,000
Management point	25,000
Distribution point (non-OSD)	4,000
Distribution point (OSD)	Limited by network and disk I/O
State migration point	Limited by network and disk I/O
Software update point (WSUS)	25,000
Fallback status point	100,000
Branch distribution point	Limited by OS license, network, and disk I/O

To achieve numbers in the ranges listed in Table 2.2, you must perform proper sizing of the ConfigMgr hardware and allocation of ConfigMgr resources. A great difference exists between the types of traffic, such as patch management, application distribution, and OS deployments. Sizing is also discussed in Chapter 4.

Secondary Site Servers

Given the capabilities of a primary site server, what is the role of a secondary site server?

▶ A secondary site does not have a SQL Server database.

▶ A secondary site server can only be a child of a primary site.

▶ Secondary site servers typically are used to manage a large amount of client data over WAN links.

Here are some examples when you may want to use secondary site servers:

▶ If you are concerned about network traffic between the clients and the Configuration Manager hierarchy, secondary sites can host a Distribution Point role and then throttle and limit when packages are updated on that DP.

▶ Let's say you have a large number of clients at a remote location and desire to cache client inventories and upload them to their primary site server at a more opportune time. This capability requires leveraging the proxy management point to have the secondary site server cache, compress, and then upload the data to the primary, while complying with a rate limit and schedule defined on the server's address.

You perform secondary site server administration through the parent site or some other site higher in the hierarchy, such as the parent's parent. In essence, a secondary site server can reduce the load on its parent primary site server, and it is more efficient with network bandwidth usage during peak times over a WAN link.

TIP

Distribution Points on Secondary Site Servers

Over the years, many SMS administrators have implemented distribution points on secondary site servers without configuring the SMS address for the sender, used by SMS to communicate with the site system. This results in a more complex architecture with no real benefit. If you do not configure bandwidth throttling, there is no point in having the DP belong to the secondary site.

Site Systems

Site systems are servers, and in some cases workstations, that host roles for the Configuration Manager infrastructure. Site systems include the following:

▶ **Component server**—A computer with ConfigMgr software installed on it. A component server is a ConfigMgr server that has had the ConfigMgr setup run on it locally and ConfigMgr software installed.

▶ **Site database server**—Required for primary sites only. This is the server running SQL Server and hosting the site database.

▶ **SMS provider**—Required for primary sites only. The provider is the WMI layer sitting between the ConfigMgr console and site database.

▶ **Management point**—Used for client and policy download. This is a location where Configuration Manager computer and device clients can exchange data with the ConfigMgr site services. ConfigMgr clients and the site server do not communicate directly with each other; all communication is facilitated via the management point. There must be at least one default management point for every ConfigMgr hierarchy.

- **Distribution point**—A distribution point is a share containing ConfigMgr packages for clients that will download them for installation. DPs are used with software distribution, software updates, and OSD. DPs do not require an additional ConfigMgr license.

- **Branch distribution point**—A branch distribution point allows a distribution point to be defined as a workstation. This is ideal for remote locations with fewer than 10 workstations, removing the need to install a secondary site server. (New with ConfigMgr 2007.)

- **Server locator point**—Used when the AD schema is not extended or when managing clients in workgroups or untrusted AD forests. The SLP helps clients find management points when they cannot find that information through AD and informs clients which MP to access to install the client software, completing client site assignment on the intranet.

- **Software update point**—The software update point (SUP) is assigned to the computer running WSUS, and is only required if using the Software Updates capability. New with ConfigMgr 2007 is its integration with WSUS and thus the SUP. WSUS enables administrators to deploy Microsoft updates to computers running the Windows operating system, leveraging built-in Automatic Updates technology. ConfigMgr now uses this role to distribute various updates to Microsoft client systems.

- **State migration point**—OSD uses the state migration point when migrating user state and settings from one computer OS load to another as part of operating system image deployment. The SMP can be used in both Refresh PC and Replace PC deployment scenarios. The state migration point requires Internet Information Services (IIS). You can use the state migration point for other functions, such as automating backup of the user's state to the network.

- **Fallback status point**—The fallback status point (FSP) is used to help administrators monitor client deployment and identify any problems encountered during installation or assignment. It also helps to identify clients that are unmanaged because they have problems communicating with their MP, which is particularly relevant when operating in native mode. (New with ConfigMgr 2007.)

- **Reporting point**—Hosts the Report Viewer component that provides web-based reporting functionality. The reporting point is only required if reports are run on a particular primary site.

- **PXE service point**—Responds to Preboot Execution Environment (PXE) requests from computers requesting operating system deployment. (New with ConfigMgr 2007.)

- **Device management point**—An extension to the management point or proxy management point. The device management point allows mobile devices to connect to ConfigMgr servers and receive policy and configuration settings.

- **Out of Band service point**—Used to enable out of band management for clients; can only be installed on primary site servers. (New with ConfigMgr 2007 SP 1.)

- **Reporting Services point**—Delivers integration with Microsoft SQL Server Reporting Services. (New with ConfigMgr 2007 R2.)

▶ **System Health Validator point**—Assigned to the computer running the Network Policy service. Only required if the Network Access Protection feature is being used. (New with ConfigMgr 2007.)

Site systems should always reside in the same AD forest as the site server. Spanning Active Directory forests with Configuration Manager sites is not recommended because you would span the Active Directory security boundary by allowing administration from a different forest.

Although not recommended, it is possible to have the following site systems in a remote forest:

▶ Server locator point

▶ Fallback status point

▶ Distribution point

▶ Management point

▶ Software update point

▶ System Health Validator point

▶ PXE service points

Site Hierarchy

Site hierarchies exist when there are more than one Configuration Manager site server and the servers have a parent/child relationship defined between them. Hierarchies can be very simple and flat or complex and deep to support an organization's requirements for systems management.

A parent ConfigMgr site implies there is at least one child site. A parent site can have many children, and those children can have children. Secondary sites cannot have child sites, and the parent of a secondary site is always a primary parent site, because secondary sites do not have their own database.

Only the PMP and DP roles can leverage the sender that the secondary site relies on for communication to the parent primary site.

A common hierarchical model is for a central site to manage servers and a child primary to manage workstations. This architecture provides a structure for the server administrators to manage their systems and the workstation administrators to manage their systems while segregating the management of those systems, the features enabled, schedules, and so on. Figure 2.2 illustrates an example of a three-tiered hierarchy with two branches, one of which is two-tiered.

Configuration Manager Client

Configuration Manager 2007 uses a new client, known as the *Configuration Manager client*. This client is the agent residing on all managed systems. The ConfigMgr Client agent periodically checks in with the ConfigMgr infrastructure, using an administrator-defined inter-

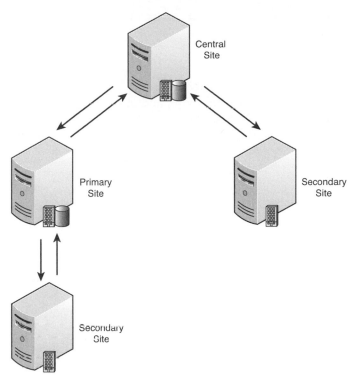

FIGURE 2.2   A three-tier Configuration Manager hierarchy, illustrating parent/child relationships

val. This interval is every 60 minutes by default, and can be set to be as wide as 1,440 minutes (every 24 hours). The client supports installation in a number of ways—preloaded into an image, manually installed, installation with a silent command line, via WSUS, or a pushed installation by the ConfigMgr server (manually or automatically) using the discovery processes defined later in the "Discovery" section of this chapter.

The ConfigMgr client is responsible for installing and removing software, running inventory, reimaging a system, performing patch management compliance scans, monitoring desired configuration compliance, software metering, remote control support, maintenance tasks, file collection, downloading policies, and uploading status messages. The client is bandwidth aware and leverages BITS to determine available network capacity and utilize that to download packages without affecting end-user performance. Chapter 5, "Network Design," describes BITS in detail.

Inventory

Installing the Configuration Manager Computer Client agent gives an administrator the ability to enable hardware and software inventory client agents to collect specific types of data and upload them to the ConfigMgr infrastructure in an efficient and compressed XML format. Hardware and software inventory run under the client SMS Agent Host service. The settings (policies) defined for the various client agents, often referred to as *sitewide settings*, affect all clients monitored by the ConfigMgr site.

Hardware Inventory

Hardware inventory enables collecting data on client systems from their motherboard, BIOS, hard disk, CPU, video card, network card, Registry, WMI, and other components. Hardware inventory uses MOF (Management Object Format) files to define what is to be inventoried and the format used to report that data. The Hardware Inventory Client agent defines hardware inventory frequency.

ConfigMgr incorporates a major shift in handling MOF files. In earlier versions, the SMS_Def.mof file was the only MOF file SMS provided natively to collect inventory. The problem was most administrators modified the file directly to extend inventory to include things such as proxy settings or antivirus definition dates and versions. Service packs and site resets overrode any customizations to the SMS_Def.mof file, making it critical to maintain backups.

ConfigMgr 2007 MOF files are functionally similar to OpsMgr management packs. The Configuration.mof file defines the data classes inventoried by the Hardware Inventory Client agent. You can create data classes to inventory existing or custom WMI repository data classes, or registry keys present on client systems.

The Configuration.mof file also defines and registers the WMI providers used to access computer information during hardware inventory. Registering providers defines the type of provider used and the classes it supports. WMI and Configuration Manager 2007 hardware inventory will only access registered providers.

The SMS_Def.mof file defines the reporting classes used by the Hardware Inventory Client agent to determine whether specific client data class information is reported. Reporting classes are based on the WMI repository data classes and the attributes of those classes; these exist on clients by default, or you can add them by customizing the Configuration.mof file.

Reporting class information in SMS_Def.mof is converted into a reporting policy provided to clients during their normal computer policy polling interval. After the client compiles the new reporting policy, the reporting policy information is stored in the client system WMI repository in the InventoryDataItem class of the Root\CCM\Policy\Machine WMI namespace.

The initial hardware inventory generated by the client is a full inventory. Subsequent inventories are *deltas*, information that has changed since the initial inventory. All of the hardware inventory data is viewable via the Configuration Manager Resource Explorer, displayed in Figure 2.3, which shows hardware for the Alamo computer system.

Software Inventory

ConfigMgr 2007's Software Inventory Client agent has the ability to scan files, inventory them, and upload this data to the site server. The Software Inventory Client agent can also

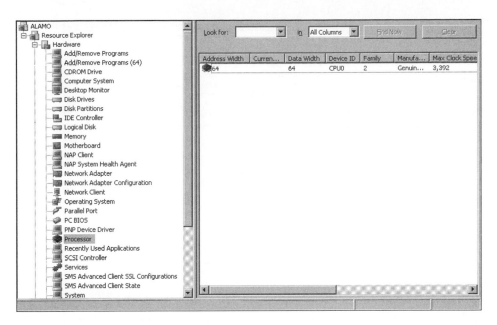

FIGURE 2.3   Configuration Manager Hardware Inventory for the Alamo system, viewed in the Resource Explorer

collect and copy files to the site server. The ConfigMgr administrator enables and configures the Software Inventory Client agent from the Configuration Manager console.

CAUTION

File Collection Warning

Be careful when you identify files to collect. If you specify collecting a 1MB file, for example, ConfigMgr will collect every occurrence of that file on each client; with 10,000 clients, you would send 10GB across the network and to the site server. Sending this amount of data will affect server storage capacity and introduce network bandwidth concerns.

Software Inventory scans the header and footer of every file with a file extension specified in the user interface (UI). By default, ConfigMgr scans only .exe files. Individual organizations may add additional file types to this list to identify specific software. When Software Inventory initially runs on a system, it performs a full scan of the drive and generates a manifest of all files the system contains. All subsequent inventories generate delta reports, thus minimizing network traffic and server processing load. Software Inventory catalogs file and product details, including a file's publisher, product name, creation date, and file version, to name a few. Figure 2.4 shows Software Inventory for the Alamo system.

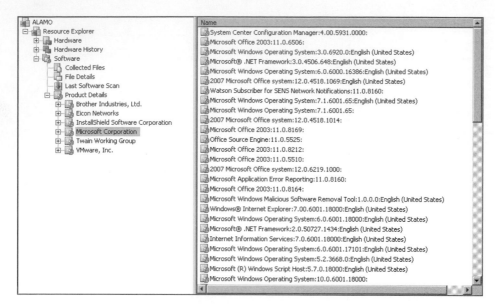

FIGURE 2.4   Configuration Manager Software Inventory viewed in the Resource Explorer

With Software Inventory, the ConfigMgr administrator can define which drives to scan, and whether to include the Windows system directory, encrypted files, or compressed files. Similar to the Hardware Inventory Client agent, a schedule can be specified determining when the Software Inventory Client agent will run.

The agent also has the ability to group various files it has scanned, which may come from the same manufacturer but show up with different names, under the same overall name. This feature is very similar to the Asset Intelligence integration introduced in SMS 2003 SP 3.

Configuration Manager Console

Configuration Manager 2007 uses the MMC, version 3.0, to provide the user interface to configure the Configuration Manager hierarchy and manage clients. An important part of ConfigMgr deployments is installing the ConfigMgr console on administrators' workstations. A best practice is to run the console from a remote system, not directly from the server.

Table 2.3 lists the platforms on which you can install the Configuration Manager 2007 console.

TABLE 2.3   Platforms Supporting the Configuration Manager 2007 Console

Operating System	x86	x64	IA64
Windows 2000 Professional SP 4	X		
Windows XP Professional SP 2	X		
Windows XP Professional for 64-bit Systems		X	

TABLE 2.3   Platforms Supporting the Configuration Manager 2007 Console

Operating System	x86	x64	IA64
Windows Vista Business Edition	X	X	
Windows Vista Enterprise Edition	X	X	
Windows Vista Ultimate Edition	X	X	
Windows 2000 Server SP 4	X		
Windows 2000 Advanced Server SP 4	X		
Windows 2000 Datacenter SP 4	X		
Windows Server 2003 Web Edition SP 1	X		
Windows Server 2003 Standard Edition SP 1	X	X	X
Windows Server 2003 Enterprise Edition SP 1	X	X	X
Windows Server 2003 Datacenter Edition SP 1	X	X	X
Windows Server 2003 R2 Standard Edition	X	X	X
Windows Server 2003 R2 Enterprise Edition	X	X	X
Windows Embedded for Point of Service (WEPOS)	X		
Windows Fundamentals for Legacy PCs (WinFLP)	X		
Windows XP Embedded SP 2	X		
Windows XP Tablet PC SP 2	X		

When upgrading to ConfigMgr 2007, many organizations have SMS 2003 and Configuration Manager 2007 coexisting to maximize end-user support. If performing an upgrade or migration from SMS 2003, you can run the SMS 2003 and the Configuration Manager 2007 consoles on the same computer in parallel. In addition, most functions an administrator can perform on a secondary site server, using the primary parent SMS Administrator console, are available with the ConfigMgr 2007 console.

Because the console now uses MMC 3.0, it can take advantage of a new feature called the *Actions pane*. This pane is context sensitive and allows administrators to quickly see and execute different tasks, based on what they selected elsewhere in the console. The console is used to configure and manage the ConfigMgr infrastructure, to execute tasks such as distributing packages and advertising packages and task sequences, to review inventory, and so on.

CAUTION

Mixed SMS/ConfigMgr Scenarios

Do not install the ConfigMgr 2007 console on an SMS 2003 secondary site server. Doing so will result in an SMS 2003 secondary site server that cannot be upgraded.

The ConfigMgr console displays what are known as *top-level objects*, also referred to as *nodes*. SMS 2003 had 12 top-level objects in the SMS Administrator's console. Microsoft substantially redesigned the ConfigMgr 2007 console to be more intuitive and logical in regard to grouping objects that work in conjunction with one another. The console now has only five top-level objects: the Site Management, Computer Management, System Status, Security Rights, and Tools nodes.

You can view an example of how this change is implemented by looking at the top-level Computer Management object, which has 12 child objects. Software Distribution is one of the child objects and contains packages and advertisements, which are two nodes where administrators spend a lot of time. Figure 2.5 displays the Configuration Manager console with the Software Distribution node highlighted.

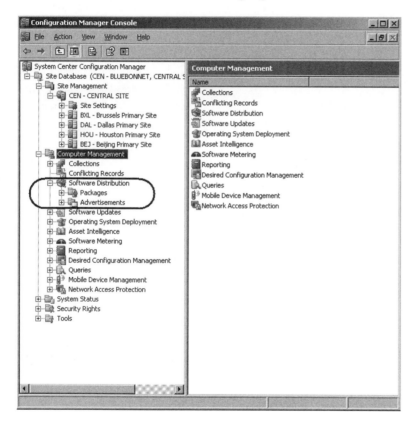

FIGURE 2.5   The Configuration Manager 2007 console

Collections

Collections are logical groupings of computer systems, users, or groups. They identify objects for a variety of purposes, such as the following:

▶ Pushing software

▶ Viewing inventory

▶ Viewing the result of a query

▶ Providing remote support via remote control and remote tools

▶ Grouping of systems with a common piece of hardware or software

You can populate collections using a direct membership or query membership rule. Both these methods allow the administrator to populate a collection. Collections are discussed in more detail in Chapter 14, "Distributing Packages."

Collections can have subcollections. This is useful for organizational reasons as well as for software distribution, due to the ability to advertise a package to a collection or its subcollections. Subcollections are also discussed in Chapter 14.

Collection security gives Configuration Manager administrators the ability to manage which administrators will have varying levels of access to specific collections. Configuration Manager 2007 uses an implementation of WBEM (Web-Based Enterprise Management) security, a standard created by the DMTF (Distributed Management Task Force). Chapter 3, "Looking Inside Configuration Manager," discusses WBEM and the DMTF. The WBEM security model leverages a class/instance model and is extremely granular. Most ConfigMgr objects have specific rights, which you can grant unique to an object.

Discovery

ConfigMgr discovers resources in a networked environment using a variety of built-in discovery methods. These discoveries create DDRs, which you can display in collections and queries. ConfigMgr has six types of discovery methods:

▶ Active Directory System Group Discovery

▶ Active Directory Security Group Discovery

▶ Active Directory System Discovery

▶ Active Directory User Discovery

▶ Heartbeat Discovery

▶ Network Discovery

The Active Directory discovery methods have the ability to specify LDAP paths for which you want to discover objects. Although some discovered objects such as users and groups are not capable of management, they are useful for reporting and using in query criteria to populate collections for application distribution.

Each discovery method has its own schedule, allowing configuration on a recurring interval and at non-peak times. See Chapter 12, "Client Management," for further information on discovery methods.

Software Metering

Software metering in ConfigMgr is passive, collecting data for a specified amount of time about the usage frequency of applications. Software metering gives administrators the ability to monitor specific application usage across the entire enterprise. Unlike in earlier versions, administrators no longer need to define most commonly used applications because ConfigMgr creates these rules automatically if an administrator-specified percentage of the environment is using an application.

Packages

ConfigMgr uses packages to distribute software and changes to clients. Think of a package as a change in a client's configuration. Historically, administrators have only thought of packages as software installs. Packages can be the silent uninstallation of an application, a remediation package from a desired configuration baseline that has been strayed from, a change to a Registry key, the startup behavior of a service, and so on. See Chapter 13, "Creating Packages," for a discussion of packaging.

Packages are distributed to DPs where they reside for clients to access. This distributed copy of the package architecture allows efficient use of bandwidth-sensitive links and minimizes the impact to the network infrastructure. Clients can download packages into their local cache and execute them later, mitigating the scenario where hundreds of clients all run an installation off a server at the same time.

Once distributed, packages are advertised to collections, which contain computer, user, or group resources. This process allows the package command line to execute according to a strict schedule and set of parameters that determines how the package will run and how the client operating system behaves, not only while the package is installing but also after it completes.

Advertisements

Advertisements are policies that ConfigMgr clients download and execute on a schedule. Advertisements define when clients can execute the program in a package and whether to run it from a distribution point or copy it to their local cache and run it locally. Chapter 13 also discusses advertisements.

By definition, advertisements require a user to initiate launching the package command. Mandatory advertisements do not require any user input and are actually a push-install, opposed to the pull-install used with advertisements in their default mode. You can use features such as Wake On LAN (WOL) in conjunction with mandatory advertisements to minimize impact to the end-user community.

TIP

Using Mandatory Advertisements with WOL

With mandatory advertisements, the ConfigMgr administrator can keep his enterprise patched to the level desired, without any user impact or interaction. Users can shut their computer down when they leave for the day to help with the company's green (energy-saving) initiative. An administrator can push a package out with a mandatory advertisement configured to shut down the computer on completion of the installation. When the user arrives the next day and turns on the machine, the startup completes the reboot cycle needed to complete the patch installation.

Distribution Points

ConfigMgr administrators can create DPs throughout an enterprise having a large number of client systems, thus minimizing network traffic over the WAN and slower links. Distribution points can utilize BITS, but not for throttling package traffic from the site server to the DP. BITS also allows checkpoint restarting. In other words, if there was an interruption to a download at 60% completion, using BITS allows the download to resume at that point instead of starting over again from the beginning, which is what happens when clients connect to DPs using Server Message Block (SMB) traffic. Distribution points can be installed on a system as either a package share or a server share. See Chapter 14 for additional information regarding the use of distribution points.

Senders

Senders are located on primary and secondary sites. Senders define how ConfigMgr sites use existing network connectivity to manage the connection, ensure the integrity of transferred data, recover from errors, and close the connection if no longer needed.

Sender types include the following:

▶ Standard sender

▶ Courier sender

▶ Asynchronous RAS sender

▶ ISDN RAS sender

▶ X25 RAS sender

▶ SNA RAS sender

The most common sender used is the standard sender, which is the only type required when there is basic network connectivity across a LAN or WAN. Microsoft designed the courier sender for sending excessively large packages across a network with slow links. The purpose of the courier sender is to create a parcel, which is a collection of files from a package, and ship the parcel on tape or CD to the remote site location where the administrator can then load the package into the site. Chapter 5 discusses the courier sender. Asynchronous RAS, ISDN, X25, and SNA senders communicate over each of those respective types of links.

Addresses

Addresses define a site code and the security account used to communicate with a remote site. Addresses also give ConfigMgr administrators the ability to schedule when traffic can flow between the two sites by priority of the traffic, as well as the percentage of bandwidth the sites may use during communications. All communication between ConfigMgr sites use SMB and travels on TCP port 445. By default, ConfigMgr secures site-to-site communication by secure key exchange, which only needs to be defined per parent/child connection. Figure 2.6 displays the Rate Limits tab for the Dallas site, limiting the transfer rate used to send data to that site.

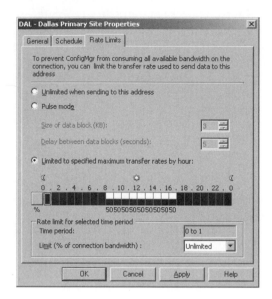

FIGURE 2.6   Properties of Configuration Manager 2007 addresses

BITS

BITS is a subcomponent of IIS, a component of Windows. Using BITS allows administrators to prioritize and throttle asynchronous file transfer between two Windows systems. BITS uses available network bandwidth to handle transfers, making them transparent to the end user's experience. BITS monitors network traffic on the local network interface and throttles itself accordingly. BITS also provides the ability to continue transferring data when network connectivity is intermittent or unreliable by leveraging checkpoint restarting.

Task Sequences

Task sequences are new in ConfigMgr 2007. Task sequences consist of a series of customizable tasks or sequentially performed steps running in an unattended fashion on a system. Task sequences often are only thought of in the context of operating system deployments. Because you can advertise task sequences directly to client systems, you can use them for a multitude of things, including chaining a series of actions together. Task sequences allow each action in the sequence to be independent of the other, let you change the order of tasks, and allow each action to have its behavior individually defined if errors occur. Task sequences consist of actions, custom and built-in actions, conditions, and steps. Task sequences also support grouping of actions for organizational purposes.

Status System

ConfigMgr maintains status on many of its technologies. Package status provides a summary of the version and time packages were copied to various distribution points. Advertisement status details when clients have received advertisements and started advertisements. It also shows the succeeded or failed status in the overall execution of the advertisement. Site status gives administrators a bird's-eye view of the health of the entire ConfigMgr site's infrastructure. ConfigMgr's component status details the health of each individual component in the site, such as discovery method's running state, sender health, DPs, MPs, and so on. Figure 2.7 shows the site status system from the ConfigMgr console.

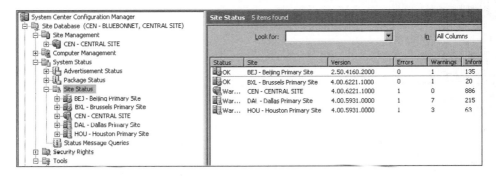

FIGURE 2.7   Configuration Manager 2007 status system example

Desired Configuration Management

DCM is a component built in to ConfigMgr that was previously provided in an SMS 2003 feature pack. DCM allows you to assess the compliance of computers with regard to a number of configurations, such as whether the correct Microsoft Windows operating system versions are installed and configured appropriately, whether all required applications are installed and configured correctly, whether optional applications are configured appropriately, and whether prohibited applications are installed. You can also check for compliance with software updates and security settings.

DCM is a framework where the ConfigMgr client has an agent, enabled at the site level, tracking baselines defined by the ConfigMgr administrator. You can also track deviations from the baseline. Each item, known as a *configuration item*, is tracked against a baseline; the item can be reported against or be corrected when the deviation occurs. System Center Configuration Packs, available from the Microsoft System Center Pack Catalog at http://go.microsoft.com/fwlink/?Linkid=71124, define Microsoft best practices for various product configurations.

You can evaluate both published and manually created baselines for compliance in your organization. Published configuration data from Microsoft and other vendors is available at http://go.microsoft.com/fwlink/?LinkId=71837. You can assign these configuration baselines to a collection, just like an advertisement, and evaluate them on a schedule independent of inventory and other agent schedules. Similar to inventory information, you can evaluate configuration baseline compliance when clients are offline; ConfigMgr sends the compliance data upon reconnection to the site hierarchy. Figure 2.8 displays the DCM home page in the Configuration Manager 2007 console.

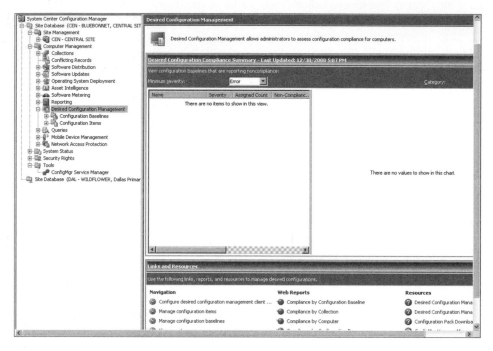

FIGURE 2.8   Configuration Manager 2007 DCM home page

See Chapter 16, "Desired Configuration Management," for a complete discussion of DCM.

Network Access Protection

NAP, new in ConfigMgr 2007, works with the Microsoft Windows Network Policy Server (NPS) on Windows Server 2008. NAP helps enforce compliance with selected software updates on clients capable of supporting NAP (NAP-capable clients). These clients include Windows XP SP 3 and Windows Vista. Using NAP, a client has restricted network access until it becomes compliant.

Configuration Manager by itself does not enforce compliance with Network Access Protection; it provides the means by which Configuration Manager clients produce a statement of health with a noncompliant status if they do not have the required software updates in the Configuration Manager NAP policies you configure. A Configuration Manager System Health Validator (SHV) point confirms the health state of the computer as compliant or noncompliant and passes this information to the Network Policy Server.

Policies on the NPS then determine whether noncompliant computers will be remediated and, additionally, whether they will have restricted network access until they are compliant.

Remediation is the mechanism of making a noncompliant computer compliant to ensure that clients conform to compliance policies. Configuration Manager remediation uses the software update packages you have already created, with the Software Updates feature. See Chapter 15, "Patch Management," for further discussion.

Reporting

Reporting in ConfigMgr is functionally very similar to that in SMS 2003. Dozens of reports, utilizing Transact-SQL (T-SQL), expose detailed hardware and software inventory data about the clients in the hierarchy. ConfigMgr 2007 adds a number of troubleshooting reports.

You can launch reports directly through the ConfigMgr console or through the reporting point site system website, and you can easily create custom reports utilizing the existing SQL views exposing the ConfigMgr site's data. Chapter 18, "Reporting," discusses ConfigMgr reporting.

Figure 2.9 illustrates ConfigMgr reports; this particular report lists all software companies collected during software inventory. With Configuration Manager 2007 R2, you can choose to use Microsoft SQL Reporting Services for reporting.

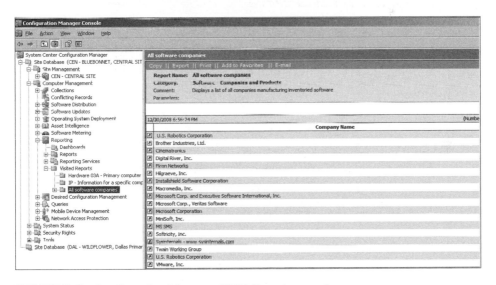

FIGURE 2.9   Configuration Manager 2007 Report example

Reports only query data from the local site server, some of which will be from child sites in the hierarchy if they exist. Because inventory and other types of data flow up the hierarchy, child sites data will show up in ConfigMgr reports run on a parent site. ConfigMgr groups reports into categories to facilitate organization, and reports may link to one another to provide an experience similar to drill-down reporting. You can configure reports to prompt the user for data, to provide lists of available options for prompts, or to be fully automated.

Security

Security in ConfigMgr is based completely on WMI, Microsoft's implementation of Web-Based Enterprise Management. WBEM allows access to providers such as Win32, WMI, SNMP, and Desktop Management Interface (DMI). In addition to collecting data, WBEM provides a method to secure the data by utilizing a class and instance model. As an example, the Packages node is a class containing a package for Microsoft Office, which would be an instance within the Packages class.

As shown in Figure 2.10, you need to permit granular rights specific to the class to individuals or groups, and then to specific instances of that class. Although a ConfigMgr administrator may have administrative rights on the ConfigMgr server and the SQL database for ConfigMgr, if not granted class and instance rights through the ConfigMgr console, the administrator cannot access any of the ConfigMgr objects within the ConfigMgr console.

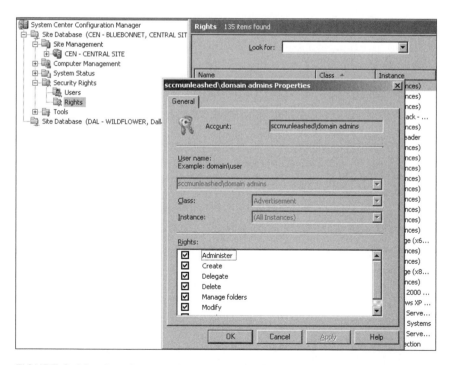

FIGURE 2.10   Granting security rights in Configuration Manager 2007

By default, only the account used to install ConfigMgr has rights to all ConfigMgr classes and instances. As a best practice, the account used to install ConfigMgr should be a service or application account.

Those topics are covered in Chapter 20, "Security and Delegation in Configuration Manager 2007."

Key Concepts

The next sections discuss how Configuration Manager 2007 can reduce IT's total cost of ownership (TCO) in a networked environment. ConfigMgr 2007 facilitates standardizing applications and the operating system, and provides methods for remotely supporting users and their systems in a fast and efficient manner. With the ability to pull data and push software across a LAN/WAN comes responsibility in understanding the impact these processes can have on the infrastructure and the end user's computing experience and overall productivity.

Standardization

The most successful implementations of SMS, or any other software distribution tool, historically have been in standardized environments. Standardizing operating systems, patch levels, application loads, hardware, and overall configuration allows administrators to test their deployments before rolling them out to the enterprise. Hardware-independent imaging, only recently a reality, allows administrators to build a single image and inject drivers on the fly during the deployment process. This process allows you to use one image for any number of hardware manufacturers and models, creating the most standardized OS deployment process available today.

Inventory allows administrators to logically group systems by any combination of hardware and software. This inventory data is useful in defining deviations from the standards created by an organization. Inventory data allows organizations to see the software installed on client systems, and software metering allows organizations to see the software executed on client systems. Analyzing these two sets of data helps organizations make educated decisions regarding software deployments and licensing.

Operating system deployments and migrations allow organizations to standardize their environment, thus controlling installations and configurations at the operating system and application level. Historically, operating system deployments have been a manual and time-consuming process, making it extremely difficult for large organizations to standardize their environment. Now operating system deployments are easier than ever, allowing levels of standardization that previously were out of reach due to technology, resources, and expense.

Remote Management

Information Technology has increasingly become a top expense in today's organizations. The ability to resolve issues quickly after they are identified requires tools that the first tier of support (usually referred to as *Tier1*) can use to perform tasks as though they were at the end user's system. These tools are critical to managing and lowering TCO of IT assets.

Tools such as Remote Control, Remote Desktop, and Remote Assistance give administrators the ability to run commands, see the hardware and software installed, and above all see the user interface the user is seeing. This type of remote control support has become an industry standard for remote user support. Branch offices and micro-branch offices, which have fewer than 10 users, have become increasingly common as corporations change and grow to stay competitive. These business models further complicate the remote management issue, making site visits not an option and remote tools critical to the support of the environment.

Software Distribution

Deploying software is one of the most primary functions of any Information Technology group. Getting users the applications, updates, security patches, and other changes required to keep an environment running is critical to a business's success. For any company to stay agile in today's market, IT must be able to adapt and meet the business's needs in a timely, efficient, and inexpensive manner. Being able to deploy software to systems, regardless of location and user's knowledge or rights of a system, is critical.

There are two primary methods to get a software update to a system—push and pull. Each of these methods ultimately gives the targeted systems the software desired for roll out, but there are many differences between the two and neither is necessarily right all the time.

Pulling Software

"Pulling" implies that the owner or recipient of the package must initiate some action. This allows the recipient to initiate the change when it is convenient, thus minimizing the impact on productivity. Allowing a user to pull down an application and install it at his or her leisure is also useful for rolling out software with user-specific settings the recipient needs to specify during installation. Even on locked-down systems where users have no rights, the end user can initiate and execute software installations as long as they were set up and approved by the IT administrative staff. Figure 2.11 illustrates the end-user notification that a program is available for installation.

FIGURE 2.11   Configuration Manager advertised program notification

The problem with a software change sent out in a "pull" fashion is that without that user initiation, the change never occurs. You can see how this will be a problem where there are changes that must take place on systems due to company policy. This could also be something a user may not want to do, such as removing a personal application from a company asset. This type of application distribution typically takes place when the users are very self-sufficient and avoiding negative impact to the end user is important.

Pushing Software

"Pushing" software speaks to the process of forcing changes to be rolled out in the enterprise. Pushing does not require user interaction, and it can be executed like policy. In fact, pushing software assumes there is no requirement for user interaction, although a need for user interaction with the installation routine does not prohibit an administrator from pushing it out. You can push software whether or not a user is logged on to a system, unlike a pull, where the user must be logged on to initiate the change. This ability to kick off a change on systems with no one logged on addresses multiple items:

▶ It eliminates file-locking issues

▶ It removes disruption to the end user's productivity

▶ Systems may be shut down afterward, allowing the user starting up the computer to complete a reboot cycle.

▶ Installation duration is not an issue because there is no user impact.

▶ Systems may be woken up using Wake On LAN technology to kick off an installation.

▶ Users are unable to interrupt the installation.

To Pull or Push

Although neither of these methods of applying changes solves all scenarios, it is easy to see how each can be used in conjunction with the other to address all types of requirements for change, configuration, and release management.

Minimizing Impact on the Network Infrastructure

Networks are critical to the daily functions of corporations today. Due to the heavy demand placed on networks, ConfigMgr utilizes several concepts and technologies to minimize the impact it places on the network infrastructure. Many of these technologies can be configured centrally, allowing other administrators to leverage the ConfigMgr architecture without needing deep knowledge of the enterprise's network infrastructure. Technologies such as BITS, distribution points, branch distribution points, download and execute, senders, and compressed XML are just a few of the technologies available.

▶ **BITS**—BITS monitors traffic in and out of the local network interfaces and throttles itself throughout a download, utilizing only the available idle bandwidth. This minimizes impact to the user experience with other network-aware applications, such as Microsoft Outlook or Internet Explorer.

As users' demand increases for more data from their applications across the network, BITS throttles itself down; as the demand drops, BITS throttles itself up to use as much bandwidth as available. Using BITS also allows an interrupted download to resume where it previously left off. BITS is covered in Chapter 5.

▶ **Distribution Points**—The "Distribution Points" section of this chapter previously touched on the DPs concept. It is important to understand that you can place distribution points anywhere, and it is not unusual to have multiple DPs on a single subnet! This is a common architectural design if there is a high demand to run packages from the distribution point or a large number of clients. A common design is to implement multiple DPs in a single location when there are concerns about router contention or high switch traffic.

▶ **Branch Distribution Points**—Branch distribution points, introduced in the "Site Systems" section, gives ConfigMgr the ability to push a package across a WAN link to a location with a very small number of clients and only traverse the WAN link one time with the package. SMS 1.x through 2003 pushed a separate package over the WAN link for every client in the remote location. Although third-party software existed to address this SMS architectural deficiency, it was costly and not well known. Now with support available for a client workstation to be a distribution point, the branch office or microbranch office model can easily be targeted and have packages pushed to it.

Whereas ordinary distribution points have packages published (also referred to as *copied* or *pushed*) to them by the ConfigMgr administrator, branch distribution points receive their package copy by updating their policy and then downloading the package source using BITS. This *pull* process is the opposite of how packages are ordinarily published to conventional distribution points.

▶ **Download and Execute**—Download and Execute is a feature introduced in SMS 2003; it leverages the BITS technology to cache a copy of the package from the DP. Many people ask, "Why would I want to cache a copy of a package if I have a local DP?"

The reason is quite simple: When packages are assigned, they are mandatory and will launch at the time stated in the advertisement. Because Kerberos tickets are time sensitive, clocks on computer systems today all synchronize with the clock on the PDC Emulator DC. This means that all clients with a mandatory advertisement will start it at exactly the same time, thus placing a heavy load on the local distribution point. The Download and Execute capability gives administrators the ability for clients to cache a copy of the package and upon execution, perform the installation from their local hard drive. BITS allows administrators to configure many things about its behavior, including how long to hold the copy of the package in its cache.

▶ **Senders**—Senders allow the throttling and prioritization of traffic by time between ConfigMgr sites. Administrators often overlook configuring senders, leaving the default of allowing all traffic at all times of the day. Without configuring senders, there is no throttling, and the network infrastructure may be utilized by traffic that could have waited until nonpeak hours of the day. Whenever parent/child relationships exist, you should experiment with senders to determine what is right for the environment in regard to time of day and workload.

▶ **Inventory**—Even at the inventory level, there are changes allowing a more efficient use of the technology now available. Hardware and software inventories are generated by their respective agents, with the output created in XML. This XML file is then compressed and sent up to the MP immediately. If the MP is not available, the client caches the inventory until the next time it is available or until the next inventory schedule, where it is rerun.

▶ **Testing**—With all this technology available to tread the network lightly, it is important to experiment with these settings in a lab environment. It is not uncommon for administrators to make mistakes that will saturate WAN links due to the nature of the product. Test whenever the ability exists to affect a network in a negative way, confirming in advance that the experience will be a positive one. Experimenting with different site configurations, package pushes, and client package execution can determine the overall load on the site, network, and distribution points.

Creating a lab for ConfigMgr is not only necessary for validating the site hierarchy and load testing, but it can also be used for package, security, patch, and upgrade testing. Figure 2.12 illustrates the lab environment used for the writing of this book. The lab incorporates a central site server (Bluebonnet) and four primary child site servers:

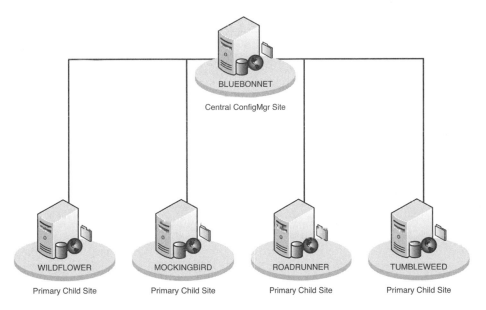

FIGURE 2.12   Configuration Manager 2007 lab example

▶ **Wildflower**—DAL site

▶ **Mockingbird**—HOU site

▶ **Roadrunner**—BEJ site

▶ **Tumbleweed**—BXL site

Mockingbird and Roadrunner are installed as SMS 2003 site servers; the HOU site, Mockingbird, is upgraded to ConfigMgr 2003 during the upgrade process in Chapter 9, "Migrating to Configuration Manager 2007."

What's New in ConfigMgr 2007

Microsoft introduces a number of new capabilities in Configuration Manager 2007. The next sections focus on the new and improved features.

Branch Distribution Points

Branch distribution points were introduced earlier in the "Site Systems" section. They have the following characteristics:

▶ While functioning similar to standard DPs, branch distribution points provide greater control over network traffic, which is necessary for branch offices that may have limited network bandwidth availability.

▶ Branch distribution points allow not only for manual content provisioning, but also provide configurable settings for scheduling and throttling network traffic to help minimize network impact.

▶ Branch distribution points allow on-demand package distributions, where packages are downloaded to the branch distribution point only when specifically requested by a client computer.

▶ Branch distribution points are limited to only being able to handle 10 concurrent connections, due to limitations in Microsoft desktop operating systems.

Figure 2.13 shows the General Properties page for a DP; there is a radial button midway down the page to enable the DP as a branch distribution point.

Software Update Point

The SUP installs as a site system role in the Configuration Manager console. Each site must have an active SUP before you can enable software updates. You can install a second SUP for communications from Internet-based client computers. You must create the software update point site system role on a server that has Windows Server Update Services (WSUS) 3.0 already installed and configured.

The software update point provides communication with WSUS and synchronizes with the WSUS database to retrieve the latest software update metadata from Microsoft Update, as well as locally published software updates. Once this is configured via the Configuration Manager console, the administrator does not need to perform any patch management in the WSUS console. Instead, all patch management configuration and

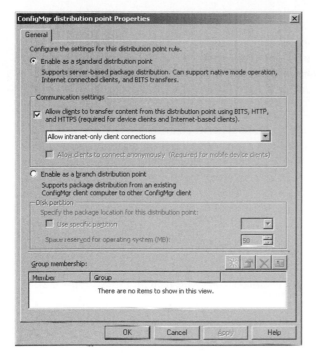

FIGURE 2.13   Configuring a branch distribution point

administration occurs in the ConfigMgr console. Figure 2.14 shows the integration between Configuration Manager and WSUS.

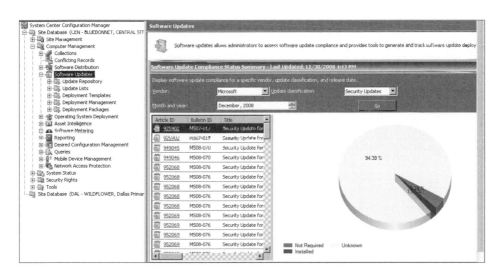

FIGURE 2.14   Software Update Compliance Status Summary

Fallback Status Point

The primary purpose of the fallback status point is to resolve client health issues. *Client health* describes the overall percentage of clients regularly checking into their designated management points, downloading policy, uploading inventory, and executing specified actions such as running an advertisement to install a package such as Microsoft Office.

The FSP in Configuration Manager 2007 always communicates with clients using HTTP, which uses unauthenticated connections and sends data in clear text, even when the site is in native mode. This makes the fallback status point vulnerable to attack, particularly when used with IBCM. To help reduce the attack surface, always dedicate a server to running the FSP and do not install other site system roles on that server in a production environment.

Install an FSP in the site if all the following scenarios exist:

▶ You want client computers to report any failures to the site database, particularly when they cannot contact an MP.

▶ You want to utilize the Configuration Manager 2007 client deployment reports that use data sent by the FSP.

▶ You have a dedicated server for this site system role and have additional security measures to help protect the server from attack.

▶ The benefits of using an FSP outweigh any security risks associated with unauthenti-cated connections and clear–text transfers over HTTP traffic.

CAUTION

Fallback Status Point Security Risk

Do not install an FSP in the site if the security risks of running a website with unau-thenticated connections and clear–text transfers outweigh the benefits of identifying client communication problems.

PXE Service Point

PXE is a technology allowing individuals to boot a computer from the network instead of a local disk. You can use this capability in situations where the disk needs to be written to in a way where no files can be in use, such as deploying an operating system.

The PXE service point must be configured to respond to PXE boot requests by Configuration Manager 2007 clients so that those clients can interact with the ConfigMgr infrastructure to determine the appropriate installation actions to take.

Other Site Systems

Other site systems new to ConfigMgr 2007 include the state migration point and branch distribution point, both introduced in the "Site Systems" section of this chapter.

Operating System Deployment

OSD in ConfigMgr is very different from the OSD Feature Pack on SMS 2003. ConfigMgr 2007 exposes a brand-new task sequencer, which sometimes is thought to be from BDD 2007 because it was available in the Business Desktop Deployment (BDD) Solution Accelerator released slightly earlier. The task sequencer from ConfigMgr was actually integrated into the BDD Solution Accelerator and Microsoft Deployment Toolkit (MDT). This integration allows for interoperability between OS deployments made in BDD/MDT and ConfigMgr. See Chapter 19, "Operating System Deployment," for a discussion of OSD.

ConfigMgr also now provides the ability to build a complete reference PC, Sysprep, and image it all using a single unattended task sequence. This new capability provides administrators a mechanism to ensure the build process across all systems, regardless of platform or image, is consistent.

Asset Intelligence

First introduced in SMS 2003 SP 3, Microsoft enhanced Asset Intelligence significantly in Configuration Manager 2007. The Asset Intelligence reports include nine new License Management reports, three new Hardware reports, and six new Software reports.

Besides tracking installed software, auto-start software, and browser helper objects, new Software reports provide information about recently used executables. In addition to the Hardware reports that track USB devices, processor age, and readiness for upgrade, these new reports identify computers that have software or hardware changes since the last inventory cycle. New Client Access License reports, added to the existing License Ledger reports, complete the ability to compare license usage with Microsoft License Statements. Figure 2.15 lists some of the Asset Intelligence reports included with ConfigMgr 2007. Asset Intelligence is discussed further in Chapter 18.

Device Management

Mobile device management has changed substantially since SMS 2003. ConfigMgr device management enables discovering, inventorying, and reporting on the following mobile device categories:

- ▶ Hardware inventory
- ▶ Software inventory
- ▶ File collection
- ▶ Software distribution
- ▶ Mobile device configuration items

ConfigMgr 2007 also adds support for the following mobile devices:

- ▶ Windows Mobile for Pocket PC 2003
- ▶ Windows Mobile for Pocket PC 2003 Second Edition
- ▶ Windows Mobile for Pocket PC Phone Edition 2003

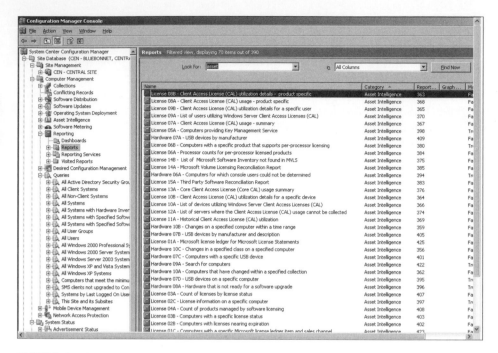

FIGURE 2.15   Configuration Manager 2007 Asset Intelligence reports

- ▶ Windows Mobile for Pocket PC Phone Edition 2003 Second Edition

- ▶ Windows Mobile Smartphone 2003

- ▶ Windows Mobile for Pocket PC 5.0

- ▶ Windows Mobile for Pocket PC Phone Edition 5.0

- ▶ Windows Mobile 5.0 Smartphone

- ▶ Windows CE 4.2 (ARM processor only)

- ▶ Windows CE 5.0 (ARM and x86 processors)

- ▶ Windows Mobile 6 Standard

- ▶ Windows Mobile 6 Professional

- ▶ Windows Mobile 6 Classic

The R2 release adds support for Windows Mobile 6.1.

SMS 2003 required connecting mobile devices to a host device running the SMS 2003 client. In ConfigMgr, mobile devices can be managed over Ethernet, wireless, or via IBCM. You can manage mobile devices when they have a standard Internet connection.

Internet-Based Client Management

IBCM allows you to manage ConfigMgr clients that are outside your network firewall. This configuration has a number of advantages, including the reduced costs of not having to run virtual private networks (VPNs) and being able to deploy software updates in a timelier manner.

Because of the higher security requirements of managing client computers on a public network, IBCM requires the site to be in native mode. Native mode ensures an independent authority mutually authenticates connections to the management point, software update point, and distribution points, and that data to and from these site systems is encrypted using Secure Sockets Layer (SSL). IBCM in essence allows ConfigMgr administrators to manage their client systems wherever they are (home, hotel, and so on) without them having to VPN in. See Chapter 6 for a discussion of IBCM.

DCM and NAP

Desired Configuration Management and Network Access Protection, both new in Configuration Manager 2007, were discussed previously in the "Desired Configuration Management" and "Network Access Protection" sections, respectively.

SQL Support

ConfigMgr 2007 requires a minimum of SQL Server 2005 with Service Pack 2 for the site database. Microsoft also supports using SQL Server 2005 SP 3 and SQL Server 2008.

The following caveats apply to using SQL Server 2008 with Configuration Manager 2007:

- ▶ There is no support for a clean installation of SQL Server 2008 with ConfigMgr 2007 RTM. You need to first install SQL Server 2005, then upgrade the database, and apply hotfix 955229.

- ▶ With ConfigMgr 2007 SP 1, Microsoft supports a clean installation of SQL Server 2008; hotfix 955262 is required.

TCP/IP is the only protocol now used for SQL Server to communicate with ConfigMgr; there is no longer a reliance on Named Pipes. The default port SQL uses is 1433, which you can change using the SQL Server Configuration Manager utility. Ports are discussed further in Chapter 5.

In most cases, Microsoft recommends having SQL Server and ConfigMgr on the same server when you install a primary site. Alternatively, Microsoft now recommends that if you are going to use a remote SQL Server, to install an additional network card in both the SQL Server and the ConfigMgr server and dedicate each card to communicate with one another, similar to a heartbeat network on a cluster.

SQL Server has supported using instances (which are multiple installations of SQL in parallel on the same server) since SQL Server 2000. Microsoft now supports the installation of the ConfigMgr 2007 database on a SQL named instance.

ConfigMgr also supports SQL replications, where you can point the MP or SLP roles at a SQL replica to improve performance in low-bandwidth scenarios. This is discussed further in Chapter 8, "Installing Configuration Manager 2007."

Client Support

Microsoft does not support the Configuration Manager client on any operating system prior to Windows 2000 Service Pack 4. Installing the Configuration Manager client explicitly is not supported on the following operating system versions:

▶ Windows 95

▶ Windows 98

▶ Windows Millennium Edition

▶ Windows XP Media Center Edition

▶ Windows XP Starter Edition

▶ Windows XP Home Edition

▶ Windows XP Professional, with less than Service Pack 2 applied

▶ Windows Vista Starter Edition

▶ Windows Vista Home Basic Edition

▶ Windows Vista Home Premium Edition

▶ Windows NT Workstation 4.0

▶ Windows NT Server 4.0

▶ Windows 2000 Server, Service Pack 3 and earlier

▶ Windows 2003 Server, with no service pack installed

▶ Windows CE 3.0

▶ Windows Mobile Pocket PC 2002

▶ Windows Mobile Smartphone 2002

Feature Dependencies

Many features of ConfigMgr are dependent on other technologies. As an example, Active Directory requires extending the schema to realize many of the benefits of client management. Without schema extensions, many of the automated tasks that clients perform would require manual workarounds.

Internet Information Services is required on several roles, such as management points, server locator points, and reporting points. Distribution points do not require IIS, but are dependent on it if they are going to use the BITS technology.

Windows Software Update Services is the underlying technology for all of Patch Management within ConfigMgr. This dependency on WSUS is why the ConfigMgr installation requirements state the WSUS console at a minimum must be installed on the site server. Having the WSUS console and binaries local to the site server allows ConfigMgr to manipulate the WSUS application and let the administrator authorize the necessary changes through the Configuration Manager console.

ConfigMgr 2007 uses certificates heavily for network access authentication because they provide strong security for authenticating users and computers and eliminate the need for less secure password-based authentication methods.

Network Access Protection is dependent on Windows Server 2008 and native mode in ConfigMgr. ConfigMgr by default installs itself into mixed mode, which means the ConfigMgr site server generates all the self-signed certificates it needs. These certificates are only used within ConfigMgr. By upgrading to native mode (discussed in Chapter 6), industry-standard PKI certificates are used. These certificates are created and managed independently from Configuration Manager, and they can be integrated with other business solutions. In native mode, clients communicate over HTTPS to the following site systems:

► Management points

► Default management point

► Network load-balanced management point

► Proxy management point

► Internet-based management point

► Standard distribution points

► Software update points

► State migration point

Table 2.4 lists the feature dependencies in ConfigMgr 2007.

TABLE 2.4　Feature Dependencies in Configuration Manager 2007

ConfigMgr Role	SQL 2005 SP 2	IIS	WebDAV	BITS Server	WSUS 3.0	.NET Framework	MMC 3.0	BITS Client	Windows Server 2008
Management points		X	X	X					
Distribution point		X	X	X					
State migration point		X							

TABLE 2.4 Feature Dependencies in Configuration Manager 2007

ConfigMgr Role	SQL 2005 SP 2	IIS	WebDAV	BITS Server	WSUS 3.0	.NET Framework	MMC 3.0	BITS Client	Windows Server 2008
PXE service point									
System Health Validator									
Branch distribution point						X		X	
Fallback status point		X							
Software update point		X		X	X				
Server locator point		X							
Reporting point		X							
SQL Server	X								
Admin console						X	X		
Client						X		X	
Network Access Protection									X

Summary

For most companies, managing IT systems is a costly endeavor, making efficiency in the field essential. ConfigMgr can help you meet the technical and management challenges facing IT departments today. Its use of an open architecture, which is distributed and scalable to the largest and most complex enterprises, builds on top of existing Microsoft technologies to help you automate configuration and release management in the enterprise.

Configuration Manager 2007 allows you to standardize your application portfolio and desktop images, release software changes to thousands of computers in minutes, reimage systems in minutes, remotely support end users in a timely fashion, track and correct configuration management deviations, and report against all these, plus detailed inventory of all clients in the enterprise. No other Microsoft product lowers the total cost of ownership (TCO) of IT assets in the enterprise.

The next chapter, "Looking Inside Configuration Manager," discusses the design concepts and working principles of Configuration Manager 2007, along with the ways that ConfigMgr utilizes core Windows technologies.

CHAPTER 3

Looking Inside Configuration Manager

Microsoft's System Center Configuration Manager (ConfigMgr) 2007 delivers a variety of configuration management and system support services via a flexible and distributed architecture. ConfigMgr 2007 takes advantage of standards-based network protocols and security for its internal working and interaction with client systems. Configuration Manager components store and use data about ConfigMgr infrastructure and activity, the environment, and managed site systems in the site database. Microsoft provides an extensive set of queries and reports based on this data, as well as facilities for extracting data for your own queries and reports.

This chapter examines the inner workings of Configuration Manager. It describes the design concepts and working principles of ConfigMgr 2007, along with the ways that ConfigMgr utilizes core Windows technologies, specifically Active Directory (AD) and Windows Management Instrumentation (WMI). It also discusses the various components of Configuration Manager, how they communicate with each other, and how they work together to implement ConfigMgr features. The chapter looks inside the site database, which is the heart of Configuration Manager. It shows how you can view the inner workings of ConfigMgr through its status messages and logs, as well as through other tools for viewing database and process activity. The emphasis of this chapter is on depth rather than breadth. The authors have chosen some of the most important feature sets and data structures to use as examples throughout the chapter, rather than try to provide a comprehensive exposition of all ConfigMgr functionality.

For those readers who are simply looking to get Configuration Manager up and running, some of the material in this chapter may not be essential. These readers may still find a quick review of the "Schema Extensions" section helpful for planning purposes. They may also find some of the methods used in the "Status Messages and Logs" section useful for troubleshooting purposes. The "Managing WMI" section provides some additional guidance on troubleshooting WMI issues. For those who desire a deeper understanding of what is going on behind the scenes with ConfigMgr, the material in this chapter will help you grasp the architectural principles of the product and guide you into exploring the inner workings of Configuration Manager.

Design Concepts

Microsoft designed Configuration Manager 2007 to deliver enhanced management services to a wide variety of Windows-based systems. Its predecessor, Systems Management Server (SMS), eases managing desktop and laptop computers in an enterprise network environment. (For information regarding the different versions of SMS, see Chapter 2, "Configuration Manager 2007 Overview.") Configuration Manager builds on the core functionality of SMS and adds an enhanced feature set that includes advanced operating system (OS) deployment capabilities and asset management features as well as support for new Out of Band (OOB) Management technologies. ConfigMgr also extends management capabilities to managed computers accessible through the Internet.

In this latest release of its systems management software, Microsoft emphasizes security and compliance, scalability and operational simplicity. To help customers meet security and compliance goals, Configuration Manager 2007 implements the following features:

- **Patch Management**—One of the most important features of ConfigMgr 2007's SMS 2003 predecessor was its capabilities for deploying patches to Windows clients and reporting on system patch compliance status. Configuration Manager improves and extends this capability by integrating with Microsoft's Windows Software Update Service (WSUS) and implementing Network Access Protection (NAP) to prevent noncompliant systems from joining the network. Chapter 15, "Patch Management," discusses patch deployment and NAP.

- **Configuration Management**—ConfigMgr's Desired Configuration Management (DCM) allows you to ensure compliance with defined standards to prevent misconfigurations and reduce the attack surface of your systems. You will find a discussion of DCM in Chapter 16, "Desired Configuration Management."

- **Active Directory Integration**—Configuration Manager 2007's integration with Active Directory provides authentication and access control. The "Active Directory Integration" section of this chapter discusses these features.

- **Security**—Configuration Manager uses certificate-based authentication, encryption, and data integrity controls to secure communications between the site systems and clients. Configuration Manager provides a new security mode, called *native mode*, which is required for some but not all certificate-based functionality. Chapter 6, "Architecture Design Planning," discusses certificates and native mode.

Microsoft has also made ConfigMgr 2007 more scalable. Some scalability enhancements include the following:

- **Distributed processing**—SMS 2003 includes the ability to distribute functional roles to other systems in the environment. ConfigMgr 2007 introduces additional roles that can be distributed, helping to balance the processing load required by any single server.

- **Scale out**—Network Load Balancing (NLB) clusters enable scaling out certain roles.

- **Flexible hierarchy**—ConfigMgr's flexible hierarchy model enables deploying its services to remote locations with limited network connectivity. This includes the branch distribution point capability, new with Configuration Manager 2007.

- **Manageability**—Configuration Manager uses Internet-standard protocols to extend management capabilities to Windows mobile devices and managed systems accessible through the Internet.

Chapter 6 includes a discussion on configuring site system roles, hierarchy design, and management of mobile devices and Internet clients.

Configuration Manager's capabilities can help simplify your operations in the following areas:

- **Planning**—Inventory and discovery data provide a central information store you can use in intelligently planning your operations. The "Inside the ConfigMgr Database" section of this chapter introduces the database and some of its potential uses.

- **Deployment**—Features for capturing, managing, and distributing system images and migrating user state information make it easier to provision new systems and upgrade existing ones. Chapter 19, "Operating System Deployment," presents ConfigMgr's Operating System Deployment (OSD) capabilities.

- **Enhancing**—Configuration Manager provides capabilities to easily deploy and maintain software applications on large numbers of client systems. Chapter 14, "Distributing Packages," discusses ConfigMgr software distribution in detail.

- **Life cycle management**—ConfigMgr 2007's improved Asset Intelligence capabilities help you track and manage hardware and software assets throughout their life cycle. Chapter 18, "Reporting," discusses the use of Asset Intelligence.

To implement these capabilities, Configuration Manager leverages key elements of the Windows platform. The two most important Windows components are AD and WMI. The next sections look in depth at how ConfigMgr uses these technologies.

Active Directory Integration

Active Directory is the central information store that Windows Server uses to maintain entity and relationship data for a wide variety of objects in a networked environment. AD provides a set of core services, including authentication, authorization, and directory services. Configuration Manager requires an Active Directory environment and takes advantage of AD to support many of its features. For more information about Active Directory in Windows Server 2003 and Windows Server 2008, see the following references:

▶ http://www.microsoft.com/windowsserver2003/technologies/directory/activedirectory/ default.mspx for information regarding Windows Server 2003 and Active Directory

▶ http://www.microsoft.com/windowsserver2008/en/us/active-directory.aspx for details on Active Directory in Windows Server 2008

In an Active Directory environment, all processes run in the security context of a user or a security context supplied by the operating system. *System accounts* are special accounts included on each Windows system used to run processes in a context supplied by the operating system. Prior to AD, the only built-in system account context was the *Local System* account. The Windows NT Local System account provided unlimited access to system resources, but you could not use it for network requests.

Using Active Directory, each system has a computer account that you can add to user groups and grant access to resources anywhere on the network. Windows Server 2003 and later operating systems add two other built-in accounts with limited access:

▶ The *Local Service* account has essentially the same rights on the local system as a nonprivileged user and no access to the network.

▶ The *Network Service* account has rights and network access similar to a nonprivileged user account.

ConfigMgr 2007 makes extensive use of system and computer accounts to run processes. Using system accounts greatly simplifies administration, eliminating the need to create and manage the large number of service accounts required using early versions of SMS.

In addition to authentication and access control services, Configuration Manager 2007 can use AD to publish information about its sites and services, making ConfigMgr easily accessible to Active Directory clients. To take advantage of this capability, you must extend the AD schema to create classes of objects specific to Configuration Manager. Although extending the schema is not required for ConfigMgr to work, it is required for certain Configuration Manager features. Extending the schema also greatly simplifies ConfigMgr deployment and operations. The "Schema Extensions" section of this chapter discusses extending the AD schema, and the "Benefits of Extending Active Directory" section covers the feature dependencies and administrative advantages provided by the schema extensions.

Configuration Manager can also take advantage of Active Directory in the following ways:

▶ Discovering information about your environment, including the existence of potential client systems. Chapter 12, "Client Management," discusses the discovery process.

▶ Assigning and installing clients through group policy, also described in Chapter 12. In addition, you can use group policy to configure basic services used by ConfigMgr.

▶ Using certificates and certificate settings deployed through AD to enhance its own security, as discussed in Chapter 6.

Schema Extensions

All objects in Active Directory are instances of classes defined in the AD schema. The schema provides definitions for common objects such as users, computers, and printers. Each object class has a set of attributes that describes members of the class. As an example, an object of the computer class has a name, operating system, and so forth. Additional information about the AD schema is available at http://msdn.microsoft.com/en-us/library/ms675085(VS.85).aspx.

The schema is extensible, allowing administrators and applications to define new object classes and modify existing classes. Using the schema extensions provided with Configuration Manager eases administering your ConfigMgr environment. The ConfigMgr schema extensions are relatively low risk and involve only a specific set of classes not likely to cause conflicts. Extending the schema is a recommended best practice for Configuration Manager because it allows you to avoid additional configuration tasks and implement stronger security. Nevertheless, you will want to test any schema modifications before applying them to your production environment.

Tools for Extending the Schema

You can extend the schema in either of two ways:

> ► Running the ExtADSch.exe utility from the ConfigMgr installation media

> ► Using the LDIFDE (Lightweight Data Interchange Format Data Exchange) utility to import the ConfigMgr_ad_schema.ldf LDIF file

If you are extending the schema on a Windows 2000 domain controller, you must use the LDIF file.

Using ExtADSch   Using ExtADSch.exe is the simplest way to extend the schema, and in SMS 2003, it was the only way to extend the schema. ExtADSch.exe creates the log file extadsch.log, located in the root of the system drive (%*systemdrive*%), which lists all schema modifications it has made and the status of the operation. After the list of attributes and classes that have been created, the log should contain the entry "Successfully extended the Active Directory schema."

Using LDIFDE   LDIFDE is a powerful command-line utility for extracting and updating directory service data on Active Directory servers, beginning with Windows 2000. LDIFDE provides command-line switches, allowing you to specify a number of options, including some you may want to use when updating the schema for ConfigMgr. Table 3.1 includes the options that you are most likely to use.

The options vary slightly, depending on the Windows Server version you are running. You can see a complete listing of LDIFDE syntax by entering the following command:

```
ldifde /?
```

TABLE 3.1 LDIFDE Command-Line Switches and Descriptions

Switch	Description
-i	Turns on Import Mode. (Required for updating the schema.)
-f	Filename. (Used to specify the location of the ConfigMgr_ad_schema.ldf file.)
-j	Log file location.
-v	Turns on Verbose Mode.
-k	Ignore Constraint Violation and Object Already Exists errors. (Use with caution. May be useful if the schema is previously extended for SMS.)

You can also find detailed information about using LDIFDE at http://technet2. microsoft.com/windowsserver2008/en/library/8fe5b815-f89d-48c0-8b2c-a9cd1d6986521033.mspx?mfr=true. A typical command to update the schema for ConfigMgr would be something like this:

```
ldifde -i -f ConfigMgr_ad_schema.ldf -v -j SchemaUpdate.log
```

The verbose logging available with LDIFDE includes more detail than the log file generated by ExtADSch.exe. The ConfigMgr_ad_schema.ldf file allows you to review all the intended changes before they are applied. You can also modify the LDF file to customize the schema extensions. As an example, you can remove the sections for creating classes and attributes that already exist as an alternative to using the –k switch referred to in Table 3.1.

> **CAUTION**
>
> **Be Careful when Editing the LDF File**
>
> Do not attempt to edit the LDF file unless you have a thorough understanding of LDF, and remember to test all modifications before applying them to your production environment.

Extending the Schema
Each AD forest has a single domain controller that has the role of schema master. All schema modifications are made on the schema master. To modify the schema, you must log on using an account in the forest root domain that is a member of the Schema Admins group.

> **NOTE**
>
> **About the Schema Admins Group**
>
> The built-in Schema Admins group exists in the root domain of your forest. Normally there should not be any user accounts in the Schema Admins group. You should only add accounts to the Schema Admins temporarily when you need to modify the schema. Exercising this level of caution will protect the schema from any accidental modifications.

The ConfigMgr 2007 schema modifications create four new classes and 14 new attributes used with these classes. The classes created represent the following:

- **Management points**—Clients can use this information to find a management point.

- **Roaming boundary ranges**—Clients can use this information to locate ConfigMgr services when they connect to the network at a location not within the boundaries of their assigned site.

- **Server locator points (SLPs)**—Clients can use this information to find an SLP.

- **ConfigMgr sites**—Clients can retrieve important information about the site from this AD object.

Real World: Tips and Techniques about Changing the Schema

You will want to exercise caution when planning any changes to the AD schema, particularly when making modifications to existing classes, because this may affect your environment.

When you modify the schema, you should take the schema master offline temporarily while you apply the changes. Regardless of the method you use to extend the schema, you should review the logs to verify that the schema extensions were successful before bringing the schema master back online. This way, if there is a problem with the schema modifications, you can seize the schema master role on another domain controller and retain your original schema!

Before actually extending the schema for ConfigMgr 2007, run the dcdiag and netdiag command-line tools, part of the Windows Support Tools. These tools validate that all domain controllers (DCs) are replicating and healthy. Because it may be difficult to validate the output of these tools, you can output the results to a text file using the following syntax:

```
dcdiag >c:\dcdiag.txt
```

Search the output text file for failures and see if any domain controllers are having problems replicating. If any failures are present, do not update the schema. Upgrading the schema when domain controllers are not healthy or replicating correctly will cause them to be orphaned as AD is revved to a higher version. The machine will then need to be manually and painfully cleaned out of AD.

Chapter 6 describes the Management Point and Server Locator Point server roles.

NOTE

Schema Extensions and ConfigMgr 2007 Updates

There are no changes to the schema extensions from the RTM (Release to Manufacturing, or initial release) version of Configuration Manager 2007 in either Service Pack (SP) 1 or Release 2 (R2) (it is unknown at the time of writing this chapter whether SP 2 will incorporate schema changes). The ConfigMgr schema extensions include previous changes from the SMS 2003 version of the schema extensions.

Although you can deploy ConfigMgr with only the SMS 2003 schema extensions applied to AD, you will not have all the functionality provided by the ConfigMgr schema extensions. Configuration Manager features not supported by the SMS 2003 Schema extensions include Network Access Protection and native mode security. The "Benefits of Extending Active Directory" section of this chapter discusses these features.

Viewing Schema Changes

If you are curious about the details of the new classes, you can use the Schema Management Microsoft Management Console (MMC) snap-in to view their full schema definitions. Before adding the snap-in to the management console, you must install it by running the following command from the command prompt:

```
regsvr32 schmmgmt.dll
```

After installing the snap-in, perform the following steps to add Schema Management to the MMC:

1. Select Start, choose Run, and then enter **MMC**.
2. Choose Add/Remove snap-in from the File menu of the Microsoft Management Console.
3. Click the Add button and then choose Active Directory Schema.
4. Choose Close and then click OK to complete the open dialog boxes.

The left pane of the schema management tool displays a tree control with two main nodes—classes and attributes. If you expand out the classes node, you will find the following classes defined by ConfigMgr:

- ▶ mSSMSManagementPoint
- ▶ mSSMSRoamingBoundaryRange
- ▶ mSSMSServerLocatorPoint
- ▶ mSSMSSite

Clicking a class selects it and displays the attributes associated with the class in the right pane. The list of attributes for each class includes many attributes previously defined in Active Directory, in addition to those attributes specifically created for ConfigMgr 2007. You can right-click a class and choose Properties to display its property page. As an example, Figure 3.1 shows the general properties of the mSSMSSite class. You can see an explanation of these properties by clicking the Help button on the Properties page.

You can see the 14 ConfigMgr attributes under the Attributes node in the schema management console. The names of each of these attributes start with *mS-SMS*. You can right-click an attribute and choose Properties to display its property page. Figure 3.2 shows the properties of the mS-SMS-Capabilities attribute.

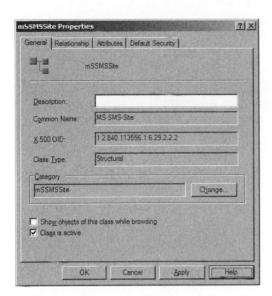

FIGURE 3.1   General properties of the schema class representing ConfigMgr sites

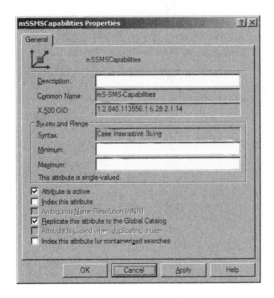

FIGURE 3.2   General properties of the schema attribute representing site capabilities

> **TIP**
>
> **Verifying the Schema Extensions**
>
> Check ExtADSch.log for failures. Seeing the Event IDs 1137 in the Directory Service Event Log alone is not confirmation that the schema was extended properly; several experiences in the field have found what seemed to be a successful schema extension to show failures in the log file.

Additional Tasks

After extending the schema, you must complete several tasks before ConfigMgr can publish the objects it will use to Active Directory:

- ▶ Creating the System Management container where the ConfigMgr objects will reside in AD. If you previously extended the schema for SMS, the System Management container will already exist. Each domain publishing ConfigMgr data must have a System Management container.

- ▶ Setting permissions on the System Management container. Setting permissions allows your ConfigMgr site servers to publish site information to the container.

- ▶ Configuring your sites to publish to AD.

The next sections describe these tasks.

Creating the System Management Container   You can use the ADSIEdit MMC tool to create the System Management AD container. If you do not already have ADSIEdit installed, you can install the tool yourself. The steps to install ADSIEdit will vary depending on the version of Windows Server you are running.

On Windows Server 2008, add ADSIEdit using Server Manager. Note that configuring the domain controller server role automatically adds ADSIEdit to the Administrative Tools program group.

To install ADSIEdit on Windows Server 2003 or Windows 2000 Server, perform the following steps:

1. Run the Windows Installer file at \SUPPORT\TOOLS\suptools.msi from the Windows Server 2003 installation media. (For Windows 2000 systems, the installer file is adminpak.msi.)
2. Select Start, choose Run, and then enter **MMC**.
3. Choose Add/Remove snap-in from the File menu.
4. Click the Add button and choose ADSI Edit.
5. Choose Close and then click OK to complete the open dialog boxes.

To create the System Management container from ADSIEdit, perform the following steps:

1. Right-click the Root ADSI Edit node in the tree pane, select Connect to..., and then click OK to connect to the default name context.

2. Expand the default name context node in the tree pane. Then expand the node showing the distinguished name of your domain (this will begin with DC=*<domain name>*) and right-click CN=System node.

3. Select New and then choose Object.

4. Select Container in the Create Object dialog box and click Next.

5. Enter the name **System Management** and then click Next and Finish, completing the wizard.

Figure 3.3 shows ADSIEdit with the tree control expanded to the CN=System node and the Create Object dialog box displayed.

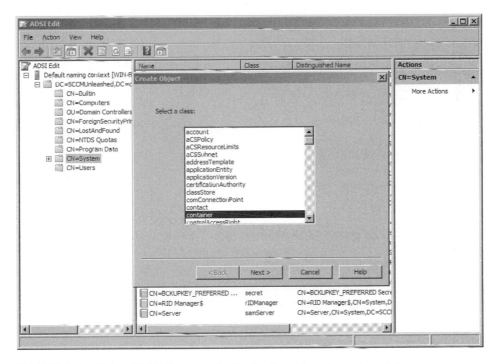

FIGURE 3.3   Using ADSIEdit to create the System Management container

Setting Permissions on the System Management Container   You can view the System Management container and set permissions on it using the Active Directory Users and Computers (ADUC) utility in the Windows Server Administrative Tools menu group. After launching ADUC, you need to enable the Advanced Features option from the View menu. You can then expand out the domain partition and System container to locate System Management.

By default, only certain administrative groups have the rights required to create and modify objects in the System Management container. For security reasons, you should create a new group and add ConfigMgr site servers to it, rather than adding them to the built-in administrative groups. Perform the following steps to grant the required access to the ConfigMgr site server security group:

1. Right-click the System Management container, choose Properties, and then select the Security tab.

2. Click the Add button and select the group used with your ConfigMgr site servers, as shown in Figure 3.4.

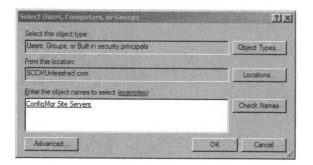

FIGURE 3.4   Selecting the Site Server security group

3. Check the box for Full Control as displayed in Figure 3.5, and choose OK to apply the changes.

Configuring Sites to Publish to Active Directory   Perform the following steps to configure a ConfigMgr site to publish site information to AD:

1. Navigate to System Center Configuration Manager -> Site Database -> Site Management -> <Site Code> in the ConfigMgr console (select Start -> All Programs -> Microsoft Configuration Manager to open the Configuration Manager console).

2. Right-click the site code and choose Properties. Click the Advanced tab and then select the Publish this site in Active Directory Domain Services check box as shown in Figure 3.6. Choose OK to apply your changes.

After extending the schema and taking the other steps necessary to enable your sites to publish to AD, you should see the ConfigMgr objects displayed in the System

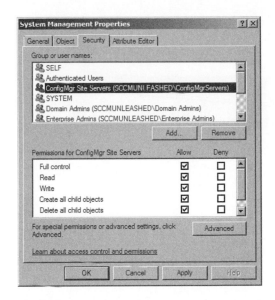

FIGURE 3.5   Assigning permissions to the System Management container

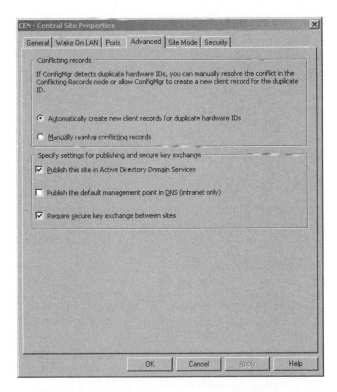

FIGURE 3.6   Configuring a site to publish to AD

Management container. Figure 3.7 shows the ConfigMgr objects viewed in Active Directory Users and Computers.

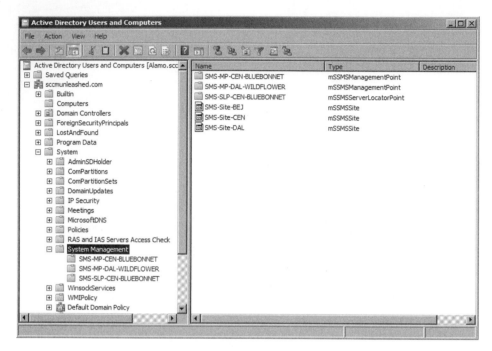

FIGURE 3.7   The System Management container displayed in Active Directory Users and Computers

Benefits of Extending Active Directory

Once you extend the Active Directory schema and perform the other steps necessary to publish site information to AD, clients in the same AD forest as your ConfigMgr sites can query AD to locate Configuration Manager services and retrieve important information about your ConfigMgr sites. Those clients in workgroups and domains without trust relationships are not able to take advantage of the schema extensions.

The following ConfigMgr features require extending the AD schema and publishing site information to AD:

▶ **Global roaming**—Roaming in ConfigMgr allows clients such as laptop computers to connect to the network at various locations and receive certain services from the local site. The schema extensions allow a client to query AD for the mSSMSRoamingBoundaryRange objects and determine whether a site exists on the IP subnet of their current network location. This is known as *global roaming*. Without the schema extensions, clients can only receive services when at their assigned site or roaming to the sites below their assigned site in the ConfigMgr hierarchy.

Global roaming can make content available to clients at network locations where it would otherwise not be available. Global roaming can also prevent unnecessary network traffic otherwise caused by those clients at remote locations requiring services from their assigned site. For more information about global roaming, see Chapter 12.

▶ **Network Access Protection**—You can use ConfigMgr's NAP capabilities to prevent clients that do not comply with specified security patch requirements from connecting to the network. NAP requires the client to retrieve health state reference information stored in the attributes of the mSSMSSite AD object. Chapter 15 discusses Network Access Protection in detail.

ConfigMgr clients can also receive a number of services through the extended schema that may be available in other ways. Chapter 12 discusses many of these features. In each case, the alternatives are more difficult to implement and some require extensive manual effort. You can use the schema extensions for the following capabilities:

▶ **Client site assignment**—To receive ConfigMgr services, you must first assign a client system to a site. The schema extensions provide an option for the client to retrieve the information from AD that it needs to identify and contact its assigned site.

▶ **Client installation properties**—A number of configurable options, such as the size of the download cache, are available through the extended schema.

▶ **Site mode settings**—The extended schema can supply information to the client about the site's security mode and certificate information required for native sites.

▶ **Server locator point and management points**—Clients can use Active Directory to identify the server locator point and management points. Without the schema extensions you must provide this information in other ways, such as manually creating special Windows Internet Naming Service (WINS) entries.

▶ **Custom Transmission Control Protocol (TCP)/Internet Protocol (IP) Port information**—If a site has been configured to use nonstandard ports for client communications, this information can be provided through the schema extensions. See Chapter 5, "Network Design," for a discussion of port customization.

In addition, the schema extensions allow for automated public key exchange, thus facilitating site-to-site communication. If you have clients assigned to your central site and do not have the schema extended, recovery from a site failure can require reprovisioning all clients manually using the trusted root key.

The AD schema extensions are a key enabling technology for Configuration Manager. You should extend the schema and take the other steps previously listed in the "Schema Extensions" section of this chapter to publish site information to Active Directory, if this is possible.

Configuration Manager and WMI

If the SQL Server database is the heart of Configuration Manager, WMI is its lifeblood. Windows Management Instrumentation has been the core management infrastructure for all Windows desktop and server operating systems beginning with Windows 2000, and it's available for download for use with earlier versions of Windows. WMI is the Windows implementation of Web-Based Enterprise Management (WBEM). WBEM is a set of standards intended to provide the basis for cross-platform interoperability of technologies to exchange management data and access management interfaces across distributed computing environments.

The Distributed Management Task Force (DMTF) supports WBEM. This group is an industry consortium created to promote standardization and integration of enterprise and Internet management technology. For more information about WBEM in general and the DMTF, see http://www.dmtf.org/about/faq/general_faq. Although much of the architectural material in this chapter is common to all implementations of WBEM, the next sections exclusively focus on WMI and its role in Configuration Manager, as follows:

▶ **WMI architecture**—This includes describing the WMI feature set, reviewing the major components of WMI, and discussing how they interact.

▶ **WMI object model**—The WMI object model and its implementation are discussed, with several tools you can use for managing WMI and looking into its inner workings.

▶ **ConfigMgr use of WMI**—Configuration Manager's use of WMI is discussed, with how you can look inside ConfigMgr through its WMI interfaces.

WMI Feature Set and Architecture

WMI serves as an abstraction layer between management applications and scripts and the physical and logical resources they manage. WMI exposes managed resources through a COM (Component Object Model) API (application programming interface). Programs written in C/C++ can call these resources directly, or you can access them through intermediate layers from applications such as scripts, Windows forms, or web forms. WMI presents a consistent and extensible object model to represent a wide variety of system, network, and other resources.

Using an object model removes much of the complexity that would otherwise be required to access and manipulate these resources. Some examples of resources you can manage through WMI include hardware devices, running processes, the Windows file system and Registry, and applications and databases.

You can invoke WMI services in several ways:

▶ Locally on a machine

▶ Remotely through a DCOM (Distributed COM) connection

▶ Remotely using a WS-Management (Web Services for Management) connection

Configuration Manager 2007 uses all three of these access methods to connect to WMI. Chapter 5 describes the use of DCOM in ConfigMgr and the network protocols used for DCOM connections.

WS-Management is a Simple Object Access Protocol (SOAP)–based specification published by the DMTF. SOAP is a standard for invoking objects remotely over a Hypertext Transfer Protocol (HTTP) or Hypertext Transfer Protocol over Secure Socket Layer (HTTPS) connection. The main advantage of SOAP is that it works across many existing network firewalls without requiring additional configuration. A complete description of WS-Management and related specifications can be found at http://www.dmtf.org/standards/wsman.

The ConfigMgr Out of Band (OOB) management point and OOB console use WS-Management to connect to the OOB management controller on systems equipped with Intel vPro technology. Chapter 6 discusses OOB Management in detail.

WMI supports requests from management applications to

▶ Retrieve or modify individual data items (properties) of managed objects;

▶ Invoke actions (methods) supported by managed objects;

▶ Execute queries against the data set of managed objects;

▶ Register to receive events from managed objects.

About WMI Query Language

WMI provides its own query language that allows you to query managed objects as data providers. WMI Query Language (WQL) is essentially a subset of SQL (Structured Query Language) with minor semantic changes. Unlike SQL, WQL does not provide statements for inserting, deleting, or updating data and does not support stored procedures. WQL does have extensions that support WMI events and other features specific to WMI. WQL is the basis for Configuration Manager queries, whereas SQL is used for ConfigMgr reports. Queries and reports are discussed in Chapters 17 and 18, respectively. One important advantage of WQL is that a WQL query can return WMI objects as well as specific properties. Because management applications such as the Configuration Manager console interact with WMI objects, WQL queries can return result sets that you can use within the ConfigMgr infrastructure. For example, Configuration Manager collections are based on WQL queries. For more information about WQL, see http://msdn.microsoft.com/en-us/library/aa394606(VS.85).aspx.

Figure 3.8 shows the basic data flow in WMI:

1. Management applications submit a request to the WMI infrastructure, which passes the request to the appropriate provider.

2. The provider then handles the interaction with the actual system resources and returns the resulting response to WMI.

3. WMI passes the response back to the calling application. The response may be actual data about the resource or the result of a requested operation.

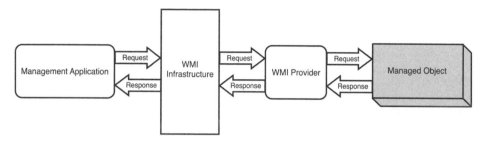

FIGURE 3.8   How WMI accepts a request from a management application and returns a response from a managed resource

WMI Providers

WMI providers are analogous to device drivers in that they know how to interact with a particular resource or set of resources. In fact, many device drivers also act as WMI providers. Microsoft supplies several built-in providers as part of Windows, such as the Event Log provider and File System provider. You will see providers implemented in the following ways:

▶ As DLLs (Dynamic Link Libraries)

▶ As Windows processes and services

Just as the WMI infrastructure serves management applications through a COM interface, providers act as COM servers to handle requests from the WMI infrastructure. When a provider loads, it registers its location and the classes, objects, properties, methods, and events it provides with WMI. WMI uses this information to route requests to the proper provider.

The WMI Infrastructure

Figure 3.9 displays the main logical components of the WMI infrastructure. The core of the WMI infrastructure is the Common Information Model Object Manager (CIMOM), described in the "Inside the WMI Object Model" section of this chapter. CIMOM brokers requests between management applications and WMI providers, and communicates with management applications through the COM API, as described earlier in the "WMI Feature Set and Architecture" section. CIMOM also manages the WMI *repository*, an on-disk database used by WMI to store certain types of data. Beginning with Windows XP, WMI also includes an XML (eXtensible Markup Language) encoder component, which management applications and scripts can invoke to generate an XML representation of managed objects.

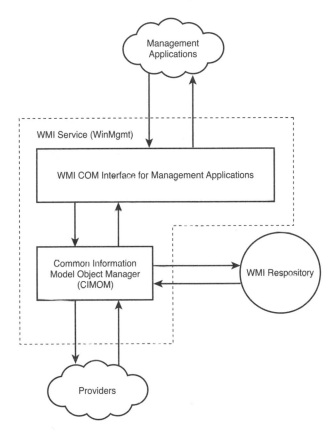

FIGURE 3.9   The major WMI infrastructure components

Most files used by WMI are stored on the file system by default under the %*windir*%\System32\Wbem folder. The executable containing the WMI service components is Winmgmt.exe. The physical implementation of the WMI infrastructure varies, depending on the version of Windows you are running. In Windows NT and Windows 2000, Winmgmt runs as a separate Windows service. In these earlier versions of Windows,

WMI providers are loaded into the Winmgmt process space, which means that a fault in one provider can crash the entire WMI process. This can cause repository corruption, which is a common cause of WMI problems in earlier Windows implementations. Using a single process space also means that providers share the security context of the Winmgmt process, which is generally the highly privileged Local System account.

Newer versions of Windows achieve greater process isolation by loading providers into one or more instances of WMIPrvse.exe. All WMI service components beginning with Windows XP run inside shared service host (SVCHOST) processes. Windows Vista introduced several significant enhancements in WMI security and stability, including the ability to specify process isolation levels, security contexts, and resource limits for provider instances. The next section of this chapter discusses WMI security. These enhancements are also available as an update for Windows XP and Windows Server 2003 systems at http://support.microsoft.com/kb/933062.

Configuration parameters for the WMI service are stored in the system Registry subtree HKEY_LOCAL_MACHINE\Software\Microsoft\WBEM. The WMI repository is a set of files stored under %windir%\System32\Wbem. The exact file structure varies slightly depending on the Windows version. WMI uses a customized version of the Jet database engine to access the repository files.

WMI also provides detailed logging of its activities. Prior to Windows Vista, log entries were written in plain text to files in the %windir%\System32\Wbem\logs folder. In Windows Vista and Windows Server 2008, most of these logs no longer exist, and Windows Event Tracing makes log data available to event data consumers, including the Event Log Service. By default, event tracing for WMI is not enabled. The "Managing WMI" section of this chapter discusses logging and event tracing options for WMI in. Some WMI providers, such as the ConfigMgr provider, also log their activity. The "Status Messages and Logs" section discusses logging by the ConfigMgr WMI provider.

Managing WMI

This section is intended to illustrate the options available for configuring WMI rather than as a "how-to" guide to administering WMI. You will rarely need to modify the WMI settings directly during day-to-day ConfigMgr administration. However, understanding the available options will help you understand the inner workings and functionality of WMI.

The Windows WMI Control is a graphical tool for managing the most important properties of the WMI infrastructure. Only members of the local Administrators group can use the WMI Control. To run this tool, perform the following steps:

1. Launch the Computer Management MMC snap-in. The exact procedure will vary depending on the version of Windows you are running. Generally you can right-click Computer or My Computer, and choose Manage.
2. Expand the Services and Applications node in the tree pane.
3. Right-click WMI Control and choose Properties.

The WMI Control opens to the General tab. As shown in Figure 3.10, the General properties confirm you have successfully connected to WMI on the local machine, display a few basic properties of your system, and specify the installed version of WMI.

FIGURE 3.10   The General tab of the WMI Control showing a successful connection to WMI on the local machine

NOTE

About Managing WMI on a Remote Machine

You can use the WMI Control tool to manage WMI on the local machine or on a remote machine. To connect to WMI on a remote machine, you follow the same procedure previously described in this section, with one additional step. Immediately after step 1, right-click the Computer Management node at the top of the tree and choose Connect to another computer. Then enter the name or IP address of the computer you want to manage and click OK. After connecting to the remote machine, complete steps 2 and 3 in the procedure.

Note that in addition to administrative privilege on the remote machine, you will need appropriate DCOM permissions (described later in this section). Also, DCOM network protocols must not be blocked on the remote machine or on any intermediary devices.

You can manage WMI security from the Security tab of the WMI Control tool. WMI uses standard Windows access control lists (ACLs) to secure each of the WMI namespaces that exist on your machine. A namespace, as described more precisely in the "Inside the WMI Object Model" section of this chapter, is a container that holds other WMI elements. The tree structure in the Security tab shows the WMI namespaces, as displayed in Figure 3.11.

FIGURE 3.11   The Security tab of the WMI Control tool, displaying the top-level WMI namespaces

It is important to note that the namespace is the most granular level in which to apply ACLs in WMI. The process of setting security on WMI namespaces, and the technology behind it, is very similar to the process of setting NTFS (NT File System) security. If you click a namespace to select it and click Security, you will see a dialog box similar to the one displayed in Figure 3.12.

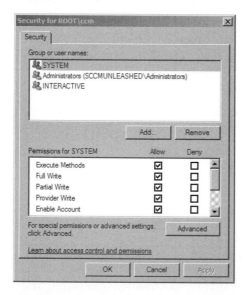

FIGURE 3.12   The WMI Security dialog box for the CCM namespace (the root namespace of the ConfigMgr client)

The dialog box in Figure 3.12 allows you to add security principals to the discretionary ACL (DACL) of the WMI namespace. The DACL specifies who can access the namespace and the type of access they have. Prior to Windows Vista, this was the only namespace access control implemented in WMI. The Vista WMI enhancements, mentioned previously in the "WMI Feature Set and Architecture" section of this chapter, add a system access control list (SACL) for WMI namespaces. The SACL specifies the actions audited for each security principal.

TIP

About Auditing

As with other auditing of object access in Windows, auditing access to WMI namespaces requires the effective value of the group policy setting Audit Object Access to be enabled. The Windows Security event log records the events specified in the auditing settings.

To specify auditing on a WMI namespace, perform the following steps:

1. From the Security dialog box shown in Figure 3.12, click the Advanced button.

2. In the Advanced Security Settings dialog box, click the Auditing tab.

3. Click the Add button and then enter the name of the user, group, or built-in security principal (see Figure 3.13). Click OK.

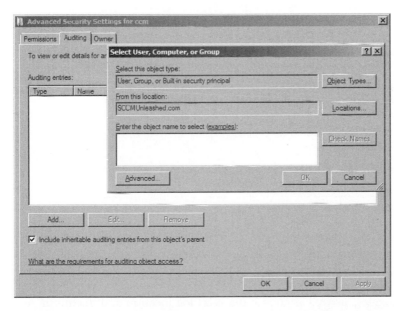

FIGURE 3.13   Specifying a user, computer, or group for WMI control security

4. Complete the selections in the Auditing Entry dialog box and click OK.

Figure 3.14 shows the entries to enable auditing for all access failures by members of the ConfigMgr Site Servers group.

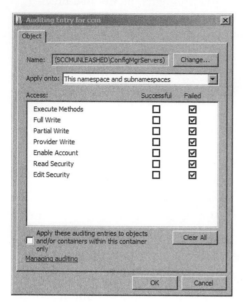

FIGURE 3.14   The WMI Auditing Entry dialog box displaying auditing enabled for all access failures by members of the ConfigMgr Site Servers group

Real World: Using Auditing to Troubleshoot WMI Connections

You can use auditing as a troubleshooting tool in the following ways:

▶ Auditing for access failures to help determine whether security problems are causing a WMI problem

▶ Auditing for access success to help determine whether there is a successful connection

Be judicious in auditing, because excessive auditing will consume unnecessary system resources and generate noise in the Security event log.

The remaining tabs of the WMI Control tool allow you to change the default namespace for WMI connections, and they provide one of several methods of backing up the WMI repository. Windows system state backups also back up the repository. Prior to Windows Vista, the WMI Control tool also contained a logging tab that allowed you to specify verbose, normal, or no logging, as well as choose the WMI log location and maximum log size. In Windows Server 2008 and Vista, you can enable logging and configure log options in the Windows Event Viewer.

To enable WMI Trace Logging in Windows 2008 and Vista, perform the following steps:

1. Open Event Viewer.
2. On the View menu, select Show Analytic and Debug Logs.
3. In the tree control, expand Applications and Service Logs -> Microsoft -> Windows -> WMI Activity.
4. Right-click Trace and then select Enable Log from the context menu. Choosing Properties from the same menu allows you to configure logging properties for WMI. You will now be able to view, filter, and manage the WMI log from this node in the Event Viewer tree.

You can read more about WMI Logging at http://msdn.microsoft.com/en-us/library/aa394564(VS.85).aspx.

You should be aware that User Account Control, also introduced in Windows Vista, applies to privileged WMI operations. This can affect some scripts and command-line utilities. For a discussion of User Account Control and WMI, see http://msdn.microsoft.com/en-us/library/aa826699(VS.85).aspx.

Additional command-line tools are available for managing WMI, which you can download from http://msdn.microsoft.com/en-us/library/aa827351(VS.85).aspx.

TIP

Using the WMIDiag Utility

SMS was one of the first applications to take advantage of WMI. At one time, SMS was often the only WMI management application running on many Windows machines. In those days, it was a common practice among SMS administrators to simply delete the repository when WMI errors were detected, and then restart WMI to re-create the repository. This is no longer a safe practice, because many applications depend on data stored in the repository. Moreover, WMI errors can result from many other problems in your environment and may have nothing to do with WMI itself.

Rather than deleting the repository, you should obtain the WMI Diagnosis Utility (WMIDiag) from the Microsoft download site (http://www.microsoft.com/downloads/details.aspx?familyid=d7ba3cd6-18d1-4d05-b11e-4c64192ae97d&displaylang=en, or go to www.microsoft.com/downloads and search for **WMIDiag**). WMIDiag can help you diagnose most WMI problems, and in many cases it provides detailed instructions on how to correct those problems.

Inside the WMI Object Model

The DMTF's Common Information Model (CIM) is the basis for the WMI object model. CIM defines a core model that provides the basic semantics for representing managed objects, and describes several common models representing specific areas of management, such as systems, networks, and applications. Third parties develop extended models, which are platform-specific implementations of common classes. You can categorize the class definitions used to represent managed objects as follows:

▶ *Core classes* represent general constructs that are applicable to all areas of management. The Managed Element class is the most basic and general class and is at the root of the CIM class hierarchy. Other examples of core classes include

    ▶ Component

    ▶ Collection

    ▶ Statistical Information

Core classes are part of the core model and are the basic building blocks from which other classes are developed.

▶ *Common classes* represent specific types of managed objects. Common classes are generalized representations of a category of objects, such as a computer system or an application. These classes are not tied to a particular implementation or technology.

▶ *Extended classes* are technology-specific extensions of common classes, such as a Win32 computer system or Configuration Manager.

WMI classes support inheritance, meaning you can derive a new class from an existing class. The derived class is often referred to as a *child* or *subclass* of the original class. The child class has a set of attributes available to it from its parent class. Inheritance saves developers the effort of needing to create definitions for all class attributes from scratch. Developers of a child class can optionally override the definition of an inherited attribute with a different definition better suited to that class. A child class can also have additional attributes not inherited from the parent.

Typically, core and common classes are not used directly to represent managed objects. Rather, they are used as *base classes* from which other classes are derived. The "Looking Inside the CIMV2 Namespace" section of this chapter presents an example of how a class inherits attributes from its parent class.

A special type of WMI class is the *system class*. WMI uses system classes internally to support its operations. They represent providers, WMI events, inheritance metadata about WMI classes, and more.

WMI classes support three types of attributes:

▶ *Properties* are the characteristics of the managed objects, such as the name of a computer system or the current value of a performance counter.

▶ *Methods* are actions that a managed object can perform on your behalf. As an example, an object representing a Windows service may provide methods to start, stop, or restart the service.

▶ *Associations* are actually links to a special type of WMI class, an association class, which represents a relationship between other objects. The "Looking Inside the CIMV2 Namespace" section examines the associations that link a file share security descriptor to the share and to the security principals specified in its access control lists.

You can also modify WMI classes, properties, and methods by the use of *qualifiers*. A qualifier on a class may designate it as abstract, meaning the class is used only to derive other classes and no objects of that class will be instantiated. Two important qualifiers designate data as static or dynamic:

▶ **Static data**—Supplied in the class or object definition and stored in the WMI repository

▶ **Dynamic data**—Accessed directly through the provider and represents live data on the system

The CIM specification also includes a language for exchanging management information. The Managed Object Format (MOF) provides a way to describe classes, instances, and other CIM constructs in textual form. In WMI, MOF files are included with providers to register the classes, properties, objects, and events they support with WMI. The information in the MOF files is compiled and stored in the WMI repository. Examples of information in MOF format are included throughout the chapter.

TIP

Acronym Usage

Chapter 1, "Configuration Management Basics," discussed the Microsoft Operations Framework, often referred to as MOF. There is no relationship between the Microsoft Operations Framework and Managed Object Format, although both use the same acronym.

Namespaces organize WMI classes and other elements. A *namespace* is a container, much like a folder in a file system. Developers can add objects to existing namespaces or create new namespaces. As already seen in the "Managing WMI" section, the *Root* namespace defines a hierarchy organizing the namespaces on a system. The "Managing WMI" section also mentions that the WMI Control tool allows you to specify the default namespace for connections to WMI. Generally, the default namespace will be Root\CIMV2. This is the namespace defining most of the major classes for Windows management. The next section looks at several of the classes in that namespace. Because Configuration Manager is all about Windows Management, it is not surprising that ConfigMgr uses this namespace extensively. ConfigMgr also defines its own namespaces, discussed in the section "Looking Inside Configuration Manager with WMI."

This section covers the major concepts of WMI and the CIM model, which will be used to look inside ConfigMgr WMI activity. If you are interested in learning about other aspects, of CIM, a good place to start is the tutorial at http://www.wbemsolutions.com/tutorials/ CIM/index.html. The full CIM specification can by found at http://www.dmtf.org/ standards/cim/cim_spec_v22. Documentation for WMI is available at http://msdn. microsoft.com/en-us/library/aa394582.aspx.

Looking Inside the CIMV2 Namespace

Windows provides a basic tool called WBEMTest that allows you to connect to a WMI namespace and execute WMI operations. There are also a number of tools from Microsoft and third parties with more intuitive graphical interfaces for displaying and navigating WMI namespaces. This section uses the Microsoft WMI Administrative Tools to look into the Root\CIMV2 namespace. These tools include the WMI CIM Studio and the WMI Object Browser. You can download the WMI Administrative Tools from http://www.microsoft.com/downloads/details.aspx?FamilyID=6430f853-1120-48db-8cc5-f2abdc3ed314&DisplayLang=en or search for **WMITools** at www.microsoft.com/ downloads. After downloading, you will need to run the WMITools.exe executable file to install the tools.

You can use CIM Studio to explore the classes in a namespace and view the properties, methods, and associations of each class. Perform the following steps to launch CIM Studio and connect to the CIMV2 namespace:

1. Select Start -> All Programs -> WMI Tools -> WMI CIM Studio.
2. CIM Studio will open a web browser and attempt to run an ActiveX control.

    If your browser blocks the control, select the option Allow Blocked Content.
3. Verify that root\CIMV2 displays in the Connect to namespace dialog box and then click OK. Notice that you can also browse to other namespaces on the local computer of a remote computer.
4. Click OK to accept the default logon settings.

When you open CIM Studio and connect to a namespace, the Class Explorer in the left pane contains a tree structure that displays the base classes in the selected namespace. Figure 3.15 displays the left pane with some of the root classes of the CIMV2 namespace.

Notice that most of the class names in Figure 3.15 begin with CIM or Win32. Class names starting with *CIM* indicate that the class is one of the core or common classes defined in the DMTF CIM schema. Extended classes are those classes with names beginning with *Win32*, which are part of the Win32 schema defined by Microsoft for managing the Win32 environment.

The Win32_LogicalShareSecuritySetting class

This section uses the Win32_LogicalShareSecuritySetting class to illustrate how you can use CIM Studio to understand a class of managed objects. Figure 3.16 shows the Win32_LogicalShareSecuritySetting class displayed in CIM Studio. This class represents the

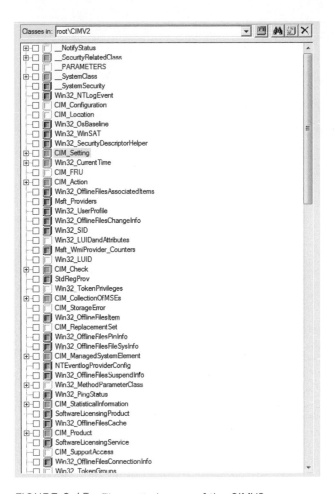

Classes in: root\CIMV2

```
__NotifyStatus
__SecurityRelatedClass
__PARAMETERS
__SystemClass
__SystemSecurity
Win32_NTLogEvent
CIM_Configuration
CIM_Location
Win32_OsBaseline
Win32_WinSAT
Win32_SecurityDescriptorHelper
CIM_Setting
Win32_CurrentTime
CIM_FRU
CIM_Action
Win32_OfflineFilesAssociatedItems
Msft_Providers
Win32_UserProfile
Win32_OfflineFilesChangeInfo
Win32_SID
Win32_LUIDandAttributes
Msft_WmiProvider_Counters
Win32_LUID
CIM_Check
StdRegProv
Win32_TokenPrivileges
CIM_CollectionOfMSEs
CIM_StorageError
Win32_OfflineFilesItem
CIM_ReplacementSet
Win32_OfflineFilesPinInfo
Win32_OfflineFilesFileSysInfo
CIM_ManagedSystemElement
NTEventlogProviderConfig
Win32_OfflineFilesSuspendInfo
Win32_MethodParameterClass
Win32_PingStatus
CIM_StatisticalInformation
SoftwareLicensingProduct
Win32_OfflineFilesCache
CIM_Product
SoftwareLicensingService
CIM_SupportAccess
Win32_OfflineFilesConnectionInfo
Win32_TokenGroups
```

FIGURE 3.15   The root classes of the CIMV2 namespace displayed in CIM Studio

security settings on a Windows file share. The expanded tree shows the root class, CIM_Setting, and the classes derived from each successive subclass.

Looking at the tree structure, you can see that Win32_LogicalShareSecuritySetting is derived from Win32_SecuritySetting, which in turn is derived from CIM_Setting. The Class View in the right pane displays the properties of the Win32_LogicalShareSecuritySetting class. To the left of each property name you will see one of the following icons:

► A yellow downward-pointing arrow indicates the property is inherited from the parent class.

► A property page indicates the property is defined within the class.

► A computer system indicates that the property is a system class. You can also recognize system classes by their names, which always start with a double underscore (__).

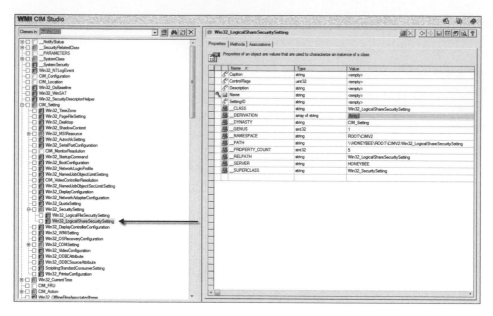

FIGURE 3.16   The Win32_LogicalShareSecuritySetting class displayed in CIM Studio

As an example, each WMI class has certain System properties, such as _PATH, _DYNASTY, _SUPERCLASS, and _DERIVATION. Here are some points to keep in mind:

▶ The _PATH property shows the location of the class in the namespace hierarchy. Management applications and scripts use the _PATH property to connect to the class.

▶ _DYNASTY, _SUPERCLASS, and _DERIVATION are all related to class inheritance and represent the root class from which the class is derived, its immediate parent, and the entire family tree of the class, respectively.

  Clicking the Array button next to _DERIVATION displays the array of parent classes from which the class is derived. The array is essentially the inheritance information already observed by traversing the tree, as shown in Figure 3.17.

The remaining properties of Win32_LogicalShareSecuritySetting are the ones that actually represent characteristics describing instances of Windows file share security settings. You can see that except for the name, all of these properties are inherited. An object that has nothing unique about it except its name would not be very interesting, but there is more to the Win32_LogicalShareSecuritySetting class than just the class properties. The most interesting attributes of Win32_LogicalShareSecuritySetting are on the remaining tabs of the CIM Studio Class View pane.

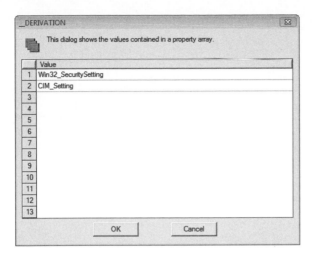

FIGURE 3.17   The array of classes from which the Win32_LogicalShareSecuritySetting class is derived, as displayed in CIM Studio

Clicking the Methods tab displays the two methods of the Win32_LogicalShareSecuritySetting class (GetSecurityDescriptor and SetSecurityDescriptor), as shown in Figure 3.18.

Getting Additional Information

These methods let you work with the permissions on the actual file share. Clicking the Help button on the toolbar in the upper-right corner of Class View in Figure 3.18 provides additional information about the class.

A Sample Help Entry

The help entry for Win32_LogicalShareSecuritySetting returns the following information:

```
security settings for a logical file

Caption

A short textual description (one-line string) of the CIM_Setting object.


ControlFlags

Inheritance-related flags.  See SECURITY_DESCRIPTOR_CONTROL


Description

A textual description of the CIM_Setting object.


Name

The name of the share
```

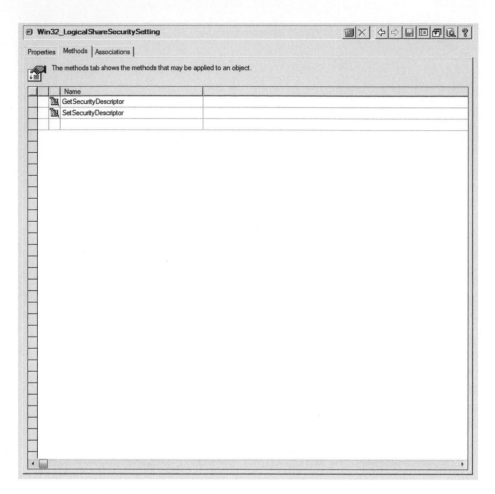

FIGURE 3.18   The Win32_LogicalShareSecuritySetting class methods, displayed in CIM Studio, allow management applications to retrieve or modify security on file shares.

```
SettingID
The identifier by which the CIM_Setting object is known.

uint32 GetSecurityDescriptor(
[out] object:Win32_SecurityDescriptor Descriptor
);

Retrieves a structural representation of the object's security descriptor.
The method returns an integer value that can be interpreted as follows:
0 - Successful completion.
```

```
2 - The user does not have access to the requested information.

8 - Unknown failure.

9 - The user does not have adequate privileges.

21 - The specified parameter is invalid.

Other - For integer values other than those listed above,

refer to Win32 error code documentation.


Descriptor

<description missing>


uint32 SetSecurityDescriptor(

[in] object:Win32_SecurityDescriptor Descriptor

);


Sets security descriptor to the specified structure.

The method returns an integer value that can be interpreted as follows:

0 - Successful completion.

2 - The user does not have access to the requested information.

8 - Unknown failure.

9 - The user does not have adequate privileges.

21 - The specified parameter is invalid.

Other - For integer values other than those listed above,

refer to Win32 error code documentation.


Descriptor

<description missing>
```

Putting It All Together

The Win32_LogicalShareSecuritySetting example in the "A Sample Help Entry" sidebar shows that the GetSecurityDescriptor method returns the current security descriptor of the file share as an object of type Win32_SecurityDescriptor. The SetSecurityDescriptor method accepts a Win32_SecurityDescriptor object as input and replaces the security descriptor on the share with information supplied in the security descriptor object. The example also lists the status codes returned by these methods.

The information on the Class View Associations tab, shown in Figure 3.19, provides the key to understanding the implementation of Win32_LogicalShareSecuritySetting.

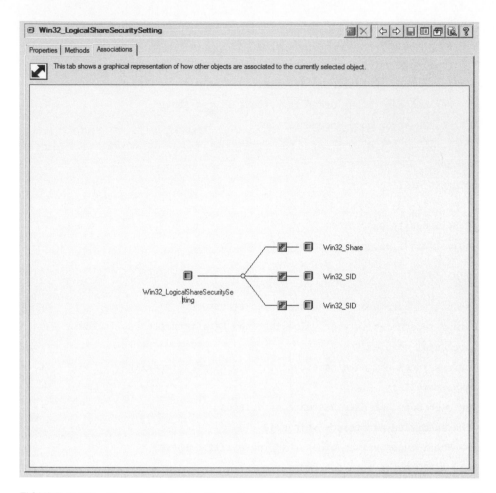

FIGURE 3.19 The Win32_LogicalShareSecuritySetting class associations, displayed here in CIM Studio, link the share security setting's objects to objects representing the share and the share's ACL entries.

The Win32_LogicalShareSecuritySetting Associations tab shown in Figure 3.19 displays an association with the Win32_Share class as well as associations with the two instances of the Win32_SID class. Class icons marked with a diagonal arrow represent the association classes linking other classes together. If you hover your mouse cursor over the Class icons for each of the association classes linking Win32_LogicalShareSecuritySetting to Win32_SID class instances, you can see that one is a Win32_LogicalShareAccess class instance and the other is a Win32_LogicalShareAuditing class instance.

▶ Instances of the Win32_LogicalShareAccess association represent access control entries (ACEs) in the DACL (that is, share permissions).

▶ The Win32_LogicalShareAuditing instances represent ACEs in the SACL (audit settings) on the share. You can double-click any of the classes shown on this tab to navigate to it in Class View.

Because objects of the Win32_LogicalShareSecuritySetting class allow you to work with live data on the system, you would expect this to be a dynamic class. You can verify this by returning to the Properties or Methods tab, right-clicking any attribute, and selecting Object Qualifiers. The Win32_LogicalShareSecuritySetting object qualifiers are shown in Figure 3.20, including the Dynamic qualifier, which is of type Boolean with a value of True.

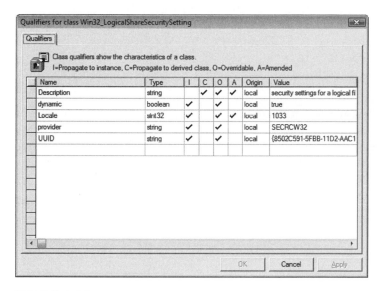

FIGURE 3.20   The Win32_LogicalShareSecuritySetting class qualifiers displayed in CIM Studio

From the Class View you can also use the Instances button to display all instances of the class, and you can open the properties of an instance by double-clicking it. The section "Hardware Inventory Through WMI" discusses how to use another of the WMI administrative tools, the WMI Object Browser, to view class instances. Just above the toolbar are icons that launch the MOF generator and MOF compiler wizards, as shown earlier in Figure 3.16. To launch the MOF compiler, you must check the Class icon next to the class and double-click the Wizard icon. The MOF language defining the Win32_LogicalShareSecuritySetting class is as follows:

```
#pragma namespace("\\\\.\\ROOT\\CIMV2")
//***********************************************************************
//* Class: Win32_LogicalShareSecuritySetting
//* Derived from: Win32_SecuritySetting
//***********************************************************************
[dynamic: ToInstance, provider("SECRCW32"): ToInstance, Locale(1033): ToInstance,
UUID("{8502C591-5FBB-11D2-AAC1-006008C78BC7}"): ToInstance]
class Win32_LogicalShareSecuritySetting : Win32_SecuritySetting
{
    [key, read: ToSubClass] string Name;
    [Privileges{"SeSecurityPrivilege", "SeRestorePrivilege"}: ToSubClass,
    implemented, ValueMap{"0", "2", "8", "9", "21", ".."}]
    uint32 GetSecurityDescriptor([OUT] Win32_SecurityDescriptor Descriptor);
    [Privileges{"SeSecurityPrivilege", "SeRestorePrivilege"}: ToSubClass,
    implemented, ValueMap{"0", "2", "8", "9", "21", ".."}]
    uint32 SetSecurityDescriptor([IN] Win32_SecurityDescriptor Descriptor);
};
```

The first line of the MOF entry, #pragma namespace ("\\\\.\\ROOT\\CIMV2"), is a
preprocessor command instructing the MOF compiler to load the MOF definitions into
the Root\CIMV2 namespace. A comment block follows, which indicates the class name
Class: Win32_LogicalShareSecuritySetting and the class derivation Derived from:
Win32_SecuritySetting. Next, a bracketed list of object qualifiers (refer to Figure 3.20
for a GUI representation of the object qualifiers):

▶ The *dynamic* qualifier indicates that the class is dynamic and will be instantiated at
runtime.

▶ The *provider* qualifier specifies that the instance provider is "SECRCW32."

▶ The *locale* qualifier indicates the locale of the class, 1033 (U.S. English).

▶ The *UUID* qualifier is a Universally Unique Identifier for the class.

Each of these qualifiers propagates to class instances, as indicated by the toinstance
keyword.

The next section contains the class declaration Win32_LogicalShareSecuritySetting :
Win32_SecuritySetting. This declaration derives the Win32_LogicalShareSecuritySetting
class from the Win32_SecuritySetting base class. The body of the class declaration declares
locally defined class properties and methods. The Name property (the name of the share)
is declared to be of type String and designated as a key value, indicating that it uniquely
identifies an instance of the class. The GetSecurityDescriptor and SetSecurityDescriptor
methods are both of type uint32, indicating that each method return an unsigned 32-bit
integer. GetSecurityDescriptor has an output parameter of type Win32_SecurityDescriptor,
whereas SetSecurityDescriptor has a corresponding input parameter of the same type.
Immediately preceding each of these method definitions you will see the following
method qualifiers specified:

▶ *Privileges* requests the access privileges required to manipulate Win32 security
descriptors.

▶ *Implemented* is a Boolean value indicating the method is implemented in the class.

▶ *Valuemap* specifies the method's return values. The "A Sample Help Entry" sidebar lists the meaning of each of these values.

In addition to the locally implemented properties and qualifiers, the Win32_LogicalShareSecuritySetting class inherits properties and qualifiers defined as part of its parent class, Win32_SecuritySetting.

Before continuing, you may want to explore several other classes in the Root\CIMV2 namespace:

▶ Work your way up the inheritance tree from the Win32_LogicalShareSecuritySetting class and see where each of the inherited properties of the class originates. In addition, notice that if you bring up the object qualifiers on the parent classes, you can see these are qualified as abstract classes.

▶ The immediate sibling of the Win32_LogicalShareSecuritySetting class is the Win32_LogicalFileSecuritySetting class. Notice the differences in the properties and associations for this class. Share security and file security have many characteristics in common but a few important differences. Seeing how they are both derived from the Win32_SecuritySetting class demonstrates the power and flexibility of class inheritance.

▶ Expand the CIM_StatisticalInformation root class and then the Win32_Perf class. The two branches of Win32_Perf show how a variety of performance counters are implemented as managed objects.

This section looked at several of the default classes in the Root\CIMV2 namespace and discussed how to use CIM Studio to explore a WMI namespace. The "Hardware Inventory Through WMI" section looks at how ConfigMgr uses the classes in Root\CIMV2 and adds some of its own classes.

The Root\CCM Namespace

The ConfigMgr client also uses WMI for internal control of its own operations. ConfigMgr 2007 creates and uses several namespaces in addition to adding classes to the Root\CIMV2 namespace.

The most important namespace created by the ConfigMgr client is the Root\CCM namespace. Together with several namespaces under Root\CCM, this namespace holds the configuration and policies that govern the operation of the ConfigMgr client. The hardware inventory process described in the next section of this chapter uses a policy stored in the Root\CCM\Policy\Machine namespace to specify what inventory data to retrieve from managed objects defined in the Root\CIMV2 namespace. "The Configuration Manager Client WMI Namespace" section discusses additional uses of the Root\CCM namespace.

Hardware Inventory Through WMI

ConfigMgr uses two MOF files to control hardware inventory:

- ▶ **SMS_Def.mof**—Specifies the information reported to the management point during the client inventory retrieval cycle. The actual SMS_Def.mof file is not downloaded to the ConfigMgr client. Instead, the client receives changes to reporting class configuration as part of its machine policy. Chapter 12 discusses client policy.

- ▶ **Configuration.mof**—Defines custom data classes the hardware inventory client agent will inventory. In addition to standard WMI classes, such as the Win32 classes, you can create data classes to provide inventory data that is accessible through WMI, such as data from the client's system Registry. ConfigMgr clients download the Configuration.mof file as part of their machine policy retrieval cycle. Any changes are compiled and loaded into the WMI repository.

The ConfigMgr client stores its machine policy in the Root\CCM\Policy\Machine WMI namespace. You can use the WMI Object Browser from the WMI Administrative Tools to examine some to the inventory-related objects in this namespace. To launch the WMI Object Browser and connect to the ConfigMgr machine policy namespace, perform the following steps:

1. Select Start -> All Programs -> WMI Tools -> WMI Object Browser.
2. The WMI Object Browser opens a web browser and attempts to run an ActiveX control.

   If your browser blocks the control, select the option Allow Blocked Content.
3. Change the entry in the Connect to namespace dialog box to **Root\CCM\Policy\Machine** and then click OK.
4. Click OK to accept the default logon settings.

You can locate objects of a specified class by clicking the Browse button (the binocular icon on the toolbar above the left pane). As an example, select InventoryDataItem from the available classes, as shown in Figure 3.21. InventoryDataItem is the class representing inventory items specified in the machine policy. Click the Browse button to display a list of InventoryDataItem instances in the Machine Policy namespace, as shown in Figure 3.22.

Figure 3.22 has the columns resized to hide the Key (1) column, which displays an object GUID (Globally Unique Identifier), and to display the more interesting information in Key (2) and Key (3).

Selecting the instance that refers to the Win32_DiskDrive class in the Root\CIMV2 namespace and double-clicking this entry displays the instance properties shown in Figure 3.23. The Namespace and ItemClass properties tell the hardware inventory agent it can retrieve inventory data for this class from Win32_DiskDrive objects in the Root\CIMV2 namespace.

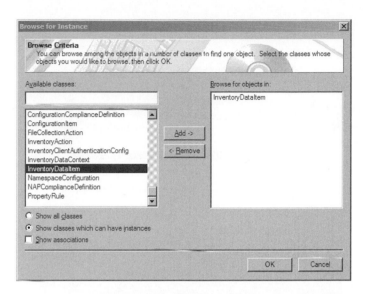

FIGURE 3.21   Browsing for InventoryDataItem in the WMI Object Browser

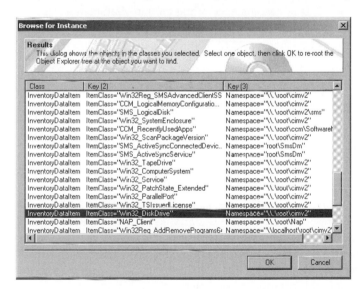

FIGURE 3.22   InventoryDataItem instances listed in the WMI Object Browser

The Properties property contains a list of properties to inventory from each instance of Root\CIMV2\Win32_DiskDrive. Here are the properties listed:

```
Availability, Description, DeviceID, Index, InterfaceType, Manufacturer,
MediaType, Model, Name, Partitions, PNPDeviceID, SCSIBus, SCSILogicalUnit,
SCSIPort, SCSITargetId, Size, SystemName
```

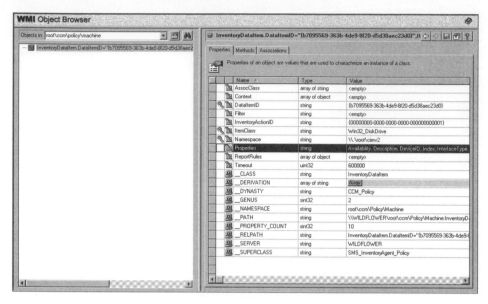

FIGURE 3.23   Properties of the Win32_DiskDrive instance of the InventoryDataItem as displayed in the WMI Object Browser

Win32_DiskDrive objects have many other properties besides these. If you examine the default SMS_Def.mof file that comes with ConfigMgr, you will find a section starting with the following:

```
[ SMS_Report    (TRUE),
  SMS_Group_Name ("Disk"),
  SMS_Class_ID   ("MICROSOFT¦DISK¦1.0") ]

class Win32_DiskDrive : SMS_Class_Template
```

This section is followed by a list of inventory properties available for the Win32_DiskDrive class. The properties listed here correspond to the ones designated with "SMS_Report (TRUE)" in the SMS_Def.mof file. SMS_Report is a class qualifier defined in the SMS_Class_Template class definition in SMS_Def.mof. If you change the SMS_Report qualifier on any of the available inventory properties in SMS_Def.mof on the site server, the corresponding WMI InventoryDataItem instance in the machine policy namespace is updated on the client during the next machine policy retrieval cycle.

Another InventoryDataItem instance in the Root\CCM\Policy\Machine namespace—Win32Reg_AddRemovePrograms—configures inventory settings for reporting on items of the Win32Reg_AddRemovePrograms class in the Root\CIMV2 namespace. Unlike Win32_DiskDrive, Win32Reg_AddRemovePrograms is not a default Win32 class; it is defined in the Configuration.mof file. The following is the MOF code for Win32Reg_AddRemovePrograms:

```
#pragma namespace ("\\\\.\\root\\cimv2")
[ dynamic,
  provider("RegProv"),
  ClassContext("local¦HKEY_LOCAL_MACHINE\\Software\\Microsoft\\Windows
\\CurrentVersion\\Uninstall")
]
class Win32Reg_AddRemovePrograms
{
    [key]
        string    ProdID;
    [PropertyContext("DisplayName")]
        string    DisplayName;
    [PropertyContext("InstallDate")]
        string    InstallDate;
    [PropertyContext("Publisher")  ]
        string    Publisher;
    [PropertyContext("DisplayVersion")]
        string    Version;
};
```

When the ConfigMgr client downloads and compiles the Configuration.mof file during its machine policy retrieval cycle, WMI adds this class to the Root\CIMV2 namespace. The class uses the Registry provider (RegProv) to retrieve the information stored under HKEY_LOCAL_MACHINE\Software\Microsoft\Windows\CurrentVersion\Uninstall in the local Registry dynamically. Each key under this location stores information about an item in Add/Remove Programs. This exposes these keys as managed objects of the newly compiled WMI class. The reporting class of the same name defined in SMS_Def.mof specifies what inventory data to report from these managed objects.

This example shows how the Configuration.mof and SMS_Def.mof files can be used together to add information from the system Registry to the ConfigMgr inventory. You can use similar methods to add data from any provider installed on the ConfigMgr client machines.

The Configuration Manager Client WMI Namespace

The Configuration Manager client creates WMI classes to represent its own components and configuration. The root of the ConfigMgr client namespace hierarchy is Root\CCM. The Root\CCM namespace contains classes representing client properties, such as identity and version information, installation options, and site information. Two of the classes in this namespace expose much of the functionality available through the Configuration Management Control Panel applet:

▶ The SMS_Client WMI class provides methods, displayed in Figure 3.24, that implement client operations such as site assignment, policy retrieval, and client repair.

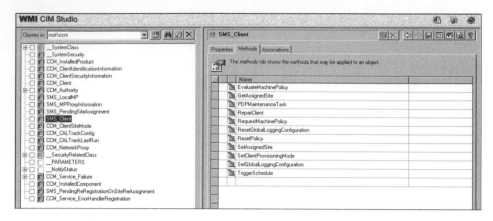

FIGURE 3.24   The SMS_Client class with the Methods tab displayed in CIM Studio

▶ The CCM_InstalledComponent class defines properties such as name, file, and version information describing each of the installed client components. Figure 3.25 displays a list of the instances of the CCM_InstalledComponent class.

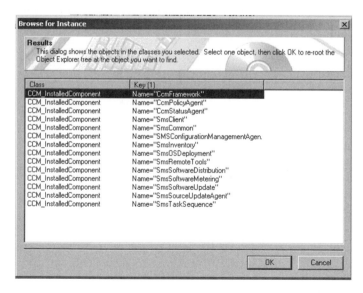

FIGURE 3.25   Instances of the CCM_InstalledComponent class listed in the WMI Object Browser

You will find managed objects for various client components in namespaces under Root\CCM. Figure 3.26 shows an instance of these classes, the CacheConfig class. The CacheConfig class in the Root\CCM\SoftMgmtAgent namespace contains settings for the client download cache, found on the Advanced tab of the Configuration Management Control Panel applet.

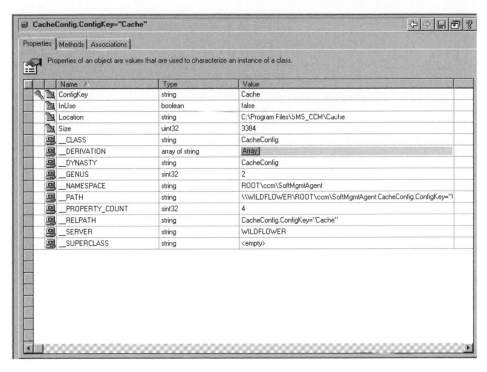

FIGURE 3.26   The properties of the CacheConfig class instance represent the client download cache settings.

The ConfigMgr client uses the Root\CCM\policy namespace hierarchy to store and process policy settings retrieved from the management point. The client maintains separate namespaces for machine policy and user policy.

TIP

Using Local Client Policy

Clients normally download and apply policy defined on their assigned site as described in this section. You can choose to override downloaded policy settings on individual clients using local client policy. As an example, the Remote Tools client agent configuration is a sitewide setting, but the needs of individual client systems may vary. If your sitewide settings require a user to accept a remote control session, you may choose to use local policy to override this on servers. The ConfigMgr SDK (Software Development Kit) documentation describes how to manage local policy at http://msdn.microsoft.com/en-us/library/cc145455.aspx. Use caution when using local policy because it can complicate troubleshooting client issues.

During the policy retrieval and evaluation cycle, the policy agent, a component of the client agent, downloads and compiles policy settings and instantiates the requested policy settings in the Root\CCM\policy\<*machine|user*>\RequestedConfig namespace. The Policy Evaluator component then uses the information in RequestedConfig to update the Root\CCM\policy\<*machine|user*>\ActualConfig namespace. Based on the policy settings in the actual configuration, the Policy Agent Provider component updates various component instances with their appropriate settings. As an example, consider some of the objects used by the client to process policy for an advertisement:

▶ **The policy agent**—The policy agent stores the policy for an assigned advertisement as an instance of the CCM_SoftwareDistribution class in the Root\ccm\policy\<*machine|user*>\ActualConfig namespace, as shown in Figure 3.27.

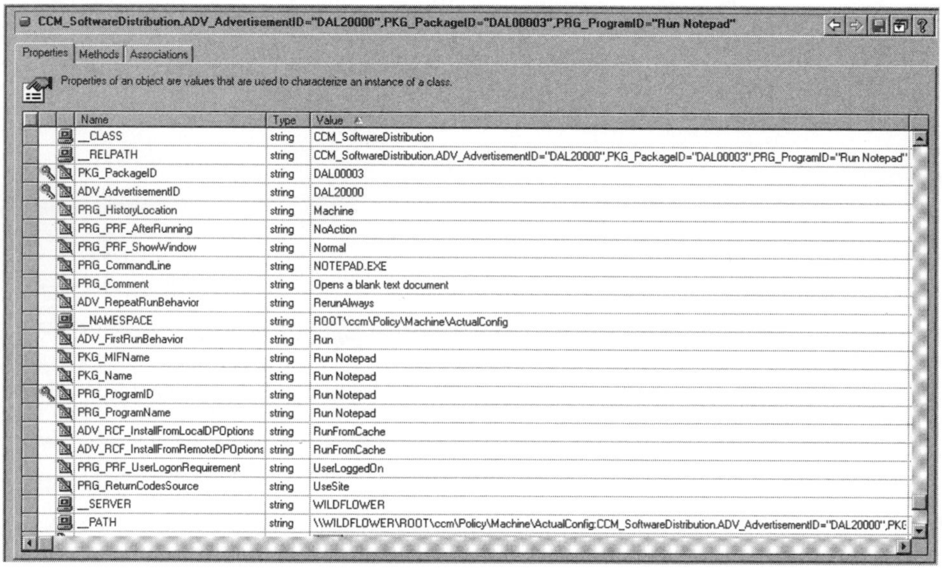

FIGURE 3.27   The properties of the CCM_SoftwareDistribution class instance for an advertisement to download and run Notepad

▶ **The Scheduler component**—The Scheduler maintains history for the advertisement in a CCM_Scheduler_History object in the Root\CCM\scheduler namespace, as displayed in Figure 3.28.

This namespace can also contain schedule information for other components, including DCM schedules, software update schedules, and NAP schedules.

▶ **The Content Transfer Manager**—The Content Transfer Management component uses the CacheInfoEx object in the Root\CCM\SoftMgmtAgent namespace, shown in Figure 3.29, to manage cached content for the advertisement.

▶ **The SoftwareDistributionClientConfig class**—Machine policy also controls the settings of various ConfigMgr client components. The SoftwareDistributionClientConfig class, shown in Figure 3.30, contains the Software Distribution client agent settings.

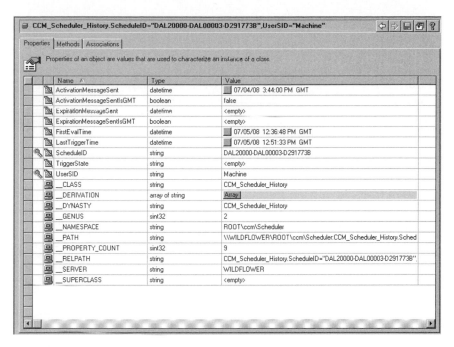

FIGURE 3.28   The Scheduler uses the CCM_Scheduler_History object to maintain history for an advertisement.

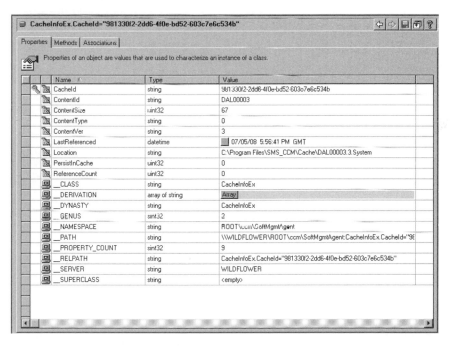

FIGURE 3.29   The CacheInfoEx object is used to manage cached content for the advertisement.

This section looked at some of the more important WMI classes the ConfigMgr client uses for its operations. This is by no means an exhaustive list; in fact, hundreds of classes are used by the client. The classes presented here are representative of some of the most important client operations. The Configuration Manager server components have an even larger set of WMI classes. The next section presents an overview of how ConfigMgr uses WMI for server operations.

WMI on Configuration Manager Servers

The SMS provider is a WMI provider that exposes many of the most important objects in the Configuration Manager site database as WMI managed objects. This provider is generally installed on either the site server or the site database server, discussed in Chapter 5. The ConfigMgr console and auxiliary applications such as the Resource Explorer, Service Manager, and various ConfigMgr tools are implemented as WMI management applications. Chapter 10, "The Configuration Manager Console," discusses the ConfigMgr console. As with other WMI providers, you can also take advantage of the SMS provider's objects in custom scripts or other management applications. The provider also implements the Configuration Manager object security model. Chapter 20, "Security and Delegation in Configuration Manager 2007," discusses the object security model and explains how to grant users access to the console and rights on various ConfigMgr objects and classes.

The SMS provider namespace is Root\SMS\site_<*Site Code*>. You can use standard WMI tools to view ConfigMgr classes and objects. You can also view the properties of SMS provider objects from within the ConfigMgr console. To enable viewing of WMI information, navigate to the AdminUI\bin folder under the main ConfigMgr installation folder and start the console with either or both of the following command-line options:

▶ `AdminConsole.msc /SMS:NamespaceView=1`—This adds a ConfigMgr Namespace node to the console tree. The Namespace node displays a list of WMI classes in the ConfigMgr namespace. You can click a class name, as shown in Figure 3.31, to display its properties, qualifiers, and methods in the details pane. You can also select a property to see its associated list of property qualifiers.

▶ `AdminConsole.msc /SMS:DebugView=1`—This allows you to view object properties as raw WMI data. With Debug view enabled, you can right-click an object in the console tree and choose ConfigMgr Object Properties View to display the WMI properties. Notice that the default console view essentially presents the same information in a Windows dialog box. Figure 3.32 shows the WMI properties of the DAL ConfigMgr site.

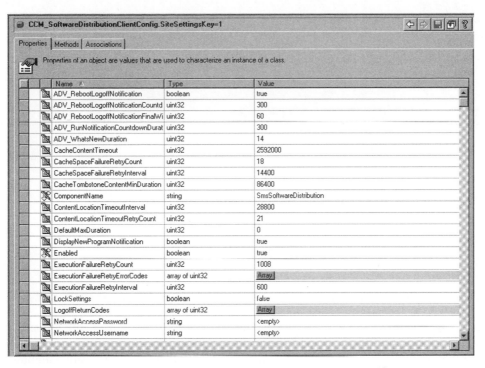

FIGURE 3.30   Some of the properties of the SoftwareDistributionClientConfig class reflect client agent settings received from the site.

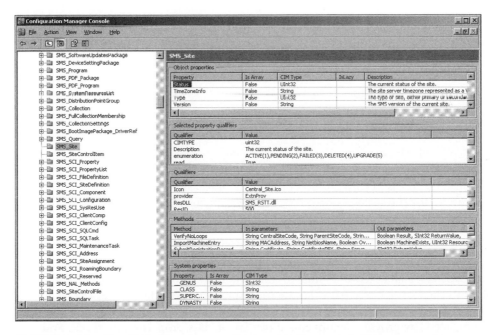

FIGURE 3.31   The SMS_Site class as displayed in the console Namespace view

Figure 3.32 displayed the property qualifiers of the Status property, showing that the status value "1" means ACTIVE.

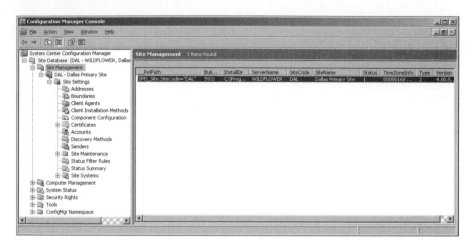

FIGURE 3.32   The properties of the DAL site displayed in the console's Object Properties view

Using the console WMI views makes exploring the SMS provider namespace much easier. To illustrate how to drill down into the underlying WMI from the console, this section uses ConfigMgr collections as an example. (Chapter 13, "Creating Packages," and Chapter 14, "Distributing Packages," discuss collections.) To explore the WMI behind ConfigMgr collections, perform the following steps:

1. Enter the following command line to open the console with both the Namespace and Debug views enabled:

   ```
   AdminConsole.msc /SMS:DebugView=1 /SMS:NamespaceView=1
   ```

2. Navigate to System Center Configuration Manager -> Site Database -> Computer Management -> Collections.

3. Right-click the Collections node, and then choose the ConfigMgr Object Properties View. Figure 3.33 displays some of the WMI properties of the collection instances.

   ▶ The RelPath property in column 1 provides the class name, SMS_Collection, and the name of each instance. You can use this information to locate the class and instances in CIM Studio of the WMI Object Browser. This is especially useful for those classes with names not easily guessed, such as the SMS_SIIB_Configuration class that represents many site settings.

   ▶ The MemberClass name of the SMS_Collection instances tells you where to find additional information about the collection members.

4. The /SMS:NamespaceView=1 command-line switch adds the ConfigMgr Namespace folder to the Console tree pane. Locate the SMS_Collection class under the ConfigMgr Namespace node in the console tree pane. As shown in Figure 3.34, the Namespace view provides a convenient display of class properties, methods, and qualifiers.

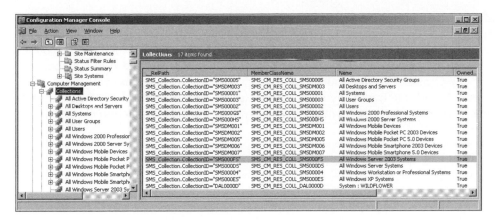

FIGURE 3.33   Some of the key properties of the ConfigMgr collections, as displayed in console's Object Properties view

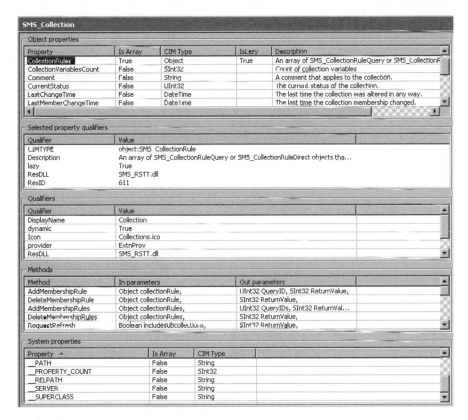

FIGURE 3.34   The Namespace view in the ConfigMgr Collections console displays the SMS_Collection class properties, methods, and qualifiers.

5. You can use CIM Studio and the WMI Object Browser to explore the SMS_Collection class and instances further. Figures 3.35 and 3.36, respectively, show the class methods and associations in CIM Studio. The SMS_Collection class methods allow you to perform operations such as pushing the ConfigMgr Client to collection members with the Create CCRs method and updating collection membership with the RequestRefresh method. When you perform these operations through the ConfigMgr console, you are actually invoking the methods of the SMS_Collection class.

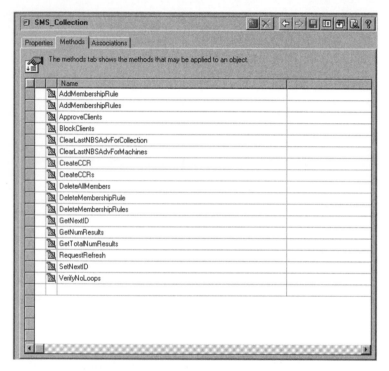

FIGURE 3.35   The Methods tab of the SMS_Collection class displayed in CIM Studio

The Smsprov.mof file contains the MOF language defining the Root\SMS namespace and the classes it contains. You can find the Smsprov.mof file in the bin\<*platform*> folder under the Configuration Manager installation folder. You can also export MOF definitions for instances of the following ConfigMgr object types directly from the console:

▶ Collections

▶ Queries

▶ Reports

To export object definitions to MOF files, right-click the parent node, choose Export Objects, and complete the wizard to choose the instances to export and the file location as well as to enter descriptive text. You can use a similar process to import objects from MOF files.

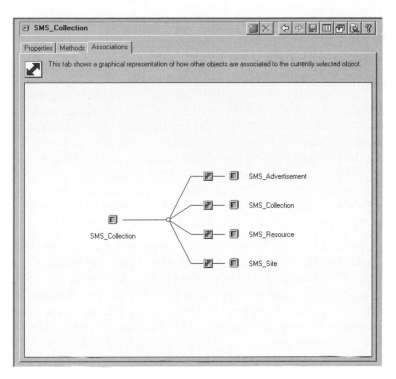

FIGURE 3.36 The SMS_Collection class associations link a collection to its subcollections, members, and advertisements for the collection.

This section showed how the SMS provider exposes Configuration Manager server components and database objects as WMI-managed objects. The "Root\CCM Namespace," "Hardware Inventory Through WMI," and "The Configuration Manager Client WMI Namespace" sections discussed how the ConfigMgr client uses WMI to maintain its configuration and policy and to gather inventory data. The Configuration Manager SDK, which you can download from http://www.microsoft.com/downloads/details.aspx? FamilyID=064A995F-EF13-4200-81AD-E3AF6218EDCC&displaylang=en (or search for **ConfigMgr SDK** at www.microsoft.com/downloads), provides extensive documentation and sample code for using WMI to manage ConfigMgr programmatically, with managed code or scripts.

Components and Communications

Configuration Manager's code design is based on a componentized architecture where sets of related tasks are carried out by logically distinct units of executable code, working together to implement higher-level functionality. Most Configuration Manager code resides in dynamic link libraries (DLLs) in the bin*<processor architecture>* folder under the Configuration Manager installation folder. Although several components run as threads of the SMS Executive service, some run as separate services. You can install all the components on the site server, or you can alternatively distribute many components to other servers.

Most of the thread components use folders known as *inboxes* to receive files from other components. Inboxes may consist of a single folder or a folder subtree. Components maintain open file system change-notification handles on their inboxes. When one component has work for another component to do, it drops a file in its inbox. The operating system then returns a file-change notification event to the component owning the inbox. Some components also use in-memory queues for faster communications with other components on the local machine. What's more, some components maintain outbox folders in which they place files to be processed by other components. Many components additionally operate a watchdog cycle, in which they wake up at regular intervals to perform specific work. Unlike early SMS versions in which watchdog cycles introduced latency into various operations, time-sensitive processing does not depend on watchdog cycles.

Table 3.2 displays many of the Configuration Manager components with a description of their principal functions, the folders they use to communicate with other components, and the log files they maintain. The Component Type column indicates whether the component runs as its own process or as a thread of the Executive service, and whether or not it is monitored by the Site Component Manager. The components installed on a Configuration Manager site system will vary depending on the site roles assigned to the server and the coder revision you are running.

Here is additional information regarding some of the components described in Table 3.2:

▶ The Site Component Manager also monitors the Site Control inbox (sitectrl.box) for changes to site properties that require adding, removing, or altering a component on a site system. This is in addition to monitoring its own inbox.

▶ The Discovery Data Manager, Inventory Data Loader, Software Inventory Processor, and State System components maintain trusted inboxes under the inboxes\auth folder for signed files.

▶ The Management Point File Dispatcher transfers files from its inboxes (MP outbox folders) to the inboxes of other components. To accomplish this, it uses the inboxes of the following components as its outboxes: Client Configuration Manager, Discovery Data Manager, Distribution Manager, Inventory Processor, Software Metering Processor, State System, and Status Manager.

The core components that maintain a ConfigMgr site are the Executive Service, Site Component Manager, Site Control Manager, and Site Hierarchy Manager:

▶ The Executive Service is the host process in which most other components run. The Executive Service exists on every ConfigMgr site system other than the site database server.

▶ The Site Component Manager is a separate service that configures and manages other components.

TABLE 3.2   Component Names and Descriptions

Component Name	Display Name	Description	Component Type	Directory Used	Log File
SMS_SITE_ COMPONENT_ MANAGER	Site Component Manager	Installs and manages components on site systems	Component not installed by Site Component Manager	INBOX: sitecomp.box.	sitecomp.log
SMS_EXECUTIVE	Executive Service	Host process for thread components	Monitored Service Component		smsexec.log
SMS_REPORTING_ POINT	Reporting Point	Executes report queries against the site database and returns record sets	Monitored Service Component		smsreporting.log
SMS_SERVER_ LOCATOR_ POINT	Server Locator Point	Handles client service location requests	Monitored Service Component		
SMS_SITE_SQL_ BACKUP	SMS Site SQL Backup Service	Backup process for site database	Monitored Service Component		smssqlbkup.log
SMS_SITE_VSS_ WRITER	SMS Writer Service	Manages volume snapshots for backups	Monitored Service Component		smswriter.log
SMS_AI_KB_MANAGER	Asset Intelligence Knowledge Base Manager	Maintains Asset Intelligence data in the site database	Monitored Thread Component	INBOX: aikbmgr.box	aikbmgr.log
SMS_AMT_PROXY_ COMPONENT	Advanced Management Technology (AMT) Proxy	Handles provisioning, maintenance, and requests for Intel AMT clients	Monitored Thread Component	INBOX: amtproxymgr.box	amtproxymgr.log
SMS_CI_ASSIGNMENT_ MANAGER	Client Assignment Manager	Manages client site assignments	Monitored Thread Component	INBOX: ciamgr.box	ciamgr.log

3

TABLE 3.2 Component Names and Descriptions

Component Name	Display Name	Description	Component Type	Directory Used	Log File
SMS_CLIENT_CONFIG_MANAGER	Client Configuration Manager	Carries out client push installation and maintains the Client Push Installation Account	Monitored Thread Component	INBOX: ccr.box	ccm.log
SMS_COLLECTION_EVALUATOR	Collection Evaluator	Updates collection membership	Monitored Thread Component	INBOX: colleval.box OUTBOX: coll_out.box (used for sending to child sites)	colleval.log
SMS_COMPONENT_MONITOR	Component Monitor	Maintains Registry setting for discovery components	Monitored Thread Component		compmon.log
SMS_COMPONENT_STATUS_SUMMARIZER	Component Status Summarizer	Processes component status summarization rules	Monitored Thread Component	INBOX: Compsumm.box	compsumm.log
SMS_COURIER_SENDER_CONFIRMATION	Courier Sender Confirmation Service	Records courier sender tasks	Monitored Thread Component	INBOX: coursend.box	cscnfsvc.log
SMS_DATABASE_NOTIFICATION_MONITOR	Database Monitor	Watches the database for changes to certain tables and creates files in the inboxes of components responsible for processing those changes	Monitored Thread Component		smsdbmon.log
SMS_DESPOOLER	Despooler	Processes incoming files from parent or child sites	Monitored Thread Component	INBOX: despoolr.box	despool.log

TABLE 3.2   Component Names and Descriptions

Component Name	Display Name	Description	Component Type	Directory Used	Log File
SMS_DISCOVERY_DATA_MANAGER	Discovery Data Manager	Processes discovery data and enters it into the site database	Monitored Thread Component	INBOXES: ddm.box; Auth\ddm.box	ddm.log
SMS_DISTRIBUTION_MANAGER	Distribution Manager	Copies packages to distribution points	Monitored Thread Component	INBOX: distmgr.box	distmgr.log
SMS_HIERARCHY_MANAGER	Site Hierarchy Manager	Processes and replicates changes to the site hierarchy	Monitored Thread Component	INBOX: hman.box	hman.log
SMS_INBOX_MANAGER	Inbox Manager	Maintains inbox files	Monitored Thread Component		inboxmgr.log
SMS_INBOX_MONITOR	Inbox Monitor	Monitors the file count in various inboxes	Monitored Thread Component		inboxmon.log
SMS_INVENTORY_DATA_LOADER	Inventory Data Loader	Loads hardware inventory data from clients into the site database	Monitored Thread Component	INBOXES: dataldr.box;Auth\dataldr.box	dataldr.log
SMS_INVENTORY_PROCESSOR	Inventory Processor	Converts hardware inventory to a binary format used by the data loader	Monitored Thread Component	INBOX: Inventry.box	invproc.log
SMS_LAN_SENDER	Standard Sender	Initiates intersite communications across TCP/IP networks	Monitored Thread Component	INBOX: schedule.box\ outboxes\LAN	sender.log

3

TABLE 3.2 Component Names and Descriptions

Component Name	Display Name	Description	Component Type	Directory Used	Log File
SMS_MP_CONTROL_MANAGER	Management Point Control Manager	Manages certificate usage for the management point and monitors management point availability	Monitored Thread Component		mpcontrol.log
SMS_MP_FILE_DISPATCH_MANAGER	Management Point File Dispatcher	Transfers files from management point outboxes to site server inboxes	Monitored Thread Component	INBOX: MP\OUTBOXES OUTBOXES: See note	mpfdm.log
SMS_OBJECT_REPLICATION_MANAGER	Object Replication Manager	Creates CIXML representations for the ConfigMgr object for replication to primary child sites	Monitored Thread Component	INBOX: objmgr.box	objreplmgr.log
SMS_OFFER_MANAGER	Offer Manager	Manages advertisements	Monitored Thread Component	INBOX: offermgr.box	offermgr.log
SMS_OFFER_STATUS_SUMMARIZER	Offer Status Summarizer	Populates advertisement status summary information in the site database	Monitored Thread Component	INBOX: OfferSum.box	offersum.log
SMS_OUTBOX_MONITOR			Monitored Thread Component		
SMS_POLICY_PROVIDER	Policy Provider	Generates policies for ConfigMgr components	Monitored Thread Component	INBOX: policypv.box	policypv.log

TABLE 3.2 Component Names and Descriptions

Component Name	Display Name	Description	Component Type	Directory Used	Log File
SMS_REPLICATION_ MANAGER	Replication Manager	Processes inbound and outbound files for intersite communications	Monitored Thread Component	INBOX: Replmgr.box	replmgr.log
SMS_SCHEDULER	Scheduler	Converts replication manager jobs to sender jobs	Monitored Thread Component	INBOX: Schedule.box	sched.log
SMS_SITE_CONTROL_ MANAGER	Site Control Manager	Maintains the site control file	Monitored Thread Component	INBOX: sitectrl.box	sitectrl.log
SMS_SITE_SYSTEM_ STATUS_SUMMARIZER	Site Status Summarizer	Processes status messages for the local site and applies summarization rules	Monitored Thread Component	INBOX: SiteStat.Box\repl	sitestat.log
SMS_SOFTWARE_ INVENTORY_ PROCESSOR	Software Inventory Processor	Loads software inventory data from clients into the site database	Monitored Thread Component	INBOXES: sinv.box; Auth\sinv.box	sinvproc.log
SMS_SOFTWARE_ METERING_ PROCESSOR	Software Metering Processor	Processes software metering information from clients and updates metering data in the site database	Monitored Thread Component	INBOX: swmproc.box	swmproc.log
SMS_STATE_ MIGRATION_POINT	State Migration Point	Maintains user state data	Monitored Thread Component		smpmgr.log
SMS_STATE_SYSTEM	State System	Processes and summarizes state messages	Monitored Thread Component	INBOX: Auth\statesys.box	statesys.log

3

TABLE 3.2   Component Names and Descriptions

Component Name	Display Name	Description	Component Type	Directory Used	Log File
SMS_STATUS_MANAGER	Status Manager	Processes status messages and writes status information to the site database	Monitored Thread Component	INBOX: Statmgr.box; SMS_EXECUTIVE to SMS_STATUS_MANAGER in-memory status message queue	statmgr.log
SMS_WSUS_CONFIGURATION_MANAGER	WSUS Configuration Manager	Maintains WSUS settings and checks connectivity to upstream server	Monitored Thread Component	INBOX: WSUSMgr.box	WCM.log
SMS_WSUS_CONTROL_MANAGER	WSUS Control Manager	Verifies WSUS component health, configuration, and database connectivity	Monitored Thread Component		WSUSCtrl.log
SMS_WSUS_SYNC_MANAGER	WSUS Synchronization Manager	Synchronizes updates with upstream server	Monitored Thread Component	INBOX: wsyncmgr.box	wsyncmgr.log
SMS_SITE_BACKUP	Site Backup Agent	Performs the site backup task	Unmonitored Service Component		Smsbkup.log (in site backup folder)
SMS_AD_SYSTEM_DISCOVERY_AGENT	AD System Discovery Agent	Performs Active Directory system discovery	Unmonitored Thread Component	This component drops DDRs in DDR.box	Adsysdis.log
SMS_NETWORK_DISCOVERY	Network Discovery Agent	Performs network discovery	Unmonitored Thread Component	Drops DDRs in DDR.box	netdisc.log
SMS_WINNT_SERVER_DISCOVERY_AGENT	Server Discovery Agent	Performs discovery on ConfigMgr site systems	Unmonitored Thread Component	Drops DDRs in DDR.box	ntsvrdis.log

▶ The Site Hierarchy Manager and Site Control Manager work together to maintain the site settings. Each Configuration Manager site maintains a site control file with basic configuration information. The site control file is an ASCII text file located in the Site Control Manager inbox. The site control file includes the parent site, sender addresses, client and server components, and various other site properties. For child sites, a copy of the site control file is replicated to the parent site and to all sites above it in the hierarchy. The site database contains a copy of the site control file for the current site and all direct and indirect child sites.

CAUTION

Do Not Edit the Site Control File Directly

The site control file is critical to the functioning of your site. Do not attempt to edit the site control file unless you are asked to do so by Microsoft support personnel. Remember to test all modifications before applying them to your production environment.

The current site control file, Sitectrl.ct0, is located in the Site Control Manager inbox. The Site Control Manager maintains a history of up to 100 versions of the site control file in the *<ConfigMgr Inboxes>*\sitectrl.box\history folder. The following is an example showing how ConfigMgr components interact; here an administrator makes a change to a site property using the Configuration Manager console:

1. The console application reads the current site control file and calculates a delta based on the settings applied by the administrator. The console code then invokes the CommitSCF method of the SMS_SiteControlFile WMI object to apply the changes in the delta site control file.

2. The SMS provider executes the method against the database, which inserts the changes into the SiteControl table.

3. Inserting data into the SiteControl table fires the SMSDBMON_SiteControl_SiteControl_AddUpd_HMAN_ins trigger. This creates a new entry in the TableChangeNotifications table.

4. The Database Monitor detects the change to the database and creates a site control update file in the Hierarchy Manager inbox.

5. The Hierarchy Manager merges the changes from the site control update file into a temporary .ct1 delta site control file. Hierarchy Manager then copies the .ct1 file to the Site Control Manager inbox.

6. The Site Control Manager receives a file system change notification from the operating system, indicating that a new file was created in its inbox. The Site Control Manager wakes up and processes the file. After applying the changes to the old site control file, Site Control Manager copies the new site control file to three locations:

   ▶ The main Site Control Manager (the sitectrl.box).

   ▶ The sitectrl.box\history subfolder (where it is renamed using the appropriate sequential version number).

▶ The sitectrl.box\outgoing folder (as a .ct2 file). Site Control Manager then copies the .ct2 file to the Hierarchy Manager inbox.

7. Hierarchy Manager commits the changes to the site database. If the site has a parent site, the Hierarchy Manager also copies the replication manager inbox. Replication between sites is discussed next.

Figure 3.37 illustrates these steps.

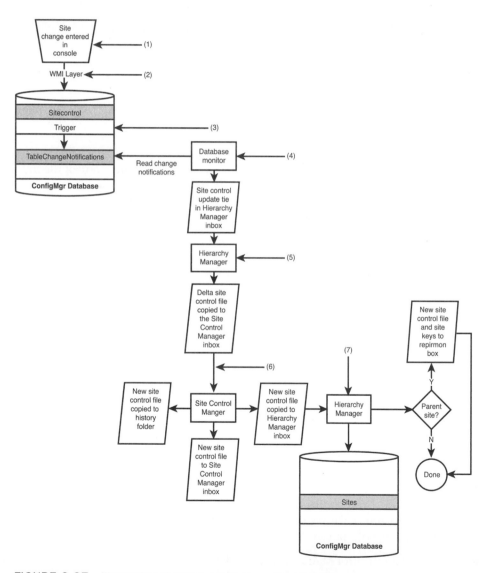

FIGURE 3.37   Illustrating changes made to a site property

Most of the remaining components work together, implementing specific feature sets. An important example of this is the components related to intersite communications.

When a change occurs to the site control file at a primary site, the Hierarchy Manager initiates the process of replicating the file to other sites that need a copy of the file. This includes the parent site and any child sites affected by the change. Various other components initiate the replication of objects (such as packages, advertisements, and queries) to child primary sites and data (such as inventory and status messages) to parent sites. When a Configuration Manager component has data to replicate to another site, the following steps take place:

1. The component with data to replicate to another site copies the file(s) to one of the subfolders of the Outbound folder in the Replication Manager's inbox. The subfolders are named high, normal, or low to indicate the priority of the replication job. The file names begin with the destination site code for routing purposes.

2. The Replication Manager compresses the file(s) to its process folder and moves them to its ready folder. Replication Manager then creates a job file under the Scheduler inbox.

3. The Scheduler processes the instruction file and creates instruction and package files in the tosend folder (inboxes\schedule.box\tosend). It then transfers the files to the appropriate sender.

4. The sender copies the files to the SMS_SITE share on the destination site server. This share is the despooler\receive inbox.

5. At the destination site, the Despooler validates the signature from of the source site server, decompresses the files, and moves them to the Replication Manager inbox.

6. The Replication Manager moves the file to the appropriate inbox of the component for which the file is intended. The Replication Manager also initiates any replication to additional sites that may be required.

The "Status Messages and Logs" section of this chapter looks into the inner workings of these processes.

Inside the ConfigMgr Database

The Configuration Manager site database is a SQL Server database that contains data about your ConfigMgr infrastructure and objects, the client systems you manage, and other discovered resources. The default name of the site database is SMS_<*Site Code*> (where <*Site Code*> indicates the primary site the database is associated with). Although the exact number of objects in a ConfigMgr site database varies, there are generally several thousand objects. Management applications, including the Configuration Manager console, use WMI to access the database.

SQL Access to the Database

Microsoft's Configuration Manager developers provide an extensive set of database views that present the underlying data tables in a consistent way. The views abstract away many of the details of the underlying table structure, which may change with future product releases. In some cases, ConfigMgr uses stored procedures in place of views to retrieve data from the tables. The reports in Configuration Manager use SQL views. Chapter 18 presents numerous examples of reports based on the SQL views. You can use the views to understand the internal structure of the database. The next sections present a subset of these views and provide information about how the views are organized and named.

Most of the Configuration Manager SQL views correspond to ConfigMgr WMI classes. In many cases, the views also reflect the underlying table structure, with minor formatting changes and more meaningful field names.

Most ConfigMgr administration tasks do not require you to work directly with SQL statements. One Configuration Manager component—ConfigMgr reporting—allows you to directly supply native SQL statements that access the site database. The ConfigMgr console also allows you to create and schedule SQL database maintenance tasks. Chapter 21, "Backup, Recovery, and Maintenance," discusses database maintenance tasks.

Using SQL Server Management Studio

The primary user interface for administering SQL Server 2005 is the SQL Server Management Studio. To access the Configuration Manager views, perform the following steps:

1. Launch the SQL Server Management Studio from Start -> Programs -> Microsoft SQL Server 2005 -> SQL Server Management Studio.

2. After connecting to the site database server SQL instance, expand *<servername>*\database\SMS_*<Site Code>*\views in the tree control in the left pane.

Viewing Collections

The "WMI on Configuration Manager Servers" section of this chapter looked in some detail at the Collections WMI object. The Collections WMI object provides access to the properties and methods of the Configuration Manager collections defined in the site database. The SQL view v_Collections provides access to much of the same data. Figure 3.38 shows the tree control expanded in the left pane to display the column definitions for v_Collections, whereas the view on the right displays some of the column values visible when opening the view. These columns correspond to the SMS_Collection WMI class properties, many of which were shown in Figures 3.33 and 3.34. Notice that the MemberClassName column provides the name of the view for the collection membership. These views correspond to the WMI objects specified in the MemberClassName property of the SMS_Collection WMI class.

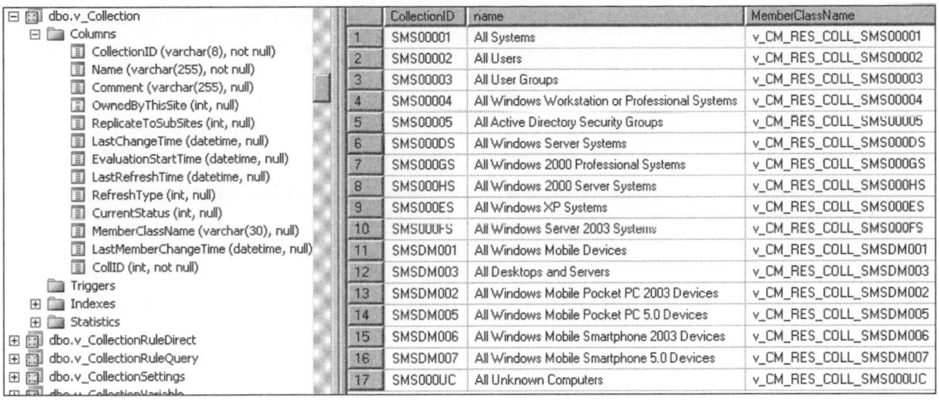

	CollectionID	name	MemberClassName
1	SMS00001	All Systems	v_CM_RES_COLL_SMS00001
2	SMS00002	All Users	v_CM_RES_COLL_SMS00002
3	SMS00003	All User Groups	v_CM_RES_COLL_SMS00003
4	SMS00004	All Windows Workstation or Professional Systems	v_CM_RES_COLL_SMS00004
5	SMS00005	All Active Directory Security Groups	v_CM_RES_COLL_SMS00005
6	SMS000DS	All Windows Server Systems	v_CM_RES_COLL_SMS000DS
7	SMS000GS	All Windows 2000 Professional Systems	v_CM_RES_COLL_SMS000GS
8	SMS000HS	All Windows 2000 Server Systems	v_CM_RES_COLL_SMS000HS
9	SMS000ES	All Windows XP Systems	v_CM_RES_COLL_SMS000ES
10	SMS000FS	All Windows Server 2003 Systems	v_CM_RES_COLL_SMS000FS
11	SMSDM001	All Windows Mobile Devices	v_CM_RES_COLL_SMSDM001
12	SMSDM003	All Desktops and Servers	v_CM_RES_COLL_SMSDM003
13	SMSDM002	All Windows Mobile Pocket PC 2003 Devices	v_CM_RES_COLL_SMSDM002
14	SMSDM005	All Windows Mobile Pocket PC 5.0 Devices	v_CM_RES_COLL_SMSDM005
15	SMSDM006	All Windows Mobile Smartphone 2003 Devices	v_CM_RES_COLL_SMSDM006
16	SMSDM007	All Windows Mobile Smartphone 5.0 Devices	v_CM_RES_COLL_SMSDM007
17	SMS000UC	All Unknown Computers	v_CM_RES_COLL_SMS000UC

Tree panel (left):
- dbo.v_Collection
  - Columns
    - CollectionID (varchar(8), not null)
    - Name (varchar(255), not null)
    - Comment (varchar(255), null)
    - OwnedByThisSite (int, null)
    - ReplicateToSubSites (int, null)
    - LastChangeTime (datetime, null)
    - EvaluationStartTime (datetime, null)
    - LastRefreshTime (datetime, null)
    - RefreshType (int, null)
    - CurrentStatus (int, null)
    - MemberClassName (varchar(30), null)
    - LastMemberChangeTime (datetime, null)
    - CollID (int, not null)
  - Triggers
  - Indexes
  - Statistics
- dbo.v_CollectionRuleDirect
- dbo.v_CollectionRuleQuery
- dbo.v_CollectionSettings
- dbo.v_CollectionVariable

FIGURE 3.38   The v_Collection SQL view displays the most important properties of the site's Configuration Manager collections.

The v_Collection view is one of several views referencing Configuration Manager objects. Similar views include v_Advertisement, v_Package, and v_Report. The naming conventions for views generally map to the corresponding WMI classes, according to the following rules:

▶ WMI class names begin with SMS_, and SQL view names begin with v or v_.

▶ View names over 30 characters are truncated.

▶ The WMI property names are the same as the field names in the SQL views.

Site Properties

Basic Configuration Manager site properties are stored in the Sites table and exposed though several views and stored procedures. As an example, v_site displays the basic configuration of the current site and its child sites. The sysreslist table stores information about the site systems. An example of a stored procedure that retrieves data from the sites and sysreslist tables is MP_GetMPListForSite, which displays management point information for the site. The SMSData table includes additional site details, exposed through v_identification.

The tables and views discussed so far relate to the Configuration Manager objects and infrastructure. The database also contains a wealth of data gathered by various discovery methods and client inventory. Chapter 12 discusses discovery and inventory. Discovery and inventory data is stored in resource tables and presented in resource views. The naming conventions for resource views are as follows:

▶ Views displaying current inventory data are named v_GS_<group name>.

▶ Views displaying inventory history data are named v_HS_<group name>.

▶ Views containing discovery data are named v_R_<resource type name> for data contained in WMI scalar properties and v_RA_<architecture name>_<group name> for data contained in WMI array properties.

▶ Inventory data for custom architectures is presented in views named v_G<resource type number>_<group name> and v_H<resource type number>_<group name>. The use of custom architectures is described in Chapter 7, "Testing and Stabilizing."

Other Views

Several views are included that present metadata on other views and serve as keys to understanding the view schema. The v_SchemaViews view, displayed in Figure 3.39, lists the views in the view schema family and shows the type of each view.

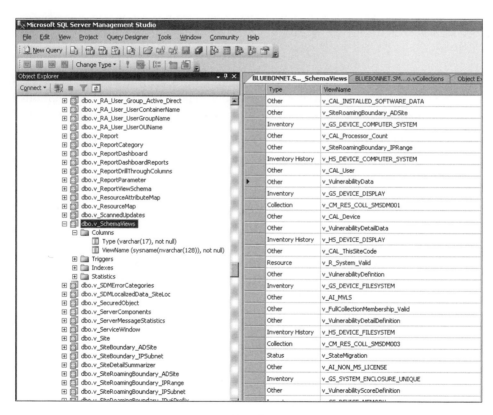

FIGURE 3.39   V_SchemaViews provides a list and categorization of Configuration Manager views.

The following SQL statement generates the V_SchemaViews view:

```
CREATE VIEW [dbo].[v_SchemaViews] As SELECT CASE
WHEN name like 'v[_]RA[_]%' THEN 'Resource Array'
WHEN name like 'v[_]R[_]%'  THEN 'Resource'
```

```
WHEN name like 'v[_]HS[_]%' THEN 'Inventory History'
WHEN name like 'v[_]GS[_]%' THEN 'Inventory'
WHEN name like 'v[_]CM[_]%' THEN 'Collection'
WHEN name like '%Summ%' THEN 'Status Summarizer'
WHEN name like '%Stat%' THEN 'Status'
WHEN name like '%Permission%' THEN 'Security'
WHEN name like '%Secured%' THEN 'Security'
WHEN name like '%Map%' THEN 'Schema'
WHEN name = 'v_SchemaViews' THEN 'Schema'
ELSE 'Other'
END
As 'Type', name As 'ViewName'
FROM sysobjects
WHERE type='V' AND name like 'v[_]%'
```

If you examine the SQL statement, you can see that the selection criteria in the CASE statement use the naming conventions to determine the type of each view.

The v_ResourceMap view presents data from the DiscoveryArchitectures table, which defines the views representing discovery data. Table 3.3 displays the data provided by the v_ResourceMap view.

TABLE 3.3   The v_ResourceMap View

ResourceType	DisplayName	ResourceClassName
2	Unknown System	v_R_UnknownSystem
3	User Group	v_R_UserGroup
4	User	v_R_User
5	System	v_R_System
6	IP Network	v_R_IPNetwork

ConfigMgr uses the fields in Table 3.3 in the following manner:

▶ The ResourceType field is the key used throughout the resource views to associate resources with the appropriate discovery architecture.

▶ The DisplayName field is a descriptive name of the discovery architecture.

▶ The ResourceClassName indicates the view that contains basic identifying information for each discovered instance of the architecture.

As an example, the v_R_System view provides the unique Resource ID of each computer system discovered by Configuration Manager as well as basic system properties such as the NetBIOS name, operating system, and AD domain. Each resource view containing system information includes the Resource ID field, allowing you to link resources such as hard drives and network cards with the system to which they belong. Chapter 18 discusses using the Resource ID to create reports using data from multiple views.

The v_ResourceAttributeMap view displayed in Figure 3.40 presents resource attribute types extracted from discovery property definition data in the DiscPropertyDefs table.

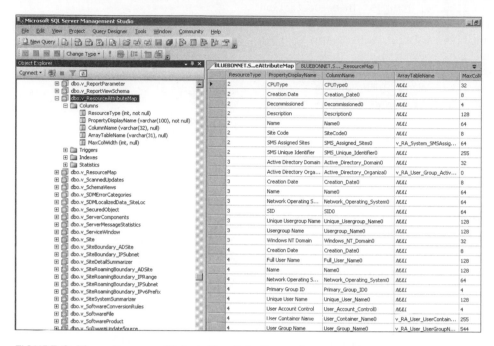

FIGURE 3.40   v_ResourceAttributeMap lists the attributes used in resource views.

TIP

Column Names Have a "0" Appended

The ConfigMgr development team appends the column names with "0" to avoid possible conflicts with SQL reserved words.

The v_GroupMap view lists the inventory groups and views associated with each inventory architecture. Table 3.4 displays some v_GroupMap entries. Each inventory architecture represents a WMI class specified for inventory collection in the SMS_Def.mof file.

Each entry in Table 3.4 specifies the resource type, a unique GroupID, the inventory and inventory history views that present the group data, and the Management Information Format (MIF) class from which the inventory data for the group is derived.

The v_GroupAttributeMap lists the attributes associated with each inventory group, and the v_ReportViewSchema view provides a list of all classes and properties.

This section examined several of the SQL views Microsoft provides. You can learn a lot about the internal structure of ConfigMgr by using the SQL Server Management Studio to explore the database on your own. You may want to look at the views, the underlying tables, and some of the stored procedures ConfigMgr uses. The examples in this section show how you can analyze and understand these objects.

TABLE 3.4 The v_ GroupMap View (Partial Listing)

Resource Type	GroupID	DisplayName	InvClassName	InvHistoryClassName	MIFClass
5	1	System	v_GS_SYSTEM	v_HS_SYSTEM	SYSTEM
5	2	Workstation Status	v_GS_WORKSTATION_STATUS		MICROSOFT|WORKSTATION_STATUS|1.0
5	3	CCM_RecentlyUsedApps	v_GS_CCM_RECENTLY_USED_APPS		MICROSOFT|CCM_RECENTLY_USED_APPS|1.0
5	41	Add Remove Programs	v_GS_ADD_REMOVE_PROGRAMS	v_HS_ADD_REMOVE_PROGRAMS	MICROSOFT|ADD_REMOVE_PROGRAMS|1.0
5	42	Add Remove Programs (64)	v_GS_ADD_REMOVE_PROGRAMS_64	v_HS_ADD_REMOVE_PROGRAMS_64	MICROSOFT|ADD_REMOVE_PROGRAMS_64|1.0
5	43	BIOS	v_GS_PC_BIOS	v_HS_PC_BIOS	MICROSOFT|PC_BIOS|1.0
5	44	CD-ROM	v_GS_CDROM	v_HS_CDROM	MICROSOFT|CDROM|1.0
5	45	Computer System	v_GS_COMPUTER_SYSTEM	v_HS_COMPUTER_SYSTEM	MICROSOFT|COMPUTER_SYSTEM|1.0
5	46	Disk	v_GS_DISK	v_HS_DISK	MICROSOFT|DISK|1.0
5	47	Partition	v_GS_PARTITION	v_HS_PARTITION	MICROSOFT|PARTITION|1.0
5	48	Logical Disk	v_GS_LOGICAL_DISK	v_HS_LOGICAL_DISK	MICROSOFT|LOGICAL_DISK|1.0

3

> **CAUTION**
>
> **Do Not Modify the Site Database Directly**
>
> The site database is critical to the functioning of your site. Do not attempt to create, delete, or modify any database objects, or to modify data stored in the database, unless asked to do so by Microsoft support personnel. Remember to test all modifications before applying them to your production environment.

Status Messages and Logs

ConfigMgr 2007 provides two built-in mechanisms for viewing and troubleshooting Configuration Manager operations:

▶ ConfigMgr components generate status messages to report milestone activity and problem occurrences. System administrators can view status messages and use them in queries and reports. You can also configure the status message system to invoke automated actions in response to specified status messages.

▶ ConfigMgr components generate extensive logs that give additional detail about their activity.

Both the status message system and logging are highly configurable and provide valuable windows into the system.

Digging into ConfigMgr logs is the best way to gain a deep understanding of ConfigMgr internals. Much of the material in this chapter is drawn from analyzing log files. Chapter 21 covers configuring the status message system. Appendix A, "Configuration Manager Log Files," discusses the various ConfigMgr logs in detail. Appendix A also presents log configuration options for capturing additional details of ConfigMgr component operations, including SQL statements and Network Abstraction Layer (NAL) operations. This part of the chapter discusses the use of status messages and logs for looking at the inner working of Configuration Manager.

The ConfigMgr logs are text files, and you can view them in Windows Notepad or your favorite text editor. One of the most popular tools for previous versions of SMS, however, has been the log viewer tool (Trace32). Most administrators prefer to use the log viewer rather than a text editor to display log files. An updated version of the log viewer is part of the ConfigMgr 2007 Toolkit. The log viewer formats log entries, provides search and highlighting features, and provides error lookup. You can optionally turn on an auto-refresh feature to update the displayed log in near real time.

The smsprov.log file shows calls to the SMS provider from management applications. The bottom pane of the log viewer displays the details of the highlighted log entry. The entry in Figure 3.41 shows that the user SCCMUNLEASHED\administrator modified an instance of class SMS_SCI_SiteDefinition. The SMS_SCI_SiteDefinition, displayed in Figure 3.42, provides an interface to binary data stored in the SiteControl table.

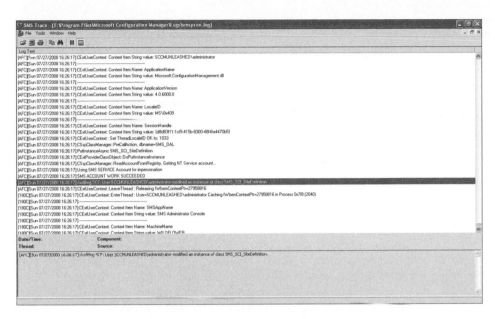

FIGURE 3.41   Smsprov.log displayed in the Log Viewer (Trace32)

FIGURE 3.42   The SMS_SCI_SiteDefinition WMI class displayed in CIM Viewer

Figure 3.41 shows a portion of the smsprov.log file as displayed in the log viewer.

The smsprov.log file later shows the following actions performed that commit the changes to the database:

```
ExecMethodAsync : SMS_SiteControlFile::CommitSCF
CSspClassManager::PreCallAction, dbname=SMS_DAL
CExtProviderClassObject::DoExecuteMethod CommitSCF
Calling SubmitDeltaSCFToDatabase for user=SCCMUNLEASHED\administrator,
computer=WILDFLOWER,component=Microsoft.ConfigurationManagement.dll
CSspSiteControl::CommitSCF - Delta was created
```

The log file provides additional details of the security context setup and database connection, not displayed here.

Using the SQL Server Profiler lets you see SQL requests sent to the SQL Server database. (For information about the SQL Server Profiler, see http://msdn.microsoft.com/en-us/library/ms187929.aspx.)

TIP

Using SQL Logging to Capture SQL Activity

An alternative to using the SQL Profiler to capture SQL activity is to enable SQL logging, as described in Appendix A. This will add details of SQL commands directly into the logs for components that access the database. Turning SQL logging on or off requires you to restart the Executive service.

The following SQL commands sent by ConfigMgr components show the SMS provider inserting data into the SiteControl table and the Database Monitor retrieving the change notification from the database:

```
[SMS Provider] insert SiteControl (SiteCode, TypeFlag, SerialNumber, BinaryData)
values ("DAL", 2, 33, 0x0)
[SMS_DATABASE_NOTIFICATION_MONITOR] exec spGetChangeNotifications
```

What connects these two events is a trigger on the SiteControl table. A *trigger* is a special SQL procedure that fires in response to specified data-modification events. The SiteControl table defines the following trigger:

```
CREATE TRIGGER [dbo].[SMSDBMON_SiteControl_SiteControl_AddUpd_HMAN_ins]
ON [dbo].[SiteControl] FOR insert AS
BEGIN
    INSERT INTO
TableChangeNotifications(Component,TableName,ActionType,Key1,Key2,Key3)
SELECT "SiteControl_AddUpd_HMAN","SiteControl",1,
IsNULL(convert(varchar(256),SiteCode),''),
IsNULL(convert(varchar(256),TypeFlag),''),''
FROM inserted
IF @@ERROR != 0 ROLLBACK TRAN
END
```

This trigger creates an entry in the TableChangeNotifications table each time a record is inserted in the SiteControl table. When the Database Monitor executes the spGetChangeNotifications stored procedure, it reads the TableChangeNotifications table and processes any new entries it finds.

Example: Joining a Site to a New Parent

As the smsprov.log and SQL Profiler trace were captured while joining a Configuration Manager site to a new parent site, the ParentSiteCode property was changed. Changing the parent site is a change to the site properties, which results in writing a new site control file. As described in the "Components and Communications" section of this chapter, the SMS provider initializes this operation, performed by the Site Control Manager, Site Hierarchy Manager, and the Database Monitor. The Site Control Manager and Site Hierarchy Manager generate milestone status messages when they have completed each major phase of processing the site control file updates. Table 3.5 displays these status messages.

TABLE 3.5   Status Messages Generated During Site Join

Component	Message ID	Description
SMS_HIERARCHY_ MANAGER	3307	SMS Hierarchy Manager detected that a change was requested by this site to the configuration of site "DAL." SMS Hierarchy Manager created a delta site control file for this request. If this site is site "DAL," SMS Hierarchy Manager submits this file to SMS Site Control Manager at this site. If site "DAL" is a child site, SMS Hierarchy Manager instructs SMS Replication Manager to deliver the file to SMS Site Control Manager at site "DAL" at high priority.

TABLE 3.5   Status Messages Generated During Site Join

Component	Message ID	Description
SMS_SITE_CONTROL_ MANAGER	2807	The delta site control file %ProgramFiles%\Microsoft Configuration Manager\inboxes\sitectrl.box\incoming\ .CT1 contains a site configuration change request submitted by the "Microsoft.ConfigurationManagement.dll" SMS Provider client running as user "SCCMUNLEASHED\administrator" on computer "WILDFLOWER" at site "DAL" at "7/27/2008 4:26:17 PM." The site configuration change request was assigned the serial number 33 at site "DAL." SMS Site Control Manager uses this serial number to ensure that it does not process the same site configuration change request from an SMS Provider client (such as the SMS Administrator console) more than once. When an SMS Provider client submits a delta site control file containing a site configuration change request, SMS Hierarchy Manager at the site submitting the file will report status message 3307. You can track the time on message 3307 and this one to determine when the site configuration change request was submitted and when it actually went into effect.
SMS_SITE_CONTROL_ MANAGER	2814	SMS Site Control Manager modified the properties of the "Site Definition" item named "Site Definition" in the actual site control file %ProgramFiles%\Microsoft Configuration Manager\inboxes\sitectrl.box\sitectrl.ct0. This modification occurred due to a site configuration change request in the delta site control file %ProgramFiles%\Microsoft Configuration Manager\inboxes\sitectrl.box\incoming\drfg12og.CT1. The change will take effect in serial number 53 of the actual site control file. You can compare the file %ProgramFiles%\Microsoft Configuration Manager\inboxes\sitectrl.box\history\00000034.ct0 with the file %ProgramFiles%\Microsoft Configuration Manager\inboxes\sitectrl.box\history\00000035.ct0 to determine which properties changed.
SMS_SITE_CONTROL_ MANAGER	2811	SMS Site Control Manager created serial number 53 of the actual site control file %ProgramFiles%\Microsoft Configuration Manager\inboxes\sitectrl.box\sitectrl.ct0. This creation occurred in response to a site configuration change request contained in the delta site control file %ProgramFiles%\Microsoft Configuration Manager\inboxes\sitectrl.box\incoming\drfg12og.CT1. The other SMS server components will detect a new actual site control file is available, read it, and reconfigure themselves accordingly.

TABLE 3.5 Status Messages Generated During Site Join

Component	Message ID	Description
SMS_SITE_CONTROL_ MANAGER	2865	SMS Site Control Manager submitted a copy of serial number 53 of the actual site control file %*ProgramFiles*%\Microsoft Configuration Manager\inboxes\sitectrl.box\sitectrl.ct0 to SMS Hierarchy Manager. This is the new actual site control file that contains the current configuration of this site. If this is a primary site, SMS Hierarchy Manager will update this site's database with the copy. If this is a child site of another site, SMS Hierarchy Manager will replicate the copy up the site hierarchy, updating each parent site's database.
SMS_HIERARCHY_ MANAGER	3306	SMS Hierarchy Manager successfully processed "%*ProgramFiles*%\Microsoft Configuration Manager\inboxes\hman.box\AVBLXF1C.CT2," which represented serial number 53 of the site control file for site "Dallas Primary Site" (DAL). If this site is a primary site, SMS Hierarchy Manager stores this site control file in the SMS site database. If this site reports to a parent site, SMS Hierarchy Manager instructs SMS Replication Manager to replicate this file to the parent site at high priority.

The third entry in Table 3.5 identified as 2814 in the Message ID column contains the following statement:

> You can compare the file C:\Program Files\Microsoft Configuration Manager\inboxes\sitectrl.box\history\00000034.ct0 with the file C:\Program Files\Microsoft Configuration Manager\inboxes\sitectrl.box\history\00000035.ct0 to determine which properties changed.

Comparing these two files shows the delta entry in the new site control file, 00000035.ct0:

```
BEGIN_PROPERTY_LIST
    <Deltas>
    <Set,"Site Definition","Site Definition">
END_PROPERTY_LIST
```

This entry indicates the change is in the Site Definition section of the file. Table 3.6 presents part of the Site Definition section of each site control file. (The parent site code entry is changed from <> to <CEN>.)

TABLE 3.6   Changes to the Site Configuration File

00000034.ct0 File	00000035.ct0 File
\<DAL>	\<DAL>
\<Dallas Primary Site>	\<Dallas Primary Site>
\<>	\<CEN>
\<WILDFLOWER>	\<WILDFLOWER>
\<SCCMUNLEASHED>	\<SCCMUNLEASHED>

To capture this activity in detail, configure the logging for these three components to write to a single log file. This log provides a detailed record of how the Configuration Manager components work together to process changes to the site. The log entry displayed in Figure 3.43 shows the Database Monitor dropping an .SCU (Site Configuration Update) file in the Hierarchy Manager inbox.

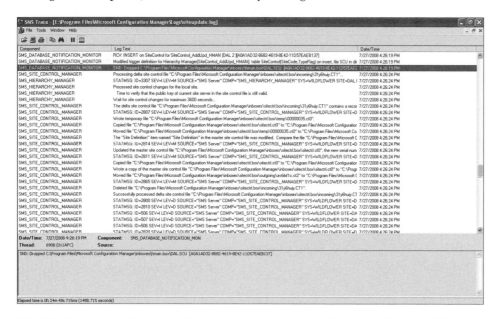

FIGURE 3.43   The Database Monitor dropping a site configuration file (Trace32)

CAUTION

Be Careful when Combining Log Files

Configuring more than one Configuration Manager component to write to a single log file can be useful when you want to see the overall flow of an operation. The resulting log files can sometimes become overwhelming, however. Be careful when you configure this type of logging.

To see even more detail of the process activity that carries out the site modification, use Process Monitor to capture the file system activity of the SMSExec process during the site join. More information on Process Monitor and a link to download this useful tool are available at http://technet.microsoft.com/en-us/sysinternals/bb896645.aspx.

Figure 3.44 shows the initial phase of the site join activity as displayed in the Process Monitor user interface. You can use some of Process Monitor's filtering options to selectively display activity related to processing the site change:

▶ Using the ConfigMgr logs, you can determine the thread identifiers (TIDs) of the three components of interest and apply a filter to show only events from these threads.

▶ Filter to include only operations that access files in the ConfigMgr inbox folders.

▶ Figure 3.44 has access to the Status Manager inbox filtered out. Components write to the Status Manager inbox to generate status messages.

▶ Filter out several other operations such as closing files.

Notice the NotifyChangeDirectory (directory change notifications) operations are highlighted. These initiate processing by a ConfigMgr component in response to a change to the component's inbox folder. The first highlighted event in Figure 3.44 shows the Database Monitor (TID 2484) creating the site control update file DAL.SCU in the Hierarchy Manager inbox.

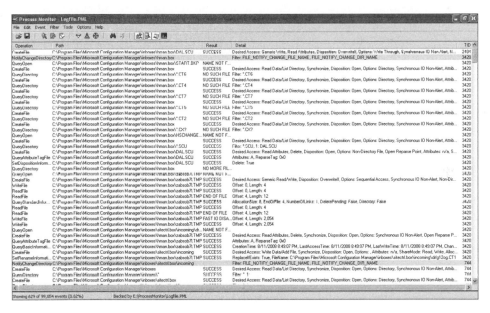

FIGURE 3.44   Process Monitor displays file operations executed by selected Configuration Manager components.

When Database Monitor creates the DAL.SCU file in the Hierarchy Manager inbox, Hierarchy Manager (TID 3420) begins reading the database for site configuration changes and preparing the delta site control (*.CT1) file.

Process Monitor can display Registry access as well as file access. You could use Process Monitor to see the details of Hierarchy Manager retrieving the Registry values it uses to construct a connection string to the site database and accessing the SQL client libraries to initiate the database connection.

The filters omit the sequence of events showing this activity. Instead, take a look at the SQL activity from the Hierarchy Manager found in the SQL Profiler data:

```
Select SiteCode, SiteName, ReportToSite, Status, DetailedStatus, TimeStamp,
SomeId, SiteType, BuildNumber,  Version, SiteServer, InstallDir, TimeZoneInfo
FROM Sites AS Sites order by ReportToSite, SiteCode
select * from SetupInfo where id = 'VERSION'
select distinct SiteCode from SiteControl where TypeFlag = 2
select SerialNumber from SiteControl where SiteCode = 'DAL' and TypeFlag = 2
order by SerialNumber asc
SELECT ISNULL(DATALENGTH(BinaryData),0), BinaryData FROM SiteControl
where SiteCode = 'DAL' and TypeFlag = 2 and SerialNumber = 33
```

This shows the actual SQL queries Hierarchy Manager uses to retrieve data from the Sites and SiteControl tables. Hierarchy Manager uses this data to construct the delta site control file. Hierarchy Manager writes the site configuration changes to a temporary file and then executes a file-rename operation to place the delta site control file in the Site Control Manager inbox. The rename operation is the last event shown prior to the next high-lighted NotifyChangeDirectory operation in Figure 3.44. At this point Hierarchy Manager logs the following single entry:

```
SMS_HIERARCHY_MANAGER    Processed site control changes for the local site.
7/27/2008 4:26:24 PM
```

Hierarchy Manager also generates the first status message shown in Table 3.5 and logs this entry:

```
SMS_HIERARCHY_MANAGER    3420 (0x0D5C)    7/27/2008 4:26:24 PM
STATMSG: ID=3307 SEV=I LEV=M SOURCE="SMS Server" COMP="SMS_HIERARCHY_MANAGER"
SYS=WILDFLOWER SITE=DAL PID=4092 TID=3420 GMTDATE=Tue Aug 12 01:49:07.063 2008
ISTR0="DAL" ISTR1="" ISTR2="" ISTR3="" ISTR4="" ISTR5="" ISTR6="" ISTR7=""
ISTR8="" ISTR9="" NUMATTRS=0
```

The directory change notification signals to the Site Control Manager (TID 744) that it has work to do. Site Control Manager generates the following log entries to record its processing of the delta site control file (some details are omitted here):

```
SMS_SITE_CONTROL_MANAGER    Processing delta site control file
"C:\Program Files\Microsoft Configuration Manager\inboxes\sitectrl.box\incoming\
drfg12og.CT1"...    7/27/2008 4:26:24 PM

SMS_SITE_CONTROL_MANAGER    The delta site control file
"C:\Program Files\Microsoft Configuration Manager\inboxes\sitectrl.box\
```

incoming\drfg12og.CT1" contains a record submitted by the
Microsoft.ConfigurationManagement.dll running as user SCCMUNLEASHED\administrator
on computer WILDFLOWER at site DAL via the SMS SDK on
Sun Jul 27 21:26:17 GMT. The record was assigned the serial number 33
at site DAL.   7/27/2008 4:26:24 PM

SMS_SITE_CONTROL_MANAGER   Wrote temporary file "C:\Program Files\Microsoft
Configuration Manager\inboxes\sitectrl.box\temp\00000035.ct0".
7/27/2008 4:26:24 PM

SMS_SITE_CONTROL_MANAGER   Copied file "C:\Program Files\Microsoft
Configuration Manager\inboxes\sitectrl.box\sitectrl.ct0" to "C:\Program
Files\Microsoft Configuration Manager\inboxes\sitectrl.box\history\
00000034.ct0".   7/27/2008 4:26:24 PM

SMS_SITE_CONTROL_MANAGER   Moved file "C:\Program Files\Microsoft Configuration
Manager\inboxes\sitectrl.box\temp\00000035.ct0" to "C:\Program
Files\Microsoft Configuration Manager\inboxes\sitectrl.box\sitectrl.ct0".
7/27/2008 4:26:24 PM

SMS_SITE_CONTROL_MANAGER   The "Site Definition" item named "Site Definition"
in the master site control file was modified. Compare the file
"C:\Program Files\Microsoft Configuration Manager\inboxes\sitectrl.box\history\
00000034.ct0" with the file "C:\Program Files\Microsoft Configuration Manager\
inboxes\sitectrl.box\history\00000035.ct0" for more information.
7/27/2008 4:26:24 PM

SMS_SITE_CONTROL_MANAGER   Updated the master site control file
"C:\Program Files\Microsoft Configuration Manager\inboxes\
sitectrl.box\sitectrl.ct0", the new serial number is 53.7/27/2008 4:26:24 PM

SMS_SITE_CONTROL_MANAGER   Copied file "C:\Program Files\Microsoft
Configuration Manager\inboxes\sitectrl.box\sitectrl.ct0" to "C:\Program
Files\Microsoft Configuration Manager\inboxes\sitectrl.box\history\00000035.ct0".
7/27/2008 4:26:24 PM

SMS_SITE_CONTROL_MANAGER   Wrote a copy of the master site control file
"C:\Program Files\Microsoft Configuration Manager\inboxes\sitectrl.box\
sitectrl.ct0" to "C:\Program Files\Microsoft Configuration Manager\inboxes\
sitectrl.box\outgoing\avblxf1c.ct2" in SMS VarFile format.   7/27/2008 4:26:24 PM

SMS_SITE_CONTROL_MANAGER   Moved file "C:\Program Files\Microsoft Configuration
Manager\inboxes\sitectrl.box\outgoing\avblxf1c.ct2" to "C:\Program
Files\Microsoft Configuration Manager\inboxes\hman.box\avblxf1c.ct2".
7/27/2008 4:26:24 PM

SMS_SITE_CONTROL_MANAGER   Deleted file "C:\Program Files\Microsoft
Configuration Manager\inboxes\sitectrl.box\incoming\drfg12og.CT1".
7/27/2008 4:26:24 PM

SMS_SITE_CONTROL_MANAGER   Successfully processed delta site control file
"C:\Program Files\Microsoft Configuration Manager\inboxes\
sitectrl.box\incoming\drfg12og.CT1".   7/27/2008 4:26:24 PM

SMS_SITE_CONTROL_MANAGER   New parent site code: CEN   7/27/2008 4:26:24 PM

SMS_SITE_CONTROL_MANAGER   Processing delta site control file "C:\Program
Files\Microsoft Configuration Manager\inboxes\sitectrl.box\incoming\
drfg12og.CT1"...   7/27/2008 4:26:24 PM

SMS_SITE_CONTROL_MANAGER   The delta site control file "C:\Program
Files\Microsoft Configuration Manager\inboxes\sitectrl.box\incoming\drfg12og.CT1"
contains a record submitted by the Microsoft.ConfigurationManagement.dll running as
user SCCMUNLEASHED\administrator on computer WILDFLOWER at site DAL via the SMS
SDK on Sun Jul 27 21:26:17 GMT. The record was assigned the serial number 33
at site DAL.   7/27/2008 4:26:24 PM

SMS_SITE_CONTROL_MANAGER   Wrote temporary file "C:\Program Files\Microsoft
Configuration Manager\inboxes\sitectrl.box\temp\00000035.ct0".   7/27/2008
4:26:24 PM

SMS_SITE_CONTROL_MANAGER   Copied file "C:\Program Files\Microsoft
Configuration Manager\inboxes\sitectrl.box\sitectrl.ct0" to "C:\Program
Files\Microsoft Configuration Manager\inboxes\sitectrl.box\history\00000034.ct0".
7/27/2008 4:26:24 PM

SMS_SITE_CONTROL_MANAGER   Moved file "C:\Program Files\Microsoft Configuration
Manager\inboxes\sitectrl.box\temp\00000035.ct0" to "C:\Program Files\Microsoft
Configuration Manager\inboxes\sitectrl.box\sitectrl.ct0".   7/27/2008
4:26:24 PM

SMS_SITE_CONTROL_MANAGER   The "Site Definition" item named "Site Definition"
in the master site control file was modified. Compare the file "C:\Program
Files\Microsoft Configuration Manager\inboxes\sitectrl.box\history\00000034.ct0"
with the file "C:\Program Files\Microsoft Configuration
Manager\inboxes\sitectrl.box\history\00000035.ct0" for more information.
7/27/2008 4:26:24 PM

SMS_SITE_CONTROL_MANAGER   Updated the master site control file "C:\Program
Files\Microsoft Configuration Manager\inboxes\sitectrl.box\sitectrl.ct0", the new
serial number is 53.   7/27/2008 4:26:24 PM

SMS_SITE_CONTROL_MANAGER   Copied file "C:\Program Files\Microsoft
Configuration Manager\inboxes\sitectrl.box\sitectrl.ct0" to "C:\Program
Files\Microsoft Configuration Manager\inboxes\sitectrl.box\history\00000035.ct0".
7/27/2008 4:26:24 PM

SMS_SITE_CONTROL_MANAGER   Wrote a copy of the master site control file
"C:\Program Files\Microsoft Configuration Manager\inboxes\sitectrl.box\
sitectrl.ct0" to "C:\Program Files\Microsoft Configuration Manager\inboxes\
sitectrl.box\outgoing\avblxf1c.ct2" in SMS VarFile format.
7/27/2008 4:26:24 PM

```
SMS_SITE_CONTROL_MANAGER     Moved file "C:\Program Files\Microsoft Configuration
Manager\inboxes\sitectrl.box\outgoing\avblxf1c.ct2" to "C:\Program
Files\Microsoft Configuration Manager\inboxes\hman.box\avblxf1c.ct2".
7/27/2008 4:26:24 PM

SMS_SITE_CONTROL_MANAGER     Deleted file "C:\Program Files\Microsoft
Configuration Manager\inboxes\sitectrl.box\incoming\drfg12og.CT1".
7/27/2008 4:26:24 PM

SMS_SITE_CONTROL_MANAGER     Successfully processed delta site control file
"C:\Program Files\Microsoft Configuration Manager\inboxes\sitectrl.box\
incoming\drfg12og.CT1".     7/27/2008 4:26:24 PM

SMS_SITE_CONTROL_MANAGER     New parent site code: CEN     7/27/2008 4:26:24 PM
```

The logs show that after detecting the delta site control file, the Site Control Manager moves the master site control file to the history folder and creates a new site control file. Site Control Manager then enumerates and validates the changes in the new file. Once the file is validated, it becomes the new master site control file and is written to the history folder as well.

In addition, Site Control Manager writes the new site control file in SMS VarFile format to the Hierarchy Manager inbox as a .CT2 file. The Hierarchy Manager updates the sites table in the database with the new site information. Hierarchy Manager then creates a .CT6 file with the site's public key information and forwards this file to the parent site to initiate the site join. The following log entries show Hierarchy Manager updating the database and triggering replication to the new parent site:

```
SMS_HIERARCHY_MANAGER     Site DAL in Sites table: Site status = 1, Detailed status
= 1 7/27/2008 4:26:29 PM

SMS_HIERARCHY_MANAGER     Processing site control file: Site DAL File C:\Program
Files\Microsoft Configuration Manager\inboxes\hman.box\AVBLXF1C.CT2
7/27/2008 4:26:29 PM

SMS_HIERARCHY_MANAGER     Update the Sites table: Site=DAL Parent=CEN
7/27/2008 4:26:29 PM

SMS_HIERARCHY_MANAGER     Attaching site DAL to site CEN     7/27/2008 4:26:29 PM

SMS_HIERARCHY_MANAGER     Creating a new CT6 file to send to the Parent Site
7/27/2008 4:26:29 PM

SMS_HIERARCHY_MANAGER     Successfully created the CT6 file C:\Program
Files\Microsoft Configuration Manager\inboxes\hman.box\pubkey\DAL.CT6
7/27/2008 4:26:29 PM

SMS_HIERARCHY_MANAGER     Created file listing all public keys, C:\Program
Files\Microsoft Configuration Manager\inboxes\hman.box\pubkey\DAL.CT6, to forward
to new parent site.     7/27/2008 4:26:29 PM
```

```
SMS_HIERARCHY_MANAGER        Successfully forwarded CT6 file to parent site.
7/27/2008 4:26:29 PM

SMS_HIERARCHY_MANAGER        Sent the actual site control image to site CEN
7/27/2008 4:26:29 PM

SMS_HIERARCHY_MANAGER        Created site notification for site DAL 7/27/2008 4:26:30 PM

SMS_HIERARCHY_MANAGER        Created site control notification for site DAL
7/27/2008 4:26:30 PM
```

At this point, the SQL Profiler trace shows a large amount of activity by the Site Hierarchy Manager updating the site database with information from the new master site control file. Here's a sampling of these queries:

```
delete SiteControl from SiteControl
where SiteCode = 'DAL' and TypeFlag = 2 and  SerialNumber <= 33

UPDATE SysResList SET ResourceType= "Windows NT Server",
ServerName = "WILDFLOWER",  ServerRemoteName = "wildflower.sccmunleashed.com",
PublicDNSName = "", InternetEnabled = 0, Shared = 0 WHERE NALPath =
"[""Display=\\WILDFLOWER\""]MSWNET:[""SMS_SITE=DAL""]\\WILDFLOWER\"
and SiteCode = "DAL" and RoleName = "SMS Component Server" and
(ResourceType != "Windows NT Server" or ServerName != "WILDFLOWER" or
ServerRemoteName != "wildflower.sccmunleashed.com" or  PublicDNSName != "" or
InternetEnabled != 0 or Shared != 0) ;

update SysResList set Certificate=<Certificate hash value>

insert SiteNotification (SiteCode, TimeKey) values ("DAL", "04/10/1970 06:35:00")

update SiteNotification set TimeKey = "07/27/2008 16:26:30" where SiteCode = "DAL"
```

The components responsible for replicating the site change to the parent site are the Replication Manager, Scheduler, and Sender. To see how Hierarchy Manager initiates the actual site join, the next section looks at some events captured with Process Monitor. It then reviews some of the key entries from the logs from the three components involved in intersite replication.

Viewing Intersite Replication

When a component requires intersite replication services, you expect to see the component write to the Replication Manager's inbox to initiate the replication process. Here the Process Monitor data is filtered to find events that indicate files are written to replmgr.box. The filtered data is sent to Microsoft Excel for analysis. Table 3.7 contains some events related to the site-join process.

TABLE 3.7   File Operations That Initiate Intersite Replication

Operation	Details	Component
CreateFile	%*ProgramFiles*%\Microsoft Configuration Manager\ inboxes\replmgr.box\outbound\normal\CENut1kg.RPL	Status Summarizer
CreateFile	%*ProgramFiles*%\Microsoft Configuration Manager\ inboxes\replmgr.box\outbound\normal\CEN1fht1.RPL	Status Summarizer
CreateFile	%*ProgramFiles*%\Microsoft Configuration Manager\ inboxes\replmgr.box\outbound\high\CENO9g8m.RPT	Hierarchy Manager
SetRename-InformationFile	%*ProgramFiles*%\Microsoft Configuration Manager\inboxes\hman.box\2vy1wrxz.TMP ReplaceIfExists: True, FileName: C:\Program Files\Microsoft Configuration Manager\inboxes\ replmgr.box\outbound\high\CENO9g8m.RPT	Hierarchy Manager

Both the Status Summarizer and Hierarchy Manager create files for Replication Manager to process:

▶ The two Status Summarizer files are normal priority jobs and are inserted in the normal folder.

▶ The Hierarchy Manager job is high priority and goes in the high folder.

Replication Manager scans its inboxes, finds the files, and processes them to create jobs for the Scheduler, as the following sequence of log entries shows:

```
SMS_REPLICATION_MANAGER  7/27/2008 4:26:29 PM  Scanning normal
priority outbound replication directory.
125

SMS_REPLICATION_MANAGER  7/27/2008 4:26:29 PM  Found 2 replication files

SMS_REPLICATION_MANAGER  7/27/2008 4:26:29 PM  There may be more
replication files coming in, wait 5 seconds and scan again.

SMS_REPLICATION_MANAGER  7/27/2008 4:26:34 PM  Found 1 replication files

SMS_REPLICATION_MANAGER  7/27/2008 4:26:34 PM  There may be more
replication files coming in, wait 5 seconds and scan again.

SMS_REPLICATION_MANAGER  7/27/2008 4:26:39 PM  Did not find any
additional replication files.

SMS_REPLICATION_MANAGER  7/27/2008 4:26:39 PM  Minijob created.
Priority 2, transfer root
(\\WILDFLOWER\SMS_DAL\inboxes\replmgr.box\ready\2_r3pltl.CEN).
```

Process Monitor shows Replication Manager creating the .JOB file in the Scheduler's inbox:

```
SetRenameInformationFile \\WILDFLOWER\SMS_DAL\inboxes\schedule.box\UID\0000088A.JOB
```

Figure 3.45 displays the log entries by the Scheduler's initial processing of these jobs, which takes place during the next Scheduler Processing cycle.

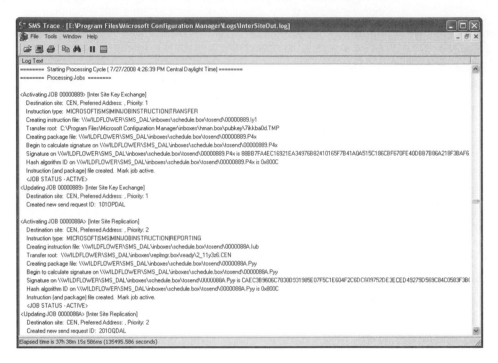

FIGURE 3.45   The Log Viewer (Trace32) shows the events logged during the sender processing cycle

After a 10-second delay, the Scheduler processes the sending requests.

```
There is direct address to site CEN, no need for routing for send request 1010PDAL.
Scheduling send request 1010PDAL.
Selected outbox.  From: C:\Program Files\Microsoft Configuration
Manager\inboxes\schedule.box\requests to
\\WILDFLOWER\SMS_DAL\inboxes\schedule.box\outboxes\LAN.
```

The following excerpts from the LAN sender log show the major phases of the sending operation. First, the sender connects to the Scheduler's outbox (\..\schedule.box\outboxes\LAN) to check for sender instructions. The sender then finds the send request and establishes a connection to the destination site.

```
Connecting to C:\Program Files\Microsoft Configuration Manager
\inboxes\schedule.box\outboxes\LAN.
```

Found send request. ID: 101OPDAL, Dest Site: CEN
We have 0 active connections
Checking for site-specific sending capacity. Used 0 out of 3.
We have 0 active connections
Created sending thread (Thread ID = C94)
Trying the No. 1 address (out of 1)
Found send request. ID: 201OQDAL, Dest Site: CEN
FQDN for server Bluebonnet is Bluebonnet.sccmunleashed.com
We have 1 active connections
The next major phase of the sender operation is to locate the package and
instruction files and verify that they are not already on the destination server:
Passed the xmit file test, use the existing connection
Package file = C:\Program Files\Microsoft Configuration Manager
\inboxes\schedule.box\tosend\00000889.P4x
Instruction file = C:\Program Files\Microsoft Configuration Manager
\inboxes\schedule.box\tosend\00000889.Iy1
Checking for remote file \\Bluebonnet.sccmunleashed.com\SMS_Site\101OPDAL.PCK
Checking for remote file \\Bluebonnet.sccmunleashed.com\SMS_Site\101OPDAL.SNI
The final major phase of the sending process is to actually transmit the data,
together with package instructions that will allow the Despooler component at the
receiving site to unpack and correctly route the files:
Attempt to create/open the remote file
\\Bluebonnet.sccmunleashed.com\SMS_Site\101OPDAL.PCK
Created/opened the remote file \\Bluebonnet.sccmunleashed.com\SMS_Site\101OPDAL.PCK
Checking for remote file \\Bluebonnet.sccmunleashed.com\SMS_Site\201OQDAL.TMP
Attempt to create/open the remote file
\\Bluebonnet.sccmunleashed.com\SMS_Site\101OPDAL.PCK
Created/opened the remote file \\Bluebonnet.sccmunleashed.com\SMS_Site\101OPDAL.PCK
Sending Started [C:\Program Files\Microsoft Configuration Manager
\inboxes\schedule.box\tosend\00000889.P4x]
Attempt to write 671 bytes to \\Bluebonnet.sccmunleashed.com\SMS_Site\101OPDAL.PCK
at position 0
Attempt to create/open the remote file
\\Bluebonnet.sccmunleashed.com\SMS_Site\201OQDAL.PCK
Wrote 671 bytes to \\Bluebonnet.sccmunleashed.com\SMS_Site\101OPDAL.PCK at position 0
Sending completed [C:\Program Files\Microsoft Configuration Manager
\inboxes\schedule.box\tosend\00000889.P4x]

TIP

Using NAL Logging to Capture Network Connection Processing

If you are interested in seeing even more detail of ConfigMgr network activity, you can
enable Network Abstraction Layer logging. Appendix A describes NAL logging.

When a site is joined to a new parent site, all site configuration, discovery, and inventory data is replicated to the parent site. The sending components continue this process until the replication is complete. Other processes not detailed here due to space considerations include the receiving end of the site join and the synchronization of objects and data between the newly joined sites.

Summary

This chapter discussed the internal working of Configuration Manager. It looked at how ConfigMgr sites publish information in Active Directory and how ConfigMgr clients use directory information. The chapter then discussed how ConfigMgr clients and servers use WMI. It examined some of the internal storage of the ConfigMgr database, and how ConfigMgr processes and threads work together to implement key features. Finally, the chapter presented an example of how you can use ConfigMgr status messages and logs along with some other tools to drill down into the inner workings of Configuration Manager.

The next chapter discusses how to leverage Configuration Manager features to design solutions and deliver value to your organization.

PART II

Planning, Design, and Installation

IN THIS PART

Configuration Manager Solution Design

Proper planning and designing of your Configuration Manager (ConfigMgr) solution is crucial to its success. No matter how small or large one's ConfigMgr deployment, there are many factors to consider to ensure the deployed solution meets its operational requirements yet does not impact the network, computers, or users in a negative fashion.

Historically, poor implementations and usage of Systems Management Server (SMS) have led to a negative perception of the product in general. SMS was frequently deployed in environments where the organization's requirements were not known. This resulted in a long learning curve as administrators and support staff often discovered product features months or years after their SMS implementation.

A goal of this book is to address mistakes made by SMS administrators worldwide and attempt to educate the reader on best practices and common misconceptions. Proper deployment and planning is required in any project for a successful deployment. This chapter discusses Configuration Manager Solution Design, emphasizing the Microsoft Solution Framework (MSF). The MSF is a deployment methodology you can use for planning your ConfigMgr deployment.

MSF Process Phases for Configuration Manager

The MSF Process Model depicts a series of high-level tasks that Microsoft recommends to deploy applications and technologies successfully. MSF is not specific to any technology; it is a broad representation of items to review and activities to perform. The purpose of the MSF Process Model is to combine industry project management guidance while overseeing the implementation of the technology from the envisioning phase, through deployment, and into production. For more information on the Microsoft Solution Framework, refer to http://www.microsoft.com/msf.

By leveraging the MSF Process Model, administrators can implement ConfigMgr in a fast and efficient manner, prepared to address any requirements or issues that arise. The model, illustrated in Figure 4.1, divides the process of creating and deploying a solution into five distinct phases:

▶ Envisioning

▶ Planning

▶ Developing

▶ Stabilizing

▶ Deploying

FIGURE 4.1   The Microsoft Solution Framework Process Model

Although Figure 4.1 illustrates MSF as a waterfall model or sequential development process, it can also be a spiral model where the deployment phase is iterative and returns to the envisioning phase, which is how the MSF typically is envisioned. This is useful in rapid software development projects where there are not clear milestones.

Envisioning the Solution

During the envisioning phase, the ConfigMgr design team identifies the high-level requirements and business goals for the project. Using this information, the team then develops a document that states the current state, project goals, and scope.

Think of the envisioning phase as a high-level whiteboard session. This is when team members discuss the pros and cons of various topologies, issues that may arise, testing scenarios that may need to be passed for a feature to be used, responsibilities, and time-lines. The product of this phase, the *Project Scope Document*, should capture this information and present it in a simple fashion that is easy to digest. During the envisioning phase, a number of areas are examined, which are discussed in the next sections.

Assessing the Current Environment

The first step in designing your solution is to understand the current environment. Knowing where you are is a first step in planning how to design your ConfigMgr solution. A detailed assessment gathers information from a variety of sources, resulting in a document you can easily review and update. A variety of sources may be used to gather information for an assessment document, including the following:

▶ Interviews with networking, support, executive management, asset management, procurement, and security IT personnel

▶ Information from business stakeholders

▶ Current documentation on the network, security, servers, and client operating systems

   Document the hardware, software, configurations, business technical and functional requirements, and overall network topology. In large-scale enterprises, these tasks may need to occur multiple times (for instance, once per physical location).

The data collected from these sources should be compiled into an architecture document describing the current state. This will serve as a reference point going forward, as well as a snapshot when looking back. This process frequently uncovers real business needs that may have not been known at the time the project was first envisioned.

Envisioning the Network Infrastructure

The network infrastructure is given consideration as part of the envisioning phase of the project. The network is one of the most fragile and complex parts of an IT infrastructure. Areas to consider should include the following:

▶ What are the networks' boundaries?

▶ What network protocols are used?

▶ What subnets make up the network?

▶ Is Active Directory (AD) in use?

▶ Are all the subnets in AD sites?

▶ Are there wide area network (WAN) links in the infrastructure and, if so, what are their speeds?

▶ Will the Configuration Manager solution span the WAN, or will you use ConfigMgr to manage the local location only?

▶ Will firewalls and routers allow the ports ConfigMgr requires to pass traffic, or is port filtering applied at this level?

▶ What will be the impact to end users when client agents or packages are pushed across the network?

▶ Are machine accounts in more than one AD domain?

▶ Are machine accounts in more than one AD forest?

▶ Will you be able to use a single service account with administrative rights on all site systems?

▶ Are there computers that are in workgroups?

▶ Is managing servers part of the plan?

▶ Can the ConfigMgr client be provisioned as part of the operating system deployment process on workstations and servers?

▶ Do users work from outside the firewall for long periods of time?

▶ How is patch management accomplished?

▶ Will remote control be deployed?

▶ Will support operators remote control users' computers without their permission and, if so, is this allowed enterprisewide?

▶ What are management's expectations of the solution?

▶ How quickly after deployment are ConfigMgr features expected to be available to the support staff?

Once there are answers to these questions, the project team will have a better idea of the solution's requirements and tasks to address with upper management and the security team to determine whether company policies may influence some of these answers.

Chapter 5, "Network Design," discusses how you can design your ConfigMgr 2007 solution to address these areas.

Envisioning the Solution Architecture

The solution architecture needs to be conceptualized at this point of the project. This is when ConfigMgr topology conversations should occur. The decisions made here become a reference point for what the initial ConfigMgr architecture and topology will look like. Here are some key items to think about and discuss:

▶ How many ConfigMgr servers are necessary?

▶ Is there a server (or servers) that meets the hardware requirements or must it be procured?

▶ How many SQL servers are required?

▶ What are the licensing costs of the solution?

▶ Who will need access to the ConfigMgr console?

▶ Does the Active Directory schema need to be extended?

▶ Will using ConfigMgr require native mode or will mixed mode be acceptable?

Chapter 6, "Architecture Design Planning," covers a number of these items. You will also want to refer to the "Site Design," "Capacity Planning," "Licensing Requirements," and "Extending the Schema" sections of this chapter for additional information.

Envisioning Server Architecture

Server architecture follows solution architecture because the decisions made in the solution architecture phase affect the server architecture. Server architecture is where the ConfigMgr team conceptualizes server requirements. This includes CPUs, RAM, and most importantly drive configuration. Decisions such as whether SQL Server is installed locally or on a separate server are critical to the drive configuration and memory required for sufficient performance. Decisions made in this phase of the ConfigMgr deployment will have an effect on licensing and procurement. The "Developing the Server Architecture," "Disk Performance," and "Capacity Planning" sections of this chapter provide additional discussion in these areas.

Envisioning Client Architecture

Client architecture is where the ConfigMgr team and sponsors conceptualize how the agents will be loaded and the settings they will have. Corporate policy often drives many of the ConfigMgr agent policy settings, such as whether or not to prompt for remote control access to a user's computer.

Frequently, the corporate legal department may have stipulations about which agents may be loaded on certain systems. Discovering these corporate policies is usually time consuming and inflexible, and they may drive a different solution and server design than initially anticipated. The "Client Architecture" section of this chapter and Chapter 12, "Client Management," discuss specifics of the client design and implementation.

Licensing Requirements

Configuration Manager 2007 is a management solution and, as such, requires licenses for both management servers and managed clients (agents). Part of the requirements your organization may have for a given solution will include its licensing costs, and licensing is frequently an item driving part of the final ConfigMgr architecture.

Configuration Manager licensing is available with and without a SQL Server license. When the SQL Server installation is used only for ConfigMgr purposes, such as when installed on primary site servers, using the combined SQL Server/ConfigMgr license offers substantial savings. When ConfigMgr is licensed with the SQL Server, no other databases other than the ConfigMgr database can use the SQL Server, and no Client Access Licenses (CALs) are required for the SQL Server.

ConfigMgr licensing consists of three types of licenses:

▶ Server license for each management server

▶ Management license (ML) for each managed operating system environment (OSE)

▶ Management license for each managed client

Microsoft provided only one version of SMS 2003. Today, with ConfigMgr 2007, there are two versions of the product:

- ▶ Standard
- ▶ Enterprise

According to Microsoft's ConfigMgr licensing page (http://www.microsoft.com/systemcenter/configurationmanager/en/us/pricing-licensing.aspx), the only real difference in the two versions is the server workload running in the OSE, which can be a single device, PC, terminal, PDA, or other device. An Enterprise Server ML is required for using the Desired Configuration Management (DCM) functionality of the Configuration Manager solution. The use of proactive management functionality in DCM is limited to the Enterprise Server ML, whereas the Standard Server ML provides operating system and basic DCM functionality.

To clarify this some, based on conversations with Microsoft, the difference between the Standard and Enterprise MLs is the ability to use DCM on SKUs other than the Windows Base Operating System. Here are some specifics:

Standard Server ML:

- ▶ Inventory for any workload
- ▶ Software distribution for any workload
- ▶ Patch management for any workload
- ▶ DCM for basic workloads
  - ▶ Base OS or system hardware
  - ▶ Storage/File/Print (including FTP, NFS, SMB, and CIFS)
  - ▶ Networking (DHCP, DNS, WINS, and RADIUS)

Enterprise Server ML:

- ▶ All Standard Server ML functionality
- ▶ Any functionality not covered by a Standard Server ML, including DCM for applications and compliance

See Chapter 16, "Desired Configuration Management," for a discussion of DCM.

More About OSEs

Microsoft discusses OSEs at http://www.microsoft.com/systemcenter/configuration-manager/en/us/pricing-licensing.aspx. Here's an excerpt:

"A Management License (ML) will need to be assigned to a device for each OSE on that device which is managed by Configuration Manager 2007 Release 2 (R2), except for

OSEs on devices functioning only as network infrastructure devices (OSI layer 3 or below). A device can be a single server, single personal computer, workstation, terminal, handheld computer, pager, telephone, personal digital assistant, or other electronic device. An OSE is all or part of an operating system instance, or all or part of a virtual (or otherwise emulated) operating system instance which enables separate machine identity (primary computer name or similar unique identifier) or separate administrative rights, and instances of applications, if any, configured to run on the operating system instance or parts identified above. There are two types of OSEs—physical and virtual. A physical OSE is configured to run directly on a physical hardware system. A virtual OSE is configured to run on a virtual (or otherwise emulated) hardware system. A physical hardware system can have either or both of the following: (1) one physical OSE and (2) one or more virtual OSEs."

During the discovery phase of the project, you will want to review your organization's Microsoft licensing agreements for desktops and servers. If your organization already has the Microsoft Core Client Access License (CAL) Suite (see http://www.microsoft.com/calsuites/core.mspx), it is possible you already own the management license for each managed client. The CAL Suite encompasses four fundamental Microsoft server product families:

▶ Windows Server

▶ Exchange Server

▶ Office SharePoint Server

▶ System Center Configuration Manager

Using the Configuration Manager licensing page previously referenced in this section, Microsoft provides a licensing guide to use in estimating the cost of the various technologies. Costs given are in U.S. dollars:

▶ **Configuration Manager Server 2007 R2—$579**

▶ **Configuration Manager Server 2007 R2 with SQL Server Technology—$1,321**

▶ **Enterprise ML—$430**

▶ **Standard ML—$157**

▶ **Client ML—$41**

To estimate the costs for a company with a single primary site server intending to do standard configuration management on the 50 servers that are clients and 950 workstation clients, use the following numbers:

▶ Configuration Manager Server 2007 R2 with SQL Server Technology: $1 \times \$1,321 = \$1,321$

▶ Standard ML: 50 × $157 = $7,850

▶ Client ML: 950 × $41 = $38,950

The total cost of this estimate comes to $48,121. This is only an estimate using a single site server and does not include any operating system or other CALs required in a networked environment. In addition, your organization's licensing costs will vary depending on the size of the organization and the type of license agreement held.

For more information on Microsoft Volume Licensing options and available discounts, visit http://www.microsoft.com/licensing/default.mspx.

Training Requirements

Implementing any new tool brings a requirement for training administrative staff, support staff, and potentially even users. ConfigMgr is a technology that touches many areas—servers, databases, networks, and users workstations. Most groups in Information Technology (IT) will require some level of training specific to their job function and the impact ConfigMgr will have on them or the technologies for which they are responsible. At this point in the project, the design team should start addressing training requirements to address the various audiences. Training should begin before implementing Configuration Manager to help facilitate its adoption, understanding of the tool, its impact on the environment from a cost- and timesaving perspective, and the technical impact it will have on the various pieces of the IT infrastructure.

Your specific environment will determine the level and amount of training required. You may need to consider both user and technical training.

User Training

If your ConfigMgr implementation will be pushing a considerable amount of software that requires user involvement, training end users will be paramount and decisions must be made regarding the type of training to provide, the medium, and so on. When end-user training is required, technologies available today make it very easy to provide web-based training in video form to users on a company intranet. This mechanism is very low cost, support for the media is inherent to the client operating systems, and most users will know how to access and use the posted video training sessions.

Real World: Video Training

For Configuration Manager deployments that involve user interaction, you can email users with a link to a company intranet portal site for IT where they can watch a 2-to-3-minute video clip showing the expected end-user experience and interaction requirements. Tools such as Microsoft LiveMeeting and other third-party screen-capture tools can help facilitate creating this training material.

Technical Training

The links at http://technet.microsoft.com/en-us/library/bb694263.aspx provide access to documents to help you get started with Configuration Manager. There is also formal training using Microsoft Official Curriculum (MOC). The MOC for System Center Configuration Manager 2007 offers IT professionals the training needed to deploy, administer, and support Configuration Manager 2007. Course 6451A, "Planning, Deploying and Managing Microsoft System Center Configuration Manager 2007," is a 5-day instructor-led course teaching students the skills needed to plan, deploy, and support ConfigMgr 2007 implementations. Course 6451A's syllabus can be found at http://www.microsoft.com/learning/en/us/syllabi/6451a.aspx. For more information about the Microsoft Official Curriculum, visit the Microsoft training website at http://go.microsoft.com/fwlink/?LinkId=80347. For other ConfigMgr 2007 training options, see Appendix B, "Reference URLs."

Microsoft offers a Technical Specialist ConfigMgr certification. The requirements and summary of Exam 70-401, "Microsoft System Center Configuration Manager 2007, Configuring," can be viewed at http://www.microsoft.com/learning/en/us/exams/70-401.mspx. Completing Exam 70-401 will grant the individual a Microsoft Certified Technology Specialist (MCTS) endorsement in System Center Configuration Manager 2007. Exam 70-401 is also available as an elective for Microsoft Certified Systems Administrator (MCSA) and Microsoft Certified Systems Engineer (MCSE) certification on Windows Server 2008.

Planning for Implementation

During the MSF planning phase, the team identifies the ConfigMgr features it will implement and decides how to implement them. These items drive what is known as the *functional specification*. The functional specification is the foundation of the design. It incorporates the current state of the environment, the business functional and technical requirements, and the proposed architecture of the solution, and it discusses how the solution will address the business requirements. The functional specification also addresses the order in which the solution is built, tested, and deployed, defining success factors for each tested scenario.

The team should include a project manager who will facilitate the validation of business requirements, log key decision factors, and log the construction and testing activities in a master project plan. The master project plan will map against a schedule known as the *master project schedule*. The master project schedule is a series of dates when key milestones should occur, such as the following:

- ▶ Server build
- ▶ Storage allocation
- ▶ SQL Server installation
- ▶ ConfigMgr installation
- ▶ Site System provisioning
- ▶ Test package creation and distribution

- ▶ Test client deployment

- ▶ Test client policies for expected behavior

- ▶ Test advertisement behavior

- ▶ Pilot client deployment

- ▶ Production deployment

In addition, the team should develop a risk management plan. Managing risk is a core discipline of the MSF, because change and resulting uncertainty are inherent in the IT life cycle. By having a risk management plan, you can proactively deal with uncertainty and continually assess risks.

When the functional specification, master project plan, master project schedule, and risk management plan deliverables are approved, the team can begin the deployment. This planning phase ends when the master project plan (MPP and not to be confused with Microsoft Project) is approved.

There often will be changes to the architecture after the MPP is approved, because assumptions are initially made for certain aspects of the proposed solution. The functional specification is referred to as a *living document*, because updates are made to it after the MPP is approved. These updates should describe the reason for modifying the initial architecture and its changes, for future reference. The project manager will own all the project-specific documentation. This documentation also includes individual test, training, pilot, communication, and release plans.

The communication plan has several purposes, paramount of which is notifying the community of the changes being implemented and the impact those changes will have on existing systems. The challenge with communications is keeping them short, to the point, and not inundating users with emails. The communication plan is often overlooked, so much so that it is common for ConfigMgr implementations to occur without users and IT staff knowing it is taking place! The communication plan for such a project has a unique audience because it includes executives, management, project teams, IT, and users with various skill levels. It is important that the communication plan "sell" the overall project and technology to the user community. By letting the various audiences know what the technology will do for the organization as well as how it will save time and money and increase the overall end-user support experience, the ConfigMgr project team will increase its chance for a successful deployment.

Planning the Proof of Concept

The proof of concept (POC) is where the solution's architecture is validated. Those architectural features, processes, or options that do not meet the business and technical requirements will be flushed out during the POC. A number of different items should be evaluated and determined whether they will be in the POC—and ultimately in the solution. The following list is not comprehensive because your business may have unique requirements beyond these, but it's a starting point for formulating the ConfigMgr solution:

- Are multiple sites in the hierarchy necessary?

- Should you extend the Active Directory schema?

- Is this an upgrade or a new installation?

- Choose between a simple or custom setup when installing Configuration Manager 2007.

- Do you require a custom website?

- Choose Configuration Manager boundaries.

- Choose a Configuration Manager client installation method.

- Choose which Configuration Manager features you need.

- Choose between local and remote Configuration Manager site database servers.

- Choose the SMS Provider installation location.

- Choose between native mode and mixed mode.

    If you will implement native mode, consider the following:

    - Determine if you can use your existing PKI (Public Key Infrastructure). For information on how PKI works, see Chapter 11, "Related Technologies and References."

    - Determine if you need to specify client certificate settings.

    - Decide how to deploy the site server signing certificate to clients.

    - Determine if you need to renew or change the site server signing certificate.

    - Determine if you need to enable Certificate Revocation Checking (CRL) on clients.

    - Determine if you need to configure a Certificate Trust List (CTL) with Internet Information Services (IIS).

- Decide if you need to configure HTTP communication for roaming and site assignment.

The proof of concept should be limited to a sandbox-type lab environment where administrators can freely manipulate settings and learn how the ConfigMgr solution can help them more effectively manage their IT assets. Key business requirements should be identified by this time; these should be verified in the POC.

Planning the Pilot

IT management, training, program management, and release management teams are typically involved in the pilot efforts. The pilot plan identifies the scope of the pilot, participants, locations, what will be tested, and success criteria. Planning the pilot phase involves project team members working out the logistics regarding the following:

▶ Who is in the pilot, and what is their contact information?

▶ Is there a timeline?

▶ Where are the servers and clients located?

▶ What will be tested?

▶ What will the communication plan say?

▶ When will the communication plan be ready?

▶ What is the rollback plan?

▶ Is staff training required?

▶ What will be expected of the pilot users?

Planning the pilot phase is essential to the success of the phase itself. The pilot phase is the first actual phase where the solution is tested in a production environment, with the user's policies, network infrastructure, and skill levels all affecting and providing insight to the overall deployment plan and processes. The success of the pilot will illustrate the project team has tested the design in the production environment where users are working and has demonstrated the business and technical requirements have been met.

Planning for Implementation

Once the project team and the business determine the pilot is successful, the next step on the road to the ConfigMgr solution deployment is its implementation. The plans made for piloting the solution should be leveraged for the production implementation. Most of the tools, lessons, and processes established as part of the testing and pilot phases can be leveraged to simplify and standardize the production rollout. This includes a list of tasks, issues encountered, their associated resolutions, and the overall monitoring of the server and client deployments. You can leverage the Microsoft Solution Framework for guidance around deliverables for various stages of MSF. Information on the MSF is available at http://www.microsoft.com/technet/solutionaccelerators/msf/default.mspx.

Developing the Solution Architecture

No two ConfigMgr implementations are the same. Between network topology, desired functionality, and requirements, each ConfigMgr implementation is unique in its own way. Some organizations have federated or distributed IT departments, lending themselves to a tiered ConfigMgr hierarchy where support personnel have ownership of the clients in their respective regions. Figure 4.2 illustrates a decentralized IT model, where sitewide management functions are typically handled at the regional level.

Alternatively, with the rising cost of IT in today's economy, the push is greater than ever before to consolidate and centralize resources. For proof of this point, look at the virtualization market leading the way in cost savings via consolidation, particularly in larger

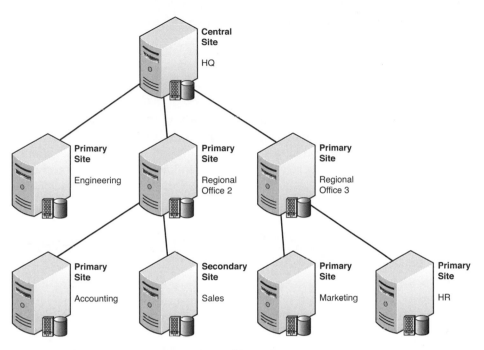

FIGURE 4.2   A heavily tiered ConfigMgr hierarchy

environments (see http://www.cio.com/article/471408/The_Tricky_Math_of_Server_Virtualization_ROI for a discussion on this). ConfigMgr scales to very large numbers, as listed in Table 4.1, which is taken from the ConfigMgr 2007 R2 help file.

TABLE 4.1   Configuration Manager 2007 Supported Scalability Numbers

Site Role	Maximum Numbers
Hierarchy (central site)	200,000 clients
Primary site	100,000 clients
Secondary site	500 secondary sites per primary site
System Health Validator	100,000 clients
Management point	25,000 clients (greater with Network Load Balancing [NLB])
Distribution point (non-OSD)	4,000 clients
Distribution point (OSD)	Limited by disk I/O and network bandwidth
State migration point	Limited by disk I/O and network bandwidth
Software update point (SUP)	25,000 clients (greater with NLB)
Fallback status point	100,000 clients

TABLE 4.1   Configuration Manager 2007 Supported Scalability Numbers

Site Role	Maximum Numbers
Branch distribution point	2,000 per site, 100 clients each; limited by disk I/O, network bandwidth, and operating system license version

With the scalability numbers as high as specified in Table 4.1, implementing a single site (which would be the central site) provides ConfigMgr administrators the ability to manage a very large number of clients. Most often, the number of site servers is driven by various demands—from the network team, management, political influences, and finally technical requirements. A centralized hierarchy is the easiest to manage if you have the bandwidth and hardware to support the client load.

NOTE

ConfigMgr Site Database Placement

Starting in the late 1990s, Microsoft has recommended loading SQL Server locally on primary site servers. The recommendation comes from the requirement for the WBEM (Web-Based Enterprise Management) provider to have "fast access" to the site database. However, if a high-speed connection is available to a remote SQL Server, performance might be better than collocating due to the more database-intensive processing required.

Centralized hierarchies, as displayed in Figure 4.3, come in several flavors. A good example of ConfigMgr centralization is a manufacturing company that has implemented one site in the United States, another in Europe, and finally a third in Asia. The requirement for a primary site server in Asia was one that falls into the technical category, because several countries in that site use native language operating systems that leverage double-byte characters.

Using three primary sites and hundreds of distribution points, the organization depicted in Figure 4.3 was able to effectively roll out patches monthly as well as operating systems on demand in refresh and new system Operating System Deployment (OSD) scenarios, provide remote support, perform detailed inventory, and use a third party add-on—asset management—for thousands and thousands of clients. This is managed using approximately six individuals around the world supporting over 100 locations.

In some cases, organizations implement a flat hierarchy to satisfy political desires within the organization yet still comply with management's desires concerning inventory management, patching, and so on. The flat hierarchy model allows for a simple hierarchy providing some measure of autonomy, while still allowing a higher level of management over child sites. This is a common approach when a complex hierarchy is required but the organization wants to isolate network communication between tiers. Flat hierarchies, such as the one illustrated in Figure 4.4, are particularly useful in situations where reliable network communications are of concern.

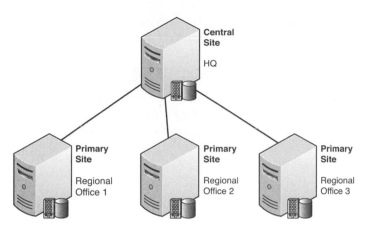

FIGURE 4.3   A centralized ConfigMgr hierarchy

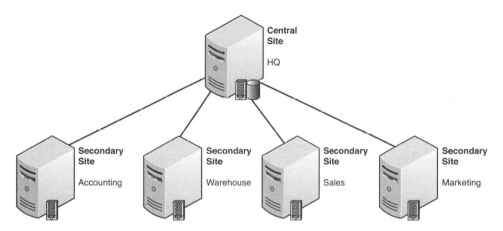

FIGURE 4.4   A flat ConfigMgr hierarchy

Regardless of the hierarchy model implemented, the overall solution will work the same and provide the same robust level of management across the organization. The key difference is in the flexibility afforded by the solution as a whole to the enterprise. It is up to the design team to determine the hierarchy that will be best for the requirements, network, and usage profile.

The next sections discuss areas to consider when developing your solution architecture.

Developing the Network Infrastructure

The design team should spend a considerable amount of time on the network infrastructure. Large amounts of data may be passed across the network, and the traffic patterns will match that which may be blocked by a variety of network intrusion detection systems (IDS), intrusion prevention systems (IPS), and firewalls. Major roadblocks in a managed client deployment often occur at the lowest layers in the Open Systems Interconnection (OSI) model, with large amounts of time spent troubleshooting it at the application level.

Real World: Beware of IDS and IPS Solutions

If your network is using solutions such as IDS and IPS between site servers and clients, you will need to work with the network group to configure these systems properly to allow ConfigMgr traffic. Due to the nature of discovery, client pushing, and the client connecting to AD and management points (MPs), the traffic pattern matches what is commonly known as a *zombie attack* and will therefore be blocked by these solutions.

The symptom is usually a ConfigMgr client that is only partially installed. In addition, many of these solutions seem to block this traffic when in passive mode and without logging it. You will need to refer to your specific solution's support information to configure it to allow this traffic.

Network mediums such as Frame, ATM, and so on are usually transparent to the ConfigMgr solution. Little regard needs to be given to the network medium, but this is not the case with the individual circuit speed. Understanding circuit speeds, the number of clients at a given location, and the expectations of software distribution are the three most substantial factors in planning where to place distribution points (DPs). If client demands are significant enough, such as a large number of systems at a location with inventory and software distribution requirements, an additional primary or a secondary ConfigMgr site may be warranted.

The following times are examples of how long a circuit could be saturated pushing software such as Microsoft Office to a distribution point:

▶ A 1GB file transferred over a 512Kbps link will take approximately 4 hours and 40 minutes.

▶ A 1GB file copied over a T1 will take only 1 hour and 33 minutes.

▶ Increase this circuit to a DS3, which is approximately 45Mbps, and the transfer time drops to just over 3 minutes.

This scenario demonstrates how additional bandwidth may be required in locations that may have previously not needed such bandwidth capacity. You can recoup the return on investment (ROI) of this additional bandwidth with lower overall administrative costs, including the following:

▶ Reducing or eliminating the need for local server resources

▶ Reducing or eliminating the need for remote backup operations

▶ Reducing travel for IT resources that travel to locations for administration or support reasons

► Consolidating voice and data services over a single circuit

► Eliminating long-distance charges due to interoffice direct dialing

The topic of multiple site servers and additional management points introduces the use of addresses and senders, where traffic can be scheduled and throttled across network segments. More information on these topics is available in Chapter 6.

Extending the Schema

Leveraging Active Directory with schema extensions provides a constant, redundant, easily accessible, and secure location when querying for ConfigMgr information. This makes extending the schema the preferred approach when implementing ConfigMgr. If you previously extended the AD schema for SMS 2003, it should be extended again because not all functionality for ConfigMgr 2007 exists in SMS 2003 schema extensions. Table 4.2 illustrates the ConfigMgr features that depend and benefit from AD schema extensions.

TABLE 4.2   Schema Extension Dependencies for ConfigMgr 2007

Feature	Schema Extension Required
Client Installation and site assignment	Recommended
Site mode setting and related settings such as client certificate selection and CRL checking	Recommended
Port configuration for client-to-server communication	Recommended
Global roaming	Required
Network Access Protection (NAP)	Required
Secure key exchange between sites	Recommended
Verifying a trusted management point	Recommended
Recovering from the failure of a central site server hosting the management point role	Recommended

When the schema is not extended, ConfigMgr administrators have to perform manual maintenance tasks that could otherwise be automated with ConfigMgr 2007. These include running scripts and maintaining group policy objects (GPOs) as well as other items required to roll out clients and have them perform with acceptable functionality. Many of the workarounds published in the ConfigMgr online help file do not even scale to support medium-size deployments. Chapter 3, "Looking Inside Configuration Manager," provides additional information about the benefits of extending the schema and discusses the process of extending the AD schema.

Secondary Site Considerations

Secondary site servers, discussed in Chapter 6, are used in ConfigMgr to lessen the load on the primary parent site and reduce network bandwidth utilization. It is extremely important to understand how to leverage secondary sites over slow links when defining the distribution point architecture across the WAN. Secondary site servers can host a role known as the proxy management point (PMP), which, to conserve bandwidth, caches a local copy of the policies stored on the parent primary site.

If you place distribution points in a secondary site, clients that are local to the secondary site and within its boundaries can request content from a local DP rather than downloading it across the WAN. The benefit here is that although multiple clients request the content, it is only sent across the slower WAN link once and then installed locally across the LAN by each client. This conserves bandwidth and improves the end-user experience.

You can also use branch DPs in this manner, which provide the added benefit of being supported on client operating systems such as Windows XP and Vista. If you're deploying secondary site servers purely for the sake of throttling transmissions to DPs, use branch DPs rather than creating secondary sites. However, although branch DPs will keep traffic down, they do not provide the ability to cache and push client inventories, status messages, and policies, as does the PMP of a secondary site server. Branch DPs are limited to 10 concurrent connections when being run from a client operating system rather than a server.

Secondary site servers have a number of advantages and limitations, which should be understood to implement them in your organization effectively. Advantages of secondary site servers include the following:

▶ Do not require a ConfigMgr Server license.

▶ Do not require a SQL Server database.

▶ Can be managed remotely.

▶ Can have PMPs to optimize WAN traffic.

▶ Can have DPs to optimize WAN traffic.

Here are some of the disadvantages of secondary site servers you will want to consider:

▶ Cannot have child sites.

▶ Can only have a primary site as a parent site.

▶ Cannot be moved in the hierarchy without uninstalling and then reinstalling.

▶ Cannot be upgraded to a primary site.

▶ Cannot have ConfigMgr clients assigned to them; hence, client agent settings are inherited from the primary parent site.

▶ Although configuring the site address allows throttling and scheduling of inventories as well as status and policy transmissions, overly restrictive settings may result in undesirable behavior.

NOTE

Secondary Site Upgrades

ConfigMgr provides the capability to upgrade SMS 2003 secondary sites to ConfigMgr 2007 secondary sites; however, this process will not upgrade a secondary site to a primary.

Site Modes

ConfigMgr provides modes of security: mixed and native. If you are familiar with SMS 2003, that version used standard and advanced site security modes. Different from SMS 2003, if you upgrade the site to the more secure mode, you can downgrade it later. ConfigMgr 2007's mixed mode is functionally equivalent to SMS 2003's advanced security. Because self-signing of transmissions by the management point or the site server using certificates is only available with ConfigMgr, Internet-Based Client Management (IBCM) is not available on ConfigMgr sites running in mixed mode, because IBCM requires manipulating the certificate templates. On the other hand, authentication between clients and site servers uses the same proprietary technology as SMS 2003 when ConfigMgr is in mixed mode.

Native mode introduces new functionality and complexity to ConfigMgr security, such as using industry-standard Public Key Infrastructure certificates and Secure Sockets Layer (SSL) authentication between clients and site systems. ConfigMgr also supports third-party certificates, as long as their template is modifiable. SSL does not encrypt transmissions of policies; these are signed by the site server and management point. Metering data, status messages, policy, and inventory are all signed and encrypted. Because IBCM requires clients to communicate over HTTPS across the Internet to the ConfigMgr hierarchy, it requires native mode. If you will be implementing IBCM, you will want to analyze carefully the various supported deployment scenarios discussed at http://technet.microsoft.com/en-us/library/bb693824.aspx. Chapter 6 provides additional information about planning for site security modes.

NOTE

Securely Publishing to the Web

When publishing HTTP or HTTPS to the Web from inside a network, you should use Microsoft Internet Security and Acceleration (ISA) Server to perform web publishing of these ports. ISA acts as a reverse proxy in this fashion and provides application layer packet inspection to protect internal systems from malicious code.

Configuration Manager 2007 Roles

ConfigMgr 2007 has numerous roles that serve various purposes. Some roles are mandatory, some are optional, and some are recommended. Table 4.3 lists the ConfigMgr 2007 roles. Chapter 2, "Configuration Manager 2007 Overview," introduces the different roles, and Chapter 8, "Installing Configuration Manager 2007," covers the specifics of installing them.

TABLE 4.3   ConfigMgr 2007 Roles

Role	Mandatory/Recommended/Optional
Site/component server	Mandatory
Management point	Recommended; mandatory if hosting clients
Server locator point	Recommended
Distribution point	Recommended
Reporting point	Recommended
State migration point	Optional
PXE service point	Optional
Software update point	Recommended
Fallback status point	Recommended
System Health Validator	Recommended
Out of Band service point	Optional
Asset Intelligence sync point	Optional
Reporting service point (R2)	Recommended

Each role has different purposes that create unique loads on the site system housing that role. You will need to plan to ensure the site system can handle the load placed on it once in production. The following sections touch on many of the common design considerations that go into a ConfigMgr deployment.

Site Servers

Site servers are the most heavily planned role in the hierarchy. They typically include a local installation of SQL Server and the reporting point, may have thousands of systems reporting to them, run queries, update collection membership, house the management point and server locator point (SLP), and provide connections for ConfigMgr administration consoles across the organization. Site servers handle updating distribution points, process discovery data, and collect inventory from client systems. When a hierarchy of sites exists, site servers also replicate bidirectionally, sending collection, query, and various package data down the hierarchy and consuming inventory data from the lower tier of the hierarchy. Inventory data is only replicated from any given child to its parent and from that site to the next parent site if one exists. Eventually all inventory data makes it to the top of the hierarchy, the central site. In large implementations, the central site does not have any clients, and it is used primarily for reporting purposes.

NOTE

Placement of the Reporting Point Role

Microsoft recommends placing the reporting point role on a dedicated system in the central site position of the hierarchy for large deployments, to offload the reporting impact on SQL Server.

Collections are updated on a schedule in ConfigMgr, which defaults to every 24 hours beginning at the time the collection was created. Depending on the size of your site and the habits of your ConfigMgr administrators, there may be hundreds to thousands of collections. With so many collections updating against the SQL Server database, you may see a negative performance impact if too many collections are updating or collections are updating too often. This is a scenario often observed in the field, when large numbers of clients in collections are updating on a very aggressive schedule, such as hourly or every 15 minutes. Although these types of intervals are sometimes required, it is important to understand the load this puts on SQL Server and Windows disks. Adequate spindle counts will allow such aggressive collection evaluation. Monitoring various disk counters, covered in the "Developing the Server Architecture" section of this chapter, will provide insight into whether or not there is sufficient hardware to handle the load.

TIP

Collection Evaluation

Take note of the collection evaluation intervals and throttle back the evaluation intervals on those collections rarely used. It is common to find many collections that only need updating on a weekly basis, thus freeing resources on the site server for other pertinent tasks.

Distribution Points

Distribution points are typically the most heavily used role from an I/O perspective in all of ConfigMgr. Hundreds to thousands of clients may download or install packages from any given distribution point. Because each environment has unique circumstances around the volume of packages they push, the frequency in which the packages are pushed, and the average size of the packages, it is difficult to create a standard recommendation for sizing distribution points. Here are several best practices for DPs:

▶ Use BITS whenever possible to download and execute packages.

▶ Protect DPs on slow links or in remote locations.

▶ Verify there are enough spindles on the DP to support the packages pulled from them.

▶ Group distribution points as possible, for simpler administration.

▶ Make sure DPs have sufficient drive space to accommodate packages.

▶ If DPs are placed on a system with multiple purposes, such as a domain controller, make sure the load will not hinder other services the system provides.

▶ When placed on systems providing other network services, the DPs should be placed on a dedicated logical drive, if possible, to segregate I/O.

If a WAN link exists between a site server and the distribution point, using a secondary site server for the remote DP has a number of advantages. The primary benefit is the scheduling and throttling of traffic between the primary site server and secondary site server in regard to package replication. Here are some points to keep in mind:

▶ When the WAN link is reliable but somewhat small (such as a T1) or the link hosts important services for users across the WAN, a secondary site server housing the DP is highly recommended, as shown in Figure 4.5.

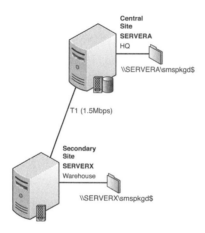

FIGURE 4.5   A DP on a secondary site server

▶ When the WAN link is unreliable or very slow (such as in a circuit under 1.5Mbps), it is best to use a branch DP, which enables leveraging BITS to replicate the package data.

System Health Validator

Network Access Protection requires Windows Server 2008. The NAP role is dependent on the Server 2008 version because it obtains the network policy data from Windows Server 2008. Windows Server 2008 has a role within the operating system itself called the Network Policy Server (NPS) role. This role defines what is deemed as healthy and unhealthy as well as the remediation actions to take when unhealthy clients are found. NAP relies extensively on NPS and the ConfigMgr System Health Validator role. If you plan to implement NAP, Windows Server 2008 and SHV will be a critical piece of your ConfigMgr topology and architecture. Although Chapters 11 and 15 discuss NAP, NPS, and SHV in more detail, it is important at the planning stage to understand the relationship of the roles, the load the systems will have, and their dependencies on each other, as well as the underlying technologies (such as IIS and Windows Server 2008).

Server Locator Point

By default, clients on the intranet query the Active Directory for their site assignment and resident management point. If the AD schema is not extended, server locator points become mandatory. SLPs are only required when you are managing clients in a workgroup or another AD forest, or have not extended the Active Directory schema. SLPs are not required when IBCM is used. Typically, only one SLP per site is necessary if implemented; the site server hosts this role in a sufficient manner.

Management Point

The management point is the most significant role in the ConfigMgr site. This role is the primary point for contact between clients and the site server. The management point requires IIS and WebDAV (Web Development Authoring and Versioning).

> **NOTE**
>
> **MPs on Server 2008**
>
> You must download, install, and configure WebDAV manually on management points running Windows Server 2008.

Management points provide the following services to clients:

- ▶ Installation prerequisites

- ▶ Client installation files

- ▶ Configuration details

- ▶ Advertisements

- ▶ Software distribution package source file locations

- ▶ Receive inventory data

- ▶ Receive software-metering information

- ▶ Receive status and state messages from clients

When provisioning an MP, the ConfigMgr wizard prompts the administrator for whether the site database (which is the default) or a database replica should be used. The database replica option should only be selected when desiring to use NLB for the MPs. (Replicas are discussed further in Chapter 8.) The site systems hosting the MP roles must have permission to update their objects in AD.

Management points can support intranet, Internet, and device clients. Management points supporting Internet clients require a web server signing certificate. By default, and as a best practice, the management point computer account is used to access site database information.

Fallback Status Point

The fallback status point (FSP) is the lifesaver of ConfigMgr 2007. It cannot be stressed enough how important it is to implement this role. The FSP lets administrators know when a client installation has failed, is having communication issues with the MP, and is left in an unmanaged state.

The FSP receives state messages from clients and relays them to the site. Because clients can be assigned to only one FSP, make sure to assign them prior to deployment.

Microsoft Documentation on the Fallback Status Point

The ConfigMgr help file (see the "Fallback Status Point" section) has this to say about FSPs:

"Examples of state messages a client might send to a fallback status point if it encountered problems during client deployment include the following:

▶ The client failed to install properly (for example, because of incorrect setup options or syntax errors, or because it failed to locate the required files).

▶ The client failed to be assigned to a site.

▶ The client failed to register with its assigned site.

▶ The client failed to locate its management point.

▶ There was a network connectivity problem between the client and the management point.

▶ The management point is not configured correctly (for example, IIS is not configured correctly for a Configuration Manager Management Point).

In addition to sending state messages when there is a problem during client deployment, the client will send a state message to the fallback status point when it is successfully installed and when it is successfully assigned to a Configuration Manager 2007 site. In this scenario, the client will also report if a restart is required to complete the installation.

Using the Fallback Status Point to Identify Native Mode Communication Problems

Because the fallback status point accepts unauthenticated communications, it accepts state messages from native mode clients when PKI certificate issues prevent communication between the client and its management point. Examples of state messages a client might send to a fallback status point to identify problems with native mode communication include the following:

▶ There is no valid client certificate.

▶ There is more than one possible valid client certificate without an appropriate certificate selection configuration specified.

▶ A server certificate needed for native mode communication fails to chain successfully to the trusted root certification.

▶ A server certificate needed for native mode communication is expired.

▶ A server certificate needed for native mode communication is revoked.

Software Update Point

Microsoft's documentation states that the software update point (SUP) role is required within the ConfigMgr hierarchy if you are deploying software updates. The SUP interacts with WSUS to configure settings, to request synchronization to the upstream update source and on the central site, and to synchronize the software updates from the WSUS database to the site server database.

NOTE

ConfigMgr SP 1 Requirements

Configuration Manager 2007 SP 1 requires WSUS 3.0 SP 1 at the time of this writing. As service packs for both Configuration Manager and WSUS evolve, this requirement may change. Make sure to refer to the release notes and requirements prior to deploying either ConfigMgr or WSUS.

Never make changes to WSUS from within the WSUS Administration console. The active software update point is controlled via the ConfigMgr console. Changes made to WSUS will be overwritten hourly by ConfigMgr's WSUS Configuration Manager component of the SMS Executive Service. More on ConfigMgr's patch management capabilities is provided in Chapter 15, "Patch Management."

Reporting Point

A reporting point (RP) is a ConfigMgr role designed to host web reports that query the database of the primary site for which they belong. Because they require SQL to run queries against, RPs can only belong to primary sites, not secondary sites. When multiple primary sites are in a hierarchy, it is a good idea to implement an RP at each primary site. This gives the individual groups who manage the site servers the ability to run reports specific to their managed environment.

Reporting points have the following requirements:

▶ The site system computer must have IIS installed and enabled.

▶ Active Server Pages must be installed and enabled.

▶ Microsoft Internet Explorer 5.01 SP 2 or later must be installed on any server or client that uses Report Viewer.

▶ To use graphs in reports, Office Web Components (Microsoft Office 2000 SP 2, Microsoft Office XP, or Microsoft Office 2003) must be installed.

NOTE

Reporting Point Prerequisite Requirements

When you install ASP.NET on a Windows Server 2008 operating system reporting point, you must also manually enable Windows Authentication. For more information, see the "How to Configure Windows Server 2008 for Site Systems" section of the ConfigMgr R2 help file.

Office Web Components is not supported on 64-bit operating systems. If you want to use graphs in reports, use 32-bit operating systems for your reporting points.

Real World: Making ConfigMgr Reports Easily Accessible

In large ConfigMgr hierarchies, management often wants to view specific reports in ConfigMgr. Instead of using the default folder name for the central site reporting point (SMSReporting_*bbn*, where *bbn* is the site code), you can remove the site code from the end of the folder name. This ultimately affects the URL used and allows management to browse to http://<*servername*>/smsreporting to access the reporting point.

An alternative for this is leaving the default RP folder names as they are and create a DNS alias to point to the server in question. If you create an alias record called smsreporting and point it at the central site server, users will be directed to the server http://bluebonnet/inetpub, for example, for the hierarchy used in this book. This is the default IIS website for the Bluebonnet site server, and does not get to the RP. By implementing a default.html file containing the following lines, you cause requests made to the server to be directed to the default IIS directory and then redirected to the SMSReporting virtual directory with the site's site code:

```
<HTML>
<META HTTP-EQUIV="REFRESH" CONTENT="0; URL=/smsreporting_bbn">
</HTML>
```

This abstracts the site code from general knowledge and lets users browse to a user-friendly record.

Not All Roles Are Available All the Time

Not every role is available all the time to clients. If you will be implementing IBCM, it is important to understand that only a few roles are available to clients out on the untrusted network. Only the following roles are available to IBCM clients:

- ▶ Management point
- ▶ Fallback status point
- ▶ Software update point
- ▶ Distribution point (if it is not a site system share), protected site system, or branch distribution point

Real World: Be Aware of Prerequisites for ConfigMgr Roles

It is important to note the requirements or prerequisites (covered in Chapter 2) that ConfigMgr roles have in a hierarchy. As an example, while planning your distribution point architecture, it may go unnoticed that IIS is required for using BITS-enabled distribution points. This requirement has been an issue in many environments where the distribution point is expected to be on remote DCs scattered across the WAN. The requirement of IIS for MPs, DPs, state migration points, fallback status points, software update points, server locator points, and reporting points places emphasis on these systems, their patching, and other services they provide to the networked systems.

Developing the Server Architecture

CPU, RAM, and disk I/O are the three most important items when planning and configuring server hardware. The size, or robustness, of the server provisioned for any given role dictates how well it will handle the load. When discussing expectations of the overall solution, some level of understanding needs to be communicated and agreed on. ConfigMgr has many dependencies, including business and user requirements in addition to the overall infrastructure and network services requirements. This makes it difficult to predict expectations for the overall solution. Because each environment is different and has different requirements, there is no "one size fits all" solution.

Database Servers

The site database server is the most memory-intensive role in the ConfigMgr hierarchy. The amount of memory used is configurable in SQL Server and limited to 3GB, unless you are running SQL Server on an x64 platform and operating system. (Covering alternatives to this, such as AWE, is beyond the scope of this book.) If SQL Server will require more than 3GB, as in instances when it is not dedicated to ConfigMgr, using a separate SQL Server running on x64 becomes a compelling solution.

Several counters are listed in Table 4.4 that you will want to evaluate on your ConfigMgr database server.

TABLE 4.4   Site Database Server Counters to Be Monitored

Object	Instance	Comments
Physical Disk	Avg. Disk Queue Length: Volume	Select one of these counters for each volume involved in Configuration Manager processes. This includes the operating system installation volume, ConfigMgr installation (inbox) volume, as well as the SQL Server tempdb, site database, and log volumes.

TABLE 4.4   Site Database Server Counters to Be Monitored

Object	Instance	Comments
Physical Disk	% Disk Time	Select one of these counters for each volume that is involved in Configuration Manager data processing. These include the operating system installation volume, ConfigMgr installation (inbox) volume, SQL Server tempdb, site database, and log volumes.
SqlServer:General Statistics	Temp Tables Creation Rate	General SQL Server statistics.
SqlServer:General Statistics	Logouts/sec	General SQL Server statistics.
SqlServer:General Statistics	Logins/sec	General SQL Server statistics.
SqlServer:SQL Statistics	SQL Re-Compilations/sec	General SQL Server statistics.
SqlServer:SQL Statistics	SQL Compilations/sec	General SQL Server statistics.
SqlServer:SQL Statistics	Batch Requests/sec	General SQL Server statistics.
SqlServer:Memory Manager	Lock Memory	General SQL Server statistics.
SQLServer:Locks	Lock Requests/sec	General SQL Server statistics.
SQLServer:Locks	Number of Deadlocks/sec	General SQL Server statistics.
SqlServer:Databases	Transactions/sec: SCCM db	General SQL Server statistics.
SqlServer:Databases	Transactions/sec: Wsus Db	General SQL Server statistics.

You will also want to understand some basic SQL Server best practices. Some of these options will vary depending on your site size, hierarchy, which roles you are using, and how you are using them.

Microsoft has posted several SQL Server best practices as well as technical white papers at http://technet.microsoft.com/en-us/sqlserver/bb671430.aspx.

Microsoft has also produced a SQL Server 2005 Best Practice Analyzer (BPA) that gathers data from SQL Server configuration settings. The SQL BPA produces a report using predefined recommendations to determine if there are issues with the SQL Server implementation. The SQL 2005 BPA can be downloaded at http://www.microsoft.com/downloads. Search for **SQL Server 2005 Best Practices**. (No BPA is planned for SQL Server 2008.)

General Performance

There is no ideal performance or target goal for a given ConfigMgr solution. Cost/benefit analysis should be performed to weigh the performance cost versus the actual requirements.

Across any ConfigMgr role, it is important to understand the overall load the role places on a system, and how the system will handle that load. Table 4.5 illustrates a general array of performance counters system administrators should be aware of and use to gauge the overall performance, or health, of their systems. These counters are not specific to servers or roles, and can be applied to any Microsoft Windows operating system.

TABLE 4.5   General System Performance Counters

Object	Counter	Instance	Notes
System	% Total Processor Time	N/A	Less than 80% is acceptable. Consistently exceeding that level means more CPU is needed or the load needs to be reduced.
System	Processor Queue Length	N/A	Two or fewer means the CPU utilization is acceptable.
Thread	Context Switches/sec	_total	Lower is better. Measure the thread counter to enable the processor queue length counter.
Physical Disk	%Disk Time	Each disk	Less than 80% is acceptable.
Physical Disk	Current Disk Queue Length	Each disk	Tells you how many I/O operations are waiting for the hard disk to become available. Opinions vary widely on this one; the common rule is to multiply the number of spindles in the array by two and make sure the value stays below this.
Memory	Committed Bytes	N/A	Should be less than the installed RAM.
Memory	Page Reads/sec	N/A	If consistently exceeding 5, add RAM.
SQL Server	Cache Hit Ratio	N/A	98% or more is acceptable; lower means SQL is being delayed by paging.

Disk Performance

Disks today are the weakest point in a computer's performance, and you will want to give serious attention to designing the right disk subsystem for the various ConfigMgr roles. Due to the increasing demand to lower server prices, vendors now make server systems available using hardware designed for the desktop-level system. This may lead to performance bottlenecks and disk failures with ConfigMgr site systems. Although performance using SCSI (Small Computer System Interface) devices may be adequate for server specs, technologies such as SATA (Serial Advanced Technology Attachment) have a much higher Mean Time Between Failure (MTBF), which is calculated during Phase 2 of a hard drive's life.

It is important to understand the implications of drive failure in servers. Although a drive may fail and the system may continue to run, if another drive fails, the entire volume goes down, ultimately creating an outage. If you are dealing with an enterprise environment, outages are never welcome. Here are the three phases of a drive's life:

▶ Phase 1 of a drive's life is the burn-in phase, and failure is very high.

▶ In phase 2, the drive is run for a length of time and the failure rate is minimal. This equates to the normal operational lifetime of the drive and is how the MTBF value is calculated.

▶ Phase 3 is where failure rates increase and the drive is reaching the end of its life, or warranty (ironically).

Table 4.6 lists characteristics of several types of drives.

TABLE 4.6   Disk Drive Characteristics

Drive Type	Rotational Speed	Average Seek/Access Time	MTBF
EIDE	5400–7500 rpm	Seek time: 8 to 10 ms	300,000–500,000 hours at 20% duty cycle.
SCSI	7500–15000 rpm	Access time: 5 to 10 ms	600,000–1,200,000 hours at 100% duty cycle.
SATA	5400–10000 rpm	Access time: 3 to 7 ms	Mostly less expensive drives than SCSI, and MTBF's defined for less than 100% duty cycle. MTBF 500,000–1,500,000 hours.

Real World: ConfigMgr and Disk I/O

Disk I/O is the biggest performance bottleneck on ConfigMgr implementations and can have a large impact on overall site health. When a site cannot keep up with client demands, a snowball effect occurs—unless the load decreases, the server cannot catch up and performance continuously deteriorates.

Modern-day best practices for disk architecture include the following:

▶ Use SCSI or SAS devices when possible.

▶ Use hardware RAID (Redundant Array of Independent Disks) instead of software RAID. Software RAID uses the CPU of the server, taking away from its ability to process computations.

▶ Use battery-backed cache controller cards. This allows the disks to run at a higher performance level due to the lack of corruption from possible power loss.

▶ More spindles with smaller size are better than fewer spindles of larger disks.

▶ Utilize eight or more drives in RAID 1+0 when serious I/O or performance concerns are present.

▶ Make sure you have adequate network bandwidth to support data transfers. As an example, it takes 2.5Gbps to equate to the transfer rate of a SCSI Ultra 320 drive.

Smaller sites may be able to run sufficiently on a small array, such as a RAID1 array, which uses two disks. However, larger implementations will falter on such a small backend disk subsystem. As scale increases in the enterprise or demand increases on the disk subsystem used by ConfigMgr, a larger array becomes necessary to support the load. Unfortunately, there is no formula where x number of ConfigMgr clients equals y number of disks—there are just too many possible implementation paths in ConfigMgr 2007 to allow a standard formula to dictate disk I/O load.

When dealing with larger enterprises or more aggressive policy evaluation intervals, such as daily or hourly inventories, know that adding spindles always increases performance of the disk subsystem. Arrays composed of many disks will yield exponentially better performance than arrays just several disks smaller. An easy way to understand this is thinking of each disk as a worker going to find information. When there are additional workers, the information is returned quicker.

If ConfigMgr console performance is important to your ConfigMgr administrators, you will want to explore SANs (Storage Area Networks) and other storage solutions for the ConfigMgr database and binaries. Although discussing SANs, iSCSI (Internet SCSI), and other disk technologies is beyond the scope of this book, you will want to explore them in large-scale enterprises with 20,000 or more clients reporting to a site server. This does not imply that if there are fewer than 20,000 clients that you should not look at using a SAN for your SQL Server databases or distribution points. Storage solutions offer a variety of other benefits, including disaster recovery, backup, and other options that are frequently vendor specific.

Disk optimization steps include the following:

▶ The ConfigMgr SQL database should be on its own array.

▶ The ConfigMgr SQL transaction log should be on its own array.

▶ The Windows operating system should be on its own array.

▶ Any distribution point should be on its own array.

▶ Any software update point should be on its own array.

Operating systems perform best when loaded on RAID 1 arrays. Consult with your company's standard on whether you use RAID1+0 or external storage solutions such as SANs. The principle here is that two disks give good performance, redundancy, and the lowest possible failure rate. (That is correct. With only two disks in a RAID1 array, you are four times less likely to have a failure than in a RAID5 array with eight disks!)

Databases typically need to be placed on RAID5 or RAID10 arrays, due to the sheer number of disks required to support the database size. Fortunately, ConfigMgr has a relatively small database size, although its size is dependent on a multitude of variables such as inventories, packages, number of clients, features in use, and such. SMS 2003's SQL sizing was based on 50MB + ($N \times$ 250KB), where N is the number of clients. This means that if there were 5,000 clients, the formula would read as follows:

50MB + (5,000 $\times$ 250KB) = 1.27GB

This sizing formula was found to be unrealistically low, and most administrators doubled or tripled the value. With ConfigMgr 2007, you can use the same rule of thumb for database sizing, but should increase the 250KB multiplier to support the new features, including patch management, configuration management, and expanded inventory. Experience has shown that 2MB per client is a more realistic value to use than 250KB as a starting point for sizing the ConfigMgr database. This means you should use the following formula to determine the required database size:

50MB + ($N \times$ 2,048KB), where N is the number of clients

Using this new formula for the same size (5,000 clients) gives a considerably higher number:

50MB + (5,000 $\times$ 2,048KB) = 9.8GB

SQL Server transaction logs can usually be a RAID1 array because it is not common for ConfigMgr requirements to do point-in-time restores. This means selecting a simple database recovery model, so the transaction log will not need to be extraordinarily large.

DPs and state migration points are the most critical in terms of disk I/O. Memory and CPU on these roles are a minor concern, and are not an issue as long as there's sufficient RAM on the system to prevent unnecessary swapping.

Distribution points can have the most widely varying requirements depending on how they are used. As an example, if a company performs routine software patching and package pushes, the size of its distribution point may be minimal, particularly if BITS is used extensively to download and execute content. Anything from a single disk to a RAID1 array could be effective in a branch DP or a conventional DP.

If you introduce the OSD functionality into your ConfigMgr solution, the requirements jump substantially. Conventional packages are relatively small, between 1MB and 200MB, depending on the average package. Microsoft Office usually is one of the largest at 1GB for the 2007 version. Operating system images, regardless of the applications being in the images or called from outside them, average around 1GB for Windows XP and 3GB to 4GB for Vista images in the ImageX WIM (Windows Imaging) format. In addition, because download-and-execute is not an option for operating system deployments, you can have a DP with a very large data demand for many machines in parallel. The best solution for this scenario is many disk spindles. You should seriously consider SANs if your ConfigMgr implementation requires supporting large operating system deployments. State migration points may have similar disk I/O requirements. Disk I/O for this role is difficult to calculate, with each user's state volume size being an unknown.

TIP

Calculating User State Volume

You can use ConfigMgr to calculate user state volume size, thus helping to define capacity requirements and expected timeframes for OS migrations. Simply query the user's dataset you desire to capture running a script deployed as a package, and store the size in Windows Management Instrumentation (WMI) on the client. The next inventory will upload data to the site server, where it can be used to populate reports. Microsoft partners such as SCCM Experts (formerly known as SMS Experts) specialize in solutions such as this.

Monitoring Performance

If available, utilize tools such as System Center Operations Manager (OpsMgr) 2007 to baseline performance and monitor ConfigMgr site health. When external monitoring solutions are not available, use a tool such as Performance Monitor (Perfmon), which is built into each version of Windows. Perfmon enables administrators to collect a myriad of performance data and log it to a file for later analysis. Realize that this method of using Performance Monitor can place a load on the system when the samples are captured at an aggressive interval! Because you only need to look at average performance over a broad period, sampling every 10 or 15 minutes is acceptable and provides a multitude of useful data to analyze when tuning the system.

TIP

Benchmarking

Consider periodically collecting performance metrics from the site systems when they are utilized during business hours. This data ultimately will provide a baseline by which you can measure performance. This data is useful for scaling out or up, depending on how the load increases on the site systems. CPU, memory, disk, and network throughput are the four areas to evaluate periodically.

Capacity Planning

Capacity requirements are frequently miscalculated in the initial planning phases of ConfigMgr deployments because adequate thought is not given to the actual amount of data that will be kept on each site server and site system. Adding storage after the fact is a rather difficult situation to deal with; it frequently requires outages, possibly moving roles around, and in general is something that could have been dealt with in advance if properly architected.

A number of items contribute to ConfigMgr capacity requirements:

▶ Software inventory has the ability to do file collection.

In a 5,000-seat environment, collecting a 1MB file will add 5GB of storage to the server, backups, and the network load while transferring the data. ConfigMgr software inventory file collection can be configured to limit the maximum amount transferred per client, but the site server and network infrastructure will need to handle this size times the number of clients reporting to the site server or hierarchy.

Adding a software file extension such as .dll to your inventory can easily double the ConfigMgr database size. Tables in the ConfigMgr database such as softwarefile can grow exponentially in size, affecting reporting and Resource Explorer performance. When designing your ConfigMgr solution, it is important to know what software file types will be inventoried to help determine backend storage requirements from a capacity and performance perspective.

▶ You can scale SUPs and MPs beyond 25,000 clients per site by implementing these site system roles with NLB, as illustrated in Figure 4.6.

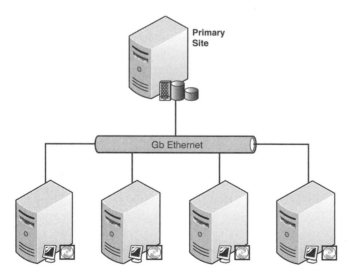

FIGURE 4.6   Network load-balanced MPs and SUPs

If you are implementing NLB on an MP in a mixed mode site, IIS does not allow clients to authenticate to the site system using Kerberos authentication. To support an NLB implementation, you must reconfigure the website application pools running under the Local System account to run under a domain user account.

▶ Distribution points have disk I/O and network I/O constraints.

Considerations affecting the size of the volume needed include how many packages are planned to be kept on distribution points year-round, and the number of packages a given distribution point is expected to support. Although the ConfigMgr documentation states that a distribution point can handle up to 4,000 clients, network speed, disk performance, and package size greatly impact this value.

TIP

Capacity Planning Calculations

DPs and state migration points are site systems with unique capacity requirements. As a rule of thumb, take the current size of your existing software library volume and then triple it to use as a starting point for DPs or package source repository requirements.

▶ The state migration point (SMP) is a Configuration Manager 2007 site role providing a secure location to store user state, data, and settings, prior to an operating system deployment.

You can store the user state on the SMP while the operating system deployment proceeds, and then restore the user state to the new computer from the state migration point, as illustrated in Figure 4.7.

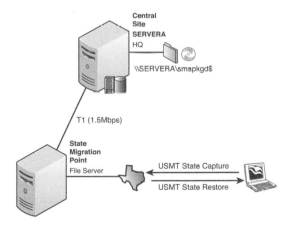

FIGURE 4.7   A state migration point role

Each SMP site server can only be a member of one Configuration Manager 2007 site. State migration points provide ConfigMgr administrators the ability to store users' data and purge it automatically after it has become stale, a period defined by the ConfigMgr administrator. The concept behind this relies on the data being restored or backed up within the allotted threshold. Figure 4.8 shows the state migration point properties.

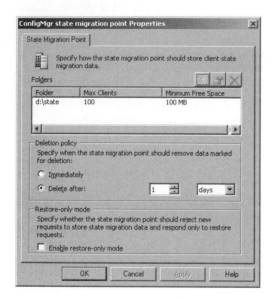

FIGURE 4.8   A state migration point properties page

Although state migration points allow for automatic scheduled deletion of data considered stale, capacity planning is still needed to handle the volume of data sent at the state migration point within the defined retention period. Chapter 19, "Operating System Deployment," discusses state migration points in more detail.

Site Boundaries

ConfigMgr boundaries, discussed in Chapter 6, are logical groupings defining where the site server has management capabilities. You can specify boundaries using AD sites, Internet Protocol (IP) subnets, IP address ranges, or IPv6 prefixes. Figure 4.9 depicts the Dallas site boundary on the Bluebonnet central site.

When defining boundaries, the ConfigMgr administrator must define whether these boundaries are slow or fast (which really means unreliable or reliable). Boundaries should be unique to each site server and ideally not overlap.

When planning your ConfigMgr site boundaries, you may discover unique requirements for some AD sites or subnets, which may often lead to creating additional ConfigMgr sites. Some client settings at a site level only may not be allowed on certain subnets or AD sites (as an example, remote controlling a computer without user interaction). This action may

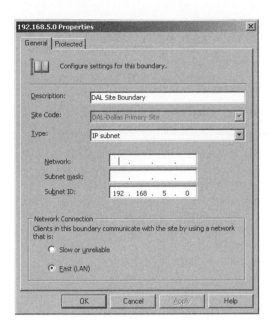

FIGURE 4.9   ConfigMgr boundaries

be prohibited in the Accounting AD site or subnet and ultimately require an additional site server with unique settings for the location.

Although settings are often sitewide, they can be overridden using local policy. Local policies are described in Chapter 3.

Roaming

Roaming in ConfigMgr is the capability allowing clients to move between sites in the hierarchy, yet still be managed, while making the best use of local network resources. ConfigMgr clients have the ability to roam throughout the hierarchy, allowing clients to leverage services from a nearby site server in the hierarchy so that traversing a WAN or "slow" network is not required. As an example, if a client is at a remote location supporting a site server the client does not belong to, the client can use the roaming feature to install packages off that site server's DP if the packages are present, thus minimizing impact to the WAN and optimizing the end-user experience of software distribution.

Figure 4.10 illustrates how a client can roam to a different network defined as a slow or unreliable network managed by another site. This is a common scenario when laptops travel, which allows ConfigMgr clients to automatically download and execute packages rather than installing them across the WAN.

How Roaming Works

The following includes information taken from the "About Client Roaming in Configuration Manager" section of the ConfigMgr help file.

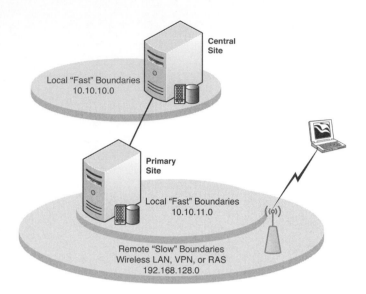

FIGURE 4.10   A roaming client

Roaming occurs when a ConfigMgr client leaves the corporate local area network (LAN) and changes to a home network environment. Roaming is often a misunderstood concept and technology—the simplest way to view roaming behavior is to understand that whenever a client changes network subnets, it is roaming. Roaming always involves an IP address change. Roaming boundaries are based on subnets in the hierarchy, which indicate where the ConfigMgr administrators want the clients to go to download content.

Global roaming, which is only available if you have extended the schema, occurs when a client first identifies the site into which it has roamed, by comparing its current IP address with the list of IP subnets that define the boundaries in the hierarchy. When the client finds a match for the boundary, it can identify which site is configured for that boundary and locate the management point for that site. The default management point for the site that the client has roamed into is referred to as the *resident management point*.

The resident management point informs the roaming client of distribution points in its site containing package source files that the client can access. However, if the package source files are not available in the site the client has roamed into, the client falls back to asking its default management point for distribution points.

If Active Directory is not available, or if the Active Directory schema is not extended, clients can roam only to the lower-level sites of their assigned site. This is called *regional roaming*. In regional roaming, the client can roam to lower-level sites and still receive software packages from distribution points.

When an advertisement is sent to the client, the client receives information about the advertised package location from its assigned management point. Alternatively, if the client has roamed into a secondary site, it receives information about the advertised package location from a proxy management point, if one is available. The client then uses the distribution points of one of its assigned site's lower-level sites. The distribution point it uses depends on which roaming boundary the client is in and whether the advertised package is available on the distribution point.

Global roaming allows the client to roam to higher-level sites, sibling sites, and sites in other branches of the ConfigMgr hierarchy and still receive software packages from distribution points. Global roaming requires Active Directory and the Active Directory schema extensions. Global roaming cannot be performed across Active Directory forests.

Regional roaming behavior occurs when clients cannot access Configuration Manager 2007 site information published to AD; these clients continue to contact the default management point in their assigned site. The clients are not aware of the site's identity that they have roamed into, or of the management points in that site.

In this scenario, when clients roam into a site that is lower in the hierarchy than their assigned site (for example, a child site or a grandchild site), the client's default management point informs the roaming client of the closest distribution points the client can access.

Site Design

Designing a site involves analyzing several items and making decisions on the settings to apply to those items. You will need to analyze items such as client agent settings or policies to determine what the best setting is for the environment the site will be managing. A great example of this is the notification options selected for users to experience when they receive advertisements to run packages on their systems.

Site design items are not specific to client agent settings; they consist of many things, including the following:

▶ Is the server physical or virtual?

▶ Where is the server?

▶ What is the storage subsystem?

▶ Is SQL Server installed on the site server or a separate system?

▶ Is the site a primary or secondary?

▶ What are the site boundaries?

▶ Which ports will be used for client communication?

▶ Is the site in mixed or native mode?

▶ What is the hardware inventory frequency?

▶ Who are the administrators and operators of this site?

▶ What is the hardware inventory collecting information on?

▶ Which discovery methods will be used?

▶ What is the discovery method's frequency?

▶ What LDAP path is being queried for discovery?

▶ What client push installation system types are selected?

▶ What client push installation account is being used?

▶ What rights does the client push installation account have?

▶ Which roles does the site hold?

▶ What site maintenance tasks are enabled, and what are their settings?

▶ What site systems are in the ConfigMgr site, and what are their roles?

▶ Is Wake On LAN (WOL) enabled, and what are its settings?

Although some settings may only be useful in a disaster-recovery scenario, many of them can have negative impacts when used incorrectly. As an example, when you're performing discovery from multiple ConfigMgr sites within a hierarchy, it is possible for a system to be discovered multiple times with its data discovery record (DDR) sent up the hierarchy and processed by each system that handles it. This not only results in duplicate DDR analysis effort, but every site will have to analyze each DDR and determine which is newer. It is best to let sites discover only resources that belong to that site, even for child sites—because discovered data flows up the hierarchy. This is easily viewable by looking at the properties of any discovered system or client in a collection.

Due to ConfigMgr's scalable design, sites may host multiple ConfigMgr roles. In most implementations of 10,000 managed clients or fewer, you can use a single site server with specifications similar to those listed in the next sections. These designs are documented by Microsoft at http://download.microsoft.com/download/4/b/9/4b97e9b7-7056-41ae-8fc8-dd87bc477b54/Sample%20Configurations%20and%20Common%20Performance%20Related%20Questions.pdf (this link is also available in Appendix B), for scaling and providing adequate performance in the listed configurations.

Site Design for a Smaller Environment

In a small ConfigMgr site, you can configure a site server containing a management point as follows:

▶ Dual Xeon 3GHz

▶ 4GB of RAM

▶ SAS drives with battery-backed cache

▶ RAID1 array for OS and SQL TempDB

▶ RAID1 array for ConfigMgr files and SQL database and log

Site Design with 25,000 Clients

In larger environments of approximately 25,000 seats, Microsoft found the following site design to be sufficient.

Site server:

▶ Dual Xeon 3GHz

▶ 4GB of RAM

▶ SAS drives with battery-backed cache

▶ RAID1 array for OS

▶ RAID1 array for ConfigMgr files

▶ RAID10 array (four disks) for SQL Server database, log, and TempDB

Management point:

▶ Dual Xeon 3GHz

▶ 4GB of RAM

▶ SAS drives with battery-backed cache

▶ RAID1 array for OS

▶ RAID1 array for ConfigMgr files

Site Design with 50,000–100,000 Clients

When you scale up to 50,000 clients, this site's physical design adds NLB management points to support the additional load. At 100,000 clients, the management points are load-balanced across four systems and the management points read from a SQL site database replica. The following configuration details the hardware recommended to achieve this client density on a single site.

Site server:

▶ Quad Xeon 2.66GHz

▶ 16GB of RAM

▶ SAS drives with battery-backed cache

▶ RAID1 array for OS

▶ RAID1 array for SQL TempDB

▶ RAID10 array (four disks) for ConfigMgr files

▶ RAID10 array (four disks) for SQL data files

▶ RAID10 array (four disks) for SQL log files

▶ RAID1 array for SQL replication distribution database

Four management points in the NLB cluster:

▶ Dual Xeon 3GHz

▶ 4GB of RAM

▶ SAS drives with battery-backed cache

▶ RAID1 array for OS

▶ RAID1 array for ConfigMgr files

▶ RAID10 array (four disks) for SQL replication distribution database

Site Design with Over 100,000 Clients

When implementing ConfigMgr with greater than 100,000 clients, use a central site with no clients reporting to it. Ever since SMS 2.0, the central site was intended for inventory rollup, status processing, centralized administration, and reporting. The key difference is that although during the SMS 2.0 timeframe hierarchies over 500 clients were recommended to implement a central site with no clients, Microsoft now baselines that architecture at hierarchies greater than 100,000 clients.

Client Architecture

When you define which agents will be loaded into the ConfigMgr client, you are actually defining the ConfigMgr client architecture. This architecture requires planning to ensure future initiatives will work without issues.

As an example, defining an initial ConfigMgr client cache value is an important task to perform before rolling out clients to the enterprise. Although you can modify the cache size on an individual client basis, initial packages may fail if they exceed the default cache size.

Another setting is choosing to have the client display a visual indicator or even generate an audible alert when the client is being remote-controlled. Enabling the audio is considered annoying by users, and systems have been known to have problems with it. Displaying a visual indicator is suggested, because it lets the user know the system is still being controlled and identifies when the remote administrator has closed the session.

ConfigMgr clients consist of multiple agents, each of which has unique settings that can be assigned to them. When the settings are defined, ConfigMgr creates XML (eXtensible Markup Language) policies, which are downloaded via the management point to clients. The following agents have policies defined that collectively make up the ConfigMgr Client architecture illustrated in Table 4.7.

TABLE 4.7   Client Agents

Agent	Settings
Hardware Inventory Client Agent	Defines which objects should be queried from the system hardware, Registry, file system, and so on, and the frequency in which they should be inventoried
Software Inventory Client Agent	Defines which file extensions should be scanned and the frequency
Advertised Programs Client Agent	Defines client behavior when advertisements run
Computer Client Agent	Used to specify the accounts ConfigMgr will use for network access, customization of balloon pop-ups, reminders for users, BITS, and restart settings
Desired Configuration Management Client Agent	Defines the interval in which compliance against the defined baselines are evaluated
Mobile Device Client Agent	Only applies to Windows Mobile devices, defined hardware, software, file collection, and software distribution settings
Remote Tools Client Agent	Defines which administrators can remote-access client systems using the Remote Desktop Protocol (RDP), and settings to manipulate the end-user experience while being remotely viewed
Network Access Protection Client Agent	Maintains settings for compliance and out-of-compliance resolution and notification to end users; works in conjunction with Windows Server 2008 Network Policy Server; requires Configuration Manager 2007 R2
Software Metering Client Agent	Specifies the schedule in which software-metering data is collected
Software Updates Client Agent	Defines the schedule for processing Windows Update deployments, reevaluation, installation behavior, and end-user experience settings

Client architecture is fairly flexible in that if a setting is not initially deployed correctly, it can be changed centrally with the clients updating to the new setting in fairly quick fashion (as fast as the setting for the Computer Client Agent Policy Polling Interval). The importance of understanding the agents and their settings is primarily to facilitate creating a correct ConfigMgr site design and to position the ConfigMgr deployment team for success.

Chapter 12 further discusses client architecture.

Multilanguage Scenarios

In today's global economy, more companies have networks spanning multiple countries than ever before. The nature of the different languages used from country to country presents new challenges for system administrators. When Microsoft Windows client operating systems are installed using the native, non-English language of the country, ConfigMgr administrators must look at available options to address their system management needs. The International Client Pack (ICP) is a specialized set of client files split across two separate downloads, supporting the following 22 languages. You can download the ConfigMgr 2007 SP 1 ICPs by searching for **ICP** at www.microsoft.com/downloads.

ICP1 contains the following languages:

- ► English
- ► French
- ► German
- ► Japanese
- ► Spanish

ICP2 contains all languages from ICP1 plus the following:

- ► Chinese (Simplified)
- ► Chinese (Traditional)
- ► Czech
- ► Danish
- ► Dutch
- ► Finnish
- ► Greek
- ► Hungarian
- ► Italian
- ► Korean
- ► Norwegian
- ► Polish
- ► Portuguese
- ► Portuguese (Brazil)
- ► Russian
- ► Swedish
- ► Turkish

ICPs are client files only. The files consist of the following:

► Client.msi

► Client.mst

► Several small supporting files, including language resource files

ICP Versioning

ConfigMgr site and service pack versions must correlate to the ICP version implemented. As an example, you should only install the Microsoft System Center Configuration Manager 2007 SP 1 International Client Packs on a ConfigMgr 2007 SP 1 site.

CAUTION

ICPs and Service Packs

When using ICPs with ConfigMgr, you cannot upgrade to a new service pack level until the associated ICP is also available. ICPs are released shortly after service packs. Once the ICP is released for a new service pack, install the service pack and then install the new ICP.

ICPs are versioned in a fashion where the client version number is greater than the service pack level of the current ConfigMgr client. You can identify service pack, ICP, and hotfix numbers from the version number, which is the last four digits of the Configuration Manager 2007 version number. Let's use a sample scenario to illustrate how clients know they need to upgrade to an ICP-versioned client. The following illustrates a current ConfigMgr 2007 RTM install that is being upgraded to SP 1:

► **ConfigMgr 2007 RTM Client version—4.0.5931.0000**

► **ConfigMgr 2007 SP 1 Prerelease version—4.00.6086.1000**

► **ConfigMgr 2007 SP 1 Client version—4.00.6221.1000**

► **ConfigMgr 2007 SP 1 ICP1 Client version—4.00.6221.1400**

► **ConfigMgr 2007 SP 1 ICP2 Client version—4.00.6221.1700**

► **ConfigMgr 2007 R2 Client version—4.00.6355.1000**

Microsoft Documentation on ICP

Microsoft TechNet at http://technet.microsoft.com/en-us/library/bb680389.aspx states the following:

"You can determine whether an ICP is installed by checking for multiple language folders, such as the 00000409 folder for English and the 00000407 folder for German on the site server. There is a folder for each client language supported by that ICP.

The first digit of the fourth part of the version number, such as *n* in n000, is the service pack release number. As an example, 2.50.2485.2000 denotes SP 2. If the Configuration Manager 2007 version number is 2.50.2485.3000 or higher, then the service pack is SP 3.

Additionally, ICP1 has a 4 as the third-to-last digit. For example, 2.50.2485.2400 indicates SP 2 ICP1, and 2.50.2485.3400 indicates SP 3 ICP1. Likewise, ICP2 has a 7 as the third-to-last digit. For example, 2.50.2485.3700 indicates SP 3 ICP2.

The last three digits are the hotfix version number, which can range from .0001 to .0299.

If you apply Configuration Manager 2007 SP 2 ICP1 to a Configuration Manager 2007 SP 2 U.S. English site that had several hotfixes installed after SP 2 was installed and files with the same name are included in ICP1, then ICP1 overwrites the newer files because the files in ICP1 do not contain the bug fixes. If the ICP overwrites new files, whatever problems caused you to apply the hotfixes might reappear. As an example, you may have previously applied a hotfix to prevent Configuration Manager 2007 APM32 from using the CPU at 100 percent. Later you apply ICP1, which does not contain the hotfix. After ICP1 installation, your site server CPU usage is back to 100 percent. To prevent this from occurring, contact Microsoft Customer Support and Services (CSS) and obtain the version of the hotfix that correctly matches the ICP you intend to install before ICP installation. After you install the ICP, immediately install the hotfixes that were released later than the ICP."

To determine the version of an ICP on a site server, check the version value of HKEY_LOCAL_MACHINE\Software\Microsoft\SMS\Setup in the Registry. To validate the management point has been updated, verify that language directories such as 00000409, 00000407, and so on, exist and contain .mst files. To verify clients have received the updated client binaries, create a custom query and include the Client Version property from the System Resource class. To verify the client has received the updates at the client, open the Configuration Manager applet in Control Panel and view the version of each client on the Components tab.

CAUTION

ICPs and Hotfixes

When you're applying a hotfix to an ICP client or site, the hotfix must support the ICP version running on the system.

ICP Scenarios and Implementations

If an ICP is installed on a site server, the only prerequisite is the operating system must be English.

End-user experience will vary depending on whether or not the ICP is deployed. The following scenarios could exist:

Scenario 1—The site server is running the English operating system without any ICP.

- ▶ Clients running native language OS will show the ConfigMgr client in English; users may not be able to read ConfigMgr dialog boxes.

- ▶ Clients running the Multilanguage User Interface (MUI) will have the same experience as those running native OS; users may not be able to read ConfigMgr dialog boxes.

Scenario 2—The site server is installed in English and ICP1 or ICP2 is installed.

- ▶ Clients running native language will be able to see the ConfigMgr client dialog boxes in their language as long as the ICP version includes their language.

- ▶ Clients running MUI will be able to see the ConfigMgr client dialog boxes in their language as long as the ICP version includes their language.

Take special considerations when deploying the ICP to ConfigMgr hierarchies. Always read the release notes and product documentation, and test thoroughly in a lab and pilot environment.

Testing

You will want to establish a lab environment and implement ConfigMgr in a completely isolated lab scenario. Labs return large amounts of ROI to those organizations that use them. Using a lab allows IT administrators to work with, experiment, and learn new technology, configurations, and scenarios needed in a production environment, while mitigating the risk by isolating the lab environment from those systems that could cause a loss in revenue or service if an outage occurred. In short, labs should mirror a production environment as closely as possible, have no risk associated with their use, and be able to be reset to allow for quickly repeating a process or testing a given scenario.

Using a lab allows several options that build on each other to guarantee the success of the ConfigMgr implementation. With a lab, you can implement ConfigMgr without interference of network devices such as firewalls, routers, IDS, and IPS. If resources allow, you can scale the solution in the lab to validate the expected performance and behavior of the design destined for the production environment.

Your ConfigMgr test plan should validate the overall solution design from client settings through site-to-site communications. This does not have to be a complete test of every ConfigMgr function, although the more thorough the test is, the more comfortable everyone on the team will be with the solution and the more prepared the team will be for the deployment. There has to be a testing balance because the sheer size of the ConfigMgr solution could take months to test feature by feature. Before piloting the ConfigMgr solution, administrators should develop a test plan specific to the features they have chosen to implement and the design components questioned during the envisioning and designing phases. Table 4.8 illustrates a sample test plan.

TABLE 4.8   ConfigMgr Deployment Test Plan

Task#	Pilot Testing Tasks	Complete (Yes/No)?	Results/Comments
1.	Determine test client group and create collection with direct rule name mapping		Allows ConfigMgr deployment team to positively identify the client involved in the test.
2.	Verify discovery and install ConfigMgr client on test computers with manual push installation		In the ConfigMgr console, under Collections, find the target computers, right-click a computer, choose All Tasks, Install Client. Upon success, enable the client push installation.
3.	Verify automated push installation		Validate a client system receives the ConfigMgr client.
4.	Verify inventory		Using the ConfigMgr console, verify that the newly installed client shows hardware inventory information.
5.	Verify client agent settings		Validate remote control works and prompts the user.
6.	Verify BITS downloaded package		Create a small test package. Ensure that all test DPs are used. Advertise it to the test computer. Ensure that the advertisement is downloaded from the assigned DP and then installed. Verify that the test computer receives the package and installs correctly.
7.	Verify reporting		Connect to http://BLUEBONNET (for the SCCMUnleashed.com environment) and verify that web reporting is operational. Run the All Software Companies report from within the ConfigMgr console Reporting node.
8.	Verify security		Validate that ConfigMgr administrators with limited rights can only perform the tasks approved.

Technologies such as Microsoft Virtual PC, Microsoft Virtual Server, Hyper-V, and VMware's ESX, Server, and Workstation allow ConfigMgr administrators to implement, test, validate, and roll back design features in minutes using a minimum of hardware. Third-party solutions for these products, as well as some crafty use of Microsoft Server and Microsoft Routing and Remote Access Service (RRAS), allow simulating individual network segments as well.

Once the ConfigMgr solution design is validated in a lab environment, keep the lab for long-term use and testing of packages, scripts, service packs, changes to the site settings, use of new roles, and so on. Using the lab will lower the overall effort associated with management of the ConfigMgr solution, provide its administrators with experience and confidence, increase productivity, and lower the chances of problems in the production environment.

Stabilizing During the Pilot

Piloting leverages all the information and lessons learned in the design and testing phases while incorporating the communication plan and implementing the solution in the production environment to a limited number of systems. Piloting the ConfigMgr solution initially lets the project team validate its design and the network infrastructure, and measure the load the solution places on the infrastructure.

TIP

Piloting Target

As a rule of thumb, use a percentage of the environment as your pilot so the project team can handle any issues that arise and the pilot does not go as expected. 1% is a good quick pilot where the audience can provide direct feedback to the project team. Once success is met, then move to a larger 5%–10% pilot group. It is also a good idea to select users or systems from dissimilar regions or departments, to ensure the pilot accurately represents production and keeps the pilot as informative as possible for the team.

The pilot is the first actual test of the communication plan, the network infrastructure, and the user's response to the deployment. Feedback from pilot users is valuable for the project team, who should address the items raised so the production deployment goes smoothly.

The ConfigMgr project team should focus on items questioned in the design or test phase. Those site roles you plan to implement should exist in the pilot; it is much easier to fix or even redesign a system where there are no other systems dependent on its use! Test each of the functions you expect to use on the various site systems and roles. If you will be using protected DPs, verify they are working correctly and clients are not pulling packages across a WAN because the local DP has boundaries defined incorrectly.

TIP

Pilot Deployment

Most problems with ConfigMgr deployments are associated with the network infrastructure or client-based security software such as client firewalls. Testing will validate the solution works as expected. Piloting should uncover these issues and allow ConfigMgr administrators the ability to develop solutions.

The pilot phase of the project is usually one of the longest phases. This is due to the issues that arise, the efforts required to resolve them, and the processes that may have to be followed. This phase will usually point out issues in the production environment that were going unnoticed. The closer the lab environment is to the production environment, the smoother the pilot will be. Labs that accurately depict the production environment are unfortunately rare and ultimately the pilot phase becomes a long and costly one.

TIP

Package Failures

The lack of time synchronization is frequently identified as the root cause of why packages are not running at their advertised time.

Release clients the exact same way you would for the production release. It is important to follow the release plan to validate the overall solution design. Deviating from the plan may lead to results that are incorrectly positive. Verify the same features are enabled, collect the data from the pilot deployments and tests, evaluate the data, and update the solution design if needed. If the project team decides a ConfigMgr feature needs to be changed from how it was originally architected, testing and piloting that agent or feature should be started over to validate the change did not cause a negative impact elsewhere or cause a requirement to no longer be met.

Changes may be required to the ConfigMgr solution at an agent, site, or hierarchy level to accommodate needs discovered only through piloting the solution. Become familiar with the Windows Event Logs and Performance Monitor tools. The "Developing the Server Architecture" section of this chapter discussed some best practices for gauging the performance of system hardware and the load placed on it.

Antivirus software is frequently lacking in a lab environment due to the isolation of the lab and the fashion in which it is built. When the ConfigMgr solution is placed into production, antivirus and other management agents are typically loaded on the system. You will want to exclude the ConfigMgr site server inboxes, logs, and client cache locations. Exclude the following list of file extensions from your antivirus software:

adc	box	ccr
cfg	cmn	ct0
ct1	ct2	dat
dc	ddr	i
ins	ist	job
lkp	lo_	log
mif	mof	nal
ncf	nhm	ofn
ofr	p*	pcf
pck	pdf	pkg
pkn	rpl	rpt
sca	scd	scu
sha	sic	sid
srq	srs	ssu
svf	tmp	udc

4

Deploying

The deployment phase should be one of the easier phases in the project life cycle. If tests were conducted in a legitimate fashion and pilot scenarios were indicative of real-world conditions, deploying the finalized solution should have no surprises. If there was no pilot phase, and the production implementation is the first actual instance of ConfigMgr in production, care should be taken to make sure no negative impacts occur to production. Three critical tasks need to be monitored when implementing ConfigMgr:

▶ Agent rollout

▶ Distributing of packages to distribution points

▶ Advertisements targeted to systems where reboots may occur, such as patch packages

Depending on the roles previously implemented, the scope of the pilot activities may require reimplementing site servers and/or site systems. When utilizing this model of test/pilot/production, it is important to validate the consistency of the site server and site systems implementations. Overlooked items can produce skewed results, disqualifying all other tests performed in the given stage or scenario. If this approach is desired, consider utilizing a scripted implementation of the specific system. Chapter 8 discusses ConfigMgr installation, configuring the site server, and multisite hierarchy creations.

> **NOTE**
>
> **ConfigMgr Scripted Installations**
>
> Unattended setups using the /Script command-line option are only supported on new installations of primary sites, secondary sites, and Configuration Manager consoles.

Because you can deploy ConfigMgr in a large variety of configurations, the technical ability required for a successful implementation of Configuration Manager 2007 is greater than average. Knowledge of basic concepts is critical, and collaborating with existing IT groups such as networking, security, and database administration will likely be key success factors. Although Microsoft provides a familiar wizard-based experience to implement the ConfigMgr site server, much of the configuration and deployment tasks occur outside this initial implementation experience.

By the time ConfigMgr is deployed into production, the ConfigMgr project team will know the permissions required to push agents, will have validated that time synchronization is successful, will know the settings to deploy at specific sites, will understand the network impact on given segments, and will have a solid concept of the site systems in the hierarchy, their roles, and the expected user experience.

After ConfigMgr is rolled out, the ConfigMgr team, which may be different from the project team, should take ownership and responsibility of the day-to-day operations and maintenance of the solution.

Summary

This chapter discussed the architectural design options ConfigMgr presents to the administrator, the impact of various ConfigMgr roles on the site server and site systems, questions to ask of the business, the importance of the impact the solution can have on the network, and how significant proper planning and testing are for these features. The chapter provided a solid framework for architecting servers capable of handling any size environment and measuring methods by which to validate these server designs. It covered the key items administrators need to be aware of when implementing ConfigMgr in international organizations. Finally, the chapter provided some metrics for testing the success of the implementation against following the Microsoft Solution Framework, taking the solution all the way through deployment.

The next several chapters dive deeper into some of the design areas introduced in this chapter. Chapter 5 focuses on the communications ConfigMgr makes between various clients, sites, and site systems. It also covers discovery, BITS, server placement, and troubleshooting network issues affecting ConfigMgr.

Network Design

Chapter 4, "Configuration Manager Solution Design," discussed how using the framework of a solutions-based architecture could help to unleash the value of System Center Configuration Manager (ConfigMgr). Since today's Information Technology (IT) solutions typically are delivered in a networked environment, effectively planning and implementing a ConfigMgr implementation is contingent on understanding your network, including the resources it offers and the limitations it imposes.

Central to the planning process is the reality that communication between systems is dependent on the network that connects them. Understanding how ConfigMgr lives within the network will help you design, deliver, and manage successful solutions to meet your business objectives. A recurrent issue with management solutions is providing the required core management services—without consuming excessive network resources or adversely affecting other network activity. When you start planning your Configuration Manager deployment, you should review all available network documentation and engage the team that supports the network in your organization. A consideration of how ConfigMgr will affect your network is critical to the success of your deployment.

This chapter discusses the ways in which Configuration Manager uses the network, with approaches for optimally delivering solutions in various network environments. The discussion includes the following areas:

▶ Discussing the network requirements for each ConfigMgr communication process.

▶ Understanding how Configuration Manager deals with fast and slow networks.

The Background Intelligent Transfer Service (BITS) is a key enabling technology in delivering Configuration Manager services. The chapter includes a detailed discussion of BITS to help in implementing and troubleshooting these services.

▶ Evaluating which network conditions to consider when designing your ConfigMgr hierarchy and server placement.

▶ Examining the special challenges around mobile, disconnected, and sometimes connected users.

▶ Considering how you can use Configuration Manager to discover network resources.

▶ Using Internet Protocol (IP) subnets and Active Directory (AD) sites to optimize delivery of services to your client systems.

▶ Discussing network communication problems that may occur and how to troubleshoot them.

After you complete this chapter, you should have a fundamental understanding of how Configuration Manager works in a networked environment. You will be able to use your knowledge of Configuration Manager networking to optimize your deployment and effectively troubleshoot network-related issues.

Configuration Manager Network Communications

Configuration Manager clients and server systems use a variety of protocols to communicate with each other across the network. The following sections discuss the network communications between server roles within a site, the communications of ConfigMgr clients with servers in the site, and communications between sites.

Intrasite Server Communications

As previously described in Chapter 2, "Configuration Manager 2007 Overview," a ConfigMgr *site* contains of a set of servers carrying out various system roles. In the simplest configuration, the ConfigMgr site server holds all deployed site system roles. Designs that are more complex may involve moving certain roles to other servers within the site. Assigning roles to multiple servers brings network considerations into play for intrasite communications. This section discusses the protocols used for network communications and the flow of information between site systems. For information on how network considerations affect your decision of how to distribute server roles, see the "Server Placement" section of this chapter.

Configuration Manager site systems use various protocols to communicate with each other. The most important protocols include the following:

▶ Configuration Manager site systems use standard SQL Server communication protocols to talk to MicroSoft SQL Server.

▶ The site server and other systems use the Remote Procedure Call (RPC) protocol to invoke remote functionality on other systems.

▶ Most file-transfer operations use the Server Message Block (SMB) protocol.

▶ BITS and various other services use Hypertext Transfer Protocol (HTTP) and/or Secure Hypertext Transfer Protocol (HTTPS).

The following sections discuss the specifics of these protocols.

Communications with SQL Server

With Configuration Manager 2007, SQL Server connectivity uses standard SQL Server TCP/IP communications. Microsoft reserved Transmission Control Protocol (TCP) port 1433 as the default port with the default SQL Server instance; for named instances, the port is dynamic and is not 1433—the SQL Browser listens on User Datagram Protocol (UDP) port 1434 and directs the connection to a dynamically chosen TCP port. You can use the SQL client network configuration tools and server setup to specify a port other than 1433 for the default instance. For additional information on changing the port used by SQL Server, see http://support.microsoft.com/kb/823938, which describes static and dynamic port allocation as well as configuring SQL Server to use a static or dynamic port. Although ConfigMgr supports Named Pipes connections to SQL Server, you should use the Named Pipes protocol for troubleshooting only.

The primary site server, SMS provider, and management point all make intensive use of SQL Server. The reporting point, PXE (Preboot Execution Environment) service point, and server locator point (SLP) also access the database directly. In Configuration Manager 2007 Release 2 (R2), the reporting services point, multicast-enabled distribution point, and client status reporting host also connect to the site database.

> **NOTE**
>
> **About Named Pipes**
>
> Named Pipes uses NT LAN Manager (NTLM) authentication only and does not support Kerberos authentication. Kerberos provides mutual authentication of the client and server, whereas NTLM authenticates the client only. TCP/IP also provides better performance under challenging network conditions such as across a wide area network (WAN) link.

The Configuration Manager console accesses the site database using the SMS provider, which is an intermediate Windows Management Instrumentation (WMI) layer used for database communication. Figure 5.1 shows the systems that communicate with SQL Server. The figure does not show other communications involving these site systems, such as communications with the site server or with clients.

Communications Using RPC

RPC is an industry-standard protocol used to invoke code across process boundaries, generally between processes on different machines. The calling process initiates an RPC call on TCP or UDP port 135 and receives a response on a dynamically allocated TCP port in the range of 1024 to 5000 (unless you have configured a custom range on your systems, which can be done using the RPC Configuration Tool [RPCCfg.exe] from the

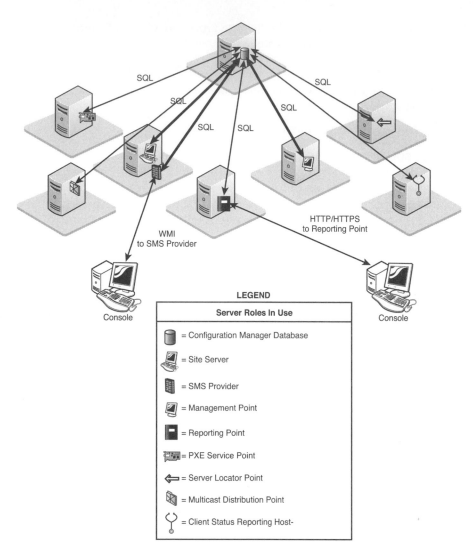

FIGURE 5.1   SQL Server communications

Windows Server 2003 Resource Kit). The site server initiates RPC connections for configuring site systems.

Communications Using SMB

SMB is the core protocol for Windows file, printer, and port sharing and for interprocess communications mechanisms such as Named Pipes and Mail Slots. Configuration Manager components rely heavily on file exchanges to communicate with each other, as described in Chapter 3, "Looking Inside Configuration Manager." Most site systems also pass status message and state message files back to the site server using SMB. SMB traffic involves a series of requests and responses, which can involve multiple roundtrips between the communicating systems. This means that network latency can substantially affect certain SMB communications.

The largest file transfers between site systems involve distributing software packages (including Operating System Deployment [OSD] image files) to distribution points. Transfers from the site server to a standard distribution point use SMB. The Distribution Manager component of Configuration Manager handles distributing packages to the standard distribution points within the site. Branch distribution points use BITS to download packages from standard BITS-enabled distribution points. Packages are sent between sites using the sender mechanism, described in the "Site-to-Site Communications" section of this chapter.

Software distribution settings are located under System Center Configuration Manager -> Site Database -> Site Management -> *<Site Code> <Site Name>* -> Site Settings -> Component Configuration in the Configuration Manager console. As shown in Figure 5.2, several parameters are available that you can tune to regulate how packages are sent to distribution points. These parameters control concurrent distribution and retry behavior. The first section (Concurrent distribution settings) allows packages to be sent in parallel to more than one distribution point, whereas the second area (Retry settings) controls how often to retry unsuccessful sending attempts as well as the delay in minutes before retrying. The settings in this figure are the default settings.

▶ **Maximum number of packages**—Specifies the maximum number of packages (from one to seven) that can be copied to distribution points in parallel.

▶ **Maximum threads per package**—Specifies the maximum number of threads (from 1 to 50) allocated to each package during distribution. The maximum total number of threads allocated to package distribution is (Maximum number of packages) × (Maximum threads per package).

▶ **Number of retries**—Specifies the number of times (from 1 to 1,000) that the Distribution Manager will retry a failed package distribution attempt.

▶ **Delay before retrying (minutes)**—Specifies the delay (from 1 minute to 1,440 minutes [24 hours]) before retrying a failed distribution attempt.

The distribution settings dialog box also provides a check box to enable the option Send package from the nearest site in the hierarchy. This option causes child sites to retrieve newly targeted packages from the nearest site at which the required packages are available, rather than from the source site for the package.

FIGURE 5.2   Distribution point settings

Although increasing the maximum packages and maximum threads per package will require more server and network resources, it results in faster package deployment. In many instances, you can increase the maximum number of threads from the default value of 5. Adjustments to these values should be based on the following criteria:

▶ The available capacity of the network connecting your site server to the distribution points

▶ Monitoring the bandwidth used by package distribution

The retry and delay settings determine the resiliency of your package distribution if you encounter intermittent connectivity problems. The reliability of your network and the Mean Time To Restore (MTTR) specified in your Service Level Agreements (SLAs) governing network outages determine the optimum settings for your environment.

CAUTION

Use Care when Adjusting Distribution Point Settings

Changing the distribution point settings shown in Figure 5.2 will have an impact on overall site function. If you are already seeing backlogs in any of the inboxes or sluggish site server processing, adjusting these settings may make overall performance worse.

Site System Communications Using HTTP and HTTPS

HTTP and HTTPS (secure HTTP) are used for communication between the site server and the software update point (SUP). Branch distribution points also use these protocols for BITS-enabled transfers of packages from standard distribution points.

At the highest-level site in your hierarchy that has a software update point configured, the SUP will need to connect to the Internet over HTTP to synchronize with Microsoft updates. If the server is not able to connect to the Internet directly, you can specify a proxy server on the ConfigMgr software update point properties page, as displayed in Figure 5.3. To access this page, expand the ConfigMgr Console tree to System Center Configuration Manager -> Site Database -> Site Management -> *<Site Code> <Site Name>* -> Site Settings -> Site Systems -> *<Site System>* and then right-click ConfigMgr software update point and choose Properties.

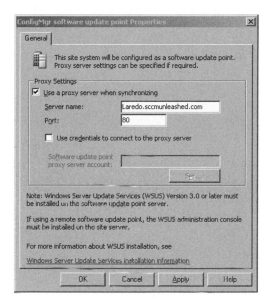

FIGURE 5.3   The software update point properties page

Software update points at downstream sites can synchronize with a Windows Software Updates Server (WSUS) at a higher level of the hierarchy.

Replication of Package Refresh Data

When you initially deploy a package to a distribution point, Configuration Manager provides two mechanisms specifically designed to minimize the amount of network traffic generated when replicating changes to the package. These mechanisms are delta replication and binary differential replication:

> ▶ Systems Management Server (SMS) 2003 introduced file-based *delta replication*. When a package is updated, a delta compressed package file—containing only the files that have changed since the previous version—is created in addition to the full compressed package file. The source site server will maintain deltas for up to five versions of a package. Only changed files are sent if the package is sent to a distribution point or site that already has one of the previous five versions of the package.

▶ A new option in Configuration Manager 2007 is *binary differential replication* of packages. Binary differential replication works similarly to delta replication, with two exceptions:

  ▶ A binary comparison of the files is made.

  ▶ Only the portions of the files that have changed are sent, not entire files.

Binary differential replication is highly advantageous for packages consisting of very large files, such as Windows Installer packages or operating system (OS) images.

For packages with many small files, binary differential replication may not be worth the overhead it incurs. You can enable the option to use binary differential replication on a per-package basis. Chapter 13, "Creating Packages," and Chapter 14, "Distributing Packages," discuss options for configuring packages and sending them to distribution points.

Other Server Communications

In addition to communications between Configuration Manager systems, the following basic network services are required:

▶ Active Directory

▶ Domain services

▶ Global Catalog (GC) services

▶ DNS (Domain Naming Service)

▶ NetBIOS name resolution (in some configurations)

If you have any of the Active Directory discovery methods configured, a high volume of network traffic will occur between the site server and domain controller (DC) while AD discovery is running. Chapter 12, "Client Management," discusses Active Directory discovery methods.

Client-to-Server Communications

Configuration Manager is designed to use Internet standard protocols for most client communications. In addition, most of the client communication ports are configurable. Configuration Manager supports both mixed and native mode sites. In mixed mode sites, most client communications are over HTTP, whereas native mode sites use HTTPS. For more information about mixed versus native mode, see Chapter 6, "Architecture Design Planning."

Customizing Client Communications

Data sent across the network using the TCP or UDP protocol is transmitted in discrete units of data called *packets*. Each packet includes the following:

▶ A body that contains the actual data

▶ A header with addressing and other control information

The header includes the IP addresses of the source and destination machines as well as the port numbers of the source and destination services or applications. A *port number* is a number from 1 to 65535 used to identify the application. An application or service "listens" on a specific port if it has registered with the operating system to receive packets addressed to that port. Like many services, Configuration Manager services have standard ports on which they listen by default.

Table 5.1 lists the communications protocols and ports used by various applications and services. You can also find information regarding the communication protocols and ports used by ConfigMgr at http://technet.microsoft.com/en-us/library/bb632618.aspx.

In addition to standard ConfigMgr 2007 traffic, Network Access Protection (NAP) generates the traffic described in Table 5.2. If you use firewalls that block this traffic, you must reconfigure them for NAP to work with ConfigMgr 2007. You will also need to identify ports used by the client to communicate with the System Health Validator point (SHV). The NAP enforcement client you are using determines the ports for system health validation.

Information online regarding ports for NAP in Configuration Manager 2007 is located at http://technet.microsoft.com/en-us/library/bb694170.aspx.

Reasons for Changing Ports

You may choose to use custom rather than standard ports for client-to-server communications for the following reasons:

▶ Custom ports may be necessary for Configuration Manager to work with your network firewall policies.

▶ You may also need to use a custom website for ConfigMgr instead of the default site on your Internet Information Services (IIS) servers. Although this is not a best practice, it may be necessary if ConfigMgr is sharing IIS servers with other applications that depend on the default site.

TABLE 5.1 Communication Paths and Ports

From Component	Direction	To Component	Description	UDP Port	TCP Port
Site server	<->	Site server	SMB	—	445
Site server	<->	Site server	Point-to-Point Tunneling Protocol (PPTP)	—	1723[1]
Primary site server	->	Domain controller	Lightweight Directory Access Protocol (LDAP)	—	389
Primary site server	->	Domain controller	LDAP (Secure Sockets Layer [SSL] connection)	636	636
Primary site server	->	Domain controller	Global Catalog LDAP	—	3268
Primary site server	->	Domain controller	Global Catalog LDAP SSL	—	3269
Primary site server	->	Domain controller	RPC Endpoint Mapper	135	135
Primary site server	->	Domain controller	RPC	—	DYNAMIC
Primary site server	->	Domain controller	Kerberos	88	—
Site server	<->[2]	Software update point	SMB	—	445
Site server	<->[2]	Software update point	HTTP	—	80 or 8530[3]
Site server	<->[2]	Software update point	HTTPS	—	443 or 8531[3]
Software update point	->	Internet	HTTP	—	80[3]
Site server	<->[2]	State migration point	SMB	—	445
Site server	<->[2]	State migration point	RPC Endpoint Mapper	135	135
Site server	->	Client	Client Push Installation	—	135
Client	->	Software update point	HTTP	—	80 or 8530[3]
Client	->	Software update point	HTTPS	—	443 or 8531[3]
Client	->	State migration point	HTTP	—	80[5]
Client	->	State migration point	HTTPS	—	443[5]

TABLE 5.1   Communication Paths and Ports

From Component	To Component	Direction	Description	UDP Port	TCP Port
Client	State migration point	->	SMB	—	445
Client	PXE service point	->	Dynamic Host Configuration Protocol (DHCP)	67, 68	—
Client	PXE service point	->	Trivial File Transfer Protocol (TFTP)	69[6]	—
Client	PXE service point	->	Boot Information Negotiation Layer (BINL)	4011	—
Site server	PXE service point	<->[2]	SMB	—	445
Site server	PXE service point	<->[2]	RPC Endpoint Mapper	135	135
Site server	PXE service point	<->[2]	RPC	—	DYNAMIC
Site server	System Health Validator	<->[2]	SMB	—	445
Site server	System Health Validator	<->[2]	RPC Endpoint Mapper	135	135
Site server	System Health Validator	<->[2]	RPC	—	DYNAMIC
Client	System Heath Validator	->[7]	DHCP	67, 68	—
Client	System Heath Validator	->[7]	IPSec	500	80, 443
Site server	Fallback status point	<->[2]	SMB	—	445
Site server	Fallback status point	<->[2]	RPC Endpoint Mapper	135	135
Site server	Fallback status point	<->[2]	RPC	—	DYNAMIC
Client	Fallback status point	->	HTTP	—	80[5]
Site server	Distribution point	->	SMB	—	445
Site server	Distribution point	->	RPC Endpoint Mapper	135	135
Site server	Distribution point	->	RPC	—	DYNAMIC

5

TABLE 5.1   Communication Paths and Ports

From Component	Direction	To Component	Description	UDP Port	TCP Port
Client	->	Distribution point	HTTP	—	80[5]
Client	->	Distribution point	HTTPS	—	443[5]
Client	->	Distribution point	SMB	—	445
Client	->	Distribution point	Multicast Protocol	63000-64000	—
Client	->	Branch distribution point	SMB	—	445
Client	->	Management point	HTTP	—	80[5]
Client	->	Management point	HTTPS	—	443[5]
Client	->	Server locator point	HTTP	—	80[5]
Branch distribution point	->	Distribution point	HTTPS	—	443[5]
Branch distribution point	->	Distribution point	HTTP	—	80 [5]
Site server	->	Provider	SMB	—	445
Site server	->	Provider	RPC Endpoint Mapper	135	135
Site server	->	Provider	RPC	—	DYNAMIC
Server locator point	->	SQL Server	SQL over TCP	1434 (for named instances only)	1433 for default instance; DYNAMIC for named instances
Management point	->	SQL Server	SQL over TCP	1434 (for named instances only)	1433 for default instance; DYNAMIC for named instances

TABLE 5.1   Communication Paths and Ports

From Component	Direction	To Component	Description	UDP Port	TCP Port
Provider	->	SQL Server	SQL over TCP	1434 (for named instances only)	1433 for default instance; DYNAMIC for named instances
Reporting point	->	Reporting Services point, SQL Server	SQL over TCP	1434 (for named instances only)	1433 for default instance; DYNAMIC for named instances
Configuration Manager console	->	Reporting point	HTTP	—	80[5]
Configuration Manager console	->	Reporting point	HTTPS	—	443[5]
Configuration Manager console	->	Provider	RPC Endpoint Mapper	135	135
Configuration Manager console	->	Provider	RPC	—	DYNAMIC
Configuration Manager console	->	Internet	HTTP	—	80
Primary site server	->	SQL Server	SQL over TCP	1434 (for named instances only)	1433 for default instance; DYNAMIC for named instances
Management point	->	Domain controller	LDAP	—	389
Management point	->	Domain controller	LDAP SSL connection	636	636
Management point	->	Domain controller	Global Catalog LDAP	—	3268
Management point	->	Domain controller	Global Catalog LDAP SSL	—	3269
Management point	->	Domain controller	RPC Endpoint Mapper	135	135
Management point	->	Domain controller	RPC	—	DYNAMIC
Management point	->	Domain controller	Kerberos	88	—

5

TABLE 5.1   Communication Paths and Ports

From Component	Direction	To Component	Description	UDP Port	TCP Port
Site server	->	Reporting point, Reporting Services point	SMB	—	445
Site server	->	Reporting point, Reporting Services point	RPC Endpoint Mapper	135	135
Site server	->	Reporting point, Reporting Services point	RPC	—	DYNAMIC
Site server	<->[2]	Server locator point	SMB	—	445
Site server	<->[2]	Server locator point	RPC Endpoint Mapper	135	135
Site server	<->[2]	Server locator point	RPC	—	DYNAMIC
Configuration Manager console	->	Site server	RPC (initial connection to WMI to locate provider system)	—	135
Software update point	->	Windows Software Update Services (WSUS) synchronization server	HTTP	—	80 or 8530[3]
Software update point	->	WSUS synchronization server	HTTPS	—	443 or 8531[3]
Configuration Manager Console	->	Client	Remote Control (control)	2701	2701
Configuration Manager console	->	Client	Remote Control (data)	2702	2702
Configuration Manager console	->	Client	Remote Assistance RDP (Remote Desktop Protocol) and Real-Time Communications (RTC)	—	3389
Configuration Manager console	->	Client	RPC Endpoint Mapper	—	135
Management point	<->[2]	Site server	RPC Endpoint Mapper	—	135
Management point	<->[2]	Site server	RPC	—	DYNAMIC

TABLE 5.1 Communication Paths and Ports

From Component	Direction	To Component	Description	UDP Port	TCP Port
Site server	->	Client	Wake On LAN	9[5]	—
PXE service point	->	SQL Server	SQL over TCP	1434 (for named instances only)	1433 for default instance; DYNAMIC for named instances
Site server	<->	Asset Intelligence synchronization point	SMB	—	445
Site server	<->	Asset Intelligence synchronization point	RPC Endpoint Mapper	135	135
Site server	<->	Asset Intelligence synchronization point	RPC	—	DYNAMIC
Asset Intelligence synchronization point	<->	System Center Online	HTTPS	—	443
Multicast distribution point	->	SQL Server	SQL over TCP	—	1433 for default instance; DYNAMIC for named instances
Client status reporting host	->	Client	RPC Endpoint Mapper	135	135
Client status reporting host	->	Client	RPC	—	DYNAMIC
Client status reporting host	->	Client	ICMPV4 Type 8 (echo) or ICMPV6 Type 128 (echo request)	n/a	n/a
Client status reporting host	->	Management point	NetBIOS Session Service	—	139

5

TABLE 5.1 Communication Paths and Ports

From Component	Direction	To Component	Description	UDP Port	TCP Port
Client status reporting host	->	Management point	SMB	—	445
Client status reporting host	->	SQL Server	SQL over TCP	—	1433 for default instance; DYNAMIC for named instances
Site server	<->[2]	Reporting Services point	SMB	—	445
Site server	<->[2]	Reporting Services point	RPC Endpoint Mapper	135	135
Site server	<->[2]	Reporting Services point	RPC	—	DYNAMIC
Configuration Manager console	->	Reporting Services point	HTTP	—	80[5]
Configuration Manager console	->	Reporting Services point	HTTPS	—	443[5]
Reporting Services point	->	SQL Server	SQL over TCP	—	1433 for default instance; DYNAMIC for named instances
Site server	<->	Out of Band service point	SMB	—	445
Site server	<->	Out of Band service point	RPC Endpoint Mapper	135	135
Site server	<->	Out of Band service point	RPC	—	DYNAMIC
AMT management controller	->	Out of Band service point	Provisioning	—	9971 (configurable)
Out of Band service point	->	AMT management controller	Discovery	—	16992
Out of Band service point	->	AMT management controller	Power control, provisioning, discovery	—	16993

TABLE 5.1   Communication Paths and Ports

From Component	Direction	To Component	Description	UDP Port	TCP Port
Out of Band management console	–>	AMT management controller	General management tasks	—	16993
Out of Band management console	–>	AMT management controller	Serial over LAN and IDE redirection	—	16995

[1]ConfigMgr 2007 can use the RAS sender with PPTP to send and receive site, client, and administrative information through a firewall using PPTP TCP port 1723.

[2]Communication between a site server and site systems is bidirectional by default. The site server initiates communication to configure the site system, and then most site systems will connect back to the site server to return status information (although reporting points and distribution points do not send back status information). Selecting "Allow only site server initiated data transfers from this site system" on the site system properties page keeps the site system from initiating communication to the site server.

[3]You can install WSUS on the default website (port 80) or on a custom website (port 8530). You can change this port after installation. If the HTTP port is 80, the HTTPS port must be 443. If the HTTP port is something other than 80, then the HTTPS port must be 1 higher (for example 8530 and 8531).

[4]You cannot configure the proxy server port, but you can route it through a configured proxy server.

[5]You can define an alternate port in ConfigMgr for this value. If you define a custom port, substitute that port when defining the IP filter information for your IPSec policies.

[6]The TFTP Daemon system service does not require a username or password and is an integral part of Windows Deployment Services (WDS). TFTP is designed to support diskless boot environments. The daemons listen on UDP port 69, but they respond from a dynamically allocated high port. Enabling this port allows the TFTP service to receive incoming requests but does not allow the server to respond to the requests. (Allowing a response requires configuring the TFTP server to respond from port 69.)

[7]The client requires the ports established with NAP, such as DHCP and IPSec. No port is required for 802.1x.

TABLE 5.2   TCP Ports Required by Firewalls to Support NAP

Function	TCP Port	Description
Site server publishing health state reference to AD domain services	389 (LDAP) or 636 (LDAPS)	Writing to AD domain services
System Health Validator point querying AD for ConfigMgr health state reference	3268 (Global Catalog lookup) or 3269 (secure Global Catalog lookup)	Reading from a global catalog server
Installing System Health Validator point and ongoing configuration	445, 135	SMBs to install; RPCs for configuration
Status messages from System Health Validator point to site server	445	SMBs

Specifying Ports

You may specify custom ports for client communications during either Configuration Manager setup or later using the ConfigMgr console:

▶ During setup, you can specify a custom HTTP port for mixed mode sites or a custom HTTPS port for native mode sites in the Port Settings dialog box, displayed in Figure 5.4.

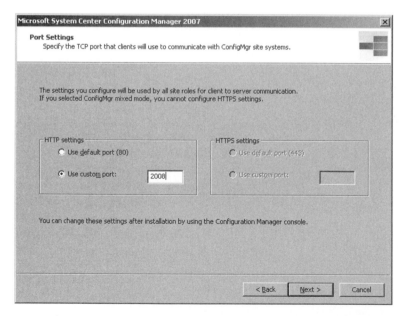

FIGURE 5.4   Specifying an alternate TCP port for client-to-server communications during setup

The port specified in Figure 5.4 is used for client-to-server communications by all site systems.

▶ After setup, you can change your selection and add alternate ports on the Ports tab of the Site Properties sheet in the ConfigMgr console. Perform the following steps:

1. Navigate to System Center Configuration Manager -> Site Database -> Site Management -> *<Site Code> <Site Name>*.

2. Right-click the site name, choose Properties, and then select the Ports tab. As shown in Figure 5.5, you can specify both default ports and alternate ports for client communications.

3. To enable a port, modify an enabled port or change the default port and then double-click the entry to bring up the Port Detail dialog box shown in Figure 5.6.

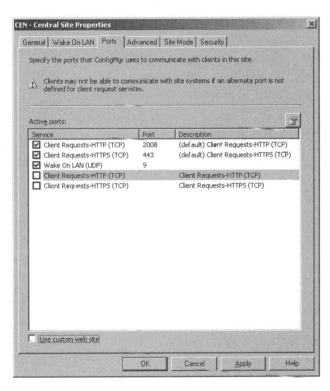

FIGURE 5.5   Specifying the TCP ports clients will use from the ConfigMgr console

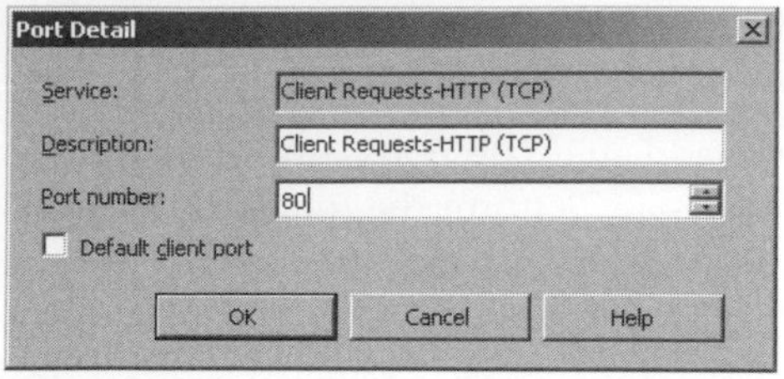

FIGURE 5.6   The Port Detail dialog box

TIP

Specifying Different Ports

If you utilize custom ports or custom websites, you should use them consistently throughout your hierarchy. Using different ports or websites at different sites can cause problems as clients roam from one site to another.

Regardless of whether you change the default HTTP and HTTPS ports, it is always a good idea to specify alternate ports to increase the availability of these services.

Initial Communication

The initial communication between the client and the ConfigMgr hierarchy occurs during client installation. The sequence of network calls depends on the client installation method used. Client installation methods are discussed in detail in Chapter 12. For purposes of this discussion, there are two general types of client installation methods:

▶ Server initiated (client push)

▶ Client initiated (all other methods)

Client push installation includes a preinstallation phase in which the site server connects to the client to initiate installation:

▶ In the client push installation method, the server makes an initial connection to the admin$ share on the prospective client computer using Windows file sharing protocols.

▶ The server also establishes a WMI connection to the client using the Distributed Component Object Model (DCOM) through TCP port 135.

  DCOM is a Microsoft standard for communication between software components, either on a local computer or across a network. This approach differs from SMS 2003, which used a remote Registry connection rather than WMI.

▶ The site server uses these connections to copy the required setup files to the client and then installs and starts the ccmsetup service. Additional requirements for client push installation are covered in Chapter 12.

Once the preinstallation phase is complete, the installation proceeds in a manner similar to other installation methods.

Regardless of the client installation method used, the first network-related task for the new client is to locate and contact a management point (MP) for its assigned site. From this point onward, the MP will be the primary point of contact between the client and its site. Unless the client installation source files are staged locally, the setup process uses BITS to pull the files from the CCM_CLIENT website on the MP. Once the client is installed, it continues to communicate with the management point using HTTP or HTTPS, and generally uses BITS to download policy and component updates and to send client information, including inventory, metering data, state messages, and status messages, to the site.

Identifying the Client's Assigned Site

There are three general ways for the client to determine the site it is assigned to as well as to locate the management point for that site:

▶ Depending on the installation method used, the site code and management point may have been supplied as command-line arguments. The management point may be specified using an IP address, a Fully Qualified Domain Name (FQDN), or a simple name.

▶ If the information is not provided via the command line, clients in the same Active Directory forest with the site server can generally retrieve this information by querying AD (assuming the schema is extended and the appropriate information is published in AD).

▶ If the required information is not available in AD, the client must contact a server locator point for site and management point information:

  ▶ The SLP may be specified in the command line.

  ▶ If the SLP is not provided through the command line, it must be resolved through NetBIOS name resolution.

    ▶ If you are using WINS server for NetBIOS name resolution, you must manually add the SLP entry to WINS following the procedure found at http://technet.microsoft.com/en-us/library/bb632567.aspx:

    Open a command prompt (Start -> Run, and then type **cmd**), type **netsh**, and then press Enter.

    Type **wins** and then press Enter.

    Type **server** and then press Enter.

Type the appropriate command to add the name. Here's an example:
```
add name Name=SMS_SLP endchar=1A rectype=0 ip=<server locator point IP
address>
```

▶ If a WINS server is not available, you can supply the SLP information using an LMHosts file. The SLP information in LMHosts is as follows:
```
<SLP IP address > "SMS_SLP        \0x1a" #PRE.
```

About HTTP Communications for Native Mode Clients

Server locator points support only HTTP communications; they do not support HTTPS. By default, intranet clients assigned to native mode sites require HTTPS for all web-based communications. If a native mode intranet client needs to contact an SLP, enable the option Allow HTTP communication for roaming and site assignment. This option can be enabled by supplying the /native:FALLBACK switch or the /native:CRLANDFALLBACK switch in the ccmsetup command line.

Enabling HTTP also allows the client to download content from mixed mode sites when roaming within the boundaries of the site. You can apply this option on a sitewide basis, allowing clients already assigned to the native mode site to use downloads from mixed mode sites. The Allow HTTP communication for roaming and site assignment option is located on the Site Mode tab of the Site Properties sheet, displayed in Figure 5.7. To access the property sheet, open the Configuration Manager console and navigate to System Center Configuration Manager -> Site Database -> Site Management -> <Site Code> <Site Name>, then right-click the site name and choose Properties and select the Site Mode tab.

If your installation requires server locator points for site assignment, enable HTTP for native mode clients. HTTP traffic is not encrypted and therefore less secure than HTTPS. If you are considering enabling HTTP for client roaming functionality, you will need to evaluate the tradeoff between security and network functionality.

For more information about security, see Chapter 20, "Security and Delegation in Configuration Manager 2007." For additional information about client roaming, see Chapter 12.

Client Protocols

The Configuration Manager client uses the HTTP or HTTPS protocol exclusively to communicate with the management point and the software update point. These two roles are among the systems having the highest volume and frequency of communication with ConfigMgr clients. Clients communicate with the management point more frequently than with any of the other Configuration Manager site systems.

▶ Client systems poll the management point regularly for policy updates. The default polling interval is every hour.

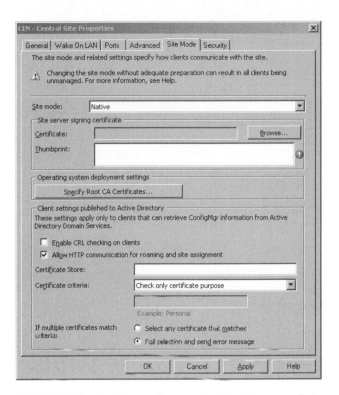

FIGURE 5.7   Enabling native mode clients to use HTTP

▶ Clients send state, status, inventory, metering, and discovery data to the management point. State information is sent every 5 minutes by default. Inventory, metering, and heartbeat discovery data is sent every 7 days by default.

▶ You can configure the schedules for clients to pull policy and send state, inventory, metering, and heartbeat discovery data as described in Chapter 12. Choosing a simple schedule for inventory causes the network load to spread over time, because not all clients will send inventory at the same time. A custom schedule provides more control over the timing of inventory collection, but may have considerable impact when inventory runs.

▶ Initial inventory on new clients is considerably larger than regular inventory updates, which only send a delta (only the files that have changed since the previous version) over the network.

The frequency and size of client downloads of software updates from the SUP depends on how you configure software updates and the client configuration. Many individual software updates are relatively small (a few megabytes or smaller). Some can be quite large, however, including service packs, which can be hundreds of megabytes or even larger.

> **TIP**
>
> **More about Software Updates**
>
> Additional information about software updates can be found in Chapter 15, "Patch Management."

Microsoft generally releases critical security updates for its products monthly on the second Tuesday of the month, known as "Patch Tuesday." Typically, once you evaluate and approve the Patch Tuesday updates for your environment, you will make them available as a group for distribution to your clients.

Some new features of Configuration Manager 2007 decrease the network impact of software updates. The Software Updates agent uses selective download technology to download only the individual files that the client requires from a software updates package. In addition, supersedence information is provided to help administrators avoid deploying updates superseded by a newer update. Even with these enhancements, software updates can require significant network bandwidth. You will want to consider this requirement when planning your software updates strategy.

Clients use HTTP/HTTPS or the SMB protocol to pull data from distribution points and state migration points:

▶ Clients downloading a package to their local cache from a BITS-enabled distribution point use BITS over HTTP or HTTPS.

▶ Clients running the package directly from the distribution point use SMB.

▶ Clients retrieving packages from branch distribution points use only the SMB protocol.

Depending on the size of the software package, downloads from distribution points can be quite large. Clients do not use either binary differential replication or delta replication; therefore, changes to a package the client has cached will trigger a full download to the client.

Clients use state migration points less frequently, generally during operating system upgrades or hardware replacement. The amount of traffic sent to and from the state migration point depends on the amount of user data to be preserved. For more information about user state migration, see Chapter 19, "Operating System Deployment."

The remaining site systems handle relatively little client traffic, but use a variety of protocols:

▶ The PXE service point responds to PXE boot requests and initiates boot image downloads. The PXE boot process is an extension of the DHCP protocol. DHCP is widely used for assigning IP addresses and TCP/IP configurations.

▶ If you enable Configuration Manager for NAP, clients will pass a statement of health (SoH) to the System Health Validator when making a new DHCP request or a new IPSec (Internet Protocol Security) connection to the network. Once connected, the client will periodically submit a new SoH to the System Health Validator. The default interval for system health to be reevaluated is 24 hours. Chapter 15 discusses NAP in detail.

▶ The fallback status point, like the server locator point, responds to client requests using HTTP communications only.

▶ The site server connects to the client when Wake On LAN functionality is required for patch deployment or other activities. The default port for Wake On LAN is UDP port 9; however, you can configure this using the dialog box shown previously in Figure 5.6.

▶ If administrators use the Configuration Manager Remote Tools, the machine on which the console is running contacts the client directly. Remote tools use the SMS/Configuration Manager Remote Control protocol (UDP and TCP ports 2701 and 2702) to connect to Windows 2000 computers, and RDP (which uses TCP port 3389) to connect to computers running Windows XP or later.

Site-to-Site Communications

Sites in a ConfigMgr hierarchy must share configuration information, client data such as inventory and discovery data, status information, and so on. Chapter 3 describes the information flow up and down the hierarchy. All data exchanges between sites are transmitted by means of *senders*. Senders use the SMB protocol to transfer files between sites.

Configuring Senders

Configuration Manager sites are configured to use networks for site-to-site communications by creating a sender corresponding to the underlying network. By default, each Configuration Manager site has one sender installed—a *standard sender*. In most cases, the standard sender is the only one you will use. A standard sender uses your primary network for communications.

To add, delete, or change the properties of senders from the Configuration Manager console, navigate to System Center Configuration Manager -> Site Database -> Site Management -> *<Site Code> <Site Name>* -> Site Settings -> Senders. If you have sites connected by any of the Remote Access Services (RAS) connection types shown in Figure 5.8, you can add senders to use those connections.

Each sender can have the following settings configured:

▶ **Maximum Concurrent Sendings (All Sites)**—Senders can use multiple threads to send more than one job at a time. This setting controls the maximum number of sendings (from 1 to 999) that the sender can execute simultaneously. Increasing this number speeds up site-to-site communications but can potentially consume more bandwidth.

FIGURE 5.8   Selecting the sender type for a new sender

▶ **Maximum Concurrent Sendings (Per Site)**—This is the number of sendings (from 1 to 999) that can execute simultaneously to a single site.

This setting should always be set to a lower value than Maximum Concurrent Sendings (All Sites) to avoid the possibility that all of a sender's threads will be occupied sending to a site that is unavailable. RAS senders are limited to one thread per site.

▶ **Number of Retries**—Specifies the number of times (from 1 to 99) that the sender will retry a failed sending.

▶ **Delay Before Retrying (minutes)**—Specifies the delay (from 1 minute to 99 minutes) before retrying a failed sending attempt.

NOTE

About Bandwidth Throttling Between Sites

If you implement bandwidth throttling between sites, the sender will send all data serially between those sites, regardless of the number of concurrent sendings you have configured on the sender. Bandwidth throttling is discussed in the "Configuring Sender Addresses" section of this chapter.

Figure 5.9 displays the default values for the standard sender configuration. If you have sufficient server resources and available network bandwidth, you may want to increase the number of threads allowed by the Maximum Concurrent Sendings setting from the default value. Before increasing this setting, you should obtain a baseline of network utilization and server performance data for key server resources such as the processor and network interface to verify that additional capacity is available. You should closely monitor the change to ensure that server and network performance are not adversely affected.

About Courier Sender

Another way of sending data between sites is through the *courier sender*. The courier sender is a virtual sender that does not actually transfer data between sites, but rather accounts for packages transferred using Out of Band (OOB) mechanisms. Courier sender is used only for software distribution, and like other senders, it requires that you configure an address at the source site for the target site. Microsoft designed the courier sender capability to allow package distribution between sites using physical media such as tape, DVD, and external hard drives. You can also use courier sender to manage packages copied by third-party replication technologies, such as SAN replication.

To manage courier sender, you use the ConfigMgr Courier Sender program in the Configuration Manager 2007 program group. This application allows you to create outgoing parcels, which creates a compressed version of the package and instruction files, and then mark them as received at the destination site.

Courier sender was a relatively unused feature in earlier versions of SMS. This capability would be more valuable as a tool with console integration and a scripting interface, which are not currently available.

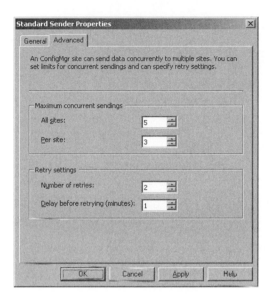

FIGURE 5.9   The Standard Sender Properties sheet showing the default values

Configuring Sender Addresses

In order to join two sites together as part of a Configuration Manager hierarchy, each of the sites must have at least one sender address configured for the other site. All information sent between sites will use these addresses and their corresponding senders. An address specifies a sender type and the site server for the destination site. You can configure additional parameters to control the behavior of sender addresses. To add, delete, or change the properties of addresses from the Configuration Manager console, perform the following steps:

1. Navigate to System Center Configuration Manager -> Site Database -> Site Management -> *<Site Code> <Site Name>* -> Site Settings -> Addresses.

2. To create a new address, right-click the Addresses node and choose New.

3. Select the appropriate sender type. Figure 5.10 shows the initial dialog box for creating a new standard sender address.

   Note that the relative address priority will be set to 1 for the first sender you create for a destination site. If you subsequently create additional addresses for the same site, their relative priorities will be 2, 3, and so on. The address with the lowest relative priority is always tried first. By default, the sender will use the security context of the computer account of the local site server. You can change the relative priority after the address is created by right-clicking the higher priority address and choosing decrement priority.

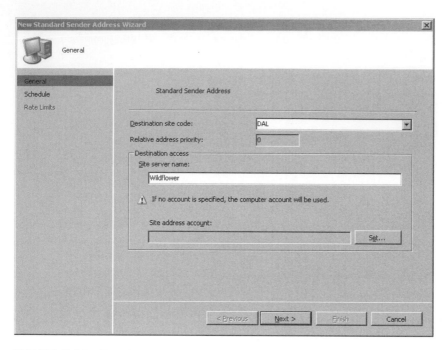

FIGURE 5.10   Entering the destination server for a new address

4. In the next dialog box, shown in Figure 5.11, you can set a schedule for the address. The schedule specifies what types of traffic are allowed to use the address during a given period. During certain hours, you may choose to limit use of the address to medium- or high-priority traffic or to high-priority data only, or you may not want to use the address at all. The priority of ConfigMgr data is discussed in the "Data Priorities" section of this chapter. The local time on the sending site server is used for scheduling purposes.

5. The final screen for creating a sender address allows you to specify rate limits for the address. As shown in Figure 5.12, you can specify the rate limits for a given time interval. The available values are limited to 0%, 10%, 25%, 50%, 75%, 90%, or 100%. Specifying a rate limit prevents the sender from using multiple threads, even if the maximum concurrent sendings settings (refer to Figure 5.9) allow multiple threads.

When sending limits are in effect, the sending site will time how long it takes to send each block of data and pause before sending the next block for an interval determined by the sending limit. In general, this results in the sender using all available bandwidth the designated percentage of time, which is roughly equivalent to using the allowed percentage of overall bandwidth. In some cases, factors other than bandwidth availability may cause a delay in receiving acknowledgements, resulting in calculations of available bandwidth that may be unrealistically low. As an example, if the destination site system is heavily loaded or if network latency is a factor, the elapsed time before an acknowledgement

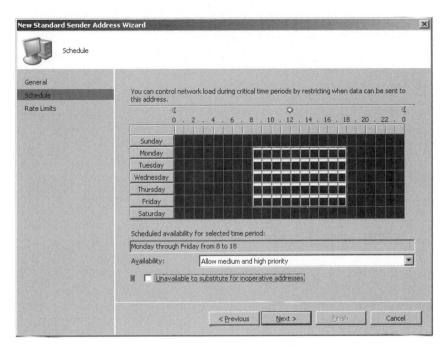

FIGURE 5.11   Setting the schedule for a new address

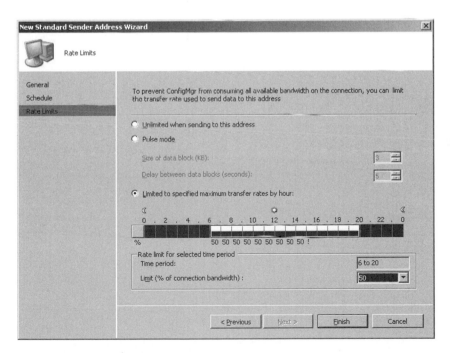

FIGURE 5.12   Specifying the maximum bandwidth utilization for a new address

is received may be high even though ample bandwidth is available. In cases of networks having very low bandwidth or those that may frequently be near saturation with other traffic, you may find the *pulse mode* option to be more useful in limiting network utilization by the sender. As shown in Figure 5.13, pulse mode sends blocks of data of a specific size at fixed intervals. The default for pulse mode is 3KB blocks at 5-second intervals.

You can choose to create more than one address to the same site. This allows you to provide different policies for different data priorities and multiple sender types.

NOTE

About Latency Between Sites

Restrictions on sending between sites during certain hours can introduce substantial latency in replicating objects and data throughout the hierarchy. It is important to keep this in mind when working with software packages. If updates are made to a package before a child site has received previous updates to the same package, redundant files may be sent between sites. Binary differential replication also does not work between sites until all targeted sites have received at least one version of the package.

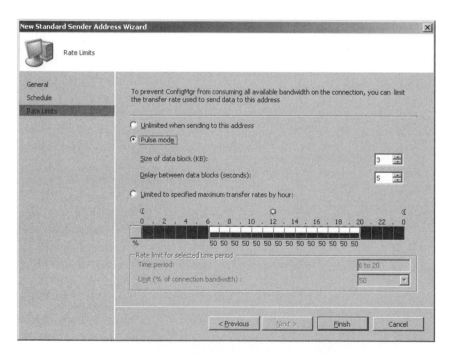

FIGURE 5.13   Limiting bandwidth utilization through pulse mode

Data Priorities

Configuration Manager data is classified by priority:

▶ High

▶ Medium

▶ Low

You can configure the priority of certain data such as status messages, packages, and advertisements. Package and advertisement priorities are discussed in Chapters 13 and 14. Replication of status messages can consume a large amount of network bandwidth. You should consider this in tuning the Status Message System, discussed in the next section.

Tuning Status Message Replication

Status messages provide one of the primary means of looking at the health of your Configuration Manager infrastructure and identifying any problems that may occur. Nearly all Configuration Manager components generate status messages to report various milestones and events. Configuration Manager clients send status messages to their management point, site systems send status messages to the site server, and child sites can replicate messages to their parent site. You can choose which messages to replicate and the data priority for each type of message sent between sites. Status messages sent up the hierarchy can account for much of the overall site-to-site traffic. This is especially true when child sites have a large number of clients. To limit the impact of status message replication, it is important to tune the Status Message System.

The most important settings for status message replication are the status filter rules. Each status message received by a site passes through the site's *status filter*, which evaluates the message to determine whether it matches the criteria of each of its status filter rules. A match invokes the action you specify for the rule. One of the actions you can specify is to replicate the message to the parent site.

You can configure status filter rules in the ConfigMgr console under System Center Configuration Manager -> Site Database -> Site Management -> <*Site Code*> <*Site Name*> -> Site Settings -> Status Filter Rules. As shown in Figure 5.14, two "Replicate all" status filter rules are among the rules enabled by default:

▶ Replicate all SMS Client messages at low priority

▶ Replicate all other messages at medium priority

The rule to replicate client settings is higher on the list in Figure 5.15, showing that it has a higher priority and will be processed before the rule to replicate all other messages at medium priority. Messages received from clients will match the first rule and are replicated to the parent site at low priority. All other status messages will be replicated at medium priority. You can modify these rules depending on your requirements. As an example, if local administrators perform all client troubleshooting at a particular site, you may decide not to replicate status messages originating on client systems from that site to its parent site.

Name	Status
Detect when the status of the site database changes to Critical because it could not b...	Enabled
Detect when the status of the site database changes to Warning due to low free space.	Enabled
Detect when the status of the site database changes to Critical due to low free space.	Enabled
Detect when the status of the transaction log for the site database changes to Critical...	Enabled
Detect when the status of the transaction log for the site database changes to Warni...	Enabled
Detect when the status of the transaction log for the site database changes to Critical...	Enabled
Detect when the status of a site system's storage object changes to Critical because i...	Enabled
Detect when the status of a site system's storage object changes to Warning due to l...	Enabled
Detect when the status of a site system's storage object changes to Critical due to lo...	Enabled
Detect when the status of a server component changes to Warning.	Enabled
Detect when the status of a server component changes to Critical.	Enabled
Write audit messages to the site database and and specify the period after which the ...	Enabled
Write all other messages to the site database and specify the period after which the u...	Enabled
Replicate all SMS Client messages at low priority.	Enabled
Replicate all other messages at medium priority.	Enabled

FIGURE 5.14   The list of status filter rules enabled in the default configuration

To stop replicating client messages, perform these steps:

1. Right-click the rule.
2. Choose Properties.
3. Select the Actions tab in the Status Filter Rule Properties page.
4. Tick the box at the bottom for Do not process lower-priority status filter rules.

By changing the action from Replicate to Parent Site to Do not process lower-priority status filter rules (as shown in Figure 5.15), you can prevent these messages from being processed by the lower-priority rule Replicate all other messages at medium priority. The result is that client messages will be discarded. This prevents using queries and reports at higher-level sites to view client status and deployment results.

Note that the modified rule is still named Replicate all SMS Client messages at low priority, although it no longer actually replicates the messages. To change the name of the rule, you would need to delete or disable the existing rule and create a new rule with the appropriate name. This information is also discussed in Chapter 21, "Backup, Recovery, and Maintenance."

You can create new rules to control replication of specific types of messages. To create a new status filter rule, perform the following steps:

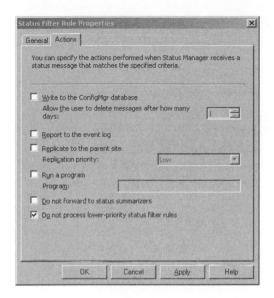

FIGURE 5.15   Modifying a status filter rule

1. Right-click the Status Filter Rules node in the console tree and then select New Status Filter Rule to initiate the New Status Filter Rule Wizard.

2. Name the rule **Replicate Milestones and Informational Messages at Low Priority** and check the Message Type and Severity boxes. With the selections shown in Figure 5.16, the filter will process all messages of type Milestone or with a severity of Informational.

3. Choose the action Replicate to Parent Site / Replication Priority: Low, as shown in Figure 5.17.

4. The wizard will display a summary page for the new rule and ask you to confirm your choice. This completes the New Status Filter Rule Wizard.

After completing the wizard, you need to change the priority of the rule so it processes in the correct order. The rule should run after the rule that discards client messages, but before the catchall rule to replicate at medium priority.

Right-click the rule in the list and choose Increment Priority. The list of rules shown in Figure 5.18 will perform the following replication actions:

▶ All client messages will be dropped.

▶ Informational and milestone messages will be replicated only during times when the sender address setting allows sending low-priority data.

▶ All other messages will be replicated during times when the sender address setting allows sending medium priority data.

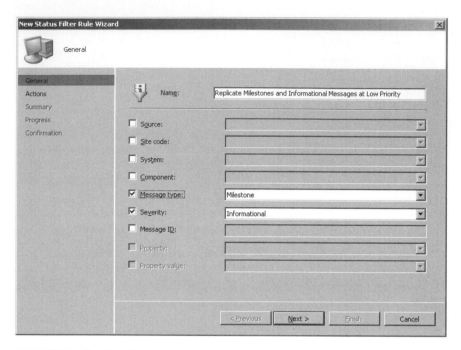

FIGURE 5.16   Specifying criteria against which the status message will be evaluated to determine if the new status filter rule will be applied

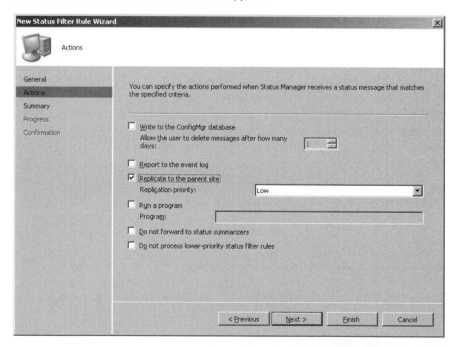

FIGURE 5.17   Specifying the action(s) that occur when a status message matches the filter criteria

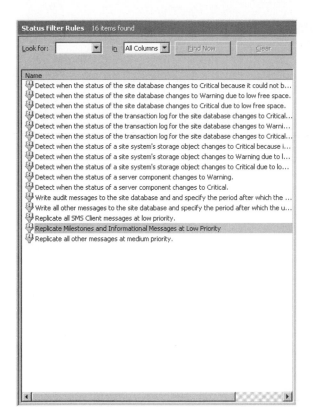

FIGURE 5.18   The list of status filter rules, including the newly created rule, in the desired order

In addition to individual status messages, each Configuration Manager site maintains status summary data. Status summary data displays the overall status of a system, component or advertisement as OK, Warning, or Critical based on the number and type of messages received. Similar to individual status messages, you can decide whether to replicate status summary data to the parent site and the data priority to assign to the replication. Chapter 21 includes the steps to configure replication of status summarizer data.

Data Compression and Site Planning

Whereas network traffic between sites is compressed, traffic within a site is not compressed. You should consider the advantages of compression, scheduling, and data priorities when deciding whether to place secondary sites at remote locations. You may want to use a secondary site to provide services that otherwise are provided by site systems belonging to the parent site, particularly distribution points. Planning for secondary sites is discussed further in Chapter 6.

Fast Networks and Slow Networks

Some Configuration Manager services such as software distribution can consume substantial network bandwidth.

Effectively delivering these services across slow, congested, or unreliable network segments requires careful planning. ConfigMgr provides a mechanism to help with this by defining each site boundary as Fast (LAN) or Slow or unreliable, as shown in Figure 5.19.

FIGURE 5.19   Site boundaries can be defined as slow or fast

Chapter 6 discusses site boundaries. If you are familiar with SMS 2003, you can think of fast site boundaries as SMS 2003 local roaming boundaries, and you can think of slow or unreliable site boundaries as remote roaming boundaries. Options are available to control the way in which software distribution and software updates take place, based on whether you have designated the client's network location as fast or slow in the site boundary properties.

As an example, an advertisement or software updates deployment might specify that clients on a fast network will run the program directly from the distribution point, whereas clients on slow networks will download the files from the distribution point and run them locally. The "download and run" option allows the client to take advantage of the BITS protocol (described in the "Use of BITS" section of this chapter). You can also configure advertisements and deployments not to run at all on slow or unreliable networks. For more information about software distribution and software updates, see Chapters 14 and 15.

Fast, slow, reliable, and unreliable are all relative terms. Although the UI (user interface) suggests that a fast network shares a local area network segment with the ConfigMgr site systems, you should take this suggestion as a general guideline and not necessarily a definitive criterion. You should base your decision of whether to define a particular boundary as fast or slow on your software distribution model and how you want clients within that boundary to behave within that model. In addition to overall speed and reliability, factors you might consider include the following:

▶ Available bandwidth, including peak usage times

▶ Potential impact of software distribution on other business processes sharing the link

▶ The business value of delivering the higher level of service you intend to provide to fast network clients

For example, the SCCMUnleashed organization supports small office and home office (SOHO) users, some of whom have very slow and unreliable connections to the corporate network. It is essential that these users receive critical security updates and other ConfigMgr services. However, it is not feasible to distribute large software packages to them across these network connections. For this reason, many advertisements will be configured not to run on slow networks.

SCCMUnleashed has a major office and data center in Houston, and a smaller office in nearby Conroe. Conroe does not have a datacenter with server class hardware, physical security, or other services. The company decides not to deploy site systems in Conroe and to make this office part of the Houston site. The Conroe office has a 4Mbps dedicated link to Houston, which is lightly utilized. The network team uses Resource Reservation Protocol (RSVP) to guarantee an acceptable quality of service across this link for critical business processes, so the company is not concerned about the impact of software distribution on these processes. The company therefore decides to designate the Conroe subnet as a fast boundary to allow users at that site to access all advertised packages from the distribution point in Houston, even though the connection is substantially below local area network (LAN) speed. Figure 5.20 shows the Houston site.

Use of BITS

The Background Intelligent Transfer Service optimizes file transfers based on network conditions. This optimization includes the following:

▶ Automatically adjusting the rate of the transfer, based on available bandwidth

▶ Suspending and resuming transfers that are interrupted

▶ Providing rudimentary consistency checking

▶ Using group policy and the Configuration Manager console to provide options for tuning BITS-enabled transfers

Let's now look in depth at the BITS feature set, its use by ConfigMgr, and configuring BITS background transfers.

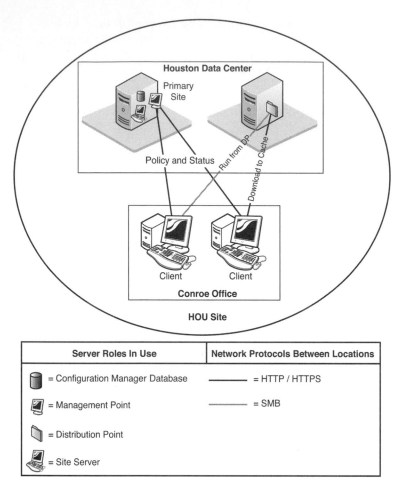

FIGURE 5.20   The Houston site includes the Houston data center and Conroe office.

Configuration Manager makes extensive use of BITS to efficiently use network bandwidth and deal with network connections that are unreliable or not always available. BITS supports downloads over both HTTP and HTTPS. SMS 2003 took advantage of BITS for downloading software from distribution points to clients. Use of BITS in Configuration Manager 2007 has increased and is integral for copying data to branch distribution points, which use BITS to download and cache software packages from other distribution points. BITS 2.0 or higher is a required ConfigMgr component. Here are the key features of all BITS versions:

▶ File transfers that occur quietly in the background, using only bandwidth that is not required by other applications

▶ The ability to suspend and resume transfers interrupted by transient network conditions

BITS Versions for Configuration Manager Clients

BITS has been a component of all Windows operating systems since Windows XP, and it is available for Windows 2000. Microsoft has released several versions of BITS, with added functionality in each revision. The versions supported by Configuration Manager 2007 include the following:

- ▶ BITS Version 2.0—Supported for backward compatibility with systems running Windows 2000 Service Pack (SP) 4. Windows 2000 clients with earlier versions of BITS are upgraded to version 2.0 during client installation.

- ▶ BITS Version 2.5—Installed on all clients which support that version during client installation unless the client already has version 2.5 or higher. BITS 2.5 or higher is included on all systems running Windows Server 2008, Windows Vista, and Windows XP Service Pack 3. Version 2.5 can also be installed on machines running Windows Server 2003 SP 1 or SP 2 or Windows XP SP 2.

- ▶ BITS Version 3.0—Available on the Windows Server 2008 and Windows Vista operating systems only.

BITS versions 2.0 and 2.5 are available as separate downloads. Because BITS upgrades require a reboot, you may want to consider deploying the required BITS versions in advance to all clients needing an upgrade, to avoid a required reboot during ConfigMgr client deployment.

TIP

Advantage of Using Background Transfers

If you have ever initiated a large file transfer and had your computer come to a crawl, you will appreciate the concept of background transfers. BITS versions 1.0–2.0 used counters from the network interface card (NIC) to determine demand for bandwidth by other applications running on the local machine. All versions of BITS throttle the bandwidth used, such that file transfers will only take bandwidth not used by other applications. Foreground applications therefore remain responsive to the user and other services are able to operate without interruption. The transfers occur asynchronously, meaning that the rate can vary over time.

Instead of a steady stream of data, you can consider the data as being "drizzled" across the network. This also allows a transfer that is interrupted to pick up where it left off when connectivity is restored.

One problem with earlier versions of BITS is that the system is only aware of the traffic passing through the NIC. Even if the network segment to which the machine is connected is quite congested, if there is little or no network activity on the local machine it would appear to BITS that most of the bandwidth supported by the card is available. Under these conditions BITS transmits data at a high rate, potentially causing additional network congestion problems. BITS 2.5 and higher versions get around this limitation by pulling usage statistics from the Internet Gateway Device (IGD). Certain conditions must be met in order to pull statistics from the IGD:

▶ Universal Plug and Play (UPnP) must be enabled.

▶ The device must support UPnP byte counters.

▶ UPnP traffic (TCP 2869 and UDP 1900) is not blocked by any firewall device or software.

▶ The device must respond to GetTotalBytesSent and GetTotalBytesReceived in a timely fashion.

▶ The file transfer must traverse the gateway.

NOTE

Error 16393 if BITS Cannot Retrieve Information from IDG

If BITS is unable to retrieve counter data from the IDG, the following event is logged:

    Event ID 16393 Source: Microsoft-Windows-Bits-Client

BITS has encountered an error communicating with an Internet Gateway Device. Please check that the device is functioning properly. BITS will not attempt to use this device until the next system reboot. Error code: %1.

Modifying BITS Functionality Through Group Policy

In most circumstances, BITS will intelligently manage the use of network bandwidth without additional configuration. If you find that BITS-enabled transfers are consuming more bandwidth than desired or if you want to provide extra protection for other business-critical network activity, group policy can limit the bandwidth BITS will consume. The setting is specified in Kbps, and its name varies depending on the version of Windows you are running.

▶ For Windows Server 2003 group policy, the setting is called "Maximum network bandwidth that BITS uses."

▶ For Windows Server 2008 group policy, the setting is "Maximum network bandwidth for BITS background transfers."

In both versions of Windows Server, this setting is found under Computer Configuration -> Administrative Templates -> Network -> Background Intelligent Transfer Service. The setting, shown in Figure 5.21 for Windows Server 2008 group policy, allows a limit for a specific time interval (such as working hours) and a different limit for outside that interval. All versions of BITS supported by ConfigMgr also have a timeout for inactive transfers (defaulting to 90 days) that is configurable through group policy.

BITS 3.0 introduces several new group policy options. These allow you to control settings such as the maximum active download time for BITS jobs, the number of jobs allowed per user and per machine, and the maximum number of files per job.

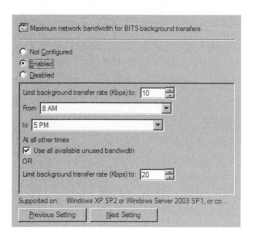

Maximum network bandwidth for BITS background transfers

○ Not Configured
● Enabled
○ Disabled

Limit background transfer rate (Kbps) to: 10

From 8 AM

to 5 PM

At all other times
☑ Use all available unused bandwidth
OR
Limit background transfer rate (Kbps) to: 20

Supported on: Windows XP SP2 or Windows Server 2003 SP1, or co...

Previous Setting   Next Setting

FIGURE 5.21   Setting the maximum network bandwidth for BITS background transfers

Group policy settings are only available in Active Directory domains. Although group policies are generally applied at the domain or Organizational Unit (OU) level, BITS-related policies are examples of a policy that you might consider implementing at the site level.

An *AD site* is generally a region of high network connectivity. By applying the BITS-related policies to the site, you can control the behavior of all systems in your AD forest based on network location, regardless of their domain or OU membership.

Modifying BITS Functionality Within Configuration Manager

You can also define the maximum network bandwidth for BITS background transfers using the ConfigMgr console. The settings are specified on the BITS tab of the Computer Client Agent property sheet, located under System Center Configuration Manager -> Site Database -> Site Management -> *<Site Code><Site Name>* -> Site Settings -> Client Agents -> Computer Client Agent - > BITS tab on the Configuration Manager console. As shown in Figure 5.22, these settings are similar to the group policy settings, but in this case they are applied either to all clients in the ConfigMgr site or to branch distribution points only.

Comparative Advantages of Group Policy and ConfigMgr Settings for BITS

Unlike group policy settings, the settings on the Computer Client agent apply to clients that are in workgroups or untrusted domains. These are global settings for all clients in the site, however, while group policy allows you to control the behavior of BITS for clients in specific domains, OUs, individual computers, or AD sites. You can achieve even more granular control of group policy by WMI filtering and/or security group filtering. These filtering techniques selectively apply group policy objects (GPOs) to users or computers based on the results of WMI queries or security group membership. An excellent resource on group policy management is available online at the Windows Server 2003 Tech Center (http://technet2.microsoft.com/windowsserver/en/library/):

▶ The section on WMI filtering is found at http://technet.microsoft.com/en-us/library/
cc779036.aspx.

▶ Security group filtering is discussed in http://technet.microsoft.com/en-us/library/
cc781988.aspx.

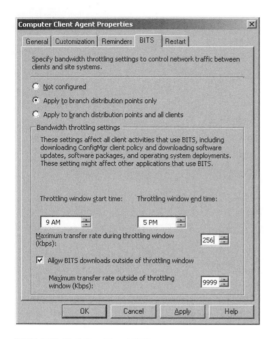

FIGURE 5.22   Use BITS throttling settings to control network traffic.

As mentioned earlier in the "BITS Versions for Configuration Manager Clients" section of
this chapter, Windows Server 2008 group policy has a wider range of BITS-related options
for BITS version 3.0 than that available through the ConfigMgr settings. Through
ConfigMgr, however, you are able to assign BITS settings specifically to branch distribution
points. Because there are different options available through group policy and ConfigMgr
settings, you may choose to use both to control BITS behavior.

CAUTION

Avoid Conflicts in Group Policy and ConfigMgr BITS Settings

If you are using both group policy and ConfigMgr settings to govern BITS functionality, be careful to avoid applying both methods to the same systems. The domain policies will override locally stored ConfigMgr settings and may produce unpredictable results. If systems requiring ConfigMgr BITS settings reside in AD containers that have BITS policies applied, you can use WMI filtering or security group filtering to block application of group policy objects containing BITS settings. In any case, you should plan and test such configurations carefully.

Other BITS Features

On client systems with multiple physical or virtual interfaces, BITS uses the GetBestInterface function to select the interface with the best route to the server it needs to access. Once the file transfer is complete, BITS verifies that the file size is correct. However, BITS does not perform a more extensive file integrity check to detect corruption or tampering that may have occurred.

Enabling a Distribution Point for BITS

In order to enable a distribution point to use BITS, the distribution point must be running IIS 6.0 or higher with ASP.NET and WebDAV (Web-based Distributed Authoring and Versioning) enabled. You can enable these features in various ways, depending on the version of Windows Server you are running. After meeting these prerequisites, you can enable a distribution point for BITS through a check box on the distribution point properties page, as shown in Figure 5.23. Note that BITS-enabled distribution points will download files to clients and branch distribution points using BITS; however, programs that run from the distribution point will use the standard SMB protocol.

TIP

WebDAV and Windows Server 2008

You must manually install WebDAV on Windows 2008.

Server Placement

To optimize Configuration Manager's use of your network, you should consider the placement of servers holding various site roles. The following guidelines should help with your planning:

▶ The site server should have a high bandwidth and highly available connection to the site database server. The site server also needs good connectivity to a domain controller, particularly if any of the Active Directory discovery methods are enabled.

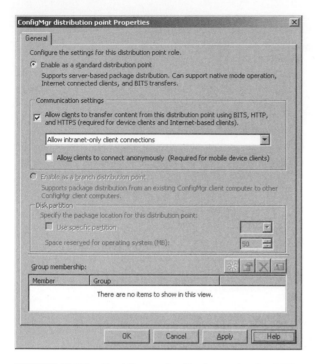

FIGURE 5.23   Enabling a distribution point for BITS on the distribution point properties page

▶ You can install the SMS provider on the site server, the site database server, or another server with highly available network connectivity to these systems and to all systems running the ConfigMgr console. Because the SMS provider uses system and network resources, you should consider the resources available when you select the provider location. For more information on choosing the provider location, see http://technet.microsoft.com/en-us/library/bb694290.aspx.

▶ The reporting point needs good connectivity to the site database server.

▶ You can configure the management point and server locator point to use the site database or a replica of the site database. In either case, good connectivity to the database is required.

▶ You should place all client-facing systems in close proximity to the clients they serve. If you support Internet-only clients, the systems these clients will access should be in a DMZ (demilitarized zone, also known as a *perimeter network*). In general, do not place the site server and site database server in an Internet-accessible DMZ.

▶ The placement of distribution points is especially important. For clients across a WAN link from the site server, consider whether to deploy a standard distribution point or a branch distribution point.

A branch distribution point uses BITS to receive packages across the WAN but requires clients to use SMB. A standard BITS-enabled distribution point uses SMB across the WAN, but is capable of providing BITS downloads to clients:

► A small office with a few clients separated from the main site location by a slow or unreliable link is an excellent candidate for a branch distribution point.

► For a larger office with a better WAN connection, you should consider a standard protected distribution point. Standard distribution points provide the advantage of allowing clients to download content using BITS. You may still decide to deploy a branch distribution point at a larger site to take advantage of "on-demand" package distribution. Another advantage of branch distribution points is you can use OOB methods such as copying files from a local source to distribute a package to a branch DP, avoiding the WAN link altogether. If you install branch distribution points at larger sites, you should place them on systems running a server operating system to avoid the connection limitations of Windows Vista or Windows XP.

► You may also decide to deploy a secondary site at the remote location to take advantage of intersite communication features such as scheduling and compression, or to provide additional site server roles such as a proxy management point or software updates point. Determining when to create additional sites is discussed in Chapter 6.

Disconnected Users and Sometimes-Connected Users

Users who do not connect to the enterprise network or who only connect occasionally present a special configuration management challenge. SMS 2003 provided limited support for intermittent network connections through BITS. When a client's network connection to its distribution point dropped while a download was in progress, the download could resume the next time the client established a connection to that distribution point. This allowed effective software distribution services to users such as home office users who intermittently establish a VPN connection to the corporate network. Those individuals using laptops both at the office and away from the office also benefit from the ability to resume interrupted downloads.

However, for some highly mobile users it is unlikely to complete a large download efficiently using a single distribution point. Airline pilots, for example, may carry laptops that they use to connect to the airline's network at various airports along their route. Each airport is likely to fall within the boundaries of a different site or distribution point. A suspended download would therefore start over from the new distribution point and might never complete. A Configuration Manager 2007 enhancement allows suspended BITS downloads to resume from any BITS-enabled distribution point. In this way, pilots and other highly mobile users are able to complete downloads as they travel.

Configuration Manager also provides Internet-Based Client Management (IBCM), which allows you to provide some services to users who never connect directly to your network.

IBCM allows you to provide services over the Internet, including software distribution and software updates to Internet-only clients. You will also receive inventory and status from those clients. Clients that sometimes connect to the corporate network can also take advantage of IBCM services, including the ability of BITS downloads to take place partially over the intranet and partially over the Internet. IBCM does not support OS deployment, client deployment, NAP, and ConfigMgr Remote Tools. For more information on Internet-based clients, see Chapter 12.

Network Discovery

Configuration Manager can use a variety of network protocols to probe your network and gather data about the objects it discovers into the site database. Network discovery can be used to identify potential ConfigMgr clients. Network discovery can also be used to add network topology data and information about non-client network devices to your database for use in queries, collections, and reports. Configuration Manager network discovery is similar to that in SMS 2003, except there is a new configuration tab for DHCP servers and support added for IPv6.

To configure network discovery, right-click Network Discovery in the Configuration Manager console under System Center Configuration Manager -> Site Database -> Site Management -> *<Site Code> <Site Name>* -> Discovery Methods -> Network Discovery and then choose Properties. As displayed in Figure 5.24, there are three levels of network discovery:

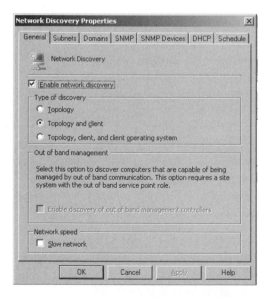

FIGURE 5.24   Choosing the type of network discovery to run

- ▶ Topology

- ▶ Topology and client

- ▶ Topology, client, and client operating systems

NOTE

About Network Discovery Resource Utilization

Network discovery can have a major impact on your network and site systems. To avoid overloading network or server resources, you should schedule network discovery to run during off-peak times. If you have a large number of machines, you should perform initial discovery in phases. You may choose to discover a few subnets at a time or you may choose to first discover topology only, then clients, and later add operating system discovery. You should limit the number of new resources you expect to discover to no more than 5,000 at a time.

If discovery will traverse slow network segments, check the Slow network box on the General tab to throttle the number of concurrent network request and adjust timeout values.

The Subnets, Domains, and SNMP Devices tabs determine the initial scope of network discovery. Figure 5.25 displays the Subnets tab. By default, the local subnet and the site server's domain will be discovered. You can add subnets, domains, or SNMP devices using the starburst icon (circled in Figure 5.25) on the respective tabs. You can also remove or modify existing subnets or domains.

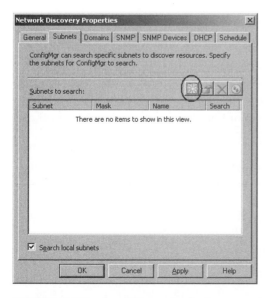

FIGURE 5.25 Specifying subnets for network discovery

Discovering Network Topology

Network discovery uses Simple Network Management Protocol (SNMP) to query network infrastructure devices for basic information about your network topology. The discovery process generates data discovery records (DDRs) for network devices and subnets. A *DDR* is a small file with identifying information about an object that is processed and stored in the ConfigMgr database. The properties for SNMP discovery are configured on the SNMP tab of the Network Discovery Properties sheet, shown in Figure 5.26.

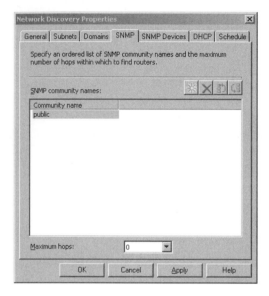

FIGURE 5.26   Specifying SNMP community strings for network discovery

All SNMP devices are configured with a community string, which by default is named *public*. To connect to an SNMP device, you must add its community string to the list of communities to discover. The maximum hops specified on the SNMP tab controls how far discovery will traverse the network. If the number of hops is set to 0, the devices on the site server's local subnet will be discovered. If the number of hops is more than 0, network discovery will query the routing tables of the local router to retrieve a list of subnets connected to it and the IP addresses of devices listed in the ipRouteNextHop of the router. These subnets and devices are considered to be one hop away. Network discovery will continue to perform the same process based on the routing data of the devices on the next hop, until it reaches the maximum number of hops. Additional subnets and devices on those subnets will be discovered if one of the following occurs:

▶ The subnet is specified on the Subnets tab.

▶ The subnet information is retrieved from a device specified on the SNMP Devices tab.

Because a router can be connected to many subnets, the scope of network discovery can increase dramatically with each higher value of the Maximum hops setting. On the local subnet, network discovery can connect to the router using Router Information Protocol (RIP) or by listening for Open Shortest Path First (OSPF) multicast addresses, even if SNMP is not available on the router.

Network discovery can also retrieve information from Microsoft DHCP servers. The Network Discovery Properties DHCP tab lists the DHCP servers to query. By default, network discovery will use the site server's DHCP server, although typically, the site server is not configured as a DHCP client and you will need to add DHCP servers manually using the starburst icon. Figure 5.27 displays an example of this.

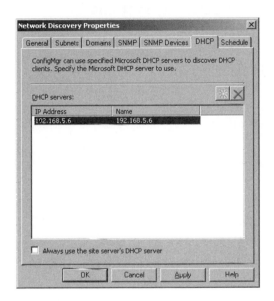

FIGURE 5.27   Specifying DHCP servers to be used by network discovery

The site server will establish an RPC connection to each of the specified DHCP servers to retrieve subnet and scope information. Subnets defined on the DHCP servers are added to the list of available subnets for future network discovery, but are not enabled for discovery by default. For each active lease on the DHCP server, the network discovery process also attempts to resolve the IP address to a name. For more information on Microsoft DHCP, see the Microsoft DHCP FAQ at http://www.microsoft.com/technet/network/dhcp/dhcpfaq.mspx#EUG.

Topology and Client Discovery

To discover potential Configuration Manager clients, network discovery attempts to identify as many devices as possible on the IP network. An array of IP addresses from the ipNetToMediaTable of SNMP devices is used to identify IP addresses in use, and network discovery pings each address to determine if it is currently active. If the device replies to the ping, network discovery attempts to use SNMP to query the device. If network discovery can access the device's management information through SNMP, it will retrieve any routing table or other information the device holds about other IP addresses it is aware of. Each IP address is resolved to a NetBIOS name if possible.

Network discovery will also retrieve the Browse list for any domains specified on the Domains tab. The Browse list is the same list used to display machines in the Windows Network Neighborhood, and can be enumerated with the Net View command. As with other discovered devices, network discovery then attempts to ping the device to see if it is active.

Discovering Topology, Client, and Client Operating Systems

In addition to the discovery process for topology and clients, if client operating system discovery is specified, network discovery will attempt to make a connection using LAN Manager calls to determine whether the machine is running Windows and, if so, what version of Windows it is running.

In order for network discovery to create a DDR for a discovered device, the IP address and subnet mask of the device must be retrieved. Network discovery retrieves the subnet mask from one of the following:

▶ **The device itself if it is manageable through SNMP**—Windows machines are only manageable through SNMP if the SNMP service is running and configured with the required community information. This will generally not be the case.

▶ **The Address Resolution Protocol (ARP) cache of a router with information about the device**—ARP is a protocol used to resolve IP addresses to the Media Access Control (MAC) addresses of the network cards. Routers keep this information cached for a finite amount of time, depending on the router configuration. The ARP cache generally will not have information about every device on the attached network segment. This makes retrieving subnet mask information from the router ARP cache a hit-or-miss operation.

▶ **The DHCP server**—If you are using Microsoft DHCP for all of your IP address assignment, retrieval of subnet mask information from the DHCP server will generally work well. Any machines with static IP addresses or any machines using non-Microsoft DHCP will need to be discovered by another method. All DHCP servers must also be listed on the DHCP tab.

There are many dependencies for network discovery to work properly. Required protocols must be allowed by firewalls, enabled, and configured properly on clients. Network discovery is an important way to discover clients, but in general you will not want to rely on it exclusively. Client discovery methods and strategies are discussed in Chapter 12. In addition to discovering potential clients, network discovery provides information about your network environment that is not available from other discovery methods.

Using Subnets in Configuration Manager

The boundaries of Configuration Manager sites and protected site systems determine the network locations from which clients can receive certain services from the site or system. Site boundaries are defined as follows:

- ▶ An Active Directory site
- ▶ An IP subnet
- ▶ An IP range
- ▶ An IPv6 prefix

You select boundaries for protected site systems from the boundaries of the site.

Active Directory sites generally correspond to a local area network. By using AD sites as site boundaries, you may be able to eliminate the duplication of effort involved in maintaining subnet information in two places. You should update the AD site configuration to reflect network topology changes, such as adding new subnets to a LAN. As long as the site structure in AD is appropriate for your ConfigMgr sites, relying on AD sites as boundaries will be a simple and effective solution.

In some cases, you may need more granular control of your site boundaries. For example, you may wish to add satellite offices to a ConfigMgr site that are not part of the same AD site. You may also want to provide a separate Configuration Manager site for particular types of systems within your AD site, such as servers. You may also need to use IP-based boundaries to support clients that are not able to retrieve site information from your Active Directory, such as workgroup clients or clients in domains that do not have a trust relationship with your site server's domain.

Protected site systems are useful for smaller offices that do not have their own Configuration Manager site but have local servers that can provide services to clients. The site systems that can be protected systems are distribution points and state migration points. Clients within the boundaries of a protected system will use that system before using another distribution point or state migration point in the site.

In SMS 2003, a client within the boundaries of a protected distribution point would use only the protected distribution point to access package content. In Configuration Manager 2007, you can specify whether the client will use another distribution point if content is not available from the protected distribution point. This behavior is specified through options in the properties of the advertisement, software update deployment, or task sequence. Advertisements, software update deployment, and task sequences are discussed in Chapters 14, 15, and 19, respectively.

Troubleshooting Configuration Manager Network Issues

Configuration Manager depends on basic network services such as connectivity and name resolution to work properly. Network-related issues are a common source of problems that can affect Configuration Manager service delivery. The next sections look at some typical issues you may encounter related to network dependencies. When troubleshooting, it is important to keep an open mind. Some issues caused by incorrect security settings, for example, can produce very similar symptoms to network issues. The last part of this chapter provides a brief overview of some general network troubleshooting methods, followed by a discussion of how to troubleshoot some specific ConfigMgr issues potentially caused by network problems.

Among the common network-related issues that can affect Configuration Manager are the following:

▶ Network configuration issues

▶ Basic connectivity problems

▶ Name resolution issues

▶ Blocked or unresponsive ports

▶ Timeout issues

The following sections briefly describe a few of the many tools and techniques for troubleshooting these types of issues.

Network Configuration Issues

If you suspect that the TCP/IP networking on one of your systems is not working correctly, you can log on to the system and enter the following at the command prompt (Start -> Run, and then type **cmd**):

```
Ipconfig /all
```

You should see a list of the installed network adapters with IP addresses and other IP configuration data. If no IP address or only an autoconfiguration IP address is displayed, the network components are either not configured or not functioning properly. If this occurs when the IP address configuration is set to obtain an IP address automatically, this means the machine was unable to contact a DHCP server. For more information on configuring TCP/IP, see http://technet2.microsoft.com/windowsserver/en/library/99f79ed8-df1e-49a6-a4f4-eb13623663011033.mspx?mfr=true.

If the machine has one or more valid IP addresses, you can test TCP/IP functioning by entering the following two commands at the command prompt:

▶ Ping 127.0.0.1

▶ Ping <IP address of this machine>

In both cases, you should see a series of replies, such as the following:

```
Reply from 127.0.0.1: bytes=32 time=9ms TTL=128
```

If you receive a request timed out message, TCP/IP networking on the machine is not working properly.

The NetDiag.exe utility, which you can download from Microsoft's website, can be used to diagnose (and in some cases fix) a wide variety of network configuration issues. For more information on Netdiag, see http://www.microsoft.com/technet/prodtechnol/windows2000serv/reskit/prork/pref_tts_nigx.mspx?mfr=true.

Basic Connectivity Problems

Basic connectivity problems occur if

- ▶ Systems are not physically connected;

- ▶ There is a hardware or software problem on one of the systems or an intermediate device;

- ▶ The packets are not correctly routed between the systems.

To start troubleshooting basic connectivity, log on to one of the affected systems and ping the system with which it has problems communicating. To do this, open a command prompt (Start -> Run, and then type **cmd**) and enter the following command:

```
Ping <IP address of target system>
```

In most cases, you should get a response showing the time it took to get a reply to the ping request and other statistics. If the system is not responding, you may get one of the following messages:

- ▶ **Request timed out**—This simply means that you did not get a response in the expected time. In some cases, the target system may have been configured not to respond to a ping. You can test this on the target system by pinging its own IP address to make sure it is responding. If you suspect that the ping request timed out because of slow network conditions, you can try increasing the timeout value from the default value of 1 second. As an example, `Ping -w 5000 <IP address of target system>` will wait 5,000 milliseconds (5 seconds).

- ▶ **Destination Host Unreachable or Destination Network Unreachable**—This is generally a response from a router indicating that no route is defined to the host or subnet.

Other return values are possible indicating specific errors. For more information on the ping command, see http://technet2.microsoft.com/windowsserver/en/library/9eaf7bddee42-4358-9b60-66c8463dbdee1033.mspx?mfr=true.

You can drill deeper into connectivity issues using commands such as tracert and pathping, which are described at http://www.microsoft.com/technet/prodtechnol/windows2000serv/reskit/cnet/cnbd_trb_dfln.mspx?mfr=true.

Name Resolution Issues

Most Configuration Manager components rely on DNS for name resolution. In some cases, ConfigMgr also uses NetBIOS name resolution. Once again, you can use the ping command as a quick test of name resolution. At the command prompt, enter

▶ **Ping** *<FQDN of target system>*

For example:

Ping bluebonnet.sccmunleashed.com

▶ **Ping** *<hostname of target system>*

For example:

Ping bluebonnet

▶ **Ping** *<NetBIOS name of target system>*

For example:

Ping \\bluebonnet

In each case, these commands should return a response showing the correct IP of the target system, such as the following:

Pinging bluebonnet.sccmunleashed.com [192.168.5.4] with 32 bytes of data:

If DNS name resolution fails, you can troubleshoot this using the NSlookup command described at http://support.microsoft.com/kb/200525. To troubleshoot NetBIOS name resolution using Nbtstat and other methods, see KB article 323388 (at http://support. microsoft.com/kb/323388). It's also useful to test pinging the known IP address of the target machine—if that works then you have narrowed the issue to some sort of name resolution–related issue.

An additional DNS problem that sometimes occurs is an incorrect referral. Incorrect referrals occur when a hostname is used instead of an FQDN, and the wrong domain name is appended due to the DNS suffix search order. This typically results in "access denied" errors. If you see unexpected "access denied" errors, try pinging the site system using both the hostname and the FQDN to make sure they resolve to the same address.

Blocked or Unresponsive Ports

A common source of connectivity problems involves ports blocked by intermediate devices such as routers or firewalls. In other cases, the port may simply not be listening on the system to which you are trying to connect. To identify problems with specific ports, first refer to Table 5.1 earlier in this chapter to determine the ports used by the failing service. You can then attempt to connect to the specific port on the target system using the telnet command. For example, to verify that you can connect to the Trivial File Transfer Protocol (TFTP) Daemon service (port 69) on PXE service point Dabney. SCCMUnleashed.com, open a command prompt (Start -> Run, and then type **cmd**) and enter the following:

Telnet Dabney.SCCMUnleashed.com 69

If telnet is successful, you will receive the Telnet screen with a cursor. If the connection fails, you will receive an error message.

When a connection to a port fails, first verify that the service is listening on the appropriate port. On the machine that should receive the connections, enter the command netstat –a to list all connections and listening ports.

▶ If the port is not shown, verify that all system requirements and prerequisites are met.

▶ If the port displays as enabled, check all network firewall logs for dropped packets.

Refer to your network team or vendor firewall documentation for procedures for checking firewall logs. Also, check the Windows Firewall logs and settings (see http://technet. microsoft.com/en-us/network/bb545423.aspx) and any third-party security software that performs intrusion detection and prevention.

Additional tools are available for troubleshooting port status issues, such as the following:

▶ The PortQry command-line utility, downloadable from http://www.microsoft.com/ downloads/details.aspx?familyid=89811747-C74B-4638-A2D5-AC828BDC6983&displaylang=en.

▶ PortQryUI, which you can download from http://www.microsoft.com/ downloads/details.aspx?FamilyID=8355E537-1FA6-4569-AABB-F248F4BD91D0&displaylang=en. PortQryUI provides equivalent functionality to PortQry through a graphical user interface (GUI).

Going to www.microsoft.com/downloads and searching for **PortQry** will bring up links for both these tools.

Testing Client–to–Management Point Connectivity

To test client connectivity to an MP, you can try entering the following URLs in the client's web browser.

For mixed mode clients:

http://<*MP*>/sms_mp/.sms_aut?mplist

http://<*MP*>/sms_mp/.sms_aut?mpcert

For native mode clients:

https://<*MP*>/sms_mp/.sms_aut?mplist

https://<*MP*>/sms_mp/.sms_aut?mpcert

Note that <*MP*> is either the IP address or the name of the management point. If a name is used, the name should be one of the following:

▶ The NetBIOS name for mixed mode clients

▶ Either the short name or the FQDN for intranet clients in native mode, depending on how the management point name is specified in the site properties

▶ The FQDN for Internet clients

In each case, the first URL (the one ending in "mplist" in the preceding examples) should return an XML-formatted list of management points or a blank page, whereas the second URL (ending in "mpcert") should return a string of characters corresponding to the management point certificate. Any error messages or other unexpected return values indicate a problem communicating with the management point.

Timeout Issues

The response times you see from the ping command can help you to confirm network performance problems that could be causing connections to time out. In some cases timeouts are configurable; however, if timeouts are a frequent problem, you should review your server placement and network configuration to see if improvements can be made.

Identifying Network Issues Affecting Configuration Manager

Almost all Configuration Manager functionality depends on adequate network services. The next sections will look at some of the features most often affected by network issues. These features include site system and client installation, software distribution, and data synchronization across the hierarchy. Chapter 3 introduced the two major features of Configuration Manager for troubleshooting:

▶ The Status Message System

▶ The ConfigMgr logs

The following sections discuss some indicators of possible network issues that you may see in the status messages and logs. In addition to troubleshooting, you can use this information to configure proactive monitoring for ConfigMgr, helping to spot many problems before they impact service delivery.

The following discussion is by no means an exhaustive list of possible network issues. It does cover some of the more common issues, and should give you an idea of how to use these tools effectively.

Network Issues Affecting Site System Installation

When there is a problem installing or configuring a site system, this will generally show up in the Site Component Manager status. In the ConfigMgr console, expand System Center Configuration Manager -> Site Database -> System Status -> Site Status -> *<Site Code> <Site Name>* -> Component Status. Right-click SMS_SITE_COMPONENT_ MANAGER and choose View Messages -> All. If network problems are preventing a site system installation, you will typically see status messages similar to the ones detailed in Table 5.3.

TABLE 5.3   Site Component Manager Status Messages Indicating Network Problems

Severity	Message ID	Description
Error	1037	SMS Site Component Manager could not access site system "\\MINEOLA." The operating system reported error 2147942453: The network path was not found.
		Possible cause: The site system is turned off, not connected to the network, or not functioning properly.
		Solution: Verify that the site system is turned on, connected to the network, and functioning properly.
		Possible cause: SMS Site Component Manager does not have sufficient access rights to connect to the site system.
		Solution: Verify that the site server's computer$ account has administrator rights on the remote site system.
		Possible cause: Network problems are preventing SMS Site Component Manager from connecting to the site system.
		Solution: Investigate and correct any problems on your network.
		Possible cause: You took the site system out of service and do not intend on using it as a site system any more.
		Solution: Remove this site system from the list of site systems for this site. The list appears in the Site Systems node of the ConfigMgr console.
Error	1028	SMS Site Component Manager failed to configure site system "\\MINEOLA" to receive SMS server components.
		Solution: Review any previous status messages to determine the exact reason for the failure.
		The SMS Site Component Manager cannot install any ConfigMgr server components on this site system until the site system is configured successfully. The Site Component Manager will automatically retry this operation in 60 minutes. To force SMS Site Component Manager to retry this operation immediately, stop and restart SMS Site Component Manager using the SMS Service Manager.
Error	578	Could not read Registry key "HKEY_LOCAL_MACHINE\SOFTWARE\Microsoft\SMS" on computer MINEOLA. The operating system reported error 11001: No such host is known.
		Resolution: Troubleshoot name resolution.

You will find additional information in the log file sitecomp.log. Network problems are indicated by errors such as ERROR: NAL failed to access NAL path....

Network Issues Affecting Client Installation

When Client Push Installation is enabled, the Client Configuration Manager component on the site server is responsible for installing the client on those systems that are discovered and targeted for installation. When an installation attempt fails, a Client Configuration Request (.CCR) file is copied to the folder *<%ProgramFiles%\ ConfigMgrInstallPath>*\inboxes\ccrretry.box (where *<ConfigMgrInstallPath>* indicates the folder in which Configuration Manager is installed, by default Microsoft Configuration Manager.

It is not unusual for a client installation to take more than one attempt, and you may see some files in the ccrretry.box folder as part of normal operations. However, a large backlog of files in this location may indicate a problem pushing out the client software. Problems will also show up under the status for Client Configuration Manager (in the console under System Center Configuration Manager -> Site Database -> System Status -> Site Status -> Component Status -> SMS_CLIENT_CONFIG_MANAGER).

NOTE

About Offline Clients

You may see a backlog of CCR retries and numerous status messages indicating client installation failures, which occur simply because the machines were temporarily disconnected or shut down when Client Configuration Manager attempted to contact them. The Client Configuration Manager may also be attempting to reach machines that are permanently offline but previously discovered by ConfigMgr 2007. This is a particularly common issue with Active Directory system discovery. If your Active Directory contains machine accounts for computers that no longer exist, AD system discovery will discover these machines, and Client Push (if enabled) will attempt to install the client on them. Your change control process should include removal of stale computer accounts from Active Directory.

See Chapter 21 for additional considerations for managing discovery data.

Table 5.4 lists some messages that indicate possible network issues.

You may find additional information in the log files ccm.log on the site server and ccmsetup.log on the client (the ccmsetup log only exists if the attempted installation progressed far enough for the setup process to start on the client).

Table 5.5 lists log entries that can help identify network issues.

Missing or Incorrect Service Principal Name Registration

Service Principal Names (SPNs) provide information used by clients to identify and mutually authenticate with services using Kerberos authentication. Services use Active Directory SPN registration to make the required information available to clients. Missing or incorrect SPN registration is a common cause of problems with client communications with site systems, such as failure to download content or client approval problems. HTTP 401 errors in client log files, including the Datatransferservice.log and ccmexec.log, may indicate problems with SPN registrations. To register the required Service Principal Names properly, refer to the following documentation:

TABLE 5.4   Client Configuration Manager Status Messages Indicating Network Problems

Severity	Message ID	Description
Warning	3014	SMS Client Configuration Manager cannot connect to the machine "MINEOLA." The operating system reported Error 5: Access is denied.
		Possible cause: The client is not accessible.
		Solution: Verify that the client is connected to the network and that the SMS Service account or (if specified) the SMS Client Remote Installation account has the required privileges, as specified in the SMS documentation.
		Possible cause: A remote client installation account was not specified in the SMS Admin console, the account is not valid, is disabled, or has an expired password.
		Solution: Ensure one or more valid and active remote client installation accounts are specified in the ConfigMgr console, that the account names and passwords are correct, and that the account has the required administrator rights on the target machines.
Warning	3010	In the past %3 hours, SMS Client Configuration Manager (CCM) has made %1 unsuccessful attempt(s) to install SMS on client %2.[1] CCM will continue to attempt to install this client.
Error	3011	SMS Client Configuration Manager (CCM) failed to complete the SMS installation on client.
Warning	3015	SMS Client Configuration Manager cannot find machine %1 on the network.

[1]*%1, %2, and so forth represent replaceable parameters. The actual values will be supplied at run-time.*

▶ If you are running the SQL Server service using a domain account on the site database server or other roles requiring SQL Server, you must follow the instructions in http://technet.microsoft.com/en-us/library/bb735885.aspx to register the SPN. If the SQL Server service is configured to run under the local system account, you do not need to manually register the SPN. However, running SQL Server in the local system context is not recommended for security reasons.

▶ For site systems that require IIS, if the system is registered in DNS using a CNAME (a DNS alias rather than the actual computer name), you will need to register the SPN using the procedure described in http://technet.microsoft.com/en-us/library/bb694288.aspx.

▶ If you are using a management point configured as a network load-balancing (NLB) cluster in a mixed mode site, refer to http://technet.microsoft.com/en-us/library/bb735879.aspx for instructions on SPN registration.

TABLE 5.5   Log File Entries Indicating Network Problems with Client Installation

Log File Name	Log File Entry	Description	Troubleshooting Steps
ccm.log	The network path was not found (Error Code 53).	Unable to resolve or contact client	Follow basic network troubleshooting between the site server and client (note: the client may simply have been offline).
ccm.log	The network name cannot be found (Error 67).	Unable to connect to client	Verify that File and Printer Sharing for Microsoft Networks is enabled on the client and not blocked by firewall or security software.
ccmsetup.log	Failed to send HTTP request (Error 12029).	Error communicating with management point	Review the LocationServices log to identify the MP. Test the connection to the MP.
ccmsetup.log	Failed to successfully complete HTTP request.	Error communicating with management point	Review the LocationServices log to identify the MP. Test the connection to the MP.

Network Issues Affecting Software Distribution

Software distribution relies on networking to send packages to distribution points and for clients to download policy from management points and content from distribution points. Figure 5.28 shows the principal network exchanges involved in software distribution. In this figure, the directional arrows indicate the principal direction of data transfer. This may differ from the direction shown in Table 5.1, which indicates the system initiating the connection.

You will find status information relating to the general functioning of package deployment under System Center Configuration Manager -> Site Database -> <System Status> -> Site Status -> Component Status -> SMS_DISTRIBUTION_MANAGER.

Table 5.6 shows Distribution Manager status messages that may indicate network problems preventing package distribution. You can also find status information for individual packages under System Center Configuration Manager -> Site Database -> System Status -> Package Status. Additional details are available in Distmgr.log.

Some general status information about advertisements is available in the Configuration Manager console. General statistics about advertisements are located under System Center Configuration Manager -> Site Database -> System Status -> Advertisement Status.

To view status messages for a particular advertisement, expand out the Advertisement Status node, select the advertisement, right-click the site of interest from the right window, choose Show Messages, and then select an interval of interest. Status message ID 10051, for example, indicates that the package was not available on the distribution point. Detailed troubleshooting of advertisement problems often requires looking at the client logs.

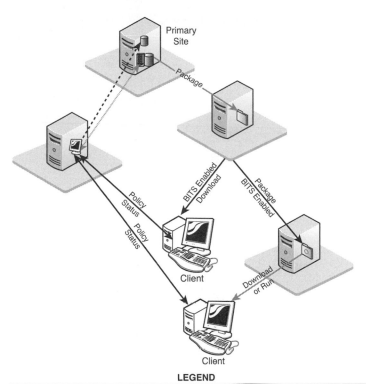

LEGEND

Server Roles in Use	Network Protocols in Use
= Configuration Manager Database	——— = HTTP / HTTPS
= Management Point	——— = SMB
= Distribution Point	······· = SQL over TCP
= Branch Distribution Point	∼∼∼∼∼ = RPC

FIGURE 5.28   The major systems for software distribution and data flow between them. The client–to–management point connection includes policy downloads and status uploads.

Table 5.7 shows some key entries to check in the client logs. Client log files are discussed in Appendix A, "Configuration Manager Log Files."

Configuration Manager provides an option to enable Network Abstraction Layer (NAL) logging, which adds detailed logging of network connection processing to the log for components that use network resources. NAL logging increases the log size substantially and logs many apparent errors that may be misleading; however, it can also be an essential tool for network troubleshooting. In general, you should only enable NAL logging when you need it to troubleshoot a specific issue. Appendix A discusses how to enable NAL logging.

TABLE 5.6   Distribution Manager Status Messages Indicating Possible Network Problems

Severity	Message ID	Description
Error	2302	SMS Distribution Manager failed to process package %1 (package ID = %2).
Error	2307	SMS Distribution Manager failed to access the source directory %1 for package %2.
Error	2328	SMS Distribution Manager failed to copy package %1 from %2 to %3.
Error	2332	SMS Distribution Manager failed to remove package %1 from distribution path %2.
Error	2344	Failed to create virtual directory on the defined share or volume on distribution point %1.

TABLE 5.7   Client Log File Entries Related to Locating and Retrieving Advertised Content

Log File Name	Log File Entry	Description	Troubleshooting Steps
LocationServices .log	Distribution Point=<server name>	Informational. Shows what DP is used for the package, based on the PackageID.	A UNC (Universal Naming Convention) path (e.g., \\<servername>\<share>\<packageID>) indicates an SMB connection. Transfer details will be in FileBITS.log. A URL (e.g., http://<servername>/<directory>/<packageID>) indicates a BITS download. Transfer details will be in DataTransferService.log.
LocationServices .log	Retrieved <local|proxy|default> Management Point	Informational. Shows the MP systems.	None.
PolicyAgent.log	Received delta policy update with <number of> assignments	Informational. Shows the policy download occurred and the number of assignments.	None.
CAS.log	Failed to get DP location...	Possible boundary issue.	Review the LocationServices log.
CAS.log	Download failed for content...	Error communicating with distribution point (DP).	Review the log for additional details. Follow basic network troubleshooting between the client and the DP.
CAS.log	Download failed for download request...	Error communicating with distribution point.	Check BITS functionality on the client; reinstall BITS if necessary.

TABLE 5.7   Client Log File Entries Related to Locating and Retrieving Advertised Content

Log File Name	Log File Entry	Description	Troubleshooting Steps
DataTransfer Service.log	ERROR (0x80070422)	BITS communication failure.	Follow basic network troubleshooting between the client and DP.
FileBITS.log	Encountered error while copying files	SMB error.	Review the log for additional details. Follow basic network troubleshooting between the client and the DP.

Keeping Boundaries Consistent with Network Changes

As changes occur in your network topology, such as new or modified IP subnets, it is important to modify the boundaries of your Configuration Manager sites and protected site systems to reflect these changes. Failure to update ConfigMgr boundaries to reflect network changes is a common cause of problems with software distribution and automatic site assignment. Use appropriate change control procedures to ensure Configuration Manager 2007 stays up to date with your network environment.

If you are using Active Directory for your site boundaries, you can monitor the Windows System event log for specific Event IDs based on the version of Windows Server:

▶ For Windows Server 2003 and Windows Server 2008 domain controllers, look for Event ID 5807, Type: Warning, Source: NETLOGON on each domain controller.

▶ On Windows 2000 domain controllers, the Event ID will be 5778.

This event indicates that one or more computers have connected to the domain controller from an IP address that is not part of a defined Active Directory site. For information on troubleshooting and remediating this issue, see http://support.microsoft.com/kb/889031.

Network Issues Affecting Site Communications

Problems with site-to-site communications can cause problems such as new or modified objects at parent sites not replicated to child sites, and data from child sites not updated at the parent site. An indication of problems with site communications is often a backlog of files in the folders used by the site-to-site communications components:

▶ *<ConfigMgrInstallPath>*\inboxes\schedule.box\outboxes*<sender name>* is the outbox for the sender (where *<sender name>* is the name of the sender; for the standard sender this will be LAN).

Files used by the sender are queued here for processing. A backlog of send request (.srq) files may indicate that the sender is having problems processing requests or a problem connecting or transferring data to another site.

▶ *<ConfigMgrInstallPath>*\inboxes\schedule.box\requests stores send requests before sending them to the sender.

▶ *<ConfigMgrInstallPath>*\inboxes\schedule.box\tosend stores package and instruction files to transfer to another site.

If you find a backlog of files in any of these folders, check the sender log (sender.log) for errors. You may also view the sender status in the ConfigMgr console, under System Center Configuration Manager -> Site Database -> System Status -> Site Status -> Component Status -> SMS_LAN_SENDER.

Summary

This chapter described how Configuration Manager 2007 uses the network. It discussed the protocols used by Configuration Manager as well as configuring the network components. It then considered how you could apply this knowledge to optimize your network utilization and server placement. The chapter looked at some of the details of BITS, a key enabling technology for Configuration Manager, and described how Configuration Manager network discovery can gather data about network resources and potential clients. Finally, it discussed network troubleshooting, and ways to identify network issues that may affect some specific Configuration Manager components and services.

The next chapter describes how to plan your Configuration Manager infrastructure, with a special emphasis on specific new features that present infrastructure planning challenges.

CHAPTER 6

Architecture Design Planning

As you may have already realized from reading Chapter 4, "Configuration Manager Solution Design," and Chapter 5, "Network Design," planning a Configuration Manager (ConfigMgr) implementation is a complex task. When it comes to architecture design planning, you will want to base your Configuration Manager design on your specific organization and the solutions you plan to deliver.

Decision points to consider regarding your environment incorporate information relating to a number of areas:

▶ The business dynamics of your solution

  ▶ Your business objectives

  ▶ The services and solutions you plan to deliver

  ▶ Geographic, language, and cultural considerations

  ▶ Organizational structure

▶ Your Information Technology (IT) environment

  ▶ Business, regulatory, and IT policies that govern operations

  ▶ Security requirements

  ▶ Administrative model

  ▶ Support considerations

▶ Your technical environment

  ▶ Network environment

  ▶ Active Directory environment

  ▶ Server and datacenter infrastructure

▶ Installed client base and hardware refresh cycle

▶ Existing SQL Server deployment

▶ Storage and backup infrastructure

This chapter focuses on infrastructure and solution delivery planning. To apply the material presented here effectively, you will need a good understanding of your environment and organization. The preplanning worksheets included with Configuration Manager product documentation (http://technet.microsoft.com/en-us/library/bb694080.aspx) provide an excellent vehicle for pulling together information about your environment. Here are some additional factors you should consider not specifically addressed in these worksheets:

▶ Regulatory compliance requirements affecting your organization

▶ Configuration management processes in place, especially if your organization has an enterprise Configuration Management Database (CMDB) with which you want to integrate data stored in Configuration Manager

▶ Release management processes that you may want to consider when planning for software distribution, software updates, and operating system (OS) deployment

▶ Enterprise storage architecture, particularly if you are considering a SAN back-end for software distribution files

▶ Enterprise services such as monitoring and backups that are necessary to support your Configuration Manager infrastructure

Microsoft's planning worksheets (http://technet.microsoft.com/en-us/library/bb694186. aspx) are designed to help with your infrastructure planning. The material in this chapter dealing with infrastructure planning is intended to complement the planning worksheets.

The chapter gives emphasis to delivering the following solutions:

▶ Patch Management and Patch Compliance

▶ Mobile Device Management

▶ Internet-Based Client Management (IBCM)

▶ Operating System Deployment (OSD)

▶ Out of Band (OOB) Management

These features either are new to Configuration Manager 2007 or have changed substantially from System Management Server (SMS) 2003. Chapter 2, "Configuration Manager 2007 Overview," presents a more extensive list of new or enhanced features. The features discussed in this chapter present special requirements that may affect your site and hierarchy planning. Proper planning can help you take advantage of these improvements more effectively.

TIP

More about Planning

Several chapters in this book discuss planning aspects. If you have not already, you will want to look at Chapters 4 and 5.

Hierarchy Planning

Once you have a good understanding of your objectives and environment, your first planning task is to design your Configuration Manager hierarchy. A hierarchy consists of one or more ConfigMgr sites, and potentially additional SMS 2003 sites. Although you can have more than one Configuration Manager hierarchy in your organization, you generally will want to organize all your sites into a single hierarchy.

About Sites

Configuration Manager clients receive their policy from their assigned site. Within a site, client agents and other components share a common configuration. As an example, Remote Tools options are enabled on a per-site basis. The site therefore defines a natural administrative boundary for those clients that share configuration options and should be managed together.

Sites also align with geographic and network boundaries. Communications within a site require a high level of network services, whereas communications between sites can take advantage of scheduling, compression, and other optimizations for remote communications. Chapter 5 discusses intersite communications.

Site Codes

Each Configuration Manager site is identified by a unique three-character site code. Site codes can consist of upper- and lowercase letters and/or numeric digits. Be aware of the following restrictions when using site codes:

▶ Avoid using reserved names such as AUX, CON, NUL, PRN (see http://msdn. microsoft.com/en-us/library/aa365247.aspx for the list of reserved filenames), or SMS when choosing site codes.

▶ Avoid reusing site codes previously used in your Configuration Manager hierarchy. Site codes are stored in the site databases of other sites in the hierarchy and in some configurations are saved in Active Directory and WINS. If you were to reuse a site code, it is possible that all references to the old site were not removed completely or are reintroduced from a restored backup. This could cause problems resolving the site.

Designing a Hierarchy

The site at the top of your hierarchy is the *central site*. In some cases, this may be the only site you need. Most large or geographically dispersed organizations will benefit from having additional sites. A simple hierarchy example is shown in Figure 6.1. This figure shows part of a proposed hierarchy design for the domain used in this book,

SCCMUnleashed.com. Not all sites in that domain are shown in Figure 6.1, and some sites may be combined in the final design.

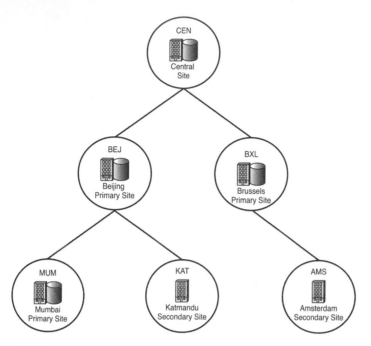

FIGURE 6.1   A possible three-tiered hierarchy for SCCMUnleashed.com sites in Europe and the Asia/Pacific (APAC) region

You may want to consider additional sites in the following instances:

▶ **Locations are separated from other existing or planned sites by wide area network (WAN) links**—Generally, a site should be within a well-connected region, such as a local area network (LAN) environment. To avoid managing an unnecessarily large number of sites, locations with small numbers of computers should generally be part of the existing site with the best connectivity.

▶ **Groups of machines require different client agent settings**—You will want to create a separate site for machines requiring different client agent settings, because client agent settings are configured on a per-site basis. It is possible to override sitewide settings on individual clients using local policy; however, this is not generally recommended because it makes troubleshooting more difficult.

▶ **Support is required for down-level clients**—If sites are in native mode, you may need a separate mixed mode site to support older clients, such as SMS 2003 Service

Pack (SP) 3 clients. Native mode and mixed mode are discussed in the "Planning for Site Security Modes" section of this chapter.

▶ **Multilingual requirements**—Locations that will be using different language versions of the Configuration Manager client and server software should generally be separate sites.

▶ **Scalability considerations**—Regardless of other considerations, very large organizations will need multiple sites for scalability reasons. The maximum number of clients supported by a single site is 100,000.

The best practice for multisite hierarchies is to have a central site with no clients other than the site server itself. All sites other than the central site are joined to a parent site. Each site may have only one parent site but may have more than one child site.

Primary Sites Versus Secondary Sites

ConfigMgr 2007 can incorporate primary and secondary sites in a hierarchy. A *primary site* is a site with its own SQL Server database. Primary sites can have secondary sites or other primary sites as child sites. Configuration Manager clients are assigned to primary sites, and they receive policy from their assigned sites. *Secondary sites* are used at remote locations to provide Configuration Manager services locally to clients assigned to primary sites in the hierarchy. Secondary sites cannot have child sites and they do not have clients assigned to them. Secondary sites are administered from their parent site.

You may decide to add primary sites for the following reasons:

▶ **Administrative advantages**—Each client is assigned to a primary site. Clients receive policies, including client agent settings, from their assigned site. If your clients need different client agent settings than those at the parent site, you may choose to deploy an additional primary site. Secondary sites are administered though their parent site. Delegating administrative privilege to local personnel, such as the ability to distribute software at the site, is simpler at a primary site than a secondary site.

▶ **Hierarchy advantages**—You can disjoin a primary site from its parent site and join it to a different site, but you must reinstall a secondary site to move it in the hierarchy. This is important if your organizational structure frequently changes due to office closures and relocations, mergers and divestitures, and so forth. A primary site can also have child sites; secondary sites cannot.

▶ **Scalability advantages**—With proper design, a primary site can support over 100,000 clients. A secondary site can support around 1,000 clients.

You may decide to use a secondary site based on the following considerations:

▶ **No need to install and support SQL Server**—Primary sites require access to Microsoft SQL Server to access the ConfigMgr database. Unless you already have a SQL Server installation at a primary site, you will need to install SQL Server either on the site server or on a separate server. In either case, this will require additional hardware resources and support efforts.

▶ **Licensing costs**—Currently, secondary sites do not require a Configuration Manager 2007 server license or a SQL Server license. Of course, all site systems require a Windows Server license. Chapter 4 includes a discussion of ConfigMgr licensing.

Planning Your Hierarchy Structure

A consistent principle in Configuration Manager is that a parent site must be at least as advanced in its software version and configuration as its child sites. This is true in terms of both code version and security mode. As an example, a Configuration Manager 2007 SP 1 site can have a child site without SP 1, but could not report to a parent site without SP 1. A Configuration Manager site can have SMS 2003 SP 2 or higher child sites, but cannot have an SMS 2003 parent site. Similarly, a native mode site can have a mixed mode child site, but not vice versa. Figure 6.2 shows some possible parent/child relationships that are allowed and others that are not allowed.

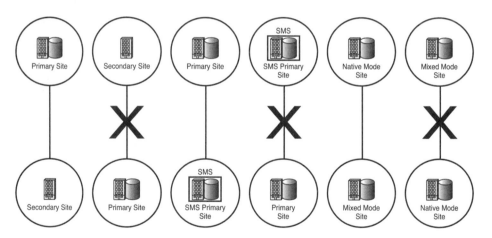

FIGURE 6.2   Examples of parent/child relationships that are allowed and others that are not allowed

You should plan your hierarchy such that upgrades, service packs, and other enhancements can be easily applied, starting from the central site and then proceeding down the hierarchy. You should also consider capacity, bandwidth, and latency issues when deciding how to structure your hierarchy. Figure 6.3 shows an alternate hierarchy for the same sites previously shown in Figure 6.1.

The flatter hierarchy displayed in Figure 6.3 has the following advantages:

▶ Less processing and storage capacity is required in the Beijing (BEJ) and Brussels (BXL) primary sites. With the original hierarchy design, these sites have to process communications and store data from their child sites as well as from local clients.

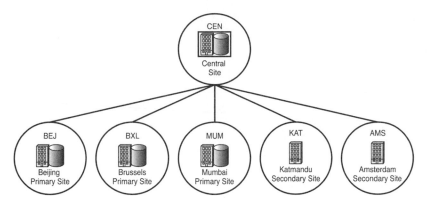

FIGURE 6.3   A possible two-tiered hierarchy for SCCMUnleashed.com sites in Europe and the APAC region

▶ Network communications between the central site and the Amsterdam (AMS), Katmandu (KAT), and Mumbai (MUM) sites as configured in Figure 6 will introduce additional latency because of the need to send data through an intermediate site. This is particularly true if sender scheduling limits the hours for sending certain data. Chapter 5 discusses latency issues.

▶ Overall bandwidth consumption may be lower because communications between the central site and the AMS, KAT, and MUM sites can take the optimum network route, rather than necessarily going through the intermediate primary site. As an example, if your sites are connected through a Multi Protocol Label Switching (MPLS) cloud, traffic between a site and its direct child site requires one trip through the cloud, whereas an intermediate site will store and forward data, which requires an additional trip.

▶ The impact of a site or communications failure affecting the BEJ or BXL site is limited to that site. Site recovery at those sites will be considerably simpler in this model. See Chapter 21, "Backup, Recovery, and Maintenance," for a discussion of site recovery.

▶ Future restructuring may be easier. As an example, if Beijing were part of a divestiture or office closing, the Katmandu site would not need to be reinstalled in the flat hierarchy model.

▶ Legal requirements such as export controls may prohibit certain software or data from traversing certain intermediate sites.

The more structured design in Figure 6.1 also has some advantages:

▶ Software packages, software updates, and operating system images can be distributed using a fan-out mechanism, which reduces the workload of the initiating site and the network link between the initiating site and other sites. For example, a package needed at the BEJ, KAT, and MUM sites can be copied once across the link from the central site to Beijing, and then copied from Beijing to Katmandu and Mumbai. This example uses a central site in North America, and Beijing, Katmandu, and Mumbai are in the Asia/Pacific region. This is an important consideration because the WAN links from the central site to the APAC sites have less available bandwidth than the connections within the APAC region.

▶ Administrators in the APAC region can connect to the BEJ site to administer the KAT secondary site rather than needing to connect to the central site. Similarly, administrators in Europe can administer the AMS secondary site through BXL. Although a relatively flat hierarchy is generally recommended, it may make sense to introduce additional layers into the hierarchy if several sites are in a region that is remote from your central site.

Using SMSMap to Document Your Hierarchy

SMSMap (described at http://technet.microsoft.com/en-us/magazine/cc137998.aspx) is a freeware utility you can use to automatically generate Visio drawings of ConfigMgr 2007 and SMS 2003 sites and site servers. You can run SMSMap from any machine with Microsoft Visio installed. Here are some key points:

▶ As shown in Figure 6.4, you can enter credentials for an account with at least read access to your Configuration Manager site database and connect to any primary site server.

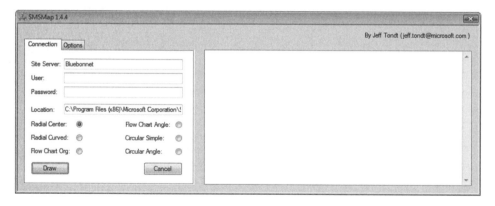

FIGURE 6.4   The SMSMap utility Connection tab

▶ To map your entire hierarchy, connect to the central site. The utility gives you a choice of six layout designs; the Options tab, shown in Figure 6.5, allows you to specify the level of site detail to gather. The program will automatically generate a map showing your site servers and the other details you specify. Once you save the drawing, you can edit it in Visio to suit your preferences.

Jeff Tondt, a Senior Consultant for Microsoft Consulting Services, developed SMSMap, which is available at http://www.tondtware.com/downloads.html. Microsoft *TechNet* magazine took an in-depth look at this valuable utility in July 2007 (http://technet. microsoft.com/en-us/magazine/cc137998.aspx). Several enhancements have been added since that article was written, including support for Configuration Manager.

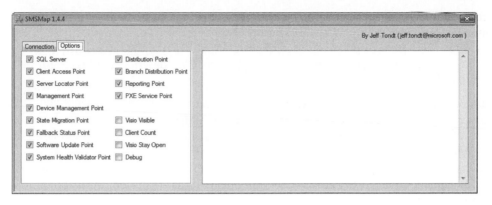

FIGURE 6.5   The SMSMap utility Options tab

Site Planning

After defining some (or all) of your primary and secondary sites, you can begin to plan the site infrastructure and services at each site. The major tasks involved in site planning include determining the site systems to deploy, sizing the hardware for each site system, and determining the boundaries and security mode for the site. These areas are discussed in the next sections.

Site Servers and Site Systems Planning

The server infrastructure is the foundation of your site. The following sections present key issues to consider as you decide how to distribute system roles among servers as well as specifications for server hardware.

Deploying Site System Roles

The minimum server requirement for a Configuration Manager site is a single site server. The site server can be configured for all the site system roles deployed at your site, or you can assign some roles to additional servers. Here are some reasons for assigning site system roles to servers other than the site server:

- ▶ **Network topology**—For sites that span WAN links, you will generally want to make distribution points available at each physical location.

- ▶ **Security**—You may want to move client-facing roles such as the management point (MP), distribution point (DP), and software update point (SUP) off the site server to prevent clients from accessing the site server directly. You will definitely want to do this if you support Internet clients, in which case you would deploy those servers accessible from the Internet in a DMZ (demilitarized zone).

- ▶ **Scalability**—For large sites you may want to distribute the computing load between multiple systems. For very large sites, you may need to use Network Load Balancing (NLB) clusters with certain site systems. Chapter 4 includes a discussion of configuring site systems in large sites. You can also configure the management point and server locator point to use a replica of the site database. Using a SQL replica distributes the load across multiple servers, but introduces replication latency, which increases the time for updates to become available to client systems. See http://technet.microsoft.com/en-us/library/bb693697.aspx for a description of configuring SQL replication for Configuration Manager.

▶ **Management**—In general, you will get sufficient performance if you install SQL Server on your primary site servers and keep the Configuration Manager database local on the site server, provided the site server has adequate hardware resources. Many organizations have SQL database servers already deployed and supported by database administrators. In this case, it may make sense to move the site database to one of these servers, particularly if that will enable you to take advantage of SQL Server clustering and use 64-bit SQL Server editions.

SQL Server is the only site system that supports failover clustering, and it's the only ConfigMgr role that Microsoft recommends running on the 64-bit versions of Windows. Configuration Manager is a database-intensive application. If the database is not on the site server, it is essential to have very good connectivity between the site server and the SQL Server system.

System Requirements

Table 6.1 displays the minimum requirements for Configuration Manager 2007 site systems.

TABLE 6.1   Site System Components and Requirements

Component	Requirement
Processor	733MHz Pentium III minimum (2.0 GHz or faster recommended).
RAM	256MB minimum (1,024MB or more recommended).
Free disk space	5GB minimum formatted with the NTFS file system (15GB or more free recommended if using Operating System Deployment [OSD]).
Operating system	Supported systems include the following:
	Windows Server 2003 Standard or Enterprise Edition Service Pack 2. Both 64-bit and Release 2 (R2) versions are supported.
	Windows Server 2003 Storage Server Edition SP 2 or higher and Windows Server 2003 Web Edition SP 2 or higher are supported for the distribution point and the Configuration Manager console only.
	Client operating systems (Windows XP Service Pack 2 or higher, excluding consumer editions) are supported for the branch distribution point and ConfigMgr console only.
	All site system roles are supported on all versions of Windows Server 2008 except for Server Core. Windows Server 2008 support requires Configuration Manager 2007 SP 1.
	Configuration requirements for Windows Server 2008 site systems are discussed in the "Windows Server 2008 Planning" section of this chapter.

As with any Windows installation, Microsoft only supports hardware components listed on the Windows Hardware Compatibility List (HCL). The HCL for each Windows version is located at http://www.microsoft.com/whdc/hcl/default.mspx. For maximum supportability, it is best to use hardware bearing the Windows Server Hardware logo. Information about Windows logo certified hardware is available in the Windows Server catalog, at http://go.microsoft.com/fwlink/?LinkID=80785.

Other installation requirements include the following:

▶ All site systems must be belong to a Windows 2000, Windows 2003, or Windows Server 2008 Active Directory domain. With the exception of the site database server, Microsoft does not support installing Configuration Manager 2007 site servers or any other site systems on a Windows Server cluster instance. Computers that are physical nodes of a Windows Server cluster instance can be managed as Configuration Manager 2007 clients.

▶ Using a Storage Area Network (SAN) is supported as long as a supported Windows server is attached directly to the volume hosted by the SAN.

Install the site database on the default instance or a named instance of SQL Server, using SQL Server 2005 Service Pack 2 or greater. You can also configure the instance used to host the site database as a SQL Server failover cluster instance.

Configuration Manager 2007 R2 introduces three new site system roles:

▶ Client Status Reporting Host System

▶ Distribution Point for Application Virtualization

▶ Reporting Services Point

The Client Status Reporting Host System role is supported on all versions of Windows Server 2003 SP 1 and above, Windows Server 2008, and on client operating systems (including Windows XP Service Pack 2 or higher, excluding consumer editions). The Reporting Services Point and Distribution Point for Application Virtualization roles are supported on Standard and Enterprise editions of Windows Server 2003 (SP 2 or higher) and Windows Server 2008. The Reporting Services Point role is also supported on the Datacenter editions of Windows Server.

The placement of distribution points (DPs) is especially important in site planning. DPs are generally implemented in the following manner:

▶ One or more standard (unprotected) DPs at the primary network location of the site. Additional distribution points will provide load balancing and redundancy. Clients at the central location and clients not assigned to a protected distribution point will use these unprotected DPs.

▶ Protected distribution points at remote locations with adequate server infrastructure.

▶ Branch DPs at smaller locations without server infrastructure. You may also choose to use a branch DP to take advantage of Background Intelligent Transfer Service (BITS) transfers across the WAN and on-demand package deployment.

Chapter 5 discusses network considerations around the placement of distribution points at remote locations. Distribution point management is discussed in Chapter 14, "Distributing Packages."

Both distribution points and software update points may require substantial storage. Storage requirements for distribution points depend on the number and size of software packages and OS images they host. The "Software Update Planning" section of this chapter discusses storage considerations for software update points.

Heavily used distribution points and software update points will handle a large amount of network traffic; you will want to provision them with the fastest network card your network infrastructure supports.

Using NAS and SAN for DPs and SUPs

Distribution points and software update points can be installed on NAS (Network Attached Storage) devices running the required Windows Server versions. You can also install these system roles on servers using directly connected SAN storage. Enterprise storage vendors offer replication technology that may provide advantages over Configuration Manager package replication or Windows Software Update Service (WSUS) replication, although integrating other replication technologies with Configuration Manager may present some challenges.

You can use third-party replication to copy content to a standard Windows file share and use a Universal Naming Convention (UNC) path to run programs from the share. This model loses some advantages of Configuration Manager software distribution, such as the download-and-run capability and the use of BITS.

When distributing packages to branch distribution points, you can specify the option that the administrator manually copies this package to branch distribution points for those packages that will be copied outside of the ConfigMgr distribution process. Once again, the BITS functionality and download-and-run option are not available for branch distribution points. It is likely that Microsoft will extend this option (that the administrator manually copy this package) to standard distribution points in future releases of Configuration Manager. Using third-party replication to fully deploy packages to child sites also requires the use of courier sender, described in Chapter 5.

Hardware Sizing and Configuration

The minimum/published ("box") hardware specs are far below what you should consider for anything more than a small lab environment. A typical site server for a moderately sized site with 1,000–5,000 clients might have two to four quad core processors and 4GB–8GB of RAM. Because Configuration Manager 2007 is a 32-bit application, Microsoft recommends running it on a 32-bit version of Windows Server for best performance. SQL Server fully supports 64-bit computing, and performs best on a 64-bit platform.

If you use System Center Operations Manager (OpsMgr) to monitor your environment and are considering deploying Configuration Manager on a 64-bit server OS, you should review the information presented at http://wmug.co.uk/blogs/cliffs_blog/archive/2009/02/14/configmgr-monitoring-configmgr-2007-with-operations-manager-2007-in-a-64-bit-environment.aspx.

The issue Cliff Hobbs discusses is that the ConfigMgr client is 32-bit only, so its performance counters are only captured by the 32-bit OpsMgr agent. However, because the OS is 64 bit, this means performance counters are only captured by a 64-bit OpsMgr agent—and you can't install both versions of the agent on a single system.

Similar considerations may apply to other monitoring applications. ConfigMgr 2007 Service Pack 2 will add native 64-bit performance counters to the ConfigMgr client, so it can be monitored along with the OS and other 64-bit applications using a 64-bit Operations Manager agent. Chapter 2 includes a discussion of the planned service pack. Using Operations Manager to monitor Configuration Manager is discussed in Chapter 21.

NOTE

About Addressable Memory for 32-bit Windows

To utilize more than 4GB of physical memory on a 32-bit Windows version, you must use the Enterprise or Datacenter Edition and enable the Physical Address Extension (PAE) feature. For more information about memory support of Windows Server versions, see http://msdn.microsoft.com/en-us/library/aa366778(VS.85).aspx. For information about PAE, see http://msdn.microsoft.com/en-us/library/aa366796(VS.85).aspx.

Configuration Manager is an I/O-intensive application, and it will benefit from the fastest disk subsystem you can provide. Here are some points to keep in mind:

▶ The volume on which you install Configuration Manager and the volume containing the site database will experience the heaviest disk utilization. For best performance using local storage, install Configuration Manager on a separate array from the OS and other applications, using a separate controller if available.

▶ If you install SQL Server locally on the site server, you should also consider separate disk arrays for the SQL Server application and the SQL log files. Corporate standards may specify the RAID (redundant array of independent disks) levels for the OS and application partitions.

Chapter 4 includes specifics on server configuration and disk placement for several site designs. Table 6.2 lists a representative storage configuration for an all-in-one site server.

TABLE 6.2   Suggested Storage Configurations for an All-in-One Site Server

Purpose	Partitions	Physical Storage
OS	C:	RAID 1 (mirrored)
Configuration Manager	E:	RAID 5 (striping with parity)
SQL Server	F:	RAID 5
SQL log files	G:	
WSUS and so on	H:	
Paging File	X:	

Microsoft describes the different RAID types in an article at http://technet2.microsoft.com/ windowsserver/en/library/cb871b6c-8ce7-4eb7-9aba-52b36e31d2a11033.mspx?mfr=true. For optimal performance, implement all RAID arrays at the hardware level. For details on implementing hardware-based RAID, consult the documentation from your hardware vendor. If using SAN storage, you should install Configuration Manager on a dedicated Logical Unit Number (LUN), if available.

NOTE

About Deploying Site Systems on Virtual Machines

All Configuration Manager 2007 site server roles are supported on virtual machines running the appropriate Windows Server versions as guest operating systems on a Microsoft Virtual Server 2005 R2 host with or without SP 1. Hyper-V is also supported, and Cliff Hobbs has an excellent article on migrating your virtual machines to Hyper-V at http://wmug.co.uk/blogs/cliffs_blog/archive/2009/02/10/hyper-v-how-to-migrate-vms-to-hyper-v.aspx.

It is important to review Microsoft's support policy before deploying any ConfigMgr site system roles to Windows Server systems running on other virtualization platforms such as VMware. There is anecdotal evidence that Configuration Manager has been successfully deployed on VMware ESX; however, Microsoft does not guarantee to fully support software running on any non-Microsoft virtualization technology. You should read and consider Microsoft's "Support policy for Microsoft software running in non-Microsoft hardware virtualization software" (http://support.microsoft.com/kb/897615) before deploying any Microsoft software on non-Microsoft virtualization platforms. Virtualization platforms listed in the Server Virtualization Validation Program (SVVP) are supported for all site system roles, subject to the terms of that program. For more information about SVVP, see http://go.microsoft.com/fwlink/?LinkId=134672.

In general, demanding applications such as a site server or a SQL Server database for a large primary site are not good candidates for virtualization. In this context, a site with more than 1,000 clients reporting to it, including clients at child sites, is a poor candidate for a virtualized site server. The authors have seen instances where even a virtualized site server at a site with a few hundred clients may present problems.

Disk defragmentation should be run on a regular basis. It is also important to use a consistent SMS_Def.mof file throughout your hierarchy to allow multithreaded processing of hardware inventory data. For more information about the SMS_Def.mof file, see Chapter 12, "Client Management."

For a detailed discussion of choosing, tuning, and benchmarking hardware, check the following references:

▶ For Windows Server 2003, see http://download.microsoft.com/download/2/8/0/ 2800a518-7ac6-4aac-bd85-74d2c52e1ec6/tuning.doc.

▶ The Windows Server 2008 version is located at http://download.microsoft.com/ download/9/c/5/9c5b2167-8017-4bae-9fde-d599bac8184a/Perf-tun-srv.docx.

Using the SCCM 2007 Capacity Planner

The section "Planning Your Hierarchy Structure" introduced the SMSMap utility by Jeff Tondt. Jeff has written another useful tool for Configuration Manager planning—the SCCM 2007 Capacity Planner. The Capacity Planner provides a set of macro-driven Excel worksheets whose objectives include the following:

► Suggesting edge locations for SCCM Server and SCCM Component Servers. Edge locations are typically the lowest tier sites.

► Suggesting hardware for SCCM Server and SCCM Component Servers.

The tool allows you to enter scenarios about your site hierarchy and assumptions about each site, and it outputs hardware recommendations and other capacity-related information. You can easily try various what-if scenarios, such as replacing a distribution point with a branch distribution point or using a replicated SQL Server database for your management point. Sample scenarios are included that let you play with many possible configurations.

The current version of the tool, available at http://www.tondtware.com/downloads.html, comes with a disclaimer that it is a work in progress. No capacity planning tool can take every factor of your environment and usage into account. The results this tool has given seem pretty realistic, though, and it is a great way to explore various possible configurations. Like SMSMap, this is definitely a tool to try.

Antivirus Scanning

To avoid performance degradation, establish appropriate virus-scanning exclusions for all inboxes on the site server. The individual inboxes are subfolders of the inboxes folder (*%ProgramFiles%*\Microsoft Configuration Manager\Inboxes by default) with .box folder names. Some enterprise antivirus products are capable of applying exclusions selectively to certain processes. In this case, the Configuration Manager processes listed in Chapter 3, "Looking Inside Configuration Manager," should be listed as low-risk processes for access to the inbox folders. You should also consider virus-scanning exclusions for the following areas:

► All server and client log files

► The client cache folders and WMI (Windows Management Instrumentation) folders

► All SQL Server databases and transaction logs

► Site backup files and volume shadow copy files

Chapter 20, "Security and Delegation in Configuration Manager 2007," discusses virus-scanning exclusions in more detail.

Planning for Very Large Sites

Very large sites, especially those with 25,000 or more clients, have some special considerations to include in your planning. Chapter 4 discusses this in detail. You may also want to check Microsoft's documentation at http://technet.microsoft.com/en-us/library/bb932180.aspx.

Planning Site Boundaries

Configuration Manager clients use site boundaries for two purposes:

▶ Automatic client assignment during installation.

▶ Locating services during normal operations. (For more information about client assignment and service location, see Chapter 12.)

It is important to plan and maintain site boundaries that are appropriate to your network topology and do not overlap. Overlapping boundaries will cause problems for Configuration Manager clients.

Automatic site assignment can have unpredictable results when a client is located within the boundaries of more than one site. Overlapping boundaries will also cause problems with software distribution. Clients access content from the distribution points of the site in which they currently reside; having conflicting site boundaries can result in the client failing to locate available content or downloading content from an inappropriate location. You can specify boundaries by Active Directory (AD) sites, Internet Protocol (IP) subnets, IP address ranges, or IPv6 prefixes.

Planning for Site Security Modes

Each Configuration Manager site can be in one of two security modes—native or mixed mode. Here are some reasons you may choose to use native mode:

▶ Native mode sites use mutual, certificate-based authentication between site systems and between clients and servers. Native mode also provides advanced encryption and signing for secure exchanges. This is the most secure option for a Configuration Manager site.

▶ Native mode is required for Internet-based client support.

Here are some reasons to choose to use mixed mode:

▶ Native mode requires a properly implemented Public Key Infrastructure (PKI). PKI design, testing, and implementation involve a major organizational investment and require proper planning. Your PKI deployment should take into account other applications and requirements you may have in addition to your Configuration Manager requirements. Chapter 11, "Related Technologies and References," includes a discussion of PKI.

▶ Mixed mode sites support SMS 2003 SP 3 or higher clients, as well as Windows 2000 clients. Native mode sites do not support these older clients.

▶ Your organization requires WINS (Windows Internet Name Service) for clients to locate their default management point. Chapter 5 explains the reasons you may need to use WINS.

Software Update Planning

All software is subject to possible bugs or design flaws that may introduce security vulnerabilities or other defects into your environment. Software vendors, including Microsoft, regularly release updates, or patches, to their software to address these problems. Software updates may also introduce new or enhanced functionality to software products. Testing software updates and deploying them to a large number of systems in a timely manner is an increasingly important challenge for all IT organizations.

The next sections present an overview of how Configuration Manager components can work together to support your enterprise patch management requirements. They also discuss the infrastructure requirements for Configuration Manager patch management. Chapter 15, "Patch Management," provides detailed guidance on using ConfigMgr software update functionality.

Software Updates Solution Planning

Patch management is a vital component of an enterprise security policy. The average time from the publication of a vulnerability to the appearance of an exploit has gone from several months in the 1990s to just several days. Zero-day exploits, which appear before a patch is released, are increasingly common. You should therefore plan for both standard releases and emergency releases of software updates.

To test patches prior to production implementation, create test collections of machines with a representative cross-section of your hardware and software configurations. Your test plan should include procedures to deploy updates to test collections and monitor both the deployment process and the impact on test machines.

> **NOTE**
>
> **About the Risk of Delaying Software Updates**
>
> Some organizations, including at least one branch of the U.S. armed forces, have determined that the risk for them of postponing patches even briefly outweighs the risk of deploying untested patches. For this reason, they immediately push all newly released patches. You need to carefully evaluate what is right for your security and availability needs.

In addition to the Software Updates capability integrated into Configuration Manager, the following Configuration Manager features are available to support a good patch management and patch compliance solution:

▶ **Collections**—In addition to test collections, you should create and maintain collections for systems that have special considerations for software updates. For example, you may decide to handle software updates to a collection of systems in scope for Sarbanes-Oxley Act (SOX) or HIPAA controls differently due to change control requirements.

▶ **Reports**—Chapter 18, "Reporting," shows some examples of how Configuration Manager reporting capabilities can provide visibility into patch management and compliance.

▶ **Maintenance Windows**—A new feature of Configuration Manager—maintenance windows—gives you the ability to specify times during which Configuration Manager will apply changes to systems. If a system belongs to a collection with defined maintenance windows, then software updates, operating system (OS) deployments, and software distribution are suppressed during times that fall outside a maintenance window. For emergency deployments, distributions can be set to ignore maintenance windows.

▶ **Wake On LAN and Intel Active Management Technology (AMT)**—These features allow you to send software updates, advertisements, and OS deployments to systems that are online but powered down. You should consider deploying these services to support your Software Updates solution.

The "Out of Band (OOB) Management Planning" section of this chapter discusses Wake On LAN and AMT.

Auditing and Regulatory Compliance

Patch management for systems that store and process financial or other regulated data is increasingly a concern for auditors and management groups responsible for regulatory compliance. The Sarbanes-Oxley Act requires all publicly traded companies in the United States to certify the integrity of controls affecting their financial statements, including controls in place on IT systems. Similar requirements are part of various other regulatory requirements. Patch management is a key control that auditors typically investigate. Patch management at U.S. government agencies is specifically identified for review by the Inspector General to ensure compliance with the Federal Information Security Management Act and Agency Privacy Management (see http://www. whitehouse.gov/omb/memoranda/fy2007/m07-19.pdf for details).

Audit concerns around patch management not only include ensuring that software is regularly patched, but also that processes are in place to appropriately identify, evaluate, and prioritize relevant patches and that proper change control procedures are followed. Patch management presents both a responsibility and an opportunity for IT professionals to work together with upper management, auditors, and other groups responsible for regulatory compliance. A perspective on patch management for financial professionals is presented in "Patch Management: No Longer Just an IT Problem," at http://www.nysscpa.org/cpajournal/2007/1107/essentials/p68.htm.

Your patch management solution should also integrate with the following IT processes:

▶ **Change management**—Deploying software updates on a scheduled or emergency basis should be subject to the controls of your change management process. The use of maintenance windows makes it simpler for you to comply with many change management policies.

▶ **Configuration management and release management**—Inputs from these two processes should help you to systematically identify vulnerabilities that may apply to your environment. They can also help you identify baselines against which patches need to be tested and to determine which systems and software store and process regulated data.

▶ **Security risk management**—Prioritizing risks and maintaining and staying current with known vulnerabilities and exploits are essential to effective patch management practices. An effective security risk management program will also help in identifying mitigating factors that may allow some patches to be deferred until regular maintenance or the release of a new build.

Software Updates Architecture

Each Configuration Manager primary site that provides software update services to clients must have an active SUP. ConfigMgr clients use the active SUP as follows:

▶ The client system connects to the SUP to run vulnerability scans.

▶ The client then retrieves any required patches from the distribution point and applies the patches to the client system.

The SUP is an optional system role in a secondary site. If a secondary site does not have an active SUP, clients residing in the boundaries of the site will use the SUP at the parent site. The advantage of configuring an active SUP at a secondary site is that it reduces network bandwidth consumption on the link between the site and its parent. The SUP system role is configured on a server with WSUS 3.0 installed.

How Software Updates Work

The active SUP at the central site synchronizes with the Microsoft Updates Internet site. The active SUP in every other site synchronizes with the active SUP at its parent site.

Intranet clients run vulnerability scans from the active SUP at their local site. If the site is in native mode and the active SUP is accessible from the Internet, you can configure the active SUP to accept connections from clients on the Internet as well as intranet clients. If your active SUP does not accept Internet connections, you can configure a separate Internet-based SUP. Internet-based SUPs at secondary sites are not supported and do not work, although the user interface allows you to configure them. Figure 6.6 shows some options for Software Updates synchronization and client support.

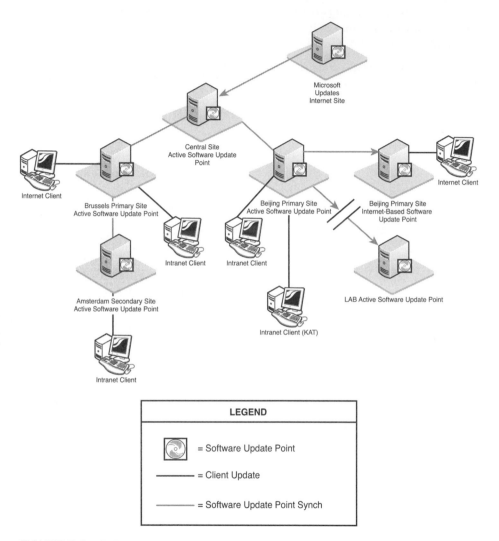

FIGURE 6.6   Software Updates synchronization architecture

In Figure 6.6, the active SUP for the Brussels (BXL) primary site is configured to accept both Internet and intranet access. Katmandu does not have an active SUP, so clients synchronize with the parent site. The LAB site shown is a separate hierarchy on an isolated network. Software updates are exported to an external hard drive and imported in the lab.

NOTE

About Environments with Standalone WSUS

Do not configure the WSUS functionality on your SUP outside of ConfigMgr. ConfigMgr will overwrite any settings configured in WSUS. You also should remove any group policy for WSUS that might affect ConfigMgr clients. Clients with WSUS settings established by group policy cannot be managed by ConfigMgr software updates. For additional information about software updates and WSUS, see Chapter 15.

The storage requirements for software update points depend on the software update point component properties. You choose which products, classifications, and languages to support:

▶ Currently supported products include all supported versions of Windows (Windows 2000 and higher), Microsoft Office products, server products such as Exchange, ISA, and SQL Server, and Microsoft security products. Microsoft does not currently provide updates for third-party products as part of the catalog. Independent software vendors and application developers can use the System Center Updates Publisher (SCUP) to integrate their updates with ConfigMgr. For information about SCUP, go to the Microsoft Downloads Center (http://www.microsoft.com/downloads) and search for **System Center Updates Publisher (SCUP) 4.0**.

▶ Here are the classifications:

  ▶ Critical Updates (non-security-related patches fixing major defects)

  ▶ Definition Updates (for items such as virus signatures)

  ▶ Drivers

  ▶ Feature Packs (for new or enhanced functionality)

  ▶ Security Updates

  ▶ Service Packs (major rollups with full regression testing)

  ▶ Tools

  ▶ Update Rollups (combine multiple fixes with basic regression testing)

  ▶ Updates (all other non-security fixes)

▶ Approximately 25 language versions are available

> **NOTE**
>
> **About Managing Malware Signature Files**
>
> The minimum synchronization time for ConfigMgr software updates is 24 hours. The 24-hour time period is not suitable for virus definition files and similar updates required by anti-malware programs, because these files may need to be updated on a more urgent basis. ConfigMgr Software Updates is therefore not a supported solution for managing signature files for Forefront Client Security and other anti-malware products.

Using WSUSutil

An alternative to configuring an SUP to participate in a synchronization hierarchy is scheduling or manually initiating export and import operations using the WSUSutil utility. See http://technet.microsoft.com/en-us/library/bb680473.aspx for procedures to synchronize updates using WSUSutil. You might choose to use WSUSutil to synchronize software update points in an isolated lab without network connectivity, or to take advantage of third-party replication tools in a SAN environment.

Device Management Planning

The proliferation of smartphones, PDAs, and other mobile devices presents a wide range of challenges and opportunities to IT organizations. Applications on these devices, along with access to corporate email, instant messaging, and line-of-business applications, are vital to the productivity of an increasingly mobile workforce. Devices such as point-of-sale systems and RFID scanners play business critical roles in many enterprises. To effectively deploy and support mobile devices, it is essential to implement device configuration standards, efficiently install applications to those devices, and secure both data on the devices and connections into the enterprise network.

A number of point products (products providing a solution to a single problem) exist for mobile device management. Using Configuration Manager for device management has several advantages over using a separate device management solution:

▶ You can leverage the same infrastructure you have deployed, licensed, and supported for computer management.

▶ Device data will be integrated into your Configuration Manager database.

▶ Configuration Manager enables you to use a consistent approach for managing all systems.

Configuration Manager 2007 device management extends a subset of ConfigMgr client services to a variety of mobile devices running the Windows Mobile and Windows Embedded CE operating systems. A complete list of supported versions is located at http://technet.microsoft.com/en-us/library/bb693782.aspx. The R2 release adds support for Windows Mobile 6.1.

Some point products offer a more extensive set of device management features than Configuration Manager provides, and they support a more extensive array of devices. You should consider the range of devices you need to support and your management needs, as well as cost, in deciding on a device management solution.

Using Configuration Manager for device management provides several benefits:

- ▶ Hardware and software inventory supply data about the mobile devices you support and the applications installed on those devices:
  - ▶ Although hardware inventory on PCs relies on configuration data exposed through WMI, because mobile devices do not support WMI, this limits the information you can collect. Basic device information gathered includes CPU, device name and ID, memory, phone number, user, and OS details. This is essential data for targeting software distribution and asset management.
  - ▶ Software inventory is similar to software inventory for PC clients.
- ▶ File collection allows you to back up files from mobile devices and acquire file-based data from mobile devices for use in enterprise systems. Typical file collection tasks include centralizing contact information and acquiring data stored in files on embedded systems.
- ▶ Software distribution enables you to deploy Windows Mobile, Windows CE, and Pocket PC–based applications needed by mobile workers.
- ▶ Mobile device configuration items allow you to enforce options such as device locking and password options on mobile devices in your enterprise.

Windows CE Operating Systems

In the early 1990s, Microsoft undertook two innovative but unsuccessful attempts to create Windows-based handheld devices. In 1994, Microsoft combined the development teams to form the Windows CE team. Two years later, Microsoft released the first version of Windows CE for the then nascent PDA market. The Windows CE kernel is not based on the Windows kernel, but is designed to provide Windows-like functionality with minimal computing resources.

Over the years a variety of operating systems and devices based on the CE kernel have been released under brands such as Windows CE, Palm PC, Pocket PC, Smartphone, and Windows Mobile. Today's Windows CE core supports component-based, embedded, real-time operating systems requiring minimal storage.

Two distinct families of operating systems are now based on Windows CE technology:

- ▶ **Windows Mobile family**—Designed for smartphones and PDAs
- ▶ **Windows Embedded CE**—Used in a wide variety of embedded applications.

For more information on Windows Mobile, see http://www.microsoft.com/Windowsmobile/default.mspx. For additional information on Windows Embedded CE, see http://www.microsoft.com/windows/embedded/products/windowsce/default.mspx.

About XP Embedded Clients

In addition to Windows CE Embedded, Microsoft offers an embedded OS based on the XP kernel. Windows XP Embedded has a much larger memory and storage footprint than the CE Embedded version, and it's designed for more capable and complex systems such as industrial robots and advanced set-top boxes. You can manage these devices with the standard ConfigMgr client. If you need to manage XP Embedded clients, consider the following specific points:

▶ XP Embedded clients will appear in the All Windows XP Clients collection by default. You should create a collection based on the Windows Management Instrumentation (WMI) attribute OS_Product Suite = 64 to manage your XP Embedded clients. For information about creating collections, see Chapter 14.

▶ Many XP Embedded clients have special attributes you will want to inventory that are not included in the standard hardware inventory. You will want to add custom classes to capture this inventory data. Chapter 3 discusses adding custom classes to your inventory.

▶ You must disable the XP Embedded Service Pack 2 Feature Pack 2007 disk protection features during software distribution and software updates. To do this securely, you should first reboot to a clean configuration to clear any malware that might be in RAM. You should also re-create the hibernation file after updates. Re-creating the hibernation file is required if the protected partition has been updated and may require manual intervention.

For more information about Windows XP Embedded, see http://www.microsoft.com/windows/embedded/products/wexpe/default.mspx.

Communicating with Site Systems

Mobile devices communicate with site systems through the HTTP/HTTPS protocol. A Configuration Manager site must be in native security mode to manage Internet-based mobile devices. Mobile devices connected through a VPN gateway can receive services from mixed mode sites; however, this configuration requires configuring Internet Information Services (IIS) for anonymous access on the distribution point.

Three Configuration Manager site systems communicate directly with mobile devices:

▶ **Mobile Device Management Point (MDMP)**—Mobile devices receive policy from the MDMP and send inventory, state, and status messages as well as collected files to the MDMP. Before configuring an MDMP, first configure the server as a management point and have IIS installed with BITS and WebDAV (Web-based Distributed Authoring and Versioning) enabled. To enable a management point for device support, check the Allow devices to use this management point box on the management point's properties page, as shown in Figure 6.7.

This page is located in the Configuration Manager console under System Center Configuration Manager -> Site Database -> Site Management -> *<Site Code> <Site Name>* -> Site Settings -> Site System -> *<Site System>*.

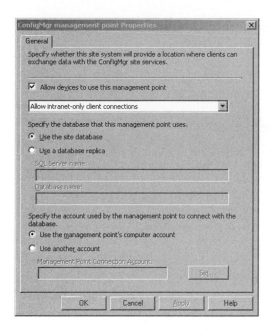

FIGURE 6.7   The device management point's properties page

▶ **Distribution Point**—Mobile devices download content from distribution points, much like standard clients. To support mobile devices, a distribution point must have the Allow clients to transfer content from this distribution point using BITS, HTTP, and HTTPS option enabled. In addition, if the site is in mixed mode, you must enable the Allow clients to connect anonymously option for device support. Enable these options on the General tab of the distribution point's properties page, displayed in Figure 6.8.

To access this page, navigate to System Center Configuration Manager -> Site Database -> Site Management -> *<Site Code> <Site Name>* -> Site Settings -> Site System -> *<Site System>* in the Configuration Manager console. Although you must enable BITS on the distribution point, devices do not actually use BITS to download content.

▶ **Fallback Status Point (FSP)**—A mobile device can contact an FSP to report status if it is unable to contact its management point.

Installing Client Software

Just as the Configuration Manager client must be installed on managed computers, client software must be installed on mobile devices before they can receive Configuration Manager services. The options available to install the mobile device client depend on whether or not your devices synchronize with a PC through Mobile Device Center for Windows Vista or use ActiveSync for Windows XP.

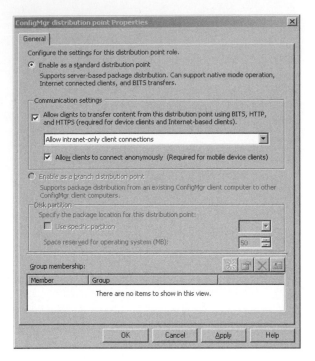

FIGURE 6.8   Device management settings on the distribution point's properties page

---

TIP

About Windows Device Synchronization Technologies

For more information about Mobile Device Center and ActiveSync, see
http://go.microsoft.com/fwlink/?LinkId=81724.

Using Mobile Device Center or ActiveSync simplifies the installation process via a platform-agnostic installation folder. The client installation program (DMClientXfer.exe) on the synching PC will automatically select and install the correct version of the mobile client for the OS on the device. To distribute the mobile device client to a device that synchronizes with a PC, the following options are available:

▶ You can copy the installation folder to the PC and manually run DMClientXfer.exe from the connected device.

▶ If the PC is a Configuration Manager client, you can use software distribution to deploy an advertisement to the PC, which will automatically initiate setup when the device synchronizes.

For those devices that do not synchronize with a PC though Mobile Device Center or ActiveSync, you will need to create a platform-specific installation folder with the correct versions of the setup files. You then place the folder on a location that is accessible to the device, such as a memory card or network share. You can initiate the platform-specific setup program (DMInstaller *<platform type>*.exe) manually from the device. Regardless of the installation method used, the installation folder must contain the following items in addition to the client setup files:

▶ The mobile client settings file, DMCommonInstaller.ini, for installations through a Mobile Device Center or ActiveSync-connected PC, or ClientSettings.ini for other installations. The settings file contains installation options, information needed to contact the Configuration Manager site, certificate metadata, and other information.

▶ Any required certificates for native or server authentication mode.

For detailed mobile client deployment procedures, see http://technet.microsoft.com/en-us/library/bb680634.aspx.

After installing the client, you can send upgrades over the air using ConfigMgr's software distribution functionality.

Configuring Client Agent Settings

The Mobile Device Client Agent settings control the schedule, options for policy downloads, and inventory. You can configure these settings on the properties page under System Center Configuration Manager -> Site Database -> Site Management -> *<Site Code>* *<Site Name>* -> Site Settings -> Client Agents -> Device Client Agent in the ConfigMgr console. Figure 6.9 shows the default settings for the General tab of the client agent properties page, which controls the policy download schedule and retry settings.

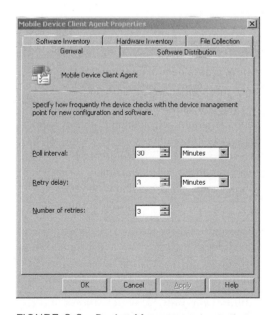

FIGURE 6.9   Device Management agent general properties

Figure 6.10 shows how to enable file collection and collect all files with the .log extension. The remaining tabs are used to enable or disable hardware and software inventory and software distribution, and to set the frequency of hardware inventory.

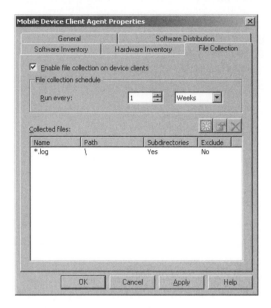

FIGURE 6.10   Configuring the Device Management agent to collect log files

Planning for Internet-Based Clients

Most organizations have users working from home or remote offices without a direct connection to the enterprise network. Mobile workers will also use laptops at locations that are on the network and at remote locations. In other cases, systems such as kiosk computers or point-of-sale systems require remote management. As long as these computers have a connection to the Internet, Configuration Manager provides two options for managing them, using either a Virtual Private Network (VPN) or Internet-Based Client Management (IBCM), as discussed in the next sections.

Choosing a Solution for Internet-Based Clients

SMS 2003 and earlier versions required a VPN connection to manage computers without a direct physical connection to your enterprise network. To establish a VPN connection, client computers or other devices authenticate with a gateway on your network across an unsecure network, generally the Internet. Once the client is authenticated, it establishes an encrypted session (or *tunnel*) through which private communications can take place. You can use VPN connections to support all Configuration Manager 2007 features.

Configuration Manager 2007 provides a new capability called IBCM, which allows you to deliver certain services directly over the Internet without requiring a VPN connection. VPN services require a significant investment in infrastructure and support. Even if you have a VPN in place and available to all client systems, there are reasons why it may not be an ideal vehicle for delivering Configuration Manager services:

▶ Client systems must make an additional connection to the gateway.

▶ Challenges in managing the VPN address space as part of your site boundaries.

However, depending on your business requirements and existing infrastructure, a VPN-based solution may be the best way to manage computers that must connect through the Internet. VPN supports all of Configuration Manager's features, whereas IBCM supports only a subset. IBCM also requires a PKI deployment and in most configurations requires deploying an additional server. You should consider the capabilities of both solutions when deciding how to meet the needs of your Internet-based clients.

IBCM Features and Requirements

IBCM supports the following Configuration Manager features:

▶ Hardware and software inventory, including file collection

▶ State and status reporting

▶ Software Distribution

▶ Software Updates

▶ Software Metering

IBCM does not support other Configuration Manager features such as client deployment, OSD, Remote Tools, and Network Access Protection (NAP).

Sites supporting Internet-based clients must be primary sites in native mode with certificates deployed to servers and clients. See the "Certificate Requirements Planning" section of this chapter for a discussion of certificate requirements planning. The systems that directly support Internet-based clients must be accessible from the Internet via HTTP/HTTPS (complete firewall requirements are provided at http://technet.microsoft.com/en-us/library/bb633122.aspx). Systems that may provide services for Internet clients include the following:

▶ **Management point**—This is the only required role, providing policy to clients and receiving inventory, state, status, and other data from clients.

▶ **Distribution points**—One or more standard distribution points are required for software deployment. These distribution points must be site systems rather than server shares. Internet-facing branch distribution points are not supported.

▶ **Fallback status point**—The FSP is recommended to allow clients that are having problems contacting the management point to report status to the site.

▶ **Software update point**—The SUP is required for software updates.

Chapter 2 previously introduced these site systems.

Each of these systems require configuration to accept connections from the Internet, and the site system properties must include a Fully Qualified Domain Name (FQDN) that is resolvable from the Internet. Internet-facing site systems cannot be protected site systems.

Deploying Servers to Support Internet-Based Clients

For security reasons, systems accessible to Internet-based clients should always be deployed in a DMZ (generally referred to in the product documentation as a *perimeter network*). Microsoft supports several scenarios for site and server placement:

▶ A site that does not support intranet clients and spans the perimeter network and intranet. The site server is in the intranet. All Internet-based site systems are in the perimeter network and accept connections for clients connecting over the Internet.

▶ A site that does not support intranet clients and is in the perimeter network only.

▶ A site supporting both Internet and intranet clients, which spans the perimeter network and intranet. All Internet-based site systems are in the perimeter network and support connections for clients connecting over the Internet. A second management point, SUP, FSP, and additional distribution points, along with other site systems, are in the intranet for those clients connecting over the intranet.

▶ A site that supports both Internet and intranet clients, and bridges the perimeter network and the intranet. There is a single management point. This is both the site's default management point and the Internet-based client's management point.

These scenarios are described in detail in http://technet.microsoft.com/en-us/library/bb693824.aspx.

When designing your solution, your primary consideration will be the level of security you need. Providing services through the Internet potentially exposes you to unauthorized access. You should involve any necessary resources to ensure that proper security risk management and secure network design principles are followed.

Each of the scenarios Microsoft supports involves three security zones:

▶ The Internet (least secure)

▶ The perimeter network (more secure)

▶ The internal network (most secure)

The purpose of the perimeter network is to protect your internal network, where your most valuable systems and data reside. If a host in the perimeter network is compromised, it is the job of the inner firewall, the one between the perimeter network and the internal network, to protect your high-value assets. One basic principle of network security is that allowing any connections to be initiated from a less secure zone to a more secure zone is a risk. As you step through the supported scenarios, focus on the allowed protocols at the inner firewall. The options that allow inbound connections are likely to be less secure than those that do not.

A special risk is introduced by solutions that bridge the perimeter network and the internal network. In this case, you do not have a dedicated inner firewall. If one of the bridging hosts is compromised, it could be used to attack the internal network. If you choose to implement this model, you should take special care to harden the systems as much as possible, monitor them closely, and verify that you have disabled routing between the network cards. Many organizations have security policies that forbid using servers to bridge security zones.

Take your own secure network architecture into account as you consider each of the scenarios Microsoft supports for deploying servers to support Internet clients, because you may need to adapt these scenarios to meet your own security requirements. Carefully consider the relative advantages of each model.

Using a Dedicated Site for Internet Clients

The first option to consider is whether to have a dedicated site for Internet clients. Using a dedicated site provides some options that simplify your security planning. If you use a dedicated Internet-only site, you should have only an Internet-based management point and not a default MP. The most secure configuration is a dedicated site, totally within the perimeter network, that is absolutely separate from the hierarchy supporting intranet clients. This configuration, shown in Figure 6.11, does not require connectivity between the Internet-accessible systems and your internal network.

Maintaining a Separate Active Directory Forest

For complete isolation, you would need a separate Active Directory forest in the perimeter network. This configuration does not support clients that connect both as Internet and intranet clients. Even if you have mobile clients that sometimes connect directly to your network, or clients that sometimes establish a VPN connection, you will need to configure them as Internet-only clients, which will have the more limited IBCM management capabilities.

Allowing Site-to-Site Communications Across an Inner Firewall

A dedicated site for Internet clients can also reside in the perimeter network but be joined to a parent site in your internal network. This configuration requires you to allow site-to-site communications across your inner firewall.

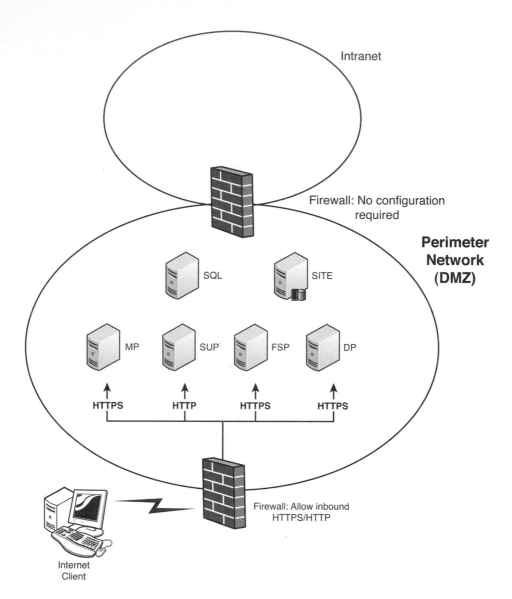

FIGURE 6.11   Server placement and firewall configuration for Internet-based client management

Having a Site Span the Internal Network and Perimeter Network

You can configure a site to span the internal network and the perimeter network. A site that spans these zones can be dedicated to Internet clients only or can have both Internet and intranet clients. In this configuration, the site server and SQL database server are in the internal network. You can provide services to intranet clients either by deploying separate client-facing systems in the internal network or by configuring site systems in your DMZ to accept connections from both intranet and Internet clients and then allowing outbound client connections though the internal firewall.

Configure Internet-facing systems using the option Allow only site server initiated data transfers from this site system. You can configure this setting on the site system properties page, found under System Center Configuration Manager -> Site Database -> Site Management -> *<Site Code> <Site Name>* -> Site Settings -> Site Systems -> *<Site System>* -> Site System, which is displayed in Figure 6.12. This configuration eliminates the need to allow inbound connections to the site server though the inner firewall.

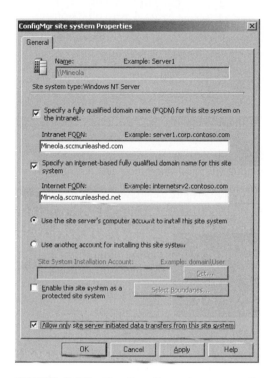

FIGURE 6.12   Use the site system properties page to specify the site server will initiate communications

You can also eliminate the need for inbound SQL connections by deploying a SQL replica in the DMZ, which requires considerable configuration but can enhance security. Configuring site database replication is described in Chapter 8, "Installing Configuration Manager 2007," and at http://technet.microsoft.com/en-us/library/bb693697.aspx.

Certificate Requirements Planning

Configuration Manager requires a properly configured Public Key Infrastructure for native mode operations. Mixed mode sites can also use certificates for a limited set of functions without a PKI implementation. The next section ("About PKI") briefly introduces basic PKI concepts. It then discusses how ConfigMgr uses PKI and how you should plan to deploy a PKI solution or leverage your existing PKI for ConfigMgr.

About PKI

Public key cryptography, discussed in depth in Chapter 11, is currently the principal cryptographic standard for secure communications on the Internet and on private networks. The algorithms behind public key cryptography allow messages to be encrypted and decrypted using a key pair. The keys in the pair are numbers that are mathematically related such that a message encrypted with one of the keys in the pair can only be decrypted with the other key. Each user (or system) that uses public key cryptography has a unique key pair. One of the keys in the pair is kept secret. This is the private key. The other key, the public key, is published to make it available to other users. You can use key pairs in two different ways:

▶ You can encrypt a message with a user's public key and send it to the user. Only the user with the matching private key can decrypt and read it.

▶ You can sign a message by encrypting it with your private key. Users who have your public key can decrypt and read the message. Because the recipients know that the message was encrypted with your private key, they can be confident that you are the sender and the message has not been tampered with.

On a small scale, it would be possible for all users to know each other's public keys. This is not practical on a larger scale. To allow the use of public key cryptography in large environments, including the Internet, PKI technology was developed. PKI provides a framework for securing both session-based and messaging communications using a hierarchy of Certificate Authorities (CAs). At the top of a PKI hierarchy is the root CA, a system whose public key is known and trusted by all parties who will participate in that PKI. A CA is used to issue binary objects known as *certificates* to other systems or users. Certificates can be issued for specific purposes and validate the identity of the certificate holder. Because a compromised root CA would compromise the integrity of an organization's entire PKI, the root CA is generally kept offline and not used to issue certificates directly to users and systems. A set of subordinate CAs receive certificates from the root, which allow them to also issue certificates.

Planning to Use PKI with Configuration Manager

In native mode, most client-to-server communications are mutually authenticated, signed, and encrypted using the HTTPS protocol. Here are the principal types of certificates used by native mode sites:

▶ Client certificates, used by the client to authenticate to site systems

▶ Web server certificates, used by site systems to authenticate to clients

▶ The document-signing certificate, used by the site server to ensure the integrity of client policy and content

All native mode ConfigMgr systems that communicate by HTTPS require PKI certificates. These systems include the following:

▶ Clients

▶ Management points

▶ Standard distribution points when using the download-and-run option

▶ Software update points

▶ State migration points

Each server supporting HTTPS requires a certificate based on the Microsoft web server template or equivalent. All computer client systems require a computer or workstation certificate. Mobile device clients require an authenticated session certificate. Detailed descriptions of the required certificates can be found at http://technet.microsoft.com/en-us/library/bb680733(TechNet.10).aspx. All communications with Internet-based clients and Internet-based device clients require PKI certificates on the clients and site systems, except for sending status messages to the FSP. Status messages sent to the FSP are essentially a call for help when a client is having problems contacting the site, so HTTP is used in case certificate-related issues are causing the problem.

> **NOTE**
>
> **About Encrypting Communications Between Servers**
>
> Server-to-server communication is not encrypted in either native mode or mixed mode sites. To secure communications between servers, you should consider using IP Security (IPSec). Chapter 20 discusses the use of IPSec on ConfigMgr.

PKI and Native Mode Sites

In addition to supporting HTTPS communications between clients and site systems, native mode ConfigMgr sites use PKI to support OSD for signing policies and task sequences, and for client certificate deployment. Here are some key points:

▶ To sign policies, the site server must have a document-signing certificate installed.

▶ For OSD task sequences, you must install a client authentication certificate to provide authentication to the management point temporarily until the client is fully provisioned with its permanent certificate.

▶ A root certificate from each root CA supporting ConfigMgr site systems must be imported into the site configuration for certificate signing. For information about configuring OSD, see Chapter 19, "Operating System Deployment."

For Configuration Manager clients and site systems to operate successfully in native mode, all systems must trust the CAs that issue the certificate, as well as any root and intermediate CAs in the certificate hierarchy. Certificates issued by certain well-known public authorities are trusted by default on all Windows computers and many mobile devices. If you use your own PKI, however, you will need to make sure that your CA certificates are added to the trusted store on all systems. In an Active Directory forest, you can use AD services to achieve this. You also need to deploy the certificates themselves to all site systems and clients. Using Microsoft Certificate Services with an Enterprise Certification Authority simplifies many of these operations; however, you can use any PKI supporting x.509 version 3 certificates. Chapter 11 discusses PKI management.

Certificates and Mixed Mode Sites

You can configure mixed mode sites to use self-signed server certificates to secure client communications with the management point and state migration point only. Mixed mode sites can also use certificates to sign policy and sign content. Clients will verify the signature if the option to download content from the distribution point and run locally is selected in the advertisement properties. Configuration Manager 2007 manages certificates used by mixed mode sites, and you cannot use these certificates outside ConfigMgr operations. Using certificates in mixed mode sites does not require a PKI infrastructure.

Windows Server 2008 Planning

Support for Windows Server 2008 clients or site systems require Configuration Manager 2007 SP 1. There are no special considerations for Windows Server 2008 client support on servers running full installations of Windows Server 2008. Microsoft supports the client on Windows Server 2008 core installations; however, Desired Configuration Management and Out of Band Management do not work with the core build. There are several items to note regarding Windows Server 2008 site systems:

▶ You cannot install site systems on Windows Server 2008 core installations.

▶ Site servers, management points, distribution points, branch distribution points, and reporting points require options not enabled by default on Windows 2008 servers.

The article at http://technet.microsoft.com/en-us/library/cc431377(TechNet.10).aspx provides step–by-step instructions on how to configure Windows Server 2008 for site system roles. Here are some specific features and settings you must enable:

▶ IIS, BITS, and WebDAV are required for management points and BITS-enabled distribution points. WebDAV is not an included component in Windows Server 2008. You can download and install WebDAV from http://go.microsoft.com/fwlink/?LinkId=108052.

▶ After installing WebDAV, use IIS Manager to enable WebDAV and to create and enable an authoring rule to allow read access to all content for all users. You also need to configure the following WebDAV settings:

   ▶ Allow anonymous property queries

   ▶ Allow property queries with infinite depth

   ▶ Allow access to hidden files (on BITS-enabled distribution points only)

   ▶ Disallow custom properties

▶ You must modify the requestFiltering options on BITS-enabled distribution points. Edit the configuration file %*windir*%\System32\inetsrv\config\applicationHost.config as follows:

  ▶ Locate the <requestFiltering> section.

  ▶ For each file extension that will be included in packages on that distribution point, change the value of the allowed attribute from False to True.

Using PowerShell to Identify Required File Extensions

If you have a set of existing packages in a source folder or on a distribution point, you can use PowerShell to obtain a list of the file extensions in your packages. Enter the following at the PowerShell prompt:

```
Get-ChildItem <pkgshare> -recurse | Select-Object Extension | Sort-Object
Extension | Get-Unique -asString
```

Here, *<pkgshare>* is the local or UNC path of your package folder. For example, if your packages were stored on \\Mineola\SMSPKGE$, you would enter the following:

```
Get-ChildItem \\Mineola\SMSPKGE$ -recurse | Select-Object Extension | Sort-
Object Extension | Get-Unique —asString
```

Windows PowerShell is a powerful and flexible scripting and shell language included on the installation disk for Windows Server 2008. PowerShell is also available for download for Windows XP, Windows Vista, and Windows Server 2003 SP 1. PowerShell offers numerous enhancements over both the MS-DOS-style command and batch file language and VBScript, and it's rapidly becoming an essential tool for administering Windows and Microsoft server applications. Microsoft has added extensions to support functionality in applications including Operations Manager 2007, Exchange Server 2007, and Virtual Machine Manager.

You can visit the Windows PowerShell Technology Center at http://www.microsoft.com/windowsserver2003/technologies/management/powershell/default.mspx for additional information about PowerShell. The article at http://www.windows7th.com/?p=22028 includes a nice description of using PowerShell V2 with the ConfigMgr provider.

▶ Site servers and branch distribution points use remote differential compression (RDC) to generate package signatures and perform signature comparison. RDC is not installed by default on Windows Server 2008 but can be installed through Server Manager.

▶ Finally, you must add ASP.NET on reporting points. This can be done through Server Manager. You should choose the Windows Authentication security option for ASP.NET.

Configuration Manager also takes advantage of the Windows Deployment Service (WDS) in Windows Server 2008. This provides advanced functionality such as multicast operating system deployments. Chapter 19 discusses Configuration Manager integration with WDS.

9

Operating System Deployment Planning

Like its SMS predecessors, Configuration Manager provides a range of useful functionality. At each point in its history, though, SMS had a "killer app" that drove its adoption.

In the early days of SMS the one thing IT departments wanted was remote control. As remote control became ubiquitous and eventually built in to Windows, it was no longer as compelling a reason to deploy SMS. The release of SMS 2003 brought a new killer app that met a critical need facing the IT community—patch management. Although the need for effective patch management has become even more critical and the Configuration Manager feature set supporting it has been improved, it may well be that the most important new feature of Configuration Manager 2007 is OSD.

Provisioning new systems to corporate standards is a repetitive chore without suitable automated tools. Deploying new operating systems with increasingly demanding hardware requirements and potential application compatibility issues can be a daunting challenge for IT departments whose resources are already stretched thin. Microsoft has made a major investment in Configuration Manager OS deployment. Driving shorter adoption cycles for new operating systems is undoubtedly a strategic goal for Microsoft, so this is one part of the product the company is particularly motivated to get right. Whether or not OSD will prove to be the killer app for Configuration Manager 2007 remains to be seen, but the product certainly has some useful and well-thought-out capabilities. Here are some of the major capabilities of OSD:

- ▶ **Image capture and deployment**—ConfigMgr uses a Windows Image Format file (.WIM) image that can be applied to a target computer. You can use an existing image, if one is available, or you can capture an image from a reference computer. A *reference computer* is a computer that you configure exactly as you would like to deploy production machines with the same base hardware configuration.

- ▶ **User state migration**—When you want to provide a new computer to an existing user, the Windows User State Migration Tool (USMT) can capture the user's environment, settings, and data for transfer to the new machine. The Configuration Manager state migration point receives user state data from the USMT and stores it for deployment to the target machine.

- ▶ **Task sequences**—A task sequence can encapsulate the entire process of configuring source computers, capturing and deploying images, migrating user state and other settings, and running any post-installation tasks such as deploying ConfigMgr packages to the new machine.

- ▶ **Application Compatibility Toolkit**—Although not strictly part of OSD, this ConfigMgr R2 feature makes the planning of a major OS rollout much simpler.

This section highlights some of the key planning issues around OSD. Chapter 19 presents this feature set in detail.

You can choose from several options for deploying images and task sequences:

- ▶ If upgrading an existing ConfigMgr client computer, you can use ConfigMgr to initiate the installation from a distribution point.

- You can initiate the installation from bootable media configured to connect to the distribution point.

- You can use PXE (Preboot Execution Environment) Boot to initiate the installation. Most network cards will initiate a PXE Boot request sequence if an operating system is not already installed. The ConfigMgr PXE service point is capable of responding to PXE Boot requests and initiating an installation from a distribution point.

- You can use standalone media containing all the necessary installation files. This avoids the network traffic generated by installing from a distribution point, but requires you to build and distribute complete images, including all drivers and other required files.

- If you are replacing a user's existing machine, you can use a state migration point to transfer user state data.

TIP

Task Sequences Are Not Just for OSD

Task sequences are not only for OSD deployments. You can advertise a task sequence to existing clients just as you would a program in a package. To advertise a task sequence, just right-click the Advertisements node in the ConfigMgr console and choose Advertise Task Sequence. This launches the New Advertisement Wizard, which allows you to select the task sequence, target collection, and specify other advertisement properties. For an interesting discussion of the possibilities provided by advertising task sequences, see http://wmug.co.uk/blogs/r0b/archive/2008/09/08/configmgr-using-task-sequences-to-deploy-more-than-operating-systems.aspx.

When preparing your boot image, you must include all necessary network card and mass storage drivers. You should inventory additional drivers in your target environment and add them to the driver catalog you make available on your distribution points. You may include applications in your OS image, provided the applications do not contain unique identifiers that cannot be generalized by Sysprep. You can also install applications separately from the image as a post-install task. Including applications in your images can increase the number of images you need to create and maintain, but can make the installation process faster. OS images are often 2GB or larger. You should consider your storage requirements when sizing distribution points.

You should also consider the bandwidth required to deploy images when planning your deployment strategy. You may choose to use courier sender to distribute images between sites on physical media rather than using the network for this task. You should also consider backing up user data to the network or using existing backups rather than migrating user data as part of the user state migration.

ConfigMgr 2007 R2 introduces multicast capability for OS image deployment. Multicast can greatly reduce bandwidth consumption when deploying images to multiple machines. For an excellent discussion of ConfigMgr multicast capability, see http://blogs.msdn.com/steverac/archive/2008/10/19/setting-up-multicasting-in-sccm.aspx.

The Application Compatibility Toolkit (App Compat), new in ConfigMgr 2007 R2, helps with two key tasks:

▶ Inventorying applications in your environment and reporting on compatibility with Windows Vista

▶ Providing reports on which devices in your environment are Vista compatible and what driver upgrades may be required

Although not a replacement for testing applications with your specific build and environment, App Compat can help to quickly identify the applications and hardware that are likely to cause problems with your migration. Chapter 18 describes how to use the Application Compatibility Toolkit.

Planning for Wake On LAN

An increasing number of organizations are using power management features to reduce energy consumption by partially or even completely shutting down idle computers. The Advanced Configuration and Power Interface (ACPI) specification, which has become the industry standard for PC power management, defines various "sleep states," ranging from S0 (On and fully functional) to S5 (Off and powered down). Wake On LAN can be used to "wake up" computers in sleep states S1 through S5.

Configuration Manager can use Wake On LAN to deploy software updates or mandatory advertisements to client computers connected to the network that are in a sleeping state. You can use this capability to deploy applications during off-hours to avoid affecting users, while ensuring critical patch deployments are not delayed by waiting for computers to power up.

Using Wake On LAN requires the following:

▶ The power supply must support Wake On LAN.

▶ The client network interface cards (NICs) must support the standard magic packet format.

▶ The Basic Input/Output System (BIOS) settings for the NIC must have wake-up packets enabled.

Windows Logo–compliant NICs are required to support the magic packet format.

TIP

About Magic Packets

The magic packet is a standard wake-up frame that targets a specific network interface. The packet is a broadcast frame sent by the data link or OSI-2 layer. The packet enables remote access to a computer that is in a power-saving state (the computer is powered off, but some power is reserved for the NIC). When the listening computer receives this packet, it checks the packet for correct information, then switches on and boots.

The Configuration Manager 2007 client is required for Wake On LAN functionality, and Wake On LAN must be deployed at a primary site with hardware inventory enabled. Limitations to Wake On LAN include the following:

▶ The functionality does not support Internet-based clients.

▶ Wake On LAN is not aware of maintenance windows.

You can use either unicast packets or subnet-directed broadcasts for Wake On LAN:

▶ Unicast packets, also known as *directed packets*, are sent to the last-known IP address for the target computer based on hardware inventory.

▶ Subnet-directed broadcasts are targeted to the last reported subnet of the target machine. This allows subnet-directed broadcast packets to reach their target even if the IP address has changed.

To support subnet-directed Wake On LAN broadcasts, your network infrastructure must allow IP-directed broadcasts between the site server and client computers. For security reasons, by default most routers do not allow subnet-directed broadcasts. Enabling subnet-directed broadcasts can expose your network to certain types of denial-of-service attacks.

To prevent attacks, if you choose to use subnet-directed broadcasts you should use a nondefault port and allow broadcasts only from the site servers. If you use unicast packets, you need to configure switches to forward User Datagram Protocol (UDP) packets. Unicast packets also may not work with all sleep states on some network adapters.

Out of Band (OOB) Management Planning

One of the most exciting developments in desktop technology in recent years is Intel's Advanced Management Technology (AMT), based on the vPro technology. For many years, server vendors have offered Out of Band (OOB) Management capability using a dedicated network connection, network card, and processor. Due to cost, this type of configuration is generally not practical for desktop systems. Intel's introduction of network cards and chipsets supporting AMT, while not providing the hardware redundancy of the server class solutions, brings the same manner of management functionality to desktop systems. This section looks at the ways Configuration Manager takes advantage of AMT features. More information about AMT and vPro technologies can be found at http://www.intel.com/ technology/vpro/index.htm.

OOB Management uses Windows remote management technology (WS-Management) to connect to the management controller on a computer. Configuration Manager 2007 SP 1 introduces support for OOB Management capabilities, including the following:

▶ **Remote helpdesk functions**—Using the Out of Band Management console, a separate management console that ships with SP 1, you can connect to systems and perform functions such as the following:

▶ Changing the power state of sleeping systems

▶ Watching the boot sequence before the operating system loads

▶ Managing system BIOS settings

▶ Redirecting IDE drives to network locations or other devices

▶ **Powering up sleeping systems**—This capability enables software distribution, software updates, and OSD.

▶ ConfigMgr updates can be scheduled or done on demand.

▶ AMT provides better security than Wake On LAN, including Kerberos authentication and encryption.

If you are planning to use OOB Management, your desktop infrastructure and PKI deployment must meet several requirements to support it. Even if you do not plan to use this functionality immediately, you may want to plan for it in your new hardware purchases. Table 6.3 lists the key dependencies to plan for if you want to use OOB Management.

TABLE 6.3   Dependencies for Using OOB Management

Requirement Type	Details
Client hardware	Intel Centrino or Core Duo vPro chipset.
	Intel AMT firmware versions 3.2.1 or later. The Intel translator supports firmware revisions 3.0 and earlier.
	A supported network card such as the Intel 82566DM.
PKI	OOB Management requires a Microsoft Enterprise Certificate Authority.
	Each AMT managed computer requires an OEM certificate installed in the management controller memory and a Web Server Certificate. Your computer supplier can install the OEM certificate, or it can be added manually to each system.
	Configuration Manager can be running in mixed or native mode. Native mode is not required for OOB Management.
Configuration Manager setup	A site system must be configured with the Out of Band Service Point role.
	An AMT Provisioning and Discovery account must be configured.
	Computers supporting OOB Management must be discovered and provisioned.

For details on configuring Out of Band Management, see http://technet.microsoft.com/en-us/library/cc161822(TechNet.10).aspx.

> **NOTE**
>
> **About the DASH Standard**
>
> The Distributed Management Task Force (DMTF) has introduced the Desktop and Mobile Architecture for System Hardware (DASH) standard to bring standardization to advanced desktop management technology. Intel AMT 3.2.1 is fully DASH compliant and has additional functionality making it a superset of the DASH specification. Other hardware vendors such as AMD have also released management technology based on the DASH standard. It seems likely that in the future Configuration Manager will work with these technologies as well.

Summary

This chapter discussed some of the key planning considerations around deploying Configuration Manager and preparing to use some of its most important features. It looked at planning your hierarchy and sites, including hardware sizing, site boundaries, and security modes. The chapter then discussed planning for software updates and supporting mobile devices and Internet clients. It considered the certificate requirements for ConfigMgr and special issues with Windows Server 2008. Finally, the chapter discussed planning for OSD and the use of Wake On LAN and OOB Management functionality.

The next chapter discusses how to test, refine, and extend your planned Configuration Manager deployment.

CHAPTER 7

Testing and Stabilizing

As with any major Information Technology (IT) project, implementing and supporting Microsoft Configuration Manager (ConfigMgr) requires a phased approach when transforming your initial vision into a working production system. Microsoft provides guidance on managing the life cycle of IT initiatives through two complementary sets of best practices, Microsoft Operations Framework (MOF) and Microsoft Solutions Framework (MSF):

▶ MOF, introduced in Chapter 1, "Configuration Management Basics," is a framework for IT operations.

▶ MSF, described in Chapter 4, "Configuration Manager Solution Design," provides guidance on developing and implementing new IT initiatives.

Together, these frameworks address the phases you need to go through to plan, build, deploy, and operate a technology-based business solution.

Chapters 4 through 6 took you through the process of envisioning, designing, and planning solutions based on Microsoft Configuration Manager 2007. Chapter 4 discussed how you might begin to envision and plan your solutions. Chapter 5, "Network Design," presented the network infrastructure considerations you should take into account during the planning phase, whereas Chapter 6, "Architecture Design Planning," provided guidelines for planning the details of your sites, hierarchy, and feature set implementation.

This chapter discusses how to test your solution before deploying it to your production environment, and how to stabilize and customize your solution as you begin the deployment phase. The latter is the stage where you are actually building, testing, and refining your solution. Even if you have not adopted the Microsoft frameworks or a similar formal set of best practices, you can still apply the principles they suggest in guiding your efforts during this critical phase of your deployment.

Building, testing, and stabilizing your solution includes several major activities:

▶ The first step is building a proof of concept (POC) implementation. A *proof of concept* is a trial deployment that implements the essential features of your solution but is not designed to be part of your production environment.

▶ Later in your implementation, you will carry out a pilot deployment in your production environment. The *pilot* is a controlled implementation to a selected subset of your production systems.

   Throughout this phase, you will monitor and test your solution. Based on the test results, you may need to make adjustments and customizations so the final solution will work well in your production environment.

Depending on the size and culture of your organization, you may follow a more or less structured approach to planning and building your solution. For any deployment, you will want to test the basic functionality you plan to use before deploying to production. You may require more or less extensive testing and formal release management processes, based on the following:

▶ **The size and complexity of your environment**—Deploying Configuration Manager in a large, complex environment calls for more extensive testing than a smaller deployment.

▶ **The feature set you plan to use**—Some ConfigMgr features such as Out of Band (OOB) Management and Operating System Deployment (OSD) have network and service infrastructure dependencies you need to consider when testing and building your solution. Similarly, some features such as Network Access Protection (NAP) and Software Updates impact clients more directly than lower impact Configuration Manager services such as inventory and reporting. Features that have a higher impact on clients introduce greater risk to your production environment. You need to account for those risk factors in testing, and incorporate risk avoidance or mitigation strategies as you build your solution.

▶ **The extent to which your solution is customized and integrated with other elements of your environment**—Relatively generic deployments may largely consist of deploying features that are well tested out of the box. These features may just need basic validation in your environment. In contrast, every customization and integration point should be thoroughly tested and documented as part of your solution build.

Proving the Concepts

To prove that your design is conceptually sound, you will need to implement the essential features of your solution in a test environment. The primary goals of the POC include the following:

▶ Providing evidence that the proposed technical solution is feasible and addresses the business requirements. It is important to validate your processes and documentation as well as the technical design.

▶ Furnishing an opportunity for the support team to gain knowledge of the product.

▶ Identifying and addressing any gaps or weaknesses in the original design.

Here are the key requirements for an effective proof of concept:

▶ A POC environment that adequately reflects your production environment.

▶ A test plan that validates each element of your functional requirements.

▶ A communications plan that allows you to effectively share lessons learned and applies the results to improving your design, documentation, and processes.

Microsoft's frameworks identify four stages of the IT project life cycle:

▶ Plan

▶ Build

▶ Deploy

▶ Operate

The build stage focuses on developing and stabilizing your solution and encompasses the activities described in this chapter. If you have followed MSF guidance during the planning phase, you will have several key deliverables that will help with the POC. As you enter the build stage for your Configuration Manager deployment project, you should have the functional specification, risk management plan, master project plan, and master project schedule in place. These planning documents will help you define clear goals as well as set entry and exit criteria for the POC. These documents will also define the requirements for the POC environment and your test plan. The documents essential to the POC include the following:

▶ **The functional specification**—This provides a detailed description of the feature set, and explains how each feature should look and behave. It also describes the overall architecture and design of each feature. This document will identify what ConfigMgr features you need to configure as well as the infrastructure requirements each feature depends on.

▶ **The master project plan (MPP)**—The MPP generally includes a deployment plan, capacity plan, security plan, and test plan, among other elements. One goal of the POC will be to validate each element of the MPP. The test plan in the MPP will be largely carried out during the POC phase.

Building the Proof of Concept Environment

To avoid delay, you can start setting up the test environment while your plans are being finalized and reviewed. Chapters 4, 5, and 6 discussed the planning process. You will want to carry out the preliminary work of providing a network, servers, workstations, and support tools in parallel with the planning phase. Be sure to establish backup and monitoring systems and processes if these are not already in place.

Ideally, your POC environment would be an exact replica of your production environment; however, in practice this is not feasible. Therefore, it becomes necessary to identify the critical systems, infrastructure, and activities that adequately represent the production environment. Organizations using MOF or other Information Technology Infrastructure Library (ITIL) practices can leverage information from the enterprise Configuration Management Database (CMDB) to help identify the relevant configuration items (CIs) that need to be replicated in the test environment. The CMDB includes details about both the individual CIs and the relationships between them. You should review your functional specification and master project plan and use the CMDB to map the dependencies relevant to the CIs in your Configuration Manager deployment. Here are a few examples of how you might use the CMDB to plan your test environment:

▶ The CMDB is the starting point for enumerating the client configurations you need to test. Although it may not be possible to test every configuration, your test environment should include as complete a sample of platforms as possible. At a minimum, you should include all operating system versions found in your production environment and the major hardware platforms you will be supporting. If you plan to use Configuration Manager to manage mobile devices such as smartphones running Windows Mobile, you should include devices on each carrier network as well.

▶ Your MPP calls for ConfigMgr sites in various locations such as Brussels and Beijing. The CMDB contains information about these sites including local area network (LAN) and wide area network (WAN) characteristics, Windows language and locale settings, the number and type of clients systems, information about the local IT and vendor support organizations, and possibly legal and regulatory requirements affecting the sites.

One way to replicate the network environment of these sites accurately in your POC would be with a distributed test environment, which would include systems physically located at these sites. An alternative method is to configure the physical or virtual network infrastructure to introduce bandwidth throttling, latency, and transient communications anomalies between sites to simulate your actual network characteristics and conditions.

▶ Your functional specification calls for delivering OOB Management to laptop and desktop computers supporting Intel Advanced Management Technology (AMT). The CMDB will help you identify all AMT-capable models in your environment so that you can include them in testing.

▶ Your functional specification includes a requirement to provide reports on software license compliance for all your standard desktop applications. You can use the

CMDB to identify those applications you will need to report on and the available license data to incorporate in the reports.

If you do not already have an enterprise CMDB, you will need to use other means to gather data about your environment. Start with the existing documentation about your network, client and server hardware, and other elements of your environment. You may want to employ an asset discovery tool to update your documentation and fill in any gaps. The information and data collection methods you assemble may be useful to you later if you decide to develop a CMDB.

You can carry out a proof of concept in a physically isolated lab or in a controlled environment with connectivity to your production network. There are advantages and disadvantages to each:

- Using an isolated lab provides the greatest safety, and frees you from the need to consider possible impact on the live environment. However, this can take longer to set up because you have to duplicate infrastructure services.

- Implementing a POC in a test environment connected to your production network can save time and money because you can leverage existing infrastructure services rather than having to duplicate them in the test environment. The downside is that caution needs to be exercised at all times to avoid making changes that will affect your live environment.

The following sections discuss each of these environments.

Proving the Concepts in a Pure Lab Environment

Generally, you will deploy the POC in a lab environment isolated from your production network. Testing in an isolated lab gives you the freedom to try things out without having to worry about risks to your production environment. If your organization does not already have a suitable lab in place, you should consider building one. The test environment should mirror your live environment as closely as possible. Here are some points to keep in mind:

▶ Ideally, you should deploy Configuration Manager server roles on hardware identical to what you will use in production. You could accomplish this by "borrowing" the actual hardware you will use for your production site systems to use as part of the POC. This approach allows the most realistic testing, but requires you to tear down at least part of the POC environment when you move the production hardware to the live environment.

In general, it is a good idea to keep the POC environment available if possible. This gives you an environment for future testing of hotfixes, service packs, upgrades, new packages and operating system (OS) images, and any additional functionality you may decide to deploy. The POC environment is also a great place for training and experimentation. If you decide to use production hardware during the POC, you may be able to preserve the environment for future use by performing a P2V (physical-to-virtual) conversion of the site systems before removing them from the POC environment.

▶ In addition to the site systems, you should have a mix of clients in the POC environment representing a cross-section of the hardware, operating systems, and applications you will encounter in your live environment. The network infrastructure and core services should also replicate the essential features of your production environment. Although this may be expensive, it can save you from greater costs later if you encounter unexpected problems in the production environment.

A properly designed lab environment allows development and testing of your solution without affecting production systems. Everyone working in the lab should understand that test systems can become unstable and require reinstallation. It is not uncommon for an unstable lab environment to be a source of frustration, but you should keep in mind that many of the problems that arise in the lab would otherwise have occurred in your production environment! Encountering problems in the lab is actually a good thing, because you have the opportunity to address them before they affect the live environment. Because it is often necessary to roll back a test server to a previous state, you should maintain frequent backups or snapshots of all servers. Here are a few approaches:

▶ For virtual machines, reverting to a snapshot of the original build or a more recent baseline snapshot is generally the most efficient way to roll back to a previous configuration.

▶ For physical machines, you may be able to leverage Configuration Manager OSD to capture configuration baselines and redeploy them as necessary.

▶ To restore your ConfigMgr site server or other site systems required for OS deployment, you will need to use other recovery methods. In this case, you may need to do a bare metal restore or apply a standard server image and reinstall SQL Server and Configuration Manager. It may be helpful to maintain images of standard server configurations on removable media because machines are often "wiped" or reformatted. Developing scripted installations will help with this process, and you can use them in your production environment as well.

Regardless of how you manage recovery in your lab environment, you will need to follow the site recovery process described in Chapter 21, "Backup, Recovery, and Maintenance," when restoring a site server that is part of a Configuration Manager hierarchy.

You can use the test environment to finalize infrastructure components, including server build specifications, service configurations, and deployment packages and scripts. You will want to develop test specifications and test cases around each of the feature sets you plan to deploy.

Virtualization in a Test Environment

When designing a test environment, you should consider the respective advantages of physical or virtual hardware. Virtualization can dramatically lower the costs of building a test environment. By running multiple virtual machines on a single physical host, you can save on hardware, power, and cooling and in some cases on software licenses as well. Virtualization technology allows you to take snapshots of a virtual machine and later roll the machine back to the exact state it was in at the time of the snapshot. Reverting a test system to a snapshot requires much less time and effort than restoring a physical machine from a backup. Virtualization enables quick and efficient provisioning of large numbers of client systems for test purposes.

If you will be using a clustered configuration for the SQL Server database server in production, you will want to test the effects of a cluster failover. For this type of testing, virtual machines may not accurately represent the functioning of physical hardware you will have in production.

Similarly, if you are using Network Load Balancing (NLB) clustering for any of your servers roles, virtual machines (VMs) sharing the same network interface card (NIC) or sharing a NIC with other VMs might not adequately reflect the behavior you will see in the live environment. OS Deployment and OOB Management are examples of functionality you will need to test on physical hardware. To test OS Deployment adequately, you should deploy images and task sequences to hardware that realistically reflect the target hardware in your production environment.

The standard methods for provisioning virtual machines and deploying base images to them differ significantly from the methods used with physical hardware. Adequate testing of driver installation requires a representative population of physical hardware devices in the test environment. OOB Management using Intel AMT requires special hardware support, as described in Chapter 6. Backup and recovery processes are also different for virtual machines and physical machines. You should make sure the backup and recovery processes you test are valid for your production environment.

An optimum test environment may include both virtual and physical systems:

▶ Use at least one physical server or server cluster to validate the hardware configuration and site maintenance procedures for critical site systems, such as the site server and site database server.

▶ Install client systems on physical hardware to test hardware-dependent functionality such as OS Deployment and OOB Management.

▶ Using virtual machines allows you to scale your test environment far beyond the limits your budget would allow if you had to build a separate physical machine for each test system.

▶ Virtual machines can allow you to test more scenarios in less time and recover your test environment to a known-good state more quickly than using a lab configuration tied to physical hardware.

Configuration Manager 2007 requires certain infrastructure dependencies for installation and for certain features to work. Chapter 2, "Configuration Manager 2007 Overview," covers feature dependencies. Your POC environment will generally need the following services to be in place:

▶ Active Directory (AD) is a required dependency for Configuration Manager 2007. The AD environment for your POC should closely resemble your production AD. The "Active Directory Considerations" section of this chapter discusses creating the AD environment for your POC.

▶ Domain Naming Service (DNS) is required for AD and for many ConfigMgr features. Using AD-integrated DNS meets this requirement when you deploy AD in the POC environment. If you use a non-AD-integrated DNS, you will need to configure similar DNS servers in the POC environment. If you want your DNS zones to mirror those in your production environment, you need to copy and edit the configuration and zone files from your production DNS. You should refer to the documentation for your DNS server software for details on completing this task.

▶ Windows Internet Naming Service (WINS) is required for certain functionality if you will not be using AD schema extensions or you have clients that cannot take advantage of AD schema extensions. For information on feature dependencies and requirements for AD schema extensions, and on how to use WINS in place of the extended schema, refer to Chapter 6.

▶ Public Key Infrastructure (PKI) is required for Configuration Manager native mode operation and for certain features such as OOB Management. Chapter 6 discusses PKI dependencies as well.

You should also deploy any security software you use in production, such as antimalware and host intrusion detection software, to the POC environment. Network-based security controls such as firewalls and intrusion detection systems should also be in place and configured consistently with those in your production environment.

Active Directory Considerations

Configuration Manager 2007 is closely integrated with Active Directory, making it important that your POC AD be as close as possible to your actual AD environment. You can use several approaches in creating a suitable AD implementation in a POC environment. The first method is often referred to as the *peel-off* method. In this scenario, you add a domain controller (DC) to each production domain you wish to replicate in your POC, peel the DC off from production, and move it to the POC environment.

To essentially clone an AD domain using the peel-off method, perform the following steps:

1. Add a new domain controller to your production domain. You can add a domain controller using the Dcpromo process, described in http://technet.microsoft.com/en-us/library/cc732887.aspx.

   Do not make the new DC a global catalog server. If you are using AD Integrated DNS, you may or may not want to install DNS, depending on whether you want a copy of your production DNS in the lab. Your production DNS may include records such as aliases for Internet-based systems that you want to preserve. If this is not the case, you may be better off to start with a clean DNS installation after bringing the DC online in the lab.

2. Shut down the newly added DC, remove it from the production network, and move it to the lab network.

3. On one of your production DCs, run the Ntdsutil command-line utility and use the metadata cleanup option to remove references to the DC you just removed from the network.

   This is necessary to prevent errors that would otherwise occur when the DC's replication partners attempt to contact it and when the Windows components responsible for AD replication attempt to generate a replication topology. You also need to remove DNS entries for the DC through the DNS console and use the ADSI Edit Microsoft Management Console (MMC) snap-in to remove File Replication System (FRS) references to the DC. This is the same process used after an unsuccessful domain controller demotion, as described in http://support.microsoft.com/kb/216498.

4. Bring the DC you moved to the lab environment online, give it a new IP configuration for the subnet it is on, and perform the same process of metadata cleanup described in step 3 to remove references to other DCs in the production environment. Install DNS services on the DC if they are not already installed, and your lab DCs act as DNS servers.

5. Seize the domain Flexible Single Master Operations (FSMO) roles on the new DC. If the domain is the forest root domain, you should also seize the forest FSMO roles. One way to seize the FSMO roles is to use Ntdsutil, as described in http://support.microsoft.com/kb/255504.

A variation on the peel-off method is to clone an existing DC instead of actually removing it from the domain and transferring it to the lab:

▶ Cloning a DC has the advantage of minimizing the impact on the production environment. In particular, the metadata cleanup in the production environment described in step 3 of the preceding procedure is not required, although the meta-data cleanup in the lab environment is still necessary.

▶ To clone a DC on physical hardware, you may be able to use your backup software following procedures described in the backup vendor's documentation. You may also be able to use imaging software or P2P (physical-to-physical) migration tools.

If you have a DC running as a virtual machine, the cloning process may be even easier. You will probably just need to shut down the DC and use your virtualization software's management tools to clone the image. You can then copy the cloned image to the lab and bring the new virtual machine online on a host connected to the lab environment.

The major alternative to the peel-off method is standing up a new AD forest in the POC environment and reproducing the essential elements of your production AD in the new forest. To accomplish this you will need to consider the following steps:

1. Create a new domain controller in the POC environment as the first domain controller in a new forest. You can create a domain controller in a new forest using the Dcpromo process, described in http://technet.microsoft.com/en-us/library/cc732887.aspx, previously referenced in this section.

2. Again using Dcpromo, add any child domains and additional DCs you will need in your environment.

3. Configure services such as DNS and Global Catalog servers in your new forest, and assign the FSMO roles to appropriately reflect your production environment.

4. On a production DC, use the LDIFDE command or other tools to export the objects you need from your production AD. Chapter 6 introduced LDIFDE, and http://support.microsoft.com/kb/555636 describes the process of exporting and importing objects with LDIFDE.

5. Transfer the output file from step 4 to the DC in the POC environment and use the same tools to import the AD objects.

6. Transfer any relevant group policy objects (GPOs) from the production environment to the POC environment. GPOs control many settings that affect Configuration Manager, such as security and network settings. At a minimum, you will want to import the default domain policy and default domain controller policy from your production environment.

You will find the Group Policy Management Console (GPMC) installed in the Administrative Tools program group on Windows Server 2008 systems when you choose the Group Policy Management role in Server Manager. You can also download the GPMC from http://www.microsoft.com/downloads/details.aspx?FamilyID=0a6d4c24-8cbd-4b35-9272-dd3cbfc81887&displaylang=en for installation on Windows Server 2003 or Windows XP systems. You can transfer group policy objects using the GPMC as follows:

a. Expand the Group Policy Management tree to locate the domain and the GPO you wish to export. Right-click the GPO and choose Back Up.... Alternatively, right-click the Group Policy Objects node and choose Back Up All....

Figure 7.1 displays the GPMC with the default domain policy for the sccmunleashed.com domain selected.

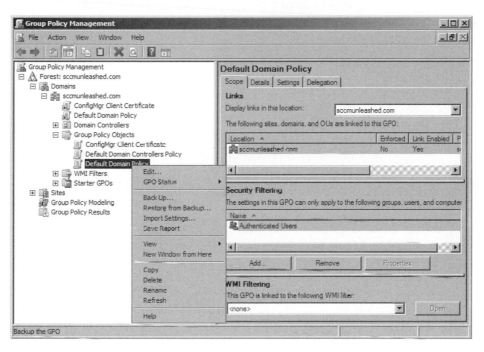

FIGURE 7.1   The GPMC with the context menu sccmunleashed default domain policy displayed

b. Complete the Back Up Group Policy Object dialog box and click Back Up. Figure 7.2 displays this dialog box.

You can also use scripts to export and import group policy. Microsoft provides sample scripts for various group policy–related tasks, including backing up and importing GPOs. You can find these sample scripts at http://technet.microsoft.com/en-us/library/cc784365.aspx.

If you are planning to use the AD schema extensions for Configuration Manager, you should include the schema extensions in your POC environment. Chapter 3, "Looking Inside Configuration Manager," describes the AD schema extensions and the benefits of extending the schema.

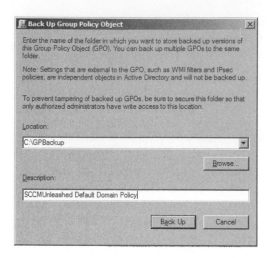

FIGURE 7.2   The GPMC Back Up Group Policy Object dialog box

TIP

Software Licensing for Your POC

If you are standing up a separate environment to evaluate Microsoft software, you may be able to take advantage of free limited-time evaluation software, or use reduced-cost licensing for full-featured evaluation software with subscription programs such as TechNet Plus and MSDN (Microsoft Developer Network). Evaluation software is not licensed for use in a production environment, and other license restrictions apply. Carefully review the licensing terms for all evaluation software before downloading and installing it. Information about evaluation software and subscription programs is available at http://technet.microsoft.com/en-us/evalcenter/default.aspx.

If your organization provides products, services, or solutions to customers based on Microsoft technology, you may also be eligible to receive licensing benefits for internal-use software by joining the Microsoft partner program. For more information about the Microsoft partner program and the licensing terms and conditions under this program, see https://partner.microsoft.com.

Proving the Concepts in an Environment Connected to Your Production Network

Although there are many advantages to having an isolated lab environment for your proof of concept, you may also consider doing POC testing on systems connected to your production network. This approach has the following advantages:

▶ The cost will be lower because you do not need to create a separate network infrastructure.

▶ The time to deploy the POC environment will be substantially less because you will typically be able to leverage existing services such as DNS, WINS, DHCP (Dynamic Host Configuration Protocol), and backup services. In a lab environment, you would need to install and configure these services independently of your production deployment.

▶ It may be difficult or impossible to adequately reproduce certain features of your environment in a test lab. Enterprise monitoring solutions, PKI infrastructure, and production security services are examples of services you may have deployed in production that would be prohibitively expensive to duplicate in a lab.

If you use a POC environment connected to production, you will generally need to create a separate AD environment for the POC. This is particularly true if you are using the schema extensions to publish site information to AD. You cannot use the peel-off method in this circumstance, so you will need to stand up a separate AD forest from scratch. If you have an existing ConfigMgr 2007 or Systems Management Server (SMS) 2003 deployment in production, you will also need to make sure that the site boundaries of your POC ConfigMgr sites do not overlap with the site boundaries of your production deployment, and that you do not use the same site code for more than one site!

Testing in the POC Phase

A successful proof of concept will demonstrate that the proposed technical solution is feasible and help identify any gaps or weaknesses in the original design. To accomplish this, you need to test all functional components of the design and demonstrate how the system performs under stress. You should begin the POC phase with a comprehensive test plan that validates all functionality and yield performance metrics that will project the performance in the live environment.

Functional Testing

Start by assembling a list of features you will implement in your ConfigMgr deployment with criteria to validate each feature. Functional testing verifies that each feature operates correctly. Some of the common areas of functional testing include the following:

▶ **Site system installation**—Chapter 8, "Installing Configuration Manager 2007," presents the success criteria for server installation. Confirm that your POC deployment successfully meets these criteria.

▶ **Client installation**—Test each client installation method you plan to use in production. To confirm that the client agent and required components are installed and enabled, open Control Panel on the client system and view the Components tab of the Configuration Management applet. Figure 7.3 shows the component status displayed in Control Panel. You should also review the Client Deployment Failure Report and run the following status message queries:

   ▶ Client Configuration Requests (CCRs) Processed Unsuccessfully

   ▶ Client Components Experiencing Fatal Errors

Both these queries should return zero systems in their output. See Chapter 18, "Reporting," for a discussion of ConfigMgr reports, and Chapter 17, "Configuration Manager Queries," for status message queries.

▶ **Client inventory**—Schedule client inventory and review the results. Again, you do not want any errors or warnings. You can run the following status message queries to view possible errors or warnings during inventory collection:

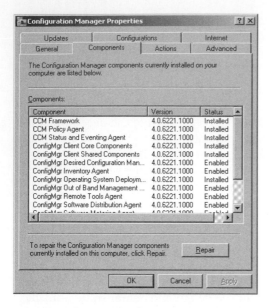

FIGURE 7.3   The Components tab of the Configuration Management Properties control panel applet

> ▶ Clients That Reported Errors or Warnings During Inventory File Collection.

> ▶ Clients That Reported Errors or Warnings While Creating a Hardware Inventory File.

> ▶ Clients That Reported Errors or Warnings While Creating a Software Inventory File.

▶ **Backup and recovery**—As part of your POC, validate your backup and recovery processes for all site systems.

▶ **Service delivery**—Design functional tests and success criteria for each service you plan to deliver, such as software deployment, software updates, or remote administration.

Stress Testing

One of the most challenging aspects of POC testing is generating a load approximating the load your systems will experience in a live environment. Client activity, which scales linearly with the number of client systems, generates much of the load on Configuration Manager site systems. As the number of clients increases, site systems will experience a heavier load from activities such as the following:

▶ Processing inventory data

▶ Processing other client data such as heartbeat discovery data, state messages, status messages, and software-metering data

▶ Processing requests to the management point for policy downloads

▶ Concurrent connections to distribution points

▶ Updating larger collections and running queries and reports against larger data sets

---

TIP

Scripting to Simulate Larger Client Loads

One way you can simulate some aspects of a larger client load is with scripting. For example, you can use a script provided by Microsoft (http://technet.microsoft.com/en-us/library/bb633207.aspx) to initiate a Machine Policy Retrieval and Evaluation Cycle from a client workstation. You could add logic to the script to invoke the policy retrieval cycle repeatedly and run the script from multiple clients, simulating the load a management point at a busy site might experience.

The System Center Configuration Manager 2007 Software Development Kit (SDK) includes a more general discussion of automating client actions and includes sample code in Visual Basic Script and C#. The relevant section in the SDK is in the chapter on "Configuration Manager Client Programming," under "Configuration Manager Client Automation." You can download the SDK from http://www.microsoft.com/downloads/details.aspx?FamilyID=064A995F-EF13-4200-81AD-E3AF6218EDCC&displaylang=en (or from Microsoft's Download Center at www.microsoft.com/downloads; search for **ConfigMgr 2007 SDK**.)

The SMS Object Generator (smsobjen.exe) is a tool Microsoft provided to simulate various objects for load-testing various versions of SMS. The SMS Object Generator is included with the SMS 2.0 Resource Kit tools, which are part of the BackOffice Resource Kit, version 4.5. Microsoft has not updated this tool for Configuration Manager 2007, and testing shows some but not all functions of this tool work with ConfigMgr. The tool is able to generate data discovery records (DDRs), which you can use to populate the ConfigMgr database with simulated client systems. These objects appear as legacy clients. However, Configuration Manager will not successfully process the inventory data generated by the tool. This is not surprising because the inventory data format for legacy clients is not supported in ConfigMgr 2007. You can use the tool to simulate the following:

▶ Discovery data

▶ Inventory data (processed as bad inventory files)

▶ Status messages

Using this tool allows stress testing the server components used for processing discovery, inventory, and status messages. By creating objects at a child primary site, you can also generate a load for the components involved in replicating data to the parent site. Populating the database with a large number of simulated client systems also enables you to create large collections for stress testing the collection evaluator. Figure 7.4 shows the SMS Object Generator user interface for generating DDRs. Enter the path of the Discovery

Data Manager inbox in the DDR path text box. In the default ConfigMgr installation, the path is C:\Program Files\Microsoft Configuration Manager\inboxes\ddm.box. Chapter 3 discusses the inbox folders for various components.

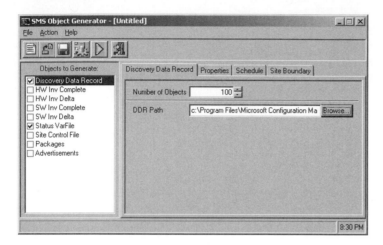

FIGURE 7.4   The SMS Object Generator user interface

POC Exit Criteria and Deliverables

The exit criteria for the POC should include completing all functional tests and stress tests and completion of required deliverables. Be sure to review any unresolved problems that occur during testing to determine whether they are "showstoppers" that prevent you from moving to the pilot phase before making adjustments. Potential showstoppers include issues that would seriously affect existing functionality in your live environment, compromise security, or prevent required functionality from working. You can note less serious issues as exceptions and continue to investigate them in the POC environment while moving forward with your pilot.

Here are the major deliverables of the POC:

▶ Updated project plans based on test results and adjustments.

▶ Detailed process documentation providing procedures for each required ConfigMgr task.

▶ Any configuration elements you plan to use in production, such as scripted installations, site settings files, and object definition files. Chapter 8 discusses scripted installations. The next two sections of this chapter describe procedures for creating and using site settings files and object definition files.

If you have customized any group policy objects to support ConfigMgr functionality, you will want to use the procedures described in the "Active Directory Considerations" section of this chapter to transfer these settings to production. Examples of group policy settings that you can use to support ConfigMgr functionality are client site assignment and BITS (Background Intelligent Transfer Service) settings. Client site assignment is discussed in Chapter 12, "Client Management," and BITS settings are covered in Chapter 5.

Transferring Site Settings

Site settings files are XML (eXtensible Markup Language) files that can be used to reliably reproduce site configuration items such as site component configuration, client agent properties, and site maintenance tasks. To create a site settings file for use in production, perform the following steps:

1. Open the Configuration Manager Console and then navigate to System Center Configuration Manager -> Site Database -> Site Management in the console.

2. Right-click the site and choose Transfer Site Settings. This launches the Transfer Site Settings Wizard. On the Welcome screen shown in Figure 7.5, click Next.

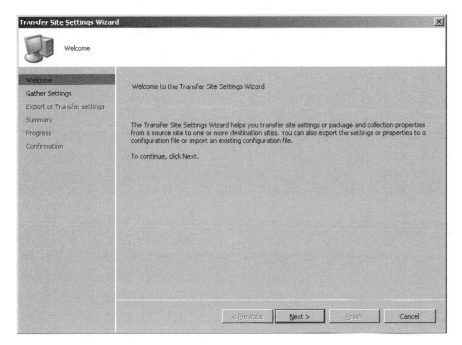

FIGURE 7.5   The Transfer Site Settings Wizard's Welcome screen

3. On the Gather Settings screen displayed in Figure 7.6, confirm that the Export settings and Site settings radio buttons are selected and then click Next.

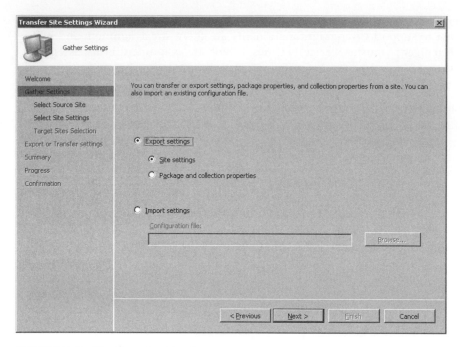

FIGURE 7.6   The Transfer Site Settings Wizard's Gather Settings screen

4. On the Select Source Site screen shown in Figure 7.7, check the box next to the site(s) you want to export settings from and then click Next.

5. On the Select Site Settings screen shown in Figure 7.8, expand the tree control and check the boxes next to the settings you want to transfer. Checking the box at the top of the tree will select all site settings.

6. Select Export or Transfer Settings from the navigation bar on the right side of the wizard. In the Export or Transfer Settings screen shown in Figure 7.9, make sure the Export settings for later use box is checked and enter the path for the destination XML file. Check the Include current values for each setting box and then click Next.

7. Review the information in the Summary screen shown in Figure 7.10. After clicking Next, you will see a progress information screen, and a confirmation screen appears when the settings transfer completes. You can now copy the XML file to your production network and use the same wizard to import the settings on your production site.

On your production site, you will use the Transfer Site Settings Wizard again to import the site settings. At step 3 of the preceding process, choose the Import Settings option instead of Export settings, and browse to the saved XML file. The rest of the process is essentially the same. For more information on the Transfer Site Settings Wizard, see http://technet. microsoft.com/en-us/library/bb632809.aspx.

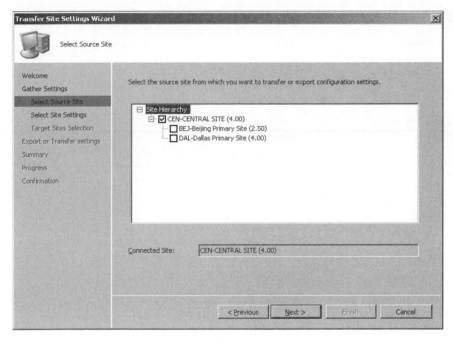

FIGURE 7.7 The Transfer Site Settings Wizard's Select Source Site screen

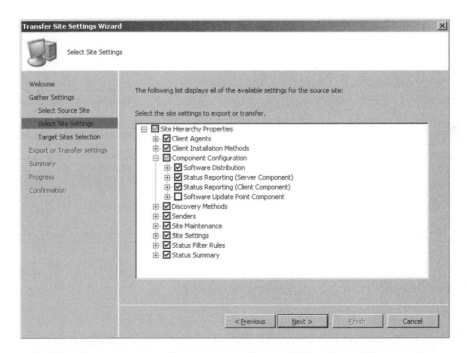

FIGURE 7.8 The Transfer Site Settings Wizard's Select Site Settings screen

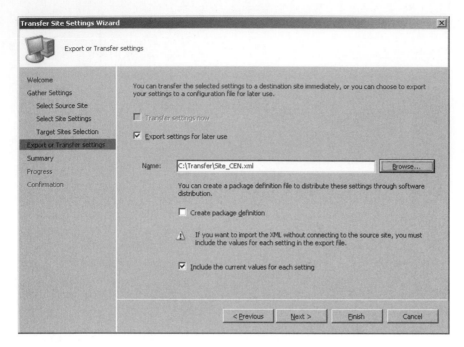

FIGURE 7.9   The Transfer Site Settings Wizard's Export or Transfer Settings Site screen

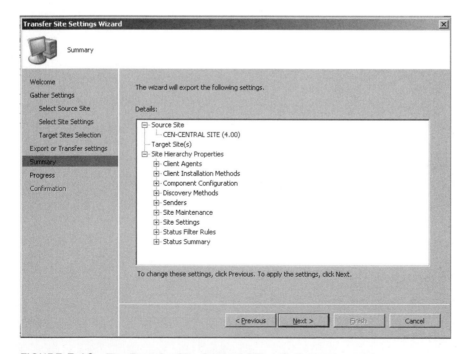

FIGURE 7.10   The Transfer Site Settings Wizard's Summary screen

Transferring Other Objects

You may have noticed the option to export packages and collections on the Transfer Site Settings Wizard's Gather Settings screen, shown earlier in Figure 7.6. Microsoft designed this option to transfer settings such as collection-refresh schedules and package priority from one object to another within your site. It does not provide a way to transfer packages and collections developed in your POC environment to production.

You can use the ConfigMgr console to export the definitions of certain objects as MOF (Managed Object Format) files that you can import into your production environment. You can export MOF definitions for instances of the following ConfigMgr object types from the console:

▶ Collections

▶ Queries

▶ Reports

To export objects' definitions to MOF files, right-click the parent node, choose Export Objects, and complete the wizard to choose the instances to export, specify the file location, and enter descriptive text. You can use a similar process to import objects from MOF files.

> **NOTE**
>
> **Which MOF Is It?**
>
> This chapter uses the acronym MOF for two things—the Microsoft Operations Framework and Managed Object Format files. Although it is confusing, both are valid.

If you're planning to use Configuration Manager OSD, you will want to develop and test your images, task sequences, and driver packages in the POC environment. You can export and import task sequences as XML files from the ConfigMgr console. Other OSD objects can be copied manually in their native file formats and imported into the production environment. Similarly, if you will be using ConfigMgr software deployment, you will want to develop and test software packages in the POC environment. To avoid introducing possible errors by manually re-creating packages, you can use package definition files to create consistent packages in the POC and production environments.

Microsoft provides information about creating and using package definition files at http://technet.microsoft.com/en-us/library/bb693959.aspx. OSD and software distribution are discussed in Chapter 19, "Operating System Deployment," and Chapter 14, "Distributing Packages," respectively.

Pilot Phase

During the pilot phase, you will work with a small subset of the users and systems in your live environment. Unlike the POC, the pilot environment is intended to become a permanent part of the production deployment of your solution. Typically, a pilot deployment begins with a single ConfigMgr site. Client systems are selectively added to the pilot. Often the initial group of clients in your pilot consists of computers in the IT department or those whose users are known as technically savvy and willing to be early adopters of new technology. It is important to keep users informed of any changes during the pilot and solicit feedback on any unusual conditions the users might experience, such as error messages or performance impact.

If you have an existing SMS implementation, you must make sure that the boundaries of your pilot site(s) do not overlap with the boundaries of any existing SMS sites. To avoid overlapping boundaries, you may need to create dedicated IP subnets and/or AD sites for your pilot deployment.

One of the essential goals of the pilot is to monitor the impact ConfigMgr has on your production systems and your network. This will be much easier if you are using an enterprise monitoring tool such as Microsoft System Center Operations Manager (OpsMgr). If you have Operations Manager in place, you should use the Base OS management pack to capture baseline data on your pilot systems before deployment. You can then track and investigate any major changes in performance or event characteristics that may occur.

If you do not have access to an enterprise monitoring tool, you can use the Windows performance monitoring tools to capture performance data on your site systems and some client systems. Here are some of the performance counters providing a general snapshot of utilization of principal system resources:

▶ Memory: Available Bytes

▶ Memory: Pages/sec

▶ Network Interface: Bytes Total/sec

▶ Network Interface: Output Queue Length

▶ Physical Disk (each instance): % Disk Time

▶ Processor (total): % Processor Time

▶ System: Processor Queue Length

For procedures for capturing this data, refer to the Windows help files for the version of Windows you are using. Capture a baseline prior to ConfigMgr deployment and capture additional data after deployment. You should consider the impact of any major changes in average system resource utilization or peak utilization that may be associated with ConfigMgr activity such as inventory collection.

You should also use any available network traffic monitoring tools to gather baseline statistics on WAN and LAN utilization prior to the pilot deployment, and compare the baselines with monitoring data gathered during the pilot. Most organizations have network monitoring in place, which may be managed by a dedicated network support team. If you do not already have network monitoring tools, you can locate a variety of tools through sites such as http://www.monitortools.com/.

Results and Adjustments

As part of the exit review for each phase, you should consider the results of that phase and make adjustments to optimize your solution. Review the results for failure conditions, network and system performance impact, and usability concerns. In the case of failure conditions, you will need to consider whether you can proceed to the next phase before correcting the issues identified in testing. You should document failures of noncritical functionality or occasional failures; however, these types of issues should not delay moving to the next deployment phase. Here are some examples of adjustments you might make based on the results of your POC and pilot deployments:

▶ Scheduling changes to reduce performance impact, such as randomizing the client inventory schedule to reduce spikes in network activity or server load. Conversely, you may find that you need to schedule inventory collection for off-peak hours to reduce the impact on end users.

▶ Modifying your hardware specifications to address performance problems found during testing.

▶ Adjusting your site hierarchy, sender configuration, and server placement should you find bandwidth utilization issues during testing. Chapter 5 discussed network design considerations.

▶ Identifying known errors and providing support staff with troubleshooting procedures and the training to address these errors.

▶ Altering user-facing functionality such as notification policies for software updates to meet the needs and preferences of your user community.

Customizing the Solution

During the proof of concept and pilot phases, place special emphasis on testing and validating any customizations and integration points of your solution. You may also decide to try various custom extensions to Configuration Manager to add value to your solution. Members of the System Center Alliance, a Microsoft partner program, offer products that extend, enhance, and connect your ConfigMgr solution. Some of the ways in which applications from alliance partners may add value to your solution include the following:

▶ Extending Configuration Manager's management capabilities to non-Windows systems such as Unix hosts and BlackBerry or Symbian mobile devices.

▶ Enhancing manageability through tools to help administrators with tasks such as software packaging and inventory customization. You can also enable end users with enhanced services such as self-service portals for requesting software packages.

▶ Connecting your ConfigMgr deployment with external systems such as an enterprise job scheduler or a federated CMDB. Coordinating your scheduled Configuration Manager tasks with other scheduled activity can help you better manage your enterprise. Similarly, the wealth of data that ConfigMgr gathers through inventory and discovery can provide the CMDB with detailed knowledge of your Windows environment.

Most major personal computer (PC) and server hardware vendors also provide inventory extensions that allow you to add vendor specific attributes, such as asset tag numbers, to ConfigMgr hardware inventory. Microsoft publishes a directory of System Center Alliance members at http://www.microsoft.com/systemcenter/en/us/alliance-members.aspx.

This book discusses various customizations you can make to Configuration Manager:

▶ Chapter 3 discusses the ConfigMgr SDK, which can be used to provide access to ConfigMgr data and functionality for external applications and scripts.

▶ Chapter 3 also describes how to customize hardware inventory by editing the SMS_def.mof and configuration.mof files.

▶ Chapter 10, "The Configuration Manager Console," discusses customizing the Configuration Manager console.

▶ Chapter 18 presents customizations used in reporting.

▶ Chapter 19 discusses custom solutions with the task sequencer.

The proof of concept phase is a great time to look at these customizations and try them in your test environment.

Summary

This chapter discussed the process of testing and stabilizing your Configuration Manager design. It described the goals of a proof of concept, how to create a POC environment, and the type of testing you can do in the POC phase. It then discussed the role of a pilot phase in your live environment. Finally, the chapter looked at how to adjust your solution based on the results of your testing, and how to use the testing phase to explore and validate customizations to your design.

In the next chapter, you will see how to install your Configuration Manager hierarchy and configure your site systems and client agent settings.

CHAPTER 8

Installing Configuration Manager 2007

Finally! By now, you have spent a considerable amount of time reading the first seven chapters of this book. You have studied the terminology, examined those components you plan to install, and carefully designed your ConfigMgr 2007 hierarchy, paying very close attention to wide area network (WAN) links and administrative requirements. You have also documented and verified your site boundaries, and have determined whether you will operate in mixed mode or "go native." Due to its nature, a successful Configuration Manager (ConfigMgr) implementation requires substantial planning.

This chapter covers installation of the central site server and basic configuration tasks. It also reviews multisite installation considerations as well as discusses the installation of primary and secondary child sites. In addition, the chapter discusses troubleshooting approaches for site installation and configuration.

You may notice the use of multiple site servers in this chapter. The lab environment used in this book has a central site (CEN) running on Bluebonnet, and four primary sites, all in the SCCMUnleashed.com domain. Here are the primary sites reporting to the central site:

- ▶ **DAL (Dallas)**—Running on the Wildflower server

- ▶ **HOU (Houston)**—Running on the Mockingbird server

- ▶ **BXL (Brussels)**—Installed on the Tumbleweed server

- ▶ **BEJ (Beijing)**—Installed on the Roadrunner server

This chapter discusses the installation of Configuration Manager 2007 on the central site server, and uses the BXL primary site for examples as well. The CEN, DAL, and BXL sites are running Configuration Manager 2007, whereas HOU and BEJ run SMS 2003. Chapter 9, "Migrating to Configuration Manager 2007," steps through the process of upgrading the HOU primary site to Configuration Manager 2007. The Configuration Manager console installs as part of your site server installation; Chapter 10, "The Configuration Manager Console," includes a discussion of installing the console on other systems.

Pre-Installation

You are almost ready to begin the ConfigMgr site installation. Before launching the installation program (setup.exe), assess the points in this section to ensure you have completed all prerequisites. If you have multiple ConfigMgr sites and/or servers in your design, verify you have that information documented, including what servers handle which ConfigMgr site roles, as well as required prerequisites for each server. Review the following questions:

▶ Will you configure the central site for mixed mode or native mode?

   Chapter 6, "Architecture Design Planning," discusses site security modes.

▶ Will your hierarchy contain all primary sites, or primary and secondary sites? Will you need any branch distribution points?

   Chapter 2, "Configuration Manager 2007 Overview," introduces primary and secondary sites as well as the use of branch distribution points.

▶ Will you install all site components on your central site, or distribute them over multiple servers?

   Chapter 6 discusses distributing components across multiple servers.

▶ How much drive space do you need on each site server?

   See Chapter 6 for disk space requirements.

▶ Do you need to extend the Active Directory (AD) schema?

   Chapter 3, "Looking Inside Configuration Manager," discusses extending the schema.

▶ Is your hardware sufficient?

   See Chapter 4, "Configuration Manager Solution Design," and Chapter 6 for hardware requirements and planning.

These are questions you will want specific answers for before deploying your first production ConfigMgr site. If the answers are not completely clear, do not pass Go! Spend some additional time reviewing the previous chapters, particularly Chapter 6.

Before starting the installation process for ConfigMgr, verify you have installed and configured all software prerequisites. The next sections briefly describe those requirements. For additional information on prerequisites when installing Configuration Manager, refer to http://technet.microsoft.com/en-us/library/bb694113.aspx.

Windows Components

Configuration Manager 2007 depends on a number of Windows components. Depending on your site design, you may not need all components on each ConfigMgr site in your hierarchy. Table 8.1 provides a brief overview of the Windows components required for each site server and site role. See http://technet.microsoft.com/en-us/library/bb680717. aspx for a complete list of ConfigMgr-supported configurations.

TABLE 8.1   Windows Components Required for ConfigMgr Roles

ConfigMgr Role	Required Windows Component
Distribution point	WebDAV (Web Distributed Authoring and Version) extensions.
To allow content transfer from the distribution point using BITS, HTTP, and HTTPS, you must also have IIS 6.0 (or later) and BITS.	BITS-enabled distribution point.
IIS (Internet Information Services) 6.0 or later.	BITS (Background Intelligent Transfer Service). WebDAV extensions.
Branch distribution point	Remote Differential Compression (RDC). This is installed by default on Windows Server 2003. BITS.
Management point	IIS 6.0 or later. BITS. WebDAV extensions.
Fallback status point	IIS 6.0 or later.
Software update point	Windows Server Update Services (WSUS version 3.0) or later, depending on the ConfigMgr service pack level. IIS 6.0 or later.
Server locator point	IIS 6.0 or later.
Reporting point	IIS 6.0 or later. ASP (Active Server Pages).
System Health Validator point	Windows Server 2008, Enterprise, Datacenter, and Standard Editions.
Site servers	All site servers must be a member of an Active Directory domain. RDC (installed by default on Windows Server 2003).
ConfigMgr console	.NET Framework 2.0. Microsoft Management Console (MMC) 3.0.
Multicast-Enabled Distribution Point	Windows Server 2008, Windows Deployment Services, and IIS with ISAPI Extensions.

8

TABLE 8.1   Continued

ConfigMgr Role	Required Windows Component
Virtual Application Streaming	BITS, IIS 6.0 or later.
Client Status Reporting	Microsoft .NET Framework 2.0, Office Web Components.
SQL Reporting Services Reporting	Microsoft SQL Server 2005 Reporting Services, IIS 6.0.

Windows Server 2008 will have some default components configured differently from Windows Server 2003. For example, WebDAV extensions require a separate download, and Remote Differential Compression is not enabled by default. For instructions on configuring these components for Windows Server 2008, review the article on configuring Windows Server 2008 for site systems at http://technet.microsoft.com/en-us/library/cc431377.aspx.

SQL Server

All primary sites use Microsoft SQL Server 2005 with Service Pack 2 or greater for the Configuration Manager database. Consider using Enterprise edition if you are planning to use clustering with more than two nodes or if you have a very large site. SQL Server Standard edition will be sufficient for almost all environments.

Microsoft now supports upgrading the site database to SQL Server 2008 if you apply a hotfix:

▶ For the base or Released to Manufacturing (RTM) version of ConfigMgr 2007, apply the hotfix discussed at http://support.microsoft.com/kb/955229. Apply the hotfix to the following servers:

  ▶ Primary site servers using SQL Server 2008 to host the site database.

  ▶ Secondary site servers reporting to primary sites that use SQL Server 2008 to host the database.

  ▶ Systems with the Configuration Manager 2007 console installed and connecting to a site that uses SQL Server 2008 to host the database.

  ▶ Servers hosting a remote Systems Management Server (SMS) provider.

▶ For ConfigMgr Service Pack (SP) 1, follow the instructions at http://support.microsoft.com/kb/955262. If applicable, apply the hotfix to the following servers:

  ▶ Primary site servers using SQL Server 2008 to host the database.

  ▶ Systems with the Configuration Manager console installed and connecting to a site using SQL Server 2008 to host the database.

  ▶ Servers hosting a remote SMS provider.

Windows Server Update Services

If you plan to use ConfigMgr to deploy Microsoft security patches, you must install WSUS 3.0 (for ConfigMgr 2007 RTM) or WSUS 3.0 SP 1 (for ConfigMgr 2007 SP 1). For information on WSUS with ConfigMgr, see http://technet.microsoft.com/en-us/library/bb693886.aspx. Chapter 15, "Patch Management," discusses using ConfigMgr 2007 for security patch management.

The Prerequisite Checker

Running the ConfigMgr prerequisite checker confirms whether your system meets the minimum installation requirements for ConfigMgr 2007. The prerequisite checker verifies requirements such as administrative rights, SQL Server version, .NET Framework version, eXtensible Markup Language (XML) version, MMC version, and required Windows updates and hotfixes. Microsoft provides a complete list of setup prerequisite checks at http://technet.microsoft.com/en-us/library/bb680951.aspx.

The ConfigMgr prerequisite checker automatically runs during site installation. You can also run it separately by using one of the following methods:

▶ Select the prerequisite checker from the ConfigMgr installation menu (Splash.hta) in the root of the installation media.

▶ Call setup.exe with appropriate command-line arguments. For example, to verify the prerequisites for a secondary site, open a command prompt (Start -> Run, and type **cmd**) and type

```
Setup.exe /prereq /sec
```

For a complete list of arguments, see http://technet.microsoft.com/en-us/library/bb681060.aspx.

Site Installation

After verifying the prerequisites and deciding whether to extend the Active Directory schema, you are ready to begin ConfigMgr site installation.

TIP

Use SMS Trace to Monitor ConfigMgr Installation

SMS Trace (also called Trace32 and introduced in Chapter 3) is a utility in the ConfigMgr Toolkit used to view log files in real time. Download the ConfigMgr Toolkit from Microsoft at http://www.microsoft.com/downloads (search for **ConfigMgr Toolkit)**, and install it on your soon-to-be primary site. After you begin the ConfigMgr installation, launch Trace32 and open the ConfigMgr installation logs (%*SystemRoot*%\ConfigMgrPrereq.log and %*SystemRoot*%\ConfigMgrSetup.log). You will see the logs dynamically update as the installation proceeds.

Installing ConfigMgr

Perform the following steps to install the primary site:

1. Browse to your installation media and launch Splash.hta, found in the root of the installation media. As shown in Figure 8.1, you have several options in the splash screen, including running the prerequisite checker, reviewing the release notes, and installing ConfigMgr.

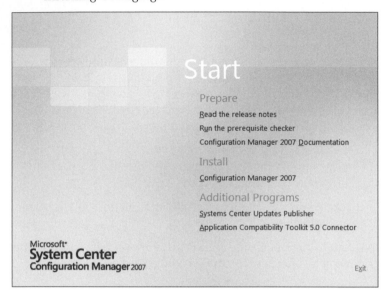

FIGURE 8.1   System Center Configuration Manager Installation splash screen

2. Review the release notes for late-breaking information about known issues, bug fixes, and other important information. When you are ready, select the option Install Configuration Manager 2007 to view the Welcome screen.

3. Verify you are ready to move forward and then click Next to choose a setup option, as shown in Figure 8.2.

Real World: Previous Installations of ConfigMgr or SMS

If you arrive at the Available Setup Options screen (shown in Figure 8.2) and see that you are unable to install a ConfigMgr site server, first confirm you are installing the site on a supported operating system. In addition, if the server previously had SMS or ConfigMgr installed, you may encounter this situation if the uninstall was not completely successful. If the Registry key HKEY_LOCAL_MACHINE\Software\Microsoft\SMS\Setup exists, delete it and retry the installation.

If the installation continues to fail, check the ConfigMgr installation logs (%*SystemRoot*%\ConfigMgrPrereq.log and %*SystemRoot*%\ConfigMgrSetup.log) for more information. You may be able to perform a little additional "clean-up." If all else fails, you may need to resort to reinstalling the operating system on the server for a clean opportunity to install ConfigMgr.

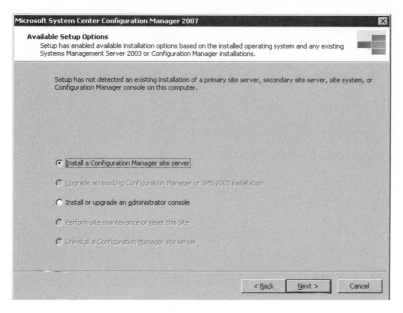

FIGURE 8.2   Available setup options for Configuration Manager installation

4. Provided you are attempting to install on a supported server operating system (OS), select the option Install a Configuration Manager site server. Then click Next to view the license terms. Read the license agreement, and if you agree to the terms, click Next to proceed.

TIP

Install the ConfigMgr Console on a Workstation for Everyday Use

Another option on the Available Setup Options screen is Install or upgrade an administrator console. A common misconception for new ConfigMgr administrators is that you must run the Configuration Manager console on the site server. You can actually install it separately on a workstation operating system (such as Windows Vista or XP). While installing the console, you will select a site to manage. After installation, you can also attach to additional ConfigMgr primary sites and manage them all from a single console, without needing explicit administrative rights to the server. Chapter 10 discusses using the ConfigMgr console.

---

5. On the Installation Settings page displayed in Figure 8.3, you finally can start selecting those decisions you reviewed in the "Pre-Installation" section of this chapter prior to starting the installation. Choose between custom settings and simple settings:

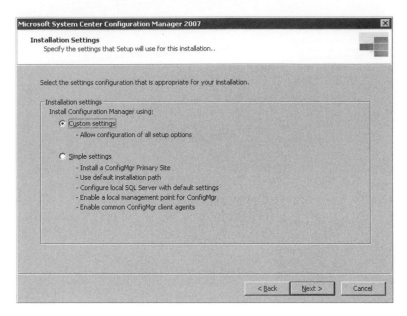

FIGURE 8.3   Choosing to install using custom or simple settings

> ▶ Custom settings allow you to specify the installation path, configure individual component settings and client agents, port settings, and more.

> ▶ Simple settings are most useful in a test environment, but the authors recommend using custom settings so you are more aware of the configuration options and the process required for production deployment.

> Choose the Custom settings option and click Next to continue.

6. On the Site Type page shown in Figure 8.4, select Primary site. Because you are installing your first site, this will also be your central site.

7. After you specify the site type, the wizard asks you to participate in the Customer Experience Improvement Program. Review the documentation at http://technet.microsoft.com/en-us/library/bb693975.aspx and be familiar with your corporate policies. Then choose whether to participate.

   Joining the Customer Experience Improvement Program can help the Configuration Manager development team understand your pain points in Configuration Manager. You can change this option after installation by using the Help menu in the ConfigMgr console.

8. Specify the product key for your Configuration Manager installation. Enter a valid product key and then click Next to continue.

9. On the Destination Folder page, select the installation directory to install the software.

10. On the Site Settings page shown in Figure 8.5, enter the three-character site code, along with a site name (or description). Use those three characters wisely, because

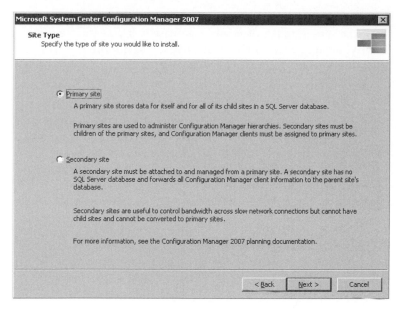

FIGURE 8.4   Specifying a site type

you will be unable to change the site code or the site name after installation
completes. Figure 8.5 uses the code CEN and the name CENTRAL SITE.

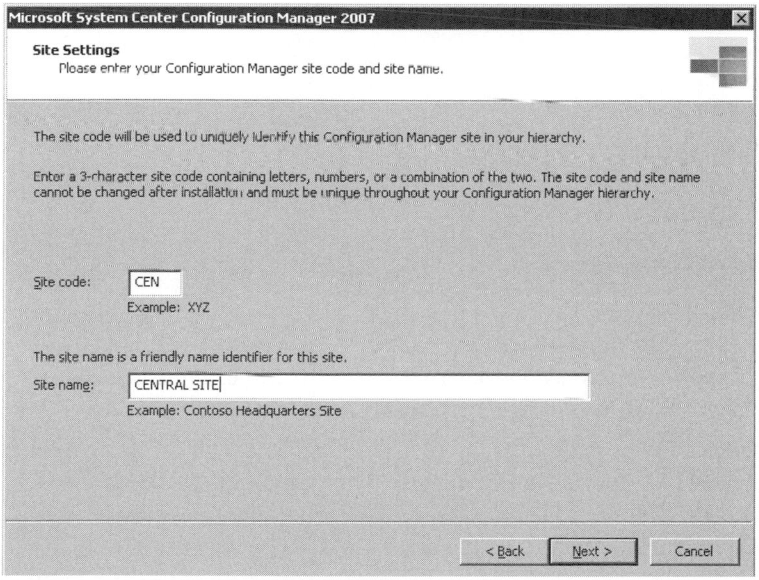

FIGURE 8.5   The Site Settings page

11. On the next page, the wizard asks you to specify the desired site mode. As discussed previously in Chapter 6, be sure to make your selection wisely. If you choose to "go native" right now, have your signed security certificate ready to import.

If you will be supporting SMS 2003 clients or Windows 2000 systems in this site, the site will need to use mixed mode. Mixed mode is also required if your site has a parent site configured for mixed mode.

It is recommended you install the first site in mixed mode (although you can always switch back and forth; see http://technet.microsoft.com/en-us/library/bb693556.aspx for details). After completing installation and confirming everything is working properly, migrate the site to native mode. For this sample installation, select mixed mode for now. The "Preparing for Native Mode" and "Enabling Native Mode" sections of this chapter give an example of configuring a site in native mode.

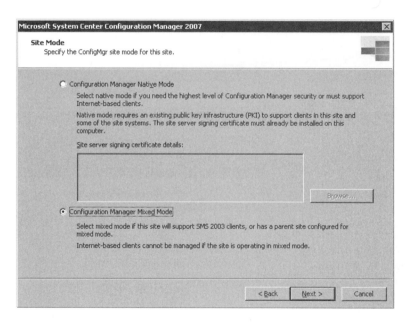

FIGURE 8.6   Specifying the site mode

12. You are now ready to enable client agents for your site. As shown in Figure 8.7, enabling client agents is as simple as checking a box. With the exception of Network Access Protection, all client agents are enabled by default.

13. On the Database Server page (shown in Figure 8.8), identify the SQL Server computer name and instance, and specify the ConfigMgr site database name. If the database name does not exist, the Configuration Manager setup program will create a new database if SQL Server is installed on the local system.

If you specified SQL on a remote server, you must first create the database manually and add the machine account of the primary site server to the local Administrators group of the remote SQL server. Also during installation, the user account that is

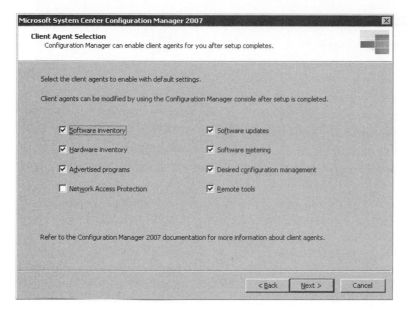

FIGURE 8.7   The Client Agent Selection page

running the ConfigMgr install must have administrative rights on the SQL server, or be assigned the sysadmin SQL Server role on the remote SQL server. Microsoft provides detailed documentation on installing ConfigMgr with a remote SQL Server at http://technet.microsoft.com/en-us/library/bb693554.aspx.

To specify a remote SQL database, simply enter the NetBIOS name of the remote SQL server and ensure that both you (as the installer) and the ConfigMgr site server have administrative rights to the SQL Server computer for installation and configuration.

Figure 8.8 shows the Database Server page with the name of the database server and the (default) site database name specified. The database will be installed on the default instance of the Bluebonnet central site server. If you want to use a named instance, simply enter it using the format specified in Figure 8.8.

TIP

Multiple Primary Sites—Use a Consistent Database Name

You may encounter a situation where it is necessary to modify your site database configuration. If you have multiple primary sites (which means you have multiple site databases, because each primary site has its own database), you may want to consider changing the database name to a consistent name (for example, "ConfigMgr"). Because using the default site database name results in a unique name for each database on each site, as shown in Figure 8.8, if you need to run a SQL script on each of your databases, you may have to change the script for each site. Using a consistent database name for all sites provides additional opportunities to automate configuration and maintenance changes.

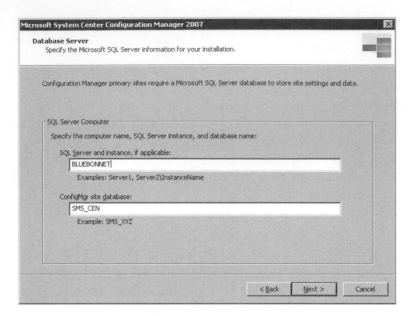

FIGURE 8.8   Specifying the database server and instance

14. The next page of the setup wizard is the SMS Provider Settings page. Specify the NetBIOS name of the server to install the SMS provider.

The SMS provider is your communication method between the ConfigMgr console and the ConfigMgr database. It is also the supported avenue to ConfigMgr data using Windows Management Instrumentation (WMI). The SMS provider is typically installed on the ConfigMgr primary site. You can also install the SMS provider on the SQL Server system or an entirely separate server. Do not install the provider on a clustered SQL Server instance or a SQL Server containing databases for multiple sites, because Microsoft does not support the provider in these scenarios. For larger sites, you may consider offloading the provider to increase performance. Microsoft provides documentation on choosing the SMS provider installation location at http://technet.microsoft.com/en-us/library/bb694290.aspx.

15. On the Management Point page, choose to install a management point (MP) if you will be assigning clients to this site. All ConfigMgr clients require access to the management point to communicate with the ConfigMgr site. You can install the management point on the site server or a separate supported server operating system. Check the management point system requirements in Table 8.1 for additional information. You can create a new management point, or move an existing management point once site installation completes.

16. On the Port Settings page, select the default port (80) or use a custom port for client communications, provided you configured the site to use mixed mode. (If you're configuring for native mode, HTTPS settings are also available for configuration.)

17. On the Updated Prerequisite Components page, you have the option to automatically connect to the Internet and download all prerequisite components, or you can specify an existing path to where you have previously downloaded the components. Setup will download several components, such as the Windows Update Agent, a WMI update, the Microsoft Remote Differential Compression Library, and a BITS update. Multiple supported languages are automatically downloaded as well.

TIP

How to Download Site Prerequisites Before Installation

Depending on your environment, you may not have access to the Internet from your ConfigMgr site, or you may have a slow Internet connection. Alternatively, you may be like us and prefer that everything you need is available before installing your site.

To download the prerequisites in advance, ensure you have Internet access, connect to your ConfigMgr installation media, and run the following command:

```
<Media Path>\SMSSETUP\BIN\I386\Setup.exe /DOWNLOAD <Destination>
```

Here, `<Destination>` is the location destination for your download—ensure this folder exists prior to running the setup command.

You can run this command from any supported Windows OS (Windows Vista, Windows XP, and so on). The download takes approximately 5 minutes with a high-speed Internet connection.

---

18. The Updated Prerequisite Component Path page will do one of two things, depending on your selection on the Updated Prerequisite Components page:

   ▶ If you selected Check for updates and download newer versions to an alternate path, specify the path to download the files.

   ▶ If you selected The latest updates have already been downloaded to an alternate path, simply specify the path so the installation can use those files.

19. Review the Settings Summary page, displayed in Figure 8.9, to ensure you entered all configuration information accurately. You can reconfigure some of these settings later, but others (such as Site Code and Site Name) are permanent. Click Next, which automatically launches the prerequisite checker.

20. The Installation Prerequisite Check page verifies installation of all prerequisites, with results displayed in Figure 8.10. The complete list of setup prerequisite checks at http://technet.microsoft.com/en-us/library/bb680951.aspx provides detailed information of all ConfigMgr prerequisites. For any items that fail the check, double-click the individual result to see additional information. You should be able to remediate most problems while leaving the setup page open. If the server must be rebooted, you will need to restart the installation process from the beginning.

21. After correcting any items that failed prerequisite checks, click Run Check to rerun the prerequisite check. After all checks pass, click OK to begin the ConfigMgr site installation. During the installation process, review the installation log located at %*SystemRoot*%\ConfigMgrSetup.log. An installation progress page appears, as displayed in Figure 8.11.

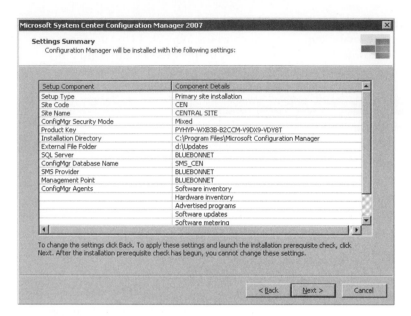

FIGURE 8.9   The Settings Summary page

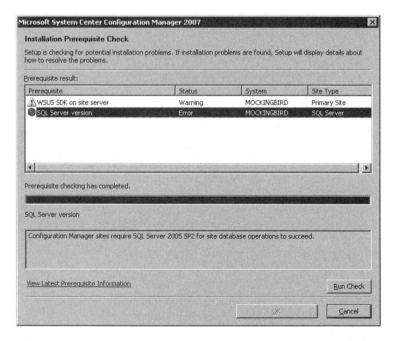

FIGURE 8.10   The Installation Prerequisite Check page, with failures

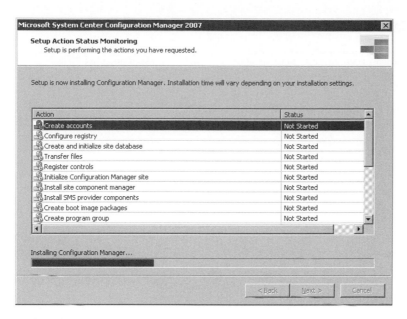

FIGURE 8.11   The Setup Action Status Monitoring page

22. The Completing the Microsoft System Center Configuration Manager 2007 Setup Wizard page appears at the end of the installation. If you haven't been watching the ConfigMgrSetup.log using SMS Trace (see the earlier note "Use SMS Trace to Monitor ConfigMgr Installation" regarding SMS Trace), click the View Log button to review the log, as shown in Figure 8.12.

TIP

Always Review ConfigMgrPrereq.log and ConfigMgrSetup.log

If you are like the authors of this book, you will be very excited when you see the message in Figure 8.12 that reads "Setup completed all operations successfully." Although there is a very good chance that this message is completely accurate, it is highly recommended you take the time to review the logs. Installations have occurred that appeared (and reported) to be successful, but were not completely successful due to problems such as improper SQL configuration or improper rights between servers. The message in Figure 8.12 gives a good indication of success, but the logs give the best indication. Browse %*SystemRoot%*\ConfigMgrPrereq.log and %*SystemRoot%*\ConfigMgrSetup.log to view additional installation information.

With the central site installed, you can use the same procedures to install other primary site servers. You would then join the sites together, as discussed in the "Attaching to Parent" section of this chapter. You will also want to upgrade your site servers to the

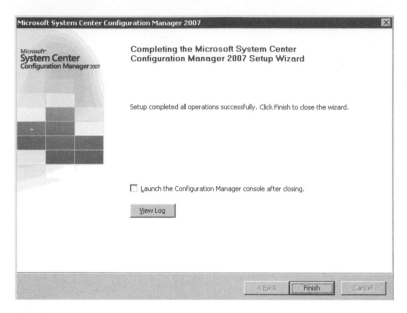

FIGURE 8.12   Completing the Microsoft System Center Configuration Manager 2007 Setup Wizard

current service pack level and ConfigMgr 2007 Release 2 (R2), as discussed in the following sections.

> **NOTE**
>
> **Performing a Silent Installation of ConfigMgr**
>
> You can perform a silent/unattended installation of ConfigMgr. The article at http://technet.microsoft.com/en-us/library/bb693561.aspx provides information on unattended setups and includes additional links to sample script files and command-line parameters.

Installing a ConfigMgr Service Pack

Before installing a service pack, read the Readme file included with the service pack media. As always, ensure you have a proper backup before attempting the upgrade. Chapter 21, "Backup, Recovery, and Maintenance," contains information about configuring ConfigMgr scheduled backups.

> **NOTE**
>
> **Disable All SQL Replication Before Performing the Site Upgrade**
>
> To upgrade successfully, you must first remove any existing database replication and subscriptions. Microsoft provides an article on disabling SQL Server database

replication at http://technet.microsoft.com/en-us/library/bb693954.aspx. The
"Disabling SQL Replication" section later in this chapter also discusses the steps to
disable replication.

Performing a Site Database Upgrade Test

Before upgrading a site, you should perform a site database upgrade test. This test is a
destructive test, so be sure to make a copy of your database, as described in the "Making a
Copy of the ConfigMgr Database" sidebar.

Making a Copy of the ConfigMgr Database

Perform the following steps to make a copy of the ConfigMgr site database:

1. Stop the following Windows Services for ConfigMgr:
   - ▶ SMS_SITECOMPONENT_MANAGER
   - ▶ SMS_EXECUTIVE
   - ▶ SMS_SITE_SQL_BACKUP
   - ▶ SMS_SITE_VSS_WRITER
   - ▶ Any other services running that begin with "SMS_"
2. Launch Microsoft SQL Server Management Studio (Start -> Programs -> SQL
   Server 2005 -> SQL Server Management Studio).
3. Expand the Databases node and right-click the ConfigMgr database (by default
   named SMS_*XXX*, where *XXX* is the site code). Now select Tasks -> Copy
   Database to launch the Copy Database Wizard.
4. Click Next after reviewing the Welcome screen.
5. Select the source server and configure the required authentication settings.
6. Specify the destination server and configure the required authentication settings.
7. Specify the transfer method—the detach and attach method is preferred.
8. Verify the ConfigMgr Site database is the selected database to copy.
9. Accept the default database name for the new test database, or specify as desired.
10. Accept the defaults on the Configure the Package page of the Copy Database
    Wizard.
11. Select Run Immediately as the start time.
12. Click Finish for the copy to proceed. (Depending on the size of the database, this
    may take several minutes to several hours.)
13. Verify successful completion and then click Close to close the Copy Database
    Wizard.
14. Refresh the Databases node in SQL Server Management Studio to see the new
    database.
15. Restart the services stopped in step 1, or simply reboot the server.

8

The database copy does not need to reside on the production ConfigMgr site—in fact, it doesn't even need to be on a ConfigMgr site! Simply attach the database copy to any SQL Server instance running the same version and service pack level as your site database.

After copying the database, perform the following steps:

1. From the installation media, run the following command line, replacing *SMS_XXX_COPY* with the name of your test database:

   SMSSETUP\BIN\I386\setup.exe /testdbupgrade *<SMS_XXX_COPY>*

   The prerequisite checker will run briefly.

2. Select Begin TestDBUpgrade.

   Once again, the log files *%SystemRoot%*\ConfigMgrPrereq.log and *%SystemRoot%*\ConfigMgrSetup.log are updated, this time with information about the database upgrade test. A message appears stating ConfigMgr has been successfully upgraded.

Successfully performing a test upgrade on your database is an indicator that the database portion of the site upgrade will run smoothly.

Performing the Upgrade

The remainder of the process of installing the latest service pack for ConfigMgr is very similar to the initial installation of your site. Follow the steps previously described in the "Installing ConfigMgr" section of this chapter:

▶ Perform the same steps for running the prerequisite checker and downloading additional prerequisites.

▶ Because your site is already a primary site, the Available Setup Options page gives you the ability to upgrade or uninstall. As shown in Figure 8.13, select the option Upgrade an existing Configuration Manager or SMS 2003 installation.

▶ You may be prompted to uninstall an older version of the Windows Automated Installation Kit (WAIK) first; if so, be certain to restart your server after removing the WAIK.

To ensure proper functionality, also upgrade all remote consoles, using the same process as when upgrading your site.

TIP

Upgrade Your New Site to the Current ConfigMgr Service Pack Before Attaching to Your Hierarchy

When installing a new site, be sure to upgrade the site to your standard service pack level for ConfigMgr before you attach the site to your hierarchy. When you attach a site, all parent sites initiate a replication to ensure that the new site has proper content. A similar process occurs when you install a service pack on a child site. By your upgrading to your standard service pack level before attaching the site, the new site only needs to process one complete replication instead of two. Save yourself, your network, and your new site some processing cycles by ensuring the new site has your standard ConfigMgr service pack installed prior to attaching. The "Attaching to Parent" section of this chapter provides information about attaching a primary to a parent primary site.

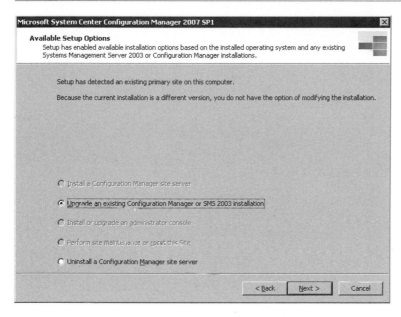

FIGURE 8.13   The Available Setup Options page

After the upgrade completes, review the installation logs *%SystemRoot%*\ConfigMgrPrereq.log and *%SystemRoot%*\ConfigMgrSetup.log. Next, launch the ConfigMgr console, expand the Site Database node, and click Site Management to view the version information for your site. Figure 8.14 shows an example of the central site with ConfigMgr with SP 1 installed—both the version and build number have changed from the base release of ConfigMgr 2007.

TIP

Order of Operations—Upgrade Central Site First

If you have a multisite hierarchy in place, be sure to upgrade the central site first and then move down the hierarchy from the top.

For additional information about upgrading a ConfigMgr site to the latest service pack, search the Microsoft TechCenter for the appropriate ConfigMgr Service Pack check list. As an example, the ConfigMgr 2007 Service Pack 1 Upgrade check list is at http://technet. microsoft.com/en-us/library/cc161792.aspx.

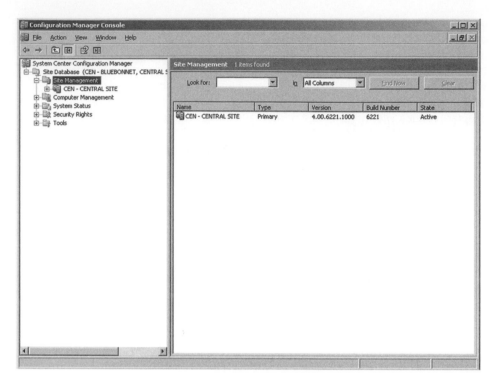

FIGURE 8.14   ConfigMgr site with Service Pack 1 installed

After upgrading the site, you must upgrade the clients attached to the site. Clients can be upgraded with the Client Push Installation Wizard, Software Updates, Software Distribution, or Software Update Point Client Installation. See Chapter 12, "Client Management," for additional information on upgrading clients.

Installing ConfigMgr 2007 R2

Installing R2 is similar to installing a service pack on a site server. Fortunately, R2 is a much smaller installation. Prior to installing R2, you must install ConfigMgr SP 1 (or the latest service pack).

NOTE

Disable All SQL Replication Before Upgrading the Site to ConfigMgr 2007 R2

Similar to when you install a service pack, remove all database replication and subscriptions. Before upgrading to R2, check Microsoft's article on disabling SQL Server database replication, located at http://technet.microsoft.com/en-us/library/bb693954.aspx. The "Disabling SQL Replication" section later in this chapter also discusses the steps to disable replication.

To upgrade to ConfigMgr 2007 R2, perform the following steps:

1. Close all instances of the MMC on the site server (this includes the ConfigMgr console, SQL Server Management Studio, Computer Management, and so on).
2. Launch Splash.hta from the R2 installation media.
3. Click to install Configuration Manager 2007 R2.
4. Review the Welcome page.
5. Review and accept the license agreement.
6. Verify the information and enter a valid product key.
7. Click Finish to complete the installation.

Unlike when you install a service pack, the site version information does not change after R2. In addition, there is no client code update with ConfigMgr 2007 R2. Remember that if you have a multisite hierarchy in place, you need to upgrade your central site first.

To verify the R2 installation, check Add or Remove Programs or right-click the site in the ConfigMgr console and select Properties to view the Site Properties, as shown in Figure 8.15 for the CEN site. For additional information about upgrading your ConfigMgr Site to R2, read the Configuration Manager 2007 R2 installation check list at http://tcchnet. microsoft.com/en-us/library/cc161948.aspx.

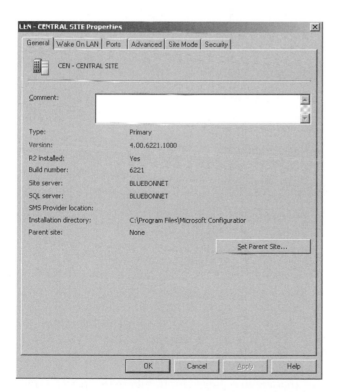

FIGURE 8.15   ConfigMgr 2007 site with R2 installed

NOTE

Installing ConfigMgr on Windows Server 2008

Windows Server 2008 requires additional configuration changes when you install a ConfigMgr site or ConfigMgr site system. The document on configuring Windows Server 2008 for site systems at http://technet.microsoft.com/en-us/library/cc431377.aspx provides more information.

Configuring Site Properties

Site Properties is one of the first objects to configure after you install a new site. To access the Site Properties from the ConfigMgr console, select Site Database -> Site Management. Right-click the desired site (BXL is selected in this example) and select Properties, as displayed in Figure 8.16.

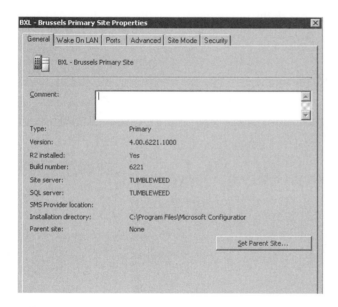

FIGURE 8.16   The General tab of the Site Properties dialog box

General

As Figure 8.16 shows, the General tab of the Site Properties dialog box provides important information about the BXL site installation, including the type and version, whether R2 is installed, and the build, site server, SQL server, and so on. You may also attach or detach from a parent site from this tab by selecting the Set Parent Site button. The "Attaching to Parent" section of this chapter demonstrates how to attach to a parent site.

Wake On LAN

ConfigMgr is able to "wake up" systems that are in a powered-off, hibernate, or sleep state. Once this is set, you can configure the wake-up on a per-advertisement or per-mandatory software update deployment (that is, a software update deployment configured with a deadline, as discussed in Chapter 15). The Wake On LAN tab of the Site Properties dialog box enables you to configure Wake On LAN, as shown in Figure 8.17.

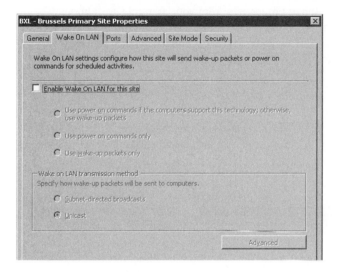

FIGURE 8.17   The Wake On LAN tab of the Site Properties dialog box

To enable any support within ConfigMgr for Wake On LAN, first enable the Enable Wake On LAN for this site check box. (If a ConfigMgr 2007 service pack is not installed, the options are slightly different.) Select from the three available options, depending on the type of clients you will manage:

▶ The first two options describe power-on commands. These are primarily for managing Intel Active Management Technology–provisioned systems. AMT uses a different method for waking up systems than traditional wake-up packets, often referred to as *magic packets* in documentation and on the Internet.

   ▶ If all systems you intend to manage are AMT-provisioned, select the option Use power on commands only.

   ▶ If you have traditional wake-up packets, choose Use wake-up packets only.

▶ If you have a mixture of AMT and traditional wake-up packets, select the first option, Use power on commands if the computers support this terminology. Otherwise, use wake-up packets.

Remember that simply having systems with AMT support in the BIOS does not provision them for enterprise management. Review the information in Chapter 15 to ensure your clients are properly provisioned.

If you select the first or third option in Figure 8.17, you must also specify the Wake On LAN transmission method—either subnet-directed broadcasts or unicast—at the bottom part of this page.

> **TIP**
>
> **About Subnet-Directed Broadcasts**
>
> To use subnet-directed broadcasts, you may need to work with your network teams to configure network hardware to allow these broadcasts from your primary site. Although subnet-directed broadcasts comprise the easiest method, your network team may consider this method the least secure. The ConfigMgr integrated help contains additional information regarding subnet-directed broadcasts versus unicast.

Click the Advanced button in Figure 8.17 to configure additional site settings for the wake-up process. The Advanced properties allow you to configure the retry count and delay, the number of systems woken up before a pause, and how much time in advance to wake up a system before a mandatory advertisement (or software update deadline) is scheduled to occur.

> **NOTE**
>
> **Configure Clients to Support Wake On LAN**
>
> Configuring your ConfigMgr site to support Wake On LAN is pretty straightforward and is half of the required configuration. The other half is dependent on the client, which also must be configured to allow Wake On LAN. This is a BIOS configuration, and you can change it manually. Most computer manufacturers allow it to be configured by running an executable or script. Check with your computer manufacturer for specifics. If you still have problems after configuring the BIOS, verify you are using the vendor-provided network interface card driver, as the Windows-provided driver may have limited functionality. The article at http://technet.microsoft.com/en-us/library/bb932199.aspx includes information on troubleshooting Wake On LAN issues.

Ports

Use the Ports tab to customize ports the client will use to communicate with the site, as well as the port used by the site for Wake On LAN. As shown in Figure 8.18, you can configure both HTTP and HTTPS ports for client communications, and for each of these you can create an alternate port should you decide to change from the default ports.

If you want (or need) to use a different website than the default IIS website, enable the Use custom web site check box at the bottom of the dialog box in Figure 8.18. Enabling this check box requires previously configuring a custom website named **SMSWeb** on all site systems that require IIS for this site and any secondary sites attached to this site. The article at http://technet.microsoft.com/en-us/library/bb693482.aspx provides additional information on configuring custom websites for ConfigMgr sites.

Advanced

The Advanced tab of the Site Properties dialog box allows additional configuration of your ConfigMgr site. Figure 8.19 shows the available options for the Advanced tab.

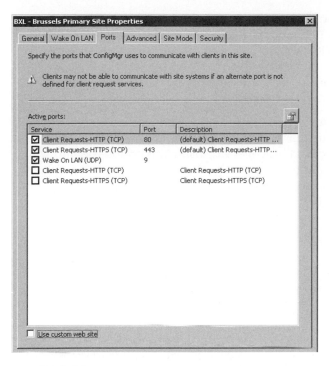

FIGURE 8.18   The Ports tab of the Site Properties dialog box

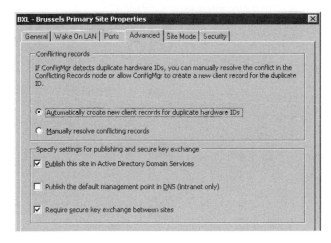

FIGURE 8.19   The Advanced tab of the Site Properties dialog box

These options can have significant impact on the health of the ConfigMgr clients assigned to this site. The first part of this page deals with conflicting records.

▶ **Automatically create new client records for duplicate hardware IDs**—This is the default setting, and it should not be changed. Exceptions would be if you have a small site or a site requiring close monitoring of ConfigMgr client reinstalls or operating system reinstalls and if you need to preserve ConfigMgr client inventory history. (Automatically creating new client records was the only configuration available in SMS 2003, and it could not be modified.)

▶ **Manually resolve conflicting records**—This option gives the ConfigMgr administrator more power to determine how to handle duplicate hardware IDs. (Duplicate hardware IDs are discussed further in Chapter 21.) Using this option, systems with duplicate hardware IDs appear in the Conflicting Records node of the ConfigMgr console. To resolve conflicting records manually, you can choose which process to apply to the conflicting records:

  ▶ **Merge the record**—Merging combines the new record with the existing record. This can be an excellent option if you know the old resource is the same as the new resource, and you want to preserve hardware and software inventory. An example of this would be if you needed to reinstall the ConfigMgr client on a system.

  ▶ **Create a new record**—Creating a new record makes the newer record the official record and marks the old record as obsolete.

  ▶ **Block**—This process creates a new record for the client and marks it as blocked. ConfigMgr does not manage systems in the blocked state, and the older record remains in the database. You may want to consider blocking a system while investigating the reason for the record conflict.

When a new record is created, the old record is marked obsolete and purged from the ConfigMgr database, based on configured maintenance tasks. Remember that as long as a system appears in the Conflicting Records node of the ConfigMgr console, it is in an unmanaged state.

NOTE

Client Records and Direct Membership Rules in Collections

When a new record is created (automatically or manually), the client also receives a new ResourceID. The ResourceID is a key property of the client and is used to create direct membership rules for collections. When the client receives a new ResourceID, although all direct membership rules that referenced the ResourceID with the old computer account still exist, they will not apply to the new client record. This is very important to remember when troubleshooting software distribution problems.

The client membership is typically retained for query-based membership rules, because the query-based rule is generally dependent on a specific hardware configuration, NetBIOS name, or other static information on the client.

The second section of the Advanced tab of the Site Properties dialog box allows you to specify settings for publishing and secure key exchange:

▶ **Publish this site in Active Directory Domain Services**—Use this option to leverage Active Directory for content location requests and site assignment for ConfigMgr clients. If you previously published to Active Directory and then choose to clear this check box, the information is not removed from Active Directory and you must delete it manually.

▶ **Publish the default management point in DNS (intranet only)**—This choice will publish the default management point in DNS as a Service Location (SRV) record. Consider this option only if the site system is configured with the management point role.

TIP

Publishing the Default Management Point to DNS

If you are not leveraging Active Directory and do not use WINS, consider enabling the option to publish to DNS. Review the information at http://technet.microsoft.com/en-us/library/bb633035.aspx to determine if you need to publish to DNS. Information on configuring ConfigMgr clients to find their MP using DNS publishing is available at http://technet.microsoft.com/en us/library/bb633030.aspx.

▶ **Require secure key exchange between sites**—Leave this option enabled to maintain a higher level of security for site-to-site communications. With this option enabled and site data published to Active Directory, no additional configuration is required. If the site is not publishing site data to Active Directory, use the Preinst.exe hierarchy maintenance tool from the ConfigMgr toolkit to copy the child site's public key to the parent site.

Chapter 3 provides information on Active Directory schema extensions for ConfigMgr, and http://technet.microsoft.com/en-us/library/bb632936.aspx includes instructions on manually publishing the default management point to DNS.

Site Mode

The Site Mode tab allows you to configure native mode or mixed mode and provides additional settings required for each mode. At first glance, the Site Mode tab appears to be simple, in that you can easily switch from mixed mode to native mode. Chapter 6 includes a complete discussion of when to switch to native mode.

Configuring Mixed Mode   Figure 8.20 shows there are several settings to configure while in mixed mode.

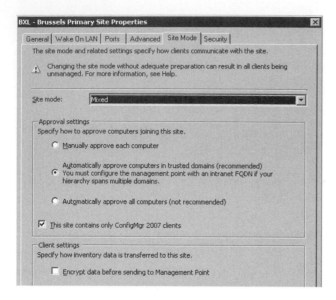

FIGURE 8.20   The Site Mode tab of the Site Properties dialog box, in mixed mode

The Approval settings section allows you to determine how ConfigMgr will approve systems. Every system (except mobile device clients) that installs the ConfigMgr client must be approved before it can be managed in a mixed mode site. Select one of the three available options to manage approval for computers joining the site:

▶ **Manually approve each computer**—This is obviously the most labor-intensive approach, and requires the administrator to approve each new client. The manual approval process occurs at the ConfigMgr site to which the client is assigned.

▶ **Automatically approve computers in trusted domains (recommended)**—This is the suggested setting, because it is the most secure. The setting allows ConfigMgr to approve all computers joined to domains trusted by the site server. For this setting to be secure, processes should be in place to prevent untrustworthy computers from joining trusted domains. If you have multiple trusted domains, you must configure the sites'default management point with a Fully Qualified Domain Name (FQDN).

▶ **Automatically approve all computers**—This setting is the least secure, and allows all assigned computers to join the site.

TIP

Reverting from Native to Mixed Mode?

In native mode, approval is not required because client authentication using PKI certificates takes the place of approval. It is common to see clients with a state of "unapproved" in the ConfigMgr console while in native mode. If you must revert to mixed mode, you will need to approve the unapproved clients manually to manage them.

Other settings in Figure 8.20 include the following:

▶ If you have ConfigMgr clients only (meaning there are no SMS 2003 clients), keep the default enabled setting of This site contains only ConfigMgr 2007 clients. This setting enables a more secure method of communication, but is not compatible with SMS 2003 clients.

▶ The final mixed mode setting, Encrypt data before sending to the management point, is used to encrypt hardware inventory, software inventory, and other client data to prevent easy viewing of intercepted client data.

Preparing for Native Mode   Chapter 6 discusses planning for site security modes. Migrating to native mode requires significant knowledge of your Public Key Infrastructure (PKI), so be sure to know that infrastructure (or know someone who does). Chapter 11, "Related Technologies and References," includes information on PKI management. Migration to native node at this time is relatively simple, because only the first site is deployed, site properties are not configured, and clients are not yet installed.

You can find a detailed check list with the steps to migrate a site to native mode at http://technet.microsoft.com/en-us/library/bb632727.aspx. You will also find links from that document that provide more detail for each step (and any additional required steps).

Three types of certificates are required for native mode:

▶ **Site server signing certificate**—Use this certificate to sign client policies. The certificate must be created and deployed to the ConfigMgr site before switching to native mode. In a multisite environment, you must configure this certificate directly on each primary site database. You cannot use the console on a parent site; to make the configuration changes, you must be directly connected to that site.

▶ **Web server certificate**—Use this certificate to encrypt data and authenticate the server to clients. The certificate must reside on ConfigMgr site systems such as the management point and distribution point.

▶ **Client certificate**—Install this certificate on computers that will be ConfigMgr clients to allow the client to authenticate to ConfigMgr site systems. Installing this certificate on the management point enables monitoring management point health.

See http://technet.microsoft.com/en-us/library/bb680733.aspx for additional information on certificate requirements for native mode.

Enabling Native Mode   To enable native mode, perform the following steps:

1. Navigate to the Site Mode tab of the Advanced properties dialog box of the connected site. (Remember, you must be logged in to the site you are converting to native mode, and using the ConfigMgr console on that local site.)
2. Change the Site Mode selection from Mixed to Native. Click Browse.

3. From the Available Certificates dialog box, select the certificate issued to the name The site code of this site server is *xxx*. Verify it has an intended purpose of Document Signing and then click OK. (This example uses BXL as the site code. Your certificate must contain the site code under Issued to name; otherwise, ConfigMgr will refuse it.)

After you select the certificate, native mode settings will appear similar to those displayed in Figure 8.21 for the SCCMUnleashed.com BXL site.

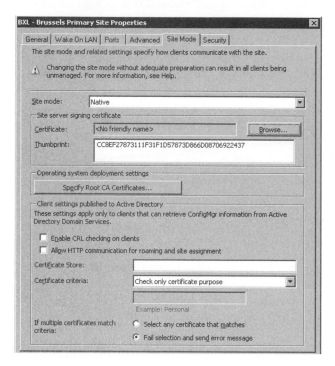

FIGURE 8.21   Enabling Native Mode on the ConfigMgr Site and specifying the Site Server Signing Certificate

4. Click OK to apply the configuration. ConfigMgr will start the process of migrating the site to native mode. The time to complete the migration will vary, depending on the number of policies that require signing. For this fresh install of ConfigMgr, the migration was complete in less than 5 minutes.

5. To verify the migration is complete, expand System Status in the ConfigMgr console and then click Status Message Queries. Right-click All Status Messages and select Show Messages. Accept the default of 1 hour for the prompted value so that status messages from the last hour display. Search the results for the following status messages:

▶ **SMS_MP_CONTROL_MANAGER MessageID 4629**—The management point has successfully reinstalled.

> ▶ **SMS_POLICY_PROVIDER MessageID 5116**—The site server has signed all
> policies with the site server signing certificate.

The site is now migrated to native mode.

The next step is enabling client communication to the native mode site, which is straightforward because there are no existing clients and the ConfigMgr components are not yet
configured. You will need to configure IIS to use the web server certificate to allow client
communications.

The steps to configure IIS vary, depending on the version of Windows Server that is
running:

> ▶ For Windows Server 2003, perform the following steps:
>
>   1. Open IIS Services Manager, expand the Web Sites node, right-click the Default
>   Web Site, and select Properties.
>   2. Select the Directory Security tab and then click Server Certificate.
>   3. Follow the wizard and select Assign an existing certificate.
>   4. Select the proper certificate; verify the Intended Purpose field has a value of Server
>   Authentication.
>   5. Verify the SSL port is configured to number 443 and then finish the wizard.

> ▶ Perform the following steps if you are using Windows Server 2008:
>
>   1. Open IIS Services Manager, expand the Sites node, right-click on Default Web Site,
>   and select Edit Bindings.
>   2. Select the https entry and click Edit.
>   3. Select the appropriate certificate and verify that the Intended Purpose field has a
>   value of Server Authentication.
>   4. Click OK and then click Close to complete the configuration.

NOTE

Enabling IIS with Distributed Site Systems

If management points, distribution points, or other client-facing roles are configured on
multiple servers, you must configure IIS on each server to use the web server certificate.

The final native mode migration step is to ensure clients have a proper certificate for
communications to your management point, distribution point, and other roles that interface with the client (the fallback status point and server locator point roles do not require

certificate-based communication). Work with your PKI team to force clients to receive the required certificate automatically. For additional information on deploying PKI certificates for native mode, see http://technet.microsoft.com/en-us/library/bb680312.aspx.

You now have a healthy ConfigMgr site in native mode. The next task is to install site systems, which is covered in the next section of this chapter. Chapter 2 introduces the different types of site systems.

Installing Site Systems

Site systems "make the world go 'round" in the ConfigMgr world. As with most site configuration, almost all of these settings are configured once and typically do not require later modification. Each ConfigMgr site contains a site server and one or more site systems. Site systems are components of ConfigMgr, a number of which you may or may not desire to use. Although some components are required, most are optional, depending on the specific configuration. In smaller sites, all site systems (also called site *roles*) may be installed on a single server. Earlier in the "Installing ConfigMgr" section of this chapter, we selected Custom Settings for the installation type, and accepted the default configuration for a custom installation. Based on the options selected during site installation, ConfigMgr installs the following site systems automatically:

▶ **Component server**—This site system does not have configurable options. Any site server running a site system requiring the ConfigMgr 2007 service will have the component server listed as a site system.

▶ **Distribution point**—A distribution point is used to stage source installation files, driver package files, operating system images, and software updates for client use. By default, this is a standard distribution point, meaning that when clients request a location for content (installation files), ConfigMgr forwards a Universal Naming Convention (UNC) path to allow the client to access the data via service message blocks (SMBs).

   If you want to use Download and Execute for installation packages, you must enable the check box to allow clients to transfer content using BITS, HTTP, and HTTPS. This is often referred to as a *BITS-enabled DP*. When this check box is enabled, the client will access content from the distribution point using HTTP and use BITS to "trickle" the installation files to the local system. Chapter 14, "Distributing Packages," contains additional information about distribution points.

   You also can create a branch distribution point for a new site. Branch distribution points are described later in this section.

   Use the Group Membership section at the bottom of the Distribution Point Properties dialog box to create distribution point groups. This capability allows you to group DPs easily and becomes very helpful when sending content to distribution points. As an example, you can make a DP group of all your DPs in Europe, and then any time you need to send content to the Europe DPs, simply select the group rather than the tedious process of selecting each DP manually.

The Multicast tab appears when ConfigMgr 2007 R2 is installed, and it's only used during Operating System Deployment (OSD). From this tab, you may specify the User Datagram Protocol (UDP) ports to use, the transfer rate, and the maximum clients. You can also enable scheduled multicast. With scheduled multicast, you can configure the start delay from the time the first system requests content, as well as specify the minimum session size. When scheduled multicast is enabled, the multicast begins either when the Start Delay time is exceeded or the number of session requests to the DP is larger than the minimum session size, whichever comes first. Multicast requires distribution points that are BITS enabled. For additional information, check Microsoft's documentation discussing multicast configurations for OSD at http://technet.microsoft.com/en-us/library/cc431383.aspx.

The Virtual Applications tab also appears with ConfigMgr 2007 R2 installed. Enable this option to configure application streaming to target computers. You must BITS-enable the distribution point to enable virtual application streaming.

▶ **Management point**—If you will be assigning clients to this site, the MP role must be enabled. The management point is the primary connection point between clients and the ConfigMgr site. Depending on how many systems will use this MP, you may want to consider offloading the MP role from the site server. Each primary site has one active MP, which clients use to obtain policy, forward inventory, and the other client communication requirements. If you plan to manage mobile devices from this site, enable the check box to allow devices to use this management point.

The MP can be configured to use a database replica. If the SQL database on your primary site is very busy all the time, you may consider configuring a SQL database replica and configuring the MP to use the replica for content information. By default, the MP computer account is configured to connect to the database. You may need to grant rights to allow this communication. Alternatively, you can specify an MP connection account to establish this communication if desired. The "Using Replicas and Offloading Site Roles" section of this chapter contains information for creating a database replica.

▶ **Site server**—This is a standard role added during every site server installation. No configuration is required.

▶ **Site system**—A site system can be a server or share that supports the site. The site system may perform more than one role. It is highly recommended that you specify the FQDN for intranet clients (the FQDN must be specified for Internet-based clients).

If you have multiple domains and do not use a fully replicated WINS or have a disjointed namespace, you may see errors in client logs where the client is unable to obtain content for a distribution. One of the first places to look to resolve this issue is whether you have specified an intranet FQDN. When the site is in native mode, the FQDN specified in the server certificate subject name must match the intranet FQDN specified in the Site System Properties page, as displayed in Figure 8.22.

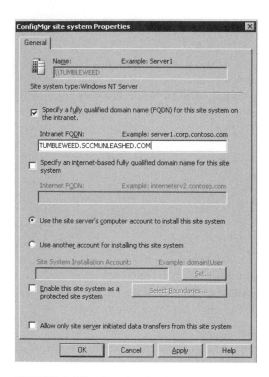

FIGURE 8.22   The ConfigMgr Site System Properties dialog box

By default, the site server's computer account is used to install the site system, although you can specify a different account on this page if desired.

You can also specify the option Enable this site system as a protected site system. By checking this box, you then select the boundaries that can use this site system. For example, you may have a DP on a remote WAN, and you want to ensure that only systems in that remote site have the ability to access content from the DP, enable the protected site system, and select the boundaries to protect. Protected systems are used for DPs and state migration points.

The final check box, Allow only site server initiated data transfers from this site system, can be used for systems that are configured for site system roles that are supported across forests. Checking this box forces the ConfigMgr site to use the Site

System Installation account to connect to the remote site system. Even if a trust exists, the Site System Installation account will be used.

▶ **Site database server**—This site system displays the SQL Server name and the SQL database name used by this ConfigMgr site. No configuration is required for the site database server.

As this discussion shows, Configuration Manager automatically configures many site systems, even when using a custom configuration for the ConfigMgr installation. Let's look at the other site roles and using additional servers for site roles.

Use the Site Role Wizard to add more roles to an existing site system. Right-click the server name and then select New Roles to initiate the Site Role Wizard. The first step in the wizard allows you to configure the same options visible in Figure 8.22, which shows the Site System Properties dialog box. Verify the settings for this site and then click Next in the wizard to select additional roles. The rest of this section describes each of the remaining roles you can configure from the Site Role Wizard:

▶ **Fallback status point**—Configure a fallback status point (FSP) before you begin to deploy clients. The FSP helps you verify successful client installation, identify client installation failures, and provide a method for clients to report when they are not able to contact a management point. The FSP also helps identify communication problems with clients in native mode.

You can configure how many state messages to forward to your ConfigMgr site each throttle interval, thus preventing the FSP from overwhelming your ConfigMgr site. If your site is configured in native mode and you have specified an Internet FQDN, you can configure the FSP to allow intranet-only connections or both intranet and Internet connections.

You may need to perform additional configurations to ensure that your clients use the FSP. The section "How to Assign the Fallback Status Point to Client Computers" in the ConfigMgr integrated help file provides additional information.

▶ **PXE service point**—Use a PXE service point to leverage the Preboot Execution Environment (PXE) for ConfigMgr Operating System Deployment (OSD). When you enable the PXE service point, you receive notification that ConfigMgr will open UDP ports 67, 68, 69, and 4011 on the site system so it can respond to PXE requests.

If you have ConfigMgr 2007 R2 installed, you also have the option to enable Unknown Computer Support. This allows you to deploy imaged systems not currently managed by ConfigMgr.

8

CAUTION

Unknown Computer Support and the PXE Service Point

Use extreme caution when using Unknown Computer Support and the PXE service point. When Unknown Computer Support is enabled, any unknown computers that boot to PXE will attempt to run mandatory task sequences. If you have mandatory task sequence advertisements for OSD, you may encounter unexpected results on a new (unknown) system, or an unhealthy ConfigMgr client. Automatically deploying an image to an unknown computer (which happens to be a critical web server for your company) may cause you to quickly dust off your resume. On the lighter side, it may also help you standardize on Windows! To prevent an unintentional operating system deployment to one or multiple systems, create a text file that contains the Media Access Control (MAC) addresses (one per line in the text file) for the systems to exclude and then store it on each PXE service point. Separate the MAC address elements with colons (for example, ab:cd:01:23:45:67). Also, in the Registry on each PXE service point, add a string value named MACIgnoreListFile at HKEY_LOCAL_MACHINE\Software\Microsoft\SMS\PXE and point it to the full path to the text file. See http://technet.microsoft.com/en-us/library/cc431378.aspx for more information.

You can also enable the option Require a password for computers that boot to PXE, which allows you to restrict PXE OS deployment to users who know the password (this typically is your service desk and on-site support teams).

One final important step for configuring PXE is that you must either create a self-signed certificate or import a certificate. If your site is configured for native mode, you must import a certificate from a trusted root Certificate Authority.

▶ **Reporting point**—Create a reporting point to view reports and dashboards for your site. Many ConfigMgr administrators also refer to this as *web reporting*. ConfigMgr contains over 300 built-in web reports. If you install ConfigMgr R2, you will have nearly 400 built-in web reports. You can also create additional web reports as required. You must install IIS prior to installing the reporting point.

Review Figure 8.23 for reporting point configuration. The information shown is the default settings. Because the site code in Figure 8.23 is BXL, the report folder is SMSReporting_BXL by default. The report folder name will be part of the URL used to access the web reporting site.

Two types of rights are required for access to view web reports:

▶ Add users and user groups to the local SMS Reporting Users security group on the server to grant them access to the Web Reporting site.

▶ Grant the users or user groups class rights to view all web reports, or instance rights on specific reports, as needed.

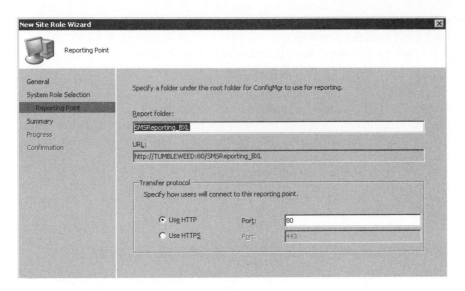

FIGURE 8.23   Creating a new reporting point

Chapter 18, "Reporting," contains additional information about reporting points.

▶ **Reporting services point**—With ConfigMgr 2007 R2, you can optionally install a reporting services point as well. Install SQL Reporting Services (SRS) before attempting to configure a reporting services point.

NOTE

Multiple Instances of SQL Reporting Services May Cause Issues

If multiple instances of SRS exist on the same site, you may encounter unexpected results when installing a reporting services point. During installation, ConfigMgr queries WMI on the server for all instances of SQL Reporting Services, and it *always* installs the reporting services point on the first instance returned.

▶ **Asset Intelligence synchronization point**—If you have Microsoft Software Assurance (SA), you can create an Asset Intelligence synchronization point to download Asset Intelligence catalog information and upload custom software title catalog information (if desired). To configure the synchronization point, you must obtain a certificate from Microsoft and import it during configuration. You can also specify a proxy server and proxy server account if your network requires proxy authentication. By default, the synchronization schedule runs every 7 days. See Chapter 18 for additional configuration information.

▶ **Out of Band service point**—If you have systems with Intel Active Management Technology (AMT), enable the Out of Band service point to improve control of Wake On LAN and other remote management needs. AMT is a technology used in vPro;

systems with vPro installed can be managed using the Out of Band (OOB) service point. OOB in this instance refers to systems that are connected on the LAN, but not running Windows (or you don't have access remotely to Windows on the system). Using vPro, you can remotely connect to these systems, even while the system is powered off, provided all configurations are completed in advance.

As displayed in Figure 8.24, you can configure the properties of the Out of Band service point role to increase or reduce the network and CPU utilization of the site due to the OOB service point. As an example, when you create and enable Wake On LAN for an advertisement, the OOB service point will wake all targeted vPro-enabled systems using the settings specified in Figure 8.24. Review the ConfigMgr help file for additional information regarding each property in Figure 8.24.

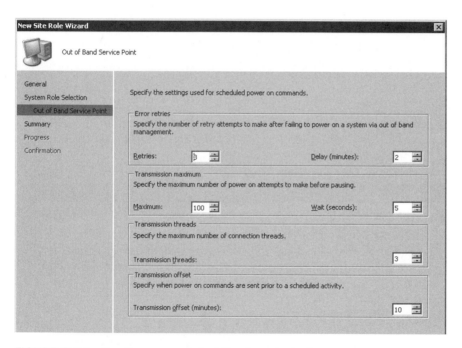

FIGURE 8.24 Creating a new Out of Band service point

NOTE

Provision Computers for AMT

You must set up and configure (provision) AMT-based computers so ConfigMgr can manage them with the Out of Band service point. There are two types of provisioning:

▶**Out of Band**—A system without a ConfigMgr 2007 SP 1 client

▶**In Band**—A system with a healthy ConfigMgr 2007 SP 1 client

Check the document at http://technet.microsoft.com/en-us/library/cc431371.aspx for a discussion of the provisioning process. The check list at http://technet.microsoft.com/en-us/library/cc161943.aspx specifies the steps to enable Out of Band Management in ConfigMgr 2007. Chapter 11 discusses AMT.

▶ **Server locator point**—Create a server locator point (SLP) for clients to complete site assignment and find management points when they cannot find that information in Active Directory. As discussed in Chapter 4, those scenarios requiring an SLP include the following:

  ▶ You have workgroup clients or clients from another Active Directory forest.

  ▶ You have not extended Active Directory.

  ▶ You have extended Active Directory, but have not configured all ConfigMgr sites to publish information to Active Directory.

You do not need to install an SLP if all sites are configured for Internet-based client management (IBCM).

Configure IIS on the site system before installing the SLP. When installing the SLP, you can choose to use the site database or a database replica. You can also specify a server locator point connection account if you require a different account than the SLP computer account. See the "Using Replicas and Offloading Site Roles" section for information on creating a database replica.

Specifying the Server Locator Point

You can specify the server locator point for clients using one of the following methods:

  ▶ Manually publish the server locator point in WINS so that clients can automatically locate it. Client computers search WINS for the server locator point if the client.msi Installation property SMSDIRECTORYLOOKUP=NOWINS has not been specified.

  ▶ Assign the server locator point to clients during client installation, using the client.msi property SMSSLP=*<server locator point name>* on the CCMSetup command line.

    If the SLP needs to be added manually to WINS, such as when Computer Browsing in the domain is disabled, perform the following steps:

    1. Open a command prompt (Select Start -> Run, and then type **cmd**).

    2. At the command prompt, type **netsh** and then press Enter.

    3. Type **wins** and press Enter.

    4. Type **server** and then press Enter.

       To manage a remote WINS server, type **server** <***<servername>** or ***XXX.XXX.XXX.XXX***>, specifying the NetBIOS name or IP address.

5. Type the appropriate command on a single line, as in the following example:

```
add name Name=SMS_SLP endchar=1A  rectype=0
ip={<server locator point IP address>}
```

Perform the following steps to validate the SLP was added to WINS successfully:

1. Open a command prompt.

2. At the command prompt, type **netsh** and then press Enter.

3. Type **wins** and then press Enter.

4. Type **server** and then press Enter.

   To manage a remote WINS server, type **server** <****_**servername**_> or
   **XXX.XXX.XXX.XXX**>, specifying the NetBIOS name or IP address.

5. Type the appropriate command, as in the following example:

```
show name Name=SMS_SLP endchar=1A
```

▶ **Software update point**—Create a software update point (SUP) to use the Software Updates feature of ConfigMgr. Configure IIS and install WSUS 3.0 SP 1 prior to adding this role. Your first SUP (usually installed on your central site) synchronizes with Microsoft Update over the Internet to obtain patch detection and download information. If you have multiple sites in your hierarchy, all child site SUPs will synchronize with the parent SUP. All primary sites must have an active SUP. Clients also connect to the active SUP (for its assigned site) to perform updates scanning to determine patch applicability.

When creating the SUP role, specify the proxy server name and configure an SUP proxy server account if needed. You can configure this for both the central site to access Microsoft Update and for child sites to access SUP on their parent site. Also, be sure to enable the new SUP as the active SUP, so that clients can use it.

You must configure the SUP component after installing the SUP role. Refer to Chapter 15 for additional information about configuring the SUP.

▶ **State migration point**—Create a state migration point (SMP) to store user state migration data during reimaging or hardware replacement. Figure 8.25 shows configuring an SMP. You can see the directory D:\UserData is specified on the local drive of the ConfigMgr site. The Max Clients setting indicates the maximum number of clients that can be saved to the folder at any given time. Minimum Free Space prevents additional migration data from writing to the disk, if the drive falls below minimum free space.

Also in Figure 8.25, you can see the deletion policy is configured as 10 days, so that once the data has been successfully restored (and marked for deletion), the data is automatically removed after 10 days. If you check the box Enable restore-only mode, all requests for user state store will be refused for this SMP, although the SMP will remain operational for restore operations. Chapter 19, "Operating

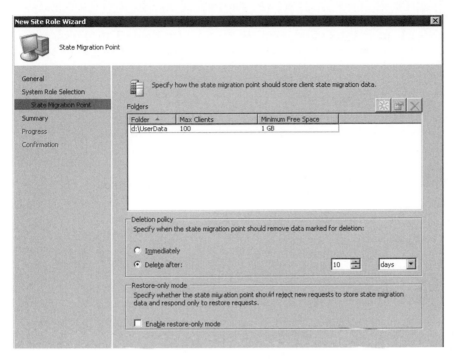

FIGURE 8.25   Creating a new state migration point

System Deployment," contains additional information about state migration point configuration.

▶ **System Health Validator point**—Install a System Health Validator point if you will use ConfigMgr for Network Access Protection (NAP). Installing the role is very easy because there are no settings to configure! However, you must install this site system role on Windows Server 2008 configured with the Network Policy Server (NPS) role. Refer to Chapter 15 for more information.

▶ **Branch distribution point**—Create a branch distribution point (BDP) on a branch office computer to allow clients in that office to access content locally. Think of a small office with 10 computers—you may not want to install a dedicated server and primary or secondary ConfigMgr site. When you install a branch distribution point, systems in the branch office will still traverse the WAN for management point traffic (ConfigMgr machine policy, submitting inventory, and so on), which is nominal traffic. The branch distribution point allows systems to install software and software updates from a local distribution point, thus removing WAN traffic for those installations without incurring the overhead of another site at the remote location. You can install a branch distribution point on Windows XP, Windows Vista, Windows Server 2003, Windows Server 2008, and newer Windows operating systems.

Create a new site system (as described in the next section, "New Site System Server Wizard") on a new server or workstation and then select Distribution Point as the role. (In order to create a branch distribution point, the target system must be a healthy ConfigMgr client.) Configure the next page of the wizard as shown in Figure 8.26 to create a branch distribution point. The example in Figure 8.26 allows ConfigMgr to determine which partition to use on the site system. If the site system has multiple partitions, you can specify a specific partition if desired. You can also reserve space on the drive for the operating system, to prevent ConfigMgr from using the entire drive. Figure 8.26 shows reserved space configured as 500MB. For additional information about configuring multicast and enabling virtual application streaming, review the bullet at the beginning of this section regarding distribution points.

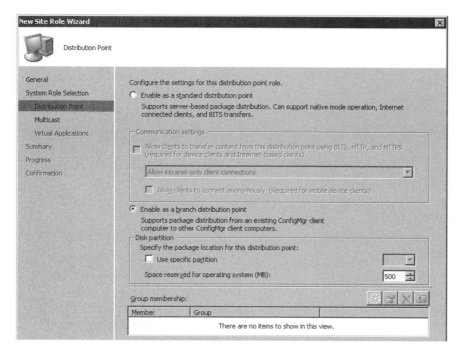

FIGURE 8.26   Creating a new branch distribution point

Branch distribution points use BITS to download content from a standard BITS-enabled distribution point. If the standard BITS-enabled DP is configured with protected boundaries, the boundaries of the BDP must be included or else the BDP will not be able to download content from the standard DP. Another important consideration is that when a client accesses a BDP for content, the content is only accessed via SMB (not BITS).

NOTE

Comparing Distribution Points to Branch Distribution Points

After reviewing the information for both distribution points and branch distribution points, you may wonder which is best for you. And as almost all things technical, *it depends*. Consider BDPs for small-office scenarios. Here are a few points to consider:

▶The BDP depends on the ConfigMgr client to be installed and properly configured.

▶The BDP must be a member of the domain, and not a Windows 2000 system.

▶BDPs are not supported on Internet-based clients.

▶BDPs do not support multicast for OSD.

▶If a BDP is installed on a workstation operating system (for example, Windows XP or Vista), it is limited to 10 concurrent client connections.

Microsoft provides information about standard and branch distribution points at http://technet.microsoft.com/en-us/library/bb680853.aspx. Another helpful document is at http://technet.microsoft.com/en-us/library/bb932184.aspx.

Now that you know how to configure each site role, it's important to know that you can offload site roles to reduce the load on your primary site server. For many environments, offloading roles may not be required. However, if you notice one role is using a large amount of bandwidth, or CPU cycles, consider offloading it by creating a new site system, as described in the next section.

New Site System Server Wizard

Use the New Site System Wizard to enable additional servers (or workstations in the case of branch distribution points) for your site. As discussed in Chapter 4, many site system roles can be offloaded from the ConfigMgr site. The site server that you add will typically be a server operating system. The current exception is for a branch distribution point, which is a supported site role on any valid operating system higher than Windows 2000 SP 4.

To create a new site system, perform the following steps:

1. Right-click Site Systems in the ConfigMgr console and select New -> Server.

2. In the new Site System Wizard, enter a name for the site server (usually the server name) and enter an FQDN if possible, as shown in Figure 8.27.

   You can also specify an alternate account for installing the site system, if the ConfigMgr Site computer account does not have administrative rights on the new server.

3. Click Next in the wizard and then select any valid role for the new site server. The role(s) selected in this page determines the remainder of the configuration pages for the wizard. Each selected role will have its own configuration page to complete the wizard. You may also choose not to select any roles at this time, and just configure it as a site system.

New Site System Server Share Wizard

Use the New Site System Server Share Wizard to create a distribution point on a share on a server. Using this method lets you control exactly where ConfigMgr places source files on the drive. Also with a server share, no ConfigMgr components are installed on the server—it's simply a share clients connect to for obtaining content. If you enable the server share for BITS, ConfigMgr will automatically configure a website on the server. Virtual application streaming is also available (for R2 sites), but multicast is not.

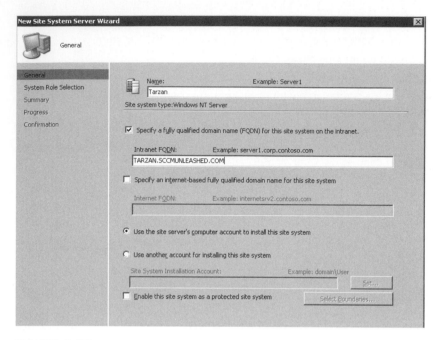

FIGURE 8.27   The New Site System Server Wizard

Create a share on the desired server and then grant the site server's computer account control of the share. This is displayed in Figure 8.28.

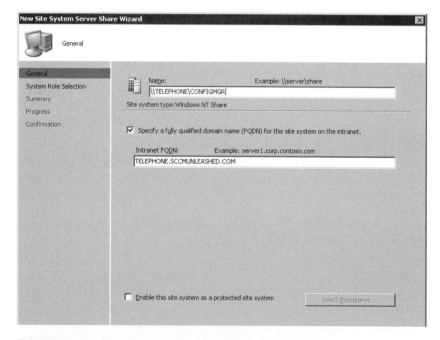

FIGURE 8.28   The New Site System Server Share Wizard

Using Replicas and Offloading Site Roles

A number of ConfigMgr activities can affect the performance of your site server; these include the number of clients, the frequency of machine policy polling intervals, the frequency of hardware and software inventory, software updates, and so on.

Chapter 4 introduced an approach for improving performance known as *offloading site roles*. You can offload site roles such as distribution points and the management point in larger sites. This helps site server performance in the following ways:

▶ Offloading the distribution point results in fewer connections to the site server, because all clients connect to the DP to download and install software.

▶ Offloading the management point means clients no longer need to connect directly to the site server.

You may also want to consider offloading other site roles such as the reporting point, software update point, proxy management point, device management point, and server locator point.

When you offload the management point to another server, clients in your site will connect to that offloaded server to forward inventory, query for machine and user policy, and perform other MP functions. However, offloading the management point may not relieve as much activity from the site server as you had hoped. Every time a client queries the MP for policy, the management point queries the site database to determine policy information for the client. (You can see this traffic by running SQL Trace on the site server ConfigMgr database and enabling verbose and debug logging for the management point logs.) You may want to offload this often resource-intensive function by creating a SQL database replica. In ConfigMgr 2007, you can use a replica for the management point, proxy management point (PMP), device management point (DMP—part of a management point), and server locator point.

Using Database Replicas

SQL Server replication uses a *publisher* (this is the source database, typically your ConfigMgr primary site) and a *subscriber* (the destination of data replica, a server with SQL Server installed). Before setting up replication, ensure your primary site is configured properly and is healthy. Next, install SQL Server on the Windows system that will be the subscriber. (You can have multiple subscribers, although the examples in this chapter only refer to a single subscriber.) You will also create a snapshot publication, which is typically used to publish data when data changes are infrequent and there is a small amount of data. This data is read-only on the replica, and does not have to be synchronized back to the publisher. The next sections discuss the process of creating a replica and offloading the management point to the replica server.

8

Pre-Replication Setup Tasks

Before setting up replication, you must configure both the publisher and the subscriber. Perform the following steps:

1. Run the SQL Server 2005 Surface Area Configuration Wizard (Start -> Programs -> Microsoft SQL Server 2005 -> Configuration Tools -> SQL Server Surface Area Configuration Wizard). This tool configures required services and connections, and Common Language Runtime (CLR) integration. Click the link near the bottom of the page for Surface Area Configuration for Services and Connections, displayed in Figure 8.29.

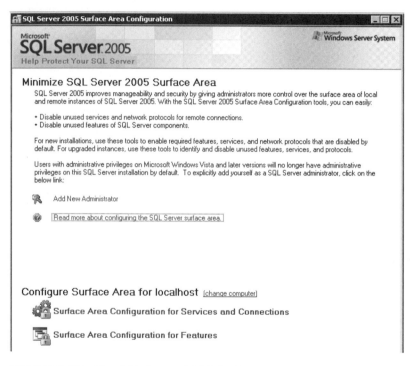

FIGURE 8.29   The SQL Server 2003 Surface Area Configuration Wizard

2. Expand the Database Engine node and select Remote Connections. Select Local and remote connections and then choose Using TCP/IP only. Click OK and then select the link for Surface Area Configuration for Features, also shown in Figure 8.29.

3. Expand Database Engine and select CLR Integration. Check the box Enable CLR Integration, select OK, and then exit the utility.

4. Modify SQL Server so that data larger than the default size of 64KB will replicate successfully. The length of some data to be replicated may be longer than the default maximum. Open SQL Server Management Studio on the publisher (site server

database) and open a new query. Be sure to select your ConfigMgr database as the source database in the dropdown at the top. Execute the following command:

```
EXEC sp_configure 'max text repl size', 2147483647
```

5. Review the Messages window for any reported issues. Next, run the following command to commit the configuration changes to SQL Server:

```
RECONFIGURE WITH OVERRIDE
```

6. Verify the command completed successfully.

7. Use SQL Server Management Studio to create a new database for the subscriber. A logical name would be the site database name appended with "_REP" at the end. This example uses SMS_BXL_REP to indicate the database is a replica database from the ConfigMgr BXL primary site.

Replication Setup Tasks

Now it is time to perform the tasks to set up replication. These consist of setting up the publisher and the subscriber and creating a publication. Configuring the publisher computer can be time consuming. Before performing these steps on a production server, it is best to create your first replica on a test site.

Perform the following steps to configure the publisher to publish the site database for replication:

1. Create a share on the publisher (the server with the ConfigMgr site database). Grant the proper access for SQL Server to properly read and write to that share. This example creates a directory named D:\SQLData\Repl with a share named \\TUMBLEWEED\REPL.

2. Launch SQL Server Management Studio on the server containing the ConfigMgr site database. Right-click Replication in the left node and then select Configure Distribution to start the wizard.

3. After the Welcome page, select the default option '<servername>' will act as its own Distributor, as displayed in Figure 8.30. Click Next, and SQL Server will create a distribution database and log.

4. On the Snapshot Folder page, enter the UNC path to the share previously created. For this example, enter \\TUMBLEWEED\REPL.

5. On the Distribution Database page, specify the name and location of the database and database log file. Take the defaults as shown in Figure 8.31.

6. On the Publishers page, select the SQL Server computer that hosts the ConfigMgr site database.

7. On the Wizard Actions page, check the Configure Distribution box and then click Next. Verify the settings and then click Finish.

8. Wait several minutes for the Configure Distribution Wizard to finish configuring the distributor and enabling the publisher. The wizard will display "Success" or "Fail." Close the wizard.

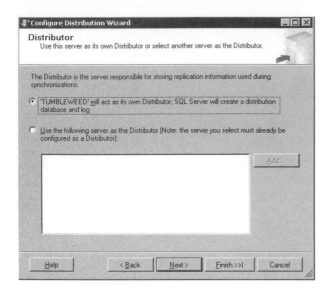

FIGURE 8.30 The Select Distribution page of the Configure Distribution Wizard

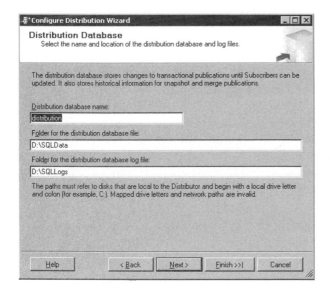

FIGURE 8.31 The Distribution Database page of the Configure Distribution Wizard

The next task is to configure a new local publication of the required ConfigMgr tables. Fortunately, only a small number of objects (approximately 100) in the ConfigMgr database require replication. Because each environment can vary, there is no exact rule regarding size, but you can expect the size of a SQL replica database to be approximately 80% to 90% smaller than the ConfigMgr site database. Perform the following steps:

1. On the server running the ConfigMgr site database, launch SQL Server Management Studio and then expand the Replication node. Right-click Local Publications and then select New Publication to start the New Publication Wizard.

2. After the Welcome page, select the ConfigMgr site database as the publication database, as shown in Figure 8.32.

FIGURE 8.32   Select the BXL ConfigMgr database in the New Publication Wizard

3. For the publication type, select Transactional Publication. In a transactional publication scenario, a replica database pulls an entire snapshot the first time it connects, and then the publisher streams transactions to the subscribers.

4. The next page of the New Publication Wizard is the Articles page, where you select database tables and other objects (views, functions, stored procedures, and so on) required for replication. This will be the most time-consuming page of the entire replication process. Be sure to take your time, and select all necessary objects.

Additional Steps for Replicating Objects

The objects in the tables may change from one service pack to the next (as an example, the ConfigMgr original release requires 48 tables, whereas ConfigMgr SP 1 requires 49 tables for replication), so perform the following procedures each time you upgrade or install a new ConfigMgr site:

8

1. In SQL Server Management Studio, open a new Query Window and select the ConfigMgr database as the current database. Execute one of the following commands, depending on the role of your replica:

   ▶ If your replica is for a management point, execute this command:

   ```
   Select ObjectName from ReplicatedObjects where SiteSystemType = 'MP'
   ```

   ▶ If the replica is for a server locator point, execute

   ```
   Select ObjectName from ReplicatedObjects where SiteSystemType = 'SLP'
   ```

   Information contained in the MP query is inclusive of the information for the SLP query, so if you are creating one replica for both the MP and SLP, run the first command only.

2. Copy the results into your favorite spreadsheet program for easy reference. At this point, you will need to browse through tables, views, stored procedures, and functions in the wizard to select all required objects.

   Functions generally start with *fn*, views generally start with *v_*, and stored procedures generally start with *sp*, *MP*, or *DMP*. Just about everything else is a table.

3. Click Next to continue. Figure 8.33 shows the Articles page of the New Publication Wizard.

FIGURE 8.33   Select database objects in the New Publication Wizard

4. Review the information on the Article Issues page and click Next to continue.
5. Click Next on the Filter Table Rows page, because no filters are required.

6. On the Snapshot Agent page, displayed in Figure 8.34, check the box Create a snapshot immediately and keep the snapshot available to initialize subscriptions.

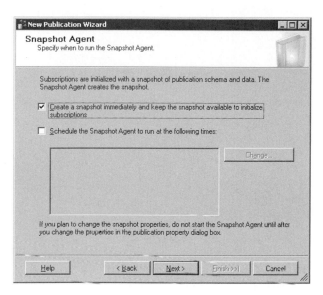

FIGURE 8.34   Snapshot agent configuration In the New Publication Wizard

7. On the Agent Security page, click the Security Settings button and enter a valid Windows account, or select the option to run the agent under the SQL Server Agent service account.

8. On the Wizard Actions page, select the option Create the publication and then click Next. Enter a publication name (**BXL_Publisher** in this example) and click Finish. The Creating Publication dialog box may appear for several minutes while creating the snapshot. Verify "Success" in the dialog box and then close the wizard.

You have successfully created the publisher. A single publisher can provide replication for many subscribers. As an example, you could have five secondary sites with proxy management points, all using a SQL replica of the primary site database.

With the publisher created, it is time to configure the subscriber. Perform the following steps:

1. On the server intended to host the subscriber, launch SQL Server Management Studio, expand the Replication node, right-click Local Subscriptions, and then select New Subscriptions.

2. After the Welcome page, enter the name of the SQL Server running the publisher you previously created and select that publisher, as displayed in Figure 8.35.

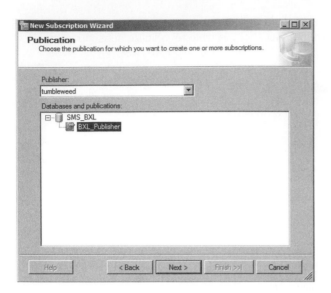

FIGURE 8.35   Choosing the publication in the New Subscription Wizard

3. On the Distribution Agent Location page, leave the default of Run each agent as its Subscriber (pull subscriptions). Click next.

4. On the Subscribers page, select the replica database name (SMS_BXL_REP).

5. On the Distribution Agent Security page, click the ellipsis (...) either to configure a process account or to configure the agent to run under the SQL Server Agent service account.

6. On the Synchronization Schedule page, configure the agent to run on a schedule. Click the dropdown box and select Define Schedule.

7. On the New Job Schedule page, configure the job to run every 15 minutes.

8. On the Initialize Subscriptions page, configure the initialization to occur immediately.

9. On the Wizard Actions tab, check the box Create the subscriptions. Click Next.

10. Review the Summary page and then select Finish to start the subscription process.

The replication will complete within several minutes. To monitor status, expand the SQL Server Agent, right-click Job Activity Monitor, and then select View Job Activity. If the Job Activity displays an error for the replication job, you can view the logging for that job by expanding SQL Server Agent -> Jobs, right-clicking the job in question, and selecting View History to display the Job Activity Monitor, as displayed in Figure 8.36.

Post-Replication Setup Tasks

SQL replication is now configured. Several post-replication setup configuration tasks are necessary to allow ConfigMgr site systems to use the replica. Perform the following steps:

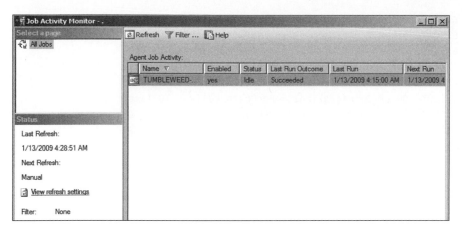

FIGURE 8.36   The Job Activity Monitor

1. Start by creating database roles. Three roles are required, with proper permission granted to those roles. Using SQL Server Management Studio, execute the following statement on the site replica (subscriber) database:

```
CREATE ROLE [smsdbrole_MP] AUTHORIZATION [dbo]
CREATE ROLE [smsdbrole_DMP] AUTHORIZATION [dbo]
CREATE ROLE [smsdbrole_SLP] AUTHORIZATION [dbo]
```

2. After successfully creating the roles, grant each role proper access to the replica. The following SQL statements (listed at http://technet.microsoft.com/en-us/library/bb633288.aspx) are specific to ConfigMgr 2007 SP1. Execute these statements on the site replica (subscriber) database (you can also find these statements in the article referenced in the previous sentence, which will make it easy to copy/paste):

```
GRANT SELECT ON Sites TO [smsdbrole_SLP]
GRANT SELECT ON SysResList TO [smsdbrole_SLP]
GRANT SELECT ON RoamingBoundaryIPSubnet TO [smsdbrole_SLP]
GRANT SELECT ON RoamingBoundaryIPv6Prefix TO [smsdbrole_SLP]
GRANT SELECT ON RoamingBoundaryIPRange TO [smsdbrole_SLP]
GRANT SELECT ON RoamingBoundaryADSite TO [smsdbrole_SLP]
GRANT EXECUTE ON MP_GetAllInventoryClasses TO [smsdbrole_MP]
GRANT EXECUTE ON MP_GetClientIDFromMacAddress TO [smsdbrole_MP]
GRANT EXECUTE ON MP_GetClientIDFromSmbiosID TO [smsdbrole_MP]
GRANT EXECUTE ON MP_GetInventoryClassProperties TO [smsdbrole_MP]
GRANT EXECUTE ON MP_GetSiteInfoFromADSite TO [smsdbrole_MP]
GRANT EXECUTE ON MP_GetSiteInfoFromIPAddress TO [smsdbrole_MP]
GRANT EXECUTE ON MP_GetSiteInfoFromIPv6Prefix TO [smsdbrole_MP]
GRANT EXECUTE ON MP_GetSiteInfoUnified TO [smsdbrole_MP]
GRANT EXECUTE ON MP_GetContentDPInfoProtected TO [smsdbrole_MP]
```

8

```
GRANT EXECUTE ON MP_GetContentDPInfoUnprotected TO [smsdbrole_MP]
GRANT EXECUTE ON MP_GetProtectedSMPSites TO [smsdbrole_MP]
GRANT EXECUTE ON MP_GetUnprotectedSMPSites TO [smsdbrole_MP]
GRANT EXECUTE ON MP_GetStateMigClientInfo TO [smsdbrole_MP]
GRANT EXECUTE ON MP_GetStateMigAssocInfo TO [smsdbrole_MP]
GRANT EXECUTE ON MP_GetMigrationInfoForRestoreClient TO [smsdbrole_MP]
GRANT EXECUTE ON MP_GetMigrationInfoUsersForRestoreClient TO [smsdbrole_MP]
GRANT EXECUTE ON MP_GetSelectiveDownloadMap TO [smsdbrole_MP]
GRANT EXECUTE ON MP_GetPeerDPList TO [smsdbrole_MP]
GRANT EXECUTE ON MP_GetWSUSServerLocations TO [smsdbrole_MP]
GRANT EXECUTE ON MP_GetPendingPackagesForBranchDP TO [smsdbrole_MP]
GRANT EXECUTE ON MP_GetPolicyBody TO [smsdbrole_MP]
GRANT EXECUTE ON MP_GetPolicyBodyAfterAuthorization TO [smsdbrole_MP]
GRANT EXECUTE ON MP_IsPolicyBodyAuthorized TO [smsdbrole_MP]
GRANT EXECUTE ON MP_IsClientRegistered TO [smsdbrole_MP]
GRANT EXECUTE ON sp_GetPublicKeyForSMSID TO [smsdbrole_MP]
GRANT EXECUTE ON MP_GetEncryptionCertificateForSMSID TO [smsdbrole_MP]
GRANT EXECUTE ON MP_GetProvisioningModePolicyAssignments TO [smsdbrole_MP]
GRANT EXECUTE ON MP_GetMachinePolicyAssignments TO [smsdbrole_MP]
GRANT EXECUTE ON MP_GetUserAndUserGroupPolicyAssignments TO [smsdbrole_MP]
GRANT EXECUTE ON MP_GetListOfMPsInSite TO [smsdbrole_MP]
GRANT EXECUTE ON MP_GetHINVLastUpdateTime TO [smsdbrole_MP]
GRANT EXECUTE ON MP_GetLocalSitesFromAssignedSite TO [smsdbrole_MP]
GRANT EXECUTE ON MP_GetMPSitesFromAssignedSite TO [smsdbrole_MP]
GRANT EXECUTE ON MP_GetMPListForSite TO [smsdbrole_MP]
GRANT EXECUTE ON MP_GetSdmPackageBody TO [smsdbrole_MP]
GRANT EXECUTE ON MP_MatchDrivers TO [smsdbrole_MP]
GRANT EXECUTE ON sp_GetPublicKeySMSUID TO [smsdbrole_MP]
GRANT EXECUTE ON DMP_GetMachinePolicies TO [smsdbrole_DMP]
GRANT EXECUTE ON DMP_GetPackageVersion TO [smsdbrole_DMP]
GRANT EXECUTE ON DMP_GetSettings TO [smsdbrole_DMP]
GRANT EXECUTE ON DMP_GetSoftwareDistBody TO [smsdbrole_DMP]
GRANT EXECUTE ON DMP_GetSoftwareDistIDs TO [smsdbrole_DMP]
GRANT EXECUTE ON DMP_GetHinvTranslations TO [smsdbrole_DMP]
GRANT EXECUTE ON DMP_GetDiscoveryTranslations TO [smsdbrole_DMP]
```

Note that these SQL statements were updated for SP 1, and the SQL statements may need to be updated at a future date. Review http://technet.microsoft.com/en-us/library/bb633288.aspx for current information.

3. Now it is time to grant the appropriate rights for the site systems to access the site database replica. Use the Local System account or create connection accounts. This example uses the Local System account. Execute the following SQL statement against the subscriber server:

```
CREATE USER [SCCMUNLEASHED\Telephone$] FOR LOGIN
[SCCMUNLEASHED\Telephone$] WITH DEFAULT_SCHEMA=[dbo]
```

In this case, SCCMUNLEASHED is the domain name and Telephone$ is the name of the computer account.

4. Add the roles for the MP, DMP, and SLP by executing the following SQL statements:

```
EXEC sp_addrolemember 'smsdbrole_MP' , '<sccmunleashed\telephone$>'
EXEC sp_addrolemember 'smsdbrole_DMP' , '<sccmunleashed\telephone$>'
EXEC sp_addrolemember 'smsdbrole_SLP' , '<sccmunleashed\telephone$>'
```

Congratulations! You have configured your SQL database replica for use by ConfigMgr. For additional information on configuring SQL Server site database replication, refer to http://technet.microsoft.com/en-us/library/bb693697.aspx.

Disabling SQL Replication

When planning to upgrade a site to a new ConfigMgr service pack (or upgrading to a newer version of ConfigMgr), you must first disable SQL Server replication. Perform the following steps:

1. To disable replication from the publisher, open SQL Server Management Studio, right-click Replication, and then select Disable Publishing and Distribution. Follow the wizard, and select the option in Figure 8.37 to disable publishing. Click Finish to disable replication from the publisher.

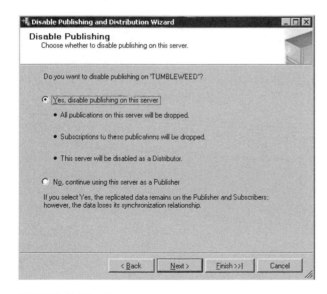

FIGURE 8.37   The Disable Publishing and Distribution Wizard

CAUTION

Disabling Publishing Drops All Publications and Subscriptions Associated with That Distributor

Note the information in the Disable Publishing page in Figure 8.37. This process will drop all publications and subscriptions as well as disable the distributor. If your ConfigMgr site shares a database with another application, verify that the only replication used on this server is for ConfigMgr before you disable replication.

2. To delete local subscriptions from the subscriber, open SQL Server Management Studio, expand Replication, and select Local Subscriptions. Right-click the subscription to your site database (see Figure 8.38) and select Delete. Click Yes to confirm subscription deletion.

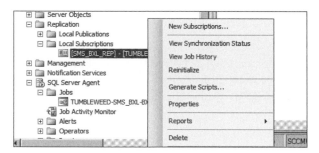

FIGURE 8.38   Disabling SQL replication from the subscriber

3. After performing the required ConfigMgr upgrades or service pack installations, review the steps earlier in the "Replication Setup Tasks" section to re-create your replica.

Offloading the Management Point

If you have a very busy site with a very large number of systems assigned to it, you will want to consider both offloading the MP and using a SQL replica to alleviate some of the stress on your primary site. If you offload the MP without creating a replica, each time a client polls for new policy, the offloaded MP queries the primary site database. Configuring the MP to use a database replica results in that traffic no longer going to the primary site database, thereby relieving stress on the primary site.

After creating a database replica on a new server (the subscriber), perform the following steps to install your management point to this new server and use the database replica. For this example, the new server (Telephone) has the replica configured, and is not currently used by ConfigMgr for any roles. Similar to installing the roles on the site server, ensure the new server meets the required prerequisites listed in Table 8.1 for the role. For example, the MP role requires IIS. Here are the steps to follow:

1. In the ConfigMgr console, expand Site Management -> Site Database -> Site Systems. Right-click Site Systems and then select New -> Server. Enter a valid name and the intranet FQDN, as shown in Figure 8.39. Also, grant the proper rights for the site

server to install the site system. To use the site server's computer account to install this site system, add the site server's computer account to the local Administrators group of the new server.

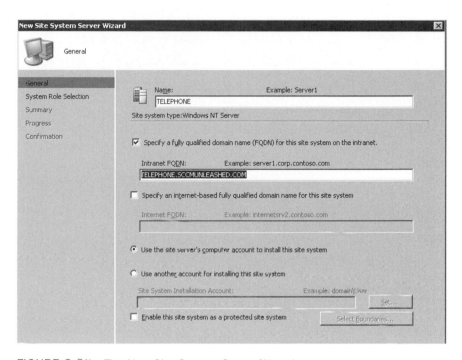

FIGURE 8.39   The New Site System Server Wizard

2. Click Next in the New Site System Server Wizard, select Management Point for the role to install on the new site server, and click Next. The Management Point configuration page is shown in Figure 8.40.

3. Click Next and then Finish, thus completing the wizard. Review the Site Status messages as well as the \SMS\Logs directory on the new site system server. MPSetup.log provides additional information about the MP installation on the new server.

Configuring Site Boundaries

As you worked through Chapter 6, you documented the desired site boundaries for your ConfigMgr site. To add a site boundary, navigate to the desired site in the ConfigMgr console and then expand Site Settings -> Boundaries. Right-click Boundaries and then select New Site Boundary. Enter and select the correct properties for the site, as shown in Figure 8.41, and then click OK to set the boundary.

You have the option to select an IP subnet, Active Directory site, IPv6 prefix, or IP address range for the site boundary.

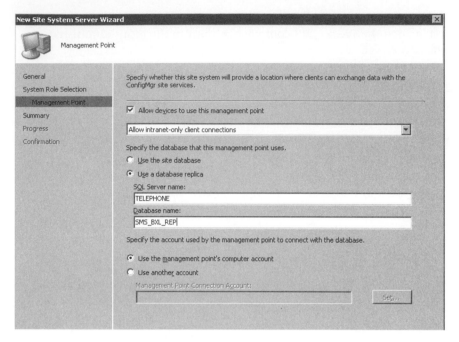

FIGURE 8.40   Configuring the MP with a database replica in the New Site System Server Wizard

FIGURE 8.41   Adding a new site boundary

NOTE

About Protected Boundaries

You have the ability to "protect" boundaries on distribution points and state migration points. By creating protected boundaries, you allow only client systems within those boundaries to access the content. A common scenario for this would be a distribution point located across the WAN for your primary site. You may install a distribution point at a remote office so that systems in the office can obtain content locally. To prevent systems from the main office from obtaining content from that remote DP, add protected boundaries to the DP to "protect" it from WAN traffic.

To protect a distribution point, configure a valid site boundary on the site server for the remote office. Depending on your environment, this could be an IP subnet, Active Directory site, or any other validated site boundary. Next, in the ConfigMgr console, navigate to the server name under Site Systems, right-click the ConfigMgr site system role, and select Properties, as shown earlier in Figure 8.22. Check the box Enable this site system as a protected site system. Finally, click the Select Boundaries button to select the desired boundaries.

Multisite Configuration

Larger or more distributed environments typically have multiple ConfigMgr sites. Chapter 6 includes information to help determine which type of sites you require for your enterprise. The next sections will help you configure communication between sites and create child sites.

Configuring Addresses

ConfigMgr uses sender addresses for site-to-site communication. When you create a secondary site, you will automatically configure the address during the site-creation process. You must manually create addresses when creating a primary site. There are several different types of sender addresses:

▶ **Standard sender address**—Standard senders are used for LAN and WAN communications, when routers connect through multiple LANs.

▶ **Courier sender address**—This capability is installed and configured by default. You will find the Courier Sender Address option in the Start Menu in the ConfigMgr program group. Courier sender is very useful when you have large packages that require excessive time or bandwidth to send over the network. You simply create the offline media (CD, DVD, portable hard drive, and so on), deliver it to the destination site (via postal mail or another delivery process), and use courier sender at the remote site to import the packages properly.

▶ **Various RAS sender addresses**—RAS sender addresses are used for RAS communication. These include the following:

▶ Over an asynchronous line

▶ Over an Integrated Services Digital Network (ISDN) line

▶ Over a System Network Architecture (SNA) link

▶ Over an X.25 line

You can control the network load for each address, to prevent ConfigMgr from using all available bandwidth for that connection. You can also create multiple addresses to the same site for redundancy, if desired. The following steps go through the process of creating a standard sender address from the central site (CEN) to a child primary site (BXL):

1. From the central site, expand Site Settings, right-click Addresses, and select New -> Standard Sender Address.

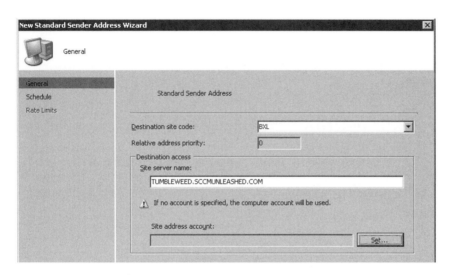

FIGURE 8.42   Creating a standard sender address

2. Specify the site code of the destination site and then enter the name of the child site server, as shown in Figure 8.42. You can enter the NetBIOS name or FQDN.

   By default, communications occur using the computer account, so ensure that the computer account of the parent site has admin access to the new child site. As an example, the following command run from the Tumbleweed (BXL) site server will give the computer account administrative access:

   ```
   NET LocalGroup Administrators /Add SCCMUNLEASHED\BLUEBONNET$
   ```

   This command adds the central site server (Bluebonnet) to the local administrators group on Tumbleweed. If you prefer not to use the local computer account, you can specify a site address account.

3. The next page of the New Standard Sender Address Wizard allows you to configure a schedule for handling multiple priority levels differently. By default, all priorities are open 24 hours a day. Figure 8.43 shows a schedule configured to be open for all priorities during off-business hours (in this case, Monday through Friday 7:00

a.m.–6:00 p.m.), and to only allow medium and high priority communications during the defined business hours.

NOTE

About Throttling Site Addresses

By default site addresses are not throttled—they are configured as "Open for all Priorities," which allows the ConfigMgr sender to use the maximum number of threads as configured in the "Concurrent distribution settings" section of the Distribution Point tab of Software Distribution Properties. If you create an address schedule as shown in Figure 8.43, all traffic from the sender to a site will become serial, which may slow the amount of time it takes to send software to new distribution points at the target site.

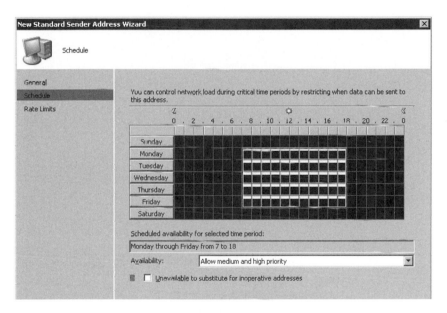

FIGURE 8.43   Creating a standard sender address schedule

If you have multiple addresses for this site, use the check box on the Schedule screen in Figure 8.43 to define whether this address can be used as a substitute if another address to the destination site fails.

4. The Rate Limits page of this wizard allows you to configure rate limits to manage network load between sites during specific hours of each day. By default, rate limits are configured as unlimited. You can also manage the rate limits by pulse mode, or limit it to a maximum transfer rate by hour.

Select Pulse mode and then specify the size of the data block (in KB) that ConfigMgr sends to the address. Also, specify the delay between data blocks (in seconds).

Alternatively, specify the maximum transfer rates per hour. In Figure 8.44, the rate limit is configured as unlimited during off-business hours, and to utilize only 50% of available connection bandwidth during the business day.

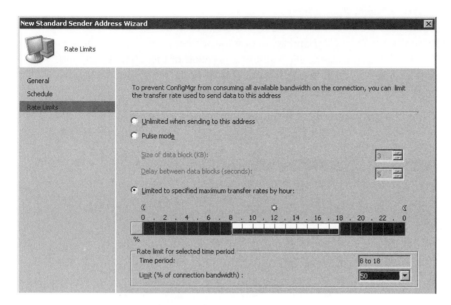

FIGURE 8.44   Creating standard sender address rate limits

Perform the same steps to configure a sender address from the child site to the parent.

Configuring Senders

By default, standard and courier senders are installed automatically on every site server. To configure additional senders, refer to http://technet.microsoft.com/en-us/library/bb694245.aspx, which discusses preparing servers for different senders.

Depending on the number of child sites, you may need to modify the sender properties. Figure 8.45 displays the default settings for the standard sender.

The Advanced tab allows you to specify the maximum number of concurrent connections the ConfigMgr server can make, the number of retries allowed, and how often the sender may retry a failed attempt.

The "Maximum current sendings" section allows you to specify the maximum number of simultaneous communications allowed for this sender and each destination site:

▶ **All sites**—Specifying a number here will set the total number of simultaneous connections. This number should always be larger than the Per site setting.

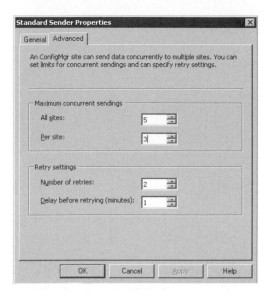

FIGURE 8.45   Configuring standard sender properties using the Advanced tab

> **Per site**—This setting determines how many simultaneous connections are permit-
> ted to a single site.

For a smaller hierarchy, the default settings may be sufficient. If you have more than two
or three child sites, you may want to consider increasing these numbers, provided there is
available bandwidth from the parent site. See http://technet.microsoft.com/en-us/library/
bb632976.aspx for additional information on sender properties.

Attaching to Parent

After installing the primary site and configuring the addresses and senders, you are ready to
attach to a parent site. Perform the following steps:

1. To attach a primary child site to a parent, connect to the ConfigMgr console of the
   child site, expand Site Management, right-click the primary site name, and select
   Properties.

2. In the General tab of the Site Properties dialog box, click the Select Parent Site
   button.

3. Because you have already created the proper addresses, simply click the Report to
   parent site radio button displayed in Figure 8.46 and select the parent site from the
   dropdown list. (If you have an Asset Intelligence synchronization point configured
   on the child site, you must remove this role before attaching to the parent site.)

FIGURE 8.46   Setting the parent site

Once you complete the wizard, replicating objects from the parent site to the child site may take from a few minutes to several hours, depending on the number of objects (packages, programs, collections, software updates, and so on) on the parent site. Review sender.log on both the parent and child site to verify site connectivity. Also, when you attach your site to a parent site, you may experience backlogs in some of your inbox folders (for example, ddm.box, dataldr.box, sinv.box, statmgr.box\statmsgs, and statesys.box, to name a few). During the attachment process, local inbox processing is paused until the child site has forwarded all site and client information to its new parent site.

Installing Child Primary Sites

This chapter has discussed the process of installing a ConfigMgr site. The steps outlined apply to configuring both the central site and any child primary site.

To install a primary site, follow the steps in the "Site Installation" section for installing a ConfigMgr site.

When installing a ConfigMgr site that will be a child site, install the site and then apply the same level of service pack (and R2 and hotfixes, if applicable) on the parent site before attaching the child site to the parent site.

After attaching the child primary site to the parent site, perform any additional configurations necessary. You will also want to review the "Transfer Site Settings Wizard" and "Copy Packages Wizard" sections of this chapter—these two tools can help simplify (and standardize) configuring child sites.

Installing Secondary Sites

Two methods are available for installing secondary sites:

▶ Installing directly from the ConfigMgr installation media

▶ Installing the secondary from the ConfigMgr console of the parent site

If you choose to install using installation media, you will also need to ensure you apply the appropriate service pack (and R2, if required). Installing the secondary site from the ConfigMgr console will install the same version of ConfigMgr that is on the parent site. Regardless of the method you choose, you should run the prerequisite checker first, as described earlier in "The Prerequisite Checker" section of this chapter.

To install a secondary site from its parent, perform the following steps:

1. From the ConfigMgr console of the parent site, expand Site Database -> Site Management, right-click the parent site name, and then select New Secondary Site to begin the Secondary Site Creation Wizard.

2. After the Welcome screen, specify the site code and site name. Click Next.

3. At the Site Server page, specify the site server name (NetBIOS name) and installation directory (for example, C:\ConfigMgr). Click Next.

4. Select Copy installation source file over the network from the parent site server. If the secondary site is on a very slow link, you may want to consider pre-staging the source files on the new server and then specify the path.

5. Specify a new sender address (use the FQDN if possible). Also, specify a site connection account, or ensure that the system account of the parent site has administrative access to the new secondary site server.

6. Specify the sender address from the secondary site to the primary (use the FQDN if possible).

7. Complete the installation wizard, and monitor the following log files on the new secondary site:

   ▶ SMS_BOOTSTRAP.log

   ▶ ConfigMgrPrereq.log

   ▶ ConfigMgrSetup.log

   After ConfigMgrSetup.log indicates the installation is complete, several background processes will continue to complete the configuration. You can view the installation and configuration status in the ConfigMgr console from the parent site, as shown in Figure 8.47, which shows the state as "Pending." Review the ConfigMgrSetup.log for any potential problems.

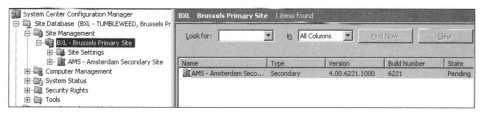

FIGURE 8.47 Secondary site installation

8. After installation completes, install R2 (if applicable).

Troubleshooting Secondary Site Installation

Several common deployment issues may occur with secondary sites, including the following:

▶ Failure to exchange secure keys between parent/child and child/parent.

▶ Secondary site status stays in pending state, with the site control file not making it up from the secondary site.

▶ Establishing an address from the primary to the secondary but not having one from the secondary to the primary.

The next sections discuss these issues.

Secure Key Exchange

You can configure parent and child sites to require secure key exchange for communication. When you're installing a secondary site configured to use secure key exchange to communicate with its primary site, the key transfer may occasionally fail.

Although the secondary site installation will be successful, communication between the sites will fail, because the primary parent site will reject communication until there is a secure key exchange. This is evidenced by entries in the despool.log file at the parent site server, the despooler inbox folder at the parent, and status messages regarding secure key exchange issues:

▶ **Despool.log**—The despool.log file is located on the parent site server—the default location is *%ProgramFiles%*\Microsoft Configuration Manager\Logs. The Despooler component is responsible for all incoming and outgoing communications between sites. The despool.log file logs all site-to-site communication, including communication failures.

When site communications fail due to the missing secure key, despool.log will contain the following entries:

```
Cannot find a public key for instruction
%ProgramFiles%\Microsoft Configuration Manager\inboxes\despoolr.box\receive
incoming from site <secondary site code>, retry it later
Cannot find valid public key for key exchange instruction coming from
site <secondary site code>
```

Both entries state that Configuration Manager tries to locate the key. It retries this every 5 minutes, for a maximum of 100 times.

▶ **Despooler inbox folder at the parent site**—Secure key exchange communication failures can also be identified when the \inboxes\despoolr.box\receive folder becomes backlogged with files. These files have extensions of .ins and contain site instructions. When site communication is successful, these files are sent, processed, and then deleted from the \receive folder. When the key is missing, those files remain in the folder at the parent site.

▶ **Status messages**—The SMS_Despooler will generate the following status messages for the receiving site:

  ▶ **Message ID 4404**—The Despooler component received an instruction and package file from a site that will not be processed because the site does not allow unsigned key exchange between sites.

  ▶ **Message ID 4405**—The site has received an instruction file containing inter-site replication data that will not be processed and retired because a valid public key cannot be located for the sending site.

To resolve the public key exchange issue, you must exchange the keys between the sites manually with the hierarchy maintenance tool (preinst.exe). This tool is installed by default with Configuration Manager 2007. The following procedure discusses the steps to manually exchange the public keys using the hierarchy maintenance tool.

Perform these steps at the child/secondary site:

1. Go to Start -> Run and then type **CMD** to open a command prompt.

2. At the command prompt, navigate to the location of the preinst.exe tool. The tool is located in the *<ConfigMgrInstallPath>*\bin\i386*<language code>* folder on the site server.

3. Type **preinst /keyforparent** to export the public key of the child site server. The key file is *<Site Code>*.ct4, and is stored at the root of the system drive.

4. Move the *<Site Code>*.ct4 key to the *<ConfigMgrInstallPath>*\inboxes\hman.box folder at the parent site.

Perform these steps at the parent site:

1. Go to Start -> Run and then type **CMD** to open a command prompt.

2. At the command prompt, navigate to the location of the preinst.exe tool. The tool is located in the *<ConfigMgrInstallPath>*\bin\i386*<language code>* folder on the site server.

3. Type the command **preinst /keyforchild** to export the public key of the parent site server. This key file is *<Site Code>*.ct5 and will be stored at the root of the system drive.

4. Move the *<Site Code>*.ct5 key to the *<ConfigMgrInstallPath>*\inboxes\hman.box folder at the child site.

Communication will start within 5 minutes once the keys are exchanged. To monitor the process, check the contents of the despool.log file.

Secondary Site Status Remains in Pending State after Upgrade or Installation

If the site control file is not created successfully, the secondary site may remain in a pending status and never go active.

When you install or upgrade a secondary site, the final installation step is for the Site Control Manager service at the secondary site to copy the .ct2 control file to its parent. This file contains the information that the installation or upgrade was a success.

To force the Site Control Manager service to create the .ct2 control file, perform the following steps:

1. Verify that the secondary site server is indeed successfully installed, and that all services and components are up and running.

2. At the secondary site, browse to the *<ConfigMgrInstallPath>*\inboxes\sitectrl.box folder. Copy the SiteCtrl.ct0 file to a temporary location (for example, c:\temp).

3. At the temporary location, change the name of the earlier copied Sitectrl.ct0 file to 00000000.ct2.

4. Copy the 00000000.ct2 file to the *<ConfigMgrInstallPath>*\inboxes\hman.box at the parent site.

This procedure informs the parent site that there is an updated site control file, and it will process this file immediately.

Addresses

When you deploy a secondary site through the console of the primary parent site, the Secondary Site Creation Wizard enables you to configure the address for the primary and secondary sites. However, the configuration of the sender address for the primary site at the secondary site may occasionally fail. If the sender address is missing, site communication fails and sender.log at the parent site server will contain the following entries:

```
Cannot connect to server <secondary site server name> at remote site
<secondary site code>, won't try send requests going to site
<secondary site code>, for an hour or until there are no active send requests.
There is no existing connection
Could not establish connection
Attempt to connect failed
```

When this occurs, you can create the sender address manually. Use the ConfigMgr console to configure the address. Because secondary sites do not have a database, you must manage them through a console connected to the primary site database in the console. Refer to the "Configuring Addresses" section of this chapter for the steps to add a standard sender address.

Transfer Site Settings Wizard

Use the Transfer Site Settings Wizard to transfer site settings between sites. You can transfer settings down the hierarchy, or you can export configuration settings to an XML file and import them to a different site. Perform the following steps:

1. Right-click any site in the ConfigMgr Admin console to start the Transfer Site Settings Wizard. At the Welcome page, click Next to continue.

2. You have the option to export or import settings. For this example, select Export settings. Then, on the next screen, select the site to transfer settings from (the source site).

3. Click Next to select the site settings to transfer (or export), as shown in Figure 8.48.

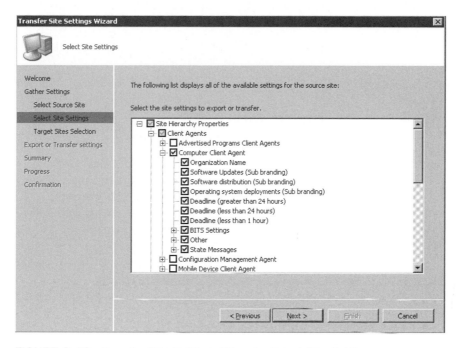

FIGURE 8.48   Transfer Site Settings Wizard – Select Site Settings

4. Select the destination site(s) or click Next to export the site settings. If you selected one or more destination sites, the wizard will automatically begin applying the site settings to each site.

5. A success dialog box will appear upon completion.

CAUTION

Verify Settings for Transfer Site Settings Wizard

The Transfer Site Settings Wizard will do exactly what you tell it to do—so if you tell it to transfer discovery methods and include Active Directory containers, you may begin discovering duplicate objects from different sites, thus causing additional backlog and confusion at your central site.

If you chose to export the settings to an XML file, you can later import those settings to any site.

Copy Packages Wizard

The Copy Packages Wizard allows you to easily add multiple packages to a distribution point. You can copy four different types of packages, each requiring that you initiate the wizard from a different location:

▶ The Packages node, under Software Distribution

▶ The Deployment Packages node, under Software Updates

▶ The Boot Images node, under Operating System Deployment

▶ The Driver Packages node, under Operating System Deployment

Right-click any of the nodes listed here and then select Copy Packages. In the Copy Packages Wizard displayed in Figure 8.49, select the destination distribution point. The next page of the wizard allows you to select multiple packages. You can also click the Source button to select an existing distribution point. This allows you to easily select all packages for the new distribution point that are on the source distribution point.

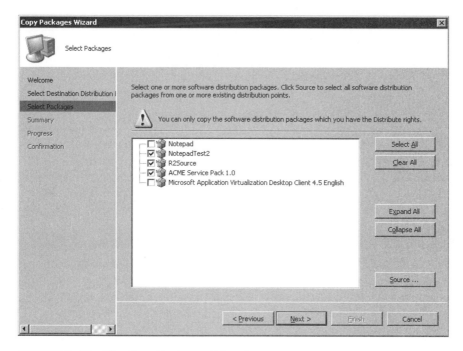

FIGURE 8.49   The Copy Packages Wizard

The process begins when you complete the wizard. This process uses the same process as if you manually added distribution points, so monitor the distribution status for each package selected, if desired.

Preload Package Tool

Another useful tool is the Preload Package tool, also known as the package loader tool. This tool allows you to manually copy compressed Software Distribution package source files to the new site. You can also use the tool to import the package properly into ConfigMgr at the remote site. You can download the Package Preload tool from Microsoft's download site at http://www.microsoft.com/downloads (search for **PreloadPkgOnSite.exe**).

Troubleshooting Site Installation

Troubleshooting site installation may appear overwhelming at first, but take your time and go step by step to identify problems. Keep in mind that first you have a site installation, and then component installation/configuration. Almost all site installation information will appear in the logs on the root of the system drive, namely ConfigMgrPrereq.log, ConfigMgrSetup.log, and SMS_BOOTSTRAP.log (this appears on secondary site installations when initiated from its parent site). Install the ConfigMgr toolkit prior to site installation. Open Trace32.exe from the toolkit to associate .log files with Trace32. Trace32 makes ConfigMgr log files easier to read.

Always verify prerequisites using the latest information from Microsoft. You can find this information in the release notes of the installation media and updated information with service packs and R2. If you are able to access the ConfigMgr Admin console, navigate to System Status -> Site Status to review site component information. SMS Executive is a good place to begin.

See http://technet.microsoft.com/en-us/library/bb693526.aspx for additional information when verifying a successful site installation. You will also want to review Appendix A, "Configuration Manager Log Files," for a comprehensive list of ConfigMgr log files.

ConfigMgr Service Manager

Depending on the specific components installed on a server, there may be as many as nine different Windows services running specifically for ConfigMgr 2007, with many threads running under those services. The ConfigMgr Service Manager, installed as a tool with Configuration Manager 2007, enables you to manage all services and each thread in those services independently.

Perform the following steps to access the ConfigMgr Service Manager:

1. Expand the Tools node in the ConfigMgr console.
2. Right-click ConfigMgr Service Manager.
3. Select Start ConfigMgr Service Manager to open the ConfigMgr Service Manager console.

The ConfigMgr threads are grouped by components and by servers:

▶ If you have only one server supporting all site roles, the list of components will look identical.

▶ If you are using multiple servers to distribute the components, the Servers view may provide additional functionality for you.

Clicking the Components node provides additional detail about each component (or thread) for ConfigMgr. Figure 8.50 shows components in the BXL primary site.

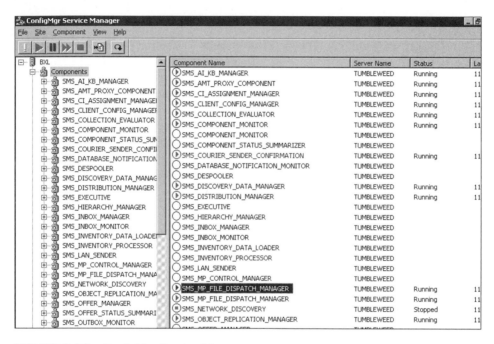

FIGURE 8.50   ConfigMgr Service Manager

Each component listed in the Service Manager has either a green arrow, red box, or an empty circle to its left. When you first open ConfigMgr Service Manager, it displays only empty circles. Here are some points to keep in mind:

▶ To query a component, right-click the component on the detail pane and select Query to see the current status of that component.

▶ To query all components, right-click a component and then choose Select All. Right-click again and select Query to see the status for all components. When querying all components, you may wait several minutes for the results to display.

After querying a component, you can right-click to start, stop, resume, or pause the component. After you click one of the actions, you just requery the component to display the current state. ConfigMgr generally does a great job of managing the components required for the site to run properly. It is only necessary to adjust components when troubleshooting your site. As an example, you may find that the Discovery Data Manager log (ddm.log) is reporting errors reading discovery data, but the files are processed from the inbox (\inboxes\auth\ddm.box) so quickly that you are unable to inspect them. To disable this process temporarily, stop the SMS_DISCOVERY_DATA_MANAGER thread using ConfigMgr Service Manager. After inspecting the files, restart the thread.

TIP

Managing Components (Threads) Using the Registry

Microsoft recommends using ConfigMgr Service Manager to manage the ConfigMgr components. If you are unable to open the ConfigMgr console, you can use the Registry to manage the ConfigMgr threads. On the site server, run Regedit (Start -> cmd, and then type **regedit**). Navigate to HKEY_LOCAL_MACHINE\Software\Microsoft\ SMS\Components\SMS_Executive\Threads and select the thread you wish to manage.

As an example, select SMS_Despooler. You can see the current state and startup type. To stop the thread, simply change the value of Requested Operation from None to Stop. Refresh the Registry key information and, in several seconds, you will see the Current State has changed from Running to Stopped, and the Requested Operation is reset to None. To restart the service, change the Requested Operation value to Start.

Another important feature in ConfigMgr Service Manager is the Logging property for each component. By right-clicking and selecting Logging on a specific component, you can enable or disable logging, specify the path and filename for the log, and specify the maximum log size (in MB).

Highlighting multiple components and right-clicking Logging allows you to configure the properties for multiple logs at the same time. Exercise caution, because you may inadvertently specify the same log filename for multiple components. Although supported, this may cause confusion when troubleshooting.

Summary

This chapter walked you through the basic process of installing a ConfigMgr 2007 site. As you can see from the multiple installation and configuration procedures, a thoroughly documented process customized for your environment will provide a valuable reference when moving from a test environment to production.

Spend the necessary time up front to plan your hierarchy, to ensure you build the infrastructure required to support the needs of your environment.

The next chapter takes an existing SMS 2003 primary site and upgrades it to Configuration Manager 2007.

CHAPTER 9

Migrating to Configuration Manager 2007

The previous chapter (Chapter 8, "Installing Configuration Manager 2007") discussed installing a new Configuration Manager (ConfigMgr) 2007 hierarchy. If you already have an existing Microsoft Systems Management Server (SMS) deployment, you will almost certainly want to preserve much of the work put into that SMS implementation when you upgrade to ConfigMgr 2007. This chapter presents the options that are available when migrating an existing SMS environment to Configuration Manager. It then explains in detail how to carry out the migration and deal with interoperability issues with a mixed SMS and ConfigMgr environment. The chapter also discusses some specific issues you may encounter during or after migration, and how you might deal with them.

Planning Your Migration from SMS 2003

When planning a migration to Configuration Manager, you should first assess your current environment. Here are the key questions you need to consider when looking at your SMS 2003 environment:

▶ Is your environment working well today? You should consider the services you are currently delivering with SMS and the success rate you are achieving.

▶ Is your server hardware adequate to support the ConfigMgr deployment you envision, or does the hardware need replacing?

▶ Does your hierarchy fit your current network environment?

You should also determine what new features you will support and how they will affect your requirements. Chapter 2, "Configuration Manager 2007 Overview," presents the new capabilities of Configuration Manager 2007.

There are two basic strategies for migrating from an SMS 2003 environment to Configuration Manager 2007:

▶ Perform an *in-place* upgrade on sites running SMS 2003 Service Pack 2 (SP 2) or higher to upgrade directly to Configuration Manager.

▶ Carry out a *side-by-side* migration to replace your existing SMS sites with ConfigMgr sites.

Although an in-place upgrade is simpler than a side-by-side migration, there are circumstances under which you may want to consider the side-by-side approach:

▶ **Restructuring**—You want to restructure your hierarchy during migration. This is the most compelling reason to choose a side-by-side migration.

▶ **Mixed environment**—You plan to maintain a mixed environment for an extended period. One reason you may need to do this is to maintain compatibility with older clients not supported under ConfigMgr 2007, such as Windows 98 or Windows NT systems.

▶ **Hardware upgrades**—You plan to upgrade site server hardware. Although a side-by-side migration is not necessary for hardware upgrades, the extra work of replacing hardware and upgrading to ConfigMgr makes the advantages of an in-place upgrade less compelling.

Choosing your migration strategies is not an all-or-nothing decision. You may find that it makes sense to upgrade some of your sites in place, while replacing other sites in a side-by-side fashion.

> **NOTE**
>
> **About Supported Upgrade Paths**
>
> You cannot upgrade directly to Configuration Manager 2007 from any version of SMS earlier than SMS 2003 SP 2. If you are running an earlier product version, you must upgrade to SMS 2003 SP 2 or SP 3 before upgrading to ConfigMgr.

You may recall from the hierarchy planning discussion in Chapter 6, "Architecture Design Planning," that a Configuration Manager site cannot report to an SMS 2003 parent site. This restriction means that you must always begin your upgrade with the central site and progress down the hierarchy. If you want to introduce ConfigMgr at a child site before upgrading the central site, you must detach the site from your hierarchy and perform an upgrade or side-by-side migration to create a standalone ConfigMgr site. You can later integrate that site into your hierarchy.

Planning Hierarchy Changes During Migration

Before determining a migration strategy, review your current hierarchy to determine whether you will make any changes to it as you move to a Configuration Manager environment. There are two major reasons you may decide to modify your hierarchy during migration:

▶ **Business requirements**—You may find that your current SMS hierarchy is no longer optimal to meet the needs of your organization and match the requirements of your environment. It is likely that there have been changes to your business, your network, or your administrative model since you first deployed SMS to your organization. Your migration to Configuration Manager 2007 presents a good opportunity to review and improve upon your current hierarchy design.

▶ **Product capabilities**—The new features of Configuration Manager provide options and requirements not present in SMS 2003 and earlier versions. As an example, the new branch distribution point server role can replace a secondary site in many scenarios. Similarly, if one of your goals is to support Internet-only clients (a new feature of ConfigMgr 2007), you may decide to add a dedicated site for Internet-based client management (IBCM).

You might start by reviewing the material on hierarchy design in the planning chapters of this book (Chapters 4–6) as well as in the product documentation, asking yourself how you would plan a new implementation from the ground up to meet your goals and fit your environment. You can then compare the hierarchy you would envision to your current model and decide what changes to make.

Conducting an In-place Upgrade

You can upgrade an SMS 2003 SP 2 or SP 3 primary site to Configuration Manager 2007 by running the Setup program from the ConfigMgr 2007 installation media. Use the slipstreamed SP 1 version of ConfigMgr for upgrades wherever possible. Using a slipstreamed version saves the extra effort of applying the service pack after the upgrade; in addition, SP 1 has an enhanced prerequisite checker. The prerequisite checker is described in the next section of this chapter, "Running the Prerequisite Checker."

In some cases, you may not be able to upgrade to SP 1 directly. In such a case, upgrade from a supported service pack level of SMS 2003 to the Release-to-Manufacturing (RTM) version of ConfigMgr 2007 and then upgrade again to SP 1.

> **NOTE**
>
> **About Backing Up Your Site**
>
> As with any software upgrade, verify that you have a complete backup of your site server before upgrading the site server, site database server, or site database. You should also confirm you have all required installation media and supporting documentation available in the event you need to recover your site. For a complete list of requirements for recovering an SMS 2003 site, install and run the Recovery Expert from the SMS 2003 installation media.
>
> You should also note that the upgrade removes any custom files you have added to the SMS folder structure. If you wish to retain these files, you should copy them to another location and restore them to their original location after the upgrade.

Feature Packs

Microsoft released several feature packs for SMS 2003 that add functionality not included in the original product. If you installed any of the SMS 2003 feature packs, uninstall them before upgrading each site. The only exception to this is the Inventory Tool for Microsoft Updates (ITMU), used for patch deployment to SMS clients. (See Chapter 15, "Patch Management," for a discussion of patch management for ConfigMgr 2007.) You should keep ITMU installed and upgrade it as part of your upgrade to Configuration Manager.

If you are using the Operating System Deployment (OSD) Feature Pack, your existing OS images will display under the OSD FP Packages node in the ConfigMgr console. You will need to deploy each of those images to a reference machine prior to the upgrade and capture them as part of your Configuration Manager OSD if you want to continue to use the images in Configuration Manager 2007 OSD. Chapter 19, "Operating System Deployment," discusses Configuration Manager OSD.

Upgrade Prerequisites

The prerequisites for upgrading to Configuration Manager 2007 include the following requirements:

- ▶ All SMS 2003 sites being upgraded must be at SMS 2003 SP 2 or above.

- ▶ All site server systems must be running Windows Server 2003 SP 2 or above with .NET Framework 2.0 installed.

- ▶ All primary sites must be running SQL Server 2005 SP 2 or above.

- ▶ All sites you will be upgrading need to be in advanced security mode.

- ▶ Microsoft Management Console (MMC) 3.0 is required for the ConfigMgr console.

- ▶ SMS 2003 supported two types of clients: legacy clients and advanced clients. ConfigMgr sites support SMS 2003 advanced clients, but legacy clients do not work in ConfigMgr 2007 sites and are not supported by Microsoft. You should install the advanced client on SMS 2003 client systems running Windows 2000 Service Pack 4. ConfigMgr 2007 sites do not support clients running earlier versions of Windows.

The Configuration Manager installation media includes a prerequisite checker that looks for these and many other requirements. The next section of this chapter describes how to use this tool. Some additional considerations for site upgrades include the following:

▶ Running the prerequisite checker on the site server only verifies the readiness of the site server itself. You can run the prerequisite checker separately on management point servers to verify that your management point meets the requirements for Configuration Manager. You should also verify that any site system roles you have distributed to other systems meet the minimum requirement for those system roles. Chapter 6 discusses the requirements for site systems.

▶ If you modified the membership rules for any of the default SMS collections, the upgrade preserves those modifications. If you removed any of these collections, they are re-created unless you run Setup with the /NODEFAULTCOLL switch.

Running the Prerequisite Checker

Before running the actual site setup, run the prerequisite checker from the Configuration Manager installation media; then download the required files and resolve any issues reported. To run the prerequisite checker, launch splash.hta from the root folder of the ConfigMgr installation media. The splash screen, shown in Figure 9.1, offers several options.

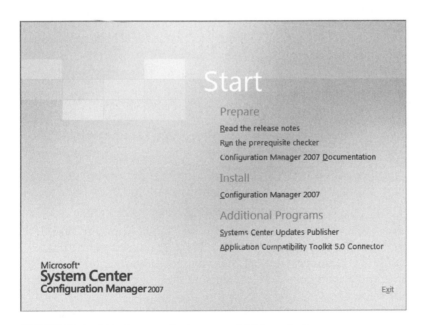

FIGURE 9.1   The Setup splash screen (RTM version)

Choosing Run the prerequisite checker brings up the Microsoft System Center Configuration Manager 2007 Installation Prerequisite Check Options screen, displayed in Figure 9.2.

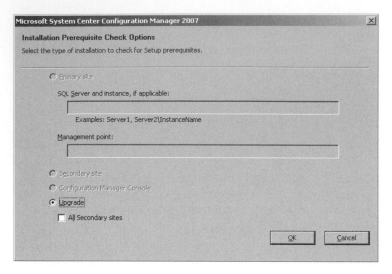

FIGURE 9.2   The Prerequisite Check Options screen

Notice that the options for installing a new site are grayed out and the only available option in Figure 9.2 is Upgrade. There is also a check box allowing you to check the readiness of all secondary sites. You will want to select this option if you are running the prerequisite checker on a site server of a primary site with immediate child secondary sites. After verifying the appropriate options are selected, click OK to run the prerequisite checks. The checks may take a few minutes, after which you will see a screen displaying the results of the prerequisite check. Figure 9.3 shows an example of the prerequisite check results.

The output may show two types of results:

▶ A red circle with an X indicates a critical error, which is likely to cause Setup to fail. You must correct any critical issues before continuing.

▶ A yellow warning symbol with an exclamation mark indicates a possible problem that will not prevent you from upgrading your site but should be fixed prior to the upgrade.

Notice the text in the lower pane, which tells you that you can double-click any item to display details about how to resolve the problem or view the ConfigMgrPrereq.log file to help identify problems. Ensure you understand each issue presented by the prerequisite checker before continuing. The results screen also includes a link to view the latest prerequisite information. Use this link to access a complete list of prerequisite check rules with the severity level of each rule (warning or failure), a description of the prerequisite the rule is checking, and detailed information about the check. Figure 9.4 shows an example of the details displayed in the Results pane by double-clicking the "WSUS SDK on site server" result.

Chapter 15 discusses the prerequisites for ConfigMgr Software Updates. For this particular rule, the information displayed by the wizard is essentially the same as what you will find

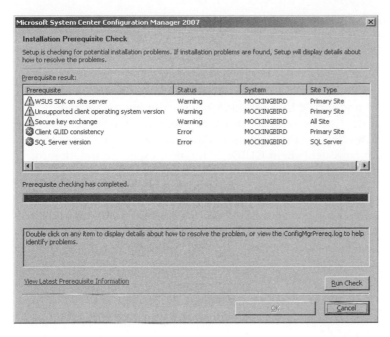

FIGURE 9.3   The Installation Prerequisite Check screen with resulting output

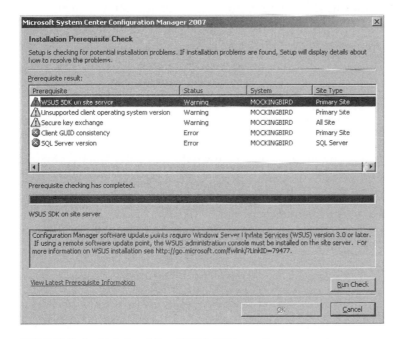

FIGURE 9.4   Details of the WSUS SDK on site server rule

in the ConfigMgrPrereq.log file. In some cases, you will find additional information on the Setup Prerequisite Checks web page (located at http://technet.microsoft.com/en-us/library/bb680951.aspx) and in the log file.

As an example, if you double-click the "Client GUID consistency" error displayed in Figure 9.4, the text displayed in the user interface simply states "Inconsistent client GUIDs can lead to SQL Server errors and should be resolved before continuing the upgrade process." The Setup Prerequisite Checks web page provides a somewhat more detailed description of the rule "Verifies that the Configuration Manager 2007 site database to be upgraded does not contain inconsistent client GUIDs." The most useful information for resolving this problem is in the ConfigMgrPrereq.log, located in the root of the C drive:

```
<10-26-2008 17:19:41> Rule Name: Client GUID consistency
<10-26-2008 17:19:42> Query select Netbios_Name0, SMS_Unique_Identifier0,
➥GUID from System_DISC sys join MachineIdGroupXRef xref on
➥sys.ItemKey=xref.MachineID where IsNULL(SMS_Unique_Identifier0,'')
➥!= IsNULL(GUID,'') returned one or more rows.
<10-26-2008 17:19:42>          Result: Error
<10-26-2008 17:19:42>          Inconsistent client GUIDs can lead to SQL
➥Server errors and should be resolved before continuing the upgrade process.
```

You can copy the SQL query shown in the log and run it against your site database to find out which client GUIDs (Globally Unique Identifiers) are causing the problem. The exact steps for running the query will vary depending on the version of SQL Server you are running. If you are running SQL Server 2005, you can execute the query as follows:

1. Launch Microsoft SQL Server Management Studio from the Microsoft SQL Server 2005 program group.
2. Click the New Query button at the upper left, just below the menu bar.
3. Enter the query text in the new query window. Be sure that your site database is selected in the database dropdown control, as shown in Figure 9.5.

The results show the system SMS-000005 has an inconsistent SMS GUID. In this case, the problem can be corrected by deleting this system from the database, removing the SMS client software on the system, or by deleting the smscfg.ini file from the Windows folder and reinstalling the client.

The detail of the unsupported client operating system version rule included in the ConfigMgrPrereq.log contains the following SQL query:

```
select Netbios_Name0, ip.IP_Addresses0, Operating_System_Name_and0, os.CSDVersion0
from System_DISC as sd left join Operating_System_DATA as os
on sd.ItemKey = os.MachineID inner join System_SMS_Assign_ARR as assign
on assign.ItemKey=sd.ItemKey left join System_IP_Address_ARR as ip
on sd.ItemKey = ip.ItemKey
where Netbios_Name0 in
(select Netbios_Name0 from System_DISC as sd2
left join Operating_System_DATA as os2 on sd2.ItemKey = os2.MachineID    inner join
System_SMS_Assign_ARR as assign2
```

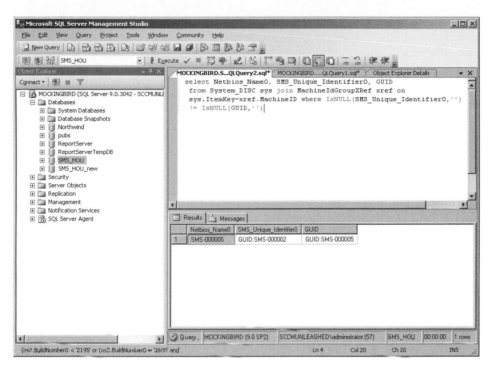

FIGURE 9.5   Using SQL Server Management Studio to execute the check for the inconsistent
client GUIDs prerequisite checker rule

```
on assign2.ItemKey=sd2.ItemKey
where (os2.BuildNumber0 < '2195'
or (os2.BuildNumber0 = '2600' and os2.CSDVersion0 < 'Service Pack 2')
or (os2.BuildNumber0 = '2195' and os2.CSDVersion0 < 'Service Pack 4') )
and  sd2.Client0='1' and assign2.SMS_Assigned_Sites0="HOU")
```

This query illustrates the fact that you may need to make some minor adjustments to the
SQL syntax. In this example, the site name appears in the log enclosed in double quotes
("HOU"). You will need to replace this with the site name in single quotes ('HOU') before
executing the query. The additional details of this rule indicate the following:

```
Configuration Manager clients are only supported on Windows 2000 SP4 or
later operating systems.
```

After running the SQL query to identify those clients running unsupported operating
system versions, you will need to either upgrade these clients to a newer operating system
or exclude them from the Configuration Manager migration.

The prerequisite checker shown in Figures 9.2 through 9.4 is from the Configuration
Manager 2007 RTM version. Microsoft has enhanced the prerequisite checker shipped

with Configuration Manager Service Pack 1 with a number of additional checks. Figure 9.6 shows the results when using the SP 1 prerequisite checker on the same SMS 2003 site server. Notice the scroll bars, which indicate you can see additional results by scrolling down on the results list.

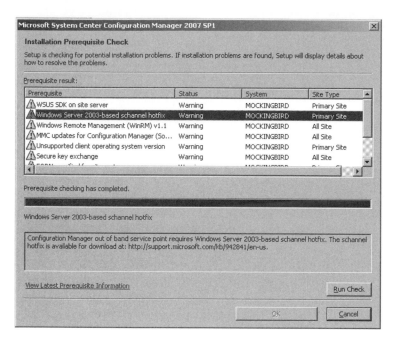

FIGURE 9.6   The SP 1 prerequisite checker with details of the schannel hotfix rule

The Details pane shows that the particular rule selected in Figure 9.6 applies only to Out of Band service points (a new feature in SP 1). However, some of the added checks also apply to the RTM version. It is therefore advantageous to run the SP 1 prerequisite checker, even if you are upgrading only to Configuration Manager 2007 RTM.

Upgrading SQL Server

SMS 2003 SP 2 and above versions provide support for both SQL Server 2000 SP 4 and SQL Server 2005. If your site database server is running SQL Server 2000, you will need to upgrade to SQL Server 2005 and apply Service Pack 2 before you can upgrade your SMS primary site. The next sections of this chapter step through a sample SQL Server upgrade. For additional information about upgrading SQL Server, you can refer to the SQL Server documentation and the release notes on the product installation media.

Running the Upgrade Advisor

Before upgrading SQL Server, download and run the latest SQL Server 2005 Upgrade Advisor from http://www.microsoft.com/downloads/details.aspx?familyid=1470e86b-7e05-4322-a677-95ab44f12d75&displaylang=en (at www.microsoft.com/downloads, search for

SQL Server 2005 Upgrade Advisor). After the download is complete, execute the SQLUASetup.msi Installer package to install the Upgrade Advisor. Once it is installed, you can launch the Upgrade Advisor from Start -> Programs -> Microsoft SQL Server 2005. The welcome screen shown in Figure 9.7 includes the option Launch Upgrade Advisor Analysis Wizard.

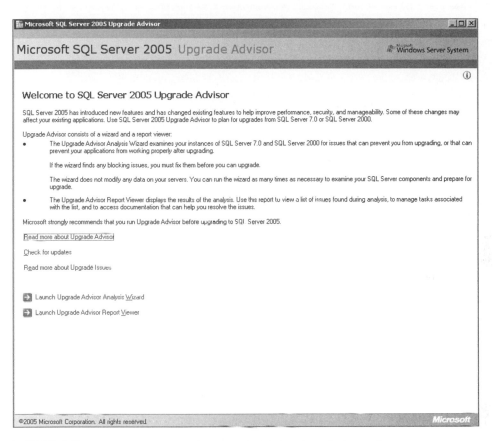

FIGURE 9.7   The SQL Server 2005 Upgrade Advisor installation welcome screen

The Analysis Wizard allows you to select the components and databases to analyze, and it generates a report. You can view the report from the launch report button when the wizard completes, or you can use the Launch Upgrade Advisor Report Viewer link on the Upgrade Advisor welcome screen. Be sure to investigate any potential problems indicated in the Upgrade Advisor report.

The report shown in Figure 9.8 identified an issue with one of the extended stored procedures registered by SMS. The links in the report indicated that the affected object was the extended stored procedure xp_SMS_notification. Following the instructions on the "Tell me more about this issue and how to resolve it" link, the issue was corrected by executing the following SQL queries to re-register the procedure with the full path:

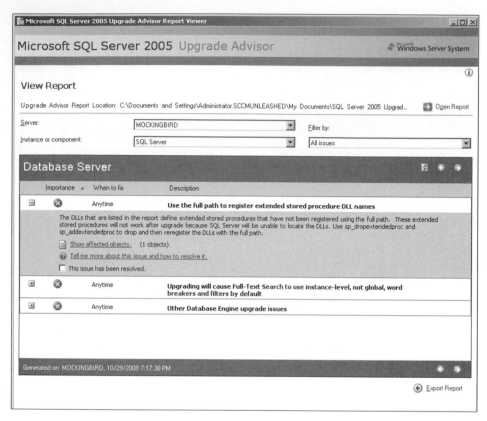

FIGURE 9.8   The SQL Server 2005 Upgrade Advisor report

```
sp_dropextendedproc xp_SMS_notification
sp_addextendedproc xp_SMS_notification, 'C:\WINDOWS\system32\smsxp.dll'
```

Performing the Upgrade

After preparing your database server for the SQL Server upgrade, you can launch the Setup from SQL Server installation media splash screen. Perform the following steps:

1. To access the splash screen, insert the CD if autoplay is enabled, or launch the screen from \servers\default.hta on the installation media.

2. Setup first installs the Microsoft SQL Native Client and Microsoft SQL Server 2005 Setup Support Files. You can install the server components after this step completes. In most cases, you will simply choose to upgrade the default SQL Server instance and select all options to match your existing configuration.

3. You will have the option to install additional components, as shown in Figure 9.9. For example, you might want to install the Reporting Services component if you plan to install a reporting services point at the site and use SQL Reporting Services for your reports. Chapter 18, "Reporting," discusses Configuration Manager reporting and the use of SQL Reporting Services (SRS).

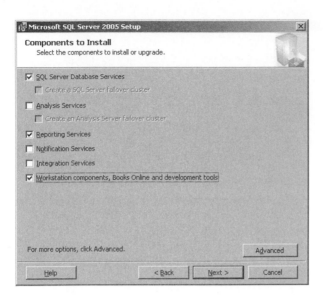

FIGURE 9.9   The SQL Server 2005 installation Components to Install screen

4. When Setup completes, you can run the optional Surface Area Configuration Tool. You may want to run the tool at this time to enhance security by reducing the attack surface of your SQL Server. Chapter 20, "Security and Delegation in Configuration Manager 2007," describes the Surface Area Configuration Tool.

5. After upgrading to SQL Server 2005, you will need to download and apply Service Pack 2. It is generally a good idea at this point to visit the Windows Update site and apply any recommended SQL Server 2005 post–SP 2 updates.

Database Upgrade Tips and Tricks

Before upgrading an SMS 2003 primary site to Configuration Manager 2007, test the database upgrade to ensure there are no incompatibilities. To test the database upgrade, perform the following steps:

1. Make a copy of your site database to use for the test upgrade. It is essential to test the upgrade with a copy of the database rather than the actual site database, because running the test upgrade against your production database could render the database incompatible with SMS 2003.

   You can copy the database using SQL Server Management Studio by right-clicking the site database and choosing Tasks -> Copy Database, as shown in Figure 9.10. This launches the Copy Database Wizard. The wizard is straightforward, and you can generally accept the default options. Note that the SQL Server Agent service must be running for the database copy to succeed. When the copy completes, you should record the size of the newly copied database files. You will need this information to estimate the space requirements for the database upgrade.

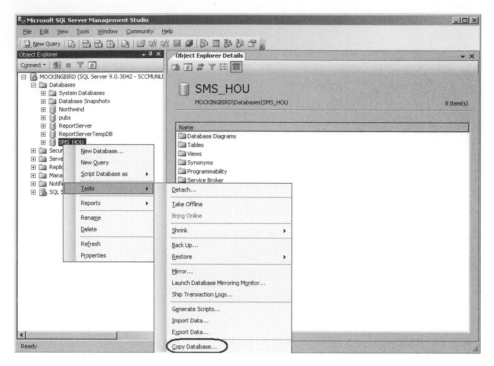

FIGURE 9.10   Copying the SMS site database

2. Test the database upgrade using the following syntax:

```
setup /testdbupgrade <databasename>
```

Run this from the smssetup\bin\<*processor architecture*> folder of the ConfigMgr installation media, where <*databasename*> is the name of your copied database and <*processor architecture*> is generally i386.

3. At the Installation Prerequisite Check screen shown in Figure 9.11, click Begin TestDBUpgrade.

4. When the test database upgrade completes, you should see a message that Configuration Manager was successfully upgraded. To verify there were no errors, review the log files c:\ConfigMgrPrereq.log and c:\ConfigMgrSetup.log. Resolve any problems indicated in the logs before upgrading your site to ConfigMgr 2007.

You should also compare the size of the upgraded database files with the initial database size you recorded in step 1. This provides an estimate of the additional space required when you upgrade the database.

Before upgrading your database, export any custom objects you created outside of SMS. Any custom tables created in the SMS database, for example, are removed by the upgrade,

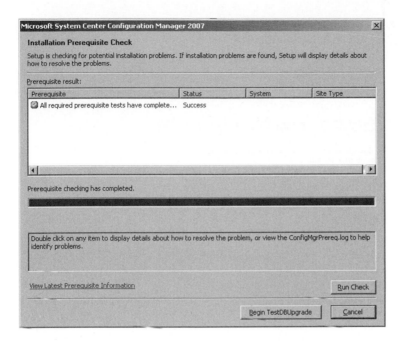

FIGURE 9.11   Launching the database upgrade test

although the upgrade preserves custom views based on the default SMS tables. You should also be prepared to re-create any customizations made to default SMS reports, because the upgrade process overwrites changes made to the default reports.

Any custom objects you have created within SMS, such as custom collections or cloned reports, are preserved through the upgrade.

Upgrading a Primary Site

After completing the prerequisites outlined in the previous sections, you are ready to upgrade your primary site.

You should also verify client push installation is disabled on your site prior to the upgrade. This will allow you more control over the client upgrade process. The "Upgrading SMS 2003 Clients" section of this chapter discusses upgrading clients.

Perform the following steps to upgrade your primary site:

1. Launch an upgrade to Configuration Manager 2007 by choosing Install Configuration Manager 2007 from the splash screen of the installation media.

   ▶ You can access the splash screen by double-clicking splash.hta from the installation CD or other location where you have the installation files available.

▶ You can also run setup.exe directly from the SMSSETUP\bin*<processor architecture>* directory on the installation media.

2. After reviewing the important reminders on the Setup Wizard welcome screen shown in Figure 9.12, click Next.

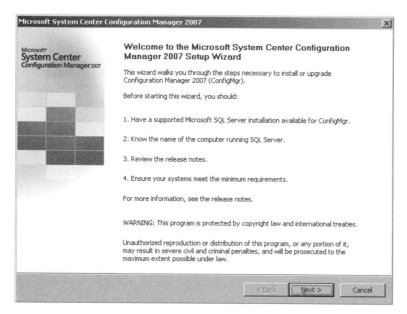

FIGURE 9.12   The Configuration Manager 2007 Setup Wizard welcome screen

3. Setup will detect that you have an existing SMS or ConfigMgr primary site on your server and provide the available options to upgrade or remove the site, as displayed in the Available Setup Options screen in Figure 9.13. Make sure that Upgrade an existing Configuration Manager or SMS 2003 installation is selected and then click Next.

4. Review the license terms in the Microsoft Software License Terms dialog box shown in Figure 9.14. Then select "I accept these license terms" if you wish to continue. You may also choose to print the license terms. Click Next to continue.

5. You have the opportunity to participate in the Customer Experience Improvement Program. This is an optional program to provide feedback to Microsoft, and your choice does not affect the upgrade process.

6. After entering your selection, you will need to enter your 25-digit product key, generally found on the installation CD case or supplied as part of your volume license agreement.

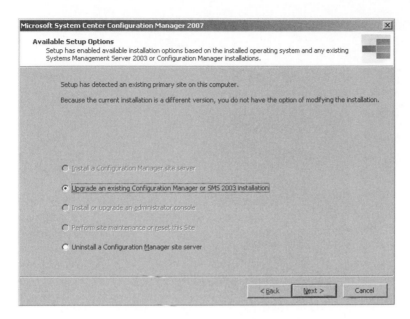

FIGURE 9.13   The Configuration Manager 2007 Setup Wizard installation options

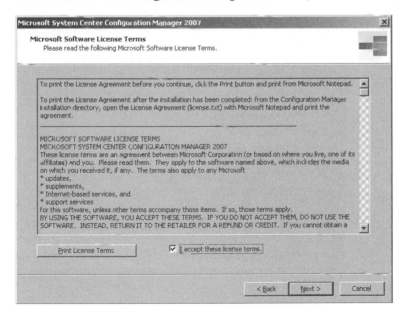

FIGURE 9.14   The Microsoft Software License Terms dialog box

7. After you provide the product key, the wizard will prompt you to download the latest prerequisite updates. The download can take a considerable amount of time, so you may want to download the updates in advance. Make the appropriate selection in the dialog box shown in Figure 9.15, and choose Next to enter or browse to the updated prerequisite components location.

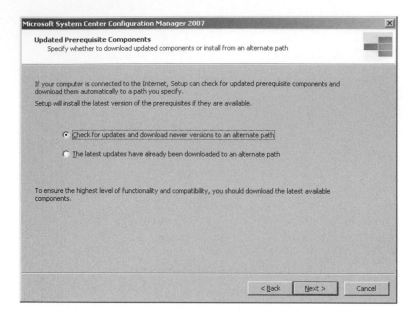

FIGURE 9.15   The Updated Prerequisite Components dialog box

8. Once you download the updated prerequisites or supply the path to the existing files, Setup runs a prerequisite check to verify your site meets all required prerequisites.

9. When the prerequisite check completes successfully, click Begin Install to upgrade your site. This will take some time—the actual time depends largely on your installation settings and the size of the site database. Figure 9.16 shows the Setup Actions Status Monitoring screen, which provides a detailed view of the actions Setup is performing and the status of each action.

10. If you have ITMU installed, Setup detects its presence and launches the ITMU Setup Wizard displayed in Figure 9.17. You can either complete the ITMU upgrade now, or cancel it and use the SMSITMU.MSI installer file located in the \SMSSETUP\SUMSCANTOOLS\<processor architecture> folder on the Configuration Manager installation media to upgrade the scan tools after completing your Configuration Manager upgrade. If you do not upgrade ITMU during the upgrade, it will be necessary to upgrade it later for it to work properly for SMS clients with ConfigMgr 2007.

If you choose to upgrade ITMU at this point, the ITMU upgrade process prompts you to download the latest security updates catalog from the Web or supply an alternate location for the catalog, as shown in Figure 9.18.

Once you complete this dialog box and click Next, Setup finishes the ITMU upgrade and displays the Setup Complete dialog box, shown in Figure 9.19.

The upgraded ITMU can deliver patches to SMS 2003 clients in your ConfigMgr site. As the message in the dialog box in Figure 9.19 indicates, you will need to ensure that your clients have Microsoft Installer (MSI) 3.1 or later if you use ITMU to deliver updates for Microsoft Office or other Windows Installer–based updates to

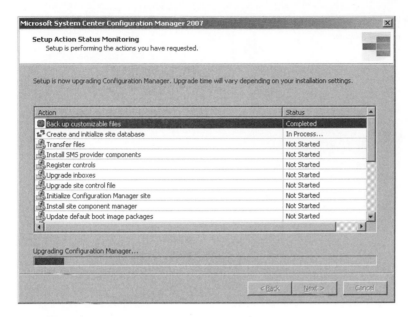

FIGURE 9.16   The Setup Actions Status Monitoring dialog box

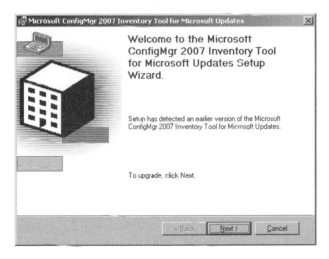

FIGURE 9.17   The ITMU Setup Wizard welcome dialog box

those clients. To provide continuity of service, you should plan to deploy the appropriate MSI version to your clients before upgrading your site.

For Configuration Manager clients, you will need to install WSUS and complete the additional steps required for ConfigMgr software updates. Chapter 15 discusses software updates and patch management. The "Migrating WSUS to Configuration Manager" section of this chapter discusses migrating from standalone WSUS to ConfigMgr WSUS. Chapter 15 also discusses using ITMU to support SMS 2003 clients in your ConfigMgr environment.

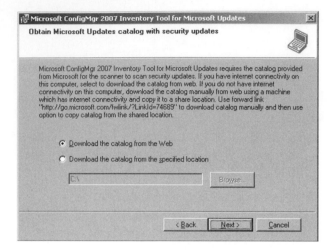

FIGURE 9.18   The ITMU security updates catalog download dialog box

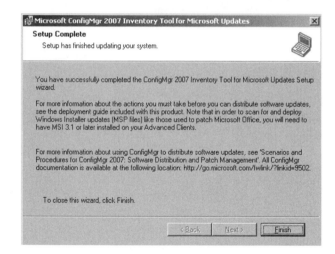

FIGURE 9.19   The ITMU Setup Complete dialog box

11. After ITMU Setup completes, the focus returns to the Configuration Manager Setup Action Status Monitoring dialog box previously displayed in Figure 9.16. The Next button is enabled when all actions complete; at this time, all the actions should now show a green success indicator.

12. Clicking Next brings up the completion dialog box shown in Figure 9.20. Click the View Log button to check for any errors and confirm the end of the log includes the message "Installation and configuration processes are done."

13. Confirm that the following services have started:

   ▶ SMS_EXECUTIVE

   ▶ SMS_SITE_COMPONENT_MANAGER

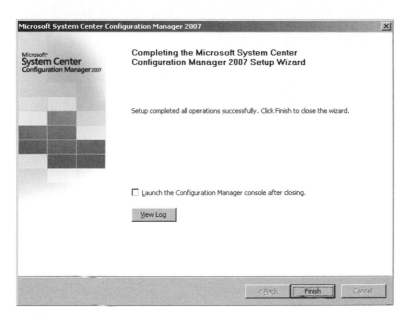

FIGURE 9.20   The completing Configuration Manager setup dialog box

▶ SMS_SITE_SQL_BACKUP

▶ SMS_SITE_VSS_WRITER

14. Finally, you should open the Configuration Manager console and review the site system status and component status. Chapter 21, "Backup, Recovery, and Maintenance," describes how to check ConfigMgr status.

Upgrading Secondary Sites

You can upgrade a secondary site after you upgrade its parent primary site. Before upgrading your secondary sites, run the prerequisite checker on the parent primary site server again—this time check the All Secondary Sites box on the Installation Prerequisite Check Options page, previously displayed in Figure 9.2, to verify the sites meet all prerequisites for the Configuration Manager upgrade. The prerequisite checker displays any errors or warnings in the results screen and generates the log file c:\ConfigMgrPrereq.log on the secondary site server.

To upgrade a secondary site, perform the following steps:

1. Run the Upgrade Secondary Site Wizard from its parent site. One way to start the wizard is to open the Configuration Manager console, expand the tree control in the left pane to System Center Configuration Manager -> Site Database -> Site Management and then click the parent primary site's site code. Figure 9.21 shows

this node of the Configuration Manager console, displaying Beaumont as a
secondary site under the Houston primary site.

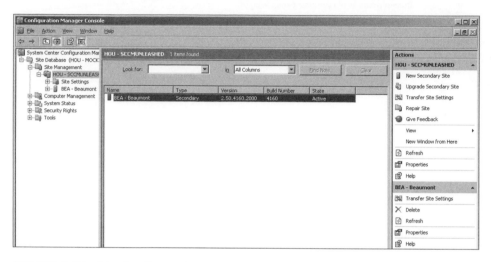

FIGURE 9.21   The Configuration Manager console focused on the parent primary site

2. Choose Upgrade Secondary Site from the Actions pane on the far right side of the
   console to launch the wizard. Figure 9.22 shows the Upgrade Secondary Site Wizard's
   Welcome screen.

3. Clicking Next at the Welcome screen brings up the Secondary Sites page displayed in
   Figure 9.23. This page shows a list of secondary sites available for upgrade. Select the
   site(s) you wish to upgrade and click Next.

4. The Installation Source Files page, displayed in Figure 9.24, allows you to choose
   whether to copy the required files from the parent site or point to a location on the
   local server. The option to use a local CD or installation point allows you to
   conserve network resources and reduces the time required for Setup to run. If you
   use a local copy of the installation media, you must copy the files to the \SMSSetup
   folder in the root of one of the local drives. After indicating the location of the
   installation files, click Finish to complete the secondary site upgrade.

5. The primary site server now makes an RPC connection to the secondary site server
   and installs the SMS_Bootstrap service, which copies the necessary files for Setup and
   launches the setup process. The bootstrap and setup processes create the
   c:\SMS_BOOTSTRAP.log and c:\ConfigMgrSetup.log files, respectively, on the secondary site server. When the upgrade completes successfully, you should see entries
   similar to the following in the ConfigMgrSetup.log:

```
SMS Setup full version is 4.00.5931.0000
Installing SMS Site Component Manager ...
```

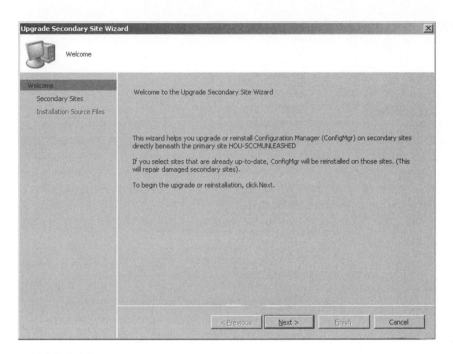

FIGURE 9.22   The Upgrade Secondary Site Wizard's Welcome screen

```
Installing Site Component Manager under acct <NT AUTHORIIY\SYSTEM>
➥path <C:\SMS\bin\i386\sitecomp.exe>
Started Site Component Manager service
SMS Site Component Manager installation completed.
Done with service installation
Starting WMI.
Using default Timeout value.
Checking status of WinMgmt...
Verified that WinMgmt is running.
SMS Setup full version is 4.00.5931.0000
```

The upgrade will take several minutes to complete—longer if you are copying files across a wide area network (WAN) link with limited available bandwidth. You can view the site properties in the ConfigMgr console to verify that the version is now 4.00.5931.000 (ConfigMgr 2007 RTM) or higher. You can also use the console to view the site status for any errors that may have occurred.

Upgrading SMS 2003 Clients

Unless you have client push installation enabled, your SMS 2003 clients will not automatically upgrade to the Configuration Manager client during your site upgrade. Here are some points to keep in mind:

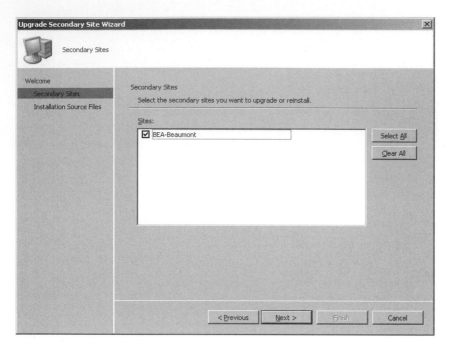

FIGURE 9.23   The Upgrade Secondary Site Wizard site selection page

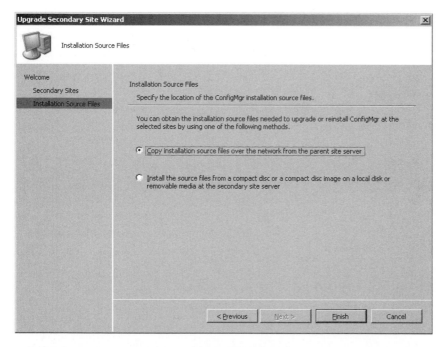

FIGURE 9.24   The Upgrade Secondary Site Wizard's Installation Source Files page

▶ You can use any of the supported discovery and client deployment methods to deploy the client agent. Chapter 12, "Client Management," describes discovery and client deployment.

▶ You can use software distribution to selectively deploy the upgrade to selected collections of clients. To use software distribution to deploy the client upgrade, you will first need to create the Microsoft Configuration Manager Client Upgrade 4.0 ALL package, using the Package Definition option in the Create Package from Definition Wizard, as shown in Figure 9.25.

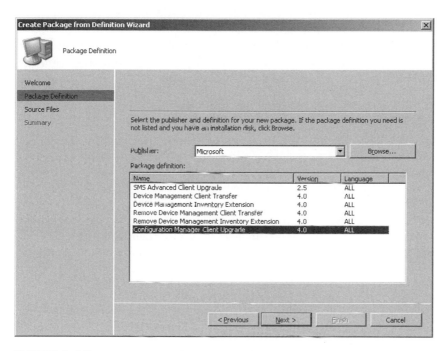

FIGURE 9.25   Selecting the definition file for the ConfigMgr Client upgrade package

To complete the wizard, you will need to choose This package contains source files option and then specify the package source location as the \client folder under your ConfigMgr installation folder. For more information about software distribution, see Chapter 14, "Distributing Packages."

Post-Upgrade Considerations

Once your site upgrades successfully, you will need to configure any new site systems and make any changes required for site maintenance tasks, updated boundaries, discovery methods, client agent settings, and client installation methods. Chapter 8 discusses these configuration tasks. Other post-upgrade considerations include the console, site boundaries, and the SMS SQL Monitor, which are discussed in the next sections.

Consoles

During the upgrade, the existing SMS Administrator console on the site server is upgraded to the ConfigMgr console. You cannot use the ConfigMgr console to manage SMS 2003 primary sites, or the SMS 2003 Administrator console to administer ConfigMgr sites. When you initially launch the console after upgrading to Configuration Manager 2007, you may need to connect to the site database using the Connect to Site Database Wizard. Chapter 10, "The Configuration Manager Console," describes this wizard.

You will need to separately upgrade the console on administrative workstations. Running Setup on a remote console installation installs the Configuration Manager console alongside the SMS 2003 Administrator console. If you prefer to upgrade the console to the ConfigMgr version only, run Setup with the /UPGRADE switch. Once the ConfigMgr console is installed on a machine, you will not be able to install the SMS 2003 console or apply a service pack to an existing SMS console installation. Although the two console versions can coexist on a machine, you cannot uninstall one without also removing the other.

Site Boundaries

Most site properties and settings will be preserved in your Configuration Manager site, although any site boundaries defined in SMS 2003 will be migrated as read-only. You will not be able to edit these boundaries, and will need to delete and re-create the boundaries to make any changes.

SMS SQL Monitor

SMS 2003 implemented the SMS SQL Monitor as a separate service. This component runs as an SMS Executive thread in Configuration Manager 2007. Although Setup should remove the SQL Monitor service, in some cases this service is not cleanly removed and still shows up as an installed service set to start automatically (although it will fail to start). If the SMS SQL Monitor service is still installed after your upgrade, you should disable the service.

Migrating WSUS to Configuration Manager

If you are currently using standalone WSUS for patch deployment rather than deploying patches with SMS 2003, you will need to disable any Active Directory (AD) group policies you have configured for managing WSUS clients. Configuration Manager clients receive policies from their assigned ConfigMgr site rather than from AD. If you need to keep the AD group policies in place to manage other WSUS clients in your environment, you can accomplish this in several ways, although each method can involve a substantial amount of work:

▶ Move your ConfigMgr clients and your WSUS clients to separate Organizational Units (OUs) in Active Directory, and apply the WSUS policies only to the WSUS clients.

▶ Use security groups to filter the application of GPOs so the WSUS policies will not apply to ConfigMgr clients. To accomplish this, you will need to be able to add the ConfigMgr clients to a security group that has the apply group policy right on the GPO set to denied. For information on using security group membership to filter GPO applications, see http://technet.microsoft.com/en-us/library/cc779291.aspx.

▶ Use WMI to filter the application of GPOs so that the WSUS policies will not apply to ConfigMgr clients. For information on WMI filtering, see http://technet.microsoft. com/en-us/library/cc781936.aspx.

Here's a WMI filter to exclude Configuration Manager clients:

```
Root\CCM;Select * from SMS_Client where ClientVersion not like '4.%'
```

A WMI filter to exclude all clients assigned to the HOU site would look like this:

```
Root\CCM;Select * from SMS_Client where SMS_Authority not like 'SMS:HOU'
```

If you decide to adopt any of these methods, you should carefully test them during your proof of concept and pilot phases before deploying them to your live environment. Chapter 7, "Testing and Stabilizing," discusses the proof of concept and pilot phases.

You will need to install WSUS on each system you plan to use as a software update point (SUP), and install the WSUS administration components on your site servers. Exit the WSUS setup without configuring synchronization settings or update classifications, categories, and languages, because you will configure these settings in the ConfigMgr console.

You can use an existing WSUS server as an SUP; however, you should delete the software updates metadata from the database prior to configuring the system as an SUP. Failure to do so can cause a number of problems, including clients scanning for and reporting on update classifications, categories, and languages not configured for your site.

Chapter 15 discusses installing and configuring software update points.

Side-by-Side Migrations

Whereas an in-place upgrade provides the advantage of preserving your SMS 2003 sites and settings, a side-by-side migration may be more appropriate if you plan major changes to your SMS environment. Carrying out a side-by-side migration includes the following tasks:

▶ Standing up new Configuration Manager 2007 sites with new site codes alongside your existing SMS 2003 sites.

▶ Migrating site boundaries, clients, and database objects from your existing SMS hierarchy to the new ConfigMgr sites.

▶ Removing any entries published by the old sites from Active Directory and WINS. If you will continue to use your old site systems for other purposes, you should review their Active Directory group memberships and remove them from any groups that are no longer required.

Microsoft provides a very useful flowchart describing the major activities for a side-by-side migration, available at http://technet.microsoft.com/en-us/library/bb681052.aspx.

Migrating Site Boundaries

As part of a side-by-side migration, you will need to assign site boundaries manually to your ConfigMgr sites and remove the corresponding boundaries from your SMS sites. The important point is that site boundaries should never overlap, because overlapping boundaries will cause serious problems for both SMS and ConfigMgr clients. Clients use site boundaries to determine their site assignment and to receive policy and content from the appropriate sites. Overlapping boundaries can cause unpredictable results for operations that depend on clients correctly determining what site they are located in, such as software distribution.

You should first remove site boundaries from the SMS sites you plan to decommission, and allow time for replication before adding the boundaries to your new ConfigMgr sites. Chapter 8 describes the procedure for adding boundaries to a Configuration Manager site. Before adding boundaries to one of your ConfigMgr sites, remove any boundaries from your SMS sites that would contain any part of the IP address space or AD sites that will comprise the ConfigMgr site boundaries. To delete a site boundary in SMS 2003, perform the following steps:

1. Open the SMS 2003 Administrator console and navigate to the Systems Management Server -> Site Database -> Site Hierarchy -> *<Site Code> <Site Name>* node in the tree control.

2. Right-click the site name and choose Properties. Then click the Site Boundaries tab.

3. Highlight the boundary you wish to delete and click the Delete button.

4. Repeat this process for each site boundary you wish to delete; then click the Roaming Boundaries tab and delete any roaming boundaries that will conflict with your ConfigMgr site boundaries.

Figure 9.26 shows the SMS 2003 Site Boundaries dialog box.

Migrating Clients

Several methods are available to migrate your existing SMS 2003 clients to your new ConfigMgr sites. Here are the major options:

▶ Use any of the client deployment methods that allow you to specify a site code to assign the clients to the new site at the same time they are upgraded. For example, you might run the command CCMSETUP.EXE /noservice SMSSITECODE=*xyz,* where *xyz* is the client's new site code. You can also use client push installation to upgrade clients and assign them to their new site code. Chapter 12 describes client push installation.

▶ Use SMS 2003 software deployment to advertise a package for reassigning the clients. One way to create a package for site assignment is to use a Visual Basic script (VBScript) similar to the following:

```
On Error Resume Next
dim oSMSClient
set oSMSClient = CreateObject ("Microsoft.SMS.Client")
oSMSClient.SetAssignedSite "ABC",0
set oSMSClient=nothing
```

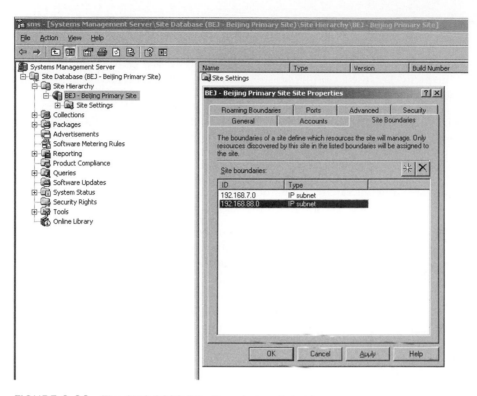

FIGURE 9.26   The SMS 2003 Site Boundaries dialog box

Your program command line will then be `cscript.exe <path to vb script><script name>.vbs`. The `<path>` is not required if your package includes source files and the script is in the root of the package source directory.

Because you have probably already removed the boundaries from your SMS site, your clients will treat your distribution points as remote. You will therefore need to select the option in your advertisement settings to either download or run from a remote distribution point when the package is not available on a local distribution point.

▶ If the SMS console ("Right Click") tools are installed, you can right-click a collection or individual SMS client and use the tools to reassign all clients in the collection. The console tools will attempt to connect to each system in the collection and initiate the site change; therefore, any clients that are offline or otherwise inaccessible will not receive the site change.

▶ Log on to an individual client machine and change the site code on the Advanced tab of the Control Panel Systems Management applet.

You will generally want to use one of the first two methods listed here to migrate most of your client systems. The last two methods are useful for picking up any clients missed by your primary migration method.

Migrating SMS Database Objects

The most common way to preserve the objects you have created in SMS database, such as packages and collections, is to temporarily join your new ConfigMgr central site to the existing SMS hierarchy. Because a ConfigMgr site cannot be a child of an SMS 2003 site, this means you will need to do one of the following:

▶ Upgrade your existing SMS 2003 central site to ConfigMgr before joining the new site to it. Although this should not affect the rest of your SMS hierarchy, it does require that the existing central site meet all the ConfigMgr system requirements.

▶ Install your new ConfigMgr central site as an SMS 2003 SP 2 or higher site, join it to the existing SMS 2003 hierarchy, allow the objects to replicate, and then detach the site. You can then upgrade the site to Configuration Manager 2007.

Alternatively, you can use a temporary site to transfer the objects. You can build an SMS 2003 site, perhaps as a virtual machine (VM), join it to your production SMS hierarchy, allow replication to complete, and then detach it from the SMS hierarchy. You will then upgrade the temporary site to ConfigMgr, remove any objects you no longer need, and make your new ConfigMgr production site a child of the temporary site. After the objects replicate to your permanent ConfigMgr site, detach your permanent ConfigMgr central site from the temporary site and decommission the temporary site. This method is a bit more work but allows you to have a clean ConfigMgr installation for your permanent site rather than upgrading, and it does not require you to upgrade your production SMS central site.

Queries and reports do not replicate down the hierarchy. You must export these objects from the SMS sites where they are defined and import them into your ConfigMgr site, as described in Chapter 7. Microsoft also has tools available for migrating SMS objects to ConfigMgr. These tools are not publicly available; contact your Microsoft support representative if you are interested in using these tools.

Migrating Hardware Inventory Customizations

SMS and Configuration Manager use Managed Object Format (MOF) files for hardware inventory. These files are substantially different in Configuration Manager from those in SMS 2003. As discussed in Chapter 3, "Looking Inside Configuration Manager," the data classes defined by ConfigMgr 2007 are now defined in the configuration.mof file, whereas the reporting classes are specified in the SMS_Def.mof file. This means that you will need to separate out any custom classes defined in your SMS 2003 SMS_Def.mof or mini-MOF files and then add the appropriate MOF language to each of the ConfigMgr .mof files.

Before the upgrade, copy your SMS_Def.mof file and any mini-MOF files you are using to a separate location to avoid them being overwritten. After the upgrade completes, use a text editor to open and edit the .mof files.

If you have custom classes defined in your SMS 2003 SMS_Def.mof file or in mini-MOF files, you can use the `#pragma namespace` compiler directives in the file to locate the data and reporting classes for these definitions. The SMS 2003 SMS_Def.mof file uses a `#pragma` *namespace* compiler directive to instruct the compiler to use a particular namespace. Most custom data classes extract data from the root\CINV2 WMI (Windows Management Instrumentation) namespace.

In general, you can locate data classes in the SMS_Def.mof or mini-MOF by searching for the #pragma *namespace root\CINV2* directive. You should append the block of text following this directive to the end of the configuration.mof file (without the #pragma *namespace* directive itself). You will find the corresponding reporting class definitions under the #pragma *namespace root\CINV2\sms*. These should be copied to the SMS_Def.mof file.

Interoperability Considerations

Although you can upgrade SMS 2003 SP 2 sites directly to ConfigMgr 2007, you should upgrade them to SP 3 if you plan to maintain SMS 2003 sites for a significant period. ConfigMgr clients running Windows Vista will not function correctly if they roam to SMS 2003 SP 2 sites. In addition, SMS 2003 SP 2 clients cannot roam to ConfigMgr sites in native mode.

SMS 2003 SP 2 is no longer supported based on the Microsoft support life cycle. You should therefore upgrade any SP 2 sites and clients to SP 3 or ConfigMgr 2007 as soon as possible to continue to receive support and software updates.

In a mixed environment, you will use the SMS 2003 Administrator console to administer SMS 2003 primary sites and the ConfigMgr console to administer ConfigMgr primary sites. If you have secondary sites running SMS 2003, you will be able to administer them through the parent primary site; however, you will not be able to change the accounts or passwords used by these secondary sites. You will also not be able to create or configure Remote Access Service (RAS) senders or configure Active Directory Security Group Discovery on SMS 2003 secondary sites with ConfigMgr parent sites.

Troubleshooting Upgrade Issues

If you encounter any failures during the setup process, you should check the setup log at c:\ConfigMgrSetup.log for any error messages. Some common upgrade issues include the following:

▶ You receive the following error message: Cannot insert the default site control image to the database. ConfigMgrSetup.log contains the entry "error xp_SMS_notification not found."

This generally occurs when you have reinstalled SQL Server on the site database server and the xp_SMS_notification extended stored procedure was removed during setup. To correct this problem, use the procedure described in http://support. microsoft.com/kb/556084 to re-create the extended stored procedure.

▶ Setup fails while attempting to install the SMS Provider. ConfigMgrSetup.log contains the entry "CompileMOFFile: Failed to compile MOF."

This generally results from an incorrect AD Service Principal Name (SPN) registration. See Chapter 5, "Network Design," for a discussion of Service Principal Name issues.

▶ Upgrading a secondary site may fail when using local source files if the bootstrap process is unable to locate the installation files in the correct path or if there is a version mismatch.

SMS_Bootstrap.log will show errors locating the install.map file or an incorrect build number in install.map.

▶ Setup fails to correctly detect the type of site you have installed.

This may be the result of previous failed upgrade attempts or incorrect information in the site server registry.

▶ The SMS SQL Monitor service is no longer required in Configuration Manager 2007 SP 1. You should disable or delete this service after the upgrade to avoid misleading error messages at logon, in the system event log, and in the ConfigMgr status message system.

One way to delete the service is to use the SC.EXE Windows Resource Kit tool with command line `SC delete SMS_SQL_Monitor`. For information about SC.EXE, see http://technet.microsoft.com/en-us/library/bb490995.aspx. After you delete the service, you can manually remove the following Registry keys:

  ▶ HKEY_LOCAL_MACHINE\Software\Microsoft\SMS\COMPONENTS\SMS_ SITE_COMPONENT_MANAGER\Component Servers\<servername> \Components\SMS_SQL_MONITOR

  ▶ HKEY_LOCAL_MACHINE\Software\Microsoft\SMS\Tracing\SMS_SQL_ MONITOR

If Setup completes successfully, you should review the site status to make sure all systems and components have an OK status, or investigate any errors or warnings that have occurred. Chapter 21 discusses the status system.

Summary

This chapter discussed how to upgrade an existing SMS 2003 hierarchy to Configuration Manager 2007. The next chapter presents the interface through which you will administer your ConfigMgr environment, the Configuration Manager console.

PART III

Configuration Manager Operations

IN THIS PART

The Configuration Manager Console

The Administrator console is a key element of any Configuration Manager (ConfigMgr) 2007 environment. The console is the interface administrators use to maintain the site and hierarchy as well as to perform daily tasks to manage and configure sites, the site database, clients, and monitor the status of the hierarchy.

This chapter describes how to deploy the console, console features, and how to use those features.

Using Microsoft Management Console 3.0

The ConfigMgr console has a new fresh look, with a different look and feel from the older Systems Management Server (SMS) 2003 console. This new look and feel is because the console is based on the new Microsoft Management Console 3.0 (MMC) framework.

Using the MMC, an administrator can load multiple tools, known as *snap-ins*. A snap-in is an application built to run within the MMC. Adding snap-ins themselves has much improved with MMC 3.0; instead of having to use a tedious procedure involving two dialog boxes to build a separate console, version 3.0 provides a single dialog box, thus making it much easier to create custom consoles. You can then make these consoles available to individuals when you want to delegate specific management tasks.

The capability to add these custom consoles is of particular interest to ConfigMgr administrators, because the ConfigMgr Administrator console itself is actually a snap-in hosted by the MMC. Using the MMC allows ConfigMgr admins to create consoles easily that allow users to see only a specific part of the ConfigMgr functionality. As an example, you may want to create a custom console for helpdesk users where they only have the ability to use the ConfigMgr Remote Tools feature.

Touring the Console

When opening the ConfigMgr 2007 console, you will notice it contains the following three panes:

- ▶ **Console tree**—The console tree is on the left side of the console. It allows you to browse the multiple nodes to manage your site and clients.

- ▶ **Result pane**—The result pane is the middle section of the console. When you select a tree object, this pane displays the results.

- ▶ **Actions pane**—The Actions pane is the pane displayed at the right side of the console. This is the only pane that you can hide. The Actions pane contains options and tasks, which are available as well when you right-click an object in the console tree or the result pane.

Figure 10.1 shows the ConfigMgr console.

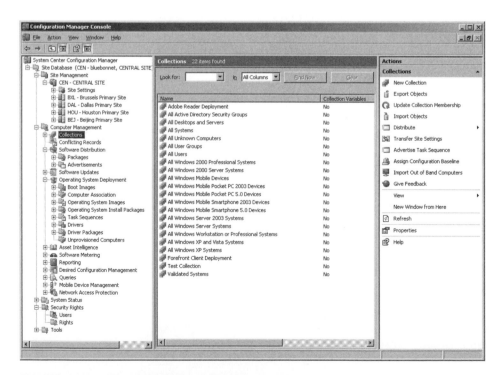

FIGURE 10.1   The Configuration Manager console

The ConfigMgr 2007 console includes search folders, a search bar, allows drag and drop, can replicate folders down the hierarchy, and incorporates home pages. The next sections discuss several of these features.

New Console Features

As described earlier, the MMC 3.0 framework introduces many new features and capabilities in the Configuration Manager console:

- ▶ **Drag and drop**—The ConfigMgr 2007 console allows you to drag and drop objects. As an example, you can drag a program and drop it onto a collection to create an advertisement. This saves much time and keystrokes, and can help you keep things organized.

- ▶ **Home pages**—When you select a main node such as Software Distribution or Desired Configuration Management, a home page will display in the result pane. These home pages give you a quick overview of the status of a certain feature when you select the root node of that feature. As an example, you can view the status of deployed packages or the percentage of compliant systems with Desired Configuration Management.

- ▶ **Sort columns**—This is not exactly a new feature because it was also an option with SMS 2003, although the SMS 2003 version did not work and was very buggy. This feature now functions with ConfigMgr 2007. You can also sort the columns to find information more quickly.

- ▶ **Search bar**—Sites can grow very fast with custom collections, packages, programs, and advertisements. Also, over 300 reports come with the ConfigMgr 2007 product. The search bar at the top of the results pane will help you to find all your objects in multiple columns.

- ▶ **Search folders**—Search folders comprise another new feature. Although search folders do not ship with the console, you can create your own search folder in most nodes. Search folders are not available in the Collection nodes and on several of the main nodes such as Software Distribution and Operating System Deployment. You can define a query criterion for each search folder, which filters the results that will display in the folder. Search folders provide a great way to arrange different objects, and they make things much easier for those individuals who want to organize their admin consoles.

Creating a Search Folder

Search folders work great for filtering and organizing the objects and information in the console. As an example, you can create a search folder for all your packages with a specific manufacturer. To create this search folder, perform the following steps:

1. Navigate to the Computer Management node, expand Software Distribution, and then right-click Packages.

2. Select New and choose Search Folder.

3. In the Search Folder Criteria dialog box, choose the object Manufacturer.

4. In the Edit the property's search criteria box, click the *<text to find>* hyperlink.

5. Specify a manufacturer to define your search criteria (such as Microsoft). Click Add and then OK.

6. Repeat steps 4 and 5 to define multiple combined criteria, as displayed in Figure 10.2.

7. By default, the search folder will only search in the current folder. You can mark the "Search all folders under this feature" option in the bottom of Figure 10.2 to let Configuration Manager search in all subfolders.

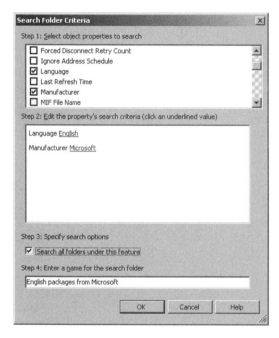

FIGURE 10.2   A search folder for English packages from Microsoft

8. The last step is to define a friendly name for the search folder, such as **English packages from Microsoft**.

In addition to organizing and filtering information in the console, you can combine search folders with an action (for example, with software updates).

You can create a search folder containing a criterion that filters required updates released in a previous month for client computers or servers. The use of search folders is part of the Software Updates workflow. This allows you to add the resulting updates from the search folder to an update list, to create reports to display compliancy, and eventually to create a deployment based on the software update list.

Perform the following steps to create a search folder to locate updates released on a specific date:

1. In the Configuration Manager console, navigate to Site Database -> Computer Management -> Software Updates -> Update Repository.

2. The Update Repository contains a search folder by default. Right-click Search Folders and then select New Search Folder.

3. To define the criteria, select Date Released to specify the date the software update was released.

4. Check the box Search all folders under this feature.

5. Enter a name for the folder (as an example, **Updates released in March**) and click OK.

6. Back in the console, click the folder you created. The software updates are displayed by article ID and are based on the criteria you specified for this search folder. In the folder, you can check if the software update is required for computers and create an update list based on the results.

Home Pages

Another new feature in the ConfigMgr 2007 console is home pages. The goal of the home page is to deliver a complete status overview specific to the selected node. Home pages are available for the following nodes:

▶ **Software Distribution**—This home page shows the status of all package advertisements. For each advertisement, you can see how many have started, succeeded, failed, retried, or are waiting.

▶ **Software Updates**—Here you can see the status of required, deployed, and already installed updates. It also shows the update compliancy percentage of the site.

▶ **Operating System Deployment**—The Operating System Deployment home page also shows the status of advertisements, but only for those task sequences that are advertised.

▶ **Asset Intelligence**—This home page shows the inventoried software titles, categories, and software families.

▶ **Desired Configuration Management**—The compliancy of Desired Configuration Management items is shown in this home page.

▶ **Network Access Protection**—This home page also shows compliancy and remediation errors, and the total number of computers in remediation.

When you select any of these main nodes, the home page appears in the result pane.

As an example, the Software Distribution home page by default shows the status of the top-10 active advertisements in the last 7 days.

Home pages are divided in three sections.

10

▶ On each home page, the first section enables you to configure the filters for the results shown in the middle section.

Every home page has different types of filters you can apply. As an example, with the Desired Configuration Management home page, you can set filters such as time-frames and severities. The Software Updates home page provides you with filters such as Vendor and Update classifications as well as the ability to apply a filter for the month and year the update was released.

▶ When the filters are applied, the middle section displays the results, with the number and a chart for a quick status overview.

▶ The bottom of each home page has a Links and Resources section. This section contains shortcuts to other nodes such as Advertisements, enabling you to navigate quickly through the console. It also contains links to web reports and help resources.

To run web reports, you must configure a reporting point. This is discussed in Chapter 18, "Reporting."

Figure 10.3 displays the home page of Software Updates.

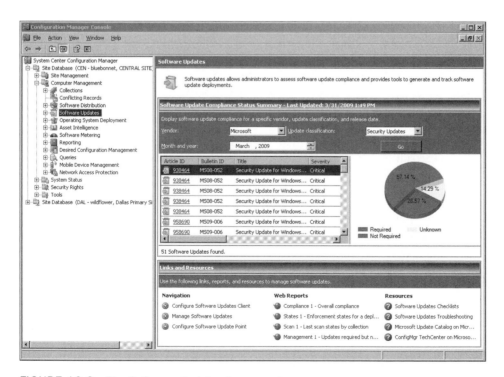

FIGURE 10.3   The Software Updates home page

The results in the home pages are automatically refreshed. This is also known as home page *summarization*. Except for the Asset Intelligence node, each node has a summarization interval. Table 10.1 shows the interval for each node.

TABLE 10.1   Default Refresh Interval for Each Home Page

Home Page	Summarization Interval
Software Distribution	1 hour
Software Updates	4 hours
Operating System Deployment	1 hour
Desired Configuration Management	2 hours
Network Access Protection	30 minutes

If you prefer a tighter or specific interval, you can configure a custom schedule with the Schedule Home Page Summarization link provided in the Actions pane. To apply the new custom schedule, click Run Home Page Summarization, also provided in the Actions pane.

Console Nodes

In addition to the new, improved look provided with MMC 3.0, Microsoft wanted to create a more user-friendly console with ConfigMgr 2007. The ConfigMgr team reorganized the console tree, which now consists of five main nodes, rather than the 12 nodes you had with the SMS 2003 console.

Here are the five main nodes:

▶ **Site Management**—The Site Management node shows the site hierarchy and the site components, such as boundaries, client agents, addresses, site maintenance tasks, and roles.

▶ **Computer Management**—This is the main node for the administrator. It contains all the components to manage the clients in the site.

▶ **System Status**—This node shows the overall health of the site, and includes tasks for troubleshooting a site.

▶ **Security Rights**—Security rights can be set here on entities of ConfigMgr, such as collections, remote tools, packages, and advertisements.

▶ **Tools**—The Tools node contains the ConfigMgr Service Manager, which can be used to start and stop services and components.

10

When you deploy a site, the Computer Management and System Status nodes are the most commonly used nodes for daily administration and management of your clients.

Table 10.2 describes the nodes and subnodes in more detail.

TABLE 10.2   Configuration Manager Console Nodes

Node	Subnode	Description
Site Database		Here you can select the site database for the site you want to manage. You can customize the console by connecting to multiple site databases.
Site Management		This main node displays the site hierarchy. The central site will display at the top, with all primary and secondary sites shown below. The Site Management node allows you to configure sitewide settings for that particular site or any child sites in the hierarchy.
		Using the console, you can configure properties such as boundaries, site roles, addresses, client agents, discovery methods, certificates, status filters, and summarizers. To keep the site healthy, there is a site maintenance folder with tasks and SQL commands.
Computer Management		This node enables you to use Manager 2007 features to manage ConfigMgr 2007 clients. It includes a number of subnodes.
Computer Management	Collections	In this subnode, you can create, delete, or modify collections. Collections are used to group clients for distributing packages and other tasks. Chapter 14, "Distributing Packages," discusses collections in detail.
Computer Management	Conflicting Records	Sometimes there will be duplicate records. This subnode allows you to manage those records, create new records, and block them. Chapter 21, "Backup, Recovery, and Maintenance," discusses conflicting record management.
Computer Management	Software Distribution	This subnode displays all the packages and advertisements to distribute software to the clients in the collections. Chapter 14 discusses software distribution.

TABLE 10.2   Configuration Manager Console Nodes

Node	Subnode	Description
Computer Management	Software Updates	Software Updates allows administrators to deploy updates to the clients. Chapter 15, "Patch Management," discusses Software Updates.
Computer Management	Operating System Deployment	A new capability in ConfigMgr 2007, Operating System Deployment allows the administrator to create and deploy operating system images based on task sequences. Chapter 19, "Operating System Deployment," discusses this functionality.
Computer Management	Asset Intelligence	You can use Asset Intelligence, discussed in Chapter 18, to create reports and inventory showing software usage.
Computer Management	Software Metering	You can create metering rules in this subnode to monitor the program usage of the clients. Chapter 12, "Client Management," discusses software metering.
Computer Management	Reporting	This subnode allows you to create and run reports based on WQL queries. Chapter 18 covers ConfigMgr reporting.
Computer Management	Desired Configuration Management	ConfigMgr 2007 includes the ability to configure desired configuration management rules and baselines, and use configuration packs to keep your clients compliant with company policy. Chapter 16, named appropriately, "Desired Configuration Management," discusses this capability.
Computer Management	Queries	By default, some basic queries such as All Systems are installed with ConfigMgr. Administrators can create and run their own queries to collect information from the ConfigMgr database. Chapter 17, "Configuration Manager Queries," discusses the use of queries.
Computer Management	Mobile Device Management	Configuration items and packages can be created to manage mobile devices. Chapter 12 discusses managing mobile devices.

10

TABLE 10.2 Configuration Manager Console Nodes

Node	Subnode	Description
Computer Management	Network Access Protection	This subnode enables you to configure ConfigMgr as a remediation server for software update deployment. Chapter 15 discusses Network Access Protection.
System Status		This node displays the health of the site, packages, and advertisements. You can use this node for troubleshooting and maintenance tasks. Chapter 21 discusses System Status.
System Status	Advertisement Status	Shows the status of all advertisements for the site.
System Status	Package Status	Shows the status of all packages for the site.
System Status	Site Status	Shows the overall health of the site hierarchy and tasks for troubleshooting a site.
System Status	Status Message Queries	Queries collection status information of client and site components.
Security Rights		Use this node to set security rights for ConfigMgr security objects, including collections, packages, and advertisements.
Security Rights	Users	This subnode allows you to add, delete, and clone users or groups who need access to ConfigMgr.
Security Rights	Rights	In the Rights subnode, you can set the permissions a specific user has. This subnode also displays an overview of all rights currently set. ConfigMgr rights are categorized under Class and Instance rights. The Manage User Wizard also allows you to configure the rights for the user. Chapter 20, "Security and Delegation in Configuration Manager 2007," describes security rights.
Tools		The Tools node allows you to start and stop ConfigMgr 2007 service and thread component activity.

TABLE 10.2   Configuration Manager Console Nodes

Node	Subnode	Description
Tools	ConfigMgr Service Manager	The ConfigMgr Service Manager is located under this subnode. You can use the Service Manager to start, stop, pause, and resume components in Configuration Manager. The "Configuration Manager Service Manager" section later in this chapter describes the ConfigMgr Service Manager in more detail.

Console Keystrokes

Although you can use the mouse to navigate through all the nodes in Configuration Manager, it also has a number of keystrokes you can use. The combination of those keystrokes and the mouse enables you to browse through the console very quickly. Table 10.3 displays a list of the available keystrokes.

TABLE 10.3   Configuration Manager Keystrokes

Keystroke	Description
F1	Pressing the F1 key displays the Configuration Manager Documentation Library. Help is "location aware," meaning if you press the F1 key while the Query node is selected, the library will open at the "Query" section in Online Help.
F3	The F3 key automatically moves the cursor to the "Look for" section in the top bar of the result pane.
F5	To refresh items in a console pane or to refresh the results of components, press the F5 key.
F6	To move between the console tree pane and the result pane, use the F6 key. When you move from the console tree pane to the result pane, the cursor is automatically placed in the "Look for" section in the top bar of the result pane. Moving works both ways, so you can also move from the result pane to the console tree pane.
Shift+F10	Holding down the Shift key and pressing the F10 key will display the action menu of the selected item. This is the same menu as when right-clicking the item with the mouse.
Tab, Shift+Tab	Using the Tab key, you can move the focus from the console tree pane to the result pane and the available boxes in the top bar of the result pane. Holding down the Shift key while pressing the Tab key allows you to change the focus to the opposite direction.
Up arrow	Moves the cursor up in the tree or the items in the result pane.
Down arrow	Moves the cursor down in the tree or the items in the result pane.

10

TABLE 10.3   Configuration Manager Keystrokes

Keystroke	Description
Right arrow	Pressing the right arrow expands the selected items, displaying all child items.
Left arrow	Pressing the left arrow collapses all child items of the selected item. This also applies to the main nodes in the console. As an example, when the Software Distribution node is selected, the left arrow key moves the cursor to the parent (the main Computer Management node).

About the SMS Right Click Tools

The SMS "Right Click" tools were introduced as SMS Administrator console additions, provided free of charge at http://offshore-it.co.uk/smstools.html. You can download enhancements, described at http://myitforum.com/cs2/blogs/rhouchins/archive/2008/04/09/sccm-right-click-tools.aspx, including support for ConfigMgr 2007.

Launching Reports

With Configuration Manager 2007 Release 2 (R2), you have the capability to view either classic or SQL Reporting Services (SRS) reports using the Configuration Manager console.

The ConfigMgr Report Viewer allows you to navigate the reporting site, enter parameters for reports, and render the reports for viewing in a web browser. Accessing this functionality either from the console or from a web browser requires IE 5.01 Service Pack (SP) 2 or later to host the Report Viewer ActiveX control.

Microsoft provides over 300 ready-made reports that you can use or modify for your reporting requirements; these reports are described in Chapter 18. The next sections discuss viewing classic and SQL Reporting Services (SRS) reports available with ConfigMgr 2007 R2.

Viewing Classic Reports from the ConfigMgr Console

To view ConfigMgr classic reports from the console, perform the following steps:

1. Expand the Configuration Manager console tree to System Center Configuration Manager -> Site Database -> Computer Management -> Reporting -> Reports. The Reports pane on the right displays a list of available reports.

    The "Look for" list box allows you to filter the list of reports.

2. Right-click the report you wish to run and choose Run from the context menu.

3. The console now invokes the Report Viewer, which permits you to enter any required or optional parameters for the selected report and launch the report. Notice that the Report Viewer, displayed in Figure 10.4, provides a Values button, allowing you to view and select from the list of values corresponding to the parameters that are stored in the database. You can enter a partial string using the wildcard characters _ (to match a single character) and % (to match zero or more characters) to narrow the list.

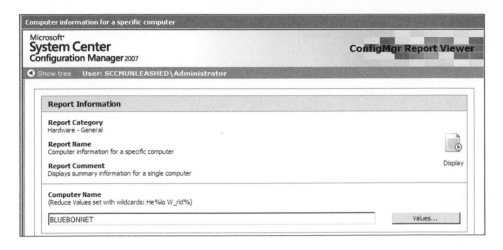

FIGURE 10.4   The Report Viewer

By default, the Report Viewer displays a list of up to 1,000 values. The DWORD Registry value HKEY_LOCAL_MACHINE\Software\Microsoft\SMS\Reporting\Values Rowcount on the reporting server specifies the maximum number of values returned in the values list. This DWORD value does not exist by default. To specify that Report Viewer should display all values, set Values Rowcount to 0xffffffff.

4. Click the Display icon in the upper-right section of Report Viewer to display the report. By default, the Report Viewer will display up to 10,000 rows of data in the report. The DWORD Registry value HKEY_LOCAL_MACHINE\Software\Microsoft\SMS\Reporting\Rowcount on the reporting server specifies the maximum number of rows returned by Report Viewer. To specify that reports should display all values, set Rowcount to 0xffffffff.

5. You can use the Show Tree button in the upper-left corner of Report Viewer to display the reporting hierarchy as a tree control. This is the same tree displayed by IE when you open the reporting point URL.

Viewing SRS Reports from the ConfigMgr Console

To view ConfigMgr SRS reports from the console, perform the following steps:

1. Expand the Configuration Manager console tree to System Center Configuration Manager -> Site Database -> Computer Management -> Reporting Services -> *<servername>*, where *<servername>* represents your reporting services point.

2. The All Reports folder displays a list of reports similar to that in the Reports console tree node used for classic reporting. SRS also provides a folder called Report Folders containing reports arranged in subfolders by folder category. Locate the report you wish to run under either folder structure, right-click the report, and choose Run from the context menu.

3. The report viewer pane displayed in Figure 10.5 is functionally equivalent to the Report Viewer control provided with classic reporting. Enter the required parameters and any optional parameters you choose to supply, or use the Values links to use the selection list, and then click View Report to open the report.

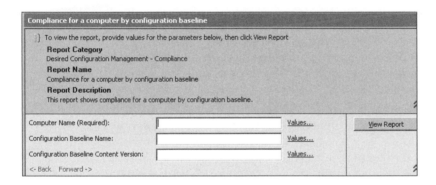

FIGURE 10.5   The SRS report viewer pane with the compliance for a computer by configuration baseline report selected

Using Internet Explorer to View Reports

You can also use a web browser (Internet Explorer 5.01 SP 2 or later) to view reports. This enables individuals to view reports who do not otherwise need access to the ConfigMgr console.

Perform the following steps to view ConfigMgr classic reports using Internet Explorer (IE):

1. Launch Internet Explorer and enter the reporting point URL. The default URL is http://<servername>/SMSReporting_<Site Code>, where <servername> is the name of your reporting point server and <Site Code> is the ConfigMgr site code.

2. The Report Viewer tree control will open as shown in Figure 10.6. You can use the tree control to navigate to the reports in your reporting folder. The reports are arranged in folders under the Reports node of the tree control (Chapter 18 includes a list of those categories). Figure 10.6 shows the reporting point website as displayed in Internet Explorer.

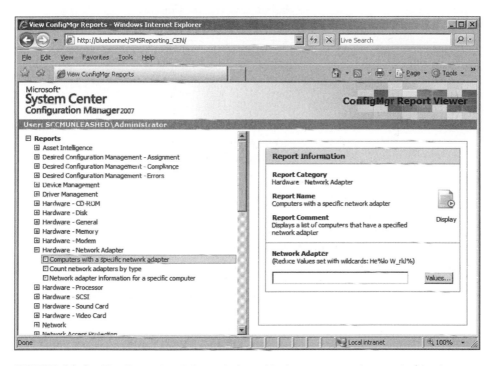

FIGURE 10.6   The Reporting Point website, with the tree control expanded to the report Computers with a specific network adapter

Perform the following steps to view ConfigMgr SRS reports using Internet Explorer:

1. Launch IE and enter the SRS URL. The default URL is http://<servername>/reports/, where <servername> is the name of your reporting services point server. (Chapter 18 discusses configuring the reporting services point.) The default report folder name is ConfigMgr_<Site Code>.

2. The SRS home page will open, as displayed in Figure 10.7. You can click the category links to open the corresponding report folders.

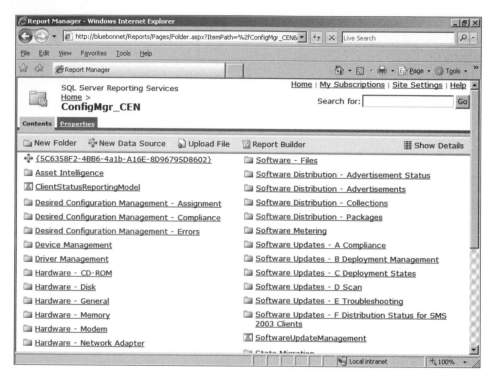

FIGURE 10.7   The Reporting Services page for the central site server (Bluebonnet), displayed in Internet Explorer

Console Deployment

Now that you have been introduced to the console, let's spend some time discussing its installation. When you install a new primary site, the ConfigMgr console is also installed on that system by default. However, organizations typically require multiple consoles to manage the site hierarchy; this is particularly true in enterprise organizations. In these scenarios, you will also want to install the console on the desktops of ConfigMgr administrators. The next sections discuss the platforms on which the console is supported, installation prerequisites, the steps to install the ConfigMgr console using the setup wizard, and performing an unintended console installation.

Supported Platforms

Microsoft supports the Configuration Manager console on the following Microsoft platforms:

▶ Windows XP Professional with Service Pack 2 or above.

▶ Windows Vista, all editions.

▶ Windows Server 2003, all editions with Service Pack 1 or above.

▶ Windows Server 2008, all editions other than Server Core. Server Core is only supported with Configuration Manager 2007 with SP 1 or higher.

Prerequisites

Prior to installing the console, ensure the intended system has met the following prerequisites:

▶ Microsoft Management Console 3.0

▶ .NET Framework 2.0 or higher

▶ At least 100MB (megabytes) free disk space

To make sure you meet all the prerequisites before you start the installation wizard, you can choose to run the prerequisite checker from the splash screen initiated from the Configuration Manager 2007 installation media.

Installation Using the Configuration Manager Setup Wizard

After meeting the prerequisites discussed in the previous section, start installing the console by running the Configuration Manager Setup Wizard. If you are using the ConfigMgr installation CD, the wizard will automatically start. If installing from the file system, you can start the setup manually by opening the splash.hta file, found in the root of the installation media. Perform the following steps to install the console:

1. The first screen presents several options, including running the prerequisite checker, reviewing the release notes, and installing ConfigMgr. Figure 10.8 displays this screen.

2. Select Install Configuration Manager 2007 to proceed to the welcome screen. This screen suggests steps you should take prior to starting the installation wizard. When you are ready, click Next in the welcome screen, displayed in Figure 10.9.

3. The next screen shows the available setup options, displayed in Figure 10.10. Select Install or upgrade an administrator console. Click Next to continue.

4. The following screen, displayed in Figure 10.11, is the Microsoft Software License Terms screen. Ensure you read the license agreement, and select the option "I accept these license terms." Click Next to advance to the next screen.

5. On the Customer Experience Improvement Program Configuration page displayed in Figure 10.12, you can choose to join the program. Microsoft uses the Customer Experience Improvement Program to gather information regarding your ConfigMgr installation. You can read the documentation at http://technet.microsoft.com/en-us/library/bb693975.aspx for more information.

   When you participate in the program, information regarding the health and performance of ConfigMgr components and your server is sent to Microsoft in a summary file. Microsoft uses this information for analysis and future releases of ConfigMgr.

10

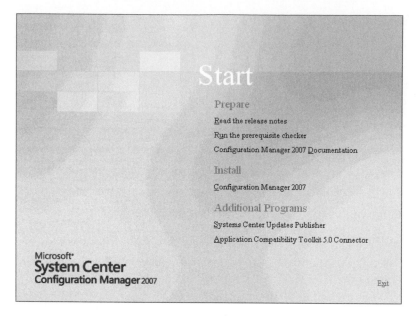

FIGURE 10.8   The Configuration Manager 2007 splash screen

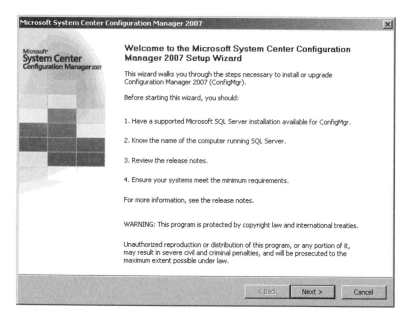

FIGURE 10.9   The Configuration Manager 2007 welcome screen

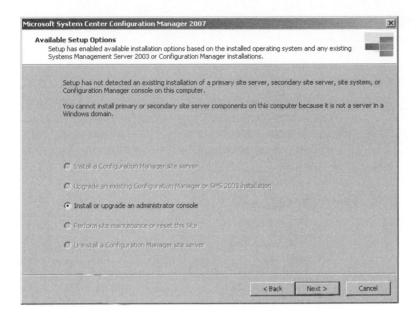

FIGURE 10.10   Choose one of the available setup options.

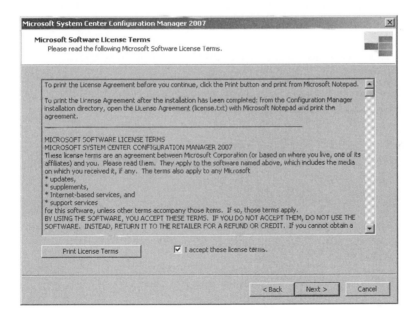

FIGURE 10.11   Microsoft software license terms

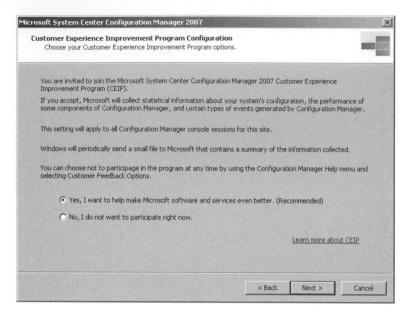

FIGURE 10.12   The Customer Experience Improvement Program Configuration screen

Select whether or not to participate in the program, and click Next to continue. You can always decide to opt out later.

6. You now are requested to specify a destination folder for installing the console, as displayed in Figure 10.13. Type the path or select the Browse option to specify the location where setup will install the console installation files. Click Next.

7. The next screen, shown in Figure 10.14, is the Site Server screen. Specify the name of the primary site server you want to connect to in the console and then click Next to continue.

8. You now advance to the Settings Summary screen, displayed in Figure 10.15. Verify the details you specified in the previous steps, and either click Back to change the information or click Next to proceed to the next step.

9. Once you verify your settings, the wizard automatically performs an installation prerequisite check. Notice in Figure 10.16 that the prerequisite checker is displaying two warnings. You can double-click any prerequisite listed to display details regarding that problem, with information on how to resolve outstanding issues.

   You can also troubleshoot by checking the ConfigMgrPrereq.log, located in the root of the system drive. When all the prerequisites are met (or there are only warnings), the Begin Install button becomes available. Click Begin Install to start installing the console.

10. The Setup Action Status Monitoring screen shows the progress and status of all the installation actions (see Figure 10.17). When all actions are complete, click Next to continue.

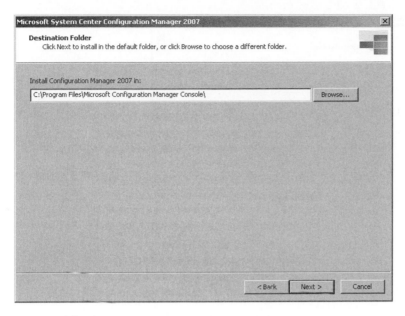

FIGURE 10.13   Specifying the destination folder

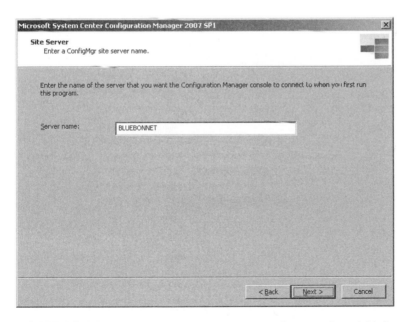

FIGURE 10.14   Specifying the server you want the console to initially connect to

10

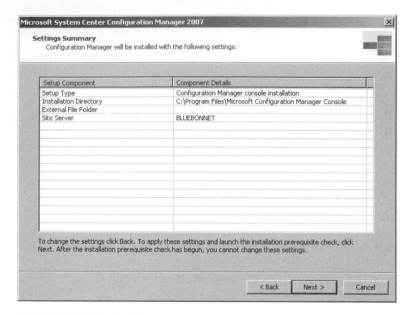

FIGURE 10.15   Verifying your settings

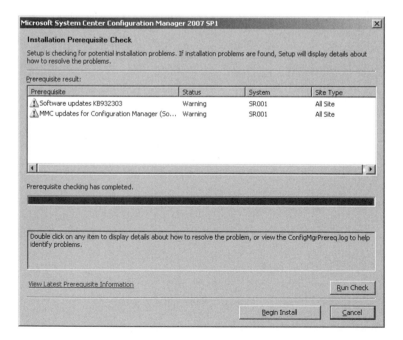

FIGURE 10.16   Installation Prerequisite Check results

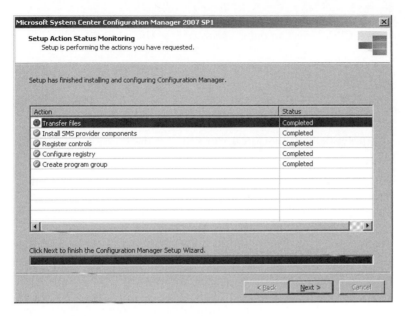

FIGURE 10.17   Displaying installation status

11. Figure 10.18 shows the final page of the wizard, which displays the installation completion status. If the installation failed, you can review ConfigMgrSetup.log by clicking the View Log button. This log file is located in the root of your system drive.

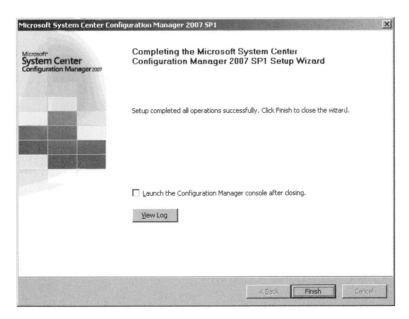

FIGURE 10.18   Completing the Configuration Manager Setup Wizard

When the installation is successful, you can select the option Launch the Configuration Manager console after closing. Click Finish to complete and close the wizard.

Unattended Console Installation

Instead of using the Configuration Manager Setup Wizard, you can install the console in unattended mode. An unattended installation can be used to deploy the console silently to multiple systems at once, potentially using ConfigMgr software distribution, or with a group policy object (GPO).

Before installing the console to multiple systems, verify that every targeted system is on a supported platform and that all the required prerequisites, described earlier in the "Prerequisites" section, are met. You can choose to check these requirements using the ConfigMgr hardware and inventory functions.

When you install the console using the setup wizard, as in the previous section, the wizard asks you to specify a number of settings. For an unattended installation, you can use an initialization file to specify these settings in advance.

The initialization file is a text file and can be created using Windows Notepad. The following information is required in the initialization file:

```
[Identification]
Action=InstallAdminUI
[Options]
SMSInstallDir=<Specify the installation directory>
ParentSiteServer=<Specify the primary site the console must connect to>
SDKServer=<Specify the SMS provider>
```

Specify the required options, and save the initialization file with an extension of .ini. As an example, you might name the file **AdminConsole.ini**.

To start the unattended setup and combine the initialization file with the setup installation files, run the following command from the command prompt or in a batch file:

```
<installation media location>\SMSSETUP\BIN\I386\SETUP.EXE
/script <path to your .ini file>
```

The installation will run in silent mode, meaning no installation screens will display during setup. To check for errors, review ConfigMgrSetup.log, which is located at the root of your system drive.

Finding Console Information on an Installed Server

Two areas are used to populate information for the console—the Windows Registry and the file system.

Registry information related to the console is located under

▶ HKEY_LOCAL_MACHINE\Software\Microsoft\MMC\Snapins\FX:{6de537a5-7a1c-4fa4-ac3a-1b6fc1036560}

▶ HKEY_LOCAL_MACHINE\Software\Microsoft\ConfigMgr

The console files are located in several places on the file system:

▶ %ProgramFiles%\Microsoft Configuration Manager\AdminUI.

▶ %ProgramFiles%\Microsoft Configuration Manager\AdminUI\bin\adminconsole.msc.

▶ The cache is stored at %HOMEPATH%\Application Data\Microsoft\MMC\admin-console.

This file retains custom settings for the console, as well as connections to site databases.

You can find an additional discussion on this subject at http://wmug.co.uk/groups/articles/pages/configmgr-console.aspx.

Customizing the Console

Using MMC technology gives you the ability to create your own custom console. You can use custom consoles to hide those features you do not use or features you want to restrict to certain individuals, because not everyone may require access to the full console. Custom consoles are also useful when you have multiple administrators with specific roles. Those administrators can create their own consoles with their most commonly used features.

To create a custom console, perform the following steps:

1. Open a new MMC by going to Start -> Run, type **mmc**, and then click the OK button. This brings up an empty console root, as displayed in Figure 10.19.

2. In the new console, select File -> Add/Remove Snap-in, as shown in Figure 10.20.

3. In the Add/Remove Snap-in dialog box, click Add and choose the System Center Configuration Manager snap-in. Click the Add button at the bottom of Figure 10.21.

4. The next screen begins the Database Connection Wizard. Click Next at the Welcome screen, displayed in Figure 10.22.

5. In the Locate Site Database screen shown in Figure 10.23, verify you selected the correct site database (this example shows the Bluebonnet site server, the central site server for the SCCMUnleashed hierarchy) and then choose the Select console tree

10

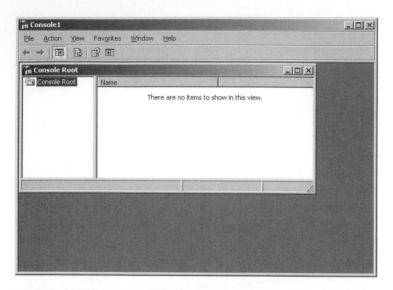

FIGURE 10.19   A new Microsoft Management Console

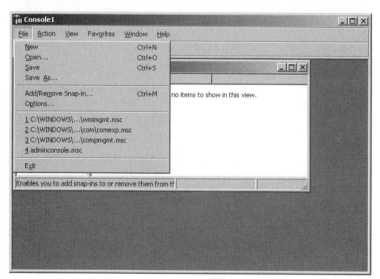

FIGURE 10.20   Adding a snap-in to the console

items to be loaded (custom) option at the bottom of the screen. Click Next to continue.

6. The next screen of the Database Connection Wizard, shown in Figure 10.24, allows you to select the items you want to appear in the console tree. Check the items you want to be available in the console and click Next to continue.

7. Figure 10.25 displays the Summary screen. To change any of your selections, click the Previous button. Otherwise, click Finish to complete the wizard.

FIGURE 10.21   Adding the System Center Configuration Manager snap-in

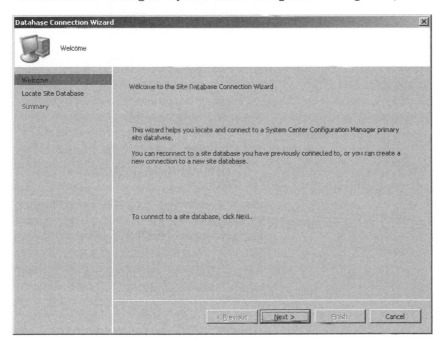

FIGURE 10.22   The Database Connection Wizard Welcome screen

You can now close the Add/Remove Snap-in dialog box and click OK to open the custom snap-in. The custom console, displayed in Figure 10.26, will now load. To save the console, select File -> Save.

When you create a custom console, be aware you can only add a single Configuration Manager snap-in to the console. However, this does not limit you in managing multiple

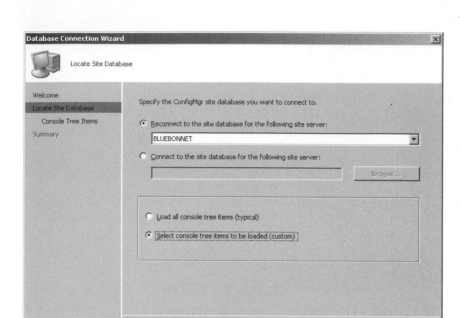

FIGURE 10.23   Specifying the site database

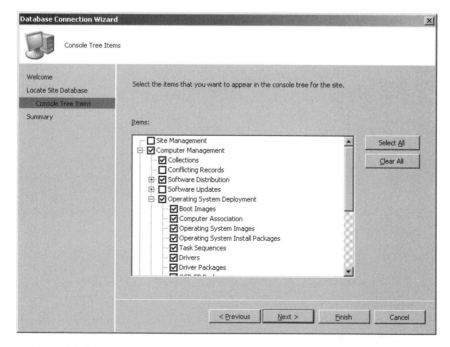

FIGURE 10.24   Selecting console tree items

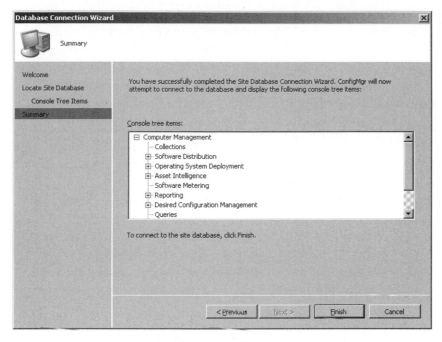

FIGURE 10.25   Summary screen of the Database Connection Wizard

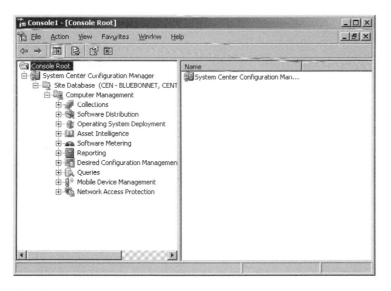

FIGURE 10.26   A newly created custom console

sites in a hierarchy. You can manage child sites by connecting to them directly, or from their parent site. When managing a child from its parent, you are not connecting directly to the child, but to the database of the parent.

If you face any site communication issues, you can also directly connect to a child site by adding a separate site database connection. Figure 10.27 shows the central site with a separate connection to a primary child site.

To add a site database connection with a custom console tree to a previously created custom console, perform the following steps:

1. In your current custom console, right-click the main System Center Configuration Manager node and select Connect to Site database.

2. The Database Connection Wizard will start. Click Next at the Welcome screen.

3. In the Locate Site Database screen, select the option Connect to the site database for the following site server. Then choose the Select Console tree items to be loaded (custom) option at the bottom of the screen. Click Next to continue.

4. The next screen of the Database Connection Wizard allows you to select the items you want to appear in the console tree. Check the items you want to be available in the console and click Next to continue.

5. At the Summary screen, check your configuration. To change any of your selections, click the Previous button. Otherwise, click Finish to complete the wizard.

Figure 10.27 displays a single console containing a custom configuration for two sites.

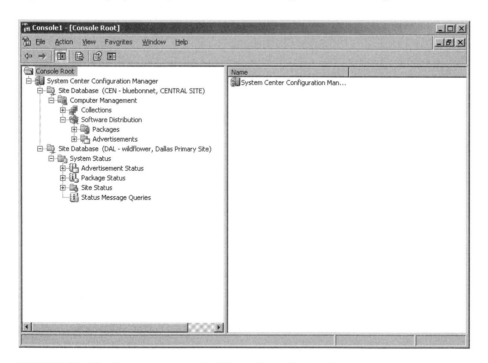

FIGURE 10.27 A custom console with multiple-site databases

Security Considerations

As mentioned earlier in the "Console Deployment" section, the console is installed during the site server setup process. After installation, by default only the administrator who ran the setup has access to the console.

Special permissions are required when other users want to install and use the console from their workstations. These permissions can be divided into two categories:

▶ Distributed Component Object Model (DCOM)

▶ Windows Management Instrumentation (WMI)

The next sections discuss these areas.

Configuring Required DCOM Permissions for the ConfigMgr Console

Administrators running the console from their workstation require Remote Activation DCOM permissions. These permissions are required on the site server and the SMS provider.

The SMS provider is the interface between the Configuration Manager console and the site database. The console uses WMI to connect to the SMS provider, and WMI itself uses DCOM. Due to these dependencies, DCOM permissions are required when running the console on a system other than the SMS provider.

Access to the SMS provider is delivered through the SMS Admins group, which is a local security group on every site server. All users running the console must be members of this group. By default, members of this group do not have administrator rights in Configuration Manager. Specific class and instance rights are still required. In the following procedure, DCOM permissions are linked to the SMS Admins group:

▶ If the SMS provider is installed on a computer other than the site server, you must perform this procedure on both the site server and the SMS provider computer.

▶ When the SMS provider is installed on the site server, you need to perform this procedure only on the site server computer.

Perform the following steps to configure Remote Activation permissions for the SMS Admins group:

1. To open the Component Services Management console, click Start -> Run and then type **dcomcnfg.exe**.

2. In the Component Services Management console, select the Console root and then expand the Component Services node.

3. Under the Component Services node, expand Computers and then click My Computer.

4. In the Component Services menu bar, click Action and then select Properties from the menu.

5. In the Properties dialog box, click the COM Security tab.

6. In the Launch and Activation Permissions section, click Edit Limits.

7. In the Launch and Activation Permissions dialog box, click Add.

8. In the Select Users, Computer or Groups window, click the Locations button.

9. In the Locations dialog box, select the computer account (rather than the domain) and click OK.

10. In the Select Users, Computer or Groups window, type **SMS Admins** in the Enter object names to select section. Click OK.

11. In the permissions area for SMS Admins, check the Remote Activation box. Figure 10.28 shows this selection.

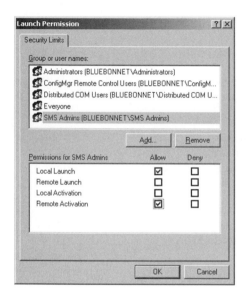

FIGURE 10.28   Establishing DCOM permissions for the SMS Admins group

12. Click OK twice and close the Component Services Management console.

Verifying and Configuring WMI Permissions

The SMS provider is the main communication interface between the site servers and the Configuration Manager console. The console itself uses a combination of DCOM and WMI.

In addition to the DCOM permissions, WMI permissions are also required. By default, the SMS Admins group has the required WMI permissions. Use the following procedure if you are using a security group other than the SMS Admins group, or if you face issues connecting due to misconfigured WMI permissions.

> **NOTE**
>
> ### Identifying Connection Problems
>
> If you face connection problems, you can identify them by the following entry in the SMSAdminUI.log:
>
> ```
> Error(ConnectServer):
> Possible UI connection error code is -2147217405 [0x80041003]
> ```
>
> To log the entry, you must enable verbose logging. The steps to enable verbose logging are described in Appendix A, "Configuration Manager Log Files." Verbose logging is described in more detail in the "Troubleshooting Console Issues" section in this chapter. After verbose logging is enabled, the log file is located in the *<ConfigMgrInstallPath>*\AdminUI\AdminUILog folder.

To verify or configure WMI permissions, perform the following steps:

1. On the server running the SMS provider, click Start -> Run, type **wmimgmt.msc**, and then click OK.
2. In the WMI Control console, right-click the WMI Control node and then click Properties in the menu.
3. In the Properties dialog box, select the Security tab.
4. Expand the Root and then click the SMS folder.
5. To verify the configured permissions, click the Security button.
6. The SMS Admins group or a custom group requires the Enable Account and Remote Enable permissions, as configured in Figure 10.29.

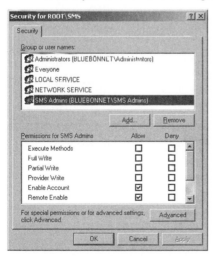

FIGURE 10.29   Enabling WMI permissions for the SMS Admins group

7. When you have configured all permissions correctly, click OK twice.
8. Close the WMI Control console.

Configuration Manager Service Manager

The Configuration Manager Service Manager, introduced in Chapter 8, "Installing Configuration Manager 2007," allows you to easily control the Configuration Manager services. A service runs in the background for nearly all components and features. The Service Manager provides you with a tool to check the status of each service or component.

Whereas most Configuration Manager services run by default, others only run when a job is assigned to them (for example, the SMS_SITE_BACKUP service).

Starting the Configuration Manager Service Manager

The Configuration Manager Service Manager can only be started through the Configuration Manager console. To start the Service Manager, navigate to the Tools node in the ConfigMgr console, expand it, and right-click ConfigMgr Service Manager. Choose Start ConfigMgr Service Manager. A new window will open, as displayed in Figure 10.30.

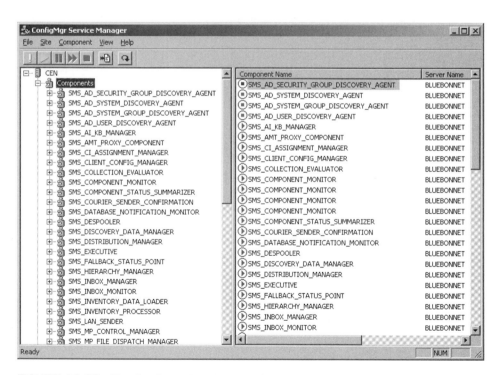

FIGURE 10.30   The Configuration Manager Service Manager console

Using the Configuration Manager Service Manager

Within the Service Manager, you can perform several actions. Although the ConfigMgr services do not display in the regular Windows Services console (services.msc), they are threaded in a similar manner as standard Windows services. You can start, stop, pause, resume, or query a service. The query action is always the first step before performing the other actions, because the query action determines the status of the component. The following options are available:

▶ **Query**—The Query action is used to determine the status of the selected component. The possible actions you can perform will be based on the state of the component. As an example, the only available action for a component in a stopped state is to start it.

▶ **Start**—Use the Start action to start a stopped component.

▶ **Stop**—This action stops a running component. Stopping a component also shuts down its runtime environment and clears the log files and other related files.

▶ **Pause**—Use this action to pause a running component. Pausing a component preserves its runtime environment. You can pause most components to observe the behavior and the created data in the log files. Several components cannot be paused, including SMS_REPORTING_POINT and SMS_SERVER_LOCATOR_POINT.

▶ **Resume**—When a component is paused, the Resume action will resume the component so it is running again.

To run actions on Configuration Manager components, perform the following steps:

1. In the ConfigMgr Service Manager, expand your site by double-clicking the site code. Then expand Components to view a list of components. To display a list of servers running one or more Configuration Manager components, expand the Servers node.

2. Select a component. From the menu bar choose Component and then click Query to determine the status of the component.

3. To perform an action such as Start, Stop, Pause, or Resume, select Components in the menu bar and then choose the appropriate action.

Troubleshooting Console Issues

This section of the chapter describes how to troubleshoot issues with the ConfigMgr console. The MMC 3.0 console itself is very stable, and issues are generally due to configuring the required permissions or issues with WMI.

Enable Verbose Logging

The first step in troubleshooting issues related to the console is to look at the log file. ConfigMgr by default provides many log files regarding the health of the site and its components.

This differs for the console log file. Because the log file generates a considerable amount of information requiring system resources, logging is not enabled by default.

To enable verbose logging, perform the following steps:

1. Close all active Configuration Manager 2007 consoles.

2. Browse to the *<ConfigMgrInstallPath>*\AdminUI\bin\ folder.

3. In the bin folder, locate the adminui.console.dll.config file and open this file using Windows Notepad.

4. Within the file, navigate to the line

   ```
   <source name="SmsAdminUISnapIn" switchValue="Error" >
   ```
   Change this line to read

   ```
   <source name="SmsAdminUISnapIn" switchValue="Verbose" >
   ```

5. Close the file and save your changes.

   Note that in Windows Server 2008, unless you are a member of the Domain Admins group, you have only read and execute permissions on this file. To modify the file, at least write permission is required.

6. Start the Configuration Manager 2007 console.

7. Navigate to the *<ConfigMgrInstallPath>*\AdminUI\AdminUILog\ folder and verify a log file named SMSAdminUI.log was created.

By default, only administrators and SMS admins have permissions to read the SMSAdminUI.log log file.

The logging starts immediately when you start the console. When the console starts, any navigation through the console is logged as well. Therefore, it is recommended you disable verbose logging when it is no longer required for troubleshooting.

To disable verbose logging, undo the line change described in step 4.

Common Issues

Table 10.4 describes the most common issues related to the Configuration Manager console.

TABLE 10.4   Common Issues and Resolutions

Error	Description
Cannot connect to the site database.	When starting the Configuration Manager console, you may get an error stating that a connection with the site database could not be established. Verify that the SQL Server hosting the database as well as the SMS provider are both available and healthy.
	You may also receive this error if your user account does not have the required Remote Activation permissions on the site server and the SMS provider. The "Security Considerations" section of this chapter discusses how to grant users the required privileges.

TABLE 10.4   Common Issues and Resolutions

Error	Description
User does not see all console objects.	When a user is missing some components in the console, there may be no object rights assigned for that user or he or she is using a custom console. Users only see those components to which they have rights. In addition to object rights, users running the console must be a member of the SMS Admins group or a custom group running with equivalent rights. Custom consoles are described in more detail in this chapter in the "Customizing the Console" section.
Error: This function is not supported on this site system.	Configuration Manager 2007 uses files and Registry keys like any other application. A user without permission to the files or Registry keys Configuration Manager is using can receive this error. When a user receives this error, verify that user is a member of the SMS Admins group or a custom group with equivalent rights.
After an upgrade, administrators don't have assigned rights to new Configuration Manager 2007 objects.	When an in-place upgrade from SMS 2003 to Configuration Manager 2007 is performed, not all administrators are assigned rights to all objects. In a new installation, the user running the installation has all the assigned rights to all objects; this is the same when running an upgrade. The user running the upgrade has all assigned rights. Other administrators have assigned rights to the objects as they existed in the SMS 2003 site. The administrator running the upgrade must manually assign the appropriate rights to the administrators.
The ConfigMgr console hangs when a connection is lost.	If the Configuration Manager console loses its connection with the site database and SMS provider, it stops responding. No error is displayed. When the console hangs, try to close it with the Windows Task Manager by terminating the mmc.exe console process. To open the console with the default view, start the console with the /sms:NoRestore option.

Preventing the Console from Hanging when Running Large Queries

By default, the Configuration Manager console stops responding when creating queries that return more than 2,000 results. This is the same as when creating collections with a query-based membership rule that returns more than the maximum of 2,000 results.

If you require such large queries, perform the following procedure to adjust the maximum threshold through the Registry. Follow these steps:

1. Go to Start -> Run and type **regedit**. Click OK.

2. In the Registry, browse to HKEY_LOCAL_MACHINE\Software\Microsoft\ ConfigMgr\AdminUI\QueryProcessors.

3. Right-click QueryProcessors, select New, and choose the option DWORD Value.

4. Name the new DWORD value **ValueLimit**.

5. Configure ValueLimit with a value that is large enough to return the results of the query. As an example, use a value of **3000** to set the maximum allowed query results to 3,000.

Configuration Manager Console Command-Line Options

When the console is installed, the setup program creates a file named adminconsole.msc in the *<ConfigMgrInstallPath>*\AdminUI\Bin directory. This is the console MMC snap-in; launching the console will start this file. As described in the "Customizing the Console" section of this chapter, you can also create and save custom consoles.

The console has several parameters (command-line options) that you can use to modify how the console starts. Table 10.5 describes the available options and their functions.

TABLE 10.5   Configuration Manager Console Parameters

Parameter	Function
sms:debugview	This parameter adds more detail regarding the record in the database of a selected object. This information is displayed in the Actions pane.
sms:ResetSettings	To start the console with default settings and views, you can use this parameter to reset settings such as views, column width, and column order.
sms:providerlocale=<*LocalID*>	This parameter is mostly used in combination with the <*culture*> parameter to change the code page used by the SMS provider.
sms:culture=<*culture*>	Use this parameter to force a specific regional option. This parameter overrides the configured Regional settings in the Control Panel. For a list of available culture options, see http://go.microsoft.com/fwlink/?LinkID=93069.
sms:NoRestore	To start the console more quickly (or when the console stops responding), you can use this parameter to open the console at the default top System Center Configuration Manager node.
sms:ignoreExtensions	When facing issues with console extensions, you can use this parameter to start the console without any extensions.
sms:NamespaceView=1	For SDK programmers, this parameter can be used to display a class name view.

To start the console with a parameter, use the following syntax:

```
<ConfigMgrInstallPath>\AdminUI\Bin\adminconsole.msc /parameter
```

Summary

This chapter introduced the Configuration Manager 2007 console, an MMC 3.0 application. It described the console nodes, discussed launching reports, and stepped through the process of deploying the console. It also discussed security considerations. The chapter ended with a discussion of troubleshooting various console issues.

The next chapter discusses a number of the technologies used in ConfigMgr 2007.

Related Technologies and References

This chapter discusses a number of technologies used in Configuration Manager (ConfigMgr) 2007. These include the significance of certificates and their use in ConfigMgr 2007, with some basic information that will help when troubleshooting communication issues within the hierarchy. The chapter also reviews the technologies associated with Network Access Protection (NAP), specifically Windows Server 2008 and its Network Policy Server role. It then moves into the area of operating system (OS) deployment technologies, reviewing ImageX and associated technologies. The chapter also discusses Intel's Active Management Technology (AMT), its relationship with vPro, and ConfigMgr's Out of Band Management capabilities, introduced with ConfigMgr 2007 Service Pack (SP) 1. You will learn how these technologies work, how they complement Configuration Manager, and best practices to leverage these OS deployment tools.

Although none of these technologies is required to implement a ConfigMgr site, having a good understanding will only help ConfigMgr administrators when implementing these features and functionality. Here are the key ConfigMgr capabilities these technologies support:

▶ Operating System Deployment, known as OSD

▶ Internet-based client management, known as IBCM

▶ Out of Band (OOB) Management, which allows an administrator to connect to a computer when the system is turned off, in sleep or hibernate mode, or otherwise unresponsive through the operating system

OSD and IBCM provide ConfigMgr administrators the capability to create huge amounts of return on their investment in ConfigMgr licensing and its overall cost in implementation and administration. In other words, if you are not utilizing these two capabilities, you will want to look into them extensively—you will be upgrading Windows at some point, and clients are more mobile now than ever before. Either of these ConfigMgr capabilities can save your organization considerable money. OOB enables remote administration of client systems that were previously inaccessible due to the new management standards and technologies.

PKI Management References

You can implement ConfigMgr in either mixed mode or native mode. Native mode, the more secure of the two, requires several certificates from the PKI (Public Key Infrastructure) for it to handle operations such as IBCM. A PKI is an implementation of certificate technology that allows binding a public key with some identity via a Certificate Authority (CA). ConfigMgr leverages the PKI to encrypt the transmission of data between the management point (MP) and the client itself, and authentication of the client to the MP. For ConfigMgr, these identities are machine accounts. The certificate is bound via a registration process and then carried out by Active Directory group policy objects (GPOs) and the CA auto-enrollment process. You can also implement the certificates manually, depending on your environment and deployment processes. ConfigMgr does not perform any of the certificate deployment or management for the PKI or itself; the PKI's Registration Authority ensures the certificates are correctly bound. Each account, identity, public key, binding, and validity condition allow the CA to generate and issue certificates that cannot be duplicated.

> **NOTE**
>
> **ConfigMgr PKI Requirements**
>
> ConfigMgr 2007 can only leverage template-based certificates issued by an enterprise Certificate Authority running on the Enterprise edition or Datacenter edition of Windows Server 2003 or Windows Server 2008. Running a PKI on the Standard edition of Windows Server 2003 or 2008 does not give administrators the ability to modify the templates per ConfigMgr's requirements.

Microsoft specifies certificate requirements for native mode at http://technet.microsoft.com/en-us/library/bb680733.aspx. Unfortunately, this topic was not well documented in the base release (also known as Released-to-Manufacturing [RTM]) of ConfigMgr 2007, and many administrators struggled trying to get PKI certificates to work while the CA was running on Windows Server 2003 Standard edition.

Cryptography Basics

Cryptography is the practice of hiding information, commonly used in security scenarios such as ATM cards and passwords. Two cryptographic functions are supported:

▶ Symmetrical encryption

▶ Asymmetrical encryption

Encryption is the process of transforming information (referred to as *plain text*) using an algorithm (a *cipher*) to make it unreadable to anyone except those possessing special knowledge, usually referred to as a *key*. The result of the process is encrypted information (referred to as *cipher text* in cryptography). In many contexts, the word *encryption* also implicitly refers to the reverse process, decryption (such that "encryption software" will also perform decryption), that is, to make the encrypted information readable again by making it unencrypted.

Symmetrical encryption uses a single key for encryption, which both the sender and receiver will leverage to decrypt the transmissions. When data is encrypted with a symmetric algorithm, the sender generates a random symmetric key. The algorithm and the application determine the bit-length of the key. Figure 11.1 illustrates the symmetrical encryption process.

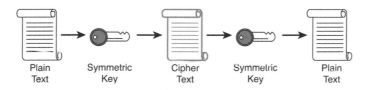

FIGURE 11.1   The symmetrical encryption process

Asymmetric encryption uses a key pair. The keys that make up the key pair are mathematically related and referred to as the *public* and *private* keys. Public keys are distributed freely. You can publish them to Active Directory (AD) and install them via auto-enrollment. The "Deploying Certificates" section of this chapter covers auto-enrollment. The use of this key pair ensures that only the recipient has access to the necessary private key to decrypt the data. Figure 11.2 illustrates the asymmetrical encryption process.

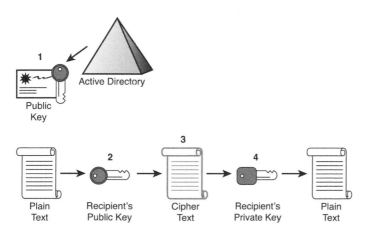

FIGURE 11.2   The asymmetrical encryption process

The following points define the process illustrated in Figure 11.2:

1. The sender obtains the recipient's public key.

2. Data is passed an asymmetrical encryption algorithm. It is encrypted with the recipient's public key, producing encrypted cipher text.

3. Cipher text is sent to the recipient, who already has the private key.

4. The recipient decrypts the cipher text with his or her private key back into the original format.

NOTE

Using Symmetric and Asymmetric Encryption

Applications will generally use both encryption algorithms to encrypt data by first encrypting the data with a symmetric algorithm and then encrypting the symmetric encryption key using an asymmetric algorithm.

Two inputs are required when encrypting data:

▶ The algorithm

▶ The key

The algorithm defines how to convert the data to the cipher text, and the key is used to input the data into the algorithm. Figure 11.3 illustrates the asymmetrical signing process.

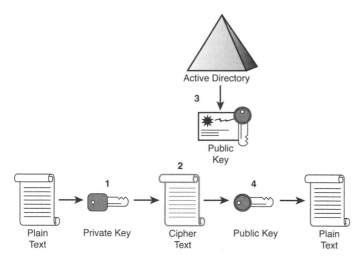

FIGURE 11.3   The asymmetrical signing process

The following steps demonstrate how in Figure 11.3 you can validate the sender's identity and that the data was not altered:

1. The data passes though an asymmetrical encryption algorithm, using the private key as the encryption key.

2. Cipher text is sent to the recipient.

3. The recipient obtains the sender's public key.

4. The recipient decrypts cipher text with the sender's public key back to original format.

This encryption process protects the data, or payload, from being intercepted and read, viewed, or altered. If it were intercepted, the decryption process would fail, thus letting the recipient know there was a breach.

Digital signing is used to prove the source and integrity of the data. Using a hash algorithm, digitally signed data can be trusted to be the original content. Hash algorithms such as MD5 (Message Digest 5) and SHA1 (Secure Hash Algorithm 1) apply a mathematical formula to an object, resulting in output known as a *hash value*, *message digest*, or just *digest*. Hashes cannot be reversed, making them very useful in verifying data integrity.

Refer to Chapter 6, "Architecture Design Planning," for specific detail on how ConfigMgr utilizes certificate services.

How SSL Works

Both SSL (Secure Sockets Layer) and TLS (Transport Layer Security), which is replacing SSL, are cryptographic protocols providing security and data integrity for communications over TCP/IP (Transmission Control Protocol/Internet Protocol). SSL encrypts the segments of the Transport layer protocol, which is Layer 4 of the Open Systems Interconnection (OSI) model. An SSL client and server negotiate a stateful connection by using a handshaking procedure. During this handshake, the client and server agree on various parameters used to establish the connection's security:

▶ The initiation of the secure session begins when a client connects to an SSL-enabled server requesting a secure connection.

▶ The server then picks the strongest cipher and hash function that it supports, and notifies the client of the decision.

▶ The server sends back its identification in the form of a digital certificate, which contains the server name, the trusted Certificate Authority, and the server's public encryption key.

The client may contact the server that issued the certificate (the trusted CA, as before) and confirm the certificate is authentic before proceeding:

▶ In order to generate the session keys used for the secure connection, the client encrypts a random number with the server's public key, and sends the result to the server. Only the server can decrypt it (with its private key). This is the one fact that makes the keys hidden from third parties, because only the server and the client have access to this data.

▶ From the random number, both parties generate key material for encryption and decryption.

This concludes the handshake and begins the secured connection, which is encrypted and decrypted with the key material until the connection closes. If any one of the preceding processes fails, the SSL handshake fails and the connection is not created.

TLS and SSL have a variety of security measures:

▶ The client may use the Certificate Authority's public key to validate the CA's digital signature on the server certificate. If the digital signature can be verified, the client accepts the server certificate as a valid certificate issued by a trusted CA.

▶ The client verifies that the issuing CA is on its list of trusted CAs.

▶ The client checks the server's certificate validity period. The authentication process stops if the current date and time fall outside of the validity period.

▶ Protection is provided against a downgrade of the protocol to a previous (less secure) version or a weaker cipher suite.

▶ All the application records are numbered with a sequence number. Using this sequence number in the message authentication codes (MACs) provides additional security.

▶ The message digest is enhanced with a key, so only a key holder can check the MAC, as specified in RFC 2104. (TLS only.)

▶ The message that ends the handshake (Finished) sends a hash of all the exchanged handshake messages seen by both parties.

▶ The pseudorandom function splits the input data in half and processes each one with a different hashing algorithm (MD5 and SHA1). It then XORs them together to create the MAC. This provides protection even if one of these algorithms is found vulnerable. (TLS only.)

▶ SSL v3 improved upon SSL v2 by adding SHA1-based ciphers and support for certificate authentication. Additional improvements in SSL v3 include better handshake protocol flow and increased resistance to man-in-the-middle attacks.

Establishing a PKI

Microsoft provides native support for PKI in Windows Server 2003 and 2008 Active Directory. If you are running Windows 2000 Active Directory, special considerations are necessary because you must upgrade the schema to the Windows Server 2003 schema. This requires Windows 2000 domain controllers to be on SP 3 at a minimum. If you are running Windows 2000 Active Directory, refer to http://support.microsoft.com/kb/325379 and http://support.microsoft.com/kb/314649 for steps and precautions before upgrading the schema or Active Directory to the 2003 version.

With Microsoft Windows 2003 or 2008 Active Directory, the only configuration required for an Enterprise CA is if you have an Active Directory forest with multiple domains. In this scenario, you must add the CA's computer account to each domain's built-in Cert Publishers local group.

Configuration Manager Certificate Requirements

There are multiple certificate requirements for ConfigMgr to leverage PKI. If you already have a PKI in place in the organization, you must verify it meets the ConfigMgr requirements:

▶ The PKI Root CA is running on the Enterprise or Datacenter edition of Windows Server 2003 or 2008.

▶ Systems in any domain in the forest can recognize the Root CA as being trusted.

▶ The site servers, site systems, computers, and devices must all have a certificate from the CA.

▶ Certificates for the site servers, site systems, computers, and devices must reside in the personal store in the computer certificate store.

▶ Clients must have a copy before they can accept the policies from the management point that is signed with this certificate.

▶ Primary site servers cannot support key lengths greater than 8,096 bits.

▶ Site systems do not have a published maximum key length.

▶ Both computers and mobile device clients cannot support key lengths greater than 2,048 bits.

CAUTION

Encryption Key Length

Older network components used to have issues handling 2,048-bit (and higher) encrypted traffic. Although this is no longer an issue with today's hardware, issues may still arise with some technologies. With IBCM being a focus of certificate usage, unknown home and Internet service provider (ISP) networks will need to support whatever key length you choose. Validate the bit length you are using will traverse all network mediums in your environment before rolling out to all systems.

If your organization does not have a PKI, it must determine what the architecture for the CA will look like, how many tiers it will have, what security measures will be put in place, the types of certificates it will issue, and whether the CA is published via AD or through a website. Microsoft provides valuable systematic guides for deploying certificates in the following environments:

▶ **Windows Server 2003**—http://technet.microsoft.com/en-us/library/bb694035.aspx

▶ **Windows Server 2008**—http://technet.microsoft.com/en-us/library/cc872789.aspx

When establishing a CA, it is best to use Windows Enterprise edition due to its advanced features not available in other versions of the OS. The issuance of version 2 certificate templates, private key archival, and role separation enforcement are only available when Certificate Services is installed on Windows Enterprise edition or Datacenter edition, the latter not being cost effective in most cases. You will need to issue certificates based off modified version 2 templates.

To install Certificate Services, execute the following steps on Windows Server 2003. Log on as a member of the Enterprise Admins security group with local Administrator rights on the server where the install is being performed. Then follow these steps:

1. From the Start menu, select Control Panel and then click Add or Remove Programs.

2. In the Add or Remove Programs window, click Add/Remove Windows Components.

3. Scroll down and check the Certificate Services box.

4. You also want to check the Application Server box, because this will open the details selection for that component. Verify that IIS (Internet Information Services) is selected and then click OK.

5. In the Microsoft Certificate Services dialog box, click Yes to the warning about not changing domain membership after Certificate Services is installed.

6. Click the Certificate Services Web Enrollment Support subcomponent.

7. Click OK and then click Next.

8. On the CA Type page, click Enterprise Root CA, check the Use Custom Settings to Generate the Key Pair and CA Certificate box, and then click Next.

9. On the Public and Private Key Pair page, set the following options:

    ▶ **CSP**—Microsoft Strong Cryptographic Service Provider

    ▶ **Allow the CSP to interact with the desktop**—Disabled

    ▶ **Hash algorithm**—SHA-1

    ▶ **Key length**—2,048

10. On the Public and Private Key Pair page, click Next.

11. On the CA Identifying Information page, enter the following information:

    ▶ **Common Name for this CA**—*ServerName*

    ▶ **Distinguished name suffix**—DC=*mydomain*,DC=*com*

    ▶ **Validity Period**—5 Years

12. On the CA Identifying Information page, click Next.

13. On the Certificate Database Settings page, accept the default settings and click Next.

14. Click Yes on the Microsoft Certificate Services dialog box informing you Active Server Pages must be enabled on IIS if you wish to use the Certificate Services Web enrollment site.

15. In the Microsoft Certificate Services dialog box, click Yes to create the necessary folders.

11

16. If prompted, insert the Windows Server 2003 Enterprise Edition CD in the CD-ROM drive and choose the \i386 folder.

If prompted to insert the CD for the i386 folder, ensure you reapply whatever service pack the OS is running after installing Certificate Services.

17. If prompted with a dialog box informing you Internet Information Services must be temporarily stopped, click Yes.

18. On the Completing the Windows Components Wizard page, click Finish.

To install Certificate Services, execute the following steps on Windows Server 2008. You must be logged on as a member of the Enterprise Admins security group with local Administrator rights on the server where the install is being performed.

1. Open Server Manager, click Add Roles, and click Next.

2. Click Active Directory Certificate Services and then click Next two times.

3. On the Select Role Services page, click Certification Authority and then click Next.

4. On the Specify Setup Type page, click Enterprise and then click Next.

5. On the Specify CA Type page, click Subordinate CA and then click Next.

6. On the Set Up Private Key page, click Create a new private key. Click Next.

7. On the Configure Cryptography page, select a cryptographic service provider, key length, and hash algorithm. Click Next.

8. On the Request Certificate page, browse to locate the root CA (if the root CA is not connected to the network, save the certificate request to a file so that it can be processed later). Click Next.

9. On the Configure CA Name page, create a unique name to identify the CA. Click Next.

10. On the Set Validity Period page, specify the number of years or months that the CA certificate will be valid. Click Next.

11. On the Configure Certificate Database page, accept the default locations or specify a custom location for the certificate database and certificate database log. Click Next.

12. On the Confirm Installation Options page, review all the configuration settings you have selected. If you want to accept these options, click Install and wait until the setup process has finished.

Deploying PKI for ConfigMgr Native Mode

If you are deploying PKI for native mode, verify the following items:

1. Confirm your PKI can support the various certificates required by Configuration Manager 2007 (see http://technet.microsoft.com/en-us/library/bb680733.aspx for details).

2. Ensure the following computers in the Configuration Manager 2007 site have a trusted root Certificate Authority in common and intermediate Certificate Authorities as needed:

    ▶ The site server

- ▶ Management points (the default management point, proxy management point, Internet-based management point, and network load balanced management points)

- ▶ Distribution points

- ▶ Software update points

- ▶ State migration points

- ▶ All client computers and mobile client devices

3. If you will use a Certificate Revocation List (CRL), publish it where all computers can locate it.

4. Deploy the site server signing certificate to the site server, and determine how clients will retrieve it.

5. Deploy the web server certificates to the following site systems and then configure IIS with the certificates:

- ▶ Management points (the default management point, proxy management point, Internet-based management point, and network load balanced management points)

- ▶ Distribution points

- ▶ Software update points

- ▶ State migration points

6. This step is optional but recommended. On the site systems with the deployed web server certificates, create or modify a Certificate Trust List (CTL) in IIS to contain the root Certificate Authorities used by clients.

7. Deploy client certificates to clients and management points.

8. If you have mobile client devices, deploy the client device certificates.

9. If you are using the Operating System Deployment feature, perform the following tasks:

- ▶ Export root CA certificates that operating system clients will use during the deployment process so these can be imported into the Configuration Management console as a site setting.

- ▶ Prepare and export one or more client certificates into a PKCS #12 file so that these can be included in the operating system deployment.

Certificate Templates

Certificate templates do just what you would expect: They let the CA issue certificates preconfigured with specific settings or information. Windows Server 2003 supports version 1 and 2 certificate templates. Windows Server 2008 supports version 3, although ConfigMgr does not currently support this version. Certificates templates are stored in the configuration naming context in the following location:

```
CN=Certificate Templates,CN=Public Key
➥Services,CN=Services,CN=Configuration, ForestRootDomain.
```

Version 1 certificate templates are only capable of having their permissions modified. Version 2 certificate templates allow you to create new templates by duplicating existing version 1 or 2 templates.

ConfigMgr requires the use of the following certificate templates:

▶ Web Server

▶ Computer or Workstation

▶ Authenticated Session

Detailed requirements for the certificate templates and the data the templates must contain can be found at http://technet.microsoft.com/en-us/library/bb680733.aspx, in the "Certificate Requirements for Native Mode" section.

Certificate Validation

Certificate validation guarantees that the information contained in the certificate is authentic, what the certificate is to be used for, and that the certificate is trusted. When you enable Certificate Revocation List checking, the Windows OS using the certificate validates each certificate in the chain until it reaches the CA.

CRL checking is the process of searching for revoked certificates on a server. The default setting for ConfigMgr in native mode is that the clients validate their certificate against the CRL. Although disabling CRL checking is not a best practice, some technologies offer scenarios where CRL checking may not be necessary or ideal. As an example, Windows mobile devices cannot perform CRL checking. You can disable CRL checking using one of two methods:

▶ Configuring the setting as a site property

▶ Using the /Native or /Native:FALLBACK switches with CCMSctup.exe at client installation time

Certificate validation also includes certificate discovery and path validation:

▶ Certificate discovery is used to build or enumerate the certificate chain at the client while the issued certificate is being validated.

▶ Path validation is the process of running checks against each certificate discovered in the chain until the root CA is reached.

These checks include verifying Authenticode signatures, determining if the issuing CA certificate is already in the certificate store, and checking for policy object identifiers.

Deploying Certificates

Once the PKI is built and the certificate templates are in place, ConfigMgr administrators can begin issuing certificates to sites, site systems, and clients. There are a number of ways to deploy the certificates to each.

Deploying to Site Servers

ConfigMgr site servers can obtain their certificates in one of five ways:

▶ If Microsoft's PKI is used, the ConfigMgr administrator can modify a version 2 template that can be requested online.

▶ If Microsoft's PKI with web enrollment is used, the certificate can be requested from the website of the CA. A template can be created with the necessary configuration, which can also be requested from the website.

▶ If IIS is installed on the site server, site servers will always have one role available, because the certificate request can be initiated through IIS.

▶ The certificate can be requested using the Microsoft Certreq command-line utility included with Windows 2000 Server, Windows XP, Windows Server 2003, and Windows Server 2008.

▶ The certificate can be created using the certificate management tools and then imported on the site server.

NOTE

Site Server Signing Certificate

Every site in the Configuration Manager 2007 hierarchy configured for native mode requires that each site server have its own site server signing certificate. This includes a central site used for reporting that has no clients assigned to it.

Deploying to Site Systems

ConfigMgr site systems can obtain their certificates in a number of ways:

▶ Using Microsoft's PKI with an enterprise CA, you can create the certificates based off a version 2 template and assign them to the servers using group policy and auto-enrollment.

▶ Using Microsoft's PKI with web enrollment, the certificate can be requested from the website of the CA.

▶ If IIS is installed on the site server, site servers will always have one role available, because the certificate request can be initiated through IIS.

▶ The certificate can be requested using the Microsoft Certreq command-line utility included with Windows 2000 Server, Windows XP, Windows Server 2003, and Windows Server 2008.

▶ The certificate can be created with the certificate management tools and then imported on to the site server.

Deploying to ConfigMgr Clients

ConfigMgr clients can obtain their certificates in one of three ways:

▶ Automatically through Active Directory Domain Services.

▶ Manually when the client is installed via ccmsetup.exe using the client.msi parameter SMSSIGNCERT with the path and filename of the exported certificate.

▶ Automatically from the management point.

Certificate Auto-Enrollment

The process of certificate auto-enrollment handles certificate enrollment, certificate renewal, and certain other tasks, including removing revoked certificates and downloading trusted root CA certificates. Fortunately, Windows 2003 PKI extends certificate auto-enrollment for users to all certificate types.

Microsoft's PKI uses certificate auto-enrollment in several ways:

▶ Every Windows DC automatically receives a DC certificate when the machine joins a domain with an enterprise CA defined.

▶ Administrators can use a group policy object (GPO) setting that automatically enrolls machines for IP security (IPSec) or SSL certificates.

▶ An administrator can use a GPO setting that automatically enrolls several users.

▶ A CA administrator who wants to change a property of a particular certificate type can duplicate the old certificate template to create a new certificate template and let the new template supersede the old one. Auto-enrollment then automatically distributes to the appropriate PKI users a new certificate based on the new template.

User and machine auto-enrollment requires that the machine and user be part of an AD domain.

Certificate and PKI References

Here are some good reference materials for certificates and PKI:

▶ *Microsoft Windows Server 2003 PKI and Certificate Security* (Microsoft Press, 2004).

▶ Microsoft Official Curriculum, Course 2821, "Designing and Managing a Windows Public Key Infrastructure" (www.microsoft.com/traincert/syllabi/2821afinal.asp).

▶ For best practices when implementing a Microsoft Windows Server 2003 PKI, see the article at http://www.microsoft.com/technet/prodtechnol/windowsserver2003/technologies/security/ws3pkibp.mspx.

▶ PKI enhancements in Windows XP Professional and Windows Server 2003 are described at http://technet.microsoft.com/en-us/library/bb457034.aspx.

▶ Knowledge Base Article 219059 discusses that an enterprise CA may not publish certificates from child or trusted domains (http://support.microsoft.com/kb/219059).

Network Access Protection in Windows Server 2008

Network Access Protection is a ConfigMgr process in which NAP-capable clients evaluate their compliance with predefined policies and send this data in as a client Statement of Health (SoH) to the System Health Validator point (SHV) site system. This evaluation consists of comparing the updates specified in the NAP policy with what is installed on the client. ConfigMgr administrators can choose actions to perform when clients are found to be out of compliance; this process is known as *remediation*. Remediation uses existing software update packages to update the client with the software updates feature.

The systems responsible for the policies, health evaluation, and remediation are often confused due to ConfigMgr relying on Windows Server 2008's Network Policy Server (NPS). ConfigMgr by itself does not enforce compliance with NAP; it provides a mechanism by which ConfigMgr clients can produce an SoH with a noncompliant status if they lack software updates required by the ConfigMgr NAP policies you configure. A ConfigMgr SHV confirms the health state of the computer as compliant or noncompliant, and passes this information to the NPS. Policies on the NPS then determine whether noncompliant computers will be remediated and, additionally, whether they will have restricted network access until they are compliant.

NAP is only supported on the following operating systems:

▶ Windows XP with SP 3 and above

▶ Windows Vista

▶ Windows Server 2008

Here are 10 things you should know about ConfigMgr NAP:

▶ The technologies required for NAP are built in to Windows Server 2008 and Windows Vista.

▶ Deploying NAP does not require additional licenses (check with your Microsoft representative for current information on licensing).

▶ The NAP agent is really a service running on the box and can be managed via group policy.

▶ The agent for XP shipped as part of Service Pack 3 for XP in April of 2008.

▶ NAP is *not* a security solution; it is a network health solution.

▶ There is no NAP agent for Windows Server 2003; Microsoft is not developing an NAP agent for any platform older than Windows XP Service Pack 3.

▶ NAP interoperates with Cisco's Network Admission Control framework.

▶ NAP interoperates with practically every switch/access point in the market and uses industry-standard protocols.

▶ NAP is currently deployed to thousands of desktops inside and outside of Microsoft.

▶ The NAP Statement of Health protocol has been accepted as a TNC/TCG standard.

NPS Overview in Windows Server 2008

Network Policy Server is Microsoft's replacement technology in Windows Server 2008 for Internet Authentication Service (IAS) in Windows Server 2003. IAS only provided a subset of NPS's capabilities. Both IAS and NPS allow administrators to route traffic authentication against AD for remote access and enforcement of network access. Both technologies offer these capabilities:

▶ VPN services

▶ Dial-up services

▶ 802.11 protected access

▶ Routing and Remote Access (RRAS)

▶ Authentication through AD

▶ Control of network access with policies (GPOs)

NPS now lets administrators centrally configure and manage network policies with the following three features: RADIUS (Remote Authentication Dial-In User Service) server, RADIUS proxy, and NAP policy server. NPS also allows centralized connection authentication, authorization, and accounting for many types of network access, including wireless and virtual private network (VPN) connections.

NPS's full suite on functionality and capabilities includes the following:

▶ Microsoft's implementation of the RADIUS protocol.

▶ Configurable as a RADIUS server.

▶ Configurable as a RADIUS proxy that forwards connection requests to other RADIUS servers for processing.

▶ A required component of NAP. When you deploy NAP, NPS functions as an NAP health policy server.

▶ Configurable to perform all three functions (RADIUS server, RADIUS proxy, NAP health policy server) at the same time.

▶ Compatible with user account databases in Active Directory Domain Services (AD DS).

NPS is available on all Windows Server 2008 editions except Microsoft's Web Server 2008.

ConfigMgr NAP Policies

NAP policies in ConfigMgr evaluate clients and verify if they have the required updates. ConfigMgr then sends the NPS the SoH from the client and a list of remediation servers. NPS then determines whether the client will be granted full network access or restricted network access, and whether the computer can be remediated if found to be out of compliance. NPS supports the following policies for NAP clients:

▶ NAP-capable clients that are compliant have full network access.

▶ NAP-capable clients that are noncompliant have restricted network access until remediated.

▶ NAP-capable clients that are noncompliant have full network access for a limited time and are immediately remediated.

▸ NAP-ineligible clients have full network access.

▸ NAP-ineligible clients have restricted network access but are not remediated.

▸ All error conditions, by default, result in computers having restricted access (with remediation if supported by the client), but they can be configured for full network access.

CAUTION

ConfigMgr NAP Remediation Requirement

If health policies are not enforced in the network policy on the NPS, NAP in Configuration Manager cannot remediate noncompliant computers. Compliance in this case can be achieved through the defined Configuration Manager Software Updates functionality. If health policies are enforced in the network policy on the NPS, NAP in Configuration Manager always attempts to remediate noncompliant computers, even if the option to auto-remediate noncompliant computers is not enabled in the network policy.

NAP in ConfigMgr 2007 builds on the capabilities and automation routines offered natively in NPS. The integration of NPS in ConfigMgr creates some very sophisticated possibilities for administrators to secure their network environment. The value of NAP increases exponentially as the number of mobile systems in an environment increase.

ConfigMgr NAP Evaluation

ConfigMgr NAP is a feature that allows administrators the ability to enforce compliance of software updates, or restrict access, on client computers to help protect the integrity of the network. NAP is managed via policies that the clients download. Administrators define their requirements for connectivity to the environment. The client checks its configuration against that which is defined, and generates a client Statement of Health. This SoH is sent to the SHV, a ConfigMgr role. The SHV evaluates what is required if the client is out of compliance and offers options defined by the administrator for remediation. The remediation process may be user interactive or completely silent, depending on the administrative desires for the specific deviation from compliance. If the client does not have current NAP policies, the agent will kick off a machine policy refresh, which includes the latest NAP policies, and then reevaluate its health and send a more current SoH.

CAUTION

NAP SoH Time Validation

Although NAP SoH time validation can be set as wide as every 7 days, the default is every 26 hours, which could lead to poor user experience due to clients being restricted from the network after long weekends or holidays. Finding an acceptable threshold for your environment will require a balance between user acceptance and security risk mitigation. A good starting point is 4 or 5 days.

NAP's success hinges on software update management (SUM). If SUM is not working correctly, clients can be accidently quarantined without the capability of remediation. Do not NAP-enforce software updates without approving and distributing those updates, because clients will otherwise be unable to remediate. An exception to this is for those highly critical patches, where the risk of infection is greater than network access by the non-compliant user or system.

NAP Health State

ConfigMgr clients generate an SoH when the NAP agent requests it from the ConfigMgr client. The ConfigMgr client sends the SoH to the ConfigMgr SHV for verification. The SHV then sends a Statement of Health Response (SoHR) containing the client health state to the NPS. The NPS then sends the client heath state back to the client as an SoHR. The SoH always contains the following items:

▶ The client's compliance status

▶ The client's site

▶ A timestamp reference to identify the Configuration Manager NAP policies that the client used to evaluate its compliance

All NAP-capable clients generate an SoH with a compliant status, even when the site is not NAP enabled. Once NAP is enabled on the site, clients will evaluate their SoH against the NAP policies defined on the NPS.

CAUTION

Forcing Fresh Scans for NAP Evaluations

Perform thorough testing when using the Force a fresh scan for each evaluation option on the NAP agent within ConfigMgr. This feature will generate excessively long authentication times and may lead to an unfavorable boot-up/logon experience.

This is another setting to use with caution, but it may be of value in situations where a specific patch is required. Experiment with these enforcement settings in a lab environment, so the end user experience is clearly understood.

The SHV will accept a cached statement of health from clients If it is within the configured validity period and it does not conflict with the optional Date setting specified on the General tab of System Health Validator Point Component Properties. SoH messages may also contain failures when a client cannot determine its own health status. Figure 11.4 illustrates the System Health Validator Point Component configuration within the ConfigMgr console.

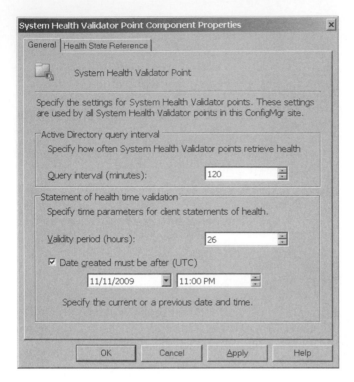

FIGURE 11.4   SHV component properties

When clients generate an unknown response state failure, the NPS may not be able to auto-remediate the client. ConfigMgr clients may return a compliant SoH when they actually are noncompliant, and the SHV will send a noncompliant SoH to the NPS. This can occur when the client has not downloaded the new policies for compliance and is sending a cached SoH. When a client's SoH is sent to the SHV/NPS with a noncompliant status and it is remediated, the client will generate another SoH and re-send it, with a list of the client's MP, DP, and SUP, to the SHV, where it will be reevaluated and eventually granted access to the network.

Windows Imaging and Image Management

Imaging is the process of deploying computer operating systems with the necessary settings and applications by overwriting the hard drive structure with a file that is a clone of another PC, usually referred to as the *reference PC* or *master*. Typically, companies have used one image for each hardware platform, and sometimes even one per department. This generally was because imaging technology was sector based, and swapping HAL (Hardware Abstraction Layer) types was not possible and not supported. The total cost of ownership (TCO) to image computer systems this way is very high, because it requires administrators to update numerous images (often dozens in large environments) as frequently as there are software changes, new patches, and so on. Image management therefore has been a full-time job in many enterprise environments.

In recent years, due to evolving hardware and software technology, imaging is again "sexy." Administrators can create hardware-independent images, layering on dozens of applications, build those applications into the image, and perform maintenance on images in minutes. Previously, image deployments took between 30 minutes to 1 hour. Today, with ImageX (discussed in the "ImageX" section of the chapter), PCs are turned on, booted into WinPE, imaged, set up, and at the sign-on screen within several minutes. Sending users to go get a cup of coffee is now a viable window to perform a PC refresh for them!

In discussing imaging, a few key scenarios cover 99% of the imaging performed by system administrators. These are the New PC, Refresh, and Replace PC scenarios, which are covered in the following sections.

New PC Scenario

In the New PC scenario, there is no data backup. The system boots from PXE, CD/DVD, USB, or a locally installed bootable operating system such as WinPE. Once booted, the system then has the hard disk overwritten entirely with an image written to the drive. This scenario is sometimes referred to as "bare metal."

> **TIP**
>
> **New PC Scenario and Disk Wiping**
>
> It is a best practice to include a wipe of the disk and the MBR in the New PC scenario. This eliminates the hidden partitions most OEMs place on the hard drive and allows the administrator to reclaim that space for the OS. It is also common to implement this step if there is a need to image systems previously using a file format other than NTFS, such as Linux.

Several conditions may warrant the use of the New PC scenario:

▶ A PC is brand new, and it needs the corporate image put on it.

▶ The user of an existing system is no longer with the company, and the system needs reimaging for a new user.

▶ There is no concern with backing up the current user's state or data of an existing system and it needs reimaging. This scenario could exist in a training room, lab, kiosk, and so on.

Refresh PC Scenario

In the Refresh PC scenario, the PC has an existing user and it needs reimaging. This is sometimes called an *in-place migration*. The scenario requires backing up the user's state using some automated process, such as the User State Migration Tool (USMT). The USMT allows the backup and storage of the user's state to a network location or locally on a part of the hard drive. By default, OSD will use the state migration point (SMP) to store user state during an OS migration. The Refresh PC scenario can use the SMP, a folder on the hard drive, or a network share to store data from the OS the user was initially running. WinPE is copied to this same hard drive location, which the PC boots into and downloads the image into. It then applies the image to the disk, reboots again, and finally in the destination OS performs the necessary deployment tasks. In short, the Refresh PC scenario is the New PC scenario, but with a user state backup in front and no possibility of doing a disk wipe because of the minint folder.

Several conditions may call for the use of the Refresh PC scenario:

▶ The organization is upgrading from one version of Windows to another.

▶ The organization is deploying a new desktop due to implementing a large number of configuration changes or a standardization effort.

▶ The system is having problems, and the amount of time already spent troubleshooting makes reimaging cost effective.

Replace PC Scenario

The Replace PC scenario is the most complicated because it is similar to the Refresh PC scenario, but the user state backup occurs on the user's old PC and the rest of the deployment occurs on the new PC. This may also be referred to as a *side-by-side migration*. The Replace PC scenario is used in the following situations:

▶ Replacing old hardware for newer hardware

▶ Hardware failure

Table 11.1 reflects the high-level phases of the three primary types of imaging scenarios. This does not reflect task sequences or all scenarios, but rather to clarifies how the scenarios differ.

TABLE 11.1 OS Deployment Scenario Phases

Phase	New PC Scenario	Refresh PC Scenario	Replace PC Scenario
Validation/initialization		X	Old PC
State capture		X	Old PC
Pre-installation	X	X	New PC
Installation	X	X	New PC
Post-installation	X	X	New PC
State restore	X	X	New PC

ImageX

Microsoft's Windows imaging utility, ImageX.exe, is a file-based imaging technology that is hardware independent and highly compressed. ImageX, introduced in Windows Automated Installation Kit (WAIK) 0.9, allows for the capturing, maintenance, and deploying of Windows Imaging Format (WIM) images. Unlike sector-based imaging technologies, which make images of the 1's and 0's on the drive, ImageX copies all the files into its image, a WIM file. Because ImageX is file based, it has the ability to make only a copy of a file one time, no matter how many instances of that same file exist. This intelligence, along with file exclusion, allows WIM images to be substantially smaller than other sector-based imaging or cloning tools. It is not uncommon for ImageX WIM images to be one-third to one-half the size of other utilities' images.

WIM images have the ability to hold multiple WIM images inside a single WIM image. For instance, the Windows Vista WIM has seven different versions or SKUs of Windows Vista in it. You can mount WIM images on an NTFS file system and customize them. This means there is no need to redo an image when most administrative types of changes need to occur. After you mount a WIM image, the following items can be modified within the image:

- Settings
- Modules
- Language packs
- Drivers
- Packages
- Files

Here's the ImageX capture syntax:

```
imagex /config config.ini /capture [source] [image file] "IMAGEDESCRIPTION"
```

Here's the ImageX append syntax:

```
imagex /append  [source]    [image file] "IMAGEDESCRIPTION"
```

Here's the ImageX apply syntax:

```
imagex /apply [image file] [Destination Path] [Index]
```

And, finally, here's the ImageX info syntax:

```
imagex /info img_file  [img_number | img_name] [new_name] [new_desc] {/boot |
/check | /logfile}
```

Here's the process in which WIM images are edited offline:

1. Execute the ImageX command to mount the image in a Read/Write fashion.

2. Extract the image to an existing file system.

3. Make the necessary modifications to the extracted image.

4. Commit the changes made to the image with the `apply` switch.

File Versus Sector Imaging

Sector-based imaging has many issues that are time consuming and costly to work around. Sector-based technologies have a number of stipulations:

▶ The target for the image deployment must be the same HAL type as the reference PC.

▶ The same mass storage controller must be present on the target and reference PCs.

▶ The contents of the disk are destroyed in the process by writing over the destination disk Master File Table (MFT) and data, making it very difficult to handle many required migration tasks.

Although several sector-based imaging technologies allow you to edit an image after creating it, there are very few tasks that the administrator is capable of performing, and the file-deletion capability deletes the files without reclaiming the space. The significance of this last point means that a laptop image made from a reference PC with 4GB of RAM will most likely have a several GB page file and a 4GB hibernation file. That is approximately 6GB going into an image that is unnecessary, because it will be re-created on the first boot. The deletion of these files will not reclaim the space, but leaves the administrator with lots of room to add other items that usually are not needed in this volume. ImageX excels in this area, because it ignores the hibernation and page files during the capture phase.

Because sector-based imaging technologies image the disk at the "1's and 0's" level, a file such as winword.exe, which may be located on the system numerous times, is copied into the image as many times as it is present. ImageX, on the other hand, will only copy winword.exe once per version and place pointers for the other instances it finds. This single-instance file imaging allows for even greater efficiencies during the capture and apply phases, and produces smaller images in general. Because ImageX works at the file level, it provides the following capabilities:

▶ More flexibility and control over the deployed media.

▶ Rapid extraction of images to decrease setup time.

▶ A reduction in image size because of single instancing, which means the file data is stored separately from the path information. This enables files that exist in multiple paths or in multiple images to be stored once, and then shared across the images.

▶ Nondestructive application of images. ImageX does not perform an all-inclusive over-write of the contents of your drive. You can selectively add and remove information.

▶ The ability to work across any platform supported by Windows.

▶ Two different compression algorithms, Fast and Maximum, to further reduce your image size.

▶ The ability to treat an image file like a directory. For example, you can add, copy, paste, and delete files using a file-management tool such as Windows Explorer.

Boot Images

ConfigMgr uses WinPE as its boot device for clients undergoing an OS deployment. The WinPE image is stored on the ConfigMgr server as a WIM file. It's approximately 120MB in size and is named boot.wim. The ConfigMgr administrator provides these WIM files; they are not created by performing captures. In both the New PC and Replace PC scenarios, boot.wim is downloaded to the client PC from PXE, USB, or a CD/DVD. In the Refresh PC scenario, the client has boot.wim downloaded to the minint folder, and boot.ini is redirected to point at this location. This allows the reboot occurring after the user state capture to boot the system into WinPE, and for the OS deployment to commence the replacement.

ConfigMgr provides two default boot.wim images: one for x86 and one for x64. As with any other package, you must deploy these boot images to distribution points for clients to be able to download and use them. The boot.wim files that come with ConfigMgr will require customization to support the network drivers and storage controller drivers utilized throughout the deployments.

TIP

Customizing WinPE

ConfigMgr administrators have found it very useful to add a variety of tools to WinPE for troubleshooting deployments. Some of the tools found beneficial include SMS Trace32, Sysinternals tools, Microsoft's Diagnostic and Recovery Toolkit (DART) tools, and other scripting tools. Anything you can use on a system to troubleshoot a failed deployment can be added to WinPE and made available on the client system this way. Keep in mind, though, that the more tools added, the larger the size of the boot.wim PE build.

Updating the boot images is a fairly simple process. Perform the following steps to update any boot image:

1. Open the ConfigMgr console.
2. Navigate to System Center Configuration Manager -> Site Database *<Site Code>* -> *<Site Name>* ->Computer Management -> Operating System Deployment -> Boot Images.
3. Select the boot image desired, right-click, and select Properties.
4. Select the Windows PE tab to add drivers.
5. Select the Image tab to add/change an image property.

Another approach would include the following:

1. Open the ConfigMgr console.

2. Navigate to System Center Configuration Manager -> Site Database <*Site Code*> -> <*Site Name*> -> Computer Management -> Operating System Deployment -> Drivers.

3. Select the driver to add, right-click, and select Add or Remove Drivers to Boot Images.

Alternatively, simply select the driver to add and drag it to the boot image under the Boot Images node.

TIP

WinPE Updates

If you update WinPE, the distribution points it resides on must also be updated. This same process must occur when there are updates to package source files, and is frequently overlooked.

Driver Injection

ConfigMgr can maintain a driver catalog. This catalog keeps drivers external to the images and enables a centralized, easily administered location to store drivers. The driver catalog allows storing multiple versions of the same device driver to support systems that may still require older versions for support. The driver catalog is broken up into drivers and driver packages. A *driver* is an INF file, as well as several other files, that defines how an operating system is supposed to use a specific piece of hardware. The operating system matches the driver to the hardware by the Plug and Play ID (PnPID). The driver package is merely a grouping of drivers for a specific purpose that later can be deployed to distribution points.

As images are being built without drivers installed locally, the OS deployment process will have to provide the drivers to the target PC at the appropriate time. This occurs through the task sequencer by leveraging the WinPE Auto Apply Drivers task sequence step. This step automatically detects and installs all applicable Plug and Play device drivers it can locate in the driver catalog. For ConfigMgr to search in the driver catalog for the new device drivers, you should add the Auto Apply Drivers task sequence step to an existing task sequence. Auto Apply Drivers contains the following options:

▶ **Name**—A short user-defined name that describes the action taken in this step

▶ **Description**—More detailed information about the action taken in this step

▶ **Install only the best matched compatible drivers**—Specifies that the task sequence step will install only the best matched driver for each hardware device detected

▶ **Install all compatible drivers**—Specifies that the task sequence step will install all compatible drivers for each hardware device detected and allow Windows setup to choose the best driver

▶ **Consider drivers from all categories**—Specifies that the task sequence action will search all available driver categories for appropriate device drivers

▶ **Limit driver matching to only consider drivers in selected categories—** Specifies that the task sequence action will search for device drivers in specified driver categories for the appropriate device drivers

▶ **Do unattended installation of unsigned drivers on versions of Windows where this is allowed—**Allows this task sequence action to install unsigned Windows device drivers

Image Capture

Capturing an image is the first of three steps required to deploy an operating system. The second task is to create the task sequence, and the third task is the advertising of the task sequence to a collection. There are two possible methods for capturing an image:

▶ Build the reference PC and capture the image using capture media

▶ Create a task sequence to build and capture an operating system image

Many find the manual build method to be the easiest and least prone to errors from a capturing perspective, but it allows human error to occur on the build of the reference PC. Capturing a PC image using media requires the following steps:

1. Build the reference computer.

    ▶ Place the computer in a workgroup.

    ▶ The local Administrator password must be blank.

    ▶ Do not require password complexity in the local system policy.

2. In the Configuration Manager console, navigate to System Center Configuration Manager -> Site Database *<Site Code>* -> *<Site Name>* -> Computer Management -> Operating System Deployment -> Task Sequences.

3. On the Action menu, select Create Task Sequence Media Wizard. Select the Capture Media option and click Next.

4. On the Media Type page, specify the type of media you want to use for the capture media.

5. On the Media file line, enter the save path and filename of the media that will be used to perform the installation.

6. Select the boot image that should be associated with the media.

7. Create a bootable CD that contains the .ISO file you created by using an appropriate software application.

8. Boot the computer into the full operating system and insert the capture CD.

9. Run the Image Capture Wizard and identify the location for the captured image to be stored.

10. Add the captured image to Configuration Manager 2007 as an image package:

    ▶ Navigate to System Center Configuration Manager -> Site Database *<Site Code>* -> *<Site Name>* -> Computer Management -> Operating System Deployment -> Operating System Images.

▶ On the Action menu, or from the Actions pane, select Add Operating System Image to launch the Add Operating System Image Wizard. Complete the wizard to add the operating system image.

The other method of capturing an image is to create a task sequence to build and capture an operating system image. You can use a task sequence to build an operating system from scratch in an unattended format. This ensures consistency as the build is updated over time and removes the human error factor, because all tasks that occur to configure the OS are placed in the task sequencer as tasks. To create a new build-and-capture task sequence, perform the following steps:

1. In the Configuration Manager console, navigate to System Center Configuration Manager -> Site Database *<Site Code>* -> *<Site Name>* -> Computer Management -> Operating System Deployment -> Task Sequences.

2. Right-click the Task Sequences node and then click New/Task Sequence.

3. On the Create a New Task Sequence page, select Build and capture a reference operating system image. Click Next.

4. On the Task Sequence Information page, specify a name for the task sequence and add an optional comment. Specify the boot image that will be associated with the task sequence. Click Next.

5. On the Install Windows Operating System page, specify the operating system install package to use for installing. Install the operating system by clicking the Browse button to launch the Select an Operating System Install Package dialog box and then selecting the operating system install package.

6. On the Install the Windows Operating System page, specify the Windows product key and server license. By default, the local administrator account will be disabled. If you want to always use the same administrator account for the computers that will run this task sequence, select the Always use the same administrator password option and provide the password that will be used. Click Next.

7. On the Configure the Network page, specify if the target computer will join a workgroup or a windows domain.

▶ If you are adding the target computer to a workgroup, you must type the name of the workgroup in the space provided.

▶ If you are adding the target computer to a Windows domain, click the Set button to launch the Windows User Account dialog box and specify the user account and password that are used to add the computer to the domain. The account you specify must have domain join permissions in the Windows domain or Organizational Unit (OU) to which you want to add the computer. You must also specify the name of the domain and OU to add the target computer. Click Next.

8. On the Install ConfigMgr page, click the Browse button to launch the Select a Package dialog box. Then select the Configuration Manager 2007 package to use to install the Configuration Manager 2007 client. Specify the Configuration Manager

2007 client installation properties that will be used in the Installation properties window. Click Next.

9. On the Include Updates in Image page, specify how the target computer will install assigned software updates by selecting the appropriate option.

10. On the Install Software Packages page, click the New button to launch the Program Select dialog box. Click the Browse button to launch the Select a Package dialog box. Select the ConfigMgr packages you want to include and then click OK. Use the drop-down to select the associated programs to use.

11. On the System Preparation page, specify the Configuration Manager 2007 package that contains the Sysprep tool. The Sysprep tool specified must support the operating system install package version selected in step 5.

12. On the Image Properties page, specify identifying information that will be associated with the task sequence you are creating.

13. On the Capture Image page, specify where the captured operating system image will be saved on the network. Click the Set button to launch the Windows User Account dialog box, and specify the network account to use to access the specified operating system image output location.

14. To complete the creation of the new task sequence, on the Summary page, click Next.

15. To confirm that the new task sequence was created using the properties specified, review the confirmation on the Confirmation page.

16. Click Close to close the New Task Sequence Wizard.

Because ConfigMgr uses WinPE as the boot media to deploy an operating system, in theory you can use any type of image with the ConfigMgr deployment process. In addition, task sequences are the actual ConfigMgr objects advertised to a collection, which allows an infinite number of possibilities to be deployed to clients.

Windows Deployment Integration

Windows Deployment Services (WDS), which is included with Microsoft WAIK and Windows Server 2003 SP 2, is the new version of Microsoft Remote Installation Services (RIS). WDS, similar to RIS, is used to deploy Windows operating systems to client PCs without requiring an administrator present. WDS uses a hook into DHCP to allow PXE booting of PCs, and it leverages the Trivial File Transfer Protocol (TFTP) to network boot clients into WinPE and apply images to them.

Windows Deployment Services provides the following benefits:

▶ Reduces the complexity of deployments. Also, the cost is built in to the licensing of Microsoft Windows Server.

▶ Empowers users to reimage their own PC.

▶ Allows network-based installation of Windows operating systems.

▶ Supports the New PC scenario.

▶ Supports mixed environments that include Windows XP/Vista and Microsoft Windows Server 2003/2008.

▶ Provides an end-to-end solution for the deployment of Windows operating systems to client computers and servers.

▶ Builds on standard Windows Server 2008 setup technologies, including WinPE, WIM files, and image-based setup.

When ConfigMgr 2007 shipped, it lacked a method of supporting the New PC scenario without IT administrators having to touch the ConfigMgr Administrator console for each PC they needed to image. ConfigMgr 2007 Release 2 (R2) resolved this issue. The issue was that an administrator could not image a PC using the New PC scenario without ConfigMgr first knowing about the PC. This meant that new PCs—either coming right from the OEM or without having had the ConfigMgr client on them—could not be imaged without a ConfigMgr admin going into the ConfigMgr console and creating the computer association.

Although PXE booting a PC and connecting to WDS works as expected, another issue arises when you introduce ConfigMgr into the equation. If the computer is unknown to the local ConfigMgr site, ConfigMgr will not respond to the PXE request. MDT offers a PXE filter, which hooks into WDS and ConfigMgr, allowing WDS to add PCs to the ConfigMgr database prior to ConfigMgr seeing the request.

Several other integration points exist between WDS/MDT and ConfigMgr. You can customize WinPE builds in the Deployment Workbench within MDT and then use them in ConfigMgr. You can use task sequences from the Workbench in ConfigMgr, but not without some modifications. Keep in mind the environment used for deployments in MDT does not exist in ConfigMgr, nor does a ConfigMgr client know about the MDT environment.

AMT and vPro

Intel Corporation, the world's largest semiconductor company and inventor of the vast majority of computer processors in PCs today, has created a technology known as vPro. vPro is a set of features and logic built in to a PC motherboard, similar to how the MMX instruction set was built in Intel's processors. Intel vPro is a combination of processor technologies, hardware enhancements, management features, and security technologies that allow remote access to the PC. This includes monitoring, maintenance, and management—all accomplished independently of the state of the operating system or power state of the PC. Intel vPro is intended to help businesses gain certain maintenance and servicing advantages, improve security, and reduce costs.

Intel systems that support vPro technology were originally branded with the logo depicted in Figure 11.5.

FIGURE 11.5   The original Intel vPro logo

Since the vPro release, Intel has updated its processors and motherboards, also known as *system boards*, to include vPro technologies. The Core 2 Duo or Quad processors are the most recognizable new processors released by Intel. Since these new technologies have come out, Intel has released a new logo in 2008 for vPro, which is illustrated in Figure 11.6.

FIGURE 11.6   The new Intel vPro logo

Intel has also created Active Management Technology, known as AMT. Intel AMT is a hardware-based technology for remotely managing and securing PCs that are "out of band." Currently, Intel AMT is available in

▶ Desktop PCs with an Intel Core 2 processor with vPro technology

▶ Laptop PCs with a Centrino processor with vPro technology or a Centrino 2 proces-sor with vPro technology

ConfigMgr 2007 with Service Pack 1 supports the AMT vPro clients, leveraging the integra-tion between the Intel OOB Management console and the ConfigMgr console. Intel's AMT and vPro technology make it possible for ConfigMgr to provision vPro clients without an OS deployed in scenarios where the client is down, the hard drive is corrupt, and so on— all while the PC is powered off.

Intel AMT is part of the Intel Management Engine, built in to PCs with Intel vPro technol-ogy. Intel AMT is built in to a secondary processor located on the motherboard. AMT is not intended for use by itself; it is intended for use with software management applica-tions such as ConfigMgr. AMT performs hardware-based management over the TCP/IP protocol, which is unlike software-based management in ConfigMgr, because there is no dependency on the operating system. Examples of hardware-based management include DHCP (Dynamic Host Configuration Protocol), BOOTP (Bootstrap Protocol), and WOL (Wake On LAN).

Intel AMT includes hardware-based remote management features, security features, power-management features, and remote-configuration features. These features allow an IT technician to access an AMT PC when traditional techniques such as Remote Desktop or WOL are not available. Intel AMT operates on an independent hardware-based OOB communication channel, which operates regardless of whether the OS is running, functional, or even powered on. The hardware-based AMT features in laptop and desktop PCs include the following:

▶ Encrypted, remote communication channel between the IT console and Intel AMT.

▶ Ability for a wired PC outside the company's firewall on an open local area network (LAN) to establish a secure communication tunnel (via AMT) back to the IT console. Examples of an open LAN include a wired laptop at home or at an SMB (small/medium business) site without a proxy server.

▶ Remote power up/power down/power cycle through encrypted WOL.

▶ Remote boot via integrated device electronics redirect (IDE-R).

▶ Console redirection, via serial over LAN (SOL).

▶ Hardware-based filters for monitoring packet headers in inbound and outbound network traffic for known threats and for monitoring known/unknown threats based on time-based heuristics. Laptops and desktop PCs have filters to monitor packet headers. Desktop PCs have packet-header filters and time-based filters.

▶ Isolation circuitry to port-block, rate-limit, or fully isolate a PC that might be compromised or infected.

▶ Agent presence checking, via hardware-based, policy-based programmable timers. A "miss" generates an event; you can specify that the event generate an alert.

▶ OOB alerting.

▶ Persistent event log, stored in protected AMT memory for software tools such as ConfigMgr to access while the OS is down.

▶ Access (preboot) the PC's Universal Unique Identifier (UUID).

▶ Access (preboot) hardware asset information, such as a component's manufacturer and model; this is updated every time the system goes through Power-On Self-Test (POST).

▶ Access (preboot) to a third-party data store (TPDS), a protected memory area that software vendors can use for version information, .DAT files, and other information.

▶ Remote configuration options, including certificate-based zero-touch remote configuration, USB key configuration (light-touch), and manual configuration.

Additional AMT features in laptop PCs include the following:

▶ Support for IEEE 802.11 a/g/n wireless protocols

▶ Cisco-compatible extensions for Voice over WLAN

Intel vPro platform features include the following:

- Support for IEEE 802.1x, Cisco Self Defending Network (SDN), and Microsoft Network Access Protection (NAP)

- Gigabit network connection or network wireless connection (on laptops)

- Intel Trusted Execution Technology (Intel TXT) and an industry-standard Trusted Platform Module (TPM), version 1.2

- Intel Virtualization Technology (Intel VT)

- 64-bit processors optimized for multitasking and multithreading

- 64-bit integrated graphics to provide enough performance that the PC does not need a discrete (separate) graphics card, even for graphics-intensive operating systems such as Microsoft Windows Vista

- Industry standards, such as ASF, XML, SOAP, TLS, HTTP authentication, Kerberos (Microsoft Active Directory), DASH (based on draft 1.0 specifications), and WS-MAN

- Quiet System Technology (QST), formerly called *advanced fan speed control (AFSC)*

- Architecture, package design, and technologies for power coordination and better thermals, in order to operate at very low voltages, use power more efficiently, and help meet Energy Star requirements

Because Intel AMT allows access to the PC below the OS level, security for the AMT features is a key concern. Security for communications between Intel AMT and the provisioning service and/or management console can be established in different ways, depending on the network environment. Security can be established via certificates and keys (TLS public key infrastructure, or TLS-PKI), pre-shared keys (TLS-PSK), or administrator password. Security technologies that protect access to the AMT features are built in to the hardware and firmware. As with other hardware-based features of AMT, the security technologies are active even if the PC is powered off, the OS has crashed, software agents are missing, or hardware (such as a hard drive or memory) has failed.

Summary

As you can tell from reading this chapter, the tools discussed will run independently from ConfigMgr. Also, ConfigMgr 2007 does not require these tools for its core functionality. Many of the tools and technologies mentioned are far more capable than can be covered in a single chapter. Several of the technologies are actually standalone technologies designed to address a specific need in the market for which Microsoft received feedback. Together, all these tools create a comprehensive solution and allow ConfigMgr to continue to be the best-of-breed solution for OS deployments, managing clients outside the firewall, enforcement of network access policies, and imaging in general.

CHAPTER 12

Client Management

Now that you have your Configuration Manager (ConfigMgr) environment installed and configured, it is time to begin client management. The context in which the word *client* is used refers to any system that has the ConfigMgr client installed and configured. A ConfigMgr client can be a workstation or server operating system, or a mobile device or cash register using Windows Embedded systems. ConfigMgr site servers can also (and usually do) have the ConfigMgr client installed.

ConfigMgr clients communicate with the site server via management points (MPs) and proxy management points (PMPs). When a client communicates with a management point, it may be receiving ConfigMgr policy, forwarding inventory information, updating deployment state, or addressing other client details. This chapter discusses how to configure a management point, configure client agents (hardware inventory, software inventory, and other agents), discover and deploy clients, and troubleshoot client problems.

TIP

Check Privacy Issues in Regards to Configuration Manager

Companies (and employees) are becoming more aware of privacy issues every day. Take time to read Microsoft's documentation on security best practices and privacy information for ConfigMgr features at http://technet.microsoft.com/en-us/library/bb632704.aspx.

Configuring the Management Point

Configure a management point for any site to which you plan to assign clients. Before installing an MP, review the prerequisites discussed in Chapter 8, "Installing Configuration Manager 2007." Use the following steps to install the management point on a primary site:

1. In the ConfigMgr console, navigate to Site Management -> Site Database -> Site Management -> <Site Code> <Site Name> -> Site Settings -> Site Systems. Expand Site Systems, right-click the site server, and select New Roles.

2. The first page of the New Site Role Wizard should already be configured. Click Next and then select the Management Point role.

3. After clicking Next, configure the MP, an example of which is displayed in Figure 12.1. Specify the following options:

    ▶ Select "Allow devices to use this management point" if you have devices that you want to manage.

    ▶ Select the type of connections to allow from clients—intranet only, Internet only, or both.

    ▶ If you are using a SQL Replica, specify the database information.

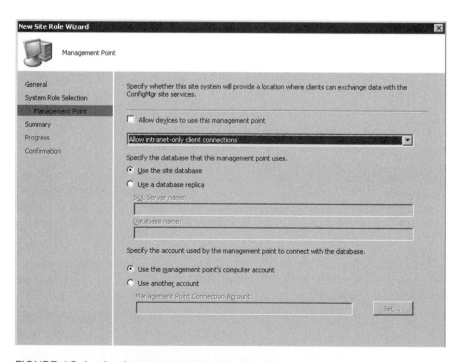

FIGURE 12.1   Configuring the MP in the New Site Role Wizard

> ► You will need to specify an MP connection account if you cannot configure the management point's computer account to access content.

> If the MP needs access to a site database in a different domain (regardless of forest), you must use an MP connection account.

4. Review the Summary page. Click Next and then Finish to complete the setup.
5. Review mpsetup.log and mpmsi.log on the ConfigMgr site server to check for any errors.

Real World: Searching the MSI Installer Logs for Errors

When looking for errors in the mpmsi.log file, open the file and search for **value 3**. If it exists, look several lines above that for the error. The text will provide a beginning point for troubleshooting.

The process just completed described creating a management point on a primary site server. Depending on the size of your site, you may consider offloading the management point to a second server to remove some of the processes required of your primary site. Chapter 8 includes information on offloading the management point and enabling you to configure the MP to work with a replica of the SQL database for the site.

Configuring Client Agents

You configure client agents to enable specific client features such as hardware inventory, software updates, and software distribution. Client agents are always configured at the primary site level, which means that all clients assigned to that site will receive the same client agent settings. All ConfigMgr clients are assigned to a primary site—although clients may use a secondary site for proxy management points and other client communication, the client agent configuration is from the primary site.

Real World: Managing Client Settings for Multiple Sites

Most environments with multiple primary sites attempt to configure client agents consistently throughout the hierarchy; you can manage this easily using the Transfer Site Settings Wizard, described in Chapter 8.

Alternatively, some environments implement a new primary site just to configure the clients assigned to that site differently. As an example, you may have an office in a country that prohibits collecting user information. You could configure a new primary site in that office and disable the hardware inventory client agent, but still collect hardware inventory from client computers in other locations.

Figure 12.2 displays all the client agents, which are described in the next sections, along with configurations for consideration.

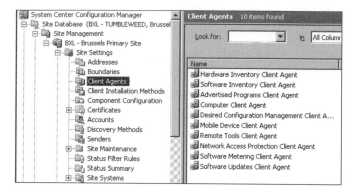

FIGURE 12.2   ConfigMgr client agents

After the client agents are configured, all clients assigned to that site will receive policy to enable (or disable) the appropriate agents. Most agents have a schedule for when they should perform an operation on the client. The "Client Troubleshooting" section covers methods to manually force actions to occur on the client.

Hardware Inventory

To a new ConfigMgr administrator, *hardware inventory* sounds like collecting specific hardware information for a client. Although true, that is only a small subset of the information you can collect in hardware inventory. Hardware information is collected from Windows Management Instrumentation (WMI) and the Windows Registry (via WMI). Refer to Figure 12.3, which displays the standard hardware inventory queried from a Windows XP Professional client named Tarzan in the SCCMUnleashed domain.

As the Resource Explorer in Figure 12.3 shows, ConfigMgr inventories a significant amount of hardware by default, such as network adapters, SCSI controllers, disk drives, and partitions. You also see information such as Add/Remove Programs (software that appears in Add/Remove Programs), Services (Windows services on the inventoried system), and various operating system information. To launch the Resource Explorer, simply right-click a computer object in a collection and select Start -> Resource Explorer.

Once you are introduced to hardware inventory, you will probably find it to be vital information you want to collect in your environment. Perform the following steps to enable hardware inventory:

1. Right-click Hardware Inventory Client Agent and then select Properties to view the General tab, displayed in Figure 12.4.

2. Simply check the box "Enable hardware inventory on clients" to enable hardware inventory for the site. Most administrators will select the simple schedule for inventory.

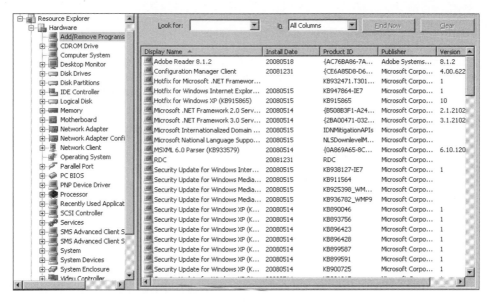

FIGURE 12.3   Resource Explorer for a Windows XP Professional client

FIGURE 12.4   The Hardware Inventory Client agent

Using a Simple Schedule

Some client agents (such as hardware inventory) perform actions on a recurring schedule. When you configure the client agent, you have the ability to determine the frequency of that recurrence. The two types of recurring schedules are simple and custom.

▶ With a simple schedule, you specify the frequency that hardware inventory will run. By default, inventory will run every 7 days. The start time is configured from the ConfigMgr client install time. This means that if a client was installed at 7:00 a.m. on a Monday, and inventory is configured to run on a simple schedule every 7 days, hardware inventory will run every Monday at 7:00 a.m. Because not all clients were installed at exactly the same time, each client will have its own schedule for executing hardware inventory, which helps reduce peak usage times.

▶ The alternative schedule is the custom schedule, which allows you to specify the exact time and day that inventory will run. When you configure a custom schedule for hardware inventory, it forces all clients to report inventory at the same time. This can cause an overload on your site, depending on the number of clients assigned to that site.

3. The last option on the General tab of Figure 12.4 (Maximum custom MIF file size) is a bit confusing, because it really applies to the settings on the MIF Collection tab. You can specify the maximum size of MIF or NOIDMIF files that the site can process (choose between 1KB and 5,000KB). ConfigMgr moves MIF files that are larger than the specified size to the \inboxes\auth\dataldr.box\badmifs folder. For the MIF file size configuration to be used at all, you must enable at least one of the check boxes on the MIF Collection tab displayed in Figure 12.5.

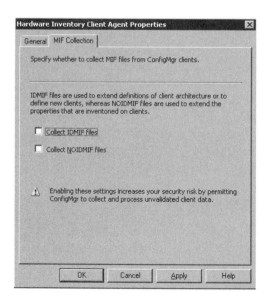

FIGURE 12.5   The MIF Collection tab of the Hardware Inventory Client agent

Figure 12.5 shows you can collect IDMIF and NOIDMIF files. Both these file types are legacy, and should be avoided if possible. The documentation at http://technet.microsoft.com/en-us/library/cc180618.aspx provides additional information on IDMIF and NOIDMIF files.

Modifying the SMS_Def.mof File

Figure 12.3 shows hardware inventory is configured by default to inventory a significant amount of data. You may find that you need more or less information. Use the SMS_Def.mof file to enable or disable the inventory of specific classes as well as properties within those classes. The SMS_Def.mof file is located in *<ConfigMgrInstallPath>*\inboxes\clifiles.src\hinv. Make a backup copy of the file, and then edit the original file using a standard text editor such as Windows Notepad.

The following example modifies the SMS_Def.mof file to inventory ConfigMgr http ports configured on the client. This class is disabled by default, as shown in Figure 12.6.

```
[ SMS_Report     (FALSE),
  SMS_Group_Name ("SMS Advanced Client Ports"),
  SMS_Class_ID   ("MICROSOFT|ADVANCED_CLIENT_PORTS|1.0") ]

class Win32Reg_SMSAdvancedClientPorts : SMS_Class_Template
{
    [SMS_Report (TRUE), key ]
        string InstanceKey;
    [SMS_Report (TRUE)     ]
        uint32 PortName;
    [SMS_Report (TRUE)     ]
        uint32 HttpsPortName;
};
```

FIGURE 12.6   Default inventory configuration for Win32Reg_SMSAdvancedClientPorts from SMS_Def.mof

To change SMS_Def.mof to inventory the http ports, perform the following steps:

1. Using Notepad, open SMS_Def.mof, located in *<ConfigMgrInstallPath>*\inboxes\clifiles.src\hinv.

2. Notice all the properties of the Win32Reg_AdvancedClientPorts class (InstanceKey, PortName, and HttpsPortName) are configured to report inventory, because SMS_Def.mof specifies the TRUE value for each. However, notice that the class reporting is disabled (the very first line in Figure 12.6 is for class reporting).

3. To enable reporting, simply change FALSE in the first line of Figure 12.6 to TRUE, as shown in Figure 12.7.

```
[ SMS_Report     (TRUE),
  SMS_Group_Name ("SMS Advanced Client Ports"),
  SMS_Class_ID   ("MICROSOFT|ADVANCED_CLIENT_PORTS|1.0") ]

class Win32Reg_SMSAdvancedClientPorts : SMS_Class_Template
{
    [SMS_Report (TRUE), key ]
        string InstanceKey;
    [SMS_Report (TRUE)     ]
        uint32 PortName;
    [SMS_Report (TRUE)     ]
        uint32 HttpsPortName;
};
```

FIGURE 12.7   Inventory enabled for Win32Reg_SMSAdvancedClientPorts from SMS_Def.mof

You must enable reporting of a class to inventory any of its properties. You can disable the inventory of properties within a class by setting the respective TRUE to FALSE.

4. Save the SMS_Def.mof file, and view Dataldr.log to see ConfigMgr compile the MOF.

5. Because the SMS_Def.mof is a sitewide setting, copy your new SMS_Def.mof file to the proper location on all primary sites in your hierarchy to enable the modified inventory for each site.

ConfigMgr hardware inventory is very extensible. All data located in WMI or the Windows Registry can be easily collected using ConfigMgr hardware inventory. If the desired data does not currently exist in WMI or the Registry, you can always use ConfigMgr's software distribution component to run a script or executable on each system to populate the Registry with desired data and then collect it using hardware inventory.

For additional information, Microsoft provides documentation on extending hardware inventory at http://technet.microsoft.com/en-us/library/bb680609.aspx. You may also want to consider purchasing the *SCCM Expert's* book *Start to Finish Guide to MOF Editing*, by Jeff Gilbert, available at http://www.smsexpert.com/MOF/Guide.aspx. This book provides an in-depth look at modifying and customizing hardware inventory.

For information on how SMS_Def.mof and Configuration.mof are used in Configuration Manager 2007, see Chapter 3, "Looking Inside Configuration Manager."

TIP

Best Practices for Inventory Security

Collecting inventory can expose potential vulnerabilities to attackers. You will want to read Microsoft's documentation on inventory security best practices and privacy information at http://technet.microsoft.com/en-us/library/bb680795.aspx.

Software Inventory

Software inventory collects information about files and file locations. The General tab for the Software Inventory Client Agent Properties dialog box is very similar to the General tab for hardware inventory, previously described in the "Hardware Inventory" section of this chapter. Enable the software inventory agent, and select to use a simple or custom schedule (review the "Using a Simple Schedule" sidebar). On the Inventory Collection tab, select the file type and path for files to inventory. As Figure 12.8 shows, ConfigMgr 2007 inventories .exe files by default.

To add an additional file type, click the orange starburst in Figure 12.8 to open the Inventoried File Properties tab shown in Figure 12.9.

Figure 12.9 shows a new rule being created to inventory all pre–Access 2007 databases (*.mdb extension) located in the %*PUBLIC*% path environment variable. Options specified

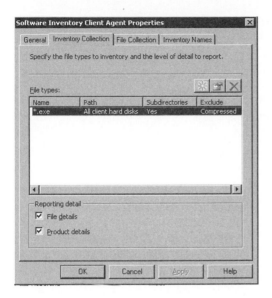

FIGURE 12.8   The Inventory Collection tab of the Software Inventory Client Agent Properties dialog box

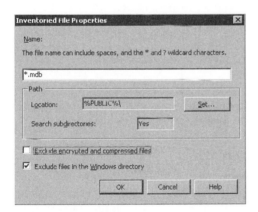

FIGURE 12.9   Defining a new filename to inventory

include searching subdirectories and including compressed and encrypted files. Although this example uses a file extension, you can also inventory for an exact filename (budget.mdb) or partial filename (budget*.mdb). The ConfigMgr integrated help provides additional assistance on wildcard usage.

Use the File Collection tab, visible in Figure 12.8, to collect a file (or files) from each client. Click the orange starburst on that page to create a new file collection entry. Figure

12.10 shows a sample file collection entry. Similar to software inventory, file collection allows you to specify an exact filename or use wildcards. You can also specify a specific path, or accept the default that queries all local hard disks for the file. You will also notice that there is a Maximum Size (KB) option—this specifies the maximum size of all files this rule will collect. As an example, if you specified *.ini as the rule, an attempt would be made to collect all .ini files, but if the sum of the size of those files is greater than the Maximum size, none of the files will be collected.

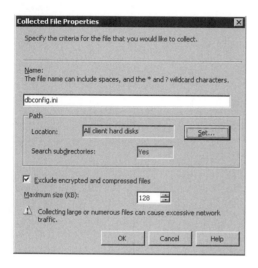

FIGURE 12.10   Creating a new file collection entry

File collection occurs during a scheduled software inventory cycle. Once files are collected, you can use Resource Explorer to view the files.

The last tab of the Software Inventory Client Agent Properties dialog box (Figure 12.8) is Inventory Names. You can use this to help make more sense out of software inventory data. The header properties in files are not always consistent, which often makes reporting of this data confusing. A name is often listed in multiple ways; as an example, Microsoft can be represented as Microsoft Corp., Microsoft Corporation, Microsoft, and so on. Microsoft has already prepopulated some data for Microsoft products to help make inventory more concise, as shown in Figure 12.11.

Figure 12.11 shows that each name specified in Inventoried Names will be grouped and considered as the display name of Microsoft Corporation. By clicking on the starburst by Display name, you can easily add to this list to group other software as well.

As an example, say you have six different programs from Acme Corporation and notice that different names are inventoried for Manufacturer (Acme Corp., Acme, Acme

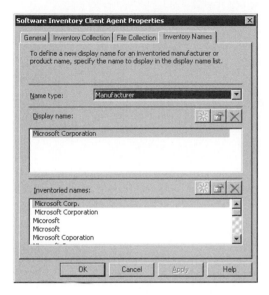

FIGURE 12.11   Configuring inventory names

Corporation, Acme Corp. International, and so on). You can add a new display name of **Acme Corporation** and then enter each inventoried name into the Inventoried Names section in the Software Inventory Client Agent Properties dialog box. You can perform this same grouping for the Product property by changing the Name type option in Figure 12.11.

> **NOTE**
>
> **More About ConfigMgr Inventory**
>
> As discussed in Chapter 2, "Configuration Manager 2007 Overview," the initial inventory generated by the client is a full inventory, with subsequent inventories reflecting changes only, as deltas. In addition, ConfigMgr's Asset Intelligence capability, discussed in Chapter 18, "Reporting," will match collected hardware and software inventory to its catalog of known devices and applications to convert the inventory data into useable information about the assets in your environment.

Advertised Programs

Configuring the Advertised Programs Client agent enables software distribution for the site. Software distribution is one of the core functions of ConfigMgr. Check the first box in Figure 12.12 to enable software distribution.

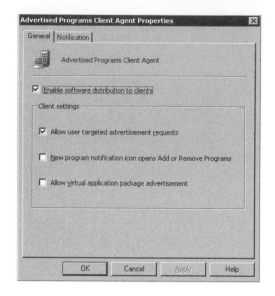

FIGURE 12.12   The General tab of the Advertised Programs Client Agent Properties dialog box

The three check boxes in the Client Settings frame help you customize software distribution:

▶ **Allow user targeted advertisement requests**—Check this box if you will target users for advertisements. If you only target computers, clear this check box to reduce policy data transmitted from server to client. This reduces network bandwidth.

▶ **New program notification icon opens Add or Remove Programs**—This check box is tied to the Notification tab of the Advertised Programs Client agent as well as individual program properties. If you enable client notifications, the user will see a notification in the system tray to indicate that a new optional program is available to install. When this box is checked, if the user clicks the new program notification, Add or Remove Programs opens, allowing the user to select the option to install a program from the network.

▶ **Allow virtual application package advertisement**—If ConfigMgr 2007 Release 2 (R2) is installed, this check box is visible and you can enable it to support virtual application deployment for the site.

The Notification tab of the Advertised Programs Client agent gives you the ability to display a notification message and play a sound if desired when new programs become available. You can also configure a countdown for when a mandatory advertisement will run.

Computer Client

The Computer Client agent provides many general settings. Figure 12.13 shows the General tab of the Computer Client Agent Properties dialog box. Specify a Network Access Account to allow ConfigMgr clients to access network resources during software distribution and Operating System Deployment (OSD). This should be a low-rights user account, which simply has access to file shares you may require.

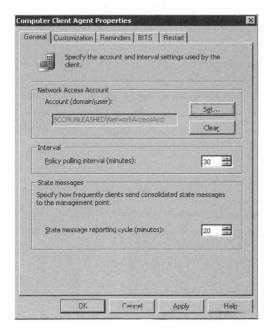

FIGURE 12.13   The General tab of the Computer Client Agent Properties dialog box

You also specify the default policy polling interval on this tab. The polling interval is the interval that the ConfigMgr client checks its management point for new or updated client policy (including software update deployments and software distribution). Depending on your environment, you may have reason to increase or decrease this interval:

▶ You may consider increasing the polling interval if advertisements and update deployments are not updated frequently and there is no demand for immediate availability.

▶ If there is high demand for immediate availability of new programs, you may want to decrease the polling interval. Decreasing the interval will cause additional load on your management point. If in doubt, leave the default of every 60 minutes, and change it later if required.

You can also modify the polling interval on a per-collection basis if desired.

The final option on the General tab is configuring the state message reporting cycle (in minutes). Software Updates deployment, task sequence advertisements, and Desired

Configuration Management (DCM) use state messages to send state information to the ConfigMgr site. During these operations, the client may create several state messages. Leave the default of 15 minutes, and extend this interval if you start to receive backlogs of state messages.

The Customization tab of the Computer Client Agent Properties dialog box allows you to add customized branding to Software Updates deployments. This can provide a better user experience, and helps your end users know that updates are being deployed by your Information Technology (IT) organization.

The Reminders tab allows you to configure the interval for system tray balloon notifications for software updates, mandatory software distributions, and task sequence advertisements. Gently remind users of possible disruptions to their schedule, and allow them to install mandatory distributions in advance of deadlines when possible.

Configure the BITS tab to manage client communications and the maximum transfer rates for each client. As shown in Figure 12.14, BITS (Background Intelligent Transfer Service) throttling can be configured three different ways:

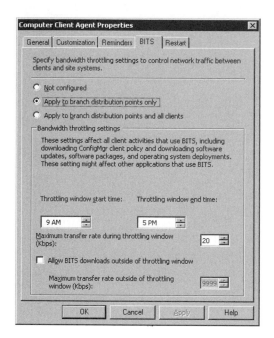

FIGURE 12.14   The BITS tab of the Computer Client Agent Properties dialog box

▶ **Not configured**—No throttling is managed using ConfigMgr.

▶ **Apply to branch distribution points only**—This setting will only configure throttling for branch DPs, allowing you to control the bandwidth used by the branch DP when copying source files from its parent site.

▶ **Apply to branch distribution points and all clients**—Just as the description implies, this setting will control BITS throttling for all ConfigMgr client agents.

As you can see in Figure 12.14, you specify a throttling window start and end time, as well as the transfer rate during that window. You can set the maximum transfer rate during the throttling window between 0 and 9999 Kbps.

> **NOTE**
>
> **Group Policy Settings Supersede ConfigMgr Settings**
>
> Any group policy settings configured to manage BITS will override ConfigMgr settings.

You can also check the box to allow BITS downloads outside the throttling window, and specify the maximum transfer rate outside the window. This gives you the flexibility to restrict transfers during peak hours of network traffic, and then relax your transfer rules during off-peak hours, thus allowing the branch distribution point (and all other clients, if desired) to download content faster from the ConfigMgr site.

The Restart tab of the Computer Client Agent Properties dialog box allows you to specify how much notice a user receives before a restart occurs.

Desired Configuration Management

Simply check the box to enable Desired Configuration Management. By default, the compliance evaluation schedule will be a simple schedule of every 7 days. Similar to configuring hardware inventory, you can create a custom schedule if desired. Chapter 16, "Desired Configuration Management," provides additional information on DCM.

Mobile Devices

Mobile Device Client Agent Properties is your one-stop-shop to configure those mobile devices that ConfigMgr will manage. From this single dialog box, you define the polling interval, inventory properties, software distribution, and file collection. Figure 12.15 displays the default configuration of the Mobile Device Client agent. The article at http://technet.microsoft.com/en-us/library/bb693474.aspx provides more information about managing mobile devices with ConfigMgr.

The mobile client performs operations similar to the ConfigMgr client. Table 12.1 lists several differences to consider.

TABLE 12.1   Mobile Client Nuances

Mobile Client Setting	Additional Information
Polling Interval	For a mobile client, consider a polling interval of 6 hours, because you will not make changes as frequently on a mobile client as a workstation.

TABLE 12.1 Mobile Client Nuances

Mobile Client Setting	Additional Information
Retry Delay	If the mobile client cannot connect to the management point at its polling interval, you can specify an interval for retrying the connection. You also specify the number of retry attempts. The polling interval must be less than the retry delay multiplied by the number of retries.
Software Inventory	You may use wildcards, but use caution, because inventorying a large number of files may impact the performance of the device.
Hardware Inventory	Mobile device hardware inventory is not extensible like the workstation client. Data such as owner name, phone number, user name, certificates, International Mobile Equipment Identity (IMEI) number, battery status, memory, and other device information is collected. See the ConfigMgr integrated help for additional information.

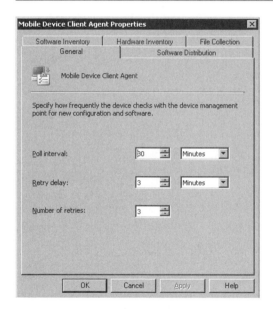

FIGURE 12.15 The Mobile Device Client agent

Remote Tools

You enable the Remote Tools Client agent to connect to remote systems so you can control the user's desktop. Figure 12.16 displays the General tab of the Remote Tools Client Agent Properties dialog box.

Check the first box to enable Remote Tools. Use the configuration settings on the General tab to manage the level of access. Some companies prefer not to ask for permission for remotely accessing clients; other companies require that a user is asked for permission before granting remote access.

FIGURE 12.16   The Remote Tools Client Agent Properties dialog box

You can grant rights to users and Active Directory groups to use remote control on a sitewide level or on a collection level. For example, you could grant the Server Operations group Remote Control rights to a collection containing servers, and grant the Service Desk group Remote Control rights to a collection containing workstations. Chapter 20, "Security and Delegation in Configuration Manager 2007," contains additional information regarding Remote Tools security.

Use the Notification tab to configure if and how you will notify an end user a remote control session is active. This setting applies only to Remote Tools.

You can also control the Remote Assistance and Remote Desktop settings of ConfigMgr clients from the respective tab on the Remote Tools Client Agent Properties dialog box. The settings you configure are sitewide, and they override any local policy configured on the client. Domain policy takes precedence over these settings.

NOTE

About Remote Tools in ConfigMgr 2007

ConfigMgr has a new version of the Remote Tools Client agent that uses the Microsoft RDP protocol. This is the same protocol that supports Remote Desktop and Remote Assistance. All ConfigMgr-supported operating systems support the RDP protocol except Windows 2000 operating systems. ConfigMgr uses an updated version of the SMS 2003 Remote Tools Client agent on Windows 2000 operating systems in order to support remote control.

The biggest advantage to the new version of Remote Tools (for Windows XP, Windows Server 2003, and newer) is that it is more secure. Unfortunately, due to the enhanced security, you also lose the functionality to manipulate the Ctrl+Alt+Delete screen. For Windows 2000, you still have this functionality by clicking the gold key on the toolbar after initiating a Remote Tools session.

Network Access Protection

Enable the check box on the General tab of the Network Access Protection Client Agent Properties dialog box to configure Network Access Protection (NAP). On the Evaluation tab, specify the frequency of NAP reevaluation after the client has successfully connected to the network. You can also force a fresh scan for each evaluation instead of allowing clients to offer a cached Statement of Health, as displayed in Figure 12.17.

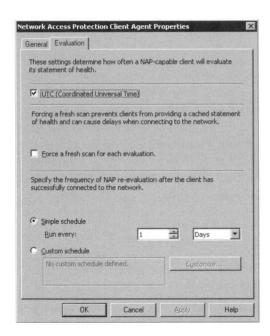

FIGURE 12.17   The Evaluation tab of the Network Access Protection Client Agent Properties dialog box

---

NOTE

Statement of Health, Cached or Fresh?

You may be trying to determine whether you should enable the check box to force a fresh scan for each evaluation. This option is added for environments that must ensure a fresh compliance scan is performed at every evaluation cycle. Although this option may be needed for some environments, requiring a new Statement of Health to be generated at each scan can be resource intensive, and may take a few minutes to complete on a client. Although forcing a fresh scan for each evaluation is more secure, it will also create a slower user experience, because the user may not be able to access corporate network resources until the evaluation completes.

For more information, review these Microsoft documents:

▶http://technet.microsoft.com/en-us/library/bb632844.aspx

▶http://technet.microsoft.com/en-us/library/bb680833.aspx

Software Metering

Use software metering to monitor and collect software usage data on ConfigMgr clients. Once this is enabled, you can identify users who use a certain application, the peak usage times of the application, and more.

The default schedule collects data from each client every 7 days. After enabling the agent, right-click the Software Metering node in the ConfigMgr console and then select Properties, as shown in Figure 12.18.

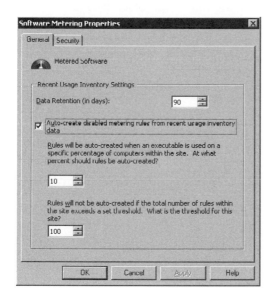

FIGURE 12.18   Software Metering Properties dialog box

The Data Retention property in Figure 12.18 specifies how many days the data obtained from the metering rules will be stored in the database. The 90-day default setting should be sufficient, unless you plan to trend usage data for over 3 months. (When using Asset Intelligence, you will need to enable software metering to identify and report on various assets. This is discussed in Chapter 18.)

Enable the check box to auto-create metering rules from recent usage inventory data. The rules ConfigMgr creates require that you enable them. The two additional settings in this frame allow you to configure the requirements for auto-creating rules. By default, rules are auto-created when an executable runs on 10% of the computers in the site, unless the total number of rules for the site exceeds 100. To view rules, simply click the Software Metering node. To enable a rule, right-click a disabled rule and select Enable. By allowing ConfigMgr to auto-create metering rules, you will get a better idea of the software that is installed on a large number of systems in your environment, and have the ability to easily enable metering for the software.

A classic example of using this feature is to find a large number of systems with software such as Microsoft Visio installed. When you see this new rule, you enable it, and from software metering web reports, you find that only 20% of the systems that have the software installed use it on a regular basis. You can now use this information to support the removal of the licensed application on nearly 80% of the installation base, thus reducing your software costs.

To create a new rule, right-click the Software Metering node and select New -> Software Metering Rule to launch the New Software Metering Rule Wizard, as shown in Figure 12.19.

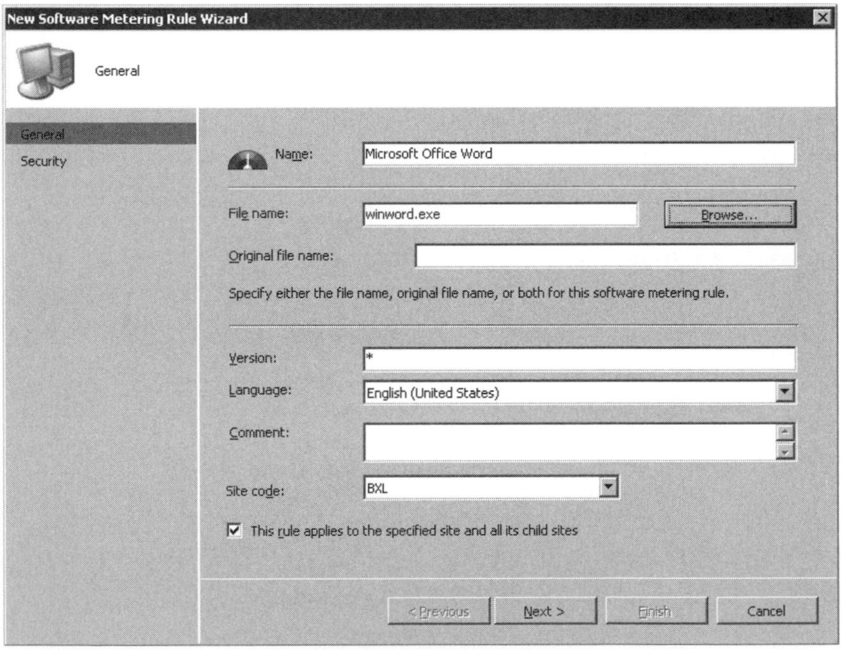

FIGURE 12.19   The New Software Metering Rule Wizard

Figure 12.19 shows a basic rule to meter Microsoft Office Word. Specify the name of the rule and the exact filename (no wildcards). You can manually enter the filename, or you can click the Browse button, navigate to the file, and select it to populate the details automatically on this page. Alternatively, you can specify the original filename, obtained by reading the filename from the header of the file. You can enter a version number to meter a specific version, or use an asterisk to inventory all versions.

TIP

Do Not Leave the Version Property Blank in the New Software Metering Rule Wizard

Leaving the Version property blank results in only metering where the file version is blank in the file header. You may encounter a file in this situation, but not normally.

The default language in the wizard is English. If you are uncertain whether the file you desire to meter will have a consistent language (or if it doesn't have a language at all), select -**Any**- from the dropdown. Specify the site code that this rule applies to, and determine whether you want to apply the rule to all child sites of the specified site code.

TIP

Information About Software Metering Privacy

Metering data is encrypted during transfer to the management point but is not stored as encrypted in the site database. Additional information regarding software metering privacy is available at http://technet.microsoft.com/en-us/library/bb680486.aspx.

Software Updates

Configure the Software Updates Client agent to leverage one of the most popular (and most important) features of ConfigMgr 2007 —patch management.

NOTE

Activate the Software Update Point

You must have an active software update point (SUP) in the ConfigMgr site in order to use the Software Updates Client agent. Chapter 8 and Chapter 15, "Patch Management," contain information about enabling an active SUP.

Simply enable the check box on the General tab for the default configuration of the Software Updates Client agent, as shown in Figure 12.20.

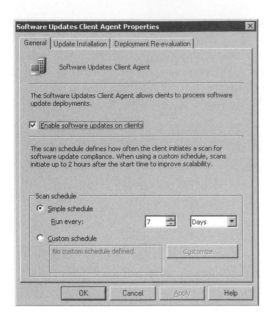

FIGURE 12.20   The Software Updates Client Agent Properties dialog box

You can then choose for the scan to run a simple or custom schedule. The "Using a Simple Schedule" sidebar earlier in this chapter discusses choosing a simple or custom schedule. On the Update Installation tab, you can choose the client to install all mandatory deployments, even if a deployment has a deadline in the future. In this situation, you have multiple deployments targeting a system, with multiple deadlines. If you enable this check box, all mandatory updates will be deployed when the first deadline is reached. This helps to eliminate multiple reboots, and provides a better end-user experience. You can also choose to hide all display notifications from end users if desired—this is a sitewide setting, meaning all Software Updates notifications will be hidden from the user. To hide notifications on a per-deployment basis, modify the properties of the desired deployment. The Deployment Re-evaluation tab allows you to configure enforcement of a patch that was uninstalled. By default, the client will reevaluate every 7 days to ensure compliance. Chapter 15 includes information about patch management.

Client Discovery

With the agents configured, it is time to begin discovering potential clients. Before you enable client discovery, verify that Client Push Installation is configured properly. If you have Client Push enabled and run a system discovery, you will immediately begin to install the ConfigMgr client on all systems assigned to the site (based on site boundaries). Client Push is not a requirement for discovery. It is suggested you first use the Client Push Installation Wizard to install clients, and then enable Client Push. The "Client Deployment" section of this chapter provides additional information about Client Push and the Client Push Installation Wizard.

Two common settings will appear through most discovery methods:

▶ **Recursive**—When enabled, this specifies that the discovery method searches child objects.

▶ **Include Groups**—Discovers objects within groups. When this is enabled, you will probably discover more objects, but this also increases the likelihood of discovering the same object more than once.

Another common element between most discovery methods is the Polling Schedule tab. Use this tab to create a recurring schedule. You can also enable the check box to run the discovery as soon as possible.

Active Directory System Group Discovery

Active Directory (AD) System Group Discovery is a discovery method that polls the domain controller for System Group objects in the domain or Lightweight Directory Access Protocol (LDAP) path specified on a schedule configured by the ConfigMgr administrator. Here are the default group account attributes returned by Active Directory System Group Discovery:

▶ Organizational Unit

▶ Global Groups

▶ Universal Groups

▶ Nested Groups

▶ Nonsecurity Groups

AD System Group Discovery will only discover these attributes for systems that have previously been discovered by some other method (AD System Discovery, Heartbeat Discovery). After enabling AD System Group Discovery, click the starburst to configure the desired container to search. As displayed in Figure 12.21, you have the ability to select the local domain or local namespace or use a custom LDAP or GC query.

FIGURE 12.21   Active Directory System Group Discovery

Review the log file adsysgrp.log for detailed information when the discovery method executes.

Active Directory Security Group Discovery

Active Directory Security Group Discovery is a discovery method that polls the domain controller for Security Group objects in the domain or LDAP path, based on a schedule configured by the ConfigMgr administrator.

Configuring this discovery method is very similar to configuring AD System Group Discovery. AD Security Group Discovery will only discover these attributes for systems previously discovered by some other method (AD System Discovery, Heartbeat Discovery). Specify the container to discover, and determine if you want to discover recursively, and within groups. Finally, set a polling interval. Review the adsgdis.log file for detailed information when the discovery method executes.

Active Directory System Discovery

Active Directory System Discovery is the key discovery method used to create data discovery records (DDRs) for computers. DDRs contain data such as operating system (OS) name and version, Internet Protocol (IP) addresses and subnets, and AD site names. You can use these DDRs to target installations for client deployment. Active Directory System Discovery is agentless, and you can use it to discover what is in your environment before installing client agents on computers. This capability gives the administrator an understanding of the network infrastructure and deployment challenges in advance.

Configuring this discovery method is very similar to configuring AD System Group Discovery. Specify the container to discover, and determine if you want to discover recursively, and within groups. Finally, set a polling interval.

If you used Systems Management Server (SMS) 2003, you will also notice a new tab named Active Directory Attribute. This tab allows you to add more Active Directory attributes to the system discovery process. You can add any computer object attribute from Active Directory, such as OperatingSystemServicePack and terminalserver. You can find all available attributes using the ADSIEdit MMC snap-in. Microsoft provides documentation on ADSIEdit at http://technet.microsoft.com/en-us/library/cc773354.aspx. You can find a list of AD search computer property attributes at http://www.winzero.ca/Active-Directory-computers.htm. Review the adsysdis.log log file for detailed information when the discovery method executes.

Active Directory User Discovery

Active Directory User Discovery is a discovery method that polls the domain controller for user objects in the domain or LDAP path specified on a schedule configured by the ConfigMgr administrator. Here are the default user attributes returned by Active Directory User Discovery:

- ▶ User name

- ▶ DNS host name

- ▶ Object class

- ▶ Active Directory domain

- ▶ Active Directory container name

The first two tabs are configured the same as the other Active Directory discoveries—simply specify the container and polling interval. The most interesting tab is the Active Directory Attribute tab, shown in Figure 12.22.

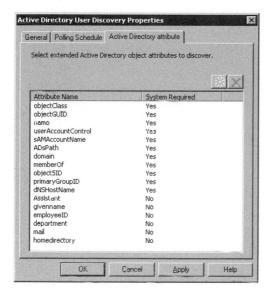

FIGURE 12.22   Active Directory User Discovery Properties dialog box

The System Required column indicates whether the Attribute name is a required attribute. All the attributes where System Required is equal to No in Figure 12.22 are attributes manually added to discovery. As you can see, it is possible to discover much more information about users than the defaults. You can identify employeeID, mail (email address), manager, department, and more. You can find all available attributes using the ADSIEdit MMC snap-in.

Review the adusrdis.log file for detailed information when the discovery method executes.

> **Real World: Active Directory Discovery Methods**
>
> For all the AD discovery methods, if the Active Directory environment used by ConfigMgr is not well maintained, you can end up with a lot of garbage in your collections. Moreover, if you enable Push Install, your site will "spin" on those garbage systems when trying to install the ConfigMgr client. Because most AD environments are not copasetic, it is important to discover only those Organizational Units (OUs) that are known to be clean, or not enable Push Install.

Heartbeat Discovery

Heartbeat Discovery is a ConfigMgr capability that enables deployed ConfigMgr clients to send DDRs to their management point. This enables clients to keep the ConfigMgr database current with discovery-related data that often changes, such as IP addresses. Heartbeat Discovery is the only required discovery method and the only one that must be enabled.

Configure a simple schedule, ensuring the schedule is configured to run more frequently than the client rediscovery period of the Clear Install Flag task in Site Maintenance. The Clear Install Flag task relies on accurate data that is forwarded from Heartbeat Discovery. If a heartbeat is not forwarded within the client rediscovery period, the install flag is cleared, causing a new attempt at installing the client and unnecessary utilization of your site and clients.

Network Discovery

Network Discovery allows ConfigMgr administrators to collect discovery data by IP subnet, domain, Simple Network Management Protocol (SNMP) community, SNMP device, or DHCP server (which must be a Microsoft-based DHCP server).

Enable Network Discovery and then choose the type of discovery to perform:

▶ **Topology**—Discovers routers and IP subnets. Specify the Maximum hops option on the SNMP tab to allow additional router hops to discover additional systems. Refer to the documentation at http://technet.microsoft.com/en-us/library/bb680992.aspx for additional information regarding router hops.

▶ **Topology and client**—In addition to discovering topology as described in the previous bullet, this type also discovers potential client computers using an IP address. Specify one or more DHCP servers on the DHCP tab for Network Discovery to query DHCP servers (Microsoft DHCP only) for clients that have an IP address lease. Depending on the size of your network, you may want to limit the number of hops to reduce network traffic.

▶ **Topology, client, and client operating system**—In addition to topology and client information, the client operating system is also identified by using this network discovery type. Client operating system information is obtained using SNMP, DHCP, the Windows browser, and Windows networking calls.

Figure 12.23 shows Topology selected as the discovery type.

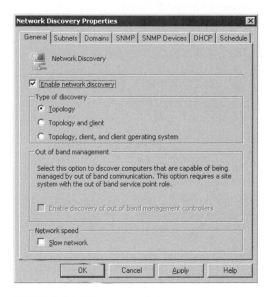

FIGURE 12.23   Network Discovery Properties dialog box

Figure 12.23 also shows the Out of Band (OOB) Management frame currently disabled—you must have ConfigMgr Service Pack (SP) 1 installed to even see this frame at all. You must configure the OOB service point and configure a provisioning account before you can enable discovery of Out of Band management controllers. Here are some points to keep in mind:

▶ If you are on a slow network, enable the check box on this dialog box to reduce the number of SNMP sessions and increase the SNMP timeout.

▶ Specify subnets to discover by adding them to the Subnets tab. The desired subnet will not be searched if it exceeds the number of hops specified on the SNMP tab. In addition, the local subnet to the site server will be searched by default.

▶ Specify specific domains using the Domains tab. By default, local domain search is enabled.

▶ Specify all community names (they are case sensitive) in the SNMP community names property of the SNMP tab. Take the time to identify all community names used on your network, so that network discovery can search as many routers as possible. Specify the maximum number of router hops from the site server. You can choose from 0 to 10. Microsoft provides documentation about router hops at http://technet.microsoft.com/en-us/library/bb680992.aspx.

Microsoft's document at http://technet.microsoft.com/en-us/library/bb693986.aspx contains additional information about Network Discovery. You will also want to review netdisc.log for detailed information when the discovery method executes.

Discovery Methods—Which Should I Choose?

As with answers to many Microsoft-related questions, *it depends*. That answer seems to be a cop-out, but sometimes it is necessary. After reading the "Client Discovery" section of this chapter, you should have a better understanding what each method consists of and what it can do for you. Here are some pointers to keep you on track:

▶ **Heartbeat Discovery**—Always enable this method of discovery for every site that has assigned clients. Unlike other discovery methods, Heartbeat Discovery is executed at the client, and information is forwarded to the site. This "heartbeat" updates the ConfigMgr site with updated client information. Ensure the intervals for the Delete Inactive Client Discovery and Delete Aged Discovery Data site maintenance tasks are set larger than the heartbeat interval setting. Heartbeat Discovery does not discover new clients, but keeps existing clients healthy in the ConfigMgr site.

▶ **Active Directory System Discovery**—If you have Active Directory, this will probably be your primary method of discovery and client installation. In addition to discovering computers, you can discover additional computer attributes from Active Directory.

▶ **Active Directory System Group Discovery**—This discovery method queries Active Directory for group membership and Organizational Unit information on computer systems that are existing clients assigned to the ConfigMgr site. The discovery method will not discover new systems, but will discover additional information about existing systems.

▶ **Active Directory User Discovery**—This discovery method queries Active Directory for user resources and includes objects such as user domain, AD container name, and username. Additional user attributes can be queries, such as manager, telephone number, and more. Because this is user discovery, client installation does not occur. This discovery method is very valuable if you plan to target users with software distribution.

▶ **Active Directory Security Group Discovery**—This discovery method queries Active Directory for groups. It is not used for client installation, but can be used when targeting AD groups for software distribution.

▶ **Network Discovery**—If all systems are in Active Directory, you may not need to use Network Discovery. If you use workgroups, or also want to discover routers, printers, and other network-connected devices, Network Discovery is for you. Client installation will only target those systems discovered using this method (not printers, routers, and such).

Client Deployment

You are now ready to dive into one of the most important configuration steps of ConfigMgr—client deployment. (Actually, just about every step of configuring ConfigMgr is the most important step!) By this point, you have completed many critical tasks, such as installing a site, selecting boundaries, configuring site systems and components, and discovering potential clients. The next sections present several alternatives for deploying the ConfigMgr client agent. More than likely, your environment will require at least two of these methods, and probably more.

Site boundaries are a very important part of client deployment. Your potential clients should be part of a boundary (IP subnet, AD site, IP address range, and so on), and have access to a server locator point (SLP) or Active Directory (and you should have published information to Active Directory according to the discussion in Chapter 8). Once these settings are configured, client deployment will flow quite nicely. For further reading, review Microsoft's documentation on sample assignment scenarios for Configuration Manager primary sites at http://technet.microsoft.com/en-us/library/bb680334.aspx.

One more document worth mentioning is Microsoft Knowledge Base (KB) article 925282, "How to Troubleshoot Advanced Client Push Installation issues in Systems Management Server 2003," at http://support.microsoft.com/kb/925282. Although it is an SMS 2003 document, the client installation process is the same as ConfigMgr 2007. Jeff Gilbert also provides a great blog post describing Client Push Installation and common scenarios with primary and secondary sites at http://myitforum.com/cs2/blogs/jgilbert/archive/2007/02/22/sms-2003-client-push-installation-method-explained.aspx.

As you will see throughout all installation methods, command-line options are required to install the ConfigMgr client properly.

Command-Line Properties

When you install the ConfigMgr client, you have more than 50 command-line properties to choose. This section covers the most popular commands. The article at http://technet.microsoft.com/en-us/library/bb680980.aspx provides a complete list.

ConfigMgr uses CCMSetup.exe and CCMSetup.msi as the main programs for client installation. Other files are required (Windows Update Agent, XML Parser, and so on), but only CCMSetup.exe and CCMSetup.msi are called directly with command-line options.

In almost all scenarios, you will call CCMSetup.exe with the appropriate command-line options. CCMSetup.exe then downloads and installs the required components and launches CCMSetup.msi with the proper command-line options. The only exception to this is when you are deploying the ConfigMgr client using Active Directory. Table 12.2 lists popular command-line options for CCMSetup.exe, and Table 12.3 lists popular command-line options for CCMClient.msi. As mentioned previously, you generally will not call CCMClient.msi directly; you will simply execute CCMSetup.exe and pass command-line options for both CCMSetup.exe and CCMSetup.msi.

TABLE 12.2   Popular CCMSetup.exe Command-Line Properties for Client Installation

Property	Description
/noservice	By default, CCMSetup runs as a service logged on as the local system account, which may not have access to network resources during client installation. Use the /noservice switch to force the installation to occur running as the user who launched CCMSetup.exe.
/uninstall	Uninstalls the ConfigMgr client.
/mp:	Specifies a valid ConfigMgr management point that CCMSetup will use to download required installation files.
/native:	Use the /native switch to install a client for Internet-only communication.

TABLE 12.3   Popular CCMSetup.msi Command-Line Properties for Client Installation

Property	Description
CCMALWAYSINF	Set this property to 1 to configure the client to always be an Internet-based client. Use CCMHOSTNAME when CCMALWAYSINF is used, to specify the FQDN of the Internet-based management point. Also, review the information for CCMCERTSEL and CCMCERTSTORE in the ConfigMgr integrated help. (CCMALWAYSINF=1)
CCMHTTPPORT	Specifies an alternate HTTP port for client communications. Unless specified, the default port of 80 is used. (CCMHTTPPORT=357)
CCMHTTPSPORT	Specifies an alternate HTTPS port for client communications. Unless specified, the default port of 443 is used. (CCMHTTPSPORT=483)
CCMDEBUGLOGGING	Use CCMDEBUGLOGGING=1 to enable debug logging. Use this for troubleshooting. Due to the large amount of data logged when in debug logging mode, avoid making this a standard for client installation.
DISABLESITEOPT	Set this value to true (DISABLESITEOPT=TRUE) to prevent all users (including local admins) from changing the ConfigMgr-assigned site through the Configuration Management control panel applet.
DISABLECACHEOPT	Set this value to true (DISABLECACHEOPT=TRUE) to prevent all users (including local admins) from changing the ConfigMgr cache size through the Configuration Management control panel applet.
SMSCACHESIZE	Specifies the maximum size of the client cache in either MB or as a percentage (if used with PERCENTDISKSPACE or PERCENTFREEDISKSPACE). If you do not specify the SMSCACHESIZE option, the default value of 5,120MB is used. (SMSCACHESIZE=2048)
SMSSITECODE	Specifies the site in which to assign the client. Use a valid three-character site code, or use the word AUTO to auto-assign the site. Do not use AUTO if the client will find its default MP using DNS. (SMSSITECODE=AUTO or SMSSITECODE=BXL)
SMSSLP	Specifies the SLP for site assignment. (SMSSLP=BLUEBONNET.SCCMUnleashed.COM)

TABLE 12.3   Popular CCMSetup.msi Command-Line Properties for Client Installation

Property	Description
FSP	Specifies the fallback status point for clients to send state messages in regard to client installation success or failure. (FSP=Mockingbird)

The command-line options in Tables 12.2 and 12.3 are used throughout the various client installation methods appearing in this chapter.

One other aspect of client installation that is consistent is the client installation logs ccmsetup.log (appears when ccmsetup.exe is used to install the client) and client.msi.log (appears for every client installation). Review these log files in the %*windir*%\system32\ccmsetup directory for x86 systems, and in %*windir*%\ccmsetup\ for x64 systems. Also, check ClientIDManagerStartup.log to verify that the client has successfully registered with its site. A client will not successfully pull policy until it is registered with the site. Additional information on common registration issues is available at

▶ http://blogs.technet.com/configurationmgr/archive/2009/01/14/configmgr-2007-client-registration-fails-and-clients-cannot-pull-any-policies.aspx

▶ http://support.microsoft.com/kb/938009

▶ http://support.microsoft.com/kb/961663

Manual Installation

Although manual client installation is probably not the method you will use to install all clients, it is a method that all environments will use, most often in service desk or on-site support scenarios. Having a well-documented process for reinstalling a ConfigMgr client is essential.

First, you must locate the installation files. By default, you will find these files in the %*ProgramFiles*%\Microsoft Configuration Manager\Client folder. CCMSetup.exe is the file you will use to initiate the installation, and depending on the operating system version, additional windows components (XML Parser, Windows Update Agent, BITS, and so on) are installed from this folder. ConfigMgr requires these additional components for a healthy client. Fortunately, you don't have to manage the installation of each of these components. There are three primary methods to install the client manually:

▶ The most basic method to install the ConfigMgr client is to copy the entire Client folder (and subfolders) to the local system and then launch CCMSetup.exe from the local drive. By using this method, CCMSetup automatically obtains the dependent source files from the local source. Alternatively, you could map a drive to a remote server and run CCMSetup. Typically, running CCMSetup from a UNC path will be unsuccessful.

▶ Execute CCMSetup.exe (either remote or local) and specify the /source: command-line switch. For example, if you have a share named \\TUMBLEWEED\ConfigMgrClient that contains the client installation files, you could execute the following statement:

```
\\TUMBLEWEED\ConfigMgrClient\CCMSETUP.EXE
/source:"\\TUMBLEWEED\ConfigMgrClient"
```

You can use the /source: switch multiple times to give CCMSetup alternative locations to download installation files. Also, verify the user account that launches CCMSetup.exe has read access to the share.

▶ Execute CCMSetup.exe (either remote or local) and specify the /mp: command-line switch with a valid management point. Note that this switch simply specifies access to client installation source files—it has no impact on site assignment. For example, using the same share mentioned in the previous bullet, you could execute the following statement:

```
\\TUMBLEWEED\ConfigMgrClient\CCMSETUP.EXE /mp:TUMBLEWEED.SCCMUnleashed.com
```

Similar to the /source: switch, the /mp: switch can be specified multiple times for alternative download locations.

Now that you have seen these three options, you may ask which one is the best. As with all things technical, *it depends*. The authors prefer the /mp: switch for almost all manual installation scenarios. Using this switch means you need access to CCMSetup.exe (and of course a healthy management point). ConfigMgr handles the source file folder, and the files are accessed by the client via HTTP.

Client Push Installation

Enable Client Push Installation to deploy the client agent automatically to those systems discovered and assigned to the site. Before enabling Client Push Installation, it is highly recommended you use the Client Push Installation Wizard for testing individual systems and individual collections. The only configuration difference between Client Push Installation and the Client Push Installation Wizard is the first check box in Figure 12.24. Figure 12.24 shows the General tab of the Client Push Installation Properties dialog box.

FIGURE 12.24   The General tab of the Client Push Installation Properties dialog box

As you can see in Figure 12.24, the Enable Client Push Installation to assigned resources box is checked. When you enable this check box, you can then determine the system types to target. Servers and workstations are enabled by default; domain controllers and site systems are disabled. Click the Accounts tab to configure Client Push Installation accounts, as displayed in Figure 12.25.

FIGURE 12.25   The Accounts tab of the Client Push Installation Properties dialog box

Use the Accounts tab to add accounts to install the ConfigMgr client. To add a local account, simply follow the same pattern shown in Figure 12.25. For the local administrator account, simply enter .**Administrator** and the appropriate password. Enter multiple accounts to ensure you have at least one administrator account for each system you desire to install. To configure installation settings, use the Client tab, as shown in Figure 12.26.

FIGURE 12.26   The Client tab of the Client Push Installation Properties dialog box

By default, the SMSSITECODE public property is visible. You can add Windows Installer command-line properties (see Table 12.3) to configure the client at install time. As an example, to modify the cache size, add the property SMSCACHESIZE=1024, where 1024 is the size (in MB) to configure. The ccm.log file on the site server provides client installation information.

If the site is unable to install the client (because of rights, the system not being on the network, and so on), the site attempts to install the client every hour for 168 hours (1 week). See Microsoft's document on Client Push at http://technet.microsoft.com/en-us/library/bb632380.aspx for additional information. Note that Client Push does not need to be enabled to push clients, as discussed in the next section.

Client Push Installation Wizard

The Client Push Installation Wizard uses the same process as Client Push Installation. The title makes it obvious that the only difference is the wizard itself. It is highly recommended you test deployments using the Client Push Installation Wizard prior to enabling Client Push Installation, because you have more control.

To configure the Client Push Installation Wizard, simply configure the Accounts and Clients tabs (Figures 12.25 and 12.26, respectively). To use the wizard, perform the following steps:

1. Right-click a collection or computer object and then select Install Client.

2. Click Next to continue the Client Push Installation Wizard.

3. Review the following options, as shown in Figure 12.27:

   ▶ **Include domain controllers**—This selection includes domain controllers.

   ▶ **Include only clients in this site's boundaries**—This is a default setting. Clear this check box to install the client on systems discovered but not assigned to this site (clients that are not included in your specified site boundaries).

   ▶ **Include subcollections**—This check box is enabled if you are using the Client Push Installation Wizard to target a collection. Enable this check box to target the current collection and all subcollections.

   ▶ **Always install (repair or upgrade existing client)**—This option allows you to force a reinstallation of the ConfigMgr client. This option also helps when upgrading clients. If you install a new service pack to ConfigMgr, Client Push Installation will not automatically upgrade clients. Use the Client Push Installation Wizard to upgrade clients or send using standard software deployment. The "Client Upgrade" section of this chapter discusses alternatives.

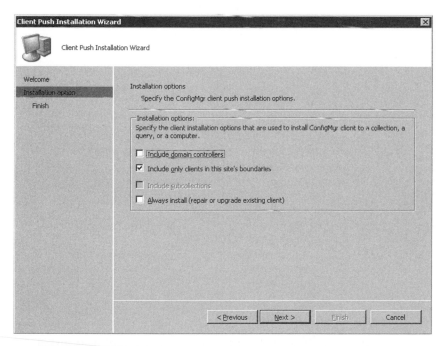

FIGURE 12.27   Client Push Installation Wizard installation options

4. Review the Summary page to confirm that you have targeted the intended collection or computer object, and then click Finish. Review ccm.log on the site server for client installation information.

You can use the Client Push Installation Wizard even after you have enabled Client Push to force a reinstall on a client or multiple clients, or to upgrade clients.

Client Installation in Image Deployment

Pre-installing the ConfigMgr client into an operating system allows you to get your ConfigMgr client up and running as soon as the image is deployed.

NOTE

Use ConfigMgr Operating System Deployment

If you use ConfigMgr to capture and deploy the operating system image, all steps described in this section are automatically performed for you during image capture and restore.

To install the ConfigMgr client, follow the steps described in the "Manual Installation" section of this chapter, and omit the SMSSITECODE property. When the SMSSITECODE property is omitted, the client does not attempt assignment. Delete the SMS section in the Computer Account Certificates Store, displayed in Figure 12.28.

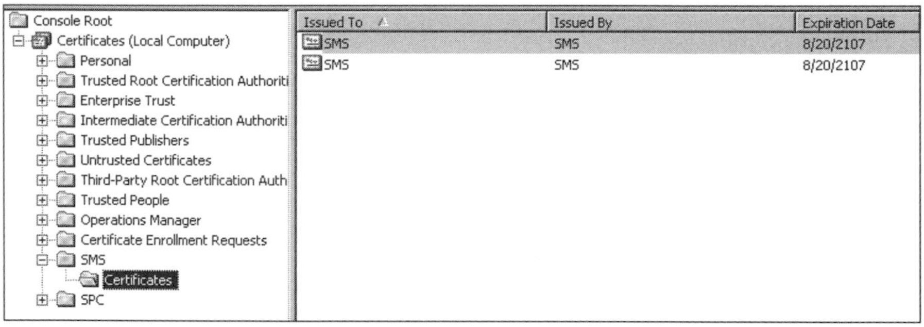

FIGURE 12.28   ConfigMgr client certificates

Microsoft provides additional information for installing ConfigMgr clients using imaging at http://technet.microsoft.com/en-us/library/bb694095.aspx.

Software Update Point Client Installation

You can use group policy and the SUP to install the ConfigMgr client. With this installation method, you are not able to specify Windows Installer properties on the command-line settings, but you can specify the properties using group policy. If you have extended the Active Directory schema, clients will be able to discover their assigned site properly.

A key point to remember with this installation method is that once the ConfigMgr client installation succeeds, it will verify the client is configured to use the correct SUP (according to ConfigMgr Site assignment and site boundaries) and modify it if required. If the deployed group policy configures the client to use a different SUP, the client configuration (of the SUP) will fail and generate errors in the ConfigMgr client logs. See http://technet. microsoft.com/en-us/library/bb633194.aspx for complete details.

Client Uninstall

To uninstall the client, simply run `ccmsetup.exe /uninstall`—you can use ccmsetup.exe in the client installation directory or copy ccmsetup from a site (there is no need to copy the entire installation directory).

You may encounter failures on some corrupted clients (mostly from WMI errors) when attempting to uninstall. In extreme cases, installations may be successful if you use ccmclean.exe from the SMS 2003 Toolkit. Technically, this is not supported on ConfigMgr, but if you have a corrupt client that you cannot reinstall, or uninstall, try using ccmclean.exe.

Client Upgrade

Say you have successfully deployed ConfigMgr, and you have a healthy site. A few months later, you now have a service pack for ConfigMgr. You have successfully upgraded your site(s) to the new service pack, and now you need to upgrade the clients, because clients do not automatically upgrade.

If you have a small, single site, the easiest method to upgrade clients is to use the Client Push Installation Wizard. Simply right-click the desired collection and then select Install Client. Follow the remaining steps in the "Client Push Installation Wizard" section of this chapter, and force a reinstall/upgrade on targeted clients.

A great method to perform this upgrade in larger environments is to use ConfigMgr software distribution (see Chapter 13, "Creating Packages," and Chapter 14, "Distributing Packages," for information on creating and distributing packages). Simply create a package and specify the package source as the ConfigMgr client installation files (by default, %*ProgramFiles*%\Microsoft Configuration Manager\Client). Then send this package to your distribution points. Create a program that executes ccmsetup.exe. Do not specify the SMSSITECODE property, unless you want to change the site code. You can add other Windows Installer properties, such as FSP and the SMSSLP (http://technet.microsoft.com/ en-us/library/bb680980.aspx) to change the current configuration of the existing client. Finally, create an advertisement targeting desired systems.

Using either the Client Push Installation Wizard or traditional software distribution, you will not need to specify a different installation for x86, x64, or IA64. CCMSetup.exe will handle the need to install the appropriate client on the appropriate platform.

Client Patches

A client patch is somewhat different to deploy than a client upgrade:

▶ A client patch may be required when you install a hotfix on the site, or it may even be a client-only patch.

▶ A client upgrade will normally occur when a ConfigMgr service pack is released.

A client patch will typically be a Windows Installer patch (with an .msp extension). To deploy this patch, create a new package and use traditional software distribution methods. A sample command line for Microsoft Knowledge Base article 955955 would be

```
msiexec.exe /P SCCM2007AC-SP1-KB955955-X86.msp /L*v %temp%\SCCM2007AC-SP1-KB955955-
X86.log /q REINSTALL=ALL REINSTALLMODE=mous
```

Although the command line appears as more than one line here, it is actually one line. KB article 955955 at http://support.microsoft.com/kb/955955 provides an example of how to deploy a ConfigMgr client patch.

Client Troubleshooting

ConfigMgr has evolved from the old SMS 1.2 days, where software distribution (using the good old Package Command Manager) and inventory seemed to be the key components of the product. Today, software distribution and inventory are very important, but just part of the full suite. Operating System Deployment, Software Updates management, and DCM are several of the new components of ConfigMgr. Fortunately, the ConfigMgr client has over 30 log files for different client components. Appendix A, "Configuration Manager Log Files," contains detailed information about log files. The next sections discuss general troubleshooting scenarios, online resources (typically the best method for troubleshooting assistance), common issues such as resolving conflicting hardware IDs and dealing with duplicate records, and using the ConfigMgr Toolkit.

General Scenarios

This section discusses several general troubleshooting scenarios. Table 12.4 lists several common issues to help get you started.

TABLE 12.4   Common Client Issues and Suggestions for Solutions

Issue	Comments
ConfigMgr client doesn't have an assigned site.	Launch the Configuration Manager control panel applet, and from the Advanced tab click Discover. If automatic site assignment fails, verify the client is in a designated site boundary and has access to Active Directory (or the SLP, specified during client installation). If you're using AD sites for your site boundaries, verify the AD site includes the client subnet. Review ClientLocation.log and CCMExec.log.
Client unable to download content for software distribution/patch management.	Review execmgr.log, CAS.log, and LocationServices.log for more information from the client. Verify the client should be able to obtain content (local/remote DPs, protected boundaries on site systems, and so on). Also verify content for the package has the correct source version by verifying the source version in package properties. Also, check the distribution points in Package Status to verify package source version and verify that the desired distribution point is targeted and installed for the package source.
Software updates scan failing.	Verify the client's primary site has a valid and healthy software update point. Verify that there is no group policy enforced that specifies the WSUS location (ConfigMgr needs to manage this location). Review WUAHandler.log, ScanAgent.log, UpdatesStore.log, and %windir%\windowsupdate.log.
Software Updates deployment failing.	Verify the client has successfully scanned with the latest catalog (compare the latest content version in ScanAgent.log with the latest content version in wsyncmgr.log on the ConfigMgr site). Clients that have not scanned with the latest content may not see the latest patches. Review UpdatesDeployment.log, WUAHandler.log, UpdatesHandler.log, %windir%\windowsupdate.log, UpdatesStore.log, and execmgr.log.

Online Assistance

The Internet is your best friend for both ConfigMgr documentation and ConfigMgr troubleshooting. Table 12.5 provides some favorite tools and sites for online assistance.

TABLE 12.5   Online Assistance for ConfigMgr Client Troubleshooting

Website/Utility	Comments
myitforum.com	Developed and maintained by Rod Trent, and considered the premier independent site for ConfigMgr assistance.
	Subscribe to blogs at http://www.myitforum.com/cs2/blogs.
	The very popular ConfigMgr email discussion lists can be found at http://www.myitforum.com/lists/. You will learn a lot just by monitoring this list. You can also post your question to some of the best ConfigMgr experts on the planet.
	The Community forums are located at http://www.myitforum.com/forums/. Great forums on System Center products, as well as Windows, VBScript, and more.
	Spend some time on www.myitforum.com to experience many of the other resources, such as myitforum.tv, myitwiki, and more.
Microsoft Configuration Manager Document Library	The ConfigMgr Document Library at http://technet.microsoft.com/en-us/library/bb680651.aspx contains almost the same documentation as the ConfigMgr integrated help (the F1 key in the console). The major difference is that the content online is updated almost every month!
	You can also upgrade the ConfigMgr integrated help using the ConfigMgr 2007 Help File Update Wizard at http://www.microsoft.com/downloads/details.aspx?FamilyID=71816b0f-de06-40e0-bce7-ad4b1e4377bb&displaylang=en.
Troubleshooting ConfigMgr documentation	The troubleshooting documentation at http://technet.microsoft.com/en-us/library/bb632812.aspx can provide a bit of insight into processes and error messages. The Microsoft TechCenter has also recently added a Community Content section on the bottom of each web page that allows you to submit your own content.
Troubleshooting Client Push Installation	Although the document at http://support.microsoft.com/kb/925282 was created for SMS 2003, most of the troubleshooting steps and techniques apply in ConfigMgr also.
System Center Content Search gadget	This gadget allows you to easily search for System Center information because it uses Live Search macros to search specific sites instead of the entire Internet. The gadget is available for download at http://gallery.live.com/LiveItemDetail.aspx?li=49e26ad0-113d-4f3d-a711-57f6530c75d9.
ConfigMgr Toolkit	Use the toolkit to view logs, inspect client policy, and manage Desired Configuration Management baselines. The "ConfigMgr Toolkit" section in this chapter contains additional information about the ConfigMgr Toolkit. Download the current ConfigMgr Toolkit from http://www.microsoft.com/downloads/details.aspx?FamilyID=948e477e-fd3b-4a09-9015-141683c7ad5f&DisplayLang=en (or at www.microsoft.com/downloads, search for **ConfigMgr Toolkit**).

Conflicting Hardware IDs

ConfigMgr creates unique hardware IDs to define unique computers. Based on 10 computer properties (SCSI adapter, processor serial number, MAC address, and so on), a unique hardware ID is created. If a system is reimaged (and no hardware replaced), the hardware ID will be consistent from the previous install to the new install.

When this occurs, ConfigMgr will have two records for the same resource, often called *duplicate hardware IDs*. As discussed in Chapter 8, the Advanced tab of the Site Properties provides the option to create new client records manually or automatically.

ConfigMgr Toolkit

The ConfigMgr Toolkit is available from Microsoft's download center at http://www.microsoft.com/downloads/details.aspx?FamilyID=948e477e-fd3b-4a09-9015-141683c7ad5f&DisplayLang=en (or at www.microsoft.com/downloads, search for **ConfigMgr Toolkit**). It includes seven tools to help you manage and troubleshoot Configuration Manager 2007. Table 12.6 describes these tools.

TABLE 12.6   ConfigMgr Toolkit tools

Tool	Description
Client Spy	Client Spy helps you troubleshoot client issues related to software distribution, inventory, and software metering.
Policy Spy	Policy Spy provides a policy view that helps you review and troubleshoot ConfigMgr client policies.
Trace32	Trace32, introduced in Chapter 3, gives you the ability to view and monitor the log files created and updated by ConfigMgr servers and clients.
Security Configuration Wizard Template (SCW)	Discussed in Chapter 20, the SCW is an attack surface reduction tool for Windows Server 2003 SP 1 and 2. SCW determines the minimum functionality for a server's role(s) and disables any functionality not required.
DCM Model Verification	Discussed in Chapter 16, this tool validates and tests configuration items and baselines authored externally from the ConfigMgr console.
DCM Digest Conversion	This tool converts existing SMS 2003 DCM Solution templates to DCM 2007 configuration items.
DCM Substitution Variables	Used to author configuration items that use chained setting and object discovery.

In troubleshooting ConfigMgr, Trace32 (also known as SMS Trace) will be your best friend. You may be used to reading log files using Windows Notepad or another log reader such as Tail. For ConfigMgr, nothing beats Trace32. In addition to being customized to read ConfigMgr logs, it allows you to view those logs in real time, meaning as ConfigMgr writes new data to the log, the data will appear in Trace32. You can open log files using Trace32 on both local and remote systems. Figure 12.29 shows Trace32 viewing the execmgr.log log file.

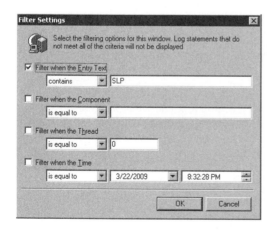

Log Text	Component
CExecutionManager::HandleMessage received message: '<?xml version="1.0' ?>▥<SoftwareDeploymentMessage MessageT₃	execmgr
Received creation notification for user 'S-1-5-18'.	execmgr
OnPolicyActivation package GCS0025E program Install	execmgr
Policy arrived for parent package GCS0025E program Install	execmgr
Raising event:▥[SMS_CodePage(437), SMS_LocaleID(1033)]▥instance of SoftDistProgramOfferReceivedEvent▥{▥Advertiser	execmgr
In CExecutionManager::Notify	execmgr
Policy is updated for Program: install, Package: GCS000BB, Advert: GCS20091	execmgr
In CExecutionManager::Notify	execmgr
Policy is updated for Program: Install, Package: GCS001BB, Advert: GCS201B8	execmgr
In CExecutionManager::Notify	execmgr
Policy is updated for Program: Install, Package: GCS001C8, Advert: GCS201F1	execmgr
In CExecutionManager::Notify	execmgr
Policy is updated for Program: Install, Package: GCS0008C, Advert: GCS201AE	execmgr
In CExecutionManager::Notify	execmgr
Received creation notification for user 'S-1-5-18'.	execmgr
Policy arrived for child program Qfiniti 3.5 with Patch 5	execmgr
In CExecutionManager::Notify	execmgr
Policy is updated for Program: Qfiniti 3.5 with Patch 5 and Hotfixes, Package: GCS0008C, Advert: GCS201AE	execmgr

FIGURE 12.29   Viewing execmgr.log from Trace32 (a.k.a. SMS Trace)

If you have viewed sitecomp.log using Notepad, you will see a significant difference in human readability with Trace32. Trace32 is configured to automatically parse date/time stamps as well as format the data to make it easier for the administrator to view. By default, Trace32 highlights keywords such as *Error* and *Warning*. You can also define additional keywords to highlight. Figure 12.30 shows the Filter feature.

Filter Settings

Select the filtering options for this window. Log statements that do not meet all of the criteria will not be displayed

☑ Filter when the Entry Text
[contains ▾] [SLP]

☐ Filter when the Component
[is equal to ▾] [ ]

☐ Filter when the Thread
[is equal to ▾] [0]

☐ Filter when the Time
[is equal to ▾] [3/22/2009 ▾] [8:32:28 PM ⬍]

[OK]   [Cancel]

FIGURE 12.30   Filtering content using Trace32

Filter (from the Tools option) allows you to customize the view to see only specific words or phrases, and even a specific date/time. You can also open multiple log files in one view, which may help you see the bigger picture when troubleshooting.

Also from the Tools option, you will find Error Lookup. Error Lookup prompts you to enter a Windows error message, and it displays the description for that error. As an example, entering error number 32 displays "The process cannot access the file because it is being used by another process." Spend some time with Trace32 and the reference documentation located in ConfigMgr Toolkit help.

Clispy, the SMS Advanced Client Troubleshooting Tool and part of the Toolkit, is another great tool for troubleshooting client issues. Clispy allows you to view the following for both the current computer and remote computers:

▶ Software distribution execution requests.

▶ Software distribution history. (Quickly see success or failure for software distribution.)

▶ Software distribution cache information. (Monitor items currently in a download state, items in the local ConfigMgr cache, and cache size.)

▶ Software distribution pending executions.

Use Policy Spy to view ConfigMgr client policy on either a local or a remote computer. As shown in Figure 12.31, you can view machine policy as well as user policy.

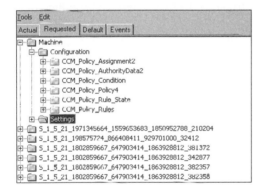

FIGURE 12.31   Policy Spy from the ConfigMgr Toolkit

Policy Spy allows you to view the complete policy, as downloaded from the client's management point. It also allows you to delete policy instances as well as reset policy (which basically removes all nondefault client policy and then queries the management point for all assigned policies). Check the ConfigMgr Toolkit documentation for more information.

General Troubleshooting Information

Many techs will uninstall and reinstall the ConfigMgr client at the first sign of trouble. It is really best to avoid this process, because it is often more time consuming and does not always solve the problem. Software Updates is a great example. Just because patches are failing to install does not mean that the client is corrupt—it could be that the Automatic Updates agent is not working properly. Before uninstalling the client, perform some basic tests to determine what is working, if anything. Here are several basic functionality tests to try, which may help you narrow the scope of the problem at hand.

▶ **Try to install software**—This is easiest if you are using Run Advertised Programs, because you can simply launch a test installation to see if it works. By performing this test, you can confirm that the client is talking to its management point and is able to obtain content as well as install software.

▶ **Try the same task on another computer in the same locale**—It is very important to see if the reported issue is isolated to one computer. One of the easiest ways to confirm this is to verify whether the problem exists on a different computer. Be sure to test using the same environment (same operating system, same IP subnet, even the same logged-on user if possible).

▶ **Check to see if other components are working**—Hardware and software inventory, as well as Discovery Data Manager (Heartbeat Discovery), are components that hardly encounter issues. Use the Configuration Manager control panel applet to launch one (or all) of these actions, and monitor InventoryAgent.log to verify success.

▶ **Rediscover the client**—From the Configuration Manager control panel applet, on the Advanced tab, click the Discover button to rediscover the client to its assigned site. If the client successfully assigns to a site, it successfully queried Active Directory (or its SLP) and is in a valid set of site boundaries.

Spend some time troubleshooting clients, and read the client logs carefully. The logs are very detailed, and usually help you determine the root cause of the problem.

The ConfigMgr Client Agent

Access the Configuration Manager applet from the control panel (on x64 systems, look in a subfolder for x86 control panel icons). Table 12.7 describes each of the tabs in the Configuration Manager control panel applet, also called the Configuration Manager Properties dialog box. (All log files mentioned in Table 12.7 are located on the ConfigMgr client.)

TABLE 12.7   Configuration Manager Properties Dialog Box

Tab	Description
General	Displays discovery information for the client. Includes information such as Active Directory site name, ConfigMgr site code, IP address and subnet, management point, and more. This information can prove very helpful when troubleshooting client issues.
Components	Displays each component of the ConfigMgr client agent, with the version. The status column will show all components as installed, and depending on client agent configuration, some components will be enabled. Click the Repair button (requires administrative rights) to force the client to reinstall using the local installation source.

TABLE 12.7   Configuration Manager Properties Dialog Box

Tab	Description
Actions	Client actions occur on a predefined schedule (some by the administrator with client agent configuration, and others defined internally by ConfigMgr). Simply highlight the action and then click Initiate Action to execute the action. Here is a brief description of each action:
	Branch Distribution Point Maintenance Task—This task verifies pre-staged packages and downloads additional packages that are targeted for the distribution point. More information is available at http://technet.microsoft.com/en-us/library/bb681046.aspx. Watch PeerDPAgent.log for details.
	Discovery Data Collection Cycle—Forces the client to forward discovery data (the same as Heartbeat Discovery data) to the client's management point. Watch InventoryAgent.log for details.
	File Collection Cycle—Watch InventoryAgent.log for details.
	Hardware Inventory Cycle—Watch InventoryAgent.log for details.
	Machine Policy Retrieval & Evaluation Cycle—Also often referred to as the *polling interval* for the client. Queries the management point for new/updated policy assignments that target computers. Watch PolicyAgent.log and PolicyEvaluator.log for details.
	Software Inventory Cycle—Watch InventoryAgent.log for details.
	Software Metering Usage Report Cycle—Gathers software metering information from the client and forwards it to the management point. Watch SWMTRReportGen.log and mtrmgr.log for details.
	Software Updates Deployment Evaluation Cycle—Triggers the client to evaluate all targeted deployments for software updates. Watch UpdatesDeployment.log, WUAHandler.Log, UpdatesHandler.log, and UpdatesStore.log for details.
	Software Updates Scan Cycle—Triggers the client to run a new scan for software updates. Watch ScanAgent.log, WUAHAndler.log, UpdatesHandler.log, and UpdatesStore.log for details.
	User Policy Retrieval & Evaluation Cycle—Similar to Machine Policy Retrieval and Evaluation Cycle, but queries the management point for new/updated policy assignments that target users and user groups. Watch PolicyAgent.log and PolicyEvaluator.log for details.
	Windows Installer Source List Update Cycle—Manages the source list for self-healing of Windows Installer–based applications. Watch SrcUpdateMgr.log for details. View http://technet.microsoft.com/en-us/library/bb892810.aspx for more details.
Advanced	Click the Discover button to force the client to rediscover its assigned site. View ClientLocation.log for details. You can also specify the DNS suffix for site assignment (if required for your environment), as well as modify the Temporary Program Download folder (also known as *client cache*).
Updates	You can configure Software Updates to install at a time more convenient for you, provided your desired time occurs before a deadline for installing software updates.

12

TABLE 12.7   Configuration Manager Properties Dialog Box

Tab	Description
Configurations	Displays DCM baselines applicable to this system. You can click Evaluate to reevaluate the baseline. You can also view the DCM report if you are an administrator on the computer.
Internet	If the client is communicating in native mode, the Internet tab appears and is configurable. Specify the Internet-based management point (using FQDN) and any required proxy information required for communication.

Out of Band Management

Out of Band (OOB) Management allows you to remotely connect to and manage a system when the operating system is corrupt or when the system is powered off or in a sleep or hibernate mode. In-band management involves managing a system as you have with ConfigMgr 2007 and SMS 2003—that is, managing a system through the Windows operating system. With Out of Band Management, you can even manage the ConfigMgr system when the hard drive has failed. Think of Out of Band Management as giving you the opportunity to troubleshoot (and hopefully resolve) a problem without sending a person onsite to fix it. Here is a list of basic functions you can perform using the OOB service point:

▶ Powering on one or many computers (for example, to apply security patches during off-peak business hours)

▶ Powering off one or many computers

▶ Restarting a computer into PXE or from a boot image file, to reimage a computer

▶ Reconfiguring BIOS settings

▶ Configuring advertisements and Software Updates to use Wake On LAN to wake up systems to apply patches

Microsoft's article at http://technet.microsoft.com/en-us/library/cc161944.aspx lists additional scenarios for using Out of Band Management.

Chapter 8 describes how to enable the OOB service point. To learn how to discover and provision systems using OOB Management, the document at http://technet.microsoft.com/en-us/library/cc161963.aspx, provides a great overview.

Fallback Status Point

If you have an FSP in your environment and specify an FSP during client installation, you can use ConfigMgr Web Reporting to view the status of client installation in your environment. Use the following reports to review client installation received from the fallback status point:

▶ Client Assignment Detailed Status Report

- ▶ Client Assignment Failure Details

- ▶ Client Assignment Status Details

- ▶ Client Assignment Success Details

- ▶ Client Deployment Failure Report

- ▶ Client Deployment Status Details

- ▶ Client Deployment Success Report

Additional information about the fallback status point is available at http://technet. microsoft.com/en-us/library/bb694178.aspx and in Chapter 2.

Client Approval

Another new feature in ConfigMgr 2007 is client approval. If your ConfigMgr site is configured in mixed mode, all clients must be approved to communicate with the assigned site. A client will successfully install and assign to a ConfigMgr site, but client approval must occur before a client can obtain content from the site. You can manually approve clients (the most secure), automatically approve all clients (the least secure), or automatically approve all clients in the trusted domain (somewhere in between the most and least secure).

Summary

This chapter described how to configure the management point, configure client agents, and customize hardware inventory. You also learned how to discover clients, install the client agent, and perform basic client troubleshooting.

Remember that when you enable Client Push Installation, automatic installation occurs on every system assigned to your site. Before enabling Client Push Installation, use the Client Push Installation Wizard to test against single clients, and use small collections to verify your push installation settings are configured properly.

CHAPTER 13

Creating Packages

One of the challenges of client/server administration is managing the software deployed to those systems. The ability to manage software includes

▶ Deploying software as required on workstations, servers, and Windows mobile devices;

▶ Updating existing software packages;

▶ Providing a comprehensive inventory of installed software packages;

▶ Removing software from systems where it does not belong.

These topics are discussed throughout the chapters of *System Center Configuration Manager 2007 Unleashed*. The first item in the list—software distribution—has been a core component of Systems Management Server (SMS) since Microsoft first released the product in 1994. This functionality has evolved over the various versions of SMS, and it continues as a core capability in Microsoft's newest release of the software, System Center Configuration Manager (ConfigMgr) 2007. However, before deploying, updating, inventorying, or removing software, you will most likely need to package it for use by ConfigMgr. Software packaging is a core component of distributing software in ConfigMgr.

This chapter discusses how software packaging works in ConfigMgr 2007 and provides examples of how to package software with ConfigMgr. Chapter 14, "Distributing Packages," continues the process by taking the packages created in this chapter and discussing their deployment.

The Case for ConfigMgr Software Packaging

In general, packages are used to install software on systems. You can also use packages to execute just a command on a system, without installing any software. If you go back far enough into the history of Windows systems, there was a time when the IT (Information Technology) staff simply used batch scripts and executable files to install software.

Real World: What About Removing Software?

The focus on software installation presents an interesting challenge—did software technicians and system administrators consider how to remove that installed software from a system? Initially, software packages tended to be inconsistent in their uninstallation methods; and in some cases, you could not uninstall them.

Software packaging has evolved such that the majority of installations are now performed using an MSI (Microsoft Installer Package) file. Using MSIs provide a more consistent installation (and uninstallation) experience and is the current industry standard.

You may be thinking, "Why do I have to package software within ConfigMgr? I already have a software package (it may even be an MSI file). Why must I repackage it to distribute it in Configuration Manager 2007?" Realize that ConfigMgr is not so much packaging software as it is *preparing* software for distribution. The packages, programs, and advertisements in ConfigMgr are designed to utilize existing packaging, or work with unpackaged software applications by directly executing an EXE or other file type—much like you might see on a raw CD or DVD. The reason one packages software in ConfigMgr is that software companies design commercial software packages for manual installation by the individual purchasing the software, and the installation process expects users to respond to configuration questions. In contrast, ConfigMgr packages are typically used with unattended installations. With Configuration Manager, you are not really repackaging the application—you are using the existing software package to automate its usage by ConfigMgr.

As an example, if you install WinZip (available at www.winzip.com), its setup program asks questions regarding preferences to install the software on a particular system. When you automate the software installation process, a fully automated WinZip software package will not prompt users with questions about how they want something installed. Instead, you must determine in advance how to install the application on all your systems.

ConfigMgr is flexible in its options for deploying software packaging. ConfigMgr 2007 provides the ability to install on a per-system or per-user basis and can also prompt the user for information or provide fully silent software installations. Although Configuration Manager can provide installations designed for user interaction, its real power in this area is its ability to deploy software silently, without any user interaction required.

Advantages of ConfigMgr software packaging include the following:

▶ Automated deployment

▶ Consistency

- ▶ Targeted deployments

- ▶ The capability to automate software removal

- ▶ Reusability

The next sections discuss these benefits.

Automated Deployment

Software deployments in Configuration Manager are typically designed for installation without user intervention, although ConfigMgr can deploy software requiring user intervention if that is necessary. Using an automated approach enables a quicker and more efficient software installation, and permits an unattended installation without the user logged in to the system. Automating software installation is one of the major benefits of using ConfigMgr to deploy software.

Consistency

Automating a software deployment includes selecting installation options in advance. Using the WinZip installation as an illustration, there is a series of questions asked during setup—from accepting a license agreement to the location to install the program. WinZip also asks whether to use the classic or wizard interface.

Packaging software with Configuration Manager lets you define how to install the software such that it will be consistent throughout your environment. As an example, ConfigMgr-installed software will use a particular directory and a specific configuration. This makes it quicker to find the program, and easier for the users (and helpdesk personnel) because there is a consistent experience with the application regardless of the particular desktop.

Consistency in software deployments also increases the uniformity of data in the reports available with Configuration Manager 2007. ConfigMgr includes software inventory functionality and reports on your installed software. (Chapter 18, "Reporting," describes the many reports available using Configuration Manager 2007.) Performing software deployments with ConfigMgr simplifies the process to provide a consistent version of that software throughout your organization. Without standard deployments, if you use software such as Adobe Reader and let users download and install it on their own, you may have several different versions to support.

Targeted Deployment

Using ConfigMgr 2007 lets you choose which systems or users will receive what software. Configuration Manager automates software deployment to these specified groups of systems or users. This capability, known as *targeting*, helps you meet the particular deployment requirements of your organization. As an example, you can target one configuration for an application to one group and a different configuration of that application to another group. This targeted approach to deployment provides increased flexibility while maintaining the ability to deploy software in an automated method.

Software Removal

An often overlooked benefit of using ConfigMgr for software packaging is the ability to automate uninstalling those software packages. An instance where this would be beneficial is a software package with a specified timeframe of when it should be available and when it needs to be removed. This might be a software package licensed only for 1 year.

Another advantage to automated software removal is the ability to deal with unwanted software. If ConfigMgr, using its software inventory functionality, determines a nonsupported software package is residing on a system, you can define a process to uninstall that software. As an example, assume your organization does not permit installing peer-to-peer (P2P) file-sharing software on the network. The general approach to shutting down these types of software packages is to block them at the network level. If that is not viable, you can use ConfigMgr to automate the process of uninstalling these software packages when found on a system. You can remove the software by using a program in a software package that performs the removal. For applications installed using MSI files, software can be removed using a program defined in the MSI package. For those applications without a predefined software removal command line, you would need to create an uninstall program to uninstall the application. This also provides a good alternative approach to controlling P2P software, in addition to blocking those applications on the network layer.

Software Package Reuse

Packages created with Configuration Manager are reusable. As an example, if you create a software package for a single location in a company, you can use that same package for other locations in the company—without having to deploy the software manually. You can also configure software packages for use with other ConfigMgr technologies such as Operating System Deployment (OSD). Chapter 19, "Operating System Deployment," discusses OSD in more detail. At a high level, the OSD function deploys operating systems through ConfigMgr. You can also take software packages created with Configuration Manager to use in the post-deployment tasks of an OSD deployment.

Comparing GPO-based Software Distribution to ConfigMgr Software Distribution

Active Directory provides a significant amount of functionality through group policy, including the ability to distribute software. A commonly asked question by organizations using group policy for software deployment is, What are the benefits in using ConfigMgr for software distribution versus using group policy?

Several functions are more robust with ConfigMgr software distribution:

▶ **More granular targeting**—Group policy enables targeting software distribution to specific sites, domains, and Organizational Units (OUs). You can further target this software by filtering it to Active Directory security groups.

ConfigMgr can be even more granular in its targeting by using collections, which can also use queries. The "About Packages, Programs, Collections, Distribution Points, and Advertisements" section of this chapter discusses collections.

Software Distribution with Collections Versus Group Policy

It is easy to say using collections provides more granular targeting, but how specifically is targeting more granular with collections instead of using software distribution through group policy?

For starters, what type of targeting can you do with group policy? Although you can define a group policy to apply to many different areas, in terms of software distribution and targeting, the policy typically is applied at an OU level. Software distributed through group policy can be either assigned (mandatory) or published (available for installation). An OU can contain either users or computers. This provides an effective way to distribute software to a specific targeted set of computers or users. Sounds powerful, doesn't it?

Okay, so what's different from that with ConfigMgr? For starters, think about what a collection is and how it is used. A collection is a custom grouping of systems (or a grouping of users) based on criteria you define. To match group policy, you can actually create a collection based on an Organizational Unit. You can also define a collection based on the name of a server (or use wildcards), or a system that has a particular software package installed on it, or a system without a particular software package installed. You can define collections based on hardware—does it have adequate free disk space? Does it meet the processor or operating system requirements to allow installation of the program?

The real power of ConfigMgr targeting is in the definition of a collection. You can define a collection based on just about any information gathered by ConfigMgr, which is extremely diverse. This includes software inventory, hardware inventory, information in Active Directory Users or Computers, and even custom information such as the existence of a particular Registry key!

You can also use collections to schedule when software is deployed, based on maintenance windows defined for the collection. ConfigMgr can even control when to reboot systems after deploying software that requires a reboot.

Consider a client environment with collections built based on a custom Registry key containing the criticality level (tier) of the server, which is then used to define a collection used as part of defining maintenance periods. This means that with a collection you can target anything you can target with a group policy object, and go far beyond that based on what is necessary for a particular environment.

▶ **Better tracking**—Although group policy allows you to check software distributed with a variety of tools, including the RSoP (Resultant Set of Policy), tracking deployed software is somewhat limited. Using ConfigMgr, you can easily track the status of the software being deployed using either the system status within the ConfigMgr console (see Chapter 17, "Configuration Manager Queries," for more information) or ConfigMgr's integrated reporting components (discussed in Chapter 18.)

▶ **Network impact**—Group policy software distribution occurs at system startup or user logon, thus increasing the likelihood that multiple software packages are deployed within a site at the same time. ConfigMgr can schedule software for deployment in a variety of methods, and use BITS (Background Intelligent Transfer Service), fan-out distribution, and compression between sites. These capabilities minimize the impact of software distribution and reduce bandwidth requirements.

▶ **Robust packaging options**—Software distribution using group policy is generally restricted to MSI software packages. You can deploy non-MSI files with group policy, but they are deployed as voluntary applications—rather than mandatory software distributed to the user. ConfigMgr provides the ability to install any software format, including MSIs, EXE files, batch scripts, Visual Basic (VB) scripts, and others. You can even create a package that just executes a set of command lines.

If you currently use group policy to distribute software, how do you migrate to ConfigMgr for your software distribution requirements? The following steps are suggested:

1. Package in ConfigMgr distribution format the software currently deployed through group policy. The majority of software deployed via GPOs uses an MSI file, which easily integrates with ConfigMgr (see the "Creating a Package" section for examples).

2. Target the software, pushing it only to those systems or users that were targets of the GPO software distribution. (Targeting is accomplished using collections, discussed in the "About Packages, Programs, Collections, Distribution Points, and Advertisements" section of this chapter.)

3. Once the functionality provided with GPO software distribution is available using ConfigMgr software distribution, shut down your GPO software distribution functionality.

About Packages, Programs, Collections, Distribution Points, and Advertisements

Having discussed software packaging in ConfigMgr, compared it with software packaging outside ConfigMgr, and compared ConfigMgr software distribution with GPO-based software distribution, it is now time to begin delving into how ConfigMgr works. Let's start with discussing some of the key terms and how these capabilities interact with each other. The next sections discuss packages, programs, collections, distribution points, and advertisements.

Packages

A software *package* consists of general information about the software to deploy, including the name, version, manufacturer, language, and where source files for the package are located (if that package has source files). Packages are created either from a package definition file (such as an MSI, SMS, or PDF file—discussed in more detail later in the "Creating a Package" section) or manually. Software packages within ConfigMgr are not actually a repackaging of the software packaged by a vendor. ConfigMgr will have the same source files used to install the software, but uses MSI files to auto-populate many of the questions required when creating packages and programs within ConfigMgr. You can also create software packages without using package definition files. ConfigMgr provides the ability to deploy executables, batch files, VBScript, JavaScript, and command files, among others. If you can execute it, you can design a package to deploy it!

A package optionally includes programs, which provide the specifics of how the software runs. The package also contains information about who can access it (security) and where it is distributed (distribution points).

ConfigMgr uses packages to distribute software, as well as to deploy changes to client configurations, such as Registry changes.

Programs

A package contains *programs*. These are commands specifying what should occur on a client when the package is received. A program can do just about anything—it can install software, distribute data, run antivirus software, or update the client configuration.

Each package must contain at least one program if the package will perform any action other than to provide a pointer to the source files. Most MSI files provide six default programs when used for software distribution, each allowing the package to run in different ways:

- ▶ **Per-system attended**—This installation causes a program to install, expects user interaction, and is run once for the system on which it is targeted to install.

- ▶ **Per-system unattended**—This installation causes a program to install that expects to run without user interaction and is run once for the system on which it is targeted to install.

- ▶ **Per-system uninstall**—This installation performs an uninstallation of the program, and is run once for the system on which it is targeted to uninstall.

- ▶ **Per-user attended**—This installation causes a program to install and expects user interaction, and is run once for the user for whom it is targeted to install.

- ▶ **Per-user unattended**—This installation causes a program to install without user interaction, and runs once for the user for whom it is targeted to install.

13

▶ **Per-user uninstall**—This installation performs an uninstallation of the program, and is run once for the user for whom it is targeted to uninstall.

Each program specifies the command-line used to run the program in the method described. As an example, a per-system unattended installation will include a switch to run the program without user intervention.

Collections

A *collection* represents resources within ConfigMgr. A collection is a logical grouping and can consist of computers, users, or security groups. Collections provide a target for ConfigMgr functions such as software distribution (see the sidebar on "Software Distribution with Collections Versus Group Policy" for additional information on the types of targeting available using collections in ConfigMgr). Collections can be either *static* (defined to specific resources) or *dynamic* (either built on a query you define or an existing query that comes prebuilt with ConfigMgr). The next two sections discuss these collection types.

Static Collections

You define static collections by manually adding a resource to a collection. An example of a static collection is a group of test workstations used to test software package deployments. As an example, the Test Workstations collection has TestWS1, TestWS2, and TestWS3 manually added to it. Static collections are useful when you need to define a limited number of systems or users to a collection and the membership in the collection does not change frequently. Membership is fixed (static) without manual changes.

Dynamic Collections

You define dynamic collections by using a query-based membership in the collection. You can achieve the same result as with the Test Workstations static collection (see the previous section) by defining a rule to add any workstations to the collection using names starting with **TestWS**. This assumes that only test workstations are named with the test workstation naming convention (such as TestWS4). The benefit to a dynamic collection is it does not require manual changes to add resources to the collection. Let's say you define a Test Workstations dynamic collection that adds all workstations starting with the name TestWS. If additional test workstations are created later, those new workstations will automatically become part of the Test Workstations collection.

Distribution Points

A *distribution point (DP)* is a ConfigMgr server role where packages are stored for later distribution, making it similar in nature to a file share containing software used for installations. The location of distribution points can be significant in terms of network impact.

As an example, if you create a package to install Microsoft Office (which is a very large software package), you would not want it to install the software from a distribution point across a wide area network (WAN) link, due to the effect on network traffic across that link. Generally, you would prefer to use a local distribution point with access to the software you want to install. To help with WAN link utilization, ConfigMgr can use BITS to transfer large amounts of data across networks, including WAN links, as discussed in Chapter 5, "Network Design." However, it is best to provide a local distribution point for any location where multiple clients will access software packages. BITS is only available for communication between the distribution point to the client. Branch distribution points only use SMB; they do not use BITS to communicate to the client.

You can arrange DPs in a manner to help simplify their management—an example of this is gathering all distribution points in the United States into a single group and those in Europe into another group. This capability gives ConfigMgr administrators the ability to group distribution points geographically or by department, or use any other method that enables easily adding or removing packages from large numbers of DPs in a timely manner.

You can configure distribution points to support various functions. One example is a *protected distribution point*, which allows ConfigMgr administrators to restrict which clients can connect to the DP from specified AD sites or subnets. Using protected distribution points ensures clients do not access content on a distribution point over a slow link.

Advertisements

An *advertisement* ties these concepts together. An advertisement says to take a specific program within a package and make it available to a collection previously defined, and it specifies the distribution point(s) to use when deploying the program. Advertisements are either voluntary (they show as available for the user to install) or mandatory.

How These Combine

Consider a package containing multiple programs. That package is sent to a distribution point and advertised to a collection. Although this looks like a relatively complex way to distribute software, it is also a very powerful approach. Let's break this down into a simple example of how these concepts work together.

You need to distribute an application called MyApp to the HR department this week. Perform the following steps:

1. Create a package for the application and then create an unattended installation and (optionally, but recommended) an uninstallation program within the package.
2. Define a collection of the workstations used by the HR department personnel.

   The users of the HR application are all located in the corporate office, which has a single distribution point used when distributing software from Configuration Manager.
3. Create an advertisement that ties this all together. Figure 13.1 displays the advertisement. The advertisement ties the package and the program (MyApp unattended installation) to the collection (the HR workstations) and the distribution point used for installing the software (corporate distribution point).

Knowing how these concepts combine is critical for understanding how Configuration Manager deploys software. Chapter 14 provides additional information on how ConfigMgr distributes software.

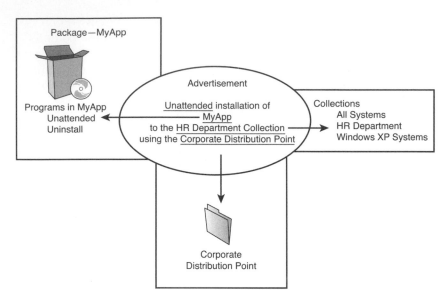

FIGURE 13.1   Combining packages, programs, advertisements, distribution points, and collections

Creating a Package

Because the focus of this chapter is software packaging, the next sections walk through the steps to create a package in ConfigMgr and provide examples of the process.

Packages can come in many flavors:

▶ Packages that use a definition file.

You can create ConfigMgr packages either with a definition file or without. A *definition file* provides the answers to the majority of the questions required to create a package.

SMS 1.x definition files had an extension of PDF (Package Definition File). With SMS 2.0, you created the definitions in files using either a PDF or SMS (Systems Management Server) extension. Although these two types of definition files still exist, and you can use them with ConfigMgr to create a package, they are relatively uncommon now.

The package definition file most commonly used by ConfigMgr 2007 is the MSI file. The "OpsMgr Client" section of this chapter includes an example of using an MSI file.

▶ Packages that you can create without a definition file, discussed in detail in the "Forefront Client" section.

▶ A package that does not even need to have source files as part of the package.

This is often used when ConfigMgr is used to run a program already stored on the system, such as the automated uninstall of the ConfigMgr client.

TIP

Remotely Uninstall ConfigMgr Agent Using PsTools

If you are looking for a quick way to uninstall the Configuration Manager agent from a remote system, try this:

```
Psexec \\<computer> -u <domain\user>
➥c:\windows\system32\ccmsetup\ccmsetup.exe /uninstall
```

A successful result is shown here:

```
C:\windows\system32\ccmsetup\ccmsetup.exe exited on (computer)
➥with error code 0.
```

PsExec is part of the SysInternal PsTools, available for download at http://technet.microsoft.com/en-us/sysinternals/bb896649.aspx. These can be invaluable when performing actions on remote systems.

The goal remains the same, regardless of how it is achieved. ConfigMgr takes these different types of packages and integrates them to create Configuration Manager packages. To illustrate how this is accomplished, the next sections step through an example using a relatively simple package to deploy that's utilized by many ConfigMgr installations—the Operations Manager (OpsMgr) 2007 client.

OpsMgr Client

Operations Manager 2007 is another member of the System Center product family. It monitors the health of applications, servers, and services. OpsMgr requires an agent installation process, which can be accomplished using ConfigMgr. The next sections discuss this process.

Using the Create Package from Definition Wizard

Creating the ConfigMgr package for Operations Manager is straightforward and requires only a few steps:

1. Locate the installation files for the OpsMgr agent installation. These are the *installation source files*.

   For this example, a share named *source* is on the D: drive of the Bluebonnet server with a subfolder named *OpsMgr*. The OpsMgr agent software was previously copied to this folder (D:\source\OpsMgr) from the OpsMgr installation media.

NOTE

Installation Source File Locations

Two different lines of thought exist for where installation files should be stored. The first is to store them on an existing network share such as a distributed file server (DFS) so they will be consistently located on the network, with only a single copy of the installation source files required. The second approach is to place copies of the files in a folder on the ConfigMgr server itself.

It is best to use a folder on the ConfigMgr site server because other individuals may rearrange and potentially remove files on a network share without realizing the impact on the ConfigMgr software packaging process. Using a dedicated folder prevents someone from inadvertently moving, changing, or deleting those installation files required for ConfigMgr.

2. Within the Configuration Manager console, navigate to System Center Configuration Manager -> Site Database -> Computer Management -> Software Distribution -> Packages.

3. Right-click Packages and choose New -> Package from Definition. This starts the Create Package from Definition Wizard shown in Figure 13.2. Click Next to continue.

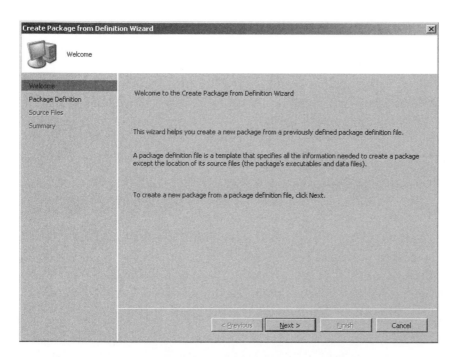

FIGURE 13.2   Create Package from Definition Wizard's Welcome screen

4. ConfigMgr displays the existing package definitions it is aware of (see Figure 13.3). Click the Browse button (circled in Figure 13.3) to locate the package definition file. For this example, create the package from a definition file by pointing it to MOMAgent.msi for the i386 version of the OpsMgr agent. This file was located on the ConfigMgr server in the d:\source\OpsMgr\agent\i386 folder.

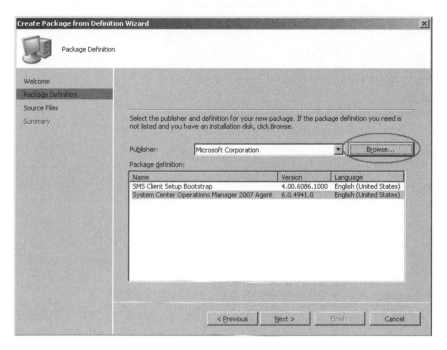

FIGURE 13.3   Defining the package as part of the Create Package from Definition Wizard

5. After you select the MSI file, it appears on the screen previously shown in Figure 13.3, which now displays the System Center Operations Manager 2007 agent. Figure 13.4 shows this screen. Click Next to continue.

6. The next page of the wizard identifies three different ways you can manage source files:

   ▶ **This package does not contain any source files**—This may be useful in a configuration where ConfigMgr is running a program already stored on the system.

   ▶ **Always obtain files from a source directory**—This option is the one most commonly used.

   ▶ **Create a compressed version of the source files**—This may be useful when you need to decrease storage requirements.

   Select the second option for this package—Always obtain files from a source directory—as shown in Figure 13.5. Click Next to continue.

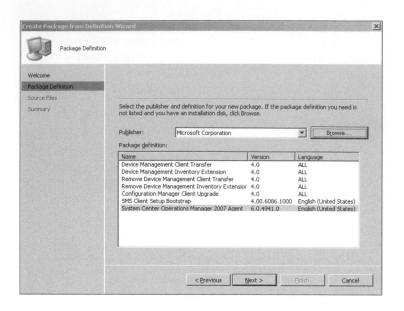

FIGURE 13.4   OpsMgr agent listed in the Create Package from Definition Wizard

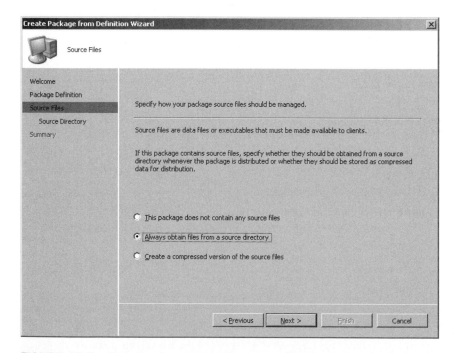

FIGURE 13.5   Choosing how to manage source files in the Create Package from Definition Wizard

> **NOTE**
>
> **Using Source File Compression**
>
> The Create Package from Definition Wizard includes a source files option to create a compressed version of the source files, as displayed in Figure 13.5. Compression is particularly helpful in environments where it is important to decrease storage requirements. Compressed packages are also useful for CD installs, because the source files may not be available after creating the package. It is important to note that compressed source files must be stored on NTFS file systems (not FAT).
>
> You should not use compressed source files if the source files are likely to change or if there's not a significant decrease in the size of the package from compressing it.

7. The wizard next verifies the location of the source files. This step appears if the option selected on the previous page of the wizard specified source files were part of the package—if the package did not contain any source files, this screen does not appear.

   The wizard defaults to the option Local drive on site server, which is the location of the source files and folder where you chose the package definition file (in this case the MOMAgent.msi file specified in step 4 of this process). This is shown in Figure 13.6. Click Next to continue.

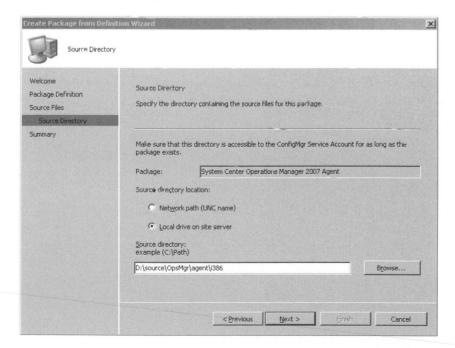

FIGURE 13.6   Source directory in the Create Package from Definition Wizard

8. The Summary page is the final screen of the Create Package from Definition Wizard (see Figure 13.7). It lists the options chosen to create the package. These include the name of the package, how to handle source files, and the location of the source directory. Click Finish to complete the Create Package from Definition Wizard.

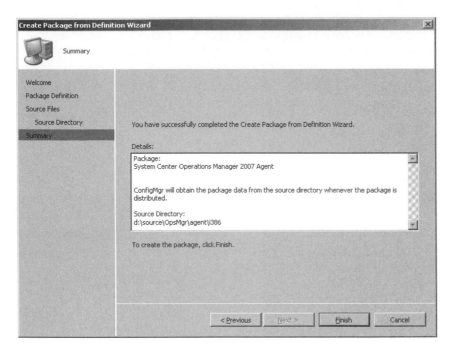

FIGURE 13.7   Summary of the Create Package from Definition Wizard

9. Using the information in the MSI file, the wizard now creates a set of installation options for the program, including Per-system attended, Per-system unattended, Per-system uninstall, Per-user attended, Per-user unattended, and Per-user uninstall, as displayed in Figure 13.8.

Using an MSI file for the package definition greatly simplifies the process of creating the OpsMgr package, because the MSI supplies the information that otherwise would have to be manually specified to Configuration Manager.

With the package created, the next step is configuring the program the package will use. In the case of the OpsMgr agent, this is the Per-system unattended program. The Per-system unattended program deploys the OpsMgr package on a per-system basis and runs without user intervention. Right-click the program (located in the Configuration Manager console -> Site Database -> Software Distribution -> Packages -> <name of the package that was created> (in this case Microsoft Corporation System Center Operations Manager 2007 Agent)) and open the Properties page.

Properties for each program include the following tabs:

▶ General

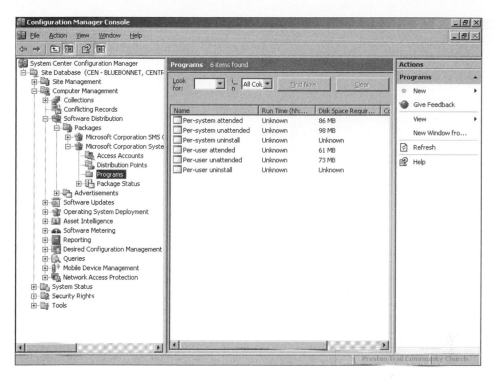

FIGURE 13.8   Programs created as part of the OpsMgr agent package creation process

- ▶ Requirements
- ▶ Environment
- ▶ Advanced
- ▶ Windows Installer
- ▶ MOM Maintenance Mode

Each of these tabs defines how the program will function. Let's review the content of each, using the OpsMgr package as an example.

The General tab (shown in Figure 13.9) has a variety of fields automatically populated with information, based on the package definition file used to create the OpsMgr package:

- ▶ **Name**—The Name field is prepopulated and cannot be changed.
- ▶ **Comment**—This is the first field you can modify. This field is a 127-character text field, used to give a description of the program.
- ▶ **Command line**—This field is a text field that can have up to 255 characters. It provides the command line that installs the OpsMgr agent. For the OpsMgr agent installation, the field uses the following syntax:

```
MSIEXEC.exe /q ALLUSERS=2 /m MSIHATJB /I "MOMAgent.msi"
```

FIGURE 13.9   General tab for the per-system unattended installation program

▶ **Start in**—An optional 127-character text field, this specifies either the absolute path to the program you are installing (such as c:\install_files\program.exe) or the folder relative to the distribution point you are installing within (such as install_files). This defaulted to blank for the OpsMgr agent program.

▶ **Run**—This dropdown specifies whether the program will run normal, minimized, maximized, or hidden:

    ▶ **Normal**—This is the default mode, and means the program runs based on system and program defaults.

    ▶ **Minimized**—Running minimized shows the program only on the task bar during installation. The window exists on the task bar during the installation process; however, it is not the active window maximized on the user's workstation.

    ▶ **Maximized**—This is a good configuration to use when installing programs that require user intervention. It's also good for package testing.

    ▶ **Hidden**—This mode hides the program during installation, and is a good option for fully automated program deployments.

The OpsMgr program defaulted to the Normal configuration.

▶ **After running**—This field is a dropdown selection determining what will occur after the program completes. Here are the options:

    ▶ **No action required**—The OpsMgr agent defaulted to No action required, which means that no restart or logoff is required for the program (the case in the OpsMgr agent installation).

- ▸ **Configuration Manager restarts computer**—The option to have ConfigMgr restart the computer is useful when you're deploying a program that requires a reboot but the reboot is not initiated as part of the program.

- ▸ **Program restarts computer**—Select this option if the program requires a reboot and the program actually performs the restart program.

- ▸ **Configuration Manager logs user off**—Use this option when the program installation requires the user not to be on the system.

It is important to note that both the ConfigMgr restarts computer and ConfigMgr logs user off options take place forcefully, after a grace period. This means that if either of these options is used, any applications running on the clients will not have the opportunity to save their data or state.

- ▸ **Category**—Category is a dropdown selection used to help find specific programs in ConfigMgr. This field defaulted to blank for the OpsMgr agent installation, but you can create a new category by typing in the text for the category's name.

Configuring the Installation Program

You will want to make several changes to the program's configuration on the General tab for the OpsMgr agent installation. First, add a comment explaining what the program will do. Next, change the properties on the Per-system attended command line, as follows:

```
MSIEXEC.exe /i MOMAgent.msi /qn /l*v MOMinstall.log
➥/m MSIHATJB USE_MANUALLY_SPECIFIED_SETTINGS=0
```

This syntax will install the MOMAgent.msi in quiet mode, save the MSI log file to a log named MOMinstall.log, and provide no configuration information to the client (because the agent configuration is discovered from Active Directory). Run the program as hidden, keep the After Running setting of No action required, and specify a Category setting of OpsMgr. Figure 13.10 displays these settings.

Now, move to the Requirements tab for the program. Figure 13.11 shows the default configuration for the OpsMgr program previously created using the package definition file.

The Requirements tab tells Configuration Manager the requirements for running the program:

- ▸ **Estimated disk space**—The estimated disk space required to run the program.

- ▸ **Maximum allowed run time (minutes)**—The amount of time the program is permitted to run.

- ▸ **This program can run only on specified client platforms**—If the program can only run on specified platforms, select the allowed platforms.

- ▸ **Additional requirements**—This is an optional field for specifying additional requirement information for users (up to 127 characters). Text will appear on client computers in Control Panel -> Run Advertised Programs.

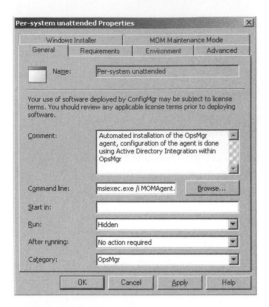

FIGURE 13.10   Configuration changes on the General tab of the OpsMgr agent installation program

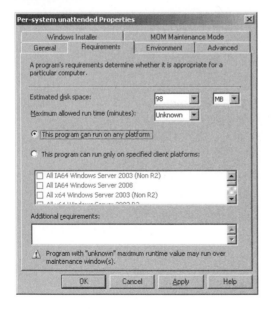

FIGURE 13.11   Requirements tab for the Per-system unattended installation program

The Estimated disk space setting defaults to 86MB when the package definition file for the OpsMgr agent is used. Although the actual amount of disk space may vary from the amount defined with the package definition file, the default can provide a good starting point. As an example, installations of the OpsMgr agent can require at least 154MB of disk space based on the management packs monitored on the agent system, so the setting here will be 200MB. Although there is a large difference between an 86MB estimate and a 200MB estimate, it is better to overestimate the required disk space ConfigMgr will check for—so when applications are distributed they do not fill the remainder of the disk space on the system. The Estimated disk space setting can be in KB, MB, or GB, and it defaults to Unknown for program installations.

The Maximum allowed run time (minutes) setting defines how long the program is expected to run. There can be considerable variation in how a program will run; this depends on the speed of the system ConfigMgr is installing it on, the size of the program, and the network connectivity between the system and the source files used for the installation. In this example, the setting defaulted to Unknown. However, based on previous installations of the OpsMgr agent, it should complete within 10 minutes. This option has direct impacts to configurations on both the Environment tab and the MOM Maintenance Mode tab (discussed later in this section) due to the addition of maintenance windows within ConfigMgr 2007. This is used to determine whether a package has the time to install before the maintenance window closes.

Two options are available for platforms on which ConfigMgr can run the program:

▶ **This program can run on any platform**—This is the default configuration and works well for programs that are not platform specific.

▶ **This program can run only on specified client platforms**—This type of installation is for client-specific platforms. As an example, the OpsMgr client actually has three different installation files based on the client platform (amd64, i386, ia64). In this situation, you would separately package each of the different program types and use this option to allow each program to run only on a specific client platform.

NOTE

Available Platforms to Run a Program On

The list of available platforms may not be up to date with current OS releases. An easy workaround for this is to create a collection of just the operating systems you want and target that collection.

Specifying that a program can run only on certain client platforms is only beneficial when a collection contains systems with multiple platforms. If an advertisement is targeted to a collection with only one platform and the program is restricted to only run on a specific client platform, this setting will be redundant.

For the OpsMgr agent, change the properties on the Requirements tab to set the estimated disk space to 200MB and the maximum allowed run time (in minutes) to 10. Also, specify that this program can only run on specified client platforms (that is, the x86 platforms this agent runs on), as shown in Figure 13.12.

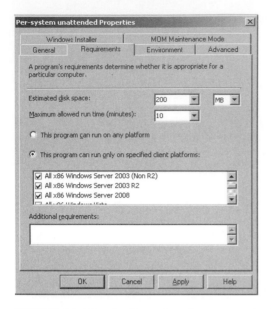

FIGURE 13.12   Configuration changes on the Requirements tab of the OpsMgr agent installation program

The Environment tab for this program identifies when a program can run. Here are the options:

▸ **Whether or not a user is logged on**—This is the default configuration, and it works for the majority of installations.

▸ **Only when a user is logged on**—This installation type is used when the program ConfigMgr is installing needs to have the user logged in to install.

▸ **Only when no user is logged on**—The installation type will not install until the user logs out of the system.

The conditions under which a program can run directly tie into the Run mode options:

▸ **Run with user's rights**—This is only available if the option "Only when a user is logged on" is chosen for when the program can be run.

▸ **Run with administrative rights**—This is the default option and is available in any of the three configurations that determine when a program can run. If you choose this option, a check box is available to allow users to interact with the program (Allow users to interact with this program). This setting causes advertisements to execute under the Local System account context.

> ### TIP
>
> **Running Advertisements with Administrative Rights**
>
> At first glance, running an advertisement with administrative rights seems like a no-brainer. Using this approach, you can install the software regardless of what level of

permissions are available to the user logged in to the system. However, this can cause some difficulties when installing a program that writes data to the Registry, or if the package tries to access files the account does not have rights to access. If this situation occurs, try running with the user's rights instead. If that does not work, create two different programs—one that runs under the user access and allows access to the Registry, and a second that runs with administrative rights. Next, link the programs together with a Run this program first option. Sometimes this will require repackaging the application (see the "Repackaging" section of this chapter for details) to determine the portion of the application that requires administrator rights to install. Another option involves using the task sequencing engine to deploy packages that need to perform Registry edits or run something in the user's context. This can be done by running a command line with a run as statement (this functionality is only available in ConfigMgr 2007 R2).

Use the Allow users to interact with this program option in those situations where the user needs to interact with the program. The option Allow users to interact with the program is also an excellent troubleshooting method to use when packages are not installing correctly. With this option selected, the user interface is visible to the user logged in to the system, and the user can interact with the program. As an example, you will choose this option if the program requires the user to make a selection or click a button. If a program runs without this option selected and the program requires user intervention, it waits for the user interaction (which will never occur) and will eventually time out when the maximum allowed runtime has occurred (defined on the Requirements tab of the program; if undefined, the program times out after 12 hours).

The Drive mode that the program runs under includes the following configurations:

▶ **Runs with UNC name**—This is the default setting, which runs the program using the UNC (Universal Naming Convention) name. As an example, \\<*smsserver*>\smspkge$\DAL00004 would be the distribution point when you create a package for the DAL site and store it on the E: drive of the system. Chapter 14 provides more information regarding distribution points and where files are stored.

▶ **Requires drive letter**—The program requires a mapped drive to install, but allows ConfigMgr to use any available drive letter.

▶ **Requires specific drive letter (example: Z):**—The program requires mapping a specific drive letter for installation (if you choose this option, an additional box is provided for specifying the letter to be mapped). If the drive letter is not available on the client system, the program will not run.

▶ **Reconnect to distribution point at logon**—This last setting specifies that the client will reconnect to the ConfigMgr distribution point when logging in to the system. This option is only available if the program runs only when a user is logged on, with the user's rights, and requires either a drive letter, or a specific drive letter (as an example, the drive letter **Z**).

For the OpsMgr agent, take the defaults, as displayed in Figure 13.13.

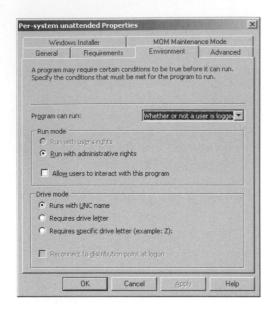

FIGURE 13.13   Environment tab for the Per-system unattended installation program

The Advanced tab for the program, shown in Figure 13.14, specifies a variety of configurations, such as whether other programs run prior to this one, whether this program is run once for the computer or for each user, where program notifications are suppressed, how disabled programs are handled on clients, and how the program integrates with install software task sequences.

- **Run another program first**—This is the first option available on the Advanced tab. These are program *dependencies*, and specifying this option causes another program to be run before this program runs. By default, the check box is cleared. As an example, there's a software package that has several separate programs requiring installation before the package can be installed. This program has five levels of dependency—our original program will not run unless program #2 has run, and program #2 will not run unless program #3 has run, and so on.

  If you choose this option, you must specify a package and a program. The option "Allow this program to be installed from the Install Software task sequence without being advertised" is relevant when discussing task sequences within ConfigMgr. Task sequences are a list of customizable tasks or steps sequentially performed. A task sequence can be advertised to a collection; as an example, a program can be advertised to a collection. Task sequences provide a more elegant solution for many situations, including those where multiple dependencies exist for a single program. Task sequences are discussed in more detail in Chapter 19.

  If you specify the option to run another program first, the Always run this program first option is also available (defaults as unchecked). If this option is checked, the program it is dependent on will run regardless of whether it previously ran on the same system.

▶ **When this program is assigned to a computer**—This is a dropdown with two choices:

   ▶ **Run once for the computer**—This is the default setting.

   ▶ **Run once for every user who logs in**—This option causes the program to run for each user who logs in to the computer.

▶ **Suppress program notifications**—This option is a check box that is cleared by default. When checked, the option causes any notification area icons, messages, and countdown notifications to not display for the program. This is useful for programs that may be running when someone is using the system, if there is no requirement for notification that the program is running.

▶ **Disable this program on computers where it is advertised**—This check box determines how ConfigMgr will handle the program. The option defaults to unchecked, but if checked, it specifies that advertisements containing this program are disabled. When checked, this option also removes the program from the list of available programs that the user can run, and the program will not run on the systems where it is assigned.

   This approach is useful when there is a need to temporarily halt a deployment because the change applies to all advertisements of the program, and the program is disabled when policies are retrieved by the client.

▶ **Allow this program to be installed from the Install Software task sequence without being advertised**—The final check box on the Advanced tab determines how the Install Software task sequence in OSD handles the program. The option is unchecked by default. You should check this option for any programs used within an OSD task sequence.

For the OpsMgr agent, accept the default configurations, shown in Figure 13.14.

The Windows Installer tab for the program provides installation source management. If the program requires repair or reinstallation, the MSI file automatically accesses the package files on a distribution point to reinstall or repair the program. This screen defaults to cleared, as displayed in Figure 13.15 for the OpsMgr package.

The available fields on the screen shown in Figure 13.15 are the Windows Installer product code and the Windows Installer file. You can define these by clicking the Import button and specifying the MSI file used for the program. Choosing the MSI file populates both of these fields.

For the OpsMgr agent, accept the default configurations as displayed in Figure 13.15.

The final tab determines the MOM maintenance mode configurations for the program. Two options are available on this tab, as displayed in Figure 13.16:

▶ **Disable Operations Manager alerts while this program runs**—Selecting this option places the computer in OpsMgr maintenance mode while the program is running. The duration of the maintenance mode is defined by the Maximum allowed run time (minutes) setting defined on the Requirements tab (refer to

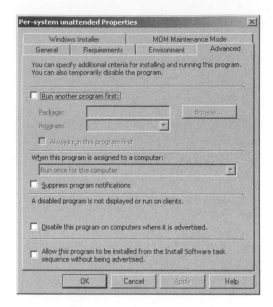

FIGURE 13.14   Advanced tab for the Per-system unattended installation program

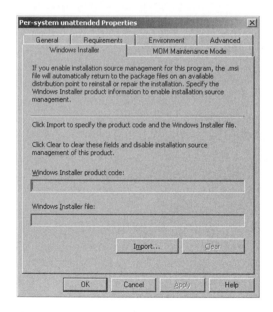

FIGURE 13.15   Windows Installer tab for the Per-system unattended installation program

Figure 13.11). Unfortunately, this option does not actually perform the steps required to truly disable Operations Manager alerts while the program is running. The option pauses the OpsMgr health service, but it does not put everything into maintenance mode, meaning heartbeat alerts are still generated. This option defaults to unchecked.

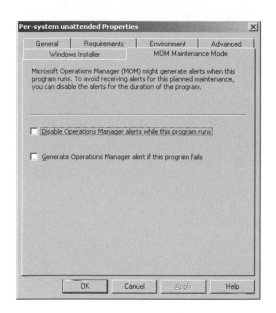

FIGURE 13.16   MOM Maintenance Mode tab for the Per-system unattended installation program

▶ **Generate Operations Manager alert if this program fails**—If this option is checked, it creates an event in the application log containing the package name, program name, advertisement ID, advertisement comment, and failure code or Management Information Format (MIF) failure description. You can configure the application event to create an alert in MOM/Operations Manager that will alert on the situation. A good example of when to use this feature is for critical software deployments such as service pack (SP) packages. This option defaults to unchecked.

Configuring the Package Used by the Package Definition File

Using a package definition file provides a solid configuration for building the program required to install the OpsMgr agent. This is just one of the configurations completed with the Create Package from Definition Wizard, which also created the package that includes the program(s) previously discussed in the "Using the Create Package From Definition Wizard" section of this chapter. To see the properties of this package, right-click the package (located in the Configuration Manager console -> Site Database -> Software Distribution -> Packages) and go to the Properties page.

The package's General tab displays the default settings created. These include the name, version, manufacturer, language, and comment for the package. Figure 13.17 shows an example of the General tab with the information populated from the package definition file.

Notice the other tabs that are part of the package properties. The Data Source tab in Figure 13.18 specifies where the files are located and shows their distribution method.

In this example, the OpsMgr package was created with uncompressed source files (see the option previously specified in Figure 13.5 to always obtain files from the source directory). You can change this setting after creating the package, and change the location of the source files using the Set button next to this field. Unchecking the option This package

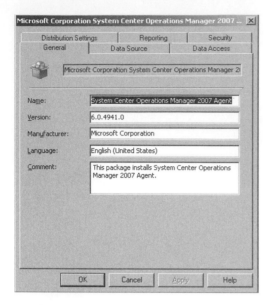

FIGURE 13.17   General tab of the package

contains source files will gray out the remaining items on this tab. Alternatively, you can also choose to make this package use a compressed copy of the source directory, which grays out the option to update distribution points on a schedule.

If you check the option Always obtain files from the source directory, there is an option to update distribution points on a schedule. This option is useful for those software packages that you expect to update source files for on a regular basis. The option is configured by using the Schedule button and then configuring the start time (which defaults to the current date and time), the recurrence (none, weekly, monthly, custom interval) and how often it will recur (in days, hours or minutes). This option is seldom used, however.

Use the option Persist content in the client cache for recurring packages such as antivirus software. This option stores the program in the client cache for an indefinite period; however, this requires that the advertisement is configured to download and execute. The option is disabled by default. Use this option with care, because it decreases the amount of available client cache and could cause a package to fail to distribute if there is insufficient space to store that package.

The last option on this tab is Enable binary differential replication, which by default is disabled. If this option is checked, the package uses binary delta comparison for the source files. This means that ConfigMgr sends only the changed portions of the file, rather than the entire file.

Checking this option can significantly decrease bandwidth requirements when creating updates for large packages already sent to distribution points. However, using this option introduces additional complexity to replicating packages and debugging issues with package distribution. For more details on binary differential replication, refer to Chapter 5 and Chapter 14.

For the OpsMgr package, leave the defaults previously configured through the package definition file, displayed in Figure 13.18.

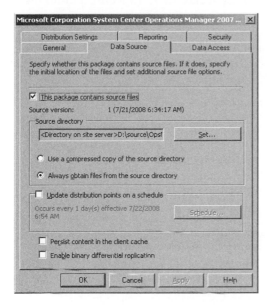

Microsoft Corporation System Center Operations Manager 2007 ... ☒

| Distribution Settings | | Reporting | | Security |
| General | Data Source | | Data Access | |

Specify whether this package contains source files. If it does, specify the initial location of the files and set additional source file options.

☑ This package contains source files

Source version: 1 (7/21/2008 6:34:17 AM)

Source directory
| <Directory on site server>D:\source\Opsf | Set... |

○ Use a compressed copy of the source directory

◉ Always obtain files from the source directory

☐ Update distribution points on a schedule

Occurs every 1 day(s) effective 7/22/2008 6:54 AM   Schedule...

☐ Persist content in the client cache

☐ Enable binary differential replication

| OK | Cancel | Apply | Help |

FIGURE 13.18   Data Source tab of the package

The Data Access tab (shown in Figure 13.19) specifies the shared folder location of the package when sent to a DP as well as the package update settings. The shared folder location section allows you to choose one of two options:

▶ **Access the distribution folder through common ConfigMgr package share—** This is the default configuration and specifies that packages are accessed through the SMSPKG$x$$ share (where x is the drive letter the distribution point is storing the data on). As an example, if you store a package on the E: drive of the Wildflower server, the package is accessed via the \\Wildflower\SMSPKGE$ share.

▶ **Share the distribution folder—**This option allows you to share the folder using a share name that you specify. The share name must be unique across all packages. Each time the package is updated or refreshed, the content of the folder (including files and subfolders) is deleted and re-created. If you created a share on the Wildflower site server for the custom application MyApp, the share name would be \\Wildflower\MyApp.

A variation of this option is specifying a share that includes the path, which might be under a shared path such as the name of the company's custom applications. For MyApp, this would be stored under \\Wildflower\OdysseyMyApp if you specified the share name of Odyssey\MyApp (it is best to create a top-level share specific to the organization to differentiate between custom and noncustom applications). These options to share the distribution folder under a nondefault name are useful if systems outside of ConfigMgr will access the share.

The Package update settings section of the Data Access tab specifies how ConfigMgr will handle access to distribution points when there are updates to the package data. If users are connected to the distribution points, there may be locked files or inconsistent results—some of the files may be updated but others not. By default, the option to disconnect users from distribution points is unchecked. If this option is checked, two additional configurations are required; these relate to the number of retries before users are disconnected and the interval between user notifications and disconnections. This option only affects standard distribution points (not branch distribution points).

▶ **The number of retries before disconnecting users**—This option specifies the number of times ConfigMgr will try to update the package source files before it disconnects users from the DP. This setting defaults to 2 and has an acceptable range of 0–99.

▶ **The interval between user notification and disconnection (minutes)**—The interval specifies the number of minutes ConfigMgr will wait after notifying users before disconnecting them from the distribution point. This setting defaults to 5 minutes and has an acceptable range of 0–59 minutes.

NOTE

Run Program from Distribution Point and Vista/Server 2008 Client Systems

If the program within the package has the option "Run the program from the distribution point" selected (defined in the advertisement on the Distribution Point tab, discussed in Chapter 14) and the clients are running Windows Vista or Windows Server 2008, those clients will not receive user notification.

For the OpsMgr package, keep the defaults configured through the package definition file, shown in Figure 13.19.

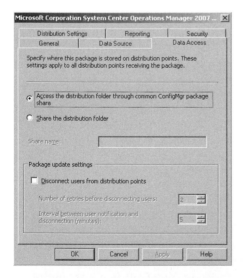

FIGURE 13.19   Data Access tab of the package

The Distribution Settings tab displayed in Figure 13.20 specifies the priority, preferred sender, and configurations for branch distribution points for the package.

- **Sending priority**—This has options of Low, Medium (default), and High. The setting determines the priority of the package when sending it to another site. ConfigMgr sends packages in priority order; if packages have identical priorities, ConfigMgr sends them in the order they were created. The Low priority option is good for packages not requiring quick distribution, such as nonmandatory packages infrequently installed. The High priority option is good for packages requiring distribution quickly, regardless of other packages available.

- **Preferred sender**—The Preferred sender dropdown specifies the type of sender used to send the package to other sites. The default setting is <No Preference>, which uses any available sender. Here are the other options available:

  - Asynchronous RAS Sender

  - Courier Sender

  - ISDN RAS Sender

  - Standard Sender

  - SNA RAS Sender

  - X25 RAS Sender

  The default configuration will work for most situations, although a good example of when to change this is for large packages that you do not want to send over the network. For these types of packages, specifying the courier sender allows distribution without sending them across the network. Courier sender is not used to distribute packages unless you choose this option.

The Branch distribution point content settings section has two options:

- **Automatically download content when packages are assigned to branch distribution points**—This is the default setting. If you choose this option, a second check box is available: Make the package available on protected distribution points when requested by clients inside the protected boundaries. This specifies whether the package is available for download to a branch distribution point not already designated as a DP. Choosing this option means the local branch distribution point will download the package when a client requests the package. Once the content is available on the DP, the next client request will be able to download and run the content (this is only available for protected branch distribution points).

TIP

Branch Distribution Points and Automatically Downloaded Content

The first time a client requests software from the branch distribution point configured to automatically download content when packages are assigned to branch distribution points, an error message displays indicating the content is not available (assuming this is an advertisement that must be triggered manually). This error is normal and indicates the distribution point does not yet have the content. Attempting to run the software from the branch distribution point will set the flag on the branch distribution point to retrieve the content.

▶ **Administrator manually copies the package to branch distribution points—** This is the other option to distribute content, and it's useful if you have your own replication mechanisms in place for branch distribution points (such as a scheduled off-hours Robocopy to the branch distribution point).

For the OpsMgr package, keep the defaults configured with the package definition file, shown in Figure 13.20.

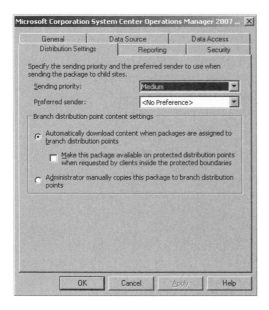

FIGURE 13.20   Distribution Settings tab of the package

The Reporting tab of the software package, displayed in Figure 13.21, specifies the configurations for the Management Information Format (MIF) configured for the package. The package's MIF file is placed in the Windows folder; ConfigMgr can find the file and use the information in it to provide package success and failure information. Two options are available on this tab:

> ▶ **Use package properties for status MIF matching**—This option specifies the settings used for the MIF filename (maximum 50 characters), name (maximum 50 characters), version (maximum 32 characters), and publisher (maximum 50 characters). This is the default option when you use a package definition file to create your software package (shown in Figure 13.21). The MIF filename is also integrated into the programs on the General tab in the command-line field using the /m parameter.

> ▶ **Use these fields for status MIF matching**—This is the default option when creating a new package without a definition file. If you choose this option, ConfigMgr uses the properties on the General tab for MIF file matching.

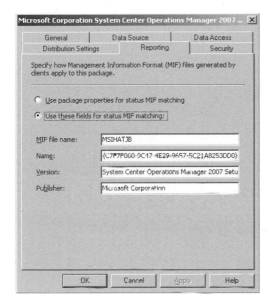

FIGURE 13.21   Reporting tab of the package

The last tab on the package properties is the Security tab. This tab defines the class and instance security for this package object. The top section shows the class security rights for the object and the bottom section shows the instance security rights. Each section has three buttons used to maintain entries in that section:

> ▶ Selecting the starburst button allows you to add security rights.

> ▶ The folder button edits the highlighted security rights.

> ▶ The red X button deletes the highlighted security rights.

Figure 13.22 shows the default security rights generated from the package definition file. Chapter 20, "Security and Delegation in Configuration Manager 2007," discusses security.

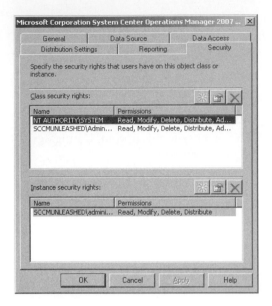

FIGURE 13.22   Security tab of the package

After completing the program configuration, your next step is to distribute the package, which is discussed in Chapter 14.

Advantages of Using a Package Definition File

Using a package definition file saves a significant amount of work by streamlining the process of creating the package and the programs. It provides a good starting point you can use when customizing software packages to specific requirements.

Packaging the Operations Manager agent with a package definition file demonstrates many of the configurations used when manually creating a package and a program. Although using a package definition file (an MSI, PDF, or MIF file) is the recommended approach, what takes place when a package definition file is not available? Drawing on the information just used to create the OpsMgr package, the next section discusses the process for creating packages and programs manually, using the Forefront client as an example.

Forefront Client

Microsoft Forefront Client Security provides unified virus and spyware protection for Windows platforms. There are several prerequisites prior to deploying the Forefront client. These include a properly installed and configured Forefront Client Security (FCS) management server, an FCS policy for the clients, a Windows update policy for the clients, and access to the Forefront client for packaging. Once these are in place, you can package the Forefront client.

The Forefront client source files are in the root folder of the FCS installation media. To make the location of these source files consistent, create a subfolder in the d:\source folder called **Forefront** (d:\source now contains OpsMgr and Forefront top-level folders). Copy the contents of the client folder from the installation media to the d:\source\Forefront folder. With the source files in the correct location, begin creating the Forefront package.

Using the New Package Wizard

Similar to when you created a package using a package definition file, open the Configuration Manager console and navigate to System Center Configuration Manager -> Site Database -> Computer Management -> Software Distribution -> Packages. Right-click Packages, and this time choose New -> Package. This starts the New Package Wizard. On the first page of the wizard (the General page), specify a variety of fields, each of which is your personal preference for the package. As long as the fields properly explain what the package is, the actual content is not critical. These fields include the following:

▶ **Name**—The name of the package. This example used **Forefront Client Security Agent**. To determine each of the fields for this package, right-click the program you are installing (clientsetup.exe, in this case) and work using the fields shown as program properties. For the name, you can choose a shortened version of the Description field shown in Figure 13.23.

▶ **Version**—The version of the software package. For this example, the version is 1.0.1703.0 which is available on the Details tab for the Properties of the Forefront Client Security client. The General tab for this is shown in Figure 13.23.

▶ **Manufacturer**—Who created the software package. Specify **Microsoft**, shortened from the Company field shown in Figure 13.23.

▶ **Language**—The language of the package (English, in this case), which is a shortened version of the language information provided as a value for the Language item.

▶ **Comment**—Additional information on the package. For consistency with the existing OpsMgr package, specify the comment shown in Figure 13.24.

Configuring the Package

Figure 13.24 shows the full set of information specified for the package. Note that the manufacturer name is automatically prepended to the name, with the version and language added at the end, thus giving the full name of the program: Microsoft Forefront Client Security Agent 1.0.1703.0 English, as shown at the top of Figure 13.24 in the field next to the package icon.

Click Next to continue and now configure the data source for this package. Specify the source folder created earlier, which is the **d:\source\Forefront** folder. Anticipating there will be regular updates to this package, configure the package to update distribution points on a schedule (daily in this case). Figure 13.25 displays this configuration.

There are no additional fields in the wizard you need to alter from the defaults (Data Access, Distribution Settings, Reporting, Security, Summary) so click the Finish button on

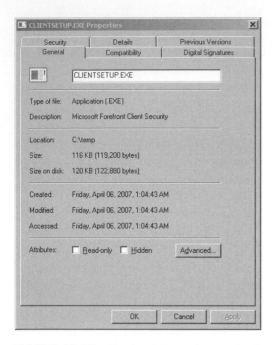

FIGURE 13.23   Version information on the Forefront Client Security client installation program

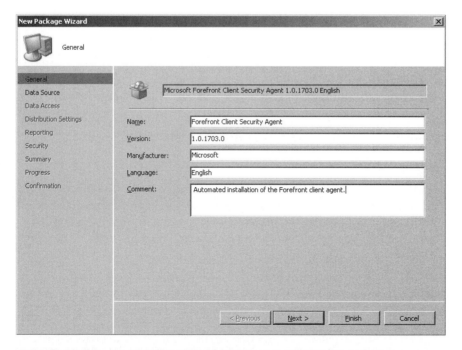

FIGURE 13.24   Packaging the Forefront client on the General screen

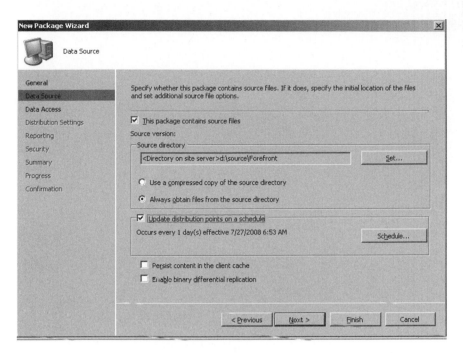

FIGURE 13.25   Packaging the Forefront client on the Data Source screen

Figure 13.25 to bypass the remaining configuration pages. Click Next on the Summary page and click Close after creating the package.

Adding Programs

The package is created, but without any programs for the package to run. To specify the program you want to create, open the Configuration Manager console and then navigate to System Center Configuration Manager -> Site Database -> Computer Management -> Software Distribution -> Packages -> Microsoft Forefront Client Security Agent 1.0.1703.0 English -> Programs. Right-click Programs and choose New -> Program to start the New Program Wizard. On the General screen, specify a name, comment, command line, and how the program will run. For this example, configure settings for the Forefront client as displayed in Figure 13.26.

The Name and Comment fields can contain whatever text is appropriate, and do not require a specific set of text as long as they properly describe the program and its function.

However, the command line needs a very specific set of information. How do you know what to put into the command line field? There are two primary methods for determining the appropriate command-line information:

- ▶ The easiest method is opening the folder containing the installation program and running the program with /? after the command. As an example, Figure 13.27 shows the output from running `clientsetup /?`. The parameters shown here indicate the parameters necessary to specify when running the program. The command

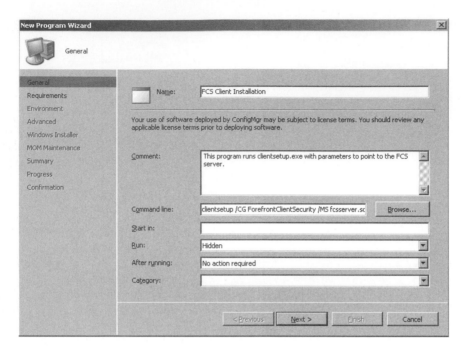

FIGURE 13.26   Creating the program for the Forefront client on the General screen

line shown in Figure 13.27 uses both the /CG and /MS parameters to install the Forefront client.

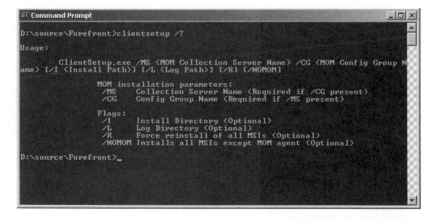

FIGURE 13.27   Output from running the **clientsetup** /? command

▶ Alternatively, you can find command-line information using the Internet to check commonly used sites, such as myITforum.com and AppDeploy.com, or just search for command-line parameters.

Figure 13.26 also shows the Run parameter set to Hidden, so the user will not see the program installing on his or her system. Keep the default "After running" selection of No action required. Click Next, and continue on to the Requirements screen.

On this page, set the estimated disk space to 350MB (based on the client requirements available at http://www.microsoft.com/forefront/clientsecurity/en/us/system-requirements.aspx). You will also want to specify the x86 platforms (this is further restricted, because for the XP platforms only Windows XP SP 2 is supported, and for the Windows 2000 platforms only Windows 2000 SP 4 is supported). Figure 13.28 displays this configuration. Click Next.

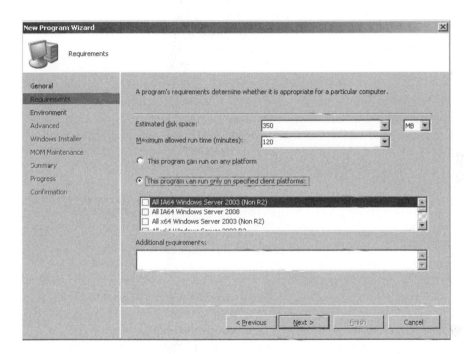

FIGURE 13.28   Creating the program for the Forefront client on the Requirements screen

On the Environment screen, change the default configuration to run whether or not a user is logged on. Take the default configurations on the Advanced, Windows Installer, and MOM Maintenance screens. Click Finish to move to the Summary page and click Next to finish creating the program, then close the wizard.

At this point, you have created a package for the Forefront client and a program that runs an unattended installation of the program. The next step would be to specify the distribution points to use to distribute the software, but that discussion takes place in Chapter 14.

Custom Packages

The majority of the packages needed for most organizations have existing package definition files, because most major packages now install from MSI files. For those packages that
do not have package definition files but do have setup files, the Forefront client example
illustrates that you can manually create packages by performing some additional steps.
You can often install simple applications with a batch file or a script.

TIP

Site for Software Packaging and Deployment Guidance

A great place for general guidance on software deployment is the AppDeploy site
(http://www.appdeploy.com). AppDeploy provides information on how to distribute software, including examples for Adobe Reader, Microsoft Office, and Visual Studio .NET.
You now can deploy nearly all software using packages that run the various command-
line configurations.

What do you do for the few applications that you cannot package using normal methods?
There are some packages you cannot package using standard processes, but you can
repackage them.

Repackaging

Software repackaging takes an existing application installation and converts it to an MSI
package. You would take a snapshot of a system before and after installing the software on
a system and then convert the results into the MSI package. Several tools are available to
help with repackaging:

▶ The SMS Installer is a command-line tool used for repackaging, and has been avail-
able since Systems Management Server 2.0. This installer's most recent update was
the Windows Installer Step-Up utility (ISU), which converts packages to MSI formats.
SMS Installer is still available for download at http://www.microsoft.com/technet/
sms/20/downloads/tools/installer.mspx, but Microsoft has not updated it for
ConfigMgr 2007. The most comprehensive source of information on the SMS
Installer is *Microsoft SMS Installer* (Computing McGraw-Hill, 2000), written by Rod
Trent from myITforum.com.

▶ Acresso Software's AdminStudio Configuration Manager Editor provides repackaging
for Configuration Manager 2007, converting applications to MSI format. A free
download of this product is available at http://www.acresso.com/promolanding/
7698.htm. The fully featured package includes the ability to create transforms (MST
files), improved integration with ConfigMgr, and integration with the ConfigMgr
Web console (available at http://www.myitforum.com/articles/19/view.asp?id=8662).

▶ Several other vendors provide repackaging options that may meet your requirements. For additional information on these vendors, go to the AppDeploy website
(http://www.appdeploy.com/tools/browse.asp) and browse for repackagers.

However, there may be software you cannot even effectively repackage to create an MSI. Although this is not common, it can happen.

Scripted Installations

A coworker had a situation where OSD was being used to deploy a large number of operating system upgrades. The client had a Wireless Configured Privacy–based wireless configuration that needed to be deployed to all systems being upgraded. Testing determined no method existed that allowed either installing the WEP configuration or repackaging the WEP configuration. Faced with that situation, the best option was to use a scripted installation.

A scripted installation uses a tool such as AutoIT (available for download at http://www.autoitscript.com), which uses a simulated set of keystrokes, mouse movements, and Windows manipulation to automate tasks. These tasks are tested on a client workstation until they reliably perform the process they were designed to perform. The tasks are compiled into an executable that ConfigMgr can deploy as a software package. The software package requires the user be logged on and can interact with the package, because the scripted installation actually performs the installation through the user interface. Although it is not recommended as an approach for providing software installation, this is a good trick for those cases where no other software packaging approaches are viable.

Integrating Virtual Applications

Moving forward, Microsoft is wrapping its new direction for packaging around another Microsoft technology— SoftGrid—and its integration with Configuration Manager 2007.

What Is SoftGrid?

On July 7, 2006, Microsoft completed the acquisition of a company called Softricity. Softricity provided an application virtualization solution that Microsoft has rebranded as Microsoft SoftGrid.

SoftGrid provides the ability to virtualize applications running on a desktop. The virtualized application does not install on the client system. These applications are streamed to the client, requiring only SoftGrid client installation to the client system. SoftGrid deployments exist in situations where the application cannot run on the standard client operating system, or where multiple versions of a single application need to exist on the same system but cannot due to conflicts.

A SoftGrid Example

Consider an environment that needs to run Microsoft Word 2003 and 2007 on the same client system. There are several ways to accomplish this:

▶ Have the users install the software locally on their system.

▶ Use ConfigMgr to deploy both software packages.

Each of these approaches includes dealing with any potential conflicts between the applications.

▶ Let SoftGrid virtualize the application.

This results in both applications packaged and available to the users, but not physically deployed to the client system. The client still sees the icons for each of the programs, and they run as if installed locally to the system—without actually going through the installation process.

How SoftGrid Works

SoftGrid runs applications in a siloed environment using virtualized versions of the operating system components, including the Registry, files, fonts, INI settings, COM configurations, embedded services, and environment variables. This siloed approach means that applications do not install directly into the client system. If the user were to open up the Registry on his or her workstation, there would not be any Registry settings for Microsoft Word, even though there is an icon for Word on the desktop and Word runs as if it was a locally installed application.

SoftGrid provides this functionality through a client- and server-based configuration. The SoftGrid architecture uses a SoftGrid Virtual Application Server for delivering applications, and it uses a client that installs on those systems that will have applications deployed.

SoftGrid-defined applications use a process called *sequencing*. Sequencing defines how a standard application will install and function as a virtualized application.

When using virtual applications with ConfigMgr, you must deploy **both** the ConfigMgr client and the App-V client to those client systems for the virtual applications to work on these systems.

App-V 4.5

Microsoft released the first Microsoft-branded version of the product formerly known as SoftGrid in 2008, naming it Microsoft Application Virtualization 4.5 (App-V 4.5 for short).

You can get App-V 4.5 several ways:

▶ Through the Microsoft Desktop Optimization Pack (MDOP) (http://www.microsoft.com/windows/enterprise/products/mdop.aspx)

▶ As part of Microsoft Application Virtualization for Terminal Services (http://www.microsoft.com/systemcenter/appv/terminalsvcs.mspx)

You can take applications sequenced using App-V 4.5 and deploy them as virtual applications with ConfigMgr 2007. Additional information on App-V 4.5 is available at http://www.microsoft.com/systemcenter/appv/default.mspx, and the App-V 4.5 FAQ is located at http://technet.microsoft.com/en-us/appvirtualization/cc664494.aspx.

Integration with SMS/Configuration Manager

When Microsoft added SoftGrid to its product line, the functionality crossings between SMS and SoftGrid were significant:

▶ One of the core functions of SMS was to deploy applications

▶ SoftGrid's core function is to provide virtualized applications

Configuration Manager 2007 Release 2 (R2) provides integration between these two programs such that you can manage App-V virtualized applications from Configuration Manager 2007.

Activating Application Virtualization in ConfigMgr 2007 R2

Although Microsoft Application Virtualization is integrated with ConfigMgr 2007 R2, ConfigMgr does not activate the application virtualization functionality by default. Several steps are required to add the Microsoft Application Virtualization components:

▶ Configure the Advertised Program Client agent to run virtual applications through the ConfigMgr console.

Navigate to -> Site Database -> Site Management *<Site Code> <Site Name>* -> Site Settings -> Client Agents -> Advertised Programs Client Agent. Right-click Advertised Programs Client Agent and then select Properties.

On the General tab, select the option Allow virtual application package advertisement. Figure 13.29 displays this configuration.

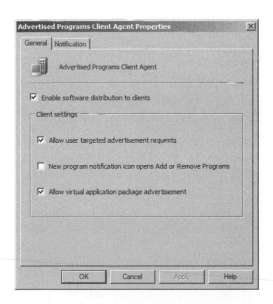

FIGURE 13.29   Configure virtual applications on Advertised Programs

Real World: Caution when Checking the Allow Virtual Application Package Advertisement

There was a situation where a site deployed SoftGrid to provide the majority of application distribution for that environment. Only those applications that could not be sequenced properly were deployed through ConfigMgr. The SoftGrid environment suddenly stopped functioning and systems that were online started to remove their applications and references to the SoftGrid server. It was eventually determined that SoftGrid integration had been enabled in ConfigMgr at the time that the SoftGrid environment stopped functioning (the Allow virtual application package advertisement setting in the Advertised Program Client Agent Properties specifically).

This change caused the Configuration Manager clients to remove *all* previously deployed virtual application packages (published through an Application Virtualization full infrastructure or standalone MSI). This occurred through a purging of the Application Virtualization Client cache and removing any existing Application Virtualization Client references to Application Virtualization Management Servers.

The lesson—if you have an existing SoftGrid environment and plan to activate this functionality in ConfigMgr 2007 (R2), be sure you fully test the impacts in a testing environment prior to making the change in production.

▶ Enable the Application Virtualization streaming server.

Open the ConfigMgr console -> Site Database -> Site Management *<Site Code> <Site Name>* -> Site Settings -> Site Systems. Then click the name of the server, right-click the ConfigMgr Distribution Point, and select Properties.

On the Virtual Applications tab, select Enable Virtual Application Streaming. See Figure 13.30 for this selection. Also verify that the distribution point supports HTTP requests (available in the properties of the distribution point on the General tab, under communication settings with the following option: Allow clients to transfer content from this distribution point using BITS, HTTP, and HTTPS).

After adding these components, you can import virtual application packages into Configuration Manager through the ConfigMgr console -> Computer Management -> Software Distribution -> Packages node.

The ability for Configuration Manager 2007 to integrate virtual applications greatly expands its functionality, because ConfigMgr can now deploy both installed and virtualized applications!

Additional Readings on App-V

Although the emphasis of this book is on Configuration Manager 2007, the new functionality added with Application Virtualization will lead to an increased focus by ConfigMgr administrators on sequencing applications for use with ConfigMgr. The example used in this chapter assumes that you already have access to sequenced applications, which may not be the case.

The following references provide additional reading on sequencing applications:

▶ Steve Rachui's blog entry presents a step-by-step example for sequencing an application in App-V and provides additional details on the App-V client, available at http://blogs.msdn.com/steverac/archive/2008/12/22/deploying-virtual-apps-with-sccm.aspx.

▶ Microsoft also provides a video discussing application sequencing, available at http://technet.microsoft.com/en-us/windows/dd459150.aspx.

▶ The Microsoft App-V documentation library is available at http://technet.microsoft.com/en-us/appvirtualization/cc843994.aspx. This library includes a white paper on virtual application management with Configuration Manager 2007 and Application Virtualization 4.5.

▶ Steve also has a good blog write-up that provides an App-V introduction highlighting components and integration with ConfigMgr, available at http://blogs.msdn.com/steverac/archive/2008/12/22/app-v-introduction-components-and-sccm-integration.aspx.

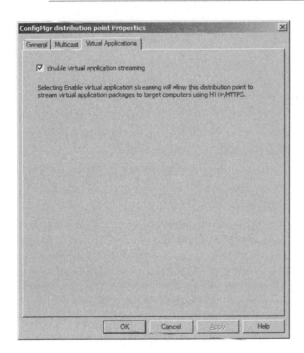

FIGURE 13.30   Configure virtual applications streaming on distribution point(s)

Creating Adobe Reader as a Virtual Application in ConfigMgr R2

Prior to creating a virtual application in Configuration Manager 2007 R2, you must activate Application Virtualization, as discussed in the previous section. The second requirement is to have an application sequenced with App-V 4.5. The steps required to sequence a virtual application are outside of the scope of this book. The article at http://technet.microsoft.com/en-us/appvirtualization/cc843994.aspx, mentioned in the "Additional

Readings on App-V" sidebar, is a good starting point for understanding virtual applications and sequencing.

Preparing a Sequenced Application for Packaging

Before creating the package, place the sequenced application on the site server. Perform the following steps:

1. Store the sequenced application and the manifest.XML file in a unique folder structure. On the primary site server, create a folder (SoftGrid). Under that folder, create an additional folder (Adobe). Copy the sequenced application files, including the manifest.XML file, into this folder (Adobe, in this case).

2. Create and share out a folder to be used later with the New Virtual Application Package Wizard. Create a folder called Adobe on the site server (this could be Bluebonnet in the SCCMUnleashed environment) under a folder called VirtualApps, and share it with permissions to allow everyone read-level access. Give ConfigMgr administrators full access.

When sequencing your next application, create a new folder under the SoftGrid folder for the new application (say, Microsoft Office) and then create a new folder under \VirtualApps for the new application as well. This approach provides a consistent way to locate the various shared folders under the \VirtualApps top-level folder.

Creating the Virtual Application

After storing the sequenced application in one folder, and creating and sharing a destination folder, you are ready to start the wizard to create the virtual application! Perform the following steps:

1. Open the ConfigMgr console -> Computer Management -> Software Distribution -> Packages. Right-click Packages and choose New -> Virtual Application Package to start the New Virtual Application Package Wizard.

2. This wizard looks for the files created when the Microsoft Application Virtualization Sequencer sequences an application. The wizard starts with defining the package source information. For this example, specify the Adobe_Reader_Adobe_9_MNT_manifest.xml file stored in the e:\SoftGrid\Adobe folder structure, as displayed in Figure 13.31.

TIP

Each Sequenced Application Requires Its Own Folder

During initial testing, a single folder stored each of the sequenced applications (the e:\softgrid folder). It was determined that if you attempt to store multiple sequenced applications in the same folder, the New Virtual Application Package Wizard will fail with an error that there are multiple sequenced applications in the same folder, and the wizard will not continue. You will want to create the unique folder structure for each application discussed at the beginning of the "Preparing a Sequenced Application for Packaging" section.

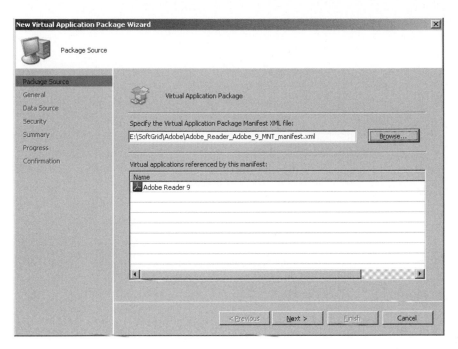

FIGURE 13.31   Configuring the package source for the Adobe Reader virtual application

3. The next screen provides the general settings for the new virtual application. The Name field prepopulates based on the manifest.XML file. Specify the version, manufacturer, and language, and leave the Comment field blank for this example, as shown in Figure 13.32. The option "Remove this package from clients when it is no longer advertised" is checked so that the package is removed if it is not advertised.

4. The Data Source screen is next. Here, you will specify the data source configuration for the Adobe Reader virtual application. The destination directory is the empty folder previously shared, specified with the UNC path (**bluebonnet\adobe**) as displayed in Figure 13.33. The package source and destination directories cannot use the same folder. These folders can exist on the same server and the same drive, just not the same folder.

5. Specify the Security settings associated with the new virtual application. The default security rights shown in Figure 13.34 should be sufficient.

6. The wizard process completes through the Summary page, which shows the information defined for this new virtual application. The Progress screen shows the state of the virtual application as it is created, and the Confirmation screen shows the success (or failure) of the virtual application creation process. Figure 13.35 displays the successful creation of the Adobe Reader virtual application.

7. Configuration Manager lists virtual applications in the same folder structure as non-virtual applications (Computer Management -> Software Distribution -> Packages). Figure 13.36 shows an example of a regular packaged application (the ACME Service Pack) and a virtual application (the Adobe Reader just created).

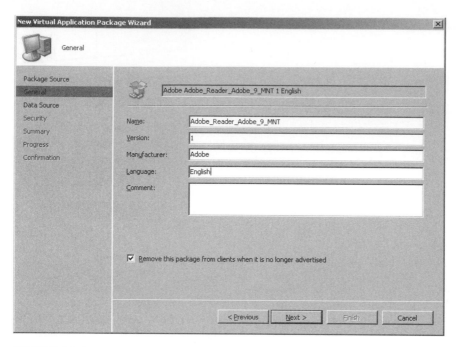

FIGURE 13.32   Configuring the General settings for the Adobe Reader virtual application

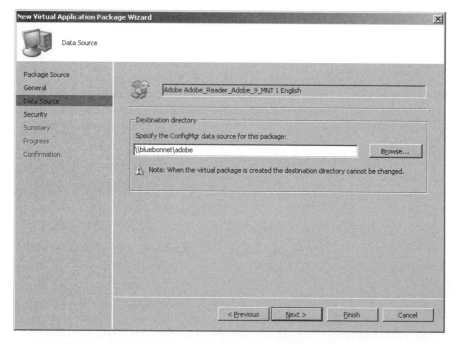

FIGURE 13.33   Configuring the Data Source settings for the Adobe Reader virtual application

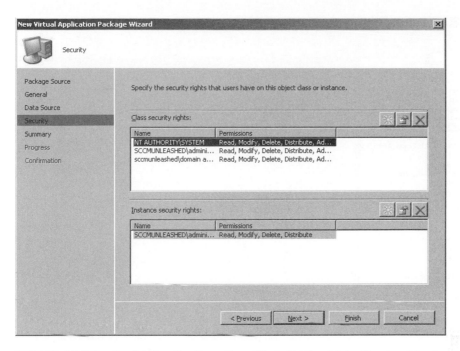

FIGURE 13.34   Configuring the Security settings for the Adobe Reader virtual application

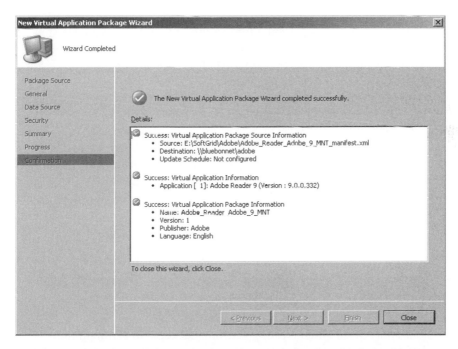

FIGURE 13.35   The successful creation of the Adobe Reader virtual application

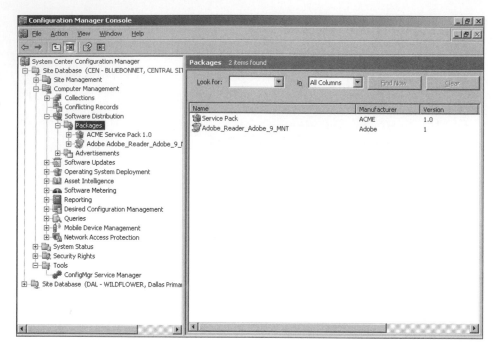

FIGURE 13.36   ConfigMgr console with a virtual application created

The integration of virtual application packaging into ConfigMgr 2007 R2 is a large step forward in providing a single platform to package and deploy software, regardless of whether it is deployed as a software package or a virtual application.

TIP

Prepackaged Virtual Applications Available for Download

The website http://www.instantapp.net has a number of applications prepackaged as App-V-enabled applications that are freely downloadable and instantly usable. These applications not only provide functional virtual applications without sequencing them, but also provide a great way to validate your ConfigMgr environment's ability to distribute virtual applications prior to testing your own virtual applications.

Avoiding Common ConfigMgr Software Packaging Issues

Several common issues may occur when creating software packages in Configuration Manager. These relate to issues in understanding the options available within ConfigMgr and when testing software packages.

Program and Package Properties

One key consideration when developing software packages in Configuration Manager are the options available when creating a package and a program. These options—such as the ability to require another package to install prior to installation, placing restrictions on the program such as the platforms it installs on, and how much free space is required for the program to install—provide increased capabilities when packaging software with ConfigMgr.

In order for you to understand these options better, the chapter includes details in the "OpsMgr Client" and "Forefront Client" sections on all available package and program configurations.

Testing, Testing, Testing

The most commonly overlooked method of avoiding issues with ConfigMgr packaging is to test for as many contingencies as possible. If you are creating a software package to deploy to 1,000 workstations, you almost certainly will run into unexpected configurations. Effective testing processes can limit the risks of program failures or unexpected complications.

To test software packages, you need a testing lab (also discussed in Chapter 7, "Testing and Stabilizing"). This lab includes computers representative of those systems to which you will deploy the software package. However, it is often very difficult to get nonproduction versions of actual systems for testing purposes.

One method to address this requirement is to use a virtual lab environment for software package testing. With a product such as Hyper-V or VMware, you can run multiple computers without requiring an entire lab of physical hardware. One of the major benefits of a virtual environment is the ability to return a computer quickly to an earlier configuration. This capability makes it easy to roll an operating system back to its previous state (prior to deploying the software package). This is beneficial when testing software packages, as they often need to go through multiple testing iterations. Although you can build computers in the virtual environment from standard images, a more representative approach would be to actually perform a physical-to-virtual (P2V) translation of existing desktops in your environment, and then change the computer's security identifier (SID) and name. Virtual lab environments also have the benefit of a smaller physical footprint, so less hardware is required for creating the lab.

Alternatively, physical lab environments provide real examples of those computers where you would deploy the package. In some cases, only a physical lab environment will identify issues such as a driver conflict existing between the software package and a set of computers running on a specific hardware platform. Your physical lab computers should be actual production systems taken from the groups where you are deploying software packages, and should represent the types of hardware that exist in your environment.

The authors' recommended approach to creating a lab environment is a hybrid between a physical lab and a virtual lab. Using some of both types of systems minimizes the number of systems required, while providing many of the benefits of a physical lab.

Another important factor to consider when testing software packages is what exactly to test. You should create a set of tests identifying the types of conditions to test before releasing the package. Here are some examples of this:

▶ Installing the software package where there is not enough disk space

▶ Deploying to an unsupported platform

▶ Deploying where the program is already installed

▶ Deploying with other software packages installed that may cause conflicts

The exact set of tests will vary depending on your package, but identifying potential failure conditions ahead of time and testing for those conditions significantly increase the likelihood of creating a functional software package.

Summary

This chapter discussed the various methods available for deploying software in a Windows environment and explained the benefits of using Configuration Manager to deploy software. It described how various components in ConfigMgr come together to provide a software deployment solution, and it provided examples for how to create packages in ConfigMgr both with and without a package definition file. The chapter also discussed programs and packages and available configuration options, as well as tips for avoiding common issues when creating packages. The chapter concluded with a discussion of Microsoft's direction for packaging in ConfigMgr, and tips for avoiding common ConfigMgr packaging issues. The next chapter will use these software packaging concepts in discussing how to deploy software with Configuration Manager 2007.

CHAPTER 14

Distributing Packages

Chapter 13, "Creating Packages," discussed several approaches for deploying software in Windows environments. It also provided details regarding the software packaging processes used in Configuration Manager (ConfigMgr) 2007. After you configure software for distribution in Configuration Manager, the next step is distributing it to client systems.

Using those packages and programs created in Chapter 13, this chapter discusses the steps necessary to move them through the software distribution process via queries, collections, distribution points, and advertisements. Figure 14.1 shows how these components combine to distribute software using Configuration Manager 2007.

The chapter also discusses distributing software using application virtualization, which is Microsoft's new direction for software distribution in ConfigMgr 2007.

About Queries

Queries, which are covered in depth in Chapter 17, "Configuration Manager Queries," are similar to collections in that you can use them to show information about resources matching specified criteria (behind the scenes a collection actually contains its own query, defined by a membership rule, which is used to specify the data that will populate the collection). From a functional perspective, you can use either a collection or a query to show what resources match the criteria you specify. However, queries run on an ad-hoc basis, whereas collections are sets of discovered resources typically based on hardware and

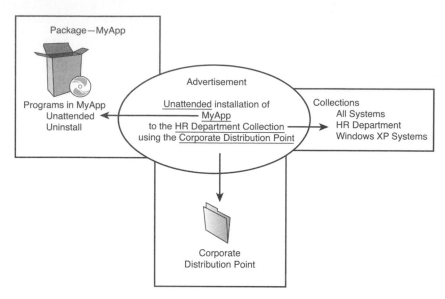

FIGURE 14.1   Combining packages, programs, advertisements, distribution points, and collections

software inventory, with the membership updated on a scheduled basis. Both queries and collections can be static, with a predefined membership. However, the results of a query always reflect the current state, whereas a collection may require updating to reflect the present state of those resources.

You can use both hardware and software inventory as criteria in queries and collections, making it important to activate both the ConfigMgr hardware and software inventory functions, and to collect that inventory information frequently to keep the information current. Hardware inventory is particularly important, because you can extend the SMS_Def.mof file to gather additional information with the hardware inventory component.

You can use queries for the following functions:

▶ **Providing information**—Queries can easily identify resources matching specified criteria. As an example, running the All Windows XP Systems query will list all Windows XP systems identified by Configuration Manager. Queries are not the same as reports (the data does not appear in a report-ready format), but can be used to gather information quickly based on the results of the query you defined.

▶ **As a basis for performing actions**—You can use queries to perform actions on the resources within the query. For instance, you can highlight a server and activate the Resource Explorer to see the current hardware and software inventory for the system, install an agent, or perform other tasks.

▶ **Creating collections**—When you create a collection, you can use existing queries to develop the criteria required for a resource to be a member of a collection. The

"Creating a Dynamic Collection" section in this chapter discusses this technique, which uses the Query Rule Properties screen of the New Collection Wizard.

Real World: Using Queries to Build Collections

There are several schools of thought about using queries as an ad-hoc tool when building collections. Conventional wisdom holds that most ConfigMgr administrators don't really do that. However, by using a query, you can check your logic, see if it works, and tune it until you like the result. Then you can create a collection based on the results. That can be more effective (and efficient) than creating a collection and continuing to tune it and update its members. It is easier to build a collection when there is something to base it off of.

What is the main difference between a query and a collection? Collections are used to organize and group systems and users together for a similar purpose, such as software distribution or to advertise task sequences. The software distribution process does not use queries. You create queries on an ad-hoc basis, meaning they reflect current resources that match the criteria. With a collection, on the other hand, you would schedule to update its resources on a daily basis.

Understanding the differences between queries and collections and the function of queries provides context to help you understand collections in Configuration Manager 2007.

Creating Collections

Collections represent resources within ConfigMgr; they consist of computers, users, or groups. You use collections to target ConfigMgr functions such as defining maintenance windows and performing software distributions, and you can define them as static or dynamic. ConfigMgr includes a set of predefined collections, providing a solid set of collections to use for targeting and presenting good templates for developing additional custom collections that you can build on. Figure 14.2 displays a set of predefined collections in ConfigMgr in the Configuration Manager console.

TIP

Identifying Predefined Collections

If you are in the habit of using the same naming convention for your collections as those supplied by Microsoft (such as All Windows 2003 Server Systems), it can become difficult to determine whether a particular collection was predefined or custom built.

To identify predefined collections, look at the Collection ID field. ConfigMgr's predefined collections start with *SMS* or *SMSDM* (for example, SMS Device Management). ConfigMgr creates custom collections using the site name, as you can see in Figure 14.2, where the collection ID for Static Collection Test starts with *CEN* (the three-letter code for the central site in the SCCMUnleashed environment).

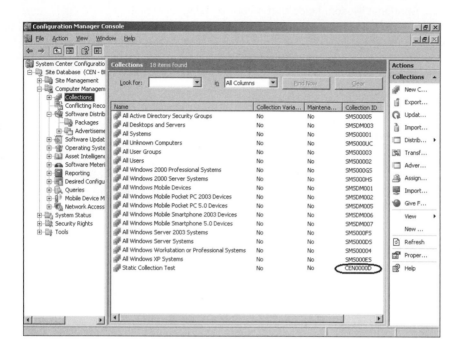

FIGURE 14.2   Collections in Configuration Manager 2007

Static Collections

Static collections are the easiest type of collection to create, and they are useful when you want to define a limited number of systems or users in a collection when the collection membership does not change frequently.

Creating a Static Collection

To understand how static collections work, you will create a static collection for a single computer system, which is one of the most common static collections. Perform the following steps:

1. Collections are defined in the ConfigMgr console. Navigate to Site Database -> Computer Management -> Collections. Right-click and choose New Collection to start the New Collection Wizard.

2. On the General screen (shown in Figure 14.3), define the name of the new collection and a description that is stored in the Comment field. A good approach to naming the collection is to use names similar to collections that already exist. For example, you would name a new collection containing Windows 2008 servers "All Windows 2008 Server Systems," and a new collection with Windows servers in the Dallas site might be "All Windows Server Systems in Dallas."

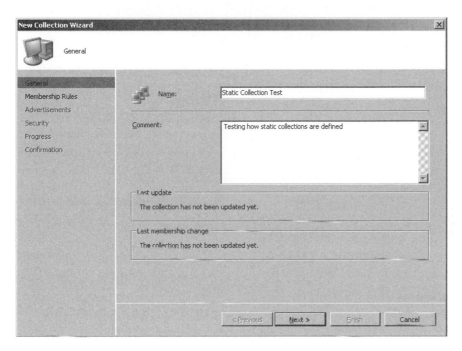

FIGURE 14.3   The General page of the New Collection Wizard

This example creates a sample collection named **Static Collection Test**, used temporarily for this environment.

3. There are no members in the collection by default. To add a static member to this collection, click the computer icon (circled in Figure 14.4) to open the Create Direct Membership Rule Wizard.

   Alternatively, clicking the query icon (next to the computer icon) opens the Query Rule Properties dialog box, discussed in the "Dynamic Collections" section.

4. After the Welcome screen of the Create Direct Membership Rule Wizard, the wizard proceeds to the Search for Resources step, asking you how to find resources to add to the collection. The Search for Resources screen in Figure 14.5 defines the following fields:

   ▶ **Resource class**—Provides the list of available resource classes, including Unknown Computer, User Group Resource, User Resource (default), System

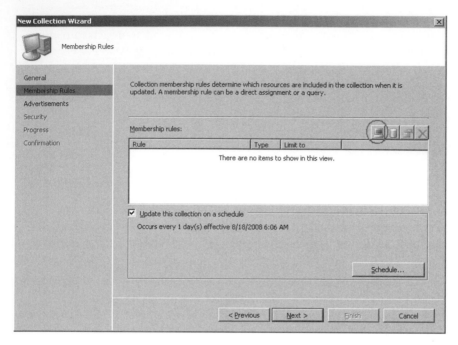

FIGURE 14.4   Membership Rules screen of the New Collection Wizard

Resource, and IP Network. This example will use System Resource to identify the name of the computer that will be a member of the static collection.

- ▶ **Attribute name**—The attributes available vary depending on the resource class previously chosen. Figure 14.5 shows the Netbios Name selected, as a means to identify the name of the computer that will be a member of the collection.

- ▶ **Value**—This field defines the potential values for this area. Wildcards are available as needed; as an example, the use of % in this field will identify all available NetBIOS names in the environment. The example shown in Figure 14.5 specifies the Bluebonnet server.

5. You can limit collections to contain only members that exist in another collection. As an example, if a collection is restricted to all Windows 2003 systems, any systems without Windows 2003 installed are not included as a potential member in the collection. Because the potential membership for this collection is already limited by using the value Bluebonnet (previously defined on the Search for Resources screen in Figure 14.5), Figure 14.6 leaves the Search in this collection field blank. Limiting the membership is also required when you are using the ConfigMgr console and do not have full rights to ConfigMgr resource database; this lets you limit your scope to the collection that your account has access to.

6. The previous pages in this wizard defined the potential membership for the collection as a specific resource—Bluebonnet (shown in Figure 14.7). If multiple resources match those restrictions already specified, they would now appear on the Select

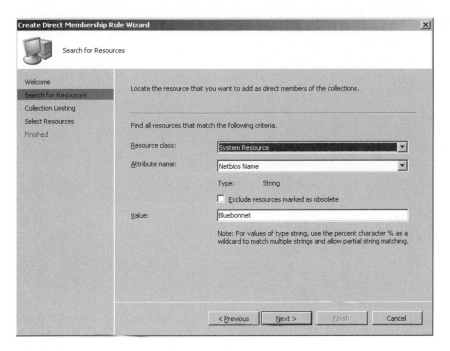

FIGURE 14.5   Search for Resources page of the Create Direct Membership Rule Wizard

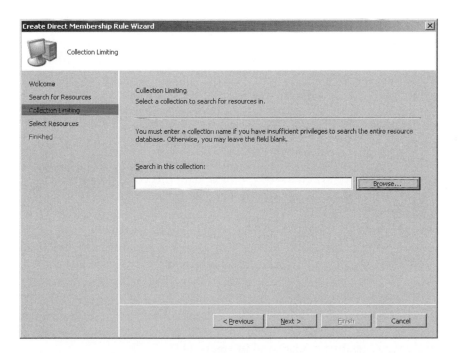

FIGURE 14.6   Collection Limiting page of the Create Direct Membership Rule Wizard

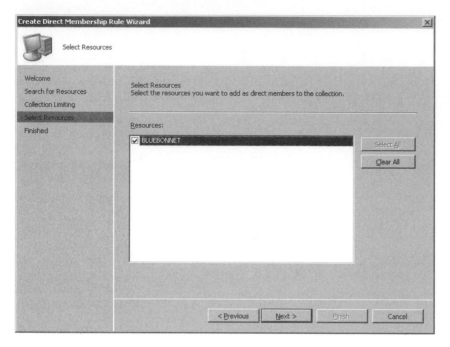

FIGURE 14.7   Select Resources page of the Create Direct Membership Rule Wizard

Resources page to select the resource(s) for the collection. As an example, if the collection was restricted to all Windows 2003 systems matching the value of SRV%, the Select Resources page would list all the Windows 2003 servers starting with a name containing SRV (SRVAD01, SRVEXCH02, and so on).

7. The Membership Rules screen shows the resources in the new collection. This example creates a new collection containing a single server named Bluebonnet. After moving to the Finished page, the wizard returns to the New Collection Wizard with a direct membership rule created for the Bluebonnet server, displayed in Figure 14.8.

   The Membership Rules screen also provides the capability to schedule when (or if) to update the collection. Notice the checked box for Update this collection on a schedule, which is the default configuration. Also notice that the collection is scheduled to update each day at the same time it was created.

   Collections will automatically update their contents on a scheduled basis, keeping the contents of the collection current with existing resources. You can also update a collection at any time by right-clicking the collection and choosing the option Update Collection Membership. (However, there is rarely a requirement to update a static membership collection manually.)

8. Next is the Advertisements screen, which shows a list of advertisements currently defined for this collection. Because you did not create any advertisements for this collection, this screen is empty, as displayed in Figure 14.9.

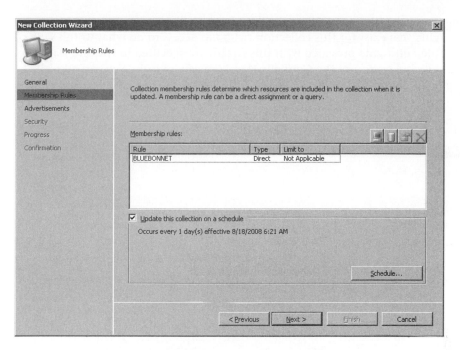

FIGURE 14.8 Membership Rules screen of the New Collection Wizard with the Bluebonnet server

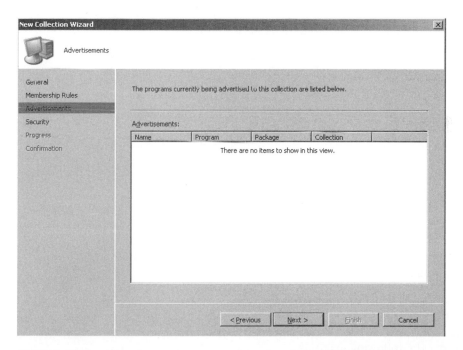

FIGURE 14.9 Advertisements screen of the New Collection Wizard

9. The Security screen (shown in Figure 14.10) provides a list of the class and instance security rights that exist for this collection (who has access to do what to this collection). The default rights provided with this wizard are specified in the Site Database -> Security Rights section of the Configuration Manager console. You can add, edit, or delete security rights using the buttons to the right, above the listed permissions.

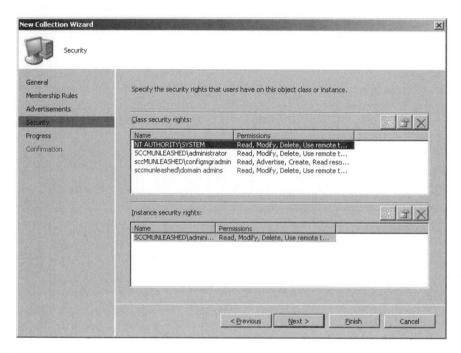

FIGURE 14.10   Security screen of the New Collection Wizard

10. The remaining screens of the New Collection Wizard display the progress as ConfigMgr creates the collection and a confirmation that the collection has been created.

Static collections have a place, particularly if you are creating test environments where you want to limit the systems involved in the tests. This differs from dynamic collections, which have the potential to add more resources to the collection based on those resources matching the criteria for the collection. For this example, a static collection provides a simple way to provide a target to use for deploying software.

Using Static Collections with Dynamic Additions

Sometimes static collections are not only static. You can interact with static collections (and dynamic collections) to add and remove members even outside of the ConfigMgr console. Consider the following example.

Real World: When a Dynamic Collection Should Be Static

Let's say there is a dynamic collection used to test packaging; the collection was created with a dynamic membership based on name (where Name equals %lab%). There is a single system called lab01, which you want to receive the test packages you are sending to the collection. However, your organization adds a new set of computers, located in the new laboratory conference room, that have names of laboratory01 through laboratory05. Based on the definition of the dynamic collection, these new systems would receive the test packages!

By defining a static collection with the exact name of the system you want the collection to contain, you limit the risk of deploying packages to systems that you do not want to receive them.

During the Systems Management Server (SMS) 2003 timeframe, a consulting organization was using SMS 2003 with the Operating System Deployment (OSD) feature pack to deploy operating systems. This organization also packaged a significant number of applications to deploy during the OSD process. Although most of these functioned as expected, a small subset of the software packages would freeze during the installation process, which caused the operating system deployment to freeze as well.

To address this situation, they created a collection (PostOSDInstall) that had a list of all the workstations deployed with OSD. As OSD completed the installation of each workstation, they added a task to run a script that added the workstation name to the PostOSDInstall collection. The collection was configured to update membership very frequently; once the workstation was added to the PostOSDInstall collection, the software packages advertised to the collection would begin to deploy shortly after the OSD process completed. Using this technique provided a way to deploy software that was failing within the OSD process through ConfigMgr—by approaching it from a different perspective.

Although this is a relatively in-depth example, it is included to show the type of functionality available through static collections that are added to dynamically.

Dynamic Collections

Now that you have gone through the process to create a static collection, let's talk about dynamic collections. A *dynamic collection* uses a query-based membership to determine the members of that collection. This means that dynamic collections change, based on the criteria defined for the collection.

Creating a Dynamic Collection

Chapter 13 created a software package for Microsoft Forefront Client Security. This section will create collections for both the Microsoft Forefront Client Security package and for the Operation Manager client. These collections are used later for targeting in the "Forefront Advertisement" and "OpsMgr Advertisement" sections in this chapter, respectively.

The SCCMUnleashed.com organization is starting the process of deploying the Forefront client to a set of workstations, but wants to limit the size of the deployment to mitigate the risk of affecting large numbers of workstations simultaneously. This can be addressed by creating a dynamic collection to target all Windows XP or Vista systems, restricted in its reach by being limited to systems only in a specific Organizational Unit (OU). To create this dynamic collection, perform the following steps:

1. The first step of this process is creating a collection containing all Windows XP and Vista systems. You create a dynamic collection in a similar manner to a static collection within the ConfigMgr console -> Site Database -> Computer Management -> Collections. Right-click and choose New Collection. Name this collection **All Windows XP and Vista Systems**, and this time use the query icon (circled in Figure 14.11) to define the collection membership.

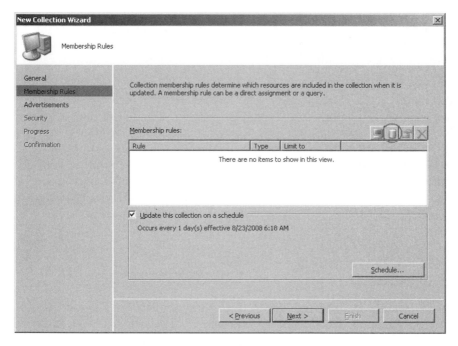

FIGURE 14.11   Membership Rules screen of the New Collection Wizard with the Query icon highlighted

Membership Rules

You can implement query membership rules independently or in conjunction with direct membership rules. As an example, you could populate a collection in the following manner:

▶ Using a query that contains all systems with *application x* (a query membership rule)

▶ Adding a second rule for those systems containing a specific name (a direct membership rule)

Direct membership rules give administrators the ability to select any of the existing resource classes (which include User, User Group, and System Resources) as the criteria for collection membership. The most common implementation of direct membership rules is the use of the NetBIOS name attribute in the System Resource class. More information is available regarding Configuration Manager resource classes and attribute names in Chapter 3, "Looking Inside Configuration Manager."

Query membership rules are more powerful than direct membership rules, and because of their dynamic capabilities, they are recommended for creating collection memberships. Collections have the ability to rerun a query configured as the membership rule on a recurring interval, so that systems that do not meet the criteria initially for the collection will show up if they meet the criteria later. In Configuration Manager 2007, the default collection's update interval is every 24 hours. You can configure this frequency in the ConfigMgr console to be more or less frequent, per collection, dependent on management needs. For information on using the nodes in the Configuration Manager console, see Chapter 10, "The Configuration Manager Console."

Use caution when setting aggressive collection update intervals, particularly in large environments or on servers with poorly performing disk subsystems. In SMS 2.0, the default collection update interval was set for every 2 hours—this was found to waste system resources and cause overall poor performance on site servers. With SMS 2003, the default collection update interval changed to 24 hours, the consensus being that if collections need more frequent updating, the admin could configure "one-off" type scenarios, as needed, using the collection properties.

2. Define the name of the collection as **All Windows XP and Vista Systems** and then use the Import Query Statement button (shown in Figure 14.12) to import an existing query. Choose the query most similar to the one you want to create—All Windows XP Systems, in this case. After selecting the query, edit it using the Edit Query Statement button.

3. Editing the query statement on the General tab shows the various attributes for the collection. The focus for this particular collection is on the Criteria tab, which is what needs to change to alter the collection to display both Vista and XP systems. To edit the criteria, either double-click the line showing the criteria or click the modify button (circled in Figure 14.13).

4. Editing the criteria opens the Criterion Properties dialog box. This dialog box (shown in Figure 14.14) allows you to define how to configure the criteria for this query. The following fields affect how the query works:

▶ **Criterion Type**—Options include Null, Simple value, Attribute reference, Subselected values, and List of values. Chapter 17 describes these fields in more detail.

▶ **Null value**—Compares the query attribute to a null value.

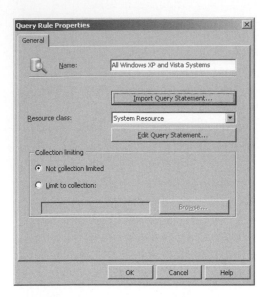

FIGURE 14.12   Query rule properties for All Vista and XP

FIGURE 14.13   Criteria for All Vista and XP

> ▶ **Simple value**—Compares to a constant value. Selecting Simple value enables the simple value settings.
>
> ▶ **Attribute reference**—Compares to another attribute. Selecting Attribute reference enables the attribute reference settings.
>
> ▶ **SubSelected values**—Compares to results returned by another query. Selecting SubSelected values enables the subselected values settings.

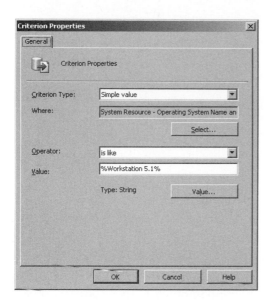

FIGURE 14.14   Criterion for All Windows XP Systems

▶ **List of values**—Compares to a list of constant values. Selecting List of values enables the list of values settings.

The All Windows XP Systems query in Figure 14.14 originally used a simple value.

▶ **Where**—The Where field is grayed out and shows the Where clause defined for the query. Use the Select button in Figure 14.14 to change the content of this field.

▶ **Operator**—This dropdown field specifies how to assess the values. Options vary, depending on the value defined for the criterion type.

The All Windows XP Systems query is using the "is like" value.

▶ **Value**—This field defines the value the criteria needs to match. As an example, the value required for the All Windows XP Systems query is %Workstation 5.1%.

5. For this example, change the Criterion Type setting to List of values (to be able to match multiple different operating systems using the query). List of values is only one of the available criteria discussed in step 4, but it most closely matches the requirements for this particular collection. This change alters the Operator field, which now defaults to a value of "is in." Use the Value button to display the values currently known for the field defined in the Where clause. In this example, this is all known operating system versions; Figure 14.15 displays these values.

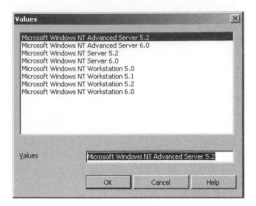

FIGURE 14.15   Operating system version listing

6. To make this query match the values for all Windows XP and Vista systems, use the Value button (shown in Figure 14.16) to add the different operating system values matching that value—Microsoft Windows NT Workstation 5.1, Microsoft Windows NT Workstation 5.2, Microsoft Windows NT Workstation 6.0. These values are selected based on the value that is selected (these do not need to be typed in if they are selected from the Values list).

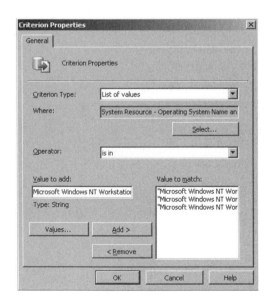

FIGURE 14.16   Criterion for all Windows XP and Vista systems

These versions match to Windows XP, Windows XP 64, and Windows Vista. A good reference for Windows version numbers is available at http://en.wikipedia.org/wiki/Windows_NT.

Here are two ways to create this collection:

- ▶ Defining a collection that would match all operating system versions that include **workstation** but also match previous operating system versions (such as Windows 2000 Professional System)

- ▶ Creating a collection that would match all operating system versions containing **%Microsoft Windows NT Workstation 5.%** or **%Microsoft Windows NT Workstation 6.%**

The second approach is more straightforward, meets the criteria, and will adapt if additional workstation versions are created that match the criteria. ConfigMgr is a flexible tool, and offers multiple ways to achieve the same result.

TIP

Approach for Creating Collections

It is best to create collections based on the criteria most logical to you so that they perform as you expect them to and are easier to debug.

To verify the membership of the collection, complete the wizard and verify that the members of the new collection match the members expected, based on the query just defined.

Creating a Dynamic Collection Limited to a Collection

After creating a collection that includes all the Windows XP and Windows Vista systems, you can use that collection to limit the available members of another collection, in this case a Forefront collection, to target the Forefront client software for deployment. Perform the following steps:

1. Create a second collection, calling it **Forefront Client Deployment**. Provide a description for the collection and move on to the Membership Rules screen. Use the Query icon (circled previously in Figure 14.11) to define the collection membership.

2. Define the name as **Forefront Client Deployment** and limit the collection to the All Windows XP and Vista Systems collection created earlier in the "Creating a Dynamic Collection" section. Figure 14.17 displays this configuration.

3. You will need to create a new query statement to limit this collection to only system resources that are part of a specific OU structure. To do this, choose the Edit Query Statement button and set the Resource class to System Resource. On the next page, choose Simple value where the System Resource – System OU Name is equal to the value of the OU used to store these resources. For this example, the value is **SCCMUnleashed/Test** (the domain name followed by a slash and then the name of the OU).

   If several different OU structures existed, you could use the List of values option, as previously discussed in the "Creating a Dynamic Collection" section. With only a single OU location, it is simpler to define this as a simple value, as displayed in Figure 14.18.

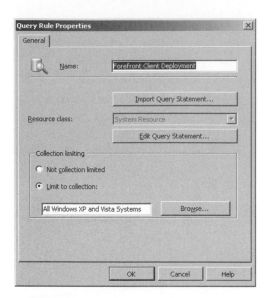

FIGURE 14.17   Criterion for the new Forefront Client Deployment collection

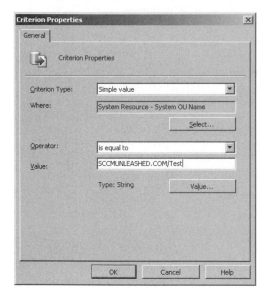

FIGURE 14.18   Limiting a collection based on the OU

4. To verify the membership of the collection, complete the wizard and verify the members of the new collection match the members expected, based on the query defined in step 3. For this example, the expected result is Windows XP or Windows Vista systems existing in the Test OU structure.

This collection is used to target the Forefront client, discussed later in the "Forefront Advertisement" section.

Subcollections

In Configuration Manager, you can use subcollections to associate one collection with another collection. There are two different types of subcollections:

- ▶ Linked subcollections
- ▶ Dependent subcollections

The next two sections discuss these types.

Linked Subcollections

Use a linked collection to tie a collection to an existing ConfigMgr collection. To create a linked subcollection, highlight the collection you want to link and then choose the New -> Link to collection option. Note that linked subcollections can exist in multiple locations in the collection structure. As an example, you could link the All Windows XP and Vista systems collection created in the "Creating a Dynamic Collection" section in this chapter to multiple locations in the ConfigMgr collection so it appears in multiple places with the same name.

Linked collections do not draw their membership from the collection they are linked under. This means you could create a collection called My Static Collection (with two hard-coded systems defined as members) and then link the All Desktops and Servers collection to it. The membership of the All Desktops and Servers collection is *not* limited to the two members of the top-level collection My Static Collection, but rather shows the full list of members that exist in the All Desktops and Servers collection.

Dependent Subcollections

You create a dependent subcollection when you highlight an existing collection and define a new collection under the original collection.

Why would you want to use dependent subcollections? A common usage is for software distribution targeting. Create a top-level collection for all systems that need the software package deployed, with subcollections for the different types of programs that will run on the systems. As an example, create the collections used to deploy the Operations Manager (OpsMgr) client, which will vary depending on whether the system is amd64, i386, or ia64. Perform the following steps:

1. Begin by creating a top-level collection called **All Client Systems**, based on the existing All Client Systems query. The next collection you define (step 2) will use this collection and limit the members to those systems that are ConfigMgr clients.

2. Create another top-level collection, named **OpsMgr Client Deployment**. Define this collection to contain all Windows Server operating systems that have ConfigMgr agents deployed to them.

    Create this collection using the same process used in the "Creating a Dynamic Collection" section of the chapter (but the criteria used is %Server% instead of %Workstation%) and limit the collection membership to the All Client Systems collection.

3. To define a different time to update this collection, select the Schedule button in Figure 14.19 to open the Custom Schedule dialog box displayed in Figure 14.20.

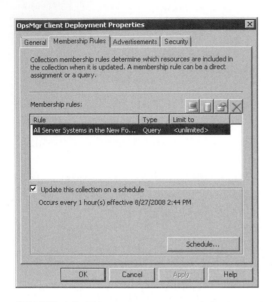

FIGURE 14.19   Setting the schedule for updates to the OpsMgr Client Deployment collection

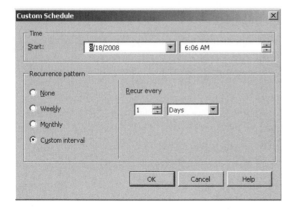

FIGURE 14.20   Defining a custom schedule for the collection

This dialog box is used with dynamic collections only; static collections do not have scheduled update times, because they will not change unless the membership is changed manually. The Custom Schedule dialog box contains several fields:

▶ **Time Start**—This is a two-part field specifying the date and time the collection updates, which defaults to the date and time you created the collection.

▶ **Recurrence pattern**—Options include None, Weekly, Monthly, and Custom Interval.

▶ **Recur every**—The value for this field varies depending on the recurrence pattern chosen:

If you choose None, there are no options for this field.

If you choose Weekly, the number of weeks can be defined (defaults to 1) and you can specify the day of the week to update the collection.

If you choose Monthly, the number of months can be defined (defaults to 1) and you can specify the day of the month as a number (default of 1) or the last day of the month. You can also specify a fixed day (such as the first Tuesday of the month).

In this case, the recurrence pattern is set to update daily. Click OK to return to the Membership Rules screen and then clear the option Update this collection on a schedule.

4. Now that you have a top-level collection for the OpsMgr software deployment, the next step is to create the dependent subcollections. Highlight the OpsMgr Client Deployment collection, right-click, and choose New -> Collection.

Name the first subcollection **OpsMgr AMD64**. Create it as a dynamic collection and specify the membership such that the criterion matches a simple value for Computer System – System Type, where it is equal to **x64-based PC**, as shown in Figure 14.21. As a reference, the OpsMgr agent has three folders for the different hardware types:

FIGURE 14.21 Limiting a collection based on the computer system type

▶ **AMD64**—Equals "x64-based PC" for the collection membership

▶ **I386**—Equals "x86-based PC" for the collection membership

▶ **IA64**—Equals "IA64-based PC" for the collection membership

---

TIP

Identifying Criteria for Collections

With all the information ConfigMgr gathers from hardware and software inventory, it can be difficult to identify which criteria to use to restrict collection membership. Although the Criterion Properties dialog box provides a list of values available for the various categories, it is often helpful to see the fields and values in a different format to find what you are looking for.

Using the Resource Explorer provides hardware and software inventory information in a format that is easy to browse. Highlight a system you know will have the value, right-click, and choose Start -> Resource Explorer.

Although this approach does not provide all available information that may be used in a collection, it does present a large quantity of information you can utilize for collection criteria.

The "OpsMgr Advertisement" section will reference these new subcollections (OpsMgr AMD64, OpsMgr I386, and OpsMgr IA64) when creating advertisements for the OpsMgr agent deployment.

NOTE

How Subcollections Become Linked Collections

The page at http://technet.microsoft.com/en-us/library/bb680976.aspx provides the following information regarding dependent subcollections:

"Dependent subcollections are created as a new collection under an existing collection. When you create a subcollection, it is dependent on the collection under which it was created, as long as you do not link other collections to it. If the subcollection is linked to other collections, the subcollection becomes a linked collection while attached to more than one collection. When you delete a collection, any dependent subcollections of that collection are also deleted. Any advertisements, queries, or collection membership rules that are dependent on the subcollection are affected by its deletion. Because of this, it is strongly recommended that you use the Delete Collection Wizard to delete any collections that may contain dependent subcollections."

Subcollections are very useful for logically gathering groups of collections, and can be nested multiple levels deep (as an example, collection1 can have subcollection1, which contains subcollection2, which contains subcollection3, and so on). Although subcollections can be to almost any depth, you should use fewer than 10 levels to mini-mize the complexity.

Exclusion Collections

An interesting situation occurs when trying to create a collection for systems that do *not* match a condition. As an example, it is easy to create a collection of systems that have a particular file deployed to them. It is more difficult to create a collection of systems without that file deployed to them. You can accomplish this by creating a custom query that uses a subselect to exclude the members of another query.

Exclusion collections are useful in situations where you want software to deploy to a large number of systems but have specific systems you want to exclude. An example of where this applies is with validated systems. A *validated system* is one that has a strict process to validate system functionality any time software is installed on it. Typically, these types of systems are patched less frequently, with larger number of patches occurring at the same time to minimize the time required to execute the validation process.

To create an exclusion collection, the first thing to do is identify the collection you want to exclude. Navigate to Collection IDs in the Configuration Manager console by going to System Center Configuration Manager -> Site Database -> Computer Management -> Collections. In this case, Validated Systems is the collection you want to exclude, and it has a Collection ID of CEN0000E, as displayed in Figure 14.22.

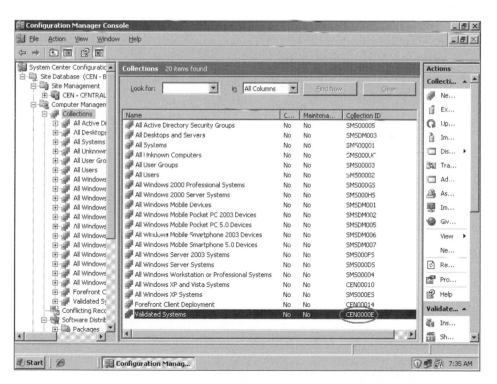

FIGURE 14.22   Determining the collection ID for the Validated System collection

The goal is to create a collection based on the Forefront Client Deployment collection that does not include the members of the Validated Systems collection. As you see in Figure 14.23, there are currently 11 systems meeting the criteria defined earlier for the original Forefront Client Deployment collection, discussed in the "Creating a Dynamic Collection Limited to a Collection" section.

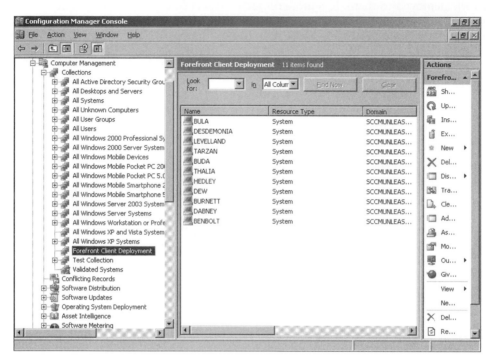

FIGURE 14.23   Members of the Forefront Client Deployment collection

In contrast to the Forefront Client Deployment collection, the Validated Systems collection displayed in Figure 14.24 is a static collection with Buda and Thalia as members (see the "Creating a Static Collection" section for the steps to create a static collection).

There now are two collections: One contains 11 members (including Buda and Thalia) and the second contains only two members (Buda and Thalia). You can modify the query that defines the Forefront Client Deployment collection to tell the first collection to exclude members of the second collection. Add the following code to the original query:

```
and SMS_R_System.ResourceID not in (Select ResourceID from
SMS_FullCollectionMembership where CollectionID="<collection ID>")
```

The query restricts this particular collection to the collection ID CEN0000E. The complete query will look like Figure 14.25.

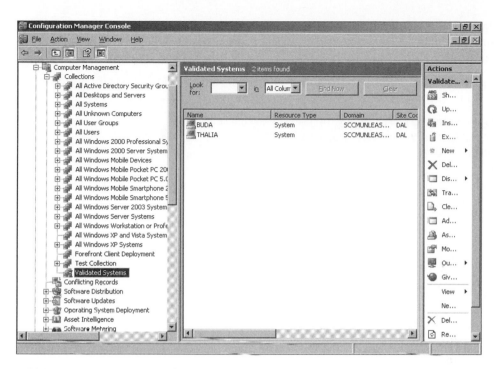

FIGURE 14.24   Members of the Validated Systems collection

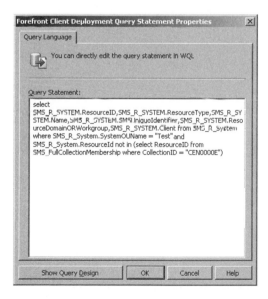

FIGURE 14.25   New query removing validated systems from the Forefront Client Deployment collection

By editing the WMI Query Language (WQL) code directly, you can create additional criteria to limit the collection. Here, System Resource – ResourceID (SMS_R_System.ResourceID) is added to the criteria list as a subselect type, and "not in" is used as the operator.

You can use the same concept to exclude multiple collections. Simply specify multiple collections to exclude, such as:

```
and SMS_R_System.ResourceID not in (Select ResourceID from
SMS_FullCollectionMembership where CollectionID="<collection ID>",
"<collection ID 2>", ...)
```

You can also add this directly via the user interface (UI) through the Criterion Properties, shown in Figure 14.26, which shows the original collection criterion changed to remove the members of the CEN0000E collection.

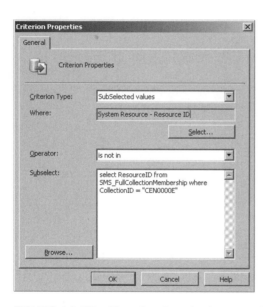

FIGURE 14.26   Changing the criterion to exclude a collection

---

TIP

Benefits of Using Two Collections

You may find it useful to have both a "not in" collection and a collection defined as "which ones are missing from the other collection." This technique allows you to define a very complicated collection for the actual membership; then the second collection is just a comparison between (as an example) all systems and the "not in" collection.

To illustrate how this can work, consider a case using antivirus systems. Here, you may want one collection that has all systems that have McAfee and another collection that has all systems that do not have McAfee. One is used to get an action (perhaps to update a date file) and the other is set with another action (deploy the McAfee software).

You can also easily create a collection that excludes members from one collection and from a second collection, such as a "servers without antivirus" collection, which is a collection containing any server without McAfee or Norton or Forefront, and so on.

The original Forefront Client Deployment collection had 11 resources, and the Validated Systems has two resources that overlap between the two collections. By excluding those resources in the second collection, the expectation is the new collection will only have nine resources and not contain the resources from the Validated Systems collection (Buda and Thalia). The contents of the new Forefront Client Deployment collection, displayed in Figure 14.27, confirm that the collection does not include the members of the Validated Systems collection.

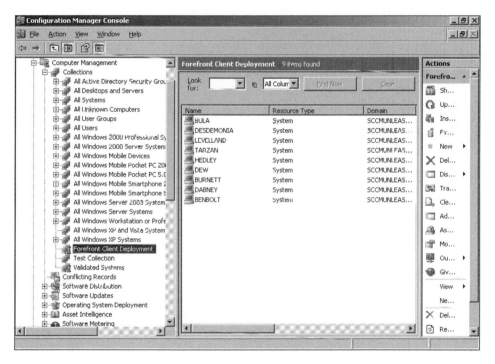

FIGURE 14.27   Forefront Client Deployment collection without Validated Systems resources

Collection Flexibility

This chapter has discussed several ways to define collections in ConfigMgr. These include collections with static members, dynamic memberships, subcollections, and exclusion collections. Each of these demonstrates the flexibility of the ConfigMgr collection functionality, which really comes down to the powerful ability to target exactly what you need to target with your collections.

Right-clicking a Collection

If you want to see the power and flexibility of Configuration Manager 2007, a great way to do so is to simply right-click a collection. The resulting list is staggering at first glance. As you would expect with a right-click, you can see the properties of the collection, delete the collection, get help, refresh the contents, and customize the view that you are seeing. However, with a simple right-click, you can also show the count of how many systems are in the collection, update the membership of the collection, install the ConfigMgr client to the systems in the collection, and modify the settings of the collection or export the objects in the collection. You can create a new collection or a new link to a collection, delete the resource in the collection, and distribute software to the collection.

Although that sounds like a long list, it is just the beginning! How about transferring site settings or clearing the last PXE advertisement, advertising a task sequence, assigning a baseline configuration, or performing Out of Band Management on the systems in the collection. The point here is that collections are extremely powerful and extremely flexible, and they are a key piece of how you can configure Configuration Manager to perform very complex and granular forms of targeting.

Using Distribution Points

After creating packages/programs and the collection you intend to advertise them to, it is important to understand how ConfigMgr distributes programs. Here are the three major types of distribution points in ConfigMgr:

▶ Standard distribution points

▶ BITS-enabled standard distribution points

▶ Branch distribution points

In addition, each type of distribution may be "protected." The next sections discuss each of these distribution points and their usage in the ConfigMgr 2007 software deployment process.

TIP

Client Roaming and Distribution Points

Client roaming allows clients to move between sites in the ConfigMgr hierarchy and still be managed while making the best use of available network resources. Roaming allows a client currently not in the boundaries of its site to find the closest distribution point to download source files for functions such as software distribution. Roaming clients can access advertisement content as long as the content is available from the distribution point if the setting "When a client is connected within a slow or unreliable network boundary: Do not run program" is unchecked on the advertisement (configured on the Advertisement Properties, Distribution Points tab). If a client is roaming to a subnet boundary outside the boundaries of a ConfigMgr site, it will be unable to access ConfigMgr resources. Details on complex roaming configurations are available at http://technet.microsoft.com/en-us/library/bb694028.aspx. This example assumes the client is roaming to a subnet boundary controlled by another site. Roaming within a site involves both regional and global roaming, as discussed in Chapter 4, "Configuration Manager Solution Design."

Standard Distribution Points

ConfigMgr deploys software using distribution points. A *distribution point* (DP) is a server role in ConfigMgr that receives packages for distribution throughout the site. DPs provide local network access to software distributed by ConfigMgr. As an example, if Microsoft Office is being deployed to an environment with locations in Dallas, Houston, Beijing, and Brussels, it is preferable for each of these locations to install from the local area network (LAN), versus copying the data across the link multiple times to install the software on the client workstations in that location.

Distribution points are server roles defined in ConfigMgr console -> Site Database -> Site Management -> *<Site Code>* *<Site Name>* Site Settings -> Site Systems. ConfigMgr adds new servers as either a new server or a new server share.

> **NOTE**
>
> **Comparing Server and Server Share Distribution Points**
>
> A distribution point is the only site system you can create as a server share; all other roles are created as servers. Server shares allow you to choose a specific drive and create a Windows share that ConfigMgr uses for the distribution point role—but the disadvantage is you have to monitor that share to ensure the drive does not fill up. When the distribution point is a server, ConfigMgr will manage the space for you by creating new SMSPKGx$ shares when more space is required. The downside with server-based distribution points is you cannot control growth; ConfigMgr can potentially take over all available NTFS drive space on the designated server. Distribution points on servers can also be configured as branch distribution points and support Internet-based clients; these DPs are not supported with server shares.
>
> For additional information, see http://technet.microsoft.com/en-us/library/bb892801.aspx.

After defining a server as a site server, you can assign the various server roles available, including the distribution point server role. To add the distribution point server role to the Wildflower site server in the DAL ConfigMgr site, perform the following steps:

1. Start by highlighting the Wildflower server under Site Database -> Site Management -> *<Site Code>* *<Site Name>* Site Settings -> Site Systems. Right-click and choose

New Roles to initiate the New Site Role Wizard. On the first page, specify the settings shown in Figure 14.28:

- ▶ **Intranet FQDN**—Specify the Fully Qualified Domain Name (FQDN) for this site system on the intranet. This setting determines the name intranet-based systems will use to connect to the server, and is required for native mode and publishing in DNS. Enter the default FQDN, which is **wildflower.sccmunleashed.com**.

- ▶ **Internet FQDN**—Specify the Internet-based Fully Qualified Domain Name for this site system. This setting determines what name Internet-based systems will use when connecting to the server. Enter the default FQDN, **wildflower.sccmunleashed.com**.

- ▶ **Account**—You can select Use the site server's computer account to install this site system or Use another account for installing this site system. Choose the default setting, which is using the site server's computer account.

- ▶ **Protected Site System**—Set this site server to be configured as a protected site system. The "Protected Distribution Points" section discusses this setting in more detail. For this configuration, leave the default setting, which is unchecked.

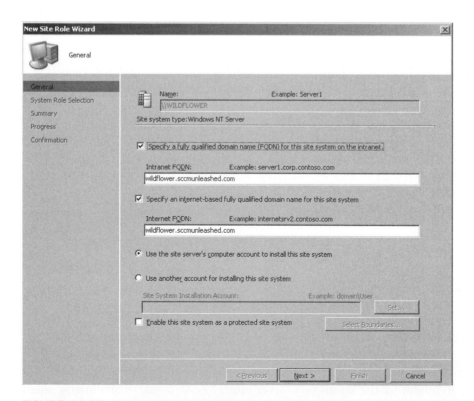

FIGURE 14.28   Configuring the settings for the new distribution point server role on Wildflower

2. On the System Role Selection screen, specify the available roles to activate on this site system. Only those site system roles not previously assigned to the site system are displayed. For this example, add the distribution point role, as shown in Figure 14.29.

3. Specify the details for the configuration of the distribution point role you are creating on Wildflower. This includes several settings, displayed in Figure 14.30:

> ▶ **Enable as a standard distribution point**—This is the default configuration, which allows configuring the Communication Settings section of the screen. Because you are creating a standard distribution point, select this option.

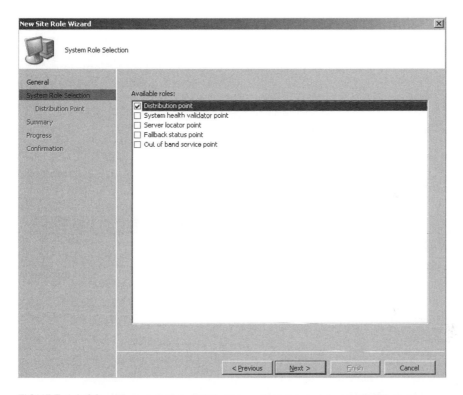

FIGURE 14.29   Choosing the distribution point server role on Wildflower

---

NOTE

Binary Differential Replication and Delta Replication in ConfigMgr

One of the benefits of Configuration Manager 2007 is its ability to update source files for a previously deployed package by only sending changes that occurred after deploying the package. As an example, the OpsMgr packages were pushed out to the various distribution points, but the agent now needs updating to include a newly released version of the software. When the new version of the package is sent to the distribution points, ConfigMgr only sends those parts of the package that changed after it was last sent to those distribution points. This approach helps minimize the network impact of updating packages in a ConfigMgr environment. Additional details on binary differential replication are available at http://technet.microsoft.com/en-us/library/bb693953.aspx.

Binary delta replication and delta replication are not the same. Delta replication is performed at the file level, whereas binary delta replication is performed at the byte level. Delta replication can work while binary delta replication is disabled. If you enable binary delta replication, standard delta replication is disabled as a result.

▶ **Communication settings**—Allow clients to transfer content from this distribution point using BITS, HTTP, and HTTPS (required for device clients and Internet-based clients). Options available for this setting include the following:

   ▶ Allow intranet-only client connections

   ▶ Allow Internet-only client connections

   ▶ Allow both intranet and Internet client connections

   See Chapter 5, "Network Design," for additional detail on BITS.

TIP

Why Does Only the Intranet Option Appear?

If your ConfigMgr environment is in native mode, three communications settings options appear on the Distribution Point page of the New Site Role Wizard:

▶Allow intranet-only client connections

▶Allow Internet-only client connections

▶Allow both intranet and Internet client connections

If your ConfigMgr environment is in mixed mode (the case with the site shown in Figure 14.30), the only option available is Allow intranet-only client connections.

Also in native mode, the box for Allow clients to connect anonymously is checked and grayed out, whereas in mixed mode this option can be checked or unchecked.

This setting indicates whether BITS will be used for the DP, and is required for connections from mobile device clients and Internet-based clients. For Windows 2008 server systems, you will need to download, install, and configure WebDAV manually if your DP will be using this setting. BITS is used on the distribution point, so check this option, as shown in Figure 14.30.

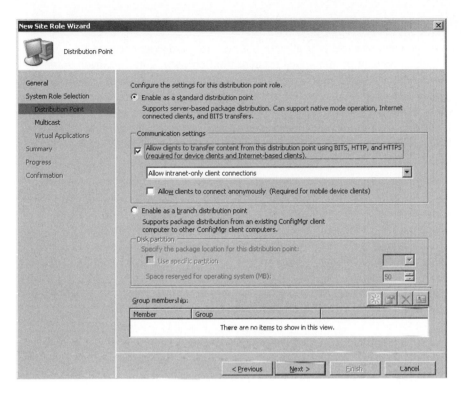

FIGURE 14.30   Configuring the distribution point server role on Wildflower

▶ **Enable as a branch distribution point**—This sets the distribution point to be a branch distribution point, discussed later in the "Branch Distribution Points" section.

For this option to be available, the site system you are configuring must be listed as a client in the collection. This is because the branch distribution is a client component (rather than a server component) and will require a healthy ConfigMgr client for activation.

▶ **Group membership**—Provides a way to group distribution points together into logical groupings. As an example, you could create a grouping for all distribution points in a site. Take the default configuration, which is not to identify any group memberships for this distribution point.

4. Finish the New Site Role Wizard process through the Summary, Progress, and Confirmation pages to complete creating the new distribution point.

Specifying Where Distribution Points Store Data

When a distribution point site role is assigned to a system, ConfigMgr chooses the drive with the largest amount of free space to store the ConfigMgr data. However, there will be situations when you need to choose where the distribution point data is stored. For these types of situations, it is best to create a new server share. This allows you to define the share on the server, which enables you to choose where you want to store the data. (See the earlier note "Comparing Server and Server Share Distribution Points" in this section for information on the difference between server and server share distribution points.)

As an example, if you create a new distribution point on the Wildflower server as a server type, ConfigMgr automatically chooses the NTFS-formatted drive with the largest amount of free space (G: in this case) and creates a SMSPKGG$ share on the G: drive. However, if you configure this new distribution point on the Wildflower server as a new server share, you can create a share called "share" (or SMSPKGF$ to be consistent with the ConfigMgr naming standard) and store data on the F: drive instead of the G: drive.

Another available option is to create a file at the root of the drive (i.e. C:\) named **NO_SMS_ON_DRIVE.sms** that you want to prevent ConfigMgr from installing any components on.

In summary, distribution points are most useful in environments where the systems will receive software deployments and a local server (part of the LAN) can provide the software distribution point role. Using regular or standard distribution points is suggested for those environments without a requirement to restrict which systems can communicate with the DP.

Protected Distribution Points

A protected distribution point (PDP) is a distribution point on a site system configured as a protected site system. You can define protected site systems for distribution points or state migration points. Using a protected site system means only clients within the boundaries defined for the site system can use that site system. In the case of a distribution point, this means only clients that are part of the boundaries defined for the protected distribution point can use the distribution point for software installation.

You can use PDPs to minimize wide area network (WAN) traffic by restricting ConfigMgr clients to use only those distribution points local to those systems. If the clients cannot access a distribution point, they cannot install software packages—so this restriction may require additional distribution points to provide redundancy. Defining additional distribution points enables a site to provide software distribution even if one of the protected distribution points is offline. Note that you cannot use protected distribution points for connections from clients over the Internet.

You can configure protected distribution points when you create the site system, or later by changing the properties of the site system. To convert the new distribution point created on the Wildflower server in the "Standard Distribution Points" section of the chapter, perform the following steps:

1. In the ConfigMgr console, navigate to Site Database -> Site Management -> *<Site Code> <Site Name>* -> Site Settings -> Site Systems -> Wildflower -> ConfigMgr Site System. Then right-click and choose Properties.

2. Enable this site system as a protected site system by checking the appropriate box on the properties of the Wildflower site system, as circled in Figure 14.31.

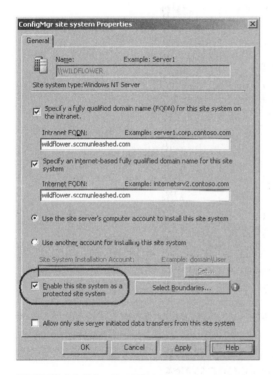

FIGURE 14.31   Enabling the protected site system setting for Wildflower

3. After enabling this setting, you need to select the boundaries for the protected site system. If no boundaries are defined for the protected site system, no clients will be able to use the site system! To determine the boundaries for this protected site system, click the Select Boundaries button (Figure 14.31) and choose from the available subnets that display. For this example, the 192.168.5.0 subnet was selected for the boundaries on the protected site system, as displayed in Figure 14.32. For more information on subnets in ConfigMgr 2007, see Chapter 5.

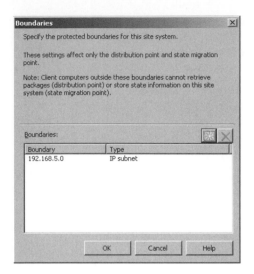

FIGURE 14.32   Configuring the boundaries of the protected site system setting for Wildflower

For those environments with a requirement to minimize the potential impact to the network, protected distribution points are highly recommended.

Branch Distribution Points

A branch distribution point (BDP) is a distribution point on a site system designed to provide distribution point functionality in those locations where a server is not available, such as a small or distributed office. You can install branch distribution points on workstation or server-class systems, which gives ConfigMgr 2007 the ability to distribute software from the local network without a local distribution point. A branch distribution point requires a BITS-enabled standard distribution point containing the content to be delivered to the BDP. If a branch distribution point is communicating with a protected standard distribution point, the boundaries of that standard distribution point need to include the branch distribution point.

You can define multiple branch distribution points for a location. This is a recommended configuration, because workstations are more likely to be rebooted during the day than server systems.

To install a branch distribution point, the system must be an existing ConfigMgr client that is not in a workgroup, running Windows 2000, or configured to use an Internet-based management point. Perform the following steps to add a branch distribution point:

1. Change the configuration for Wildflower so that it will be a BITS-enabled standard distribution point.

Set this by navigating in the ConfigMgr console to Site Database -> Site Settings -> *<Site Code> <Site Name>* -> Site Systems -> Wildflower -> ConfigMgr Distribution Point. Right-click and choose Properties.

2. Check the Communication settings box (shown in Figure 14.33) and set the drop-down option to Allow intranet-only client connections. (There are no plans to allow Internet-based clients in this site.)

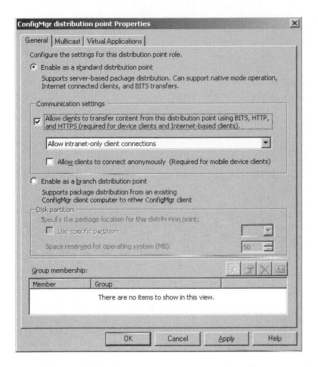

FIGURE 14.33   Enabling BITS on the Wildflower standard distribution point

3. Now that there is a BITS-enabled standard distribution point, you will create a branch distribution point to communicate with it. To create the branch distribution point, navigate in the console to Site Database -> Site Management -> *<Site Code> <Site Name>* -> Site Settings -> Site Systems. Then right-click and choose New -> Server.

4. Because the branch distribution point will be on the Dabney system, specify that system's name and FQDN, as shown in Figure 14.34. It is not a requirement in all cases to specify the FQDN on this page, although this option is checked and may be filled in by default. You must specify the FQDN if you will be using native mode and Internet-based clients, if the site has clients in different domains with automatic approval of clients, for IPv6-only environments, or for environments not using WINS.

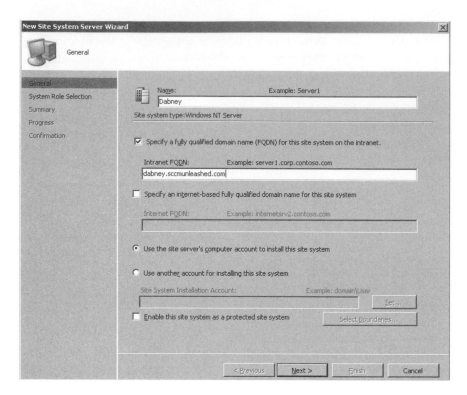

FIGURE 14.34   General settings of the New Site System Server Wizard for the Dabney branch distribution point

5. When selecting the system role, check the distribution point role, similar to Figure 14.29.

On the Distribution Point screen of the New Site Role Wizard, select the option Enable as a branch distribution point, as displayed in Figure 14.35.

After checking this option, you can choose a partition on which to store the branch distribution data, and specify an amount of space to reserve for the operating system. If you do not specify a partition for the branch distribution data, the wizard will automatically select the drive with the largest amount of free space. In Figure 14.35, the amount of space to reserve for the operating system is kept at the default of 50MB.

After you create the branch distribution point for Dabney, it is visible in the console when specifying a distribution point to use for your packages (Navigate to Site Database -> Computer Management -> Software Distribution -> Packages -> *<Package Name>* -> Distribution Points). You can also see it under the site settings (Site Database -> Site Management -> *<Site Code> <Site Name>* -> Site Settings -> Site Systems -> *<servername>*). In both cases, the console lists the standard distribution points as type Server whereas the branch distribution points show as type Branch.

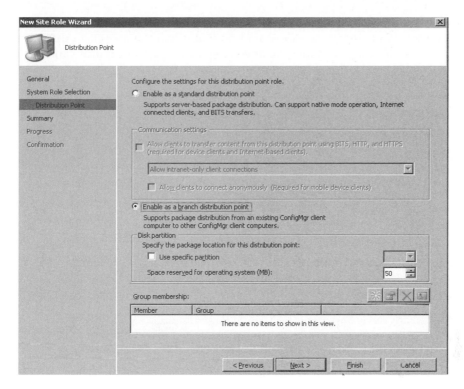

FIGURE 14.35   Distribution Point settings of the New Site Role Wizard for the Dabney branch distribution point

Branch distribution points provide an effective way to minimize network usage and increase performance when distributing software packages to locations where a standard distribution point is not viable.

Advertised Programs Client Agent

Prior to sending out any advertisements in Configuration Manager 2007, you must enable the client agent for advertised programs. Navigate in the ConfigMgr console to Site Management -> *<Site Code> <Site Name>* -> Site Settings -> Client Agents -> Advertised Programs Client Agent. Right-click and choose Properties. On the General tab, specify the following:

- ▶ **Enable software distribution to clients**—Check this option to distribute software to clients with ConfigMgr.

- ▶ **Allow user targeted advertisement requests**—If this option is checked, users can be targeted (in addition to computers) to receive software. If you will not use user targeting, uncheck this option to decrease the amount of policy data sent between the client and the ConfigMgr servers.

▶ **New program notification icon opens Add or Remove Programs**—Checking this option means that when a new program is available and the user clicks the new program notification icon, the Add or Remove Programs applet in Control Panel will display.

On the Notification tab, specify the following:

▶ **Display a notification message**—Displays a visual cue that a new advertisement is available. This appears on the task bar in the notifications area.

▶ **Play a sound**—Creates an audible cue that a new advertisement is available.

▶ **Provide a countdown**—Provides a visual countdown that a program is about to install.

▶ **Countdown length (minutes)**—If a countdown is checked, this is the number of minutes to display the countdown. This field defaults to 5 minutes.

Figure 14.36 displays the General and Notification tabs for the Advertised Programs Client Agent Properties.

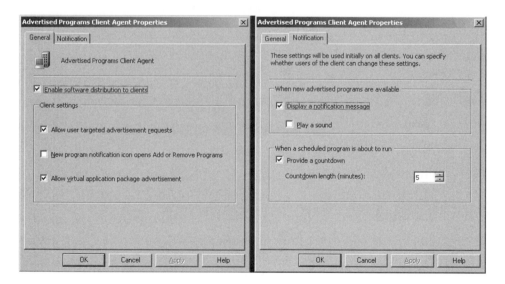

FIGURE 14.36   Advertised Programs Client Agent Properties tabs

With the Advertised Programs Client agent configured, the next step is creating advertisements.

Creating Advertisements

At this point, you have stepped through the processes to create a package/program, created a collection to distribute them to, and created distribution points, specifying the method to use when distributing the software. Now it is time to tie these together and distribute software. Distribution is achieved through advertisements, which tie all these concepts together (as displayed earlier in Figure 14.1) to distribute software using ConfigMgr.

As part of the advertisement, you will use the packages/programs defined in Chapter 13 and the collections and distribution points defined in this chapter, providing a targeted software deployment for both Forefront client software and OpsMgr client software. Let's start with deploying the Forefront client to a single collection.

Forefront Advertisement

Chapter 13 presented the steps to create a package and a program that will execute an installation for the Forefront Client Security agent (see Chapter 13 for details). This chapter then stepped through the process of creating a collection named Forefront Client Deployment (see "Creating a Dynamic Collection") that contains Windows Vista and XP systems located in a specific OU structure.

Using an advertisement ties these concepts together. There are multiple ways to create an advertisement:

- ▶ Navigate to the Advertisement section of the ConfigMgr console (Site Database -> Computer Management -> Software Distribution -> Advertisements), right-click, and select New Advertisement. This process starts the New Advertisement Wizard, where you need to specify all the settings for the advertisement you create.

TIP

Using the New Advertisement Wizard for More Control

This section discusses using the Distribute Software to Collection Wizard to deploy software. Several options are not available when using this particular wizard, including setting priority, rerun behavior, how to interact with distribution points, whether to allow manual interaction with the advertisements, whether to use a custom countdown, and configuring security. As a result, most advanced ConfigMgr users recommend using the New Advertisement Wizard to provide more control for these types of configurations. This chapter recommends the Distribute Software to Collection Wizard to provide a solid starting point for how to deploy software, but as you spend additional time distributing software, you may decide the New Advertisement Wizard is your preferred method to use.

- ▶ Navigate to the Packages section of the ConfigMgr console (Site Database -> Computer Management -> Software Distribution -> Packages), right-click, and select Distribute Software. This starts the Distribute Package Wizard, which will pass the package information and thus require less configuration information.

- ▶ Navigate to the collection previously defined for the software distribution in the ConfigMgr console (Site Database -> Computer Management -> Collections ->

Forefront Client Deployment), right-click, and select Distribute Software. This starts
the Distribute Software to Collection Wizard, passing the collection information,
again saving you from inputting much of the configuration information.

It is really a personal preference as to which approach to use, but the authors' preference
is to use the last method to create the advertisement, as long as the collection that will be
used for targeting is already defined. To create the advertisement in this manner, perform
the following steps:

1. The Distribute Software to Collection Wizard starts with a Welcome screen and then
   prompts for package information. Because this example will distribute the Forefront
   Client Security Agent package already created, choose Select an existing package.
   Then use the Browse button, as shown in Figure 14.37.

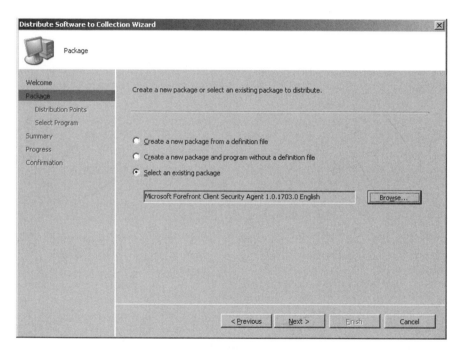

FIGURE 14.37   Choosing the package for the Distribute Software to Collection Wizard

2. The next screen specifies the distribution points where clients will access this
   package. Both distribution points are unchecked by default (see Figure 14.38). Check
   both and continue with the wizard.

3. The Select Program screen, shown in Figure 14.39, displays the program created for
   the Forefront Client Security agent (if multiple programs are available for this
   package, choose the program to run from the list displayed with the package).

4. The following screen defines the Advertisement Name setting, which defaults to a
   concatenation of the name of the package (Forefront Client Security Agent) followed

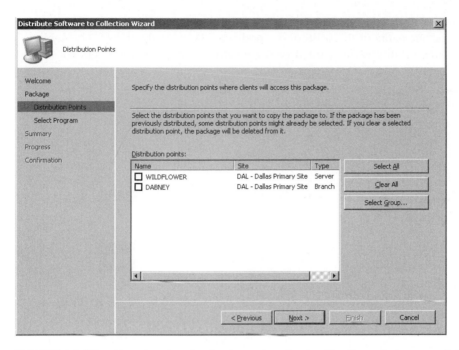

FIGURE 14.38   Choosing the distribution points for the Distribute Software to Collection Wizard

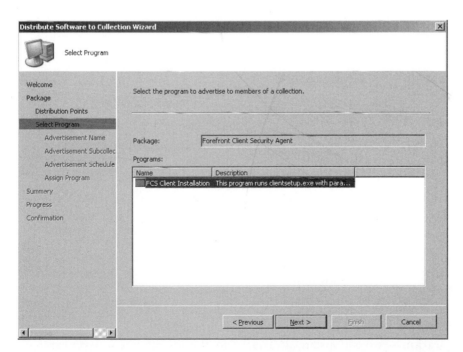

FIGURE 14.39   Choosing the program for the Distribute Software to Collection Wizard

by "–" and then the name of the program (FCS Client Installation). This is followed by "to" and the name of the collection (Forefront Client Deployment). This makes the full name for this advertisement *Forefront Client Security Agent – FCS Client Installation to Forefront Client Deployment.*

Next, on the Advertisement Subcollection screen, you choose whether the advertisement will apply to subcollections or only to the specified collection. Although no subcollections exist at this time, to avoid the chance of distributing the software to unexpected systems, select the option Advertise the program only to members of the specified collection, as displayed in Figure 14.40.

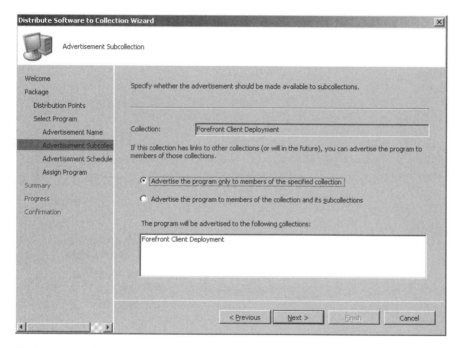

FIGURE 14.40   Advertisement Subcollection options for the Distribute Software to Collection Wizard

5. The Advertisement Schedule screen (shown in Figure 14.41) specifies when an advertisement becomes available, when or if it expires, and whether content is downloaded and run locally. The fields on this page include the following:

▶ **Advertise the program after**—Use this field to make an advertisement available beginning at a future point in time. The field defaults to the date and time the advertisement was created. For most packages, the default configuration is preferred; but this setting allows you to configure a specific time to advertise those packages requiring a later time.

▶ **Expiration**—Two options are available: "No, the advertisement never expires" and "Yes, the advertisement should expire."

The default is No, and is the preferred situation unless there is a reason why the program would no longer be viable after a certain date and time. If you choose the expiration option of Yes, define the expiration date and time here.

▶ **Download content from unprotected distribution point and run locally**—By default, this option is checked. When checked, this specifies that when the program is advertised it will download to the client before ConfigMgr attempts to run it. This option applies when the client and distribution point are connected on a fast (LAN) network boundary.

NOTE

Client Cache Settings

Configuration Manager 2007 uses the client cache if a program is configured to download and run locally to the system. The cache folder is stored on the same partition as the operating system, by default in the %*windir*%\System32\CCM\cache directory.

The default size of the client cache has increased in ConfigMgr 2007. It is now 5GB, and allocates space as required in the cache. If less than 5GB of free space is available, ConfigMgr uses a percentage of the available free space.

Take the default time to advertise the program, select no expiration date, and check the option for the content to download and run locally. See Figure 14.41 for these selections.

6. The Assign Program screen specifies whether a program is assigned and how the assignment is configured. The fields on this page include the following:

▶ **Assignment**—The two options are "No, do not assign the program" and "Yes, assign the program." This defaults to the No option, making the advertisement available for users to install, although it does not force installing the software package. The unassigned approach is useful for programs that are not mandatory and during package testing phases.

Depending on the configuration of the Advertised Programs Client agent (discussed in the "Advertised Programs Client Agent" section), users may be notified that there is software available to install. When connecting to remote systems via Remote Desktop Protocol (RDP), you must be logged in to the console session to see these notifications.

▶ **Assign after**—Configures the date and time when the advertisement is assigned to the systems in the collection.

▶ **Enable Wake On LAN**—Specifies whether to send a Wake On LAN transmission to wake up the client computer before the advertisement occurs.

This option defaults to unchecked.

▶ **Ignore maintenance windows when running program**—If this option is checked, the program will install regardless of any defined maintenance

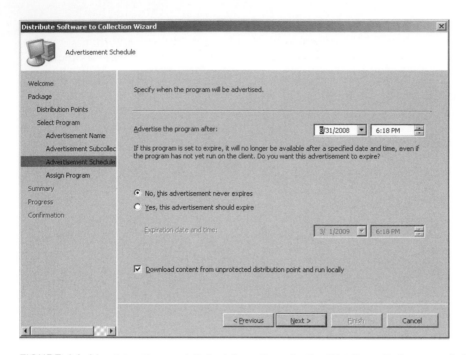

FIGURE 14.41   Advertisement Schedule options for the Distribute Software to Collection Wizard

windows. If this option is unchecked, the software will not distribute until a maintenance window occurs.

Maintenance windows are defined on the collection level. To configure a maintenance window, right-click the collection and choose Modify Collection Settings.

This option defaults to unchecked.

▶ **Allow system restart outside of maintenance windows**—If this option is checked and the program requires a reboot, the system will restart regardless of any defined maintenance windows.

This option defaults to unchecked.

The example in Figure 14.42 will deploy antivirus software as assigned, effective the time the advertisement was created. ConfigMgr will ignore any maintenance windows when running the program, although it is not using Wake On LAN and system restarts outside of the maintenance window are not allowed.

After completing the wizard process, you have distributed your first software package using Configuration Manager 2007! The next logical step is to track how the package and advertisement are functioning. You can monitor the status in the ConfigMgr console by navigating to Site Database -> System Status section. Perform the following steps:

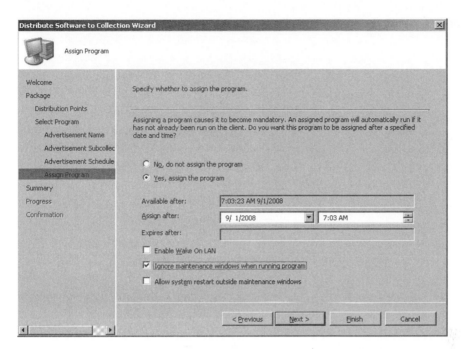

FIGURE 14.42   Program assignment options for the Distribute Software to Collection Wizard

1. The first step is to check on the status of the package being distributed. You will want to know whether the package was sent successfully to the specified distribution points. In the System Status screen, open the Package Status -> Microsoft Forefront Client Security Agent package. Here, you can track the status of the package and whether it deploys correctly to the distribution points. Figure 14.43 shows two targeted distribution points and two installed distribution points, meaning the distribution points successfully received the software package.

   If issues are referenced on this screen (such as distribution points in a retry or failed state), right-click and choose Show Messages to track either information, warning, error, or all messages related to the push of this software package to these distribution points.

2. The next step is to check on the status of the advertisement because the package was verified as successfully sent to the distribution points. Do this from the System Status section of the ConfigMgr console, this time opening Advertisement Status -> Forefront Client Security Agent. From here, you can see how many systems have received the advertisement, how many have failed, how many have started, and how many have program errors or successes.

The "OpsMgr Advertisement" section investigates the status of an advertisement in more detail.

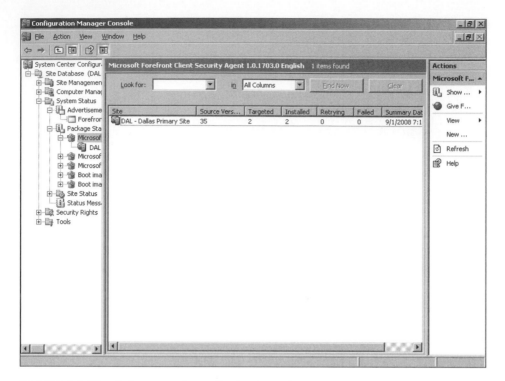

FIGURE 14.43   Software package distribution point status

OpsMgr Advertisement

The steps in Chapter 13 also created three packages that contain the programs to install the OpsMgr agent for the AMD64, I386, and IA64 platforms. This chapter then defined a top-level collection called OpsMgr Client Deployment and three subcollections, designed to contain only members of the OpsMgr Client Deployment collection and meet the defined client platform. You can use an advertisement to combine these packages/programs with the collections previously defined; this provides a targeted method for deploying the OpsMgr platform-specific client. Perform the following steps:

1. Start by creating three advertisements. The first advertisement assigns the AMD64 version of the OpsMgr client to the OpsMgr AMD64 subcollection. Navigate in the ConfigMgr console to Site Database -> Computer Management -> Collections -> OpsMgr Client Deployment -> OpsMgr AMD64. Right-click and select Distribute Software.

2. Operations Manager 2007 agents should not be distributed to root management servers, management servers, or gateway servers. Agent distribution to an existing OpsMgr server of this type can cause significant technical issues that are best avoided; you will want to consider this when distributing agents for OpsMgr. Create a new static collection named **OpsMgr Management Servers**, including the various management servers in this collection. Use the concepts discussed in the "Exclusion Collections" section to update the top-level OpsMgr collection to exclude the

OpsMgr Management Servers collection. Next, update the collection membership of the top-level and subcollections. Once this is completed, check the collections by validating that the OpsMgr Client Deployment collection does not include the members of the OpsMgr Management Servers collection and that no subcollections contain any members of OpsMgr Management Servers.

TIP

Active Directory Integration and Operations Manager

Prior to deploying the OpsMgr agents via Configuration Manager 2007, configure Operations Manager 2007 for AD Integration. *System Center Operations Manager 2007 Unleashed* (Sams Publishing, 2008) discusses AD Integration and other topics related to OpsMgr agent deployment.

---

3. The process to create an OpsMgr advertisement is the same as discussed in the "Forefront Advertisement" section. Select the AMD64 version of the package as well as the Per-system unattended installation program. Assign the program and configure it to ignore maintenance windows. Once you create the advertisement, you can validate the status of the package as it is sent to the distribution points, as discussed earlier in the "Forefront Advertisement" section.

   Create three different advertisements for these programs so the AMD64 program is sent to the OpsMgr AMD64 collection, the I386 version to the OpsMgr I386 collection, and the IA64 version is sent to the OpsMgr IA64 collection.

   When you assign an advertisement to a system, its behavior depends on how you defined the settings for the Advertised Programs Client agent (ConfigMgr Console -> Site Database -> Site Management -> *<Site Code> <Site Name>* -> Site Settings -> Client Agents -> Advertised Programs Client Agent). This particular configuration displays a notification (shown in Figure 14.44) and provides a countdown prior to launching the application.

FIGURE 14.44   Client receiving an assigned advertisement

4. Identify any errors related to the advertisement. Navigate to the System Status section of the ConfigMgr console and open Advertisement Status -> AMD64 System

Center Operations Manager Agent. This section of the console provides a high-level overview of the success or failure of the advertisement.

Right-clicking the advertisement and choosing Show Messages provides information on any updates that occurred related to this program. Common items to debug include software deployments targeted to the wrong platform (a reason to create different collections for targeting) and failures to install the program (potentially related to a variety of issues, including errors with how the package and program were created).

5. When you're debugging software advertisement issues, the Advertisement Status screen provides good high-level information, but additional detail may be necessary to identify and resolve the issues. Reviewing server and client log files helps take this to the next level.

Using the Log Files

ConfigMgr server log files for the x86 platform are located in the *%ProgramFiles%*\Microsoft Configuration Manager\Logs directory. If you are using an x64 platform, these files are stored in *%ProgramFiles(x86)%*\Microsoft Configuration Manager\Logs. ConfigMgr client log files are located in the *%windir%*\System32\CCM\Logs folder. A good quick trick to identify which file you are looking for is to sort the log files by the date they were modified, so that the most recently modified log files are at the top of the list. A list of the log files and their functions is available at http://technet.microsoft.com/en-us/library/bb892800.aspx. Appendix A, "Configuration Manager Log Files," also provides a list of log files used in Configuration Manager.

The Configuration Manager 2007 Toolkit (available for download at http://www.microsoft.com/downloads/details.aspx?familyid=948e477e-fd3b-4a09-9015-141683c7ad5f&displaylang=en, or by searching for **ConfigMgr Toolkit** at www.microsoft.com/downloads) provides a great utility called Trace32 that makes it easier to review and monitor log files for ConfigMgr. Chapter 12, "Client Management," discusses the toolkit.

Additional Advertisement Settings

Employing the Distribute Software to Collection Wizard, as was used for the Forefront and OpsMgr advertisements, provides a straightforward way to create an advertisement, but makes some assumptions regarding how you want to configure the settings of your advertisement. Knowing all the configurations available for customizing an advertisement can greatly extend the flexibility of how ConfigMgr will advertise software.

To change these configurations, review the properties available when an advertisement is created by right-clicking the advertisement (in the ConfigMgr console under Site Database -> Computer Management -> Software Distribution -> Advertisements -> *<Advertisement Name>*) and choosing Properties. The General tab has items previously configured, such as the name of the advertisement, the package, the program, the collection, and whether members of subcollections are included. However, additional tabs provide further configurations. These tabs are discussed in the next sections and include the Schedule, Distribution Points, Interaction, and Security tabs.

Advertisement Schedule

The advertisement Schedule tab provides each of the configurations shown when creating the advertisement with the Distribute Software to Collection Wizard. These include when an advertisement is scheduled to start, whether it is assigned as mandatory, whether it should use Wake On LAN, whether to ignore maintenance windows when running programs, and whether to allow system restarts outside of maintenance windows.

This tab also allows you to change either the priority or the program rerun behavior, as shown in Figure 14.45.

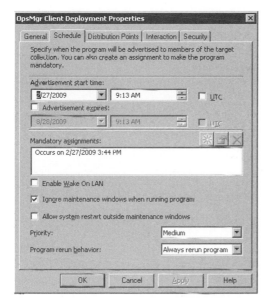

14

FIGURE 14.45   Configuring the schedule for an advertisement

- ▶ **Priority**—This includes the following options:

    - ▶ **Medium (default)**—This setting is effective for most situations.

    - ▶ **Low**—This setting is useful when the advertisement is not particularly time critical.

    - ▶ **High**—This setting is useful when the advertisement is really time critical.

- ▶ **Program rerun behavior**—Program rerun behavior includes the options to never rerun an advertised program, to always rerun the program (the default configuration), to rerun if the previous attempt failed, and to rerun if the previous attempt succeeded. This setting only has an impact on an advertisement if it is assigned, because users can run optional programs at any time and ConfigMgr does not restrict a program from rerunning.

Advertisement Distribution Points

The advertisement Distribution Points tab shows the configuration decided upon in the Distribute Software to Collection Wizard, which is the option to run the program from a distribution point or to download the content from a distribution point and run it locally.

▶ **When a client is connected within a slow or unreliable network boundary—** Three options are available for how a client will respond when connected on a slow or unreliable network boundary:

  ▶ To not run the program. (The default configuration is shown in Figure 14.46.)

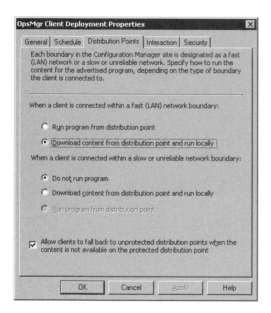

FIGURE 14.46   Configuring the distribution points for an advertisement

  ▶ To download content from a distribution point and run it locally.

  ▶ To run a program from the distribution point. (This option is unavailable and grayed out when a client is connected within a slow or unreliable network boundary.)

▶ **Allow clients to fall back to unprotected distribution points when the content is not available on the protected distribution point—**By default, this option is checked. When checked, this specifies the client should fall back to an unprotected distribution point if the content is not available on the protected distribution point. Downloading content from the distribution point and running it locally is useful when BITS is enabled on the distribution point, because the client can download all the content regardless of the network speed or reliability. If your environment is limited to only protected distribution points, this option is not bene-ficial—the client will not fail over to anything because there is nothing that is unprotected to allow the failover.

See Chapter 5 for additional information on fast and slow networks.

Advertisement Interaction

The advertisement Interaction tab (shown in Figure 14.47) provides settings that were not configurable running the Distribute Software to Collection Wizard. These include the following:

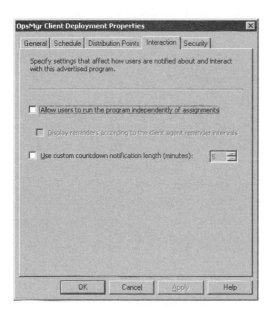

FIGURE 14.47   Configuring the user interaction for an advertisement

- ▶ **Allow users to run the program independently of advertisements**—Provides the ability to allow users to run the program independent of assignments (unchecked by default). If there is a requirement for users to be able to run the program that is advertised (whether it is assigned or not), the first box should be checked to allow this to occur. This causes the program to list as available for instal-lation in the Run Advertised Programs within ConfigMgr.

- ▶ **Display reminders according to the client agent reminder intervals**—Specify whether reminders are broadcast to the client according to the default interval configured on the Computer Client agent (grayed out unless the previous option is selected).

▶ **Use custom countdown notification length (minutes)**—Set a custom count-down notification length—as an example, for an advertisement that will run for a long time or require a reboot at the end of the installation (this option is unchecked by default).

Advertisement Security

When you use the Distribute Software to Collection Wizard to create an advertisement, the default class and instance rights are associated with that advertisement. Figure 14.48 displays these settings, which default to allow the user creating the advertisement to control the advertisement. You can change advertisement permissions by selecting the Security tab on the advertisement. You can also define advertisement permissions in the Security Rights section of the ConfigMgr console under Site Database -> Security Rights -> Rights. You can configure permissions on the class or instance level in either of these two locations, defining which users have what level of permissions to the advertisement. For more information on security, see Chapter 20, "Security and Delegation in Configuration Manager 2007."

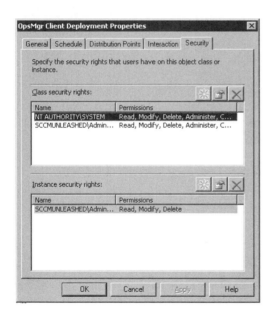

FIGURE 14.48   Configuring the security for an advertisement

Distributing Adobe Reader as a Virtual Application in ConfigMgr R2

Chapter 13 discussed creating an Adobe Reader virtual application for distribution using Configuration Manager. This virtual application was created in a ConfigMgr 2007 Release 2 (R2) environment configured to enable virtual applications. Because the application is packaged, you can follow the standard application distribution approaches discussed throughout this chapter:

- ▶ Create a collection

- ▶ Advertise the program

- ▶ Send it to a distribution point

However, before starting the process to distribute the virtual application, you should perform some preliminary steps to remove the following common virtual application issues:

- ▶ Installing the App-V 4.5 client

- ▶ Testing application distribution

After preliminary testing, you will create the test collection and distribute the virtual application.

App-V 4.5 Client

Microsoft Application Virtualization (App-V 4.5) uses both a client and a server. Although the ConfigMgr environment can provide the server functionality, the App-V client is still required for virtual applications to run on a client system. You must install both the ConfigMgr client and the App-V client on any ConfigMgr client that will run virtual applications.

App-V requires the Microsoft Desktop Optimization Pack (MDOP). MDOP is a separate download, available as part of Microsoft's Software Assurance program or purchased as part of an optional subscription license for volume license customers. More information about MDOP is available at http://www.microsoft.com/windows/enterprise/products/mdop.aspx.

During initial virtual application deployment testing, it is best to install the App-V client manually on test systems, thus eliminating problems with the client install during any troubleshooting efforts. This client is available as part of the App-V 4.5 software, and installed using the MSAppVirt_ts_client_setup_4.5.0.1485.cxe program. The App-V client has the following prerequisites you must install:

- ▶ Microsoft Application Error Reporting

- ▶ Microsoft Visual C++ 2005 SP 1 Redistributable Package

- ▶ Microsoft Core XML Services 6.0 SP 1

After completing the testing phase, you can package the App-V client (with its prerequisites) to distribute throughout the ConfigMgr environment to those systems that will run

14

virtual applications. Additional information on how to package the App-V client is available at http://scug.be/blogs/sccm/archive/2008/12/23/sccm-deploying-the-app-v-4-5-client. aspx.

To verify that the App-V client deployed successfully on a system, check the Add/Remove Programs applet (or Programs and Features on Windows Vista, as shown in Figure 14.49).

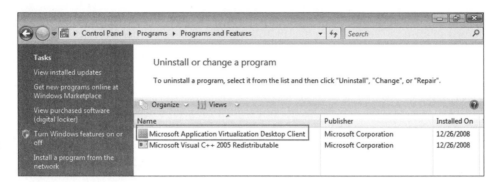

FIGURE 14.49   App-V 4.5 client successfully installed

To verify the functionality of the App-V client, a series of prepackaged applications are available on the web at http://www.instantapp.net/. Downloading and installing one or more of these applications will validate the functionality of the App-V 4.5 client.

Application Distribution Testing

To ensure things are working properly, you will want to deploy a nonvirtual application to your test systems before deploying a virtualized application. Both types of application deployment depend on many of the same ConfigMgr functions; experience shows it is easier to debug nonvirtual applications first and then deploy virtual applications. Successful distribution of the Forefront Client (see Chapter 13) or other packages to the test client will verify the functionality of both the ConfigMgr distribution point and the ConfigMgr client.

Testing application distribution prior to distributing a virtual application significantly decreases the complexity of debugging if issues occur when attempting to distribute the virtual application.

Creating the Test Collection

The test collection should be created as a static collection (see Chapter 13 for details), which will include only those systems selected for testing virtual applications. This collection should span the variety of operating systems that will be running virtual applications. For most environments, this would include at least one system running Windows XP X86,

Windows XP X64, Windows Vista X86, and Windows Vista X64. For this test, you would have previously created the Adobe Reader Deployment collection.

Creating the Advertisement

After completing initial preparation, create an advertisement that will tie the virtual application to a test collection, using a specified distribution point. Navigate in the ConfigMgr console to Site Database -> Computer Management -> Collections -> Adobe Reader Deployment (a static collection created to test deployments, similar to the one previously created in the "Static Collections" section). Right-click and select Distribute Software. Perform the following steps:

1. After the Welcome screen, select an existing package (in this case, the Adobe Reader Virtual application shown in Figure 14.50). The Distribute Software to Collection Wizard will adapt its steps to facilitate distributing virtual applications.

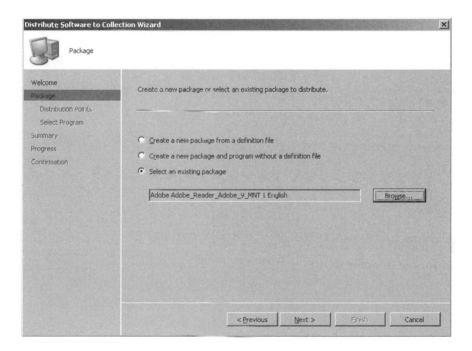

FIGURE 14.50   Distributing the Adobe Reader virtual package

2. Specify the distribution point to use for the virtual application. This example uses the Bluebonnet distribution point, because it is the only DP available within this site, as shown in Figure 14.51. When you are testing virtual application deployment,

specify those distribution points closest to the systems you are testing. Using local distribution points increases the speed of the virtual application deployment and decreases the overhead on the network when virtual applications deploy.

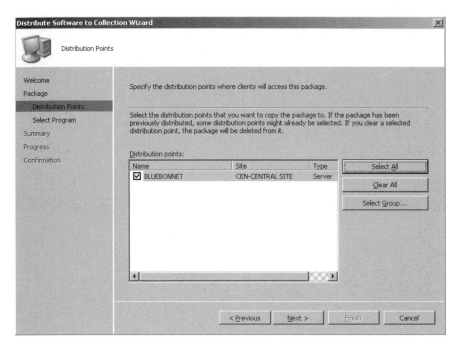

FIGURE 14.51   Specifying distribution points for the Adobe Reader virtual package

3. The next page shows the virtual program already defined, because no program configuration is required for virtual applications. The package is defined as Adobe_Reader_Adobe_9_MNT, and the virtual application is defined as [Virtual application]. Both of these fields are grayed out, as shown in Figure 14.52. You can verify this under Site Database -> Computer Management -> Software Distribution -> Packages by comparing virtual applications to nonvirtual applications.

4. Specify the name of the advertisement. This defaults to the name of the virtual application combined with the name of the target collection, as shown in Figure 14.53.

5. Take the defaults on the Advertisement Subcollection page, which will advertise to the members of the collection and its subcollections. You should also accept the defaults on the Advertisement Schedule page. This will advertise the virtual application after the time it was created, without an expiration date, and download the content from unprotected distribution points and run it locally, as shown in Figure 14.54.

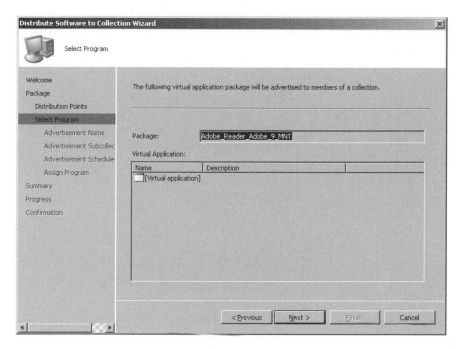

FIGURE 14.52   Specifying the program for the Adobe Reader virtual package

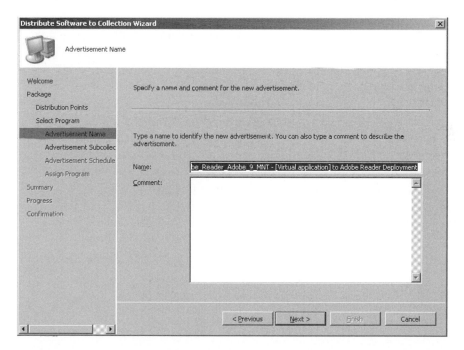

FIGURE 14.53   Specifying the advertisement name for the Adobe Reader virtual package

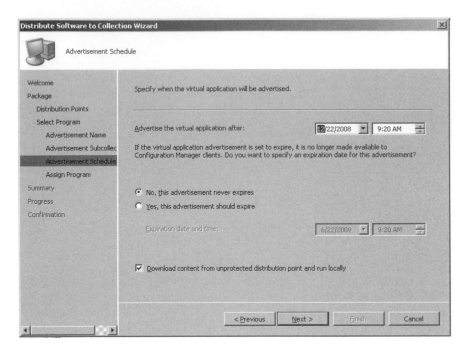

FIGURE 14.54   Specifying the advertisement schedule for the Adobe Reader virtual package

6. On the Assign Program page, you will determine whether to assign the virtual application, which makes the program mandatory for members of the collection. This will be configured with the default, which is not mandatory (see Figure 14.55). However, after testing is complete you will most likely assign the virtual application so users do not need to specify they want to install it.

7. As with other software distributions in ConfigMgr, the next page shows a summary of the advertisement you are creating. This is followed with a progress page, and then a final confirmation page. ConfigMgr will advertise the virtual application to members of the collection once the wizard completes.

   You can check the status of the package and whether it is distributed to the distribution point using the System Status section of the console under Site Database -> System Status -> Package Status. Figure 14.56 shows the Adobe Reader package has been targeted to one distribution point and installed on one distribution point.

8. After verifying the virtual application has reached the distribution point, you can monitor the status of the virtual application distribution either within the ConfigMgr console under Site Database -> System Status -> Advertisement Status or by checking the individual systems.

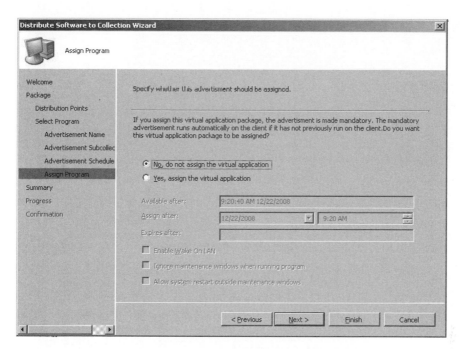

FIGURE 14.55   Specifying the assignment for the Adobe Reader virtual package

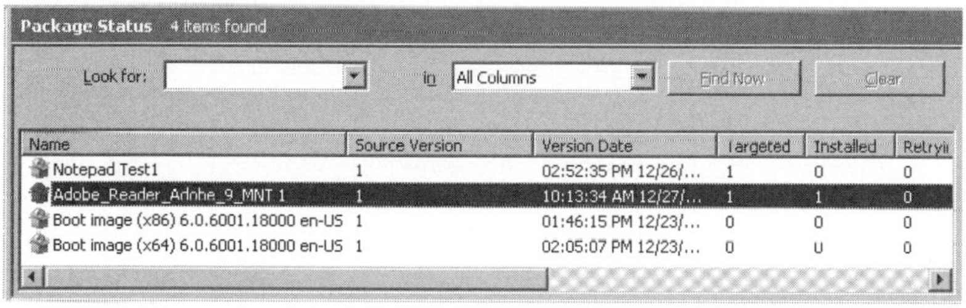

FIGURE 14.56   Checking the status of the Adobe Reader virtual application package

For debugging purposes, this was not defined as a mandatory advertisement, so you will need to choose to install the virtual application on a client system. After the advertisement is available, the application will display that it requires a download and then that it is in the process of downloading (see Figure 14.57).

9. Once distribution of the virtual application completes, the Adobe application is available on the Start menu, as highlighted in Figure 14.58.

After the Adobe Reader virtual application is available, you can run it and view PDF files, thus providing a good test of the application functionality. Figure 14.59 shows the Adobe Reader virtual application running. The building-block icon shown on the task bar (at the bottom right of the figure) indicates this is a virtual application.

FIGURE 14.57 Steps for the distribution of a nonmandatory virtual application distribution

The Adobe Reader virtual application is a good example of how you can integrate virtual applications with ConfigMgr, providing an extremely flexible method to distribute applications. The following material is recommended for additional reading on App-V and ConfigMgr:

- ▶ **App-V 4.5 documentation**—http://technet.microsoft.com/en-us/appvirtualization/cc843994.aspx

- ▶ **Raymond Chow's experiences with integrating ConfigMgr and App-V**—http://mymomexperience.blogspot.com/2008/05/marrying-sccm-r2-and-softgrid-45.html

- ▶ **Steve Rachui's post on the process of deploying virtual applications in Configuration Manager**—http://blogs.msdn.com/steverac/archive/2008/12/22/deploying-virtual-apps-with-sccm.aspx

FIGURE 14.58   The Adobe Reader virtual application on the Start menu of a client

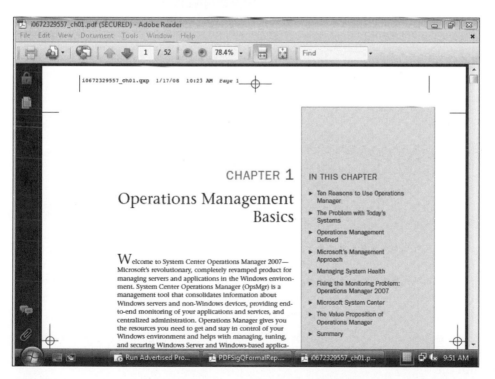

FIGURE 14.59   The Adobe Reader virtual application running on a client system

▶ **Desktop Control's blog on integrating ConfigMgr and App-V**—http://desktop-control.blogspot.com/2008/09/app-v-application-deployment-in.html

Troubleshooting ConfigMgr Software Distribution Issues

Several common issues may occur when distributing software in Configuration Manager. There are several recommended best practices to assist with troubleshooting these issues. The next sections discuss two of these approaches.

Start Simple

When distributing software with Configuration Manager 2007, you will always want to begin with simple applications and work your way up to more complex applications.

As an example, it is not a good idea to start your first software distribution with a global deployment of Office 2007. Rather, start small with a relatively simple application to package, such as WinZip or the Forefront client, and deploy it from a single distribution point to a set of test clients. You can then move to a larger number of distribution points to validate the distribution point functionality. After distributing simple applications, select ones that are more complex for this same phased approach to deployment. This process should help you identify and resolve issues more quickly.

This approach will make it easier to debug if you need to address low-level issues before they affect large numbers of systems.

Checking Status

The ConfigMgr console provides a large amount of status information that can assist with troubleshooting software distribution in an environment. This is stored under Site Database -> System Status. Chapter 17 also discusses checking system status.

▶ The Advertisement Status section assists in determining the status of the advertisements that are active and whether they are successfully deploying.

▶ The Package Status section shows the source version of the package, the number of distribution points targeted to receive the package, and the number of distribution points that already received the package. You can track the status messages for each package to determine whether there are issues with distributing the software packages to the various distribution points in the site.

▶ The Site Status section shows the overall health of ConfigMgr and can assist in determining whether low-level issues are causing software to not distribute correctly within the site.

Many low-level technical issues can be identified within the System Status section of the ConfigMgr console, and it's far more intuitive than digging through the log files on both the server and the client to determine what's going wrong during a software deployment (see Appendix A for more detail on ConfigMgr log files).

Summary

This chapter used the packages and programs created in Chapter 13 and took them through the software deployment process. It discussed queries and collections as well as created custom collections to meet the requirements of the software distribution process. The chapter also discussed distribution points and their configurations, and distributing applications with advertisements. It covered distributing virtual applications, Microsoft's new direction for software distribution in Configuration Manager 2007. Finally, the chapter discussed how to avoid common problems when deploying software with ConfigMgr. The next chapter discusses patch management using Configuration Manager 2007.

14

CHAPTER 15

Patch Management

Although patch management can be the bane of administrators and users alike due to the overall disruption it causes to computer systems, it is a key check box on any security check list. Microsoft's products have their fair share of patches to apply—and with their near ubiquitous presence in corporate America, patching Microsoft products is of utmost importance.

It is often illuminating to see how people look at the patching process. One of our coauthors remembers forwarding a story to a colleague some years ago about a Windows administrator who was bragging he had not rebooted his Windows NT 4.0 primary domain controller (PDC) in over a year and it was still running fine. Although the administrator thought this was just great, the colleague's first reaction was the administrator had not patched the system for over a year and the PDC was now a security risk!

Patching software products for security holes is an unpleasant fact for all network administrators, regardless of the operating system or software vendors involved. Fortunately, Microsoft is now ahead of the curve, both in patching its products and providing tools to simplify deployment of patches, such as Configuration Manager (ConfigMgr), Microsoft's premiere tool for patch management. The company completely rewrote the patching mechanism in ConfigMgr 2007, simplifying its use and merging the power of ConfigMgr with Windows Updates. The clunky Inventory Tool for Microsoft Updates (ITMU) used by previous versions of Systems Management Server (SMS) is completely gone (unless you must continue to support SMS 2003 clients), as are the various scan tools used to detect whether patches are necessary.

Using ConfigMgr 2007, you can seamlessly scan for and deploy updates for every supported Microsoft operating system (OS), most Microsoft server products, and selected Microsoft desktop applications such as Microsoft Office. You can also scan and deploy patches for supported third-party products using the new software update capabilities in ConfigMgr. Adobe, Citrix, and other software vendors have released update catalogs that seamlessly integrate into ConfigMgr—these are available at http://technet.microsoft.com/en-us/configmgr/bb892875.aspx.

This chapter discusses how ConfigMgr handles patching chores using its built-in Software Updates mechanism. It also touches on using Wake On LAN for delivering patches, and integrating the Network Policy Server (NPS) role built in to Windows Server 2008, which is used to ensure all your clients are up to date, including those that only touch the network occasionally. The chapter describes how to find those updates applicable to your organization, download them, and successfully deploy them in a flexible, cohesive manner using ConfigMgr.

Planning Your Software Updates Strategy

Deploying patches successfully with any tool requires planning and preparation. There are numerous aspects to consider, many of which depend on your specific environment and user requirements. This section lists items to consider when developing your patch management strategy:

▶ **Scope**—Start by determining which systems and applications to patch. Although not updating all systems or applications for a particular flaw may pose a security risk, there may be specific reasons not to patch a particular piece of software (for example, due to third-party vendor support, as described in the next bullet).

▶ **Third-party support**—Check with the vendors of your applications before applying patches. Many vendors will not support their products if you apply a Windows patch they have not tested with that product. Vendors may also issue patches to a product because a Microsoft patch caused it to break. This is vendor dependent, and varies from vendor to vendor.

Depending on the severity of the flaw a patch addresses, you may have to weigh the risk of not applying it versus the possibility of breaking the application or going out of compliance with the vendor's recommended Windows patch level. Only you, in coordination with your user population and other Information Technology (IT) support staff, can decide to apply the patch.

▶ **Patch testing**—Testing patches before deploying them to your production systems is highly recommended. Even if you do not have a full test environment at your disposal, do not let that deter you from testing. At a minimum, identify a group of systems for each patch category as your guinea pigs. You might categorize this by operating system (such as Windows Vista workstations or Windows 2008 servers) or hosted application (such as PeopleSoft servers or Finance department workstations).

Deploy patches to your identified test systems before the scheduled production rollout of the patches, leaving you sufficient time to troubleshoot and resolve any problems caused by the patches.

▶ **Coordination and scheduling**—Because Windows patches typically require a reboot, they do not lend themselves to deployment during business hours. Coordinate with other IT staff, server administrators, application administrators, your users, and management to establish maintenance windows defining acceptable times to reboot servers and workstations. Although maintenance windows are useful for all types of system maintenance, they are a definite requirement for patch management.

Do not necessarily limit yourself to a single maintenance window for all your systems, because deploying everywhere at once increases the risk of a single bad patch affecting your entire environment. Additionally, rebooting all your systems in a short period of time most likely will result in unexpected side effects from resource dependencies or other contention-type issues. As an example, if you patch your Domain Name System (DNS) servers and they all reboot at the same time, clients will not be able to resolve Internet Protocol (IP) addresses until those servers are operational. This may, in turn, cause other applications that rely on resolving IP addresses to fail.

Additionally, there may be application-specific jobs that run at particular times. Rebooting the system running the job or a remote system referenced by the job may cause that job to fail. Examples of scheduled jobs include accounting reports, payroll processing, and database maintenance.

Many organizations include patch management in their established change control process or create a process to deal with the many ramifications of updates and patches.

▶ **Notification**—Always issue fair warning to anyone potentially affected by a patch update or a system reboot. Even when you coordinate maintenance windows, sending additional notifications to other administrators and users to let them know what will transpire prevents a lot of finger pointing and many sleepless nights. Consider using multiple notifications from different sources and different channels. Notifications from an IT manager, CIO, and such are also highly recommended because they carry additional political weight and garner more attention. As an example, an email blast from the IT manager and an announcement on the company intranet or newsletter not only goes a long way in preventing the "I didn't know" excuse, but also actually invalidates it!

▶ **Political policies and support**—IT professionals all know the risks of not patching systems and applications. To implement a successful patching strategy, you must have the political support in your organization to establish a policy that dictates and enforces applying patches. Without such a top-down policy, you will continue to face opposition to patching, not only from users but also within IT. A policy enforced by your CIO (or equivalent) will eliminate any quibbling over patching.

Compliance regulations in the United States such as the Health Insurance Portability and Accountability Act (HIPAA), Sarbanes-Oxley Act of 2002 (SOX), and Gramm-Leach-Bliley Act (GLBA) are another driver for patching, eliminating any question about its necessity. Although none of these compliance laws specifically requires patching, it is one of the first things checked by auditors.

Based on the information listed, plus other factors that may be unique to your own organization or environment, consider developing a patch strategy and policy document that include things such as a timeline, rollback process, and testing procedure. Update this document every month to indicate which patches are in scope, and distribute it as part of your notification process.

The recommendations in this section are applicable no matter which tool you use to update and patch your systems, including the ITMU in SMS 2003. However, the ITMU used with SMS 2003 and Software Updates in ConfigMgr 2007 are distinctly different tools using very different ways to get the same job done. The next section discusses these differences.

Software Update Options in Microsoft Products

ConfigMgr Software Updates replaces the ITMU feature pack used in SMS 2003 and SMS 2.0. Microsoft designed ConfigMgr's Software Updates to be a first-class citizen in ConfigMgr 2007 and take advantage of the built-in Windows Updates infrastructure. The following sections discuss the Windows Update Agent used by WSUS and ConfigMgr as well as compare the ConfigMgr patching process to that in ITMU and WSUS.

The Windows Update Agent

The Windows Update Agent (WUA), in Windows operating systems since Windows 2000 Service Pack (SP) 1, provides a standard method to detect and report patch applicability for Windows and other Microsoft products—such as Office—on all Windows systems. Additionally, Microsoft updates the agent regularly to ensure it can properly detect the need for the latest available patches. You can configure the Windows Update Agent manually or through group policy to detect, download, and apply necessary patches automatically.

ConfigMgr 2007 uses the WUA to detect which patches are necessary on a system. This eliminates using separate scanning tools, which frees up the ConfigMgr administrator from maintaining these tools and Microsoft's ConfigMgr development team from creating and testing them. Using the WUA also ensures consistent patch-scanning results between ConfigMgr, Windows Server Update Services (WSUS), and manual patching.

The SMS Inventory Tool for Microsoft Updates

The ITMU is an add-on that never seemed to fit well with the rest of Microsoft's SMS product. The ITMU incorporates a separate scanning tool to detect when patches are necessary on managed systems. On occasion, Microsoft has released separate scanning tools to detect if specific patches are applicable because the base ITMU scanning tool did not detect them. Using multiple scanning utilities causes the ITMU and Windows Update to detect patch applicability differently, occasionally causing discrepancies between the two tools when identifying necessary patches.

Both the ITMU and ConfigMgr deliver and apply patches using packages. The ConfigMgr packages (called *update packages*) differ from the ITMU because they have their own branch in the Configuration Manager console, displayed in Figure 15.1. Unlike ConfigMgr software packages (discussed in Chapter 13, "Creating Packages"), update packages do not have programs, although you must install the packages on distribution points (DPs) to use them.

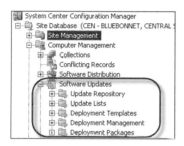

FIGURE 15.1   Software Updates in the ConfigMgr console

The ITMU and Software Updates also download Microsoft's catalog of available updates differently:

▶ The ITMU uses a separate command-line tool that runs using a Software Distribution package.

▶ Software Updates integrates with an installation of WSUS, removing from ConfigMgr the task of downloading the catalog from the Internet and instead using the standard mechanism built in to WSUS. Managed systems connect to this instance of WSUS to perform scans, although they do not actually report results to it.

Standalone WSUS

With a standalone installation of WSUS, clients are configured (either manually or with group policy) to report their status to a WSUS server and pull applicable updates from that WSUS server. Configuring when updates are installed is somewhat limited, particularly if group policy is not used. Reporting is also limited, and centrally managing and deploying patches to systems connected through a wide area network (WAN), Virtual Private Network (VPN), or the Internet is problematic.

Configuration Manager 2007

Using Software Updates in ConfigMgr 2007 addresses the shortcomings of WSUS, eliminates the requirement for ITMU, and utilizes the now ubiquitous WUA. It also provides powerful and customizable reporting that integrates with ConfigMgr's asset management and inventory capabilities. The next section begins discussing the steps required to start using this new tool.

Preparing for Software Updates

You must prepare ConfigMgr and your Windows infrastructure for the Software Updates functionality. Although it is relatively straightforward to install and configure, you must make several decisions along the way and be patient, because the initial synchronization process can take some time to complete. Preparation tasks include the following:

▶ Installing WSUS

▶ Adding software update points

▶ Preparing for synchronization

▶ Configuring the agents

▶ Establishing group policies

The following sections discuss these areas.

Software Updates Prerequisites

WSUS is the only real prerequisite to enable Software Updates in ConfigMgr. Download WSUS and (as a minimum) install the WSUS Software Development Kit (SDK) on the primary site server; you do this by installing the WSUS administrator console. You must also install the WSUS server component on either the primary site server or another accessible server that meets the requirements for WSUS, as listed at http://technet.microsoft.com/en-us/wsus/bb466188.aspx:

▶ Microsoft Windows Server 2008 (Standard or Enterprise Edition), or Microsoft Windows Server 2003 (Standard or Enterprise Edition), or Microsoft Windows 2000 Server or Advanced Server with Service Pack 4 (SP 4) or later

▶ 1GB or more RAM

▶ 1GHz Pentium III or higher processor

▶ Microsoft .NET Framework 1.1 SP 1

▶ Microsoft Background Intelligent Transfer Services (BITS) 2.0

▶ Microsoft Internet Explorer 6 SP 1

▶ Internet Information Services (IIS) 5.0 or later

WSUS also requires a SQL Server database. Generally, you use the same SQL Server installation for WSUS that you use for ConfigMgr. You can create a separate SQL Server instance for ConfigMgr to allow for granular resource control; however, this is not required as the instance of WSUS does not manage any client data and requires very little overhead on the database server, regardless of the size of the ConfigMgr installation.

WSUS 3.0 Service Pack 1 is required for ConfigMgr 2007 Service Pack 1 and Release 2 (R2) for installation on Windows Server 2008. Both 64-bit and 32-bit versions of WSUS are available.

Microsoft recommends installing WSUS on a dedicated server for larger sites. Each WSUS instance can handle up to 25,000 clients; for sites that are larger, you should deploy a Network Load Balanced (NLB) cluster to scale out the capacity of WSUS. Every ConfigMgr primary site must have a separate WSUS instance; this instance is optional for secondary sites to offload work and network traffic from the primary site WSUS server.

WSUS installation is straightforward and wizard driven, with the following guidance:

▶ Choose to store updates locally on the system rather than Microsoft Update, as shown in Figure 15.2. This setting allows WSUS to download and store license terms for specific software updates in the update content folder that you choose; ConfigMgr handles the actual download and deployment of updates. During the update synchronization process, ConfigMgr looks for applicable license terms in the content folder. If it cannot find the license terms, it will not synchronize the update. Additionally, clients must also have access to the applicable license terms in order to scan for update compliance.

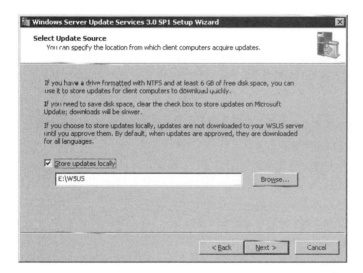

FIGURE 15.2   Choosing the content folder during WSUS installation

▶ If using a dedicated system for WSUS, use the default website to host WSUS. If you are hosting any other ConfigMgr roles on the system, create a dedicated IIS site; although this is not necessarily a standard best practice and not a technical requirement, it is the opinion of the authors that a dedicated site keeps things nice and tidy and prevents any confusion over which site handles the WSUS responsibilities. The port numbers for a dedicated site are 8530 and 8531 for Secure Socket Layer (SSL) connections. Figure 15.3 displays these options.

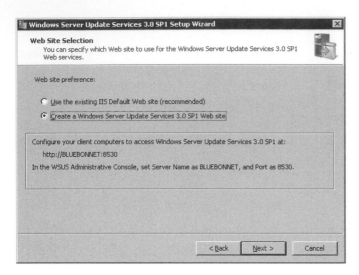

FIGURE 15.3   Choosing ports during WSUS installation

▶ Click Cancel to skip the Configuration Wizard that launches at the end of installation. WSUS does not require manual configuration because ConfigMgr 2007 takes over the control and configuration of WSUS once you install a software update point (SUP).

TIP

Setting Up a WSUS and SUP Role with NLB

A good article on configuring a ConfigMgr SUP with NLB can be found at http://blogs. msdn.com/shitanshu/archive/2008/05/13/how-to-setup-wsus-sup-role-in-nlb-in-sccm. aspx.

You may use an existing WSUS server installation as an SUP for ConfigMgr; however, you should first delete the update catalog and associated metadata from WSUS to reset WSUS back to a clean state, thus allowing ConfigMgr to properly manage and control it. In addition, because ConfigMgr takes complete control over the WSUS configuration, do not configure any clients not managed by ConfigMgr to use this WSUS installation, as this is not a supported configuration.

Creating Software Update Points

Software update points play a key role in the process of distributing updates to clients. They do not actually deliver the update files to clients like a standalone WSUS server; rather, they download the update catalog from Microsoft (or another upstream WSUS server) and make the update catalog available to clients for compliance scanning. Therefore, adding at least one SUP is required to enable software updates. Adding an SUP as a role to a site system is similar to adding any ConfigMgr role to any other site system. To do so, perform the following steps:

1. In the ConfigMgr console, start by navigating to Site Database -> Site Management -> *<Site Code> <Site Name>* -> Site Settings -> Site Systems.

   ▶ If the system running WSUS is not currently a site system, right-click Site Systems and then choose New -> Server to launch the New Site System Server Wizard, displayed in Figure 15.4. Enter the name of the site system and the intranet accessible Fully Qualified Domain Name (FQDN) of the WSUS server.

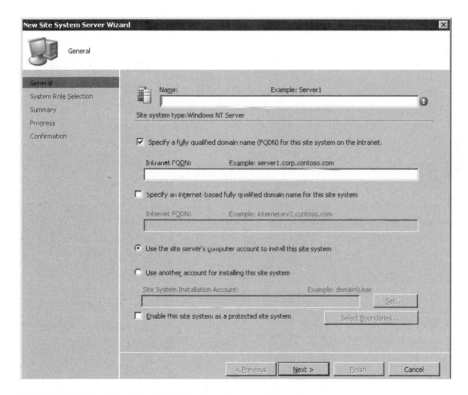

FIGURE 15.4   The New Site System Server Wizard

   ▶ If the WSUS server already is a ConfigMgr site system, right-click it and choose New Roles. This launches the New Site Role Wizard, which looks and acts exactly like the New Site System Server Wizard, except this wizard fills in the site system name and intranet FQDN for you.

2. For either wizard, choose Next and then choose Software update point from the list of available site roles.

3. At the Software Update Point screen, enter the applicable proxy server information for your environment, including credentials if necessary. WSUS uses these credentials to contact Microsoft or an upstream WSUS server to retrieve the update catalog.

4. For Active Software Update Point Properties, choose whether this SUP will be the active SUP for the site.

   There can only be one active SUP per site. An active SUP is responsible for synchronizing the updates catalog for the site from the parent site's SUP or from Microsoft if the site is the central site. Active SUPs are also responsible for communication with client systems that request the update catalog in the site where the SUP is designated active. Although it is possible to configure nonactive SUPs in any site, the only time you would not make an SUP the active SUP is if you are configuring a node to be part of an NLB SUP. It is also possible to create a nonactive SUP for redundancy purposes, although SUPs do not store any critical data you cannot easily replace (so maintaining nonactive SUPs may be considered excessive, based on your particular requirements).

   Configure the ports used by WSUS. If you used the default IIS site, these should be 80 and 443; if you used a custom site, they should be 8530 and 8531.

5. At the Synchronization Source screen, choose from where to synchronize the update catalog:

   ▶ **Microsoft Update**—This setting is used for the active SUP that is highest in the ConfigMgr site hierarchy; typically, this is the active SUP for the central site.

   ▶ **An upstream update server**—This setting is used for down-level child SUPs in the site hierarchy and Internet-based SUPs. SUPs configured with this setting configure their respective WSUS services to synchronize their updates from their parent site.

   ▶ **Do not synchronize from Microsoft Update or an upstream update server**—Configuring this setting on an SUP causes it not to synchronize automatically with any other SUP. To add updates to an SUP configured with this setting, you must manually export the updates from another WSUS system and then manually import them using WSUSutil and the export and import options.

   By default, WSUSutil.exe is located at *%ProgramFiles%\Update Services\Tools*. The syntax for the export command is `WSUSutil.exe export <exportfile> <logfile>`, where `<exportfile>` is the name of a .cab file to export the update metadata to and `<logfile>` is the name of a log file to write a record of the exported metadata to. The syntax for the import command is `WUSutil.exe import <packagename> <logfile>`. Additionally, you must copy the WSUSContent folder from the source server to the destination server. This folder, typically located at *<WSUSInstallationDrive>*\WSUS\WSUSContent\, contains license terms and potentially other downloaded content referenced by the transferred metadata.

The wizard also asks you to choose whether to send reporting events to WSUS. This is generally not required and you can leave it disabled.

6. At the Synchronization Schedule screen, configure whether you want to enable synchronization on a schedule, and if so how often and when to update the catalog from the configured source.

▶ The default simple schedule of every 7 days is usually sufficient; you do not need to change it unless there is a specific reason to do so.

▶ If you need detailed control over the download schedule, including the frequency and exact time of day, choose and configure a custom schedule.

7. Proceed to the Update Classifications screen. Microsoft categorizes updates in the catalog by classification. This page of the wizard, shown in Figure 15.5, allows you to choose all the update classifications you wish to scan for and deploy.

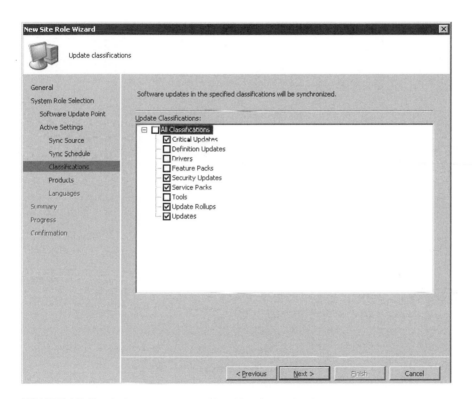

FIGURE 15.5   Software Updates classification selection

8. At the Products screen, choose the Microsoft products to include in the update catalog that WSUS will download. You can specify nearly every Microsoft server product and most Microsoft desktop products. By default, the nodes chosen include Microsoft Office and Microsoft Windows products, as displayed in Figure 15.6. This

list is not initially complete, and it is updated with additional products the first time WSUS synchronizes.

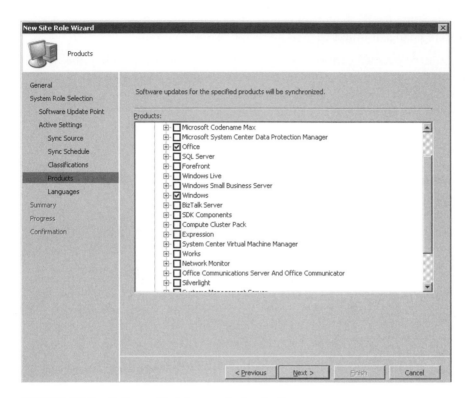

FIGURE 15.6   Software Updates product selection

9. Many Microsoft products are available in a variety of languages and require patches specific to their language. On the Languages page of the wizard, choose the language(s) in which ConfigMgr will download update files and summary details.

Only steps 1–4 are applicable for child sites. ConfigMgr automatically configures SUPs in child sites to use the SUPs in their parent site as an upstream WSUS server. The child SUP downloads its entire configuration from the upstream/parent SUP as well as the update catalog. This is not configurable.

To review or change any of these settings after installing the SUP, navigate to Site Management -> <Site Code> <Site Name> -> Site Settings -> Component Configuration in the ConfigMgr console. Right-click Software Update Point Component in the right pane and then choose Properties to launch the Software Update Point Component Properties dialog box displayed in Figure 15.7.

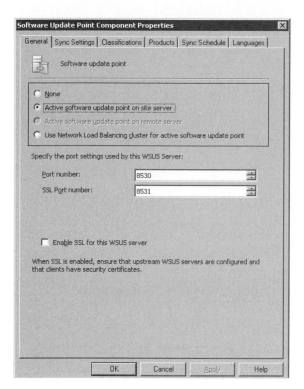

FIGURE 15.7   The Software Update Point Component Properties dialog box

After you complete the wizard, ConfigMgr installs three primary components related to WSUS, as described in Table 15.1. These components immediately go to work; if you configured everything correctly, the synchronization process will begin.

TABLE 15.1   WSUS Components

Component Name	Purpose	Log Name
WSUS Control Manager	Controls the connection to WSUS and ensures ConfigMgr can communicate with WSUS	WSUSCtrl.log
WSUS Configuration Manager	Ensures WSUS is configured according to the settings you specified	WCM.log
WSUS Sync Manager	Monitors the synchronization status and progress of WSUS and imports the update catalog from WSUS to ConfigMgr	wsyncmgr.log

Synchronization Process

An installed SUP can download the Windows Update catalog and associated metadata from Microsoft or an upstream server; the process is identical for either source. If a primary SUP cannot directly communicate with Microsoft to retrieve updates, you can manually import an update catalog from a server that downloaded the catalog from Microsoft. Both WSUS 2.0 and 3.0 use the same catalog format; this makes it possible to use either version to export the catalog manually using the same commands, as outlined here:

1. On the Internet-connected WSUS server, open a command prompt and run the following command:

   ```
   WSUSutil export <export filename.cab> <export log filename>
   ```

   WSUSUutil is typically located in the *%ProgramFiles%*\Update Services\Tools folder. The export process takes from 10 to 20 minutes to run (potentially more), depending on your hardware. WSUSutil writes to the log file after the export completes. The file is in XML format.

2. Copy the export file to the SUP using whatever method is appropriate for your environment.

3. Open a command prompt on the destination WSUS server and run WSUSutil import:

   ```
   WSUSutil import <import filename.cab> <import log filename>
   ```

   The import process is more extensive than the export process and may take over an hour to complete, so be patient. As with the export process, WSUSutil does not write to the XML log file until the import completes.

To initiate synchronization manually from Microsoft or an upstream server, navigate to Computer Management in the ConfigMgr console, expand Software Updates, right-click Update Repository, and choose Run Synchronization.

Aside from the obvious manual intervention required, there are two differences between the manual synchronization and a scheduled one:

- ▶ A manual synchronization only performs a delta synchronization, meaning it only downloads changes to the catalog of available updates. Scheduled synchronizations download the entire update catalog.

- ▶ With a scheduled synchronization, superseded updates are only marked as expired when you do a full catalog update.

After a successful synchronization, WSUS imports the update catalog into the WSUS database. The WSUS Synchronization Manager (SMS_WSUS_SYNC_MANAGER) component of ConfigMgr initiates an import of the update catalog from the WSUS database to the ConfigMgr database. Synchronization of direct child site SUPs are then initiated and the process continues down the ConfigMgr hierarchy.

The Great Disappearing WSUS

As of this writing, a known but formally undocumented issue exists that occasionally causes the WSUS website to disappear after a reboot of the site server. This typically only happens when WSUS is installed on the central site server and is not limited to a specific version of Windows or IIS. Uninstalling WSUS, leaving the content and database intact, and reinstalling WSUS with identical settings restores WSUS to a fully functioning status. However, this only fixes the symptom and not the problem, leaving the door open for it to reoccur—and based on forum input, it will continue to happen.

Although Microsoft has not issued a formal fix for this problem, an informal "fix" is located in various forums to prevent the site from being deleted. Perform the following steps:

1. Locate the cached Microsoft Installer (MSI) file for WSUS in the Registry. This is stored in the value named LocalPackage under the key HKEY_LOCAL_MACHINE\SOFTWARE\Microsoft\Windows\CurrentVersion\Installer\UserData\S-1-5-18\Products\53E7D0C2E6EE7CD4AB31C286EAED5BD9\InstallProperties.

2. Change the name of the file specified in the LocalPackage value. For example, in the SCCMUnleashed lab the file specified is c:\Windows\Installer\17bb1a3.msi. Simply changing this to 17bb1a3old.msi should prevent the website from being removed in the future.

Note that this is not an official Microsoft fix, and all the usual Registry editing precautions apply. Your mileage may vary (even if you have inflated your tires properly).

Agent Configuration

To configure specific Software Updates settings on client systems, open the ConfigMgr console and navigate to Site Database -> Site Management -> *<Site Code> <Site Name>* -> Site Settings -> Client Agents. Right-click the Software Updates Client agent and choose Properties. This opens the Software Updates Client Agent Properties dialog box, where you can configure the following settings:

▶ **Enable software updates on clients**—The first setting determines whether the agent is actually enabled. If it is not, the client does not scan for updates and ConfigMgr will not deploy updates to it. As with other ConfigMgr Client agents, disabling the agent does not remove it from the client; this simply causes it to do nothing.

▶ **Scan schedule**—This setting determines how often to scan the client system for available updates. You can use the default schedule or configure a custom schedule:

   ▶ The default schedule is a simple schedule run every 7 days. The advantage of a simple schedule is it allows update scans to catch up when the system was powered off or unable to contact an SUP.

   ▶ A custom schedule gives you granular control over when to perform update scans. Scans on a custom schedule may not start for up to 2 hours after the specified time. The actual wait time for each client after the scheduled time is random and prevents client activity from overwhelming the SUP.

The scan schedule is completely independent of actual update deployment.

▶ **Enforce mandatory deployments**—If you use multiple mandatory deployments, your systems may also be subject to multiple reboots. Enabling this setting instructs the agent to install updates from all applicable mandatory updates on a system, in effect combining the deployments and reducing the number of reboots to one. The agent combines all deployments with deadlines up to 7 days in the future by default, although this is customizable, as shown in Figure 15.8.

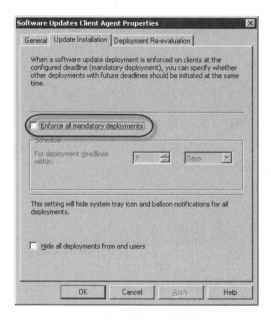

FIGURE 15.8   Enforcing mandatory deployments

▶ **Hide deployment from end users**—By default, users receive a balloon notification from the agent indicating updates are available. Depending on your organization's practices and policies, you may not want users to receive automated notifications. This setting allows you to disable the notification. You can also individually enable or disable the setting for specific update deployments.

The balloon notification allows users to initiate deploying updates at their convenience before a configured mandatory deadline. Also by default, the agent displays the notification to users at configured intervals according to Table 15.2. You can customize the intervals by navigating to the Reminders tab of the Computer Client Agent setting dialog box.

TABLE 15.2   Notification Intervals

Deployment Deadline	Interval
More than 24 hours away	Every 3 hours
Less than 24 hours away	Every hour
Less than 1 hour away	Every 15 minutes

▶ **Deployment reevaluation**—Update reevaluation scans ensure that old updates previously deployed to a system are still on that system. If ConfigMgr detects an update from a previous (but still applicable) deployment is no longer there, it immediately reinstalls the update. Reinstallation takes place without regard to maintenance windows and may be disruptive.

Group Policy Settings

Using a group policy object (GPO) is the standard way to configure WSUS and the WUA. When you're installing and configuring Software Updates, typical questions include the following:

▶ Is it necessary to create a GPO to support ConfigMgr Software Updates?

▶ What should be done with in-place Windows Updates GPOs?

You do not need to create a GPO to support ConfigMgr Software Updates. However, if you choose to create a GPO to support client installation (see Chapter 12, "Client Management," for additional information on client installations) or use an in-place GPO, you must configure the Windows Updates server option to point to the active SUP in the site. This is because ConfigMgr creates a local policy on clients, pointing them to the SUP. A domain-based GPO overrides the local policy settings, causing software updates to fail on the client if the GPO does not specify the SUP as its update server. Additionally, an effective GPO must not disable the Windows Updates service or the WUA.

To avoid any possible conflicts, Microsoft recommends not applying GPOs that enforce Windows Updates settings to ConfigMgr-managed systems. If you use a GPO to deploy clients via WSUS, you should utilize Windows Management Instrumentation (WMI) filtering, security group filtering, or another mechanism to prevent these GPOs from being applied to managed systems.

CAUTION

Disabling a Windows Update GPO

Be careful when removing or disabling a GPO that applies Windows Updates settings because the local computer's Windows Updates setting for downloading and installing updates will take effect. The local settings may cause updates to immediately download and install, or previously downloaded updates to install at the time configured in the local policy. Reboots often accompany update installation; these will be unexpected and most likely undesirable, particularly if the reboot occurs on a server. Because you do not actually approve updates in WSUS when used with ConfigMgr, this is a one-time cutover issue only.

If you are unsure of the local Windows Updates settings on your managed systems, you may want to configure a new GPO (or change an existing one) to notify users of applicable updates only; this will prevent any automatic installations. Do not use a GPO to disable Windows Updates because this will interfere with ConfigMgr Software Updates.

Software Updates Process

You can divide the actual software update process in ConfigMgr 2007 into four separate steps:

1. **Catalog synchronization**—The first step when applying patches is to define which patches are available for installation. Thankfully, Microsoft provides a catalog of all available updates for Microsoft products; it specifies how to detect whether a patch is applicable to a system. WSUS and its integration into ConfigMgr as an SUP handles the catalog-download process, as discussed in the "Synchronization Process" section earlier in this chapter. Microsoft and other third-party documentation may also refer to the update catalog as *update metadata*.

2. **Compliance scanning**—After the update catalog is downloaded and imported into ConfigMgr, a new ConfigMgr machine policy is created, informing each managed system that a new update catalog is available. Managed systems retrieve the policy according to their policy download cycle (by default every 60 minutes). After receiving the new policy, clients randomly schedule an update scan to occur within the next 2 hours, clear the previous scan history, and configure the local policy to point the WUA at the WSUS server.

   At the randomly scheduled time, the ConfigMgr Client agent invokes the local WUA to initiate a compliance scan. The WUA contacts WSUS to retrieve the catalog and scan for the updates it needs. Every 5 minutes, information about required updates is cached and forwarded en masse to the site's management point with state messages; these state messages are subsequently inserted into the ConfigMgr database. This process ensures that update compliance information is available in a timely manner.

NOTE

WUA Version

A common cause of scan compliance failures is the absence of the correct version of the WUA on clients; these are listed as "unknowns" in the console. Because the WUA is automatically updated by Microsoft Windows Update and WSUS, if you are moving clients from this type of environment your clients should all be updated to the latest version of the WUA (version 7.2.6001.788 as of May 2009 as described in KB article 949104 at http://support.microsoft.com/kb/949104).

To verify the current version of the WUA on all clients, run the Scan 1 – Last scan states by collection or Scan 2 – Last scan states by site report, use the Resource Explorer, or create a query containing the following syntax:

```
SELECT v_R_System.Netbios_Name0, v_GS_WINDOWSUPDATEAGENTVERSIO.Version0

FROM v_GS_WINDOWSUPDATEAGENTVERSIO

INNER JOIN v_R_System ON v_GS_WINDOWSUPDATEAGENTVERSIO.ResourceID =
v_R_System.ResourceID

WHERE v_GS_WINDOWSUPDATEAGENTVERSIO.Version0 <> 'ISNULL'

ORDER BY v_GS_WINDOWSUPDATEAGENTVERSIO.Version0
```

To distribute the latest WUA to all clients, download the installation package from KB article 949104 referenced above, and create a Software Distribution package to deploy it. For the program information, specify the following command-line text:

```
WindowsUpdateAgent30-<platform>.exe /quiet /norestart /wuforce
```

The Software Updates Client agent on each system classifies each update into one of four states after a compliance scan, as described in Table 15.3. Information relating to compliance status is also available at http://technet.microsoft.com/en-us/library/bb694299.aspx.

TABLE 15.3   Update Compliance State

State	Description
Required	Specifies the software update is applicable and required on the client. Any of the following four conditions can be true when the software update state is Required: The software update is not deployed to the client computer. The software update was installed on the client computer, but the most recent state message is not inserted into the site server database. The client computer will rescan for the update after installation completes—there can be a delay of up to 2 minutes before the client sends the updated state to the management point, which forwards it to the site server. The software update was installed on the client computer, but the installation requires a computer reboot before the update is complete. The software update was deployed to the client computer but not yet installed.
Not Required	Specifies the software update is not applicable on the client computer, so the update is not required.
Installed	Specifies the software update is applicable on the client computer and the client computer already has the update installed.

TABLE 15.3   Update Compliance State

State	Description
Unknown	Specifies the site server has not received a state message from the client computer, typically for one of the following reasons:
	The client computer did not successfully scan for software updates compliance.
	Although the scan completed successfully on the client computer, the state message has not been processed yet on the site server, possibly due to a backlog of state messages.
	Although the scan completed successfully on the client computer, the state message has not been received from the child site.
	The scan completed successfully on the client computer, but the state message file was corrupted in some way and could not be processed.

Forced and Unforced Scans

Compliance scans are initiated as either forced or unforced. Forced scans always happen; unforced scans may be deemed unnecessary and do not occur if the last compliance scan time, referred to as the time to live (TTL) of the last scan, is less than 24 hours old.

Additionally, clients perform compliance scans in one of two ways—online or offline:

▶ In an online scan, the full update catalog is retrieved by the client; this is typi-cally an expensive operation network-wise.

▶ An offline scan uses the locally cached catalog on the client.

If not forced to use an online scan, clients choose between an online and offline scan based on the version of the update catalog currently cached. If the cached version is the same as that on the SUP or the SUP cannot be contacted, an offline scan is performed using the currently cached copy. If the version on the SUP is newer, the client downloads the new catalog and then performs the scan.

Table 15.4 summarizes both the scan initiation types and the scan compliance types.

TABLE 15.4   Scan Initiation

Initiated By	Initiation Type	Scan Type
Client Agent Properties, general scan schedule	Forced	Online
Client Agent Properties, deployment reevaluation schedule	Unforced	Based on catalog version
Deployment, activation time	Unforced	Based on scan TTL and catalog version
Deployment, deadline time	Forced	Online
ConfigMgr Control Panel Applet, deployment reevaluation schedule	Forced	Online

TABLE 15.4   Scan Initiation

Initiated By	Initiation Type	Scan Type
ConfigMgr Control Panel Applet, software update deployment evaluation	Forced	Based on catalog version

3. **Update preparation**—In this manual step, you must determine which updates to deploy to your managed systems. ConfigMgr helps significantly by identifying how many systems are requesting specific patches, but the final determination of which updates to deploy is up to you.

   After deciding what to deploy, download the updates into update packages and create deployments to direct managed systems to install the updates. These two steps are analogous to the normal software distribution process using software distribution packages and assignments.

4. **Update distribution**—This "rubber hits the road" step is automatically handled by ConfigMgr, similar to the way it handles software distribution. Here are some key points:

   ▶ When a managed system receives a deployment policy, it immediately initiates another update compliance scan using the WUA to ensure the state of the system has not changed.

   ▶ After the scan, the systems immediately download applicable updates for mandatory deployments and schedule installation according to their maintenance windows. If there are no maintenance windows, installation occurs immediately.

   ▶ Updates for optional deployments are not downloaded until they are manually initiated.

   ▶ The client only downloads individual updates identified as necessary by the compliance scan—complete update packages are not downloaded.

   State messages communicate back to the site to ensure the update status in the database is accurate, eliminating the need to perform another compliance scan. This allows ConfigMgr to have current information about the exact patch status of a system in a short period of time rather than waiting for the next compliance scan, which may not take place until the next day or perhaps next week. Full compliance scans needlessly strain the system while obtaining the same information that simple status messages makes available.

Figure 15.9 depicts this four-step process:

1. The update catalog is downloaded from Microsoft and imported into the WSUS database.

   The update catalog is synchronized from the WSUS database to the ConfigMgr database.

15

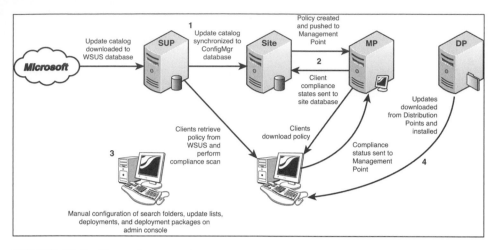

FIGURE 15.9   The software update process

2. The site creates a policy informing clients of the availability of a new update catalog; the management point downloads this policy and makes it available for retrieval by clients.

Clients download the new policy from the management point.

Clients retrieve the update catalog from WSUS and perform a compliance scan.

Clients report their compliance status to the management point.

Client compliance states are sent to the database.

3. Search folders, update lists, deployments, and deployment packages are created according to the steps outlined in the next few sections.

4. Updates, based on defined deployments, are downloaded from distribution points and installed. New client compliance information status is sent to the distribution point immediately and then to the ConfigMgr database.

ConfigMgr provides five distinct objects for you to control the deployment of updates in your environment. A subnode under Software Updates in the ConfigMgr console tree represents each of these objects:

▶ Update Repository

▶ Update Lists

▶ Deployment Templates

▶ Deployment Management

▶ Deployment Packages

The like-named sections of the chapter discuss these objects in detail, but first let's look at a step-by-step sample configuration to help get you up and running quickly.

Putting It All Together—A Quick-Start Example

Getting started with Software Updates can definitely be a bit confusing at first. The following example steps you through the initial configuration for a pilot group of workstations:

1. Create a collection for the pilot systems (called *Pilot Systems* in this example). Add the identified systems to the collection using direct rules.

2. Create a deployment template to store the settings for deployments targeted to this collection. Use the following settings:

   ▸ **Template Name**—Pilot Systems Deployment Template

   ▸ **Collection**—Pilot Systems

   ▸ **Display/Time Settings**—Allow display notification on clients; Client local time; 2-week duration

   ▸ **Restart Settings**—None selected

   ▸ **Event Generation**—None

   ▸ **Download Settings**—Do not install software updates; Download software updates from unprotected distribution point and install

   ▸ **SMS 2003 Settings**—None

3. Create a search folder to list all the updates for Windows with the following parameters:

   ▸ **Superseded**—No

   ▸ **Expired**—No

   ▸ **Products**—Windows XP, Windows Vista

   ▸ **Search all folders under this feature**—Yes

   ▸ **Name**—All Current Windows XP and Vista Updates

4. Select the search folder you just created in the console tree under Search Folders. The updates meeting the criteria just specified appear in the Details pane on the right. Select the updates, right-click, and choose Update List. The resulting Update List Wizard creates an update list and a deployment package then downloads the updates for you. Use the following settings for the Update List Wizard:

   ▸ On the first page of the wizard, create a new update list and name it **All Windows XP and Vista Updates List**. Select the Download the files associated with the selected software updates check box at the bottom of the page.

▶ On the next page of the wizard, choose to create a new package and name it **All Windows XP and Vista Updates**. Fill in the location to create the package. Note that this location should be empty, the current user must have write access to the location, and ConfigMgr creates the folders if they do not currently exist.

▶ Choose which distribution points to copy the package to.

▶ Choose Download updates from the Internet.

▶ Verify the languages selected and correct them if necessary.

5. After the downloads complete (which in this case may take more than an hour), right-click the update list All Windows XP and Vista Updates List that you just created and choose Deploy Software Updates. Use the following settings for the Deploy Software Updates Wizard:

▶ **Name**—All Windows XP and Vista Updates to Pilot Systems

▶ **Deployment Template**—Pilot Systems Deployment Template

▶ **Schedule**—Choose As soon as possible for availability and then adjust the deadline to your liking. Note that this deadline is exactly 2 weeks (to the minute) from the time you launched the wizard because the deployment template specified a 2-week deadline.

That's it. The patches you selected and put into the All Windows XP and Vista updates list are now queued for delivery to your pilot systems and are automatically deployed at the time you specified for the deadline.

Going forward, every time Microsoft releases new updates, start at step 3 of this process, creating or using a new search folder to identify the new patches. You can use the search folder shown later in Figure 15.11 and described in the "Update Repository" section as a model, creating a search folder that shows only the newest updates each month or by whatever timeframe you choose. The flow chart in Figure 15.18 (later in this chapter) also reflects this monthly, cyclical process.

Update Repository

After importing the update catalog into the ConfigMgr database, you can browse and search the catalog using the Update Repository node under Software Updates in the ConfigMgr console, displayed in Figure 15.10. Under the Update Repository node are subfolders for each update classification you chose to include in the update catalog. These folders are divided further into subfolders, based on vendor and then product. A separate subfolder also exists under the Update Repository for updates specific to WSUS Infrastructure Updates; this node is always included and you cannot disable it.

Using the Search Folders subfolder, you can define custom queries based on attributes of the patches. These attributes include the following:

▶ Release date

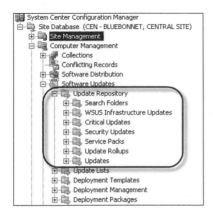

FIGURE 15.10   The Update Repository node in the ConfigMgr console

► Knowledgebase article ID

► Software product

► Update type

The search folders you create are dynamic and reevaluated each time you access them.

Search folders are the easiest way to find updates and should be your starting point for working with updates and patches. To create a new search folder, perform the following steps:

1. Right-click the Search Folders node and then select New Search Folder. This launches the Search Folder Criteria dialog box displayed in Figure 15.11, which is similar to the Rules Wizard in Microsoft Outlook.

2. You must give your new search folder a name and define the update properties for filtering.

    The following list includes the properties most commonly used to filter updates:

    ► **Date Released**—The filter for this property is not a specific date; it is the date an update was released relative to today's date. Some possible filter values include last 1 day, last 1 month, and last 1 year.

    ► **Product**—With this filter, you can limit your query to specific products. The filter list includes all products, not just the ones that you configured to include in the update catalog.

    ► **Severity**—Many updates from Microsoft, particularly security patches, are categorized according to how important Microsoft feels they are. The severity property of an update captures this information.

    ► **Superseded**—Some updates released by Microsoft are superseded by newer updates because they were either flawed or rolled into the newer update. It is usually not a good idea to deploy superseded patches; you can filter them out with this property. Possible values include Yes and No.

15

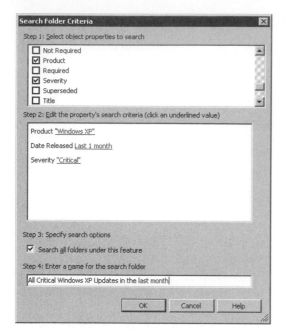

FIGURE 15.11   The Search Folder Criteria dialog box

> ▶ **Update Classification**—As this property's name implies, you can filter
>   updates based on their classification. Possible filter values include all avail-
>   able update classifications, not only the ones you chose to include in the
>   update catalog.
>
> Note that some properties cannot be used to filter updates, even though they
> appear in the Search Folder Criteria dialog box. These are marked with the
> trailing comment (property is not searchable) and include % Compliant,
> Language, License Terms, Maximum Run Time, and Nap Evaluation.
>
> Somewhat confusing in this figure is the check box labeled Search all folders
> under this feature. Here are some points to keep in mind when using this
> check box:
>
>> ▶ If the option is checked, the Search Folder queries the entire update
>>   repository. For most simple searches, you should check this option.
>>
>> ▶ If this option is unchecked, the Search Folder only searches the current
>>   folder in the ConfigMgr console, enabling you to build nested queries or
>>   a hierarchical Search Folder structure.
>>
>> The search folder displayed in Figure 15.11 queries the entire update
>> repository for all Windows XP critical updates in the last month.

After creating a search folder and selecting it from the console tree, you can view and sort
updates in the Details pane circled on the right of Figure 15.12. You can also select an
update and view extended information about it in the pane appearing at the bottom. You

can right-click an update and select Properties to view some of the same extended details in a dialog box, update the maximum runtime, and assign a custom severity. You can then use the custom severity assigned to updates to refine further the queries used for search folders.

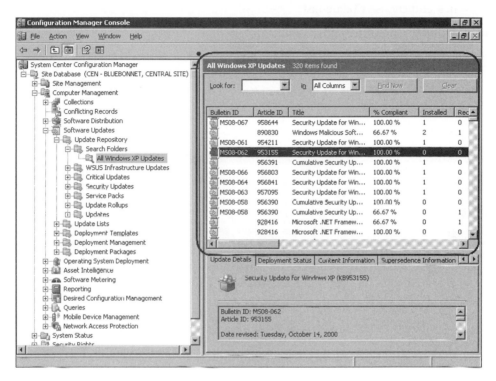

FIGURE 15.12   The Search Folder details pane

Update Lists

Update lists are intermediate objects used to build static lists of updates. Using update lists is optional but recommended. Update lists are static, rather than dynamic like search folders; this capability allows you to create a list to monitor the life cycle of a set of updates, including download status, deployment status, and compliance reporting. You can also use update lists as a delegation mechanism, allowing separate lists for different administrative use. As an example, you can create one set of lists for desktops and one set for servers, delegating the proper rights on each.

You can view the details of updates in an update list the same way you view them though the update repository—by selecting the Update List in the console tree. The result is similar to Figure 15.12. Additionally, you can customize the columns displayed in a list.

As an example, you may only want to see the Bulletin ID and percent compliance details for updates. To customize the columns, right-click the list in the ConfigMgr console tree on the left and select View -> Add/Remove columns... to launch the Add/Remove Columns dialog box, where you can move columns between the Available and Displayed lists.

To add updates to a list, select any number of updates in the update repository and do one of the following:

▶ Right-click and choose Update List.

▶ Drag the updates from the update repository to an existing list.

Both methods launch the Update List Wizard (displayed in Figure 15.13) to guide you through the process. If you add updates using the right-click method, the first page of the wizard allows you to choose to add the updates to an existing list or create a new list. This is the only method available to create a new list.

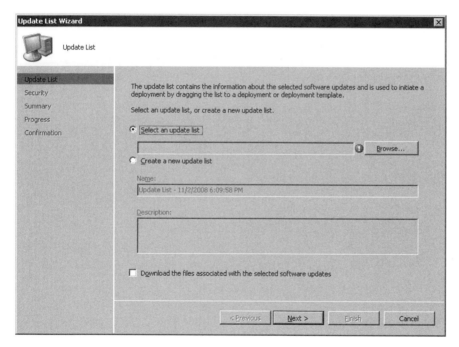

FIGURE 15.13   The first page of the Update List Wizard

In both cases, the first page of the wizard contains a check box to initiate downloading the updates. The second page varies based on whether or not you are creating a new package:

▶ If you choose to download the updates using the wizard, the next page prompts you to select an existing update package or to create a new package.

▶ If you choose to create a new package, you must name the package and specify a source location. ConfigMgr will download the applicable files for the chosen updates to the source location.

The source location must be in Universal Naming Convention (UNC) format and accessible by the current user of the ConfigMgr console. Additionally, the wizard adds a Distribution Points page, where you can specify the distribution points on which to install the package.

Update lists are also particularly useful in a multisite ConfigMgr hierarchy. Lists created at parent sites replicate to child sites; these replicated lists are read-only at the child sites. Administrators of the child sites can then use these replicated lists to expedite the deployment of the updates in those lists—they no longer have to worry about actually discovering applicable updates, just deploying them using existing collections and templates. This replication process can be used to approve updates at higher levels of the organization and push them down as "approved" patches to the lower levels for use in a delegated model of software update maintenance.

System Center Update Publisher (SCUP)

SCUP is a separate tool that third parties use to publish software update information to WSUS; this in effect expands the update catalog served by that WSUS system to include non-Microsoft updates. The main advantage of using WSUS to deploy updates over normal software distribution is that updates deployed using WSUS are subject to a compliance scan before installation. Therefore, you do not have to build any logic into the package or a collection to ensure that updates are applied only where they are needed.

A list of updates created with SCUP for products from Microsoft partners are available at the ConfigMgr TechCenter at http://technet.microsoft.com/en-us/configmgr/bb892875.aspx.

An additional use of SCUP is to publish expired or superseded Microsoft updates into WSUS for use by ConfigMgr. ConfigMgr does not allow you to download expired or superseded updates for use with Software Updates because these are viewed as a security risk. If your organization has a requirement to deploy an expired or superseded update you have not yet downloaded, one workaround is to manually download the update and publish it with SCUP. As noted, though, this is not necessarily recommended because of the security risk it may pose, but it may be required because of corporate politics or other requirements.

For complete coverage of SCUP, its capabilities and proper usage, refer to the SCUP TechNet documentation at http://technet.microsoft.com/en-us/library/bb531022.aspx.

Deployment Templates

You typically will create multiple deployments to manage distributing updates, with the only difference being the collection or the deadline for the updates. Deployment templates provide a group of common settings used to create update deployments (discussed in the section "Creating and Managing Deployments"); with templates, you can predefine the common settings for deployments, including the following:

▶ **Collection**—The collection for the deployment.

▶ **User Notification**—Suppress or allow user notification.

▶ **Deployment time interpretation**—Determines how a client interprets the deployment time—either as client local time or Coordinated Universal Time (UTC).

▶ **Duration**—The amount of time until a deployment becomes mandatory. This setting determines the actual deadline of a deployment when you use a template to create a deployment by adding the duration to the current date and time. Figure 15.14 shows the Deployment Template Wizard page to set this option.

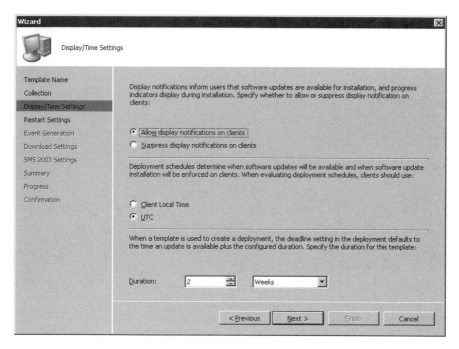

FIGURE 15.14   Deployment Template Wizard with a configured duration of 2 weeks

▶ **Restart Suppression**—You can choose to suppress restarts on servers, workstations, or both.

▶ **Ignore Maintenance Windows**—Tells the deployment to ignore any configured maintenance windows (discussed in the "Maintenance Windows" section of this chapter). This is useful when deploying critical updates or zero-day updates that need immediate installation.

▶ **Operations Manager Integration**—Unexpected restarts and update installations may generate many warnings and alerts in Operations Manager. The following are your options:

  ▶ You can instruct the ConfigMgr agent to put the Operations Manager (OpsMgr) agent on that system into maintenance mode, thus preventing unnecessary warnings and alerts.

15

> **NOTE**
>
> **Maintenance Mode**
>
> Specifying that ConfigMgr place the Operations Manager agent into maintenance mode does not truly place the OpsMgr agent health service watcher into maintenance mode; instead, it merely pauses the health service on the managed system. This should change in a future Configuration Manager service pack or maintenance release.

▶ You can also configure the deployment to generate an Operations Manager alert if an update installation fails.

Both options assume an Operations Manager environment and an Operations Manager agent installed on the client system.

▶ **Download Settings**—These settings dictate whether to download updates if the client is connected to a distribution point in a slow network, or if the client is connected to an unprotected distribution point when a protected DP is available but without the specified updates.

If you only allow content to download from distribution points in a local or fast boundary and no DPs are available to a client, the updates cannot download and the deployment will fail. This may happen with roaming clients, because they move from location to location. If you have a population of systems that roam between sites with local distribution points, be sure to define the slow boundaries and make the deployments available to the slow boundaries.

Updates in a mandatory deployment download to a client when they become available, as configured on the Schedule tab of the deployment's properties page. This capability allows clients to pre-stage the updates and ensures those updates are available when the deadline for the deployment hits, regardless of the availability on a local distribution point.

Pre-staging also prevents a distribution point from overloading with requests for updates once a deadline hits. Updates in nonmandatory deployments—those without a deadline—are not downloaded to the client until the client initiates installing updates in the deployment.

You can create new update deployments with an update template using the New Deployment Wizard. Utilizing a template makes creating deployments quicker, and ensures you can create multiple deployments using identical settings with a minimal effort. Deployment templates are optional but recommended.

To create a deployment template, launch the new Deployment Template wizard by right-clicking on the Deployment Templates node and selecting New Deployment Template. Alternatively, if you create a deployment using the New Deployment Wizard without a deployment template, you are prompted (as shown in Figure 15.15) to create a new template using the settings you just entered to create the deployment.

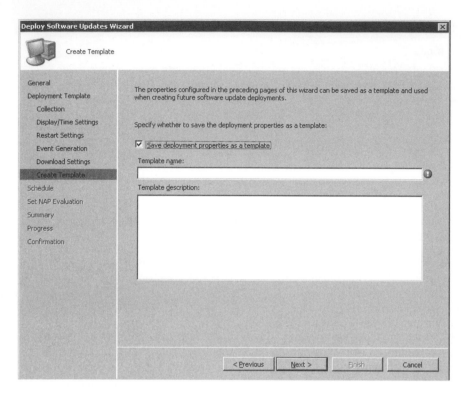

FIGURE 15.15   Creating a deployment template

There is no link between a template and deployments created using that template. ConfigMgr copies the settings from the template to the deployment but does not establish or maintain a relationship between the two.

Update Deployments

Update deployments are similar to advertisements because they control the details of actually deploying and installing updates on managed systems. The next sections discuss creating update deployments, deployment deadlines, and scheduling when using maintenance windows.

Creating Deployments

There are two methods to create a new deployment:

▶ Select a set of updates from the Update Repository, right-click them, and choose Deploy Software Updates.

▶ Right-click an update list and choose Deploy Software Updates.

The only difference between the two options is that the first uses updates you manually selected, whereas the second uses updates from a list you preconfigured. Creating deployments using a list is preferred because the list persists after you create the deployment and is available for other things, in particular reporting.

Both options launch the Deploy Software Updates Wizard. You use the wizard to configure the details of the deployment, which are the same as the details used to configure a deployment template. The wizard gives you the option to use a previously created template, in which case ConfigMgr copies all the settings from the template to the deployment. The New Update Deployment Wizard prompts for any settings not configured in the template. Additionally, you can specify the following:

▶ Start time for the deployment

▶ Whether or not the deployment is mandatory, and a deadline time

▶ To use Wake On LAN

▶ To ignore maintenance windows

Similar to update lists, deployments are replicated down a ConfigMgr hierarchy from parent sites to their children. However, instead of being available for use at the down-level sites, replicated deployments are enforced where applicable. Thus, if you create and apply a deployment at a parent site on a collection that contains systems from child sites, the deployment is enforced by the child site. This model is useful for centralized administration and enforcement of software updates in an organizational hierarchy; it forces compliance with the policy established at the top level without any intervention by down-level administrators.

Deployment Deadlines

A distinction between update deployments and advertisements is that rather than provide a mandatory time for installation, update deployments use deployment deadlines. Deployments are optionally available to users until the specified date and time, and they are enforced after this date and time. This is an oft-misunderstood concept and bears restating: Updates in a deployment are not forced to install until after the specified deadline.

Users can manually initiate the deployment until the deadline. By default, ConfigMgr prompts users to initiate deployments with a system tray balloon notification, basing the notification interval on the deadline according to Table 15.5. (You may notice these are actually the same intervals discussed in the "Agent Configuration" section of this chapter.)

TABLE 15.5   Default Deployment Notification Intervals

Deadline	Notification Interval
More than 24 hours away	Every 3 hours
Less than 24 hours away	Every hour
Less than 1 hour away	Every 15 minutes

You can customize these default intervals by going to the Reminders tab of the Computer Client Agent Properties dialog box. You get to this dialog box by navigating to Site

Database -> Site Management -> *<Site Code> <Site Name>* -> Site Settings -> Client Agents in the ConfigMgr console, right-clicking Computer Client Agent, selecting Properties from the context menu, and then clicking the Reminders tab. Figure 15.16 shows an example of this tab. If necessary, you can completely suppress notifications for specific deployments.

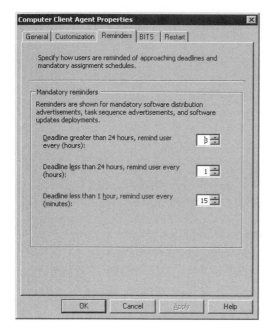

FIGURE 15.16   The Reminders tab of the Computer Client Agent Properties dialog box

At the time of the deadline, the ConfigMgr agent reevaluates compliance status of the local managed system to determine which updates are still applicable, and then schedules installing the updates.

Deployment Packages

Analogous to software distribution packages, deployment packages (Site Database -> Computer Management -> Software Updates -> Deployment Packages) are simply the collection of files needed for a defined set of updates. You manage update packages identically to software distribution packages—they must have a source folder and be available to clients by installing them on distribution points.

There are two structural differences between software distribution packages and deployment packages:

▶ Deployment packages do not have customizable programs and therefore do not have a Programs subnode in the console.

▶ Deployment packages contain specially formatted updates and accordingly have an Updates subnode, where you can add and remove updates.

Although the console does not include a specific selection to create a deployment package, there are two methods to create one:

▶ Choose to download updates on the first page of the Update List Wizard (see the "Update Lists" section of this chapter).

▶ Select updates in the update repository or an update list. Then right-click and choose Download Software Updates.

The second method launches the Download Updates Wizard, displayed in Figure 15.17. This wizard has three main pages:

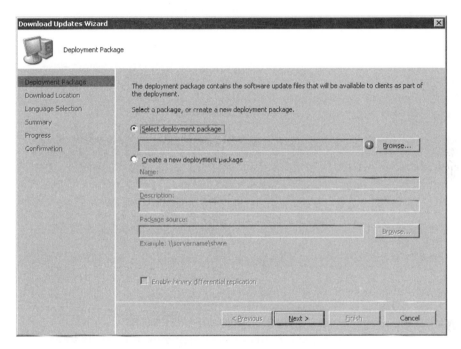

FIGURE 15.17 The first page of the Download Updates Wizard

▶ **Deployment Package**—On this page, you can choose to use an existing package or create a new one. If you create a new package, you must give it a name and specify a source location. ConfigMgr will download the applicable files for the chosen updates to the source location. The source location must be a UNC (\\<*servername*>\<*share*>) location and the current user of the ConfigMgr console must have security credentials to access that UNC location. Additionally, the wizard has some other pages for new package-specific information:

    ▶ Distribution Points

    ▶ Data Access

    ▶ Distribution Settings

NOTE

Deployment Packages Are Not Linked

Update lists and deployment packages are not linked to each other, and updates added to a list are not automatically added to any update packages you create from the list. The reverse of this is also true—updates added to a package are not automatically added to update lists used to create the package.

Similarly, deployments and deployment packages are also not linked to each other. Adding updates to a deployment package will not add them to any deployments.

▶ **Download Location**—Choose to download updates from Microsoft using an Internet location or from a network location.

▶ **Language Selection**—Many updates are localized and only applicable to corresponding localized versions of Windows. On this page of the wizard, you choose which localized updates to download. It is a best practice to select only the languages that exist in your environment, thus minimizing the amount of Internet traffic to download your selected updates.

TIP

Package Source Folder

When creating a new package, ConfigMgr creates the source folder if it does not already exist. The user account of the current ConfigMgr console user is used to create this folder and must have security credentials to do so.

Creating and Managing Deployments

The steps used to create a deployment are variable and dependent on whether you use a delegated model and either or both of the two optional components—update lists and deployment templates (both previously discussed in like-named sections). Although you have the flexibility to fit the model to your needs and requirements, it presents some ambiguity. The following section discusses implementing the third step of the four-step software update process—update preparation (previously discussed in the "Software Updates Process" section of the chapter).

A Recommended Approach

It is best to start with a recommended or generic way to set up a complex process such as Software Updates, particularly when the process offers many different paths. Figure 15.18 shows a flowchart presenting one possible path, based on best practices, for creating and managing your deployments.

The flowchart includes the following steps:

▶ **Create collections**—Similar to advertisements, update deployments are targeted to specific collections or subcollections. You can create a series of collections specifically for targeting your update deployments, where each collection has a separate

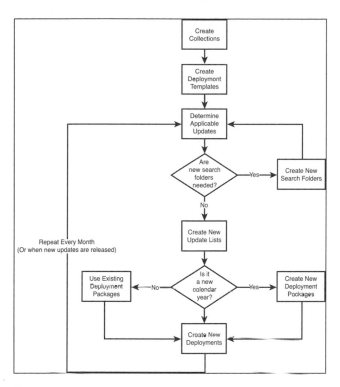

FIGURE 15.18   Showing the software update management flow

deployment targeted to it, with any differences in the deployments defined by corresponding deployment templates.

▶ **Create deployment templates**—Create a deployment template for each combination of settings needed. You can use these templates each time you create a new deployment, greatly reducing the time it takes to create a deployment and ensuring all deployments follow your defined practices for deploying updates.

▶ **Determine applicable updates**—Based on your organization's needs, requirements, and policies, you must determine which updates are applicable for your environment. You can also use compliance scan data returned from managed systems to aid in this decision. Creating search folders (previously discussed in the "Update Repository" section) will isolate updates and help you identify applicable updates.

▶ **Create or modify update lists**—Create update lists for each area of interest where compliance reporting and tracking are required. Consider creating update lists for each operating system type that exists. You may also want to create a new update list every time Microsoft releases a new batch of updates—typically the second Tuesday of every month. Using the Update Repository or Search Folders node in the console, copy updates into applicable lists. Note that updates can be part of multiple lists.

▶ **Create or modify deployment packages**—As you add updates to update lists, use the Update List Wizard to add updates to deployment packages, as described earlier in the "Update Lists" section of this chapter. You are free to create packages in whichever manner you choose.

Real World: Placing Deployment Packages on Distribution Points

The only real consideration when creating deployment packages is on which distribution point to install each package. Depending on your infrastructure, you may be able to declare that certain patches are not applicable to systems that use a specific distribution point. In this case, create a separate package for those updates and only install the package on the other distribution points. As an example, if you have a distribution point that only services servers, there is no reason to make workstation patches available on it. You should then divide your patches between two sets of packages—one for workstations, and one for servers. On the server-only DP, only install the deployment packages with server patches.

Managed systems do not download an entire package; they only download those specific updates they require from each package regardless of which package the updates are in. This capability, in combination with ConfigMgr's ability to use binary delta replication to replicate only changed bits in a package, eliminates the need for you to limit package sizes.

In general, you should create a single package containing all updates for each calendar year. This prevents numerous downloads of updates applicable to multiple systems for multiple packages. ConfigMgr uses file delta (default) or binary delta replication to install the package on distribution points, so the size of the package and its impact on network bandwidth should not be a concern.

▶ **Create or modify deployments**—Create the actual deployments used to distribute and install the updates to managed systems by right-clicking an update list and choosing Deploy Software Updates; then choose to add the updates to an existing deployment or create a new one. By creating a new deployment for each new set of updates, you can maintain the same deadline for previously created deployments. A previously created deployment template populates the actual settings for the deployment.

Perform the last four steps of the flowchart in Figure 15.18 every time Microsoft releases new updates or your organization determines there are updates requiring installation.

Maintaining Offline Virtual Machines

Many organizations now use virtual machine (VM) libraries to quickly deploy new VMs or for use with a virtual desktop infrastructure (VDI). However, you cannot directly update the VMs in the library and the master VMs used to create the new VDI guests with the latest Windows updates with an automated process, because they are not actually running and are perpetually offline.

Microsoft created a tool to deal with this exact issue—the Offline Virtual Machine Servicing Tool. This tool requires Microsoft System Center Virtual Machine Manager (VMM) and either ConfigMgr or WSUS. You create servicing jobs that specify all the details of the maintenance, including schedules and the VMs to update. The Offline Virtual Machine Servicing Tool then chooses a maintenance host to which to deploy the VM. Once deployed, the VM is updated according to the ConfigMgr policies, shut down, and copied back into the VMM library. For more details, check out the Utility Spotlight article in the October 2008 issue of *TechNet* (http://technet.microsoft.com/en-us/magazine/cc895643.aspx).

A Few Best Practices

Best practices are always tricky business—what works for one organization is not necessarily the best fit for another organization. Nevertheless, it is always good to have a starting point, a set of guidelines or recommendations from those that have been through the trenches and survived. Actually, you can learn from those who didn't survive; things like "Don't step there" or "Don't drink the water." The following list is meant to be just that, a general set of guidelines to dispel any myths and reinforce the information presented in the rest of this chapter:

▶ **Manual intervention**—Unlike the standalone version of WSUS, some manual intervention is required on an on-going basis to deploy updates with ConfigMgr. You must identify and download updates every time you want to deploy them. There is no way to automate this. Some may feel that this is a knock against the ConfigMgr Software Updates function, but this manual intervention is relatively minor and ensures that no updates are distributed in an organization without explicit, hands-on configuration.

▶ **Update packages**—Clients will pull applicable updates from any available package. Because of this, there is no specific need to separate updates into multiple packages. The only real limitation is a recommended technical limit of 500 updates per package. Some separation of updates is therefore logical, and the general guideline is to create a single update package for every calendar year of updates. Separating updates by operating system will produce duplication because some patches do cross operating system boundaries or are not operating system specific.

▶ **Update lists**—Update lists are the perfect way to track what updates were actually deployed in a given update deployment cycle. Because Microsoft sticks to its monthly update release rather vigorously, it makes sense to create a new list every month to contain the newly released updates. In addition, update lists only contain references to updates, so creating multiple update lists based on operating systems or some other criteria does not create any duplication.

▶ **Deployments**—After the deadline for a deployment passes, the need to have a separate deployment for the updates referenced in that deployment goes away. Therefore, on a regular cycle, something like every 3, 6, or 12 months, it makes sense to collapse the updates referenced in individual deployments with past deadlines into larger deployments. This simplifies deployment management and minimizes the number of individual deployments listed in the console.

▶ **Initial setup**—When you are first setting up Software Updates, it makes sense to create one large list for all updates before a given date. You can then create a deployment for this list to ensure that any new systems introduced into the environment and any existing ones are fully patched with all updates issued before you started using Software Updates. You can store updates for this list in one large package as long as it does not break the 500-update barrier.

▶ **Naming conventions**—Unlike the rest of the nodes in ConfigMgr, subfolders cannot be created under Update Lists, Deployment Management, and Deployment Packages. For this reason, you should establish and stick to a strong naming convention for these object types. This naming convention should clearly describe the criteria used to choose the updates contained in the given object, and ensure that objects are sorted chronologically. Table 15.6 contains a sample naming convention for each of these types of objects.

TABLE 15.6   Example Software Update Object Names

Object Type	Sample Names
Update List	Windows XP Updates - Pre 2008
	Windows Vista Updates - Pre 2008
	Windows XP Updates - 12/08
	Windows XP Updates - 01/09
	Windows Vista Updates - 01/09
Deployment	Windows XP Updates - 2008
	Windows Vista Updates - 2008
	Windows XP Updates - 01/09
	Windows Vista Updates - 01/09
Deployment Package	All Updates - 2009
	All Updates - Pre 2009

Maintenance Windows

Deployments are somewhat limited in that they do not define an exact time that updates should or must be installed; they merely define a time when updates become mandatory. This limitation could easily cause disruption to your users and your servers if updates install at various times after the deadline.

Maintenance windows are the perfect solution to this dilemma. In general, maintenance windows prevent the ConfigMgr client from undertaking any action that could disrupt the end user on a system. This includes preventing Software Updates deployments, Software Distribution advertisements, and restarts initiated by ConfigMgr for software updates.

Because they are set on a per-collection basis, you can create maintenance windows for specific recurring and nonrecurring start and stop times. You edit these schedules by right-clicking any collection and choosing Modify Collection Settings. This displays the Collection Settings dialog box, where the first tab, Maintenance Windows, manipulates these windows. The interface for creating maintenance window schedules, displayed in Figure 15.19, is quite flexible and allows you to specify settings such as every third Tuesday of the month.

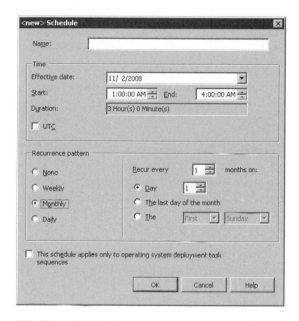

FIGURE 15.19   Creating maintenance window schedules

NOTE

Maintenance Windows and Software Distribution

Maintenance windows also affect Software Distribution advertisements. In the same way that they delay the distribution of updates in a deployment, they also delay the execution of mandatory advertised programs. Be aware of this when setting up your collections and maintenance windows. If necessary, you can configure your mandatory advertisements to ignore maintenance windows using the Schedule tab on the advertisement.

Scheduling with Maintenance Windows

If the collection where the deployment is effective has a maintenance window, the agent schedules installation for the start of the next occurrence of that maintenance window. The agent also calculates how much time it will take to install all the identified updates, ensuring the updates will not break the maintenance window. Additionally, 15 minutes are also added to this calculated window of time to account for a system restart. If installing the updates will exceed the window, the agent chooses a subset of the updates. If no applicable maintenance window exists, the agent immediately starts installing all updates.

After a deployment completes on a managed system, an additional compliance scan occurs to ensure successful installation of all updates. ConfigMgr forwards the results for this scan to the management point using state messages. This process is significantly expedited compared to the ITMU process and ensures the compliance data in the ConfigMgr database is always current.

TIP

Updating Deployments

You can add more updates to a previously created deployment by dragging them from either the update repository or an update list. This technique allows you to reuse deployments for future update installations.

Using Multiple Maintenance Windows

Maintenance windows affect software updates; they prevent updates in a mandatory deployment from installing on a system outside configured maintenance window times. This causes any mandatory deployment past its deadline to wait until the next configured maintenance window before installing its updates.

You can create multiple maintenance windows on a single collection. Any system belonging to multiple collections is also subject to the maintenance windows of those collections, because multiple maintenance windows on a single system do not cancel each other.

Maximum Runtimes

Another check performed by the Client agent is the maximum runtime for each applicable update in a deployment. If the sum of these maximum runtimes is greater than the maintenance window allows for, the Client agent will not install all applicable updates. The updates will be culled based on their maximum runtime, ensuring they complete before the window ends. To view or edit the maximum runtime for any update, find the update (in the update repository, an update list, a deployment, or even a deployment package), right-click it, and choose Properties. This opens a Properties dialog box for the update with a Maximum Run Time tab, shown in Figure 15.20; the value listed is editable. You can also multiselect updates to change their maximum runtimes in the same way. By default, all updates have a maximum runtime of 20 minutes.

Note that clients begin downloading updates as soon as deployments are available to them. This prevents the time required by clients to actually download updates from affecting the time available in the maintenance window.

Bypassing Maintenance Windows

Configure specific deployments to ignore configured maintenance windows by selecting the Ignore maintenance windows and install immediately at deadline check box on the Schedule tab of a deployment. Use this option very carefully if you have gone through the

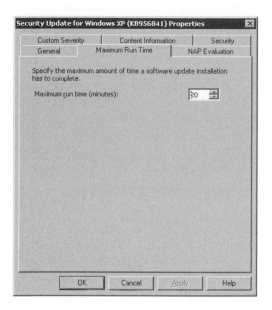

FIGURE 15.20   Maximum runtime for an update (in this case 20 minutes)

trouble of defining and setting up maintenance windows, because it will disrupt your care-fully planned update scheduling. However, in the case of zero-day updates, the disruption may be necessary.

SMS 2003 Clients

ConfigMgr 2007 continues to support down-level SMS 2003 clients to varying degrees; this support includes software update functionality. This support is critical during a large, in-place upgrade from SMS 2003, when it may be impossible to transition the entire client base quickly. This section discusses deploying updates to these SMS 2003 clients; the infor-mation assumes a knowledge and understanding of software updates in SMS 2003.

TIP

Upgrading SMS Site Servers

For information on upgrading your SMS site servers to Configuration Manager 2007, see Chapter 9, "Migrating to Configuration Manager 2007."

The upgrade maintains the following data in the site database:

▶ **Software updates metadata**—Includes items such as name, description, applicabil-ity rules, and article ID

▶ **Compliance information**—Includes the number of scanned clients for which a software update is required or not required

▶ **Client status information**—Includes the revision for the Microsoft Update catalog used by clients when scanning for software updates compliance

The SMS 2003 upgrade process automatically upgrades the actual ITMU scan tool to a new, ConfigMgr-compatible version. ConfigMgr 2007 does not support other separately released supplementary scan tools such as the Inventory Tool for Dell Updates or the February 2005 Security Update Scan Tool; any data pertaining to these tools is removed from the database after the upgrade.

SMS 2003 update advertisements are also migrated during the ConfigMgr upgrade; these continue to function as expected. The upgrade moves the advertisements in the console to the SMS2003 Advertisements node, under Site Database -> Computer Management -> Software Updates -> Deployment Management.

Because the SMS 2003 Client agent does not have the same tight integration with the WUA as the ConfigMgr Client agent, SMS 2003 clients must continue to receive their update catalog by means of an ITMU-based scan advertisement. Ensure you are only targeting SMS 2003 clients with this advertisement! Targeting ConfigMgr clients will produce unexpected results and is unsupported.

Similarly, you must download the updates catalog from Microsoft using a separate catalog synchronization advertisement—this process is identical to the process existing in SMS 2003. All updates migrated from SMS 2003 to ConfigMgr have (LEGACY) appended to their title until the initial ITMU catalog synchronization completes. Do not create new deployments using updates marked with (LEGACY), because these only exist to support migrated deployments and for reporting.

After synchronizing the ITMU update catalog and scanning SMS 2003 clients with the ITMU scan tool, you are once again ready to deploy updates to those clients. The actual process for deploying updates to SMS 2003 clients is nearly identical to the process outlined previously for ConfigMgr clients, with a few minor differences or exceptions:

▶ **Software repository**—A searchable attribute exists on all updates called Deployable to SMS2003. As this name implies, the attribute identifies updates that you can deploy to SMS 2003 clients. Using this attribute, you can build search folders specific to your SMS 2003 clients.

▶ **Deployments and deployments packages**—The loose association of deployments and deployment packages does not apply to those created for SMS 2003 clients; they roughly revert to the behavior of ITMU-based update packages and advertisements in SMS 2003.

Each deployment package used for SMS 2003 clients contains a legacy program, listed under the SMS2003 Programs subnode of the package, to deploy the updates in that package. Each of these programs is then advertised to clients using an advertisement listed under the SMS2003 advertisements subnode of deployment management.

Because this pertains to legacy SMS 2003-based clients, the programs are specific only to the updates in the package that contains the program. Additionally, the SMS

2003 agent is not intelligent enough to download only the updates that it requires and instead downloads the entire package.

▶ **Deployment templates and deployments**—SMS 2003–specific settings exist for both these objects. Choose these settings while running either the Deployment or the Deployment Template Creation Wizard, or after creation using the SMS 2003 tab of the Properties dialog box. The settings include the following:

 ▶ **Collect Hardware Inventory Immediately**—In SMS 2003, software update compliance information is stored locally on clients in the WMI repository and returned to the site using hardware inventory. It may be desirable to return this information immediately to the site database rather than waiting for the next hardware inventory cycle; this option initiates a new hardware inventory, which returns the software update compliance information to the site database immediately after update installation.

 ▶ **Distribution Point Locally Available**—This option allows you to specify downloading updates first from the local distribution point or directly access them from that DP if it is locally available.

 ▶ **No Distribution Point Locally Available**—This option allows you to specify to first download updates from a remote distribution point, or directly access them from a remote distribution point if a distribution point is not locally available. You can also specify not to install updates at all if a distribution point is not available locally.

Once you eliminate all SMS 2003 clients in your infrastructure, you can uninstall the ITMU. Until then, the hybrid approach outlined here offers a seamless and relatively painless path to managing updates for both types of clients.

Native Mode and Software Updates

As with other site roles, some special configuration is required to configure an SUP for use with a native mode ConfigMgr site. This involves configuring the WSUS IIS site to use SSL-secured communication and telling WSUS itself to use the SSL certificate. Adding this certificate authenticates the SUP to the clients and secures all communication between the SUP and the clients. Perform the following steps:

1. Begin by acquiring the SSL certificate from your Public Key Infrastructure (PKI). You must install this certificate into the Personal certificate store of the computer account on the SUP; this process is dependent on your PKI implementation.

   The requirements for this certificate are as follows:

   ▶ The Enhanced Key Usage value must contain Server Authentication (1.3.6.1.5.5.7.3.1).

   ▶ If the site system accepts connections from the Internet, the Subject Name or Subject Alternative Name must contain the Internet FQDN of the SUP.

▶ If the site system accepts connections from the intranet, the Subject Name or Subject Alternative Name must contain either the intranet FQDN (recommended) or the computer's NetBIOS name, depending on configuration of the site system.

▶ If the site system accepts connections from both the Internet and the intranet, you must specify both the Internet FQDN and the intranet FQDN (or computer NetBIOS name) using the ampersand (&) symbol delimiter between the two names.

2. Configure the WSUS site in IIS to use the certificate. The steps differ between Windows Server 2008 and Windows Server 2003. For IIS 7.0 on Windows Server 2008, follow these steps:

▶ Open the IIS 7 Administration console.

▶ Expand Sites and select the website used by WSUS (Default Web Site if you installed WSUS into the default site, or WSUS Administration if you used a custom site).

▶ Select Edit Bindings.

▶ Configure HTTPS to use the appropriate certificate.

For IIS 6.0 on Windows Server 2003, use the following steps:

▶ Open the IIS 6 Administration console.

▶ Edit the properties of the website used by WSUS (Default Web Site if you installed WSUS into the default site, or WSUS Administration if you used a custom site).

▶ Click Server Certificate on the Directory Security tab.

▶ The Web Server Certificate Wizard launches, prompting you to select the web server certificate to use.

3. Next, configure the following WSUS virtual folders to allow only SSL communication:

▶ APIRemoting30

▶ ClientWebService

▶ DSSAuthWebService

▶ ServerSyncWebService

▶ SimpleAuthWebService

You will perform this differently in Windows 2003 and Windows 2008. For IIS 7.0 on Windows Server 2008, complete these steps in the IIS 7 Administration console:

▶ Expand Sites and select the website used by WSUS (Default Web Site if you installed WSUS into the default site, or WSUS Administration if you used a custom site).

▶ For each of the virtual folders listed previously, double-click SSL Settings in Features View, select Require SSL on the SSL Settings page, and then click Apply in the Actions pane.

For IIS 6.0 on Windows Server 2003, use the following steps:

▶ Edit the properties of the website used by WSUS (Default Web Site if you installed WSUS into the default site, or WSUS Administration if you used a custom site).

▶ For each of the virtual folders listed previously, click the Directory Security tab. Then click Edit in the Secure Communications section, select Require secure channel (SSL), and then click OK and click OK again to close the properties for the virtual root.

4. Finish by configuring WSUS to use SSL. To do this, run a single command from the command prompt:

```
<WSUS Installation Folder>\Tools\WSUSutil.exe
➥configuressl <subject name in the signing certificate>
```

In this case, `<subject name in the signing certificate>` is typically the FQDN of the system hosting WSUS based on the certificate requirements listed previously.

Using Wake On LAN Capability

One hindrance to updating systems with the latest updates is the power status of the system; specifically, if the system is not powered on, how can you or a tool maintain that system? Traditionally, the best time to update systems in an organization is when no one is using them—at night. However, many users turn off their desktop systems when they leave for the day, even if instructed not to, and some systems may go into a power-saving hibernation mode. Powered-down systems present an obvious problem with no easy workaround and give us systems that either are not patched or are slammed with patches the moment users log into the network in the morning.

The solution to this is Wake On LAN (WOL). WOL is an industry-standard method of sending a remote signal over the network to a system to "wake" it up when the system is powered off or hibernating. It does this by sending a specially crafted network packet known as a *magic packet* to the destination system. The network interface card (NIC) of the destination system receives this magic packet (also referred as a *wake-up packet* in the ConfigMgr console) and proceeds to wake up the system. Chapter 6, "Architecture Design Planning," discusses magic packets.

WOL Prerequisites

There are two ConfigMgr-specific prerequisites and three external prerequisites to fully enable WOL capabilities in ConfigMgr.

ConfigMgr Prerequisites

▶ Enable hardware inventory.

▶ Install the ConfigMgr agent on destination systems.

External Prerequisites

▶ Network interface cards must support WOL and the use of the magic packet.

▶ Enable WOL on NICs and in the BIOS of destination systems.

▶ If subnet-directed broadcasts (discussed in the next section) are used, configure the network infrastructure to forward subnet-directed broadcasts.

Two Types of WOL

ConfigMgr supports two types of WOL:

▶ **Unicast**—With unicast WOL, a single magic packet is sent to the IP address of the system that needs to be woken up. The IP address is taken from the hardware inventory of the destination system (thus the requirement for hardware inventory to be enabled).

You do not have to make changes to most network infrastructures for this type of WOL to function. The magic packet is simply a specially crafted UDP (User Datagram Protocol) packet sent directly to the destination system's IP address.

The magic packet includes the Media Access Control (MAC) address of the system. The destination NIC compares the MAC address to its own before actually waking up the system; if the MAC address in the magic packet does not match the MAC address on the destination NIC, the NIC does not signal the system to wake up. This prevents a situation where the desired destination system changes its IP address, but the magic packet is sent to a different system that acquired the old IP address of the destination system. In this case, there is no way to actually wake up the destination system because its new IP address is unknown to ConfigMgr!

▶ **Subnet directed**—With subnet-directed WOL, ConfigMgr broadcasts the magic packet to the IP subnet of the destination system. All NICs on that subnet receive the magic packet. Each compares the MAC address specified in the magic packet to its own; if there is a match, the NIC wakes up its system. This allows ConfigMgr to wake up those systems with changed IP addresses that remain on the same subnet.

Subnet-directed WOL requires support from your network infrastructure; specifically your network infrastructure must support subnet-directed broadcasts. These broadcasts are often disabled due to overhead. Additionally, it is a security best practice to change the default port used by subnet-directed WOL packets and configure the network infrastructure to allow only subnet-directed broadcasts from your ConfigMgr site server.

Configuring WOL

Several configuration options are available for WOL in ConfigMgr. You perform all customizations from the Wake On LAN and Ports tabs of the *<Site>* Properties dialog box (see Figure 15.21). Right-click Site Database -> Site Management -> *<Site Code> <Site Name>* and then choose Properties to get there.

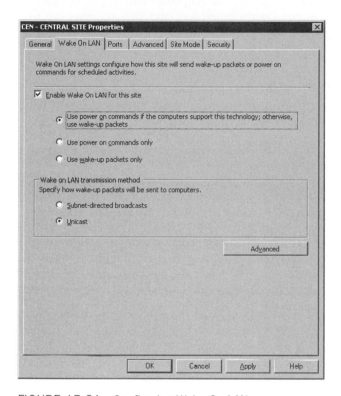

FIGURE 15.21   Configuring Wake On LAN

Enable WOL on the Wake On LAN tab and configure whether you want to use unicast or subnet-directed broadcasts. New in R2 is the ability to use the power-on functionality of the Intel AMT technology. This is an alternative to the magic packets used by traditional WOL, but requires Out of Band (OOB) management support (discussed in Chapter 6) on the destination system; OOB also must be fully configured and enabled in ConfigMgr. To support the AMT power-on capability, R2 includes three new options:

▶ Use power-on commands if the computers support this technology; otherwise, use wake-up packets.

▶ Use power-on commands only.

▶ Use wake-up packets only.

You can also access advanced options from the Wake On LAN tab by clicking the Advanced button displayed in Figure 15.21. These options are mainly network and ConfigMgr throttling controls; only change them if you are experiencing issues.

To view the port used by ConfigMgr for the magic packet, switch to the Ports tab of the *<Site>* Properties dialog box. ConfigMgr uses UDP port 9 by default. To change the port, select the Wake On LAN entry in the list box and click the Properties button (the button looks like a hand pointing to a box). The Port Details dialog box launches, allowing you to change this port number. Only a single port number is supported.

Using WOL

ConfigMgr takes care of all the details for actually implementing WOL. You simply have to tell the system when to use it. ConfigMgr 2007 supports WOL for the following three activities:

▶ Software distribution mandatory advertisements

▶ Task sequence mandatory advertisements

▶ Software update mandatory deployments

A check box is present on the Schedule tab of the Properties dialog box for each of these activities. Once one is selected, ConfigMgr sends the WOL request to each applicable destination system at the scheduled mandatory time. When the destination system wakes up, it initiates the mandatory advertisement or deployment.

WOL is a great addition to the ConfigMgr toolset. Although third-party tools were previously available to fill this gap, having the capability built in is always better—and cheaper. WOL is not complicated, and Microsoft maintains this simplicity by seamlessly integrating WOL into the console and functionality of ConfigMgr.

Using NAP to Protect Your Network

A Windows 2008 server installed with the NPS role implements system health checks against Windows systems on the network. Those systems failing these health checks are subject to various actions, including the following:

▶ Reported on

▶ Denied access to the network

▶ Placed into a quarantine status with limited network access

The Network Access Protection (NAP) functionality included in ConfigMgr 2007 extends the NAP functionality built in to Windows Server 2008, implementing a system health check based on the mandatory software updates configured in ConfigMgr. The next sections discuss this process.

NAP Prerequisites

ConfigMgr implements NAP using a new site system role—the System Health Validator (SHV) point. Install this new role on a Windows Server 2008 system that has the NPS role already installed. (Installing and configuring the NPS role is beyond the scope of this book; for detailed information see http://technet.microsoft.com/en-us/network/bb545879.aspx.) Perform the following steps on this system to install the SHV:

1. In the ConfigMgr console, navigate to Site Database -> Site Management -> *<Site Code>* *<Site Name>* -> Site Settings -> Site Systems.

    ▶ If the system running NAP is not currently a site system, right-click Site Systems and then choose New -> Server to launch the New Site System Server Wizard. Enter the name of the site system and the intranet-accessible FQDN of the NAP server.

    ▶ If the NAP server already is a ConfigMgr site system, right-click the server and choose New Roles from the context menu. This launches the New Site Role Wizard, which looks and acts exactly like the New Site System Server Wizard, except the wizard has already filled in the site system name and intranet FQDN for you.

2. For either wizard, choose Next and then choose System Health Validator Point from the list of available site roles.

3. Click Next on each subsequent wizard page. There are no configuration options inside ConfigMgr itself.

Additionally, you must extend Active Directory for ConfigMgr (see Chapter 3, "Looking Inside Configuration Manager," for details). Extending AD is required because NAP uses the System container to store Health State References. The site server publishes Health State References used during client evaluation to ensure the most current policies are used. If you plan to use NAP in a multiforest environment, you must prepare each forest and the NAP site server role according to the instructions at http://technet.microsoft.com/en-us/library/bb694120.aspx.

On the client side, NAP only works with Windows Vista, Windows Server 2008, and Windows XP SP 3 (and above) clients. This is because only these operating systems include the NPS agent. Unfortunately, no download is available to make any other version of Windows work with NPS or NAP.

Agent Settings

By default, the NPS Client agent is disabled in a ConfigMgr site and must be enabled. Perform the following steps:

1. In the ConfigMgr console, navigate to Site Database -> Site Management -> *<Site Code>* *<Site Name>* -> Site Settings -> Client Agents.

2. Right-click Network Access Protection Client Agent and then select Properties.

    The first page of the Network Access Protection Client Agent Properties dialog box has a single check box allowing you to enable (or disable) the agent.

15

On the Evaluation tab, displayed in Figure 15.22, you can configure three settings:

▶ **UTC (Coordinated Universal Time)**—This configures the client agent to assess computer system health according to UTC time rather than client local time. This setting is beneficial for those clients that roam between time zones, and ensures reevaluations are performed on a fixed time scale rather than a variable one caused by the client moving between the time zones.

▶ **Force a fresh scan for each evaluation**—This option ensures cached evaluation results are not used when a client reconnects to a network in between configured evaluation times. Forcing an additional scan can cause delays in connecting to the network, which can adversely affect mobile systems.

▶ **Schedule**—This section of the page lets you set either a simple or a detailed schedule of when you want to perform a system health check.

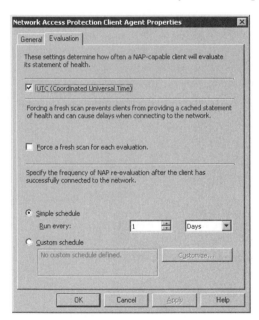

FIGURE 15.22   Configuring NAP Client agent properties

Similar to other ConfigMgr Client agents, the NPS Client agent settings are sitewide without a direct way to override them for individual systems.

System Health

Those clients subject to the policies of the NPS will report to the NPS using their built-in NPS client. The NPS Client agent retrieves policies from the NPS and evaluates the health of a system against the checks defined in the policy encapsulating the results, known as a Statement of Health (SoH). The SoH contains results from all the checks performed on the system, and the NPS Client agent submits the SoH to the NPS. The NPS receives the SoH and compares it against the NPS policies:

▶ If the system appears compliant with the policies, it is allowed on the network.

▶ If deemed noncompliant, the system can be granted limited access to the network, allowing for correction of any issues that caused it to be considered noncompliant.

NPS policies, known as *health policies*, are based on server-side components called System Health Validators. These SHVs plug in to the NPS server and enable performing specific checks on a client to validate its health. As an example, the built-in Windows Security SHV defines checks for the status of the Windows Firewall, existence of antivirus software, and other settings typically associated with the Windows Security Center. Each check results in one of two states: Pass or Fail. The status of a client as a whole may also be reported in one of three different states:

▶ **Transitional**—This state indicates that the client is not ready to report its status. In the ConfigMgr context, this could mean the client agent is not yet enabled on the system.

▶ **Infected**—This state is primarily used by antivirus SHVs and is not used by the ConfigMgr client.

▶ **Unknown**—This is a catchall state often used to indicate client credential issues.

The health policies define which SHVs to use and what conditions must be met for a system to match a health policy. The following conditions are possible in a health policy:

▶ Client passes all SHV checks

▶ Client fails all SHV checks

▶ Client passes one or more SHV checks

▶ Client fails one or more SHV checks

▶ Client reported as transitional by one or more SHVs

▶ Client reported as infected by one or more SHVs

▶ Client reported as unknown by one or more SHVs

The ConfigMgr SHV point implements the SHV that plugs in to an NPS. The policies produced by this SHV instruct the NPS Client agent to compare the exact patch status of a system against the applicable mandatory updates configured in the NAP policies in the ConfigMgr console (Site Database -> Computer Management -> Network Access Protection -> Policies). See the "Compliance" section of this chapter for a description of these policies.

A System Health Agent (SHA) is a component that plugs in to the NPS agent on the client; each server-side SHV has a corresponding client-side SHA. SHAs perform the actual checks on a system and produce the Pass/Fail results that go into the client's SoH.

The ConfigMgr client implements the ConfigMgr SHA. This SHA performs the actual comparison of the current update status on the client with the mandatory deployments applicable to the system, adding the results to the SoH for that system.

Client Compliance

The ConfigMgr SHA first performs a series of nonconfigurable checks to determine the compliance state of the client. These checks include the following:

- **Is this a new client?** If a new client has not downloaded the policies yet, the client is marked as compliant.

- **Are the site code and site ID invalid?** If yes, the client is marked as Unknown.

- **Is the NAP Client agent disabled?** If yes, the client is marked as compliant.

- **Is the SoH older than the "Date created must be after" date?** If yes, mark the client as noncompliant.

If any of these checks succeed, the status updates in the SoH and the series of checks ceases. If the client makes it through these checks, the SHA compares the configured NAP polices against the client. Each NAP policy must define two things:

- **Updates**—This is the set of updates that, if applicable to a client system, must be installed on that system for it to be marked as compliant. As an example, if an update is not applicable to a client system because it is for a different version of Windows, it is not considered. Update status is based on the last successful software updates scan of the system.

- **Effective Date**—This is the date when the updates defined in an NAP policy are considered mandatory. If the updates in the policy are not installed on a client system after this date, the system is considered noncompliant.

See http://technet.microsoft.com/en-us/library/bb680968.aspx for a detailed flowchart of the checks performed by the SHA.

You can configure multiple NAP policies, allowing for multiple sets of updates and effective dates. These policies are not targeted in any way and are applied to all systems equally. You can create an NAP policy in one of two ways:

- Right-click the Policies node (Site Database -> Computer Management -> Network Access Protection -> Policies) in the ConfigMgr console and select New. This action opens the New Policies Wizard displayed in Figure 15.23, with two primary pages— one to choose updates, and one to set the effective date for the policy. You can only choose updates from Deployment Packages.

- Right-click any single update or multiselected updates in the Update Repository, an Update List, Deployment, or Deployment Package and then select Properties from the context menu. This launches a Properties dialog box with an NAP Evaluation tab, displayed in Figure 15.24. Here, you can enable NAP evaluation and configure an effective date by the selected updates. This creates a new NAP policy under the Policies node, which you can later modify or delete.

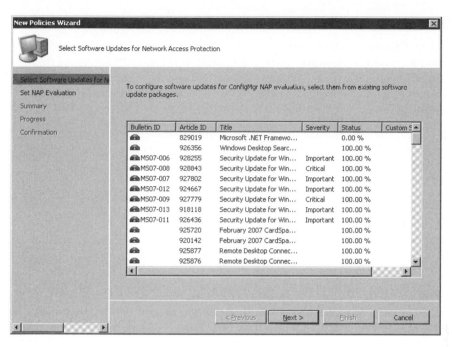

FIGURE 15.23   Selecting software updates for NAP in the New Policies Wizard

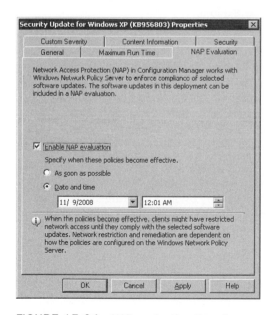

FIGURE 15.24   NAP evaluation time for an update

Remediation

If the ConfigMgr SHV deems a client system noncompliant, the system may be placed in a quarantine status based on the Network Policy configuration on the NPS server. In this quarantine status, the client system has limited access to network resources. This limited network connectivity, known as *remediation*, allows the client to correct conditions that caused it to be noncompliant.

With ConfigMgr 2007, the remediation process is automatic—the client automatically requests updates from ConfigMgr and installs them based on the NAP policies. The only required configuration is to add specific infrastructure servers to a remediation server group in the NPS. This group identifies which servers are accessible by systems placed into the quarantine status. You should add the following types of servers that host critical network services into this group:

▶ DNS servers for name resolution

▶ Domain controllers for authentication and group policy

▶ A global catalog server for locating Configuration Manager 2007 services

Do not place Configuration Manager servers in the remediation server group, because access to these systems is dynamically granted.

TIP

Utilizing Remediation to Protect Against Zero-Day Exploits

Although the obvious purpose for remediation is to prevent systems from accessing the network that are not patched up to a defined level, a not-so-obvious purpose is to deploy updates for zero-day exploits. In this case, you can use NAP to deploy updates by configuring a specific NAP policy for the update and making it effective immediately. As clients check in with your NPS infrastructure, they will immediately be out of compliance and fall into remediation, and automatically install the update. You must also ensure that the patch is available in a deployment package in this scenario.

Although it comes with some overhead in the form of the Windows Server 2008 NPS role, NAP increases the security posture of your network greatly by interrogating systems as they try to connect to the network and enforcing a minimum patch level. It can also help you deploy updates for those annoying (and upper-management attention-getting) zero-day exploits.

Troubleshooting Software Updates

The entire software update process can break at many different points. Multiple components coordinate their efforts to make the process hum along normally; however, when something goes wrong, the first step is identifying which component is having issues. Depending on the exact failure point, you can review a variety of log files for error messages. It is also important to track and report on the status of software updates to "the powers that be" or the "senior partners," whichever you are subject to. The next sections discuss how to monitor software updates as well as those areas that typically have issues and how to diagnose and (hopefully) fix them.

Monitoring Software Updates

There are two primary ways to monitor your software update status in ConfigMgr. The first and traditional way is to use reporting. As of ConfigMgr 2007 R2, there are 34 reports out of the box specific to tracking various aspects of Software Updates, including client scan states, update applicability, deployment progress, and compliance. Like all ConfigMgr reports, you can copy and customize these to fit your exact needs.

The second way to monitor Software Updates is using the Software Updates home page, accessible by directly selecting the Software Updates node in the ConfigMgr admin console tree (Site Database -> Computer Management -> Software Updates). This page provides a dashboard for finding summary information concerning your Software Updates stance. Figure 15.25 displays an example of this home page.

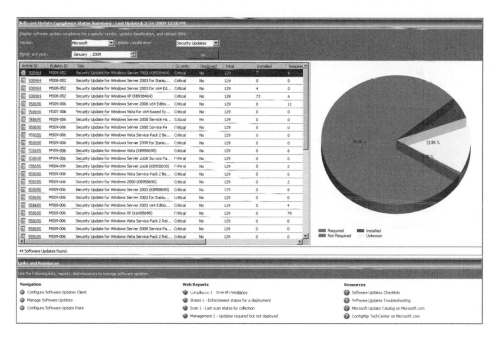

FIGURE 15.25   Software updates home page

You can select a subset of updates from the update repository by defining filter criteria for the Vendor, Month and Year, and Classification. This populates the list box on the left with updates matching the specified filter criteria. For Microsoft Updates, the listed Article IDs are actually hyperlinks that take you directly to the TechNet knowledge base article describing the update. The % Compliant column also contains hyperlinks that launch the specific software update states report, which details the count and percentage of computers in each compliance state for the specified software update. In addition to the list of updates on the left, a pie chart summarizing the compliance state of updates selected in the list is displayed on the right. You can select multiple updates in the usual way to update the pie chart with aggregate data from all the updates selected.

Links at the bottom of the page take you to other nodes in the admin console, significant reports, and applicable help documentation.

WSUS and SUP

The first component in Software Updates is WSUS. WSUS is significant because it acquires all information about available updates and distributes that catalog of updates to clients. Luckily, ConfigMgr takes over control of WSUS using an SUP and creates detailed log files of the WSUS operation. Here are the three main log files for WSUS and an SUP, located in *<ConfigMgrInstallPath>*\Logs:

- ▶ **WCM.log**—Provides information about the software update point configuration and connecting to the WSUS server for subscribed update categories, classifications, and languages.

- ▶ **WSUSCtrl.log**—This log file provides information about the configuration, database connectivity, and health of the WSUS server for the site.

- ▶ **wsyncmgr.log**—Provides information about the software updates synchronization process.

Most errors experienced with WSUS are configuration errors, including not matching the ports configured during installation of WSUS and then configured in the SUP (Site Database -> Site Management -> *<Site Code> <Site Name>* -> Site Settings -> Site Systems -> ConfigMgr software update point).

Also common are Internet connectivity issues due to firewalls, proxy servers, or other mitigating factors. Always confirm that the system running WSUS has Internet connectivity if you are downloading the update catalog directly from Microsoft, and ensure that you have properly configured the proxy account if one is required (Site Management -> *<Site Code> <Site Name>* -> Site Settings -> Component Configuration -> Software Update Point Component).

Downloading Updates

It is possible for the update downloads from Microsoft to fail. Recall that WSUS does not download the updates in ConfigMgr; you must manually initiate download of all updates. This is an interactive process; the ConfigMgr console connects to the Microsoft download servers using the credentials of the user currently logged in to the console. You can easily test connectivity for the current user by opening Internet Explorer and navigating to http://www.microsoft.com/downloads. (If a proxy server is required to connect to the Internet, configure the settings in Internet Explorer.) If the logged-in user does not have permission to perform the action, the download will not take place.

The PatchDownloader.log file logs download activity for updates. This log contains information about every patch the console attempts to download. The file is located in one of two places:

- ▶ **%*ProgramFiles*%\Microsoft Configuration Manager\Logs**—If you are running the console on the site server

- ▶ **%*ProgramFiles*%\Microsoft Configuration Manager Console\AdminUI\AdminUILog**—If you are running the console remotely

Client Update Scanning and Deployment

WUA on the local system handles the process of scanning a client for applicable updates. The ConfigMgr agent initiates the scanning according to the defined schedules or any on-demand requests; the WUA will in turn report back to the ConfigMgr agent. The following client-side log files, located in the %*SystemRoot*%\System32\CCM\logs folder on 32-bit clients and %*SystemRoot*%\SysWOW64\CCM\logs on 64-bit clients, can help when investigating failures:

- ▶ **ScanAgent.log**—Provides information about the scan requests for software updates, the tool requested for the scan, the WSUS location, and so on

- ▶ **UpdatesDeployment.log**—Provides information about the deployment on the client. This includes software update activation, evaluation, and enforcement

- ▶ **UpdatesHandler.log**—Provides information about software update compliance scanning as well as download and installation of software updates on the client

- ▶ **UpdatesStore.log**—Provides information about the compliance status for software updates assessed during the compliance scan cycle

- ▶ **WUAHandler.log**—Provides information regarding when the Windows Update Agent on the client searches for software updates

---

TIP

ConfigMgr Log Files

An excellent utility is included with the ConfigMgr 2007 Toolkit (available through Microsoft's download site at http://www.microsoft.com/downloads/details.aspx?FamilyID=948e477e-fd3b-4a09-9015-141683c7ad5f&DisplayLang=en or go to www.microsoft.com/downloads and search for **System Center Configuration Manager 2007 Toolkit**) to view log files—Trace32, also called the SMS log viewer. This utility, introduced in Chapter 3, provides a real-time view of a selected log file.

One of the main issues that can affect the scanning process is having a domain-based GPO override the Windows Updates settings. The WUAHandler.log file will clearly indicate if this issue exists in your environment.

Summary

Although many tools exist for maintaining and deploying updates to Windows systems, Configuration Manager Software Updates takes this process to a new level by integrating the process into a robust, cradle-to-grave, systems management tool. By using existing software tools such as WSUS and the WUA, ConfigMgr 2007 is able to leverage existing, known-good processes and code while extending them to new levels. This chapter discussed the new ConfigMgr Software Update functionality, implementing it successfully within your organization, and taking advantage of supplementary tools such as WOL and NAP. The combination of these tools gives you the flexibility to deploy updates in a manner that is user friendly and meets the needs of your organization, big or small.

The next chapter discusses using Desired Configuration Management, which enables you to assess compliance of computers in regard to specified configurations.

CHAPTER 16

Desired Configuration Management

Desired Configuration Management (DCM) is another exciting new feature of Configuration Manager (ConfigMgr) 2007. Using DCM enables you to monitor, report on, and take action regarding configuration of your managed systems. Unlike the Desired Configuration Monitoring feature pack for Systems Management Server (SMS) 2003, Microsoft has completely integrated DCM into ConfigMgr.

> **NOTE**
>
> **Desired Configuration Management Is Not Desired Configuration Monitoring 2.0**
>
> Although the names and functionality are similar, DCM is a completely new component in Configuration Manager 2007. The SMS 2003 Desired Configuration Monitoring feature pack, authored outside Microsoft's ConfigMgr team, uses the same engine as the popular and useful best-practices analyzers. Conversely, the ConfigMgr development team wrote DCM in its entirety, and it uses its own engine. Thus, the two components are not compatible.
>
> Microsoft provides a conversion tool, converting from the older SMS feature pack to DCM in the ConfigMgr 2007 Toolkit, available at http://www.microsoft.com. downloads. Search for **System Center Configuration Manager 2007 Toolkit**.

DCM is written to handle four general scenarios that all Information Technology (IT) organizations deal with in one form or another:

▶ **Regulatory compliance**—Given the impact of new regulatory laws in the United States covering privacy and corporate responsibility, regulatory compliance is a key scenario for many IT organizations. Examples of these laws include the Sarbanes-Oxley (SOX) Act of 2002, the Gramm-Leach-Bliley Act (GLBA), and the Health Insurance Portability and Accountability Act (HIPAA).

Each of these regulations requires IT organizations to set specific security and privacy standards for corporate and user data, as well as for IT systems. The difficult part for IT occurs when trying to enforce and report on the enforcement of the standards set. Most IT organizations simply have no way to do so, and rely on ad-hoc custom scripts or tools that provide on-demand results. In addition, these laws are not technical in nature. This leads to the actual technical requirements to fulfill the standards being subject to interpretation and varying between organizations—SOX for you is not necessarily SOX for someone else.

Even if your organization is not subject to specific regulatory compliance laws, it should still be subject to internal policies and standards. Validating your infrastructure's compliance against this internal governance is the same as validating it against governmental standards.

▶ **Pre- and post-change verification**—This scenario involves verifying the configuration of a system before and after planned changes. It is typically a good idea to verify you are only applying changes to systems in a specific state, that the planned changes occurred, and unintended changes did not take place.

▶ **Configuration drift**—Although obvious when pointed out to most IT administrators, typical IT organizations do not account for configuration drift or its implications on the state of the network.

Configuration drift starts the moment a system goes into production and is difficult to control. No matter how rigorously standard your build process is, as soon as multiple administrators begin logging in to a system to install applications, troubleshoot issues, "tweak" performance, or just make it look like they want it to, the system begins its drift from the standard. Over time, the drift for a particular system is unpredictable and has the potential to cause technical issues.

▶ **Time to resolution**—An overwhelming number of problems in the IT world are due to human error. These problems ultimately become the dreaded problem ticket that every on-call administrator loathes, particularly the one in the middle of the night or the one halfway through the fourth quarter of the Super Bowl, the American championship game in professional football. Stopping human error is all but impossible; however, identifying that human error quickly so that it can be resolved is the key to reducing the impact of such errors.

Individually or in combination, each of these scenarios places a burden on IT. There is little reward in successfully handling these scenarios, because they do not directly address or contribute to business objectives. These are typically considered the "un-fun" things in IT, and administrators do not look forward to addressing them.

Although DCM does not necessarily change the nature of these four scenarios, it goes a long way in making the scenarios more manageable and less time consuming, and integrating them into the existing process. This chapter explores the great potential of DCM, how to set it up, configure it, and use it to address these scenarios.

Configuring Desired Configuration Management

Desired Configuration Management setup is considerably simpler than other features of ConfigMgr because there is no formal site role. The client performs all processing and returns the results to the site server. This section discusses the quick setup of DCM and the rather straightforward configuration options available.

Prerequisites for DCM are client-side only:

▶ Clients must have the ConfigMgr 2007 Client agent installed

▶ Clients must have the .NET Framework 2.0 installed

To enable DCM, perform the following steps on the site server:

1. Navigate to Site Database -> Site Management -> *<Site Code> <Site Name>* -> Site Settings -> Client Agents in the ConfigMgr console tree. The middle pane displays all the available client agents, including the Desired Configuration Management Client agent, as shown in Figure 16.1.

FIGURE 16.1   Client agents in the ConfigMgr console

2. Right-click the Desired Configuration Management Client agent and choose Properties from the context menu, or simply double-click it to reveal the single-page Properties dialog box for this agent, displayed in Figure 16.2. This page has two options:

   ▶ The first option on this page is to enable DCM; it may already be checked depending on the option chosen during initial site installation. That's all there is to actually enabling DCM—it is either on or off, based on this one little check box.

   ▶ The second option is to set the default evaluation schedule for assigned baselines (the "Configuration Baselines" section covers baselines in detail).

   As with many other configurable schedules in ConfigMgr, you can choose to use a "simple" schedule that allows the client to determine exactly when the action occurs using a minimum interval. Alternately, you can set a "custom" schedule that defines exactly when to perform the action.

   The schedule set here is only the default schedule for newly assigned baselines; you can set a separate schedule for each baseline after you create it.

3. Once enabled on the server, the client DCM component will also be enabled on clients after the next policy refresh.

Amazingly, that is it as far as actually configuring the ConfigMgr site and server to use DCM. By itself, DCM will work properly, although it does not include a method to monitor the results. Consequently, you should also set up reporting as described in Chapter 18, "Reporting." Of course, just turning DCM on and enabling reporting doesn't tell DCM what to monitor or report on, so you will need to configure the settings and

FIGURE 16.2   DCM Client agent properties

other discrete units of configuration you would like DCM to monitor and report on using configuration baselines and configuration items, as introduced in the next section. You will also want to refer to both Chapter 18 and the "Reporting" section of this chapter for information regarding DCM reports.

Configurations

DCM operations in ConfigMgr are defined by two object types:

- ▶ **Configuration items**—Those constructs grouping the rules instructing DCM what to monitor and look for on systems

- ▶ **Configuration baselines**—Groupings of multiple configuration items

Instances of these two object types are often called *configurations* collectively because they define a specific system configuration.

Microsoft built DCM knowing that every IT environment is unique and that configuration standards and requirements in each IT environment are different. Thus, DCM gives you the tools to create configuration items and baselines from scratch according to your individual needs and wants. The built-in editor is straightforward and easy to use, allowing you to create simple to complex configuration items and anything in-between. The following two sections define the details of baselines and configuration items, and the "Console Authoring" section of this chapter discusses using the built-in editor to create and modify them.

Configuration Items

Configuration items encapsulate the checks that DCM makes against a system to determine its compliance. Collectively, these checks are called *evaluation criteria*. To view or edit the configuration items present in a site, navigate to Site Database -> Computer Management -> Desired Configuration Management -> Configuration Items in the ConfigMgr navigation tree. There are four types of configuration items:

- ▶ **Application**—A configuration item of this type checks for the existence of an application and its associated settings. The application's existence can be assumed, checked by Windows Installer detection, or determined by a custom script.

- ▶ **Operating Systems**—This type of configuration item checks for a specific operating system version and settings relevant to that version. The operating system version can be set by choosing from a drop down list of pre-configured operating systems or by directly setting the version values.

- ▶ **Software Updates**—These configuration items check the patch or update level of a system.

- ▶ **General**—You can use this open-ended configuration item type for any purpose.

Software update configuration items are a special type of configuration item, as they are not listed with the rest of the configuration items in the console and you cannot directly create them like the three other types. These are created when defining a baseline, with their only evaluation criteria the installation status of a specific software update chosen from the update repository. To use software update configuration items, the ConfigMgr Software Update feature, discussed in Chapter 15, "Patch Management," must be properly configured and working not only to define the software update configuration item, but also to detect its installation status.

There are two property types used to represent the evaluation criteria implemented by a configuration item:

▶ **Objects**—Objects check for the existence of discrete entities including files, registry keys, and assemblies in the Global Assembly Cache (GAC), which is the machine-wide cache used to store assemblies designed for sharing by multiple applications on a system. Additionally, objects can also check for the existence of specific permissions on registry keys, files, and attributes on files.

▶ **Settings**—These evaluate the return value of queries made against Active Directory, the Internet Information Services (IIS) metabase, the Windows Registry, SQL Server databases, the Windows Management Instrumentation (WMI) repository using WMI Query Language (WQL), or an eXtensible Markup Language (XML) file.

Settings can also use custom VBScript, JScript, or PowerShell scripts to determine compliance. In addition to validating specific values, settings can check the number of values returned from the query or script; referred to as the *instance count* of criteria validation.

Although not a perfect analogy, you can think of objects as "physical" or tangible items that the operating system uses and manipulates. Settings on the other hand describe how or with what parameters the operating system or an application goes about its many tasks.

NOTE

Using PowerShell Scripts

Unlike VBScript and JScript, PowerShell is not a core component on all versions of Windows. Thus if you use a PowerShell script, be sure that it is in fact installed on all of the systems where the configuration item will be applicable.

The validation of each criterion and instance count is configured individually to contribute to the compliance status of the configuration item as a whole. Each configuration item has four potential severity levels of non-compliance:

▶ Information—no Windows event message

▶ Information

▶ Warning

▶ Error

If any criterion fails, the configuration item as a whole is marked as non-compliant for that system. The highest severity level for any failed check, including instance count checks, is used as the severity level for the configuration item. Results of these checks are sent back to ConfigMgr for reporting. Each failed check also produces an event message in the Windows Application Event Log, except for the Information—no Windows event message level.

The combination of the Objects and Settings property types provide a wide range of criteria that DCM can check to determine compliance. The addition of custom scripts, often used with Microsoft sample baselines, gives DCM unlimited customizability and flexibility. The "Console Authoring" section includes a detailed discussion on creating and editing configuration items using the ConfigMgr console.

DCM can restrict the evaluation of application and general configuration items based on Windows platform applicability. This configuration checks for specific Windows platforms and prevents evaluating the configuration item on platforms not specified.

You can organize configuration items in several ways. This includes categories and hierarchies and combining them into baselines:

▶ **Assigning categories**—You can assign categories to configuration items (and baselines) to improve filtering and searching in the console and reports, but they ultimately serve no functional purpose. These categories cannot be exported or imported and only exist on the server. Four default categories are created at installation time:

  ▶ Client

  ▶ IT Infrastructure

  ▶ Line of Business

  ▶ Server

  You can use these categories, delete them, or add new ones; no special functionality is associated with these categories.

▶ **Creating hierarchies**—You can organize configuration items into hierarchies by creating child configuration items. Child configuration items inherit all the evaluation criteria of their designated parent; these inherited criteria cannot be changed or removed in the child. You can add additional criterion, differentiating the child item from its parent.

  One common use of child configuration items includes specialization of a more general configuration item. As an example, you may create a generic configuration item that checks for organizationwide security standards. You could then create child configuration items to check for the more rigorous security standards of the Accounting and Human Resource departments. This scenario prevents duplication and reduces effort when an organizationwide setting requires changing, because you only need to update the parent to update all the child configuration items. If you are familiar with object-oriented programming, then this concept is very similar to class specialization through inheritance.

▶ **Combining CIs**—You can combine configuration items into configuration baselines and then assign the configuration baselines to collections for evaluation. Configuration items can be part of multiple baselines, and multiple configuration items typically combine to create a baseline. The next section discusses baselines.

Configuration Items Are Not Just for DCM

DCM and configuration items are foundational for software updates management and the drivers catalog in operating system deployment; software updates and drivers are actually stored as configuration items in the database. This is most evident when setting granular permissions on classes and instances in the console—there are no entries for software updates, because these are all encapsulated by the generic configuration item type.

Configuration Baselines

As stated earlier in the "Configurations" section, configuration baselines group configuration items together; the baselines are then assigned to collections for evaluation. Configuration items are assigned to baselines using rules. Each rule is a list of a specific type of configuration item. Rules available include the following:

▶ Operating system configuration items present and properly configured

▶ Application and general configuration items required and properly configured

▶ Optional application items that are properly configured

▶ Software updates present

▶ Application configuration items not present

In addition to the configuration item rules, an additional rule exists to include other baselines. This essentially groups the baselines together and combines their evaluation.

To create a new baseline, perform the following steps:

1. Right-click Site Database -> Computer Management -> Desired Configuration Management -> Configuration Baselines in the ConfigMgr console navigation tree and select New Configuration Baseline. This launches the Create Configuration Baseline Wizard.

2. The first page, the Identification page, allows you to specify a name for the baseline and choose a category.

3. The second page of the wizard, titled "Set Configuration Baseline Rules" (shown in Figure 16.3), allows you to define the rules previously introduced in this section. You set them by clicking the blue underlined hyperlinks. These launch one of three dialog boxes, depending on the rule you clicked:

   ▶ Choose Configuration Items

   ▶ Choose Configuration Baselines

   ▶ Add Software Updates

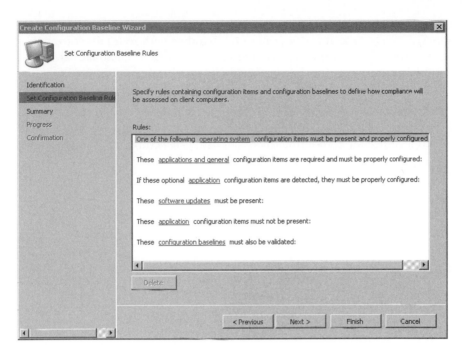

FIGURE 16.3   The Set Configuration Baseline Rules page

Each of these dialog boxes allows you to specify the object indicated by its name using sorting and filtering.

To modify an existing baseline, navigate to Site Database -> Computer Management -> Desired Configuration Management -> Configuration Baselines. Right-click the desired baseline in the Details pane and then choose Properties from the context menu. The baseline properties dialog box contains the following pages:

▶ **General**—Displays general metadata about the baseline, including creation and modification times. This page also allows you to set or remove categories from the baseline.

▶ **Rules**—Similar to the Set Configuration Baseline Rules page used during the creation of the baseline, this page displays the configuration items and baselines included and allows you to add more by clicking hyperlinks.

▶ **Relationships**—This page displays the names of other baselines that include the currently viewed baseline.

▶ **Assignments**—This page displays all collections to which the baseline is assigned. You also use the Assignments tab to modify and delete previously created assignments for the baseline.

▶ **Security**—This page displays the class and instance security rights for the baseline and is identical to every other security page in ConfigMgr.

You can also view information from all these tabs by selecting any baseline in the Details pane. This displays a Details pane at the bottom of the window with four tabs corresponding to those listed previously (with the exception of the Security tab). These tabs are view-only and offer a quick way to view the details of a baseline without opening the Properties dialog box.

In addition to using the Rules tab of a baseline's Properties dialog box to add rules, you can select Add from the context menu of a baseline. This gives you a flyout menu (shown in Figure 16.4) with a choice for each of the rule types listed. Selecting one of these works the same as selecting a hyperlink under the Rules tab.

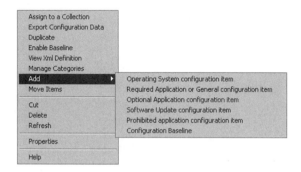

FIGURE 16.4   Baseline context menu

Assigning a baseline is what triggers its evaluation against a set of systems. Collections, being the standard targeting mechanism for ConfigMgr, are what baselines are assigned to. To assign a baseline to a collection, right-click it and then choose Assign to a Collection. This launches the Assign Configuration Baseline Wizard, as displayed in Figure 16.5. This wizard contains the following pages:

- ▶ **Choose Baselines**—Although you launch this wizard by clicking a single baseline, you can select additional baselines for assignment on this first page of the wizard.

- ▶ **Choose Collection**—Using this typical ConfigMgr page, you select which collection to assign the baselines to and whether or not to include subcollections.

- ▶ **Set Schedule**—This last page of the wizard includes two choices:

  - ▶ Simple schedule

  - ▶ Custom schedule

  By default, the value is set according to the schedule chosen on the Desired Configuration Management Client agent, as described in the "Configuring Desired Configuration Management" section.

Using DCM, configuration baselines are assigned to ConfigMgr collections. The settings and values defined in each configuration item in a baseline are compared against the current configuration of the systems in the collection, according to the evaluation

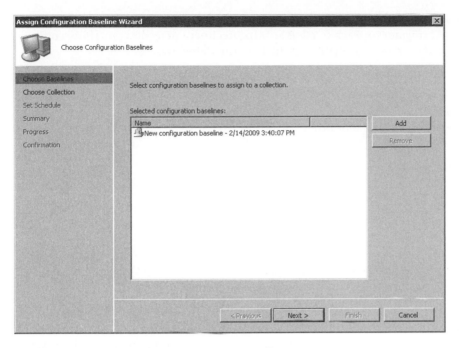

FIGURE 16.5   Assign Configuration Baseline Wizard

schedule for that baseline. The results of this comparison are returned to ConfigMgr, where you can run a variety of reports to determine how the systems fared on these comparison tests; this is also known as the *compliance status* of the system.

In addition to simply reporting on the compliance status of systems and collections, you can build collections using this same data to create remediation mechanisms. Because automatic remediation of discrepancies is not a function of DCM, you must implement some other mechanism to correct the configuration of systems. The synergistic functions of ConfigMgr 2007 allow you to create software distribution packages and programs to make these corrections.

As an example, if you create and assign a baseline that checks for the existence of an antivirus product on every workstation in a collection, any systems that fail this check are deemed noncompliant. Typically, an organization reporting the noncompliant status of systems will want to correct those as soon as possible. The approach then is to create a new collection that queries the compliance status of systems against this baseline, and use a software distribution package to install the preferred antivirus product and assign the package to the collection. The "Remediation" section later in this chapter presents an example of this. For complete details of software distribution, see Chapter 14, "Distributing Packages."

Microsoft understands there are many similarities and common requirements between IT organizations, and has released a large number of configuration baselines to use as a starting point, as a reference, or as complete solutions. These baselines are encapsulated in configuration packs (CPs). Analogous to management packs (MPs) in Operations Manager

(OpsMgr), CPs are freely downloadable from Microsoft's System Center Configuration Manager 2007 Configuration Pack Catalog at http://technet.microsoft.com/en-us/config-mgr/cc462788.aspx. Types of available CPs include the following:

▶ **Regulatory compliance**—Configuration packs intended for regulatory compliance, such as SOX, HIPAA, and the European Union Data Protection Directive (EUDPD).

▶ **Best practice**—CPs based on best-practice configurations used by Microsoft's internal IT department for major products such as Exchange, SQL Server, and Windows Server.

▶ **Third-party software and hardware**—As with the development of OpsMgr management packs, many third parties are starting to create and release CPs to help with your configuration enforcement efforts while using their products.

To import a baseline downloaded from the catalog, you must first extract it from the downloaded Microsoft Installer package. These installer packages do not actually install the configuration pack; they merely extract the necessary cabinet (.CAB) compressed file (similar to a self-extracting executable) to a folder of your choosing. Once this is extracted, perform the following steps to import the CP into ConfigMgr:

1. Navigate to and expand Site Database -> Computer Management -> Desired Configuration Management in the ConfigMgr navigation tree.

2. Right-click either Configuration Baselines or Configuration Items and choose Import Configuration Data. This launches the Import Configuration Data Wizard displayed in Figure 16.6.

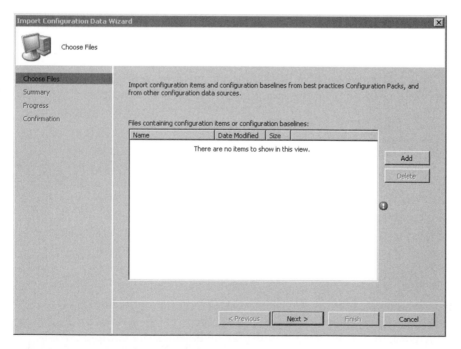

FIGURE 16.6   Import Configuration Data Wizard

3. Click Add to launch an Open dialog box. Find and select the CAB file for the CP you previously extracted and click Open.

   You can add CABs from additional configuration packs by clicking Add again.

   To remove a previously chosen CP, select it in the list box and choose Delete.

4. Clicking Next takes you to a summary page listing the configuration items and base-lines that will be imported.

5. Finally, click Finish to import the chosen CPs.

Configuration items in imported CPs are locked, preventing you from modifying them in any way. Locked configuration items are displayed with a lock icon. To use one of these configuration items as a starting point, duplicate it by right-clicking it and choosing Duplicate from the resulting context menu. The duplicated configuration item will be fully editable. It is also recommended to duplicate an existing, known-good configuration item or baseline before editing it. (*Known-good* refers to an item that has already success-fully worked in an environment.) Using this approach provides a solid rollback and baselining mechanism.

Although the CPs available from Microsoft's Configuration Pack Catalog are quite useful, they do not cover every possibility and are somewhat generic at times. Eventually, you will want to create your own criteria by modifying the CPs provided by Microsoft, or creating your own to evaluate your systems. The next sections discuss this activity, known as *authoring*.

Creating and Modifying Configurations

Customizing configuration baselines and items may be a full-time task, depending on the role set for DCM in an organization. The toolset included with ConfigMgr 2007 provides a rich environment for authoring these objects, although it is not the only way to author them. The following sections discuss how to go about authoring baselines and configura-tion items using the console as well as a few alternative methods.

Console Authoring

The main purpose of the ConfigMgr console in DCM is to organize, assign, create, and edit configuration baselines and configuration items. The built-in toolset for these last two activities—creating and editing—is fairly complete; it allows you to define a wide range of evaluation criteria covering most of the scenarios needed.

To create a new configuration item, navigate to Site Database -> Computer Management -> Desired Configuration Management -> Configuration Baselines in the ConfigMgr console navigation tree and then select New. This results in a flyout menu where you can select to create one of the three creatable types of configuration items. The resulting Configuration Item Creation Wizards for all these types are similar to each other; each has the pages listed in Table 16.1.

16

TABLE 16.1   Configuration Item Configurable Properties

Configuration Item Type	Configurable Property Types
Application	Identification
	Detection Method
	Objects
	Settings
	Applicability
General	Identification
	Objects
	Settings
	Applicability
Operating System	Identification
	Objects
	Settings
	Microsoft Windows Version

Here are descriptions of the wizards:

▶ **Identification**—On this page, you set the name of the configuration item and assign any desired categories.

▶ **Detection Method**—This page, specific to only application configuration items and shown in Figure 16.7, allows you to configure how the installation of an application is detected. There are three methods:

   ▶ **Assumption**—When this method is selected, DCM simply assumes that the application is installed without a check. Choosing this option is essentially the equivalent of creating a general configuration item.

   ▶ **Windows Installer (MSI) Detection**—This method uses the list of products installed by Windows Installer to determine if an application is installed. If an application was not installed using an MSI, this method is not applicable.

   Expected data for this method includes the Globally Unique Identifier (GUID) and the version number for the application. The easiest way to get this information is to click the Open button and select the MSI originally used to install the application. This automatically populates the fields. You can also instruct DCM that the installation was installed "per user" by checking the corresponding box shown in Figure 16.7. This check box is grayed out until you select Use Windows Installer (MSI) detection.

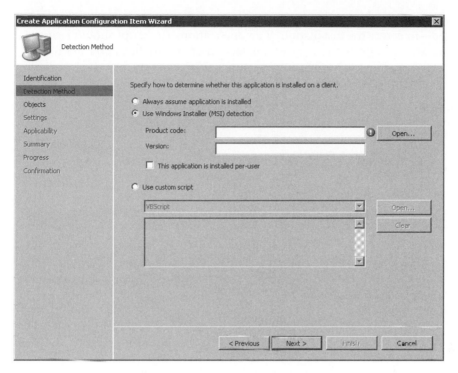

FIGURE 16.7   Configuration Item Detection Method page

NOTE

Manually Determining a Product's GUID

Although not always apparent, most software applications today are installed using an MSI. The MSIs are typically hidden inside of executables and are not directly accessible. During installation, the MSI is extracted from the executable to a temporary folder and then installed from that folder. The easiest way to determine the application's GUID and version if the MSI is hidden in this way—or not readily available for any reason—is to use WMI, and the easiest way to query WMI is the WMI console (WMIC).

WMIC is part of every Windows installation and invoked from the command line. The September 2006 issue of *TechNet* contains an excellent article on WMIC, titled "Gathering WMI Data without Writing a Single Line of Code," available at http://technet. microsoft.com/en-us/magazine/2006.09.wmidata.aspx.

Here's an example of a WMIC command to query for the GUID and version of all Microsoft Live products:

```
wmic product where "caption like '%Live%'" get name, IdentifyingNumber, version
```

This command outputs the product name, GUID, and version for every product that has Live in its name.

▶ **Script**—This method uses a custom script—VBScript, JScript, or PowerShell based—to detect the installation of an application. The script should return some text to indicate the successful detection of an installed application and no text to indicate failure. A simple example VBScript to detect the installation of the Internet Explorer Administration Kit 7 follows:

```
folderPath = "C:\Program Files\Microsoft IEAK 7"
Set fso = CreateObject("Scripting.FileSystemObject")
If fso.FolderExists(folderPath) Then
WScript.Echo "IEAK 7 Found"
End If
```

NOTE

Script Success

Scripts used in DCM are considered to be successful if they output anything to the standard output—often referred to as *StdOut*. The exact contents of the output are not evaluated; it's just that something is output. Conversely, if nothing is output, the script is considered unsuccessful.

▶ **Objects**—On this page, displayed in Figure 16.8, you choose which objects to evaluate for compliance on a system. To add a check for an object, click New at the bottom of the page (circled in the figure) and choose the type you would like to check for from the pop-up menu. Objects are discussed in the "Objects" section of this chapter.

▶ **Settings**—Shown in Figure 16.9, you choose which settings to evaluate for compliance on a system. To add a check for a setting, click New at the bottom of the page and choose which type you would like to check for from the pop-up menu. The "Settings" section discusses possible settings.

▶ **Applicability**—Only available on general and application configuration items, this page (displayed in Figure 16.10) sets the Windows platforms for which the configuration item is applicable. If the Windows version does not match, the configuration item is not evaluated. The list of Windows platforms includes all ConfigMgr-supported platforms and is broken down by version, service pack, and hardware platform. You can specify All Windows platforms, or use the list to select one or multiple platforms, making the configuration item applicable to specific Windows platforms.

▶ **Microsoft Windows Version**—Shown in Figure 16.11, this page is only available to operating system configuration items, but is very similar in function to the Applicability page described in the previous bullet. The primary difference is you can only specify a single Windows version. You can choose a Windows version from the drop-down at the top of the page or explicitly define the Windows version using the text boxes. If you chose a version from the list box at the top, the text boxes for the version are automatically populated.

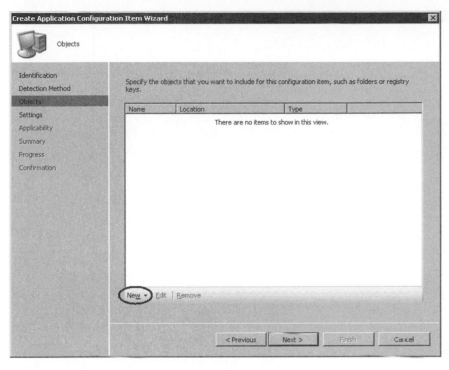

FIGURE 16.8   Configuration Item Objects page

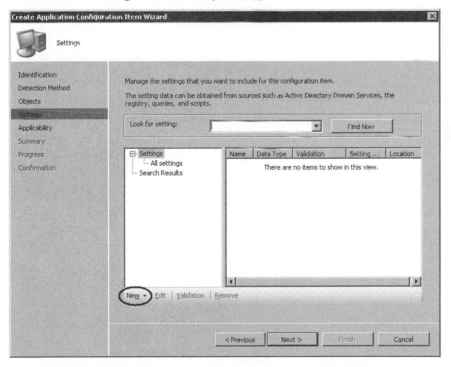

FIGURE 16.9   Configuration Item Settings page

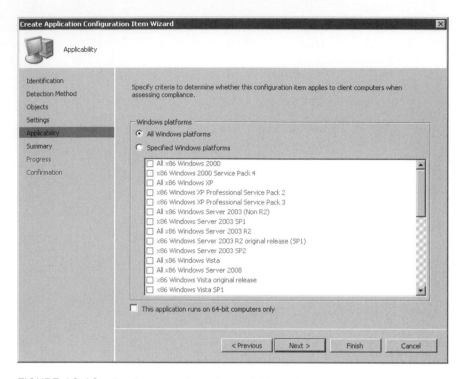

FIGURE 16.10   Configuration Item Applicability page

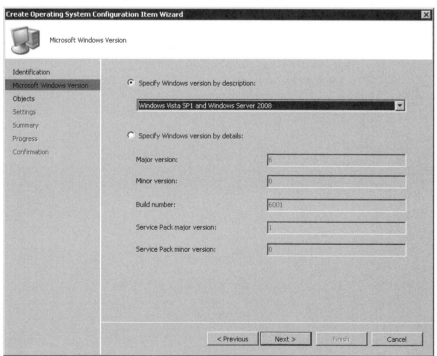

FIGURE 16.11   Configuration Item Windows Version page

The primary evaluation criteria used in configuration items is defined using the Objects and Settings tabs. These are described in detail next.

Objects

As discussed earlier in the "Configuration Items" section, objects represent the existence of an assembly, a file or folder, or a Registry key. Each type of check has the definable properties listed in Table 16.2.

Settings

As discussed in the "Configuration Items" section, settings are the result of queries against Active Directory, the IIS metabase, the Windows Registry, SQL Server databases, WMI WQL, an XML file, or a custom script. Each of these query types has the configurable properties listed in Table 16.3.

64-bit Redirection

Several caveats come with 64-bit Windows. The one most administrators notice right away is the existence of a new folder called Program Files (x86). All 32-bit applications resolve the environment variable *%ProgramFiles%* to this new Program Files folder. To see this on a 64-bit system, launch the 64-bit command prompt by typing **%windir%\SysWoW64\cmd.exe** on a run line. Type **echo %ProgramFiles%** and examine the output. You can see that 64-bit applications, such as the default command prompt, resolve *%ProgramFiles%* to the traditional Program Files folder. The same behavior occurs when a 32-bit application tries to access *%windir%*\System32—the application is transparently redirected to *%windir%*\SysWOW64. This 64-bit redirection also happens in the Registry.

The exact why's and how's of this redirection in 64-bit Windows are detailed at http://msdn.microsoft.com/en-us/library/bb427430(VS.85).aspx. You do not really need to know these details; just that it takes place. ConfigMgr typically presents you with a check box or radio button to disable the redirection any time this redirection can have an adverse effect. This is the case with File or Folder objects, Registry objects, Registry settings, and XML settings.

16

TABLE 16.2   Configurable Properties for Objects

Object Type	General
Assembly	This tab, shown in Figure 16.12, contains fields for the Assembly name as it is registered in the GAC, and an optional description.
File or Folder	This tab, shown in Figure 16.13, contains fields for the type (file or folder), path, file or folder name, search depth, and an optional description. Both the object path and object name can contain environment variables such as %SYSTEMROOT%. If %USERPROFILE% is used in the path, all user profiles on the system are searched, possibly resulting with multiple instances of the file or folder found. There are three search depths to choose from in the Name pattern search depth dropdown selection: **Specified Path**—Specifies that searches for file and folder objects will only be performed in the specified path. **Specified path (pattern)**—Searches for file and folder objects will only be performed in the specified path. **Specified path and all subfolders**—Searches for file and folder objects will be performed in the specified path and all folders below this path in the folder tree. Wildcards (* and ?) must be used in the File or Folder Name field if Specified path (pattern) or Specified path and all subfolders is selected. Wildcards cannot be used when Specified path is selected. The final choice on this tab is to enable or disable 64-bit file redirection. This option is only applicable to 64-bit operating systems and indicates whether both %windir%\system32 and %windir%\syswow64 are searched or just %windir%\syswow64.
Registry Key	This tab, shown in Figure 16.14, contains fields for the Registry hive and the key. Note that this object setting checks for the existence of a Registry key, not a value stored in the Registry. Using the radio buttons in the middle of the page, you set whether or not to look in 64-bit Registry keys. As with the similar option for file and folders, this option only has an effect on systems running 64-bit Windows.

Validation	Attributes	Permissions
Acceptable validation criteria for assemblies include Version, Culture, and Public Key Token.		
Validation criteria include Size, Product Name, File Version, Date Modified, Date Created, Company name, and SHA-1 Hash for files and Date Modified and Date Created for folders.	On this tab, you specify whether to check for specific file attributes, such as Archive, Compressed, Encrypted, Hidden, Read Only, and System.	This tab allows you to specify checks for the presence of permissions on the file or folder object. You can specify exclusive or nonexclusive permissions. Nonexclusive permissions allow for other permissions to be present on the file or folder; exclusive permissions do not.
		This tab is identical to the one for file and folder objects; it configures checks for specific permissions on the Registry key being evaluated.

16

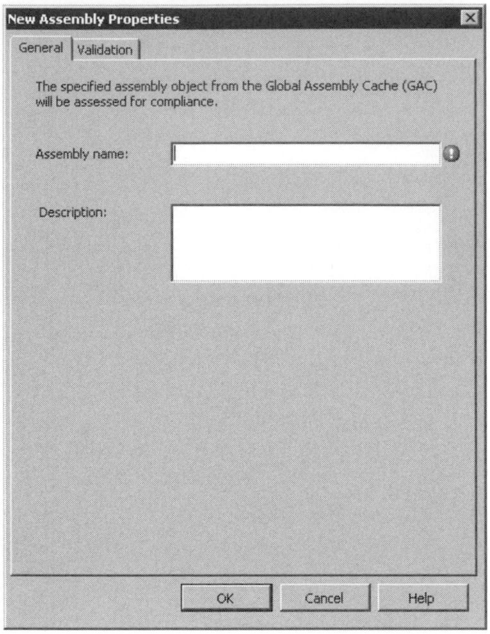

FIGURE 16.12   Assembly object type

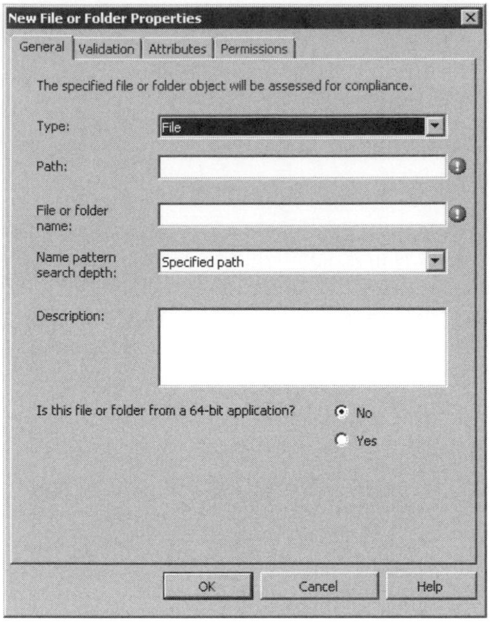

FIGURE 16.13   File or Folder object type

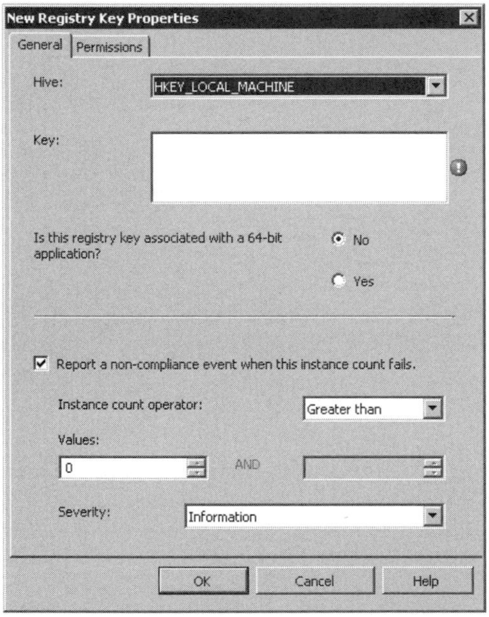

FIGURE 16.14   Registry object type

TABLE 16.3   Configurable Properties for Settings

Query Object   General Tab

Active
Directory

This tab, shown in Figure 16.15, contains fields for the display name of this object, a description (optional), the LDAP prefix (either LDAP:// to connect to a domain controller or GC:// to connect to a global catalog), the distinguished name (DN), an optional LDAP filter, the search scope, and the property to query.

You have three search scopes to choose from:

Specified path—Queries only the object specified.

Specified path and the first level of subfolders—Not valid in this version of ConfigMgr.

Specified path and all subfolders—Queries the object specified and its complete subtree in that folder.

The Query field at the bottom of the page is read-only and built for you from the other information you supply.

IIS Metabase   This tab, shown in Figure 16.16, contains fields for the display name of this object, a description (optional), the metabase path, and the property ID.

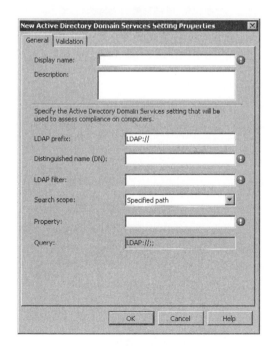

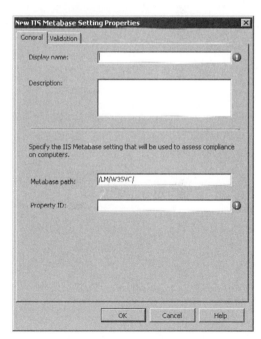

FIGURE 16.15   Active Directory setting type

FIGURE 16.16   IIS metabase setting type

TABLE 16.3   Configurable Properties for Settings

Query Object	General Tab
Registry	This tab, shown in Figure 16.17, contains fields for the display name of this object, a description (optional), the hive, the key, and the value name. By checking the box "The value name is a .Net regular expression," you can use a .NET regular expression instead of a hardcoded value to search for a particular value or set of values. .NET regular expressions provide a powerful pattern-matching syntax based on Perl regular expressions. For more information about .NET regular expressions, see http://msdn.microsoft.com/en-us/library/hs600312(VS.71).aspx. Similar to Registry objects, 64-bit Registry values can be checked by using the radio buttons at the bottom of the page.
Script	This tab, shown in Figure 16.18, contains fields for the Display name of this object, Description (optional), Script language, and the Script itself. Valid choices for the script language are VBScript, JScript, or PowerShell. To load the script from a saved file, use the Open button at the bottom of this page.

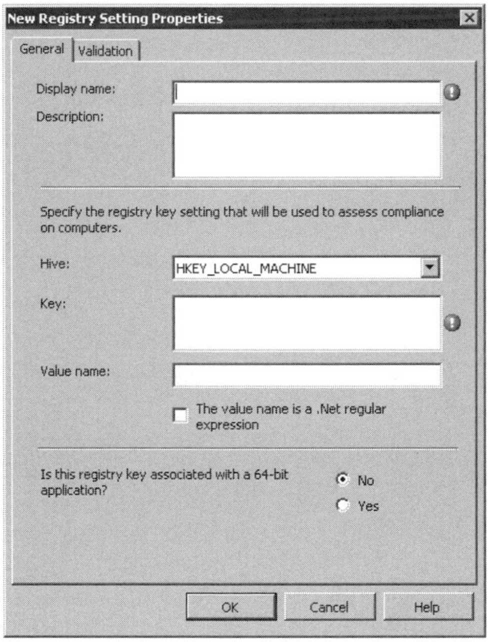

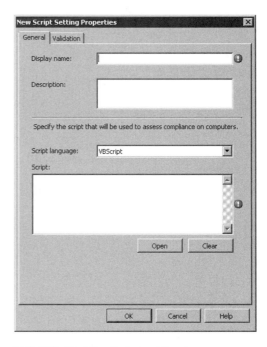

FIGURE 16.17   Registry setting type

FIGURE 16.18   Script setting type

TABLE 16.3 Configurable Properties for Settings

Query Object	General Tab
SQL Query	This tab, shown in Figure 16.19, contains fields for the display name of this object, a description (optional), instance selection, database, column, and T-SQL statement.
	Valid instance selections include the default instance, all instances, and a specific instance.
	Using the Open button at the bottom of the page, you can load a T-SQL statement from a saved file.
WMI Query	This tab, shown in Figure 16.20, contains fields for the display name of this object, a description (optional), namespace, class, property, and WQL WHERE clause.
XML Query	This tab, shown in Figure 16.21, contains fields for the display name of this object, a description (optional), the path to the XML file, XML filename, name pattern search depth, and XPath query.
	The Name pattern search depth options are identical in name and use as those of the File and Folder object setting in Table 16.2. The choice of 64-bit file redirection is also the same.
	Using the Namespaces button at the bottom of the page, you can specify the namespace for the query. To load an XPath query from a saved file, use the Open button.

16

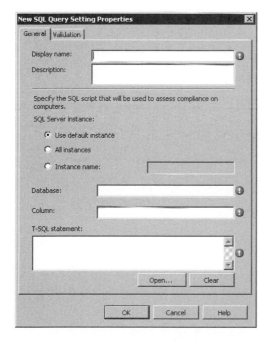

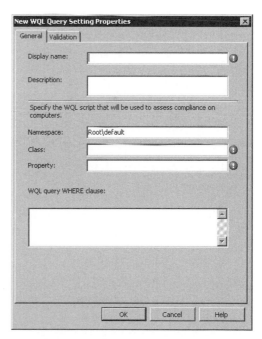

FIGURE 16.19 SQL query setting type

FIGURE 16.20 WMI query setting type

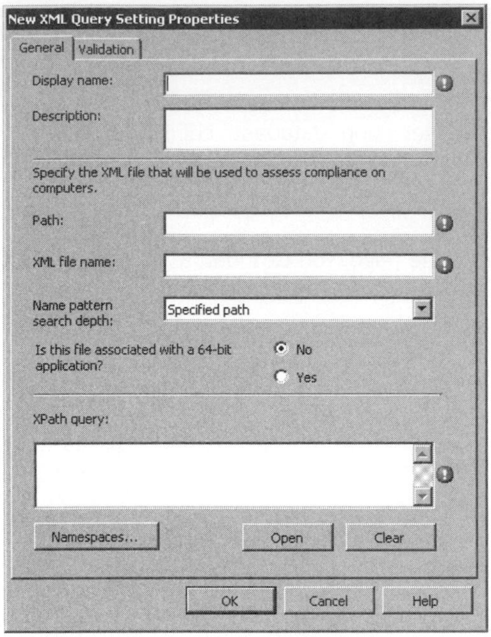

FIGURE 16.21   XML setting type

Validation Criteria

Each object, other than the Registry object, has a validation tab; by using this tab, you specify the criteria for validating that the object exists. Add criteria in the top list box by clicking the New button. This results in a pop-up menu where you choose from one of the validation properties, as specified in Table 16.2. This opens the Configure Validation dialog box shown in Figure 16.22.

The Name field is a display name for the rule and the Description field is optional. The Setting/Property field is read-only and already filled in based on the selection you made on the New pop-up menu. You have nine operators to choose from for numbers, dates, and versions:

▶ Between

▶ Equals

▶ Greater than

▶ Greater than or equal to

▶ Less than

▶ Less than or equal to

▶ None of

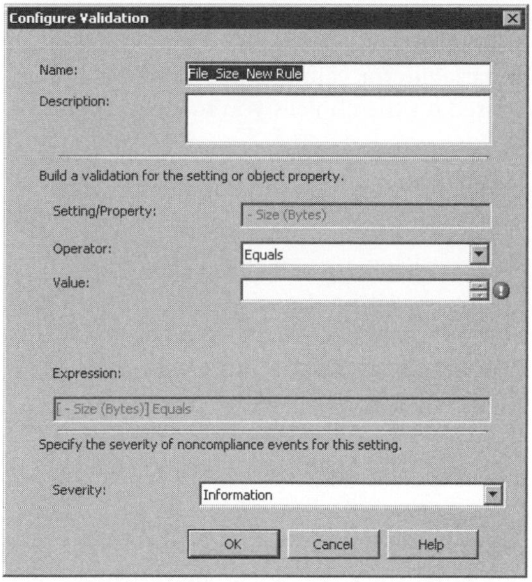

FIGURE 16.22   Configure Validation dialog box

  ▶ Not equals

  ▶ One of

String values have 13 possible operators:

  ▶ Equals

  ▶ Not equals

  ▶ One of

  ▶ Begins with

  ▶ Ends with

  ▶ Contains

  ▶ Matches

  ▶ All Of

  ▶ None Of

  ▶ Does not begin with

  ▶ Does not end with

  ▶ Does not contain

  ▶ Does not match

For One of, All of, or None of, the Value field can contain a comma-separated list of values. For the Between operator, the second Value field is added to the tab to specify the maximum value. Using Windows environment variables for values is not valid. The Expression field is read-only and built for you based on the choices you make in the tab.

At the bottom of the dialog box on the Validation tab, you set the severity associated with this check failing (also known as a *noncompliance event*); these are the same levels previously described in the "Configuration Items" section.

Similar to the object validation criteria, every setting also has a validation tab. The primary difference is that with settings, you are not validating the existence of the setting; you are validating the value of the setting and specifying the expected value or values against which to validate the setting. This means you do not choose from a predefined set of properties to validate against; instead, the validation criteria specified are compared against the setting itself as defined on the General tab. As an example, for a Registry setting, the validation criterion that you specify on the Validation tab evaluates the Registry value you specify on the General tab.

One additional property to set for validation criteria on settings is the data type. With objects, you choose from a predefined list of properties so DCM knows what the data type is. With settings, there is no way for DCM to predetermine the data type to decide how the value is compared to expected values. Possible data types include the following:

▶ String

▶ Integer

▶ Date/Time

▶ Floating Point

▶ Version

The choice of data type also affects the operators available for the validation criteria, as noted earlier in this section.

The final section at the bottom of the Validation page is wholly enabled or disabled by checking Report a non-compliance event when this instance count fails. This setting performs an additional validation check by counting the number of objects that match the criteria specified on the General tab, and it raises another noncompliance event if the count does not fall within the criteria specified.

An example of this is definitely in order. Suppose that per organizational standard, each server must have at least two and no more than four SCSI drives, and these must be formatted with 512 bytes per sector. This is a check you will want in a DCM baseline. The following steps outline setting this up:

1. Navigate to Site Database -> Computer Management -> Desired Configuration Management -> Configuration Items in the ConfigMgr console tree.

2. Right-click the configuration item to add the check to and select Properties, or you can create a new one by right-clicking the Configuration Item in the tree and selecting New.

3. Open the Settings tab.

4. Click New near the bottom left of the tab and choose WQL Query from the pop-up menu.

5. On the General tab of the New WQL Query Settings Properties dialog box, fill in the criteria as follows (and as shown in Figure 16.23). This query returns a list of all the disk drives attached to the local system that are connected using a SCSI interface.

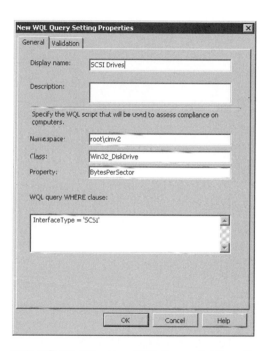

FIGURE 16.23   New WQL Query Settings Properties dialog box example

- ▶ **Namespace**—root\cimv2
- ▶ **Class**—Win32_DiskDrive
- ▶ **Property**—BytesPerSector
- ▶ **WHERE clause**—InterfaceType = 'SCSI'.

6. Open the Validation tab.

7. Select Integer for the Data Type setting at the top.

8. Choose New at the bottom left of the Details list.

9. Configure the Configure Validation dialog box as follows (and as shown in Figure 16.24):

   ▶ **Name**—Check for 512 Bytes Per Sector

   ▶ **Operator**—Equals

   ▶ **Value**—512

   ▶ **Severity**—Error

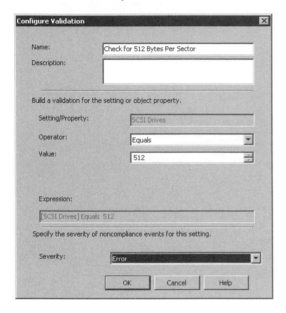

FIGURE 16.24   Configure Validation dialog box example

10. Check the box labeled Report a non-compliance event when this instance count fails.

11. Change the Instance count operator to Between and enter **2** and **4** in the Values boxes.

12. Change the Severity to Error. Figure 16.25 displays the completed Validation tab.

This criterion causes a noncompliance event, with a severity of Error raised according to the stated criteria in step 12.

The biggest challenge when creating custom configuration items is translating the business requirement or user interface–based setting into items DCM expects and can act on. The most common place to store and query settings from is the Windows Registry. Other locations include WMI, Active Directory, and SQL Server. DCM, using one of the object or setting types can evaluate all of these and more.

However, how do you determine where to look in the first place? Many resources can help you with this endeavor. First and foremost is experience with Windows. An intimate knowledge of the Registry and of where Windows stores values will make your task much easier. The ability to write custom scripts and use WMI will also help tremendously. As the old cliché goes, "There's no substitute for experience."

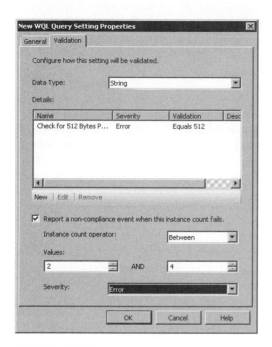

FIGURE 16.25 Validation example

Of course, even an intimate knowledge of these things does not mean you know every single Registry key or WMI class available. For that, there is TechNet and the World Wide Web in general. A number of excellent books are also available on these subjects.

Using Microsoft Tools

An excellent resource is the Microsoft-provided configuration packs. Microsoft has put a lot of work into creating them, and they provide great examples of how and where to find settings. Even if you do not actually intend to use them, it is still a good idea to download and install these CPs just to dissect them and use them as a reference. Many of the evaluation criteria are checked using custom scripts. You can easily copy these scripts and use them in your own configuration items as is or with simple modifications—it is usually much easier to modify someone else's working script than create your own from scratch.

Registry Monitor (RegMon) and Process Monitor (ProcMon) are some of the greatest all-around Windows utilities available—these are available as free downloads from Microsoft's Sysinternals site at http://technet.microsoft.com/en-us/sysinternals/default.aspx. (Note that the capabilities of RegMon are rolled into ProcMon and that RegMon does not run on Windows Vista or Windows 2008.) These tools monitor the Registry and record every change made to it, letting you identify the exact location of any modification occurring to a system. As an example, suppose you wanted to create an evaluation criteria to determine if Remote Desktop is disabled but don't know where this setting is stored in the Registry. After starting ProcMon, simply make the change in the GUI, and the Registry change will be displayed in the ProcMon window. Detailed use of ProcMon is beyond the scope of this book but is straightforward. The help file provided with ProcMon is excellent and an in-depth, on-demand TechNet webcast titled "Advanced Windows Troubleshooting with Sysinternals Process Monitor" is available at http://www.microsoft.com/emea/spotlight/sessionh.aspx?videoid=346.

Third-party Tools

Profiling a current system is an obvious way to create new configuration items. This involves surveying a system's current configuration and building configuration data from that configuration. Unfortunately, the built-in ConfigMgr toolset does not have this capa-bility. You will have to resort to a third-party tool to get this functionality. One such tool, CP Studio from Silect Software, is discussed in the "Authoring with CP Studio" section of this chapter.

Configuration and Content Versions

When editing baselines and configuration items, you can modify one of two parts—the administrative or informational part that does not play a role in evaluation, or the content criteria part that does play a role in evaluation. The properties that make up the administrative part include the following:

▶ Display name and description

▶ Categories

▶ Dependencies (not applicable to configuration items)

▶ Collection assignments (not applicable to configuration items)

▶ Auditing information, such as creation times

▶ Security rights

Only configuration items have a content version; properties that are part of the content include the following:

▶ The objects and settings assessed by clients

▶ The validation and validation criteria used during compliance evaluation

▶ The detection method used for application configuration items

▶ The applicability criteria for application and general configuration items

Both these parts have separate, independent version numbers that are tracked by ConfigMgr. These version numbers are incremented as you make changes to their respec-tive properties; and it is important to distinguish between the two areas when reviewing the results of an evaluation. The version numbers are displayed in most reports.

Exporting the Baseline

A final step after creating a new baseline is to export it. Exporting the baseline gives you a way to share it with others, copy the baseline to a separate ConfigMgr site, edit it in its native Service Modeling Language (SML) format, and back up the baseline. Exporting the baseline creates a CAB file in the folder you specify and includes any contained configuration items. To export a baseline, right-click it and choose Export Configuration Data from the context menu.

Inside the CAB file of an exported baseline is an XML file for each configuration item and the baseline itself. You can actually create or edit these files outside of ConfigMgr, as discussed in the next section, "External Authoring."

External Authoring

Configuration items and baselines are stored in the SML XML format. SML is an industry-standard language specification that provides a rich method for modeling complex IT systems and services—see http://technet.microsoft.com/en-us/manageability/bb738088. aspx for in-depth coverage of SML, including the SML schema. Not all criteria modeled in SML can actually be displayed or edited with the built-in DCM toolset. However, because SML is the native language of DCM, these criteria are still evaluated and reported on properly.

DCM Digest is another XML format that DCM can use to define configuration items and baselines. DCM Digest is a Microsoft-proprietary modeling language that is dedicated to DCM; complete details of DCM Digest, including the schema, are available in the "DesiredConfigurationManagement_DigestAuthoring.doc" Microsoft Word document in the ConfigMgr SDK (downloadable from http://www.microsoft.com/downloads/ details.aspx?FamilyId=064A995F-EF13-4200-81AD-E3AF6218EDCC&displaylang=en%20; you can also find the SDK by searching for **ConfigMgr 2007 SDK** at www.microsoft. com/downloads). ConfigMgr takes configuration data imported from DCM Digest, converts it, and stores it in the site database.

Authoring using one of these XML formats is beyond the scope of this book; please reference the links provided in this section for detailed information on this activity.

NOTE

Configuration Manager Toolkit

The Configuration Manager Toolkit, which is available for download at http://www.microsoft.com/downloads/details.aspx?FamilyID=948e477e-fd3b-4a09-9015-141683c7ad5f&DisplayLang=en (or search for **Configuration Manager 2007 Toolkit** at www.microsoft.com/downloads), includes three tools to help author outside of ConfigMgr:

▶**DCM Model Verification**—Used to validate and test configuration items and baselines authored externally from the ConfigMgr console.

▶**DCM Digest Conversion**—Used to convert existing SMS 2003 Desired Configuration Management Solution templates to Desired Configuration Management 2007 configuration items.

▶**DCM Substitution Variables**—Used to author configuration items that use chained setting and object discovery. Substitution variables cannot be created or used by the ConfigMgr built-in toolset but are part of DCM Digest specification.

16

Why would anyone want to use SML or DCM Digest rather than the built-in editor? Here are several reasons:

▶ The ConfigMgr toolset cannot model every conceivable evaluation criteria. You may have to resort to one of these languages to implement the checks you want to implement.

▶ You may be comfortable working with XML. Working with XML gives you fine-grain control over the implementation of criteria and eliminates any abstraction present in the ConfigMgr console.

▶ Using an XML format provides the ability to create and edit configuration data outside of the console.

The responsibility for creating the configuration data may not lie with a user who has access or should have access to the ConfigMgr console. Although using an XML format is a bit more cumbersome, these types of users can author without being granted privileges within ConfigMgr.

Authoring with CP Studio

The ability to author configuration data outside of the console definitely has some advantages, as discussed in the "External Authoring" section of this chapter. However, working directly with XML is fraught with issues and not an attractive option to most administrators or to individuals responsible for creating the baselines who may not even be technically inclined. This is where third-party products can be particularly useful; one particular product recommended by Microsoft and the authors of this book is Silect Software's CP Studio (http://www.silect.com/).

CP Studio offers all the advantages of authoring configuration data outside the console without the requirement of needing to know XML. CP Studio also gives you the ability to create configuration data from an existing system using a profiling process that converts the current state of the system into a baseline. This profiling process enables you to configure a system to your organization's exact standards and use CP Studio to create a baseline matching that configuration. After importing the created baseline into DCM, you can now verify that all your systems are identically configured with little effort.

CP Studio has three major features:

▶ **Golden Master Creation Wizard**—This wizard creates a configuration item from the current configuration of a specified system. The wizard prompts you to select which parts of the system to consider in creating the new baseline. The wizard cannot review every setting on a system because there are countless possibilities, but it does a very good job nonetheless. Figure 16.26 shows this wizard and the possible settings it can use to build the configuration item.

▶ **Criteria Builder**—Perhaps the lengthiest part of actually developing a configuration item using the ConfigMgr built-in toolset is jumping around to other tools to build and verify criteria. As an example, to create Registry key object or settings checks, you need to use regedit (or some other Registry editor); for WMI queries you need to

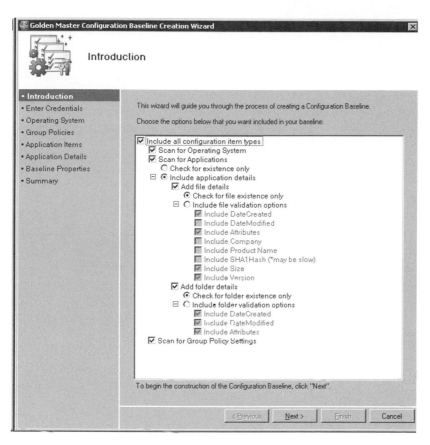

FIGURE 16.26   Validation example in CP Studio

use WBEMTest, the Microsoft WMI tools, WMIC (or another tool); and the same goes for each other type of possible criteria.

CP Studio includes built-in criteria builders and browsers for each type of criteria listed in Tables 16.2 and 16.3. Therefore, you do not have to use an external tool to browse for values or create criteria. The built-in criteria builders connect to the local system or remote systems and greatly speed the process. Figure 16.27 displays the WMI query builder.

▶ **Baseline Testing**—CP Studio has a built-in testing module that applies a selected baseline, on demand to the local or remote systems, which gives you instant results. This also greatly speeds the development life cycle of a baseline, because using the ConfigMgr toolset you first have to assign the baseline to a test collection, wait for the policy to be downloaded, and then manually log in to the system.

CP Studio does not enable you to build criteria that you cannot build with the ConfigMgr toolset. What it does, however, is offer a layer of abstraction that makes building the criteria easier and much quicker. With the addition of the testing module and Golden Master

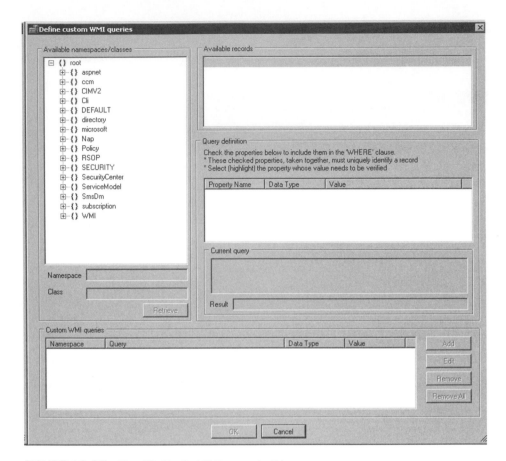

FIGURE 16.27   The CP Studio WMI query builder

Creation Wizard, CP Studio can significantly reduce your development cycle for baselines and configuration items.

Building baselines and configuration items—using the built-in toolset, raw XML, or CP Studio—are technical tasks in DCM. Deciding how to use the baseline and configuration items best in your organization is more of a conceptual task that requires planning and forethought. The next section covers some strategies for doing so.

DCM Strategies

The actual functionality of DCM is relatively straightforward—create a baseline of settings and assign those to a set of systems. However, what do you do then? It really depends on what you are going to do with the data DCM provides.

What are your business goals for using DCM? Are you simply filling a check box for the auditors? Do you want to use reports to help in troubleshooting? Are you wanting to notify the on-call admin when something is amiss? Or do you want nonstandard configurations corrected? Each baseline you create may fulfill one or more of these goals; therefore, the first step for each baseline is to identify its purpose, the target audience, and the delivery method for results. These criteria will define what criteria to include in the baseline.

After you identify these requirements, you can then set out defining the evaluation criteria (as discussed previously in the "Console Authoring" section) and how you enable the target audience to consume the results of the baseline evaluation. The following sections discuss this last mile for the results after performing an evaluation.

Reporting

Reporting is the only built-in way to view the results of DCM evaluation and the compliance status of your systems according to your baselines. A variety of reports is included out of the box to assist with this, including the following:

- ▶ Noncompliance details for a configuration item on a computer
- ▶ Compliance for a computer by baseline
- ▶ Summary compliance by configuration baseline
- ▶ Summary compliance by configuration item
- ▶ Summary compliance for a collection by computer

Baseline and configuration item evaluation is a completely client-side task. The results of this task are returned to the site using the new state message mechanism built in to ConfigMgr. State messages are asynchronous messages sent from the client to the management point to report information back to the site. State messages for DCM include XML attachments to report specific details about the evaluation of configuration baselines and items. ConfigMgr consolidates these state messages in the database and makes the results available to end users in reports. See Chapter 18 for an in-depth look at reporting in ConfigMgr. With the excellent flexibility of the built-in classic reporting and the new SQL Reporting Services (SRS) reporting, rich reporting is available through a web browser without giving any type of access to the console. This is great for middle and upper management or those annoying auditors who interrupt you every time they need to see this data.

16

NOTE

DCM Scenarios

Of the four scenarios DCM addresses (regulatory compliance, pre- and post-change verification, configuration drift, and time to resolution), only one is not clearly addressed by the reports included out of the box with ConfigMgr—and that is configuration drift. Results from every compliance scan are stored in the ConfigMgr database, so the data for a configuration drift report is indeed available.

However, because of the simplistic single query-based approach, it would be difficult, if not impossible, to use the legacy reporting component to actually create a configuration drift report. The new SRS-based reporting included with ConfigMgr 2007 R2 introduces the ability to create sophisticated and complex reports, including a configuration drift report. Implementation of this report (or set of reports) is left as an exercise for the reader (or a hint to the ConfigMgr development team).

Knowing is half the battle; therefore, reporting is also typically only half the battle. What you do with the information in a report is the other half. Actions can include alerting to make everyone aware of the issue and using an automated mechanism to correct the reported issues.

On-demand Results

In addition to using the server-side reporting functionality in ConfigMgr, administrative users can also trigger client-side report generation. After you enable DCM in the console, as described in the "Configuring Desired Configuration Management" section of this chapter, a new tab is available in the ConfigMgr Control Panel applet on all clients, titled Configurations (shown in Figure 16.28). Each baseline assigned to the client is included in the list box. Using the Evaluate button at the bottom of the page, users can trigger the evaluation of selected baselines. Using the View Report button, administrative users can display a report showing the most current evaluation results of the selected baseline. A typical use of this on-demand reporting is for IT personnel to locally troubleshoot or remediate identified noncompliance issues.

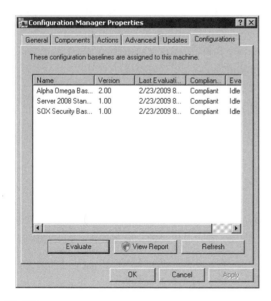

FIGURE 16.28   Configurations Control Panel applet tab

Alerting

DCM, like ConfigMgr as a whole, is not designed to be a real-time reporting or alerting system. However, it is perfectly reasonable to want the results of DCM to raise a real-time alert. The easiest way to accomplish this is in conjunction with Operations Manager.

Three of the four noncompliance severity levels for evaluation criteria drop events into a system's application event log as well as reporting back to ConfigMgr (as discussed earlier in the "Configuration Items" section of this chapter). One of OpsMgr's bread-and-butter functions is to skim the event logs of monitored systems. Thus, it is simply a matter of creating a monitor and alert in OpsMgr to look for specific noncompliant events reported by DCM. The steps to create such a monitor and alert are discussed in detail in *System Center Operations Manager 2007 Unleashed* (Sams, 2008).

If OpsMgr is not present in your environment, you could also utilize custom scripts, another product that skims the event logs, or the great new ability in Windows Server 2008 to perform an action in response to an event.

Remediation

Simply knowing about an issue using an on-demand report or receiving an alert doesn't help if the issue identified is causing a security hole or service interruptions for users—what you want is to fix the issue as quickly as possible without human intervention. As was briefly touched on in the "Configurations" section of this chapter, remediation refers to the process of correcting an issue identified, and auto-remediation is having the issue corrected in an automated manner. In both cases, DCM identifies the issue using a baseline assigned to a system in your organization.

The following example creates a ConfigMgr collection based on the noncompliant events raised by a baseline:

1. Create a new collection by right-clicking Collections in the console tree (navigate to Site Database -> Computer Management -> Collections) and selecting New Collection from the resulting context menu.

2. In the New Collection Wizard, name your new collection and add an optional comment. Click Next.

3. On the Membership Rules page, click the new query rule button to create a new query membership rule.

4. On the resulting Query Rule Properties page, name the query and click the button labeled Edit Query Statement.

5. On the Query Statement Properties dialog box, click the Show Query Language button at the bottom.

6. Paste the following query into the text box:

```
select SMS_R_System.ResourceId,
SMS_R_System.ResourceType,
SMS_R_System.Name,
SMS_R_System.SMSUniqueIdentifier,
SMS_R_System.ResourceDomainORWorkgroup,
SMS_R_System.Client
from
SMS_R_System inner join SMS_G_System_CI_ComplianceState on
➥SMS_G_System_CI_ComplianceState.ResourceID = SMS_R_System.ResourceId
```

16

```
Where
SMS_G_System_CI_ComplianceState.ComplianceStateName = "Non-Compliant"
and SMS_G_System_CI_ComplianceState.LocalizedDisplayName = "<BaselineName>"
```

7. Replace *<BaselineName>* with the name of the baseline or configuration item you want to remediate.

8. Click OK on the Query Statement Properties dialog box and OK again on the Query Rule Properties dialog box.

9. Finish the New Query Wizard by clicking Next and then Finish.

10. Finish the New Collection Wizard by clicking Next until the Finish button is enabled. Then click Finish.

ConfigMgr populates this new collection with systems that have a noncompliant evaluation result from the specified baseline or configuration item.

You can modify the preceding criteria to query for the severity of the compliance failure by using the ComplianceStateName property of the SMS_G_System_CI_ComplianceState class. For complete details of this class, see http://msdn.microsoft.com/en-us/library/cc143662.aspx.

After creating the collection, you create a software distribution package that corrects the issue and assign that package to the collection. The package could be as simple as setting a Registry key to a correct value or reinstalling the antivirus software that an application administrator accidentally on purpose uninstalled. The actual actions performed by the package are up to you and should correct any noncompliant issues that the baseline can identify. Those systems failing the compliance checks in the baseline populate the collection, which assigns them to the package correcting the issue.

NOTE

Auto-remediation Capability

At first glance, the lack of a built-in auto-remediation capability in DCM may seem like a huge missing piece. However, the question to pose here is, Do you really want the configuration of your working, production systems automatically changed?

In most cases the answer is *no*, at least not without restrictions. Although group policy does indeed affect changes to systems, the extent of what DCM can check is far greater than group policy and the ramifications are therefore larger. Additionally, for those configuration items such as the existence of an antivirus product, using this approach may not always be straightforward to remediate.

Although the next version of DCM will hopefully include some built-in auto-remediation enablers, the lack of auto-remediation in the current version does not take away from its usefulness and power.

Troubleshooting

As with all automated systems, many assumptions are made about the environment where the system is functioning. When these assumptions no longer hold true, the system fails to operate as expected. DCM is an automated system and therefore operates on certain assumptions. When issues arise, troubleshooting is necessary to determine which assumption or assumptions are no longer true.

Troubleshooting DCM, like the rest of ConfigMgr, is largely a log file review exercise. Because DCM is a client activity, the logs for DCM processing are on the client in the client logs folder (*%SystemRoot%*\System32\CCM\Logs on 32-bit systems and *%SystemRoot%*\SysWOW64\CCM\Logs on 64-bit systems). Five log files are used by DCM to store activity; Table 16.4 describes these files.

TABLE 16.4   DCM Log Files

Filename	Description
Dcmagent.log	Provides high-level information about the evaluation of assigned configuration baselines plus information regarding desired configuration management processes
Ciagent.log	Provides information about downloading, storing, and accessing assigned configuration baselines
Sdmagent.log	Provides information about downloading, storing, and accessing configuration item content
Sdmdiscagent.log	Provides high-level information about the evaluation process for the objects and settings configured in the referenced configuration items
Discovery.log	Provides detailed information about the Service Modeling Language processes

Debug and Verbose Logging

In addition to the normal logging available by default in the preceding logs, you can enable verbose and debug logging:

▶ Verbose logging adds extra detail and increases the descriptiveness of the log entries made. Verbose logging also adds one additional client log file that is specific to DCM, SmsClrHost.log, and one management point log file, MP_GetSdmPackage.log. SmsClrHost.log includes details about ConfigMgr's use of the .NET Framework, which is required for DCM, and MP_GetSdmPackage.log lists details about a management point's retrieval of DCM-specific package information.

▶ Debug logging is similar to verbose logging, but is typically meant for the developers of the component.

Enabling one or both of these can often provide you with that one extra clue that helps you solve an issue you are having. Appendix A, "Configuration Manager Log Files," includes procedures to enable verbose and debug logging.

You can also enable an extra debug log file for DCM on the client. This debug log file is not for the faint of heart, but can provide that extra information needed to troubleshoot an issue. The format of this file is XML. To enable this log file, add a REG_SZ value to HKEY_LOCAL_MACHINE\Software\Microsoft\CCM\SDMAgent named DebugFile and set the value to the name of an output file (as an example, DCMdmp.xml).

None of the preceding logging options should be enabled for normal operation because they add overhead that can bog the client down.

In addition to troubleshooting DCM itself, you will often have to troubleshoot issues with the baselines and the configuration items they contain. Issues involving the ability for DCM to evaluate a baseline or configuration item are reported through the ConfigMgr status message reporting mechanism. To view these status messages, perform the following procedure:

1. Navigate to Site Database -> System Status -> Status Message Queries in the ConfigMgr tree.

2. In the resulting details pane on the right, right-click All Status Messages and select Show Messages.

3. In the All Status Messages dialog box, enter the desired timeframe for which you would like to see status messages.

4. Review the displayed messages looking for the message IDs listed in Table 16.5.

TABLE 16.5   DCM Status Message IDs

Message ID	Description
11800	Indicates a download failure for a configuration item
11801	Indicates a hash failure for a configuration item
11802	Indicates that the .NET Framework 2.0 is not installed
11850	Indicates a download failure for SML content
11851	Indicates the policy could not be uncompressed
11853	Indicates the client computer has evaluated one or more assigned configuration baselines but cannot send the compliance results to its management point
11854	A compliance change from noncompliant to compliant or from unknown to compliant
11855	A compliance change to noncompliant with a noncompliance severity level of Information

11856	A compliance change to noncompliant with a noncompliance severity level of Warning
11857	A compliance change to noncompliant with a noncompliance severity level of Error
11858	Indicates that packages for SML content could not be uncompressed
11859	Indicates a failure in evaluating a configuration item
11860	Indicates a failure in evaluating SML content
11861	Indicates a failure in the SML discovery type process
11862	Indicates the SML discovery type is halted
11859	Indicates a failure in evaluating a configuration item
11860	Indicates a failure in evaluating SML content

Using the message IDs listed in Table 16.5, you can narrow down issues DCM has when evaluating baselines and configuration items. These status messages also provide the ability to track and monitor the evaluation status of baselines in your site.

> **NOTE**
>
> **.NET Framework**
>
> Not having the correct version of the .NET Framework installed on a client system can cause strange results that are difficult to troubleshoot. The lack of the .NET Framework can clearly be identified by the status messages returned by the client, but these are not always the first place you look to troubleshoot issues.

Information needed for DCM compliance scans often takes more than one client policy refresh cycle to be fully staged to the client. During this period, the status of the scan will not match your expectations for the result of the scan; this is to be expected and should not be cause for alarm or an extensive troubleshooting exercise. Patiently wait for an extra policy refresh cycle, and DCM will dutifully report its results in full.

It is often advantageous to trigger a DCM evaluation cycle on a remote system without interactively connecting to that system and initiating it from the Control Panel applet. The following code shows an example of how to trigger every applicable baseline on a remote system using VBScript:

```
system = "remote-system-name"
set objDCM = GetObject("winmgmts:{impersonationLevel=impersonate}!\\" &_
➥system & "\root\ccm\dcm:SMS_DesiredConfiguration")
➥Set objSWbemServices = GetObject("winmgmts:\\" & system & "\root\ccm\dcm")
➥Set colSWbemObjectSet = objSWbemServices.ExecQuery("SELECT * FROM
➥SMS_DesiredConfiguration")
```

```
For Each objSWbemObject In colSWbemObjectSet
  objDCM.TriggerEvaluation objSWbemObject.Name,objSWbemObject.Version
Next
```

This simple VBScript can easily be extended to connect to multiple systems or to allow the choice of which baseline to trigger an evaluation on.

Summary

DCM, with a little expertise, creativity, and hard work on your part, is an excellent tool that provides feedback about the configuration of Windows systems. It does this while seamlessly integrating with the rest of ConfigMgr, providing a "single pane of glass" to manage your systems from cradle to grave, top to bottom, and every other cliché you can think of (or the editor will allow). Just having the ability to provide consistent and timely compliance reports to auditors is always critical for any type of review. DCM does this and more.

The current DCM incarnation does have a few shortfalls, however. You can overcome some of these, such as external authoring and system profiling, through use of third-party tools. Others, such as auto-remediation, can be surmounted by using DCM in conjunction with the rest of ConfigMgr.

Even with these deficits, DCM efficiently fills a major blind spot in most organizations—configuration verification—without having to implement any additional enterprise tools. With the growing burden of IT audits and compliance regulations, DCM is a welcome addition to ConfigMgr and Microsoft System Center.

Configuration Manager Queries

While you were collecting inventory, distributing packages, managing patches, and performing the other activities covered in this book, a significant amount of data has made its way to the Configuration Manager (ConfigMgr) 2007 site database. As part of the discussion of creating and distributing packages in Chapter 13, "Creating Packages," and Chapter 14, "Distributing Packages," you were introduced to queries, which are data requests performed against the site database to obtain information about resources.

You can use ConfigMgr queries for a variety of purposes. You can create a query to return information regarding certain hardware and software prerequisites before sending a package to selected client systems. You can also create a query to display the status of an advertisement. Queries are also used to define collection memberships, as discussed in Chapter 14. You can use queries to retrieve any information stored in the site database.

This chapter discusses using queries as a means to obtain information. It steps through using the Query Builder, introduces WQL, discusses querying the Status Message System, and using query results.

Viewing Queries and Query Results

ConfigMgr queries are located in the ConfigMgr console, under System Center Configuration Manager -> Site Database -> Computer Management -> Queries. By default, the Queries node displays the name, resource class, and query ID for each query. The *resource class* is the type of Windows Management Instrumentation (WMI) object returned in the result set. Predefined queries have a query ID beginning with Systems Management Server (SMS), whereas those you create, similar to collections, will begin with the site code.

To customize the columns displayed in the query list, right-click the Queries node and choose View -> Add/Remove Columns. Here are the available columns not displayed by default:

▶ **Comments**—This is self-explanatory.

▶ **Expression**—This is the WMI statement for the query.

▶ **Limit to collection ID**—This is the ID of the collection from which the query will retrieve results. If you do not specify a collection ID, the query is not limited to a specific collection.

Figure 17.1 displays the default view of the Queries node.

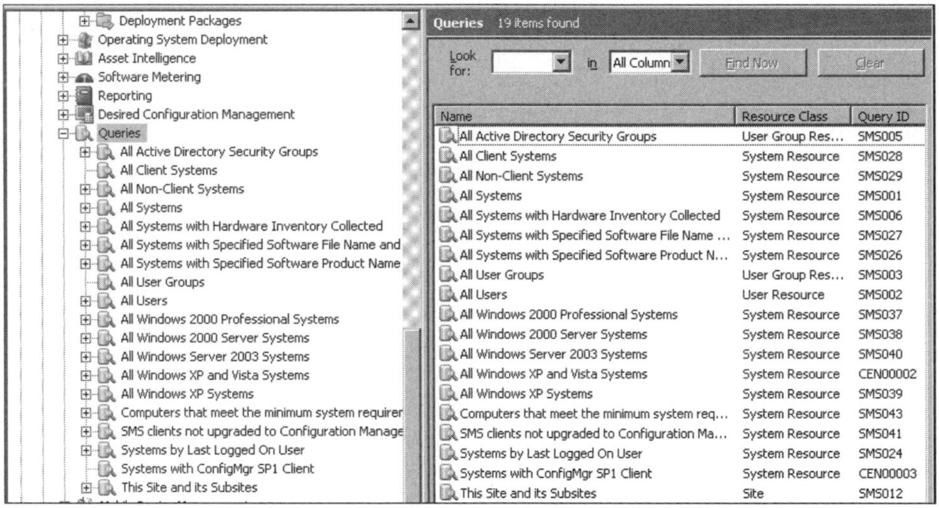

FIGURE 17.1   The ConfigMgr console Queries node displays a list of available queries

You can click a query to retrieve and display its results. Figure 17.2 displays the results for the Systems with ConfigMgr SP1 Client query. Notice the search bar at the top of the results pane; this allows you to enter a search term and choose the columns to search. You can also export the displayed data to a tab or comma- delimited text file by right-clicking the query name in the console tree and choosing View -> Export list. The "ConfigMgr Query Builder" section of this chapter shows how the Systems with ConfigMgr SP1 Client query was created.

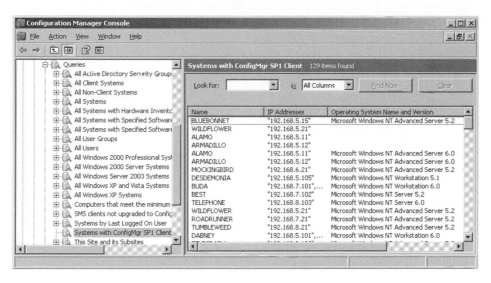

FIGURE 17.2   Query results for this site and its subsites

Creating Queries

The built-in queries are just a sample of the data available in ConfigMgr. You will want to review the properties of the built-in queries to get a better idea of how they are created, and then begin building your own queries!

Creating queries is a safe way to obtain data from ConfigMgr. When you use the Query Builder, the class joins are automatically created, thus reducing the risk of an improper join that could be resource intensive. The following sections provide additional insight into the query language, as well as the types of objects you can query.

The Query Language

ConfigMgr queries use the WMI Query Language (WQL) to gather information from the site database. In this way, queries differ from Configuration Manager reports (discussed in Chapter 18, "Reporting"), which use standard SQL syntax to access database information. ConfigMgr uses WMI for much more than just ConfigMgr queries. The ConfigMgr Software Development Kit (SDK) is a great place to learn more about WMI and WQL as well as Configuration Manager's use of these technologies.

About WQL

As Microsoft states at http://msdn.microsoft.com/en-us/library/aa394606(VS.85).aspx, WQL is a subset of the American National Standards Institute Structured Query Language (ANSI SQL) with minor semantic changes. This MSDN site lists WQL keywords. The keywords built with WQL are used to control the WMI service. Think of it as a repository of properties and methods related to the system environment that you would access similar to accessing a database.

Chapter 3, "Looking Inside Configuration Manager," introduced WQL, discussed its providers, and described how WMI maps to views in the ConfigMgr database. WMI providers are analogous to device drivers in that they know how to interact with a particular resource or set of resources.

If you are familiar with SQL, you will find adjusting to WQL is fairly simple.

Objects, Classes, and Attributes

Prior to building queries, let's discuss the terminology and the objects you will use. When selecting data in a query, you select an *object type*, one or more *attribute classes*, and one or more *attributes*. These terms are defined in the following list:

▶ **Object type**—A set of attributes that represents a ConfigMgr database object, such as a client, package, or advertisement. Table 17.1 shows the object types available for queries.

TABLE 17.1   Object Types Available for ConfigMgr Queries

Object Type	Description
Advertisement	A single attribute class that contains the data in a ConfigMgr advertisement, such as advertisement name, advertisement ID, package ID, package name, and more. This class will not tell you the advertisement status, but describes the properties of an advertisement.
Software Metering Rules	A single attribute class containing the data in a ConfigMgr software metering rule, such as rule name, filename to meter, and whether the rule is enabled. This class will not tell you metering rule summary information, but will tell you the properties of the rule.
Package	A single attribute class that contains the data in a ConfigMgr package, such as package name, package ID, source path, and more.
Program	A single attribute class containing the data in a ConfigMgr program, such as program name, package ID (to associate the program with a package), dependent program package information, and more.
Site	A single attribute class that contains the data in a ConfigMgr site, such as server name, build number, and site version.
System Resource	Many attribute classes containing the data for a computer system, such as discovery information, hardware and software information, and so on, are System Resource objects. The "Querying Inventory Data" section later in this chapter provides additional examples of inventory classes in the System Resource object type. You will find that System Resource is the object type you use more than all the others combined.

TABLE 17.1   Object Types Available for ConfigMgr Queries

Object Type	Description
User Resource	A single attribute class that contains the discovery data for user objects, such as user name, full user name, and user Organizational Unit (OU). Use this class when building queries that can be imported into collections for user-targeted advertisements.
User Group Resource	A single attribute class containing the discovery data for user group objects, such as user group name and domain. Use this class when building queries that can be imported into collections for user group–targeted advertisements.

▶ **Attribute class**—A container object that groups related attributes. For example, the Processor attribute class contains attributes such as Device ID, Manufacturer, Resource ID, and more. You can control many of the attributes in the attribute class by modifying the attributes collected in inventory by modifying the SMS_Def.mof file. Most attributes you will use in ConfigMgr queries are members of the System Resource Object type, because all hardware and software inventory information is a member of this object type. The "Querying Inventory Data" section of this chapter includes additional examples of inventory classes in the System Resource object type. If later you decide to build a web report (which uses SQL instead of WQL), you will find a SQL view with a similar name. As an example, the Computer System attribute class in WQL has a corresponding SQL view named v_GS_COMPUTER_SYSTEM.

▶ **Attribute**—The specific property that the query searches in criteria and/or displays for query results.

Figure 17.3 provides an example of object types and their relationships discussed in this section. It shows the selected object type System Resource. Within the System Resource object type, three attribute classes (Processor, Operating System, and Add/Remove Programs) are selected. The lines between each object type represent the joins that are required between classes. Here is the WQL equivalent of Figure 17.3:

```
select SMS_G_System_PROCESSOR.MaxClockSpeed, SMS_G_System_PROCESSOR.Name,
SMS_G_System_OPERATING_SYSTEM.OSLanguage,
SMS_G_System_OPERATING_SYSTEM.Version,
SMS_G_System_ADD_REMOVE_PROGRAMS.Publisher from  SMS_R_System inner join
SMS_G_System_PROCESSOR on SMS_G_System_PROCESSOR.ResourceId =
SMS_R_System.ResourceId inner join SMS_G_System_OPERATING_SYSTEM on
SMS_G_System_OPERATING_SYSTEM.ResourceId = SMS_R_System.ResourceId inner join
SMS_G_System_ADD_REMOVE_PROGRAMS on
SMS_G_System_ADD_REMOVE_PROGRAMS.ResourceId = SMS_R_System.ResourceId
```

As you can see from this code, WQL looks very similar to SQL. You will also notice that no criterion is specified (the query does not contain a WHERE clause). This particular example did not specify criteria, which is another feature of ConfigMgr queries—you may want to

17

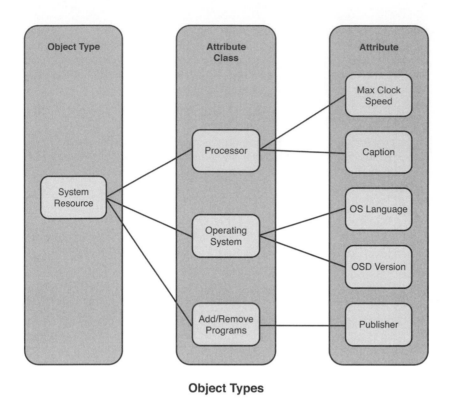

Object Types

FIGURE 17.3   Example of Query object types, attribute classes, and attributes

see all the data on occasion. You will learn in the next section how you can easily create a WQL query with criterion.

ConfigMgr Query Builder

Creating a query in ConfigMgr is fairly simple. The easiest way to create and run a query is by using the New Query Wizard, which is built in to the ConfigMgr console. Perform the following steps:

1. To launch the wizard, right-click the Queries node and then choose New -> Query. Figure 17.4 displays the New Query Wizard's General page. This example shows the name **Systems with ConfigMgr SP1 Client** entered, along with a description for the query. The default object type of System Resource is selected from the dropdown Object Type list box.

2. The General page includes the Import Query Statement button, which allows you to browse the existing queries and select one to use as a starting point for your new query. The Collection Limiting section of the page lets you select objects only from a collection you specify or a collection supplied by the user at runtime. The Systems with ConfigMgr SP1 Client query will be a new query statement created from scratch, and will not limit the results to a specific collection.

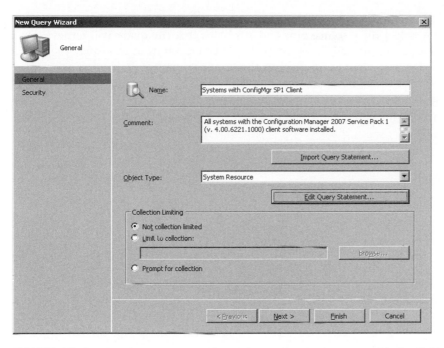

FIGURE 17.4   New Query Wizard's General page for the Systems with ConfigMgr SP1 Client query

To create the query statement, click the Edit Query Statement button. The New Query Wizard now displays the Query Statement Properties dialog box, displayed in Figure 17.5.

FIGURE 17.5   The Systems with ConfigMgr SP1 Client Query Statement Properties dialog box

3. You can click the New button to display the Result Properties dialog box, which allows you to select the resource type and attributes that the query will retrieve. On the Result Properties dialog box, you can click the Select button to display the Select Attribute dialog box. Figure 17.6 displays the Result Properties dialog box, with the Select Attribute dialog box in the foreground.

Figure 17.6 also shows the System Resource attribute class and Name attribute selected. Optionally, you could supply an alias to use as the column header for the Name column.

FIGURE 17.6   Choosing an attribute to display in the query results

After clicking OK to return to the Result Properties dialog box, add three additional system resource attributes to the query results:

▶ IPAddresses

▶ OperatingSystemNameandVersion

▶ OperatingSystemServicePack

4. After you determine that the query will display system resources and have selected those attributes you want to see, the next step in designing the query is to specify criteria for the systems you want to display.

On the Query Statement Properties dialog box's Criteria tab, click the New button to display the Criterion Properties dialog box. On the Criterion Properties dialog box, choose Simple Value from the Criterion Type list box and then click the Select button to select the attribute to use in the criterion. Figure 17.7 displays the Criterion Properties dialog box with the Select Attribute dialog box in the foreground. The attribute class used here is SMS Advanced Client State, and the specific attribute is Version.

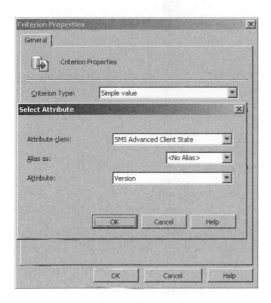

FIGURE 17.7   Choosing an attribute to use in a selection criterion for query results

5. After choosing the criterion attribute and clicking OK to return to the Criterion Properties dialog box, you can choose the operator and value for the selection criterion. Figure 17.8 shows the full criterion used: SMS Advanced Client State – Version is equal to 4.0.6221.1000. This is the client version for Configuration Manager 2007 Service Pack (SP) 1.

6. To complete the wizard, click OK to accept the criterion properties and OK again to complete the query properties. Click Next to return to the New Query Wizard's General page. You will now have an opportunity to modify security on your query. Chapter 20, "Security and Delegation in Configuration Manager 2007," discusses security. You can click Finish on the Security page to complete creating the query.

Reports Versus Queries in ConfigMgr 2007

You may be asking yourself whether you should use a report or a query. As usual, *it depends*. The main reason to use one technology over the other is the intended audience. For data used only by the ConfigMgr administrator, a query may be sufficient. However, for data that must be available to a very large audience, a web report will probably be preferred.

If you plan to build a query-based collections, you may want to consider creating a ConfigMgr query first. By creating a query, you can see the data on which you based your criteria in the WQL statement. As an example, you need to create a collection of systems that have a specific piece of software installed. When you create a query-based collection

FIGURE 17.8   The completed Criterion Properties dialog box

based on an installed file, the collection members will appear in the collection, but not the specific criteria built in the WQL statement. If you create that same WQL statement in a ConfigMgr query, you will be able to see the value of your criteria, which enables you to verify visually that your query is returning exactly what you intended. After verifying the data, insert the WQL into a query-based rule for the desired collection. The "Creating a Collection Based on Query Results" section later in this chapter contains additional information.

Table 17.2 lists some points to consider when deciding between queries and reports.

TABLE 17.2   Comparing Usage of Queries to Reports

Capability	Query	Report
Access to data	Requires access to the ConfigMgr console or the use of script	Access data from any web browser.
Export data	Ability to copy data from the ConfigMgr console and paste it into Excel	Ability to copy/paste data, as well as export to comma-separated value (.csv) file. Using SQL Reporting Services (SRS), you can also subscribe to reports, so they are sent directly to your email.
Building queries	Provides an intuitive query builder that automatically creates the necessary joins between classes of data	Provides a basic query builder, and requires you to define the proper joins, which can be complicated. You can use SQL Management Studio to build the queries, but are still required to define the joins.

Criterion Type, Operators, and Values

The previous section, "ConfigMgr Query Builder," briefly described criterion, operators, and values (each displayed in Figure 17.9). However, each of these elements of a query deserves additional detail:

▶ **Criterion**—Specify the type of criterion to use for comparison. The options follow:

▶ **Null value**—Compares a query attribute to a null value. An example of where you may find a null value would be for a system that is discovered but has not yet reported inventory. The System class would have valid data, but the Computer System class would have no information, which would be a null value. Another example would be when looking for systems that are not ConfigMgr clients. You see that SystemResource contains the Client attribute. Simply setting `SystemResource.Client is not equal to 1` will not provide the expected results, because that attribute only exists if the site knows that the system is not a client. The proper query would include `SystemResource.Client is NULL Or SystemResource.Client is 0`.

▶ **Prompted value**—This is a placeholder for a simple value that prompts the user at runtime. Using a prompted value provides additional flexibility to a query. As an example, if you are querying information for a specific computer, instead of statically entering the computer name into the query, you can elect to use a prompted value. This capability allows you to easily run the query for multiple systems without the need to create additional queries. Another example is creating a query such as "C: drive has less than x MB free." Here, using a prompted value allows you to define the value of x when running the query. The prompted value type exists in queries, but not in collections.

▶ **Simple value**—Compares to a constant value. Selecting Simple value enables the simple value settings. This is the most basic of operators. Use Simple value when you are looking for a single criterion.

▶ **Attribute reference**—Compares to another attribute. Selecting Attribute reference enables the attribute reference settings. In this case, you compare two different attributes. One example is to find out all the PCs in which the processor's current clock speed is less than the maximum clock speed.

▶ **SubSelected values**—Compares to results returned by another query. Selecting SubSelected values enables the subselected values settings. You can use this when you want to compare an attribute with the results of another query. One good example is to find out all the computers that do not have specific software. Jeff Gilbert's blog posting at http://myitforum.com/cs2/blogs/jgilbert/archive/2008/07/22/subselect-queries-the-easy-way.aspx provides additional information.

▶ **List of values**—Compares to a list of constant values. Selecting List of values enables the list of values settings. A classic example is listing all systems where the chassis is classified as a notebook. For additional information on chassis types, review information on the Win32_SystemEnclosure at http://msdn. microsoft.com/en-us/library/aa394474.aspx.

Figure 17.9 shows the Criterion Properties dialog box, where List of values is specified as the Criterion Type setting. Cross-referencing the values shown in Figure 17.9 with the Chassis Types property of the Win32_SystemEnclosure class will show you that this query is for Portable, Laptop, Notebook, and Sub Notebook chassis types.

FIGURE 17.9   Using List of values as the Criterion Type setting

▶ **Operator**—This dropdown field specifies how to assess the values. Options vary, depending on the value defined for the criterion type. When the criterion type is Simple, these values include the following:

Is equal to

Is greater than

Is greater than or equal to

Is less than

Is less than or equal to

Is like

Is not equal to

Is not like

Lowercase is equal to

Lowercase is greater than

Lowercase is greater than or equal to

Lowercase is less than

Lowercase is less than or equal to

Lowercase is like

Lowercase is not equal to

Lowercase it not like

Uppercase is equal to

Uppercase is greater than or equal to

Uppercase is less than

Uppercase is less than or equal to

Uppercase is like

Uppercase is not equal to

Uppercase is not like

▶ **Values**—Specify a value by entering it into the Value text box. You can also click the Values... button, which will query ConfigMgr for a list of possible values and allow you to select a value. If the number of possible values is very large, the list is truncated. You can use wildcards with strings by selecting one of the operators that uses the Like clause:

   ▶ **_ (underscore)**—Matches any one character

   ▶ **% (percent)**—Matches any zero or more characters

You can also use this information when building query-based rules for a collection, as discussed in Chapter 14.

Advanced Queries

A favorite feature of the Query Builder is that it automatically creates the joins for you. As an example, say you want a list of all computers and the total amount of physical memory. To make things a little more complex, your boss also wants this listing to display the Active Directory Site Name, as well as a date/time stamp of when the ConfigMgr client inventoried the information. Using the Query Builder, you simply select the classes and properties you want to display (this example will use the classes of System Resource, Memory, and Workstation Status) and then run the report. The Query Builder creates all the joins for you. To see the detail, simply click the Show Query Language button (displayed previously in Figure 17.5) after you write your query. For additional information on converting WQL to SQL, see the "Converting WQL to SQL" sidebar later in this chapter.

In addition to using the Query Builder, you can write the query statements yourself. Using WQL, you specify the WMI object classes and attributes the query will use to search the ConfigMgr site database. As an example, perhaps you want to display all systems that have reported hardware inventory in the past 30 days. There is no native way to do this using the Query Builder. Luckily, ConfigMgr supports Extended WMI Query Language, which allows you to use the following functions:

▶ **GetDate()**—This function returns the current date and time on the system. The data is returned in date-time format (for example, 12:56 AM 12/02/2009).

▶ **DateDiff()**—This function returns the difference between two date-time values in the increment you specify (for example, minute, hour, day). The DateParts listed in Table 17.3 are supported when using DateDiff in a WHERE clause in SMS WQL. Here's the proper syntax for DateDiff:

```
DateDiff ( DatePart, StartDate, EndDate )
```

    ▶ DatePart is the part of the date you want to calculate (minute, day, month, and so on).

    ▶ StartDate is the begin date.

    ▶ EndDate is the ending date.

▶ **DateAdd()**—Returns a new date-time value based on adding an interval to the specified date. Testing validated that the DateParts listed in Table 17.3 are supported when using DateAdd in a WHERE clause in SMS WQL. The proper syntax for DateAdd follows:

```
DateAdd ( DatePart, Number, Date )
```

    ▶ DatePart is the part of the date you want to calculate (minute, day, month, and so on).

    ▶ Number is the value to increment DatePart.

    ▶ Date is a valid date-time value used to calculate the new date.

Table 17.3 shows the DataParts and their abbreviations.

TABLE 17.3   DateParts and Abbreviations

DatePart	Abbreviation
Year	yy
Month	mm
Day	dd
Hour	hh
Minute	mi
Second	ss

As you can see, ConfigMgr provides a considerable amount of power in configuring queries. If you plan to create a custom query-based collection, first try to create a query using the Query Builder. Then take the next step, if necessary, to incorporate your custom query details. The next sections provide examples of using Extended WQL.

Example: Querying for Systems with a Hardware Scan in the Last 30 Days

Use this query to retrieve all systems that have reported a LastHardwareScan date within the last 30 days:

```
SELECT SMS_R_System.ResourceID,SMS_R_System.ResourceType,
SMS_R_System.Name,SMS_R_System.SMSUniqueIdentifier,
SMS_R_System.ResourceDomainORWorkgroup,SMS_R_System.Client
FROM from SMS_R_System inner join
 SMS_G_System_WORKSTATION_STATUS on
SMS_G_System_WORKSTATION_STATUS.ResourceID  = SMS_R_System.ResourceId
WHERE DATEDIFF(dd,SMS_G_System_WORKSTATION_STATUS.LastHardwareScan,GetDate()) < 30
```

Notice the WHERE clause in the WQL statement, which is using the DateDiff function. The query uses dd to specify the difference in days, then the LastHardwareScan property is compared to the current date using GetDate(). If the difference in days is less than 30, the system is included in the query.

Example: Querying for Systems Discovered Since Midnight

The following example includes all systems discovered since midnight, based on the CreationDate property in the discovery record.

```
SELECT SMS_R_System.ResourceID,SMS_R_System.ResourceType,
SMS_R_System.Name, SMS_R_System.SMSUniqueIdentifier,
SMS_R_System.ResourceDomainORWorkgroup,SMS_R_System.Client
FROM SMS_R_System
WHERE (DateDiff(day, CreationDate, GetDate()) < 1)
```

Converting WQL to SQL

Now that you understand how to create queries using the Query Builder, you may also want to create these queries in ConfigMgr web reports. If you have built any web reports, you probably know that there is no query builder type of tool. It is not well known, but you can easily translate your WQL queries to SQL. As an example, look at the query created in Figure 17.10, which shows you the system name, AD site, total physical memory, and last hardware scan. The WQL looks like this:

```
select SMS_R_System.Name, SMS_R_System.ADSiteName,
SMS_G_System_X86_PC_MEMORY.TotalPhysicalMemory,
SMS_G_System_WORKSTATION_STATUS.LastHardwareScan from SMS_R_System inner join
SMS_G_System_X86_PC_MEMORY on
SMS_G_System_X86_PC_MEMORY.ResourceId = SMS_R_System.ResourceId
```

17

```
inner join SMS_G_System_WORKSTATION_STATUS on
SMS_G_System_WORKSTATION_STATUS.ResourceId = SMS_R_System.ResourceId
```

To convert this WQL to SQL, simply execute the query. Next, review the smsprov.log on the site server, looking for a line that contains Execute SQL =. For this example, you would find a log entry similar to this:

```
[1398][Thu 03/26/2009 06:00:24]:Execute SQL =select
all SMS_R_System.Name0,SMS_R_System.AD_Site_Name0,
SMS_G_System_X86_PC_MEMORY.TotalPhysicalMemory0,
System_WORKSTATION_STATUS0.LastHWScan from System_DISC
AS SMS_R_System INNER JOIN PC_Memory_DATA AS SMS_G_System_X86_PC_MEMORY ON
SMS_G_System_X86_PC_MEMORY.MachineID = SMS_R_System.ItemKey  INNER JOIN
WorkstationStatus_DATA AS System_WORKSTATION_STATUS0 ON
System_WORKSTATION_STATUS0.MachineID = SMS_R_System.ItemKey
```

This log entry gives you the SQL syntax! For additional information on converting WQL to SQL, review Brian Leary's article at
http://www.myitforum.com/articles/8/view.asp?id=9908.

Relationships, Operations, and Joins

As discussed in the "ConfigMgr Query Builder" section of this chapter, the Query Builder automatically creates the relational joins between different attribute classes. You can view these joins by looking at the WQL statement directly (using the Show Query Language button in Figures 17.10 and 17.11) or by viewing the Joins tab on the Query Statement Properties dialog box. ResourceID is the attribute generally used for joins. You may occasionally find that MachineID and ItemKey in one attribute class map to ResourceID in another attribute class. You can also use relationships, operations, and joins to query discovery and inventory data, as discussed in the following sections.

Querying Discovery Data

You can use the following classes to query discovery data:

▶ **System Resource**—Use the System Resource class for system properties such as System Container Name, System OU Name, AD Site Name, ConfigMgr Client Version, System IP Address, System Name, and more. If you are building queries manually, join classes in WQL using the ResourceID property of the SMS_R_System class. For example, for a simple WQL query to include the Active Directory site named TestLab, enter the following query:

```
Select * from SMS_R_System where SMS_R_System.ADSiteName = "TestLab"
```

▶ **User Resource**—This class is used for user properties, such as User OU Name, User Group Name, and User Name.

▶ **User Group Resource**—The User Group Resource class is used for AD user group properties, such as User Group Name, Unique User Group Name, and Domain.

The most important piece of information to remember about discovery data is that most of it is available to you even before the computer system has a ConfigMgr client installed. As an example, you will be able to query for systems in an Active Directory site even if you have not installed clients. This is an important step when deploying ConfigMgr to a new environment. Use this data to enable discovery methods, and build queries and reports to obtain a better idea of the locations of your enterprise systems—prior to installing clients.

Querying Inventory Data

The "ConfigMgr Query Builder" section of this chapter provided detailed information on creating a basic query. This section provides additional information for selecting inventory data classes and attributes.

All hardware and software inventory will appear through the System Resource object type. If you extend SMS_Def.mof (described in Chapter 12, "Client Management"), the hardware inventory classes and attributes will also appear in the System Resource object type. Figure 17.7 showed an example of querying the hardware inventory class named SMS Advanced Client State. The SMS Advanced Client State class is inventoried using WMI during a hardware inventory cycle. Several favorite inventory classes appear in Table 17.4, along with a brief description.

TABLE 17.4 Popular Hardware and Software Inventory Classes

Name	Description
Add/Remove Programs	Contains hardware inventory information based on information found in Add or Remove Programs (a.k.a. Programs and Features in Windows Vista). If you have x64 systems, you may also need to include Add/Remove Programs (64).
Computer System	Contains information based on the Win32_ComputerSystem WMI class, which includes time zone information, computer manufacturer and model, and more.
Disk Drives	Contains information based on the Win32_DiskDrive WMI class, which includes hard drive manufacturer information, the number of partitions, the size of the drive, and more. Disk Partitions is also a popular class.
Last Software Scan	Contains the last software inventory scan date, which can be helpful when troubleshooting systems. It also provides a better perspective of the "freshness" of your data.
Network Adapter Configuration	Contains static IP configuration information.
Operating System	Based on the Win32_OperatingSystem WMI class. This class contains Windows and system directory information, operating system version and service pack, as well as virtual and physical memory information.

17

TABLE 17.4   Popular Hardware and Software Inventory Classes

Name	Description
PC BIOS	Contains BIOS version, release date, and manufacturer information.
Services	Based on Win32_Service WMI class. Contains all Windows service information such as current status, executable path, and more.
Shares	Lists the shares configured on the operating system.
Software Files	Query this class by .exe filename. Based on Software Inventory.
Software Products	Query this class based on information in the .exe file header information. Based on Software Inventory.
USB Device	Displays information for USB devices attached to the system.
Virtual Machine and Virtual Machine Details	Contains information for a virtual machine's host operating system and computer name.
Workstation Status	Contains the last hardware inventory scan date, which can be helpful when troubleshooting systems. It also provides a better perspective of the "freshness" of your data.

If any of the inventory attributes do not appear in your environment, you may need to review the classes and attributes you have configured to inventory using SMS_Def.mof, as described in Chapter 12. If you find this information is missing for a specific system, you need to verify that system is healthy, because you need a healthy ConfigMgr client to send its inventory to the ConfigMgr site. If you do not see any inventory for any system, you may need to confirm that hardware/software inventory is configured for your site.

Using Query Results

Building queries is a great way for administrators to review inventory data, discovery data, advertisement data, and other site information. You can also use information in query results to create collections as well as export data to a text file. The next sections discuss these topics.

Exporting Query Results to a Text File

Execute the query so the results display in the results pane. Then right-click the query name and select View -> Export List. You can then specify to export to tab-delimited or comma-delimited files. You can also specify to use Unicode, if required.

Importing and Exporting Queries Between Sites

You can also import and export queries between sites, and share with your favorite ConfigMgr administrators. To export a query, right-click the query object and then select Export Objects. Follow the Export Objects Wizard, and specify a filename (with an .mof extension) to save the exported query.

To import a query at the receiving site, simply right-click the Queries node and select Import Objects. Follow the prompts in the wizard to complete the import process.

Creating a Collection Based on Query Results

Collections and queries both use WQL, making moving from a query to a collection fairly simple. It is a best practice to create a query to "test" the WQL before creating a query-based collection. When you create a query, you can review the values of the attributes that you used for the query criteria. If you build a collection, you probably will not be able to see the values of those attributes. So create the query, and verify that it performs exactly as expected, and then you can copy (or import) that query into a collection.

To use the WQL from a query in a collection, you must not specify any attributes to display. As an example, Figure 17.10 shows the General tab of a query to display memory information.

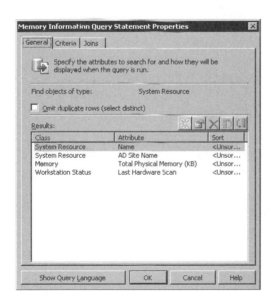

FIGURE 17.10   The General tab of a query to display memory information

Figure 17.11 shows the Criteria tab of this query. Notice that the query has a criterion specified to display only systems with more than 2,000,000KB of total physical memory.

FIGURE 17.11   The Criteria tab of a query to display memory information

Here's the WQL for this query:

```
select SMS_R_System.Name, SMS_R_System.ADSiteName,
SMS_G_System_X86_PC_MEMORY.TotalPhysicalMemory,
SMS_G_System_WORKSTATION_STATUS.LastHardwareScan from
SMS_R_System inner join SMS_G_System_X86_PC_MEMORY on
SMS_G_System_X86_PC_MEMORY.ResourceID = SMS_R_System.ResourceId inner join
SMS_G_System_WORKSTATION_STATUS on SMS_G_System_WORKSTATION_STATUS.ResourceID =
SMS_R_System.ResourceId where
SMS_G_System_X86_PC_MEMORY.TotalPhysicalMemory > 2000000
```

Simply remove all attributes from the General tab so that only criteria information remains. Next, click the Show Query Language button to reveal the updated WQL statement, which appears as follows:

```
select *  from  SMS_R_System inner join SMS_G_System_X86_PC_MEMORY on
SMS_G_System_X86_PC_MEMORY.ResourceID = SMS_R_System.ResourceId
inner join SMS_G_System_WORKSTATION_STATUS on
SMS_G_System_WORKSTATION_STATUS.ResourceID = SMS_R_System.ResourceId
where SMS_G_System_X86_PC_MEMORY.TotalPhysicalMemory > 2000000
```

Finally, paste this new WQL into a query rule for a collection.

Status Message Queries

Use ConfigMgr status message queries to view information about ConfigMgr components, audit messages, and changed objects (such as advertisements). Status messages allow you to see a little deeper into the ConfigMgr site for tasks that occur on your site. You can create custom status messages, as well as use one of more than 60 standard status message queries. To view status message queries, perform the following steps:

1. Expand Site Database -> System Status and then click Status Message Queries.

2. You will now see all the standard status messages. Simply select a status message, right-click it, and select Show Message.

   If the status message query requires additional information, you will receive a prompt. As an example, execute the All Audit Status Messages from a Specific Site status message query. You will be prompted for information, as shown in Figure 17.12.

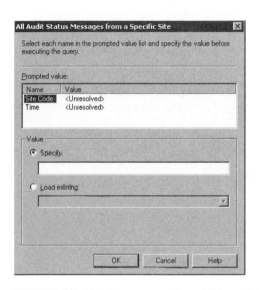

FIGURE 17.12   The prompt for additional information on a status message query

3. As shown for the Site Code value in Figure 17.12, you can directly specify the site code, or you can select the Load Existing radio button and ConfigMgr will populate the dropdown box with valid selections. (Use caution when selecting the Load Existing radio button—if the number of selections is large, such as for computer name, this process could take several hours!) Specify or select a site code and then click the Time option. For Time options, you can select an exact date and time, or you can use the built-in options for 1 hour ago, 12 hours ago, and other intervals.

Although the names of the status message queries are fairly descriptive, it is helpful to point out several queries that tend to be particularly beneficial when troubleshooting issues. Table 17.5 lists some favorite status message queries.

TABLE 17.5   Popular Status Message Queries

Query Name	escription
Advertisements Created, Modified, or Deleted	Allows you to see advertisement changes in your environment. This status message query also tells you who performed which operations, as well as the computer from which the task ran.
All Status Messages	Returns every status message reported to the site. Use caution, because this can be a very large amount of data. It can also be handy in an "emergency" situation, where you need to quickly see everything that has changed in the site in the past hour.
All Audit Status Messages for a Specific Site	For auditing purposes, this displays which user performed what action on the ConfigMgr site.
Collections Created, Modified, or Deleted	Returns collection modification information, so you can see who deleted/modified what collection, and when.
Packages, Programs, Advertisements	Each of these status message queries allows you to see changes to each of these ConfigMgr objects.

You may also want to review the following Microsoft TechCenter articles:

▶ Information discussing using status messages for ConfigMgr troubleshooting can be found at http://technet.microsoft.com/en-us/library/bb632870.aspx.

▶ An overview of the ConfigMgr status message viewer is available at http://technet.microsoft.com/en-us/library/bb632357.aspx.

Summary

This chapter provided an overview for how to create standard and custom queries, and how to create a collection based on a query. You learned about the differences between ConfigMgr queries and ConfigMgr web reports. Queries are a great tool for the ConfigMgr admin to gather data, as well as to test the query rules used in a collection. Reports are preferred for large amounts of data, and for data that you want to make available to a larger number of users on a regular basis. You learned how to convert WQL queries to SQL queries using log files. You also learned how to use status message queries (soon to be one of your new best friends).

Reporting

Your Configuration Manager (ConfigMgr) 2007 site databases contain a wealth of information regarding your network environment and ConfigMgr site. ConfigMgr's reporting capabilities allow you to tap into that data and use it to display detailed reports about your Microsoft Windows systems and ConfigMgr activities, such as software deployment and software updates. Here are some of the areas ConfigMgr allows you to report on:

▶ **Discovery data**—You can use ConfigMgr to discover and report on network resources and Active Directory (AD) user and computer objects. Chapter 12, "Client Management," discusses discovery methods.

▶ **Inventory data**—ConfigMgr hardware and software inventory provide detailed information about client computers. Chapter 2, "Configuration Manager 2007 Overview," introduced ConfigMgr inventory features.

▶ **Software metering data**—Also introduced in Chapter 2, you can use software metering to track the usage of specific software on your client systems.

▶ **Asset Intelligence data**—The new Asset Intelligence features of ConfigMgr 2007 use an extensive catalog of hardware devices and software products to help you identify, track, and manage the assets in your environment. Chapter 2 introduced Asset Intelligence; this chapter discusses Asset Intelligence data in more detail and presents its use in reporting.

▶ **Configuration Manager site data**—The configuration and relationships of your ConfigMgr sites, components, and client agents are stored in the site database. ConfigMgr reporting enables you to view and analyze the essential aspects of your ConfigMgr environment.

▶ **Configuration Management data**—You can use reporting to review the usage and progress of ConfigMgr features, such as software deployment, software updates, device management, Operating System Deployment (OSD), task sequences, Desired Configuration Management (DCM), and Network Access Protection (NAP).

▶ **Configuration Manager status data**—Reports based on status messages provide a useful tool for viewing the health of your ConfigMgr environment.

This chapter describes how to configure reporting and use ConfigMgr's reporting features to plan and assess your ConfigMgr operations and to present an in-depth picture of your Microsoft Windows environment.

ConfigMgr Classic Reports Versus SQL Reporting Services

Systems Management Server (SMS) 2003 (and earlier versions of SMS) provided a product-specific reporting implementation capable of rendering discovery, inventory, and management data from the site database as web-based reports. Microsoft also provided an extensive variety of preconfigured reports that you could use or modify according to your needs. ConfigMgr 2007 continues to support this reporting interface, and Microsoft has provided more than 200 new reports in addition to those available with SMS 2003. With ConfigMgr 2007 Release 2 (R2), Microsoft also integrates ConfigMgr with Microsoft SQL Server 2005 Reporting Services (SRS). This chapter refers to the reporting implementation based on SMS 2003 reporting technology as "classic" reporting to distinguish it from SRS reporting.

Here are several advantages Microsoft's SQL Reporting Services provides over the ConfigMgr web reports:

▶ SRS is an industry standard for reporting used by other System Center applications such as System Center Operations Manager (OpsMgr) 2007.

Reporting Trends in System Center

The evolution of reporting in Microsoft's Operations Manager product might provide some clues as to the direction of reporting in ConfigMgr.

Microsoft Operations Manager (MOM) 2005 used the SRS interface to display reports and the Report Writer for authoring, similar to ConfigMgr 2007 R2. This changed somewhat in OpsMgr 2007, which continued to use SRS as the reporting engine but integrated reporting into the OpsMgr console.

OpsMgr 2007 R2, available in mid-2009, supports use of SQL Server 2008 for the database components. The SRS in SQL Server 2008 does not use Internet Information Services (IIS); as a workaround, the OpsMgr development team wrote software that enables OpsMgr reporting to maintain its previous functionality and continue using SRS.

The next version of ConfigMgr is anticipated to support SQL Server 2008 components for reporting. It will be interesting to see the ConfigMgr development team's approach to the changes in SRS.

▶ SRS provides a user interface for those users unfamiliar with ConfigMgr 2007 reporting to generate ad hoc reports. Users can build SQL Reporting Services reports using SQL queries directly just as with classic ConfigMgr reports, or with reporting models that abstract away much of the detail of the underlying data source.

▶ SQL Reporting Services provides subscription services for reports. Using subscriptions, you can schedule regular updates to reports and distribute them by email or by placing them on a Windows file share. One advantage of publishing to a file share is the capability to easily maintain a report history.

▶ Classic ConfigMgr reporting allows you to export reports only to comma separated value (CSV) files. SQL Reporting Services additionally allows you to render reports to the following industry standard formats: eXtensible Markup Language (XML), Adobe Portable Document Format (PDF), Tagged Image File Format (TIFF), web archives (MHTML) and Microsoft Excel (XLS).

▶ SRS provides more flexible security options than available with classic reporting. Chapter 20, "Security and Delegation in Configuration Manager 2007," discusses security for both SRS and classic reporting.

▶ The SQL Reporting Services Report Builder interface provides drag-and-drop functionality to design report layout and add graphical elements to reports. These graphical designs provide the capability to produce richer reports.

Classic ConfigMgr reporting has some advantages as well:

▶ Report design and administration are consistent with SMS 2003, so there is almost no learning curve for SMS 2003 administrators. Links to any existing reports you distributed to users continue to work when you upgrade your reporting point from SMS 2003 to ConfigMgr.

▶ Classic reporting provides the capability to link to the Computer Details page. The Computer Details page provides an Explorer-like interface listing the available reports for a particular computer. The "Viewing Computer Details" section of this chapter discusses linking to Computer Details.

▶ You are more likely to get adequate performance without a dedicated server for the reporting role if you use classic reporting. If you do use a dedicated server, SRS requires a SQL Server instance (and license) for the reporting services role whereas the classic reporting point does not.

18

▶ Although ConfigMgr provides a wizard for easily migrating existing reports to SRS, any dashboards you created using classic reporting require re-creating in SRS. The "Dashboards" section of this chapter discusses dashboards.

Each reporting interface also has its own look and feel. Figures 18.1 and 18.2 display the same report as rendered in the default web format by the classic reporting engine and SRS, respectively.

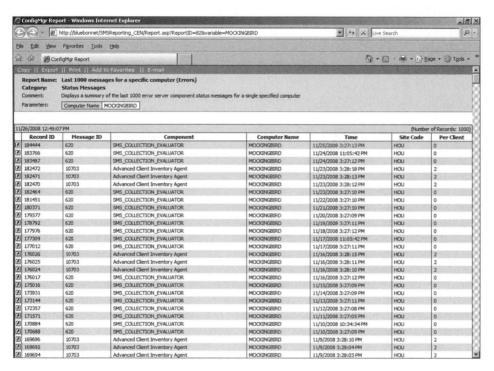

FIGURE 18.1   **The Last 1000 Messages for a Specific Computer (Errors)** Report displayed in the classic web report format

Reporting Configuration

When choosing a site to host either classic or SRS reporting, keep in mind that data flows up the ConfigMgr hierarchy and management flows down the hierarchy. This means that all data in your hierarchy is available at the central site, including discovery data, client inventory, status messages, and metering data. The central site is, therefore, the most useful location when reporting on your ConfigMgr environment. If you use child primary sites for administration, you may decide to enable reporting at these sites as well. Because management objects such as packages, advertisements, and task sequences created at child sites are not available for reporting at higher levels of the hierarchy, you must run those reports that track local management operations at the child sites.

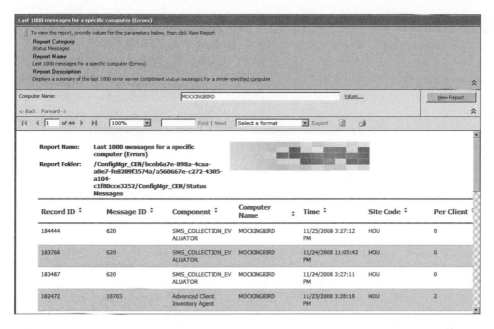

FIGURE 18.2   **The Last 1000 Messages for a Specific Computer (Errors)** Report displayed in the SQL Reporting Services format

To provide reporting capability on your site, you must first configure the appropriate site systems. Chapter 8, "Installing Configuration Manager 2007," discusses adding site systems and assigning site system roles.

- ▶ For classic reporting, you need to configure the Reporting Point site system role.

- ▶ For SRS reporting, you need to configure the Reporting Services Point site system role.

The next two sections discuss these configurations. You need to add any users that need to view reports and are not local administrators on the reporting point server to the Reporting Users local group on the reporting point server, and ensure users have either class or instance rights to view the appropriate reports. See Chapter 20 for a description of class and instance rights.

Configuring the Reporting Point for Classic Reporting

The reporting point site system computer must have IIS and Active Server Pages (ASP) installed and enabled. To enable rendering graphs in reports, install Microsoft Office Web Components (Microsoft Office 2000 SP 2, Office XP, or Office 2003) on your reporting point server.

18

> **CAUTION**
>
> **Special Considerations for Windows Server 2008 and 64-Bit Operating Systems**
>
> If you use a computer running Windows Server 2008 as your reporting point server, additional steps are required to enable the required IIS options. Chapter 6, "Architecture Design Planning," describes these steps. Also, 64-bit versions of Windows do not support Office Web Components. If you use a computer running a 64-bit operating system as your reporting point server, graph-rendering functionality is not available.

Here are the options you can specify when you configure a reporting point role:

▶ **The report folder**—ConfigMgr creates a folder with the specified name under the default website. The default name for the report folder is SMSReporting_*<Site Code>*. In Figure 18.3, the folder used for classic reporting is **SMSReporting_DAL** on the SCCMUnleashed Dallas site server.

▶ **Transfer protocol**—You can specify whether to use Hypertext Transfer Protocol (HTTP) or Secure Hypertext Transfer Protocol (HTTPS), and specify the port on which the reporting point should listen.

Based on the options you specify, ConfigMgr constructs and displays the reporting Uniform Resource Locator (URL). Figure 18.3 displays the options for configuring a reporting point.

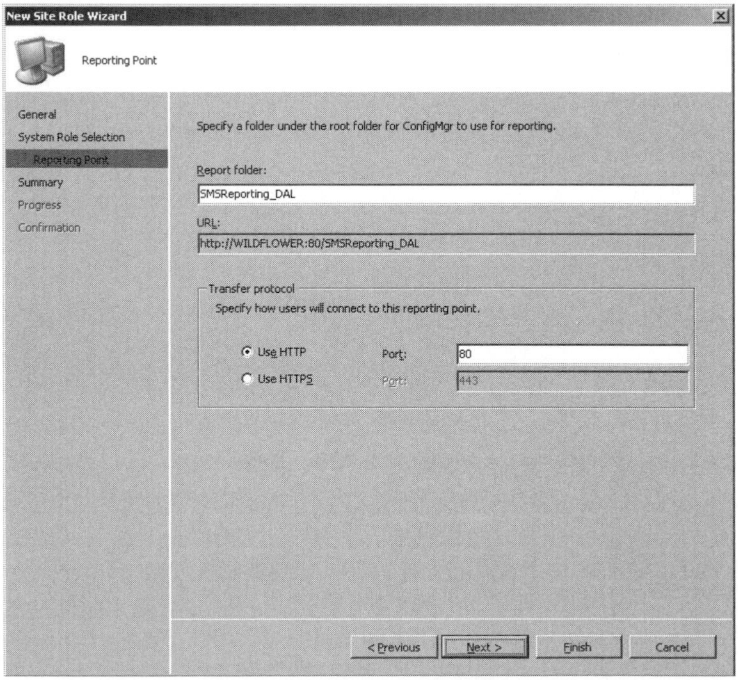

FIGURE 18.3   The Reporting Point configuration page with the default options displayed

Configuring the Reporting Services Point for SRS Reporting

You can assign the Reporting Services Point site system role to the site server or a remote server. For performance reasons, you generally want to move this role off the site server. The major prerequisites for the Reporting Services Point site system role include the following:

▶ The computer holding this role must have Microsoft SQL Server 2005 and its Reporting Services component installed. You must also configure the default report server and report manager virtual directories, the Windows service and web service identities, and the report server database.

For information about installing and configuring SQL Reporting Services, visit the SQL Reporting Services website at http://go.microsoft.com/fwlink/?LinkId=111840.

Be sure to test for a successful installation of SRS prior to configuring the reporting services point. You can do this by browsing to both http://localhost/reports and http://localhost/ReportServer from the SRS server.

  ▶ http://localhost/reports should display the SQL Server Reporting Services home page, including a toolbar for managing reports.

  ▶ http://localhost/ReportServer should display a page with the SRS installation date and version information.

▶ The computer containing the reporting services point must have IIS 6.0 installed.

▶ Your site must be running ConfigMgr 2007 R2 before you configure a reporting services point.

The only option to specify when creating the reporting services point is the report folder name. The default name for the report folder is ConfigMgr_<*Site Code*>. ConfigMgr creates the report folder under the ReportServer website on the SRS website. After creating the reporting services point, you need to configure several SRS options in the ConfigMgr console. To configure Reporting Services options, expand the Configuration Manager console tree to System Center Configuration Manager -> Site Database -> Computer Management -> Reporting -> Reporting Services. Right-click your reporting services point server, and choose Properties. The General tab displays the location, status, size, and a summary of the objects the reporting services point contains. You can use the remaining tabs to configure SRS options as follows:

▶ The Data Source Settings tab settings specify the database that supplies data to your reports. This generally is your site database or a replica of the site database. Figure 18.4 displays the Data Source Settings tab. In this figure, the Server name is **Bluebonnet** and the Database name is **SMS_CEN**.

18

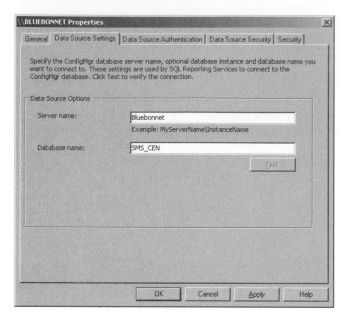

FIGURE 18.4   The Reporting Services Properties page Data Source Settings tab

▶ The Data Source Authentication tab settings specify the credentials used to access the data source.

Supported Options for ConfigMgr R2

Although the Data Source Authentication shows the option Credentials supplied by the user running the report, ConfigMgr 2007 R2 does not actually support this option.

Here are the supported options for data source authentication:

▶ **Credentials stored securely in the report server**—This option allows you to specify credentials for either a Windows or SQL Server user account, which is stored in encrypted form in the SRS report server database and used to authenticate to the data source. For more information about authentication in SQL Server, refer to the SQL Server 2005 product documentation available online at http://msdn.microsoft.com/en-us/library/ms130214.aspx. You generally choose this option if you plan to schedule unattended reports to support the SRS subscription feature.

▶ **Windows Integrated Security**—SRS uses the credentials of the user executing the report to authenticate to the data source.

▶ **Credentials are not required**—You can select this option if you do not need to restrict access to the reporting data.

Figure 18.5 shows the Data Source Authentication tab configured to store Windows account credentials in the report server database and allow the use of delegation. Delegation enables the server to use the credentials to connect to additional systems if required.

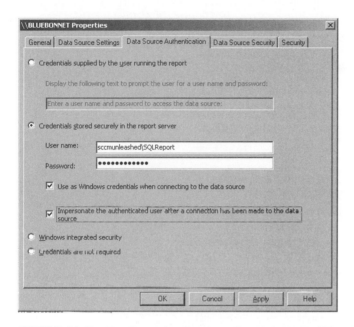

FIGURE 18.5   The Reporting Services Properties page Data Source Authentication tab

The remaining tabs specify SRS security settings. Chapter 20 discusses SRS security.

CAUTION

Reestablishing Console Report Links When Replacing a Reporting Services Point

If you enable the report option to Use Reporting Services Reports for Admin console report links and later remove the default reporting services point, console report links no longer work. To avoid this problem, select the report option to use classic reporting for console report links or specify a different default reporting services point prior to removing the reporting services point. You can reenable this option after you configure the new reporting services point. The "Console Reporting Links" section of this chapter discusses report options.

Copying ConfigMgr Classic Reports to SQL Reporting Services

You must copy your existing classic reports to Reporting Services because establishing SRS does not automatically generate these reports. To copy ConfigMgr classic reports to Reporting Services, perform the following steps:

1. Expand the Configuration Manager console tree to System Center Configuration Manager -> Site Database -> Computer Management -> Reporting -> Reporting Services. Right-click the reporting services point server, and choose the option to Copy Reports to Reporting Services.

2. On the Data Source Settings page, enter the site database server name and database name from which you will copy the reports. Figure 18.6 displays the Data Source Settings page for the Bluebonnet server and the SMS_CEN database.

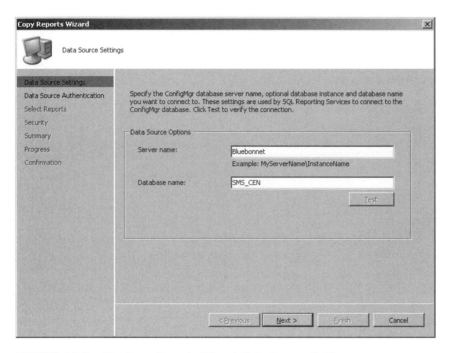

FIGURE 18.6   The Copy Reports Wizard Data Source Settings page

3. On the Data Source Authentication page, choose the option that Reporting Services uses to authenticate to the data source. By default, the data source authentication you configured on the report server Properties page is used. If you select the credentials stored securely in the report server option, you need to reenter the password to complete this dialog box.

4. The Select Reports page, shown in Figure 18.7, allows you to choose the reports you want to copy to SRS. You can include any custom reports you created in addition to those reports supplied with Configuration Manager.

5. The Security page allows you to modify the security settings for the copied reports. By default, the reports inherit the security from the SRS report folder. Chapter 20 discusses SRS security.

6. The Summary page displays the options you selected. Click Next to initiate the copy operation. The wizard now displays the progress for copying each report, as shown in Figure 18.8.

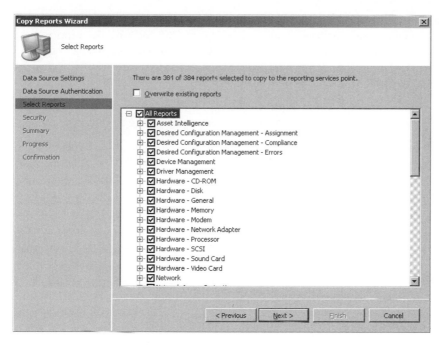

FIGURE 18.7   The Copy Reports Wizard Data Select Reports page

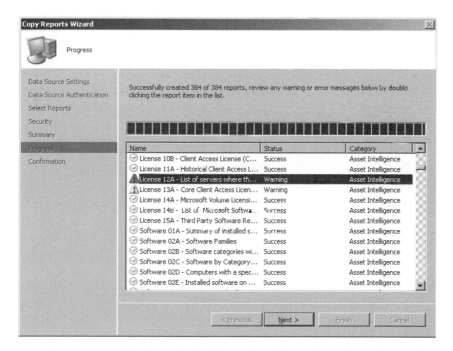

FIGURE 18.8   The Copy Reports Wizard Copy Progress page

You can double-click each item showing a warning or error status to review the associated messages. The warnings displayed in Figure 18.8 indicate the report descriptions have been truncated to conform to the SRS maximum of 512 characters. Click Next to view a confirmation page displaying the overall results of the Copy Reports Wizard.

After copying the reports to SRS, you can use the ConfigMgr console to view and administer both types of reports. You can also view either type of report using a web browser, such as Microsoft Internet Explorer (IE).

Report Categories

Microsoft provides more than 300 ready-made reports that you can use directly or modify to meet your reporting requirements. Table 18.1 shows the report categories and the number of reports in each category available with ConfigMgr 2007 R2.

TABLE 18.1   Predefined Reports Available in ConfigMgr R2

Report Category	Number of Reports
Asset Intelligence	70
Desired Configuration Management – Assignment	2
Desired Configuration Management – Compliance	17
Desired Configuration Management – Errors	6
Device Management	18
Driver Management	13
Hardware – CD-ROM	4
Hardware – Disk	8
Hardware – General	2
Hardware – Memory	5
Hardware – Modem	3
Hardware – Network Adapter	3
Hardware – Processor	5
Hardware – SCSI	3
Hardware – Sound Card	3
Hardware – Video Card	3
Network	6
Network Access Protection	13
Operating System	9

TABLE 18.1   Predefined Reports Available in ConfigMgr R2

Report Category	Number of Reports
SMS Site – Client Information	21
SMS Site – Discovery and Inventory Information	10
SMS Site – General	2
SMS Site – Server Information	3
Software – Companies and Products	11
Software – Files	5
Software Distribution – Advertisement Status	8
Software Distribution – Advertisements	4
Software Distribution – Collections	3
Software Distribution – Packages	9
Software Metering	13
Software Updates – A. Compliance	9
Software Updates – B. Deployment Management	8
Software Updates – C. Deployment States	7
Software Updates – D. Scan	4
Software Updates – E. Troubleshooting	4
Software Updates – F. Distribution Status for SMS 2003 Clients	2
State Migration	3
Status Messages	12
Status Messages – Audit	4
Task Sequence – Advertisement Status	11
Task Sequence – Advertisements	11
Task Sequence – Progress	5
Task Sequence – References	1
Upgrade Assessment – Windows Vista	4
Upgrade Assessment – Windows XP	2
Users	3
Virtual Applications	7
Wake on LAN	5

18

Chapter 10, "The Configuration Manager Console," discusses viewing classic and SRS reports.

Console Reporting Links

In addition to the report viewing functionality found under the ConfigMgr console's Reporting subtree, Microsoft provides a number of links throughout the console to reports relevant to the task at hand. As an example, the Software Distribution home page found under Configuration Manager -> Site Database -> Computer Management -> Software Distribution presents links to several reports related to software distribution. Perform the following steps to configure the behavior of these links:

1. Right-click the System Center Configuration Manager -> Site Database node in the Configuration Manager console tree, and choose Report Options.

2. The Report Options dialog box provides check boxes to use SRS for the ConfigMgr console report links and to open reports in a new window. By default, report links open inside the console window and use the classic reporting engine. If you have multiple reporting points or reporting services points, you can also use this dialog box to specify which site systems to use when launching reports from the console. Figure 18.9 displays the Report Options dialog box.

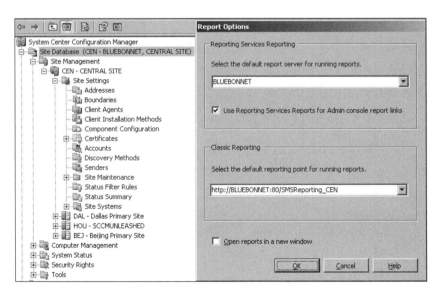

FIGURE 18.9   The Report Options dialog box used to set options for console report links

Relational Database Concepts

The heart of each report is a Structured Query Language (SQL) statement that retrieves data from the site database. SQL is the standard language for managing and querying relational databases. If you are not familiar with the basic concepts of relational databases and the SQL language, it is worth taking some time to learn about them. You don't need to be a SQL expert to administer ConfigMgr, but to get the most out of the product, it helps to know a little SQL. If you are already familiar with SQL, you might want to skip the rest of this section and proceed directly to the "Available Reports and Use Cases" section in this chapter.

Database Tables

A relational database management system (RDBMS) such as Microsoft SQL Server organizes data into logical storage containers called *tables*. You can think of a table as being similar to a spreadsheet, with data arranged in rows and columns. Table 18.2 shows a simple example of a database table.

TABLE 18.2   A Database Table Showing Available Cars

Stock Number	Color	Body Style	Engine Type
12345	Blue	Coupe	4-Cyl
12350	Red	Convertible	V-6
12399	Black	Sedan	V-6
12401	Blue	Sedan	4-Cyl

Database Views

Database developers use *views* to gather data from one or more tables and present that data to users. Using views gives developers the ability to choose which data to make available and how to arrange and format that data, without needing to reorganize the underlying tables. For the purpose of developing reports, views are essentially equivalent to tables. Microsoft provides an extensive set of views in the Configuration Manager database. Chapter 3, "Looking Inside Configuration Manager," discusses these views. The reports Microsoft provides in Configuration Manager are based on the database views, and you should use these views wherever possible when designing or customizing reports.

> **CAUTION**
>
> **Working with the Site Server Database**
>
> Many ConfigMgr administrators already have some degree of familiarity with the site server database, which is the repository of all data used by ConfigMgr. Microsoft strongly suggests using the look-but-don't-touch approach, as direct modification of the database is not supported and might render your site unusable.
>
> Microsoft provides views to use when developing queries and reports because the underlying table structure might change from version to version, and even from one service pack to another. Building queries that pull data directly from the base tables is not recommended because those queries might not work in a future version of ConfigMgr.

The Select Statement

The SQL language contains a rich set of statements for manipulating data and managing databases. For reporting purposes, it is necessary to look at only one statement of the SQL language, the SELECT statement. The SELECT statement retrieves data from a database. The SELECT statement is an extremely powerful and flexible language construct, and this chapter covers some of its basic features.

In its most basic form, the SELECT statement looks like

```
SELECT select_list FROM table_source
```

Table_source specifies the database tables or views from which the data will be retrieved, and the *select_list* is the list of columns you want to retrieve. As an example, if the data presented in Table 18.2 were stored in a table named cars, you would use the following statement to retrieve the stock number, color, and body style of the available cars:

```
SELECT [stock number], color, [body style] FROM cars
```

Notice the column names containing spaces are enclosed in square brackets []. The brackets also allow you to include SQL reserved words in your column names if you choose to do so. The preceding query would return all the data shown in Table 18.2 except the engine type.

The WHERE clause   You can limit the results of your SELECT statement to rows meeting specific criteria by adding a WHERE clause to your statement. As an example, the statement

```
SELECT [stock number], color, [body style] FROM cars WHERE [Engine Type] = 'V-6'
```

returns only the rows for cars with V-6 engines. Table 18.3 shows the results of this statement.

TABLE 18.3   The Result Set from the SELECT Statement Example

Stock Number	Color	Body Style
12350	Red	Convertible
12399	Black	Sedan

Table Joins   Database platforms such as Microsoft SQL Server are called *relational databases* because they take advantage of relationships in the data to reduce redundant storage and provide more flexibility in working with the data. If the cars in the cars sample table are rental vehicles, for example, you can use a separate table to store the rental history of each vehicle without duplicating all the information in the cars table each time a vehicle is rented. Table 18.4 shows a portion of the rentals table.

Now suppose you want to see the rental information for blue cars for the week ending 11/22/2008. Use the following SQL statement to retrieve that information, using both tables:

```
SELECT c.[stock number], c.[body style], r.CustNo AS [Customer Number], r.[Date],
(r.MilesOut - r. MilesIn) AS [Miles Driven]
FROM cars c INNER JOIN rentals r ON cars.[stock number] = rentals.[stock number]
WHERE c.color = 'Blue' AND r.[Date] BETWEEN '11/16/2008' AND '11/23/2008'
```

TABLE 18.4   Rentals Table Entries – Week Ending 11/22/2008

Stock Number	CustNo	Date	MilesOut	MilesIn
12345	7741	11/16/2008	12105	12200
12399	8806	11/17/2008	21241	21249
12345	14101	11/19/2008	12200	12233
12350	14102	11/19/2008	8888	8903
12399	9364	11/20/2008	21249	21304
12401	14103	11/21/2008	24808	24831

The key to this statement is the INNER JOIN clause, which causes this SELECT statement to pull only the data from the rows in the two tables where the stock numbers match. The results of this statement are displayed in Table 18.5.

TABLE 18.5   Blue Car Rentals–Week Ending 11/22/2008

Stock Number	Customer Number	Body Style	Date	Miles Driven
12345	7741	Coupe	11/16/2008	95
12345	14101	Coupe	11/19/2008	33
12401	14103	Sedan	11/21/2008	23

This covers enough SQL syntax to understand the SQL statements used in ConfigMgr reports. This chapter introduces several other details of the SELECT statement as necessary, but even so, it barely scratches the surface of what is possible with the SELECT statement and other features of the SQL language. The Microsoft SQL Server implementation of SQL, known as *Transact-SQL*, is fully documented in the Transact-SQL Reference, available online at http://msdn.microsoft.com/en-us/library/ms189826.aspx. You may also want to read *Microsoft SQL Server 2005 Unleashed* (Sams, 2006) for additional information regarding SQL Server 2005.

Available Reports and Use Cases

The next several sections discuss a number of the report categories previously listed in Table 18.1 and their use in understanding your environment and supporting your ConfigMgr solution. Out of the box, these predefined reports are available only as classic ConfigMgr reports, although you can easily make these reports available through SRS as well. The process of migrating reports to SRS is briefly described in the "Copying ConfigMgr Classic Reports to SQL Reporting Services" section of this chapter, and Chapter 10 discusses how to view both classic and SRS reports.

Reporting on Inventory and Discovery Data

One of the most valuable and often overlooked features of ConfigMgr is the data it gathers about your network and Windows environment. This section looks at some of the reports in the Hardware, Software, Operating System, and Network categories listed in Table 18.1 and how they use ConfigMgr inventory and discovery data.

Computer Information for a Specific Computer

One of the most basic ConfigMgr reports provided by Microsoft is the Computer information for a specific computer report. Figure 18.10 displays the output of this report for the Bluebonnet system.

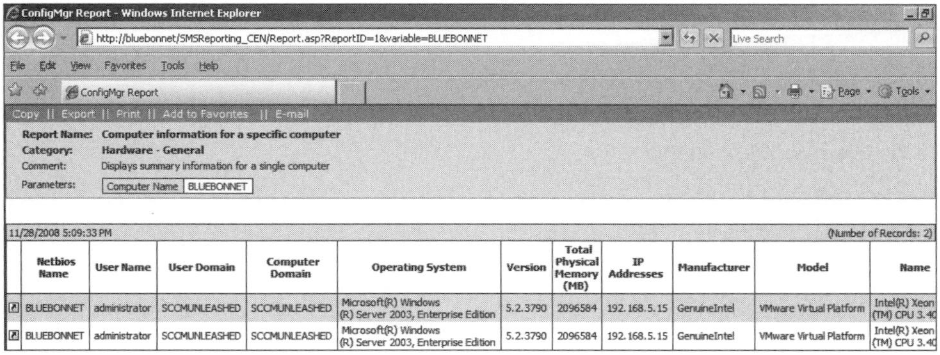

FIGURE 18.10   The **Computer information for a specific computer** report for BLUEBONNET

Let's look at the details of how this report is constructed. From the System Center Configuration Manager -> Site Database -> Computer Management -> Reporting -> Reports node of the Configuration Manager console tree, you can right-click the report and choose Properties to view and edit the report properties. Figure 18.11 displays the General tab of the report's Properties page.

The General tab shows the report's name, category, and the optional comment associated with the report. This tab also displays the SQL statement on which the report is based and provides an option to edit the SQL statement. Clicking on the Edit SQL Statement button launches the Query Builder. Figure 18.12 displays the SQL statement for the Computer information for a specific computer report in the Query Builder. The "Customizing Configuration Manager Reports" section discusses the Query Builder interface in more detail. Notice that the Display in Computer Details check box is enabled. The "Viewing Computer Details" section of this chapter shows how the Computer Details page displays data from this report.

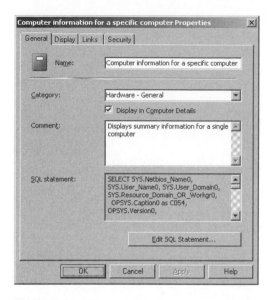

FIGURE 18.11   The **Computer information for a specific computer** report General Properties

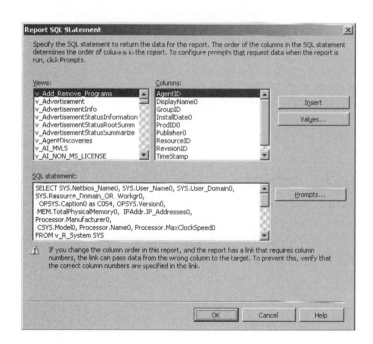

FIGURE 18.12   The Query Builder interface displaying the SQL statement for the **Computer information for a specific computer** report

The SQL statement for the **Computer information for a specific computer** report is as follows:

```
SELECT SYS.Netbios_Name0, SYS.User_Name0, SYS.User_Domain0,
SYS.Resource_Domain_OR_Workgr0,
  OPSYS.Caption0 as C054, OPSYS.Version0,
  MEM.TotalPhysicalMemory0,  IPAddr.IP_Addresses0, Processor.Manufacturer0,
  CSYS.Model0, Processor.Name0, Processor.MaxClockSpeed0
FROM v_R_System SYS
  LEFT JOIN  v_RA_System_IPAddresses IPAddr on SYS.ResourceID = IPAddr.ResourceID
  LEFT JOIN  v_GS_X86_PC_MEMORY MEM on SYS.ResourceID = MEM.ResourceID
  LEFT JOIN  v_GS_COMPUTER_SYSTEM CSYS on SYS.ResourceID = CSYS.ResourceID
  LEFT JOIN  v_GS_PROCESSOR Processor  on Processor.ResourceID = SYS.ResourceID
  LEFT JOIN v_GS_OPERATING_SYSTEM OPSYS on SYS.ResourceID=OPSYS.ResourceID
  WHERE SYS.Netbios_Name0 = @variable
  ORDER BY SYS.Netbios_Name0, SYS.Resource_Domain_OR_Workgr0
```

Here's how the statement functions:

▶ The SELECT list specifies the columns that displayed in the report; for example, SYS.Nebios_Name0 is the Nebios_Name0 column from the view v_R_System, to which the SQL statement assigns the alias SYS. The report rendering engine reformats the column header to NetBIOS Name.

▶ The data is pulled from six resource views joined together on their ResourceID. Microsoft uses the ResourceID column in each of the views to identify the computer system that each data record represents. As Chapter 3 discusses, views with the v_R or v_RA prefix represent discovery data, and those with the v_GS prefix represent inventory data.

▶ The LEFT JOIN is used in this query so that partial results are returned even if some of the requested data is not available. As an example, if the discovery data in the System and System IPAddresses views is available but the inventory data is not, the report displays the discovery data. If an INNER JOIN were used, no data would be returned unless all the views contained the corresponding ResourceID. The join also explains why there are two essentially identical records in the report. The computer has two processors; therefore, the join on v_GS_PROCESSOR matches two distinct rows. A record will be returned for each of these rows.

Many ConfigMgr reports prompt the user to supply one or more parameters at run-time. For example, the **Computer information for a specific computer** report requires the user to enter the computer name. Chapter 10 describes how to enter these values. To view details behind this prompt, click the Prompts button on the Query Builder screen (Figure 18.12), then right-click the Computer Name prompt, and choose Properties. Figure 18.13 shows the properties for the Computer Name prompt.

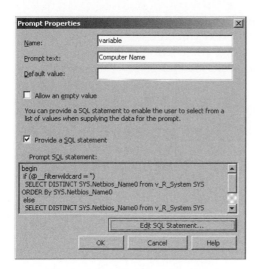

FIGURE 18.13   The Computer Name Prompt Properties page

CAUTION

Use Caution When Creating Joins

Using the wrong type of join or joining views on the wrong column can cause the query to retrieve large amounts of data, which is likely to cause your reports to time out and might create an excessive load on your Report Server and Site Database.

The Name text box on Prompt Properties page contains the name variable, which indicates that the prompted value populates the @variable parameter. This parameter appears in the WHERE clause of the report SQL statement (WHERE SYS.Netbios_Name0 = @variable). Chapter 10 describes the Report Viewer and shows how you can click the Values button to retrieve a list of available values from the site database for a prompted parameter. To edit the query that returns this list, click the Edit SQL statement at the bottom of the Prompt Properties page displayed in Figure 18.13. The query for the Computer Name prompt is

```
Begin
 if (@__filterwildcard = '')
  SELECT DISTINCT SYS.Netbios_Name0 from v_R_System SYS
  ORDER By SYS.Netbios_Name0
 else
  SELECT DISTINCT SYS.Netbios_Name0 from v_R_System SYS
  WHERE SYS.Netbios_Name0 like @__filterwildcard
  ORDER By SYS.Netbios_Name0
End
```

18

If you entered any text in the Computer Name text box before clicking the Values button, the @__filterwildcard variable represents the text you entered. This value is used to match only the values that are "like" the text string you entered. The *like* operator is a standard SQL relational operator that supports wildcard matching.

Returning to the Properties page for the **Computer information for a specific computer** report and clicking the Link tab displays the information shown in Figure 18.14.

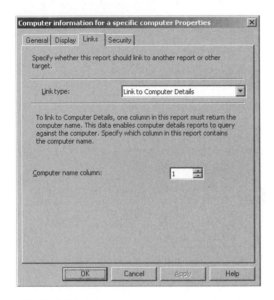

FIGURE 18.14   **Computer information for a specific computer** report Properties page Link tab shows a Link to the Computer Details.

This page indicates that the report contains a link to the Computer Details page for the computer named in column 1 of the report.

TIP

Using ConfigMgr Reports in Spreadsheets

As with any web page, you can place hyperlinks to your Configuration Manager reports in email messages, Word documents, and so on. One way you might want to use reports on specific computers is to include them in any spreadsheets you maintain with system information. To add links to the **Computer information for a specific computer** to an Excel spreadsheet, add a column to your sheet, and enter a link similar to the one here to the first cell of that column.

```
=HYPERLINK("http://<Reporting_URL>/Report.asp?ReportID=1&variable="&xxxx
,"ConfigMgr Data")
```

<Reporting_URL> is the URL of your ConfigMgr reporting point and *xxxx* is the cell containing the NetBIOS name of the computer in the initial row. Now, copy the cell and paste it into the rest of the column.

Viewing Computer Details

You might have noticed the small square containing an arrow at the beginning of each row of the report shown earlier in Figure 18.10. This is the link to the Computer Details page. Figure 18.15 displays the Computer Details page for the Bluebonnet computer.

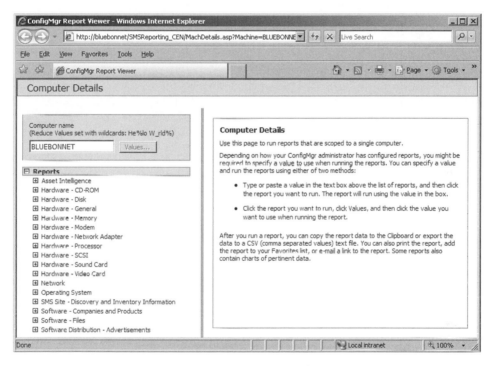

FIGURE 18.15   Computer Details page for BLUEBONNET

The tree control in the left pane displays the report categories for all reports that have been linked to Computer Details. Figure 18.11 showed the Display in Computer Details check box enabled for the Computer information for a specific computer report, and that the report category is Hardware – General.

When you expand the Computer Details Hardware – General node, you see the Computer information for a specific computer report for the selected computer. Computer Details provides convenient access to the additional reports including hardware, software, and

operating system (OS) information; data about the ConfigMgr client and software advertised to the client; and asset intelligence data. For example, Figure 18.16 shows how you
can quickly access information about Windows services from the Computer Details page.

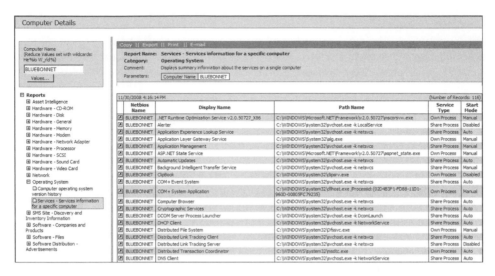

FIGURE 18.16   The **Service Information** report displayed in BLUEBONNET Computer Details

The Computer Details drill down interface is available in classic reporting but is not
included with the SRS reports.

Finding Reports That Link to Computer Details

To display information about which reports contain links to Computer Details, perform
the following steps:

1. Expand the ConfigMgr console tree to System Center Configuration Manager ->
   Site Database -> Computer Management -> Reporting.

2. Right-click the Reports node and choose View -> Add/Remove columns from the
   context menu.

3. In the Add/Remove columns dialog box, select Status Message Detail Source
   from the available columns list.

4. Click the Add button to move the selection to the displayed columns list, and
   then click OK.

You now see the Machine Source column in the list of reports.

▶ A value of True in the Machine Source column indicates a report that contains
   links to the Computer Details page.

▶ A value of False indicates there is no link to Computer Details in the report.

You can sort on this column by double-clicking the column header, which moves all
reports with Machine Details to the bottom of the list. Similarly, you can add the

Machine Detail column to display which reports are available from the machine details control. A value of True in the Machine Source column indicates a report that appears in the Computer Details page, and a value of False indicates that the report does not appear in Computer Details.

Reporting on Computers Based on Specific Criteria

One of the most useful applications of ConfigMgr inventory data is to report on computers matching specific characteristics. Some typical uses for this type of report are to identify machines needing hardware upgrades, find all computers with a specific software product installed, or enumerate the machines on a specific Internet Protocol (IP) subnet. An example of a report commonly used for computer maintenance is the Computers with low free disk space report shown in Figure 18.17. In this case, specify **2000** MB at the Disk Space Amount prompt.

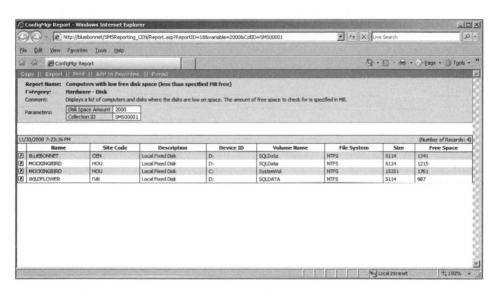

FIGURE 18.17   **Computers with low free disk space** report

Figure 18.18 shows another commonly used report: Computers with a specific product name and version. This report is an example of the Software – Companies and Products category. Most of the reports in this category use property data that the ConfigMgr software inventory process extracts from the file headers—the same data that you view when you right-click a file and view the product properties entered by the software vendors. This data might be more or less complete, depending on the information the vendor has chosen to supply. The reports in the Software – Files category focus primarily on file system information—the information you would see in a directory listing in Windows Explorer or at the command prompt.

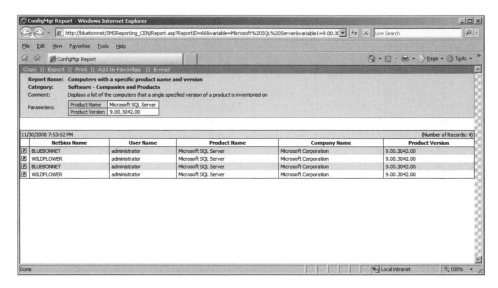

FIGURE 18.18   Computers with a specific version of Microsoft SQL Server

Reporting on Networks and Users

You can also use ConfigMgr 2007 to report on network segments and users in your environment:

▶ Network reports list the IP subnets in your environment, enumerate the client computers and other devices on each subnet, and allow you to drill down to see detailed information about the networking components of each client computer.

▶ User reports give an overview of the users in your AD domains.

▶ The Computers for a specific user name report can help identify computers used by a specific user, although it is dependent on the user having been the last person to log on at the time inventory ran.

Some of the reports in the Network and Users categories require enabling Network Discovery or Active Directory User Discovery to gather the required data.

Reporting on Sites

ConfigMgr reporting can report on your ConfigMgr 2007 hierarchy and sites. Although the SMS Site – General and SMS Site – Server Information report categories together only contain five reports, these reports provide a high-level overview of some of the most important site attributes and site status information. Here are the reports in the SMS Site – General category:

- **Sites by hierarchy with time of last site status update**—As the report description states, this report displays the list of sites in hierarchy order and shows the last time the site status was updated. The ConfigMgr status system does not automatically display a degraded site status in the ConfigMgr console tree when a site has not recently reported any status. This report is therefore a good starting point for checking the health of the hierarchy. Figure 18.19 shows the **Sites by hierarchy with time of last site status update** report.

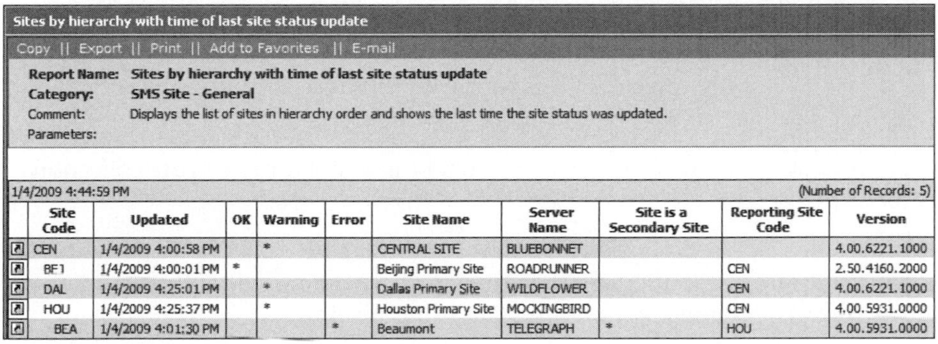
Sites by hierarchy with time of last site status update

Copy || Export || Print || Add to Favorites || E-mail

Report Name: **Sites by hierarchy with time of last site status update**
Category: **SMS Site - General**
Comment: Displays the list of sites in hierarchy order and shows the last time the site status was updated.
Parameters:

1/4/2009 4:44:59 PM (Number of Records: 5)

Site Code	Updated	OK	Warning	Error	Site Name	Server Name	Site is a Secondary Site	Reporting Site Code	Version
CEN	1/4/2009 4:00:58 PM		*		CENTRAL SITE	BLUEBONNET			4.00.6221.1000
BE1	1/4/2009 4:00:01 PM	*			Beijing Primary Site	ROADRUNNER		CEN	2.50.4160.2000
DAL	1/4/2009 4:25:01 PM		*		Dallas Primary Site	WILDFLOWER		CEN	4.00.6221.1000
HOU	1/4/2009 4:25:37 PM		*		Houston Primary Site	MOCKINGBIRD		CEN	4.00.5931.0000
BEA	1/4/2009 4:01:30 PM			*	Beaumont	TELEGRAPH	*	HOU	4.00.5931.0000

FIGURE 18.19 **Sites by hierarchy with time of last site status update** report

- **Computers in a specific site**—This report displays basic information about all computers in the site.

Reports in the SMS Site – Server Information category display the site system roles and provide status information for distribution points and branch distribution points.

Reporting on Configuration Manager Operations

Reporting is an essential part of day-to-day operations in your ConfigMgr sites. You can utilize ConfigMgr reporting to describe the operation of ConfigMgr activities including software distribution, software updates management, device management, software metering, DCM, OSD, and NAP. The next sections discuss several of these areas.

Reporting on Software Distribution

You can use ConfigMgr reports to help you plan, manage, and assess your software distribution services. Here are the report categories Microsoft provides, related to each major step of the software distribution process:

- Software Distribution – Packages
- Software Distribution – Collections
- Software Distribution – Advertisements
- Software Distribution – Advertisement Status

The **All Packages** report provides summary information for all packages available at the site. One of the most challenging aspects of software distribution is ensuring packages are available and up to date at the correct distribution points. ConfigMgr reporting provides a number of reports in this area:

▶ Several reports relating to packages allow you to view information such as all packages on a specific distribution point, distribution status for a particular package, and all active distribution activity.

▶ Two new reports with ConfigMgr 2007 R2 support virtual application distribution, reporting on streaming store distribution status for virtual application packages on a per package and per distribution point basis.

A second challenge in software distribution is ensuring the targeted collections have the correct membership, and the collection's maintenance window schedule does not conflict with the distribution. Here are two reports to assist with this:

▶ The All resources in a specific collection report is useful for reviewing collection membership.

▶ The Maintenance Windows Available to a Particular Client report is useful for planning software distribution and helping you determine whether the maintenance window feature prevented an advertisement from running.

TIP

Evaluating Collection Membership Locally

Although collection membership rules are replicated down the ConfigMgr hierarchy, each primary site evaluates collection membership based on the inventory and discovery data in its local site database. Although the **All resources in a specific collection** report is a useful way to look at collection membership at the site containing your reporting point, keep in mind that collection membership might be evaluated differently at the client's assigned site.

Clients receive policy, including advertisements, from their assigned site. If you troubleshoot a software distribution issue and the client's site does not have a reporting point, you can use the ConfigMgr console to connect directly to the assigned site and view the collection membership as it is evaluated locally.

The Advertisements category includes reports about all advertisements, advertisements based on a particular package, and advertisements to a particular client or collection. These reports help answer questions such as

▶ "Who has a particular package been advertised to?"

▶ "What software has been advertised to a user's machine?"

The Advertisement Status category helps you assess the ultimate results of software distribution and troubleshoot any issues with advertised software. This set of reports provides an excellent example of ConfigMgr reporting's drill through functionality. The All advertisements report provides an overview of your ConfigMgr advertisements. From the All advertisements report, you can drill down into the status of an individual advertisement by clicking the link in the left column. This link opens the Status of a specific advertisement report, which shows the count and percentage of clients for each acceptance status and status. Clients might have the following acceptance statuses:

▶ Accepted

▶ Expired

▶ No Status

▶ Rejected

Those clients that have accepted the advertisement also report a last status, which can have the following values:

▶ Accepted – No Further Status

▶ Cancelled

▶ Failed

▶ No Status

▶ Reboot Pending

▶ Retrying

▶ Running

▶ Succeeded

▶ Waiting

For each status category, the Status of a specific advertisement report provides a link to the All system resources for a specific advertisement in a specific state report, which lists the systems in the specified state and provides some system and status details. Finally, the All system resources for a specific advertisement in a specific state report provides a link to the Advertisement status messages for a particular client and advertisement report for each system, which displays the status messages in detail. Together these reports comprise a powerful tool for tracking the progress of your advertisements. The "Creating Classic Reports" section in this chapter provides an example of a report you can use to view the drill through sequence starting from a specified report.

For advertised task sequences, reports in the Task Sequences categories provide additional details on the progress and status of the task sequences. The Task Sequence – References report also gives the packages references by each task sequence.

ConfigMgr 2007 R2 adds the Virtual Applications report category, including reports on software you distribute as virtual applications using the new R2 application virtualization capabilities. These reports provide a comprehensive summary of your virtual applications and information about virtual application launch failures.

Reporting on Software Updates
ConfigMgr includes an extensive and highly organized set of reports for tracking software updates. Here are the categories used for the software updates reports:

▶ The Compliance category contains nine reports that display compliance information on a per system, per product, and per update basis, and overall compliance summaries.

▶ The Deployment Management category provides eight reports on the contents of your deployments and the systems they target.

▶ The Deployment States category includes seven reports on the state of each deployment and on specific systems. Microsoft defines 24 possible deployment states, such as installed, not required, and various detailed pending, downloading, or failure states.

▶ The Scan category consists of four reports with details of the last time your clients were scanned, and the scan results.

▶ The Troubleshooting category provides four reports on scan errors and deployment errors that you can use to quickly identify problems with your software update services.

▶ The Distribution Status for SMS 2003 Clients category contains two reports on the status of deployments to SMS 2003 clients in your sites.

ConfigMgr reporting is one of the major advantages for using ConfigMgr software updates over a standalone WSUS implementation in enterprise environments.

Reporting on Operating System Deployment

You can use reporting to help plan and track your OS deployment operations. Reports you can use to support OS deployment include the following:

▶ Upgrade Assessment reports for Windows Vista specify the systems meeting the minimum or recommended requirements for Vista upgrades, and those that do not.

▶ Driver Management reports list the drivers in your packages and boot images, match drivers to computers and collections, and display driver installation failures.

▶ State Migration reports track the activity of your state migration points and the details of state migration for individual computers.

▶ Some of the report categories used with software distribution also provide visibility into OS deployment operations. The Task Sequence – Progress category includes the Progress of OS deployment task sequences report. You can use additional reports in the Task Sequence and Software Distribution categories to view details and status information for advertisements and distribution operations supporting OS distribution.

Reporting on Desired Configuration Management

Reporting is an essential part of DCM. Reports in the Desired Configuration Management – Compliance category are at the heart of an effective DCM implementation:

▶ You can use the compliance reports at a high level to assess regulatory compliance or compliance with internal standards.

▶ You can use drill-through functionality to view details about compliance issues that you can use to guide your remediation efforts.

As you deploy configuration baselines, you want to view reports such as the **Summary compliance by configuration baseline** report to see an overview of how your systems measure up against the baseline. From this report, you can select a configuration item you are interested in and drill down to the **Compliance details for a Configuration baseline by configuration item** report. You then see the compliance for the selected configuration item by system and can use the link for an individual computer to view the **Summary compliance for a configuration item by computer** report. Finally, you can open the links for **Non-compliance details for a configuration item on a computer** report to view the details of compliance issues related to the selected item.

DCM reporting provides flexibility in viewing compliance data. An alternative to analyzing compliance with respect to specific baselines and configuration items is to begin with the **Summary compliance for a collection by computer** report and analyze compliance on a per system basis.

While reports in the Compliance category help manage compliance in your environment, DCM reporting provides two additional categories to assist with managing DCM itself:

▶ The Desired Configuration Management – Assignment category displays the baseline assigned to a collection or an individual computer.

▶ You can use reports in the Desired Configuration Management – Errors category to identify and evaluate errors for troubleshooting DCM.

TIP

Using SQL Reporting Services to Provide Historical Data

The ConfigMgr database maintains historical data for some items, such as inventory, but not for others such as DCM. One way to maintain a history for DCM baseline compliance or other items that do not maintain history is to create an SRS subscription delivering reports to a file share using incrementally named files. The "Creating SQL Reporting Services Subscriptions" section in this chapter provides an example of this type of subscription.

Reporting on Other Configuration Manager Operations

In addition to those reports in the preceding sections, Microsoft provides report categories to assist with implementing the following ConfigMgr features:

▶ **Device Management**—Reports in the Device Management category provide details about devices connected to client computers via ActiveSync, device client agents, and device issues such as low battery state and low disk space.

▶ **Network Access Protection**—An important planning step for deploying NAP includes reporting on NAP-capable and NAP-upgradable computers, then using the **List of computers that would be non-compliant based on selected software** updates report to assess the impact of enforcing NAP in your environment. After deploying NAP, you can use reports to list NAP policies and view remediation details.

▶ **Software Metering**—ConfigMgr gathers usage data for any application you specified in software metering rules. Reports on software metering data allow you to verify license compliance and analyze usage trends to help you plan software purchases. Reporting on computers with a metered program installed that have not run the program since a specified date can help reclaim licenses by identifying applications that are not in use and can be removed.

▶ **Wake On LAN**—You can report on Wake On LAN (WOL) activity in your ConfigMgr environment, including a history of WOL activity, pending activity and errors that have occurred.

Status Message Reporting

Status messages are one of the primary troubleshooting tools in ConfigMgr 2007. ConfigMgr server components and client systems generate status messages to report on errors, warnings, or important milestone activities that take place during ConfigMgr operations. You have already seen how reports such as the Advertisement status messages for a particular client and advertisement report display status message information related to particular ConfigMgr operations (see the "Reporting on Software Distribution" section in this chapter). Reports in the Status Message category provide a more comprehensive view of the status of your ConfigMgr sites, site components, and computer systems. Here are some reports you can use to provide an overview of how your site is functioning:

▶ Count errors in the last 12 hours

▶ Component messages for the last 12 hours

▶ Fatal errors (by component)

▶ Last 1000 messages for a specific server component

You can also use status messages reports to view status information about the computers in your hierarchy and about specific computers. Some reports that assess computer status include the following:

▶ Fatal errors (by computer name)

▶ Last 1000 messages for a specific computer (Errors)

▶ Last 1000 messages for a specific computer (Errors and Warnings)

A particularly valuable report is All messages for a specific message ID. Microsoft Knowledge Base (KB) articles and other documentation often refer to message IDs to look for when troubleshooting specific problems or confirming normal operational milestones.

The **All messages for a specific message ID** report helps you quickly locate all occurrences of a specific message in your environment.

Reports in the Status Messages – Audit category allow you to track the usage of these sensitive operations that touch ConfigMgr clients:

▶ Remote Control

▶ Out of Band Management Console Activity

Both types of operations allow administrative users to interact directly with client systems. You can view reports on all audited activity or on activity by a specific user. Audit reports also include console activity such as adding, modifying, or deleting ConfigMgr objects.

NOTE

Effect of Status Filter Rules and Maintenance Tasks on Audit Reports

When a ConfigMgr site receives a status message, it processes the message according to settings specified in the site's status filter rules. Chapter 5, "Network Design," discusses the use of status filter rules to reduce the volume of network traffic due to status message replication, and Chapter 21, "Backup, Recovery, and Maintenance," describes how to configure status filter rules. The Write audit messages to the site database and specify the period after which the user can delete the messages status filter rule is enabled by default and determines the handling of audit messages. Using the default settings for this rule, the ConfigMgr status message system writes all audit messages to the site database with a minimum retention period of 180 days and does not replicate audit messages to the parent site.

For reporting purposes, verify that the rules are configured so that all status messages in the audit reports are replicated to the reporting site and written to the site database at that site. The Delete Aged Status Messages site maintenance task removes status messages from the site database when the minimum retention period has expired. If you have this task enabled, you should make sure that the minimum retention period specified on the status filter rule's Actions tab complies with your organization's audit retention requirements. Chapter 21 discusses site maintenance tasks.

18

Viewing Status Message Details

Figure 18.14 previously showed how to use the report Properties Links tab to link a report to the Computer Details for each client machine displayed in the report. On the same tab, you can choose the Link to Status Message Details option. This option provides a link next to each row of the report, which opens the details of the status message associated with that row. On the Links tab, you must specify the column that contains the status message record ID, which uniquely identifies the specific message. An example of a report that links to status message details is the **All messages for a specific message ID** report displayed in Figure 18.20.

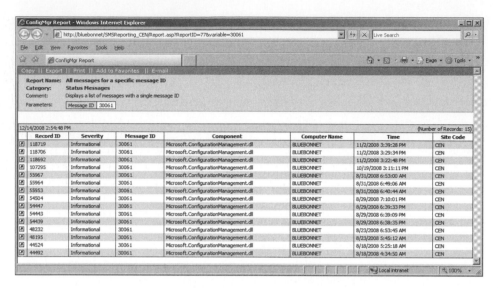

FIGURE 18.20   The **All messages for a specific message ID** report for message ID 30061

The first row of the report in Figure 18.20 displays summary information for the status message with record ID 118719. Clicking the link next to this row displays detailed information for that event occurrence. Figure 18.21 displays the details for this status message.

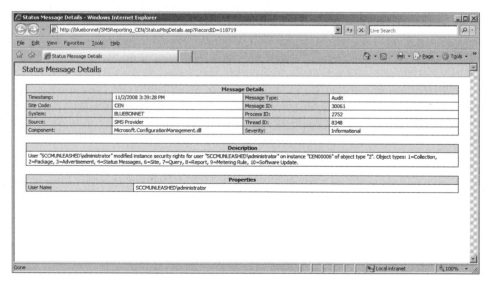

FIGURE 18.21   Status message details for a particular occurrence of message 30061

The description provides sufficient information to tell us that the Administrator account changed the permissions on the package with ID CEN00006, which turns out to be

Adobe_Reader_Adobe_9_MNT. The message does not describe what specific permissions were changed.

Finding Reports that Link to Status Message Details

To display information about which reports contain links to status message details, perform the following steps:

1. Expand the ConfigMgr console tree to System Center Configuration Manager -> Site Database -> Computer Management -> Reporting.

2. Right-click the Reports node and choose View -> Add/Remove columns from the context menu.

3. In the Add/Remove columns dialog box, select Status Message Detail Source from the available columns list.

4. Click the Add button to move the selection to the displayed columns list, and then click OK.

You now see the Status Message Detail Source column in the list of reports with a value of True for reports that implement this feature and False for those reports that do not. You can sort on this column by double-clicking the column header, which moves all reports with Status Message Details to the bottom of the list.

Client Status Reporting

The effectiveness of your ConfigMgr-based solutions is highly dependent on the client deployment coverage and the health of the ConfigMgr client components on your managed systems. All releases of ConfigMgr 2007 provide a variety of reports that use client inventory, discovery, and status message data to report on client operations and functionality. ConfigMgr 2007 R2 includes a new client status reporting (CSR) application, which gathers additional data from the management point and the clients themselves to provide enhanced client status reporting capabilities. The next sections look at how you can use both the standard reporting capabilities and the new features of R2 to help manage client operations and detect problems with client functioning.

Using Standard ConfigMgr Reports for Client Management

You can use many of the reports in the Client Information and Discovery and Inventory report categories to track your client deployment and management operations and help troubleshoot problems with potential or existing clients.

The SMS Site – Client Information report category includes a number of reports that can help you plan and manage the client deployment at your sites. Here are some particularly useful reports for planning purposes:

▶ Computers assigned but not installed for a particular site

▶ Computers with a specific SMS client version

- ▶ Clients incapable of native mode communication

- ▶ Summary information of clients capable of native mode communication

- ▶ Computers with out of band management controllers

Some of the reports specifically designed to help you monitor the status of client deployment operations include the following:

- ▶ Client Deployment Failure

- ▶ Client Deployment Success

- ▶ Client Deployment Status Details

- ▶ Client Assignment Status Details

- ▶ Client Assignment Detailed Status

- ▶ Summary information of clients in native mode

- ▶ Status of client out of band management provisioning

- ▶ Issues by incidence summary

- ▶ Issues by incidence detail for a specified site

TIP

Determining Which Clients Are Ready for Native Mode

The **Clients incapable of native mode communication, Summary information of clients in native mode,** and **Summary information of clients capable of native mode communication** reports provide details on which clients have all certificates required for native mode. Before running these reports, you should run the Sccmnativemodereadiness.exe utility on each client computer to populate the site database with client readiness data. http://technet.microsoft.com/en-us/library/bb680986.aspx describes the Sccmnativemodereadiness.exe utility and provides steps to use ConfigMgr software distribution to assign the utility on client machines.

The Issues by incidence reports show issues reported by clients that connect to fallback status points due to problems communicating with the ConfigMgr site.

The SMS Site – Discovery and Inventory report category includes several reports that you can use to identify problems with existing clients. These reports include the following:

- ▶ Computers not discovered recently (in a specified number of days)

- ▶ Computers not inventoried recently (in a specified number of days)

▶ Clients that have not reported recently (in a specified number of days)

▶ Computers that may share the same SMS Unique ID

Client Status Reporting in Configuration Manager 2007 R2

ConfigMgr 2007 R2 includes a new set of client status reporting tools for adding in-depth data about client status and health to the site database for reporting purposes. In addition to leveraging existing site data, R2 client status reporting pulls data from management points and directly from the clients. Client status reporting uses the following mechanisms to gather this data:

▶ **Client Pulse**—The CSR service connects to the management point, gathers management point logs, and extracts client policy request events. Clients normally request policy from their default management point at regular intervals, every hour by default.

▶ **Client Ping**—The CSR service attempts to ping inactive clients to determine whether the client's name resolves successfully and the client responds to an ICMP (Internet Control Message Protocol) echo request. The service then attempts to connect to the client to check the status of the ConfigMgr client service and the Background Intelligent Transfer Service (BITS). Client ping requires that the clients are configured to respond to ping requests and the CSR service account has administrator rights on the client to connect to the service control manager. Internet-based client management does not support client ping.

To use client status reporting, you must set up a client status reporting point for your ConfigMgr site. The client status reporting point system must be running Windows XP SP 2 or higher, Windows Vista, Windows Server 2003 SP 2 or higher, or Windows Server 2008 (other than Core), with the .NET Framework 2.0 installed. ConfigMgr supports all editions of these operating systems except home editions of Windows XP and Windows Vista.

The client status reporting point does not require the ConfigMgr executive service and therefore is not required to be a ConfigMgr site system. Unlike site system roles, you do not configure the client status reporting point through the ConfigMgr console. Instead, you run ClientStatusReporting.msi from the Client Status Reporting folder of the ConfigMgr 2007 R2 installation media. The Installation Wizard is straightforward and only requires you to accept the license agreement and specify the client status reporting installation path. The Installer package creates a Microsoft ConfigMgr 2007 R2 Client Status Reporting program group with links to the configuration utility and the documentation. To configure client status reporting, perform the following steps:

1. Launch Configure Client Status Reporting from the Microsoft ConfigMgr 2007 R2 Client Status Reporting program group.

2. On the Site Setting tab, specify the site database server, database name, and the client status reporting service logon account. Figure 18.22 shows the Configure Client Status Reporting Site Settings tab.

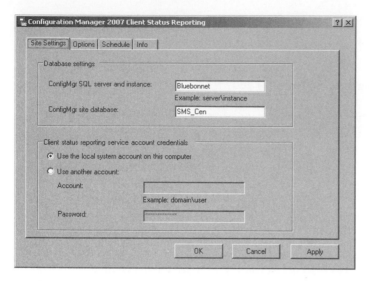

FIGURE 18.22   The Configure Client Status Reporting Site Settings tab

In this example, the CSR tools are installed on the management point server, and the service runs under the local system account, which has administrative access. If the CSR service does not have administrative access on the management point, you need to perform additional steps to configure the management point to support client pulse functionality as described in the CSR documentation in the ConfigMgr help file.

3. On the Configure Client Status Reporting Options tab, select the intervals after which you will consider a client inactive if the site has not received discovery data, inventory, status messages, or policy requests from the client. The default interval is 7 days for each type of client activity. Figure 18.23 shows the Options tab.

4. On the Configure Client Status Schedule tab, specify whether to use client pulse and client ping and the schedule for these actions. You can schedule each of these actions for specific days of the week and specify the time of day for the action to occur. You can also use this tab to specify whether the client status reporting point is for the local site only or for the entire hierarchy. Figure 18.24 shows the Schedule tab.

Asset Intelligence

Microsoft acquired AssetMetrix, an asset management software company, in 2006. They have used the technology from this acquisition to greatly enhance ConfigMgr asset recognition and reporting capabilities.

Microsoft introduced Asset Intelligence (AI) 1.0 functionality in SMS 2003 SP 3. The ConfigMgr 2007 RTM and SP 1 releases have included enhanced functionality with AI 1.1 and 1.5, respectively. This discussion focuses on support for Asset Intelligence 1.5 in ConfigMgr 2007 SP 1. You can find a comparison between the SMS 2003 version and Asset Intelligence in ConfigMgr 2007 at http://searchwindowsserver.techtarget.com/tip/ 0,289483,sid68_gci1301339,00.html, and Microsoft provides a datasheet at

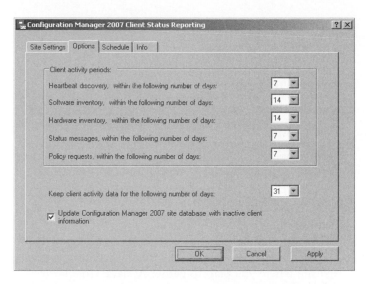

FIGURE 18.23   The Configure Client Status Reporting Options tab

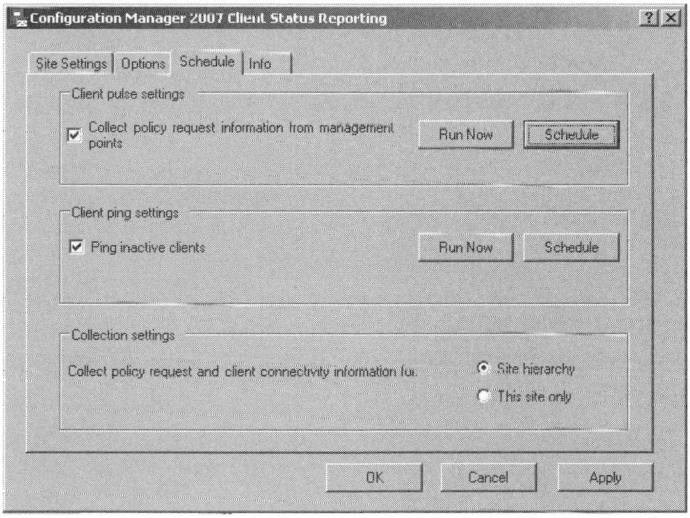

FIGURE 18.24   The Configure Client Status Reporting Schedule tab

http://download.microsoft.com/download/5/9/8/598662ce-61db-474f-80a5-7b1dafc31843/
Configuration%20Manager%20Asset%20Intelligence%20Datasheet.pdf. (These links are
also provided in Appendix B, "Reference URLs.")

ConfigMgr hardware and software inventory gather raw data about the components and
files present on client computer systems. AI matches hardware and software elements to
its extensive catalog of known devices and applications to convert inventory data into
usable information about the assets in your environment. AI also integrates usage and
license data to provide reporting capabilities on how information technology (IT) assets

are used in your environment and compliance with licensing requirements. Here are some questions Asset Intelligence reports can help you answer:

▶ What IT hardware and software assets are deployed in the environment?

▶ Who is using IT assets, and what are the usage patterns and trends?

▶ What changes have occurred in the IT asset base?

▶ How are software licenses and Microsoft Client Access Licenses (CALs) used?

▶ What hardware is compatible with operating system and application software in use or proposed for deployment?

Configuring Asset Intelligence

Asset Intelligence information collection is not enabled by default in ConfigMgr 2007. AI uses specific hardware inventory classes and software metering data to identify and report on various assets. Before enabling AI, you need to enable the hardware inventory agent and software metering agent at each site where you plan to gather AI data. Chapter 8 describes how to enable and configure client agents. To enable AI in ConfigMgr 2007 SP 1, perform the following steps:

1. Expand the Configuration Manager console tree to System Center Configuration Manager -> Site Database -> Computer Management -> Asset Intelligence.

2. Right-click the Asset Intelligence node and choose Edit Asset Intelligence Reporting Class Settings from the context menu.

3. On the Asset Intelligence Reporting Class Settings page, select the reporting classes you want to enable, and then click OK. Figure 18.25 displays this dialog box with the Enable all Asset Intelligence reporting classes option selected. Before making your selection, click the Help button and review the information about which reporting classes are required for each AI report. You can also view the list of reports using data from each class by hovering your mouse pointer over the class name. Enable only the AI reporting classes you need, to avoid increasing computer and network resource usage during the hardware inventory cycle.

Asset Intelligence uses logon events from the local Windows security event log to monitor Client Access License usage. If you plan to use AI to monitor CALs, complete the following tasks:

1. Enable auditing of success logon events on client computers. Generally, you can accomplish this through Active Directory Domain Security Policy. For clients in workgroups or downlevel domains, you need to configure this setting in the local group policy on each system. The help files for your version of Windows describe how to accomplish these tasks.

2. Edit the Configuration.mof file for each ConfigMgr site at which you collect CAL data to add appropriate settings to the CCM_CALTrackConfig WMI data class. The article at http://technet.microsoft.com/en-us/library/cc161947.aspx describes the CCM_CALTrackConfig WMI data class. Chapter 3 discusses editing the Configuration.mof file.

FIGURE 18.25   Enabling all AI reporting classes through the Asset Intelligence Reporting
Class Settings page

One of the most exciting new features in AI 1.5 is the ability to synchronize your Asset
Intelligence catalog with System Center Online. This feature is available only to Microsoft
Software Assurance (SA) customers who carry SA on ConfigMgr. For more information
about the Microsoft Software Assurance program, see http://www.microsoft.com/licensing/
sa/default.mspx. Previous versions of AI provide only a static catalog, which quickly
becomes out of date. In addition to synchronizing with the latest online catalog, SA
customers may submit data about unrecognized software to Microsoft for analysis, upload
custom applications to share with the System Center community, and maintain local
customizations of their own catalog.

To configure AI to synchronize with System Center Online, you must first install and
configure an asset intelligence synchronization point in your ConfigMgr central site. Prior
to installing your AI synchronization point, obtain a System Center Online authentication
certificate file (.pfx) from your Microsoft representative and confirm that the site system
on which you install the synch point can communicate with the Internet on port 443.
Perform the following steps to configure the Synchronization Point site role:

1. Add the asset intelligence synchronization point as a new server role for the appro-
    priate site system. Chapter 8 describes adding site system roles.

2. Enter the path to the certificate file (.pfx) on the New Site Role Wizard Asset
    Intelligence Synchronization Point Connection Settings page, and click Next.

3. Configure the synchronization schedule on the Asset Intelligence Synchronization
    Point Schedule page.

ConfigMgr 2007 SP 1 allows you to import license information from a Microsoft Volume
Licensing Software (MVLS) spreadsheet or custom spreadsheet in the appropriate format.
MVLS customers can obtain this spreadsheet from their software reseller. For information

about creating a custom spreadsheet for non-MVLS license information, see http://technet. microsoft.com/en-us/library/cc431362.aspx. To import license information, perform the following steps:

1. Open the spreadsheet in the same version of Excel used to create it and save the spreadsheet as an .xml file. (You must use Microsoft Office Excel 2003 to convert spreadsheets with the .xls file extension and Microsoft Office Excel 2007 for spreadsheets with the .xlsx extension.)

2. Expand the Configuration Manager console tree to System Center Configuration Manager -> Site Database -> Computer Management -> Asset Intelligence.

3. Right-click the Asset Intelligence node and choose Import Software Licenses from the context menu.

4. Browse to the location of your .xml license file, select the file, and click Finish to complete the License Import Wizard.

Microsoft provides a white paper on Configuration Manager 2007 Asset Intelligence at http://download.microsoft.com/download/d/0/f/d0f027ac-501c-415a-ba28-85c051d57da4/ ConfigMgr%20Asset%20Intelligence%20Whitepaper%20FINAL%20v4.pdf. (This link is also included in Appendix B as a live link.)

Viewing Asset Intelligence Reports

When you configure Asset Intelligence and allow time for the inventory collection process to populate AI data in the site database, you can view AI reports from the Reporting node of the ConfigMgr console similar to viewing any other reports. You can also view AI reports in the console, under System Center Configuration Manager -> Site Database -> Computer Management -> Asset Intelligence -> Asset Intelligence Reports. Within the Asset Intelligence report category, there are three subcategories, each of which provides extensive reporting capabilities:

▶ **Hardware**—Asset Intelligence reports in the Hardware category include reports on upgrade readiness of computers and reports that identify USB (Universal Serial Bus) devices attached to client systems. By recognizing specific hardware devices, AI gives you the capability to report on readiness for OS and application upgrades. Several reports in this category use logon information from the Security event log to report on the users who have logged on to the machine, and attempt to identify the primary user of each computer.

Identifying the primary user of a computer has been an ongoing challenge for SMS and ConfigMgr administrators. While the AI method is not perfect, it is another tool to help meet this challenge. The AI Hardware category also includes reports that detail changes made on client systems.

▶ **Licensing**—By leveraging licensing data along with software inventory data, AI provides extensive reporting capabilities on the licenses you own, license usage, and license expiration. AI licensing reports can help you solve some of the more difficult challenges in license compliance reporting, such as Client Access License (CAL) tracking and identifying Microsoft Developer Network (MSDN) software. You can use reports on per-user and per-device CAL usage to help determine how many client access licenses are in use.

AI can distinguish between different licensing SKUs (stock keeping units) such as retail or MSDN. The terms and conditions specified in MSDN license agreements differ from those in retail licenses, and the ability to recognize MSDN software is essential for determining whether your organization is appropriately and fully utilizing software used under this program. For more information about MSDN, see http:// msdn.microsoft.com/.

Another license compliance challenge is distinguishing between different editions of software such as Microsoft SQL Server. The executable names are the same, for example, for SQL Server Standard Edition and SQL Server Enterprise Edition. AI matches file details with its asset catalog, presenting accurate information on SQL Server editions in your environment.

▶ **Software**—Reports in the AI Software category provide a far more detailed and meaningful picture of the software deployed in your enterprise than reporting on raw software inventory data. AI uses its catalog of more than 300,000 software products and versions to accurately identify applications and provide details about those applications.

AI categorizes software by family, such as application development software, industry-specific software, and software used by system components and peripherals. AI further distinguishes software titles by specific categories such as software for the mining industry or software for educational services. You can also add custom labels to software titles to provide additional information relevant to your business.

All this information is available though AI software reports. AI also provides reports on software configured as auto-start and browser helper applications. AI uses software metering data to report on software usage patterns such as recently used or infrequently used programs.

There is an active TechNet forum on Asset Intelligence at http://social.technet.microsoft. com/Forums/en-US/configmgrai/threads/.

Reporting on Application Compatibility

One of the major challenges of deploying operating system upgrades, service packs, and patches is identifying potential application and hardware compatibility issues and device driver upgrade requirements. To help system administrators address these issues, Microsoft provides the Application Compatibility Toolkit (AppCompat or ACT). The Microsoft ACT connector for Configuration Manager uses AppCompat data to help you plan for Vista and Windows Server 2008 upgrades or service pack deployments for Windows XP and higher versions of Windows. To use the ACT connector, you must complete the following tasks:

1. Download and install the Application Compatibility Toolkit. The ACT toolkit is available from http://technet.microsoft.com/en-us/library/cc507847.aspx.

18

2. Install the ACT connector by running setup from the ConfigMgr 2007 installation media and selecting System Center Configuration Manager Application Compatibility Toolkit Connector from the installation options.

3. Create and deploy the appropriate ACT data collection packages (DCPs). The ACT documentation describes how to create the DCPs. You can use ConfigMgr software deployment to deploy the DCPs. Chapter 14, "Distributing Packages," describes software deployment.

   You should deploy the Inventory Collector DCP to collections of up to 5,000 systems at one time to identify the applications on your target systems. After developing an application inventory, deploy a Windows Vista Compatibility Evaluator DCP to a representative collection of machines to evaluate possible compatibility issues such as User Account Control (UAC) compatibility issues, applications using deprecated application programming interfaces (APIs), systems with a non-Microsoft Graphical Identification and Authentication (GINA) and applications requiring access to session 0.

4. Expand the Configuration Manager console tree to System Center Configuration Manager -> Site Database -> Computer Management -> Application Compatibility Toolkit Connector. Click Run Device Driver Synchronization from the Actions pane. This task retrieves the latest driver compatibility information from the Microsoft online database.

NOTE

Processing Time for Data Collection Packages

It can take up to 7 days for the ACT toolkit to retrieve and analyze application compatibility data from 5,000 machines.

After completing the steps in this section, you can use reports in the following categories to analyze your systems for issues related to Vista or Windows 2008 Server upgrades:

▶ Upgrade Assessment – Windows Server 2008

▶ Upgrade Assessment – Windows Vista

▶ Upgrade Assessment – Windows XP

Each report category includes reports that can help you determine which of your systems meet minimum and recommended hardware requirements for the relevant upgrades, and identify systems needing additional free disk space or hardware upgrades. Additional reports in the Windows Vista category display application and driver-compatibility information and availability status for driver upgrades.

Dashboards

ConfigMgr 2007 uses dashboards to present several related reports on a single page. This section creates a dashboard to display the overall status of the sites in your hierarchy, the number of errors reported by each site in the past 12 hours, and the fatal errors by component and by computer. To create the dashboard, perform the following steps:

1. Expand the Configuration Manager console tree to System Center Configuration Manager -> Site Database -> Computer Management -> Reporting.

2. Right-click the Dashboard's node and choose New Dashboard.

3. On the New Dashboard Wizard General page, enter the name for your dashboard, an optional comment, and the maximum height in pixels for the cells that contains individual reports. The default value for the maximum cell height is 250 pixels. Click Next to continue. Figure 18.26 shows the New Dashboard Wizard General page.

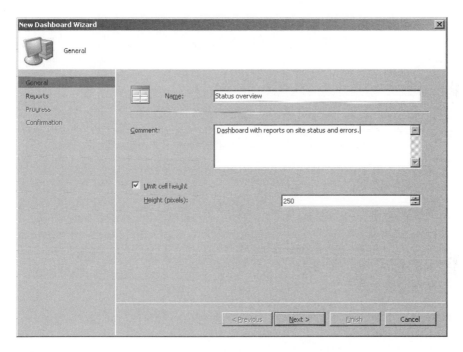

FIGURE 18.26   The New Dashboard Wizard General page for the Status overview dashboard

4. On the Reports page, select the dimensions of the dashboard in rows and columns and the reports you want to include in the dashboard. Click Next to complete the Reports page, and Close when you receive confirmation the dashboard has been successfully created. The Reports page provides buttons to select reports and move

them up or down in the display order. Dashboards can include only those reports that do not require prompted values. Figure 18.27 shows the New Dashboard Wizard Reports page.

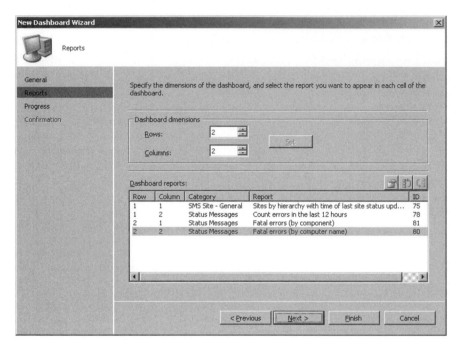

FIGURE 18.27   The New Dashboard Wizard Reports page allows you to select dashboard reports.

You can view the dashboard by navigating to the Configuration Manager console Dashboards node, right-clicking the dashboard and selecting Run. Alternately, you can open the Reporting Site home page in your web browser and navigate to the dashboards node of the Report Viewer. Figure 18.28 shows the Status overview dashboard as rendered in the ConfigMgr console.

Customizing Configuration Manager Reports

The ready-made reports Microsoft includes with ConfigMgr provide extensive capabilities for reporting on your environment and operations. However, you might sometimes need to customize these reports to get just the right report to fit your requirements. Here are several ways you can customize reports:

▶ Change layout and display characteristics of a report. For example, you can re-order the columns, add a chart or modify the existing chart, or add or modify a link.

▶ Change which data rows or columns are included in the report.

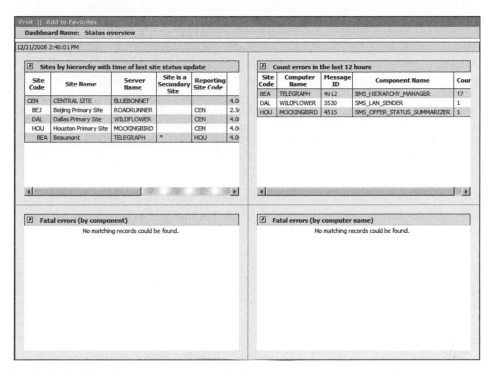

FIGURE 18.28   The Status overview dashboard presents reports on site status and errors.

▶ Add data from additional Configuration Manager database tables or add data ConfigMgr does not capture by default through inventory or discovery customizations.

▶ Add data from sources outside the Configuration Manager database.

The following sections present examples of each of these types of customization.

NOTE

Cloning Reports

For purposes of discussion, some examples in this section modify the default Configuration Manager reports. In reality, you generally want to clone the original report and make your modifications to the cloned copy.

To clone a report, expand the Configuration Manager console tree to System Center Configuration Manager -> Site Database -> Computer Management -> Reporting -> Reports. Right-click the report and choose Clone. You need to supply a new name for the cloned report.

18

Customizing Report Layout and Display

To customize the order the columns appear in a report, you can edit the report's SQL statement and simply re-order the items in the selection list. The "Dashboards" section in this chapter shows how to create a dashboard to display critical status information. One of the reports used was **Sites by hierarchy with time of last site status update**. This report provides a useful view of your sites, including their hierarchical relationships and status. The most relevant data for the status dashboard, however, is in the columns on the right of the report. You cannot view the status information in the report in the upper-left quadrant of the dashboard (as shown in Figure 18.28) without scrolling to the right. To change the column order so that the status information appears earlier in the report, perform the following steps:

1. Expand the Configuration Manager console tree to System Center Configuration Manager -> Site Database -> Computer Management -> Reporting -> Reports. Right-click the **Sites by hierarchy with time of last site status update** report, and choose Properties.

2. On the Properties page for the report, select the General tab and click the Edit SQL Statement button. A portion of the report's SQL statement is:

```
select SPACE(3*(SiteLevel-1))+so.SiteCode as SiteCode, s.SiteName,
s.ServerName,
    CASE s.Type WHEN 1 THEN '*' ELSE ' ' END as C085, s.ReportingSiteCode,
    s.Version, stat.Updated,
    CASE stat.Status WHEN 0 THEN '*' ELSE ' '  END As 'OK',
    CASE stat.Status WHEN 1 THEN '*' ELSE ' '  END As 'Warning',]
    CASE stat.Status WHEN 2 THEN '*' ELSE ' '  END As 'Error'
```

3. Edit the SQL Statement by moving the SiteName, ServerName, C085 (this is the secondary site indicator), ReportingSiteCode, and version columns to the end of the selection list. The resulting SQL statement will be:

```
select SPACE(3*(SiteLevel-1))+so.SiteCode as SiteCode, stat.Updated,
    CASE stat.Status WHEN 0 THEN '*' ELSE ' '  END As 'OK',
    CASE stat.Status WHEN 1 THEN '*' ELSE ' '  END As 'Warning',
    CASE stat.Status WHEN 2 THEN '*' ELSE ' '  END As 'Error', s.SiteName,
    s.ServerName,
    CASE s.Type WHEN 1 THEN '*' ELSE ' ' END as C085, s.ReportingSiteCode,
    s.Version
```

4. Click OK to close the Edit SQL Statement dialog box and again to close the report Properties page. You can now run the report or the dashboard to view the results of your changes. Figure 18.29 displays the Status Overview dashboard reflecting the report modifications.

You can also use the report Properties dialog box to add a chart or link to an existing report or to modify an existing chart or link. Chapter 6 introduces Jeff Tondt's SMSMap utility. You can add a link to the **Sites by hierarchy with time of last site status update** report, which displays a map of your hierarchy as follows:

1. Use SMSMap to create the hierarchy map and save it as a graphical interchange format (gif) file in a file system directory under your SMS reporting folder. The reporting folder in this example is http://bluebonnet/SMSReporting_CEN. You can

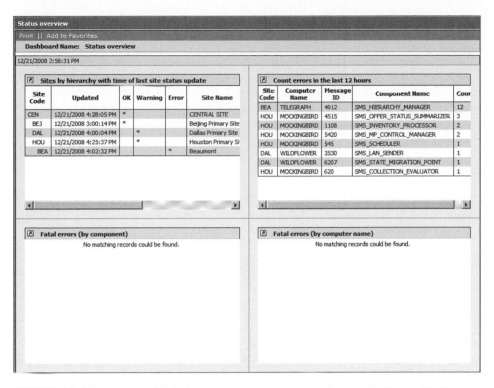

Status overview

Print || Add to Favorites

Dashboard Name: Status overview

12/21/2008 2:56:31 PM

Sites by hierarchy with time of last site status update

Site Code	Updated	OK	Warning	Error	Site Name
CEN	12/21/2008 4:28:05 PM	*			CENTRAL SITE
BEJ	12/21/2008 3:00:14 PM	*			Beijing Primary Site
DAL	12/21/2008 4:00:04 PM		*		Dallas Primary Site
HOU	12/21/2008 4:25:37 PM		*		Houston Primary Si
BEA	12/21/2008 4:02:32 PM			*	Beaumont

Count errors in the last 12 hours

Site Code	Computer Name	Message ID	Component Name	Cour
BEA	TELEGRAPH	4912	SMS_HIERARCHY_MANAGER	12
HOU	MOCKINGBIRD	4515	SMS_OFFER_STATUS_SUMMARIZER	3
HOU	MOCKINGBIRD	1108	SMS_INVENTORY_PROCESSOR	2
HOU	MOCKINGBIRD	5420	SMS_MP_CONTROL_MANAGER	2
HOU	MOCKINGBIRD	545	SMS_SCHEDULER	1
DAL	WILDFLOWER	3530	SMS_LAN_SENDER	1
DAL	WILDFLOWER	6207	SMS_STATE_MIGRATION_POINT	1
HOU	MOCKINGBIRD	620	SMS_COLLECTION_EVALUATOR	1

Fatal errors (by component)

No matching records could be found.

Fatal errors (by computer name)

No matching records could be found.

FIGURE 18.29   The modified dashboard is the same as the one in Figure 18.28, except the first report now displays status date and overall site status.

use the Internet Information Service (IIS) Manager in the Administrative Tools program group on Bluebonnet to view the properties of the SMS_Reporting folder under the default website and see that the file system path for the folder is c:\inetpub\wwwroot\SMSReporting_CEN. The SMSMap is saved as c:\inetpub\wwwroot\SMSReporting_CEN\images\SMSMap.gif. (See the Windows Server help files for information about using IIS Manager.)

2. Open the report Properties by following step 1 of the previous procedure and click on the report Properties page Links tab. Choose Link to URL from the Link type drop-down list and enter **http://bluebonnet/SMSReporting_CEN/images/smsmap.gif** in the URL box; then click OK to save your changes. The report now displays a link icon next to each of the site codes, allowing you to reference the site hierarchy map.

Customizing Report Data Selection

ConfigMgr reports are based on the ConfigMgr database views. You can add columns to your report or remove columns from the report by changing the selection list in the report SQL statement. You can also filter which rows display in the report, by modifying the WHERE clause of the report SQL statement or by specifying additional qualifiers.

18

Modifying Report Columns

The "Reporting on Computers Based on Specific Criteria" section in this chapter discusses the **Computers with low free disk space (less than specified MB free)** report, shown in Figure 18.17. To add or remove columns from this report, perform the following steps:

1. Expand the Configuration Manager console tree to System Center Configuration Manager -> Site Database -> Computer Management -> Reporting -> Reports. Right-click the **Computers with low free disk space (less than specified MB free)** report and choose Properties.

2. On the report Properties page General tab, click the Edit SQL Statement button. A portion of the report's SQL statement is:

```
SELECT SYS.Name, SYS.SiteCode, LDISK.Description0,LDISK.DeviceID0, LDISK.
VolumeName0,LDISK.FileSystem0, LDISK.Size0,LDISK.FreeSpace0
  FROM v_FullCollectionMembership SYS
  join v_GS_LOGICAL_DISK LDISK on SYS.ResourceID = LDISK.ResourceID
  WHERE
  LDISK.DriveType0 = 3 AND
  LDISK.FreeSpace0 < @variable AND
  SYS.CollectionID = @CollID
  ORDER BY SYS.Name= @CollID
  ORDER BY SYS.Name
```

3. The SQL statement's FROM clause on the third and fourth lines of the code listing in step 2 indicates that the report is based on data from the v_FullCollectionMembership and v_GS_LOGICAL_DISK views. Figure 18.30 displays the Query Builder interface, which you can use to select columns from these views to display in the report. This figure shows v_GS_LOGICAL_DISK in the views list and VolumeSerialNumber0 in the columns list as selected. After clicking the Insert button, add the view alias LDISK as a column prefix and a comma after the column name. You should also add the LDISK.Compressed0 column from the same view and SYS.Domain0 from the v_FullCollectionMembership view. The modified selection list is as follows:

```
SELECT SYS.Name, SYS.SiteCode,SYS.Domain,LDISK.Compressed0,LDISK.
  VolumeSerialNumber0,
  LDISK.Description0,LDISK.DeviceID0, LDISK.VolumeName0, LDISK.FileSystem0,
  LDISK.Size0,LDISK.FreeSpace0
  FROM v_FullCollectionMembership SYS
  join v_GS_LOGICAL_DISK LDISK on SYS.ResourceID = LDISK.ResourceID
```

The modified report now includes domain information from the system view, and the volume serial number and compression attribute from the logical disk view. Figure 18.31 displays the new report.

Filtering Report Data to Select Specific Rows

The "Reporting on Computers Based on Specific Criteria" section also discusses the **Computers with a specific product name and version** report. Notice that the example of this report displayed in Figure 18.18 contains two identical rows for each entry. This is common in ConfigMgr reports and occurs because one or both views contain records that are identical with respect to the data selected for the report but differ on some characteristic that

FIGURE 18.30 The Query Builder interface with view and column selections highlighted

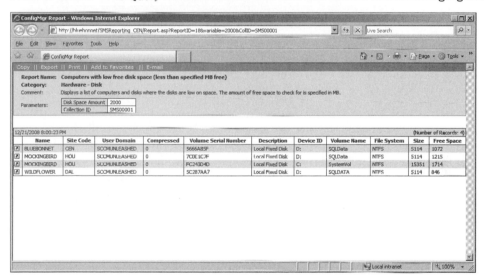

FIGURE 18.31 The modified **Computers with Low Disk Space** report includes additional information not shown in Figure 18.17.

is not of interest. This example contains two entries for Microsoft SQL Server version 9.00.3042.00 on each computer. Let's look at the SQL code used for the **Computers with a specific product name and version** report:

```
Select SYS.Netbios_Name0, SYS.User_Name0, SP.ProductName, SP.CompanyName,
SP.ProductVersion
```

```
FROM v_GS_SoftwareProduct SP JOIN v_R_System SYS on SP.ResourceID = SYS.ResourceID
WHERE SP.ProductName = @variable AND SP.ProductVersion = @variable1 Order by
SP.ProductName, SP.ProductVersion
```

Chapter 3 introduces the native SQL Server 2005 Query Tool. It is often easier to use the Query Tool rather than the Query Builder interface when you want to quickly experiment with a number of changes to SQL statements and see the results. To find the source of the apparent duplicate entry, paste this SQL statement into the Query Tool and change the selection list in the first line of the statement by replacing the specific columns from the v_GS_SoftwareProduct view (alias SP) with the wildcard **SP.***. This returns all available columns from v_GS_SoftwareProduct. You also want to replace the variables in the WHERE clause with the literal strings **'Microsoft SQL Server'** and **'9.00.3042.00'** to avoid having to populate the report prompt parameters at run time. The resulting SQL statement is

```
Select SYS.Netbios_Name0, SYS.User_Name0,  SP.*
  FROM v_GS_SoftwareProduct SP JOIN v_R_System SYS on SP.ResourceID = SYS.ResourceID
  WHERE SP.ProductName = 'Microsoft SQL Server' AND SP.ProductVersion = '9.00.3042.00'
  Order by SP.ProductName, SP.ProductVersion
```

Running the modified query in the SQL Query tool generates the results shown in Figure 18.32.

	Netbios_Name0	User_Name0	ResourceID	ProductID	CompanyName	ProductName	ProductVersion	ProductLanguage
1	BLUEBONNET	administrator	2	10	Microsoft Corporation	Microsoft SQL Server	9.00.3042.00	0
2	WILDFLOWER	administrator	53	10	Microsoft Corporation	Microsoft SQL Server	9.00.3042.00	0
3	BLUEBONNET	administrator	2	59	Microsoft Corporation	Microsoft SQL Server	9.00.3042.00	1033
4	WILDFLOWER	administrator	53	59	Microsoft Corporation	Microsoft SQL Server	9.00.3042.00	1033

FIGURE 18.32   The query results for computers with SQL Server version 9.00.3042.00

The data in rows 1 and 3, for example, is identical with the exception of the ProductID and ProductLanguage columns. The product information is gathered from file headers by the software inventory process, and the database contains inventory from files that show the product language code as 0 and from files showing the product language code as 1033. Each language version is also distinguished by Product ID. Product language information is not necessary for this report, so filter the data by adding the keyword distinct to the selection list in the original SQL statement:

```
Select distinct SYS.Netbios_Name0, SYS.User_Name0, SP.ProductName, SP.CompanyName,
SP.ProductVersion
```

This example has the prompt variables in the SQL statement replaced with literal strings to make the query easier to work with using the Query Tool. You might also want to use this technique to modify reports so that you can use them in dashboards or send to users with prepopulated parameters. You cannot use the Computers with a specific product name and version report in a dashboard because it contains prompts. However, the modified SQL statement that explicitly specified the product name 'Microsoft SQL Server' and product version '9.00.3042.00' could be used to create a dashboard report, or could be sent to your database administrators to provide specific information about that SQL Server version.

Another common issue with reports is seeing stale data included in the report. The site database often includes data about inactive computers, which are not reporting heartbeat discovery, or obsolete records about computers that have been re-imaged or replaced. To exclude this data from your reports, add the following conditions to the WHERE clause of your SQL statement:

```
SYS.Obsolete0 <> 1
SYS.Active0 = 1
```

TIP

Removing Old Data from the Site Database

ConfigMgr provides maintenance tasks that can periodically remove various types of outdated data from the site database. You can greatly improve the quality of data in many of your reports by enabling these tasks and optimizing them for your environment. Chapter 21 describes how to configure database maintenance tasks. If you use AD discovery methods, you also need to make sure old data is regularly removed from your AD to avoid ConfigMgr rediscovering objects from AD that no longer exist on your network.

In some cases, you might want to filter data based on criteria not in the base views for the report you work with. As an example, the Computers with a specific product name and version report is based on software inventory data, so you might want to ensure you are looking only at data from systems that have recently reported software inventory. The last software inventory scan date is in the v_GS_LastSoftwareScan view, which is not part of the report. To add the view to the report and filter for only those systems with inventory scans in the last 30 days, perform the following steps:

1. Add the v_GS_LastSoftwareScan to the JOIN clause of the report's SQL statement. Using the Query Builder or the SQL Query Tool, you can list the columns of v_GS_LastSoftwareScan.

   Like all ConfigMgr resource views, v_GS_LastSoftwareScan contains a ResourceID column. Use this to add this view to the report by changing

   ```
   FROM v_GS_SoftwareProduct SP JOIN v_R_System SYS on SP.ResourceID =
   SYS.ResourceID
   ```

   to

   ```
   FROM v_GS_SoftwareProduct SP JOIN v_R_System SYS on SP.ResourceID =
   SYS.ResourceID
   JOIN v_GS_LastSoftwareScan LSS on SP. ResourceID = LSS. ResourceID
   ```

2. The columns from v_GS_LastSoftwareScan are now available for the report, so add the following condition to the WHERE clause:

   ```
   LSS.LastScanDate > (getdate ()-30)
   ```

The final SQL statement looks like this:

```
Select distinct SYS.Netbios_Name0, SYS.User_Name0, SP.ProductName, SP.CompanyName,
SP.ProductVersion
```

```
FROM v_GS_SoftwareProduct SP JOIN v_R_System SYS on SP.ResourceID = SYS.ResourceID
JOIN v_GS_LastSoftwareScan LSS on SP. ResourceID = LSS. ResourceID
WHERE SP.ProductName = @variable AND SP.ProductVersion = @variable1
And SYS.Obsolete0 <> 1 and SYS.Active0 = 1 and s.LastScanDate > (getdate ()-30)
Order by SP.ProductName, SP.ProductVersion
```

The report now includes modifications to show only distinct rows and exclude data from obsolete records and machines that are inactive or have not reported software inventory in the past 30 days.

Reporting on Custom Data

With their default settings, ConfigMgr discovery and inventory methods gather a wide variety of data that you can use to report on your environment. If you need additional information about your client systems or discovered AD objects, there is a good chance ConfigMgr can get the data you need. The following sections present examples of customizing AD discovery and hardware inventory to extend your reporting capability.

Reporting on Custom Discovery Data

The Configuration Manager AD discovery methods import information about computers, users, and security groups from the AD database. Each method has a default set of attributes that it retrieves from the directory. You can specify additional attributes you want to include in the AD system discovery and AD user discovery methods. As an example, add the department, telephone number, and title to the AD user discovery method, and then display these attributes in a customized report. Perform the following steps to add attributes to the AD user discovery method:

1. Expand the Configuration Manager console tree to System Center Configuration Manager -> Site Database -> Site Management -> *<Site Code> <Site Name>* -> Discovery Methods. Right-click Active Directory User Discovery and choose Properties.

2. In the Active Directory User Discovery Properties dialog box, select the Active Directory attribute tab, click the new (starburst) button, enter the name of the attribute you want to add, and click OK. Figure 18.33 displays the dialog box for adding the **Title** attribute.

TIP

Using ADSIEdit to View Object Attributes

Chapter 3 introduces the ADSIEdit MMC snap-in, which you can use to view and edit Active Directory objects. To view the available attributes for user or computer objects, run ADSIEdit, expand the domain naming context, and select an object of the appropriate type. Right-click the user or computer object and choose Properties. This launches the Attribute Editor, which displays a complete list of available attributes for the object type.

When the discovery method runs, it generates data discovery record (DDR) files for each object it discovers. When the ConfigMgr Discovery Data Manager (DDM) component processes a DDR containing a new property, the DDM updates the WMI resource class and

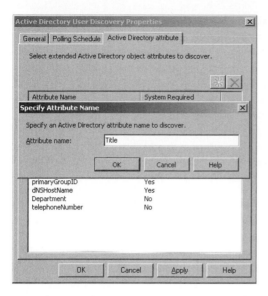

FIGURE 18.33   Adding an attribute to Active Directory User Discovery

the site database with the new property. ConfigMgr automatically adds the new property to the appropriate resource view, which makes it available for reporting. The resource view for user data is v_R_User. Having specified the attributes you want in the user resource view, let's see how to add them to a report.

The Asset Intelligence report category includes a number of reports on user activity, such as the systems, software, and licenses the user has used. Including additional user details might make these reports more useful in understanding who the user is and how to contact them. Figure 18.34 shows the Hardware 05A – Console users on a specific computer report, which displays all users who have logged on to the machine's console.

18

Report Name: Hardware 05A - Console users on a specific computer
Category: Asset Intelligence
Comment: The report displays all of the console users on a specific computer
Parameters: Computer Name DABNEY

1/1/2009 6:27:15 PM   (Number of Records: 9)

User Name	SMS Site Name	Serial Number	Asset Tag	Manufacturer	Model	Console Logons	Percent Console Time	Total Minutes on Console	Last Console Use	Log Start Date
sccmunleashed\administrator	Dallas Primary Site	None	No Asset Tag	VMware, Inc.	VMware Virtual Platform	1	98.98	14679	1/1/2009 1:42:00 PM	5/20/2008 8:25:00 PM
sccmunleashed\emartinez	Dallas Primary Site	None	No Asset Tag	VMware, Inc.	VMware Virtual Platform	1	0.69	103	1/1/2009 5:30:00 PM	5/20/2008 8:25:00 PM
sccmunleashed\hshan	Dallas Primary Site	None	No Asset Tag	VMware, Inc.	VMware Virtual Platform	1	0.18	27	1/1/2009 3:42:00 PM	5/20/2008 8:25:00 PM
sccmunleashed\ghouston	Dallas Primary Site	None	No Asset Tag	VMware, Inc.	VMware Virtual Platform	1	0.05	8	1/1/2009 5:39:00 PM	5/20/2008 8:25:00 PM
sccmunleashed\plumar	Dallas Primary Site	None	No Asset Tag	VMware, Inc.	VMware Virtual Platform	1	0.03	5	1/1/2009 5:46:00 PM	5/20/2008 8:25:00 PM
sccmunleashed\jsmith	Dallas Primary Site	None	No Asset Tag	VMware, Inc.	VMware Virtual Platform	1	0.02	3	1/1/2009 5:56:00 PM	5/20/2008 8:25:00 PM
sccmunleashed\vmcclure	Dallas Primary Site	None	No Asset Tag	VMware, Inc.	VMware Virtual Platform	1	0.02	3	1/1/2009 6:00:00 PM	5/20/2008 8:25:00 PM
sccmunleashed\bparker	Dallas Primary Site	None	No Asset Tag	VMware, Inc.	VMware Virtual Platform	1	0.02	3	1/1/2009 5:49:00 PM	5/20/2008 8:25:00 PM
sccmunleashed\tjones	Dallas Primary Site	None	No Asset Tag	VMware, Inc.	VMware Virtual Platform	1	0	0	1/1/2009 6:02:00 PM	5/20/2008 8:25:00 PM

FIGURE 18.34   Console users for the computer DABNEY

An abridged version of the SQL statement for this report is as follows:

```
Select  v_GS_SYSTEM_CONSOLE_USER.SystemConsoleUser0 as [User Name],
...
FROM v_GS_SYSTEM_CONSOLE_USER
INNER JOIN v_R_System_Valid on
v_R_System_Valid.ResourceID =
v_GS_SYSTEM_CONSOLE_USER.ResourceID
...
 WHERE v_R_System_Valid.Netbios_Name0 = @Name
...
```

To create a report showing details about the users that have logged on to a particular computer, you can clone the Hardware 05A – Console users on a specific computer report and modify the SQL statement as follows:

▶ In the FROM clause, add the following join to the user resource view.

```
INNER JOIN v_R_User U on v_GS_SYSTEM_CONSOLE_USER.SystemConsoleUser0 =
U.Unique_User_Name0
```

▶ In the select list, remove columns you are not interested in and add details from the user resource view. The list of columns added from the user resource view include the telephoneNumber, Department and Title AD attributes added to the AD User Discovery method in Figure 18.33, as follows:

```
U.Full_User_Name0 AS [Full Name], U.telephoneNumber0 AS [Telephone],
U.Department0 AS Department, U.Title0 As Title
```

Figure 18.35 displays the modified console users report.

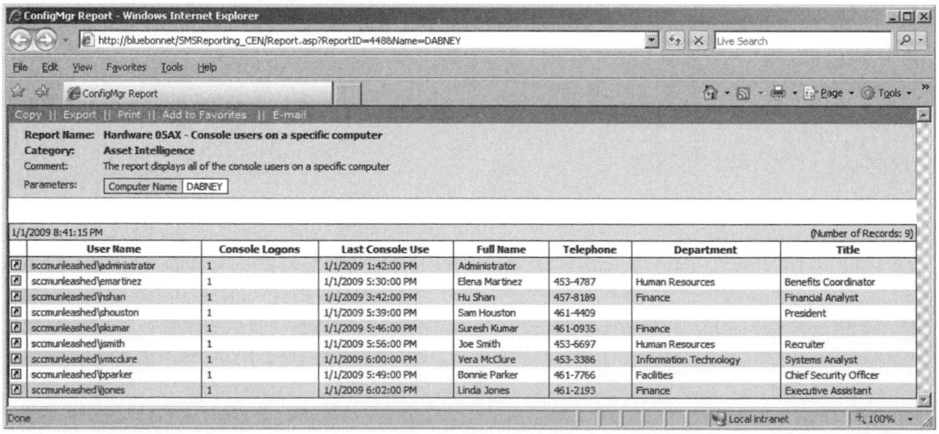

FIGURE 18.35   Console users for the computer DABNEY with additional user details

Reporting on Custom Inventory Data

Chapter 3 discusses the role of the SMS_Def.mof file in hardware inventory, and Chapter 12 explains how to enable additional inventory data items by editing this file. This section demonstrates how to use these additional classes in ConfigMgr reports. The hardware inventory process gathers basic data about each network adapter's IP configuration by default. Figure 18.36 displays the IP – Information for a specific computer report for the computer Bluebonnet, which shows the basic network adapter inventory data.

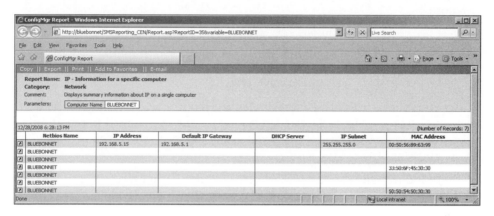

FIGURE 18.36   The **IP – Information for a specific computer** report for Bluebonnet

The next example adds the DNS server and DNS suffix search order to this report. Perform the following steps:

1. Use a text editor such as Windows Notepad to locate the following lines in class Win32_NetworkAdapterConfiguration section of the SMS_Def.mof file:

```
[SMS_Report (FALSE)      ]
    string      DNSDomainSuffixSearchOrder[];
[SMS_Report (FALSE)      ]
    string      DNSServerSearchOrder[];
```

2. Change SMS_Report value for each of these items from FALSE to TRUE:

```
[SMS_Report (TRUE)      ]
    string      DNSDomainSuffixSearchOrder[];
[SMS_Report (TRUE)      ]
    string      DNSServerSearchOrder[];
```

This change causes the hardware inventory agent on computers in the site to collect and report the DNS server and DNS domain suffix search order values for each configured network adapter. When the site server processes inventory files containing this information, it appends two new rows to the Network_DATA table in the site database:

- ▶ DNSDomainSuffixSearchOrde0
- ▶ DNSServerSearchOrder00

Remember that Microsoft bases Configuration Manager reports on SQL views rather than the underlying tables. Here is the SQL statement for the **IP – Information for a specific computer** report:

```
Select Sys.Netbios_Name0, NETW.IPAddress0, NETW.DefaultIPGateway0,
NETW.DHCPServer0, NETW.IPSubnet0, NETW.MACAddress0
FROM v_R_System Sys JOIN v_Network_DATA_Serialized NETW ON NETW.ResourceID=Sys.
ResourceID WHERE Sys.Netbios_Name0 like @variable
```

The FROM statement in the third line above reveals the report uses network information from the view v_Network_DATA_Serialized. Unlike the resource views used to report on discovery data, the inventory views are not updated automatically when you add new attributes to ConfigMgr inventory.

Chapter 3 also introduces the SQL Server Management Studio. You can use SQL Server Management Studio to examine and edit the v_Network_DATA_Serialized view. Perform the following steps:

1. Launch SQL Server Management Studio from Start -> Programs -> Microsoft SQL Server 2005 -> SQL Server Management Studio.

2. After connecting to the site database server SQL instance, expand *<servername>* -> database -> SMS_*<Site Code>* -> views in the tree control in the left pane.

3. Right-click the v_Network_DATA_Serialized view and choose Edit. This opens a query window that displays the SQL statement required to alter the view. V_Network_DATA_Serialized is based on the following select statement:

```
SELECT nd.MachineID As 'ResourceID', nd.InstanceKey As 'GroupID',
nd.RevisionID, nd.AgentID,
  nd.TimeKey As 'TimeStamp', nd.DefaultIPGateway0, nd.DHCPEnabled0,
  nd.DHCPServer00 As 'DHCPServer0', nd.DNSDomain00 As 'DNSDomain0',
  nd.DNSHostName00 As 'DNSHostName0', nd.Index0, ip.SubStr1 As
  'IPAddress0',
  nd.IPEnabled00 As 'IPEnabled0',ip.SubStr2 as 'IPSubnet0',
  nd.MACAddress0,
  nd.ServiceName0
  FROM Network_DATA as nd
  CROSS APPLY fnSplitStringsAndMerge(nd.IPAddress0, nd.IPSubnet0, ',') as ip
```

4. Add the following attributes to the SELECT list; then click the Execute button from the SQL Server Management Studio toolbar:

```
nd.DNSDomainSuffixSearchOrde0, nd.DNSServerSearchOrder00
```

The v_Network_DATA_Serialized view now includes the DNS domain suffix search order and DNS server configuration information.

NOTE

About Changes to Default Views

Future upgrades to ConfigMgr might overwrite customizations you make on default ConfigMgr objects, including views. You should document all customizations and be prepared to re-create your custom views following a service pack or upgrade.

To display this information in the **IP – Information for a specific computer** report, edit the SQL statement for the report and add the DNSDomainSuffixSearchOrde0 and DNSServerSearchOrder00 columns to the SELECT list. You also need to remove NETW.DHCPServer0 from the list. Figure 18.37 displays the resulting report for the computer Bluebonnet.

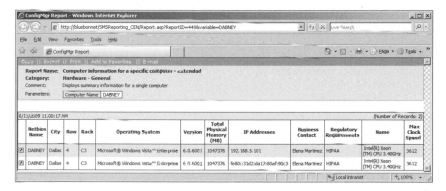

FIGURE 18.37   The modified **IP – Information for a specific computer** report for Bluebonnet, including the DNS domain suffix search order and DNS server information

Including External Data Sources in Reports

You undoubtedly have other applications and data stores in your environment that contain information related to your ConfigMgr client systems and other objects in the site database. Although reports linking to external data sources are not strictly ConfigMgr reports in that they are not based exclusively on the ConfigMgr views, linking in external data can be useful for a variety of purposes. This section presents an example of a report that uses data from the v_R_System view and from an external spreadsheet. The example imports the spreadsheet data into the ConfigMgr database. You can also use data in a separate database on a local server or on another SQL Server.

NOTE

About Fully Qualified Object Names in SQL Server

Up to now, the discussion has focused exclusively on objects in the ConfigMgr site database. When objects such as tables and views are in the site database, you can refer to them by the simple object name, and ConfigMgr reporting will know where to find them. To reference data stored in other databases or on other servers, use the four part or fully-qualified name in the form `server.database.schema.object`. For example, the fully qualified name for the sites table in central site database for SCCMUnleashed.com is `bluebonnet.sms_cen.dbo.sites`. The dbo schema is the default schema for objects created by the database owner. The server, database, and schema qualifier are optional but must be supplied if the appropriate values differ from the defaults.

For more information on SQL Server object naming, see the Transact-SQL Syntax Conventions topic in the Transact-SQL Reference, part of the online books that you can install from the SQL Server installation media.

Figure 18.38 shows a portion of a spreadsheet in which the SCCMUnleashed IT department keeps information about systems in the company data centers.

	A	F	G	H	I	J
1	Name	City	Row	Rack	Business Contact	Regulatory Requirements
2	ALAMO	Dallas	1	A4	IT Operations	SOX
3	ARMADILLO	Dallas	1	A5	IT Operations	SOX
4	BEST	Beijing	1	A6	Vera McClure	
5	BLUEBONNET	Dallas	3	E4	IT Operations	
6	BUDA	Beijing	1	B3	Suresh Kumar	SOX
7	DABNEY	Dallas	4	C3	Elena Martinez	HIPAA

FIGURE 18.38   Sample system data from an IT department spreadsheet

To add the sample data to the Computer information for a specific computer report, perform the following steps:

1. Open the spreadsheet in Microsoft Excel, then choose File -> Save As from the Excel menu, and save as a file of type text (tab delimited). Save this file as **systeminfo.txt**.

2. Open SQL Server Management Studio and connect to the site database server. Expand the Databases node in the Object Explorer (the tree on the left side), right-click the site database, and choose Tasks -> Import Data. This launches the SQL Server Import and Export Wizard.

3. Click Next on the wizard's startup page. On the Choose a Data Source page, choose Flat File Source from the data source list box and browse to the location of the saved

text file. Click the Column names in the first text row checkbox, and then click Next. Figure 18.39 shows the Choose a Data Source page with the appropriate options selected.

FIGURE 18.39   Specifying the data source in the SQL Server Import and Export Wizard

4. On the next page of the wizard, verify that the row delimiter is {CR}{LF} and Tab {t} is the column delimiter; then click Next.

5. On the Choose a Destination page, the default options should show the destination as SQL Native Client and the servername and database name for your site database. Verify that the options are correct and click Next.

6. The Select Source Tables and Views page shows your file mapped to a database table with the same name. Click Next to accept this mapping.

7. The wizard's Save and Execute Package page offers options to execute the import immediately to save the data import package. If you plan to update the data in the future, you can use a saved package to import your updated data on demand or on a scheduled basis.

   After selecting the appropriate options, click Next and then Finish, which completes the wizard.

8. Expand the Tables node under the site database in the Object Explorer tree. Right-click the newly created table and choose Properties, and then select the Permissions page. Click the Add button and add webreport_approle to the list of users and roles. Check Select in the Grant column of the list of explicit permissions for

webreport_approle and click OK. Figure 18.40 shows the Permissions page for the systeminfo table.

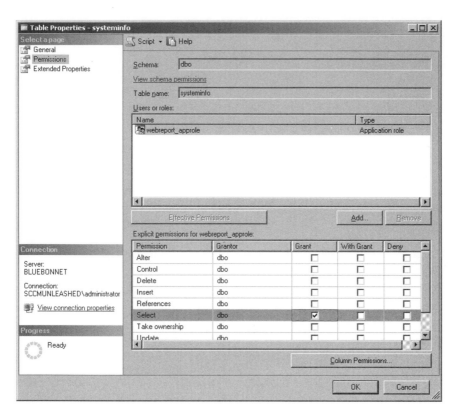

FIGURE 18.40   The Permissions page for the systeminfo table grants select permission to the webreport_approle role.

9. Open the Configuration Manager console and navigate to the Reports node. Right-click on the **Computer information for a specific computer** report, choose Clone, and enter the name for the new report. Name the new report **Computer information for a specific computer – extended**.

10. Right-click the new report, choose Properties, and then edit the report's SQL statement. Locate the following portion of the statement:

```
FROM v_R_System SYS LEFT JOIN  v_RA_System_IPAddresses IPAddr
on SYS.ResourceID = IPAddr.ResourceID
```

Insert an additional join condition for the systeminfo table. The edited section will be

```
FROM v_R_System SYS LEFT JOIN systeminfo INFO on SYS.Name0 = INFO.[Name]
LEFT JOIN  v_RA_System_IPAddresses IPAddr on SYS.ResourceID =
IPAddr.ResourceID
```

Edit the selection list at the beginning of the SQL statement and replace the following column names:

```
SYS.User_Name0, SYS.User_Domain0, SYS.Resource_Domain_OR_Workgr0,
Processor.Manufacturer0, CSYS.Model0
```

with:

```
INFO.City, INFO.Row, INFO.Rack,  INFO.[Business Contact], INFO.[Regulatory
Requirements]
```

Figure 18.41 shows the Computer information for a specific computer – extended report for the computer DABNEY.

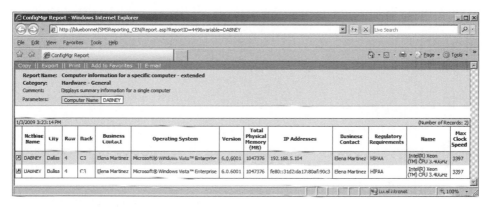

FIGURE 18.41   The Computer information for a specific computer – extended report for the computer DABNEY

Microsoft Visio 2007 Pro Add-Ins for System Center

Microsoft Visio is arguably the most popular tool used by IT professionals to create and share visual representations pertaining to IT infrastructure. Microsoft provides an extensive array of tools and add-ins for Visio through the Visio Toolbox site http:// visiotoolbox.com. The System Center Configuration Manager and System Center Operations Manager add-ins for Microsoft Visio 2007 Professional enable you to extend your reporting capability by connecting ConfigMgr and OpsMgr data to existing Visio diagrams or auto-generating Visio drawings based on database queries. Some examples of how you can use the Visio add-ins are connecting data to rack diagrams, network diagrams, and application maps to dynamically display visual cues based on configuration data. As an example, you might enhance an existing rack diagram with labels displaying the server hardware model and OS revision, or you could auto-generate a display of web servers color-coded to indicate compliance with a DCM baseline.

Additional information about the Visio add-ins for System Center and download links are available at http://visiotoolbox.com/en-us/articles1.aspx?ArticleId=6&aid=80.

Microsoft provides guidance and examples for developing custom reports at http:// technet.microsoft.com/en-us/library/dd334620.aspx, and you can download additional documentation including a Visio diagram of the ConfigMgr SQL views by accessing Microsoft's download center, http://www.microsoft.com/downloads and searching on **Creating Custom Reports By Using Configuration Manager 2007 SQL Views**.

Custom reporting is also one of the most active topics on the myITforum SMS/ConfigMgr email discussion list. For information regarding the discussion list and subscribing to the list, see http://www.myitforum.com/lists/#Microsoft_Systems_Management_Server_(SMS)_List.

Creating New Reports

Given the wide variety of ready-made reports Microsoft provides, it is generally easier to clone a report that is close to what you need and modify it than to create a new report from scratch. There might be times, however, when you want to start with a blank slate and create an entirely new report. The next sections discuss how to create new reports both in classic reporting and in SRS.

Creating Classic Reports

To create a new classic report, perform the following steps:

1. Expand the Configuration Manager console tree to System Center Configuration Manager -> Site Database -> Computer Management -> Reporting -> Reports. Right-click the Reports node and choose New -> Report.

2. On the New Report Wizard General page, enter the name, category, and an optional comment for your report. Figure 18.42 shows the New Report Wizard General page for the report named **Drill Through Sequence for a Specific Report**, created using this wizard. This report displays a sequence of reports you can open through links, beginning with an initial report selected by the user.

3. Click Edit SQL Statement to launch the Query Builder dialog box, and enter the following SQL statement for the report:

```
select R1.Name AS [Initial Report Name], R2.Name AS [First Linked Report],
R3.Name AS [Second Linked Report], R4.Name AS [Third Linked Report],
R5.Name AS [Fourth Linked Report]
  FROM v_Report R1 left join  v_Report
  R2 ON R1.DrillThroughReportID =  R2.ReportID
  left join v_Report R3 ON R2.DrillThroughReportID = R3.ReportID
  left join  v_Report R4 ON R3.DrillThroughReportID = R4.ReportID
  left join  v_Report R5 ON R4.DrillThroughReportID = R5.ReportID
  WHERE R1.Name = @ReportName
```

The user is prompted at run time to supply the value of the @ReportName parameter. To define the properties for the prompt, select Prompts to launch the prompts dialog box, and then click the New Prompt (starburst) icon to access the Prompt Properties page shown in Figure 18.43.

4. On the Prompt Properties page, enter the prompt name to use in the report SQL statement (**ReportName** in this example) and the prompt text you want displayed

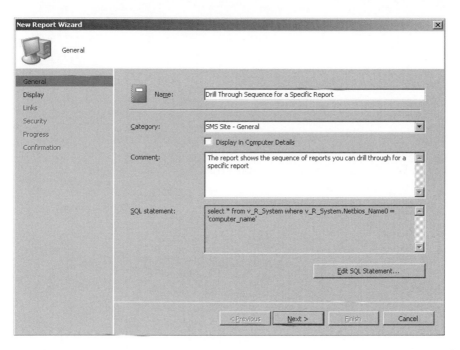

FIGURE 18.42   The New Report Wizard General page for the **Drill Through Sequence for a Specific Report**

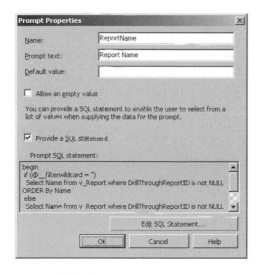

FIGURE 18.43   The Prompt Properties page for the ReportName prompt

to users. Click the Edit SQL Statement button to launch the Query Builder dialog box, and enter the SQL statement used to provide the list of available values to the user:

```
begin
 if (@__filterwildcard = '')
```

```
Select Name from v_Report where DrillThroughReportID is not NULL ORDER By
Name
else
Select Name from v_Report where DrillThroughReportID is not NULL
and Name like @__filterwildcard
ORDER By Name
end
```

5. After completing the SQL Statement dialog boxes, click Next to complete the wizard's General page and again to accept the defaults on the Display, Links, and Security pages. When you receive confirmation that the report creation was successful, click Close to complete the wizard.

Figure 18.44 shows the **Drill Through Sequence for a Specific Report** showing the sequence of linked reports beginning with the **All Software Companies** report.

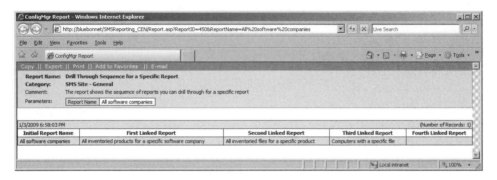

FIGURE 18.44   The **Drill Through Sequence for a Specific Report** for the **All Software Companies** report

Creating SQL Reporting Services Reports

Perform the following steps to create a new ConfigMgr 2007 R2 SQL Reporting Services based report:

1. Expand the Configuration Manager console tree to System Center Configuration Manager -> Site Database -> Computer Management -> Reporting -> Reporting Services. Right-click on the report server name and choose Create Report.

2. The Create Report Wizard Information page allows you to select either a model-based report or a SQL-based report. SQL–based reports allow you to enter SQL statements directly, as in the previous example in the "Creating Classic Reports" section. Figure 18.45 displays choosing to create a model–based report.

3. Microsoft provides the ClientStatusReporting and SoftwareUpdateManagement reporting models for Configuration Manager. Figure 18.46 shows the Model Selection page with the SoftwareUpdateManagement model selected. Click Finish to complete the wizard, or if you prefer to view a summary page and confirm your selections click Next, and then click Next on the Summary page and Close on the Confirmation page.

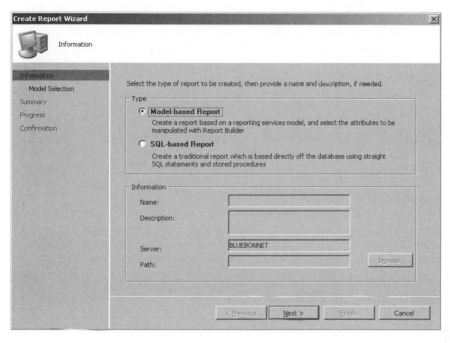

FIGURE 18.45   The Create Report Wizard Information page

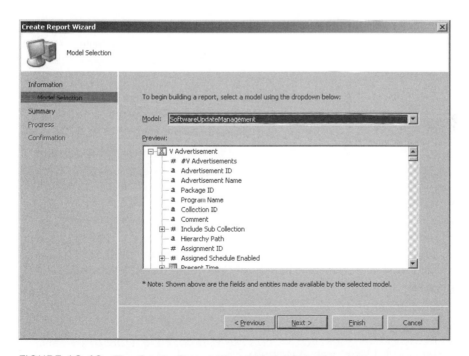

FIGURE 18.46   The Create Report Wizard Model Selection page

4. When the Create Report Wizard finishes, the Microsoft Report Builder launches automatically. The Report Builder is a graphical development environment that allows you to create, edit, and test SRS reports. For more information about using the Report Builder to design ConfigMgr reports, see http://technet.microsoft.com/en-us/library/cc678431.aspx.

Creating SQL Reporting Services Subscriptions

One of the most useful SRS features is the ability to create subscriptions. Subscriptions allow you to publish the latest version of a report on a scheduled basis to email recipients or save to a Windows file share.

> **NOTE**
>
> **Prerequisites for SRS Subscriptions**
>
> If you plan to use email delivery for SRS report subscriptions, you need to configure the SMTP (Simple Mail Transport Protocol) server and other email settings using the Microsoft SQL Server 2005 Reporting Services configuration tool. Depending on the option selected on the Data Source Authentication tab when you configure the Reporting Services Point site system role, you might also need to use the SRS configuration tools to configure an unattended execution account used to render reports for subscription-based delivery. If you chose the Credentials stored securely in the report server data source authentication option, it is not necessary to configure an execution account. The "Configuring the Reporting Services Point for SRS Reporting" section of this chapter discusses data authentication options. For information about installing SRS and using the SRS configuration tool, see http://technet.microsoft.com/en-us/library/cc512033.aspx.

To create a subscription, perform the following steps:

1. Expand the Configuration Manager console tree to System Center Configuration Manager -> Site Database -> Computer Management -> Reporting -> Reporting Services -> <servername> -> All Reports. Right-click the report you want to create a subscription for, and choose New Subscription.

2. Figure 18.47 shows the New Subscription Wizard – Subscription Delivery page for the Computers with a specific product name and version report. The options selected sends a report in Adobe PDF format to the email recipient **hu.shan@sccmunleashed.com**. The subject line will be **Visual Studio installation report** and the email will be delivered as a Normal priority message.

3. Use the New Subscription Wizard – Subscription Schedule page to create a delivery schedule for the subscription. Figure 18.48 shows the Subscription Schedule page. The report delivery is specified for a weekly basis at 8:00:00 PM Sunday to avoid rendering the report during peak usage hours.

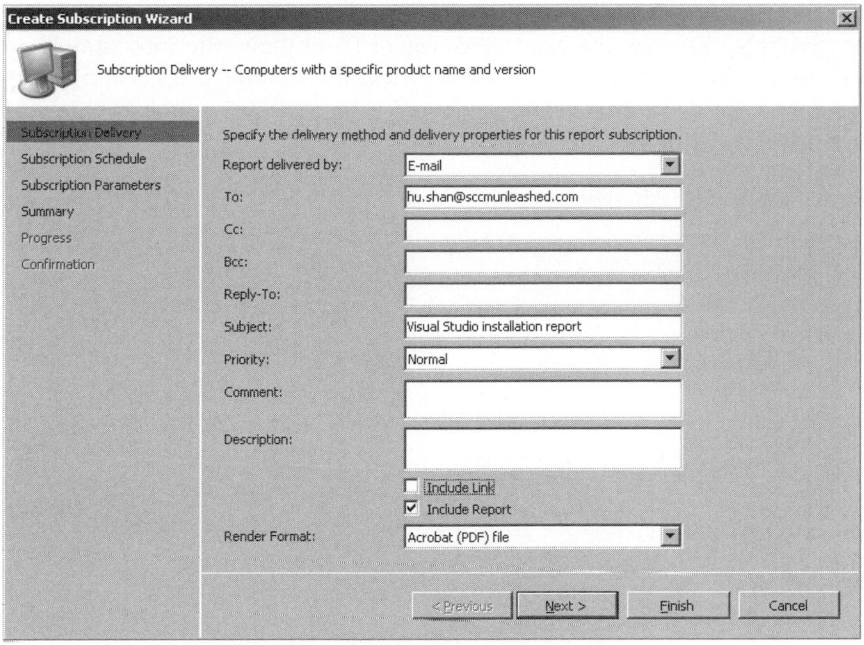

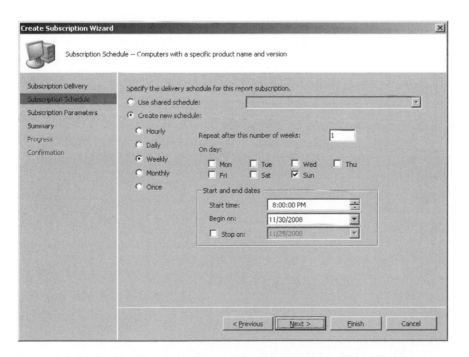

FIGURE 18.47   The New Subscription Wizard Subscription Delivery page allows you to select the subscription's delivery method, delivery options, and report format.

FIGURE 18.48   The New Subscription Wizard Subscription Schedule page

4. If your subscription is based on a report containing prompts, use the Subscription Parameters to supply values for the parameters. Figure 18.49 shows the Subscription Parameters page for the **Computers with a specific product name and version** report.

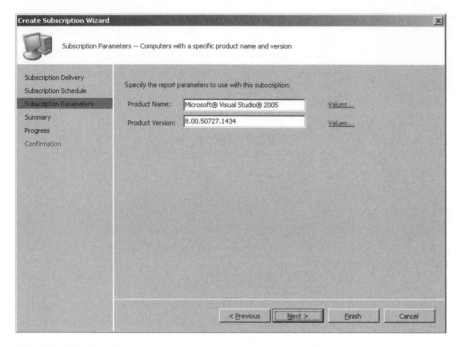

FIGURE 18.49   The New Subscription Wizard Subscription Parameters page specifying the version of Microsoft Visual Studio that will be reported on

5. To complete the New Subscription Wizard, click Next on the Summary page. Click Close when you receive confirmation that the subscription was successfully created.

The process is essentially identical for delivery to a file share, other than the options entered on the Subscription Delivery page. Figure 18.50 shows those options required to post a series of regularly incremented versions of the Visual Studio report to a file share. To use file share delivery, you must specify an account with at least Change permission on the specified share at both the share and file system level.

Troubleshooting

Some common issues with ConfigMgr reports include the following:

▶ Classic web reports, SRS reports, or dashboards not displayed correctly in Internet Explorer. If you have problems viewing reports, verify that the client has IE 5.01 SP 2 or later installed and the ConfigMgr reporting site is in the trusted sites or local intranet zone in your browser security settings. If charts and graphs in classic reports

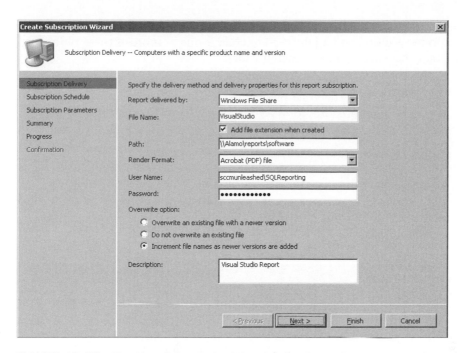

FIGURE 18.50   The New Subscription Wizard Subscription Delivery page with options to maintain a historical sequence or reports in Adobe PDF format

do not display correctly, verify that Microsoft Office Web Components (Microsoft Office 2000 SP 2, Microsoft Office XP, or Microsoft Office 2003) are installed on your reporting point server.

▶ You receive an Access Denied error when trying to view reports. Verify the user account has appropriate rights on the report you are attempting to view and is a member of the Report Users or local Administrators group on the reporting point server. For troubleshooting purposes, you might want to log on with an administrative account and attempt to view the same report.

▶ Running SRS reports from the Configuration Manager console fails with an insufficient privileges message. Make sure you have the SRS My Reports privilege, or as a workaround run the report from the SRS web page rather than the console. Chapter 20 discusses SRS privileges.

▶ Rerunning a SQL Reporting Services report in the Configuration Manager console does not reflect recent changes to the report. As a workaround, right-click the System Center Configuration Manager -> Site Database node in the Configuration Manager console tree, choose Report Options, and enable the Open reports in a new window option.

▶ You receive timeout errors when running reports. IIS uses several timeout values that govern report execution. You might need to change one or more of these timeout values if you experience frequent timeout issues:

  ▶ Use IIS Manager in the Administrative Tools program group to modify the ASP script timeout value. The exact procedure varies depending on the version of IIS you run. The procedures for IIS 6 and IIS 7 are available at http://technet. microsoft.com/en-us/library/bb632464.aspx.

  ▶ Use a text editor to modify the DBConnectionTimeout and DBCommandTimeout values in the Global.asa file in the report folder virtual directory. These settings specify the time that an ActiveX control waits for a database connection and a result set, respectively, before timing out. The default settings are 30 seconds for the connection timeout and 300 seconds for the command timeout.

TIP

Optimizing Report Queries

The majority of report execution time generally is spent executing queries and retrieving results. To avoid timeout issues and provide better report performance, you can use tools such as the Query Analyzer and SQL Profiler to optimize your queries. In some cases, you might also need to tune SQL Server to provide better performance and avoid timeouts.

Query optimization and SQL Server performance tuning are major topics of interest for database administrators, and there is a vast amount of information available on these topics. A good place to start is the SQL Server Query Processing Team blog, at http:// blogs.msdn.com/sqlqueryprocessing/default.aspx. Detailed information on SQL Server query optimization and performance tuning is also included in another volume in this series, *Microsoft SQL Server 2005 Unleashed* (Sams, 2006), which is available at http://www.mypearsonstore.com/bookstore/product.asp?isbn=0672328240.

Summary

This chapter discusses Microsoft Configuration Manager 2007 reporting features. It includes a discussion of both classic ConfigMgr reporting and the new SQL Reporting Services reporting introduced with Configuration Manager 2007 R2. The chapter describes reporting related site and site system configuration, use cases for reporting, and creating and modifying reports. The next chapter describes one of the most compelling feature sets in Configuration Manager 2007, Operating System Deployment (OSD).

Operating System Deployment

Is Operating System Deployment (OSD) the "killer app" of Configuration Manager (ConfigMgr) 2007? That depends on the specific challenges in your environment; but eventually, you will have to implement Windows Vista, Windows 7, or deploy a new batch of hardware—and then you will be glad to have OSD at your disposal.

Unlike many competitive products and the OSD Feature Pack for Systems Management Server (SMS) 2003, OSD in ConfigMgr 2007 is far more than a limited imaging solution. OSD provides a framework and a set of tools that fully automates system deployment and provisioning. It enables hardware-agnostic system images; and because OSD is part of a capable system management product, system deployment and configuration do not necessarily stop with the image itself. Using OSD minimizes and potentially eliminates image sprawl in an environment.

The main differentiator for OSD in ConfigMgr 2007 is its automation of the entire deployment process. OSD automates deployment of system images and additionally automates creating the image. Typically, most system images are manually created using a paper-based checklist. This process is time-consuming, error-prone, and subject to the interpretation and whim of the technician creating the image— factors preventing the process from being 100% reproducible or reliable. OSD eliminates these problems.

This chapter begins by introducing many of the tools used by OSD. Although a number of these tools are transparently incorporated into OSD, others require some administrative knowledge and manipulation. After discussing exactly what

OSD is and what you can do with it, the chapter launches into a walk-through of each of the OSD relevant nodes in the ConfigMgr console.

At its heart, OSD is an open-ended framework for deploying Windows operating systems. With some creativity, you can take it well beyond what Microsoft ever intended and what might be imagined. This chapter provides a considerable amount of information on how to best utilize OSD, but it cannot cover every detail or chase every rabbit hole. However, it presents information that is relevant for nearly every situation and offers a considerable amount of experienced-based knowledge.

Tools Overview

Although it is completely integrated into ConfigMgr, OSD uses and takes advantage of multiple separate tools. Knowing how OSD uses these tools and each tool's function is beneficial when setting up a deployment and troubleshooting problems. Microsoft also provides complementary tools that can enhance your deployment experience. The following sections discuss a number of these tools.

Sysprep

Sysprep, short for System Preparation, is one of the primary tools used for unattended setup of all flavors of Windows. Essentially, when used for imaging, Sysprep removes the unique Security Identifiers (SIDs) specific to a particular installation of Windows. Sysprep then configures the installation to run a brief, GUI-based, *mini-setup* when the system restarts. This mini-setup provides the following benefits:

▶ Generates new and unique SIDs for the system

▶ Enables the input of a new Windows product key

▶ Reruns the plug-and-play hardware detection

▶ Reruns the driver installation process

Sysprep in OSD
OSD fully automates the mini-setup process with a configuration file. The name of the file varies based on the version of Windows used:

▶ Sysprep.inf for Windows XP

▶ Unattend.xml for Windows Vista

OSD either builds the appropriate file on-the-fly or uses one supplied to it, inserting the information automatically into the Sysprep configuration file. This information includes the product key, organization name, networking information, and domain credentials. Incorporating this functionality adds to OSD's flexibility by eliminating the need to maintain multiple sysprep files supporting multiple deployment scenarios.

Version-Specific Flavors
Each version of Windows has its own specific version of Sysprep. For versions of Windows before Vista, you must make Sysprep available to the setup process separately by creating a

package or placing the files in *%SystemRoot%*\sysprep. You can find these files in the deploy.cab compressed file located in the \Support folder on the installation media, or you can download them from the Microsoft download site, www.microsoft.com/downloads.

For Windows Vista and later, the sysprep files come with the operating system and are located in *%windir%*\System32.

User State Migration Tool

The User State Migration Tool (USMT) is an extensive tool, deserving its own dedicated chapter if not an entire book! In short, USMT searches a system for all user data and settings, packaging them into a single archive file. You can then import this archive onto another system, restoring the user data and settings. USMT's default configuration captures all known Microsoft-centric settings and data, such as wallpaper, color scheme, Microsoft Office documents, favorites, and all files in the \My Documents folder. You can customize these defaults based upon the requirements of your environment. Microsoft provides further documentation on USMT at http://technet.microsoft.com/en-us/library/cc722032.aspx.

Incorporating XML Capabilities

The information USMT captures from a source system is highly customizable by modifying or creating a series of eXtensible Markup Language (XML) configuration files. These XML configuration files describe the files, folders, and Registry entries that USMT captures; you can either specify exact filenames and Registry locations, or perform wildcard searches to locate data or settings in these XML configuration files. USMT then uses these configuration files to capture all specified data and settings and put them into an archive for later use in restoring to a destination system.

The Tools in USMT

USMT actually consists of two tools:

▶ LoadState.exe

▶ ScanState.exe

As their names imply, ScanState.exe captures the data and settings whereas LoadState.exe restores them. Although the use of these two tools is mostly hidden from OSD in ConfigMgr 2007, it is worth noting.

Microsoft Deployment Toolkit

The Microsoft Deployment Toolkit (MDT) is a separate, yet complementary, set of tools for OSD. The MDT is available in one of two ways:

▶ As a completely stand-alone solution for deploying operating systems in a similar manner to OSD

▶ As an add-on to OSD

The Microsoft Solution Accelerator team developed the MDT, and MDT 2008 is the latest revision of the Business Desktop Deployment (BDD) Toolkit.

19

When installed as a complementary tool to ConfigMgr, the MDT provides a wizard that helps create the multiple packages required for OSD. It adds ten new tasks available for task sequences (the "Task Sequences" section in this chapter discusses task sequences), and adds a Preboot eXecution Environment (PXE) filter supporting unknown computers when deploying an image. The MDT is not required for ConfigMgr OSD but is a potentially valuable addition.

Windows Automated Installation Kit

The Windows Automated Installation Kit (WAIK) installs as part of your ConfigMgr installation and is available as a separate download from Microsoft. The version you use depends on the version of ConfigMgr you run:

▶ **Version 1.0**—Installed with ConfigMgr 2007 RTM (Release to Manufacturing)

▶ **Version 1.1**—Installed with ConfigMgr 2007 Service Pack (SP) 1

The primary difference between the two versions is that Microsoft updated the Windows PE (Windows Preinstallation Environment) boot images to Windows PE 2.1.

The WAIK is a set of tools designed to automate a Windows installation. ConfigMgr 2007 automatically uses some of the WAIK tools such as Sysprep and ImageX during the deployment process. The WAIK also includes user guides on how to use these tools, reference documents on the various unattended setup files, and Windows PE. Chapter 11, "Related Technologies and References," introduced WAIK.

Using OSD fully automates and completely integrates the many details of using the tools in the WAIK. You can also manipulate images outside of OSD using WAIK tools; this was not allowed in earlier versions of OSD.

ImageX

ImageX is a stand-alone tool that creates and deploys Windows Image Format (WIM) files from a Windows volume; because the tool is completely integrated into ConfigMgr, you do not need to install additional software. ImageX is also part of the WAIK and can be installed and used separately by installing the WAIK. Because of the tight integration, you can seamlessly use images created using ImageX outside of ConfigMgr in OSD; the opposite is also true.

Additionally, ImageX can "mount" previously created WIM files for read or read/write access. This allows you to access the files and folders stored in a WIM using a previously existing empty folder on the system. You can then add or modify files using Windows Explorer or any other tool, just as if they are part of the host system.

WIM files are the next generation of Microsoft's proprietary archive Cabinet files (often referred to as .CAB files). Using WIMs adds the ability to store metadata about the files and directories it contains; this capability allows you to restore a complete volume. Here are the advantages WIMs have over alternative, sector, or bit-based imaging tools:

▶ **File system independent**—You can capture WIMs from or deploy them to either NTFS (NT File System)- or FAT (File Allocation Table)-based file systems.

▶ **Volume size independent**—WIMs do not store any information about the volume from which they are captured. You can deploy WIMs if enough room is available on the destination volume.

▶ **Processor architecture independent**—ImageX works identically on x86, x64, and Itanium processors. The WIMs created on each are the same format and interchangeable.

▶ **File-based compression**—Files are independently compressed inside the WIM; this often leads to better compression ratios than bit-based images.

▶ **Multiple images in one file**—Multiple distinct volume images can be contained in a single WIM file.

▶ **Single instancing of files**—Multiple identical files are stored only one time. This leads to huge space gains when a WIM contains multiple images.

▶ **Nondestructive image application**—Images can be applied to a volume without destroying existing files and data.

The WIM file has proven to be so useful and versatile that Microsoft chose to drop the previous method of installing Windows with a file copy and instead uses a WIM file! Installation media for Vista and Windows 2008 contain single WIM files, taking advantage of all the items listed in this section.

System Image Manager

The System Image Manager (SIM) is part of the WAIK tools. SIM is a new GUI tool that builds unattended answer files for Windows Vista and Windows Server 2008. Instead of having to worry about the syntax of the answer file (particularly because the Vista/2008 answer file is now stored in XML), this tool graphically presents all available options and generates the unattend.xml file for you. This same file format is utilized for Sysprep equivalent files (sysprep.inf in Windows XP) used by the mini-setup to complete the setup of a Vista system when Sysprep is used.

SIM also allows you to service a Vista WIM file by adding drivers and published updates from Microsoft.

Windows PE

The Windows Preinstallation Environment is a mini-operating system currently based on Windows Vista. It includes support for networking, Windows Management Instrumentation (WMI), VBScript, batch files, and database access. Most things that run on a full-blown Vista system also run in Windows PE. The advantage of PE is that it is much smaller than the full-blown OS (typically around 100MB), and runs from a read-only disk. This makes PE suitable for booting from a CD/DVD, or over the network using PXE. OSD uses Windows PE as a boot environment, ensuring the native operating system will not interfere with the deployment process.

Many competitive imaging products traditionally used a DOS-based operating system for their boot environment. Using a DOS-based OS leads to several issues:

▶ Most hardware vendors no longer create or distribute DOS network drivers.

▶ DOS does not natively support advanced scripting languages, such as VBScript or Jscript.

These two factors greatly limit what you can accomplish during a DOS-based deployment. In contrast, Windows PE not only uses all Windows-based network drivers but also uses scripting languages, such as VBScript or JScript.

What Works Best for You

As with most things Microsoft, there are multiple paths to the same destination, none of them specifically wrong or right. For example, if you want to lock your screen—always a good idea when you step away from your desk—there are a number of ways you can accomplish this:

▶ Simultaneously press the Windows Key and L.

▶ Press Ctrl-Alt-Del and select Lock this computer.

▶ Create a desktop shortcut with the command line `RUNDLL32 USER32.DLL,LockWorkStation`.

OSD includes similar flexibility, allowing disparate organizations to use the same tool differently to meet their needs. Nearly every step of the process is customizable, and you can tailor it as necessary. Although this flexibility sometimes leads to uncertainty and conflicting opinions as to the best way to get things done, ultimately the only thing that matters is if it works for you and fits your organization's goals and requirements.

Having discussed tools used by OSD, the next section covers OSD.

OSD Scenarios

Here are the three main scenarios for operating system deployment, and OSD addresses all three:

▶ New system (also known as bare metal)

▶ In-place migration

▶ Side-by-side migration

The next sections describe these scenarios.

New System

The *new system* scenario is the easiest to deal with because you do not have to worry about user state—a user's *state* includes all the data, documents, and configuration of the system and applications that are unique to that user. This scenario simply involves wiping a system, whether it is straight from the vendor or previously used inside your organization, and deploying the image and applications to it.

In-Place Migration

An *in-place migration* is one where the system is currently in use but needs to have its operating system reloaded. This reload can be the result of a variety of reasons:

- An upgrade such as Windows XP to Windows Vista.

- The current operating system installation is broken beyond repair.

- The operating system installation does not meet current standards.

After a process is in place to quickly rebuild systems using OSD, organizations typically choose to re-image a system when the helpdesk spends a set amount of time troubleshooting without resolving an issue. This approach provides a way to decrease those helpdesk costs spent on fixing operating systems.

Side-by-Side Migration

A *side-by-side migration* usually occurs as the result of a hardware refresh. In this scenario, a new system physically replaces a user's system and might involve an operating system switch. Both in-place and side-by-side migration scenarios add the complexity of user state migration.

Official Microsoft Scenarios

For the record, there are five scenarios in existing Microsoft documentation:

- **New System**—This is the same as the New System scenario just described in the "New System" section.

- **Refresh**—This is an in-place migration without upgrading the operating system.

- **Replace**—This is a side-by-side migration without upgrading the operating system.

- **Upgrade**—This is either an in-place or a side-by-side migration, including the upgrading of the operating system.

- **OEM**—This is a scenario available to Original Equipment Manufacturers (OEM) using the MDT to prepare systems for customer or end-user delivery.

The primary difference in these scenarios from the ones previously presented in the "OSD Scenarios" section is the distinction made for upgrading the operating system. This distinction, although significant to the end-user, does not affect the actual operation of OSD, which does not change how it operates based upon the starting and ending operating system. It is affected however, by the change of physical hardware, and thus these scenarios were collapsed in this chapter to be more descriptive of the actual operation of OSD.

The OEM scenario is not covered in any detail because it is formally part of the MDT and not generally applicable to the primary audience of this book.

Imaging Goals

The core building block, which OSD builds on, is an image of a fully installed reference Windows system. *Reference systems* are systems used to build baseline images for deployment to the rest of the systems in the organization. Because hardware differences between a reference system and target deployment systems can cause issues, you must often use multiple reference systems to model your environment and thus create multiple images.

Enabling creation and deployment of this image is what OSD focuses on. However, OSD cannot automate the actual choice or definition of what goes into an image because this is not a technical decision.

A general definition of an image is *a single file that stores all the files and information for a specific disk drive volume on a computer system.* This file is portable and can be copied or deployed to a destination system.

Deploying the image file creates an exact duplicate of the original source volume. This allows you to easily copy the content of a disk drive volume containing an operating system, installed applications, and customizations to multiple other destination systems. In effect, the image clones the source system and allows rapid deployment of an operating system on a large scale. The process of copying the image to multiple machines is much quicker than doing a native Windows install and requires little manual intervention relative to a full Windows installation that includes applications and other miscellaneous configurations.

A prerequisite to the imaging process is inventorying all software and hardware in your organization. This helps ensure you take into account all possible variations—you must know all the possibilities to create the best possible images.

A question often asked is whether to include applications in the image and which ones. Do you include Microsoft Office? Microsoft Silverlight? Questions like these abound and fuel the continuing debate between using a thick or a thin image. The distinction between thick and thin images is somewhat subjective, so let's start with some simplistic definitions:

▶ **Thick image**—An image including the OS, OS updates and patches, miscellaneous components, drivers and applications

▶ **Thin image**—An image containing the OS with only a minimal set of updates and patches

Conventional wisdom is that a thin image is the better choice—why is this the case? A thin image is easier to maintain; it contains a minimal set of components and thus a smaller set of components that require updates. Like many theories, this one sounds great, but reality gets in its way; because you want to automate maintenance of images, this should be a minor concern.

Offline Image Maintenance

If you forget to add something in an image or need to add something simple to an image without having to create it again, never fear, ImageX is here.

Using ImageX, you can mount a WIM image file into an empty folder using the command `imagex /mountrw <image_path> <image index> <mount path>`, where the mount path is an empty folder. This loads an image to that empty folder, where you can access the entire file system contained in the image file as if it were part of the file system of the host operating system.

For example, if you have a WIM file called XPSP3.wim at the root of your C: Drive, you can load that WIM file to an empty folder on your C: drive named mount with the following command:

```
imagex /mountrw c:\XPSP3.wim 1 c:\mount
```

This mounts the image in a read-write mode; if you want to mount the image in a read-only mode, use /mount instead of /mountrw. Now you can open either Windows Explorer or a command prompt and manipulate the contents of the WIM file by navigating to C:\Mount. Figure 19.1 shows a folder listing of a sample captured Vista WIM file mounted in this fashion.

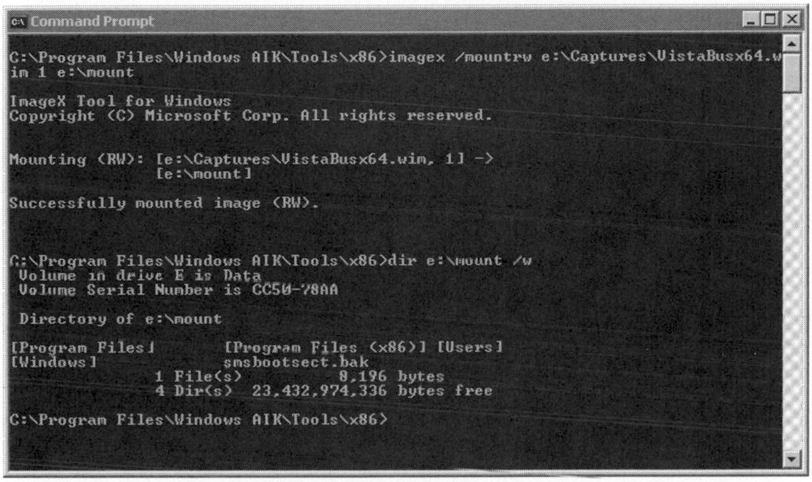

FIGURE 19.1   Mounting a captured WIM file

For example, you can add a bitmap file to the Windows folder (accessed at c:\mount\windows) or add a ReadMe.txt file to the All Users desktop (accessed at c:\mount\Documents and Settings\All Users\Desktop). You can make changes to the default user's Registry hive using reg.exe (see http://technet.microsoft.com/en-us/library/bb490984.aspx for a complete list of the reg.exe syntax). The following example shows setting the wallpaper for the default user:

1. Load the default user's Registry hive: **reg.exe load HKU\Mount c:\mount\Documents and Settings\Default User\ntuser.dat.**

2. Modify the desired setting: **reg.exe add HKU\Mount\Control Panel\Desktop /v Wallpaper /t REG_SZ /d %SystemRoot%\CompanyLogo.bmp.**

3. Unload the Registry hive: **reg.exe unload HKU\Mount.**

If you mount a Windows Vista WIM, you can also use the Windows SIM and Windows Package Manager from the WAIK to manipulate the image further, including performing the following tasks:

▶ Adding drivers

▶ Adding language packs

19

▶ Adding or removing packages such as security updates or service packs

Microsoft discusses each of these methods in detail at http://technet.microsoft.com/en-us/library/cc732695.aspx.

To save changes that you make to a file system contained in the WIM file using this mounting method, use the following command: imagex /unmount /commit c:\mount. Note the /commit option in the command line; without this option, no changes made to the mounted WIM are saved.

The WAIK must actually be installed on the host system to use ImageX to mount images. You cannot simply copy the ImageX executable to a system and use it to mount an image.

Here are several goals for the deployment images:

▶ **Hardware agnostic**—Few organizations can actually standardize on a single hardware system for all their desktops, so this goal should be obvious. What might not be as readily obvious is that it is achievable! The main obstacles to this goal are drivers and the Hardware Abstraction Layer (HAL) in Windows XP. Windows Vista (and Windows 7) change the way mass-storage drivers are handled and automatically change HALs as needed, so these concerns are no longer valid for the newer operating systems.

▶ **Universal**—Images should be a baseline for all deployments in an organization; they should contain the greatest common denominator of all the desktop needs in an organization. If not everyone requires a specific application, component, driver, and so on, it should not go into the image—you want to layer it on after deploying the image. This simple but important goal greatly affects your success with OSD. Creating an optimal universal baseline relies on your knowledge of the hardware and software in use at your organization and the accuracy of your inventory.

▶ **Deployment speed**—Although not as important as the previous goals, deployment speed is still a valid goal and becomes important if the network is not as fast as it should be or a wide area network (WAN) is involved. Applications and components included in an image only slightly increase the time it takes to deploy a system, because they are already installed and do not have to be pulled across the network separately. Applications and components layered on after the deployment might increase overall deployment time significantly because they are pulled over the network. Typically, installations include some files not even installed on the system, such as setup.exe or alternate language resource files (in the form of Dynamic Link Libraries or DLLs), which are installed only on systems supporting those languages. This can have a greater impact than is first realized.

▶ **Ease of maintenance**—In traditional, image-only deployment systems, ease of maintenance is typically the most important factor. Creating and updating images is often an intensive and lengthy manual process. Images created for these systems are typically thinner, to avoid putting in any components that might need updating. This ultimately increases overall deployment time and can increase the complexity of the deployment. ConfigMgr automates creating images, greatly easing this burden and freeing you from making decisions about your images that are based solely on maintaining the images.

An additional consideration is whether you can install an application generically or have its internal unique identifiers stripped. Sysprep does this for Windows, and OSD properly prepares the ConfigMgr Client if installed, but you must also think about the applications in the image. Some centrally managed antivirus products have trouble when installed in an image; they customize themselves to the specific system they are installed on and do not behave well when copied to another system as part of an image. This is something to verify with the vendors of the products you plan to incorporate into the image and is an area you should test.

Ultimately, thin versus thick is a moot argument. Every deployment image will probably be somewhere in the middle, and what is right for one organization might not be right for another. Having a thin image, just for the sake of having a thin image, should not be a primary goal. Maintaining images, if it is automated and done correctly, is a minor concern.

Hardware Considerations

Sometimes, hardware differences between references systems can cause problems. If you create the image properly, it can truly be hardware-agnostic. This task is sometimes more difficult in Windows XP than Windows Vista because of HAL issues and SATA (Serial Advanced Technology Attachment) drivers, but it is not impossible. To implement OSD successfully, you should derive a full inventory of all hardware used in the targeted environment. From this inventory, it can be determined if any anomalies exist, if all the drivers are still available from the manufacturer, or if all the systems meet the minimum requirements for the operating system you deploy.

When deploying Windows XP and Windows Server 2003, different HAL types are potentially the biggest obstacle to creating a hardware agnostic image. Here are the six HAL types available:

- ACPI Multiprocessor PC

- ACPI Uniprocessor PC

- Advanced Configuration and Power Interface (ACPI) PC

- MPS Multiprocessor PC

- MPS Uniprocessor PC

- Standard PC

The non-ACPI HALs in the preceding list are legacy types and normally needed only for very old hardware. Based on your hardware inventory, you probably can rule out their use completely.

19

TIP

Identifying the HAL

The Microsoft TechNet article "Identifying Hardware That Impacts Image-based Installations" (http://technet2.microsoft.com/windowsserver/en/library/942aaa8c-016f-4724-9a0f-04871abadd1a1033.mspx?mfr=true) describes how to identify what HAL a running system uses. Briefly, you must inspect the properties of the hal.dll file located in *%systemroot%*\system32 and compare the file details to the chart in the article.

You can identify the exact HAL in a captured image by right-clicking the image in ConfigMgr and choosing Properties. In the resulting dialog box, choose the Images tab at the top; see Figure 19.2 for an example.

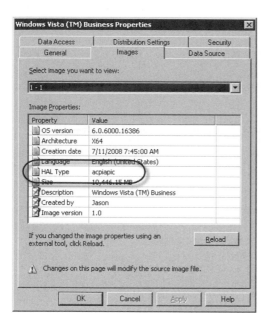

FIGURE 19.2   Identifying an image's HAL type

Eliminating legacy hardware typically leaves the three ACPI HAL types that follow three rules for imaging:

- **Images created with ACPI Uniprocessor PC HAL**—You can deploy these images to hardware requiring either ACPI Uniprocessor or ACPI Multiprocessor HALs.

- **Images created with ACPI Multiprocessor PC HAL**—You can deploy these images to hardware requiring either ACPI Uniprocessor or ACPI Multiprocessor HALs.

- **Images created using the Advanced Configuration and Power Interface (ACPI) PC HAL type**—You cannot use these images on systems requiring either of the other two HAL types. Luckily, hardware requiring this HAL type is outdated and no longer common.

This means you have to create only one image to support all your systems because they all require either ACPI Uniprocessor or ACPI Multiprocessor HALs. If through trial and error or through your hardware inventory you discover that another HAL type is in use, the only currently supported method of deploying images is to create multiple images, each containing a different HAL.

Mass storage drivers present a similar challenge; because they are essential to booting a system, they are referred to as *boot critical*. Neither Windows XP nor Windows Server 2003 includes a huge variety of the modern boot critical drivers; this includes a lack of SATA drivers, which are becoming more and more popular. You add boot-critical drivers to Windows XP and Windows Server 2003 in a different way than all other hardware drivers; you see this when manually installing a system requiring a boot-critical driver because you need to push F6 to install the driver during the blue screen pre-installation phase. OSD gracefully handles this situation with little overhead or extra work. Some trial and error testing may be involved, though.

Both Windows Vista and Windows Server 2008 include the most popular SATA drivers out of the box. If you do encounter a drive controller requiring a driver not included out of the box, you can load the driver the same way as other hardware drivers—this is due to an architectural change made by Microsoft in the handling of boot critical drivers in Windows Vista and Server 2008.

Although creating multiple images initially sounds like a hassle, it should not be. If you have properly automated your image build process using a Build and Capture task sequence (discussed in the "Task Sequences" section in this chapter), creating the multiple images is as simple as running that sequence on a system supporting each type of HAL in your inventory. The task sequence is automated, so the images will be identical except for the HAL type that they contain.

In addition, using the magic that is ImageX, these images can be merged into a single file using the /append option: `imagex /append <image_path> <image_file> <"image_name"> [<"description">]`. Because of the single instancing of WIM images, the resulting WIM file contains only one copy of each file in common between the images (which will be every file except one, the hal.dll). The result is that the WIM file will be only slightly larger than maintaining separate WIM files for each version.

The only real pain point with this solution is finding a reference system for each type of HAL. Because most of these HALs are legacy and only used on aging or outdated hardware, chances are that you do not have any in your lab and must be creative in procuring one from an active user.

Site Systems

Site systems, introduced in Chapter 2, "Configuration Manager 2007 Overview," divide the functionality and workload of the various ConfigMgr tasks. OSD, being part of ConfigMgr, also utilizes site systems. Aside from a DP and the ever-present MP, there are also two optional site system roles used by OSD: a PXE service point and a state migration point. DPs serve the same role for OSD that they do in software distribution: to deliver software packages to client systems and are required for OSD to work properly. A site MP is also required to facilitate communication between clients and ConfigMgr, although this chapter does not discuss it because this functionality is not specific to OSD.

The next sections discuss the use of these site systems with OSD.

Distribution Points

Distribution points provide clients with all packages defined for use in ConfigMgr. This includes packages specific to OSD including drivers, applications, images, and operating system installs. These packages must be made available on distribution points just like any software distribution package.

Utilizing Multicasting

Multicasting is a new feature provided by Windows Deployment Services (WDS) in Windows Server 2008; ConfigMgr 2007 Release 2 (R2) can take advantage of multicasting if the DP is installed on a Windows Server 2008 system with the WDS role also installed. Multicasting enables transporting a single stream of data over a network. Clients can then subscribe to this stream of data. The main advantage of multicasting over the traditional unicast model is this single stream of data for multiple destination systems. Unicast communication requires a separate stream of data for every client system.

In addition to WDS, you must install Internet Information Services (IIS) on the site system, including Internet Server Application Program Interface (ISAPI) extensions and IIS 6 management compatibility. Multicasting also requires support and configuration from the network infrastructure; this is beyond the scope of this book and highly dependent on the equipment used in your environment.

A downside for many multicast implementations for image deployment is that you must manually coordinate the start of the data stream. All client systems that you want to receive the stream must be waiting for the stream prior to it being sent. With WDS multi-casting in Windows Server 2008, Microsoft implemented a catch-up feature. This enables clients that join a stream midway through to continue to receive the entire stream. WDS tracks when clients join the image stream and replays the stream until all clients subscribed to the stream have received the entire image.

Multicasting is used only for image deployment in OSD; it is not used for any type of package delivery including driver, application, or operating system install. If you plan to use multicasting heavily, this might affect the decisions you make about what to put into the actual image. It might make more sense to make the image fatter to improve distribution times by using multicasting.

Installing Multicasting

To enable and configure multicasting, perform the following steps:

1. Install ConfigMgr 2007 R2. (See Chapter 8, "Installing Configuration Manager 2007," for additional information.)

2. In the ConfigMgr console, navigate to Site Management -> *<Site Code> <Site Name>* -> Site Systems -> *<Site System>* where *<Site System>* is the name of the system with a distribution point installed.

3. In the results pane, right-click the ConfigMgr distribution point; then select Properties. The ConfigMgr distribution point Properties dialog box opens.

4. Click the Multicast tab (shown in Figure 19.3), and select the Enable multicast check box. You can configure the following from this tab:

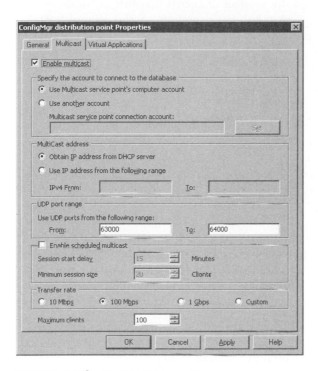

FIGURE 19.3   Multicast Properties

> **Specify the account to connect to the database**—As the text implies, you can specify an alternate account to use to connect to the site database if the Local System account cannot be used.

> **Multicast Address**—This allows you to specify a specific multicast address according to Request for Comment (RFC) 3171 (http://www.ietf.org/rfc/rfc3171.txt) or obtain one from a DHCP server.

> **UDP Port Range**—Specify which User Datagram Protocol (UDP) ports to use for multicasting.

> **Enable scheduled multicast**—Scheduled multicast configures a multicast session to wait for a specific number of clients to join a session or a number of minutes to wait before starting a session. This allows you to coordinate the client systems and ensure they are all online and available before the session

19

starts. The use of the catch-up feature described in the "Utilizing Multicasting" section reduces the importance of this functionality, but it is still available.

▶ **Transfer rate**—This setting optimizes the performance of the multicast data stream for the selected network type.

▶ **Maximum clients**—This caps the number of clients that this distribution point serves using multicast. This number is cumulative across all multicast sessions.

PXE Service Point

PXE service points enable the distribution of OSD boot images to clients via PXE (see the "Boot Images" section later in this chapter for details regarding boot images). PXE service points are actually dependent on an installation of WDS; a PXE service point essentially just takes over control of WDS. You can install WDS on Windows Server 2003 and Windows Server 2008 only, and it does not need to be collocated with any other site roles. WDS in Windows Server 2008 adds the ability to multicast images over a network enabled for multicast.

▶ To install WDS in Windows Server 2003, use Add/Remove Windows Components from the Add/Remove Programs applet in the Control Panel—WDS is listed near the bottom. WDS in Windows Server 2003 actually has multiple modes to support legacy Remote Installation Service (RIS) images; ensure you install WDS in mixed or native mode to support WIM based images.

▶ To install WDS in Windows Server 2008, use the Add Roles functionality of Server Manager. WDS is typically the last listed role and offers two subservices: Deployment Server and Transport Server. You should select both of these.

You do not need to configure WDS in any way after installing it. ConfigMgr seizes control over WDS after you install the PXE Service Point. If you do configure WDS, conflicts often arise and cause you endless hours of troubleshooting.

Multiple PXE Providers on the Same Network Subnet

A question often fielded by ConfigMgr OSD implementers is how an organization can have multiple PXE providers on the same network subnet. Usually, the client organization already has a PXE server in place to support a legacy imaging product. The real answer to this question is that it depends on the network infrastructure, not on ConfigMgr.

PXE is a standards-based protocol based on DHCP and network broadcasts. The network card installed on a system controls the actual booting of a system; this is completely independent of ConfigMgr. Generally, the first PXE provider to respond to a PXE request is chosen by the network card being booted from. On a network level, it is best to segregate PXE providers on separate subnets to control the broadcasts.

It is also possible to specify a specific PXE server using DHCP options 60, 66, and 67; however, these options are specific to a single network subnet and cannot be made more granular for PXE booting purposes. There are other options including a newer PXE specification, but this problem is completely outside the bounds of ConfigMgr and WDS.

Two excellent resources for detailed PXE information are at http://technet.microsoft.com/en-us/library/cc732351.aspx and http://support.microsoft.com/kb/244036. The second reference is a dated KB article referring to RIS, but the general PXE information is still valid.

Adding a PXE Service Point role to a site system is similar to adding any ConfigMgr role to any other site system. Perform the following steps:

1. In the ConfigMgr console, start by navigating to Site Database -> Site Management -> *<Site Code> <Site Name>* -> Site Settings -> Site Systems.

   ▶ If the system running WDS is not currently a site system, right-click Site Systems; then choose New -> Server. This launches the New Site System Server Wizard. Enter the name of the site system and the intranet accessible fully qualified domain name (FQDN) of the WDS server.

   ▶ If the WDS server already is a ConfigMgr site system, right-click the server and choose New Roles. This launches the New Site Role Wizard which looks and acts exactly like the New Site System Server Wizard, except that the wizard has already filled in the site system name and intranet FQDN for you.

2. On the System Role Selection page, choose PXE service point.

3. Note the information given in the PXE Service Point Configuration dialog box, as shown in Figure 19.4, and click Yes.

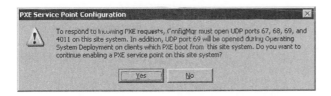

FIGURE 19.4   The PXE Service Point Configuration dialog box

4. On the PXE – General wizard page, you have the following choices:

   ▶ **Allow this PXE service point to respond to incoming PXE requests—** This first check box does exactly what it says, enables or disables PXE booting.

▶ **Enable unknown computer support**—This option only exists if you have installed ConfigMgr 2007 R2. It enables exactly what the name implies. The "Unknown Computer Support" section describes this capability in more detail.

▶ **Require a password for computer to boot to PXE**—This check box requires entering a password during the PXE boot process on the client. If enabled, you must also enter a password.

▶ **Interfaces**—On a multihomed system, this section allows you to limit which interfaces listen for PXE boot requests.

▶ **Specify the PXE server response delay**—This setting determines how long to wait before responding to PXE boot requests. The setting might help in situations where multiple PXE servers exist on the same subnet.

5. On the PXE – Database wizard page, you can choose an alternate account to use to connect to the site database and a certificate to provide mutual authentication during the OSD process. If your ConfigMgr site is not in native mode, the wizard automatically generates a self-signed certificate. If in native mode, you must supply a single certificate that all PXE booted clients can use. See the "Native Mode" section in this chapter for further details.

To review or change any of these settings after you install the PXE Service Point, navigate to Site Management -> *<Site Code> <Site Name>* -> Site Systems -> *<Site System>* in the ConfigMgr console, right-click ConfigMgr PXE service point in the right pane, and choose Properties.

PXE service points also become pseudo distribution points, listed alongside all other distribution points when copying packages. You can tell the difference between standard DPs and PXE service points by the addition of "\SMSPXEIMAGES$" to the name of the PXE service point as listed in distribution point selection list boxes. You should distribute boot images to PXE service points only because this is the only type of image provided by PXE service points with ConfigMgr OSD.

TIP

Make 32-Bit and 64-Bit Images Available

You should make both a 32-bit and 64-bit boot image available from the PXE distribution point. This enables WDS to deliver boot images to systems with either architecture. The properties of a task sequence determine the actual boot image regardless of the physical architecture of the target system; however, if the target system is a 64-bit system and a 64-bit boot image is not available, the PXE boot will not succeed.

For a complete discussion of troubleshooting WDS and PXE service points, see http://blogs.technet.com/smsandmom/archive/2008/09/17/configmgr-2007-troubleshooting-pxe-service-point-issues-and-wds-service-not-starting.aspx.

State Migration Point

The other optional site system role is the state migration point. These site systems store user state data captured from a system. A complete discussion of User State Migration is in the "User State Migration" section in this chapter.

State migration points are simply shared folders on a designated site system. Multiple state migration points are allowed in a site to provide some load balancing and better availability based on connectivity. State migration points are required only if you make use of state migration tasks, described in the "Tasks" section. These tasks automatically contact a state migration point to store and retrieve user state data.

Adding a state migration point to a site system is similar to adding any ConfigMgr role to any other site system. Perform the following steps:

1. In the ConfigMgr console, start by navigating to Site Database -> Site Management -> *<Site Code> <Site Name>* -> Site Settings -> Site Systems.

    ▶ If the system is not currently a site system, right-click Site Systems; then choose New -> Server. This launches the New Site System Server Wizard. Enter the name of the site system and the intranet accessible FQDN of the server.

    ▶ If the system already is a ConfigMgr site system, right-click the system and choose New Roles. This launches the New Site Role Wizard, which looks and acts exactly like the New Site System Server Wizard, except that the wizard has already filled in the site system name and intranet FQDN for you.

2. On the System Role Selection page, choose State migration point.

3. On the State Migration Point Wizard page, you have the following choices:

    ▶ **Folders**—This list box allows you to designate specific folders on the site system to use. You must specify a specific local path, the maximum number of clients to serve, and the minimum amount of free space on the drive hosting the folder to consider the state migration point healthy.

    ▶ **Deletion policy**—In this section you specify how long to save user state on a state migration point after it is restored.

    ▶ **Restore-only mode**—This mode prevents this state migration point accepting new user state but allows retrieval of previously saved user state data.

To review or change any of these settings after you install the state migration point, navigate to Site Management -> *<Site Code> <Site Name>* -> Site Systems -> *<Site System>* in the ConfigMgr console, right-click ConfigMgr state migration point in the right pane, and choose Properties.

19

Boot Images

From the perspective of a client system involved in OSD, Windows PE is the initial engine of the entire process, making its delivery to a client system critical. Windows PE is contained in the boot images and delivered to a client system in one of three ways:

▶ PXE during a network boot

▶ Removable media such as a CD or DVD-ROM

▶ A direct copy from a DP

The next sections discuss these delivery methods.

PXE Booting

PXE booting is typically used for bare-metal or new hardware installations when the system does not have a ConfigMgr client agent installed. Using PXE booting requires meeting the following list of criteria:

▶ A DHCP server must be available for use.

▶ The network must allow the PXE broadcast packets to reach the PXE server. PXE and DHCP use BOOTP (Bootstrap Protocol), which is a broadcast based protocol. Layer 3 network devices do not pass broadcast traffic by default; the PXE server must be on the same network segment as the client attempting to PXE boot, or you must configure the Layer 3 network devices to forward the broadcasts to the PXE server.

Most organizations already have BOOTP broadcasts forwarded on their Layer 3 devices to support DHCP; configuring them to forward BOOTP broadcasts to support PXE is a nearly identical process with the only difference being a different destination server.

▶ You must install the boot images on the PXE distribution point. This is a commonly forgotten and misunderstood step. When you add a PXE service point to your hierarchy, ConfigMgr takes over the installation of WDS on the PXE service point system. When installed, the PXE service point then registers an additional PXE-based distribution point, listed along with the other DPs in the hierarchy.

Removable Media

Typically, you use removable media for bare-metal installation of new hardware where PXE booting is not feasible. This includes the following situations:

▶ Over a WAN because the network will not forward the PXE broadcasts.

▶ Unavailable because the target system does not support it. (It has been a long time since network cards did not support network boot using PXE, but it is possible.)

▶ When you want to be absolutely certain that a system does not connect to the network prior to being fully loaded and fully patched to a designated baseline.

▶ The target system is in a protected subnet such as a DMZ (demilitarized zone, also referred to as a *perimeter network*) and cannot communicate back to the site system.

You can create images for removable media by right-clicking a task sequence and choosing Create Task Sequence Media. This launches the straightforward Task Sequence Media Wizard, allowing you to choose which type of media to create. You can burn the resulting image to a CD or DVD or place it on a bootable USB device.

You can create three types of task sequence media:

▶ **Stand-alone**—Creates a self-contained image that contains Windows PE and all the packages and information specific to a task sequence—except for software updates. Using stand-alone media allows you to run a task sequence on a target system without connectivity to a ConfigMgr site system.

When you create a stand-alone image, the system prompts for a distribution point from which to copy packages. You can set task sequence variables specific to this media image, allowing you to customize the task sequence while knowing that it will not connect to the site server during installation.

The system also prompts you to choose a media size during the creation of the image: 650MB (CD), 4.6GB (DVD), or 8.5GB (DL-DVD). Depending on the size of packages included in the task sequence, there may be multiple images created; choosing the CD image size of 650MB guarantees multiple images. When you boot a system to stand-alone media, it acts as if the task sequence used to create the media was advertised to the system with a mandatory advertisement.

▶ **Bootable**—Creates a burnable image of the chosen boot image. This allows the target system to boot into Windows PE as if you delivered the Windows PE image using PXE. You can also initiate the task sequence in a bootable media image from within Windows using the autorun feature of the image. This allows the bootable image to behave as if delivered using a ConfigMgr software distribution.

A new ConfigMgr R2 option in the Task Sequence Media Wizard relevant to bootable media is to enable unknown computer support. This enables the new unknown computer support functionality of R2, as described in the "Using Unknown System Resources in R2" section in this chapter.

▶ **Capture**—Creates a CD that allows you to capture a reference system outside of a task sequence; the image is not bootable, and you must initiate it from within an installed operating system using the Autoplay function.

The capture media option launches a wizard that copies Windows PE to a hidden, bootable, file-based partition. It syspreps the system and then reboots into Windows PE where it captures an image of the system. Note that the proper sysprep files must already exist on the target system. The wizard also prompts for a target location, filename, and credentials. Figure 19.5 shows the first screen of the Image Capture Wizard.

19

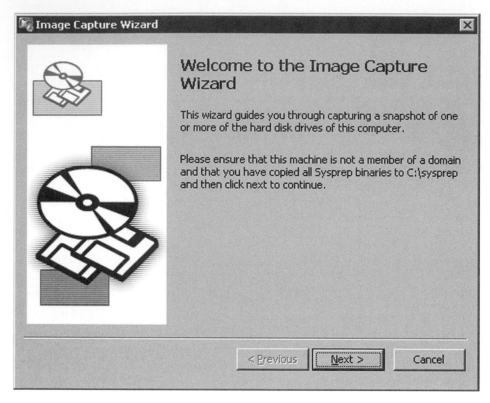

FIGURE 19.5   The Image Capture Wizard in action

The capture media can be useful in a variety of circumstances, such as if you already have a perfect reference system or a perfect process for creating the reference system. Another use of the capture media would be to import an image from a competitive imaging system; you would first deploy the image to a suitable reference system and then recapture it into a WIM format using the image capture media.

Using a Distribution Point

The final method of delivering Windows PE is through ConfigMgr itself! If a system already has a ConfigMgr client agent installed and an OSD task sequence is advertised to the client and initiated, ConfigMgr downloads the boot image containing Windows PE to a special pseudo-partition on the hard drive. This pseudo-partition is then set to be the active partition. An automatic reboot is initiated, and the system is booted into the Windows PE image contained in the active pseudo-partition.

The "Task Sequence Targeting" section discusses advertisements further.

Incorporating Windows PE

Each of the methods just described in the previous sections causes the target system to boot into a boot image containing Windows PE. When in Windows PE, an advertised task sequence is initiated or continued. (The "Task Sequence Targeting" section later in this chapter discusses advertising a task sequence.) The primary reason for using Windows PE is to perform those tasks on the system you cannot perform while the host operating system runs, such as deploying or capturing an image. Windows PE is a robust environment that supports most things available in Windows Vista, including advanced techniques and tools such as scripting and plug-and-play driver detection.

Network access is critical to the success of the task sequence in Windows PE (except for the stand-alone media option). For Windows PE to connect to the network, it must have the proper network drivers installed. OSD uses Windows PE 2.0 (ConfigMgr 2007 RTM) or Windows PE 2.1 (ConfigMgr 2007 Service Pack 1); both versions are based on Windows Vista and use Windows Vista drivers. Integrating new drivers into the boot images is straightforward, and you can accomplish this in several different ways:

▶ The Import Driver Wizard includes a page allowing you to add drivers to selected boot images.

▶ You can right-click an already imported driver and choose Add to Boot Image from the context menu.

▶ The properties of each boot image include a Windows PE page, which contains a list box for drivers. You can click the starburst button at the top to add drivers, as shown in Figure 19.6.

  This last method is difficult to use because it only lists simple driver names and not versions or other identifying information.

Computer Associations

The Computer Associations node under Operating System Deployment in the ConfigMgr console contains mappings used for User State Migration. These organize the migration of user state and settings from a source to destination computer. The mappings specify source and target systems identified by Media Access Control (MAC) address and the type of migration. There are two types of migrations:

▶ In-place (which has the same source and destination MAC addresses)

▶ Side-by-side

The mapping entries also record the date that state data was captured and restored, the location where state data is stored, and the encryption key for the state data.

For side-by-side migrations, you manually create computer associations. Right-click Computer Association (Site Management -> Computer Management -> Operating System

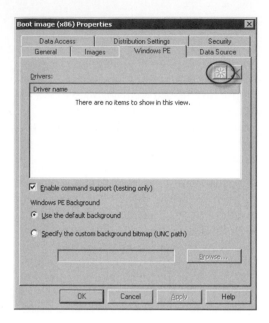

FIGURE 19.6   Adding a driver to a boot image

Deployment -> Computer Associations) and choose New -> Computer Association to launch the New Computer Association dialog box, shown in Figure 19.7. This dialog allows you to specify the source and destination computer. You can use the User Accounts tab to specifically limit which profiles are captured. You must create a side-by-side computer association manually before an applicable task sequence is run on a system. If one does not exist, ConfigMgr automatically creates an in-place computer association.

After creating an association, you can right-click it to view the following information:

- ▶ Source Computer Properties

- ▶ Destination Computer Properties

- ▶ User Accounts

- ▶ Recovery Information

The next sections discuss recovering previously captured user data and importing computers previously unknown to Configuration Manager.

Recovery

To recover previously captured user data manually, you must first extract the encryption key and the user state store location from the computer association. These display by selecting View Recovery Information from the context menu of an association used to capture data, as shown in Figure 19.8. You can then pass the key and the state location on a command line to USMT using the /decrypt option. Sample syntax would be

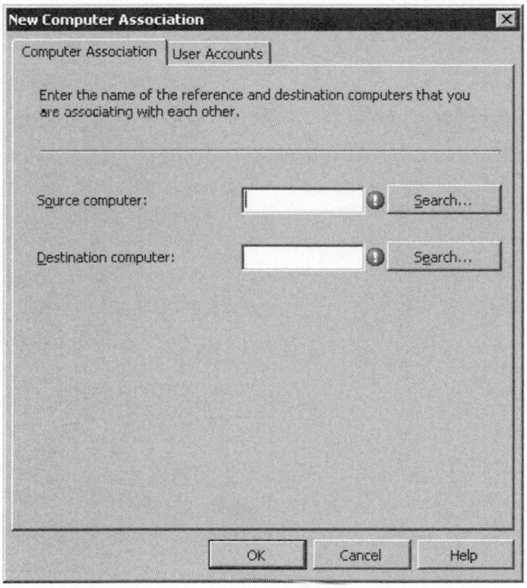

FIGURE 19.7   The New Computer Association dialog box

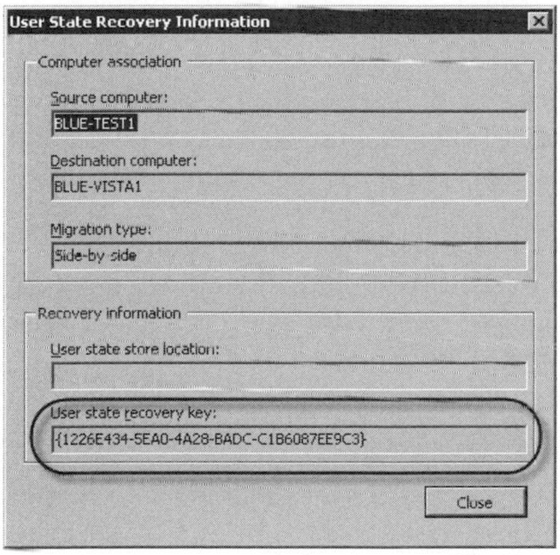

FIGURE 19.8   User state recovery key from a computer association

```
loadstate <state store path> /i <migapp.xml> /i <miguser.xml> /i  <migsys.xml>
/decrypt /key:<encryption key>
```

Miguser.xml, migapp.xml, and migsys.xml are the xml configuration files used to capture the state.

> **CAUTION**
>
> **Possible Data Loss**
>
> Recovering previously captured user data restores the data contained in the state store to the system where the command is run, which might cause local data to be overwritten.

Unknown Computer Support

If you want to use a new system as a reference computer or deploy an image to a new system using PXE that does not have a client agent on it, you must make the system known to ConfigMgr; this capability is known as *unknown computer support*. You can do this using a computer association or the MDT, or with the unknown system resources functionality available in R2.

Using Computer Associations

When PXE or a boot disk initiates a deployment, the MAC address or System Management BIOS (SMBIOS) GUID is passed to ConfigMgr. To allow ConfigMgr to respond to an unknown system, create a new system resource specifying either the MAC address or SMBIOS GUID of the unknown system. You do this, in the ConfigMgr console in the Operating System Deployment node, by right-clicking Computer Association and choosing Import Computer Information to launch the Import Computer Information Wizard. The wizard allows you to add a single or multiple computers:

▶ To add a single computer, choose Import single computer from the first page of the wizard. The next page is the Single Computer page, shown in Figure 19.9. Enter the desired computer name and either the MAC address or SMBIOS GUID of the new system. You can obtain this information when PXE booting a system from the PXE boot screen or by checking the smspxe.log. You can also get this information shipped to you by the computer manufacturer when it sends you the hardware. (Although ConfigMgr administrators often don't see the shipment manifest.)

> **TIP**
>
> **Locating the smspxe.log**
>
> If the PXE deployment point is on a site server, the smspxe.log is located in *%ProgramFiles%*\SMS_CCM\Logs; otherwise, you can find it in *%windir%*\system32\ccm\logs.

You can also specify a source computer to import user and system state settings from; this creates a computer association with the specified computer as the source and the new system as the target.

▶ Importing computers one at a time can be time-consuming; alternatively, you can import multiple computers at once using a file formatted with comma-separated

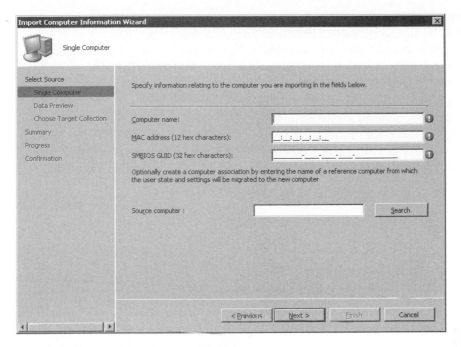

FIGURE 19.9   Importing a single computer using the Import Computer Information Wizard

values (CSV). You can create this file with Microsoft Excel, Notepad, or any other text editor and save the file using plain text format. The file must contain the desired names of the systems and either their MAC addresses or SMBIOS GUIDs, comma-separated. Optionally, you can specify the source computer for user and system state migration.

To import multiple computers, choose the Import computers using a file option from the Import Computer Information Wizard. The wizard prompts you for the CSV file to use and allows you to map the data in the file to the correct columns.

The last page of the wizard is the same whether you import a single or multiple computers: You can choose to add the new systems to the All Systems collection or to one that you specify. You should choose to import the new systems into one of your OSD collections so that the appropriate task sequence-based advertisements also apply to your new systems.

TIP

SMBIOS GUID

The way most PXE boot screens display the GUID does not correspond to the way ConfigMgr expects it; the GUID is the same but displayed differently. The result is ConfigMgr will not find the system, causing the task sequence to be unavailable or the PXE boot to fail. If you choose to use SMBIOS GUIDs, the best place to get them is from the smspxe.log on the PXE service point.

Using the MDT

The MDT offers an alternative way to handle unknown systems when PXE booting; it installs a VBScript-based PXE filter that automatically creates a resource in ConfigMgr for systems that do not already have one. This resource is identical to that created with the method just described in the "Using Computer Associations" section.

Using Unknown System Resources in R2

ConfigMgr 2007 R2 introduces a new method to handle unknown systems: an *unknown system resource*. You can place this resource in collections using direct membership rules like any other resource in ConfigMgr. ConfigMgr then applies advertisements applicable to this resource to any unknown systems encountered. There are actually two unknown system resources:

- ▶ One for x64
- ▶ One for x86

In addition to these two new resources, ConfigMgr creates a new collection, called All Unknown Computers. These two resources are initially members of this collection, so you can use it to target OSD deployments.

Unknown computer support in R2 is enabled by checking a check box on the ConfigMgr PXE service point properties dialog box as described in the "PXE Service Point" section in this chapter. You can also enable unknown computer support for removable boot media by checking the Enable unknown computer support check box on the security page of the Task Sequence Media Wizard.

NOTE

Unprovisioned Computers

Installing ConfigMgr 2007 R2 also adds a new node to the Operating System Deployment subtree in the ConfigMgr console, called Unprovisioned Computers. When ConfigMgr begins an OSD deployment to an unknown computer, it creates a new system resource for the new unknown computer and assigns it a unique identifier. When the deployment finishes successfully, the resource is removed from the Unprovisioned Computers node. If the deployment fails, the resource remains in this node.

In general, the resources in this node are informational only and used to track deployments to previously unknown computers using the new unknown computer resources.

Operating System Install Packages and Image Packages

Deployments are based off imported Windows source files or a captured image. You import the source files for Windows into ConfigMgr to create an Operating System Install Package or import a captured image to create an Image Package.

Operating System Install Packages are typically used only to automate creating images and cause the target system to go through a full Windows installation. You create images from a sample reference system as discussed in the "Imaging Goals" section in this chapter. Install and configure this reference system based upon the goals also outlined in the "Imaging Goals" section and the needs of your organization. ConfigMgr is about automation, and OSD is about automating the entire process of deploying a system.

Automated Image Creation and Capture

The intent is to automate image creation completely, ensuring the process is repeatable and requires little or no manual intervention. The image you create can make or break the entire process, and this image greatly depends upon the system where you build it.

The *reference computer*, unlike the software you load on it, should be the least common denominator in your organization. The best system to choose is one that requires no additional third-party drivers (or only one or two at the most); this has become more difficult with Windows XP because its built-in set of drivers are aging but should not be an issue with Vista.

"Real World:" Using Virtual Machine Technology for the Reference Computer

Sometimes finding a free system to use as a reference computer is difficult; many organizations do not like to keep spare systems on the shelf. Even if you do have a spare system sitting around, it might quickly be cannibalized or have parts that fail just because it has been sitting in a corner doing nothing! A perfect solution to this dilemma is to use a virtual machine (VM); whether it is hosted on your local desktop or laptop or in the data center on a server does not matter. This system is a VM with a small footprint; it rarely contributes any load to the host system. Additionally, the system is portable, easily reproducible, and has little or no associated hardware costs. You can even have multiple VMs running simultaneously to test variations of a specific scenario in parallel.

VMs created on Microsoft Hyper-V and VMWare virtualization products require no additional drivers. Each product line has optional integration components you can install that do include some drivers, but these drivers are not required for basic functionality of the VM. This helps because it keeps the image free from drivers, adding to the reasons for using a VM to build and capture an image. Unfortunately, Microsoft Virtual PC 2007 is not a good candidate for this task, because it uses the Advanced Configuration and Power Interface (ACPI) PC HAL discussed in the "Hardware Considerations" section.

The easiest and recommended way to create an image is to use a ConfigMgr task sequence, built using the Build and capture a reference operating system image option available with the New Task Sequence Wizard. The next sections discuss these steps.

19

Preparing for the Task Sequence

There are a series of things to prepare before creating and using the task sequence. Perform the following tasks:

1. **Create an Operating System Install Package**. You can use this package to perform a full automated installation of the operating system to the reference system using the source files provided, and it is based upon the source files from a Windows CD (XP or Server 2003) or DVD (Vista or Server 2008). Generally, it is best to use installation media that has the latest service packs slipstreamed into it or manually integrate the latest service pack into the source files. Additionally, you can integrate most XP patches directly into the XP source files, eliminating or reducing the need to install them during the deployment process.

   Unfortunately, there is no supported way to slipstream Vista SP 1 or SP 2 into the WIM distributed on the RTM Vista DVD. You must either obtain a DVD from Microsoft containing Vista with the desired service pack already integrated or deploy the service pack as part of the post installation process.

   As with all software packages in ConfigMgr, deploy the resulting package or image to the applicable distribution points using the New Package Wizard; because these packages and images tend to be quite large, you should plan accordingly to minimize any impact on the network. Also, allow the appropriate amount of time for these to actually be copied to the proper distribution points before trying to use them.

2. **Import drivers and create driver packages**. The "Image Deployment" section covers drivers in detail.

3. **Create software distribution packages**. The basic Build and Capture task sequence requires several packages, along with some optional ones. The New Task Sequence Wizard prompts you for each of the package types.

Adding Packages

The first required package is for the ConfigMgr client. Create this package with the Package from Definition Wizard, using the Configuration Manager Client Upgrade package definition, as highlighted in Figure 19.10. Set the package to Always obtain files from a source directory. The source files for this package are located at \\<*Site Server*> \SMS_<*Site Code*>\client.

The second required package is actually for Windows XP/2003 only. This package is for the sysprep files; no programs are necessary. Sysprep is included as part of Windows Vista and Windows Server 2008, and thus a separate package is not necessary to deploy these two operating systems.

Optional packages include any baseline software deployment packages that you want to include in your image and one for your unattended setup files. Here are the unattended setup files:

▶ Unattend.txt and/or sysprep.inf for Windows XP/Windows Server 2003

▶ Unattend.xml for Windows Vista/Windows Server 2008

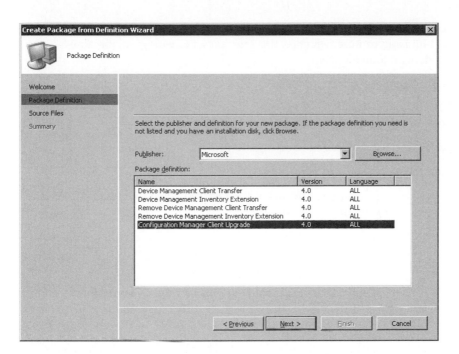

FIGURE 19.10   Choosing the Configuration Manager Client Upgrade definition in the Create Package from Definition Wizard

OSD modifies these setup files to include configuration items specified in the task sequence including the product key, username, organization, time zone, domain or workgroup to join, Administrator password, and licensing mode. If you do not supply a package with unattended setup files, ConfigMgr builds them on-the-fly using default settings and settings configured in the task sequence. Packages used for unattended setup files or Sysprep should not have any programs defined in them. These packages are strictly used to make the files available for OSD's use during the deployment.

Creating the Task Sequence

When the packages are in place, you can launch the New Task Sequence Wizard from the Task Sequences context menu and create a Build and Capture task sequence. The wizard prompts for the following information:

- ▶ **Task Sequence Name**—This is purely aesthetic.

- ▶ **Boot image**—The boot image is the WinPE image, which delivers the task sequence.

- ▶ **Operating System Installation Package**—Previously created package containing the OS source files.

- ▶ **Product key**—Not required if using Vista because this can be supplied after the installation is complete using a KMS (Key Management Service) or manually.

- ▶ **Administrator Account Status**—You can set the local Administrator account to be disabled by default.

19

▶ **Join a workgroup or domain**—If you choose a domain, you must supply credentials. For a typical build and capture sequence, this must be set to workgroup because Sysprep will fail on a domain joined system.

▶ **Configuration Manager client package**—This is the ConfigMgr client package previously created.

▶ **Software updates installation**—Specify all, mandatory only, or none.

▶ **Software deployment packages**—Packages to include in the image.

▶ **Sysprep package**—Sysprep is not required on Vista and Server 2008.

▶ **Image Properties**—These are descriptors of the task sequence including the creator of the package, its version, and a description.

▶ **Image Destination**—The Universal Naming Convention (UNC) path and filename to the image you create. You must supply credentials for an account capable of writing to the UNC path.

Be aware that this path and filename are static; if you run the same capture task sequence multiple times, it overwrites the same image file. This might be the desired result and should be taken into account.

After creating the task sequence, you can modify it by right-clicking and choosing Edit. It is always a good practice to open the task sequence to verify all steps were created automatically, enter any other optional information, and change the default settings as appropriate. Some things that typically are changed or added include the time zone, the disk format type (by default a full format of the destination volume is performed) and the addition of the unattended files package.

Formatting the Destination Volume

Leaving the disk format type as the default full format can add significant time to deploying the image. A full format of a typical 80GB hard drive takes around 10 minutes. If you have systems with larger drives, this time is increased. To change the format type to Quick, edit the Partition Disk 0 task in the task sequence. Update the volume properties at the bottom of the dialog box by highlighting the Default (Primary) volume and clicking the properties button. From the resulting dialog box, enable the Quick format check box and click OK (see Figure 19.11).

The End Product

The result of these processes is a baseline image containing an operating system, applications, and customizations you can deploy to any system and layer on top of with further applications and customizations. If set up properly, the image creation process on average-performing hardware should take around an hour for XP/2003 and about 90 minutes for Vista/2008; it will also be completely automated other than turning the reference system on—although this could also be automated using Wake On LAN. Modifying the image in the future is just a matter of updating the task sequence and kicking it off again. This process minimizes the

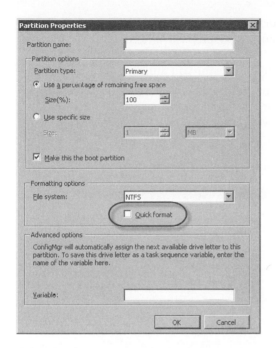

FIGURE 19.11   Selecting the option to quick format a partition

hands-on time involved to create or update your images and ensures that multiple image builds are consistent with each other—making this a completely repeatable process.

Manual Image Creation

It is also possible to create and capture an image manually. The downside to this is it is labor-intensive and prone to human error; the upside is that building the system does not require you to predefine and automate every detail. It also sidesteps some issues involving poorly packaged drivers or applications that are difficult or impossible to install in a silent or automated fashion. Manually configuring a reference system is well beyond the scope of this chapter or book and left to the expertise of the reader.

The best way to capture the system to an image is to use an image capture CD and the following steps:

1. **Install Windows**—Manually install Windows, updates, and any desired applications and drivers, and apply every last tweak to a reference system. The system should also conform to the following rules:

   ▶ Not joined to a domain.

   ▶ Does not have the ConfigMgr client installed. This is not a strict requirement but is a best practice.

   ▶ Has a blank local Administrator password.

▶ Windows XP systems require a folder named sysprep in the root of the system partition with the appropriate versions of sysprep.exe and setupcl.exe. You can also include a sysprep.inf file in the folder, but this is not required because you can inject one later or ConfigMgr builds one for you during deployment.

2. **Create the capture media**—Right-click the Task Sequences node under Operating System Deployment in the ConfigMgr console and choose Create Task Sequence Media. This launches the Task Sequence Media Wizard, shown in Figure 19.12, which creates either a bootable USB drive or ISO image (which you can burn to CD or DVD) from a boot image.

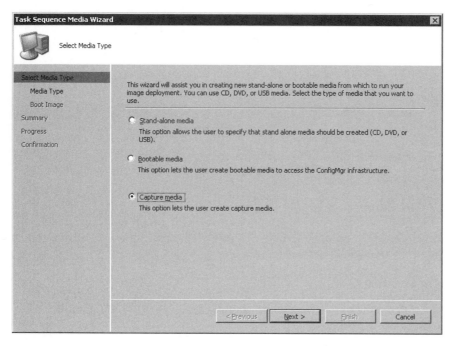

FIGURE 19.12   The Task Sequence Media wizard

3. **Run Capture**—Insert the capture media into the reference system and from within Windows; autorun the media to initiate the capture wizard. The wizard checks for the existence of the sysprep folder and files and then prompts you for a UNC path to create the image at and credentials to access the UNC.

It is also possible to boot into a custom version of Windows PE and manually initiate ImageX:

1. **Create a bootable Windows PE Image**—See Microsoft's walk-through at http://technet.microsoft.com/en-us/library/cc766385.aspx for complete details. Be sure to include ImageX in the image.

2. **Install Windows**—Install Windows according to the Install Windows step (step 1) in the previous procedure.

3. **Sysprep Windows**—Run Sysprep from the command line with the following options: `sysprep -mini -quiet -reseal -reboot`.

4. **Boot PE**—Boot the reference system into Windows PE using the image you created.

5. **Map Network Drive**—From the PE command line, map a drive letter to the destination share, for example, `net use Z: \\<computer>\<share>` and enter the proper credentials when prompted.

6. **Run ImageX**—From the same PE command prompt, run ImageX to capture the image using the following syntax: `imagex /capture [image_path] [image_file] ["name"] <"description">`, for example, `imagex /capture c: z:\MyImage.wim "My Image Name"`.

Either method creates a WIM file containing an image of your reference system, which is fully compatible and usable by OSD, which also supports images created for use with WDS because they share the same WIM format. OSD does not support RIS images.

Image Deployment

Deploying an image is similar in nature to building and capturing one. You start by creating a new task sequence using the New Task Sequence Wizard. Instead of choosing Build and capture a reference operating system image, choose Install an existing image package from the New Task Sequence Wizard. The resulting task sequence contains steps for capturing the current user state, restarting the system in Windows PE, preparing the system, deploying an image, deploying additional applications, and finally restoring user data. Figure 19.13 shows the task sequence produced by running the wizard.

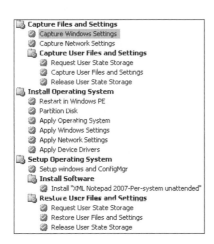

FIGURE 19.13   A Default Image Deployment Task Sequence

As with the build and capture choice from the New Task Sequence Wizard, there are a series of prerequisite items to create and set up before the wizard can complete successfully.

1. **Create an Operating System Image.** The deployment uses a WIM file that contains a Syspreped operating system image. This WIM file is one that was

previously captured and imported. Simply right-click Operating System Images and choose New to start the New Image Wizard.

2. **Create software distribution packages.** The only package the basic Image Deployment task sequence requires is the ConfigMgr Client package, which you should have already created when creating the Build and Capture task sequence.

   If you use this task sequence to capture or restore user state using the built-in user state related tasks, you need a package containing the USMT files. The best way to create the user state migration tools package is to install USMT on the site system and specify the installation path as the source path for the package, typically *%ProgramFiles%*\USMT301 for USMT version 3.01. The package does not need programs (nor does the ConfigMgr package); it simply makes the files available for use by the task sequence.

As with the Build and Capture task sequence, optional packages include software distribution packages and a package for the unattended setup files. Software distribution packages in Image Deployment task sequences are delivered after the image is applied to the system. This includes any applications not part of the common baseline of applications already included in the image, or updates or customizations to applications included in the baseline image.

Because Windows is already installed, the only unattended setup file that can be used is a sysprep.inf for Windows XP or unattend.xml for Windows Vista. This file, if present in the package specified, is updated to include the information specified in the task sequence (product key, time zone, domain, and so on) and used for the mini-setup process.

The New Task Sequence Wizard prompts you for each of the package types except for the unattended files package; edit the task sequence to add this package after the wizard completes.

3. **Import drivers and create driver packages.** Although not strictly required, adding drivers to a deployment is highly desirable and is the primary method to make your images hardware agnostic. The upcoming "Drivers" section covers drivers in detail.

You can now launch the New Task Sequence Wizard using the Task Sequences context menu and create an Image Deployment task sequence. The wizard prompts for the following information.

- ▶ **Task Sequence Name**—This entry is purely aesthetic.

- ▶ **Boot image**—This is the WinPE image used to deliver the task sequence.

- ▶ **Operating System Image**—This is the previously captured operating system image.

- ▶ **Product key**—Not required if using Vista because you can supply this after the installation completes using a KMS or manually.

- ▶ **Administrator Account Status**—You can set the local Administrator account as disabled by default.

- ▶ **Join a workgroup or domain**—If you specify a domain, you must supply credentials.

- ▶ **Software distribution client package**—This is the ConfigMgr Client installation package previously created.

- ▶ **User state migration options**—These include whether to capture user state and the package that contains the USMT files, and whether to capture current network and Windows settings.

- ▶ **Software updates installation**—Options are all, mandatory only, or none.

- ▶ **Software deployment packages**—Packages to layer on top of those already included in the image.

After the wizard creates the task sequence, you want to edit the task sequence to ensure it fits your needs. Typically, the first thing to change (as with the Build and Capture task sequence previously covered in the "Creating the Task Sequence" section) is the format type for the partition. In addition, if you want to use an XP-only unattended sysprep.inf file, you should edit the Apply Operating System task to specify which package contains this file.

Depending on a few factors such as destination hardware speed, network speed, image size, user state size, and application installation time, it can take from 10 to 60 minutes (or potentially longer) to deploy an image and have a system up and running ready for the end user. This of course happens in an efficient, zero or limited touch manner.

User State Migration

"Where's my data?" "Where's the spreadsheet I worked 20 hours on for the CEO?" "Where's my irreplaceable wallpaper of my darling grandson Johnny hitting the game-winning homerun?" These are the last questions any helpdesk technician or system administrator wants to hear, especially right after a migration.

User data is the reason that we all exist, and we want to handle it with special care. Adding users' settings to their data gives us the users' state. A major goal in any system migration is to prevent users from losing any productive time because they do not have or cannot find their data. Although it is definitely a best practice to have users store their data in a central location, such as a server-based file share or a SharePoint site, this might not be possible for a variety of reasons because your organization might not enforce a centralized storage model. Additionally, central data storage schemes tend to overlook things such as wallpaper, Outlook settings and configuration, and desktop shortcuts, letting these remain local to each system. When performing a migration, you want to capture and restore the users' state to their new system as seamlessly as possible.

In Configuration Manager 2007, the data archive produced by USMT can be stored locally, useful (but not required) for an in-place migration, or stored on a state migration point. The main benefits of local storage are that it minimizes network traffic and eliminates the need for server-based storage. This allows potentially quicker migrations and indefinite storage of the data archive.

However, in the case of a side-by-side migration, you must use the state migration point. This is essentially a secure file share for storing the USMT-produced archive. ConfigMgr encrypts and tags archives placed here for a specific destination system, using a computer association. If you did not create a computer association before running USMT, USMT creates it specifying the same destination and source systems. ConfigMgr automatically purges the archives placed on a state migration point, based on the settings of the state migration point.

TIP

Capturing User State

You cannot capture user or system state from a system if you boot the system from PXE or directly from bootable media. Both of these methods boot the system directly into Windows PE and not into the existing operating system. This means USMT cannot gather the existing state of the system and its users. The next version of USMT, dubbed USMT 2010, is slated to have this capability, but for now, you must make do without.

The best part about state migration in ConfigMgr is that it is simple and straightforward to set up. The only overhead truly incurred by state migration is storage space, and this is automatically maintained and cleaned. By default, the built-in wizard to create Image

Deployment task sequences adds the steps to provision space on the state migration point, capturing user state data and transferring it to the state migration point. It also adds the necessary tasks to retrieve the state from the state migration point and apply it to the destination system.

This default behavior is perfect for an in-place migration and works for a side-by-side migration with several small additions:

▶ Create a computer association to specify the source and destination systems by choosing New -> Computer Association from the Computer Association context-menu.

   If no association exists when storage is provisioned from the state migration point, a computer association is created with the same source and destination as the system being imaged—this is the desired scenario for an in-place migration. Alternatively, for a side-by-side migration, you must manually create a computer association before capturing the user state data; this computer association configures a pre-existing source system and a new or different destination system.

▶ You also create a new task sequence to capture the user state data. You can create this abbreviated task sequence using the New Task Sequence Wizard, choosing to create either a custom task sequence or an Install an existing image package task sequence, and deleting everything except the three relevant capture state tasks.

Here are the four tasks associated with user state:

▶ Request State Store

▶ Release State Store

▶ Capture User State

▶ Restore User State

The Request State Store and Release State Store are always used, regardless of whether you capture or restore the user state. These tasks deal with the storage space on the state migration point where the user state data is stored.

The Release State Store task has no options, and the main option for the Request State Store task is determining whether user state is retrieved or stored. This task also either creates or retrieves the encryption key that protects the user state data; the encryption key is stored along with and is specific to a single computer association. As stated earlier in this section, this computer association is created automatically with the same source and destination system if the association does not already exist during a user state capture. If you perform a user state restoration and no computer association exists, the user state tasks are gracefully skipped.

The Capture User State and Restore User State tasks do exactly as their names imply. The two main configuration options for both of these tasks are a required package containing the USMT files and an optional package containing the custom USMT configuration files. Neither package requires any program files because they both just make the necessary files available for ConfigMgr to use. The "Image Deployment" section in this chapter describes creating the USMT tools package.

19

Task Sequences

Task sequences are the core driver for any OSD operation. They consist of a series of customizable tasks or sequentially performed steps. ConfigMgr 2007 advertises task sequences to a collection in a similar fashion to software distribution packages. Many task types are built into ConfigMgr, and the Microsoft Deployment Toolkit adds a handful of useful tasks as well. Additionally, you can create your own tasks using the SDK if you cannot find one that fits your needs.

The New Task Sequence Wizard, available from the context menu of the Task Sequences node, quickly builds one of two default task sequence types or a custom task sequence:

- ▶ Build and Capture
- ▶ Deploy an Image

These two task sequence types take care of a majority of the scenarios in OSD; however, task sequences are flexible and not limited to what is produced by default. The task sequence editor allows easy customization of the task sequences; you can tailor sequences to the specific OSD needs of an organization—and with a little imagination, software deployment.

The wizard also presents the option to build a custom task sequence; task sequences built using the custom option are initially blank. Figure 19.14 shows the first screen of the New Task Sequence Wizard.

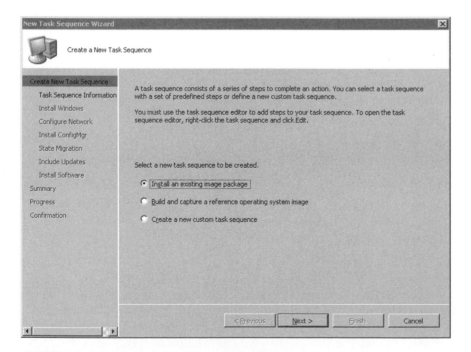

FIGURE 19.14   The New Task Sequence Wizard

The wizard guides you through creating one of the two sequence types: Build and Capture or Image Deployment, discussed in detail in the sections "Image Creation and Capture" and "Image Deployment." To edit a task sequence, right-click it and choose Edit; choosing Properties from the context-menu results in the Properties dialog box of the task sequence and not the task sequence editor. Adding a task is simply a matter of choosing the Add drop-down menu, choosing a task category, and then selecting the task. Each task is customizable and has its own configurable parameters.

Note that the capture media type discussed in the "Removable Media" and the "Manual Image Creation" sections is also a task sequence, but you cannot directly view or edit it. It is predefined and embedded in ConfigMgr and only available when you actually create the capture media.

Variables

Tasks and task sequences are similar to a macro-based programming language or a storyboard where you put together high-level steps and instructions using a graphical tool, without having to know or learn the syntax of the underlying language to take advantage of it fully. Additionally, third parties can add, and have added, tasks extending this pseudo-macro language enhancing what you can do with task sequences.

A major advantage that task sequences have over the traditional software delivery mechanism used in Systems Management Server and now ConfigMgr is that they maintain a state between steps. This state is embodied in a series of built-in variables and custom variables that survive reboots, allowing you to pass data or configuration items from one step to the next. In fact, the task that the task sequence is currently executing is also part of the task sequence's state. Variables are encrypted for security when transmitted between ConfigMgr and the target system.

Here are the three types of variables available:

- ▶ **Action**—Specify parameters for specific tasks. Nearly all are directly editable using the task sequence editor.

- ▶ **Custom**—Simple name and value pairs that you can define as you see fit.

- ▶ **Built-in**—Mostly read-only, start with an underscore, are generated automatically by the task sequence, and generally describe the environment where the task sequence executes.

The full list of task sequence action and built-in variables is available at http://technet.microsoft.com/en-us/library/bb632442.aspx. Action variables and custom variables can be set in a number of ways:

- ▶ Using a Set Task Sequence Variable task.

- ▶ Statically assigning them to a specific computer resource.

- ▶ Statically assigning them to a collection.

▶ Using the Microsoft.SMS.TSEnvironment COM object in a script or other COM compliant language. See http://msdn.microsoft.com/en-us/library/cc145669.aspx for more information on using this COM object.

▶ Leaving the value of a collection or computer variable blank (new with ConfigMgr 2007 R2). The built-in task sequence UI prompts the user for values for these empty variables. See http://myitforum.com/cs2/blogs/jsandys/archive/2008/12/04/blank-task-sequence-variables.aspx for a detailed description of this capability.

Task sequence variables set by a Set Task Variable task take precedence over computer-specific variables, which in turn take precedence over collection variables. Collection variables propagate down the site hierarchy with other collection settings. You can assign computer variables only at the site the computer is a member of, and they do not propagate up or down a site hierarchy.

You can use variables for the following tasks:

▶ Conditionally execute tasks. (See an example of this in the "Conditions and Groupings" section.)

▶ Perform string replacement in command lines. (See the example later in this section and Figure 19.15.)

▶ Provide task-specific parameter values. (See the example in this section and Figure 19.16.)

▶ Perform string replacement in unattended files. (See Ronni Pedersen's article at http://myitforum.com/cs2/blogs/rpedersen/archive/2008/07/01/using-task-sequence-variables-to-customize-deployments.aspx for a detailed example.)

For string replacement and parameter values, surround the name of the variable with % symbols; for example for a variable named *MyCustomVar*, use %*MyCustomVar*%. The task sequence engine replaces this with the value of the variable. As an example, Figure 19.15 shows the Run Command Line task. This figure demonstrates adding an entry to the Registry that you can later utilize to track the deployment version used when creating the system. You can supply the actual version by a collection variable or a preceding Set Task Sequence Variable task.

Figure 19.16 shows an example of replacing a parameter in a task. This example shows how you can use multiple product keys in a deployment. You can supply the actual product key in a collection variable or a preceding Set Task Sequence Variable task.

The next section in this chapter gives an additional example of using custom variables.

Task Conditions and Grouping

You can apply conditions to the execution of a task allowing execution only when certain conditions exist or statements evaluate to true—for example, if the operating system type equals Windows XP. This makes task sequences flexible and allows you to build complex, multipurpose task sequences. Add conditions to a task by going to the Properties tab of a task and using the Add Condition drop-down button.

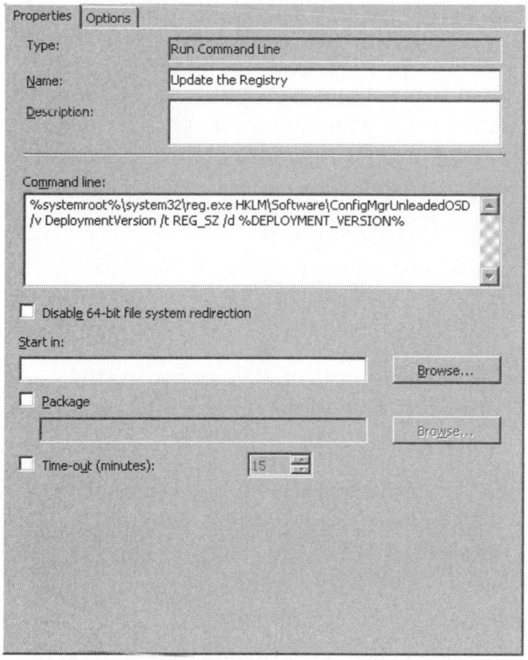

FIGURE 19.15   Using String replacement in a Run Command Line task

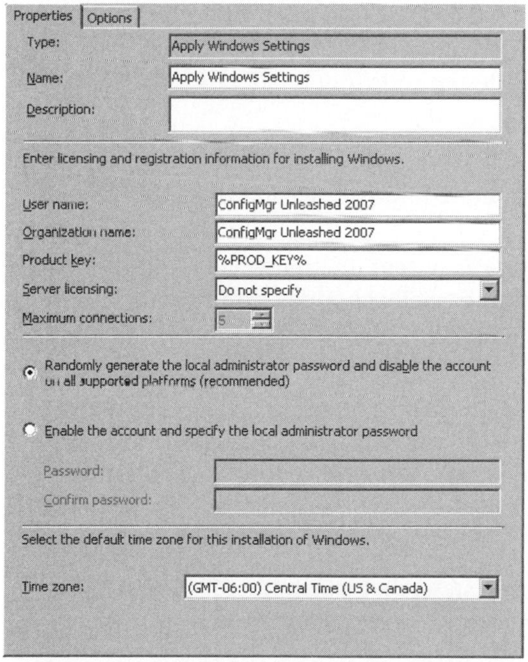

FIGURE 19.16   String replacement in a task parameter

A condition evaluates to either true or false; if all listed conditions evaluate to true, the task executes normally. The task is skipped if any condition evaluates to false.

Conditions can be combined using If statements forming a master conditional statement. Master statements are a collection of substatements; they evaluate to either true or false based upon the logical evaluation of their substatements. There are three types of master statements—each type of evaluation affects how the master statement is evaluated:

- All child statements must be true.
- Any child statement is true.
- No child statements are true.

You can chain If statements to form complex logical statements. If statements in this context closely resemble the traditional logical operators *and* and *or*, and can be used in a similar way.

Conditions can be built based on the value of a task sequence variable, the operating system version, a file's version or timestamp, a folder's timestamp, a value from the Registry, a WMI Query, or installed software. One thing to be aware of is that conditions are evaluated at the point they are defined in the task sequence. What this means is that if you want to perform a task based on the state of the current operating system after the initial reboot of the system into Windows PE, you must set a conditional variable before the reboot and use that conditional variable to execute the desired task conditionally.

For example, perform the following steps to install Microsoft XML Notepad in an in-place migration, using a task that executes only if the software was installed previously on the system:

1. Create a Set Task Variable task before the Restart in Windows PE task.
2. Set a variable, such as InstallXMLNotepad, to true.
3. Go to the Options tab of this task and add an Install Software condition; use the installation MSI for the product when prompted, XMLNotepad.msi in this case. Figure 19.17 shows the result.
4. Highlight the Install "XML Notepad 2007-Per-system unattended" task in the task tree on the left to edit it; this task is shown partially chopped off in Figure 19.17. Change to the Options tab for this task and add a new Task Sequence Variable condition. Set this condition to check for the value of **InstallXMLNotepad** equal to **True**.

You can collect tasks into a hierarchy of groups. This allows tasks to be aesthetically organized, and also gives the flexibility of conditionally executing tasks in a group and discontinuing the execution of a group of tasks if one fails, without affecting the entire task sequence. You can add separate execution conditions to each group in the exact same way that you add them to an individual task.

ConfigMgr evaluates each task for its completion state; that is, whether it completed successfully and performs the following actions for an unsuccessful task:

- If a task does not complete successfully, the group containing the task is also set to unsuccessful, and ConfigMgr discontinues processing tasks in the group.

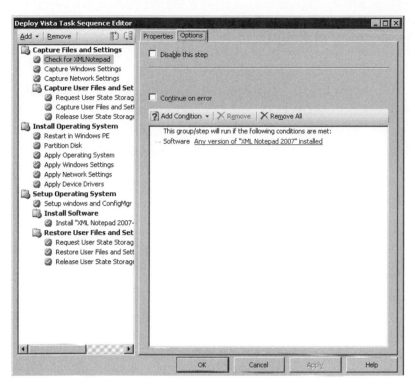

FIGURE 19.17   Checking for XML Notepad task in the Deploy Vista Task Sequence Editor

> ▶ If the task is not contained in a parent group, then the task sequence itself is set to unsuccessful and terminated.

You can override the default behavior using the Continue on Error option available on the Options tab of each task and group. If the Continue on Error option is set, ConfigMgr ignores the error state of the task or group and processing continues sequentially as if no error occurred. You can find an excellent example of grouping tasks together to control the flow of a task sequence and handling errors at http://blogs.msdn.com/steverac/archive/2008/07/15/capturing-logs-during-failed-task-sequence-execution.aspx.

Tasks

Here are the six built-in categories of tasks:

> ▶ General

> ▶ Disks

> ▶ User State

> ▶ Images

> ▶ Drivers

> ▶ Settings

Under each category is a set of tasks corresponding to that category. Each task is discussed briefly in the following sections. Note that some tasks must be combined with others and in a specific order for them to make sense—when this is required, it is noted in the discussion of that particular task.

You can disable each task independently using the Options tab; this allows you to disable tasks during troubleshooting.

General Category

Options under the General category (shown in Figure 19.18) include the following:

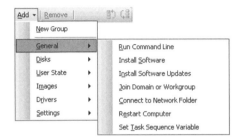

FIGURE 19.18   General tasks

▶ **Run Command Line**—This task allows you to run any valid command line that you want in your task sequence, including batch files and VBScripts. If the files referenced in the command line do not exist on the target computer, you can specify a package containing those files. Additional options include specifying a working directory for the command line, and a timeout to ensure that a command does not continue executing if it falls into an infinite loop or becomes otherwise hung.

Because it is possible for multiple return codes to be considered as a successful execution of a given command line, there is an additional option on the Options tab, displayed in Figure 19.19, allowing you to configure numeric return values that should be considered a success. This field should contain integers separated by spaces. Note that only the first value listed can be negative. The typical success code of 0 is listed by default, along with 3010—denoting success with a reboot required.

TIP

DOS Commands

To use a DOS command such as md or copy, you must call the command as a parameter to the command interpreter cmd.exe, for example, cmd.exe /c md NewDirectory.

New in ConfigMgr 2007 R2 is the option to specify the user account that runs the command, which allows greater flexibility. Prior to R2, the command uses the security credentials of Local System.

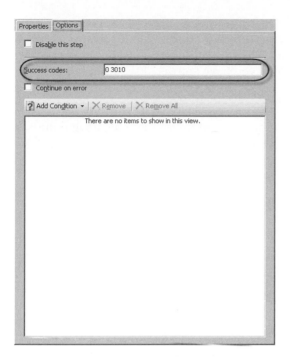

FIGURE 19.19   Run Command Options tab

▶ **Install Software**—With this task, you can call any program from any package that you defined as part of software distribution. (See Chapter 13, "Creating Packages," and Chapter 14, "Distributing Packages," for information on defining packages for software distribution.) The program must meet three distinct qualifications:

   ▶ It must run silently and not interact with the desktop.

   ▶ It must run with administrative privileges.

   ▶ It must not initiate a reboot; reboots can be handled within a task sequence if needed.

A caveat with program execution is that program dependencies are honored, but programs in the dependent chain are not automatically initiated. For example, if you configure program A to run program B with the Run Another Program First option, program A does not automatically run program B and fails to install unless program B already ran on the system (presumably using another task). This occurs because the Run Another Program First option sets up a dependency chain that is checked before a program is run. In this example, program A depends upon program B. During Software Distribution, this setting automatically causes ConfigMgr to run program B before program A. However, this does not happen with OSD; the dependencies for program A execution are not met, thus causing program A to fail when it executes.

An advanced use of this task is to install multiple applications based on the value of a series of task sequence variables. You must name the variables with a single base name and then append a three-digit, sequential numeric suffix (such as Software001, Software002, Software003, and so on). Each variable should contain a value matching the pattern PackageID:Program Name. A break in the sequence number stops the evaluation of the variables; for example, if you have Software001, Software002, and Software004 and omit Software003, execution of programs stops at Software002.

▶ **Install Software Updates**—This task allows you to incorporate software updates into an image, limiting the amount of time spent on updates after deploying the image. The task is also used to layer on updates not included in the image, allowing you to deploy fully patched systems. Updates used for this task are pulled directly from the ConfigMgr Software Updates facilities; these must be configured and performing properly and the ConfigMgr client installed on the target system prior to the task's execution. You cannot use this task to pull updates from any other source.

There are two options available for this task:

▶ **Install Mandatory Software Updates**—These are those options advertised to a collection containing the resource with an installation deadline specified.

▶ **Install All Software Updates**—This installs all updates advertised to the collection where the task sequence is advertised.

▶ **Join Domain or Workgroup**—Joining a domain or workgroup is a required step during a Windows installation; this task allows you to configure this behavior. If you specify a domain name, you must also specify credentials capable of joining a system to the domain and an Organizational Unit (OU) to place the computer object.

CAUTION

Do Not Use a Domain User Account to Join a Domain in a Task

Note that by default all Domain Users can only join 10 computers to a domain (see Microsoft KB number 251335 for further details: http://support.microsoft.com/kb/251335). Because of the 10-computer limitation, ensure that the account used in the Join Domain or Workgroup task has higher privileges than a Domain User because that causes unexpected failures in the task sequence after it successfully runs 10 times.

You can use this task to join a system to a domain instead of using the domain join functionality of Windows setup configured using a sysprep.inf or unattend.xml. You can also use this task to unjoin a system from a domain before syspreping.

▶ **Connect to Network Folder**—With this task, you can map a drive letter to any shared folder using a UNC while specifying alternate credentials to make this connection. This drive letter is available in subsequent tasks to access resources available in that share.

One common use for this task is to map a drive later used by another task to copy the task sequence logs to that shared folder, and then use it for troubleshooting or tracking purposes. An excellent discussion of this specific troubleshooting step is at http://blogs.msdn.com/steverac/archive/2008/07/15/capturing-logs-during-failed-task-sequence-execution.aspx.

▶ **Restart Computer**—As its name clearly states, this task restarts the host computer where the task sequence is currently running. After the restart, the system can be set to boot either into the task sequence's specified boot image or into the currently installed default operating system. You can specify a message to display on the screen, providing feedback to anyone observing the task sequence's progress, along with a timeout allowing the observer to initiate the restart manually.

▶ **Set Task Sequence Variable**—Setting task sequence variables allows you to configure available OSD-specific deployment options, configure variable application deployments with the Install Software task category, or execute future tasks in the task sequence conditionally.

Conditions can be applied to this step so that the variable is set only when specific conditions exist; you can then configure a future task to be performed based on this variable being set. The "Conditions" section gives an example of this.

Disks Category

A number of configurations are possible under the Disks option (shown in Figure 19.20):

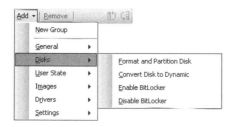

FIGURE 19.20   Disk tasks

▶ **Format and Partition Disks**—This flexible task allows you to configure the partitioning and formatting of all disks in the target system and is a notable improvement over OSD in SMS 2003, which could only easily handle the C: drive. If you plan to handle multiple physical disks, each must have its own instance of this task. Configuration options include specifying the physical disk number and the type of disk to create

  ▶ A standard disk using a master boot record (MBR)

  ▶ A disk using a Globally Unique Identifier (GUID) partition table, known as a GPT

    GPT disks are relatively new to Windows and not supported for boot disks, except on Itanium systems.

19

In addition to specifying which disk to use and its partitions, you can create individual volumes:

- ► Each volume can be set to a percent of total space on the disk or hard-coded to a specific size.

- ► The format type can be specified (NTFS, FAT32, or none).

- ► The partition can be set to be a boot partition.

By default, a full format of the volume takes place. A full format can add unnecessary time to the task sequence when a quick format is normally sufficient.

The last option for this task allows you to store the drive letter used in a task sequence variable. This allows you to reference files on this volume or use the file system on this volume in future tasks by referencing this task sequence variable.

- ► **Convert Disk to Dynamic**—This task converts a specified disk to a dynamic disk. The only configuration option for this task is to specify the disk number to convert.

- ► **Enable BitLocker**—Only applicable to systems running Windows Vista or later, this task enables BitLocker on a specified disk. BitLocker encrypts the contents of an entire disk at a low-level. Additional configuration options include the following:

  - ► Where to store the startup key (Trusted Platform Module [TPM], USB drive, or both).

    Choosing USB startup key storage requires attaching a USB drive to the system during the execution of the task sequence.

  - ► Where to store the recovery key (Active Directory, or no storage).

  - ► The final BitLocker configuration option chooses whether to wait for full encryption of the drive before the task sequence continues.

    Depending on the current contents of the drive, this could be a lengthy process and greatly increase the running time of the task sequence. If you do not choose this option, drive encryption takes place dynamically in the background.

  BitLocker requires two NTFS partitions: one for the system volume and one for the operating system volume. The system volume partition must be at least 1.5GB in size and set as the active partition. Create these partitions in a Format and Partition Disk task prior to executing the Enable BitLocker task in the task sequence.

- ► **Disable BitLocker**—The exact opposite of enabling BitLocker, this task simply disables BitLocker on a specified drive. Decrypting the drive contents is dynamic and in the background; the task sequence does not wait for completion of this activity before continuing.

User State Category

A number of tasks are available under User State, displayed in Figure 19.21:

- ► **Request State Store**—The Request State Store task attempts to connect to a state migration point prior to capturing or restoring a user's state data.

FIGURE 19.21   User State tasks

If there are multiple state migration points in an environment, the task uses the first one listed on the site's management point with space available for the capture; for a site with multiple state migration points, each migration point is searched looking for the one with a computer association where the destination system is listed as a target.

You can specify the number of times to retry the connection and the delay between retries, and whether to capture or restore a user's state. An additional option allows using the Network Access account rather than the Computer account for connecting to the state migration point.

This task creates a computer association if one does not already exist and the Request State Store task is configured to capture the user's state; this created association lists the target system as both the source and destination, which is perfect for an in-place migration. If you do not want an in-place migration, you must manually create the computer association before the task sequence runs by using the Computer Associations node (Site Management -> Computer Management -> Operating System Deployment -> Computer Associations).

If the task is used to capture user state data, it creates an encryption key that stores the data securely; this key is stored with the computer association. If used to restore the user state data, this task retrieves the encryption key from the computer association.

The computer association also stores the exact path where the files are stored on the state migration point, and the times they were captured and restored. An additional option while creating a computer association is the ability to choose which user profiles to capture—either by using the User Accounts tab or by right-clicking an association after it is created and choosing Specify User Accounts. To recover captured user state data, see the discussion in the "Computer Associations" section in this chapter.

▶ **Capture User State**—This task initiates the use of USMT (described in the "User State Migration Tool" section) and captures the user state data using ScanState. A prerequisite for using this task is the existence of a software distribution package containing the files from an installation of USMT. In addition, you would use this task after successful execution of a Request State Store task configured to use for capturing user state.

Additional options for this task include the following:

▶ Using custom USMT configuration files

▶ Skipping EFS encrypted files

▶ Continuing without raising an error if some files cannot be captured

▶ Verbose logging

You can customize the options passed to ScanState by setting the OSDMigrateAdditionalCaptureOptions task sequence variable. It is also possible to use a Run Command Line task to invoke ScanState manually. Use a Set Task Sequence Variable task to set OSDStateStorePath to the value of _SMSTSUserStatePath and pass OSDStateStorePath to ScanState as the location of the state store; for example, `cmd /c scanstate.exe %OSDStateStorePath% /i:migapp.xml /i:miguser.xml /i:migsys.xml /ui:DOMAIN\* /v:1 /l:c:\temp\loadstate.log`.

▶ **Restore User State**—This is the mirror task for Capture User State and has similar options: a USMT package must exist, specify if using nondefault configuration files, continuation without raising an error when files cannot be restored, and verbose logging.

The one option that is different from a Capture User State task is the addition of a password for migrated local accounts. The password for these accounts cannot be migrated even though their data might be, so you must supply a password to use for all the accounts. You must use this task after a Request State Store task configured for restoring user state.

You can customize the options passed to LoadState by setting the OSDMigrateAdditionalRestoreOptions task sequence variable. It is also possible to use a Run Command Line task to invoke LoadState manually, by using a Set Task Sequence Variable task. Set OSDStateStorePath to the value of SMSTSUserStatePath— the same as when manually invoking ScanState—and pass OSDStateStorePath to LoadState as the location of the state store; for example, `cmd /c scanstate.exe %OSDStateStorePath% /i:migapp.xml /i:miguser.xml /i:migsys.xml /ui:DOMAIN\* /v:1 /l:c:\temp\loadstate.log`.

▶ **Release State Store**—This task has no options and must be preceded by a Request State Store task and either a Capture User State or a Restore User State task.

▶ If used with a successful Capture User State task, this task tells the state migration point that the capture was completely successful and is ready to restore. The state migration point then marks the user state data as read-only.

▶ If used with a successful Restore User State task, the task also communicates with the state migration point telling it that a successful restore took place. The state migration point then applies the configured retention settings on this data, allowing the storage space used by the data to be cleaned up.

Images Category

Tasks in the Images category focus on capturing and deploying images, operating system configuration, Sysprep, and the ConfigMgr client agent. Figure 19.22 displays these tasks.

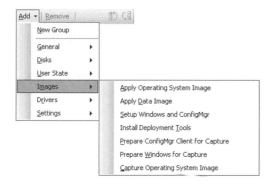

FIGURE 19.22   Images tasks

▶ **Apply Operating System Image**—This is the central task in any OSD task sequence and performs one of two things:

> ▶ It applies an operating system captured in an image to the target system from an operating system image. This is a destructive operation; OSD wipes the entire partition before delivering the image. You can preserve a single folder from being wiped by setting the _SMSTSUserStatePath task variable.

TIP

Storing User State Locally

To store user data on the local file system without using a state migration point, you must set two task sequence variables:

▶ _SMSTSUserStatePath

▶ OSDStateStorePath

_SMSTSUserStatePath must appear before the Apply Operating System Image task to prevent this path from being wiped during the image deployment. OSDStateStorePath actually controls where OSD stores user state data and must be set before executing any user state tasks; it needs to be set to the same path as, or a subfolder of, _SMSTSUserStatePath. To restore user state data from a locally source, set OSDStateStorePath to the correct local path before any user state tasks are executed.

> ▶ It installs an operating system on the target system using the original source files from an operating system install package.

The options for this task are to specify a package containing unattended setup files and select a destination—Next available formatted partition, Specific disk and partition, Specific logical drive letter, or Logical drive letter stored in a variable.

If you specify an unattended files package for Windows XP and deploy an image, you should specify a sysprep.inf file. If you deploy an XP setup, use an unattend.txt file. Vista uses the same file format regardless of the type of deployment. If you do not specify an unattended file, ConfigMgr uses an applicable default one.

If you need to create one (or more) of these unattended setup files, Microsoft has kindly provided a couple of tools to facilitate this, depending on the OS you are deploying:

> **Windows XP**—Setupmgr.exe for Windows XP is contained in the deploy.cab compressed file along with Sysprep. Also contained in deploy.cab is deploy.chm—a help file containing a complete reference to the valid schema and possible settings of the unattended setup files for Windows XP.

> **Windows Vista**—SIM for Windows Vista is part of the WAIK. A help file is also installed with the WAIK, Unattended Windows Setup Reference.chm, containing a comprehensive reference to the schema of Windows Vista setup files.

> **Apply Data Image**—This task uses a preexisting image listed as an operating system image and applies it to a data partition. The same options for specifying a destination for the Deploy Operating System task are available for the Apply Data Image task.

> **Setup Windows and ConfigMgr**—This task initiates Windows setup for build and capture task sequences or reboots the computer into the deployed, Syspreped image for deployment task sequences. Once the OS setup is finished, it then installs the ConfigMgr client on the target system. The only prerequisite is the package containing the ConfigMgr client, which you must select for this task. Additional command-line options used to install the ConfigMgr client can also be specified, such as /mp and /native.

> **Install Deployment Tools**—The main job of this task is to make the sysprep files available to the task sequence. The task typically is used only in Build and Capture task sequences. If the operating system version installed is XP (or earlier), a package containing the sysprep files from the corresponding deploy.cab file must be specified. Sysprep is included in the installation of Vista, so this task does not need a separate package when installing Vista.

> **Prepare ConfigMgr For Client**—This task is required before capturing an operating system image from a target system. It prepares the ConfigMgr client agent to be part of an image by stripping it of any unique identifiers. There are no options for this task.

> **Prepare Windows for Capture**—This task runs the actual Sysprep on an installed operating system, stripping it of any uniqueness and preparing it for capture in an image. There are only two options available for this task:

- ▶ Automatically build mass storage driver list.

  The build mass storage driver list option is equivalent to using the bmsd option with Sysprep; it is a rarely used advanced option.

- ▶ Do not reset activation flag.

  The Do not reset activation flag option is equivalent to the activate option of Sysprep and is used only when you capture an image of an operating system that has already been activated. This option is also rarely used.

- ▶ **Capture Operating System Image**—This task captures an image of the installed operating system on the target system to a WIM file using ImageX. Two parameters are required:

  - ▶ The first parameter is a filename for the destination WIM file. This filename needs to be fully qualified to include the destination UNC and can be on any accessible folder share; for example, \\<*servername*>\Captures\XPBaseline01.wim.

  - ▶ The second parameter is an account and its associated password with permissions to write to the specified location.

  Optional parameters are metadata to associate with the image including the creator, version, and description.

CAUTION

WIM Capture

If you hard-code the WIM filename and location, ensure you copy or move the WIM file from the folder where it was captured to prevent another execution of this task from overwriting it.

Drivers Category

There are two driver-specific tasks, as shown in Figure 19.23. Both tasks inject drivers into an image or operating system during its deployment.

FIGURE 19.23   Drivers tasks

▶ **Auto Apply Drivers**—Using this task, you tell the task sequence to first run a plug-and-play check on the target system's hardware generating a list of plug-and-play IDs; this check emulates the plug-and-play check that Windows setup performs.

The task compares the list of IDs to the driver catalog maintained by OSD; copying those best matched to the target system. In addition, the unattended setup file is modified to reference the copied drivers for usage during the full Windows setup or mini-setup on Syspreped images.

Options for this task include the following:

- ▶ Copying the best matched drivers

- ▶ Copying all compatible drivers and choosing the categories of the drivers to consider for matching

- ▶ Bypass checking of a signature on drivers on operating systems that allow it

▶ **Apply Driver Package**—Use this task to tell the task sequence to copy all the drivers in a particular driver package to a target system and update the unattended setup files with those drivers. The Apply Driver Package task skips the plug-and-play pre-check performed by the Auto Apply Drivers task and forces ConfigMgr to copy the specified drivers.

Using this task, you can deploy mass-storage drivers such as SATA drivers to Windows XP and Windows 2003. You would also use this task in cases where the plug-and-play pre-detection used by the Auto Apply Drivers task is not picking up the proper driver or the hardware is not yet attached to the system, as is the case for locally attached printers and scanners.

Options include choosing a particular package, choosing the specific mass-storage device driver to use from the package, and overriding the requirement to use signed drivers.

TIP

Using Mass Storage Drivers

The ConfigMgr development team chose a narrow definition of which driver classes are eligible for deployment as mass storage drivers, also known as boot critical device drivers. As a result, only drivers of the class SCSIAdapter can be considered for mass-storage devices. To use a device with the class hdc, you must edit the oemsetup.txt file and change the class from hdc to SCSIAdapter before you import the driver into ConfigMgr. This is actually a known oversight fixed in ConfigMgr 2007 Service Pack 1.

Settings Category

Settings tasks capture specific settings from a source system and restore them during an in-place migration or allow you to specify the specific settings during a side-by-side migration or new installation. Figure 19.24 shows available settings tasks.

▶ **Capture Network Settings**—This task, used for an in-place upgrade, captures the network settings of a source system before wiping the system. These settings are

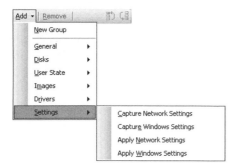

FIGURE 19.24   Settings tasks

automatically migrated to the system after deploying the operating system and override any settings specified in an Apply Network Settings task. The two network settings that can be migrated are the domain and workgroup membership and the network adapter configuration. If neither option is selected, the task is benign.

▶ **Capture Windows Settings**—Similar to the Capture Network Settings task, this task captures specific Windows settings and migrates them during an in-place upgrade; these settings override any settings specified in an Apply Windows Settings task. The Windows settings that can be migrated are the computer name, username and organization name, and the time zone. If you do not select any options, this task does nothing.

▶ **Apply Network Settings**—This task sets network settings on a target system including joining a domain or workgroup and network adapter settings. If joining a domain, an account and password must be set that has privileges to join the domain. You can configure multiple network adapters individually; each can be set to use DHCP or a statically assigned Internet Protocol (IP) address. You can also specify static DNS and WINS settings and advanced filtering settings. Settings specified in this task are overridden by those captured using a Capture Network Settings task.

▶ **Apply Windows Settings**—This task sets specific Windows settings on the target system including username, organization name, product key, server licensing model, local administrator password, and time zone. Settings specified using this task are added to the unattended setup file in use. A product key is not required for Vista or Windows Server 2008 because these products automatically operate in an evaluation mode that does not require a product key for 30 days. Settings specified in the task are overridden by those captured using a Capture Windows Settings task.

CAUTION

Do Not Disable the Administrator Account

Do not set the local Administrator account to disabled when deploying an image to a system that will not be part of a domain; you will at this point have a system that you cannot access because the only account on the system will be disabled.

19

Custom Commands

The Run Command Line task is your ticket to infinite customization of a task sequence. It provides the ability to run any command already available in Windows or that you include in a package. Figure 19.15, displayed previously, is an example of how to update the Registry. You can also import a Registry file using regedit.exe, run a custom script, or install an otherwise annoying device driver from a vendor-supplied .exe.

Using a Run Command Line task, you can add a user interface that enables users to provide input into your task sequence. An excellent example of this is the OSDAppChooser, available at http://osdappchooser.codeplex.com.

Another example of using a custom executable from a Run Command Line task is presented by Hewlett Packard (HP) in "Deployment of HP ProLiant Servers Using System Center Configuration Manager 2007 White Paper," available at http://h20392.www2.hp.com/portal/swdepot/displayProductInfo.do?productNumber=HPS CCMOSDWP. The document details the use of the SmartStart Scripting Toolkit to provision ProLiant server hardware automatically during a deployment. This includes things such as firmware upgrades, BIOS settings, and physical drive preparation.

The Microsoft Deployment Guys (http://blogs.technet.com/deploymentguys/default.aspx) present a handful of very useful scripts to run using a Run Command Line task. Many examples are geared toward the MDT, but are applicable to OSD with some minor tweaking in a few cases.

The possibilities are limited only by your resourcefulness and ability. With a little elbow grease and an example or two, you should be able to find or create a script or executable that automates anything and everything required by your deployment.

Task Sequence Targeting

Task sequences are advertised to collections in a manner similar to software distribution packages. To create a task sequence advertisement, right-click the desired task sequence and select Advertise; this launches the New Advertisement Wizard (shown in Figure 19.25), which is nearly identical to the Software Distribution New Advertisement Wizard. Reinforcing their similarity is the fact that task sequences advertisements are actually stored under the Software Distribution -> Advertisements node in the ConfigMgr console.

The wizard steps you through the process of creating the advertisement by prompting you for the following information:

- ▶ Target collection
- ▶ Include subcollections
- ▶ Advertisement start time
- ▶ Advertisement expiration time
- ▶ Mandatory advertisements times
- ▶ Priority (for site-to-site task sequence distribution)

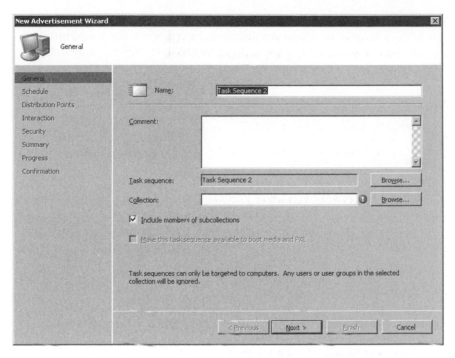

FIGURE 19.25   The New Advertisement Wizard for task sequences

- ▶ Distribution point retrieval method; you can download content locally when needed, download all content before starting, access content directly

- ▶ Use remote distribution point when no local one is available

- ▶ Use an unprotected point when no protected one is available

- ▶ Display reminders

- ▶ Show task sequence progress

- ▶ Security

TIP

Multicasting and Distribution Points

If you use multicasting to deliver an image, be sure the distribution point retrieval method is set to download all content before starting the task sequence. Multicasting is not an on-demand delivery system and cannot be used with the option to access content directly from a distribution point, which essentially is on-demand.

A good approach is creating a set of collections with permanent advertisements. When you need to use a specific task sequence, you can just add the resource to the collection.

For example, in a simple scenario where you plan to use a build and capture task sequence, such as a task sequence to deploy an image and a task sequence to capture user settings only, you can build a parent collection with three child collections named for the task sequence advertised to it, as displayed in Figure 19.26.

FIGURE 19.26   Sample collections for OSD

This technique works well for systems that have a ConfigMgr client agent on them already; you simply use a direct membership rule to add them to the collection. For those systems without a ConfigMgr agent, the "Unknown Computer Support" section discusses several approaches.

Using nonmandatory advertisements requires user intervention because a prompt appears forcing the choice of which task sequence, if any, to run. This might be desirable and is something to consider when designing your collections. To maintain the zero-touch approach, it is best to create one collection per task sequence and use mandatory assignments for each task sequence. If some user or technician intervention is acceptable, using nonmandatory assignments can simplify your collection hierarchy. A menu displays all task sequences available to a system, and the current operator of the system can choose which one to run.

You must create an advertisement for a task sequence regardless of which method you choose to deploy the task sequence: PXE, media, or ConfigMgr. If you use PXE and mandatory advertisements, subsequent PXE-based boots of the same system ignore the advertisement. If this is not desired and there is a need to rerun the advertisement, right-click the computer resource and select the Clear Last PXE Advertisement option. You can also do this for an entire collection.

Change Control and Portability

Nothing is specifically built-in to assist in managing changes for task sequences, although there are several things you can do to avoid losing work:

▶ Always duplicate a task sequence for backup purposes after it is created, and any time you are about to edit. This is an easy and quick step you can perform by right-clicking any task sequence and clicking Duplicate. You can also set up a dedicated folder to move your duplicates into to avoid clutter.

▶ Export the task sequence from the ConfigMgr console by right-clicking it and choosing Export. This exports the task sequence to an XML file that you can enter into a source control system or just store in a file system. You can re-import exported task sequences by clicking on the Task Sequences node and choosing Import. Note that passwords and Windows product keys are stripped from the exported XML files.

Exporting task sequences to XML files is also an approach for copying a task sequence to an unconnected ConfigMgr site. You simply need to copy the exported XML file to a location accessible by the destination site and import it. Copying a task sequence to an unconnected site does add a few complexities though because task sequences depend on packages. The exported XML file contains references to packages and their IDs on the source site; these will, of course, not exist on the destination site and must be created. You also need to update the task sequence to reference the proper Package IDs and add in any necessary passwords and product keys.

For connected ConfigMgr sites, task sequences, like most other objects created in ConfigMgr, flow down a hierarchy of child sites. This allows you to create a master task sequence at a parent site for use at child sites. You must also ensure that the packages referenced in the task sequence are available to child sites.

Customizing Task Sequences

The two default task sequence types, Build and Capture and Deployment, are useful when beginning your use of OSD and task sequences. However, do not lock yourself into the tasks the New Task Sequence Wizard places into these default task sequences. These two task sequences are just starting points for all but the most basic deployments. Remember that they are fully editable, allowing you to customize them as much or as little as you want. Ultimately, using these two task sequence types is not even required. You could start from a blank task sequence by choosing Custom in the New Task Sequence editor and start with a completely clean slate.

Interestingly enough, although task sequences are built for OSD, you can use them for software deployment or any other system configuration activity requiring multiple steps and possibly state maintenance during those steps. This gives rise to the scenario of allowing the activity to continue even after a reboot.

Many in-house or legacy applications require installing multiple packages or performing other configuration tasks in a specific sequence while also surviving a single or multiple intervening reboots. Repackaging these installations often proves challenging if not impossible because of their nature. Task sequences are a perfect way to accomplish the many steps involved in these types of installations.

19

Tips and Techniques

Successful use of OSD, similar to using ConfigMgr in general, requires some time to become familiar with all the capabilities of the tool and the prerequisites for each step. When you know what each step in the process is for and the mechanics behind each step, proper setup and configuration becomes second nature. (A good reference book always helps, too.) The following sections discuss some items to verify in your environment, ConfigMgr setup, and configuration to try to prevent OSD issues.

Confirm Packages Are Available

When you set up your task sequences, ensure each package referenced in a task is available on a DP. For any package to be available for client use in ConfigMgr, you must install it properly on a distribution point that is accessible by the destination client. This includes installing packages for the boot images, operating system image, operating system install package, USMT, ConfigMgr client agent, Sysprep, unattended setup files, drives, and software. At the beginning of the execution of each task sequence, each package referenced in the task sequence is checked to ensure it is available to the client. If it is not available, the task sequence fails and terminates.

To determine quickly the packages required by a task sequence, select it in the console. The lower half of the pane displays two tabs—General and References. The References tab lists all the required packages, as shown in Figure 19.27.

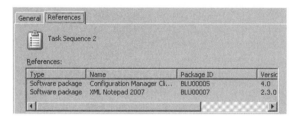

FIGURE 19.27   Packages referenced by a Task Sequence

Control PXE Network Boots

True zero-touch deployments using PXE deployment and Windows PE might cause major problems. If users accidentally set network boot as their default boot option, their system might boot straight into Windows PE using PXE and begin deploying an image, wiping their system! Although this scenario assumes a few details (including the use of either Unknown Computer support in R2 or the MDT PXE filter), it is possible—and stories are floating around Microsoft of this situation coming to fruition and wiping an executive's laptop! If you use PXE, make sure you limit it to a controlled subnet or put other measures in place to ensure this situation does not cause you to have to update your resume.

Don't Add Unnecessary Windows XP Drivers

A mistake often made is adding Windows XP drivers to the boot images. This typically will not work because ConfigMgr 2007 uses a version of Windows PE based on Vista. In addition, there is generally no need to add drivers other than network drivers and sometimes mass-storage drivers to the boot images. The only critical functionality during the PE deployment phase is network and local drive access. The built-in Vista drivers handle everything else necessary including mouse, keyboard, video, and standard disk access.

Conflicting Hardware IDs

If you previously used a desktop or laptop in your organization, you might need to resolve the conflicting hardware IDs. ConfigMgr builds unique hardware IDs for each system it manages based upon the installed hardware. ConfigMgr also assigns a random GUID to each managed resource when the resource is assigned to a site. The hardware ID does not change if a system is reloaded or reimaged, but ConfigMgr has no way of discerning your intentions with the system and does one of two things:

▶ Creates a new GUID and resource record

▶ Drops the resource into the Conflicting Records section

Chapter 12, "Client Management," discusses resolving conflicting hardware IDs.

Test Task Sequences

When a task sequence is about to begin, it verifies that all dependencies are accessible from an available distribution point. The task sequence will end if dependencies are not accessible:

▶ If you used a mandatory advertisement for the task sequence, the system simply reboots without warning (possibly causing an endless cycle with Windows PE starting and then rebooting).

▶ Nonmandatory task sequences display an error message and a 15-minute countdown before rebooting. As of SP 1, the error message does usually indicate which dependency is inaccessible.

Another way to determine which dependency is inaccessible is to review the smsts.log file (discussed later in the "Troubleshooting" section) on the target system.

Beware the Überbug

A continual problem with Windows XP deployments is the dreaded Überbug. This Windows XP-only problem is the result of the new way Windows Vista partitions disks and a conflict with some system BIOSes. The Überbug causes a blue screen with the error code 0x000000ED, which appears after successfully deploying the image and completing mini-setup. Microsoft KB article 931760 (http://support.microsoft.com/kb/931760) describes two methods and a hotfix to fix this bug. The hotfix described in the article is only applicable to Windows XP with Service Pack 2 because it is included in Service Pack 3. You can let ConfigMgr automatically apply the registry fix described in the KB article in a task sequence by setting the OSDDiskpartBiosCompatibilityMode to True, using a Set

19

Task Sequence Variable task, as shown in Figure 19.28. You must place this task before the Format and Partition task.

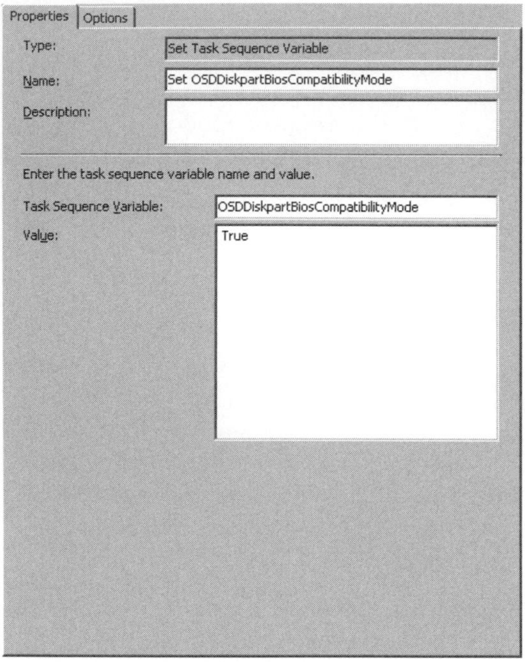

FIGURE 19.28   Setting OSDDiskpartBiosCompatibilityMode

Test Thoroughly

Always test, test, and test some more. Because there are so many different variables in a deployment process, some under your control and some not, you should test your deployments thoroughly. Here are some things you can do:

▶ Test each model of workstation, laptop, and server you plan to use.

▶ Test each time that you change a package or add a task to a task sequence.

▶ Test to ensure that USMT is functioning properly and as expected.

Drivers

One of the nicest features of OSD in Configuration Manager 2007 is the driver catalog, which stores all applicable drivers for all identified hardware in an organization. The deployment process uses this catalog to identify which drivers to copy to a system. Entries are made to the unattended setup file in use, which effectively adds the drivers to the internal Windows driver catalog. When added to the internal driver catalog, the drivers copied to the system are available for the setup or mini-setup plug-and-play device detection, driver installation processes, and any new hardware additions made to the system.

Adding drivers to the catalog is a matter of right-clicking the Drivers node and selecting Import from the context menu, which launches the Import Driver Wizard that guides you through the process. As you must import drivers from a UNC path, it is a good idea to create a driver repository somewhere on your network to store all the driver files. ConfigMgr 2007 searches all subdirectories of the specified path for valid drivers; the list, displayed by the Import New Driver Wizard, allows you to choose the drivers to import. Figure 19.29 shows the Driver Details page of the wizard.

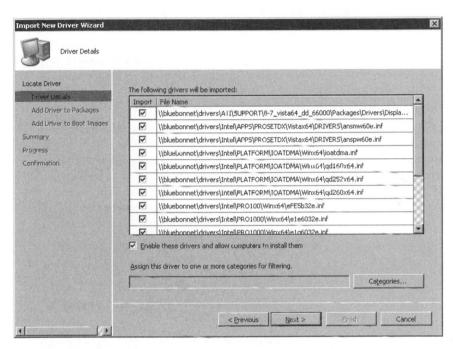

FIGURE 19.29   The Driver Details page of the Import New Driver Wizard

The Driver Details page of the wizard also allows you to assign the drivers to a specific category. Although you are free to create categories as you want, categories are an optional classification tool because drivers might be members of multiple categories. Categories can be used to version drivers or separate and classify them in some other logical way that makes sense for your organization. You can use categories in the Auto Apply Drivers task to filter those drivers considered for installation but without any other specific function within ConfigMgr.

All drivers must be stored in a driver package, regardless of the task type used to deploy them to a target system. You can create a new package during the Import New Driver Wizard or specify an existing one. These packages are identical to normal software distribution packages—they are containers for files that you must install onto a distribution point for use. One potentially confusing point is that you must specify a source folder when creating the driver package. Although this is equivalent to the source folder of a software distribution package, you do not populate the folder with source files because the Import Drivers Wizard does this. You can also add drivers to a driver package after importing drivers into the catalog by dragging and dropping them from the catalog to a specific package.

TIP

Check Share Permissions

ConfigMgr uses the Local System account of the system hosting the SMS provider to copy driver files to the source folder during the driver import process. Because you must specify a UNC path for the source files when creating the package with the wizard, ensure the share permissions allow the Local System account access if the share is local or the Computer account of the site system has access when the share is remote.

You can organize driver packages in any way that makes sense for your deployments. A recommended approach is to create a package for each PC model to which you deploy a system. Using separate packages allows you to use the Apply Driver Package task to force the use of all drivers for a specific model. Additionally, you should create a package for your Windows XP mass-storage (SATA) drivers and packages for any devices existing in your organization but not necessarily connected to the system during deployment. This includes direct-connected printers, biometric readers, card readers, or scanners.

Here are the two task types used to add drivers to a system during OSD deployment:

▶ **Auto Apply Drivers**—Smartly deploy drivers to a target system using a plug-and-play device detection. This plug-and-play detection is separate from the Windows plug-and-play device detection and enables the deployment process to inject only drivers that are applicable to the target system.

▶ **Apply Driver Package**—Inject drivers without any detection. The main uses for this task type are to force certain drivers onto a system because the OSD plug-and-play process is not properly detecting devices when you want to add drivers for devices either not connected to the system during deployment, or for Windows XP mass-storage device drivers.

These two task types were described previously in the "Drivers Category" section. The two task types are not mutually exclusive; you can mix-and-match multiple instances of each task type using different options to achieve your desired result.

TIP

Drivers Not Installing

A recent issue plaguing Windows XP SP 3 deployments involves drivers properly identified and copied to the destination system but not installed by the Windows XP minisetup process. To overcome this issue, add a custom Run Command Line task to the Deployment task sequence after the Setup Windows and ConfigMgr task with the following command line:

```
rundll32.exe Syssetup.dll,UpdatePnpDeviceDrivers
```

This command initiates a full Windows plug-and-play detection cycle that installs drivers for unknown devices if they are available.

Note that just because you added a driver into a deployment does not mean that Windows will use it. Windows goes through its own plug-and-play process to identify devices and then uses suitable drivers from its internal catalog; the internal catalog includes drivers you injected using one of the two task types. Insiders have described the Windows plug-and-play process as a black art. OSD attempts to replicate it as closely as possible, but there are many complicating factors, including parent-child relationships that hide child devices until the parent drivers are installed. Although the Auto Apply Drivers task works well most of the time, there are times where it simply will not identify and inject the proper driver. In these cases, you can add the problem driver to a driver package of its own and use a separate Apply Driver Package task to inject the driver for use by Windows.

Acquiring device drivers is typically a straightforward process: You visit the hardware vendor's website and download those drivers listed for the hardware models of interest. Occasionally you will find the drivers are packaged in an installation program. Here are two options for these cases:

▶ Extract the driver files for the installation program. This is the best option but not always available because extracting them may be an undocumented or unsupported process.

▶ Create a software distribution package and install the drivers using a Software Install task. If you resort to this technique to install drivers, ensure you use the proper switches to install the drivers silently. You may also want to verify the drivers installed in this fashion are installed only on specific hardware models: Use a WMI query conditional on the task, such as the following example:

```
SELECT * FROM Win32_ComputerSystem WHERE Model like "%760%"
```

Use the ROOT\CIMV2 WMI namespace for this query and replace the text in the quotes with the appropriate model number. Note that the percent sign indicates the wildcard in WMI Query Language (WQL) and represents zero or more of any character.

To quickly determine what the model attribute is on any system, run the following from a command prompt:

```
wmic computersystem get model
```

Drivers in the Image

Because you want your image to be as generic as possible and include only those items existing on every system in your organization, you want to minimize additional third-party drivers in the image itself. Minimizing drivers limits the size of the image; however, it is completely unavoidable to include some drivers—particularly those distributed with the operating system and those required for the reference system itself. This is quite acceptable, and you should not worry too much about additional drivers; most drivers are relatively small, and Windows does not use or load them if they are not for a device currently installed.

There might be occasions when you want to force certain drivers into every image; for example, when users use locally attached devices such as printers, scanners, card readers, or biometric devices not attached to the system during its deployment. If this is the case, then you should make the same choice with these drivers as you do with software. Is the device going to connect to all (or nearly all) systems? If so, then it makes perfect sense to include it in the image. If not, then it should be layered on after the image is deployed using an Apply Driver Package task.

Another common concern voiced is that if you do not include a driver in the image, it will not be available to systems where you deploy the image. This particularly comes up as a concern for the built-in drivers. This is a false assumption. All drivers that come with Windows will still be part of the image unless you go through a lot of pain and effort to remove them.

Drivers After the Image

Few, if any, organizations use the exact same desktop and laptop hardware for all their users. Although this is a desirable goal, it is unrealistic for most organizations because of many factors—the ever-changing model lineup delivered by hardware vendors, the diversity of user requirements, merges and acquisitions, hardware refresh cycles, and so on. Because of this, you end up with a wide range of hardware in your organization and many different drivers. As with software that is not ubiquitous throughout your organization, after deploying the image you need to layer on various drivers by using one of the two driver task types, described previously in the "Drivers Category" section of this chapter:

▶ Auto Apply Drivers

▶ Apply Driver Package

Driver management is an oft-discussed topic in the various forums on the Internet, including the main Microsoft Configuration Manager forums. Many different opinions exist on this topic and can be placed on a spectrum with "Control Freak" at one end and "Chaos" at the other:

▶ Control Freaks only use the Apply Driver Package tasks in combination with the WQL conditional presented in the "Drivers" section to ensure only specific drivers are deployed to systems in a controlled manner.

▶ Subscribers to the Chaos methodology use only an Auto Apply Drivers task and let chaos reign with driver deployment.

Although neither methodology is necessarily wrong, the reality is that most OSD deployments fall somewhere in the middle depending on the drivers and systems you are deploying. As long as it works for you and enables you to deploy your systems successfully, the methodology you adopt cannot be wrong. An excellent blog post reinforcing some of the information presented here is available at http://blogs.technet.com/deploymentguys/ archive/2008/02/15/driver-management-part-1-configuration-manager.aspx.

Post Deployment Tasks

Because OSD is part of ConfigMgr, deploying a system does necessarily end after deploying the image. This allows a lot of flexibility in choosing what should and should not be part of an image. This was a major point of emphasis for Microsoft when building OSD into ConfigMgr 2007. Deploying an image is a relatively simple task; the true power of OSD is its capability to perform pre- and post-deployment tasks and allow you as the administrator to customize them for your environment.

ConfigMgr Software Deployment

For those organizations without a robust software deployment solution, the ability to include more things in the reference image or create multiple reference images might be the only way to deploy software and other customizations. ConfigMgr is a robust software deployment platform, letting you distribute software and other customizations in an automated and controllable way after deploying the image.

You can implement customizations in many different ways, including task sequence variables, static collection membership, and dynamic collection membership.

Group Policy

One of the mistakes often made when creating a reference image is to pack all the registry tweaks and customizations into the image. This is a manual process using .reg files or scripts. There are multiple problems with this approach:

▶ The customizations are not enforced in any way. Users can undo or change the customization.

▶ The customization does not uniformly apply to all systems in an organization, specifically those not deployed with OSD or those that might have a different image on them.

▶ Manual processes are subject to the skill and opinion of the person applying them.

▶ Script and .reg files are potentially difficult to maintain for those not familiar with them, and you cannot change them after deploying the image to a system.

Using group policies and preferences have none of the disadvantages just listed. By using the built-in policies or a customized ADM or ADMX file, you can change any Registry setting and enforce it uniformly across the organization, using the native Windows GUI policy editor.

19

Troubleshooting

Finding and correcting problems in OSD is similar to fixing issues elsewhere in ConfigMgr—look in the logs. The trick, as always, is to find the correct log. You can find a complete list of all OSD logs as part of the log file listing in Appendix A, "Configuration Manager Log Files," and at http://technet.microsoft.com/en-us/library/bb932135.aspx. OSD has expanded on this by including robust status messages and the OSD home page, which summarizes available information.

Operating System Deployment Home Page

The OSD home page is a good place to start reviewing and troubleshooting deployments; you access it by selecting the top-level Operating System Deployment node in the Configuration Manager console. The right pane displays a list of all OSD deployments, their status, and some valuable statistics including running, success, and failure counts. Selecting a specific advertisement in the list displays a summary graph to the right.

The bottom of this home page includes links to other sections of OSD, valuable Web reports, and links to topics in the help system.

Check Advertisement Status

Another valuable source of information is the Advertisement Status node under System Status in the ConfigMgr console. Each advertised task sequence has its own entry; these are no different from advertised software distribution entries. Perform these steps:

1. In the ConfigMgr MMC, select System Status -> Advertisement Status.
2. Drill-down all the way on the tree node and right-click the corresponding site node in the right detail pane.
3. From the resulting context-menu, choose Show messages -> All.
4. Each task in the task sequence has an entry along with other task sequence status messages. Unfortunately, if the target system does not yet have a ConfigMgr client agent installed, it cannot send status messages back to ConfigMgr. The system caches the messages until there is an installed agent.

The Smsts.log File

After checking advertisement status, the next place to look is in the smsts.log on the target system. This log file lives in various places depending on the stage of the deployment, as listed in Table 19.1. the smsts.log file is a detailed log of every task sequence-related action that takes place on a target system. It usually indicates exactly why a task sequence fails.

You might also want to check http://blogs.technet.com/inside_osd/archive/2007/12/13/troubleshooting-tips.aspx for additional information. Steve Rachui of Microsoft discusses an excellent method for copying the OSD log files, including smsts.log, at http://blogs.msdn.com/steverac/archive/2008/07/15/capturing-logs-during-failed-task-sequence-execution.aspx.

TABLE 19.1   Smsts.log Locations

Deployment Finished?	Status	ConfigMgr Client Installed?	Location
No	Windows PE running	N/A	Windows temp folder on the RAM-disk—usually x:\windows\temp\smsts.log
No	Deployed OS running	Yes	Smstslog sub folder in the ConfigMgr client logging folder—usually %windir%\system32\ccm\logs\smstslog
No	Deployed OS running	No	Windows temp sub folder—usually %windir%\temp\smstslog
Yes	Windows PE running	N/A	Smstslog folder on the largest available volume
Yes	Deployed OS running	Yes	ConfigMgr client logging folder—usually %windir%\system32\ccm\logs
Yes	Deployed OS running	No	Windows temp folder—usually %windir%\Temp

Error Codes

There is no complete list of error codes that can be returned by a task sequence. This is because ConfigMgr and OSD use a variety of tools and Windows APIs to perform their work. Here are several suggestions in diagnosing error codes:

▶ A good place to start is the ever-handy Trace32 log viewer. A built-in error lookup function in this tool available from the menu, Tools -> Error Lookup, attempts to look up an error number and return a friendly message. This message is often informative and can lead you down the path to finding the actual issue.

▶ You can also find a list of common OSD-relevant error codes and possible solutions available on TechNet, at http://technet.microsoft.com/en-us/library/bb735886.aspx.

Status Reports

Running task sequences send status messages back to the server for each step in the task sequence. You can find the last 1,024 characters of stdout/stderr text from each action in these status messages. You can use this information to remotely diagnose a task sequence issue; this is particularly useful if an error occurred in Windows PE and the debug shell is not enabled. The report History – Specific task sequence advertisements run on a specific computer provides a list of these status messages for a specific advertisement and computer; you can open this report from the Reports node in the ConfigMgr console.

Command Line Support

A highly recommended troubleshooting step is to enable command line support in Windows PE. When enabled, you can start a separate command line by pressing F8 while a target system is booted into Windows PE. From this command line, you can launch Windows Notepad to view the smsts.log file or otherwise inspect the target system. A common use of this command line is to run `ipconfig /all` to verify that network drivers have been loaded with proper configuration of IP-related network information. To enable command line support, edit the properties of your boot images by right-clicking them and selecting Edit. Go to the Windows PE tab and check the option to Enable command support, as highlighted in Figure 19.30.

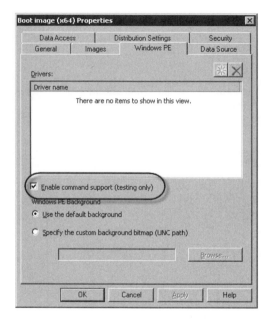

FIGURE 19.30   Enable Windows PE command support

It is possible for a user to intentionally or unintentionally press F8 during the process and gain access to the file system or subvert the process altogether. Because of this, Microsoft recommends that you disable command line support for production deployments.

Native Mode

OSD in a native mode ConfigMgr environment requires one additional certificate. Systems use this certificate when they are booted using PXE or physical media. It allows these systems to authenticate and securely communicate with the ConfigMgr site systems. You can share a single certificate for all OSD deployments; this certificate is used only during the deployment process and not actually installed on the target system.

The requirements for this certificate are as follows:

▶ The Enhanced Key Usage value must contain Client Authentication (1.3.6.1.5.5.7.3.2).

▶ The Subject Name or Subject Alternative Name field must be unique.

▶ The certificate must be stored in a Public Key Certificate Standard (PKCS #12) format file, which must also contain the private key.

▶ The maximum key length is 2,048 bits.

When you create a PXE service point or task sequence media, ConfigMgr prompts you to create a self-signed certificate or import a certificate. For a native mode site, you must choose to import a certificate and supply the password protecting the certificate file.

You can view imported certificates under the Site Management -> *<Site Code>* -> *<Site Name>* -> Site Settings -> Certificates in the Boot Media and PXE nodes. Only two options are available from the context menu of imported certificates: Block and Unblock.

In addition to the new certificate, you must also specify the Root Certificate Authority (CA) certificate to ConfigMgr. You do this on the Site Mode tab of the Site Properties configuration dialog by pressing the Specify Root CA Certificates button, as shown in Figure 19.31.

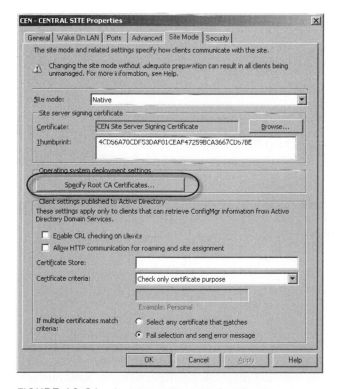

FIGURE 19.31   Specifying Root CA Certificates

Certificate Revocation Lists

By default, ConfigMgr enables Certificate Revocation List (CRL) checking. Depending on your PKI implementation, you can publish the CRL to multiple, various locations including Active Directory and a website. OSD targets booted using PXE or media cannot access CRLs published to Active Directory. Thus if your CRLs are published only to Active Directory, OSD cannot access them and will fail.

In addition, if the first CRL distribution point listed in your certificates is Active Directory, you might experience a delay during the Windows PE startup process. This happens because Windows PE tries to access each CRL distribution point in the order listed in the certificate.

Although it is possible to change your CRL distribution points, certificates already issued will not reflect this change; you have to revoke the existing certificates and issue new ones. Disabling CRL checking in ConfigMgr is another option but is discouraged.

The recommended solution is to carefully plan your PKI infrastructure and ensure that your CRLs are accessible to all systems that need them.

Upgrading from SMS 2003

Although Microsoft supports both in-place upgrades and side-by-by-side migrations from SMS 2003 to Config 2007, you cannot directly transfer any work done in the OSD Feature Pack of SMS 2003. In fact, you must uninstall the OSD Feature Pack from SMS 2003 before you perform an upgrade. Here are some of the limitations:

▶ The upgrade process creates a new node named OSD FP Packages under the Operating System Deployment node in the ConfigMgr console, with all existing operating system feature pack packages placed under this new node. The node appears until you delete the existing operating system packages.

▶ You cannot create new advertisements in this node or distribute down-level feature pack operating system images to distribution points.

▶ Down-level image packages are not available as a choice when choosing an Operating System Image package in the Apply Operating System Image task, although existing advertisements and package deployments for down-level images are upgraded intact and still usable after the upgrade.

▶ Images created using the OSD Feature Pack are not compatible with OSD in ConfigMgr, and you cannot directly import them. Your only choice here is to re-create the image using one of the methods previously described in the "Operating System Install Packages and Image Packages" section. This could be as simple as deploying the legacy image and manually recapturing it using capture media. However, if the down-level image contains the SMS 2003 client, you should remove the client first.

For the long-term, you should definitely consider revamping your imaging process and use a full-fledged Build and Capture task sequence to create your image.

Summary

Is OSD the "killer app" of ConfigMgr? That is ultimately for you to decide based upon your needs. There is no doubt however, that OSD is a serious step up from OSD in SMS 2003 and over any competitive imaging product.

OSD gives you the power and flexibility to deploy server and workstation images regardless of the hardware that you have in your organization. It allows you prepare the hardware and layer on applications, drivers, and other customizations after deploying the image. Infinite customization allows it to fit your every need while also reducing the maintenance overhead involved with manually creating and maintaining multiple images.

The next section of this book moves into administering Configuration Manager 2007, with Chapter 20 discussing Configuration Manager security.

19

PART IV

Administering Configuration Manager 2007

IN THIS PART

Security and Delegation in Configuration Manager 2007

In the early days of computing and data communications, security concerns were often afterthoughts—that is, if any thought was given at all. Today, in a world where new threats emerge at an ever-increasing rate, the stakes are much higher as financial transactions, personal data, business records, intellectual property, military secrets, and vital infrastructure all require secure and reliable information systems. Every organization should develop and implement a security program that meets regulatory requirements and aligns with business needs. Compliance with security policies should be a fundamental consideration and measurable objective throughout the life cycle of every information technology (IT) initiative.

This chapter discusses the security-related issues you need to consider as you apply your organization's security policies and objectives to your Configuration Manager (ConfigMgr) deployment. Configuration Manager 2007 presents both a set of opportunities and challenges in terms of organizational security. Previous chapters present a number of ConfigMgr features that you can use to enhance the security of your environment. Here are some of these features:

▶ **Patch Management**—A large number of exploits take advantage of unpatched systems that remain vulnerable even after a fix is available from the software vendor. ConfigMgr facilitates patch management for Microsoft operating systems and applications through its software updates feature set. Chapter 15, "Patch Management," discusses patch management.

▶ **Network Access Protection (NAP)**—Keeping unpatched or otherwise inadequately protected systems from accessing your network and remediating those systems where possible provides a strong line of defense against threats that might use these systems to breach network security. Chapter 15 also includes a discussion of NAP.

▶ **Desired Configuration Management (DCM)**—Misconfigured systems are another major category of vulnerabilities that can expose your network to attack. DCM provides you with the ability to evaluate your systems against baselines, which represent recommended best practices. Chapter 16, "Desired Configuration Management," discusses DCM.

This chapter considers how these and other ConfigMgr features can support your overall IT security efforts. The emphasis, however, will be on the other side of the security equation—securing the ConfigMgr infrastructure itself. Remember that a ConfigMgr agent running on a client system is capable of executing any code it is instructed to run, either in the privileged system context or in the context of the logged-on user. Using ConfigMgr remote tools and Out of Band (OOB) Management allows you to reach out and touch client systems throughout your environment. If these features are misused, either deliberately or accidentally, the consequences to your organization can be far-reaching. The ConfigMgr database also includes data about your environment that might be of value to a potential attacker, such as information about network infrastructure, missing patches, and possible misconfigurations. To minimize the possibility that your own ConfigMgr infrastructure will be used against you, it is essential you implement an appropriate strategy to deal with the following issues:

▶ **Securing administrative access to Configuration Manager**—Allocate administrative rights on ConfigMgr sites and the underlying technologies your sites depend on (such as Active Directory and SQL Server) on the principle of least privilege, and closely monitor them to minimize the chances of misuse.

▶ **Securing ConfigMgr Accounts**—Configuration Manager uses a number of user accounts, machine accounts, and security groups for its own operations. It is important to understand how these accounts and groups are used, assign rights to them on the principle of least privilege, and implement effective account life cycle management practices.

▶ **Securing the Configuration Manager hierarchy**—It is critical to maintain the security of your ConfigMgr site systems. A compromised site server or distribution point, for example, could be used to subvert systems throughout your environment. This chapter discusses security issues you should consider in your hierarchy design and server placement. It also discusses physical security, operating system (OS) hardening, and application level security for your site systems, and looks at how to securely deploy and manage client agents.

▶ **Securing Configuration Manager communications**—As many attacks today are network-based, protecting network communications is vital to protecting your systems and data. The chapter looks at how to protect site-to-site, server-to-server, and client-to-server communications throughout your hierarchy.

▶ **Security in day-to-day operations**—You should design the processes you use to support your infrastructure and deliver ConfigMgr services with security in mind. This chapter discusses security issues relevant to administering infrastructure services such as site backups and ConfigMgr features such as software distribution.

Basic Security Concepts

IT departments often address information security through a set of tactical initiatives, such as carrying out a network vulnerability scan or deploying antivirus programs. Although these are important tools for securing your IT environment, their effectiveness can be limited unless they are part of an overall security program.

A security program is an ongoing organizational effort to align security policies and practices with your business goals and regulatory requirements. An effective security program requires involvement and support from upper-management. In a corporate environment, ultimate responsibility for information security and regulatory compliance rests with the executive management and board of directors. The security program defines an enterprise security architecture including policies, standards, and practices for addressing security within your organization. The enterprise security architecture should form the basis of your strategic, tactical, and operational initiatives to address information security. Organizations today are at various stages of maturity in terms of implementing a security program. Many are just starting or have not started at all, whereas other organizations have made extensive efforts and have robust security programs.

Security Programs and the Infrastructure Optimization Model

Similar to other aspects of IT, security programs tend to go through the steps portrayed in Microsoft's Infrastructure Optimization Model (IO Model), introduced in Chapter 1, "Configuration Management Basics," used to assess the maturity of organizations' IT operations.

The Infrastructure Optimization Model categorizes the state of one's IT infrastructure, describing the impacts on cost, security risks, and the ability to respond to changes. Using the model in Figure 20.1, you can identify where your organization is, and where you want to be.

▶ **Basic**—Reactionary, with much time spent fighting fires

▶ **Standardized**—Gaining control

▶ **Rationalized**—Enabling the business

▶ **Dynamic**—Being a strategic asset

Although most organizations are somewhere between the basic and standardized levels in this model, typically you should prefer to have a strategic asset rather than fighting fires. This is as true in managing security as in managing desktops.

As an IT professional, you should become familiar with your organization's security program and engage the appropriate resources to support your efforts to implement security effectively within the scope of your responsibility. To implement ConfigMgr security

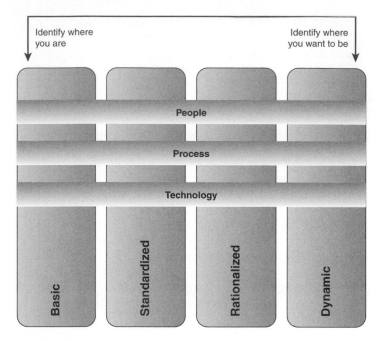

FIGURE 20.1   The Infrastructure Optimization Model

in a way that is appropriate and beneficial to your organization, you need to understand ConfigMgr security issues and apply them according to the policies and methodology of your enterprise security program.

The principal objectives of information security are to protect the Confidentiality, Integrity, and Availability (known as the CIA or AIC triad) of information assets. A fourth objective included by many security experts is alternately called accountability or auditability. These objectives can be described as follows:

▶ **Confidentiality**—Protecting company secrets, private employee information and information belonging to customers, partners and suppliers is essential to avoid potential legal sanctions and financial losses. Confidentiality is even more important in military organizations. Configuration Manager 2007 provides access to data stored on client machines through its inventory and remote management capabilities. The site database also contains configuration data that an attacker can use to find vulnerabilities in your network and systems. Protecting your ConfigMgr infrastructure is, therefore, vital to ensuring confidentiality for sensitive data.

▶ **Integrity**—In addition to protecting data from unauthorized disclosure, effective security must protect information and systems from unauthorized modification. A poorly designed software package or malicious use of ConfigMgr tools can easily compromise the integrity of your environment. Protecting the integrity of information systems is, therefore, a paramount concern in ConfigMgr security.

▶ **Availability**—In many cases, an interruption of vital services might cause business losses equal to or greater than a lapse in confidentiality or integrity. For example, a customer-facing website might not store or process sensitive information, but if it is down, the company's Internet presence is lost until the service is restored. Even in military settings where confidentiality and integrity are generally the foremost concerns, disruption of vital command, communications, or intelligence systems during combat operations can have catastrophic consequences. Your ConfigMgr infrastructure needs to be resilient enough to provide services reliably while at the same time avoiding any negative effects on other network or system functionality. Although ConfigMgr service availability often is not considered mission critical, if your patch management infrastructure is down when you need to deploy a critical patch, your entire environment could be at risk. If you enforce Network Access Protection (NAP), clients might need to access ConfigMgr services for remediation to gain access to your network.

▶ **Accountability**—To demonstrate you follow security policies and that allow you to take corrective action if a breach of security occurs, you must maintain effective audit logs to track security sensitive operations on a per user basis. With increasing emphasis on regulatory compliance, the completeness and integrity of audit logs and records of user activity is an integral part of any security program. ConfigMgr provides the ability to track user actions, and additional audit capabilities are available within Windows, SQL Server, and in many cases through your network infrastructure devices.

A guiding principle in security is the concept of *risk management*. It is not possible for any organization to keep its assets absolutely secure. Some basic risk management concepts include

▶ A *vulnerability* is a weakness that could result in compromise of the confidentiality, integrity, or availability of your information or systems.

▶ A *threat* is a potential danger to your information systems. Keep in mind that threats include both malicious and inadvertent actions. Good security helps protect against honest mistakes by users and deliberate breaches by hackers and malware creators.

▶ A *risk* is the likelihood of a threat being realized and the associated business impact if the threat is realized.

There are four possible approaches for dealing with risk, and your organizational policies determine how you choose or recommend a strategy for each set of potential risks:

▶ **Risk avoidance**—You might decide that the business value of undertaking a technology initiative simply does not justify the risk. For example, you might decide that the value to your company of Internet-based client management (IBCM) is not sufficient to justify exposing your ConfigMgr infrastructure to the Internet.

▶ **Risk mitigation**—You might decide to implement countermeasures to address potential threats to reduce risk. For example, you might decide to implement a Public Key Infrastructure (PKI) and deploy Configuration Manager 2007 in native mode to reduce the chances of a network-based attack on ConfigMgr communications.

▶ **Risk acceptance**—You might decide to accept certain risks if both the business value of the activity and the cost of implementing additional controls to mitigate risk outweigh the potential losses posed by the risk. For example, you might decide to accept the risk of using a system as a branch distribution point (BDP) that does not meet the normal security standards of your server infrastructure. You would choose to accept this risk if you determine the value of the services the BDP provides is sufficient to justify the risk, and the cost of implementing a higher level of security is not justified by the risk mitigation it would provide.

▶ **Risk transfer**—In some cases you can purchase insurance to protect your organization from losses due to certain risks. Risk transfer is mentioned here for completeness, but this strategy is generally not applicable to the security choices you make in your ConfigMgr deployment.

Every organization must assess the value of its assets and weigh the probable losses from threats to those assets against the costs of implementing additional security measures to counter those threats. Much of the discussion in this chapter focuses on the vulnerabilities that might be present in your ConfigMgr hierarchy and operations, and the risk mitigation strategies available to you. Risk mitigation strategies, also known as *controls*, fall into three categories:

▶ **Technical**—Technical controls are often the first things that come to mind when thinking of information security. Firewalls, antimalware programs, access controls, and cryptography are examples of tools you can use to implement technical controls. Microsoft provides extensive guidance on technical controls relevant to ConfigMgr under the Security and Privacy for Configuration Manager 2007 topic at the System Center TechCenter (http://technet.microsoft.com/en-us/library/bb680768.aspx). This chapter reviews many of the principles presented in the documentation and provides additional context and discussion, although it does not present every detail provided in the Microsoft documentation. Reading the Microsoft discussion in its entirety is highly recommended in addition to the material in this chapter.

▶ **Administrative**—Administrative controls are every bit as essential to information security as technical controls. These controls include policies, standards, and procedures that integrate sound security practices into the way your organization does business and how you provide IT services.

▶ **Physical**—Physical controls prevent unauthorized physical access to your IT assets. These controls include building access systems, cameras, guards, and alarm systems. Physical security is an integral part of information security, and there is a growing trend to unify information security and physical security, although most IT professionals are not directly responsible for physical security services. Although this chapter therefore does not discuss physical controls in detail, it is imperative to ensure that your ConfigMgr infrastructure servers are in physically secure locations. If you want to learn more about physical security, the SANS Institute white papers located at http://www.sans.org/reading_room/whitepapers/physcial/ are a good place to start.

TIP

Applying Industry Best Practices

This book emphasizes the value of applying industry best practices such as the IT Infrastructure Library (ITIL) and Microsoft Operations Framework (MOF) to guide you in designing, deploying, and managing solutions with ConfigMgr. It is equally important to apply best practices when implementing security for information systems. The Control Objectives for Information and related Technology (COBIT) is a widely accepted standard for implementing an IT governance framework. The International Organization for Standardization (ISO)/International Electrotechnical Commission (IEC) 27000 series provide standards and best practices for information security.

You can find information about COBIT at http://www.isaca.org/template.cfm?section=home. Information about the ISO/IEC standards is available at http://www.iso.org/iso/home.htm.

Securing Administrative Access to Configuration Manager

An administrator with full access to your ConfigMgr hierarchy has the ability to perform an almost unlimited range of actions within your managed environment. Here's what a person with the requisite permissions can do:

▶ Distribute and run any code of his choosing on any ConfigMgr client system, using either the privileged system account or the credentials of the logged-on user. This singular ability gives the administrator virtually unlimited control over the managed environment.

▶ Collect and view any file from client systems. This makes all data stored in the file systems of your client systems potentially accessible to the ConfigMgr administrator.

▶ Interact directly with client systems through remote tools or OOB Management. On Windows 2000 systems, an administrator can use the gold-key functionality to simulate the Ctrl+Alt+Delete key combination and log on to the computer. With OOB Management, an administrator can reboot a client and interact with the system during boot sequence—potentially booting to an ISO image. This gives the administrator potential ways to view and control user activity or access the machines in an unauthorized manner.

To mitigate the risks of someone with administrative access to ConfigMgr misusing her privileges, you should follow these principles as you develop your ConfigMgr administrative model and procedures:

▶ Employ separation of duties wherever possible to make it more difficult to abuse administrative access. When a person is able to carry out malicious or unauthorized activity on his own, the level of effort and risk of being caught is much lower than it would be if collusion with others were necessary.

For example, packaging software is a highly sensitive operation because malicious code can be bundled with the software package. If a separate individual tests the package, the chances of detecting the malicious code will be higher. If another person is in charge of creating advertisements to distribute the package, the administrator who introduced the malware cannot target-specific systems for attack. Having a separate individual monitoring the deployment provides a final check on the software distribution activity, because unusual activity can be detected during deployment. Although it might not be feasible to assign each of these tasks to separate individuals, involving more than one person in the process can significantly reduce your risk.

▶ Grant the least privilege necessary for each administrator to carry out his responsibilities. Assigning overly broad privileges to users or administrators greatly increases the chances of compromising systems or data. A common example of this is adding a user to a local Administrators group on a Windows system instead of delegating the specific rights the user needs. In the "Administrative Access within Configuration Manager" section of this chapter, you see how to provide granular access rights to ConfigMgr features and objects to individual users. Although granular assignment of rights increases the administrative overhead of managing your ConfigMgr hierarchy, this is one of the most important controls on administrative access.

▶ Ensure audit trails for all security sensitive actions are properly preserved and that regular audits of your IT environment include a review of ConfigMgr activity. It is true that in any environment there will be some group of individuals with authority to carry out those actions required to administer information systems. Although you cannot generally block the administrative group from all opportunities to misuse their authority, increasing the chance of detection acts as a strong deterrent and reduces the chances of repeated or ongoing breaches of security taking place. Auditing is also an area in which separation of duties should be strictly enforced; you should not ask the administrators responsible for normal operations to provide data or reports used for auditing purposes.

Your organization should maintain sound practices around the management of job roles requiring administrative access. It is important that Human Resources (HR) departments have adequate pre-employment screening practices including background checks on prospective employees. Only give this type of administrative access to those employees whose job descriptions explicitly describe systems or application administration responsibilities. Employees receiving privileged accounts or access to sensitive information should sign forms accepting the conditions for this access and acknowledging potential consequences for misuse of privileged access. Develop these forms in consultation with the Legal department to ensure compliance with applicable laws.

Recommended practices include requiring employees to take vacation time and rotating responsibilities because this can often lead to detecting unauthorized activity. High turnover in security sensitive positions greatly increases risk, and your organization should make every effort to attract and retain high-quality, stable individuals for systems administration positions. Adequate and ongoing training of system administrators that includes an emphasis on security issues is essential to ensure they follow sound practices.

Offshoring can present particular challenges in terms of obtaining reliable background information on prospective employees and prosecuting legal action if required. This must be considered in any decision to transfer administrative roles to offshore locations. Outsourcing does not alleviate a company of its duty to protect customer, employee, and other sensitive data. You should, therefore, make sure that any service providers you engage follow security practices meeting or exceeding your organizational baselines.

Keep in mind that any individual or program that gains access to the administrative user's session or account has the same privileged access the administrator has. To reduce the chances that an intruder or piece of malicious code hijacks an administrator's credentials, you should take the following precautions:

▶ All administrators should use a separate, nonprivileged account for routine activities such as checking email and accessing the Internet. Use nonprivileged accounts as the primary logon to any machine other than servers or dedicated administrative workstations. To enforce this practice, consider blocking administrator account access to mailboxes and Internet connections. Windows Vista facilitates this practice through User Access Control (UAC). You should implement UAC settings to at least prompt the user and consider requiring a password for administrative access on Vista workstations used by administrators. If administrators use workstations running earlier versions of Windows, they need to use the "run as" functionality to launch the ConfigMgr console or access a terminal server to run the console instead of running it locally.

▶ Pay extra attention to securing administrative workstations. The security practices discussed in the "Securing Site Systems" section of this chapter apply to administrative workstations and to servers. It is especially important to disable password caching on administrative workstations and to locate these systems in areas that are physically secure and not easily accessible to "shoulder surfing."

Administrative Access at the Operating System Level

Administrative rights to your ConfigMgr systems begin with the Active Directory (AD) forest where you deploy ConfigMgr and the individual host operating systems of your site systems. As discussed throughout the "Administrative Access within Configuration Manager," "Securing Site System Local Administration," and "SQL Server Administrative Security" sections in this chapter, the access rights to ConfigMgr, the site systems, and the site database generally are assigned to AD users and groups. Access to the ConfigMgr infrastructure should be limited to only those personnel with direct responsibility for ConfigMgr operations or security.

For all practical purposes, it is impossible to prevent a domain administrator in the domain in which these users or accounts are defined from usurping administrative rights on your ConfigMgr hierarchy. However, you can make it difficult for this to happen without being noticed. You should consider the following measures to protect groups and user accounts with privileged access to any security sensitive infrastructure, including ConfigMgr:

▶ Restrict rights to manage administrative accounts and groups to a small group of senior administrators. You should remove any delegated rights to groups such as helpdesk personnel.

▶ Set auditing to record any changes to these user accounts and groups. Specify auditing of changes to AD in the highest precedence group policy that applies to your domain controllers. This is generally the Default Domain Controllers policy. Chapter 7, "Testing and Stabilizing," introduces the Group Policy Management console (GPMC). You can use the GPMC to edit the auditing settings for your AD domain. The auditing policies are defined in the Default Domain Controllers policy under Computer Configuration -> Policies -> Windows Settings -> Security Settings -> Local Policy -> Audit Policy. The events you specify through the audit policy are recorded in the local security log of the domain controller on which the event occurs. Some specific auditing settings you might consider include

  ▶ **Audit account management**—Events in the account management category include such sensitive operations as setting the password on a user account or adding a member to a group. Auditing account management is discussed at http://technet.microsoft.com/en-us/library/cc737542.aspx.

  ▶ **Audit directory service access**—Events in the directory service access category include modifications to specific AD objects such as users or groups.

When you enable the directory service access auditing category through group policy, you also need to turn on auditing of the specific objects. There are several methods available to enable auditing on directory services objects. One way is to use the Active Directory Users and Computers (ADUC) tool. In general, you set the auditing at the Organizational Unit (OU) level rather than on individual objects. To enable auditing on an OU using ADUC, perform the following steps:

1. Open Active Directory Users and Computers from the Windows Server Administrative Tools menu group.

2. Expand the directory tree to the OU you want to audit. Right-click on the OU, and choose Properties.

3. Click on the Security tab of the properties page; then click the Advanced button.

4. On the Advanced Security Settings page, click on the Auditing tab and click the Add button.

5. Enter **Everyone** in the Select User, Computer, or Group dialog box and click OK.

6. In the Auditing Entry dialog box, select Descendant Group objects from the Apply onto drop-down list. Check the Successful column under Write all properties, Add/remove self as member, and any other operations you want to audit. Figure 20.2 displays the Auditing Entry dialog for the ConfigMgrAdmins OU in the foreground, with auditing enabled for all actions that successfully modify groups in the OU.

To track Windows and AD administration, you generally want to audit successful changes. You might also want to audit failure events of attempts to perform directory

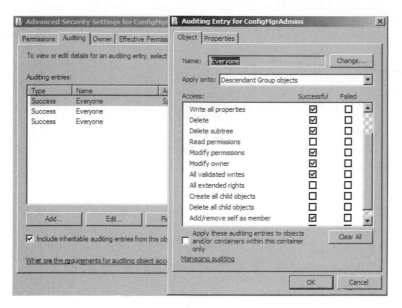

FIGURE 20.2   Enabling auditing for all users modifying groups in the ConfigMgrAdmins OU

operations, to detect attempts to breach directory security by users who are not authorized administrators.

CAUTION

Plan and Test Before Changing Audit Policies

Some audit settings can generate a large number of events in the security logs. Intensive auditing can have a server performance impact. More important, logging too many events can cause the allocated log space to fill up and events to be lost.

Securing the Audit Trail

One of the challenges for any security program is preserving the integrity of the audit logs. Attackers commonly try to cover their tracks by erasing or altering logs that might reveal their activities. If your system is in scope for regulatory compliance, it is essential you take measures to prevent any accidental or deliberate alterations of the audit record. For Windows security logs, the following audit settings can help detect events that might indicate a gap in audit log integrity:

▶ **Audit policy change**—Because group policy controls many of the most important security settings in your domain, you generally need to audit all policy changes. You need to review the security logs regularly for event ID 612 (An audit policy was changed). By changing audit policy, an administrator can prevent other actions from appearing in the audit logs. An unauthorized change to audit policy is a serious security breach, and you need to investigate it thoroughly.

▶ **Audit system events**—System events are events on individual servers such as startup or shutdown. Two system events of interest in protecting the integrity of audit logs are

> ▶ **Event ID 516**—Internal resources allocated for the queuing of security event messages have been exhausted, leading to the loss of some security event messages.
>
> This event can indicate a server that is overloaded or a Denial of Service (DoS) attack against the audit subsystem. Regardless of the cause, it is an indication that your audit record is incomplete.
>
> ▶ **Event ID 517**—The audit log was cleared.
>
> Clearing the audit log is an operation reserved to system administrators unless you have granted the right to manage auditing and security logs to other users through group policy. Clearing the audit log without backing it up creates a gap in the audit record. Even if the log is backed up when cleared, there is a slight window of opportunity for an administrator to perform unauthorized actions and then clear the audit log a second time without backing it up. You might detect this type of activity by comparing the timestamp on the log backup with the timestamp on the first event in the new log, and reviewing the new log for event 520. (The system time was changed.) Because of the risk of log tampering, it is best to avoid practices that require clearing the security log manually.

The maximum size of the Security log is finite, and you should carefully consider your options for setting Security log policies. You can set the event log policies locally using the Event Viewer application in the Administrative Tools program group or through group policy. To manage event log setting through group policy, edit the appropriate policy in the GPMC and navigate to Computer Configuration -> Policies -> Windows Settings -> Security Settings -> Event Log. Here are some available options for the event log:

▶ **Maximum security log size**—This is the maximum log size in kilobytes with a range of possible values from 64 through 4,194,240 (4GB). This value must be a multiple of 64. The average size of an event is approximately 500 bytes. You should, therefore, choose a value that is adequate to hold the number of events per day you estimate will occur, multiplied by the number of days in your desired retention period. For Windows 2003 Server 32-bit editions, the maximum recommended event log size is approximately 300MB. For Windows Server 2008 and all 64-bit Windows Server editions, the maximum recommended size is 4GB.

▶ **Retain security log**—This specifies the minimum age that an event in the security log can be overwritten if the retention method (discussed in the next bullet) for the security log is By Days. If you use this method, you should set this policy to a large enough value to ensure the logs will be backed up before events are overwritten.

▶ **Retention method for security log**—This setting allows you to choose one of three options:

   ▶ **Overwrite events by days**—This setting allows events to be overwritten only after the number of days specified in the Retain security log policy setting. This setting might cause events not being written if a large number of audited events have filled up the log, and is susceptible to an attack on the audit record by flooding the system with a large number of meaningless audit events before committing an actual security breach.

   ▶ **Overwrite events as needed**—This setting is the default method and causes the oldest events to drop from the logs in a first in, first out (FIFO) fashion. Overwriting security events might cause a loss of information if there are a large number of audited events, and is susceptible to an attack on the audit records from flooding the system with a large number of meaningless audit events after an actual security breach occurs.

   ▶ **Do not overwrite events (clear log manually)**—This setting prevents events from being overwritten. This setting might prevent events from being written if a large number of audited events fills up the log, and is susceptible to an attack on the audit records by flooding the system with a large number of meaningless audit events before committing an actual security breach. Generally, you only use this setting if you also set the Audit: Shut down system immediately if unable to log security audits policy under Computer Configuration -> Windows Settings -> Security Settings -> Local Policies -> Security Options. Setting the policy to shut down the system when unable to log security audits should only be considered in highly secure environments where audit requirements outweigh availability concerns!

Windows Server 2008 and Windows Vista provide additional group policy options for event log management, found under Computer Configuration -> Policies -> Administrative Templates -> Windows Components -> Event Log Service. These options allow you to automatically archive the event log when it reaches its maximum size. You are still limited by the available storage capacity of the partition where the security log is stored. For additional information about event log policy options, see http://technet.microsoft.com/en-us/library/cc778402.aspx. For information about recommended size settings for event logs and relocating your event logs, see http://support.microsoft.com/kb/957662.

Managing Security Logs with System Center Operations Manager

Window's native event logging capabilities might be adequate to meet the needs of smaller organizations and those with relatively low audit requirements. A centralized event logging solution such as the Audit Collection Services (ACS) in System Center Operations Manager (OpsMgr) 2007 provides several advantages over only logging information on individual servers. ACS inserts itself into the audit logging process to capture events and send them to a central repository. ACS allows you to monitor, query, and report on audited events across your Windows server environment and is more resistant to tampering or system failure than stand-alone event logging.

For more information about Operations Manager and the Audit Collection Services, see http://technet.microsoft.com/en-us/library/bb310604.aspx. A companion volume in this series, *System Center Operations Manager 2007 Unleashed* (Sams, 2008), available at http://www.amazon.com/System-Center-Operations-Manager-Unleashed/dp/0672329557 and elsewhere, can help you get the most out of Operations Manager and ACS.

Securing Site System Local Administration

The built-in local Administrators group on any Windows system has complete and unrestricted access to the computer. Even without specific administrative rights within ConfigMgr, a member of the Administrators group on a ConfigMgr site system could potentially alter files, Registry settings, or other items related to system configuration in ways that would affect ConfigMgr services. By default, the Domain Admins group for the local domain is part of the local Administrators group. You should consider removing the Domain Admins group and replacing it with the appropriate AD group that has direct responsibility for server administration of the site system. For non-client facing site systems, you might also consider removing the Domain Users group from the local Users group. The remaining built-in groups, such as Backup Operators and Power Users, should not contain any members unless required for your administrative processes. You should generally not create local users or groups on site systems other than those required by ConfigMgr. As with all Windows systems, you should rename the built-in Administrator account, set a strong password for that account, and use appropriate procedures to manage access to the account password. You should also disable the built-in Guest account.

You can use the Computer Management tool to manage local users and groups. You can also use domain-based group policy to enforce consistent settings for most local account settings across multiple servers. To manage local accounts through the computer management tool, perform the following steps:

1. Launch the Computer Management MMC snap-in. The exact procedure will vary depending on the version of Windows you run. Generally you can right-click on Computer or My Computer, and choose Manage.

2. Expand the System Tools node in the tree pane, and then expand Local Users and Groups.

3. Choose the Users or Groups node, double-click on the user group or account you want to manage, and make the appropriate changes.

To control local account and group settings though group policy, you can use the GPMC to edit either the Default Domain Policy or a policy linked to the appropriate OU for your site systems. The following nodes in the group policy tree contain settings controlling the behavior of local accounts and groups:

▶ Computer Configuration -> Windows Settings -> Security Settings -> Local Policies -> Security Options includes settings such as Accounts: Rename administrator account, which you can use to apply changes to all systems on which the policy is applied.

▶ Computer Configuration -> Windows Settings > Security Settings -> Restricted Groups allows you to specify restricted groups, such as Administrators, and specify the membership of those groups.

CAUTION

Local Administration of Machines Disjoined from the Domain

The local Administrator account is often needed to log onto a machine that was removed from the domain. In this case, the account name reverts to its state before domain group policy was applied. You should always maintain accurate records of the local Administrator account name on each system independent of the group policy setting.

Although Microsoft does not supply a tool to automate changes to the local Administrator account password across multiple systems, a number of third-party tools and scripts are available that supply this functionality.

Just as auditing AD administration helps detect and deter misuse of domain level administrative privileges, auditing actions by administrators on site systems is an important part of your control framework. You can use group policy settings in the Default Domain Policy, a policy linked to the appropriate OU for your site systems or local group policy to enable the appropriate auditing. The most important auditing categories you should enable include the following:

▶ **Audit account management**—Local user accounts and groups should rarely change, so auditing local account management on site systems will generate relatively little overhead.

▶ **Audit policy change**—As with account management, policy changes should rarely occur locally on servers. When changes do occur, you want to know about it.

▶ **Audit object access**—On the site system itself, you will be interested in auditing changes that might affect ConfigMgr functioning, such as modifications to files or server configuration. These might generate a considerable amount of audit events, so you need to set the audit policies carefully.

As with the directory service access, auditing object access requires the policy to be set and auditing to be applied to specific objects. There are various ways to set object level auditing; for example, you can use Windows Explorer to set auditing on file system objects, and you can use the Registry Editor to set auditing on Registry keys. Here are some objects you might want to audit on ConfigMgr site systems:

▶ Package source files

▶ Site control file

▶ Client source files

▶ The HKEY_LOCAL_MACHINE\Software\Microsoft\SMS\MP\Certificates registry subtree

20

As with any auditing, you should use caution and test your local audit settings thoroughly to avoid excessive auditing. Auditing large numbers of Registry keys can have a severe performance impact. You should also consider the strategies previously discussed in the "Securing the Audit Trail" section in this chapter to secure the audit trail on site systems.

Administrative Access Within Configuration Manager

Nearly all tasks you perform using the Configuration Manager console or through other administration tools and scripts use the Windows Management Instrumentation (WMI) provider to perform the requested operations. Chapter 3, "Looking Inside Configuration Manager," discusses WMI. You can apply WMI access controls to namespaces, object classes, and individual objects and assign permissions to Windows users and groups. In virtually all cases, you use the Configuration Manager console to apply permissions to ConfigMgr objects and classes rather than directly modifying WMI permissions. You might also use custom scripts to manipulate object permissions. You can assign each set of object permissions using one of two ways:

▶ *Class permissions* grant the user rights on all objects of the class. For example, class permissions on the Collections class apply to all collections.

▶ *Instance permissions* apply only to a specific instance, such as the All Windows Server Systems collection.

Most classes allow you to assign both class permissions and instance permissions; however, some classes such as the status message class do not support permissions on individual instances. The principle of least privilege suggests you should use instance permissions unless a user needs permissions on all instances of a class. Assigning permissions on a per-instance basis can become quite cumbersome, however. You need to evaluate the risk associated with assigning permissions at the class level and decide what model works best for your organization. For example, you might decide that assigning Read permissions on the package class is acceptable, but Modify permissions need to be more tightly controlled using instance permissions.

Granting Access to the Namespace

Before granting permissions to a user on object classes or individual instances of objects, you need to grant the user remote enable permission on the ROOT\SMS\site_<*Site Code*> namespace. You can generally do this by adding the user to the SMS Admins local group on the site server. The SMS Admins group does not have any administrative rights within ConfigMgr by default; adding a user to the SMS Admins group only grants them sufficient rights to launch the console and connect to the site database. Members of the local Administrators group have full access to all WMI namespaces by default. You do not, therefore, need to add members of the local Administrators group to the SMS Admins group.

As with any user access administration in Windows, the best practice is generally to add users to groups and assign permissions to the groups. As you plan your ConfigMgr administration model, you should create AD groups corresponding to each administrative role or identify existing AD groups containing the appropriate members. For example, you might create a ConfigMgr Software Packagers group for users needing rights to create and manage packages, or you might identify the existing Helpdesk group as needing access to remote tools. In general, you should assign the minimum permissions to each group to allow them to carry out their required functions and avoid creating overly broad groups that have more rights than they need. Add each AD group that needs access to the ConfigMgr console to the SMS Admins local group.

Managing Permissions Through the ConfigMgr Console

When you first install a ConfigMgr site, the user who installed the site and the Local System account have Full Control on the entire site and all objects it contains. No other users have access to the site. If you upgrade a site from SMS 2003, users retain their existing class and instance rights; however, only the system and the user who performs the upgrade have rights on object classes that are new to ConfigMgr. If you have a group of administrators who require Full Control on the site, one of the first tasks you should do is to copy the rights of the Local System account (NT AUTHORITY\SYSTEM) to the ConfigMgr administrative group. Perform the following steps:

1. Add the AD group with your ConfigMgr administrators to the SMS Admins local group on the site server. If the ConfigMgr administrators are already members of the local Administrators group on the server, this step is not required.

2. Open the ConfigMgr Console and navigate to System Center Configuration Manager -> Site Database -> Security Rights.

3. Right-click Users and choose Manage ConfigMgr Users to launch the ConfigMgr User Wizard; then click Next at the Welcome screen.

4. On the User Name page, select the option to add a new user and enter or browse for the appropriate group; then click Next. Figure 20.3 shows the User Name page with the name of the ConfigMgr administrative group entered.

5. On the User Rights page, select Copy rights from an existing ConfigMgr user or group, as displayed in Figure 20.4; then click Next.

6. On the Copy Right page, select an existing administrator account from the Source user drop-down list, as shown in Figure 20.5 and click Next. This returns you to the User Rights page, which now displays the set of rights to be copied. Click Next to view a summary of your choices and Next again to initiate the user creation. When the operation completes you receive a confirmation that the wizard has completed successfully. Click Close to return to the ConfigMgr console.

Microsoft recommends you restrict full ConfigMgr rights to a small group of trusted senior administrators. This model is likely to be appropriate for most organizations. In high-security settings, you might want to go a step further and strictly enforce the separation of duties principle. The ConfigMgr User Wizard allows you to modify existing users' rights. You could, for example, assign a security administrator Administer rights on all classes and remove all rights that are not part of the Administer permission. The security administrator could then assign rights to operational personnel based on their job roles.

To modify the rights of an existing user, perform the following steps:

1. Choose Modify an existing user on the User Name page (shown in Figure 20.3), and select the appropriate user from the drop-down list.

20

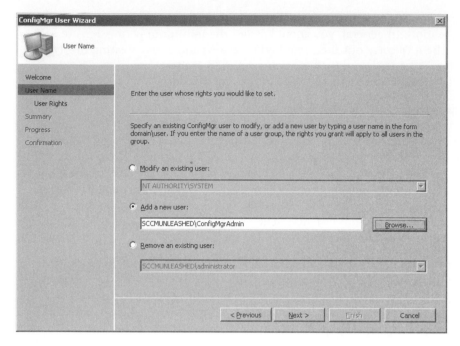

FIGURE 20.3   Adding the ConfigMgrAdmin Group as a ConfigMgr user principal

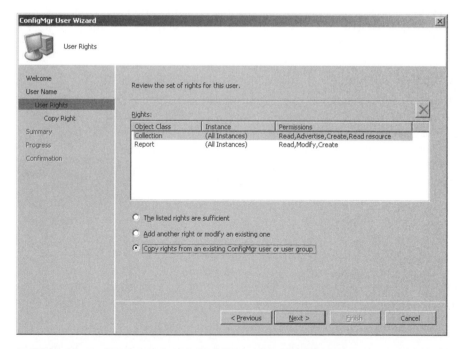

FIGURE 20.4   Choosing to copy rights from an existing user

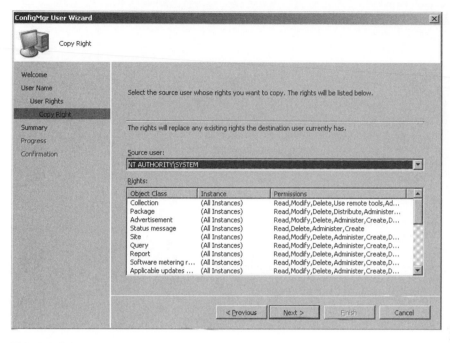

FIGURE 20.5   Copying rights from the Local System account

2. On the Copy Rights page (Figure 20.4), choose Add another right or modify an existing one. Figure 20.6 shows the Add Right page with the Package class rights selected.

3. The exact set of permissions included with Administer varies, depending on the individual class. To see the minimum set of rights required for Administer permission on the package class, click on the Clear All button, and then select Administer from the Rights list. You cannot remove the Administer right for a class or instance from all users because that would effectively orphan the affected objects.

In addition to the user node under System Center Configuration Manager -> Site Database -> Security Rights in the ConfigMgr console, there is a Rights node where you can view and edit all class and instance rights defined in your site. Figure 20.7 displays the Rights node with the rights list sorted by class.

Not only can you manage users and rights through the Security Rights console nodes, you can also view and set permissions using the Security tab on the object's Properties page. For example, you can right-click the System Center Configuration Manager -> Site Database -> Computer Management -> Collections node and choose Properties to manage security for the collections class. Right-clicking on an individual collection lets you display its Properties page and manage instance permissions for that collection. This is often the most convenient way to manage object permissions.

20

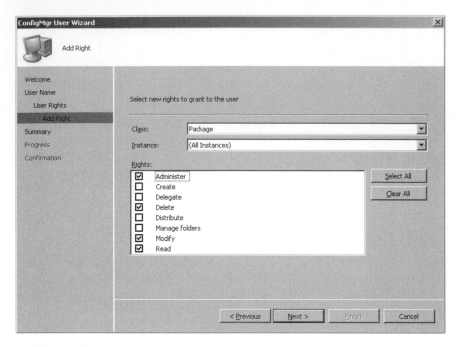

FIGURE 20.6   Assigning rights on the Package class

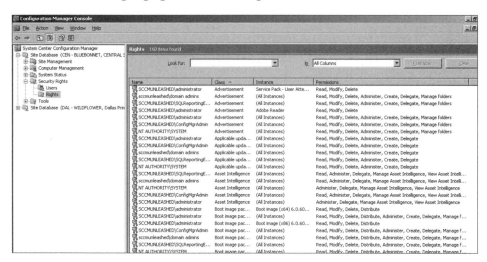

FIGURE 20.7   The ConfigMgr Console Rights node displays a list of assigned rights.

Characteristics of ConfigMgr Object Permissions

Keep in mind the following characteristics of ConfigMgr object permissions:

▶ Permissions are local to the site.

Sites form an important security boundary in ConfigMgr. Objects propagated from parent sites are read-only at child sites, indicated by the padlock icon displayed in the user interface. Class rights, rights on local objects, and access through the local SMS Admins group are all determined locally on a primary site. This enables you to divide administrative responsibilities on a per-site basis and by feature or object set. This capability provides a convenient way to restrict administrators to a portion of the hierarchy, based on the scope of their responsibilities. This can also be useful if some sites have particular requirements such as the need to meet Payment Card Industry (PCI) standards. It might be much easier to meet such requirements by isolation at the site level than through delegation of permissions within a site.

▶ Permissions are cumulative across user groups, object hierarchies, and collections.

Cumulative permissions across user groups means that if a user is in more than one group with access to a particular instance or class, that user has all rights assigned to any of the groups, and any rights explicitly assigned to the user. Cumulative permissions across object hierarchies indicate that a user with permissions on an instance and on its class has all rights assigned at either the class or the instance level. Cumulative permissions across collections means that if a resource, such as a computer or user, is a member of more than one collection, then the rights each administrator has on the resource will be the union of the rights assigned through each collection. The ConfigMgr console does not provide a way to display effective permissions on objects, so to determine the effective permissions a user has, you must consider each way in which permissions can accumulate.

▶ The available rights vary, depending on the object class.

Microsoft lists the rights applicable to specific ConfigMgr classes and instances in the Technical Reference for Configuration Manager Security, located at http://technet.microsoft.com/en-us/library/bb632791.aspx.

▶ A user with Read access on a collection can view the collection membership and discovered properties of the collection members.

Read resource rights are required to view inventory data.

▶ A user with Administer rights on a class can manage permissions on all instances of the class.

You can allow users to create objects and manage permissions only on the objects they create by assigning them class level Create and Delegate rights.

▶ There is no way to explicitly deny access to a class or instance.

Some ConfigMgr object permissions are particularly important. Pay close attention to permissions on the following objects:

▶ The site object is by far the most important ConfigMgr object. All administrative users need Read access to the site to access other objects within the site. Other rights on the site should be restricted to a small group of senior administrators. A few particularly sensitive rights are

▶ **Modify**—The right to modify the site allows users to change things such as client agent settings and site system properties.

20

▶ **Manage SQL commands**—SQL commands declared as part of site maintenance tasks run directly against the site database, bypassing the WMI layer. Because nearly all site configuration settings and ConfigMgr objects are stored in the database, direct database access enables you to perform almost any operation possible in a ConfigMgr environment.

▶ **Manage status filters**—Status filter rules can invoke actions including running a program in the context of the SMS Executive Service.

▶ Software distribution enables you to run any program or command on client machines in the context of Local System or the logged-on user. The Local System account has complete access to all resources on the machine. The logged-on user might have access to local or network resources that administrators are not allowed to touch, such as sensitive financial data or intellectual property. A program or script executing in the context of an authorized user could copy or alter data without producing a suspicious audit trail. Keep in mind that ConfigMgr can run software silently in the background, so the user is not aware of what is taking place. ConfigMgr can also run software when no user is logged on. To reduce the chances of unauthorized ConfigMgr software distribution, restrict access to the following classes:

▶ Packages are the most sensitive object in software distribution. The package properties specify the location of the source files. The package's program settings include the command line to run, and if it runs in the system or user context. Program settings also provide the capabilities to run the program hidden and to suppress program notifications. Taken together, these options allow an administrator to introduce any software of his or her choosing into your environment and control the deployment scope and the manner in which it deploys.

▶ Advertisements and collections control the targeting of software distribution. A user with Read and Advertise rights on a collection can advertise any existing package to the collection, provided the user also has Read rights on the package. A user with the right to modify a collection that is the target of an advertisement or the ability to link collections to other collections can change the targets for an existing advertisement. A user with the right to modify an existing advertisement can change the properties of the advertisement, including the package and program that will execute.

▶ Other sensitive features with client impact include software updates and OS deployment. Some examples of why access to these classes needs to be restricted include:

▶ A user with rights to modify deployment packages could prevent systems from receiving specific updates, leaving them vulnerable to attack.

▶ A user with rights to modify operating system images, driver packages or other OS deployment objects could embed code into your newly deployed systems to provide backdoor access to the systems.

The above list is by no means an exhaustive compilation of the threats posed by ConfigMgr administrative access in the wrong hands, but should give you a good idea of the types of issues to consider when assigning rights within ConfigMgr.

Security for Remote Administration

Access to the ConfigMgr remote administration tools is granted through the permitted viewer's list property of the Remote Tools Client Agent. To edit the permitted viewers list, perform the following steps:

1. Expand the Configuration Manager console tree to System Center Configuration Manager -> Site Database -> Site Management -> *<Site Code> <Site Name>* -> Site Settings -> Client Agents.

2. Right-click Remote Tools Client Agent, choose Properties, and then click the Security tab. You can use the starburst (new) icon to add groups to the permitted viewers list. To avoid ambiguity, you should enter group names using the domain\groupname format.

The "Securing Configuration Manager Operations" section in this chapter discusses additional considerations for secure use of remote tools.

Auditing Configuration Manager Administration

ConfigMgr generates status messages of type Audit to provide an audit record of certain security sensitive operations. Audit messages are generated for remote control of client systems and OOB Management console activity. The SMS provider also generates audit messages when a user creates or modifies an object or makes security changes on a ConfigMgr class or instance. The audit messages for security changes indicate the user making the change, the target user or group whose rights are modified, the object class, and the object ID for specific instances. The specific permissions assigned or removed are not included. Similarly, audit messages record a user making changes to an object, such as modifying a program in a software package but do not provide details such as the command line the user entered for the program. You can use the following status message queries to view audit messages:

- ▶ All Audit Status Messages from a Specific Site
- ▶ All Audit Status Messages from a Specific User

Chapter 18, "Reporting," discusses using reports to view audit messages and describes how to configure your audit message retention policy.

SQL Server Administrative Security

You should strictly limit direct access to the site database to a small number of administrators considered necessary to support and maintain the database itself. As a best practice, you should assign the system administrator role only to a specific AD group and use AD to manage and audit group membership. Because a database administrator could potentially create, modify, or delete any ConfigMgr object, bypassing the WMI provider, direct SQL access is the most sensitive right in ConfigMgr.

Consider auditing database changes. SQL Server auditing capabilities are described in the security audit event category of the SQL Server Books Online (downloadable at www. microsoft.com/downloads; search for **SQL Server 2005 Books Online**). You can use SQL trace functionality to capture selected SQL statements to a file or database. Chapter 3 introduces the SQL Profiler, which provides a graphical interface for capturing and viewing SQL trace data. For performance reasons, you should use stored procedures to capture SQL trace data to a file to meet your audit requirements rather than using the Profiler. You should also apply filters to avoid capturing excessive amounts of data and minimize performance impact. Information on configuring SQL Trace is at http://msdn. microsoft.com/en-us/library/ms191443.aspx.

The Center for Internet Security (CIS) provides benchmarks for configuring various operating systems, applications, and devices, located at http://www.cisecurity.org/benchmarks. html. The CIS benchmarks for SQL Server include detailed recommendations for using SQL Trace to monitor access to cardholder data for PCI compliance. Many of these recommendations apply to protecting any kind of sensitive data. Auditing capabilities are also enhanced in SQL Server 2008. Information about the new auditing features of SQL Server 2008 is available at http://msdn.microsoft.com/en-us/library/dd392015.aspx. There are also third-party tools available to provide even more extensive and tamper-resistant auditing for SQL Server.

Securing the Configuration Manager Infrastructure

An earlier section, "Securing Administrative Access to Configuration Manager," discussed how to provide appropriate levels of access to authorized ConfigMgr administrators. The chapter now looks at protecting your ConfigMgr infrastructure from unauthorized access. Critical infrastructure components that could be subject to attack include ConfigMgr site systems, accounts used by ConfigMgr, communications between sites, site systems and clients, and the file base and infrastructure services ConfigMgr depends on for its operations. Before considering each of these infrastructure components individually, let's look at how you should consider security when designing and planning your ConfigMgr infrastructure.

Building Security into Your Hierarchy

You should consider your organization's security requirements throughout the life cycle of your ConfigMgr implementation. During the hierarchy design phase, keep the following considerations in mind:

> ▶ **Active Directory considerations**—Although it is possible for a ConfigMgr site to span more than one AD forest, doing this might compromise your AD security design. The forest is a security boundary in AD. Allowing a site server in one forest to configure site systems or administer clients in a second forest could violate the

autonomy of the forest in which the managed systems reside. You can also have a child primary site report to a parent site in a different forest. Again, this might compromise the security boundary between the forests. By design, administration flows from the parent site to the child site. There are also attack vectors through which a child site could constitute a threat to other sites in the hierarchy. The strongest protection for the integrity of your AD forests is to isolate each ConfigMgr hierarchy within a single forest. You should weigh this decision against the possible administrative advantages of using a single ConfigMgr hierarchy to manage multiple forests.

▶ **Configuration Manager site selection**—In general, the fewer sites you have, the easier it is to maintain site security. Additional sites increase the number of site servers, site databases for primary sites, and intersite communications links you need to administer and secure. In some cases, however, you might consider using dedicated sites for specific security needs. A dedicated site might allow you to restrict administrative access to a smaller group and configure site-wide settings appropriately for the security requirements of the target environment. As an example, if you use remote tools elsewhere in your organization, you can choose not to enable the remote tools client agent in a specific site, protecting those systems from the threat of misuse of remote tools functionality.

▶ **Site system role assignment**—Microsoft recommends using role separation to reduce server attack surface and avoid creating a single point of failure. It is important to consider both the advantages and disadvantages of this approach from a security standpoint. Reducing the attack surface of your site systems is an important security consideration. The "Securing Site Systems" section in this chapter discusses methods for reducing the attack surface of individual site systems. Although you might reduce the attack surface of each site system by using dedicated servers with one site role per server, distributing site roles across a large number of systems might actually increase the overall attack surface of your site. Each system, account, and network communications path you add represents a potential point of attack that can lead to the compromise of the entire site.

Carefully consider the administrative and physical resources you have available to support the security of distributed site roles. It is most important to move client-facing roles, such as the management point and distribution point, off the site server. You can greatly reduce the risk of a network attack by restricting client access to only those server roles that require it. The site server and site database server are the most important roles in your site, and allowing clients to establish a network connection to these systems is a risk you need to consider eliminating.

Installing Internet Information Services (IIS) on a server greatly increases the server's attack surface. For that reason, you should generally separate server roles requiring IIS from those that do not. Chapter 4, "Configuration Manager Solution Design," discussed the requirements for Configuration Manager 2007 server roles. You need to also separate the Fallback Status Point (FSP) server role from all other system roles.

The FSP must be configured to accept unauthenticated client data. Accepting unauthenticated client data presents a risk you should avoid exposing other site roles to. One exception to Microsoft's recommendations to separate server roles is the site database server. The best security practice is to locate the site database on the site server to simplify security administration. Perhaps the most important security consideration for assigning system roles is to avoid using systems that host other applications as site systems, especially those with applications based on IIS or SQL Server. Poorly written or vulnerable web and database applications are favorite targets of attackers and could be exploited to gain control of a site system. Placing a distribution point on a server that provides file and print services is a much lower risk.

▶ **Server placement**—All site systems should be deployed in locations that are as secure as possible in terms of physical and network access. An attacker with physical access to a site system or administrative workstation could compromise your system—for example, the attacker could install a hardware device such as a keystroke logger or boot the system to an insecure operating system. You might want to consult with the team responsible for physical security to help determine the most secure locations consistent with the functional requirements of each system. Network traffic should be restricted to that necessary for ConfigMgr operations and basic server functions. Chapter 5, "Network Design," discusses ConfigMgr network traffic. The material in Chapter 5, along with the port references and diagrams Microsoft provides at http://technet.microsoft.com/en-us/library/bb632618.aspx and http://go.microsoft.com/fwlink/?LinkID=123652, can help you determine how to restrict network traffic and how to assign server roles to allow you to restrict network traffic.

Effective management and monitoring can greatly enhance the security of your environment. Potential compromise of a management application, however, is a threat you cannot afford to ignore. After all, why should an attacker go to the trouble of deploying and managing malware agents in your environment if he can just use the highly capable agents you have deployed for him?

Many organizations deploy management applications in a separate, highly secure network zone to protect them from network attacks. Chapter 6, "Architecture Design Planning," presents several network topologies you can use for IBCM. Each of these scenarios involves placing sites or systems in a perimeter network to provide services to Internet clients. You can apply the same principles to your hierarchy by placing your highest value sites and systems in more secure zones within your internal network. For example, you can adapt the model for having a site span the internal network and the perimeter network to create a hierarchy that spans your secure management network zone and the zone in which your application servers typically reside. In this instance, you would place the site server and site database server in the secure management zone. In the same manner, you can place a central site or a site with high-security requirements in a higher security network zone and configure communications with less secure sites, similar to the models for dedicated sites for Internet clients. In each case, if administrative workstations reside in the less secure network zones, they should use a Virtual Private Network (VPN) to connect to systems in the higher security zone.

Securing Site Systems

Consider your ConfigMgr site server and site systems as among the most security-sensitive assets in your organization, on a par with domain controllers. All basic controls applicable to such systems should be applied to your site systems. The next sections discuss some of the types of controls you can use to protect site systems.

Physical Security and Hardware Selection

Choose the most secure possible location and most secure hardware available for your site systems. Site servers and site database servers should be located in secure data centers. You need to balance security concerns with your other requirements as you consider the placement of client-facing systems such as distribution points. If possible, ensure that cameras are oriented to monitor access to server hardware, while protecting keyboards and monitors from being viewed through those cameras. Server-class hardware often provides functionality such as alarms that alert when detecting an open chassis or modifications to hardware. Newer hardware implements protection features such as processor-based data execution prevention (DEP). Choose hardware with the maximum reliability and redundancy for systems with high availability requirements.

System Software Security

Choose the most recent version of Microsoft Windows consistent with your system requirements, and keep up to date on all service packs and security patches. Evolving security awareness and technology is reflected in the design of modern operating systems, and each version of Windows has contained numerous security enhancements over its predecessor. Often the accumulation of small enhancements can make as much or more difference as the more highly publicized features. In addition to OS patches, you should keep system components such as the Basic Input Output System (BIOS) and firmware up to date and regularly update all drivers and applications installed on your systems.

A number of resources are available that provide current information on software and hardware vulnerabilities, threats, and countermeasures. The United States Computer Emergency Response Team (US-CERT) site, http://www.us-cert.gov/cas/alldocs.html, is a great place to start. US-CERT provides security bulletins, alerts, and a wide range of security-related information. Many software and security vendors provide additional vulnerability alerts and threat information services. Microsoft provides security bulletins related to Microsoft software, guides for securing Microsoft Windows platforms, and additional security information at http://www.microsoft.com/security/default.mspx.

Attack Surface Reduction and Server Hardening

One of the most basic and important principles for securing any system is to reduce the number of potential vulnerabilities by eliminating unnecessary services, accounts, applications, network shares, open network ports, and so on. The key to reducing the attack surface without reducing required functionality is determining those features unnecessary on a particular system so that you can turn them off. In addition to reducing the attack surface of your servers, you can "harden" the server by modifying default settings such as requiring the use of more secure network protocols and limiting access to certain Graphical User Interface (GUI) features. Microsoft provides a set of tools that greatly simplifies attack surface reduction and server hardening for the Windows operating system and for ConfigMgr and SQL Server systems:

- ▶ Windows Security Configuration Wizard (SCW)
- ▶ SQL Server Surface Area Configuration
- ▶ Configuration Manager 2007 Desired Configuration Management

Windows Server 2003 Service Pack 1 introduced the Security Configuration Wizard for Windows Server 2003. You can install the SCW through Control Panel -> Add/Remove Programs -> Windows Components. The SCW is an attack surface reduction tool that helps you identify and disable unnecessary ports and services and harden the network stack. On Windows Server 2008 systems, the SCW is installed automatically with updated functionality to configure IPv6 settings. Although you can use the Windows Server 2008 Server Manager to configure server roles, SCW provides more advanced settings, including granular control over security settings.

The Security Configuration Wizard Template for Configuration Manager 2007, included in the Microsoft System Center Configuration Manager 2007 (ConfigMgr) Toolkit, provides SCW templates for the following ConfigMgr server roles:

- ▶ Primary and secondary site servers
- ▶ Server locator points
- ▶ Management points
- ▶ Reporting points
- ▶ Fallback status points
- ▶ State migration points
- ▶ PXE service points
- ▶ Software update points
- ▶ System health validator points

To apply the appropriate security settings to a site system role, run SCW on the appropriate system after you have installed and configured all appropriate ConfigMgr roles. To apply security policies based on the template, perform the following steps:

1. Download and run ConfigMgr2007ToolKit.exe from http://go.microsoft.com/fwlink/?LinkId=93071; then install the CCM tools (CcmTools.msi).

2. Copy the ConfigMgr07.xml template file from %*ProgramFiles*%\ConfigMgr 2007 Toolkit\CCM Tools\SCW Template to the security\msscw\kbs folder under your Windows folder.

3. Enter the following command at the Windows command prompt to unregister the SMS 2003 template:

```
scwcmd register /kbname:SMS /d
```

4. Enter the following command at the command prompt to register the ConfigMgr 2007 template:

```
scwcmd register /kbname:CM07
/kbfile:%windir%\security\msscw\kbs\ConfigMgr07.xml
```

5. Launch the Security Configuration Wizard from the Administrative Tools program group and click Next on the Welcome page.

6. Figure 20.8 displays the SCW Configuration Action page. Select Create a new security policy and click Next. Note that you can also use the tool to edit or apply existing policies or roll back a security policy.

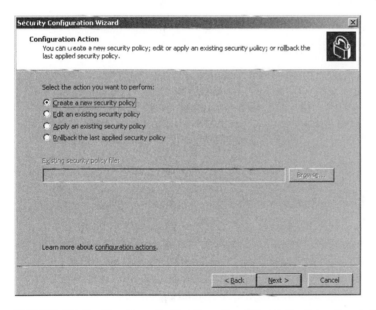

FIGURE 20.8 The Security Configuration Wizard Configuration Action page with the Create a new security policy option selected

7. Enter your server name on the Select Server page and click Next. The wizard now processes the configuration database. When processing completes, click Next and then Next again to begin Role-Based Service Configuration. Figure 20.9 displays the Select Server Roles page. Verify the appropriate roles are selected, and then click Next.

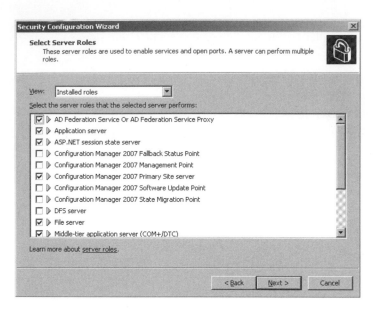

FIGURE 20.9   The Security Configuration Wizard Select Server Roles page with the detected roles on a primary site server

8. The next three pages ask you to select client features, administrative and other options, and additional services. On each of these pages, verify that the appropriate features are selected, and then click Next. On the Handling Unspecified Services page, you generally accept the default option to leave the services unchanged and click Next. Although choosing the Disable the service option for handing unspecified services provides slightly better security, you need to rerun the wizard each time you apply the policy to a new server or install new software.

NOTE

About Administrative and Other Options

Enable the appropriate options on the Administrative and Other Options page of the SCW if you plan any of the following activities:

▶ Running the Configuration Manager 2007 console on the server

▶ Using the server as a Configuration Manager 2007 distribution point

▶ Supporting Background Intelligent Transfer Service (BITS)

▶ Connecting to the server using Configuration Manager 2007 Remote Control

▶ Implementing remote WMI (required for remote ConfigMgr administration)

▶ Remotely administering IIS on the server

---

9. Figure 20.10 shows the Confirm Service Changes page. Review the list of proposed changes and navigate back to the previous pages if you need to change any of the selections. If you are satisfied with the proposed changes, click Next.

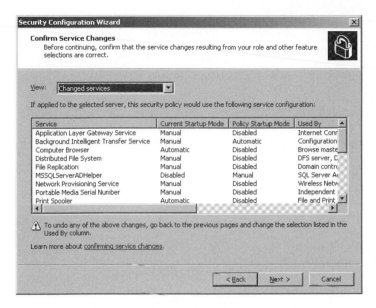

FIGURE 20.10   The Security Configuration Wizard Confirm Service Changes page with proposed changes for the primary site server

10. On the Network Security page, click Next to review and modify the list of open ports. Figure 20.11 shows the Open Ports and Approve Applications page. When you complete your port selection, click Next and then Next again to confirm your choices.

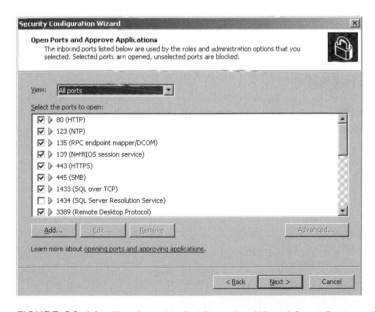

FIGURE 20.11   The Security Configuration Wizard Open Ports and Approve Applications page showing proposed changes for the primary site server

11. On the Network Security page, click Next to launch the Registry settings section of the wizard. The Registry settings need to be consistent with your network environment. The available registry settings govern

- ► Server Message Block (SMB) Security Signatures

- ► Lightweight Directory Access Protocol (LDAP) Signing

- ► Outbound and Inbound Authentication Methods

You should disable connections from computers that require LAN Manager authentication and computers not configured to use NTLMv2 (NT LAN Manager version 2) authentication unless these are required in your environment. If you enforce the signing and authentication settings in the group policy, you can choose to skip this section of the wizard.

12. The Audit Policy section of the wizard suggests changes to the local Windows audit policy. The Internet Information Services section restricts IIS features and removes unnecessary virtual directories such as help and samples. After you complete (or skip) each section of the wizard, you can save your policy selections as an .xml file that you can apply to the local server or other servers through the SCW. You also have an option to apply the policy setting locally now, which generally requires a reboot.

You can also apply the policies through AD group policy using the `scwcmd /configure` command line option for the Windows Server 2003 SCW or the `scwcmd /transform` option for Windows Server 2008. This section has only discussed a fraction of what you can do with the Security Configuration Wizard.

- ► For more information about the SCW for Windows Server 2003, see http://www.microsoft.com/windowsserver2003/technologies/security/configwiz/default.mspx.

- ► For additional information about the SCW for Windows Server 2008, see http://technet.microsoft.com/en-us/library/cc771492.aspx.

CAUTION

Test All Security Policies Before Applying Them to Production Systems

Blocking a required service, network port, or connection type can cause your server to fail to perform required functions. Be sure to test your security policies thoroughly in your proof of concept environment before deploying them to production systems.

Configuration Manager 2007 DCM can help you to reduce the attack surface and identify other configuration issues on site systems. DCM provides additional monitoring and reporting capabilities that help you maintain the configuration baseline. Microsoft provides two DCM configuration packs (CPs) for specific ConfigMgr site system roles:

- ► The System Center Configuration Manager 2007 Vulnerability Assessment CP provides baselines to help you identify vulnerabilities in you Windows, IIS, and SQL Server configurations.

▶ The System Center Configuration Manager 2007 CP provides a baseline for management points, distribution points, and software update points.

You can download the configuration packs from http://technet.microsoft.com/en-us/configmgr/cc462788.aspx. For more information about DCM, see Chapter 16.

You can install the SQL Server Surface Area Configuration tool from the SQL Server 2005 Setup program. For SQL Server 2008 environments, you can import the tool into SQL Server Management Studio from %*ProgramFiles*%\Microsoft SQL Server\100\Tools\Policies\Surface Area Configuration for Database Engine 2008 Features.xml. Using The Surface Area Configuration tool allows you to turn off unnecessary SQL Server features and functionality. For more information about SQL Server Surface Area Configuration, see http://msdn.microsoft.com/en-us/library/ms173748(SQL.90).aspx.

Security Software

You should run antivirus software on all systems in your environment and update virus signatures regularly. Relatively little hacker activity today is carried out by interactively accessing systems and manually exploiting system vulnerabilities. Instead, hackers deploy malware with sophisticated capabilities to detect and exploit known vulnerabilities. Traditional antivirus software compares files and processes against a database of signatures used to recognize known malware. Signature-based malware detection is reasonably effective against widely deployed viruses, spyware, and other malware and is an essential part of an antimalware strategy. Some antivirus programs also use behavior-based detection that responds to suspicious activity such as a program opening a network port. Software firewalls, including the Windows firewall, provide protection from network-based attacks. In high-security environments, you might choose to use specialized host intrusion prevention (HIP) software to provide an additional layer of protection by detecting and blocking a more extensive range of suspicious process activity. File Integrity Monitoring (FIM) software protects critical files from alteration. You might consider using FIM to alert you if key ConfigMgr files such as the service executables, site control file, and client source files are altered.

Security programs are by their nature intrusive. They often consume significant amounts of system resources and sometimes block legitimate activity. You should test and adjust your security software settings in your proof of concept environment and continue to monitor the impact of security software in your pilot and production environments. To improve system performance and availability, it is sometimes advisable to exclude certain directories from virus scanning. Exclusions are typically applied to files frequently accessed or generally locked during normal operations that are not common vectors for introducing malware into the environment, such as log files or the Windows paging file. Any scanning exclusions you create can introduce a potential weakness in your protection framework that could be exploited by malware. You should follow your organization's risk policy when considering any exclusions or exceptions in your controls framework. Microsoft recommends certain exclusions for all Windows systems as described in http://support.microsoft.com/kb/822158. Here are some additional virus scanning exclusions you might want to consider for ConfigMgr site systems:

▶ All files of type *.log.

20

▶ The Windows paging file, pagefile.sys.

▶ Any mapped network drives or Storage Area Network (SAN) storage mounted as drives. You can use antivirus software specifically designed for SAN environments to scan SAN storage.

▶ All files under the *<ConfigMgr Install Path>*\Inboxes folder on ConfigMgr site servers, other than those in the clifiles.src sub folder.

▶ All files under the SMS_CCM\ServiceData folder on management points.

▶ The IIS Temporary Compressed Files and inetsrv folders on servers with IIS installed.

▶ The SQL Server database, backup and log files on the site database server (*.mdf, *.ldf, *.ndf, *.bak, *.trn). If SQL Server is installed on a clustered SQL Server instance, you might also need to exclude the cluster folder and the quorum drive.

▶ The backup folder on the site server.

▶ The WSUS and MSSQL$WSUS folders on your SUP.

You should also consider any vendor-recommended exclusions for installed components such as backup software or host-based adapters (HBAs). Keep in mind, however, that vendors are typically more concerned with the functioning of their products than the security of your systems and might publish overly broad recommendations for excluding their software.

Review the logs created by your security software for malware detection and blocked actions. If you find false positive detections, evaluate the impact on system functionality and modify security software settings as required. Chapter 3 introduces the Process Monitor. If you suspect that on-access virus scanning is affecting system or application stability or performance, you can use Process Monitor to determine what files your virus scanner is opening. If you see files that are frequently scanned, you might consider them for exclusions. Some enterprise antivirus applications allow you to apply on-access scanning exclusions to files opened by specific processes you designate as low risk or low priority. This is a much safer practice than allowing all processes to read from or write to the excluded files without scanning. If your antivirus software supports this, you should designate the ConfigMgr processes as low risk and apply exclusions for specific site roles only to low risk processes. Here are some processes you might want to designate as low risk:

▶ ccmexec.exe (on management points)

▶ sitecomp.exe

▶ smsexec.exe

▶ smsrph.exe (on reporting points)

▶ smswriter.exe

▶ sqlservr.exe (on site database servers)

▶ sqlwriter.exe (on site database servers)

With any exclusion, you should be sure to scan all downloaded files for malware before copying them to locations where they are excluded from scanning.

Securing the Site Database

The site database server is the heart of your ConfigMgr site. Its security is at least as important as that of the site server. You should use a dedicated SQL Server for each primary site or locate the database on the site server itself.

Use a low privilege domain account for the SQL Server startup account, rather than running SQL Server under Local System. When you run SQL Server in a low privilege account context, you need to manually register the Service Principal Name (SPN) for the server in AD. Clients use the SPN to locate SQL services. You can use the procedure described at http://technet.microsoft.com/en-us/library/bb735885.aspx to register the SPN.

Configure SQL Server to use Windows authentication only and enable logging for at least failed logon attempts. Be sure to drop the sample databases. You can run the SQL Server Surface Area Configuration from the SQL Server program -> Configuration Tools program group to eliminate unnecessary features. Be sure to test any changes you make with the SQL Server Surface Area Configuration in your Proof of Concept environment before applying them in production. For more information about SQL Server security, see http://go.microsoft.com/fwlink/?LinkId=95071.

Securing Configuration Manager Communications

Many of the attacks we see today are network-based attacks. ConfigMgr sites, site systems, and clients communicate across network links and are potentially susceptible to the following types of attacks:

- ▶ **Misdirection attacks**—Where a client or site system is provided with the wrong name or Internet Protocol (IP) address for the partner with which it needs to communicate. To avoid misdirection attacks, you must secure service advertisement and name resolution services.

- ▶ **Spoofing attacks**—Where a rogue system impersonates the actual system with which a client or site system needs to communicate. To defeat spoofing attacks, all communications must be properly authenticated.

- ▶ **Eavesdropping or sniffer-based attacks**—Where an attacker intercepts network communications, gaining access to confidential information. Data encryption is the primary defense against breach of confidential communications.

- ▶ **Man-in-the-middle (MITM) attacks**—Attacks in which an attacker steals, alters, or interrupts communications by routing data through an intermediate node that is under the attacker's control. You can often defeat MITM attacks by using mutual authentication. Digitally signing files can help you detect alterations due to MITM attacks.

▶ **Denial of service attacks**—When an attacker uses large amounts of data or malformed data packets to crash systems or clog communication links. A resilient network infrastructure and fault tolerant service delivery design are your best defenses against DoS attacks.

Microsoft provides several security features to protect the confidentiality, integrity, and availability of ConfigMgr communications. The next sections consider how you can use these features to secure communications between ConfigMgr clients and their site, and communications between ConfigMgr sites and site systems.

CAUTION

Don't Let Attackers Use Encryption to Bypass Other Security Controls

Cryptographic controls such as encryption and digital signatures are among the most important security mechanisms you can use to protect the confidentiality and integrity of data. Encryption can be something of a double-edged sword, however, because many other security controls do not work on encrypted data. For example, antivirus programs are typically unable to scan encrypted files. Similarly, network Intrusion Detection Systems (IDS) or Intrusion Prevention Systems (IPS) cannot inspect encrypted packets for attack signatures. You should consider procedures to make sure any files and packets that bypass one control are inspected by another, such as quarantining inbound encrypted files until they can be decrypted and scanned, or using a host-based IDS or IPS at each endpoint of an encrypted tunnel.

Securing Client to Server Communications

The integrity of the policy and content your clients receive is the paramount consideration when considering client-to-server communications. An attacker who can direct client policy requests to a rogue management point or tamper with client policy can instruct the ConfigMgr agent to execute instructions of the attacker's choosing. Similarly, an attacker who can cause clients to use forged or altered content such as software packages or OS images could gain control of client systems. Data sent by the clients to the servers is generally less critical than policy and content received by the clients; however, you should consider the importance of the confidentiality and integrity of inventory and discovery data and status messages in your environment.

ConfigMgr native mode provides much stronger security for client-to-server communications than mixed mode. Native mode uses PKI certificates to provide mutual authentication and Secure Sockets Layer (SSL) encryption for most communication between clients and servers. Mutual authentication ensures that clients and servers are communicating with the correct systems and protects against man-in-the-middle attacks. If your site provides support for mobile device management in mixed mode, distribution points must allow anonymous access. The anonymous access allows unauthenticated clients access to ConfigMgr content. Even in native mode, there is no encryption or authentication of Server Message Block (SMB) communications. You should therefore configure all distribution points to use BITS to avoid having clients download content using SMB. As branch distribution points and server shares use SMB for all content access, they are less secure than standard BITS-enabled distribution points.

ConfigMgr uses a signing certificate to protect the integrity of policy downloads. In mixed mode, the management point signs client policy. In native mode, the site server signs the policy. Management points are generally less secure systems than the site server is because they must accept connections from clients and run IIS. Keep in mind that if you enable the HTTP communication for roaming and site assignment site property, clients will communicate with management points and distribution points without encryption or mutual authentication when they roam at mixed mode sites. See Chapter 5 for a discussion of the HTTP communication for roaming and site assignment option. For maximum security, enable Certificate Revocation List (CRL) checking. CRL checking causes the client to check a list of revoked certificates when communicating with site systems. Note that CRL checking requires that your CRL be available at all times and introduces a significant delay in client to server communications. You can enable CRL checking as either as a site property or a client setup property, as described in http://technet.microsoft.com/en-us/library/bb680540.aspx.

Native mode requirements include a PKI infrastructure and exclude any support for SMS 2003 clients. Chapter 6 discusses the requirements for native mode in more detail. If your site meets all native mode prerequisites, you still need to plan for native mode and deploy all required certificates. Microsoft provides a workflow for migrating to native mode at http://technet.microsoft.com/en-us/library/bb680838.aspx. If your sites meet the native mode requirements, you should strongly consider making the investment of migrating to native mode for optimal security, whether or not you require native mode features, such as IBCM. Keep in mind that you can easily revert to mixed mode if you encounter problems after enabling native mode.

If you are not ready to enable native mode on your sites, there are several steps to take to secure client-to-server communications within mixed mode sites:

▶ If possible, upgrade all clients to ConfigMgr 2007 and enable the This site contains only ConfigMgr 2007 clients check box in the site properties. This setting limits downloading of policy containing sensitive information only to approved clients.

▶ Do not automatically approve all clients. Clients can be used to attack the site, for example by sending excessive or malformed inventory as a DoS attack. Clients can also retrieve policy from the site, which might expose sensitive information about your site's configuration and operations. The option to manually approve all clients gives you the most control but requires substantial administrative overhead and is, therefore, not suitable for most installations. The automatically approve clients from trusted domains is the preferred option in most situations.

▶ In mixed mode, client inventory is signed but not encrypted by default. To provide confidential uploading of inventory data, enable the Encrypt data before sending to Management Point option in the site Properties.

The client agent downloads policy from its management point and executes instructions specified in the policy. Control of the policy is, therefore, control of the client. This makes it essential that clients verify that they are communicating with the correct management point. All communications from the management point to the client are signed using the management point's self-signed certificate. Before the client can trust the management

20

point's certificate, the client must have a list of management points it should trust and a copy of the certificate signed by a trusted authority. If you have extended the Active Directory schema and enabled AD publishing of site information, clients in the same AD forest with the site server can retrieve a list of management points from a global catalog server. (Chapter 6 discusses the AD schema extensions.) If the client cannot retrieve management point information from AD, the client can use Windows Internet Name Service (WINS) to retrieve its default management point and then obtain the management point list from the default management point. You can use the SMSDIRECTORYLOOKUP client installation property to specify one of three modes the client uses to retrieve management point information:

▶ **Active Directory Only (NOWINS)**—This mode specifies the client uses only AD to retrieve management point information. This is the most secure mode; however, management point communications can fail if the client cannot obtain the information from the global catalog.

▶ **Secure WINS (WINSSECURE)**—Using this mode specifies the client attempts to use AD first and failover to the WINS method if required. The client communicates only with the management point after validating its certificate. Secure WINS is the default mode in Configuration Manager 2007.

▶ **Any WINS (WINSPROMISCUOUS)**—Using Any WINS also specifies the client attempts to use AD first and failover to the WINS method if required; however, in this mode the client trusts management points without checking their certificate with a trusted authority. The Any WINS method is the least secure and should be avoided.

In native mode, the management point establishes trust with the client by providing a copy of its certificate signed by a certificate authority (CA) from the PKI you use to support your native mode deployment. In mixed mode, the management point presents a copy of its certificate signed with the trusted root private key. The trusted root key pair is similar to the public keys used in a PKI infrastructure, but maintained by the central site server in your ConfigMgr hierarchy for the limited purpose of supporting ConfigMgr communications. If your site is publishing to AD clients within the AD forest, it can retrieve the trusted root public key from AD. You must provision those clients that cannot retrieve the trusted root key from AD with the trusted root key using the procedure described at http://technet.microsoft.com/en-us/library/bb680504.aspx. If you have clients in mixed mode sites not provisioned with the trusted root key and unable to retrieve the key from AD, they will trust the first management point they contact.

Securing Site to Site and Server to Server Communications

All communication between ConfigMgr sites is signed with the sending site server's private key. Sites must exchange public keys to verify the signed data from other sites. To ensure this key exchange is done securely, verify the Require secure key exchange option is enabled on all sites in your hierarchy. Require secure key exchange is the default in ConfigMgr. Sites within the same AD forest can securely exchange keys automatically if the schema is extended and all sites are publishing to AD. Secure exchange between sites in separate forests or without AD publishing enabled requires the administrator to manually export each site's keys to a file and import them at the destination sites.

Communications between sites are not encrypted. Communications between site systems within a site use a variety of network protocols, discussed in Chapter 5. Most communications between site systems are also not encrypted. You might want to consider using Internet Protocol security (IPSec) to encrypt site-to-site and server-to-server communications. IPSec is the standard encryption protocol for IP networks. For more information on IPSec, see http://technet.microsoft.com/en-us/network/bb531150.aspx. IPSec encryption is processor-intensive. For those systems that encrypt a large amount of network traffic using IPSec, consider installing a network card that supports IPSec offloading. Microsoft provides specific guidance for using IPSec to secure ConfigMgr communications at http://technet.microsoft.com/en-us/library/bb632851.aspx.

In addition to cryptographic controls, ConfigMgr uses Windows access controls to secure communications between sites and between site systems. Intersite communications are secured using sender accounts, described in the "Accounts to Support ConfigMgr Infrastructure" section in this chapter. There are two ways you can configure communications between the site server and other site systems:

▶ If the site system is in the same AD forest with the site server, you can add the site system to the Site System to Site Server Connection (SMS_SiteSystemToSiteServerConnection_sitecode) local group on the site server. This group has the necessary permissions to connect to the site server and transfer data. Not all site systems require membership in the Site System to Site Server Connection group. For more information about this group, see http://technet.microsoft.com/en-us/library/bb680864.aspx.

▶ If you enable the Allow only site system initiated data transfers from this site system option in the properties for the site system, the site server uses the Site System Installation account to initiate communications with the site system. The "Accounts to Support ConfigMgr Infrastructure" section in this chapter discusses the Site System Installation account. This option is preferred for better security and required if the site system is not in the same AD forest as the site server.

Securing Configuration Manager Accounts

ConfigMgr uses are variety of accounts as part of its operating framework. Many of these accounts are required in specific situations, such as accounts to support clients or site systems in untrusted domains. Other accounts are required to support only specific services, such as Out of Band Management. You should use only the accounts required by your environment or to support specific ConfigMgr features you use. Follow best practices for configuring and managing accounts. Some general principles for managing ConfigMgr accounts include

▶ Use strong passwords and change those passwords regularly. If you have an enterprise password management application, you should use it to secure ConfigMgr passwords. At a minimum, keep the passwords in a secure location protected by access controls and encryption, only allow administrators access to the passwords on a

20

nced to know basis, and keep track of who knows the passwords. If a person with access to ConfigMgr passwords leaves the company or you suspect a password is compromised, change the affected passwords immediately.

▶ Keep track of which accounts are used where, and deprovision any accounts no longer needed. If possible, integrate account life cycle management with your enterprise change and configuration management processes.

▶ Configure each account with the minimum rights it needs to accomplish its job.

▶ Whenever you use AD accounts in ConfigMgr, allow time for newly created accounts to replicate throughout the domain before you add the accounts to ConfigMgr.

▶ Do not grant these accounts interactive logon rights. Occasionally you might need to log on with one of the accounts used for ConfigMgr operations for troubleshooting purposes. In such cases, grant interactive logon rights on a temporary basis and document this step in your trouble ticketing system. The Task Sequence Run As account also needs interactive logon rights on systems where a task sequence configured to use this account runs.

Microsoft provides detailed descriptions of all ConfigMgr accounts in the online documentation. To help you sort out these accounts, the next sections present ConfigMgr accounts organized into functional groups. You can find additional details about ConfigMgr accounts at http://technet.microsoft.com/en-us/library/bb693732.aspx.

Accounts to Support ConfigMgr Infrastructure

ConfigMgr uses accounts to install components on site systems and for intersite communications. Within the site server's AD forest or in domains trusting the site server's domain, you should use the site server machine account for these purposes rather than configuring separate accounts.

TIP

Assigning Rights to Machine Accounts

Any time you use the site server machine account for ConfigMgr operations, you need to ensure that the machine account has the required access rights for the task. In most cases, you can provide rights by adding accounts to groups. When you use Active Directory Users and Computers to add users to groups, only users, groups, and other objects such as contacts are available by default through the user interface. You can use ADUC to add machine accounts to groups by clicking the Object Types button in the Select Users, Computers, or Groups dialog box and checking the selection next to Computers. You can also specify machine accounts when using command line tools or scripts by entering the computer name with a **$** appended to the end.

Two types of accounts are used for installation purposes:

▶ Site System Installation accounts are used to install and configure site systems. You specify the Site System Installation account used to manage a particular site system on the New Site System Server Wizard, General page. Chapter 8, "Installing Configuration Manager 2007," discusses the New Site System Server Wizard.

▶ Client Push Installation accounts are used to install and configure client systems if you use the client push installation method. See Chapter 12, "Client Management," for a discussion of client installation methods. You specify Client Push Installation accounts on the Accounts tab of the site properties page. Setting site properties is also discussed in Chapter 8.

You can use either Active Directory or local accounts for site system installation and client push. These accounts need to be in the local Administrators group on the target systems. You should not add these accounts to the Domain Admins group because this would provide excessive privileges to the accounts. Instead, create groups that include the appropriate accounts and use group policy or local computer management to add those groups to the local Administrators group. The Computer Configuration -> Policies -> Windows Settings -> Security Settings -> Restricted Groups setting allows you to administer local group membership through group policy. To limit the administrative scope of these accounts, consider using multiple accounts and granting each account access only on those systems on which you use it.

The accounts used for site-to-site communications are

▶ The Site Address account is used by the LAN sender to send data to other sites in your ConfigMgr hierarchy.

▶ The Remote Access Services (RAS) Sender Phone Book account is used to initiate connection for the RAS sender.

You can specify these accounts on in the Address properties for the destination site. Chapter 5 describes how to configure Address properties. These accounts require modify rights on the SMS_Site share (<*ConfigMgr Install Path*>\Inboxes\Despoolr.box\Receive folder) on destination site servers. You should provide this access by adding the accounts to the Site to Site Connection local group (SMS_SitetoSiteConnection_<*Site Code*>) on the destination site server. The RAS Sender Phone Book account also needs rights to initiate a RAS connection. You should generally use the same account for both of these roles.

Database Connection Accounts

If you have site systems that do not reside in the same AD forest as the site database server or in a domain trusted by the site database server's domain, you need to configure accounts these systems can use to connect to the database. Within the site database server's AD forest or in trusted domains, use the site system machine's accounts for database connectivity. If you need database connection accounts, you should create these accounts as low privilege local accounts on the database server. You can specify a database connection account on the site system role Properties page. Chapter 8 discusses the Properties pages used for configuring site system roles. You will then add the accounts to predefined database roles to provide the access they require. Table 20.1 displays a list of these accounts and the database roles they require.

TABLE 20.1   Database Roles for Connection Accounts

Account Name	Database Role
Management Point Database Connection account	smsdbrole_MP
Multicast Service Point Connection account	smsdbrole_MCS
PXE Service Point Database Connection account	smsdbrole_PSP
Server Locator Point Database Connection account	smsdbrole_SLP

Accounts Used for OS Deployment and Software Distribution

ConfigMgr operating system deployment (OSD) requires accounts to carry out several specific task sequence actions. These accounts are specified in the task sequence properties. Chapter 19, "Operating System Deployment," discusses configuring task sequences. Table 20.2 displays the task sequence accounts with information about their usage and required permissions.

TABLE 20.2   Accounts Used in Task Sequences

Account Name	Where Used	How Used	Required Permissions
Capture Operating System Image account	Task sequences with the Capture Operating System Image step	To access the folder where captured images are stored	Read/Write permissions on the network share where the captured image is to be stored.
Task Sequence Editor Domain Joining account	Apply Network Settings task sequence OR Join Domain or Workgroup task sequence	To join newly imaged computers to the domain	Right to join computers to the target domain.
Task Sequence Editor Network Folder Connection account	Connect to Network Folder task sequence	To connect to network shares	Access to content.
Task Sequence Run As account	Run Command Line task sequence	To provide a context for running commands during a task sequence	Interactive logon rights and other rights required by the specific command.

OSD accounts are generally AD domain accounts; however, you have the option to use local accounts for the Capture Operating System Image account and the Task Sequence Run As account.

In addition to the accounts listed in Table 20.2, both OSD and software distribution use the Network Access account to access network resources when the client computer account and/or current user does not have access. You can configure the Network Access account in the ConfigMgr console on the General tab of the Computer Client Agent property sheet, found under System Center Configuration Manager -> Site Database -> Site Management -> *<Site Code> <Site Name>* -> Site Settings -> Client Agents. Generally, you need this account only for client computers in workgroups or untrusted domains, or for use during operating system deployment before the computer has joined the domain. Grant the account domain user permissions only. By default Domain Users have access to package shares on distribution points. If you remove this access or use a Universal Naming convention (UNC) path to specify the content location, you must grant the Network Access account Read permission if clients will use this account to access the content.

For granular access to packages, you can specify one or more Package Access accounts on a per package basis. Package Access accounts can be in any Windows user or group, or the built-in Users, Administrators or Guests groups. You generally use existing groups as Package Access accounts rather than creating accounts for this purpose. You can configure a Package Access account in the ConfigMgr console, under System Center Configuration Manager -> Site Database -> Computer Management -> Software Distribution -> Packages -> *<package name>* -> Access Accounts. The default Package Access accounts are Users with Read permission and Administrators with Full Control. In general, you change these defaults only to restrict packages to which you do not want all users to have access. Occasionally you might also need to grant Modify permission to the Users group if a setup program needs to write back to the source folder. Unless your security requirements are extremely low, you should not allow Guests access to anything on your network.

Accounts Used for Out of Band Management

Because the management controller (a vPro chipset, see Chapter 11, "Related Technologies and References," for further information regarding vPro) has low-level system access on managed clients, it is critically important that OOB management access should be as secure as possible. The Intel Active Management Technology (AMT) Management Engine uses three accounts that reside in the AMT BIOS extension (MEBx) firmware to provide OOB management functionality on client systems with supported OOB management controllers. These accounts are used for provisioning and remote administration. In addition, ConfigMgr uses a set of AD user accounts or groups to manage permissions for OOB Management.

You can configure your site to use the three accounts that reside in the BIOS extensions through the Out of Band Management Properties sheet, located under System Center Configuration Manager -> Site Database -> Site Management -> *<Site Code> <Site Name>* -> Site Settings -> Component Configuration in the ConfigMgr Console. Here are the three accounts:

▶ **MEBx account**—This account is used for initial authentication to the AMT firmware. The MEBx account is named *admin*, with the default password admin. If you or your computer manufacturer has configured the management controller with a different password, you need to use the AMT Provisioning and Discovery account for provisioning instead of the MEBx account. ConfigMgr sets the MEBx account password during the provisioning process. You can specify the password on the OOB Properties General tab, or you can specify specific values for each computer in a comma-separated values (CSV) file and import them with the Import Computer for Out of Band Management Wizard. For instructions on running the Import Computer for Out of Band Management Wizard, see http://technet.microsoft.com/en-us/library/cc161950.aspx.

▶ **AMT Provisioning and Discovery account**—You can use this account to provision those computers provisioned previously using a different AMT management solution. Specify the account name and password on the OOB Properties Provisioning Settings tab. You might need to specify more than one AMT Provisioning and Discovery account if you have computers provisioned with different usernames and passwords.

▶ **AMT Remote Admin account**—This account is used by the OOB service point to manage AMT network interface features. The AMT Remote Admin account is named *admin*, with the default password admin. During provisioning ConfigMgr resets the default password to a random strong value. If the password was previously changed locally, ConfigMgr sets the password to match the MEBx account password. If the password was reset through another AMT management solution, see http://technet.microsoft.com/en-us/library/cc161983.aspx for options for migrating to ConfigMgr.

You can delegate administrative access to OOB Management by specifying AD users or groups as AMT User accounts on the OOB properties AMT Settings tab. Figure 20.12 shows the AMT User Account Settings dialog box with permissions selected to allow the user to view general information and hardware information from clients and read the AMT event log. Click the AMT User Accounts Settings dialog box Help button to see a description of each access type. You can add up to eight AMT users or groups.

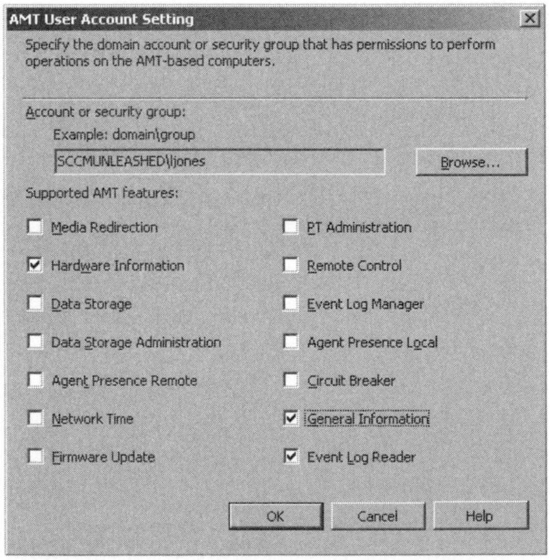

FIGURE 20.12   Adding an AMT User Account

Accounts Used for Software Updates

ConfigMgr uses two accounts for software updates:

▶ **Software Update Point Proxy Server account**—The SUP uses the Software Update Point Proxy Server account to authenticate to a proxy server or firewall to synchronize with Microsoft Updates or an upstream WSUS server. You can use any account that can authenticate to your proxy server or firewall and access the site for WSUS synchronization for this account. To specify a Software Update Point Proxy Server account, expand the ConfigMgr console to System Center Configuration Manager -> Site Database -> Site Management -> *<Site Code> <Site Name>* -> Site Settings -> Site Systems -> *<Software Update Point>*, right-click the ConfigMgr software update point, and choose Properties. On the General tab, check the boxes for Use a proxy server when synchronizing and Use credentials to connect to the proxy server, and then click the Set button to enter the account information.

▶ **Software Update Point Connection account**—WSUS services use the Software Update Point Connection account to configure settings and request synchronization. This account is required only if the SUP role is assigned to a remote server or Network Load Balancing (NLB) cluster. This account must be a member of the local Administrators group on the software update point server. To specify a Software Update Point Connection account, expand the ConfigMgr console to System Center Configuration Manager -> Site Database -> Site Management -> *<Site Code> <Site Name>* -> Site Settings -> Component Configuration. Right-click on Software Update Point Component, and choose Properties. If you selected the option for the active software update point on either a remote server or NLB cluster, the page displays a Software Update Point Connection account section. Use the Set button to enter the account credentials.

Accounts Used with Health State References

If you use Configuration Manager NAP and have system health validator points in a separate forest from the site server, ConfigMgr uses two accounts to manage health state references:

▶ **Health State Reference Publishing account**—ConfigMgr uses the Health State Reference Publishing account to publish health state references to AD. The Health State Reference Publishing account requires Read/Write permissions on the AD Systems Management container in the forest in which Health State References are stored.

▶ **Health State Reference Querying account**—The system health validator points uses the Health State Reference Querying account to read health state references from AD. The Health State Reference Querying account requires Read permission on the AD Systems Management container in the forest in which Health State References are stored.

You can configure both of these accounts on the Health State Reference tab of the System Health Validator Point Component Properties dialog box, under System Center Configuration Manager -> Site Database -> Site Management -> *<Site Code> <Site Name>* ->

20

Site Settings -> Component Configuration in the ConfigMgr console. If the system health validator points are in the same AD forest as the site server, these accounts are not required.

Miscellaneous Accounts

Configuration Manager 2007 uses additional accounts to authenticate Internet-based clients to a proxy server or firewall and for ConfigMgr Release 2 (R2) client status reporting. These accounts are

▶ **Proxy Account for Internet-Based Clients**—Clients authenticating to a proxy server or firewall to access an Internet-based management point use the Proxy Account for Internet-Based Clients. You can use any account that can authenticate to your proxy server or firewall and access the management point for this account. You can configure the Proxy Account for Internet-Based Clients on the client through the Internet tab of the Configuration Management Control Panel Applet.

▶ **Client Status Reporting Service account**—Configuration Manager 2007 R2 Client Status Reporting (CSR) uses the Client Status Reporting Service account for its core functionality. You can use either the Local System account on the client status reporting point or a domain or local user account for this role. You specify the Client Status Reporting Service account when you install Client Status Reporting, as described in Chapter 18. The Client Status Reporting Service account must be a local Administrator on the client status reporting host system and also must have the smsdbrole_CH role in the site database and Read access to the management point policy request log files. If you use the client ping feature, the Client Status Reporting Service account must also be a local Administrator on each client system.

Securing Service Dependencies for Configuration Manager

ConfigMgr depends on Domain Name System (DNS) and/or WINS to provide name resolution for site systems. Secure name resolution is an important security consideration to keep clients or other site systems from being redirected to a rogue site system. WINS has several known vulnerabilities that can be exploited to compromise client systems. You should also use DNS instead of WINS for name resolution. If possible, use Active Directory-integrated DNS to provide high availability and enable the option to allow only secure dynamic updates. A number of exploits exist that target DNS, so it is especially important to apply the latest patches to your DNS servers. For more information about securing DNS, see http://technet.microsoft.com/en-us/library/cc770432.aspx. You should also enable fully qualified domain names (FQDN) for all site systems. Using the FQDN avoids the possibility that the name will be resolved to the wrong domain or the client will fall back to NetBIOS name resolution.

ConfigMgr clients also use information published in AD or WINS to identify site systems and learn other information about sites. If a client receives incorrect site information, it could be redirected to the wrong site or server for ConfigMgr services. You should extend the Active Directory schema if possible and publish site information to AD instead of using WINS. If you configure AD publishing, you need to grant all site servers Read/Write access to the AD System Management container. Chapter 3 describes how to assign permissions on the System Management container. To avoid granting overly broad permissions, you should create a security group consisting of your ConfigMgr site servers and grant that group access to the System Management container, rather than adding the site servers to the built-in groups such as Domain Admins.

For maximum security, you can remove access for the site systems group from each site object after creating it, and add permissions for the individual site server responsible for the site instead. Managing permissions for individual servers adds significantly to your administrative overhead.

Securing Configuration Manager Reporting

ConfigMgr reports and queries provide access to information contained in the site database. The site database does not generally contain confidential business information or intellectual property; however, this type of information might be present if you collect files as a part of software inventory. The site database does contain a wealth of information about your systems and infrastructure that could be of potential value to a hacker. There might also be some privacy concerns around software metering data or data obtained through AD user discovery. Reporting security is therefore an important consideration, although generally less critical than security around services with client impact such as software distribution.

Security in Classic Reporting

To view classic reports, a user needs access to the reporting website and Read permissions on the report class or the report instances she runs. To provide access to the website, add the appropriate AD users or groups to the Reporting Users local group on each reporting point. You can assign class and instance permissions on reports just as on any ConfigMgr objects. The "Managing Permissions Through the ConfigMgr Console" section in this chapter describes how to assign class and instance permissions.

To allow users to create and modify reports, you must add them to the SMS Admins local group on the site server. You can then use the ConfigMgr console to grant the users create rights on the reports class or modify rights on the class or on specific instances. As the report builder interface performs some validation of the report SQL statements, it is not possible for a user to enter statements such as INSERT or UPDATE into the report's SQL query. You should nevertheless use caution when assigning rights to create or modify reports, because poorly written SQL queries can expose your database to attack.

Security in SQL Reporting Services

SQL Reporting Services (SRS) uses a role-based model to assign permissions to Windows users and groups. You generally assign roles to AD groups. To assign users to a reporting services role, perform the following steps:

1. Expand the Configuration Manager console tree to System Center Configuration Manager -> Site Database -> Computer Management -> Reporting -> Reporting Services. Right-click on the report server name and choose Properties.

2. On the Security tab, clear the Inheriting rights from the parent object check box and use the New, Properties, and Delete buttons to invoke the User Properties dialog box. You can use this dialog box to create, modify, or delete role assignments.

Figure 20.13 displays the User Properties dialog box, which includes descriptions of the available roles. By default, all report folders inherit the role assignments you set in the Reporting Services properties. To assign users different roles on individual report folders, expand the Report Folders node under Reporting Services, right-click the appropriate folder, and choose Properties. The Security tab on the folder property sheet provides the same options as the Reporting Services Properties Security tab described in step 2 of the preceding procedure.

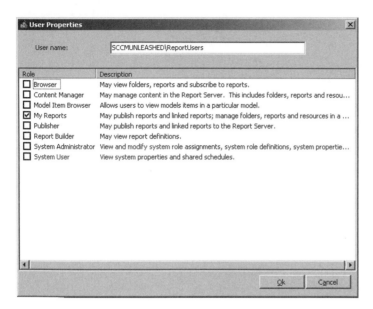

FIGURE 20.13   The SRS User Properties dialog box with the My Reports role selected

The browser role allows users to view reports. Each of the other roles provides some ability to create and manage reports. You cannot assign the same user or group to more than one role, although a user whose group memberships include more than one group with an assigned role has the cumulative set of permissions for the assigned roles. You can create new roles or customize existing roles using SQL Server Management Studio. Keep in mind that if you modify an existing role, the permissions available to all users assigned to that role reflect the changes. For instructions on how to create, delete, or modify a role, see http://msdn.microsoft.com/en-gb/library/ms156293(SQL.90).aspx.

Best Practices for Reporting Security

To provide the maximum confidentiality for data stored in your site database, grant each user only those permissions necessary to view the reports they need. Many ConfigMgr reports include details about computer hardware, software, and network configuration that can provide valuable information to a potential attacker. Here are some of the most sensitive report categories:

▶ Asset Intelligence

▶ Desired Configuration Management – Compliance

▶ Operating System

▶ Software – Companies and Products

▶ Software – Files

▶ Software Updates – A Compliance

You can use SSL to secure communications between users and your reporting points or reporting services points. Before enabling SSL on your site systems, you must install an SSL certificate as described in http://support.microsoft.com/kb/299875. When you have the certificate installed, use the ConfigMgr console to enable SSL for your reporting point. The SSL option is available on the reporting point property sheet under System Center Configuration Manager -> Site Database -> Site Management -> *<Site Code> <Site Name>* -> Site Settings -> Site Systems -> *<Reporting Point>*. To configure SSL for SQL Reporting Services, use the Report Server Virtual Directory page in the SQL Server 2005 Configure Report Server tool.

Securing Configuration Manager Operations

You should take security considerations into account as you design those processes and procedures you use to carry out day-to-day operations in your ConfigMgr environment. The next sections present some of the security issues involved in administering your hierarchy and security sensitive operations such as software distribution, DCM, and the use of remote tools.

Best Practices for Configuration Manager Administration

Only those users responsible for server administration should be able to log on locally to the site server or other site systems. Other users requiring access to the ConfigMgr console should install and run the console on secure administrative workstations or terminal servers dedicated to IT systems administration. Chapter 10, "The Configuration Manager Console," describes how to deploy the console to remote systems, including security requirements for remote administration.

You should also consider limiting web browsing from those systems with the Configuration Manager console installed, including site servers. Configuration Manager 2007 displays reports, online help, and other content as web pages hosted in the console's Microsoft Management Console (MMC) window. You can use group policy to restrict browsing on systems running the console. Group policy settings to control browsing behavior in Internet Explorer are explained in http://support.microsoft.com/kb/182569.

It is particularly important to implement controls on files used in ConfigMgr operations not managed by ConfigMgr. Some examples of these files include the following:

▶ eXtensible Markup Language (XML) files created if you use the Transfer Site Settings Wizard to copy site settings from one site to another. These files contain details about your ConfigMgr site settings; alteration of the files could result in applying inappropriate settings at the target site.

▶ Managed Object Format (MOF) files used to copy queries, collections, or reports between sites. Unauthorized changes to these files could result in a variety of issues including improper targeting of advertisements and changes to object permissions.

▶ Files created by site backup operations. Backup files contain all data from your site database and configuration information from the site control file and site server registry. Alteration of backup files could result in unauthorized changes to the site in the event of a site restore operation.

You should use Windows access lists and possibly other controls such as FIM to protect the integrity of these files. If you use external media to store or transfer files used in ConfigMgr operations, you should implement procedures to control physical access to media at all times and consider cryptographic controls on media to prevent tampering with the files. Network file transfers should also be done in a secure manner, using the most secure network available and cryptographic controls such as IPSec. Chapter 7 discusses the Transfer Site Settings Wizard and copying objects. Chapter 21, "Backup, Recovery, and Maintenance," describes backup operations.

In addition, you should digitally sign internally developed DCM configuration data and only import configuration data that has a valid signature from a trusted publisher. Configuration data from Microsoft is always digitally signed.

Operational Security for Software Distribution

To ensure only authorized software is deployed to your ConfigMgr clients, you need to build security into all phases of your software deployment life cycle. You should carefully protect package source files throughout their development, testing, deployment, and maintenance to make sure that only authorized changes occur. ConfigMgr has no way to verify the integrity of the package source folders you point it to, so it is up to you to implement the necessary controls.

You should consider the same types of controls as for other operational files to protect the source directories and provide for secure file transfer. You might want to have your Quality Assurance (QA) team digitally sign all package files before you deploy them to production. If at all possible, you should avoid embedding sensitive information such as passwords and data source connection strings in scripts, settings files, or other files within your package source folders. If it is absolutely necessary to use embedded passwords or other confidential information, always use strong encryption and Windows access controls to protect this information.

Whenever possible, use the Download content from distribution point and run locally option when you deploy software. The client calculates a hash of the downloaded content and verifies that the hash matches the value provided in the advertisement policy before running the program. This verification is not available if you use the run from distribution point option. Keep in mind that branch distribution points and programs that directly specify a UNC path do not support the download and run option.

Another important consideration for software distribution is preventing users from leveraging advertised programs to gain elevated privileges. Figure 20.14 shows the Environment tab of the program Properties page with the Run with administrative rights option selected and the Allow users to interact with this program check box enabled. This combination of settings is generally not recommended except when troubleshooting a program. With these options enabled, the user can influence the execution of a program running in an administrative context, generally Local System. In some cases, the user might break out of the user interface provided by the setup program and spawn another program, such as a command shell, which would provide unlimited access to the system.

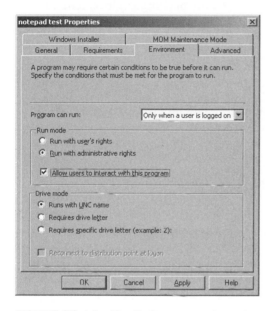

FIGURE 20.14   The Environment tab on the program properties page can allow users to interact with programs running in the Local System context.

The need to install software is probably the most common reason for granting administrative access to those users who do not have system administration responsibilities. Although allowing nonprivileged users to interact with programs running in a higher privilege context is not a best practice, in some cases it might be a better practice than granting users administrative rights to allow them to install software! Depending on your business needs and security requirements, you might consider this as a convenient way to effectively provide temporary administrative access during software installation. If you have adequate resources, package all software to run silently, or use alternate software deployment methods.

If you use ConfigMgr's Wake On LAN (WOL) functionality, use Unicast wake-up packets rather than subnet-directed broadcasts for maximum security. If you choose to use subnet-directed broadcasts, be sure to follow the recommendations presented in http://technet. microsoft.com/en-us/library/bb632486.aspx. Use Out of Band Management rather than WOL if your environment supports it.

20

If you implement Configuration Manager 2007 R2 Application Virtualization, you should enable encrypted mode for any application virtualization streaming–enabled distribution points.

Operational Security for Operating System Deployment

The considerations that apply to securing OS deployment are similar to those for software deployment. In addition, you should pay close attention to the following points:

▶ Secure the reference computer by placing it in a secure network environment, blocking unauthorized access, and keeping patches and antivirus software up to date.

▶ Secure all boot images, OS images, drivers, and driver packages as you would secure package source files.

▶ Password protect all boot media, and keep media physically secure.

▶ User state migration can present privacy and confidentiality issues. Consider these issues as you determine the data and settings to migrate and how to protect user state data. If you decommission a user state migration point, you should manually delete all user content from the system.

▶ Enable encryption for all multicast packages to prevent tampering and exclude rogue computers from multicast sessions.

Operational Security for Remote Tools Administration

Remote tools access gives administrators possible opportunities to breach user privacy or obtain confidential information. To minimize the potential for abuse of remote tools functionality, consider the following measures:

▶ Enable notification for remote sessions to prevent users from being spied on without their knowledge. Enable the Display a visual indicator and Play a sound options on the Notification tab of the Remote Tools Client Agent property sheet. You can configure Remote Tools Client Agent properties in the console, under System Center Configuration Manager -> Site Database -> Site Management -> *<Site Code>* *<Site Name>* -> Site Settings -> Client Agents.

▶ Enable Ask for permission when an administrator tries to access clients on the General tab of the Remote Tools Client Agent property sheet. The Ask for permission setting provides a level of protection, but it might be circumvented on Windows 2000 computers.

Enabling Ask for permission is a site-wide setting and prevents administrators from connecting to unattended servers or workstations. This setting might, therefore, not be appropriate for all sites.

▶ Windows 2000 Computers use an older and less secure technology for remote tools than Windows XP and later systems. In particular, the remote tools interface for Windows 2000 provide buttons that simulate Ctrl+Alt+Delete, Ctrl+Esc, Alt+Tab and other Alt+Key key combination to the remote computer. This functionality has been removed from the remote tools for Windows XP and later systems to limit access to unattended machines.

▶ To maintain consistency, do not use both group policy and ConfigMgr client agent settings to configure Remote Assistance settings. This can lead to possible conflicts and unpredictable results.

▶ A user who is in the permitted viewers list on the client computer can connect to the computer in various ways without using the ConfigMgr console. This bypasses collection level security. The only way to control access to remote tools is through the permitted viewers list. The "Security for Remote Administration" section of this chapter describes the permitted viewers list.

▶ Avoid entering passwords during a remote administrative session. Passwords could be intercepted by malicious software, or cached on the local machine.

Operational Security for Configuration Manager Inventory

Client inventory allows you to collect virtually any information about client machines through WMI. The most security sensitive capability of ConfigMgr inventory is its capability to collect files from ConfigMgr clients, which could expose any data stored in files to potential compromise if inventory functionality is misused. If you collect files containing sensitive information from clients, you should carefully monitor all collections containing these systems to ensure read resource rights are limited to the required group of administrators. You should also verify the file system permissions on the location where the files are stored adequately protect sensitive content. For maximum security, consider encrypting sensitive files on client systems to prevent exposure of sensitive data even if you collect the files.

You should also consider security issues around the file types you include in software inventory. By default, only .exe files are inventoried. Inventorying file details such as the filename might reveal confidential information, even if you do not collect the files themselves. For example, if you inventory .pst files and a user in your Finance department has a file called AAA acquisition.pst, any user with read resource rights on the client system or rights to view certain reports might learn that a proposed acquisition is under consideration.

Chapter 3 describes how you could modify the Configuration.mof in conjunction with the SMS_Def.mof file to customize and extend hardware inventory collection. Systems Management Server (SMS) 2003 and earlier versions of SMS did not support the use of the Configuration.mof file. Instead, Management Information Format (MIF) files were used for custom inventory collection. ConfigMgr also supports the use of MIF files for backward compatibility and addressing specialized requirements. Two distinct categories of MIF files are sometimes used for inventory collection:

▶ IDMIF files contain complete metadata to uniquely identify an inventory class. You can use IDMIFs to add devices to inventory that are not associated with existing client architectures, such as network printers or point of sale systems.

▶ NOIDMIF files allow you to inventory additional classes on existing clients, such as data collected from the system Registry or manually input by the user.

When ConfigMgr processes IDMIF and NOIDMIF files, the inventory processor component adds or modifies database tables as required to accommodate the data. However, ConfigMgr does not perform the same validation process on IDMIF and NOIDMIF files as on standard inventory files. To protect the integrity of the site database, you should consider disabling the collection of IDMIF and NOIDMIF files and replacing any required inventory customization with custom MOF files.

Operational Security for Mobile Device Management

The growing use of mobile devices to connect to enterprise information systems and store and process data presents a unique set of challenges to IT organizations. Mobile devices generally connect over networks and from physical locations not under the organization's control. Mobile device hardware and software is less standardized than PC hardware and software, and the controls framework around mobile devices is less mature. Mobile devices can easily be lost or stolen, which can lead to compromise of any data stored on the device and provide an attacker access to email and other network content. As part of your strategy for allowing mobile devices to access network resources and data, you should always consider the risks involved and the available strategies for mitigating risk. You can use ConfigMgr mobile device management to apply several important controls to enhance device security. To enable configuration items for mobile devices and set applicable options, expand the console tree to System Center Configuration Manager -> Site Database -> Computer Management -> Mobile Device Management, right-click Configuration Items, and choose New Configuration Item. This launches the New Configuration Item Wizard. Keep in mind that not all configuration items might be applicable, depending on the mobile device OS. You can select the configuration item type you want to enable from the New Configuration Item Wizard's Select Configuration Type page. The wizard then displays the appropriate property pages for the selected item type. Some configuration items you can use to enhance device security include

▶ The certificate installation configuration item specifies the certificate ConfigMgr distributes to mobile devices and the device certificate store.

▶ Password policies for the Windows Mobile Messaging and Security Feature Pack (MSFP) allow you to specify minimum password length, complexity requirements, and other password related parameters. You can require that the device will be wiped, meaning all data stored on the device will be erased, after a specified number of failed password attempts. Password management for Pocket PC 2003 provides some password controls but does not include device wipe capability.

▶ The Security Policies configuration item lets you specify policies to control running unsigned applications, cab files, or theme files, and to control autorun behavior for memory cards.

▶ The WiFi Properties: Authentication tab provides a number of options for controlling the behavior of devices when connecting to WiFi access points. You should enable WiFi Protected Access (WPA) or WPA preshared key (PSK) and use Temporal Key Integrity Protocol (TKIP) encryption if possible. Do not rely on wired equivalent privacy (WEP) for security. WEP is a notoriously insecure protocol.

- VPN settings allow you to configure VPN access to your corporate network.

- Registry settings allow you more granular control over device security.

Some additional controls you might consider for mobile devices include

- Full device encryption to protect all data on the device.

- Remote wipe capabilities to allow administrators to wipe lost or stolen devices.

- Bluetooth lockdown to control connections to other Bluetooth devices.

Because ConfigMgr Device Management does not provide these options, you need to use other means to implement these controls if you require them.

ConfigMgr uses cryptographic controls to protect communications with mobile device clients and ensure the integrity of policy and content downloads to those clients. The cryptographic controls require you to deploy the required certificates to these clients. For information about deploying certificates to mobile device clients, see http://technet. microsoft.com/en-us/library/bb633088.aspx. Native mode provides additional security through mutual authentication, which prevents unauthorized devices from connecting to your ConfigMgr site and can help mitigate man-in-the-middle attacks on device communications. For information about specific certificate requirements for mobile device clients in native mode sites, see http://technet.microsoft.com/en-us/library/bb693603.aspx. The Microsoft System Center Configuration Manager Mobile Device Management whitepaper provides additional information about secure communications with mobile device clients. You can find the whitepaper at http://download.microsoft.com/download/5/5/6/556544f5-b09e-4818-953d-087e08a8303a/Mobile%20Device%20Whitepaper.pdf. (This link is also included in Appendix B, "Reference URLs.")

Summary

This chapter discusses security issues related to your ConfigMgr deployment. Management applications such as ConfigMgr can greatly enhance the overall security of your environment, but you need to deploy and operate these in a secure manner to prevent their misuse. The goal of this chapter is to make you aware of key ConfigMgr security issues you need to consider throughout your involvement with the product, and how to align your security program with business needs. The discussion tries to supplement and highlight Microsoft's recommendations, not to replace them. It is highly recommended that you read and regularly review the material Microsoft provides. Remember that in security, you work against human intelligence (and human error) and you need to continually review and improve your processes and controls. The next chapter considers how to back up your sites, how to recover them if necessary, and how to maintain optimal operations of your ConfigMgr solution.

20

Backup, Recovery, and Maintenance

Chapter 20, "Security and Delegation in Configuration Manager 2007," discussed security accounts, groups, requirements, and topics such as how to delegate security rights within Configuration Manager (ConfigMgr) 2007 and secure ConfigMgr. Security is certainly a critical piece of maintaining a healthy and functional environment. Another critical piece of maintaining a healthy and functional system is ensuring its integrity through backup and recovery processes. All production systems should have established backup and recovery procedures in place, and ConfigMgr 2007 is no exception. It is also important to maintain the currency of your data, and ConfigMgr 2007 provides a number of maintenance tasks to help with this. This chapter discusses best practice approaches to backup, recover, and maintain your Configuration Manager environment.

Site and SQL Server Backups

Out-of-the box, ConfigMgr 2007 includes a number of tasks to assist in maintaining your environment. One of these, the Backup ConfigMgr Site Server maintenance task, can greatly simplify the process of backing up your ConfigMgr environment. The next sections discuss backing up and restoring your ConfigMgr database and site.

Backing Up ConfigMgr

Site maintenance tasks are located in the ConfigMgr console at Site Database -> Site Management -> *<Site Code> <Site Name>* Site Settings -> Site Maintenance -> Tasks.

The "Site Maintenance Tasks" section in this chapter contains information regarding each of these tasks.

The first task in the list, Backup ConfigMgr Site Server (selected in Figure 21.1), defaults as not enabled. The Backup ConfigMgr Site Server task provides an automated method to backup the site including the site database, ConfigMgr files, Registry keys, and system configuration information. Using the Backup ConfigMgr Site Server task is the recommended approach for backups versus using third-party vendor solutions because this is the only supported backup when restoring the ConfigMgr environment using the Configuration Manager Site Repair Wizard.

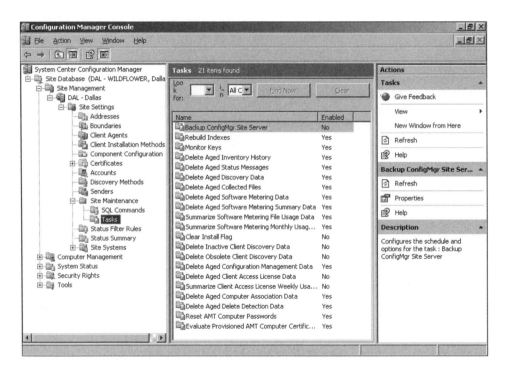

FIGURE 21.1   Default configuration for the Backup ConfigMgr Site Server task

Perform the following steps to enable the Backup ConfigMgr Site Server task and configure it to backup your site.

1. Right-click on the task shown in Figure 21.1 (Site Database -> Site Management -> *<Site Code> <Site Name>* Site Settings -> Site Maintenance -> Tasks) and choose Properties.

2. The first option on the Backup ConfigMgr Site Server Properties is to enable the task, which you can check on the top part of the dialog box in Figure 21.2.

   After that is checked, click the Set Paths button to define the path to which to back up the site and SQL information. The default configuration is to back up the information to a local drive on the site server, although the Set Paths option allows you to back the information up to a network path.

A commonly used configuration accepts the default backup timeframe to start between 12:00 AM and 5:00 AM and perform the system backup to the local drive on the site server (in this case a c:\backup directory), as shown in Figure 21.2.

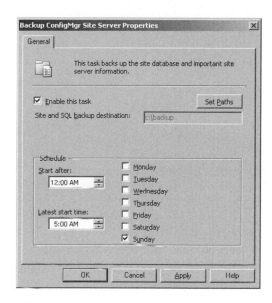

FIGURE 21.2   Sunday backup to the local drive on the ConfigMgr Site Server

3. You can configure the schedule for ConfigMgr backups to run more frequently if that is a requirement for your environment.

A successful backup creates the following folders, shown in Figure 21.3:

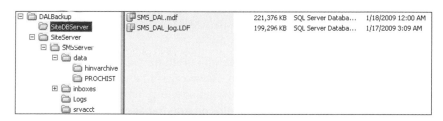

FIGURE 21.3   File structure created from a successful ConfigMgr backup task

▶ *<Site Name>*Backup. (This is DALBackup for the DAL site in the SCCMUnleashed environment.)

▶ A subfolder called SiteDBServer (which contains the mdf, ldf, and xml files).

▶ A SiteServer subfolder, containing:

   ▶ SMSServer folder—includes backups of ConfigMgr inboxes, logs, and the files that control the information collected during hardware inventory (configuration.mof and SMS_Def.mof). Also included in the inbox backup is the site control file (Sitectrl.ct0), which contains many of the settings used by the ConfigMgr site.

   ▶ ConfigMgrPrereq.log

   ▶ ConfigMgrSetup.log

   ▶ SMSbkSiteRegNAL.dat

   ▶ SMSbkSiteRegSMS.dat

Both of the two log files—ConfigMgrPrereq.log and ConfigMgrSetup.log—backed up during this process are generated during site installation and upgrades.

NOTE

Troubleshooting ConfigMgr Backups

ConfigMgr uses the Volume Shadow Copy service. Verify this service is not disabled, or your ConfigMgr backup will not run.

A recommended backup approach uses a daily backup timeframe but sends the backup information to a Universal Naming Convention (UNC) path, specifying a location that is not on any of the ConfigMgr server systems. Data backups are daily, with the backup retained for at least one month. Using this approach minimizes the risk that if the site server's drive fails, it would cause the loss of all information for ConfigMgr including the backup copy of the information. Performing this task on a daily basis minimizes the amount of information lost in comparison to restoring from a backup that might have occurred a week earlier.

TIP

Protecting Yourself Further with Backups

The default approach of backing up to a local drive (shown in Figure 21.2) is commonly used as a quick way to back up ConfigMgr information. However, this provides little benefit by itself because the backed up information resides on the same drives as the site server. To augment this approach, schedule a weekly backup to back up the information stored on the local site server into an offsite rotation using a backup product such as System Center Data Protection Manager (DPM) or third-party backup solutions.

You also need to back up the files required to restore the operating system on the site server in case of a full operating system (OS) crash. Using DPM or third-party products to provide a full backup of the OS is critical for system restores in the case where the operating system no longer functions. Performing monthly operating system backups is recommended for all ConfigMgr site server systems.

Restoring ConfigMgr Backups

With your ConfigMgr information backed up, let's discuss the process of restoring it. There are two common scenarios where recovering ConfigMgr might be required:

▶ Site Server operating system crash

▶ ConfigMgr functional crash

The next sections discuss these situations.

Site Server Operating System Crash

If a server operating system crashes, the first step is to restore the server from a backup. The "Backing Up ConfigMgr" section in this chapter discussed the requirement to back up the operating system on a monthly basis. After installing the OS, the process can then continue through the steps required to restore from a ConfigMgr functional crash.

ConfigMgr Functional Crash

In the situation where ConfigMgr is no longer functional (or the site server operating system is no longer functional as discussed in the "Site Server Operating System Crash" section), you can use the Configuration Manager Site Repair Wizard to recover your ConfigMgr environment. This wizard is installed on the site server and all computers with the ConfigMgr console and is available by navigating to Start -> Programs -> Microsoft System Center -> Configuration Manager 2007 -> ConfigMgr Site Repair Wizard. Perform the following steps:

1. Launch the wizard, which by default runs recovery on the same site server as the wizard. The example displayed in Figure 21.4 shows repairing (recovering) the Wildflower server.

2. On the next screen, tell the wizard the location of the backup files it needs to use for the site restore. You can also choose to repair or reconfigure a site and specify whether to restore the database when performing a site restore. This example performs a simple restore of files stored to a local hard drive in the c:\backup directory, as shown in Figure 21.5. In this case, the database backup is not restored, so leave the Do not restore database check box in the default configuration, which is unchecked.

   The other option available on this screen provides a way to either repair or reconfigure an existing site and do so without creating a new site and without restoring database files from backup.

3. During the repair process, several steps execute and provide status while they are restored, as shown in Figure 21.6.

4. After the restore process completes, the next step involves determining if the system is a central site or the child of another ConfigMgr site. This example is restoring the CEN site (the central site in the SCCMUnleashed environment), so the restoration

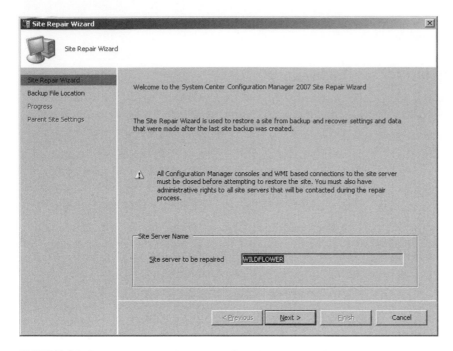

FIGURE 21.4   Starting the ConfigMgr Site Repair Wizard

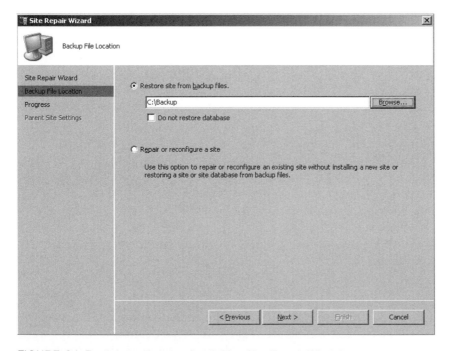

FIGURE 21.5   Configuring the ConfigMgr Site Repair Wizard

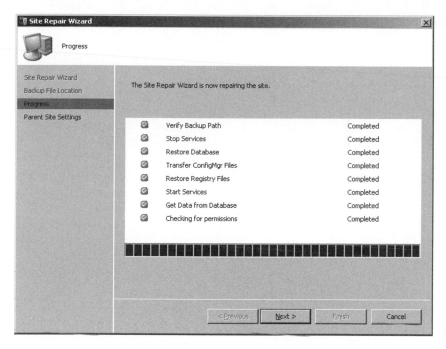

FIGURE 21.6   The Restore process in the ConfigMgr Site Repair Wizard

would include checking the option indicating that This is a central Site, as displayed in Figure 21.7.

Select this first option for those environments with a single site or when restoring the central site. If however a child site is being restored, such as the DAL site in the SCCMUnleashed environment, choose the second option in Figure 21.7, specifying that this is a child site of and identifying the parent site. (For the DAL site, the parent is the CEN site.)

5. The following screen, Verify Site Hierarchy, provides the opportunity to validate the site hierarchy information you are restoring is correct. You can add additional sites and configure addresses for the selected sites. For a single site restoration or restoration of a central site, the only site shown would be the one specified on the previous screen, as displayed in Figure 21.8.

6. Clicking Next takes you to the Package Recovery step of the Site Repair Wizard. Several options are available:

   ▶ You can specify here whether to verify the package source files are accessible, and if so, whether to update the distribution point on the site server.

   ▶ You can choose to skip package verification completely.

The distribution point in the ConfigMgr SCCMUnleashed environment is already populated, so accept the default configuration to verify that the source files are accessible, as shown in Figure 21.9.

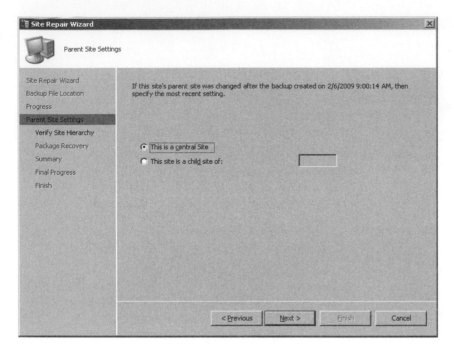

FIGURE 21.7   Specifying the site configuration in the ConfigMgr Site Repair Wizard

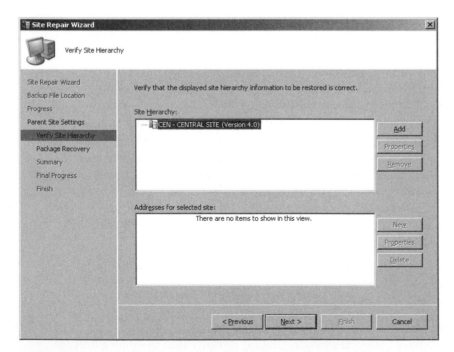

FIGURE 21.8   Configuring the hierarchy in the ConfigMgr Site Repair Wizard

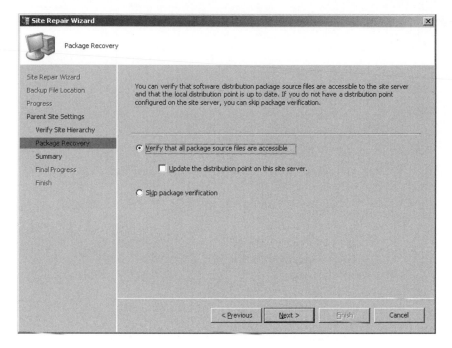

FIGURE 21.9   Verifying Packages in the ConfigMgr Site Repair Wizard

7. The restoration process continues through a series of processes (displayed in Figure 21.10), shows a summary of the actions performed, and provides a screen indicating that the restoration process is complete.

Performing a Site Reset

After successfully restoring the ConfigMgr environment, the next required step is to perform a site reset. A site reset reapplies default file and registry permissions. It also ensures that accounts used by ConfigMgr components are correct, resets the access control lists used by remote site systems, restores ConfigMgr registry keys, and restores the ConfigMgr directory tree. Take the following steps to perform a site reset:

1. Run the ConfigMgr Setup program (Start -> Programs -> Microsoft System Center -> Configuration Manager 2007 -> ConfigMgr Setup).

2. Click Next on the Welcome screen. On the Available Setup Options page, choose the option to Perform site maintenance or reset this Site, as shown in Figure 21.11.

3. On the next screen, check the option to Re-apply default file and registry permissions on this site server, displayed in Figure 21.12. On the following screen, confirm you want to perform the site reset by choosing Yes.

4. The setup program performs a series of tasks, and when they are completed (shown in Figure 21.13), you can validate the functionality of the ConfigMgr environment.

5. The final screen of the site reset provides an option to review the log file for the site reset and a check box to launch the ConfigMgr console after closing. Select the

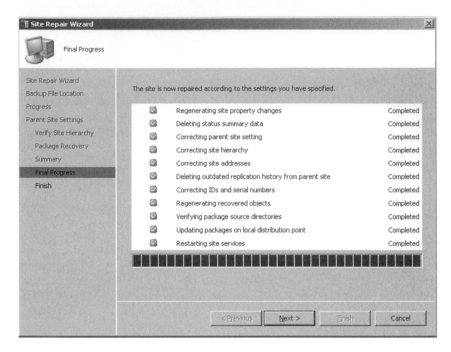

FIGURE 21.10   Completing the ConfigMgr Site Repair Wizard

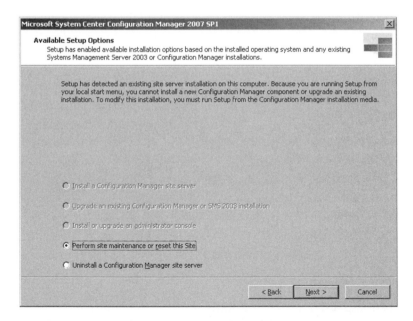

FIGURE 21.11   Setting options for the site reset

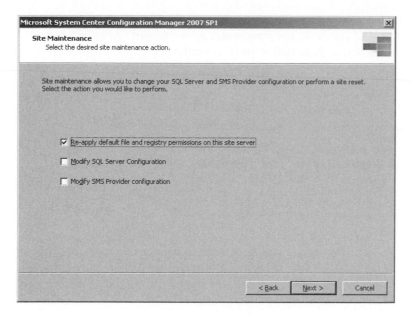

FIGURE 21.12   Setting the site maintenance configuration for the site reset

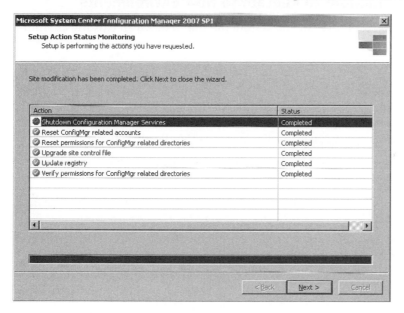

FIGURE 21.13   Tasks completed for the site reset

option to launch the ConfigMgr console because you need to validate functionality of the ConfigMgr environment after resetting the site. You also need to review the log file if you encounter any errors.

Valldating Functionality After the Restore Process

After completing the process of restoring the ConfigMgr environment, you need to validate that it is functional. There are three major areas to verify:

▶ **Checking site addresses**—Navigate to Site Database -> Site Management -> *<Site Code> <Site Name>* Site Settings -> Addresses. If you have a multiple ConfigMgr site hierarchy, verify that the appropriate site addresses still exist.

▶ **Checking site settings**—Navigate to Site Database -> Site Management -> *<Site Code> <Site Name>* Site Settings. Validate the configurations of each of the major sections and change any settings that might not be correct for your environment (Boundaries, Client Agents, Client Installation Methods, Component Configuration, Certificates, Accounts, Discovery Methods, Senders, Site Maintenance, Status Filter Rules, Status Summary, and Site Systems).

▶ **Monitoring site processes**—Navigate to Site Database -> System Status -> Site Status -> *<Site Code> - <Site Name>* -> Component Status. Check the status of all components. Review the messages on any status that does not display as healthy. You also need to address any issues identified that exist after completing the restore and site reset.

Using Back Up and Restore to Migrate to New Environments

You can utilize the steps used to back up and restore the site to move an existing environment to new hardware or build out a new environment. The next sections discuss each of these scenarios.

Moving ConfigMgr to New Hardware

A frequently asked question is how to move an existing ConfigMgr environment to new physical hardware. This often happens if the original hardware for ConfigMgr was not assessed adequately or the scope of what ConfigMgr is has significantly increased.

If the server name does not need to be changed, a backup, re-install, and restore process can be done. Here are the high levels steps required to perform this type of migration:

1. Back up the existing ConfigMgr server. When the backup is completed, shut down the ConfigMgr server.

2. Install a new server with the same name and configuration as discussed in Chapter 8, "Installing Configuration Manager 2007."

3. Restore the ConfigMgr database using the steps discussed in the TechNet article on how to move a ConfigMgr database available at http://technet.microsoft.com/en-us/library/bb680707.aspx.

4. Additional site settings might need to be transferred; these are discussed in the TechNet article available at http://technet.microsoft.com/en-us/library/bb633056.aspx.

New ConfigMgr Environment

Sometimes it is necessary to build out a new ConfigMgr environment to replace an existing one. This can occur if a ConfigMgr server cannot retain the same name and needs to be put on new hardware (see the section "Moving ConfigMgr to New Hardware"). A new environment might also be required when there are significant issues in an existing ConfigMgr environment to the point where replacing it is the most reasonable solution.

Here are the high level steps required to perform this type of migration:

1. Install the new ConfigMgr server as discussed in Chapter 8, using a different site code than used by the original ConfigMgr site.

2. Set the ConfigMgr server environment to the settings you require, including AD system discovery. Set the site boundaries to overlap with the original ConfigMgr environment.

3. When all systems are listed in the All Systems collection, right-click on the collection and select Install Client to the collection to deploy the client.

Site Maintenance

In addition to having a solid backup and recovery procedure in place, you also want to maintain the data in your site and site database. There are a variety of concepts to consider when performing site maintenance, including site maintenance tasks, DDR retention, and dealing with obsolete database records.

Site Maintenance Tasks

Site maintenance tasks are a vital part of maintaining your site. After installation and performing other initial configurations, it is imperative you understand and configure these tasks to best suit your particular ConfigMgr hierarchy.

Before making any changes to site maintenance tasks, there are several points about the tasks in general:

▶ Site maintenance tasks are set at each individual site and not automatically transferred to any other sites in your ConfigMgr hierarchy.

▶ The Transfer Site Settings Wizard, discussed in Chapter 8, has the capability to copy site maintenance task settings from one ConfigMgr site (or an exported copy of those settings) to any other ConfigMgr site.

▶ Some of the site maintenance tasks can cause unnecessary and conflicting processing on the ConfigMgr site. These pitfalls are noted with each task.

▶ Several of the tasks perform maintenance on the database, such as deleting old data or summarizing current data. Balance the amount of data manipulated at one time by scheduling the tasks to run more frequently.

Table 21.1 lists the site maintenance tasks in ConfigMgr 2007. Additional information is also available at http://technet.microsoft.com/en-us/library/bb632595.aspx.

TABLE 21.1   Site Maintenance Tasks in ConfigMgr

Task	Enabled by Default	Configuration Defaults	Description
Backup ConfigMgr Site Server	No	No default schedule	Backing up the ConfigMgr site server is easily one of the most important tasks. After installation, determine the appropriate schedule and configure this task. See the "Backing Up ConfigMgr" section for more information on what is stored and "Restoring ConfigMgr Backups" for performing a restore if necessary.
Rebuild Indexes	Yes	Every Sunday between 12:00 AM and 5:00 AM.	Database indexes speed the execution of searches in the SQL database, and most tables in the ConfigMgr database have at least one index. This task evaluates those indexes, and rebuilds them if more than 50% of the data is unique to keep your ConfigMgr site running at peak efficiency. The task drops indexes if the data in the table drops to less than 50% uniqueness. This task is also discussed in the "Database Maintenance" section.
Monitor Keys	Yes	Every Sunday between 12:00 AM and 5:00 AM.	Primary keys in the ConfigMgr database maintain relationships between the various SQL tables. This site maintenance task checks the keys to ensure that the associations are valid. The task is discussed further in the "Database Maintenance" section.
Delete Aged Inventory History	Yes	Delete data older than 90 days, Saturday after 12:00 AM until 5:00 AM.	The Delete Aged inventory History task removes data from the ConfigMgr database after the specified number of days. After a client inventory agent is enabled, clients perform the specified actions and report it back to the ConfigMgr database. This task examines that data and determines if it is older than the number of days specified in the days. Data removed by this task includes data from the Hardware and Software Inventory client agents.

TABLE 21.1   Site Maintenance Tasks in ConfigMgr

Task	Enabled by Default	Configuration Defaults	Description
Delete Aged Status Messages	Yes	Every day after 12:00 AM until 5:00 AM.	This is potentially one of the largest tasks the site server runs. The number of status messages generated by the myriad of site and client components can be high; this task is designed to keep that number in check.
			This task might run for a long time due to the number of status messages that can be deleted. It is recommended you run this task more frequently to reduce the number of status messages deleted in each pass, and shorten the length of each individual run. The task is discussed further in the "Maintaining Status Data" section of the chapter.
Delete Aged Discovery Data	Yes	Delete data older than 90 days, Saturday after 12:00 AM until 5:00 AM.	When discovery data has reached a specified age, this task removes it from the ConfigMgr database. The task deletes any system that has not been discovered in the specified threshold.
			A common thought on this is that it refers to a system that has not been discovered by heart-beat discovery; however, that is incorrect. If any discovery method (network, active directory) has discovered the system within the threshold, the system will not be deleted. For example, you can have a system that has been gone from the site for a while but still remains in the collections because Active Directory discovery found it in AD. This can happen in environments where Active Directory is not well maintained.
Delete Aged Collected Files	Yes	Delete data older than 90 days, Saturday after 12:00 AM until 5:00 AM.	The Software Inventory client agent has the capability to collect specific files and store them on the ConfigMgr site server. This task deletes files over a certain age, saving disk space. It also removes data about the collected files from the ConfigMgr database.
			Collected files are stored in the FileCol subfolder of the sinv.box inbox. If you do not collect files during software inventory, this task is irrelevant.

TABLE 21.1   Site Maintenance Tasks in ConfigMgr

Task	Enabled by Default	Configuration Defaults	Description
Delete Aged Software Metering Data	Yes	Delete data older than 5 days, every day after 12:00 AM until 5:00 AM.	When both the Software Metering client agent and a Software Metering rule are enabled on a ConfigMgr site server, clients begin to gather and report that data on the specified schedule. This task removes the data from the site server when it reaches a certain age.
Delete Aged Software Metering Summary Data	Yes	Delete data older than 270 days, Sunday after 12:00 AM until 5:00 AM.	The Summarize tasks take software metering data and summarize it in the ConfigMgr database. This task removes summarized data over a certain age, keeping only the most current dataset.
Summarize Software Metering File Usage Data	Yes	Every day after 12:00 AM until 5:00 AM.	When this task runs, it combines multiple entries in the ConfigMgr database down to a single record. This saves space in the ConfigMgr database and ultimately helps performance.
Summarize Software Metering Monthly Usage Data	Yes	Every day after 12:00 AM until 5:00 AM.	When this task runs, it combines multiple entries in the ConfigMgr database down to a single record. This saves space in the ConfigMgr database and ultimately helps performance.
Clear Install Flag	No	Clear client install flag for clients not discovered by heartbeat discovery within past 21 days, every Sunday between 12:00 AM and 5:00 AM.	The Clear Install Flag is designed to help clear out stale records from the ConfigMgr database. When a client is installed, a flag is set in the database—marking the computer as installed and current. The task clears that flag if a Heartbeat DDR is not received in the configured amount of time. As this task is closely tied to Heartbeat discovery, enable the task only if Heartbeat discovery is also enabled. If the Client Rediscovery period is set lower than the Heartbeat discovery cycle, you can cause clients to reinstall if the Client push installation method is also set. This can lead to unnecessary churn on the clients (as they reinstall over a presumably healthy client) and the site server (DDRs, MIFs, and so on).

TABLE 21.1   Site Maintenance Tasks in ConfigMgr

Task	Enabled by Default	Configuration Defaults	Description
Delete Inactive Client Discovery Data	No	Delete data older than 90 days, Saturday after 12:00 AM until 5:00 AM.	Clients can be marked inactive when the Client Health Tool marks it as such or when a client is marked obsolete. This task removes the discovery data associated with clients marked inactive; this commonly happens when a client does not heartbeat within the required time frame.
			This is a discovery method that acts specifically on heartbeat data. If heartbeat data hasn't been received, then the system is marked as inactive and is a candidate for deletion.
			Similar to the Clear Install Flag task, this task is closely tied to Heartbeat discovery. It is recommended that the Delete data older than (days) option be set higher than your ConfigMgr Heartbeat Discovery cycle.
			Because clients are marked inactive via other mechanisms, this particular task can be set to a fairly low number of days without risking data loss. If a client is marked inactive, it was already marked as such by the Client Health Tool, or via normal obsolete client processing.
Delete Obsolete Client Discovery Data	No	Delete data older than 7 days, Saturday after 12:00 AM until 5:00 AM.	When a client is marked obsolete, this task removes that client's discovery data from the ConfigMgr database. A client is marked obsolete if superseded in the ConfigMgr database by another record. See the "Obsolete Clients" section for details.
			Obsolete records are not deleted until this task runs but there is no impact on software deployment, and so on.
Delete Aged Configuration Management Data	Yes	Delete data older than 90 days, Saturday after 12:00 AM until 5:00 AM.	The ConfigMgr database stores metadata about configuration items from Software Updates, Desired Configuration Management, and Operating System Deployments. If part of that data changes, ConfigMgr marks the previous version as old when all clients are using the new data.

TABLE 21.1   Site Maintenance Tasks in ConfigMgr

Task	Enabled by Default	Configuration Defaults	Description
Delete Aged Client Access License Data	No	Delete CAL data older than 180 days. Runs on Saturday between 12:00 AM and 5:00 A.M.	Client Access License (CAL) data is stored in the ConfigMgr database when Asset Intelligence is enabled. This task cleans out the old CAL data, ensuring that the ConfigMgr license information is accurate and timely.

Set the Delete data older than days option sufficiently high to avoid deleting data that is still accurate. As an example, setting it below Hardware Inventory cycle causes CAL license data to be deleted before new data has arrived from the client.

Data deleted by this task has no effect on data at other sites in the ConfigMgr hierarchy.

The 180-day setting is sufficient for most sites. |
Summarize Client Access License Weekly Usage Data	No	Saturday after 12:00 AM until 5:00 AM.	Along with the other summarize tasks, this task is used to keep historical data points in the ConfigMgr database for reporting after the raw data is purged. This task gathers user and device CAL data and creates a weekly summary. The task does not remove information from the database, just summarizes it.
Delete Aged Computer Association Data	Yes	Delete data older than 30 days, Saturday after 12:00 AM until 5:00 AM.	ConfigMgr creates a computer association during operating system deployments that transfer user data. These associations are marked as ready for deletion after the user state restore has completed. This task removes those old associations.
Delete Aged Delete Detection Data	Yes	Delete data older than 30 days, Saturday after 12:00 AM until 5:00 AM.	New with Service Pack (SP) 1, for future integration with System Center Server Manager.

TABLE 21.1   Site Maintenance Tasks in ConfigMgr

Task	Enabled by Default	Configuration Defaults	Description
Reset AMT Computer Passwords	Yes	Password reset interval (days) is set to 2.	New with SP 1. This task resets the remote password used by ConfigMgr to manage AMT-based computers. For security purposes, computer account passwords are regularly changed every 30 days, unless the Windows functionality is disabled (say by using group policy).
			If the computer account password is reset and the AMT remote password is not reset, ConfigMgr will be unable to connect to the AMT-based computer by using out of band communication.
			Do not disable this task without disabling the Windows functionality of automatic password changes for computer accounts.
Evaluate Provisioned AMT Computer Certificates	Yes	Saturdays between 12 AM and 5 AM.	New with SP 1. The task checks the validity period of the certificate issued to AMT-based computers and automatically requests a new certificate before it expires.
		Pending days to expiration: 42.	Requesting a certificate renewal 42 days (default) before it expires allows plenty of time if there are issues, such as the issuing certification authority is not available, or there are connectivity issues.

Data Discovery Record (DDR) Retention

After installing a ConfigMgr site, you add clients and resources to the site. These objects are added using a discovery method. (The only required discovery method is the heartbeat discovery method.) Various discovery methods can be used that search Active Directory or the network for resources. Those resources include computers, Active Directory (AD) objects, site systems, routers, hubs, printers, and Internet Protocol (IP)-addressable devices. Chapter 12, "Client Management," covers discovery in detail, and Chapter 5, "Network Design," provides information on network discovery.

As ConfigMgr 2007 discovers resources, it creates records in the Configuration Manager database and files with a .DDR extension. These discovery records are called data discovery records (DDRs), which refer to the .ddr file format and the actual file used by ConfigMgr to report discovery data to a Configuration Manager site database. You can use these DDRs to target installations for client deployment. DDRs are the main method to tell a ConfigMgr site crucial details about clients. Without DDRs, no clients would be in the database for your administrators to manage!

DDRs are generated based upon the type of discovery method used and based upon a polling schedule that indicates when ConfigMgr performs the actions required to execute the discovery, such as querying Active Directory for systems in the container specified within the discovery method. Heartbeat discovery is unique because the ConfigMgr server does not poll these systems; the discovery configuration only specifies how frequently the clients send their heartbeats to ConfigMgr. The specific information contained in each record can vary depending on the particular resource.

As discussed earlier, Chapter 12 covers discovery in detail, but as a reminder, here are the different discoveries available in ConfigMgr 2007:

- ▶ **Active Directory System Discovery**—Not enabled by default; default polling schedule is daily.

- ▶ **Active Directory Security Group Discovery**—Not enabled by default; default polling schedule is daily.

- ▶ **Active Directory System Discovery**—Not enabled by default; default polling schedule is daily.

- ▶ **Active Directory User Discovery**—Not enabled by default; default polling schedule is daily.

- ▶ **Heartbeat Discovery**—Enabled by default; default polling schedule is once a week. Heartbeat discovery is unique in that it is the only discovery method that returns a client Globally Unique Identifier (GUID) as part of the discovery record; it also is the only discovery method to dictate whether clients are displayed as "installed" in the ConfigMgr console. Heartbeat discovery is responsible for letting the site know a client is still healthy.

- ▶ **Network Discovery**—Not enabled by default; no default schedule.

Data collected can include things such as the NetBIOS name of the computer, the IP address, the MAC (Media Access Control) address, and the IP subnet of the discovered computer or device.

You can configure each type of discovery method on its own custom schedule. When ConfigMgr runs discoveries, it generates resource DDRs to keep discovery data current in the database and inform ConfigMgr that the resource is still valid for the site.

DDRs are not intended for use as extended inventory; they contain basic information that gives the ConfigMgr site enough information to place the client in the database and determine if it were reported previously.

The following is a sample of a heartbeat DDR file created for the Alamo server shown in eXtensible Markup Language (XML) format. Note the NetBIOSName information for the Alamo server, IP Address information, AD Site, ConfigMgr Site, and Domain information:

21

```
<?xml version="1.0" encoding="UTF-16" ?>
- <Report>
- <ReportHeader>
- <Identification>
- <Machine>
  <ClientInstalled>1</ClientInstalled>
  <ClientType>1</ClientType>
  <ClientID>GUID:F35CA434-E9FE-41D0-870A-EF7712F3A63A</ClientID>
  <ClientVersion>4.00.6221.1000</ClientVersion>
  <NetBIOSName>ALAMO</NetBIOSName>
  <CodePage>437</CodePage>
  <SystemDefaultLCID>1033</SystemDefaultLCID>
  </Machine>
  </Identification>
- <ReportDetails>
  <ReportContent>Inventory\x0020Data</ReportContent>
  <ReportType>Full</ReportType>
  <Date>20090322125813.000000-300</Date>
  <Version>62.0</Version>
  <Format>1.1</Format>
  </ReportDetails>
- <InventoryAction ActionType="Predefined">
  <InventoryActionID>{00000000-0000-0000-0000-000000000003}</InventoryActionID>
  <Description>Discovery</Description>
  <InventoryActionLastUpdateTime>20081223140235.000000+000
  </InventoryActionLastUpdateTime>
  </InventoryAction>
  </ReportHeader>
- <ReportBody>
- <Instance ParentClass="Win32_NetworkAdapterConfiguration" Class=
  ➡"Win32_NetworkAdapterConfiguration" Namespace="\\ALAMO\root\cimv2" Content="New">
- <Win32_NetworkAdapterConfiguration>
  <Index>8</Index>
  <IPAddress>192.168.0.184</IPAddress>
  <MACAddress>00:15:5D:00:BF:10</MACAddress>
  </Win32_NetworkAdapterConfiguration>
  </Instance>
- <Instance ParentClass="Win32_ComputerSystemProduct" Class=
  ➡"Win32_ComputerSystemProduct" Namespace="\\ALAMO\root\cimv2" Content="New">
- <Win32_ComputerSystemProduct>
  <IdentifyingNumber>3461-0380-3136-6267-8632-1958-27</IdentifyingNumber>
  <Name>Virtual\x0020Machine</Name>
  <UUID>84910F83-3948-451E-9A58-A970C2ADC908</UUID>
  <Version>5.0</Version>
  </Win32_ComputerSystemProduct>
  </Instance>
```

```
- <Instance ParentClass="CCM_Client" Class="CCM_Client" Namespace=
➥"\\ALAMO\ROOT\ccm" Content="New">
- <CCM_Client>
  <ClientIdChangeDate>12/26/2008\x002020:55:41</ClientIdChangeDate>
  <PreviousClientId>Unknown</PreviousClientId>
  </CCM_Client>
  </Instance>
- <Instance ParentClass="CCM_DiscoveryData" Class=
➥"CCM_DiscoveryData" Namespace="\\ALAMO\root\ccm\invagt" Content="New">
- <CCM_DiscoveryData>
  <PlatformID>Microsoft\x0020Windows\x0020NT\x0020Server\x00205.2</PlatformID>
  </CCM_DiscoveryData>
  </Instance>
- <Instance ParentClass="SMS_Authority" Class="SMS_Authority"
Namespace="\\ALAMO\ROOT\ccm" Content="New">
- <SMS_Authority>
  <Name>SMS:DAL</Name>
  </SMS_Authority>
  </Instance>
- <Instance ParentClass="CCM_ExtNetworkAdapterConfiguration" Class=
➥"CCM_ExtNetworkAdapterConfiguration" Namespace="\\ALAMO\root\ccm\invagt" Content
➥="New">
- <CCM_ExtNetworkAdapterConfiguration>
  <FQDN>alamo.SCCMUNLEASHED.COM</FQDN>
  </CCM_ExtNetworkAdapterConfiguration>
  </Instance>
- <Instance ParentClass="CCM_ClientIdentificationInformation" Class=
➥"CCM_ClientIdentificationInformation" Namespace="\\ALAMO\ROOT\ccm" Content="New">
- <CCM_ClientIdentificationInformation>
  <HardwareID1>2:268C7D8FEBAD3A8AABAAA8A66BDC4B622B917EB6</HardwareID1>
  </CCM_ClientIdentificationInformation>
  </Instance>
- <Instance ParentClass="Win32_ComputerSystem" Class=
➥"Win32_ComputerSystem" Namespace="\\ALAMO\root\cimv2" Content
➥="New">
- <Win32_ComputerSystem>
  <Name>ALAMO</Name>
  <UserName>SCCMUNLEASHED\Administrator</UserName>
  </Win32_ComputerSystem>
  </Instance>
- <Instance ParentClass="CCM_ADSiteInfo" Class="CCM_ADSiteInfo"
Namespace="\\ALAMO\root\ccm\invagt" Content="New">
- <CCM_ADSiteInfo>
  <ADSiteName>Default-First-Site-Name</ADSiteName>
  </CCM_ADSiteInfo>
  </Instance>
```

```
- <Instance ParentClass="CCM_ComputerSystem" Class=
➥"CCM_ComputerSystem" Namespace="\\ALAMO\root\ccm\invagt" Content="New">
- <CCM_ComputerSystem>
  <Domain>SCCMUNLEASHED</Domain>
  </CCM_ComputerSystem>
  </Instance>
- <Instance ParentClass="CCM_NetworkAdapterConfiguration" Class=
➥"CCM_NetworkAdapterConfiguration" Namespace="\\ALAMO\root\ccm\invagt"
Content="New">
- <CCM_NetworkAdapterConfiguration>
  <IPSubnet>192.168.0.0</IPSubnet>
  </CCM_NetworkAdapterConfiguration>
  </Instance>
  </ReportBody>
  </Report>
```

TIP

Capturing Heartbeat Discoveries

If you want to preserve the data collected in the discovery record for troubleshooting purposes, create an empty folder named archive_reports.sms on the agent system at the ccm\inventory\temp directory (stored at c:\windows\system32 on x86 systems and c:\windows\syswow64 on x64 systems). You can verify this location by checking the registry entry setting located at

▶ HKEY_LOCAL_MACHINE\Software\Microsoft\SMS\Mobile Client\Inventory\Temp folder for x86 systems

▶ HKEY_LOCAL_MACHINE\Software\WOW6432Node\Microsoft\SMS\Mobile Client\Inventory\Temp folder for x64 systems.

After this file is created, the discovery and other inventory records are stored in XML format in this temp folder as they are processed.

The following section shows a sample of an Active Directory system discovery DDR file created for the Wildflower server. (Note the sample includes the NetBIOS name, domain of SCCMUNLEASHED, Active Directory site name, IP address, the discovery method used, and other fields that would be relevant to discovery on a Windows-based server.)

```
 MFV    :    <System>
BEGIN_PROPERTY
<8><NetBIOS Name><11><32><WILDFLOWER>
END_PROPERTY
BEGIN_PROPERTY
<1><Operating System Name and Version><11><32><Microsoft Windows NT Server 5.2>
END_PROPERTY
BEGIN_PROPERTY
<0><Resource Domain OR Workgroup><11><32><SCCMUNLEASHED>
```

```
END_PROPERTY
BEGIN_PROPERTY
<0><AD Site Name><11><32><Default-First-Site-Name>
END_PROPERTY
BEGIN_PROPERTY
<16><IP Addresses><11><64>
BEGIN_ARRAY_VALUES
<192.168.0.183>
END_ARRAY_VALUES
END_PROPERTY
BEGIN_PROPERTY
<24><Resource Names><11><256>
BEGIN_ARRAY_VALUES
<wildflower.SCCMUNLEASHED.COM>
END_ARRAY_VALUES
END_PROPERTY
BEGIN_PROPERTY
<0><Primary Group ID><8><4><515>
END_PROPERTY
BEGIN_PROPERTY
<0><User Account Control><8><4><4096>
END_PROPERTY
AGENTINFO<SMS_AD_SYSTEM_DISCOVERY_AGENT><DAL><02/06/2009 16:51:47>
FEOF  FV
```

The retention period for obsolete records is defined by settings in the Delete Obsolete Client Discovery Data task. The retention periods of DDRs are a function of whether the system is a current system, meaning that it is sending heartbeats. If the system is not current, the settings are defined in either the Delete Aged Discovery Data task (assuming that the system is not discovered by another method) or the Delete Inactive Client Discovery Data task.

Obsolete Records

Obsolete records can occur if ConfigMgr detects a duplicate machine in the database. All clients in the ConfigMgr database have several unique identifiers that tell ConfigMgr which machine is which. When two or more of those identifiers come into conflict, an obsolete record can occur.

How a Record Can be Marked as Obsolete

Consider the following scenario that might generate an obsolete record:

1. Machine XYZ is a current ConfigMgr client and is healthy.
2. Machine XYZ has a resource ID (one of the unique ids) of 1234 and a hardware ID (another unique ID) of ABCD. (In reality, the hardware ID is a long string of fixed length but is short and simple for the purpose of this example.)
3. Machine XYZ is reimaged from Windows XP to Windows Vista. A new client is installed during the imaging process.

4. Machine XYZ sends a Heartbeat DDR to its ConfigMgr site.

5. ConfigMgr processes the DDR and notices that this machine has the same hardware configuration as an already existing record with the hardware ID ABCD.

6. ConfigMgr creates a new resource ID of 1235 for the client and marks the old resource ID of 1234 as obsolete.

7. ConfigMgr now only updates information from that machine in accordance with resource ID of 1235—unless of course it is reimaged again!

Although this is just one example of how a record in the ConfigMgr database can be marked as obsolete, it is a common one.

ConfigMgr's default configuration is to automatically create a new client record for duplicate hardware IDs. This setting is configured on the properties of the site that is at -> Site Management -> *<Site Code> <Site Name>*; then right-click on Properties on the Advanced tab. There is also an option available to resolve conflicting records manually. If this setting is used, you can choose what happens when a conflicting record is detected. Any conflicting records are shown at *<Site Code> <Site Name>* -> Computer Management -> Conflicting Records. Right-clicking on a record listed here presents several options:

▶ Merge the data into the old record (this is a good option if you know that the system is the same and want to retain historical data for the system)

▶ Create a new record

▶ Block this record from any further use until the block is removed

For additional details on discovery intervals, duplicates, and how ConfigMgr handles duplicates, check Steve Rachui's blog entry at http://blogs.msdn.com/steverac/archive/2008/05/12/discovery-internals-how-duplicates-are-created-handles-obsoletes.aspx.

Obsolete discovery data continues to persist in the database until the Delete Obsolete Client Discovery Data site maintenance task runs. If that task is not enabled, the data persists until the client is marked inactive and the Delete Inactive Client Discovery Data task runs. An obsolete client is, by its nature, inactive, so these records would also be removed when the Delete Inactive Client Discovery Data task runs. If that task is also disabled, or the appropriate steps are not performed to ensure inactive clients are marked, the data remains.

These tasks are available in the ConfigMgr console, at Site Database -> Site Management -> *<Site Code> <Site Name>* Site Settings -> Site Maintenance -> Tasks. By default, both tasks are not enabled.

TIP

Setting the Retention Period for the Delete Site Maintenance Task

When configuring the Delete Site Maintenance task, it is important to set the retention period of the task to a time frame that is higher than the discovery frequency. Removing discovery data that is not aged sufficiently causes undo churn on the ConfigMgr site. A good rule of thumb is to set this to twice the heartbeat discovery interval or 7 days; whichever is longer.

For example, the Delete Obsolete Client Discovery Data task deletes the obsolete client database records related to the DDR records discussed in the "DDR Retention" section of this chapter. Obsolete client records are generally marked as such because a newer record that discovered the same client has replaced them. The new client record becomes the current client record, and the previous discovery record is now obsolete. By default, this task is not enabled. To remove obsolete records, enable this task and give it an interval that is greater than the heartbeat discovery schedule (which defaults to once a week) as shown in Figure 21.14, which specifies deleting data older than 7 days and running each Saturday morning.

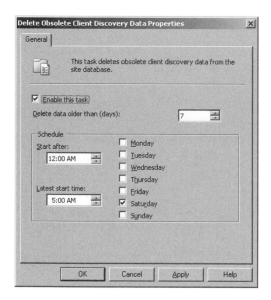

FIGURE 21.14   Enabling the task to delete obsolete client discovery data

---

NOTE

Delete Obsolete Client Discovery Data Task Thresholds

Because a client is marked as obsolete when a new record is processed for the same client, it is fairly safe to run the Delete Obsolete Client Discovery Data task with a fairly low threshold. Nondiscovery data from obsolete clients is removed by the various other site maintenance tasks.

Database Maintenance

When maintaining the ConfigMgr 2007 site database, it is vital to back up the database, as previously discussed in the "Backing Up ConfigMgr" section in this chapter. An effective backup strategy is crucial to providing a functional database environment for ConfigMgr; however additional tasks also need to occur to maintain your ConfigMgr database effectively.

TIP

Why Do a Separate Database Backup?

Are there situations where an administrator would want to do a separate database backup if the site maintenance task is handling the backup? A common reason for performing a separate database backup is that by default the maintenance task overwrites the previous backup file. There are ways to deal with this situation by adding the after-backup.bat file to specify which commands should be run after a backup (such as moving the backup file so that it would not be overwritten and stored for longer periods of time), but a simpler solution might be to perform a separate database backup.

Database maintenance is performed using two tasks defined during site installation. These tasks are available in the ConfigMgr console, at Site Database -> Site Management -> *<Site Code> <Site Name>* Site Settings -> Site Maintenance -> Tasks. The two tasks of note for database maintenance are the Monitor Keys and Rebuild Indexes tasks:

▶ **Monitor Keys**—This task is enabled by default and runs on Sunday mornings between 12:00 AM and 5:00 AM. ConfigMgr works like other database applications in that it uses primary keys to identify unique records in a table quickly. A primary key is a column (or multiple columns) that uniquely identifies one row from any other row in a database. The ConfigMgr Monitor Keys task monitors the integrity of these keys within the ConfigMgr database. As ConfigMgr runs this task itself, the responsibility of the ConfigMgr administrator is to audit this task is occurring and completing successfully when it executes.

▶ **Rebuild Indexes**—By default, the task is enabled. This task runs every Sunday between 12:00 AM and 5:00 AM. ConfigMgr, similar to other database applications, uses indexes to speed up data retrieval. As the data in the ConfigMgr database constantly changes, this task improves performance by creating indexes on database columns that are at least 50% unique. The task also drops indexes on columns that are less than 50% unique and rebuilds all the existing indexes to maximize the performance when accessing these columns.

TIP

Running Rebuild Indexes with a Large Amount of Database Data

If your ConfigMgr site database holds a large amount of data, the Rebuild Indexes task can take a considerable amount of time to run. This task is different from most tasks in that running it more frequently does not guarantee a shorter execution time but ensures your ConfigMgr site uses the database in the most efficient manner.

If there are additional database maintenance tasks required beyond the Monitor Keys and Rebuild Indexes tasks, you can add them through the SQL Commands section of the ConfigMgr console (at Site Database -> Site Management -> *<Site Code> <Site Name>* Site Settings -> Site Maintenance -> SQL Commands). To add new SQL commands to run custom maintenance tasks against the ConfigMgr 2007 site database, right-click on SQL Commands in the console and choose New SQL Commands. The New SQL Command screen (shown in Figure 21.15) provides a dialog box to define the name of the task, the SQL command to execute, where to log status information to, and a section to schedule when the maintenance task would occur.

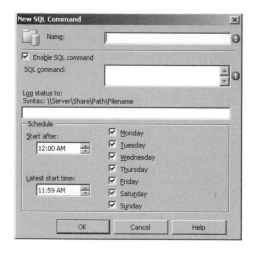

FIGURE 21.15   Configuring a custom SQL command to provide maintenance for the ConfigMgr database

You can use custom SQL commands to run a SQL command (up to 255 characters) or execute an existing stored procedure. There are several SQL commands available that provide maintenance functionality. Some examples of the types of SQL maintenance you can run include the following:

- ▶ **DBCC CHECKDB (Database Consistency Check in SQL Server 2005)**—This is a stored procedure that checks the logical and physical integrity of all objects in the site database. Here are some of the tasks the DBCC CHECKDB stored procedure performs:

    - ▶ Executing a DBCC CHECKALLOC on the database

    - ▶ Performing DBCC CHECKTABLE on every table and view in the database

    - ▶ Executing a DBCC CHECKCATALOG on the database

    - ▶ Validating the contents of every indexed view in the database

    - ▶ Validating the Service Broker data in the database

- ▶ **sp_monitor**—This system procedure displays SQL Server activities and statistics.

- ▶ **sp_spaceused**—This command displays the number of rows, disk space reserved, and disk space used by a table in the current database. It also displays the disk space reserved and used by the entire database.

▶ **sp_who**—This system procedure determines the number of SQL Server connections currently in use by ConfigMgr 2007 and other processes.

▶ **xp_sqlmaint**—This command runs database maintenance tasks.

Properly maintaining your ConfigMgr database environment can go a long way toward maintaining the functionality and performance of your ConfigMgr environment.

Making the Status Message System Work for You

Status messages provide one of the primary means to look at the health of your ConfigMgr infrastructure and identify any problems that might occur. Nearly all ConfigMgr components generate status messages to report various milestones and events. ConfigMgr clients send status messages to their management point, site systems send status messages to the site server, and child sites can replicate messages to their parent site.

You can choose which messages to replicate and the data priority for each type of message sent between sites. Status messages sent up the hierarchy can account for much of the overall site-to-site traffic. This is particularly true when child sites have a large number of clients. To limit the impact of status message replication, it is important to tune the Status Message System.

The most important settings for status message replication are the status filter rules. All status messages received by a site pass through the site's status filter, which evaluates the message to determine if it matches the criteria of each of its status filter rules. A match invokes the action you specify for the rule. One of the actions you can specify is to replicate the message to the parent site.

You can configure status filter rules in the ConfigMgr console, at System Center Configuration Manager -> Site Database -> Site Management -> *<Site Code> <Site Name>* -> Site Settings -> Status Filter Rules. As shown in Figure 21.16, two status filter rules for replication are already enabled, by default:

Name	Status
Detect when the status of the site database changes to Critical because it could not b...	Enabled
Detect when the status of the site database changes to Warning due to low free space.	Enabled
Detect when the status of the site database changes to Critical due to low free space.	Enabled
Detect when the status of the transaction log for the site database changes to Critical...	Enabled
Detect when the status of the transaction log for the site database changes to Warni...	Enabled
Detect when the status of the transaction log for the site database changes to Critical...	Enabled
Detect when the status of a site system's storage object changes to Critical because i...	Enabled
Detect when the status of a site system's storage object changes to Warning due to l...	Enabled
Detect when the status of a site system's storage object changes to Critical due to lo...	Enabled
Detect when the status of a server component changes to Warning.	Enabled
Detect when the status of a server component changes to Critical.	Enabled
Write audit messages to the site database and and specify the period after which the ...	Enabled
Write all other messages to the site database and specify the period after which the u...	Enabled
Replicate all SMS Client messages at low priority.	Enabled
Replicate all other messages at medium priority.	Enabled

FIGURE 21.16   The List of status filter rules enabled in the default configuration

▶ Replicate all SMS Client messages at low priority

▶ Replicate all other messages at medium priority

The rule to replicate client settings is higher on the list in Figure 21.16—showing it has a higher priority and will be processed before the rule that replicates all other messages at medium priority. Messages received from clients match the first rule and replicate to the parent site at low priority. All other status messages are replicated at medium priority. You can modify these rules depending on your requirements. For example, if local administrators perform all client troubleshooting at a particular site, you might decide not to replicate status messages originating on client systems from that site to its parent site.

To stop replicating client messages, perform these steps:

1. Right-click on the rule.
2. Choose Properties.
3. Select the Actions tab in the Status Filter Rule Properties page.
4. Check the box at the bottom for Do not process lower-priority status filter rules.

By changing the action from the default of Replicate to Parent Site to Do not process lower-priority status filter rules (as shown in Figure 21.17), you can prevent these messages from being processed by the lower priority Replicate all other messages at medium priority rule. This action results in client messages being discarded. As that data is not forwarded, it eliminates data within some reports at higher-level sites and any centralized view of deployments.

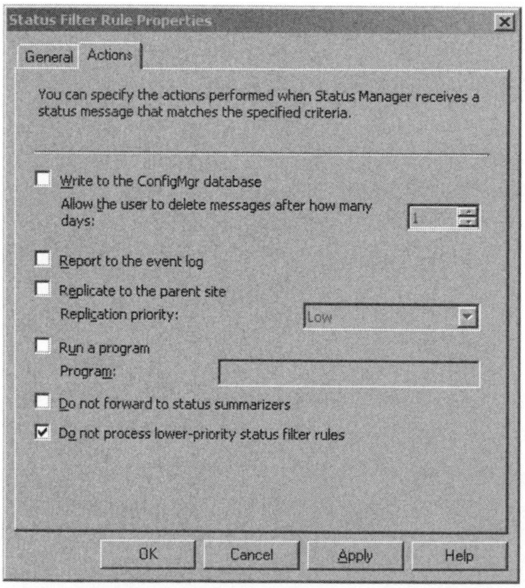

FIGURE 21.17   Modifying a status filter rule

Note that the modified rule is still named Replicate all SMS Client messages at low priority, although it no longer actually replicates the messages. To change the name of the rule, you need to delete or disable the existing rule and create a new rule with the appropriate name.

You can create new rules to control replication of specific types of messages. To create a new status filter rule, perform the following steps:

1. Right-click the Status Filter Rules node in the console tree; then select New Status Filter Rule to initiate the New Status Filter Rule Wizard.

2. Name the rule **Replicate Milestones and Informational Messages at Low Priority** and check the Message Type and Severity boxes. With the selections shown in Figure 21.18, the filter processes all messages of type Milestone or severity Informational.

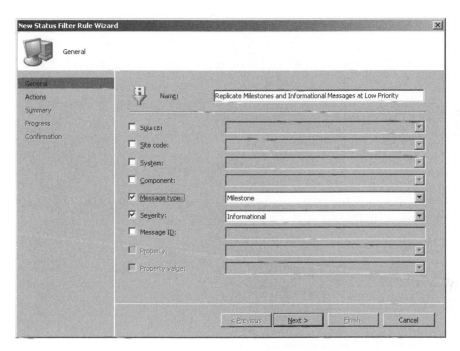

FIGURE 21.18   Specifying Criteria against which the Status Message will be evaluated to determine if the new status filter rule will be applied

3. Next, choose the action Replicate to parent site / Replication priority and select Low from the drop-down list, as shown in Figure 21.19.

4. The wizard displays a Summary page for the new rule and asks you to confirm your choice. This completes the New Status Filter Rule Wizard.

After completing the wizard, you need to change the priority of the rule so that it processes in the correct order. The rule should run after the rule that discards client messages, but before the catchall rule to replicate at medium priority.

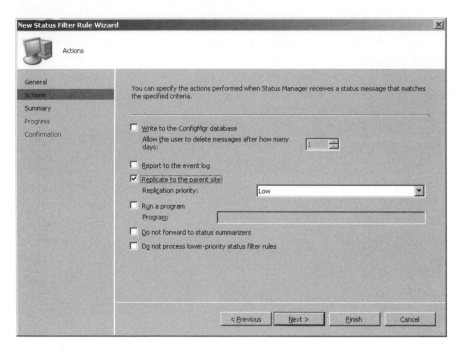

FIGURE 21.19   Specifying the actions that occur when a Status Message matches the filter criteria

Right-click the rule in the list and choose Increment priority. Figure 21.20 shows the sixteen rules. This discussion focuses on the last three rules, which configure how status messages replicate within ConfigMgr. As a summary, these are the actions now defined for ConfigMgr:

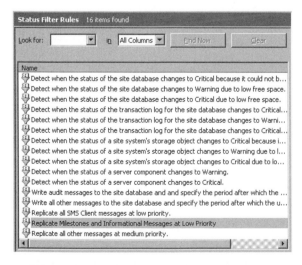

FIGURE 21.20   The list of status filter rules, including the newly created rule, in the desired order

- ▶ All Client messages will be dropped because of the steps taken to stop replicating client messages.

- ▶ Informational and Milestone messages will be replicated only during times when the Sender Address setting allows sending low priority data.

- ▶ All other messages will be replicated during times when the Sender Address setting permits sending medium priority data.

In addition to individual status messages, each ConfigMgr site maintains status summary data by default. This status summary data displays the overall status of a system, component, or advertisement as OK, Warning, or Critical based on the number and type of messages received. Similar to individual status messages, you can decide whether to replicate status summary data to the parent site and the data priority to assign to the replication.

Perform the following steps to configure replication of status summarizer data:

1. Navigate to System Center Configuration Manager -> Site Database -> Site Management -> *<Site Code> <Site Name>* -> Site Settings -> Status Summary.

2. Right-click the summarizer you want to configure.

3. Select Properties.

4. You can now choose if you want to enable status summarization, replicate to the parent site, and replication priority.

Figure 21.21 shows the default settings for the Advertisement Status Summarizer.

Effectively configuring your status filtering rules can help to direct your ConfigMgr environment to show only the status information relevant to your particular ConfigMgr site.

FIGURE 21.21   Advertisement Status Summarizer properties

Maintaining Status Data

ConfigMgr retains two different types of status data, which are set in the ConfigMgr console, at Site Database -> Site Management -> *<Site Code> <Site Name>* Site Settings -> Status Filter Rules:

- ▶ **Audit messages**—Audit messages retention is configured within the Write audit messages to the site database and specify the period after which the user can delete the messages rule. This status filter rule has a default setting of 180 days before the user can delete messages.

- ▶ **All other messages**—Other message data retention is configured within the Write all other messages to the site database and specify the period after which the user can delete the messages rule. This status filter rule has a default setting of 30 days before the user can delete messages.

These messages are removed from the ConfigMgr database through the Delete Aged Status Messages task (navigate in the ConfigMgr console to Site Database -> Site Management -> *<Site Code> <Site Name>* Site Settings -> Tasks). This task runs daily between midnight and 5:00 AM. The task deletes status messages older than seven days.

As an example, in a default configuration all audit messages are retained 180 days, and all other messages are retained 30 days. Even though the task deletes messages older than 7 days, the actual data is retained in the database for 30 (or 180) days. If you decrease the All other messages setting from 30 days down to 14 days and rerun this task, it does not have what might be the expected results, which is to delete messages older than 14 days (other than audit messages).

This is because when status messages are written to the database, the date they are scheduled to be deleted is written based on the setting on the status filter rule at that point in time. The date is calculated based upon the settings that existed for the appropriate message retention task. When the retention period is changed, the new messages remain for the time defined when they are written. Therefore, by following the example in the previous paragraph, the status messages written with the 14-day retention would be deleted and then the status messages written under the 30-day retention would be deleted.

It is recommended to retain the status messages as long as is required to diagnose the status of your ConfigMgr 2007 system. If you need to minimize the amount of space used by status messages, you can decrease the retention periods within the two rules listed in this section—although making this change is not suggested, unless it is necessary to decrease the amount of data retained.

Status Filter Rules

Status filter rules allow a ConfigMgr administrator to control which status messages are both forwarded to parent sites and which ones are written to the ConfigMgr database. These rules can be a critical method of tuning performance and eliminating unneeded information.

Rules are set in a top-down ranking, meaning that rules listed at the top of the list are processed first, followed by those listed next. This assumes that a higher-level listing does not stop processing of lower priority rules. Think of status filter rules as a series of gates that each status message must pass through. Each gate has a set of criteria against which each message is checked.

▶ If the message doesn't match the criteria, it passes through the gate to the next rule.

▶ If it matches, a set of actions can be taken, including either allowing the message to continue on its path, or stopping all further activity for the message.

ConfigMgr 2007 comes with a number of status filter rules predefined and enabled by default. These status filter rules provide actions that occur when various conditions are met, as shown in Table 21.2.

TABLE 21.2   Status Filter Rules in ConfigMgr

Status Filter Rule Name	Default Condition	Default Action
Detect when the status of the site database changes to Critical because it could not be accessed.	Source: ConfigMgr Server, Component: SMS_SITE_SYSTEM_STATUS_SUMMARIZER, Message ID: 4703	Report to the event log.
Detect when the status of the site database changes to Warning due to free disk space.	Source: ConfigMgr Server, Component: SMS_SITE_SYSTEM_STATUS_SUMMARIZER, Message ID: 4713	Report to the event log.
Detect when the status of the site database changes to Critical due to free disk space.	Source: ConfigMgr Server, Component: SMS_SITE_SYSTEM_STATUS_SUMMARIZER, Message ID: 4714	Report to the event log.
Detect when the status of the transaction log for the site database changes to Critical because it could not be accessed.	Source: ConfigMgr Server, Component: SMS_SITE_SYSTEM_STATUS_SUMMARIZER, Message ID: 4706	Report to the event log.
Detect when the status of the transaction log for the site database changes to Warning due to low free space.	Source: ConfigMgr Server, Component: SMS_SITE_SYSTEM_STATUS_SUMMARIZER, Message ID: 4716	Report to the event log.
Detect when the status of the transaction log for the site database changes to Critical due to low free space.	Source: ConfigMgr Server, Component: SMS_SITE_SYSTEM_STATUS_SUMMARIZER, Message ID: 4717	Report to the event log.
Detect when the status of a site system's storage object changes to Critical because it could not be accessed.	Source: ConfigMgr Server, Component: SMS_SITE_SYSTEM_STATUS_SUMMARIZER, Message ID: 4700	Report to the event log.

TABLE 21.2   Status Filter Rules in ConfigMgr

Status Filter Rule Name	Default Condition	Default Action
Detect when the status of a site system's storage object changes to Warning due to free disk space.	Source: ConfigMgr Server, Component: SMS_SITE_SYSTEM_STATUS_SUMMARIZER, Message ID: 4710	Report to the event log.
Detect when the status of a site system's storage object changes to Critical due to free disk space.	Source: ConfigMgr Server, Component: SMS_SITE_SYSTEM_STATUS_SUMMARIZER, Message ID: 4711	Report to the event log.
Detect when the status of a server component changes to Warning.	Source: ConfigMgr Server, Component: SMS_SITE_SYSTEM_STATUS_SUMMARIZER, Message ID: 4610	Report to the event log.
Detect when the status of a server component changes to Critical.	Source: ConfigMgr Server, Component: SMS_SITE_SYSTEM_STATUS_SUMMARIZER, Message ID: 4609	Report to the event log.
Write audit messages to the site database and specify the period after which the user can delete the messages.	Message Type: Audit	Write to the ConfigMgr database. Allow the user to delete messages after 180 days.
Write all other messages to the site database and specify the period after which the user can delete the messages.	(No settings)	Write to the ConfigMgr database. Allow the user to delete messages after 30 days.
Replicate all SMS Client messages at low priority.	Source: ConfigMgr Client	Replicate to the parent site. Replication Priority: Low.
Replicate all other messages at medium priority.	(No settings)	Replicate to the parent site. Replication Priority: Medium.

Using the ConfigMgr console, you can create new status filter rules or update existing ones. Utilize these status filter rules to either change how these configurations function, or add matching and actions for additional configurations not predefined within ConfigMgr.

Monitoring Configuration Manager with Operations Manager

Chapter 1, "Configuration Management Basics," introduces the Microsoft System Center product line including products such as Operations Manager, Essentials, Service Manager, Data Protection Manager, Capacity Planner, and Virtual Machine Manager. An important part of a server maintenance strategy should include effective monitoring of what is occurring on the servers and applications within your organization.

System Center Operations Manager 2007 (OpsMgr) provides proactive server and application monitoring and displays the information into a centralized console. OpsMgr provides a way to identify issues before they affect the environment, enabling a quicker resolution for issues when they are identified.

ConfigMgr provides its own method of status reporting through the Status Message System (discussed in the "Making the Status Message System Work for You" section of this chapter), so at first glance it would appear that using OpsMgr to monitor ConfigMgr would be redundant. The status system within ConfigMgr provides a great level of details related to the internals of what is occurring within ConfigMgr; however, it is not designed to provide proactive monitoring or alert when critical events occur. The status system is designed to only provide information that determines what occurs within ConfigMgr.

Operations Manager provides the ability to monitor the physical hardware, operating system, and core functionality such as DNS, DHCP, and Active Directory; and it provides the ability to monitor applications such as ConfigMgr 2007. OpsMgr's functionality is available through management packs (free with the product) that are available from the System Center Operations Manager 2007 Catalog on the Microsoft website. The ConfigMgr management pack is available by accessing http://technet.microsoft.com/en-us/opsmgr/cc539535.aspx and searching for **System Center Configuration Manager 2007**.

The ConfigMgr management pack provides the health state for all ConfigMgr servers and services and provides performance and availability reports for ConfigMgr. It also provides alerting for critical ConfigMgr 2007 status messages and tracks the processing rates and metrics such as the processor, memory, and disk system usage. The management pack includes product knowledge to assist with resolving alerts identified for the ConfigMgr environment.

For more information on System Center Operations Manager, the authors of this book recommend the Microsoft website for Operations Manager (http://www.microsoft.com/opsmgr) and/or *System Center Operations Manager 2007 Unleashed* (Sams, 2008), available at http://tinyurl.com/27mqnm.

Services and Descriptions

Configuration Manager 2007 uses a variety of maintenance services, which run either on the agent or on the various site servers. Knowing what services ConfigMgr uses and the functions they provide can assist with debugging issues that occur in the ConfigMgr environment. This can be critical when identifying issues that might occur after performing a ConfigMgr recovery. Table 21.3 provides a list of these services and their descriptions.

TABLE 21.3   Services Used in ConfigMgr

Service Name	Description
CCMSetup.exe	Runs on the client agent systems. Temporary service used to install the SMS Agent Host service on client systems.
SMS Agent Host	Runs on the client agent systems. Provides change and configuration services for computer management systems. Set to Automatic.
SMS Task Sequence Agent	Runs on the client agent systems. SMS client agent for task sequence execution. Set to Manual.
SMS_EXECUTIVE	Runs on the ConfigMgr server systems. Provides the primary service, which executes the ConfigMgr functions. Set to Automatic.
SMS_REPORTING_POINT	Runs on the ConfigMgr server systems. Provides the reporting services functionality when the Reporting Point site role is added. Set to Automatic.
SMS_SERVER_LOCATOR_POINT	Runs on the ConfigMgr server systems. Provides HTTP interface to locate Microsoft ConfigMgr sites and site roles when the Server Locator Point role is added. Set to Automatic.
SMS_SITE_BACKUP	Runs on the ConfigMgr server systems. This service executes the backup task functionality. Set to Manual; activates when the backup task executes.
SMS_SITE_COMPONENT_MANAGER	Runs on the ConfigMgr server systems. Installs and removes server components at a ConfigMgr site and installs any necessary server components. Set to Automatic.
SMS_SITE_SQL_BACKUP	Runs on the ConfigMgr server systems. Performs the SQL backup for the Backup ConfigMgr Site Server task. Set to Automatic.
SMS_SITE_VSS_WRITER	Runs on the ConfigMgr server systems. Creates the backup snapshot for the Backup ConfigMgr Site Server task. Set to Automatic.
SMS_SERVER_BOOTSTRAP_<servername>	Runs on the ConfigMgr server systems. Installs secondary sites that are created from the ConfigMgr console. Set to Automatic.

Summary

This chapter focuses on the steps required to backup, recover, and maintain your Configuration Manager 2007 environment. It discusses DDR retention, obsolete records, and database records. It also discusses the ConfigMgr Status Message System and using OpsMgr to monitor ConfigMgr. The chapter finishes by listing the maintenance services used within ConfigMgr.

This chapter completes the last part of the book, which focuses on how to administer Configuration Manager 2007. We hope that this has been a useful guide to ConfigMgr and provides you with an in-depth level of understanding of the product.

PART V
Appendixes

IN THIS PART

Configuration Manager Log Files

Since the early days of Systems Management Server (SMS), the application has used numerous log files for tracking and troubleshooting purposes. This appendix discusses how to enable logging as well as listing the log files used by specific Configuration Manager (ConfigMgr) 2007 components.

Related Documentation

Microsoft-related articles on log files are available in a number of places, including the following:

▶ General information is available at http://technet.microsoft.com/en-us/library/bb892800.aspx.

▶ Additional detail on client log files is found at http://technet.microsoft.com/en-us/library/bb693897.aspx.

▶ For information on mobile devices, http://technet.microsoft.com/en-us/library/bb680409.aspx discusses the log files on managed mobile devices and those computers used to deploy the mobile device client.

▶ Information on Operating System Deployment–related log files is located separately at http://technet.microsoft.com/en-us/library/bb932135.aspx.

▶ Information regarding the smsts.log file is located at http://blogs.technet.com/carlossantiago/archive/2009/01/19/how-can-i-increase-the-size-of-the-smsts-log-file.aspx.

Enabling Logging

Some logs are initially enabled, whereas others are not.

▶ To conserve server resources, server-based log files are not enabled by default. To enable site server component logging, use the ConfigMgr Service Manager, discussed in the "Using ConfigMgr Service Manager" section of this appendix. The site server components are located on the machine with the SMS_Executive service installed, in the Registry under HKEY_LOCAL_MACHINE\Software\Microsoft\SMS\Tracing\ where you can view the configuration by each component. However, Microsoft prefers you use ConfigMgr Service Manager rather than making modifications directly to the Registry.

▶ Client-based files are enabled by default, and can be disabled through the Registry on the client under HKEY_LOCAL_MACHINE\Software\Microsoft\CCM\Logging.

Those logs enabled by default may include only high-level information, to try to reduce overhead. Enabling more detailed logging produces low-level information that might be useful for troubleshooting problems, although Microsoft recommends you avoid this in production sites because it can lead to excessive logging, which may make it difficult to find relevant information in the log files. If you need to log for troubleshooting purposes, turn off detailed logging once you are through!

Debug and Verbose Logging

The level of logging enabled determines whether all the files listed on the client and management point actually exist. To enable debug or verbose logging after installing Configuration Manager 2007 for the client or management point, run the Registry editor (Start -> Run, and type **regedit.exe**) and then make the following Registry changes:

▶ For debug logging, stop the SMS Agent Host service; then create the HKEY_LOCAL_MACHINE\Software\Microsoft\CCM\Logging\debuglogging key.

Restart the SMS Agent Host service (this is also described in Microsoft TechNet knowledgebase article 833417 at http://support.microsoft.com/kb/833417).

▶ For verbose logging, change the value of Loglevel to 0 at HKEY_LOCAL_MACHINE\Software\Microsoft\CCM\Logging.

A reboot is not required.

Using ConfigMgr Service Manager

To toggle logging off or on for individual server components, perform the following steps:

1. In the ConfigMgr console, select Tools -> ConfigMgr Service Manager. Right-click and select Start ConfigMgr Service Manager.
2. Open ConfigMgr Service Manager.
3. Navigate to those components for which you want to change the logging settings.
4. In the right pane, select one or more components.
5. Right-click and select Logging.

6. In the ConfigMgr Component Logging dialog box, check or uncheck the Logging enabled option, as appropriate.

7. Click OK.

To expand log file size, run ConfigMgr Service Manager and in step 6 select the log size in MB.

SQL Logging

To enable logging for the SQL component, edit the Registry and go to HKEY_LOCAL_MACHINE\Software\Microsoft\SMS\Tracing. Change SQLEnabled to 1 and restart the SMS_EXECUTIVE service. SQL Logging will dump every SQL call for any component that interacts with the database on the server side to its associated log file. This logging tends to be rather verbose.

NAL Logging

NAL logging shows network connection processing as the server runs. When enabled, it adds entries to any server-side log that has to negotiate a network connection, such as the Distribution Manager. The logging produces a sizeable amount of error messages in the logs that may be misleading; the system is trying to work through all the different connectivity options and determine the best one—so the "errors" are not necessarily all errors.

To turn on NAL logging with all verbosity levels for the client, make the following Registry changes. You may need to add the Logging subkey.

▶ HKEY_LOCAL_MACHINE\Software\Microsoft\NAL\Logging\

Verbosity(DWORD)value=00000007

▶ HKEY_LOCAL_MACHINE\Software\Microsoft\NAL\Logging\

Log To(DWORD)value=00000003

Reporting Point Logging

To configure logging for the reporting point server, modify the HKEY_LOCAL_MACHINE\Software\Microsoft\SMS\Tracing\SMS_Reporting Point Registry key.

This key contains information regarding the log file name, maximum file size allowed, and whether it is enabled (default) or disabled. Microsoft recommends you do not disable reporting point logging.

To change the maximum file size, change the MaxFileSize DWORD value as needed. The default value is 280000 (Hex) or 2621440 (Decimal).

To modify the location of this log file, change the TraceFileName value as needed.

The SmsReporting.log file captures a great deal of information about the reporting components, site database connections, and reporting query requests, and it monitors the dashboard use and a host of other items and components. This log file can be very verbose or "chatty" and thus can grow exponentially. If you decide to temporarily disable it for one reason or another to stop the influx of information, simply change the Reporting Point Logging Enabled DWORD value from 1 (On) to 0 (Off). Change it back when you have completed your tasks.

Reporting point installation information is recorded at *%ProgramFiles%*\Microsoft Configuration Manager\Logs\SMSReportingInstall. (*%ProgramFiles%*\Microsoft Configuration Manager\) is also referred to within this appendix as *<ConfigMgrInstallPath>*.

ConfigMgr Setup Logs

This section lists setup-specific log files for the ConfigMgr installation. Setup logs for individual components are included in the section documenting log files for that component.

Almost all site installation information appears in the logs on the root of the system drive, making the log files a primary source of help when you're troubleshooting installation issues. Install the ConfigMgr toolkit prior to site installation and use Trace32.exe from the toolkit to associate .log files with Trace32. Trace32 makes ConfigMgr log files easier to read. Setup logs include the following:

- ▶ **%*SystemRoot*%\ConfigMgrPrereq.log**—Shows the results of the prerequisite checker, created in the root of the system drive.

- ▶ **%*SystemRoot*%\ConfigMgrSetup.log**—Installation log, updated with results from running ConfigMgr setup program and upgrades.

- ▶ **%*SystemRoot*%\SMS_BOOTSTRAP.log**—Installation log for secondary site servers when the installation is initiated from the parent site.

- ▶ **%*SystemRoot*%\ExtAdSch.log**—Created from the ExtADsch utility to extend the Active Directory Schema.

- ▶ **%*SystemRoot*%\ComponentSetup.log**—Shows the results of installing site components.

- ▶ **<*ConfigMgrInstallPath*>\Logs\SLPSetup.log**—Installation log for server locator point. The server locator point is used during client installations to locate an appropriate management point. Only one server locator point is required, and it should be located on the central site.

Client Log Files

Client log files are used to track various problems occurring on the ConfigMgr client. The location of these files varies when the client is also a management point.

- ▶ If the client is a management point and the management point is created prior to the client being installed, the client log files are located in the *%SystemDrive%*\SMS_CCM\Logs folder.

▶ If the client is not a management point or the client was installed prior to the management point being added, the client log files are located at %*windir*%\System32\CCM\Logs. (For 64-bit systems, these files are located at %*windir*%\SysWOW64\CCM\Logs.)

Client log files are a great place to begin troubleshooting efforts. Files include the following:

▶ **CAS.log**—Content Access service for the local machine's package cache.

▶ **CcmExec.log**—Tracks the client's activities and SMS Agent Host service information.

▶ **CertificateMaintenance.log**—Records Active Directory (AD) certificates for the directory service and management points.

▶ **ClientIDManagerStartup.log**—Used for maintenance of the resource's Globally Unique Identifier (GUID).

▶ **ClientLocation.log**—Tracks site assignments.

▶ **ContentTransferManager.log**—Records scheduling information for the Background Intelligent Transfer Service (BITS) or the Server Message Block (SMB) to download or to access ConfigMgr packages.

▶ **DataTransferService.log**—Records all BITS communication for policy or package access.

▶ **Execmgr.log**—Records advertisement information as it is run.

▶ **FileBITS.log**—Used to record SMB package access tasks.

▶ **Fsinvprovider.log**—WMI provider for software inventory and file collection tasks.

▶ **InventoryAgent.log**—Creates data discovery records (DDRs) as well as hardware and software inventory records.

▶ **LocationServices.log**—Locates management points and distribution points.

▶ **Mifprovider.log**—Management Information Format (MIF) file WMI provider.

▶ **Mtrmgr.log**—Tracks software-metering processes.

▶ **PolicyAgent.log**—Requests policies by using the Data Transfer service.

▶ **PolicyAgentProvider.log**—Records any policy changes.

▶ **PolicyEvaluator.log**—Records any new policy settings.

▶ **Remctrl.log**—Logs when the remote control component starts.

▶ **Scheduler.log**—Records schedule tasks for all client operations.

▶ **Smscliui.log**—Records usage of the Systems Management tool in Control Panel on the client.

▶ **StatusAgent.log**—Logs status messages created by the client components.

▶ **SWMTRReportGen.log**—Generates a usage data report that is collected by the metering agent. (This data is logged in Mtrmgr.log.)

Site Server Log Files

All server log files are located in the *%ProgramFiles%*\Microsoft Configuration Manager\Logs folder on the server where the role is installed. Log files for particular components are listed in those respective sections. The server log files are as follows:

▶ **Adsgdis.log**—Active Directory Security Group Discovery log.

▶ **Adusrdis.log**—Active Directory User Discovery log file showing when the discovery method runs as well as its results.

▶ **Adsysdis.log**—Active Directory System Discovery log. Active Directory System Discovery is the key discovery method used to create DDRs for computers.

▶ **Adsysgrp.log**—Information on Active Directory System Group Discovery.

▶ **Aikbmgr.log**—Maintains a record of asset intelligence data in the site database.

▶ **Ccm.log**—Logs information regarding client Configuration Manager tasks.

▶ **Cidm.log**—Records changes to the client settings by the Client Install Data Manager (CIDM).

▶ **Colleval.log**—Logs when collections are created, changed, and replicated to child sites as well as deleted by the Collection Evaluator.

▶ **Compmon.log**—Maintains Registry setting for discovery components.

▶ **Compsumm.log**—Records Component Status Summarizer tasks.

▶ **Cscnfsvc.log**—This log records Courier Sender confirmation service tasks.

▶ **Dataldr.log**—Processes MIF files for hardware inventory in the Configuration Manager 2007 database.

▶ **Ddm.log**—Saves data discovery record (DDR) information to the Configuration Manager 2007 database by the Discovery Data Manager and processes PDR (Windows Port Driver) information.

▶ **Despool.log**—Records incoming site-to-site communication transfers.

▶ **Distmgr.log**—Records package creation, compression, delta replication, and information updates.

▶ **Hman.log**—Records site configuration changes as well as publishes site information in Active Directory Domain Services.

▶ **Inboxast.log**—Records files moved from the management point to the corresponding *<ConfigMgrInstallPath>*\INBOXES folder.

▶ **Inboxmgr.log**—Records file maintenance. This log confirms inboxes were successfully created on the site server and the management point.

▶ **Inboxmon.log**—Monitors the file count in various inboxes.

▶ **Invproc.log**—Records processing of delta MIF files for the Dataloader component from client inventory files.

▶ **Mpcontrol.log**—Records the registration of the management point with Windows Internet Naming Services (WINS) and records the availability of the management point every 10 minutes.

▶ **Mpfdm.log**—Management point component that moves client files to the corresponding *<ConfigMgrInstallPath>*\INBOXES folder.

▶ **MPMSI.log**—Management point .msi installation log.

▶ **MPSetup.log**—Records the management point installation wrapper process and provides information about management point installation. Resides on the site server.

▶ **Netdisc.log**—Shows activity regarding network discovery.

▶ **Ntsvrdis.log**—ConfigMgr 2007 server discovery information. Server discovery is a "hidden" discovery method that has no user-configurable properties. It runs by default on the site server every 24 hours and its only role is to "discover" any system configured as a site system and create a DDR for it.

▶ **Offermgr.log**—Records advertisement updates.

▶ **Offersum.log**—Records summarization of advertisement status messages.

▶ **Policypv.log**—Records updates to the client policies to reflect changes to client settings or advertisements.

▶ **Replmgr.log**—Records replication of files between the site server components and the Scheduler component.

▶ **Rsetup.log**—Reporting point setup log.

▶ **Sched.log**—Records site-to-site job and package replication.

▶ **Sender.log**—Records files that are sent to other child and parent sites.

▶ **Sinvproc.log**—Records client software inventory data processing to the site database in Microsoft SQL Server.

▶ **Sitecomp.log**—Records maintenance of installed site components. This log verifies successful installation of the ConfigMgr components (or reinstallation in the case of a site reset).

▶ **Sitectrl.log**—Records site setting changes to the Sitectrl.ct0 file.

▶ **Sitestat.log**—Records the monitoring process of all site systems.

▶ **Smsdbmon.log**—Records responses to database changes related to software updates.

▶ **Smsexec.log**—Records the processing of all site server component threads.

▶ **Smsprov.log**—Records WMI provider access to the site database.

▶ **SMSReportingInstall.log**—Records the reporting point installation. This component starts the installation tasks as well as processes configuration changes.

▶ **Srvacct.log**—Records the maintenance of accounts when the site uses standard security.

▶ **Statesys.log**—Processes and summarizes state messages.

▶ **Statmgr.log**—Writes all status messages to the database.

▶ **Swmproc**—Processes metering files and maintains settings.

Backup Log Files

The following files are related to backup activity:

▶ **Smssqlbkup.log**—Records the backup process for the site database.

▶ **Smsbkup.log**—Used with the site backup task, located in the site backup folder.

▶ **Smswriter.log**—Manages volume snapshots for backups.

Management Point Log Files

You will find the management point log files at %*ProgramFiles*%\SMS_CCM\Logs on the management point if the management point was created prior to the client being installed. Otherwise, they are at %*windir*%\System32\CCM\Logs (on 64-bit systems, at %*windir*%\SysWOW64\CCM\Logs). These files include the following:

▶ **MP_ClientID.log**—Used to generate the client ID.

▶ **MP_ClientREG.log**—Used at client registration during the initial installation to verify it is an approved system.

▶ **MP_Ddr.log**—Records the conversion of XML.ddr records from clients as well as copies them to the site server.

▶ **MP_DriverManager.log**—Provides information about the management point when it responds to a request from the Auto Apply Driver task sequence action. The log is generated on the management point.

▶ **MP_GetAuth.log**—Records the status of the site management points.

▶ **MP_GetPolicy.log**—Records policy information.

▶ **MP_Hinv.log**—Converts eXtensible Markup Language (XML) hardware inventory records from clients and copies the files to the site server.

▶ **MP_Location.log**—Records location manager tasks. Useful for troubleshooting problems accessing Internet Information Services (IIS) and Windows Management Instrumentation (WMI). For OSD, provides information about the management point when it responds to request state store or release state store requests from the state migration point. The log is generated on the management point.

▶ **MP_Policy.log**—Records policy communication.

▶ **MP_Relay.log**—Copies files that are collected from the client.

▶ **MP_Retry.log**—Records the hardware inventory retry processes.

▶ **MP_RegistrationManager.log**—Records the client registration process.

▶ **MP_Sinv.log**—Converts XML hardware inventory records from clients and copies them to the site server.

▶ **MP_Status.log**—Converts XML.svf status message files from clients and copies them to the site server.

Admin User Interface Log Files

The following log files for the Admin User Interface (UI) are located in the %*ProgramFiles*%\Microsoft Configuration Manager\AdminUI\AdminUILog folder:

▶ **AdminUI.log**—Console log file

▶ **RepairWizard.log**—Records errors, warnings, and information about the process of running the Repair Wizard

▶ **ResourceExplorer.log**—Records errors, warnings, and information about running the Resource Explorer

▶ **SMSAdminUI.log**—Records the local Configuration Manager 2007 console tasks when you connect to Configuration Manager 2007 sites

Mobile Device Log Files

Log files for mobile devices include those on the mobile device management point and client logs.

Mobile Device Management Log Files

If you have enabled mobile device management in your site hierarchy, the following mobile device management log files are typically stored in the <*ConfigMgrInstallPath*> \Logs folder of the mobile device management point computer:

▶ **DmClientHealth.log**—Records the GUIDs of all mobile device clients communicating with the device management point

▶ **DmClientRegistration.log**—Records registration requests from and responses to the mobile device client in native mode

▶ **DmpDatastore.log**—Records all the site database connections and queries made by the device management point

▶ **DmpDiscovery.log**—Records all the discovery data from the mobile device clients on the device management point

▶ **DmpFileCollection.log**—Records mobile device file collection data from mobile device clients on the device management point

▶ **DmpHardware.log**—Records hardware inventory data from mobile device clients on the device management point

▶ **DmpIsapi.log**—Records mobile device communication data from device clients on the device management point

▶ **DmpMSI.log**—Records MSI data for device management point setup

▶ **DmpSetup.log**—Records the mobile device management setup process

▶ **DmpSoftware.log**—Records mobile device software distribution data from mobile device clients on the device management point

▶ **DmpStatus.log**—Records mobile device status messages data from mobile device clients on the device management point

▶ **FspIsapi.log**—Records fallback status point communication data from mobile device clients and client computers on the fallback status point

Mobile Device Management Client Logs

See http://technet.microsoft.com/en-us/library/bb680409.aspx for the locations of log files on managed mobile devices and those computers used to deploy the mobile device client; these settings are configurable. The default setting on the client is *%temp%*\DMClient\Logs. On Window Mobile Smartphone 2003, this location is redirected to \Storage\temp\DMClientLogs.

▶ **DmCertEnroll.log**—Records certificate enrollment data on mobile device clients.

▶ **DMCertResp.htm (in \temp)**—This log file records the HTML response from the certificate server when the mobile device Enroller program requests a client authentication certificate on mobile device clients.

▶ **DmClientSetup.log**—Records client setup data on mobile device clients.

▶ **DmClientXfer.log**—Records client transfer data for Windows Mobile Device Center and ActiveSync deployments.

▶ **DmCommonInstaller.log**—Records the client transfer file installation for setting up mobile device client transfer files on client computers.

▶ **DmInstaller.log**—Records whether DMInstaller correctly calls DmClientSetup, and whether DmClientSetup exits with success or failure on mobile device clients.

▶ **DmInvExtension.log**—Records the Inventory Extension file installation for setting up Inventory Extension files on client computers.

▶ **DmSvc.log**—Records mobile device management service data on mobile device clients.

OSD Log Files

The following OSD log files are located at *<ConfigMgrInstallPath>*\SMS_CCM\Logs unless otherwise noted:

▶ **CCMSetup.log**—Provides information about client-based operating system actions. Located at *%windir%*\system32\ccmsetup.

▶ **Client.msi.log**—Setup log file for the client. Located at *%windir%*\system32\ccmsetup.

▶ **CreateTSMedia.log**—Information about task sequence media when it is created. The log is generated on the computer running the Configuration Manager 2007 administrator console. Located at *<ConfigMgrInstallPath>**%temp%*.

▶ **DriverCatalog.log**—Provides information about device drivers that have been imported into the driver catalog. This file is found at *<ConfigMgrInstallPath>*\Logs.

▶ **MP_ClientIDManager.log**—This log file provides information about the Configuration Manager 2007 management point when it responds to Configuration Manager 2007 client ID requests from boot media or the Preboot Execution Environment (PXE). This log is generated on the Configuration Manager 2007 management point.

▶ **MP_DriverMGR.log**—Provides information about the ConfigMgr 2007 management point when it responds to a request from the Auto Apply Driver task sequence action. The log is generated on the Configuration Manager management point.

▶ **MP_Location.log**—Provides information about the Configuration Manager management point when it responds to request state store or release state store requests from the state migration point. This log is generated on the ConfigMgr 2007 management point.

▶ **Pxecontrol.log**—Provides information about the PXE Control Manager and is located at *<ConfigMgrInstallPath>*\sms\Logs.

▶ **PXEMsi.log**—PXEMsi.log provides information about the PXE service point. It is generated when the PXE service point site server has been created. The log file is found at *<ConfigMgrInstallPath>*\sms\Logs.

▶ **PXESetup.log**—Provides information about the PXE service point and is generated when the PXE service point site server has been created. It can be found at *<ConfigMgrInstallPath>*\sms\Logs.

▶ **Setupact.log**—This log file provides information about Windows Sysprep and setup logs. It is located at *%windir%*.

▶ **Setupapi.log**—Provides information about Windows Sysprep and setup logs. It is located in *%windir%*.

▶ **Setuperr.log**—Provides information about Windows Sysprep and setup logs. It is located in *%windir%*.

▶ **SmpIsapi.log**—Provides information about the state migration point Configuration Manager 2007 client request responses.

▶ **Smpmgr.log**—Provides information about the results of state migration point health checks and configuration changes. The log file is found at *<ConfigMgrInstallPath>*\sms\Logs.

▶ **SmpMSI.log**—Provides information about the state migration point and is generated when the state migration point site server has been created. The log file is found at *<ConfigMgrInstallPath>*\sms\Logs.

▶ **Smsprov.log**—Provides information about the SMS provider. The log file is located at *<ConfigMgrInstallPath>*\Logs.

▶ **Smspxe.log**—Provides information about the Configuration Manager 2007 PXE service point.

▶ **SMSSMPSetup.log**—Provides information about the state migration point and is generated when the state migration point site server has been created. The log file is found at *<ConfigMgrInstallPath>*\sms\Logs.

▶ **Smsts.log**—The smsts.log is used for operating system deployment and task sequence log events. smsts.log describes all task sequencer transactions and is used to help troubleshoot OSD issues. Depending on the deployment scenario, it may exist in one of the following locations:

  ▶ ***%temp%*\SMSTSLOG**—Used if the task sequence completes when running in the full operating system without an agent installed in the computer.

  ▶ ***<CCM Install Dir>*\Logs**—Used if the task sequence completes in the full operating system with a ConfigMgr client installed on the computer.

    <CCM Install Dir> is typically *%windir%*\System32\CCM\Logs, although it is *<Configuration Manager 2007 installation drive>*\SMS_CCM for the site server and *%windir%*\SysWOW64\CCM\Logs for 64-bit operating systems.

  ▶ ***<largest fixed partition>*\SMSTSLOG**—Used if the task sequence completes when running in Windows PE.

Unlike all other ConfigMgr components, you cannot configure its size in the Registry. To increase the size of smsts.log, create a file named smsts.ini in the Windows folder (*%windir%*), with the following contents:

```
[Logging]
        LogMaxSize=<maximum log file size in bytes>
        LogMaxHistory=<number of history files to maintain>
```

If you are booting up from media or using PXE, edit your boot image for the smsts.ini file to be in the Windows folder.

▶ **TaskSequenceProvider.log**—Provides information about task sequences when they are imported, exported, or edited. The log file is found at *<ConfigMgrInstallPath>*\Logs.

▶ **USMT Log loadstate.log**—USMT Log loadstate.log provides information about the User State Migration Tool (USMT) regarding the restore of user state data. It is located at *%windir%*system32\CCM\Logs.

▶ **USMT Log scanstate.log**—Provides information about the USMT regarding the capture of user state data. It is located at *%windir%*system32\CCM\Logs.

Multicast for OSD Log Files

Multicasting with OSD applies only to Configuration Manager 2007 R2. Unless otherwise noted, the following log files may be found at *<ConfigMgrInstallPath>*\SMS_CCM\Logs:

▶ **McsMgr.log**—Provides information about multicast availability and changes to multicast configuration. Located at *<ConfigMgrInstallPath>*\Logs.

▶ **McsSetup.log**—Provides information about the multicast service point role setup. The log file is generated when the multicast service point site server has been created. It confirms the environment has been successfully set up and runs the .msi file. Located at *<ConfigMgrInstallPath>*\Logs.

▶ **McsMSI.log**—Provides information about the .msi setup for the multicast service point. It is generated when the multicast service point site server has been created. Located at *<ConfigMgrInstallPath>*\Logs.

▶ **McsExec.log**—McsExec.log provides information about multicast packages, namespace management, session creation, and health checking for multicast.

▶ **McsISAPI.log**—Provides information about the multicast service point Configuration Manager 2007 client request responses.

▶ **McsPrv.log**—This file provides information about the interaction between multicast components and the Windows Deployment Service (WDS) components, such as the creation, reading, and distribution of namespaces.

▶ **McsPerf.log**—MCSPerf.log provides information about the multicast performance counter updates.

Network Access Protection Log Files

The default location for client log files related to Network Access Protection (NAP) is *%windir%*\CCM\Logs. For those client computers that are also management points, the log files are found in *%ProgramFiles%*\SMS_CCM\Logs. The log files include the following:

▶ **Ccmcca.log**—Logs the processing of compliance evaluation based on Configuration Manager NAP policy processing, and contains the processing of remediation for each software update required for compliance.

▶ **Ciagent.log**—Tracks the process of remediation and compliance. (The software updates the log file Updateshandler.log, which provides more informative details on installing the software updates required for compliance.)

▶ **Locationservices.log**—Used by other Configuration Manager features (such as information about the client's assigned site), but also contains information specific to NAP when the client is in remediation. This log records the names of the required remediation servers (management point, software update point, and distribution points that host content required for compliance), which are also sent in the client statement of health.

▶ **Sdmagent.log**—Shared with the Configuration Manager feature Desired Configuration Management (DCM), and contains the tracking process of remediation and compliance. (The software updates the log file Updateshandler.log, which provides more informative details about installing the software updates required for compliance.)

▶ **SMSSha.log**—The main log file for the ConfigMgr NAP client, this contains a merged statement of health information from the location services (LS) and configuration compliance agent (CCA) ConfigMgr components.

   SMSSha.log also contains information about the interactions between the ConfigMgr System Health Agent and the operating system NAP agent, and also between the ConfigMgr System Health Agent and both the configuration compliance agent and the location services. It provides information about whether the NAP agent successfully initialized, the statement of health data, and the statement of health response.

System Health Validator (SHV) point log files are located in *%systemdrive%*\SMSSHV\SMS_SHV\Logs. The SHV log files include the following:

▶ **Ccmperf.log**—Contains information about initializing the System Health Validator point performance counters.

▶ **SmsSHV.log**—The main log file for the System Health Validator point; logs basic operations of the System Health Validator service, including the initialization progress.

▶ **SmsSHVADCacheClient.log**—Contains information about retrieving ConfigMgr health state references from AD.

▶ **SmsSHVCacheStore.log**—Information about the cache store used to hold the ConfigMgr NAP health state references retrieved from AD, such as reading from the store and purging entries from the local cache store file. The cache store is not configurable.

▶ **SmsSHVRegistrySettings.log**—Records any dynamic changes to the SHV component configuration while the service is running.

▶ **SmsSHVQuarValidator.log**—Records client statement of health information and processing operations. To obtain full information, change the Registry key LogLevel from 1 to 0 at HKEY_LOCAL_MACHINE\Software\Microsoft\SMSSHV\Logging\@Global

▶ **SMSSHVSetup.log**—Records the success or failure (with failure reason) of installing the System Health Validator point. This log is located at *<ConfigMgrInstallPath>*\Logs.

Desired Configuration Management Log Files

The following files are located with the ConfigMgr 2007 client computer log files (*%windir%*\System32\CCM\Logs or *%windir%*\SysWOW64\CCM\Logs). For those client computers that are also management points, the client log files are located in the *%SystemDrive%*\SMS_CCM\Logs folder.

▶ **Ciagent.log**—Provides information about downloading, storing, and accessing assigned configuration baselines.

▶ **Dcmagent.log**—Provides high-level information about the evaluation of assigned configuration baselines and desired configuration management processes.

▶ **Discovery.log**—Provides detailed information about the Service Modeling Language (SML) processes.

▶ **EventLogForwarder.log**—Used for writing events to the event log when DCM flags a configuration item (CI) as out of compliance. These events are potentially available for Operations Manager (OpsMgr) to generate an alert to flag a problem condition.

▶ **MP_GetSdmPackage.log**—Lists details about a management point's retrieval of DCM-specific package information.

▶ **Sdmagent.log**—Provides information about downloading, storing, and accessing configuration item content.

▶ **Sdmdiscagent.log**—Provides high-level information about the evaluation process for the objects and settings configured in the referenced configuration items.

▶ **SmsClrHost.log**—Client log file that includes details about ConfigMgr's use of the .NET Framework (required for DCM).

Wake On LAN Log Files

The site server log files related to Wake On LAN (WOL) are located in the folder *<ConfigMgrInstallPath>*\Logs on the site server. There are no client-side log files for Wake On LAN.

▶ **Wolmgr.log**—Information about wake-up procedures, such as when to wake up advertisements or deployments that are configured for WOL

▶ **WolCmgr.log**—Contains information about which clients need to be sent wake-up packets, the number of wake-up packets sent, and the number of wake-up packets retried

Software Updates Log Files

Log files for software updates are maintained on both the site server and client. The next two sections discuss these files.

Software Updates Site Server Log Files

By default, these files are found in *<InstallPath>*\Logs:

▶ **Ciamgr.log**—Provides information about the addition, deletion, and modification of software update configuration items.

▶ **Distmgr.log**—Replication of software update deployment packages.

▶ **Objreplmgr.log**—Provides information about the replication of software updates notification files from a parent site to its child sites.

▶ **PatchDownloader.log**—Provides information about the process for downloading software updates from the update source specified in the software updates metadata to the download destination on the site server. The location will vary:

> ▶ On 64-bit operating systems and 32-bit operating systems without the Configuration Manager 2007 client installed, PatchDownloader.log is created in the server logs folder.

> ▶ On 32-bit operating systems with the ConfigMgr 2007 client installed, PatchDownloader.log is created in the client logs folder.

▶ **Replmgr.log**—Provides information about the process for replicating files between sites.

▶ **Smsdbmon.log**—Provides information about when software update configuration items are inserted, updated, or deleted from the site server database, and creates notification files for software updates components.

▶ **SUPSetup**—Provides information about the software update point installation. When the software update point installation completes, "Installation was successful" is written to this log file.

▶ **WCM.log**—Information about the software update point configuration and connecting to the Windows Server Update Services (WSUS) server for subscribed update categories, classifications, and languages.

▶ **WSUSCtrl.log**—Provides information about the configuration, database connectivity, and health of the WSUS server for the site.

▶ **Wsyncmgr.log**—Information about the software updates synchronization process.

Software Updates Client Computer Log Files

The following files are located with the ConfigMgr 2007 client computer log files (*%windir%*\System32\CCM\Logs or *%windir%*\SysWOW64\CCM\Logs). For those client computers that are also management points, the client log files are located in the *%SystemDrive%*\SMS_CCM\Logs folder.

▶ **CAS.log**—Provides information about the process of downloading software updates to the local cache and cache management.

▶ **Ciagent.log**—Provides information about processing configuration items, including software updates.

▶ **LocationServices.log**—Provides information about the location of the WSUS server when a scan is initiated on the client.

▶ **PatchDownloader.log**—Provides information about the process for downloading software updates from the update source to the download destination on the site server.

This log is only on the client computer configured as the synchronization host for the Inventory Tool for Microsoft Updates.

▶ **PolicyAgent.log**—Provides information about the process for downloading, compiling, and deleting policies on client computers.

▶ **PolicyEvaluator**—Provides information about the process for evaluating policies on client computers, including policies from software updates.

▶ **RebootCoordinator.log**—Information about the process for coordinating system restarts on client computers after software update installations.

▶ **ScanAgent.log**—Provides information about the scan requests for software updates, what tool is requested for the scan, the WSUS location, and so on.

▶ **ScanWrapper.log**—Provides information about the prerequisite checks and the scan process initialization for the Inventory Tool for Microsoft Updates on SMS 2003 clients.

▶ **SdmAgent.log**—Provides information about the process for verifying and decompressing packages containing configuration item information for software updates.

▶ **ServiceWindowManager.log**—Provides information about the process for evaluating configured maintenance windows.

▶ **SmscliUI.log**—Information about the Configuration Manager Control Panel user interactions. This includes initiating a Software Updates Scan Cycle from the Configuration Manager Properties dialog box, opening the Program Download Monitor, and so on.

▶ **SmsWusHandler**—Provides information about the scan process for the Inventory Tool for Microsoft Updates on SMS 2003 client computers.

▶ **StateMessage.log**—Provides information about when Software Updates state messages are created and sent to the management point.

▶ **UpdatesDeployment.log**—Provides information about the deployment on the client. Deployment information includes software update activation, evaluation, and enforcement. Verbose logging shows additional information about the interaction with the client user interface.

▶ **UpdatesHandler.log**—Provides information about software update compliance scanning and about the download and installation of software updates on the client.

▶ **UpdatesStore.log**—Provides information regarding the compliance status for the software updates that were assessed during the compliance scan cycle.

▶ **WUAHandler.log**—Information about when the Windows Update Agent on the client searches for software updates.

▶ **WUSSyncXML.log**—Provides information about the Inventory Tool for the Microsoft Updates synchronization process.

This log is only on the client computer configured as the synchronization host for the Inventory Tool for Microsoft Updates.

WSUS Server Log Files

You will find the following WSUS log files running on the software update point site system role in *%ProgramFiles%*\Update Services\LogFiles:

▶ **Change.log**—Captures data about the WSUS server database information that has changed

▶ **SoftwareDistribution.log**—Provides information about the software updates that are synchronized from the configured update source to the WSUS server database

Windows Update Agent Log File

The Windows Update Agent log file is found on the ConfigMgr client computer in *%windir%*. This file, WindowsUpdate.log, provides information about when the Windows Update Agent connects to the WSUS server and retrieves the software updates for compliance assessment, and whether there are updates to the agent components.

Out of Band Management Log Files

Out of Band (OOB) Management applies only to systems running ConfigMgr 2007 Service Pack (SP) 1 and above. The log files are found in the following locations:

- ▶ On the OOB service point site system server
- ▶ On any computer running the OOB Management console from the Configuration Manager console
- ▶ On client computers running the Configuration Manager 2007 SP 1 client that are managed out of band

Out of Band Service Point Log Files

The following logs are located at *<ConfigMgrInstallPath>*\Logs on the site system server selected to host the OOB service point role:

- ▶ **AMTSPSetup.log**—Shows the success or failure (with failure reason) of installing the OOB service point.
- ▶ **Amtopmgr.log**—Shows the activities of the OOB service point relating to the discovery of management controllers, provisioning, and power control commands.
- ▶ **Amtproxymgr.log**—Shows the activities of the site server relating to provisioning, which include the following:
  - ▶ Publishing provisioned computers to Active Directory Domain Services
  - ▶ Registering the service principal name of provisioned computers in Active Directory Domain Services
  - ▶ Requesting the web server certificate from the issuing Certificate Authority (CA)

  It also shows the activities of sending instruction files to the OOB service point, which include the following:
  - ▶ Discovery of management controllers
  - ▶ Provisioning
  - ▶ Power control commands

  Finally, it shows the activities related to OOB Management site replication.

Out of Band Management Console Log File

Oobconsole.log shows the activities related to running the OOB Management console. It is located at *<ConfigMgrInstallPath>*\AdminUI\AdminUILog on any computer running the OOB Management console from the ConfigMgr console.

Out of Band Management Computer Log File

Oobmgmt.log shows OOB Management activities performed on workstation computers, including the provisioning state of the management controller. It is found at *%windir%*\System32\CCM\Logs on workstation computers running the ConfigMgr 2007 SP 1 client that are managed out of band.

APPENDIX B

Reference URLs

This appendix includes a number of reference URLs associated with Configuration Manager 2007. These links are also available "live" from the Pearson website, at http://www.informit.com/store/product.aspx?isbn=0672330 237, under the Downloads tab. URLs do change—although the authors have made every effort to verify the references here as working links, they cannot guarantee those links will remain current.

The Visio template used for the graphics in this book is also at the same location.

General Resources

A number of websites, including Microsoft's, provide excellent resources for System Center Configuration Manager 2007 (ConfigMgr). This section lists some of the more general resources available:

▶ **myITforum.com**—http://www.myITforum.com is a community of worldwide Information Technology (IT) professionals and a website established in 1999 by Rod Trent. First known as swynk.com, myITforum has concentrated on Systems Management Server (SMS) and now Configuration Manager (ConfigMgr). It also includes topics on other aspects of System Center and IT.

The list of blogs and other ConfigMgr-related articles at myITforum.com is enormous. This appendix includes some specific links to pertinent information, but it does not include everything.

▶ **FAQShop.com**—http://www.faqshop.com/configmgr2007/ is the home page for the System Center Configuration Manager 2007 section of the site.

FAQShop.com provides hints, tips, and answers to frequently asked questions (FAQs) relating to Microsoft's various systems management technologies.

▶ **SystemCenterCentral.com**—Launched at the Microsoft Management Summit (MMS) in April 2009, http://systemcentercentral.com focuses exclusively on the technologies included in the System Center suite of products. This new site touts itself as the site to visit for "Everything System Center." Webmaster is *System Centre Configuration Manager 2007 Unleashed* contributor Pete Zerger.

▶ **SystemCenterForum.org**—http://www.systemcenterforum.org was also established by contributor Pete Zerger. SystemCenterForum offers news, articles, solutions, and learning resources for Operations Manager, Essentials 2007, and the System Center product suite. System Center Forum was first established as momresources.org in 2006 and renamed to SystemCenterForum.org in 2007. New postings are now at SystemCenterCentral.com.

▶ **http://www.techlog.nl**—All about everything Microsoft, maintained by Maarten Goet, Kenneth van Surksum, Steven van Loef, and Aad Noman.

▶ **System Center Virtual User Group**—A user group dedicated to providing educational resources and collaboration between users of System Center technologies worldwide. Microsoft Live Meeting is used for regular meetings. You can join the user group at http://www.systemcentercentral.com/.

▶ If you are not already receiving email notifications of new articles in the Microsoft Knowledge Base from kbalertz, you can sign up at http://kbalertz.com/ for them! You just need to create an account and select those technologies you want to be alerted about.

▶ **TechNet Manageability Center**—Links to resources and *TechNet* magazine articles can be found at http://go.microsoft.com/?linkid=7280963.

▶ Microsoft has published white papers on performance-tuning guidelines for Windows Server:

    ▶ The Windows Server 2008 version can be downloaded from http://www.microsoft.com/whdc/system/sysperf/Perf_tun_srv.mspx.

    ▶ The Windows Server 2003 version is available at http://www.microsoft.com/windowsserver2003/evaluation/performance/tuning.mspx.

▶ The Windows Server 2003 Tech Center is located at http://technet2.microsoft.com/windowsserver/en/library/.

▶ To configure SQL Server site database replication, check out http://technet.microsoft.com/en-us/library/bb693697.aspx. http://technet.microsoft.com/en-us/library/bb693954.aspx discusses disabling database replication.

▶ Michael Pearson has an excellent article discussing SRS recovery planning, available online from the SQL Server Central community (SQLServerCentral.com) at http://www.sqlservercentral.com/articles/Administration/ recoveryplanningforsqlreportingservices/1655/. You must register with SQLServerCentral to view the full article.

▶ For information on SQL Server best practices, see http://technet.microsoft.com/en-us/ sqlserver/bb671430.aspx.

The SQL Server 2005 Best Practice Analyzer is available for download at http://www.microsoft.com/downloads/details.aspx?displaylang=en&FamilyID=da053 1e4-e94c-4991-82fa-f0e3fbd05e63 (or at www.microsoft.com/downloads, search for **SQL Server 2005 Best Practices Analyzer**).

▶ To virtualize or not to virtualize? *CIO* magazine presents a discussion of potential cost savings from virtualization and consolidation at http://www.cio.com/article/ 471408/The_Tricky_Math_of_Server_Virtualization_ROI.

▶ An article by Microsoft on using SQL Server 2005 in a virtual environment can be found at http://download.microsoft.com/download/a/c/d/acd8e043-d69b-4f09-bc9e-4168b65aaa71/SQLVirtualization.doc

▶ Trying to set up a virtual server cluster? An excellent two-part write-up that provides step-by-step processes is available at http://www.roudybob.net/?p=118 and http://www.roudybob.net/?p=119.

The information is also available in PDF format at http://www.roudybob.net/ downloads/Setting-Up-A-Windows-Server-2003-Cluster-in-VS2005-Part1.pdf and http://www.roudybob.net/downloads/Setting-Up-A-Windows-Server-2003-Cluster-in-VS2005-Part2.pdf.

▶ Did you know you could back up a running virtual server VM (virtual machine)? See http://redmondmag.com/columns/print.asp?EditorialsID=2324 for information.

▶ The Virtual Machine Manager (VMM) 2007 scripting guide is available for download at http://go.microsoft.com/fwlink/?LinkId=104290. (At the time of writing this appendix, a similar guide for VMM 2008 is not yet available.)

▶ For information on the Microsoft Solution Framework (MSF), refer to http://www. microsoft.com/msf.

▶ The MSF Process Model is documented at http://download.microsoft.com/download/ 7/7/7/777104c9-506e-47c9-9da4-9e23138be493/MSF%20Process%20Model%20v. %203.1.pdf.

▶ Microsoft's white paper on MSF Risk Management is available at http://www. brightwork.com/file/PDF/MSF%20Risk%20Management%20Discipline%20v.1.1.pdf.

This paper is also downloadable from Microsoft at http://www.microsoft.com/downloads/details.aspx?familyid=6C2F2C7E-DDBD-448C-A218-074D88240942&displaylang=en.

▶ An IDC white paper sponsored by Microsoft that quantifies how businesses can reduce costs by managing the Windows desktop is available for download at http://download.microsoft.com/download/a/4/4/a4474b0c-57d8-41a2-afe6-32037fa93ea6/IDC_windesktop_IO_whitepaper.pdf.

▶ Read about proactive desktop management in Greg Shield's article in *Redmond* magazine on best practices for desktop management at http://redmondmag.com/columns/article.asp?editorialsid=2635.

▶ For information regarding the Active Directory schema, see http://msdn.microsoft.com/en-us/library/ms675085(VS.85).aspx.

▶ Information on LDIFDE is located at http://technet2.microsoft.com/windowsserver2008/en/library/8fe5b815-f89d-48c0-8b2c-a9cd1d6986521033.mspx?mfr=true.

▶ http://support.microsoft.com/kb/555636 describes the process of exporting and importing objects using LDIFDE.

▶ To troubleshoot port status issues, you can use the Portqry command-line utility (http://technet.microsoft.com/en-us/network/bb545423.aspx) or its graphical equivalent, PortQryUI at http://www.microsoft.com/downloads/details.aspx?FamilyID=8355E537-1EA6-4569-AABB-F248F4BD91D0&displaylang=en.

▶ Interested in learning more about the Microsoft Operations Framework? Check out the MOF at http://go.microsoft.com/fwlink/?LinkId=50015.

▶ Information on the IO (Infrastructure Optimization) model is available at http://www.microsoft.com/technet/infrastructure.

▶ Details about the Microsoft Solutions Framework (MSF) is located at http://www.microsoft.com/technet/solutionaccelerators/msf.

▶ You may want to implement the Windows Server 2003 Resource Kit tools if you have not already done so. You can download them from http://go.microsoft.com/fwlink/?linkid=4544.

The individual utilities are available at http://technet.microsoft.com/en-us/windowsserver/bb405955.aspx.

▶ An excellent resource on group policy management is available online at the Windows Server 2003 Tech Center: http://technet.microsoft.com/en-us/library/cc706993.aspx.

The section on WMI filtering is found at http://technet.microsoft.com/en-us/library/cc779036.aspx.

Security group filtering is discussed in http://technet.microsoft.com/en-us/ConfigMgr/cc462788.aspx.

▸ For information on using PowerShell with ConfigMgr, check out http://www.windows7th.com/?p=22028.

▸ Microsoft's System Center website is located at http://www.microsoft.com/system-center/.

▸ The System Center catalog, Microsoft's multiple pages for all things ConfigMgr and OpsMgr, incorporates the following section for Configuration Manager 2007—https://www.microsoft.com/technet/prodtechnol/scp/configmgr07.aspx.

This is the Configuration Pack Catalog, also accessible at http://go.microsoft.com/fwlink/?LinkId=71837. Approximately 70 configuration packs were in the catalog at the time of writing this appendix.

▸ Virtual labs for the System Center family can be found at http://technet.microsoft.com/en-us/configmgr/bb539977.aspx.

More Specific Information

This section provides a list of more specific ConfigMgr-related resources.

▸ Want a concise list of the site system roles? Check out http://faqshop.com/configmgr2007/desplan/dsitesytems/what%20are%20configmgr%20site%20system%20roles.htm, contributed by Cliff Hobbs, a ConfigMgr MVP.

▸ Garth Jones, a ConfigMgr MVP, provides updates us on System Center Configuration Manager in his interview at http://www.runasradio.com/default.aspx?showNum=54.

▸ Thinking about hardware configurations for your site servers? http://go.microsoft.com/fwlink/?LinkId=28617 provides a description of the most widely used RAID configurations and part of the Windows Server 2003 Deployment Kit.

▸ Microsoft has published a white paper on ConfigMgr 2007 sample configurations and performance-related questions, available at http://download.microsoft.com/download/4/b/9/4b97e9b7-7056-41ae-8fc8-dd87bc477b54/Sample%20Configurations%20and%20Common%20Performance%20Related%20Questions.pdf.

▸ You may also want to view Microsoft's best practices for central and primary site hardware and software configuration, available at http://technet.microsoft.com/en-us/library/bb932180.aspx.

▸ For information on configuring Windows Server 2008 for site system roles, check the article at http://technet.microsoft.com/en-us/library/cc431377(TechNet.10).aspx.

▸ Information regarding configuring site systems to use NLB clustering is found at http://technet.microsoft.com/en-us/library/bb633031.aspx.

▶ http://technet.microsoft.com/en-us/library/bb680733.aspx lists the Public Key Infrastructure (PKI) certificate requirements for native mode, and http://technet. microsoft.com/en-us/library/bb632727.aspx provides a detailed check list for migrating a site to native mode.

▶ Configuring Out of Band Management is discussed at http://technet.microsoft.com/en-us/library/cc161822(TechNet.10).aspx.

▶ If you want to check your knowledge of ConfigMgr dependencies and requirements for key ConfigMgr 2007 components, Microsoft has compiled a number of quizzes to help raise your level of awareness of some of the "nuances" of the product. Download the quizzes at http://www.microsoft.com/downloads/details.aspx? FamilyID=b9fb478a-ec98-47f2-b31e-57443a8ae88f&DisplayLang=en (or go to http:// www.microsoft.com/downloads and search for **configuration manager quiz**).

▶ After taking the ConfigMgr quiz, are you looking for training?

http://technet.microsoft.com/en-us/library/bb694263.aspx contains links to documents to help you get started with ConfigMgr.

The syllabus for the Microsoft-developed course "Planning, Deploying and Managing Microsoft System Center Configuration Manager 2007" (course 6451A) is located at http://www.microsoft.com/learning/en/us/syllabi/6451a.aspx.

A great ConfigMgr trainer who teaches 6451A is Michael Head. His current course schedule is located at http://www.HeadSmartGroup.com/.

Infront Consulting Group offers a 5-day course on Operating System Deployment (OSD); check the syllabus at http://www.infrontconsulting.com/docs/ SCCM2007OSD.pdf. Infront is also developing a 3-day course on Desired Configuration Management (DCM); check http://www.infrontconsulting.com/ training.php for status. http://www.infrontconsulting.com/training.php also lists the current training schedule.

▶ As the world moves towards 64 bit, the ConfigMgr client remains a 32-bit client. Cliff Hobbs has a nice write-up of the issues this creates when trying to monitor with OpsMgr at http://wmug.co.uk/blogs/cliffs_blog/archive/2009/02/14/configmgr-monitoring-configmgr-2007-with-operations-manager-2007-in-a-64-bit-environment. aspx. A Service Pack (SP) 1 hotfix is planned to address this, along with an updated ConfigMgr management pack for Operations Manager 2007 R2. In addition, ConfigMgr 2007 SP 2 will come with native 64-bit performance counters.

▶ Garth Jones, a ConfigMgr MVP, posts articles at http://www.myitforum.com/contrib/default.asp?cid=116. He also is affiliated with the SMS User Group in Canada—those blogs are at http://smsug.ca/blogs/.

▶ Configuring a software update point with NLB is nicely documented at http://blogs. msdn.com/shitanshu/archive/2008/05/13/how-to-setup-wsus-sup-role-in-nlb-in-sccm.aspx.

► http://technet.microsoft.com/en-us/library/cc779036.aspx discusses Windows Management Instrumentation (WMI) filtering using GPMC.

► WMI documentation is available at http://msdn.microsoft.com/en-us/library/aa394582.aspx.

► http://msdn.microsoft.com/en-us/library/aa394564(VS.85).aspx discusses WMI logging.

► See http://msdn.microsoft.com/en-us/library/aa826699(VS.85).aspx for a discussion of User Account Control and WMI.

► Command-line tools to manage WMI can be downloaded at http://msdn.microsoft.com/en-us/library/aa827351(VS.85).aspx.

► The WMI Diagnosis utility (WMIDiag) is available at the Microsoft download site, http://www.microsoft.com/downloads/details.aspx?familyid=d7ba3cd6-18d1-4d05-b11e-4c64192ae97d&displaylang=en.

► The WMI Administrative Tools are downloadable at http://www.microsoft.com/downloads/details.aspx?FamilyID=6430f853-1120-48db-8cc5-f2abdc3ed314&DisplayLang=en.

► CIM is the Component Information Model that WMI is based on. To learn more about CIM, use the tutorial located at http://www.wbemsolutions.com/tutorials/CIM/index.html. The full CIM specification can be found at http://www.dmtf.org/standards/cim/cim_spec_v22.

► Trying to understand licensing? Microsoft discusses current ConfigMgr licensing at http://www.microsoft.com/systemcenter/configurationmanager/en/us/pricing-licensing.aspx.

   Operating System Environment (OSE) licensing information is located at http://www.microsoft.com/systemcenter/configurationmanager/en/us/pricing-licensing.aspx.

   General licensing information is at http://www.microsoft.com/licensing/default.mspx.

► To update your ConfigMgr help files to the latest version, download the Configuration Manager 2007 Help File Update Wizard from http://www.microsoft.com/downloads/details.aspx?FamilyID=71816b0f-de06-40e0-bce7-ad4b1e4377bb&displaylang=en. Information on this is also available at http://blogs.technet.com/configmgrteam/archive/2009/02/03/need-the-latest-configuration-manager-2007-help-file.aspx.

► Microsoft's TechNet reference on security best practices and privacy information for ConfigMgr features is located at http://technet.microsoft.com/en-us/library/bb632704.aspx.

► To download the ConfigMgr SDK, go to http://www.microsoft.com/downloads/details.aspx?FamilyID=064A995F-EF13-4200-81AD-E3AF6218EDCC&displaylang=en.

▶ Create custom reports using ConfigMgr 2007 SQL Views. Microsoft documentation is downloadable at http://www.microsoft.com/downloads/details.aspx?familyid= 87BBE64E-5439-4FC8-BECC-DEB372A40F4A&displaylang=en.

▶ For information regarding WMI Query Language (WQL), see http://msdn.microsoft.com/en-us/library/aa394606(VS.85).aspx.

▶ For a discussion of User Account Control and WMI, see http://msdn.microsoft.com/en-us/library/aa826699(VS.85).aspx.

▶ Command-line tools for managing WMI are available for download at http://msdn.microsoft.com/en-us/library/aa827351(VS.85).aspx.

▶ A nice tool provided by Microsoft to search TechNet, the Knowledge Base, and TechNet Blogs for troubleshooting information related to Configuration Manager is available at http://technet.microsoft.com/en-gb/configmgr/bb625748.aspx.

▶ Microsoft provides preplanning worksheets for Configuration Manager to help you gather information about your environment, available at http://technet.microsoft. com/en-us/library/bb694080.aspx.

▶ Microsoft also provides planning worksheets, which you can download at http://technet.microsoft.com/en-us/library/bb694186.aspx.

▶ A useful flowchart describing the major activities for a side-by-side migration to ConfigMgr 2007 is available at http://technet.microsoft.com/en-us/library/bb681052. aspx.

▶ Microsoft documents prerequisites for installing Configuration Manager 2007 at http://technet.microsoft.com/en-us/library/bb694113.aspx, and http://technet. microsoft.com/en-us/library/bb680951.aspx discusses the specific checks made by the prerequisite checker.

▶ For starting the prerequisite checker from the command line, http://technet. microsoft.com/en-us/library/bb681060.aspx documents the specific arguments you can use.

▶ http://technet.microsoft.com/en-us/library/bb693561.aspx provides an overview of running a ConfigMgr 2007 unattended setup.

▶ http://technet.microsoft.com/en-us/library/bb680980.aspx discusses client installation properties, including the different switches you can specify.

▶ Information on the Transfer Site Settings Wizard is located at http://technet. microsoft.com/en-us/library/bb632809.aspx.

▶ Information regarding extending hardware inventory is available at http://technet. microsoft.com/en-us/library/bb680609.aspx.

▶ For information about package definition files, Microsoft provides documentation at http://technet.microsoft.com/en-us/library/bb693959.aspx.

▶ A great article by Raymond Chou, an Operations Manager (OpsMgr) MVP, on integrating App-V with the R2 release of ConfigMgr 2007 is located at http://mymomexperience.blogspot.com/2008/05/marrying-sccm-r2-and-softgrid-45.html.

▶ For information on converting WQL to SQL, Brian Leary has a nice article at http://www.myitforum.com/articles/8/view.asp?id=9908.

▶ Here are several links for information on Asset Intelligence:

  ▶ **Microsoft's Asset Intelligence data sheet**—http://download.microsoft.com/download/5/9/8/598662ce-61db-474f-80a5-7b1dafc31843/Configuration%20Manager%20Asset%20Intelligence%20Datasheet.pdf.

  ▶ **Comparison between Asset Intelligence in ConfigMgr 2007 and the SMS 2003 version (in particular more control over assets and licensing)**—http://searchwindowsserver.techtarget.com/tip/0,289483,sid68_gci1301339,00.html.

  ▶ **ConfigMgr 2007 Asset Intelligence white paper**—http://download.microsoft.com/download/d/0/f/d0f027ac-501c-415a-ba28-85c051d57da4/ConfigMgr%20Asset%20Intelligence%20Whitepaper%20FINAL%20v4.pdf.

▶ Deployment scenarios for IBCM (Internet-based client management) are discussed at http://technet.microsoft.com/en-us/library/bb693824.aspx.

▶ Prerequisites for IBCM are located at http://technet.microsoft.com/en-us/library/bb633122.aspx.

▶ The communication protocols and ports used by Configuration Manager 2007 are described at http://technet.microsoft.com/en-us/library/bb632618.aspx.

▶ Information online regarding ports for Network Access Protection in Configuration Manager 2007 is located at http://technet.microsoft.com/en-us/library/bb694170.aspx.

▶ Microsoft's white paper on using Configuration Manager with mobile devices is located at http://download.microsoft.com/download/5/5/6/556544f5-b09e-4818-953d-087e08a8303a/Mobile%20Device%20Whitepaper.pdf.

▶ See http://technet.microsoft.com/en-us/library/bb632442.aspx for the full list of task sequence action and built-in variables.

Blogs

This section lists some of the more interesting blogs available related to Configuration Manager. It is not intended to be a complete list; blogs come and go, and new blogs seem to spring up overnight!

▶ The Configuration Manager Team blog is located at http://blogs.technet.com/configmgrteam/.

▶ Carlos Santiago, a Premier Field Engineer at Microsoft, has a blog at http://blogs.technet.com/carlossantiago.

▶ Garth Jones, ConfigMgr MVP, blogs at http://myitforum.com/cs2/blogs/gjones/.

▶ Don Hite's blog is at http://myitforum.com/cs2/blogs/dhite/.

▶ See http://configmgr.com/ by Anthony Clendenen, a ConfigMgr MVP. He also has a myITforum blog at http://myitforum.com/cs2/blogs/socal/default.aspx.

▶ Sherry Kissinger, ConfigMgr MVP, blogs at http://myitforum.com/cs2/blogs/skissinger/.

▶ The Microsoft IT (MSIT) blog on ConfigMgr 2007 is located at http://blogs.technet.com/configmgr/.

▶ Paul Thomsen, senior SMS/ConfigMgr engineer at Microsoft, blogs at http://myitforum.com/cs2/blogs/pthomsen/.

▶ Rick Jones blogs at http://myitforum.com/cs2/blogs/rjones/.

▶ You can find Ronni Pedersen's blog at http://myitforum.com/cs2/blogs/rpedersen/. Ronni is a ConfigMgr MVP.

▶ Scott Moss's blog is at http://myitforum.com/cs2/blogs/smoss/.

▶ Chris Mosby, ConfigMgr MVP, blogs at http://myitforum.com/cs2/blogs/cmosby/.

▶ Andrius Kozeniauskas maintains a blog on ConfigMgr and SMS 2003 at http://andrius.kozeniauskas.com/blog/category/microsoft/sccmsms2003/.

▶ Kerrie Meyler, lead author for *System Center Configuration 2007 Manager Unleashed*, maintains a blog at www.networkworld.com/community/meyler.

▶ Greg Ramsey, one of our coauthors and a ConfigMgr MVP, has a blog at http://myitforum.com/cs2/blogs/gramsey/.

▶ Contributor Cameron Fuller blogs at http://cameronfuller.spaces.live.com.

▶ A blog by contributor Jason Sandys can be found at http://myitforum.com/cs2/blogs/jsandys/.

▶ Contributor Jannes Alink has his blog at www.jannesalink.com.

▶ Steve Rachui is a CSS guru on ConfigMgr and our technical reviewer. Check out his blog at http://blogs.msdn.com/steverac/.

▶ This book's blog is located at http://configmgr.spaces.live.com/.

▶ http://blogs.msdn.com/shitanshu/ is a blog by Shitanshu Verma, ConfigMgr Production Manager at Microsoft.

▶ http://www.msfaq.se/ is Stefan Schörling's blog on Microsoft System Management.

▶ http://www.feedghost.com/UserArea/LinkBlog/Htm.aspx?id=63 provides links to articles on Configuration Manager.

▶ Kim Oppalfens, MVP, blogs about Configuration Manager at http://blogcastrepository.com/blogs/kim_oppalfenss_systems_management_ideas/.

▶ http://desktopcontrol.blogspot.com/ is a blog by Ment van der Plas on desktop control.

▶ http://www.blogcatalog.com/blogs/don-hite/posts/tag/configmgr%202007/ is a collection of postings by Don Hite.

▶ Jeff Gilbert's ConfigMgr blog is located at http://myitforum.com/cs2/blogs/jgilbert/.

▶ Cliff Hobbs, ConfigMgr MVP, blogs at http://myitforum.com/cs2/blogs/chobbs/ and http://wmug.co.uk/blogs/cliffs_blog/default.aspx.

▶ http://blogs.technet.com/configurationmgr/ is the Configuration Manager Support Team blog.

▶ Kevin Sullivan's Management blog is located at https://blogs.technet.com/kevinsul_blog/. Kevin is a Technology Specialist at Microsoft focusing on management products.

▶ http://www.mcalynn.com is a blog by Duncan McAlynn that includes articles on Configuration Manager, SMS, and OpsMgr.

  Duncan now concentrates his blogging activity at systemcenterguide.com. He has transferred the articles from mcalynn.com to www.systemcenterguide.com.

▶ http://myitforum.com/cs2/blogs/jnelson/ is maintained by John Nelson, a ConfigMgr MVP.

▶ Rob Marshall, another ConfigMgr MVP, blogs at wmug.co.uk. His blog is located at http://wmug.co.uk/blogs/r0b/default.aspx.

▶ John Marcum, ConfigMgr MVP, blogs at http://myitforum.com/cs2/blogs/jmarcum/.

▶ http://blogcastrepository.com/level5/sccm/default.aspx is maintained by Brian S. Tucker, a ConfigMgr trainer.

▶ Steve Thompson, ConfigMgr MVP, blogs at http://myitforum.com/cs2/blogs/sthompson/.

▶ Always interesting to look at is the PSS Manageability Official Blog at http://blogs.technet.com/pssmanageability/default.aspx.

The System Center Family

Here are some references and articles regarding other components of Microsoft's System Center family:

- System Center Essentials combines the functionality of ConfigMgr and OpsMgr in a product designed for use by smaller organizations. For information on deployment planning and installation, see http://go.microsoft.com/fwlink/?LinkId=94444.

- Here are some blogs on System Center Essentials (Essentials):

   Simplifying IT Management—http://blogs.technet.com/caseymck/

   Managed Services blog—http://blogs.technet.com/dustinj/

   The System Center Essentials Team Blog (by the product group)—http://blogs.technet.com/systemcenteressentials/

   SCE Setup, Policy, and Reporting—http://blogs.technet.com/rtammana/

- System Center Essentials Techcenter is located at http://technet.microsoft.com/en-us/sce/bb677155.aspx.

- Can't talk about Essentials (or ConfigMgr 2007 for that matter) without thinking about WSUS? See the WSUS 3.0 blog at http://msmvps.com/blogs/athif/.

- Introducing System Center's Service Manager at http://www.microsoft.com/systemcenter/en/us/service-manager.aspx (in beta when this appendix was written). Service Manager is envisioned as an integration point for service management workflows across ConfigMgr and OpsMgr.

   Earlier articles (the product was initially code-named "Service Desk") include the following:

      http://searchwinit.techtarget.com/originalContent/0,289142,sid1_gci1184995,00.html

      http://www.eweek.com/article2/0,1759,1954020,00.asp?kc=EWRSS03119TX1K0000594

- You can find Microsoft's information on Operations Manager at http://www.microsoft.com/opsmgr, with the TechCenter located at http://technet.microsoft.com/en-us/opsmgr/default.aspx.

Public Forums

If you need an answer to a question, the first place to check is the Microsoft public forums. It is best to see if the question has already been posted before you ask it yourself!

A list of available TechNet forums is maintained at http://social.technet.microsoft.com/forums. The ConfigMgr forums (in English) are listed here:

- Configuration Manager – General (http://social.technet.microsoft.com/forums/en-US/configmgrgeneral/threads/)

- Configuration Manager – Announcements (http://social.technet.microsoft.com/forums/en-US/configmgrannouncements/threads/)

- ▶ Configuration Manager – Admin Console (http://social.technet.microsoft.com/forums/en-US/configmgradminconsole/threads/)

- ▶ Configuration Manager – Asset Intelligence (http://social.technet.microsoft.com/forums/en-US/configmgrai/threads/)

- ▶ Configuration Manager – Backup and Recovery (http://social.technet.microsoft.com/forums/en-US/configmgrbackup/threads/)

- ▶ Configuration Manager – Desired Configuration Management (http://social.technet.microsoft.com/forums/en-US/configmgrdcm/threads/)

- ▶ Configuration Manager – Documentation (http://social.technet.microsoft.com/forums/en-US/configmgrdocs/threads/)

- ▶ Configuration Manager – Internet Clients and Native Mode (http://social.technet.microsoft.com/forums/en-US/configmgribcm/threads/)

- ▶ Configuration Manager – Inventory (http://social.technet.microsoft.com/forums/en-US/configmgrosd/threads/)

- ▶ Configuration Manager – Operating System Deployment (http://social.technet.microsoft.com/forums/en-US/configmgrosd/threads/)

- ▶ Configuration Manager – SDK (http://social.technet.microsoft.com/forums/en-US/configmgrsdk/threads/)

- ▶ Configuration Manager – Setup/Deployment (http://social.technet.microsoft.com/forums/en-US/configmgrsetup/threads/)

- ▶ Configuration Manager – Software Distribution (http://social.technet.microsoft.com/forums/en-US/configmgrswdist/threads/)

- ▶ Configuration Manager – Software Updates Management (http://social.technet.microsoft.com/forums/en-US/configmgrsum/threads/)

- ▶ myITforum also has a discussion list for Configuration Manager at http://www.myitforum.com/lists/#Microsoft_Systems_Management_Server_(SMS)_List. myITforum has a number of other discussion lists as well.

Free Utilities

Everyone likes "free stuff." Here's where you can find some:

- ▶ Right Click tools for the ConfigMgr console can be found at http://myitforum.com/cs2/blogs/rhouchins/archive/2008/04/09/sccm-right-click-tools.aspx.

- ▶ Matthew Hudson, a ConfigMgr MVP, posts ConfigMgr tools at http://www.sccm-tools.com/.

▶ The Sysinternal PsTools allow you to perform tasks easily on remote systems. They are available for download at http://technet.microsoft.com/en-us/sysinternals/bb896649.aspx and are discussed in the March 2007 issue of *TechNet* magazine, available online at http://technet.microsoft.com/en-us/magazine/cc162490.aspx.

▶ A number of other tools are available at the Sysinternals area of Microsoft.com (http://technet.microsoft.com/en-us/sysinternals/default.aspx). This includes utilities such as Registry Monitor (RegMon) and Process Monitor (ProcMon). (An in-depth, on-demand TechNet webcast discussing advanced Windows troubleshooting with Process Monitor is available at http://www.microsoft.com/emea/spotlight/sessionh.aspx?videoid=346.)

▶ Another link providing information on Process Monitor and a link to download the tool can be found at http://technet.microsoft.com/en-us/sysinternals/bb896645.aspx.

▶ Microsoft provides an extensive array of tools and add-ins for Visio through the Visio Toolbox site, http://visiotoolbox.com. This includes a System Center add-in at http://visiotoolbox.com/en-us/articles1.aspx?ArticleId=6&aid=104.

▶ Ron Crumbaker's Web Remote Console 3.21 can be found at http://www.myitforum.com/articles/19/view.asp?id=8662 for SMS 2003.

For updates for ConfigMgr 2007, see http://myitforum.com/cs2/blogs/rcrumbaker/archive/2007/10/12/web-remote-tools-and-system-center-configuration-manager.aspx.

▶ Roger Zander's stuff, specifically SMS Client Center, can be found at these locations:

> http://www.myitforum.com/articles/8/view.asp?id=11268

> http://sourceforge.net/users/rzander/

> http://myitforum.com/cs2/blogs/rzander/

▶ Don't forget to take advantage of SMSMap, which will help you generate drawings of your sites and site servers. You can download SMSMap at http://www.tondtware.com/downloads.html.

Further information about the utility is available at http://technet.microsoft.com/en-us/magazine/cc137998.aspx and http://www.microsoft.com/technet/technetmag/issues/2007/07/.

▶ The System Center Content Search Gadget allows you to easily search for System Center information. The gadget uses Live Search macros to search specific sites instead of the entire Internet. You can download this utility at http://gallery.live.com/LiveItemDetail.aspx?li=49e26ad0-113d-4f3d-a711-57f6530c75d9.

▶ http://www.instantapp.net/ provides a number of applications that are prepackaged and available as App-V-enabled applications.

Other Utilities

A number of third-party utilities address specific issues in ConfigMgr. Here is a partial list:

- ▶ www.1e.com
- ▶ www.dudeworks.com
- ▶ www.enhansoft.com
- ▶ www.sccmexpert.com
- ▶ www.systemcentertools.com
- ▶ www.silect.com

Index

Numbers

A

B

clients

J-K

N

O

How can we make this index more useful? Email us at indexes@samspublishing.com

modes, developing, 193

planning, 306

policies, applying, 1008-1012

selecting, 1005

server hardening, 1007

software, 1007, 1013-1015

servers

databases, configuring, 845

defined, 56

PKI certificate deployment, 518

primary, 56-57

role, 194-195

secondary, 57-58

shares, 401

site system installations, 391

settings, transferring, 351-352

SQL replication, 403

disabling, 413-414

distributers, configuring, 405

management points, offloading, 414-415

post-replication setup tasks, 410-413

pre-replication setup tasks, 404-405

publishers, 406

setup tasks, 405-410

subscribers, 409-410

SUP role, adding, 713-716

system installations, testing, 347

upgrading, 374

Sitestat.log, 1085

sitewide settings, 62

Six Sigma, 25

size

client caches, 683

databases, 206

site servers, 302-304

slow networks, site boundaries, 262-263

Small Computer System Interface (SCSI), 204

SMB (Server Message Block) protocol, 231-232

SMFs (Service Management Functions), 43

SML (Service Modeling Language), 19

configuration items/baselines, editing, 797

IT Service Management, 19

resources, 19

SDM, compared, 17

website, 797

Smplsapi.log, 1090

Smpmgr.log, 1090

SmpMSI.log, 1090

SMS (Systems Management Server), 47

1.1, 47

1.2, 48

2.0

DDR processing, 49

inventory, 49

license enforcement, 49

overview, 48

service packs, 50

software metering, 49

software updates/patches, 49

2003, 50

Active Directory integration, 50-51

Advanced Client, 51-52

Asset Intelligence, compared, 868

changes, 50

clients, upgrading, 455-457

ConfigMgr 2007, compared, 53-55

DCM feature pack conversion, 765

OSD Feature Pack, 976

R2 (Release 2), 53

service packs, 52-53

Site Boundaries dialog box, 460

software updates, 747-749

Admins group, Remote Activation permissions, 497

database objects, 462

Map, hierarchy documentation, 298

Object Generator, 349-350

provider namespace, WMI views, 134

How can we make this index more useful? Email us at indexes@samspublishing.com

How can we make this index more useful? Email us at indexes@samspublishing.com

UNLEASHED

Unleashed takes you beyond the basics, providing an exhaustive, technically sophisticated reference for professionals who need to exploit a technology to its fullest potential. It's the best resource for practical advice from the experts, and the most in-depth coverage of the latest technologies.

Microsoft SQL Server 2008 Reporting Services Unleashed
ISBN-13: 9780672330261

OTHER UNLEASHED TITLES

ASP.NET 3.5 AJAX Unleashed
ISBN-13: 9780672329739

Windows Small Business Server 2008 Unleashed
ISBN-13: 9780672329579

Silverlight 2 Unleashed
ISBN-13: 9780672330148

Windows Communication Foundation 3.5 Unleashed
ISBN-13: 9780672330247

Windows Server 2008 Hyper-V Unleashed
ISBN-13: 9780672330285

LINQ Unleashed
ISBN-13: 9780672329838

C# 3.0 Unleashed
ISBN-13: 9780672329814

Ubuntu Unleashed 2008 Edition
ISBN-13: 9780672329937

Microsoft Expression Blend Unleashed
ISBN-13: 9780672329319

Windows PowerShell Unleashed
ISBN-13: 9780672329883

Microsoft SQL Server 2008 Analysis Services Unleashed
ISBN-13: 9780672330018

Microsoft SQL Server 2008 Integration Services Unleashed
ISBN-13: 9780672330322

Microsoft XNA Game Studio 3.0 Unleashed
ISBN-13: 9780672330223

SAP Implementation Unleashed
ISBN-13: 9780672330049

WPF Control Development Unleashed: Building Advanced User Experiences
ISBN-13: 9780672330339

Microsoft Dynamics CRM 4 Integration Unleashed
ISBN-13: 9780672330544

SAMS

informit.com/sams

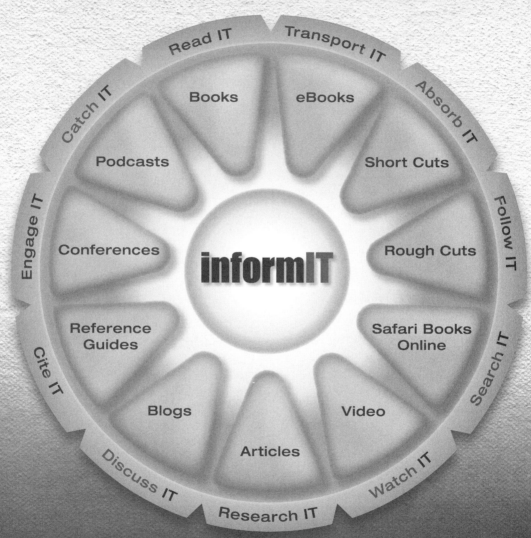